THE CAMBRIDGE HISTORY OF LAW IN AMERICA

VOLUME III

The Twentieth Century and After (1920–)

Law stands at the center of modern American life. Since the 1950s, American historians have produced an extraordinarily rich and diverse literature that has vastly expanded our knowledge of this familiar and vital yet complex and multifaceted phenomenon. But few attempts have been made to take full account of law's American history. *The Cambridge History of Law in America* has been designed for just this purpose. In three volumes we put on display all the intellectual vitality and variety of contemporary American legal history. We present as comprehensive and authoritative an account as possible of the present understanding and range of interpretation of the history of American law. We suggest where future research may lead.

In 1941, Henry Luce of *Time Magazine* named the twentieth century "the American Century." For our purposes it begins after World War I: the war was a watershed that foreshadowed a new American state form and role, confirmed the dominance of the new American corporate economy, and gave rise to a new range of international ambitions and relationships. Each arena saw such an intensification of the role of law that by its end, "the American Century was being called 'Law's Century.'" Not everything that seemed new was, but by and large this final volume of the *History* is about accelerating change: innovation in the state, in legal thought and education, in professional organization and life, and in American federalism and governance; innovation at the intersection of law with explosive struggles around race, gender, class, and sexual liberation and the full emergence of "rights" discourse, along with its limitations and blind spots; and the mobilization of "rights" and "law" to "legalize" the world. In the early twenty-first century, about the only prediction we can confidently make is that change is not yet done with us.

The Cambridge History of Law in America has been made possible by the generous support of the American Bar Foundation. Volumes I and II cover the history of law in America, respectively, from the first moments of English colonizing through the creation and stabilization of the republic; and from the foundation of the republic until the immediate aftermath of World War I.

Michael Grossberg is the Sally M. Reahard Professor of History and a Professor of Law at Indiana University. His research focuses on the relationship between law and social change, particularly the intersection of law and the family.

Christopher Tomlins is Senior Research Fellow at the American Bar Foundation in Chicago. His research encompasses the relationship among labor, colonization, and law in early America; the conceptual history of police in Anglo-American law and politics; and the place of historical materialism in legal theory.

THE CAMBRIDGE HISTORY OF
LAW IN AMERICA

VOLUME III

The Twentieth Century and After (1920–)

Edited by

MICHAEL GROSSBERG
Indiana University

CHRISTOPHER TOMLINS
The American Bar Foundation, Chicago

CAMBRIDGE
UNIVERSITY PRESS

CAMBRIDGE UNIVERSITY PRESS
Cambridge, New York, Melbourne, Madrid, Cape Town, Singapore, São Paulo, Delhi

Cambridge University Press
32 Avenue of the Americas, New York, NY 10013-2473, USA

www.cambridge.org
Information on this title: www.cambridge.org/9780521803076

First published 2008

Printed in the United States of America

A catalog record for this publication is available from the British Library.

Library of Congress Cataloging in Publication Data

The Cambridge history of law in America / edited by Michael Grossberg,
Christopher Tomlins.
    p.   cm.
Includes bibliographical references and index.
ISBN   978-0-521-80307-6 (hardback)
1. Law – United States – History.   I. Grossberg, Michael, 1950–   II. Tomlins,
Christopher L., 1951–   III. Title.
KF352.C36   2007
349.73–dc22   2007017606

ISBN   978-0-521-80307-6 hardback

CONTENTS

EDITORS' PREFACE

In February 1776, declaiming against the oppressive and absolute rule of "the Royal Brute of Britain," the revolutionary pamphleteer Tom Paine announced to the world that "so far as we approve of monarchy . . . in America THE LAW IS KING"! Paine's declaration of Americans' "common sense" of the matter turned out to be an accurate forecast of the authority the legal order would amass in the revolutionary republic. Indeed, Paine's own fiery call to action was one of the stimuli that would help his prediction come true. We know ourselves that what he claimed for law then mostly remains true now. Yet, we should note, Paine's claim was not simply prophecy; it made sense in good part because of foundations already laid. Long before 1776, law and legal institutions had gained a place of some prominence in the British American colonies. The power and position of law, in other words, are apparent throughout American history, from its earliest moments. The three volumes of *The Cambridge History of Law in America* explain why Paine's synoptic insight should be understood as both an eloquent foretelling of what would be and an accurate summation of what already was.

The Cambridge History of Law in America belongs to a long and proud scholarly tradition. In March 1896, at the instigation of Frederick William Maitland, Downing Professor of the Laws of England at Cambridge University, and of Henry Jackson, tutor in Greek at Trinity College, the syndics of Cambridge University Press invited the University's Regius Professor of Modern History, Lord John Dalberg Acton, to undertake "the general direction of a History of the World." Six months later Acton returned with a plan for a (somewhat) more restrained endeavor, an account of Europe and the United States from *The Renaissance* to *The Latest Age*. Thus was born *The Cambridge Modern History*.

Acton's plan described a collaborative, collectively written multi-volume history. Under general editorial guidance, each volume would be divided among "specially qualified writers" primed to present extensive and authoritative accounts of their subjects.[1] They were to imagine themselves writing less for other professional historians than for a more general audience of "students of history" – anyone, that is, who sought an authoritative, thoughtful, and sophisticated assessment of a particular historical subject or issue. Acton envisioned a history largely clean of the professional apparatus of reference and citation – texts that would demonstrate the "highest pitch of knowledge without the display," reliant for their authority on the expertise of the authors chosen to write them. And although it was intended that the *History* be the most complete general statement of historical knowledge available, and to that extent definitive, Acton was not interested in simply reproducing (and thus by implication freezing) what was known. He desired that his authors approach the task critically, strive for originality in their research, and take it on themselves to revise and improve the knowledge they encountered.[2]

Acton did not live to see even the first volume in print, but between 1902 and 1911 *The Cambridge Modern History* appeared in twelve substantial volumes under the editorial direction of Adolphus Ward and Stanley Leathes. The *History* quickly found a broad audience – the first volume, *The Renaissance*, sold out in a month. Other Cambridge histories soon followed: *The Cambridge History of English Literature*, which began to appear under Ward's editorship in 1907; *The Cambridge Medieval History* (1911–36); *The Cambridge History of American Literature* (1917–21); *The Cambridge Ancient History* (1923–39); *The Cambridge History of the British Empire* (1929–67); *The Cambridge History of India* (1922–60), and more. All told, close to a hundred Cambridge histories have been published. More than fifty are currently in print. Cambridge histories have justly become famous. They are to be found in the collections of libraries and individuals throughout the world.

Acton's plan for *The Cambridge Modern History* invoked certain essentials – an ideal of collective authorship and a commitment to make expertise accessible to a wider audience than simply other specialists. To these he added grander, programmatic touches. The *History* would be "an epic," a "great argument" conveying "forward progress . . . upward growth." And it would provide "chart and compass for the coming century." Such ambitions are

[1] When, early on, Acton ran into difficulties in recruiting authors for his intimidating project, Maitland gently suggested that "his omniscient lordship" simply write the whole thing himself. Acton (we note with some relief) demurred. There is humor here, but also principle. Collective authorship is a practice ingrained in the Cambridge histories from the beginning.

[2] Our account of Acton's plan and its realization gratefully relies throughout on Josef L. Altholz, "Lord Acton and the Plan of the *Cambridge Modern History*," *The Historical Journal*, 39, no. 3 (September 1996), 723–36.

characteristic of Acton's moment – the later nineteenth century – when in Britain and Continental Europe history still claimed an educative mantle "of practical utility," the means rather than science (or law) to equip both elites and ordinary citizens "to deal with the problems of their time." It was a moment, also, when history's practitioners could still imagine filling historical time with a consistent, standardized account – the product, to be sure, of many minds, but minds that thought enough alike to agree on an essential common purpose: "men acting together for no other object than the increase of accurate knowledge." Here was history (accurate knowledge) as "the teacher and the guide that regulates public life," the means by which "the recent past" would yield up "the key to present time." Here as well, lest we too quickly dismiss the vision as naïve or worse, was the shouldering of a certain responsibility. "We have to describe the ruling currents, to interpret the sovereign forces, that still govern and divide the world. There are, I suppose, at least a score of them, in politics, economics, philosophy and religion. . . . But if we carry history down to the last syllable of recorded time, and leave the reader at the point where study passes into action, we must explain to him the cause, and the growth, and the power of every great intellectual movement, and equip him for many encounters of life."

Acton's model – a standard general history, a guiding light produced by and for an intellectually confident elite – could not survive the shattering effects of two world wars. It could not survive the democratization of higher education, the proliferation of historical scholarship, the constant emergence of new fields and subdisciplines, the eventual decentering of Europe and "the West." When, amid the rubble and rationing of a hastily de-colonizing post–World War II Britain, Cambridge University Press's syndics decided a revised version was required – a *New Cambridge Modern History* for a new day – their decision acknowledged how much the world had changed. The revised version bore them out. Gone was Acton's deep faith in history's authority and grandeur. The general editor, G. N. Clark, wrote, "Historians in our self-critical age are aware that there will not be general agreement with their conclusions, nor even with some of the premises which they regard as self-evident. They must be content to set out their own thought without reserve and to respect the differences which they cannot eradicate" – including, he might have added (but perhaps there was no need) the many fundamental differences that existed among historians themselves. Cambridge histories no longer aspired to create standardized accounts of the way things had been nor to use the past to pick the lock on the future. The differences in perspective and purpose that a less confident, more self-critical age had spawned were now the larger part of the picture.

Yet the genre Acton helped found has now entered its second century. It still bears, in some fashion, his imprint. The reason it has survived, indeed prospered, has less to do with some sense of overall common purpose than the more modest but nevertheless essential precept of continued adherence to certain core principles of design simply because they have worked: individual scholars charged to synthesize the broad sweep of current knowledge of a particular topic, but also free to present an original interpretation aimed at encouraging both reflection and further scholarship, and an overall architecture that encourages new understandings of an entire subject or area of historical scholarship. Neither encyclopedias nor compilations, textbooks nor works of reference, Cambridge histories have become something quite unique – each an avowedly collective endeavor that offers the single best point of entry to the wide range of an historical subject, topic, or field; each in overall conceptual design and substance intent not simply on defining its field's development to date but on pushing it forward with new ideas. Critique and originality, revision and improvement of knowledge – all remain germane.

Readers will find that *The Cambridge History of Law in America* adheres to these core goals. Of course, like other editors we have our own particular ambitions. And so the three volumes of this Cambridge history have been designed to present to full advantage the intellectual vitality and variety of contemporary American legal history. Necessarily then – and inevitably – *The Cambridge History of Law in America* dwells on areas of concern and interpretive debates that preoccupy the current generation of legal historians. We do not ignore our predecessors.[3] Nor, however, do we attempt in the body of the *History* to chart the development of the field over their time and ours in any great detail. Readers will find a more substantial accounting of that development in the bibliographic essays that accompany each chapter, but as editors we have conceived our job to be to facilitate the presentation of as comprehensive and authoritative a rendition of the present understanding of the history of American law as possible and to suggest where future research may lead.

Cambridge histories always define their audiences widely; ours is no exception. One part of our intended audience is scholarly, but hardly confined to other legal historians; they are already the best equipped to know something of what is retailed here. So to an important extent we try to look past legal historians to historians at large. We also look beyond history to scholars across the broad sweep of law, the humanities, and the social sciences – indeed to any scholar who may find a turn to law's history useful (or simply diverting) in answering questions about law and society in America.

---

[3] See, for example, the graceful retrieval and reexamination of themes from the "imperial school" of American colonial historians undertaken by Mary Sarah Bilder in Volume I, Chapter 3.

A second part of our audience is the legal profession. Lawyers and judges experience in their professional lives something of a practical encounter with the past, although the encounter may not be one they would recognize as "historical." As John Reid has written, "The lawyer and the historian have in common the fact that they go to the past for evidence, but there the similarity largely ends." Here lawyers and judges can discover for themselves what historians do with evidence. In the process, they will also discover that not inconsiderable attention has been paid to their own lives and experiences. Legal historians have always known how important legal thought and legal education are in the formation of the professional world of the law, and both feature prominently in this *History*. Here the profession encounters the history of its activities and of the medium it inhabits from a standpoint outside itself.

The third segment of our intended audience is the general public. Our purposes in this encounter are not Acton's. We do not present this *History* as the means to educate a citizenry to deal with the problems of the moment. (Indeed, it is worth noting that in America law appropriated that role to itself from the earliest days of the republic.) Like G. N. Clark, today's historians live in self-critical times and have lower expectations than Lord Acton of what historical practice might achieve. That said, readers will find that this *History* touches on many past attempts to use law to "deal with" many past problems: in the America where law is king, it has been law's fate to be so employed. And if their accounts leave some of our authors critical in their analysis of outcomes or simply rueful in recounting the hubris (or worse) of the attempts, that in itself can be counted an education of sorts. Moreover, as Volume III's chapters show repeatedly, Americans continue to turn to law as their key medium of private problem solving and public policy formation and implementation, and on an expanding – global – stage. In that light, there is perhaps something for us to learn from Acton's acknowledgment that the scholar-expert should not abandon the reader "at the point where study passes into action." We can at the very least offer some reflection on what an encounter with the past might bring by way of advice to the "many encounters of life" lying ahead.

In reaching all three of our intended audiences, we are greatly assisted by the pronounced tendency to "demystify" and diversify its subject that has characterized American legal history for a half-century. To some, the field's very title – "legal history" – will conjure merely an arcane preoccupation with obscure terminologies and baffling texts, the doctrines and practices of old (hence defunct) law, of no obvious utility to the outsider whether historian or social scientist or practicing lawyer or just plain citizen. No doubt, legal history has at times given grounds to suppose that such a view of the discipline is generally warranted. But what is interesting in American legal history as currently practiced is just how inappropriate that characterization seems.

To read the encomia that have accumulated over the years, one might suppose that the demise of legal history's obscurity was the single-handed achievement of one man, James Willard Hurst, who on his death in 1997 was described in the *New York Times* as "the dean of American legal historians." Indeed, Hurst himself occasionally suggested the same thing; it was he who came up with the aphorism "snakes in Ireland" to describe legal history in America at the time he began working in the field in the 1930s. Though not an immodest man, it seems clear whom he cast as St. Patrick. Yet the *Times'* description was merited. Hurst's lifework – the unpacking of the changing roles of American law, market, and state from the early nineteenth to the early twentieth centuries – set the agenda of American legal historians from the 1950s well into the 1980s. That agenda was a liberation from narrower and more formalistic preoccupations, largely with the remote origins of contemporary legal doctrine or with the foundations of American constitutionalism, that had characterized the field, such as it was, earlier in the century. Most important, Hurst's work displayed some recognition of the multidimensionality of law in society – as instrument, the hallmark with which he is most associated, but also as value and as power. Hurst, in short, brought legal history into a continuing dialogue with modernity, capitalism, and the liberal state, a dialogue whose rich dividends are obvious in this *History*.

Lawyers have sometimes asked aggressively anachronistic questions of history, like – to use an apocryphal example of Robert Gordon's – "Did the framers of the Constitution confer on the federal government the power to construct an interstate highway system?" Hurstian legal history did not indulge such questions. But Hurstians did demonstrate a gentler anachronism in their restriction of the scope of the subject and their interpretation of it. Famously, for Hurst, American legal history did not begin until the nineteenth century. And when it did begin it showed a certain consistency in cause and effect. As Kermit Hall summarized the view in 1989, "Our legal history reflects back to us generations of pragmatic decision making rather than a quest for ideological purity and consistency. Personal and group interests have always ordered the course of legal development; instrumentalism has been the way of the law."[4] The Hurstian determination to demystify law occasionally reduced it to transparency – a dependent variable of society and economy (particularly economy) tied functionally to social and economic change.

---

[4] Kermit L. Hall, *The Magic Mirror: Law in American History* (New York, 1989), 335.

As a paradigm for the field, Hurstian legal history long since surrendered its dominance. What has replaced it? In two words, astonishing variety. Legal historians are aware that one cannot talk or write about economic or social or political or intellectual history, or indeed much of any kind of history, without immediately entering into realms of definition, prohibition, understanding, practice, and behavior that must imply law to have meaning. Try talking about property in any of those contexts, for example, without implying law. Today's legal historians are deeply engaged across the full range of historical investigation in demonstrating the inextricable salience of law in human affairs. As important, the interests of American historians at large have never been more overtly legal in their implications than now. To take just four popular areas of inquiry in American history – citizenship and civic personality, identity, spatiality, and the etiology of social hierarchy and subordination – it is simply impossible to imagine how one could approach any of these areas historically without engaging with law, legal ideology, legal institutions, legal practices, and legal discourse. Legal historians have been and remain deeply engaged with and influenced by social history, and as that field has drifted closer and closer to cultural history and the historical construction of identity so legal history has moved with it. The interpretive salience of race and ethnicity, of gender and class is as strong in contemporary legal historical practice as in any other realm of history. Add to that the growing influence of legal pluralism in legal history – the migration of the field from a focus on "the law" to a focus on the conditions of existence of "legality" and the competition of many alternative "legalities" – and one finds oneself at work in a field of immense opportunity and few dogmas.

"Astonishing variety" demonstrates vitality, but also suggests the benefits of a judicious collective effort at authoritative summation. The field has developed at an extraordinary rate since the early 1970s, but offers no work that could claim to approach the full range of our understanding of the American legal past.[5] *The Cambridge History of Law in America* addresses both

---

[5] The field has two valuable single-author surveys: Lawrence M. Friedman's *A History of American Law* (New York, 1973; 3rd ed. 2005) and Kermit Hall's *The Magic Mirror*. Neither approaches the range of what is on display here. The field also boasts volumes of cases and commentary, prepared according to the law teaching "case book" model, such as Stephen B. Presser and Jamil S. Zainaldin, *Law and Jurisprudence in American History: Cases and Materials* (St. Paul, MN, 1980; 6th ed. 2006) and Kermit Hall, et al., *American Legal History, Cases and Materials* (New York, 3rd ed., 2003). There also exist edited volumes of commentary and materials that focus on broad subject areas within the discipline of legal history; a preponderance deal with constitutional law, such as Lawrence M. Friedman and Harry N. Scheiber, eds., *American Law and the Constitutional Order: Historical Perspectives* (Cambridge, MA, 1978; enlarged ed. 1988). Valuable in

the vitality of variety and its organizational challenge. Individually, each
chapter in each volume is a comprehensive interrogation of a key issue in a
particular period of American legal history. Each is intended to extend the
substantive and interpretative boundaries of our knowledge of that issue.
The topics they broach range widely – from the design of British colonizing to the design of the successor republic and of its successive nineteenth-
and twentieth-century reincarnations; from legal communications within
empires to communications among nation-states within international law
to a sociology of the "legalization" that enwraps contemporary globalism;
from changes in legal doctrine to litigation trend assessments; from clashes
over law and religion to the intersection of law and popular culture; from
the movement of peoples to the production of subalternship among people
(the indigenous, slaves, dependents of all kinds); and from the discourse
of law to the discourse of rights. Chapters also deal with developments
in specific areas of law and of the legal system – crime and criminal justice, economic and commercial regulation, immigration and citizenship,
technology and environment, military law, family law, welfare law, public
health and medicine, and antitrust.[6]

Individual chapters illustrate the dynamism and immense breadth of
American legal history. Collectively, they neither exhaust its substance nor
impose a new interpretive regimen on the field. Quite the contrary, *The
Cambridge History of Law in America* intentionally calls forth the broad array
of methods and arguments that legal historians have developed. The contents of each volume demonstrate not just that expansion of subject and
method is common to every period of American legal history but also that
as the long-ascendant socio-legal perspective has given way to an increasing
diversity of analytical approaches, new interpretive opportunities are rife
everywhere. Note the influence of regionalism in Volume I and of institutionalism in Volume II. Note the attention paid in Volume III not only to
race and gender but also to sexuality. The *History* shows how legal history

their own right, such volumes are intended as specific-purpose teaching tools and do not
purport to be comprehensive. Finally, there are, of course, particular monographic works
that have proven widely influential for their conceptual acuity, or their capacity to set
a completely new tone in the way the field at large is interpreted. The most influential
have been such studies as James Willard Hurst, *Law and the Conditions of Freedom in
the Nineteenth-Century United States* (Madison, WI, 1956), and Morton J. Horwitz, *The
Transformation of American Law, 1780–1860* (Cambridge, MA, 1977).
[6] Following the tradition of Cambridge histories, each chapter includes only such footnotes
as the author deems necessary to document essential (largely primary) sources. In place
of the dense display of citations beloved of scholarly discourse that Acton's aesthetic
discouraged, each author has written a bibliographic essay that provides a summary of
his or her sources and a guide to scholarly work on the subject.

has entered dialogue with the full array of "histories" pursued within the academy – political, intellectual, social, cultural, economic, business, diplomatic, and military – and with their techniques.

The Cambridge History of Law in America is more than the sum of its parts. The *History*'s conceptual design challenges existing understandings of the field. We divide the American legal past into three distinct eras and devote a complete volume to each one: first *Early America*, then *The Long Nineteenth Century*, and last *The Twentieth Century and After*. The first volume, *Early America*, examines the era from the late sixteenth century through the early nineteenth – from the beginnings of European settlement through the creation and stabilization of the American republic. The second volume, *The Long Nineteenth Century*, begins with the appearance of the United States in the constituted form of a nation-state in 1789; it ends in 1920, in the immediate aftermath of World War I, with the world poised on the edge of the "American Century." The final volume, *The Twentieth Century and After*, concentrates on that American century both at home and abroad and peers into the murk of the twenty-first century. Within each of these broad chronological divisions occurs a much more detailed subdivision that combines an appreciation of chronology with the necessities of topical specialization.

Where appropriate, topics are revisited in successive volumes (crime and criminal justice, domestic relations law, legal thought, and legal education are all examples). Discussion of economic growth and change is ubiquitous, but we accord it no determinative priority. To facilitate comparisons and contrasts within and between eras, sequences of subjects have been arranged in similar order in each volume. Specific topics have been chosen with an eye to their historical significance and their social, institutional, and cultural coherence. They cannot be walled off from each other, so readers will notice substantive overlaps when more than one author fastens on the same issues, often to create distinct interpretations of them. History long since ceased to speak with one voice. In this *History*, readers are invited into a conversation.

Readers will notice that our chronology creates overlaps at the margins of each era. They will also notice that some chapters focus on only particular decades within a specific era[7] or span more than one era.[8] All this is

---

[7] Chronologically specific topics – the American Revolution and the creation of the republic in Volume I, the Civil War in Volume II, the New Deal era in Volume III – are treated as such. Chapters on the legal profession in Volumes II and III divide its development at the Civil War, as do those, in Volume II, on the state and on industrial organization.

[8] Volume II's chapter on the military deals with both the nineteenth and twentieth centuries, as do Volume III's chapters on agriculture and the state and on law and the environment. The latter chapter, indeed, also gestures toward the colonial period.

intentional. Historians construct history by placing subjects in relation to each other within the continuum of historical time. Historians manipulate time by creating periods to organize the placement of subjects. Thus, when historians say that a subject has been "historicized," they mean it has been located in what they consider its appropriate historical-temporal context or period. Slicing and dicing time in this fashion is crucial to the historian's objective of rendering past action coherent and comprehensible, but necessarily it has a certain arbitrariness. No matter how familiar – the colonial period, the Gilded Age, the Progressive period, and so forth – no historical period is a natural division: all are constructs. Hence we construct three "eras" in the interests of organizational coherence, but our overlaps and the distinct chronologies chosen by certain of our authors allow us to recognize different temporalities at work.

That said, the tripartite division of these volumes is intended to provide a new overall conceptual schema for American legal history, one that is broad and accommodating but that locates legal history in the contours of American history at large. Maitland never forgot that, at bottom, just as religious history is history not theology, legal history is history not law. Notwithstanding law's normative and prescriptive authority in "our" culture, it is a phenomenon for historical inquiry, not the source of an agenda. And so we take our cue, broadly, from American history. If it is anything, American history is the history of the colonization and settlement of the North American mainland, it is the history of the creation and expansion of an American nation-state, and it is the history of that state's place in and influence on the world at large. The contents and the organization of *The Cambridge History of Law in America* speak to how law became king in this America and of the multitudinous empire of people and possibilities over which that king reigned. Thus we address ourselves to the endless ramifications, across more than four centuries, of the meaning of Tom Paine's exclamation in 1776.

The Cambridge History of Law in America could not have been produced without the support and commitment of the American Bar Foundation, Cambridge University Press, and our cadre of authors. We thank them all.

The American Bar Foundation housed the project and, together with the Press, funded it. The Foundation was there at the creation: it helped initiate the project by sponsoring a two-day meeting of an ad hoc editorial consulting group in January 2000. Members of that group (Laura Edwards, Tony Freyer, Robert Gordon, Bruce H. Mann, William Novak, Stephen Siegel, Barbara Young Welke, and Victoria Saker Woeste) patiently debated the editors' initial thoughts on the conceptual and intellectual direction that the *History* should follow and helped identify potential contributors. Since then, the project has benefited from the support of two ABF directors, Bryant Garth and his successor Robert Nelson, and the sustained and enthusiastic interest of the Foundation's Board of Directors during the tenure of four Board presidents: Jacqueline Allee, M. Peter Moser, the late Robert Hetlage, and David Tang. We owe a particular debt of gratitude to Robert MacCrate for his early support and encouragement. As all this suggests, the American Bar Foundation's role in the production of *The Cambridge History of Law in America* has been of decisive importance. The part the Foundation has played underlines its standing as the preeminent research center for the study of law and society in the United States and its long tradition of support for the development of American legal history.

Cambridge University Press has, of course, been central to the project throughout. We are grateful to the syndics for their encouragement and to Frank Smith and his staff in New York for their assistance and support. Frank first suggested the project in 1996. He continued to suggest it for three years until we finally succumbed. During the years the *History* has been in development, Frank has accumulated one responsibility after another at the Press. Once we rubbed shoulders with the Executive Editor for Social Sciences. Now we address our pleas to the Editorial Director for Academic Books. But Frank will always be a history editor at heart, and he has maintained a strong interest in this *History*, always available with sage advice as the project rolled relentlessly onward. He helped the editors understand the intellectual ambitions of a Cambridge history. Those who have had the privilege of working with Frank Smith will know how important his advice and friendship have been to us throughout.

Finally, the editors want to thank the authors of the chapters in these volumes. A project like this is not to every author's taste – some took to it more easily than others. But together the sixty authors who joined us to write the *History* have done a magnificent job, and we are deeply grateful to every one. From the beginning our goal was not only to recruit as participants those whom all would identify as leading figures of our field but also to include those who, we were confident, would be leading figures of its next generation. We are delighted that so many of each were willing. We acknowledge also those who were unable for one reason or another to see an initial commitment through to the end: their efforts, too, helped us define and establish the project. And obviously, we owe a particular debt to those others who came later to take the places of the fallen.

To oversee a project in which so many people have at one time or another been involved has seemed on occasion like being the mayors of a village. People arrive and (much less frequently, thank goodness) depart. Those who settle in for the duration become a community of friends and neighbors. Over time, one learns much from one's friends and neighbors about the joys and vicissitudes of life. One learns who (and whose family) may be ailing, and who is well. One learns of hurts and difficulties; one revels in successes. And one may learn, as we did so sadly in August 2006, of an untimely death. Notwithstanding the demands of his immensely successful career in academic administration, our colleague Kermit Hall never laid down his historian's pen and was an enthusiastic participant in this project. He died suddenly and unexpectedly. His contributions to the field have been great, and he is greatly missed.

Throughout, the many authors in this project have responded courteously to our editorial advice. They have reacted with grace and occasional humor to our endless demands that they meet their deadlines. Sometimes they even sent their manuscripts too. Most important, they have striven to achieve what we asked of them – the general goals of a Cambridge history and the specific goals of *this* history, as we have described them in this preface. Their achievements are evident in the pages of each volume. In an individualistic intellectual culture, the scholarship on display here demonstrates the possibilities inherent in a collective intellectual enterprise. In the end, of course, the editors, not the authors, are responsible for the contents of these volumes. Yet, it is the authors who have given the *History* its meaning and significance.

Michael Grossberg
Christopher Tomlins

LAW AND THE STATE, 1920–2000: INSTITUTIONAL GROWTH AND STRUCTURAL CHANGE

DANIEL R. ERNST

Belief that the United States occupies an exceptional place in world history has been a persistent element of the American creed. The founding of the nation was a new birth of freedom, Americans have been taught; it delivered them from the class conflict and ideological strife that have plagued the rest of the modern world. Not infrequently, seekers of the ultimate source of the United States' exceptionalism have settled on the peculiarly fragmented nature of its government. The nation was born in a revolt against the modern state. In Europe, standing armies, centralized taxation, juryless courts, and national bureaucracies loyal to a distant sovereign were the hallmarks of the proudest monarchies. To Revolutionary America, they were evidence of tyrannous intent, "submitted to a candid world." To prevent such abominations from reappearing in the new nation, Americans shattered sovereignty into legislative, executive, and judicial fragments and embedded them in their states' written constitutions. The Federal Constitution of 1787 went further, for it also divided sovereignty between the national government and the states. The result, as John Quincy Adams observed, was "the most complicated government on the face of the globe."[1]

The new nation had plenty of law and plenty of local governments ready, willing, and able to promote private economic endeavor with grants of public land and public money. What the United States lacked, however, was centralized administration, a counterpart to the royal bureaucracies of Europe capable of consistently implementing national policies. The central government had to entrust the enforcement of an order to "agents over whom it frequently has no control, and whom it cannot perpetually direct," explained Alexis de Tocqueville. Tocqueville approved of such an arrangement for a democracy, because it prevented a tyrannous majority from imposing its will on the nation. If the American state ever became as

---

[1] John Quincy Adams, *The Jubilee of the Constitution* (New York, 1839), 115.

wieldy as its European counterparts, he warned, "freedom would soon be banished from the New World."[2]

Centralized administration finally came to the United States in the twentieth century in three waves of state-building. Each was consolidated into a durable political "regime," an amalgam of institutions, elites, social forces, and ideas that, for a time, established fundamental set of assumptions about politics for all major political actors. Each political regime emerged when war, other national emergency, or a period of unusual social ferment created a demand for a new bureaucracy or the transformation of an existing one. These administrative responses followed no master plan. The new or reformed administrative bodies were hastily assembled from whatever form of governance seemed most promising in the midst of political battles in a deeply divided state.

Administration was employed domestically in five different ways. First, it was used to conduct command-and-control regulation through administrative orders that told social or economic actors how to behave. Second, it was employed in the work of social insurance, the public provision of compensation for the misfortunes that regularly beset the members of industrial societies. Third, it was used to deploy the power of the state to collect tariffs, impose taxes, and issue public debt. Not infrequently, the ends sought were social or economic, as well as fiscal. Fourth, administration was used in the conduct of state capitalism – the public creation of economic infrastructure or the conferral of grants, loans, and other public benefits to encourage private individuals to create the infrastructure themselves. Finally, new administrative structures were created to assist or supplant the courts in the work of social police, the preservation of domestic tranquility.

Once each state-building moment passed, a period of consolidation ensued, during which older institutions, elites, and socially dominant groups reasserted themselves until an accommodation of the old and new was reached. Here, we begin with the consolidation of the 1920s, in which the new bureaucracies managed to acquire a subordinate place within a state dominated by courts and political parties. Centralized administration came into its own in a second cycle of state-building and consolidation, which commenced in the New Deal, fully emerged during World War II, and persisted well into the Cold War. We conclude with a third cycle, set off by the new "public interest" politics of the 1960s and 1970s and brought to a halt by a series of contractions in the 1980s and 1990s.

Tocqueville's warning notwithstanding, administration won a place in the American polity, but only on terms fixed by lawyers – not only those appointed to the judiciary or government legal staffs but also those in private

---

[2] Alexis de Tocqueville, *Democracy in America*, trans. Henry Reeve (London, 1862), 319–20.

law firms, corporate law departments, and public interest groups. Throughout the twentieth century, the lawyers, their clients, and their political allies demanded that bureaucrats respect an ancient ideal, that of "a government of laws and not of men." Each consolidation had its own version of the ideal, which located the sources of the "laws" that constrained the "men" (and women) of government in different entities: the bench, the needs of modern society, or the welfare of a nation of consumers. In each consolidation, political actors dominant in an earlier political regime invoked the "supremacy of law" ideal to constrain an administrative innovation that placed them at a disadvantage. But only in the last of the twentieth century's three cycles did consolidation attempt a general contraction of the administrative state. Significantly, this was the only one of the twentieth century's consolidations in which economists, the dominant profession of the market, effectively rivaled lawyers, the dominant profession of the state, as articulators of public policy.

I. ADMINISTRATION UNDER COURTS AND PARTIES

Our chronological point of departure, 1920, came just after the crest of the wave of state-building that had occurred during the Progressive era. That wave emerged at the state and local level in the 1890s and reached the federal government by World War I. During the 1920s, most of the new bureaucracies struggled to become autonomous parts of the American state. On one side they were challenged by judges, who doubted the bureaucrats' expertise and commitment to due process. On another, they faced demands for appointments and policies that promoted the interests of the nation's bottom-up, patronage-oriented political parties. Administration, then, was contained by older, more familiar political structures; in the 1920s the American state still bore more than a passing resemblance to the one Tocqueville knew.

In 1920, price-and-entry regulation by independent commission, created outside the regular departments of the executive branch, was the most salient feature of the American administrative state. Railroad commissions had been the first to arrive on the scene, established by the states after the Civil War and at the federal level, in the guise of the Interstate Commerce Commission (ICC), in 1887. Commissions limited entry into a regulated industry to firms with the requisite know-how and financial backing. They also set the rates businesses could charge for their goods and services and imposed a host of other rules. Railroad commissions, for example, developed and enforced detailed safety regulations, ordered companies to share freight cars, and decreed when railroads might abandon service to particular stations.

At the federal level, the ICC was joined in 1913 by the Federal Reserve Board, which governed the banking industry, and in 1914 by the Federal Trade Commission (FTC), which policed unfair business practices. In the states, the focus of regulation shifted away from intercity railroads (which became the ICC's exclusive preserve) to other matters. In Texas, for example, the "Railroad Commission" regulated the increasingly important oil and gas industry. More common was a turn to the regulation of municipal utilities, such as electricity, water, natural gas, streetcars, and subways. New York and Wisconsin created the first public utilities commissions (PUCs) in 1907. Seven years later all but three states had at least one PUC.

The bellwether program of social insurance, in the United States as elsewhere, was workers' compensation, a system of fixed payments to the victims of workplace injuries and their dependents. Between 1911 and 1920 forty-two American states enacted compensation schemes for industrial accidents; two more followed in the 1920s. After several false starts, federal commissions for harbor workers and the residents of the District of Columbia were created in 1927 and 1928.

American reformers argued that the United States ought to follow other industrial nations by extending the social insurance concept to cover life's other misfortunes, such as old age, unemployment, and illness. An indigenous precedent existed in pensions for Civil War veterans and their dependents, but it was a somewhat dubious one, as a series of Republican administrations had put the system to partisan use. Only in the category of "mothers' pensions" did the United States lead the world. These quite meager payments were intended to keep mothers who lacked able-bodied husbands in the home, where they could look after their children. Forty states had some form of mothers' pensions by the end of 1920. Four other states and the District of Columbia followed suit in the next decade.

The most important administrative innovations in the area of fiscal management involved taxation. State and local governments had long relied on property taxation to finance their activities, but by the end of the nineteenth century the manipulation of assessments by political machines had become a scandal. One Progressive reform was to shift responsibility from local officials to statewide "equalization boards." Another was to shift to new forms of taxation that were more difficult to use to reward political friends and punish political enemies. Income taxation soon became the reformers' tax of choice. Wisconsin implemented an income tax in 1911 as part of a broad campaign of Progressive reform. After spreading to other states, income taxes would account for 22 percent of all state revenue in 1922.

On the federal level, the ratification of the Sixteenth Amendment in 1913 was quickly followed by the adoption of a modest income tax, covering only 2 percent of the American workforce and intended as a first step in reducing federal reliance on tariffs. Coverage expanded with the United States' entry into World War I, and a new tax on profits was instituted. The staff of the Bureau of Internal Revenue (the predecessor of the Internal Revenue Service) increased from 4,000 in 1913 to 15,800 in 1920. Prominent economists and Wall Street lawyers were appointed to high positions in the Treasury Department, where they formed a tax policy group of unprecedented ability and sophistication. Although some of the wartime innovations – such as the excess profits tax – did not survive the Republicans' return to power in 1921, World War I remained an object lesson in how to use federal taxes to make economic and even social policy.

In the field of state capitalism, most conferrals of public benefits to promote economic development still followed the nineteenth-century practice of distributing grants outright, with few strings attached. Such grants might have become vehicles of planning had recipients been required to follow specific policies (such as the preservation of the environment) and some administrative body been given the job of making sure that they did. But the dominant policy in the distribution of public largess had not been planning, but rather what the legal historian Willard Hurst called "the release of individual creative energy."[3] That policy persisted into the 1920s.

More creative use of administration was evident in the construction and maintenance of public infrastructure. Road-building had long been the work of local governments, but in 1916 Washington stepped in with a "grant-in-aid" program. Public ownership of other forms of transportation was rarer, although the railroad industry was briefly nationalized during World War I and a permanent, government-owned "merchant marine" was created when transatlantic shipping became too risky for private carriers. State ownership of other public utilities was also limited. Revelations of political corruption brought an end to a late-nineteenth-century trend toward the creation of city-owned water, gas, and streetcar companies. Thereafter, urban voters preferred private ownership coupled with regulation by a statewide public utility commission. At the federal level, war again provided the impetus for an exceptional case of state ownership. In 1916 Woodrow Wilson approved the development of hydroelectric power at a government-owned dam across the Tennessee River at Muscle Shoals, Alabama, for use in the production of explosives and fertilizer. Completed in 1925, the facility's full potential was not realized until a staunch advocate of public power, Franklin Delano Roosevelt, won the presidency.

In the field of social police, administrators captured relatively little ground from the courts, which invoked the powerful constitutional

[3] James Willard Hurst, *Law and the Conditions of Freedom in the Nineteenth-Century United States* (Madison, WI, 1967), 6.

tradition that held their procedures to be the surest defender of the rights
and liberties of the subject. The settlement of labor disputes was a case
in point. Many states had created boards for the voluntary mediation and
arbitration of labor disputes after the Civil War, and a federal system for
arbitrating railway labor disputes was established after the Pullman boycott
of 1894. During World War I, the U.S. Army insisted on minimum labor
standards in its contracts for uniforms, and the federal government created
several commissions and boards to mediate labor disputes. The most powerful of these agencies, the National War Labor Board (NWLB), brought
labor leaders and businessmen together under the joint chairmanship of
a former president (William Howard Taft) and a nationally known labor
lawyer (Frank Walsh). But the state boards had no power to compel workers
or employers to accept their recommendations, and the NWLB was abolished in 1919. Criminal prosecutions and court injunctions remained the
dominant mode of policing labor disputes until the New Deal.

Only in the field of immigration, where the objects of social policing
were not citizens, did administration make major inroads on the judiciary. For most of the nineteenth century, federal courts had directed the
exclusion of aliens. Even Chinese immigrants, singled out for especially
unfavorable treatment in 1882, could remove their cases from the purview
of customs officials into federal courts. In 1891, however, Congress established a Bureau of Immigration and subsequently empowered it to decide
the citizenship status of all immigrants. The U.S. Supreme Court put some
of the Bureau's determinations beyond judicial review in the *Ju Toy* decision of 1905. Equally deferential decisions would help keep immigration
an area of extraordinary administrative discretion throughout the twentieth
century.

The administrators of the Progressive state were thus a miscellany of
officials, scattered across the social and economic landscape, who answered
to no single authority, tyrannous or otherwise. Still, their mere presence
was hard for lawyers to square with the Tocquevillean notion that Americans were exceptionally free from governmental control. They turned to an
Englishman, Albert Venn Dicey, for help. In his *Introduction to the Study of
the Law of the Constitution* (1885), Dicey contrasted the "rule of law" in common law countries with the "administrative law" that prevailed in France
and other civil law jurisdictions on the European continent. In common law
countries, Dicey argued, citizens could contest the actions of administrators
in the "ordinary courts of the land" – that is, in courts of general jurisdiction whose main work was the resolution of the disputes of private parties.
In France and elsewhere, citizens could only appeal to specialized courts
embedded in the very bureaucracies whose orders they contested. Translated

into an American idiom, Dicey taught that American could have both bureaucracy and a "government of laws," so long as administrators' actions could be challenged in courts presided over by common law judges.

Throughout the twentieth century, American judges routinely pledged their fidelity to Dicey's notion of the rule of law. Just as routinely, they departed from it in practice. One striking example involved the non-delegation doctrine, the principle that lawmaking power vested in a legislature might not be delegated to any other public institution or official. Applied strictly, the doctrine would have kept any number of administrative agencies from promulgating rules and regulations in support of their statutory missions. In a series of decisions between 1904 and 1928, however, the U.S. Supreme Court upheld sweeping delegations by employing the fiction that administrative officials were merely executing the clearly defined will of Congress. So long as a statute embodied an "intelligible principle," the Court decided, the non-delegation doctrine was satisfied. Vague standards such as the ICC's charge to set "just and reasonable" rates or the Federal Radio Commission's mandate to issue licenses in accordance with the "public interest, convenience, and necessity" easily passed constitutional scrutiny.

Courts also deferred to administrators by refusing to make their own determinations of the facts supporting administrative rulings. In 1897 the U.S. Supreme Court had crippled the ICC by permitting railroads to introduce new evidence in federal court when contesting the commission's request for an injunction. By the 1920s judges had rejected the "de novo review" of most facts and upheld agencies' findings whenever backed by substantial evidence in the record, even though the judges themselves would have decided the matter differently if free to do so. To be sure, de novo review was not abandoned totally. In *Crowell v. Benson* (1932), for example, Chief Justice Charles Evans Hughes insisted that federal courts make their own determination of the facts "upon which the enforcement of the constitutional rights of the citizen depend."[4] But other judges did not apply Hughes's "constitutional fact" doctrine widely, and soon commentators were complaining that the judiciary had abdicated in favor of the ICC, public utility commissions, and workers' compensation commissions.

Many other forms of administration were immune from even "substantial evidence" review on the ground that they dispensed "privileges" rather than determined "rights." For example, unless statutes provided otherwise, courts could not interfere with administrators as they distributed pensions, deported aliens, sold public land, awarded government contracts and loans,

---

[4] *Crowell v. Benson*, 285 U.S. 22, 56 (1932).

parceled out grants-in-aid to the states, employed public workers, or decided which periodicals were eligible for the Post Office's low-cost, "second-class" mailing privilege.

Some observers attributed the judges' infidelity to Dicey's ideal to a failure of will when confronting an avalanche of administrative decisions. Others maintained that they were simply recognizing obvious and inherent differences between adjudication and administration. The judges who staffed Dicey's "ordinary courts" were of necessity generalists. Administrators, in contrast, developed and applied the specialized expertise that modern times demanded. Courts were passive bodies that acted only when some party brought disputes before them; administrators could conduct investigations on their own initiative. Courts issued final decrees in discrete cases; administrators could continuously review prior decisions and engaged in rulemaking based on knowledge acquired by their own staffs.

Judges deferred to administrators with a reputation for employing their expertise and procedural flexibility competently and in the public interest. If they suspected that decisions were made for personal gain or to reward a political constituency, they usually found a way to avenge the rule of law. In the 1920s, the varying treatment that federal judges accorded agencies they trusted and those they did not can be seen by contrasting the ICC and the FTC. Federal judges were extremely deferential to the ICC and placed some of its "negative orders" (decisions not to proceed against the subject of a complaint) beyond judicial review. In contrast, they ran roughshod over the FTC. The U.S. Supreme Court insisted that federal judges make their own determination of what constituted "unfair methods of competition." When intermediate federal courts reversed the FTC's findings of facts, the Supreme Court usually affirmed, even though Congress had directed that the commission's determinations be considered "conclusive."

The difference in judicial treatment turned on the great disparity in the professionalism of the two agencies' staffs and the extent to which their procedures tracked those of the courts. The ICC had a tradition of non-partisanship dating from the appointment of its first chairman, the great Michigan judge Thomas Cooley. It had able economists and secretaries, and in 1916 its large legal staff was brought within the federal civil service. In most respects, its procedures were familiar to any courtroom lawyer, and its orders were backed up with published opinions that compared favorably with those of the courts. The FTC was another matter. From the start it was plagued by weak commissioners, selected more for their service to their party than their knowledge of business affairs. From 1925 onward, its chairman was William E. Humphrey, an outrageously partisan and pro-business Republican. Neither the commissioners nor their politically appointed lawyers paid any attention to the FTC's small economic staff, and the commissioners gave little indication of the reasoning behind their decisions. Senators roamed the halls at will in search of commissioners to lobby.

At the end of the 1920s, then, administration was a familiar but subordinate feature of the American state. The speed and flexibility that made it an attractive alternative to courts and legislatures also attracted the suspicions of a jealous judiciary and the unwanted attention of politicians seeking new ways to reward contributors and constituents. Many American bureaucracies had acquired administrative "capacity" – the ability to solve problems and achieve ends – but few enjoyed express judicial or legislative recognition of their "autonomy" – the ability to formulate goals and policies independently of private interests, political parties, and other arms of the state. That would be forthcoming only after an unprecedented economic crisis, a second world war, and a recasting of administrative procedure in ways that allowed lawyers greater leverage within the administrative process itself.

II. STORM OVER THE NEW DEAL

The legal history of the American administrative state did not deviate from the path of uncoordinated, sporadic growth on ground left unoccupied by courts and party-dominated legislatures until an economic catastrophe of unprecedented proportions hit the nation at the end of the 1920s. The stock market crash of 1929 and the ensuing downward spiral of business activity left nearly a quarter of the American workforce unemployed and elicited a wide range of proposals from reformers, universities, civic associations, private foundations, and government officials. The Republican president Herbert Hoover was cautious in sampling these wares, but his Democratic successor enthusiastically experimented with one innovative use of administration after another. Typically, new "emergency" or "alphabet" agencies were created as independent commissions to implement the proposals. The most successful agencies acquired the funds, staff, and procedures to formulate policies without returning to Congress and to obtain compliance with its orders with only occasional resorts to the courts.

Two vast schemes of command-and-control regulation created during the first months (the First Hundred Days) of Franklin Roosevelt's presidency showed how vital "state autonomy" was for a new agency. The National Recovery Administration (NRA) was created to reduce the overproduction of goods that was the most puzzling phase of the depression. In 1933 no profession, academic discipline, or arm of the state had the detailed knowledge of the hundreds of industries that the NRA regulated, so its administrators turned the job of drafting regulations over to "code authorities" made up of leading businessmen. In theory, the NRA's staff was to review their work, but the staff lacked the expertise and authority to second-guess the industrial representatives. By early 1935 most observers were convinced that the legislative power Congress had delegated to a supposedly independent agency was actually being exercised by the industrialists themselves. In contrast, the principal agricultural agency of the First Hundred Days, the Agricultural Adjustment Administration (AAA), was more successful in its quest for autonomy. It attacked the problem of excess supply by paying farmers to cut back on their production of wheat, corn, cotton, tobacco, rice, hogs, and milk, with the money coming from a tax on the processors of these items. Local committees of farmers were to assist in deciding whose acreage was to be reduced and how subsidies were to be distributed, but they did so under the direction of the large and well-established extension service of the U.S. Department of Agriculture and with the assistance of experts in the country's many land-grant universities.

Similar success was enjoyed by the Securities and Exchange Commission (SEC), created in 1934 after a year's experience with the regulation of the issuance of stocks and bonds by the FTC. The Securities and Exchange Commission bore a superficial resemblance to the NRA in that it asked stock dealers and exchanges to codify their best practices and relied on accountants to develop and enforce the intricate reporting requirements for each new issue of stocks and bonds. But the SEC was no rubber stamp: unusually able lawyers had drafted its organic act and served as commissioners or members of its legal staff. The agency retained a reputation for efficiency and expertise long after other New Deal agencies had slipped into quiescence. The SEC also benefited from the unusual sensitivity of securities markets to publicity. The issuance of an administrative "stop order," which blocked an offering until some discrepancy in a company's registration statement was resolved, could scare off investors. The damage was done long before the order could be challenged in court.

The New Deal also produced a landmark in the history of social insurance and social provision, the Social Security Act of 1935. One part of the statute federalized the states' mothers' pensions, but, at the insistence of Southern Democrats, it left broad discretion to state officials. In the South, officials were careful not to let these "welfare" payments upset the domination of whites. Everywhere, recipients had to submit to intrusive, stigmatizing guidelines. The statute's provisions for wage earners, such as unemployment insurance and old age insurance, were quite different. These "social security" payments were funded by the contributions of workers and their employers and were treated as unconditional entitlements. Old age pensions were exclusively administered by a federal Social Security Board; unemployment payments were distributed under strict guidelines set by federal officials.

State capitalism took a great leap forward during the New Deal. The Tennessee Valley Authority (TVA) was created in the first days of the Roosevelt presidency to use the cheap electricity generated at Muscle Shoals to promote economic development in an impoverished region. The Bonneville Power Administration, created in 1937, brought the federal generation of electric power to the Pacific Northwest. More generally, New Dealers lent on a massive scale to corporations, cooperatives, homeowners, consumers, and localities. The Reconstruction Finance Corporation was created during Hoover's administration to serve as a safety net for faltering banks. Under FDR, it became a vast and diversified lender to private business and other New Deal agencies. Smaller, more specialized programs proliferated to guarantee farm and home loans, consumer purchases of electrical appliances and equipment, rural electrical cooperatives, and municipal utilities.

Business leaders cooperated in such largess-distributing programs, but they fiercely resisted a New Deal innovation in the field of social police, the National Labor Relations Board (NLRB). A series of labor boards had been created under the NRA in response to union organizing drives in such mass production industries as electrical products and automobiles. After the NRA was declared unconstitutional, Congress created the NLRB in 1935 as a quasi-judicial, independent commission and charged it with outlawing "unfair labor practices," much as the FTC had been given the job of punishing "unfair trade practices." The NLRB's legal staff was more able than the FTC's, and many of its lawyers passionately believed in the cause of organized labor. Although employers denounced the NLRB as a radical transgression of American liberty, its powers were quite modest when compared with systems of labor governance elsewhere in the industrial world. Rather than produce detailed schedules of wages and work rules, for example, the New Deal left the terms of labor contracts to the employers and the unions themselves. Neither the NLRB nor various bodies created within the Department of Labor to oversee government contracts and enforce minimum labor standards ever developed into the national "employment courts" commonly found in other industrial countries.

The New Deal's experiments in administration may have seemed modest when compared with the centralized bureaucracies of European nations, but they were quite enough to set off a fierce debate over whether bureaucracy was compatible with the rule of law. Most of the major New Deal agencies were greeted with a barrage of injunctions challenging their constitutionality. In one eight-month period alone, the NLRB's lawyers confronted more than eighty suits inspired by a model brief prepared by a committee of lawyers affiliated with the corporate-financed American Liberty League. Such campaigns could not stop the spread of administration, but they did succeed in formalizing the hearings in which administrators passed judgment on legally protected rights. In the late 1930s, Congress increasingly showed interest in administrative reform as a way of keeping FDR from converting the alphabet agencies into an independent political base.

From the vantage point of the U.S. Supreme Court's decisions in 1935 and 1936, one would not have predicted the survival of much of the New Deal. In January 1935 prohibition of "hot oil" shipments (excess petroleum shipped across state lines) became the first major New Deal policy to fall, on the surprising ground that it violated the non-delegation doctrine. In May the U.S. Supreme Court struck down the NRA as an unconstitutional delegation of legislative power and an intrusion of the federal government into matters pertaining to the states. In January 1936, the Court declared that the AAA's tax on food processors could not be squared with the Constitution's requirement that expenditures promote "the general welfare." In May 1936 it struck down an NRA-like scheme to promote collective bargaining and fix prices in the coal industry. The TVA survived the Court's scrutiny, but otherwise the New Deal's prospects looked bleak at the end of the 1935–36 term.

Bleak, but not hopeless. The NRA and coal cases involved de facto delegations of legislative power to business groups with only modest review by public officials. Better crafted delegations to stronger agencies might well survive judicial review. The AAA had an impressive administrative staff, and the constitutional infirmity the Court identified was easily corrected by paying for crop reduction out of the general revenues of the federal government. Still, President Roosevelt was not content to hope for more favorable decisions from the Supreme Court as then constituted. Emboldened by his landslide reelection, he announced in early February 1937 a plan to appoint additional justices to the Supreme Court.

What influence the "Court-packing" plan had on the justices before its defeat in the summer of 1937 is difficult to gauge. The justices were already showing signs of greater tolerance for the alphabet agencies before the plan was announced. In December 1936, for example, a majority passed up chances to attack the SEC's power to restructure public utilities and another New Deal agency's funding of municipal power plants. More dramatic was the justices' upholding of the NLRB and the Social Security Act just months after the Court-packing plan became public. The Supreme Court upheld a reconstituted AAA in 1938, a new coal commission in 1940, and the federal minimum wage in 1941.

As the constitutional barricades fell, those who sought to restrain the federal agencies fell back on administrative law. In three cases decided in the spring of 1936, the U.S. Supreme Court seemed to reaffirm its fidelity to Dicey's notion of the rule of law. In the *Jones* decision, Justice George Sutherland denounced the SEC's refusal to let a would-be issuer of securities withdraw his registration after a stop order proceeding had commenced. In *St. Joseph Stock Yards*, Chief Justice Hughes extended his "constitutional fact" doctrine to the question of whether rates fixed by regulators were confiscatory. And in the *Morgan* case, Hughes required the U.S. Department of Agriculture to follow procedures "akin to that of a judge" when fixing rates for livestock dealers.[5]

Despite these harbingers, the anticipated Dicey revival never arrived. Too many social and economic groups counted on administration to subject the normal run of its actions to what FDR called "the stately rituals of the courts." What gained ground instead was an alternate understanding of the rule of law that provided a rationale for the growth of bureaucratic autonomy during the New Deal. It held that law was not a set of abstract, general principles, best divined by judges, but rather a set of procedures and processes that permitted all kinds of state actors to identify and articulate a socially functional result or policy. In effect, the government of laws was to become a government of social rationality. Judges still held a privileged position under the new dispensation, but they were to be more respectful of the competence of other institutions of the state. They were not to insist on their own understanding of the public good, but to ensure that other public officials exercised their power in good faith through procedures that were likely to produce socially optimal results. James Landis, dean of the Harvard Law School, magisterially reassured readers of his lectures on *The Administrative Process* that the new approach did not threaten "our ideal of the 'supremacy of law.'" Rather, it raised the ideal "to new heights where the great judge, like the conductor of a many tongued symphony ... makes known through the voice of many instruments the vision that has been given him of man's destiny upon this earth."[6]

Beginning in his second term, FDR's nominations ensured that a majority of the Supreme Court justices considered courts and agencies to be "collaborative instrumentalities of justice" – as Landis's mentor, Justice Felix Frankfurter, put it in a 1941. Federal judges insisted that agencies give the individuals and groups whose rights were directly affected by their decisions an opportunity to be heard. Whenever agencies resorted to formal adjudication, courts tended to measure their hearings against the benchmark of judicial proceedings. Most agencies proactively "judicialized"

[5] *Jones v. SEC*, 298 U.S. 1 (1936); *St. Joseph Stock Yards Co. v. United States*, 298 U.S. 38 (1936); *Morgan v. United States*, 298 U.S. 468, 481 (1936).
[6] James M. Landis, *The Administrative Process* (New Haven, 1938), 155.

their formal adjudications to avoid the courts' rebukes. Wherever this was done, lawyers and their clients acquired greater leverage over the agency's decision-making process.

The judicialization of agencies' formal procedures led administrators to develop informal ways of obtaining compliance. For example, officials at the Bureau of Internal Revenue settled most tax disputes through correspondence and conferences. If the members of the Federal Communications Commission (FCC) were scandalized by one of Mae West's double entendres, they were more likely to use a speech or press release to caution broadcasters than a lengthy revocation hearing. SEC lawyers found that a simple "deficiency letter" brought corporations to heel just by threatening the adverse publicity of a stop order proceeding. Formal adjudications were only the tip of the iceberg; informal action, the great mass below the waterline.

With the courts proving an unreliable ally, critics of the administrative process turned to Congress, where a coalition of Republicans and anti-administration Democrats had been alarmed by the Court-packing plan and FDR's attempt to purge his Congressional rivals in the Democratic primaries of 1938 and looked for ways to check the growing power of the alphabet agencies. The Walter-Logan bill, drafted by a committee of the American Bar Association, won increasing support after its introduction in January 1939. The bill sought to curb what Roscoe Pound, the former dean of the Harvard Law School, called "administrative absolutism" in three ways. First, it would mandate an "internal" separation of powers by providing for appeals of formal adjudications to independent review boards established within each commission or department. Second, it would enact a new standard for reviewing agencies' fact finding to promote more aggressive judicial oversight. Finally, it would permit the review of "any affirmative or negative decision, order, or act in specific controversies which determines the issues therein involved" – an ambiguous provision, but one that might subject even informal actions to judicial scrutiny.

Congress passed the Walter-Logan bill in 1940, but it did not do so out of a principled commitment to Dicey's rule of law. Its exemption of most agencies created before the New Deal suggested that its main goal was to deny FDR the administrative patronage he needed to build a liberal political party centered on the presidency. FDR's veto of the bill in December 1940 created a legislative stalemate that persisted for the duration of the war. In that interval, administration proved itself by helping convert the struggling prewar economy into an awesome engine of war production and economic growth. In the process, the New Deal political regime was consolidated. Programs of state capitalism that rewarded capitalists for overseeing the war machine became an inextricable part of American governance; those that targeted the persistently unemployed or regarded the long-term needs of the nation were discarded. When Congress returned to the subject of federal administrative procedure after the war, it showed more interest in bolstering the rule of lawyers within the administrative process than the rule of law through the courts.

III. WAR AND THE SHADOW OF WAR

The United States met the exigencies of World War II and the Cold War that followed with a massive expansion of the federal bureaucracy and an updating of administrative techniques pioneered during the New Deal. Civilian employment in the federal government jumped from just over 1 million civilian employees in 1940 to just under 4 million in 1945. War regulations swelled the *Federal Register* from 5,307 pages in 1940 to 17,339 pages in 1943. Not all parts of the New Deal's administrative legacy were deemed serviceable for the war and postwar states, however. Agencies charged with breaking up industries, economic planning, or the redistribution of wealth were cabined in or abolished; those that promoted growth through the distribution of government largess or the manipulation of the public finance flourished.

To be sure, a series of war agencies brought command-and-control regulation to the entire economy. The War Production Board (WPB) allocated resources through a complicated system of allowances and priorities. The Office of Price Administration (OPA) fixed retail prices, controlled rents, and ultimately rationed more than 90 percent of consumer goods, including food, gasoline, and clothing. The War Labor Board (WLB) administered a freeze on wages, and the War Food Administration directed agricultural production with procedures developed by the AAA.

But all these activities were expressly temporary and relied heavily on the cooperation of private actors. Advocates of industrial planning and wealth redistribution survived in a few agencies (notably the OPA), but as the war proceeded they became an increasingly embattled minority within the federal bureaucracy. A conservative Congressional majority dismantled the New Deal's most ambitious planning body, the National Resource Planning Board, in 1943, and Congressional committees repeatedly harried the "draft dodgers" of the OPA. Military officials acquired the upper hand in directing the war economy, and in civilian agencies leadership passed to "dollar-a-year" men who took Washington jobs with no thought of a permanent career in public service.

The expansion of state capitalism, in the guise of public contracts and loans, was even more impressive. From the summer of 1940 through the fall of 1944, the federal government awarded $175 billion in war contracts, two-thirds of which went to the nation's 100 largest corporations. At first, military and civilian procurement bureaus lacked the staff and expertise to gather data on contractors' costs, profits, finances, and subcontracting. Speed of delivery, not low prices or enlightened social policies, was the priority. In time, the WPB, Army, and Navy created cost-analysis sections and legal divisions to draft contracts, renegotiate prices when they resulted in excessive profits, and punish breaches of contractual terms. Businessmen who objected could not go straight to the courts, but had to start with boards of contract appeals created within each military branch. The lessons of wartime procurement would generally be followed in defense expenditures after VJ Day.

A revolution in the fiscal state made the massive expenditures of the war and postwar years possible. Before the war, New Dealers had used the federal income tax to target America's wealthiest. The revenue acts of 1942 and 1943 vastly expanded its coverage to reach the middle class and instituted the automatic withholding of taxes from wages and salaries. With the stroke of a pen, the federal government could take more money out of taxpayers' paychecks or add to their take-home pay. Together with other wartime innovations, such as improvements in the issuance of public debt, the federal government acquired the means to stabilize business cycles and encourage investment without intruding into the production decisions of individual businessmen. The Employment Act of 1946 made the maintenance of high levels of employment a responsibility of the federal government and created a Counsel of Economic Advisors to guide policymakers.

Existing social insurance programs, such as old age and survivors insurance, were put on a secure financial footing as revenues from war-swollen paychecks grew more rapidly than disbursements. But attempts to expand the public welfare state by creating national health insurance failed in 1943 and again in 1945, even with the backing of President Harry Truman. (Medicare and Medicaid, which covered the elderly and the poor, would not appear until 1965.) Veterans – numbering 19 million in 1950 – greatly benefited from welfare programs of their own, including unemployment insurance; job placement; grants for tuition, room, and board; and guaranteed loans. But for others the more significant development was the growth of the so-called private welfare state: pension and health plans funded by employers and managed by private insurance companies. Several firms had experimented with "welfare capitalism" during the 1920s and 1930s, but it took a resurgent economy, the demands of the labor movement, a wartime freeze on salaries (but not fringe benefits), and the favorable tax treatment of employers' contributions to spread employer-provided benefits across American industry. Once again, American policymakers counted on the private sector to provide benefits that were disbursed through wholly public schemes in other industrialized nations.

Finally, the power and the limits of the war and postwar states can be seen in the field of social police. When a real or imagined threat to social order lacked political power, the administrative state could subject it to ambitious systems of social control. The most dramatic example was the wartime internment of 120,000 first- and second-generation persons of Japanese descent residing in California and the Pacific Northwest – two-thirds of whom were American citizens. African Americans, whose labor was needed for the war economy, forced the creation of a Fair Employment Practices Committee (FEPC) to check racist whites, but the opposition of Southern Congressmen left it without adequate means of enforcement. More effective administrative systems appeared after the war, including "little" FEPCs in twenty-five states and, in 1964, the federal Equal Employment Opportunity Commission.

Of the usual targets of social policing, organized labor fared the best. Its disputes were settled by a War Labor Board (WLB), whose orders were backed by FDR's authority to seize the plants of recalcitrant employers and cancel the draft deferments of striking workers. Unions pledged not to strike and accepted a freeze on wages for the duration of the war. In return, the WLB required that employees maintain their union membership for the duration of a contract. It also provided for the arbitration of grievances, a process that produced a large body of industrial "law" beyond the domain of the courts. In 1947 Congress reacted to a strike wave with the Taft-Hartley Act, which (among other things) directed the NLRB to punish the unfair practices of unions as well as employers. Hearings on labor racketeering led to the passage in 1959 of legislation regulating unions' internal affairs. Still, the wartime bargain held into the 1970s: unions enjoyed the benefits of state-sponsored collective bargaining in return for help in organizing the industrial workforce.

A final form of social police, targeting members of the Communist Party, appeared at war's end and persisted throughout the 1950s. In 1945 the American Communist Party was in decline, weakened by internal schism. Then, the outbreak of a Cold War with the Soviet Union heightened fears of espionage, which had a factual basis in some (but very far from all) of the intelligence gathering conducted by the FBI since the 1930s. To head off action by the Republican majority in Congress, in 1947 President Truman ordered all federal agencies and departments to establish review boards to determine whether employees were disloyal to the United States. Because public employment was deemed a privilege, not a right, the boards' procedural safeguards were lower than those of the courts. For example, loyalty review boards could consider evidence that was never revealed to employees, who were thereby denied the chance to cross-examine their accusers.

The loyalty review boards, deportations of foreign-born Communists, forced resignations of union leaders affiliated with the Communist Party, trials of Communists under anti-subversion and espionage statutes, and sensational Congressional hearings transformed anti-Communism from a somewhat marginal political phenomenon into a national obsession. The administrative policing of Communists targeted real threats to national security, but it swept far too broadly and ruined the lives of many innocent persons. Further, the Red-baiting it fostered impugned the loyalty of those who advocated social reforms that were common elsewhere in the world.

The vast wartime expansion of the federal administrative state took place largely beyond the reach of judicial review. The awarding of a war contract, for example, was deemed the conferral of a privilege, not the recognition of a right, so that Congress could require recipients to pursue any disputes over contracts in administrative bodies, immune from all but the most limited judicial review. Although the OPA's enforcement suits clogged the federal district courts, the agency's preferred method of bringing businesses to heel was to deny them subsidies, another unreviewable "privilege." As during the New Deal, the overwhelming majority of disputes were resolved through negotiation and settlement without a formal hearing, a pattern that would continue into the 1950s.

On those occasions when disputes were appealed to the courts, the pre-war pattern of judicial deference continued. The Supreme Court instructed federal judges to accept departures from judicial rules of evidence and to tolerate remedies no court could order. The Supreme Court welcomed appeals that gave them the chance to rebuke agencies that had lost its confidence. (The FCC fared particularly poorly in the 1940s.) More commonly, it upheld administrators. Between 1941 and 1946 it reversed the decisions of eight leading agencies only 28 percent of the time.

If the federal judiciary thus proved an unreliable ally in resisting the wartime state, Congress beckoned as an alternative. All agencies were created under the ultimate authority of some statute, most were run by appointees subject to senatorial confirmation, and most were dependent on Congress for annual appropriations. Congress had appointed special committees to scrutinize the NLRB and other New Deal agencies before the war. More special committees were created to oversee the war effort. Some, such as the Senate committee chaired by Harry S. Truman, were temperate, but others, such as the House Select Committee to Investigate Acts of Executive Agencies Beyond the Scope of Their Authority, were openly hostile to the administrative process.

Yet, many in Congress became convinced that it lacked the tools to oversee administrative agencies in a meaningful way. True, its committees had occasionally ousted administrators who made unpopular decisions.

Further, appropriations committees had refined the practice of disciplining agencies by cutting or threatening to cut their budgets. In 1943, for example, a Congressional committee prohibited the NLRB from proceeding against employers who had entered into sweetheart, "closed-shop" contracts with company-dominated unions. But Congressional insiders knew such instances to be exceptional, and they decided that stronger measures were required. In 1946 Congress created permanent oversight committees, each supported by four professional and six clerical staffers, to police agencies within their jurisdictions.

In 1946 Congress also sought to discipline the federal agencies by passing the Administrative Procedure Act (APA), which had been drafted by a committee of the American Bar Association. It was a much milder measure than the Walter-Logan bill. The APA committed vast realms of informal agency action to administrators' discretion, with only a remote possibility of judicial review on the ground that it was arbitrary and capricious. The act's requirements for rulemaking were easily met: agencies need only give notice of an impending regulation, provide an opportunity for interested parties to submit written comments, and not behave arbitrarily or capriciously. Seemingly the APA's most significant change came in the area of formal adjudication. It declared that findings of fact in decisions made on the record after an opportunity for a hearing had to be based on "substantial evidence on the record considered as a whole." In *Universal Camera* (1951), the U.S. Supreme Court, speaking through Justice Frankfurter, announced that Congress had meant to express a "mood" in favor of closer judicial scrutiny of the factual basis of agencies' decisions.[7] Apparently lower federal judges took the hint: reversal rates in appeals from federal agencies to the U.S. Courts of Appeals were slightly higher in the 1950s than in the 1940s. Yet, in no year did the federal courts affirm agencies' actions less than 70 percent of the time, and none of the courts' decisions attacked the core of the administrative process.

Realizing that the courts could not possibly review more than a small fraction of agencies' decisions, the APA settled for "judicializing" the agencies themselves by increasing the independence and authority of the hearing examiners who took evidence, made findings of fact, and prepared recommendations for an agency's chief administrators. Under the act, hearing examiners (renamed "administrative law judges" in 1972) had to be a distinct corps within the agency; they could not be a "prosecutor" one day and a "judge" the next. The hearing examiners were not to consult with an agency's investigators or prosecutors without giving all parties notice and an opportunity to participate. Commissioners were not required to

---

[7] *Universal Camera Corp. v. NLRB*, 340 U.S. 474, 478 (1951).

accept a hearing examiner's report, but, after the *Universal Camera* decision, those who rejected a report's conclusions in cases turning on the credibility of witnesses could expect a skeptical reception in an appeal to the courts.

The legislation of 1946 completed the domestication of the New Deal's administrative state. Those without social power derived little comfort from the new regime. When the U.S. Supreme Court ruled that aliens had to be given hearings that met the standards of the APA before they could be deported, Congress promptly amended an appropriations act for the Immigration and Naturalization Service to overturn the decision. But for businesspeople buoyed by the return of economic prosperity, the system was quite satisfactory. A new breed of Washington lawyers provided inside knowledge of how administrators exercised their discretion in distributing contracts, loans, surplus defense facilities, licenses, and favorable tax rulings. Some also explained how Congressmen could be induced to hurl thunderbolts at uncooperative agencies. Should an agency persist in an unfavorable ruling or a costly regulation, these same lawyers could exploit the procedural guarantees of the APA to string out proceedings for months or even years. Delay became a chronic problem in the federal regulatory agencies of the 1950s and 1960s. For example, the FDA started to establish standards for peanut butter in 1959 but – thanks to the efforts of the masterful Washington lawyer, Thomas Austern – did not promulgate them until 1971.

In the 1950s it became increasingly obvious that something had gone terribly wrong with the administrative process in general and the independent regulatory commissions in particular. During the New Deal, James Landis had defended administration as a way to bring to bear on social problems more expertise than the courts possessed. When he revisited the regulatory commissions at the request of president-elect John F. Kennedy in 1960, Landis concluded the agencies' expertise was more fiction than fact. Agency staffs needed better pay, he announced, and their top officials ought to be appointed from the staff, rather than chosen from the ranks of campaign contributors, ex-Congressmen, and industry representatives. Landis deplored commissioners who made their decisions in secret for obscure reasons and then instructed staff members to justify the result. The staffers, he noted, could only do so on narrow grounds, because they knew they might have to defend an inconsistent result the next day.

To some extent, such charges could be sidestepped by shifting the defense of the administrative process from functionalist to pluralist grounds. Even if the commissions' procedures did not produce expert solutions to social problems, defenders argued, they gave economic groups the opportunity to press their interests on a specialized body, which then struck a balance that tolerably promoted the interests of all. Washington lawyers were particularly drawn to this rationale. Time-consuming, judicialized procedures were required for the proper presentation of their clients' needs, they maintained.

Political scientists in the 1950s had a less sanguine view. Commissions could not strike a balance of the relevant interests, they argued, because the commissioners had been "captured" by the industries they were supposed to regulate. Aloofness from partisan politics had not made commissions truly independent; it had only cut them off from popular sources of political strength. To persuade Congress to maintain their budgets and jurisdiction, commissioners needed the help of the lobbyists for the industries they regulated, and this help would not be forthcoming if they regulated too aggressively. The vigorous young agencies of the New Deal had become senile, the political scientists argued, wasting away under the debilitating disease of industry capture.

The political scientists and a parade of presidential task forces did not produce a popular demand for reform. For that, scandal was required. In 1957, at the instigation of Speaker Sam Rayburn, the House Commerce Committee created a special subcommittee on legislative oversight and provided it with a small staff, including a chief counsel, who thought he had a broad mandate to sniff out corruption. By early 1958, the staff had discovered that an FCC commissioner was taking bribes and that President Dwight Eisenhower's most trusted presidential assistant had intervened in FTC and SEC proceedings after receiving a fur coat from a targeted businessman. Most inconveniently, the chief counsel revealed that the committee chairman who appointed him had recently acquired, on very favorable terms, a large stake in a company that was then quite unexpectedly awarded a profitable television license. The chairman was not amused and fired the chief counsel. Although the subcommittee continued its investigations, the affair suggested that Congress lacked the will to oversee agencies effectively.

The search was then on for other ways to make federal regulatory agencies as independent of business interests as they were of Congress and the judiciary. The political scientists' preferred solution was to abolish independent commissions and transfer their functions to the executive departments. Such a move would place the decision makers within a hierarchy headed by the president, the one figure in Washington accountable to a national electorate. Occasionally a presidential task force or renegade commissioner endorsed the idea, but Congress had no interest in boosting presidential power at its own expense. Other opposition emerged from leading lawyers, who still believed that the commissions could regain their autonomy if they were given the right procedures, honest and expert leaders, and well-trained staffs.

That neither the political scientists' nor the lawyers' solutions would reform the administrative process became apparent during John F. Kennedy's presidency. Landis recommended that JFK ask Congress to give commissioners and their staff longer terms and better salaries, give chairmen greater authority within their commissions, and establish a White House oversight office. After Congress signaled its limited interest by rejecting three of his six reorganization plans, JFK did not bother to send over legislation for a presidential oversight office. Kennedy's appointees were vastly superior to those of Truman and Eisenhower, but for the most part Lyndon Johnson reverted to the practice of rewarding contributors and party stalwarts. In general, Kennedy and LBJ, like many postwar liberals, preferred to promote economic growth through tax cuts, rather than by expanding the regulatory state.

If neither Congress, nor the presidency, nor "the Best and the Brightest" could restore the agencies' autonomy, the judiciary at the dawn of the sixties appeared no more promising. To be sure, during the late 1950s the U.S. Supreme Court and U.S. Court of Appeals for the District of Columbia Circuit had remanded several FCC cases for hearings on whether licenses ought to be rescinded in light of Congressional revelations of corruption. Overturning the tainted decisions of a notoriously politicized agency was one thing, however; second-guessing commissioners on an ongoing basis quite another. The federal judges still saw their job as ensuring that the state treated individuals fairly, and they still tended to equate fair treatment with the procedures of the courts. Few were eager to inquire into commissioners' motives, so long as procedural niceties were observed. When, in 1957, the D.C. Circuit judge David Bazelon voted to overturn a decision of the Federal Power Commission (FPC) because its commissioners could not possibly have read, much less deliberated on, the 20,000-page record in the time they had it before them, he did so alone. The other two judges in his panel backed the FPC, and the Supreme Court rejected a further appeal.

Yet when a new cycle of state-building and consolidation commenced in the 1960s and 1970s, federal judges were in the vanguard, marching at the head of representatives of those who had lost out in the consolidation of the New Deal regime. Judges who had always thought of rights as guarantees of individual autonomy *against* a hostile state suddenly saw them as claims of individuals *on* the state for the support and protection that made autonomy possible. It was not an insight they arrived at on their own.

IV. THE RIGHTS REVOLUTION AND THE
ADMINISTRATIVE STATE

The civil rights movement of the 1950s and early 1960s showed how popular protests could be recast as rights and asserted in the courts. Among those who took note were the members of what became known as the consumer movement. Its leaders recast the capture theories of the political scientists into the language of popular protest and judicially enforceable claims on the state.

The founder of the movement was Ralph Nader, a child of Lebanese immigrants. In 1958, while still a student at the Harvard Law School, Nader started documenting the automobile industry's seeming indifference to the defective designs of its products. In 1963 he went to Washington to serve as a researcher for an executive official and a Senate investigation of the automotive industry. Two years later he won national attention by publishing *Unsafe at Any Speed*, an exposé of General Motors' concealment of a life-threatening defect in its Corvair model. Injuries resulting from the defect were, Nader charged, violations of the "body rights" of Americans, which deserved as vigorous a response as violations of civil rights.

A small army of law students and young lawyers, dubbed "Nader's Raiders," flocked to the activist's Center for the Study of Responsive Law. Between 1969 and 1970, the Center published scathing exposés of the FTC, the ICC, the FDA, the National Air Pollution Control Administration, and other agencies. The Naderites also took their charges to Congress, where they found allies among sympathetic subcommittee chairpersons, newly empowered by a series of reforms. Congress responded with more rigorous oversight and legislation that opened agencies' decision making to greater public scrutiny.

Soon other advocacy groups adopted the tactics of the consumer movement. Many originated as cadres of Washington-based activists, funded first by foundation grants and then by contributions from a dispersed, national constituency. Some of the new advocacy groups remained small, but others acquired substantial memberships. Probably the largest growth occurred in the environmental movement. "Conservationist" groups, such as the Sierra Club and the Audubon Society, saw their membership jump by one-third between 1970 and 1971. New groups, including Friends of the Earth, the Environmental Defense Fund (EDF), and the Natural Resources Defense Council (NRDC), were founded to advance a broader agenda of environmental protection. When Public Citizen, a Nader-sponsored organization, convened the first national gathering of public interest groups in 1976, more than 100 organizations sent representatives.

The public interest movement produced a distinctive style of regulation. As we have seen, before the 1960s, economic regulation commonly affected a single industry or sector by setting prices, mandating services, and limiting entry. The "new social regulation" of the 1960s and 1970s, in contrast, cut across industries to protect consumers, the environment, and the health and safety of workers. Its hallmark was a focus on quality of life issues that were more intangible than the economic concerns of the older regulatory agencies. The risks of harm to people and the environment addressed by the new laws were hard to assess, not simply for technological reasons but also because of the open-ended nature of the values at stake.

Legislation creating the new social regulation poured out of Congress until the recession of 1974–75. Consumer laws passed between 1966 and 1968 regulated automobile safety, cigarette labeling, truth in packaging, the marketing of meat and poultry, and consumer credit. A burst of environmental and health and safety legislation followed. Some of the legislation revitalized existing agencies, such as the FTC. More striking was the creation of a new administrative bodies, including, in 1970, the Environmental Protection Agency (EPA), the National Highway Traffic Safety Administration (NHTSA), and the Occupational Safety and Health Administration (OSHA) and, in 1972, the Consumer Products Safety Commission.

Just as the goals of the new regulation differed from those of the older commissions, so did its form, in two respects. First, the new statutes generally had more specific delegations of legislative power than the legislation of the early twentieth century. Instead of handing an agency a blank check to act in the public interest, advocates and their Congressional allies enacted extremely detailed provisions, even to the point of specifying numerical goals. Oversight continued after passage in the guise of subcommittee hearings and staff reports that threatened agencies with budget cuts should they fail to follow Congress's lead.

Second, the new social regulation was much more likely to take the form of rulemaking than trial-type adjudication. Most agencies created before the 1960s preferred the flexibility of case-by-case decision making, but the new social regulation required widely applicable standards with precisely specified content, something hard to produce one case at a time. In addition, the exposés of Nader and his associates revealed how corporate influence could flourish under an ad hoc approach. Rulemaking was more general in scope and was deemed harder to use to reward particular firms or industries.

Complementing the new social regulation were changes in the legal profession and administrative law. Within the legal profession, the crucial development was the emergence of public interest lawyers, paid not by clients but out of foundation grants, federal salaries, or court-awarded attorneys' fees. The new breed first appeared during the War on Poverty. In the early 1960s, a small group of lawyers, law professors, and social workers in New York and New Haven, funded by modest grants from the Ford Foundation and the federal government, developed a plan to win procedural rights for the recipients of welfare, who, under existing law, could not effectively object if administrators terminated their benefits unfairly or subjected them to demeaning supervision. For some of the lawyers,

due process was an end in itself; for others it was a way to make the existing system so burdensome that Congress would be forced to substitute a
guaranteed national income. The ranks of the anti-poverty lawyers grew
dramatically after Congress established a national legal services program in
the federal Office of Economic Opportunity. In 1965, 400 lawyers worked
in the nation's legal aid societies; in 1972, 2,660 did, thanks to federal
funding.

In their fight for welfare rights, the anti-poverty lawyers won some landmark cases, such as *Goldberg v. Kelly* (1970), which established a constitutional right to a fair hearing before welfare benefits could be terminated.
They lost others. Win or lose, they showed how litigation and publicity
could be used to reform public bureaucracies. Soon, lawyers critical of other
federal agencies followed their lead. Starting in 1970, the Ford Foundation
gave grants to a number of public interest law firms, including the Citizens
Communications Center, the Mexican American Legal Defense Fund, and
three environmental groups: the EDF, the Sierra Club Legal Defense Fund,
and the NRDC. By 1976 some seventy-five public interest law firms, law
centers, and legal clinics were in existence. They were supported by foundations, membership organizations, and (under the Clean Water Act and
some forty-five other statutes) awards of attorneys fees.

The public interest lawyers' litigation would have gone nowhere had the
courts not been willing to remake fundamental doctrines of administrative
law. The first doctrine was the law of standing, which determined whether
litigants' interests were substantial enough to justify their participation in
a suit. Before the 1960s, the right to challenge administrative agencies was
limited to companies regulated by the agency and business competitors.
Everyone else was part of the general public, which, in theory, already had
a champion in the agency itself. In the late 1960s and early 1970s, activists
won the right to appear in administrative proceedings to assert their own
notion of the public interest. An early landmark case was *Scenic Hudson*
(1965), which held that the "aesthetic, conservational, and recreational"
interests of a coalition of landowners and nature lovers gave them standing
to participate in an FPC hearing on the licensing of a hydroelectric power
plant.[8] Later courts sided with a church group that sought to participate
in the FCC's review of the racially biased programming of a television
station, the National Welfare Rights Organization in its bid to shape welfare
programs in six states, an environmental group that contested the building
of a federal highway through a park, and, in an extreme case, a group of
law students who challenged the ICC's decision to place a surcharge on the
shipment of recycled materials. (The students had advanced the somewhat

---

[8] *Scenic Hudson Preservation Conference v. FPC*, 354 F. 2d 608, 615–17 (2d Cir. 1965).

doubtful theory that the fee would lead to more litter near their homes.) Congress followed the courts by allowing "any person" to sue under the Clean Air Act of 1970 and at least fourteen other statutes.

A right to participate would have meant little had the federal judges not also decided to review the agencies' rulemaking more aggressively. The APA directed courts to uphold agencies' rules unless the process that produced them had been "arbitrary and capricious." Starting in the early 1970s, the federal judiciary, led by the D.C. Circuit, started applying the arbitrary and capricious standard with unprecedented strictness to ensure that administrators had taken a "hard look" at the environmental, health, and safety risks involved. One view, propounded by Judge David Bazelon, was dubbed the "procedural" hard look. Bazelon argued that judges could not hope to master the merits of the scientific and technical issues presented in appeals from environmental and safety agencies, but they could specify the procedures that would let public interest lawyers, who had the requisite knowledge, do the job. He argued that courts ought to impose additional procedural requirements on rulemaking, such as the right of any interested party to cross-examine witnesses at a public hearing. In contrast, Bazelon's colleague on the D.C. Circuit, Harold Leventhal, called for "substantive" hard look review, in which judges scrutinized the merits of an agency's deci-sion. Other federal judges joined the fray, until, in *Vermont Yankee* (1978), the Supreme Court seemingly endorsed substantive hard look review and unambiguously rejected Bazelon's procedural approach.[9]

Federal judges scrutinized the reasoning behind such decisions as the Department of Agriculture's refusal to ban the pesticide DDT, the Atomic Energy Commission's failure to prepare environmental impact statements, the EPA's regulation of leaded gasoline, and the National Highway Traffic Safety Administration's recission of a rule requiring automatic seatbelts and air bags in automobiles. In each case the courts acted not, as Dicey envisioned, to limit the reach of administration in the interest of private rights, but to urge agencies to regulate even more aggressively in the interest of health, safety, and the environment.

By the mid-1970s, the New Deal regime had been significantly recast. Federal agencies still engaged in command-and-control regulation, but their every move was followed by consumer-oriented legislative subcom-mittees, public interest lawyers, and the courts. New administrative bodies

---

[9] *Environmental Defense Fund, Inc. v. Ruckleshaus*, 439 F.2d 584 (D.C. Cir. 1971) (Bazelon, J.); *Greater Boston Television Corp. v. FCC*, 444 F.2d 841 (D.C. Cir. 1970) (Leventhal, J.); *Vermont Yankee Nuclear Power Corp. v. Natural Resources Defense Council, Inc.*, 435 U.S. 519 (1978).

issued regulations that crossed industrial lines with a specificity not seen since the days of the OPA. The tight administrative world presided over by the Washington lawyer was opened up to the influence of a more diffuse collection of "issue networks" composed of Congressional officials, administrative agencies, law firms, advocacy groups, foundations, and university-based experts. A new political regime had emerged and was ripe for consolidation.

V. THE CONTRACTING STATE

The early 1970s would prove to be the high-water mark of the federal administrative state in the twentieth century. Thereafter, the regulatory environment turned increasingly hostile. First, the economic prosperity that had generally prevailed since the early 1950s ended with the recession of 1973–74, to be replaced by a combination of unemployment and inflation. Fears that regulation was lessening the competitiveness of American industry in the global economy would persist throughout the remainder of the century. Second, a social and cultural backlash emerged that accused the revolution in rights of transforming individual rights into entitlements for selfish social groups. Critics charged that public interest advocates did not really represent the public, just their own, idiosyncratic agendas. Third, business leaders created their own network of Washington insiders. The number of Washington-based corporate "government affairs" offices quadrupled between 1968 and 1978; the number of Washington lawyers jumped from 16,000 to 26,000 between 1972 and 1978. Finally, the intensification of the Cold War in the 1980s revived claims that America occupied an exceptional place in world history because of its respect for freedom, especially the freedom to do business in unregulated markets.

The roots of the most dramatic of the late-twentieth-century contractions of the administrative state ran back to the 1950s when a group of economists launched an attack on the received wisdom that public utilities were "natural monopolies" requiring regulation. Nothing prevented the opening of such industries to competition, the economists argued, except the selfish interests of regulated companies and their unions, who counted on commissions to set rates that guaranteed their profits and wages. If the political scientists of the 1950s had questioned the autonomy of the federal regulatory commissions, these economists, in effect, questioned their capacity by arguing that the problem of natural monopoly they were created to address did not in fact exist and that unregulated markets would better promote social welfare. Although this heterodoxy gained adherents in the economists' ranks during the 1960s and early 1970s, even true believers doubted that deregulation would happen any time soon. The regulated industries and their unions were too influential in Congress, the consumers who stood to benefit from competitive prices too diffuse, for so dramatic a reversal of public policy to occur.

Yet, deregulation came to America in the mid-1970s in a hurry. Harbingers included the FCC's loosening of AT&T's monopoly of the manufacture of telephone equipment and a statute abolishing fixed commissions for the sale or purchase of stock. The Airline Deregulation Act of 1978 was an early, widely noted landmark. It was soon followed by the deregulation of railroads, trucking, bus transportation, banking, long-distance phone service, natural gas, and crude oil. The grand old patriarch of the federal administrative state, the ICC, barely survived with a much-diminished mandate. It was finally abolished at the end of 1995, on the eve of a second wave of deregulation affecting the transmission of electricity and local telephone service.

The campaign to abolish price-and-entry regulation triumphed because it met the needs of a variety of political actors. The consumer movement shared the deregulators' dim view of the regulatory commissions and joined their call to abolish the Civil Aeronautics Board (CAB). Congressional liberals, such as Senator Edward Kennedy, embraced deregulation to show that they could be as responsive to consumers' concerns as any Nader Raider. The two presidents plagued by the stagflation of the 1970s, Gerald Ford and Jimmy Carter, saw deregulation as a way to lower prices, increase productivity, and spur economic growth without increasing the federal deficit. Even many commissioners found deregulation to be a smart career move. The most prominent of the deregulating commissioners, the economist and CAB chairman Alfred Kahn, pursued pro-competitive policies as a matter of principle. Others, noting the acclaim lavished on Kahn, seemed motivated not so much by conviction as eagerness to jump on a political bandwagon.

Nader, Kennedy, and Carter favored not only the end of price-and-entry regulation but also the continuation of the new social regulation. Others in the late 1970s and early 1980s thought that both kinds of regulation had gone too far. They pointed to the flood of detailed regulations pouring from the environmental and safety agencies, including an incongruous OSHA rule requiring portable toilets for cowboys. The cost of enforcing and complying with the new rules soon became a major complaint. The federal government's expense in enforcing the new social regulations jumped from $539 million in 1970 to more than $5 billion ten years later. Business's compliance costs, although harder to estimate, were much higher. In 1997 the Office of Management and Budget put the cost of enforcing and complying with major federal rules at $279 billion, of which the majority was spent on environmental protection.

Rulemaking itself grew expensive and time consuming. The Administrative Procedure Act had simply required that agencies give interested parties notice of an impending rule and an opportunity to submit written comments. With the rise of hard look review, however, agencies added a series of court-like procedures and produced what became known as "hybrid rulemaking." Commonly, all interested parties were entitled to present their views orally; often each had a right to cross-examine witnesses. Courts required agencies to respond to every significant objection and to show that the rules they proposed were superior to those advanced by interested parties. To anticipate the second-guessing of the judiciary, staffs compiled mountainous records that took years to complete. By the mid-1980s, the "ossification" of rulemaking had become a common lament.

The burdens of the new social regulation set off a search for alternatives. Some agencies abandoned notice-and-comment rulemaking for adjudication. The NHTSA, for example, shifted its energies from issuing rules to individual recalls of defective automobiles. Others rediscovered the virtues of informal action, such as press releases, interpretive rules, policy statements, and emergency procedures in which their discretion was unquestioned. Finally, many added a consensus-building phase to the rulemaking process, known as "regulatory negotiation." Under traditional notice-and-comment rulemaking, interested parties could not see a rule until it was published in the *Federal Register*. In a "reg-neg" proceeding, relevant "stakeholders," including manufacturers, trade associations, and environmental and consumer groups, participated in the initial formulation of the rule. First employed in 1983 by the Federal Aviation Administration to develop a rule governing the flight time of airline personnel, reg-neg spread to other agencies and received Congress's blessing in 1990. Despite skeptics' claims that administrators sacrificed too much to gain a consensus and ended up in court anyway, negotiated rulemaking was a well-established feature in the regulatory landscape at the end of the twentieth century.

A more general consolidation of the public interest state drew on an economic concept, the cost-benefit analysis. The new social regulation established absolute standards of health and safety without suggesting that anything less was acceptable, even if the cost of compliance proved enormous. Presidents Nixon, Ford, and Carter all tried to temper rulemaking with various forms of review within the White House, without much effect. Soon after his inauguration, however, Ronald Reagan announced that agencies would be required to prepare "Regulatory Impact Analyses" for any new rule that annually cost business $100 million or more and to submit the rule to the Office of Information and Regulatory Affairs (OIRA), established in the final days of the Carter administration, for an independent review. Rules that failed OIRA's review were returned to the agencies with

a request for further study. Most of the more than 21,000 rules submitted to
OIRA in the 1980s were adopted without change, but the percentage that
passed unscathed dropped, from 87 percent in 1981 to under 71 percent
in the last four years of the decade. In several prominent cases, involving
rules on exposure to asbestos and noxious chemicals, OIRA's "return letters" made the proposed regulations politically untenable and forced their
withdrawal.

In the late 1980s and 1990s, cost-benefit analysis spread across the regulatory landscape. OIRA review continued under Presidents George H. W.
Bush and Bill Clinton, although Clinton made it somewhat more agency-
friendly. In 1994 Republican majorities in the House and Senate repealed
a "zero-tolerance" standard for pesticide residues in processed food and
required the EPA to conduct cost-benefit analyses in implementing the
Safe Water Drinking Act (1974). Clinton vetoed legislation mandating
cost-benefit analysis for all rulemaking, but did sign a bill requiring agencies to submit major rules for Congressional review at least sixty days before
their effective date. Meanwhile, cost-benefit analysis spread to the states. By
2000, more than half formally required assessments of the economic impact
of agency rulemaking, and several had created offices of regulatory reform
to conduct the reviews. An attempt in the late 1990s to require cost-benefit
analysis as a matter of constitutional law in implementing the Clean Air
Act would ultimately be turned aside in the U.S. Supreme Court's decision
in *American Trucking* (2001).[10] Still, at the end of the century cost-benefit
analysis remained a powerful means by which business groups could make
their interests felt within the public interest state.

Economists also suggested that some command-and-control regulation
be replaced with programs that provided "market incentives" to comply
with environmental or safety standards. "Pay-as-you-throw" systems, in
which municipalities billed homeowners in keeping with the amount of
solid waste they discarded, provide a simple example; "tradable permit
systems" a more complex one. Public officials set a target for the total
amount of emissions of some noxious substance and then licensed individual
polluters to produce a part of the whole. A company emitting less than its
share could sell its unused rights to a "dirtier" business. The proceeds of the
sale were a powerful incentive to create more efficient techniques of pollution
control. The tradable permit idea was incorporated into a plan to reduce
emissions of sulfur dioxide, the noxious component of acid rain. Other
applications in the 1990s included the reduction of leaded gasoline, the
phasing out of ozone-depleting chlorofluorocarbons, and the preservation
of wetlands and historic structures.

[10] *Whitman v. American Trucking Associations*, 531 US 457 (2001).

A final consolidation owed less to economists than to a reassertion of Tocquevillean tradition by a protest movement originating in the American West. Many Westerners had long resented the federal government's control of the public domain, which accounted for a great deal of the land in their states. They saw the environmental protection laws of the 1970s as a new front in Washington's war on the West. Reports of landowners imprisoned for filling in "wetlands" that were located far from any body of water but happened to be the site of vernal pools struck them as the modern equivalent of the abuses of George III. They responded by invoking the spirit of the American Revolution and launching a property rights movement. In 1995, between 600 and 1,500 property rights groups were thought to be in existence. Some were fronts for business interests, but others were authentic, grassroots organizations.

Like the public interest lawyers of the 1960s and 1970s, the property rights advocates turned to the law. Once again, foundations provided seed money, but this time the funders were conservative stalwarts, such as the John M. Olin, Sarah Scaife, and Philip McKenna foundations. A major campaign was launched to challenge federal regulation as a taking of private property without just compensation. In the 1980s and 1990s the campaign met with some success when the U.S. Supreme Court overturned regulatory actions relating to the management of coastlines and flood plains, but it would stall after the turn of the century when a majority of the Court turned its back on the earlier rulings.[11] In the meantime, the property rights movement explored legislative avenues. At least thirteen states adopted "look-before-you-leap" statutes, which required agencies to prepare "Takings Impact Analyses" before issuing regulations.

By the end of the 1990s, the property rights movement had established itself as a counterweight to the public interest movement of the 1970s, but neither its lawsuits nor other attempts to contract the regulatory state had brought an end to administration in America. To be sure, deregulation tended to shift the locus of policymaking back to the courts. As regulators exited, public prosecutors and private individuals sometimes stepped in with criminal prosecutions and class action suits. More importantly, Americans relied too heavily on administration in its various guises to ever accept a wholesale return to the nineteenth-century state of courts and parties. Thus, even when Congress ended the federal entitlement program of aid to families with dependent children, it replaced it with block grants that came with many strings attached and many administrators to pull

---

[11] *Lucas v. South Carolina Coastal Council*, 505 U.S. 1003 (1992); *Dolan v. City of Tigard*, 512 U.S. 687 (1994); *Tahoe-Sierra Preservation Council, Inc. v. Tahoe Regional Planning Agency*, 535 U. S. 302 (2002).

them. At the end of the twentieth century, Americans continued to make policy through tax laws and other tools of the fiscal state. The need for new expertise in the area of public contracts would become painfully obvious in 2001, when California was forced to make disastrous long-term agreements with the deregulated suppliers of electric power. The social policing of immigrants and other aliens remained largely beyond the reach of the courts, and a dramatic expansion of the national security state was as close as the attacks of September 11, 2001.

CONCLUSION

Tocqueville was wrong. Americans *could* have centralized administration and still be free. If, as President Ronald Reagan claimed, America was the exemplary city on a hill, pointing the way to freedom for the rest of the world, it was no less exemplary in its reliance on bureaucracy to promote the welfare of its citizens.

As the United States proceeded through the Progressive, New Deal, and public interest cycles of state-building and consolidation, centralized administration became inextricably bound up in American political life. As disparate social groups jostled for power within a new political regime, administrative bodies grew in importance. Bureaucracy held some groups together in durable, power-wielding coalitions and relegated others to the margins of public debate and policymaking. No amount of impassioned oratory could transport the United States to the stateless Eden of its mythic past. At the end of the twentieth century, abolishing administration in all of its guises would have meant the abolition of politics itself.

Lawyers were vital both to the emergence of new administrative structures and to their consolidation into stable political regimes. In time they overcame the limitations of their traditional orientation toward the courts and turned their energies to building strong and autonomous bureaucracies; they were, for example, the principal inventors of the informal means agencies used to win compliance with their wishes. Yet, lawyers were also driven, out of professional interest and their own acceptance of the "supremacy of law" ideal, to build internal checks on the administrative discretion. Lawyers judicialized the administrative process during the consolidation of the New Deal regime; they ossified rulemaking during the regime that followed.

The lawyers' dominance of the state suffered its severest challenge in the last of the twentieth century's state-building cycles. Economists were the vanguard of the deregulation movement, champions of cost-benefit analysis, and inventors of market-based alternatives to command-and-control regulation. None of these initiatives succeeded in banishing bureaucracy from America, however, and as long as it remains law and lawyers will not be obsolete. To the contrary: judging from the first years of a new political regime emerging out of the War on Terror, the need for a profession committed to the supremacy of law will be as great in the new century as at any moment in American legal history.

LEGAL THEORY AND LEGAL EDUCATION, 1920–2000

WILLIAM W. FISHER III

The overall trajectory of American legal theory during the twentieth century was as follows. At the outset, a formalist faith gripped the judiciary and the law schools. Resistance to that vision among judges, lawyers, and law teachers gradually increased, ultimately finding full expression in the legal realist movement of the 1920s and 1930s. The realist wave ebbed in the 1940s, but left behind a host of new questions concerning the nature and scope of judicial discretion, the role of "policy" in lawmaking and legal interpretation, the appropriate relationship between public and private power, which branches of government should be entrusted with which legal issues, and, most broadly, the meaning and feasibility of "the rule of law." After World War II, a new orthodoxy emerged, offering answers to those questions that seemed convincing to most legal scholars and lawmakers. Beginning in the 1960s, that new faith – dubbed by its successors, "process theory" – in turn came under attack, not from a single direction but from many angles simultaneously. The attackers, marching under the banners of "law and economics," "law and society," "Kantian liberalism," "republicanism," "critical legal studies," and "feminist legal theory," offered radically different visions of the nature and purposes of law. Each group attracted many adherents, but none swept the field. The net result is that, in the early twenty-first century, legal discourse in the United States consists of a cacophonous combination of issues and arguments originally developed by rival movements, some now defunct and others still with us.

Many aspects of the history of legal education during the twentieth century – for example, the periodic efforts to reshape law school curriculum and pedagogy and the steady increase in the importance of interdisciplinary teaching and scholarship – are best understood as outgrowths or expressions of the struggles among the competing groups of theorists. Other aspects of legal education – most importantly, the changing size and shape of the bottleneck through which students must pass to gain entry to the bar – were shaped instead by the complex relationship in American culture between exclusionary impulses (xenophobia, racism, anti-Semitism, and sexism) and inclusionary, egalitarian impulses. The net result is that the bench, bar, student bodies, and law faculties of today are by no means demographic "mirrors of America," but they are substantially more diverse than their counterparts a century ago.

In this chapter, I trace the development of these two aspects of twentieth-century American law – legal theory and legal education – identifying, when appropriate, connections between them.

I. THEORY

The Rise of Realism

"Formalism," "mechanical jurisprudence," "classical legal thought" – these are among the labels that were attached, after the fact, to the collection of attitudes and methods that dominated American legal thought and practice between roughly the 1870s and the 1930s. In the view of its critics (our primary concern here), this outlook had two related dimensions. First, it was a distinctive style of judicial reasoning. When confronted with difficult cases, judges during this period were much less likely than their predecessors during the antebellum period to seek outcomes that would advance public policy (for example, by creating incentives for economic development) or foster equity (for example, by obliging parties to abide only by commitments they had voluntarily made) and much more likely to look for guidance to precedent (decisions rendered previously by other courts in analogous cases). When directly relevant precedents were unavailable, judges commonly would seek to extract from loosely related prior decisions general principles (the more general the better) from which answers to the problems before them might be deduced. Policy considerations, if addressed at all, would be invoked only at the highest level of abstraction – when selecting the "first principles" that formed the top of a chain of deductive reasoning.

Some historians have contended that this dimension of the classical outlook was causally connected to the second: a tendency to resolve cases in socially or politically conservative ways. Between the Civil War and World War I, state and federal courts invented several new legal remedies (such as the labor injunction) and new common law rules (such as the doctrine of tortious interference with contractual relations) that strengthened the hands of employers in struggles with their employees, narrowly construed legislative efforts (such as the Sherman Act) to limit concentrations of economic power, and interpreted the Due Process Clause of the Federal Constitution in ways that shielded corporate property rights and employers' "freedom of contract" against legislative encroachment.

To be sure, even during the heyday of classicism, there were countercurrents. Some lawyers and judges persisted in openly seeking to resolve hard cases in ways that advanced and reconciled considerations of policy and justice. Businesses did not always prevail in legal contests against workers or consumers. And a small group of legal scholars – some proclaiming adherence to what they called "sociological jurisprudence" – denounced the classical reasoning style on both philosophic and political grounds.

Three of these early critics were to prove especially influential. In his judicial opinions, books, and articles, Justice Oliver Wendell Holmes, Jr. attacked his contemporaries for failing to recognize that "[t]he life of the law has not been logic; it has been experience," for purporting to derive the answers to "concrete cases" from a few "general propositions," and for reading "Mr. Herbert Spencer's Social Statics" into the Fourteenth Amendment. He urged them instead to accept "the right of the majority to embody their opinions into law" and to replace muddled natural law theories with a harshly positivist perspective: "The prophecies of what the courts will do in fact, and nothing more pretentious, are what I mean by the law." In his early writings, Roscoe Pound similarly denounced the "mechanical" mode of reasoning on which the Supreme Court had come to depend and contemporary jurisprudence's infatuation with outmoded images of the "self-reliant man." Law, he insisted, must be brought into alignment with modern "social, economic and philosophical thinking" – and, specifically, must acknowledge that justice entails not merely "fair play between individuals," but "fair play between social classes." Finally, Yale Law School's Wesley Hohfeld, in a dense but brilliant pair of articles, fought the aggregative tendencies of classicism, arguing that any legal doctrine can and should be broken down into logically independent combinations of elemental entitlements, each of which could only be justified through an examination of its "purpose" and its "effect."

In the 1920s and early 1930s, a group of young scholars, most of them affiliated with Yale, Columbia, or Johns Hopkins Universities, drew on Holmes's, Pound's, and Hohfeld's arguments to create the methodological movement that came to be known as legal realism. Two impulses, in addition to the usual desire of each generation to explode the conventions of the preceding one, help explain the force and shape of realism. First, powerful national political movements – initially Progressivism, later the New Deal – stimulated and guided the younger scholars in crafting alternatives to the conservatism of classicism. Second, recent innovations in several other academic fields helped discredit the classical mode of reasoning.

Pragmatism in philosophy, non-Euclidean geometry, theories of relativity in physics, and the rising disciplines of anthropology and psychology all called into question the value of axioms and theorems, induction and deduction, and formal rules as ways of resolving controversies and organizing social life.

From these materials, the realists fashioned two clusters of arguments – the first descriptive, the second normative. The foundation of the former was Holmes's insistence that the objective of legal analysis was to predict "what the courts will do in fact." If that is the end, the realists argued, then the "traditional legal rules and concepts" that figured so prominently in classical opinions and scholarship were largely useless. In part, their irrelevance was a function of their internal inconsistency. For almost every common law precedent, canon of statutory interpretation, and legal principle, there existed an equal and opposite precedent, canon, or principle. Even an adept logician could not derive from such contradictory propositions determinate answers to concrete questions. John Dewey and a few other realists argued that the problem ran deeper still: the analytical tools that classical writers purported to employ to reason deductively from premises to outcomes or analogically from one case or issue to another were far shakier than they realized.

In short, doctrine and logic play much smaller roles in determining how courts decide cases than is usually supposed. To the question of what then does explain judicial decisions, the realists offered various answers. Some pointed to judges' "hunches." In Joseph Hutchinson's words, "[t]he vital motivating impulse for decision is an intuitive sense of what is right or wrong in a particular case." Others, like Jerome Frank, emphasized judges' idiosyncratic personalities. Still others, like Felix Cohen, while agreeing that judges' "prejudices" were crucial, saw them as more systematic, more likely to be shaped by the worldview of the social class from which most judges were drawn, and thus more predictable.

These views, in turn, prompted the realists to regard judicial opinions with skepticism, even condescension. The ostensible function of opinions was of course to explain how courts reached their determinations and thus, among other things, to provide guidance to judges and litigants confronting similar controversies in the future. However, their real function, the realists claimed, was to "rationalize" and "legitimize" the courts' rulings, concealing from the public at large and indeed from the judges themselves the considerations, often unsavory, that truly underlay them.

Unfortunately, the realists' normative arguments – their reflections on what Karl Llewellyn referred to as "ought-questions" – were less coherent and trenchant. They did, however, develop a few major themes that, reconfigured, were to play substantial roles in subsequent schools of American

legal thought. The first may be described as "particularism." In various
contexts, realists argued, general categories should be broken down into
smaller units. For example, following Pound, they argued that scholars
should be more interested in "real" or "working" rules (descriptions of
how courts were actually resolving disputes) than in "paper" or "black
letter" rules (the norms they ostensibly invoked in justifying their decisions). Adherence to that guideline, the realists contended, would likely
reveal that judges (especially trial judges) were far more sensitive to the
peculiarities of the fact patterns they confronted than is usually supposed.
The net result: an accurate map of the landscape of the law, useful in guiding clients, would consist of more – and more specific – norms than could
be found in the standard treatises. When crafting new rules, a lawmaker
(whether a judge or a legislator) should likewise avoid the temptation to
engage in excessive generalization. Social and commercial relations vary
radically along several axes. Assuming that it was worthwhile to attempt
to formulate norms that covered more than the facts of the case at hand (a
matter on which the realists disagreed), such norms should reach no further
than the set of similar controversies. So, for example, a rule governing the
foreclosure of farm mortgages might make some sense, but probably not a
rule governing foreclosure of all mortgages, and certainly not a rule that
purported to specify remedies for breaches of contracts of all sorts.

The second theme may be described as "purposive adjudication." Wise
interpretation of a legal rule, they argued, required looking behind the
language of the norm in question to the social policy that it was designed
to advance. That conviction prompted them, when promulgating legal rules
(such as the Uniform Commercial Code) to make their purposes explicit.
In Llewellyn's words, "the rightest and most beautiful type of legal rule, is
the singing rule with purpose and with reason clear."

The realists' commitment to purposive adjudication raised a further,
more difficult question: how does a lawmaker (legislator or judge) go about
selecting the policies that should be advanced in a particular context? Their
responses were disappointing. One, Felix Cohen, made a valiant effort to
construct and defend a comprehensive utilitarian theory as a beacon for lawmakers. Most of Cohen's comrades were less ambitious, contenting themselves with an insistence on the wide variety of policies – from the creation
of incentives for productive activity, to fostering social cooperation and
"team play," to increasing the efficiency of the "legal machinery," to equalization of "men's . . . access to desired things," to providing "a right portion
of favor, of unearned aid or indulgence to those who need it" – that ought
to be considered by lawmakers. But when such goals conflict, how is one
to choose among them? By looking to custom, some realists suggested.
Immanent in extant social practices (such as the conduct of the better sort

of merchant) were standards that could and should be employed by lawmakers when selecting and enforcing norms binding on everyone. Not much of an answer.

The Legacy of Realism

By the end of the 1930s, legal realism as a coherent movement had died. In part, its demise can be attributed to increasing hostility, both from other legal scholars and from the public at large, to the views expressed by its adherents. Opponents of the New Deal resented the realists' vigorous sponsorship or defense of Roosevelt's policies. And a growing group of critics argued that the realists' positivism and tendencies toward ethical relativism had helped weaken the nation's intellectual defenses against the rising tide of Fascism in Europe. In the face of these criticisms, some realists publicly disavowed positions they had taken during the 1920s. The diminution of the scholarly output of others was probably caused as much by the lack of fresh ideas as it was by self-doubt or regret.

But the legacy of realism was powerful and durable. The Humpty-Dumpty of classicism had been irremediably broken. New conceptions of the nature and function of law and the proper responsibilities of the various participants in the legal system had to be devised.

Three implications of the realists' arguments made the task especially difficult and urgent. First, their insistence on the ubiquity of judicial lawmaking, the large zone of discretion that courts inevitably have when resolving cases, called into question the central principle of democratic theory: the proposition that the people themselves choose (either directly or through elected representatives) the laws by which they are governed. Second, the same theme, combined with the realists' emphasis on the roles played by "hunches" and "prejudices" in judges' deliberations, intensified many Americans' long-standing doubts concerning the legitimacy of judicial review – the courts' practice (nowhere authorized by the federal or state constitutions) of striking down legislation they deem inconsistent with constitutional provisions. Third, several aspects of the realists' vision of the way the legal system did and should operate were difficult to reconcile with the central Anglo-American ideal of the rule of law – in brief, the conviction that the state may legitimately impose its will on persons only through the promulgation (by lawmakers who do not know the identities of those affected) and enforcement (by judges who are free from bias and immune to pressure) of general, clear, well-publicized rules that are capable of being obeyed.

In short, the realists left their successors a formidable challenge: how to reshape or recharacterize the legal system in a way that, without relying on the discredited bromides of classicism, offered Americans reassurance that they lived in a democracy, that the exercise of judicial review was legitimate, and that the rule of law was attainable.

Legal Process

The first group to take up the task eventually came to be known as the "legal process" school. Its leading figures were Lon Fuller, Henry Hart, Albert Sacks, Erwin Griswold, Paul Freund, and Louis Jaffe at Harvard; Alexander Bickel and Harry Wellington at Yale; and Herbert Wechsler at Columbia. They surely did not agree on all things, but they shared many convictions and, more important, a sensibility – centered on the values of moderation, craft, and "sound judgment" – that would set the dominant tone of American legal theory until the middle of the 1960s.

In some respects, the legal process theorists merely reasserted (in more measured form) ideas first developed by the realists. For example, they were quick to acknowledge that there were multiple "right answers" to many of the controversies that were presented to modern courts – that the law, in short, was not determinate. The process theorists also agreed with the realists about both the importance of purposive adjudication and the multiplicity of values advanced by the typical legal norm. So, for example, Lon Fuller, in perhaps his most famous article, contended that underlying the requirement that, to be enforceable, a contract must rest on "bargained-for consideration" were several distinct social values: the need to "caution" private parties when they are about to make legally binding promises, providing judges subsequently obliged to interpret those promises with good evidence of what had been intended, and "channeling" the parties into choosing efficient and informative forms. Underlying the system of contract law as a whole were still other, more general values: respecting "private autonomy," protecting persons' reasonable reliance on promises made by others, and preventing unjust enrichment. In all cases involving the consideration doctrine, Fuller argued, judges must attend to these various purposes. In easy cases, they would all point in the same direction, and the judges would likely not even be aware of their salience; in hard cases, the purposes would conflict, and the judges would be obliged consciously to weigh and balance them. But to every case they were germane. Only one aspect of Fuller's analysis departed from the methodology developed by Llewellyn and Cohen: his insistence (of which he made much during his subsequent career) that the policies underlying the rules must be considered part of the law, not as external considerations that judges invoked only when the law "gave out."

In other respects, however, process theory deviated sharply from realism. Most importantly, while the realists' emphasis on the role of discretion and policymaking in adjudication tended to blur distinctions among the kinds of reasoning employed by the three branches of government, the process theorists were adamant that the separate branches had very different jobs and should do them in very different ways. Specifically, decisions whose resolution depended either on the expression of "preferences" or on political compromises could and should be addressed either by a legislature or by the public at large through "a count of noses at the ballot box." Decisions (such as the appointment of judges, the setting of tariff policy, or the detailed regulation of industries) with respect to which context-specific exercises of "expertise" were more important than consistency or predictability were best handled by the executive branch or by administrative agencies. Last but not least, problems "which are soluble by methods of reason" were properly allocated to the judiciary. So long as the branch to which an issue had been correctly assigned had resolved it in a procedurally proper manner, the process theorists argued, the other branches should ordinarily defer to its judgment.

The notion that the special responsibility of judges was to resolve disputes through "reason" – or "reasoned elaboration" – was the centerpiece of process theory. It encompassed at least three, related guidelines. First, "reasoned" deliberation was "dispassionate." Process theorists agreed with Felix Frankfurter that a judge must assume a posture of "intellectual disinterestedness in the analysis of the factors involved in the issues that call for decision. This in turn requires rigorous self-scrutiny to discover, with a view to curbing, every influence that may deflect from such disinterestedness." Second, when possible (typically at the appellate level), judges should consult with their colleagues before coming to conclusions. Such collegial consultation would reveal which of each judge's inclinations were idiosyncratic (and thus should be rejected) and generally would facilitate "the maturing of collective thought." Finally, judges must in their opinions explain their reasoning thoroughly, both to provide effective guidance to future litigants and to enable constructive criticism of their decisions.

The last and most controversial of the propositions associated with process theory was first developed by Herbert Wechsler – although it was subsequently adopted and applied by Archibald Cox and others. It came into play only in the special context of judicial review. When a judge was called on to determine whether a statute was consistent with a constitution, Wechsler argued, the set of considerations he or she might legitimately consider was narrower than the set appropriate in other sorts of controversies. Specifically, the judge could only rely on "reasons . . . that in their generality and their neutrality transcend any immediate result that is involved." The concept of "neutrality" was crucial but slippery. To Wechsler, it did not mean that the "value" in question must not affect different groups differently. It meant, rather, that the "value and its measure must be determined by a general analysis that gives no weight to accidents of application, finding a scope that is acceptable whatever interest, group, or person may assert the claim." What made this seemingly innocuous norm so notorious is that, in the 1959 article in which he first developed it, Wechsler argued that it could not be reconciled with the Supreme Court's decision in *Brown v. Board of Education*, which had held that the maintenance of racially segregated public schools violated the Equal Protection Clause of the Federal Constitution. Not all process theorists followed Wechsler on this issue, but some did. And this particular implication of their arguments did not bode well for the hegemony of process theory when, in the 1960s, controversies over race, voting, and sexuality increasingly assumed center stage in American politics and law.

Law and Economics

During the 1940s and 1950s, economists began with some frequency to address issues close to the hearts of legal scholars. In perhaps the most influential of those forays, Arthur Pigou argued that situations of the sort that dominate the law of torts – that is, when one party behaves in a fashion that causes an injury to another party – could and should be managed by selecting rules that forced the actors to "internalize" all of the costs of their behavior, including the losses sustained by the victims. How? Various devices might be employed, but the most straightforward would be to make the actors liable for all of the victims' injuries.

In 1960, the economist Ronald Coase published an article offering an alternative way of analyzing the same class of controversies. In "The Problem of Social Cost," Coase developed four related arguments. First, the aspiration of the legal system in cases of the sort considered by Pigou should not be merely to force actors to internalize the "social costs" associated with their activities but, more broadly, "to maximize the value of production" – taking into account the welfare and conduct of all affected parties. So, for example, a rule making each actor liable for the injuries associated with his conduct might not be socially optimal if the victims could more cheaply alter their own behavior in ways that would avoid the harms. Second, in considering possible solutions to such problems, it was important not to treat the active party as the sole "cause" of the resultant injuries – and thus presumptively the proper bearer of financial responsibility. Typically, both parties "are responsible and both should be forced to include the loss...as a cost in deciding whether to continue the activity which gives rise to" the injury. Third, in all such cases, if "there were no costs involved in carrying out market transactions," "the decision of the courts concerning liability for damage would be without effect on the allocation of resources," because the parties themselves would enter into agreements that would compel the party who could avoid the damage most cheaply to do so. (This third argument is what George Stigler subsequently dubbed the "Coase theorem.") Fourth and finally, in the overwhelming majority of cases in which transaction costs did prevent such efficiency-enhancing private arrangements, the choice of legal rule would affect the allocation of resources. In such cases, wise lawmakers should consider the relative costs of a wide variety of rules and dispute-resolution mechanisms, selecting the combination with the lowest total costs.

This cluster of arguments proved inspirational, launching a thousand scholarly ships. The largest group pursued the fourth of Coase's lines. What set of legal rules, they asked, would foster the most efficient allocation of resources in particular contexts, assuming that transaction costs would prevent the achievement of optimal solutions in such settings through free bargaining? To some doctrinal fields – contracts, torts, property, and antitrust, for example – such an inquiry seemed obviously pertinent. But the same methodology was soon applied to many fields with respect to which cost minimization might have seemed less germane – criminal law, family law, civil procedure, and constitutional law, among others. Legions of lawyer-economists set off on quests of this sort, but one, Richard Posner, towered above the others. In tens of books and hundreds of articles, he brought his particular version of the wealth-maximization criterion to bear on virtually every field of both public and private law.

Another group of scholars focused on Coase's observation that even when the absence of transaction costs made the choice of legal rule irrelevant from the standpoint of economic efficiency, that choice would affect the relative wealth of the affected parties. In the second-most influential article within the law-and-economics genre, Guido Calabresi and Douglas Melamed treated such "distributional considerations" as equal in importance to efficiency considerations when deciding not just which party to a given transaction or controversy should be given the legal entitlement but also whether a "property rule," "liability rule," or "inalienability rule" should be selected as the right mechanism for protecting that entitlement. Taking this recommendation to heart, several economists and legal scholars argued for years whether the non-waivable implied warranty of habitability that now governs residential leaseholds in most American jurisdictions did or did not improve the lot of the poor tenants it was ostensibly designed to serve. Other fields to which this approach has been extensively applied include tax and employment law.

A third group of scholars set out to refine the simplistic conception of people as rational utility-maximizers on which Coase's original arguments – and, in particular, his famous third claim – appeared to rest. Once one introduces more realistic assumptions concerning people's abilities first to discern their own desires and interests and then to determine how best to achieve them, these scholars asked, How is the selection of either efficient or distributionally fair rules affected? Their answers varied widely.

One of the factors that contributed to the enormous popularity of economic analyses of these various sorts is that they enabled their practitioners to avoid the ethical pluralism that had characterized both of the preceding two major schools of American legal theory. The realists had insisted and the process theorists had acknowledged that a diverse array of policies were relevant to every legal rule or issue. As noted above, the process theorists had argued that a wise, mature judge or other decision maker could derive from those competing considerations sensible, if not necessarily determinate answers to particular questions. But, in the 1960s, more and more participants in legal culture came to doubt that the "balancing" method commended by the process theorists had any bite at all. To some of those skeptics, economic analysis offered clarity and rigor. For Posner and his followers, the ideal of allocative efficiency offered a single beacon, the conscientious pursuit of which would make possible the socially beneficial reorganization of the entire legal system. For other economists, like Calabresi and Melamed, who were equally concerned with distributional considerations, the normative field was more complex, but nowhere near as chaotic as the sets of values associated with realism or process theory.

At the outset of the law-and-economics movement, its political valence was unclear. Although some aspects of "The Problem of Social Cost" were distinctly conservative in tone – for example, Coase's sweeping declaration that "economists, and policymakers generally, have tended to over-estimate the advantages which come from governmental regulation" – other passages expressed skepticism that unregulated private markets would foster economic efficiency. And whether exploration of the distributional consequences of legal rules will lead to liberal or conservative recommendations depends, of course, on the distributional criterion one is seeking to advance. Nevertheless, over time, economic analysis within legal scholarship came increasingly to be associated with the political Right. In part, this association was due to the notoriety and influence of a cluster of scholars centered at the University of Chicago who did indeed think that governmental intervention in private markets almost always wrought more harm than good. In part, it also resulted from most economists' insistence on the superiority of their perspective and their skepticism about the insights that could be derived from any other methodology. Whatever the cause, by the late 1970s, economists dominated the conservative end of the political spectrum at most American law schools, and their increasingly confident assaults on scholars to their left contributed heavily to bitter battles over curricula and faculty appointments.

Law and Society

The economists were not the only group of legal scholars disappointed by process theory who sought inspiration and guidance from some other academic discipline. Some turned to sociology, others to philosophy, still others to history.

The path to sociology was already reasonably well marked. Around the turn of the century, Max Weber had written provocatively about connections between law and social activity. Holmes, in "The Path of the Law," had famously predicted that "the statistics guy" would be "the man of the future." And some of the legal realists had undertaken extensive (albeit not always fruitful) empirical studies of "the law in action." In the early 1960s, a rapidly growing group of scholars, many of them professors at the University of Wisconsin Law School, built on these foundations a full-blown movement they dubbed "law and society."

Among the pioneers was Stewart Macaulay. In his most famous article, "Non-Contractual Relations in Business: A Preliminary Study," Macaulay broke sharply with the kind of legal scholarship in general and contracts scholarship in particular exemplified by Fuller's article on "Consideration and Form." A contract, he argued, is best understood as a social institution, not a legal form: "a contract, as I use the term here, involves two distinct elements: (a) rational planning of the transaction with careful provision for as many future contingencies as can be foreseen, and (b) the existence or use of actual or potential legal sanctions to induce performance of the exchange or to compensate for non-performance." Drawing on extensive empirical work concerning business practices in Wisconsin, Macaulay contended that business enterprises employ contracts, so defined, under circumstances and for reasons quite different from those presumed by traditional legal schol-ars. For example, often a firm enters into a contract more to clarify its own internal structure – say, to improve communication between production and marketing divisions – than to organize its relationship with the other party. The breach of a contract typically leads to renegotiation of the parties' relationship. Lawsuits to enforce bargains are rare and are typically moti-vated more by the thirst for revenge than by the hope of recovering damages or securing specific performance. In general, Macaulay found, contracts are less important than ongoing relationships among enterprises in organizing business and distributing their fruits.

To many scholars, the methodology exemplified by Macaulay's article seemed compelling. Detailed, empirically grounded, "bottom-up" studies of how people and enterprises actually use the law offered more insight, they believed, than the "top down" approaches of all other schools of legal theory. Many set about documenting in various contexts the gap between the "law on the books" and "the law in action." Others explored the ways in which legal norms affect the contents of bargains made in their "shadow." Still others studied the relative costs in practice of various forms of dispute resolution (often concluding that mediation and arbitration systems were superior to litigation). Finally, many explored the extent to which the regulatory and social welfare initiatives of the Great Society did (or, more often, did not) achieve their professed ends.

Like economic analysis, sociological analysis of law had no necessary political tilt. However, the large majority of empirical studies of the types just summarized terminated in criticisms of the existing legal order – specifically, in contentions that the law was biased in favor of the rich on one or more of four levels. First, the substantive rules are commonly designed to enhance or protect the interests "of those in positions of wealth and authority." Second, even when unbiased, the rules are commonly interpreted in ways that favor the powerful. Third, the legal profession is organized in ways that favor the "haves" in their struggles with the "have-nots." For example, as Marc Galanter pointed out in a seminal article, the canons of ethics permit the lawyers for "repeat players" (typically businesses) to use the litigation game strategically – settling or abandoning unpromising cases while vigorously pursuing cases with attractive facts in hopes of securing favorable precedents – but forbid the lawyers for "one-shotters" (typically individuals pressing claims against the repeat players) to do the same. Fourth, the legal system as a whole is organized in a fashion that enables "the haves" to invoke it more shrewdly and effectively than the have-nots. For example, as Galanter pointed out, the complexity and ambiguity of many of its norms and the many opportunities for appeal favor parties with access to sophisticated (expensive) counsel and the financial ability to tolerate long delays in the issuance of judgments.

The result was that while the adherents of the fading legal process school occupied the political center of most law school faculties, and the majority of the law-and-economics scholars stationed themselves on the Right, those associated with the law and society movement usually found themselves on the Left.

Law and Philosophy

In the 1970s and 1980s, significant numbers of legal scholars began to draw on moral and political philosophy to propose modifications of American legal doctrine. They fell into two reasonably distinct subgroups, each looking to a different body of argument then popular in philosophy departments.

The first subgroup was influenced most heavily by the resurgence of interest among English and American philosophers in the work of Immanuel Kant. H. L. A. Hart, writing in 1977, summarized as follows this reorientation of perspective:

We are currently witnessing, I think, the progress of a transition from a once widely accepted old faith that some form of utilitarianism, if only we could discover the right form, *must* capture the essence of political morality. The new faith is that the truth must lie not with a doctrine that takes the maximisation of aggregate or average general welfare for its goal, but with a doctrine of basic human rights, protecting specific basic liberties and interests of individuals.

Among the philosophers taking this neo-Kantian tack, the most prominent was John Rawls. Of Rawls' many arguments, the most important was his theory of distributive justice. In brief, Rawls argued that inequality in the distribution of "primary goods" is legitimate only if, by increasing incentives for productivity, it leaves the members of the lowest group in the society no worse off than they would have been under conditions of perfect equality.

Among the legal scholars who looked for guidance to Kant and (to a lesser extent) Rawls were Bruce Ackerman, Ronald Dworkin, Charles Fried, David Richards, and, in some of his work, Frank Michelman. They shared a methodology, encapsulated in the slogan: "The right is prior to the good." Less cryptically, they argued that every government has a responsibility to establish and enforce a system of basic rights and liberties, but lacks legitimate authority to encourage or compel adherence to particular ways of living. In a polity organized on those principles, people would be accorded the respect they are due as autonomous moral agents, permitted and empowered to select and pursue their own goals so long as they did not interfere with the comparable liberties of others.

From this common methodological platform, however, the members of this group derived radically different recommendations for legal reform. Michelman, for example, relied heavily on Rawls to urge the Supreme Court to increase the stringency of its review of statutes adversely affecting the poor – for example, by striking down legislation that made access to public office dependent on "economic vicissitude" or failed to abide by the principle that "each child must be guaranteed the means of developing his competence, self-knowledge, and tastes for living." Fried, by contrast, argued on Kantian premises that contract law should be refashioned so as to limit liability to situations in which a person has broken a freely made promise – that is, has violated a commitment he has imposed on him- or herself – and denounced the steadily growing roles played in American law by the idea that contractual duties should be created or construed so as to advance "the community's" goals and standards. Dworkin, in one of his many articles and books on public and private law, argued that, in determining the latitude that the state enjoys to regulate pornography, we should be sure to respect persons' "right to moral independence" – their "right not to suffer disadvantage in the distribution of social goods and opportunities ... [solely because] their officials or fellow-citizens think that their opinions about the right way to lead their own lives are ignoble and wrong." Fidelity to this principle, he concluded, requires striking down anti-pornography legislation to the extent it is motivated either by the belief that the attitudes about sexuality contained in pornographic materials are "demeaning or bestial" or by the desire to relieve people of their disgust at the knowledge that their neighbors are looking at "dirty pictures" – but does not require invalidation of legislation driven by people's desire "not to encounter genital displays on the way to the grocer" or by a demonstrated link between pornography and crime. Using standard labels, Michelman's argument might be described as progressive, Fried's as conservative, and Dworkin's as liberal. Divergence of this sort made the political cast of Kantian legal theory intriguingly ambiguous.

The members of the second of the two subgroups derived inspiration from Hegel and Aristotle, rather than Kant. They rejected their colleagues' insistence on the priority of the right over the good, arguing instead that, in Michael Sandel's words, "we cannot justify political arrangements without reference to common purposes and ends, and ... we cannot conceive our personhood without reference to our role as citizens, and as participants in a common life." Thus freed from the Kantian ban on governmental promotion of substantive visions of the good life, they set about elaborating the social and legal arrangements that would most facilitate human flourishing.

Some examples: Margaret Jane Radin of Stanford and Jeremy Waldron of Berkeley argued in separate essays that the best justification for and guide to the reform of the institution of private property are that it enables people more fully to realize their selves – for example, by forming identity-stabilizing attachments to physical objects, by cultivating the virtues of prudence and responsibility, by affording them zones of privacy, or by providing them the means of self-fulfilling acts of generosity. Dan Kahan, who would later join the Yale faculty, argued that group-libel laws (statutes that proscribe speech or expressive action designed to foster hatred of particular racial, ethnic, or religious groups) should be deemed compatible with the First Amendment because they protect the "constitutive communities" central to many people's ability to form, modify, and implement rich conceptions of personhood. Finally, Kenneth Karst of UCLA argued that "intimate associations," including marriages and non-marital partnerships, were crucial in cultivating attributes central to self-realization – "caring, commitment, intimacy, self-identification" – and thus that the courts should allow legislatures to interfere with such associations only if they have strong, non-pretextual reasons for doing so.

One variant of this general approach proved by far the most popular. The substantive vision on which it was based was the cluster of ideals now known as classical republicanism: the notions, in brief, that a good life is a virtuous life, that one component of virtue is a willingness to subordinate one's private interests to the welfare of the community as a whole, and that only through active participation in the deliberative politics of a republic is true self-realization possible. In the late 1960s and 1970s, an important group of historians had excavated this belief system, identified its roots in the writings of Aristotle and Machiavelli, and showed the important roles it had played in eighteenth-century British politics, in helping fuel the American Revolution, in shaping the Federal Constitution, and in inspiring various nineteenth-century reform movements. In the 1980s, legal scholars began to take note. Partly because many of the Founders seemed to have been steeped in republicanism, and partly because (at least if purged of its patriarchal, xenophobic, and militaristic dimensions) it offered an alternative to the time-worn ideology of liberalism, it seemed to provide a promising criterion with which to reevaluate a wide variety of doctrines in both public and private law.

In the pioneering essay of this ilk, Cass Sunstein argued that several extant doctrines – including the "rationality requirement" that the Supreme Court had derived from the Due Process Clause of the Fourteenth Amendment, the "public use" requirement in the Eminent Domain Clause of the Fifth Amendment, and the "hard-look" doctrine in administrative law – were designed at least in part to compel or encourage legislators to engage in republican-style deliberation "instead of responding mechanically to interest-group pressures." In Sunstein's view, the courts should go further in this general direction, invalidating or impeding legislation whose content or genesis conflicted with the republican ideal. In several subsequent articles, Frank Michelman invoked republicanism in more complex and tentative ways. Less confident of the substantive merits of the ideology, Michelman nevertheless emphasized its heuristic value and contended that it alone provided a plausible way of reconciling two propositions equally central to our political culture: "first, that the American people are politically free insomuch as they are governed by themselves collectively, and, second, that the American people are politically free insomuch as they are governed by laws and not men." Convinced, several other scholars began introducing republican themes into casebooks, law-review articles, and classrooms.

The heyday of this mini-movement came in 1987, when roughly a thousand law professors attended a session at the annual meeting of the Association of American Law Schools at which Sunstein and Michelman tried to address the criticisms of their arguments that had been made both by historians (who found their efforts to apply ancient ideas to modern issues troublingly anachronistic) and legal scholars who found the organicist, communitarian aspects of republicanism either naïve or repellent. Since then, this particular star in the firmament of legal theory has faded substantially, but has not disappeared altogether.

Critical Legal Studies

The first national conference on Critical Legal Studies (CLS) was held in Madison, Wisconsin, in March 1977. It attracted a wonderfully motley group of scholars (some of them former Marxists disillusioned by the sectarianism of the Left in the 1960s; many of them liberals disillusioned by the apparent failure of the civil rights movement and by the association of the Democratic Party with the war in Vietnam; and a few of them sociologists unsatisfied by the fare available at law and society conferences), legal activists (many working to improve the positions of workers or poor residential tenants), and law students. During the next few years, the number of people who attended the annual CLS meetings grew rapidly, and the body of writing they published mushroomed. After 1980, however, internecine struggles, denials of tenure to some of leading members of the movement, and the increasing disaffection of others eroded its ranks. By the early 1990s, it was moribund.

Though short-lived, CLS had a profound and lasting impact on American legal thought. As was true of legal realism, many of its most controversial claims later became widely accepted. And it helped spawn other clusters of people and ideas – critical race theory, feminist legal theory, and queer theory – that would remain vital far beyond its demise.

The central thesis of CLS was that legal discourse is highly patterned – and, more particularly, that it is organized around a series of oppositions or contradictions. The most detailed and influential map of those patterns was contained in Duncan Kennedy's pioneering 1976 essay, "Form and Substance in Private Law Adjudication." Kennedy argued that much legal argumentation could be reduced to two long-standing debates – the first over whether legal norms are best cast in the form of "clearly defined, highly administrable, general rules" or in the form of "equitable standards producing ad hoc decisions with relatively little precedential value"; the second over whether the content of legal norms should be guided by the substantive values associated with "individualism" or the values associated with "altruism." The latter pair of terms, Kennedy defined as follows:

The essence of individualism is the making of a sharp distinction between one's interests and those of others, combined with the belief that a preference in conduct for one's own interests is legitimate, but that one should be willing to respect the rules that make it possible to coexist with others similarly self-interested. The form of conduct associated with individualism is self-reliance. This means an insistence on defining and achieving objectives without help from others (i.e., without being dependent on them or asking sacrifices of them). It means accepting that they will neither share their gains nor one's own losses. And it means a firm conviction that I am entitled to enjoy the benefits of my efforts without an obligation to share or sacrifice them to the interests of others. . . .

The essence of altruism is the belief that one ought *not* to indulge a sharp preference for one's own interest over those of others. Altruism enjoins us to make sacrifices, to share, and to be merciful.

The arguments deployed in favor of any one of these positions, Kennedy argued, were "stereotyped," predictable, choreographed. For example, rules are conventionally defended on the grounds that they restrain official arbitrariness and favoritism, that they promote certainty (thus assisting private parties in planning their affairs), that they minimize judicial discretion and thus are more consistent than standards with democratic theory, and so forth. Standards are conventionally defended on the grounds that they are capable of advancing social objectives more precisely than inevitably under- or over-inclusive rules, that they are less likely to exacerbate inequalities of bargaining power, that they are less "dynamically unstable" because judges feel less need to carve exceptions out of them to favor sympathetic litigants, and so forth. Individualism is commonly buttressed with arguments that self-interestedness "is a moral good in itself," that the "invisible hand" will convert myriad uncoordinated selfish actions into collective gains, and that well-meant state efforts to curb selfish conduct typically do more harm than good. Altruism is buttressed by predictable criticisms of each of the foregoing propositions. Kennedy's most original claim was that the two rhetorical axes are connected – specifically, that the moral, economic, and political arguments associated with rules resonate with corresponding arguments for individualism and that there exists a comparable homology between the arguments for standards and the arguments for altruism. Now comes the rub. One can imagine larger argumentative structures – ways of stacking or arranging the pair of rhetorical axes – that would give lawmakers and law interpreters guidance concerning which set of claims (rules/individualism or standards/altruism) should be given precedence in which circumstances. Indeed, in both of what Kennedy dubbed the "pre-classical" period of

American law (roughly 1800–1870) and the "classical" period (roughly 1850–1940), overarching theories were in place that purported to do just that. Those theories, however, have since collapsed. The result is that, today, the two sets of arguments are on the same plane. It is no longer possible to depict one as constituting the "core" of the legal system and the other as the "periphery." Rather, "[e]very occasion for lawmaking will raise the fundamental conflict of individualism and altruism, on both a substantive and a formal level."

Other writers associated with the CLS movement emphasized other tensions within legal argumentation. Some put more weight on what Mark Kelman described as "the contradiction between a commitment to the traditional liberal notion that values or desires are arbitrary, subjective, individual, and individuating while facts or reason are objective and universal *and* a commitment to the ideal that we can 'know' social and ethical truths objectively (through objective knowledge of true human nature) or to the hope that one can transcend the usual distinction between subjective and objective in seeking moral truth." Others focused on (again quoting Kelman) "the contradiction between a commitment to an intentionalistic discourse, in which human action is seen as the product of a self-determining individual will, and a determinist discourse, in which the activity of nominal subjects merits neither respect nor condemnation because it is simply deemed the expected outcome of existing structures." But common to most CLS writing was a conviction that deep divides of this general sort were ubiquitous in American law.

This characterization of contemporary legal discourse had several important implications. The most important, perhaps, is that legal decision making – at both the legislative and the judicial levels – is highly indeterminate. Contradictory arguments of equal stature can be brought to bear on almost every issue. More subtly, many of those arguments, closely examined, consist of alloys, in which a large dollop of ideas drawn from one end of a spectrum is tempered by a few ideas drawn from the opposite end. For example, individualism is not a purely egoistic ideal, insofar as it acknowledges some duties to consider the welfare of others, just as altruism is not pure self-abnegation, but rather recognizes the legitimacy in many contexts of the pursuit of self-interest. Such tensions internal to each cluster of arguments increase the chances that a shrewd speaker of legal language could "flip" a conventional defense of any given proposition into a defense of its opposite. This is not to suggest that CLS scholars thought that legal decision making was unpredictable. Most freely acknowledged that, in Joseph Singer's words, a combination of "shared understandings of proper institutional roles and the extent to which the status quo should be maintained or altered, . . . 'common sense' understandings of what rules mean, . . . conventions (the identification of rules and exceptions), and politics (the differentiation between liberal and conservative judges)" often made it easy to predict how a court would resolve a given dispute. More fundamentally, even (or especially) Duncan Kennedy acknowledged that, for "mysterious" reasons, it is often impossible even for determined and sophisticated lawyers to construct plausible arguments for certain positions. But the zone of freedom is substantially wider than is commonly thought.

The sharply different depictions of the American legal system offered by all of the then-prominent schools of legal theory struck CLS scholars as ludicrous, pernicious, or both. They were especially scornful of process theory. Attempts to differentiate issues appropriate for resolution by the judiciary, issues best left to the legislature, and issues most sensibly decided through exercises of executive or administrative discretion in their judgment at best only separated the choices confronting lawmakers into boxes. None of the methodologies that process theorists urged on officials of the three branches – and certainly not the kind of wise "balancing" of multiple competing policy considerations that they advocated for the judiciary – seemed to CLS scholars to provide any meaningful guidance.

In the judgment of CLS scholars, the lawyer-economists should be commended for acknowledging the many choices confronting lawmakers, but their quest (or, more precisely, the quest of the subset of lawyer-economists bent on maximizing allocative efficiency) to develop a methodology that would enable determinate, socially beneficial resolution of those choices had failed. In part, that failure derived from what CLS scholars referred to as "the offer-asking problem": when measuring the "wealth" fostered by a particular legal rule, should the value of the goods or states of affairs it affected (such as habitable apartments or protection against sexual assault) be priced on the basis of the amount of money consumers would be willing and able to pay to obtain them or the amount of money consumers would demand in return for surrendering them? The economists themselves were aware that the answers to these two inquiries would sometimes diverge – for instance, when the impact of the rule in question was large in relation to the total wealth of the affected parties – but they argued that circumstances in which that divergence would render the economic inquiry indeterminate were rare. Scholars like Mark Kelman, Ed Baker, and Duncan Kennedy, drawing on recent work by psychologists like Daniel Kahneman, Amos Tversky, and Richard Thaler, contended that gaps between "offer" and "asking" prices were both larger and more common than the economists believed and thus more threatening to the methodology as a whole.

An even more serious problem was what the CLS scholars called "general indeterminacy." Suppose, to illustrate, an economist or judge wishes to determine which combination of nuisance and premises-liability rules would most promote economic efficiency. The answer is likely to hinge on the order in which she considers the two fields. If, say, she starts by determining the optimal nuisance rule and then, taking as given the entitlements produced by that analysis and the associated effects on landowners' wealth, she determines the optimal rules governing landowners' liability to injured trespassers, she is likely to select a combination of rules different from the combination she would have generated if she proceeded in the opposite order. The more numerous the issues to be considered, the more likely it is that the sequence in which they are addressed will affect the outcome. The lawyer-economists had not and could not point to any meta-criterion that would dictate one sequence rather than another.

Some of the efforts by legal scholars to glean insight from moral philosophy – in particular, the attempts by a subgroup to articulate visions of human flourishing and then to identify legal reforms that would advance those visions – struck CLS scholars as less laughable. Indeed, in the late 1980s, some scholars formerly associated with CLS embarked on projects of just that sort. But to the majority, the Aristotelian expedition, though perhaps admirable, was doomed to failure. Peer into your soul – or reflect on the best shared aspirations and commitments of your fellow citizens – and you are likely to find not the seeds of a coherent conception of the good life and the good society, but yet more contradictory impulses. In Kennedy's words,

> Most participants in American legal culture believe that the goal of individual freedom is at the same time dependent on and incompatible with the communal coercive action that is necessary to achieve it. Others (family, friends, bureaucrats, cultural figures, the state) are necessary if we are to become persons at all – they provide us the stuff of our selves and protect us in crucial ways against destruction. . . . But at the same time that it forms and protects us, the universe of others (family, friendship, bureaucracy, culture, the state) threatens us with annihilation and urges upon us forms of fusion that are quite plainly bad rather than good. . . . Through our existence as members of collectives, we impose on others and have imposed on us hierarchical structures of power, welfare, and access to enlightenment that are illegitimate, whether based on birth into a particular social class or on the accident of genetic endowment. The kicker is that the abolition of these illegitimate structures, the fashioning of an unalienated collective existence, appears to imply such a massive increase of collective control over our lives that it would defeat its purpose.

The bleakness of this outlook prompted many critics – including some on the political Left – to reject CLS as a theory of despair. To some extent, the charge is fair. Kennedy himself acknowledged that his methodology could be characterized as "tragic." Certainly, irony – a sense of the frequency with which good people are corrupted, well-meant reform efforts go awry, and in general "things fall apart" – permeates CLS writings. But the aspiration, at least, of the participants in the movement was to fuel, not enervate, projects for political and economic change by discrediting arguments that depicted the legal system as running reasonably well and susceptible of only modest adjustment, by exposing the extent to which it was designed to advance the interests of the wealthy and powerful, and by contributing to activist lawyers' awareness of the degree to which it was unstable and malleable.

Feminist Legal Theory

In the last quarter of the twentieth century, a growing group of scholars began to examine closely the relationships among law, gender, and sexuality. Their work rapidly became increasingly influential, despite (or perhaps because) of the range and depth of their disagreements.

The first of the issues on which they diverged was the ideal of equality. For centuries, successive groups of legal reformers in the United States have been striving to eliminate inequalities in the positions of women and men. In the early nineteenth century, for example, an improbable alliance of Jacksonian politicians, businessmen, and early feminists sought legislative changes that would give married women the same rights to engage in business and manage their own property that their husbands already enjoyed. The late nineteenth and early twentieth centuries witnessed a similar struggle to accord women the right to vote. In the late twentieth century, analogous campaigns were mounted to purge discrimination against women in the workplace. And so forth. Some of these reformers argued (occasionally successfully) that, to provide women true substantive equality, it was necessary to accord them "special" (i.e., unequal) treatment – for example, by providing them health benefits to cover the costs associated with pregnancy. But the ultimate goal always remained to use the law to place women on a par with men. An important line of theoretical writing, beginning with John Stuart Mill's, "On the Subjection of Women," fed and was fed by these initiatives. The primary theme of this body of writing is that women have the same capacities and deserve the same legal entitlements as men.

In the 1970s and early 1980s, more and more feminist legal theorists repudiated this liberal vision and strategy. They took the position that women are different – have different experiences, outlooks, and needs – and that both a genuine understanding of women and the identification of opportunities for progressive legal reform require taking those differences seriously. The divisions within this group, however, were just as sharp as the divide between its members and the liberal feminists.

The members of one subgroup – sometimes known as "maternal" or "cultural" feminists – were inspired by the work of Carol Gilligan, Nancy Chodorow, Jean Baker Miller, and Anne Schaef, who documented important differences in the self-conceptions and habits of mind of girls and boys, women and men. Robin West summarizes this body of work as follows:

[A]ccording to Gilligan (and her subjects), women view themselves as fundamentally connected to, not separate from, the rest of life. This difference permeates virtually every aspect of our lives. According to the vast literature on difference now being developed by cultural feminists, women's cognitive development, literary sensibility, aesthetic taste, and psychological development, no less than our anatomy, are all fundamentally different from men's, and are different in the same way: unlike men, we view ourselves as connected to, not separate from, the other. As a consequence, women's ways of knowing are more "integrative" than men's; women's aesthetic and critical sense is "embroidered" rather than "laddered;" women's psychological development remains within the sphere of "attachment" rather than "individuation."

The most significant aspect of our difference, though, is surely the moral difference. According to cultural feminism, women are more nurturant, caring, loving, and responsible to others than are men. This capacity for nurturance and care dictates the moral terms in which women, distinctively, construct social relations: women view the morality of actions against a standard of responsibility to others, rather than against a standard of rights and autonomy from others. As Gilligan puts it:

The moral imperative . . . [for] women is an injunction to care, a responsibility to discern and alleviate the "real and recognizable trouble" of this world. For men, the moral imperative appears rather as an injunction to respect the rights of others and thus to protect from interference the rights to life and self-fulfillment.

The sources of these differences were much debated by the members of the group. Were they rooted somehow in biology? The results of evolution? The byproducts of a childrearing system based on mothering – so that, in Carrie Menkel-Meadow's words, "growing up is a process of identification and connection for a girl and separation and individuation for a boy"? The byproducts of women's experiences in taking care of young children? The answers were uncertain. What was clear, however, was the presence of systematic and durable differences between the genders.

That insight, in the judgment of the cultural feminists, had various implications for law. Menkel-Meadow, for example, predicted that, once women lawyers achieved a critical mass, we would likely see several changes in the practice of law (for example, more use of mediation, more settlements, less reliance in jury arguments on rhetorical styles based on "persuasive intimidation" and more efforts on the part of advocates to create "a personal relationship with the jury in which they urge the jurors to examine their own perceptions and values and encourage them to think for themselves"); in the organization of the profession (for example, more collegiality in writing briefs, changes in the canons of ethics softening a lawyer's obligation to serve her client's needs exclusively and mandating more disclosures of information to opponents); and in legal doctrine (for example, wider definitions of relevance and admissibility in the law of evidence). Other scholars were even more explicit in urging that major fields of law should be modified to make them less male and more female. For example, Leslie Bender argued on Gilliganesque premises that the law of torts should be refashioned so as to permit a plaintiff who makes a minimal showing that a defendant has exposed her to serious risk to begin collecting from the defendant medical expenses, lost wages, and other damages – and if her claim is ultimately found to be meritorious, to force the defendant, not only to pay the plaintiff money, but to assume non-delegable responsibility to provide her direct physical care.

A second subgroup, led by Catharine MacKinnon, argued that the gender differences identified by the cultural feminists, if they existed at all, were the fruits of a socioeconomic system that enabled women to acquire status and power only through their associations with men. A reform program that celebrated and sought to generalize feminine virtues thus seemed distinctly unpromising. Rather, MacKinnon argued, we should focus on a different respect in which women are different: namely, that they are dominated by men. That dominance has many dimensions, but at base it is sexual. The nub of the matter, she argued, is that, in contemporary society, men fuck, while women are fucked. MacKinnon's claim was sweeping: "the molding, direction, and expression of sexuality organizes society into two sexes – women and men – which division underlies the totality of social relations." The central project of men, she argued, was to control all aspects of women's sexuality, from reproduction to "the social rhythms and mores of sexual intercourse." In this, they have been highly successful, not just through the establishment and enforcement of formal rules that reinforce their sexual power, but more fundamentally through the elaboration of an ideal of femininity, centered on the traits of docility, softness, passivity, nurturance, weakness, narcissism, incompetence, domesticity, and fidelity, all of which implicitly emphasize women's sexual accessibility and subordination. Females internalize that ideal in order to become women; to be a woman is to be sexually desirable to men by manifesting these features.

The mission of feminism, MacKinnon claimed, is to overturn this structure of domination. The obstacles are formidable. The infusion of contemporary institutions and culture with the male point of view is so thorough that it is extremely difficult for women to achieve an independent vantage point. In a passage that revealed at once the harshness of her diagnosis of the current situation and the ambitiousness of her hopes for the future, she argued as follows:

Feminism criticizes this male totality without an account of our capacity to do so or to imagine or realize a more whole truth. Feminism affirms women's point of view by revealing, criticizing, and explaining its impossibility. This is not a dialectical paradox. It is a methodological expression of women's situation, in which the struggle for consciousness is a struggle for world: for a sexuality, a history, a culture, a community, a form of power, an experience of the sacred.

The task of constructing such a consciousness would be made easier if we could eliminate the legal rules that sustain male dominance. Proceeding on that assumption, MacKinnon and her allies launched in the 1980s and '90s a formidable set of reform initiatives. The most successful and deservedly famous was their effort to establish the illegality of sexual harassment. Almost as notorious was their campaign to tighten prohibitions on the distribution of pornography. The city of Indianapolis did indeed adopt such an ordinance, but a federal court struck it down as a violation of the First Amendment. (Not all feminists were dismayed by the court's ruling; so-called "sex-positive" or "sex-affirmative" feminists thought the suppression of pornography would do more harm than good.) MacKinnon's most recent initiative has been an effort to secure international legal recognition of rape as a war crime.

Is there any thing, then, that feminist legal theorists have in common? Perhaps one – a methodology. Much more than any of the other groups of scholars we have considered, feminist legal theorists were and are concerned with the manner in which insights concerning the nature of law are developed and disseminated. Specifically, they emphasize *conversations* with or among women. For some, like Joan Williams, this commitment is connected to an "antifoundationalist epistemology" – the notion that our identities and our aspirations are entirely socially constructed and thus that the only way in which we can hope to identify normative criteria is to explore and debate the shared commitments of the communities to which we belong and in which we must continue to make ourselves. For others, like MacKinnon, it is rooted in appreciation of the revelatory power of the activity of "consciousness raising":

Consciousness raising is the major technique of analysis, structure of organization, method of practice, and theory of social change of the women's movement. In consciousness raising, often in groups, the impact of male dominance is concretely uncovered and analyzed through the collective speaking of women's experience, from the perspective of that experience.

Whatever its origins, this approach differs radically from the solitary, introspective methods employed by most other American legal theorists – indeed, by most scholars of all sorts.

To sum up, American legal theory in the twentieth century can be divided roughly into thirds. In the first trimester, scholars associated initially with sociological jurisprudence and then with legal realism led an ultimately successful assault on the fortress of classical legal thought. In the second, a new orthodoxy emerged, organized around the methodological commitments and political centrism of legal process theory. In the third, process theory fell from grace, succeeded not by a single revolutionary creed, but by sustained conflict between the adherents of several incompatible schools of thought: law and economics, law and society, several variants of moral philosophy, critical legal studies, and feminist legal theory. At the beginning of the twenty-first century, no resolution of this controversy was yet in sight.

II. EDUCATION

The Emergence of the Harvard System

The central event in the history of American legal education was the establishment and dissemination of the Harvard model. This transformation began in 1870, when President Charles Eliot of Harvard University appointed Christopher Columbus Langdell as dean of the law school there, and Langdell, with Eliot's aid, set in motion a set of related changes in the structure and pedagogy of the school. By 1920, the majority of American law schools – and virtually all of the elite, full-time schools – had implemented most aspects of the new system (some eagerly, some grudgingly, some after bitter internal struggles), and the increasingly powerful American Bar Association and Association of American Law Schools, formerly often divided on the issue, were now reasonably united in advocating its universal adoption.

Although the transformation in legal education was well underway before 1920, understanding the new model at its inception is crucial to comprehension of developments in legal education that occurred thereafter. So let us first briefly review its main features.

The Harvard system had five related components. First, law should be learned, not through an apprenticeship, not in an undergraduate program, but through a three or four-year formal program of study in a graduate school.

Second, the primary materials one studied in law school were appellate judicial opinions applying legal doctrines to particular sets of facts. In his pioneering casebook on the law of contracts, Langdell justified this so-called case method on the following grounds: "[L]aw, considered as a science, consists of certain principles or doctrines. To have such mastery of these as to be able to apply them with constant facility and certainty to the ever-tangled skein of human affairs, is what constitutes a true lawyer ... and the shortest and the best, if not the only way of mastering the doctrine effectually is by studying the cases in which it is embodied. ... Moreover, the number of legal doctrines is much less than is commonly supposed." Gradually, this initial justification gave way to a different theory. James Barr Ames, Langdell's successor as dean at Harvard, contended that the purpose of the case method was not to teach students the content of legal principles, which were too multifarious to be conveyed in any course of study, but rather to equip them with "the power of solving legal problems" – in other words, to train them to "think like lawyers." (The second justification, even more than the first, suggested that the jurisdictions from which the judicial opinions in question were drawn were unimportant. It thus made sense for students in schools located in different states to learn from the same casebooks – and for students to attend law schools in states other than those in which they expected to practice. Thus was born the idea of the "national law school.")

Third, classroom instruction consisted primarily of so-called Socratic questioning. The professor asked students to describe the facts of the cases and to analyze the courts' reasoning. Through repeated inquisitorial exercises, the students were expected to learn how to ferret out the principles underlying decisions and to recognize the relatively few instances in which courts had gone astray. (Interestingly, recent scholarship suggests that Langdell himself, the popularizer if not the inventor of this method, used it in a somewhat different spirit, encouraging students to think critically and frequently acknowledging "his ignorance or uncertainty about points of doctrine." But, in this respect, Langdell seems to have been atypical.)

Fourth, the subjects taught in this fashion should consist of "pure law" courses. Political science, philosophy, and economics had no place, so the proponents of the model argued, in a law school curriculum. Indeed, though the set of subjects taught in most law schools in 1920 was somewhat larger than the set taught in the middle of the nineteenth century, it did not differ in kind.

Fifth and finally, students demonstrated their competence not by writing essays expounding legal doctrine, but by applying what they had learned to hypothetical problems. Initially, those problems were brief and schematic. Over time, they became increasingly complex.

Several factors help explain why this system took root and then, like kudzu, spread so rapidly. The system rested on a particular variant of the old idea of law as a science that both resonated with the classical style of legal thought (which, as we have seen, was dominant around the turn of the century) and appealed to university administrators then in the process of refashioning American higher education along German lines. It was also, in Ames's words, "a virile system," in which learning was achieved through self-reliance, struggle, and competition, activities celebrated by the then-popular ideology of Social Darwinism. On a more practical level, it was inexpensive, enabling small faculties to teach large bodies of students. In the opinion of advocates such as Eliot and of some modern historians (such as William LaPiana), it was functional, in the senses that it did a good job of imparting to students skills they would actually need when practicing law (although many practitioners during the period were skeptical on precisely this point) and that insights gleaned through combative Socratic exchanges were more likely to be retained by students than knowledge imparted through more traditional lectures. In the opinion of other historians (such as Harry First), it served the less noble interests of a subset of law schools in controlling the market for legal education and of established practitioners in reducing competition in the provision of legal services. Finally, in the opinions of still others (such as Robert Stevens and Jerold Auerbach), it was one of many devices by which elite lawyers sought to limit the number of Irish, Italians, Poles, Jews, and African Americans who entered the profession – and to inculcate "proper principles" and respect for the American system of government in the few who were admitted. Whatever its causes, by 1920, it exerted a powerful grip on American legal education.

Criticisms (Round One)

In the first half of the twentieth century, the Harvard model was attacked from two quarters, but withstood both assaults. The first came from Alfred Reed, a non-lawyer who, under the auspices of the Carnegie Foundation, published a set of high-profile studies of legal education and the legal profession in the United States. In Reed's view, the joint aspiration of the elite university-affiliated schools, the ABA, and the AALS to create a "unitary" bar through universal adoption of the Harvard system was misguided. Instead of seeking to eliminate the rapidly growing set of unaccredited, proprietary, part-time, and night law schools, which catered to poorer students and second-generation immigrants, the bar should embrace them. Drawing loosely on the British system, which separated lawyers into barristers and solicitors, Reed argued that the United States, as a large, pluralistic society, needed more than one type of lawyer. The elite schools should train the elite; the proprietary schools should train the rest. Reed's comments on pedagogy were closely related to this vision. The case method and Socratic questioning, he acknowledged, were excellent tools in the hands of "genuine scholars" training smart, well-prepared students. But they were inferior to older, more straightforward teaching techniques when it came to training the harried students of "ordinary" abilities who filled the proprietary schools.

As one might imagine, Reed's report found favor among the deans and faculties of the proprietary schools, but did not persuade the increasingly consolidated leadership of the ABA and AALS. Elihu Root of Harvard, then chair of the ABA Section of Legal Education and Admissions to the Bar, denounced Reed's proposal for a stratified bar as undemocratic and un-American and his overall message as "reactionary," "narrow," and "unfair." Arthur Corbin of Yale, then president of the AALS, was similarly hostile. The increasingly shrill complaints of people like Gleason Archer, dean of Boston's Suffolk Law School (which, though unaccredited, was then the largest law school in the world), that the elite were conspiring to drive them out of business fell on deaf ears.

The second of the attacks came from inside the elite law schools themselves. For years, some of the faculty of major schools other than Harvard had been expressing doubts about the merits of the case method, Socratic questioning, and exclusive focus on "pure law" subjects. For example, in 1912, George Chase, formerly a professor at Columbia and by then the dean of the New York Law School, argued that "case-books take a good deal more space to set forth the law on a given subject than do text-books, and even then they may not do this with satisfactory completeness," and that "it will not seem surprising that a law school using treatises as the fundamental basis of its instruction can cover the same field of legal knowledge in a shorter time than schools which confine themselves to case-books." Legal realism threw wood onto this smoldering fire. For example, Jerome Frank, drawing directly on his views concerning the limited explanatory or predictive power of appellate opinions, argued that, if students were to learn the law through the study of cases, they should at least be provided with full information concerning the genesis of those controversies and the various factors, both "rational" and "non-rational," that shaped the conduct of the parties, lawyers, juries, and judges. More broadly, he urged law schools to recapture some of the good features of the old "legal apprenticeship system" – for example, by requiring students to visit trial and appellate courts and to participate in legal clinics, providing legal aid to the poor, to the government, or to quasi-governmental agencies. Karl Llewellyn echoed many of Frank's arguments and in addition urged law schools to abandon their misguided effort to separate pure law topics from the "background of social and economic fact and policy." History, philosophy, economics, and the like, he contended, should be introduced into the law school curriculum, not by creating courses offering interdisciplinary "perspectives" on doctrine, but by integrating serious analysis of such matters into every course.

Sentiments of these sorts, widely shared at schools where realism was well represented, generated some serious efforts to institute major pedagogic reforms. The most serious of all came at Columbia, where, with the encouragement of Dean Harlan Fiske Stone, ten faculty committees worked for two years to refashion the curriculum along "functional" lines. The effort bore some fruit – a few new courses, most pertaining to economics or trade regulation; some unconventional casebooks; and the addition of business experts, philosophers, and political scientists to the law school faculty. But the reformers lost the faculty fight over the committees' more sweeping recommendations. After the appointment in 1928 of a new, more conservative dean, the principal agitators resigned. William O. Douglas and Underhill Moore left for Yale, and Herman Oliphant and Hessel Yntema joined Walter Wheeler Cook in founding a new research center at Johns Hopkins.

Influenced in part by the arrival of Douglas and Moore, Yale Law School at the end of the decade experimented with its own curriculum a more modest scale. Dean Robert Hutchins was supportive, and some new empirically oriented courses were developed. But increasing disillusionment concerning the insights into law that could be gleaned from the social sciences and Hutchins' departure for the University of Chicago stunted the initiative. The Johns Hopkins Institute, for its part, fell prey to economic pressure. Disdaining the training of practitioners and focused exclusively on research, it was financially dependent on donors. Funded for only five years, it could not survive the philanthropic drought of the Depression.

Hegemony and Evolution

The main storyline in American legal education during the remainder of the twentieth century was the continued spread and consolidation of the Harvard model. The ABA and AALS, working increasingly collaboratively, adopted ever stricter guidelines – intended to apply to all law schools – on minimum numbers of faculty, maximum student/faculty ratios, the number of years of undergraduate study that were required for admittance (first two, then three, finally four), and the size of and funding for law libraries. For many years, these guidelines were paper tigers. Students graduating from nonconforming (and thus unaccredited) schools could still take state bar examinations and thus enter the profession. But the rules gradually grew teeth. Bar examiners acceded to pressure from the elite schools to adopt questions that resembled the problem-based questions used in the course examinations in the elite schools, and state legislatures began to make some of the guidelines (for example, two years of college study before law school and three years of law study) mandatory for admission to practice. California continued to allow graduates of unaccredited schools to become lawyers, but required them to take special tests from which students in accredited schools were exempt.

Many of the unaccredited proprietary schools responded to these growing pressures by conforming. A growing percentage adopted the case method. Some added undergraduate programs to their curricula, enabling admitted students to perform their obligatory years of pre-law study before beginning their law school courses. Others hired new faculty and expanded their libraries. But, just as the proponents of the new rules anticipated, many of the lower tier schools were incapable of complying and went out of business. The net result: the percentage of students enrolled in accredited schools steadily rose.

Yet, even as its grip was tightening, the Harvard system of legal education began to change – incrementally, to be sure, but ultimately in substantial ways. Perhaps the most obvious area of adjustment concerned the subject matter of the courses offered in the accredited schools. The absolute numbers of course offerings increased steadily. Equally important, the proportion focused exclusively on pure law topics slowly declined, whereas the proportion overtly addressing "policy" issues or drawing on disciplines other than law rose. This trend accelerated after 1970, reinforced by the addition of courses concerned with (and typically promoting) means of dispute resolution other than litigation – negotiation, mediation, and arbitration. The impact on this axis of change of the major schools of legal thought traced in the first half of this essay was obvious: More and more courses addressed such themes as the legal process, law and economics (in general or of particular subjects), law and society, critical theory, and feminist legal theory.

Even by mid-century, the number of course offerings in most schools was such that no student could take them all in three years. As a result, all schools (even Harvard, nudged by a 1947 report from a curricular reform committee chaired by Lon Fuller) reduced the number of courses students were obliged to take, increasing their freedom to pick and choose in their second and third years from a growing collection of electives. Another side effect was that the average size of upper-level classes decreased steadily. That trend, plus the proliferation of seminars, modeled loosely on those available in arts-and-sciences graduate schools, afforded some students increased contact with faculty members.

Another area of adjustment concerned the character of assigned readings. Casebooks containing nothing but appellate opinions were gradually displaced by collections of "cases and materials" – the "materials" typically consisting of bits and pieces of philosophy, sociology, political science, economics, and editorial commentary. The organization of the new books commonly reflected the schools of legal thought that their authors found most congenial. For example, Lon Fuller's 1947 contracts casebook bears many marks of legal realism. Most famously, the placement of the section on remedies at the beginning rather than at the end of the book was clearly motivated by the realist insistence that rights are derivative of remedies, not the reverse – that a right exists only to the extent that effective procedures are in place to enforce it. But it also showed the extent to which Fuller thought he had transcended realism. Specifically, the inclusion of many notes and references designed to elucidate the various policies underlying each doctrine reflected Fuller's faith that a mature judge or other decision maker could, through careful weighing of those considerations in particular contexts, resolve controversies among contracting parties in wise and reasonably determinate ways.

Pedagogy changed too. Professors continued to question students. But gradually, as the century wore on, the interrogations became less fierce, less concerned with explicating cases, and more with exploring policy issues. Professors tipped their hands more, humiliated students less, and interspersed Socratic questioning increasingly often with mini-lectures. Defenders of the new style argued that it was both more efficient and more humane than the older approach. Traditionalists, like Roger Cramton, lamented the resultant decline in "the kind of hard-nosed, analytical and disciplined thinking on which the best law schools used to pride themselves" and attributed the declension to growing "malaise" among law teachers – "uncertainty about what they are teaching and why." (Interestingly, critics from the Left offered a similar diagnosis. Roberto Unger, for example, closed his book on *The Critical Legal Studies Movement* with a harsh depiction of the mainstream law teachers that the movement was seeking to discredit and displace: "[T]hey were like a priesthood that had lost their faith and kept their jobs. They stood in tedious embarrassment before cold altars.")

Clinical legal education also rose in importance and popularity during the second half of the twentieth century. Clinical instruction has a long pedigree. The apprenticeship system by which most early nineteenth-century lawyers were trained can fairly be described as a form of clinical teaching. Around the turn of the century, a few law schools sought to recapture some of the benefits of that system by establishing legal aid clinics in which students could gain experience representing real (typically poor) clients. The University of Pennsylvania did so in 1893, the University of Denver in 1904, Harvard itself in 1912, and Yale in 1915. But several factors reduced the impact of these early programs. With rare exceptions (such as at the University of Southern California), students could not earn credit for participating in them, the instructors who guided the students lacked both tenure and prestige, and the most ambitious and competitive students usually avoided them. As we have seen, some legal realists argued that these programs should be radically expanded and made central to legal education, but their agitation had little impact.

Beginning in the 1960s, three forces combined to boost clinical education substantially. The first and probably most important was money. Between 1959 and 1965, the National Council on Legal Clinics, supported by the Ford Foundation, awarded grants totaling roughly $500,000 to nineteen law schools to enable them to create or expand clinical programs. In 1968, the Ford Foundation increased this level of support dramatically. Over the next decade, through the Council on Legal Education for Professional Responsibility (CLEPR), it granted roughly $12 million to more than 100 law schools to help them increase their for-credit clinical offerings. The second factor was social and political unrest. Starting in the 1960s, growing numbers of students became dissatisfied with the apolitical or conservative character of regular law school instruction and saw in the expanding clinics opportunities to put their skills to progressive purposes even before graduating. The growing set of clinical instructors, most of them drawn from the public interest bar, were eager to satisfy this demand. Third, the organized bar became increasingly convinced that the law schools were failing in their responsibility to provide students practical lawyering skills – facility in legal research, document drafting, counseling, initiating litigation, and so forth – and urged the schools to fill the gap through increased clinical instruction. One relatively late manifestation of this pressure was the "MacCrate Report" (named after Robert MacCrate, the chair of the ABA Task Force from which it issued), which, among other things, urged the schools to create more "opportunit[ies] for students to perform lawyering skills with appropriate feedback." By the turn of the century, the intersection of these forces had prompted the large majority of law schools to offer their students for-credit clinical instruction.

The final dimension along which the Harvard model changed was the manner in which students were differentiated. In the 1920s and 1930s, the elite schools sorted students, not at the doorstep, but after they were admitted. Even Harvard demanded of applicants nothing more than an undergraduate degree from an accredited college. But then more than half of each entering class "flunked out" before graduation. Gradually, the elite schools became ever more selective in determining which candidates they would admit while reducing the percentages they discarded after admission. This change is not to suggest, however, that the law school experience for admitted students became more egalitarian. On the contrary, the divisions drawn among the students became ever sharper.

One of the principal vehicles of stratification was the law review – an institution (puzzling to academics in other disciplines) in which students select, edit, and publish most of the articles written by law professors. The first law reviews were established in the late nineteenth century. Their number increased slowly in the first quarter of the twentieth century and rapidly thereafter. One of the reasons for their proliferation was that membership on the editorial board of a law review, typically determined entirely on the basis of first-year grades, came to function as a badge – a signal to prospective employers, among other audiences, of students' abilities and accomplishments. (Another reason, as Karl Llewellyn acidly observed, is that law review members in their second year of school could obtain from their comrades in their third year effective, personalized instruction, including close editing of their written work, that the law school faculty was unable or unwilling to provide them.) By the middle of the century, competition for such positions became fierce. Students' job opportunities, self-images, and friendship networks came to depend, to distressing degrees, on whether they had "made" law review. Starting in the 1970s, the proliferation of student-edited journals and the growing status of interdisciplinary work eroded the accreditation power of the flagship law reviews, but at the end of the century it was still formidable.

Diversity

Over the course of the twentieth century, the range of options open to people other than white men who wished to obtain legal educations expanded slowly and erratically. In 1900, no top school admitted women, although some second-tier schools – Iowa, Michigan, Boston University, and Hastings – had opened their doors to them. But the most prestigious institutions – Harvard and Yale among them – expressly refused to do so. Some proprietary schools sought to fill the resultant gap. For example, in 1908, Arthur MacLean founded the Portia Law School in Boston, initially limiting admission to women students. Over the course of the early twentieth century, the top schools, one after another, relented. Harvard, to its shame, was the last of the lot, waiting until 1950. As one might expect, the net result was that, in the second half of the century, the percentage of women among law students increased steadily. By 2000, women constituted a majority of the graduates of several schools.

In the early twentieth century, the sharply limited opportunities available to African Americans worsened even further. The campaign to "raise standards" in legal education had the predictable effect (arguably, the purpose) of constricting the number of African Americans who could gain access to the profession. In part, this constriction resulted from the increase in the number and height of the hurdles that one had to clear to be admitted, disadvantaging African Americans who, on average, had more limited educations and financial resources. And it part, it resulted from the adverse effect of the campaign on schools that specialized in training African Americans. In 1928, there were four such schools: Howard, Freylinghuysen, Simmons, and Virginia Union. A decade later, only Howard was thriving.

Only after 1950 did the situation materially improve. Some law schools (most of them in the South) were forced through litigation to abandon admissions policies that overtly discriminated against African Americans. Then, in the 1960s, other law schools adopted affirmative action admissions policies that, in one way or another, granted preferential treatment to African American, Hispanic, and Native American applicants.

In the late twentieth century, affirmative action was employed in the United States in a wide variety of economic and social contexts in efforts to remedy histories of invidious discrimination. In most of those settings, it was highly controversial, and its application to law school admissions was no exception. Some observers defended its use either as essential to affording members of minority groups access to positions of power (many of which required legal training) from which they had long been wrongly excluded or as necessary to provide all law students a learning environment in which could be found a range of views (on matters of all sorts) that was representative of the opinion spectrum of the society at large. Other observers criticized the practice either as unjust (to the whites disadvantaged by it) or as corrosive of sound pedagogy. Richard Posner, for example, traced the decreased use of Socratic questioning in the classroom in part to affirmative action, "which, virtually by definition, entails the admission of minority students less qualified on average than the law school's non-minority students, hence more likely to be embarrassed by the 'cold call' method of Socratic teaching."

To some extent, the struggle over the legitimacy of affirmative action – both in the context of law school admissions and in other settings – was a legal question. When employed by public institutions (such as law schools associated with state universities), it was challenged as violative of the Equal Protection Clause of the Federal Constitution, and when employed by private institutions, it was challenged as violative of civil rights statutes. Not surprisingly, law school faculty frequently expressed views about the merits of those challenges. In their arguments, the commentators often drew explicitly on one or another of the then-popular schools of legal thought. For example, Terrence Sandalow and John Ely both offered defenses of affirmative action grounded in process theory, and Ronald Dworkin drew overtly on his particular brand of Kantian liberalism in justifying the practice. But the connection between scholars' theoretical commitments and their views on the issue was not tight; scholars within a given school of thought sometimes disagreed. For instance, whereas some economists (like Posner) criticized the practice, others (like Robert Cooter) argued that, at least under some circumstances, it could be efficient. And while many scholars affiliated either with critical legal studies or critical race theory (such as Duncan Kennedy and Charles Lawrence) defended its use by law schools, others (such as Richard Delgado) were much more skeptical of the practice.

In the end, affirmative action survived (more or less) the legal attack on it. In the 1978 *Bakke* case, a plurality of the Supreme Court, in an opinion by Justice Powell, recognized that the promotion of diversity within its student body was "a constitutionally permissible goal for an institution of higher education." Commenting specifically on its use by law schools, Powell observed, "The law school, the proving ground for legal learning and practice, cannot be effective in isolation from the individuals and institutions with which the law interacts. Few students and no one who has practiced law would choose to study in an academic vacuum, removed from the interplay of ideas and the exchange of views with which the law is concerned." In the 2003 *Grutter* cases, the Court took much the same position, upholding reference to race in admissions decisions, so long as it is achieved not by mechanically adding points to applicants' scores to reflect their racial identities, but by taking race into account when making individualized admission decisions.

By most accounts, affirmative action, at least as employed in law school admission decisions, has been an enormous success. For example, an empirical study of the effects of the race-conscious admissions policies employed by the University of Michigan Law School since the late 1960s, concluded as follows:

By any of our study's measures Michigan's minority alumni are, as a group, highly successful in their careers. Although, as a group, they entered Michigan with lower LSAT scores and lower UGPAs [undergraduate grade point averages] than other students, in their jobs immediately after law school and in their jobs today, Michigan's minority alumni are professionals fully in the mainstream of the American economy. They are well represented in all sectors of the legal profession. They are successful financially, leaders in their communities, and generous donors of their time to pro bono work and nonprofit organizations. Most are happy with their careers, and minority alumni respond no differently than white alumni when asked about overall career satisfaction. LSAT scores and UGPA scores, two factors that figure prominently in admissions decisions, correlate with law school grades, but they seem to have no relationship to success after law school, whether success is measured by earned income, career satisfaction, or service contributions. If admission to Michigan had been determined entirely by LSAT scores and UGPA, most of the minority students who graduated from Michigan would not have been admitted even though the measures that would have worked to exclude them seem to have virtually no value as predictors of post-law school accomplishments and success.

Criticisms (Round Two)

In the last two decades of the twentieth century, the dramatic increase in the diversity of law school student bodies helped fuel another round of calls for reform of the character and content of legal education. In the judgment of the critics, the (reformed) Harvard model remained inexcusably sexist, racist, and conservative. Three clusters of criticisms loomed largest.

First, many feminists scholars argued that American law schools were inhospitable places for women students. To some extent, this was the result of overtly sexist behavior by male students or by the overwhelmingly male faculty. In class, women students were interrupted more often and were called on less often. When judging moot court competitions, faculty judges would comment on women students' dress. Criminal law professors would deliberately ask women to state the facts of rape cases. Male pronouns were commonly employed to refer to judges, lawyers, and reasonable persons; female pronouns were employed to refer to emotional or unstable persons. Casebooks and syllabi omitted or deemphasized topics of particular interest to women. The extent to which gender bias contributed to the origins or resolutions of particular controversies or to the shape of particular doctrines was typically ignored. And so forth. More fundamentally, various aspects of the prevailing pedagogy, the critics argued, disadvantaged women. The ethos of "rigor"; the privileging of general rules and arguments over context-specific considerations; the hierarchical, authoritarian Socratic method; inattention to the wisdom that can be gleaned from personal experiences – all these contributed to an environment hostile to the "female voice" and intimidating to women students.

Empirical studies lent support to these claims. The most comprehensive was conducted at the University of Pennsylvania in the early 1990s. Its principal findings were that the Socratic method made women students there feel "strange, alienated, and 'delegitimated'"; that, as a result, women participated in classroom discussions less often than men; and that, by the end of their first year of legal education, women students were three times less likely than men to rank in the top 10 percent of their class. In language that echoed one branch of feminist legal theory, the authors of the study concluded that even women who do well academically succeed in part by transforming themselves: "For these women, learning to think like a lawyer means learning to think and act like a man. As one male professor told a first-year class, 'to be a good lawyer, behave like a gentleman.'" A less formal study conducted at Harvard in 2002 came to similar conclusions: female students were less likely than males to talk in class or to graduate with honors and more likely to describe the law school experience as "alienating" – although they were more likely than men to occupy top-tier positions in student-run journals.

Critical race theorists offered analogous criticisms. The curricula of most law schools neglected racial issues, they argued, and the prevailing pedagogy erected unnecessary barriers for members of minority groups. They urged greater use in the classroom of such devices as narratives, simulations, and "reflection pieces," which would both empower minority students and highlight the racial dimensions of legal controversies and doctrines. Of special concern to many critical race theorists was the under-representation of minorities in legal scholarship. Derrick Bell, Richard Delgado, and Mari Matsuda, among others, argued that persons of color, largely because of their experiences of racial oppression, had something distinctive to contribute to scholarly debates, but had trouble finding publication outlets. Partly for that reason, they urged law schools to employ affirmative action, not just (as suggested above) when deciding which students to admit, but also when hiring and promoting faculty (although at the same time they warned of the hazards of "tokenism"). Many white professors and a few minority professors (for example, Randall Kennedy and Stephen Carter) contended, by contrast, that affirmative action was inappropriate in this context; a genuinely meritocratic standard was sufficient.

The third cluster of criticisms came from scholars associated with CLS. The most ambitious and influential essay in this genre was Duncan Kennedy's 1982 pamphlet, *Legal Education and the Reproduction of Hierarchy*. Kennedy's thesis was that, in myriad ways, law schools convey to students that "it is natural, efficient, and fair for law firms, the bar as a whole, and the society the bar services to be organized in their actual patterns of hierarchy and domination." Among the features that contribute to this message are: the "patriarchal" Socratic method, still used often in first-year classes, which inculcates ambivalence and conservatism; the technique of burying emotional or outrageous cases within casebooks dominated by run-of-the-mill cases, which pressures students to ignore their moral intuitions; the failure to provide students training in practical skills of lawyering, leaving them little choice but to seek employment after graduation in private law firms, which replicate the controlled and supervised law school experience; and a rigid grading system, which reinforces students' senses of both the inevitability and the justice of hierarchy. Only radical change in many of these dimensions could make the schools effective training grounds for lawyers interested in progressive social and political work.

As was true of the first round of criticisms, these attacks on the dominant form of legal education had relatively little impact. Overtly sexist behavior by faculty and students diminished. Some schools gave preferential treatment to minorities and, less often, to women in faculty hiring and promotion. And a few dedicated Left professors – such as Gerald Lopez at Stanford – developed courses and clinical programs intended to be more politically progressive. But, by the turn of the century, no school had developed a "radically reconceived training regimen." A chastened version of the Harvard model still ruled the waves.

CONCLUSION

In retrospect, we can see that some innovations both in American legal theory and in American legal education were shaped or provoked by developments in other dimensions of American politics and culture. For example, legal realism was inspired in part by Progressivism and was reinforced by the New Deal. Likewise, the effort during the 1960s and 1970s to achieve greater diversity in law school student bodies and the intense concern on the part of several groups of legal theorists in the various meanings of "equality" are traceable in large part to the civil rights movement. Other innovations seem more connected to developments in other academic disciplines. For example, to some extent legal realism echoed recent developments in psychology and anthropology; neo-Kantian legal theory was inspired, as the label suggests, by contemporary currents in philosophy; and CLS incorporated aspects of structuralism and postmodernism. Still other innovations seem at least partially serendipitous; a particular person with an idiosyncratic set of ideas happened to occupy a position of influence at a particular time, and much changed as a result. Examples of such figures would include Langdell, whose educational philosophy so heavily colored late-nineteenth- and twentieth-century pedagogy, and Richard Posner, whose limitless faith in the power of economics and seemingly boundless energy were crucial in launching and sustaining a variant of utilitarian analysis that continues to infuse large sectors of legal scholarship and instruction.

The result of this confluence of forces is a highly distinctive legal culture and system of legal education. Scholars and students from other countries who come to law schools in the United States are often disoriented. Much, initially, seems to them peculiar. Whether that distinctiveness will survive the twenty-first century remains to be seen.

3

THE AMERICAN LEGAL PROFESSION, 1870–2000

ROBERT W. GORDON

This chapter deals with two broad topics. One is the "legal profession," the formal institutions and organizations through which associations of lawyers seek and exercise state authority to regulate training for and admission to their guilds, to enforce their rules against members, and to protect their privileges against outsiders. The other and much broader topic is that of lawyers themselves, the people and occupational groups who make up to the profession, their work and social roles and their social standing, economic condition, and political influence. In the United States all lawyers have since the Revolution formally belonged to a single, unified profession, licensed by the states where they practice. There are no official ranks or specialties of lawyers, such as the English distinction between barristers (trial lawyers) and solicitors; the French among *avocats*, *avoués*, *conseils juridiques*, and *notaires*; or the German between the private profession of advocate and the public professions of civil servant, prosecutor, and judge, each calling for a different training, examination and career path. But in reality the legal profession is many, not one: a collection of occupational groups that work at very diverse practice tasks, enjoy very different levels of status and income, and play very different roles in the economy, politics, and society.

The chapter begins with the founding of professional organizations and institutions around 1870 and their growth and development up to 1970. It describes the "professional project" of organizational entrepreneurs from the elites of the urban bar, who launched several initiatives to create new rules to govern and organize the profession of law and new institutions to carry them into effect. Over the next hundred years these initiatives would gradually transform the profession. They were part of more general movements to organize middle-class occupations as professions – claiming a cognitive basis in science, requiring university education and credentials for entry, occupying a market niche protected from the competition of lay providers, and conferring an exalted social status and cultural authority. The lawyers who set these changes in motion believed that their society was experiencing a social and political crisis of misgovernment and class division. Their authority and status as professionals were undermined by the entry of new ethnic immigrant groups, and their dominance of public life by corrupt alliances between machine politicians and upstart corporate wealth. The movement to professionalize the legal system entailed working to create a corps and institutions – both private lawyers and public officers, such as judges, prosecutors, and administrators – capable of restoring the "rule of law," meaning governance as the applied technique of an educated elite trained and skilled in a specialized legal science and operating through procedures of which they possessed distinctive mastery. This professional reform movement required restoring respect for lawyers and the courts as independent guardians of the constitutions and legal tradition. It required excluding or disciplining ethnic newcomers. And it required replacing (in some part) governance through alliances among political parties, ethnic-immigrant urban machines, and new business interests with governance by civically virtuous professionals.

In the first section I tell the story of the mixed motives powering these professional reform movements and of their mixed achievements. As will be seen, they slowly but ultimately succeeded in their aim of closing off the profession to all but college and law school trained aspirants who passed a bar exam. They failed, however, to keep out ethnic newcomers, though they largely confined them (as well as the few African Americans and women who gained entry) to the profession's lower rungs. The ethics codes and disciplinary machinery they set up proved ineffectual to police any but the most egregious misconduct of non-elite practitioners. Their efforts to mark off and control the market for their services were partly successful, but limited by encroachments of competing professions and lay providers. They reclaimed important public legal posts for "merit" appointments, but left large enclaves such as state lower court judges and prosecutors under the influence of patronage machines and special interest politics. Before the 1970s the bar associations helped set up some charitable legal aid offices in major cities, but otherwise did little to make legal services available to the poor; thereafter they became champions of publicly funded legal services, but with meager results. Though virtually every field of law grew more specialized and technically demanding, the legal elite's aspirations to build a corpus of legal science that would legitimate their authority, as scientific medicine had done for physicians, were defeated by a lack of consensus over the content of legal science and its uncertain relevance to lawyers' work.

The next two sections shift the focus to "lawyers at work," a subject divided into two periods roughly tracking the emergence and growth of distinctive types of legal practice. The first period, 1870–1930, sees the rise of the corporate law firm, plaintiff's personal injury practice, and public interest lawyering. The second, 1930–1970, describes the new specialties emerging from the statutory and administrative innovations of the New Deal and the postwar political-economic order, as well as from the rights revolution of the 1960s and 1970s. Throughout, the emphasis is on lawyers in sectors whose practices underwent big changes, who themselves changed the world around them in significant ways, and who attracted sufficient attention from biographers and historians so that their stories can be told. (These criteria tend to leave out the largest sector of the bar in the entire long century, solo and small practitioners. Their practices did not change much over time, and they tended to be the objects and casualties of larger social forces rather than instigators of them. For both reasons, few materials exist from which to write their history.) The elite corporate bar is given special attention, because of its role in building state institutions, promoting legal and constitutional ideologies, and mediating between business and the state.

In the final section the two narratives of the "professional project" and of "lawyers at work" are combined, in an account that I call "Expansion and Upheaval," which traces the major transformation since 1970 of the demographics, institutions, and ideals of the profession and of lawyers' practices. During these years the profession tripled in size and admitted women and minorities in significant numbers. Corporate law firms multiplied, grew to enormous size, went national and international, and began to claim the largest share of total legal business. Personal injury practice entered the age of the mass-tort class action. Public interest "cause" lawyers added new constituencies and began to play a regular role in governance. All these changes in turn had a dramatic impact on the aspirations and institutions of traditional professionalism. The ideal of a single unified profession receded as social distance and income differentials widened between its upper and lower tiers. The ideals of independence and public service virtually disappeared among private lawyers, though they found a new home among public interest lawyers and non-governmental organizations (NGOs).

I. THE ORGANIZED BAR AND ITS PROFESSIONAL PROJECTS: 1870–1970

Lawyers' jobs and lives in 1870 were not very different from what they had been at mid-century. Lawyers' numbers (ca. 40,000 in 1870) in proportion to population were about the same. Only fifteen states required any formal preparation for admission to the bar, such as a cursory oral examination or three years of apprenticeship. Only about 1,600 lawyers, or 3 percent of the bar, had attended a law school, usually for one or two years at most. Nearly all lawyers were in private practice, and they usually practiced alone or in two- to three-person partnerships. The profession was highly stratified and its incomes widely dispersed. At the top, lawyers grew wealthy from retainers from merchants, manufacturers, banks, insurance companies, and especially from railroads. But even elite lawyers were rarely specialists; they still made their public reputations as trial lawyers, representing prominent clients in divorce, will, and libel contests and acting for murderers in criminal cases and for tort plaintiffs in civil suits against businesses. As they had since 1800, a small corps of elite lawyers virtually monopolized practice before the highest state and federal courts. Lawyers also dominated high elective and appointive office; two-thirds of U.S. presidents, senators, governors, and top executive appointments; and of course the entire judiciary above petty misdemeanor and probate courts were lawyers. At the bottom of the profession lawyers could not make a living at law alone; they scraped by on a practice of miscellaneous small pickings from individual clients – debt collection, real estate deals and disputes, writing and probating wills, criminal cases – combined with non-legal business on the side.

Reform movements of small groups of elite urban lawyers would eventually build the institutions that organized the modern legal profession. They began with the formation of bar associations in major urban centers – New York, Boston, Chicago, St. Louis, and Cleveland. New York's experience was copied most extensively and widely. In 1870 a group of elite lawyers signed a "call" to form a city bar association, composed of the "best men" of the bar – about 10 percent of the city's lawyers at the outset. The immediate provocation was a series of scandals. Boss Tweed's Tammany machine controlled the election of several state court judges, who at the machine's bidding immunized its associates from criminal prosecution, used their patronage powers to hire its cronies as receivers and court officers, and were suspected of taking bribes from litigants in the struggle between Jim Fisk and Jay Gould on one side, and Cornelius Vanderbilt on the other, for control of the Erie Railroad. The new bar association's aims were to purge the bench of corrupt judges, to take a leading role in reforming judicial elections by nominating capable and honest judges and lengthening their terms to make them more independent of party bosses, and to indict Boss Tweed. Interestingly, however, many of the lawyers involved in organizing the city bar association were themselves deeply implicated in the Tweed-Erie scandals; they had represented Fisk, Gould and the Erie Railroad, and similar clients. David Dudley Field, who barely escaped censure by the new city bar association for his work for the Erie Railroad, was later one of the organizers of the American Bar Association (1878), as well as a crusader for removing corrupt judges from the bench. Evidently these lawyers were trying to address the conditions of their own degradation by imposing practice standards and conditions that would limit their clients' and their own opportunities to corruption.

The same lawyers formed the backbone of general Mugwump and Progressive reform movements organized to enact anti-corruption legislation, create a merit-based civil service removed from political patronage, support non-partisan or "Fusion" candidates for state and local office, and seek electoral and jurisdictional reforms that would reduce the influence of populist and machine politics and restrict working-class voting. Their major effort was to enhance the authority and jurisdiction of federal courts and of state constitutional courts and to establish expert non-partisan administrative commissions, such as Charles Francis Adams's Railroad Commission in Massachusetts and former Judge Thomas M. Cooley's federal Interstate Commerce Commission – all seen as sources of neutral law and administration above special interest politics. Anglophile in cultural pretensions, the reformers coveted the tight guild organization, social standing, and clubby solidarity of English barristers, the elite professionalism of the English civil service, and the exalted status of English judges. From the start the professionalization movements had mixed motives – high-minded civic reform combined with exclusion and scapegoating of ethnic newcomers, especially Jews from Eastern Europe. As will be seen, they also had mixed achievements.

Building new professional institutions was a part of this broader agenda of civic and political reform. The most enduring institutions of the period were the new bar associations and the new schools of law.

The first bar associations were little more than social clubs of "the best men." By 1916 there were more than 600 bar associations, and they had developed a fairly consistent and uniform agenda. The central aim was to restrict entry to the legal profession, first by requiring passage of a bar examination and later by raising educational standards to graduation from law school and at least a high-school degree before that. These were high barriers: only 2 percent of Americans had a high-school degree in 1870 and only 8.6 percent in 1910; as late as 1940 only 6 percent had a college degree. The bar associations also sought to close down alternative routes to practice, such as apprenticeship, the diploma privilege (the admission of graduates of a state's law schools without examination), and especially the part-time night law schools proliferating in the cities. The night schools were the quickest route into practice for immigrant lawyers; by 1915 they turned out almost half the total number of new lawyers.

The spearhead of the restrictive efforts was the very unrepresentative American Bar Association – in 1910 a group of 3,700 mostly big-city lawyers comprising just 3 percent of all lawyers (by 1920 still only

9 percent.) The bar's elites looked enviously at the medical profession, which in response to the Carnegie Foundation's Flexner Report (issued in 1910) had shut down all but the few American Medical Association-approved schools as the path to a medical license. The ABA's Root Report of 1921 spelled out the same goal: to persuade licensing authorities in all the states to restrict entry to applicants who satisfied the ABA's law school and pre-legal educational requirements.

The restrictionists partly succeeded and partly failed. In the long run they won the battle for the bar exam and formal educational credentials. They gradually drove out admission through the diploma privilege and apprenticeship in almost every state; introduced written bar exams; and, in states with large cities and immigrant populations, reduced bar pass rates. By 1935 only nine states limited entry to graduates of ABA-approved law schools, by 1937 twenty states did so, and by 1979 that number increased to forty-six states. By 1949, 85 percent of new lawyers had some law school training. But the elites failed to close down the part-time night schools, which flourished and multiplied to the point of graduating over half of all new lawyers until the Depression killed most of them off. Suffolk Law School in Boston enrolled 4,000 students in 1928. By 1946 the ABA had induced every state to exclude non-citizens, though this ban was eventually struck down by the U.S. Supreme Court in *In Re Griffiths* (1973). And the nativist project to cleanse the bar of what Henry S. Drinker, a prominent legal ethicist, called "Russian Jew boys . . . up out of the gutter . . . following the methods their fathers had been using in selling shoe-strings and other merchandise," failed completely. New Jewish and Catholic immigrant lawyers flooded into the profession. In New York City, most dramatically, Jewish lawyers rose from 26 percent of new bar admissions between 1910 and 1920 to 80 percent between 1930 and 1934, stabilizing thereafter at 50 percent.

In a 1920 report on legal education for the Carnegie Foundation, Alfred Z. Reed had recommended keeping the night schools open, but using them to train the lower corps of a formally differentiated bar. The journeymen would do personal injury work, divorces, debt collection, and the like. An upper bar of university law-school educated counselors would retain practice in higher courts and complex corporate transactions.[1] Bar leaders like Elihu Root and Harlan Fiske Stone indignantly rejected Reed's report: they wanted a unified bar, but without its polluting lower half. They succeeded only in restricting the foreign born and their children to the lower rungs of the profession, not in keeping them out. Yet over time, the requirement for years of higher education – four of college, three of law school by the

---

[1] Alfred Z. Reed, *Training for the Public Profession of the Law* (New York, 1921).

post-World War II period – coupled with steeply rising tuition costs after the 1970s, undoubtedly narrowed the class background of lawyers; in 1969 only one-fifth came from families at the bottom 70 percent of occupations.

Though the bar could not control the ethnic composition of the profession, its requirements of educational credentials and bar exams played some part in restricting the number of new lawyers. The proportion of lawyers to the U.S. population was remarkably stable for three-quarters of the century. It rose between 1870 and 1900, from 1.07 per thousand to 1.5 per thousand (from 40,000 lawyers to 115,000), fell back to 1.16 per thousand in 1920, expanded again somewhat in 1920–30 to 1.35 per thousand, and then contracted in the Depression and wartime to 1.21 per thousand in 1960. In the 1970s, as we will see, controls on entry collapsed and the numbers of new entrants exploded.

The elite bar worried enough about the threat to professional standards and values from Jews and Catholics to try to limit their entry. Its own and the dominant society's gender and racial customs kept women and African Americans down to derisory numbers until the 1970s. The bar in 1900 was exclusively white and male with token exceptions: There were about 730 African American lawyers in the entire country and about 1,000 women lawyers. The ABA refused to admit African Americans to membership until 1943; they formed their own professional organization, the National Bar Association, in 1925. No Southern school after Redemption – with the prominent exception of Howard University Law School in Washington, D.C. – would admit African Americans before 1935; several states later opened all-black law schools simply to forestall integration orders.

Women fought their own long battle for admission to practice. In the most famous challenge to state laws excluding women from practice, Myra Bradwell of Illinois argued that such laws abridged the privileges and immunities of citizens to choose their professions. The Supreme Court rejected the claim in 1873, upholding discriminatory licensing laws as a valid exercise of the police power. Justice Joseph Bradley in a concurring opinion said that the "paramount destiny and mission of women are to fulfill the noble and benign offices of wife and mother" and they were thus "unfit . . . for many of the occupations of civil life."[2] Some state courts disagreed, however, and between 1869 and 1899, thirty-five states and territories, often under pressure from lawsuits, admitted women to practice – even though in most of them women could not vote or hold office. All but Delaware and Rhode Island admitted women by 1918.

Legal barriers to admission turned out to be the least of obstacles in the path of women to practice. Many schools refused to admit women as

[2] *Bradwell v. Illinois*, 83 U.S. (16 Wall) 130, 141–2 (1873).

students: Harvard held out until 1950. From 1900 to 1930, the largest numbers were graduated from schools founded specially for women, like Portia Law School in Boston and the Washington College of Law in the District of Columbia. Washington College trained women for entry into government law jobs, which discriminated less than private employers, but warned graduates they would probably have to start out as stenographers even after admission to the bar. Male lawyers viewed women as intruders on a masculine preserve, especially the courtroom. Women's gentler natures would be damaged by the rough and tumble of adversary combat and the vulgar realities of crime and civil strife, or else they would damage the cause of justice by undermining it with sentimentality or using feminine wiles to seduce juries. Judges and lawyers treated women with undisguised hostility.

Even when young Jewish men, and much more rarely, occasional women and African Americans, made their way onto the first rungs of the merito-cratic ladder – elite law schools, law review, and high class standing – almost none of them, until the 1970s, were ever hired at major law firms. The sto-ries are legendary – the future Supreme Court justices Ruth Bader Ginsburg and Sandra Day O'Connor, the African American lawyers Raymond Pace Alexander and William T. Coleman, Jr., all stars of their respective law school classes, were turned away from every law firm in the cities where they first applied. Between 1890 and 1920, all African American lawyers admitted to the Philadelphia bar practiced alone or in all-black firms or worked for the government.

Indeed the exclusion of African Americans and women from the upper bar was so taken for granted before the 1970s that it hardly raised an eyebrow except among those who suffered from it. The most glaringly visible exclusion, because the number of affected lawyers was so large, was of Jewish men. A 1939 report on Jewish lawyers in New York practice found that they made up more than half of the total number of lawyers in the city, but few of them had jobs in corporate law firms, either at the beginning or end of their careers. As late as 1960 Jerome Carlin's study of social stratification in New York City's bar concluded that "a Jewish lawyer who achieved high academic standing (that is, was selected for staff of law review) in an Ivy League school has no better chance of being in a large firm than a Protestant lawyer who did not 'make law review' and who attended a non-Ivy League school."[3] The exceptions mostly held jobs in firms that served specifically Jewish clienteles, such as banking houses and department stores, and the occasional liberal firm founded by a mixture of Gentile and Jewish partners, such as Paul Weiss Rifkind Wharton & Garrison.

---

[3] Jerome Carlin, *Lawyers' Ethics: A Survey of the New York City Bar* 30 (1966).

Blocked from the conventional pathway to success – big-firm transactional practice on behalf of corporate clients – what did marginal lawyers do to advance in their profession? Their motto might have been, "If you can't join 'em, sue 'em." The usual choice of occupation was litigation representing the other side from the elite bar's corporate clients. This was often simply routine personal injury work – tort plaintiffs' suits against railroads and streetcar companies or worker's compensation claims – but could also be fairly complex litigation, such as derivative suits or proxy fights against corporations. Labor law was often a Jewish specialty as well, attracting lawyers from immigrant socialist families to the workers' cause. Women were steered away from the courtroom: a survey of 1920 found that most women thought their best opportunities were in office practices, such as trusts and estates, domestic relations, real estate, and social welfare law. In fact, they were mostly confined to general office practice. As will be seen, Jewish, African American, and women lawyers also dominated what we now call public interest and cause lawyering.

Ethics and Discipline

Prominent among the historical ambitions of the newly organized profession was the development of ethical standards and disciplinary machinery to improve the ethics of lawyers and judges and to police or expel the deviants. At the start the reformers took a broad view of the offenders, targeting their own kind as well as immigrant parvenus. Lawyers debating the first Canons of Ethics chastised corporate lawyers for tutoring wealthy clients in how to skirt or evade the law. The Boston Bar Association, for example, drafted comments for the ABA's 1908 Ethics Committee arguing that it was "a scandal to the profession that unscrupulous businessmen can find able lawyers who devise or perfect schemes for evading the law, for imposing on investors, and for working injuries to the public; who assist in the work of improperly influencing legislature and city counsel; and nevertheless, contrive to maintain a high standing among their brethren. We think it is the duty of the bar to hold to obloquy and contempt lawyers who thus prostitute their calling."[4]

Bar association speakers and writers on ethics delivered hundreds of jeremiads between 1890 and 1920 lamenting the increasing commercialization of the bar and its growing dependence on corporate clienteles; they continued to hold out the ideal of the lawyer as an independent objective advisor. As a practical matter, however, the new grievance committees of

---

[4] Lucien Alexander, *Memorandum for Use of ABA's Committee to Draft Canons of Professional Ethics* (Chicago, 1908), 123.

the elite bar associations focused their crusades almost entirely on lower tier attorneys, the personal injury plaintiffs' bar. Elite lawyers always disdained contingency fee arrangements as "mere ventures . . . no better than a lottery ticket,"[5] but could not regulate them without taking on the principle of free contracting between lawyer and client. With increasing frequency in the 1920s and 1930s, bar committees disciplined or disbarred lawyers for "ambulance chasing," soliciting clients by going to hospitals and funerals, or using policeman and doctors to refer clients involved in accidents. Defense practice in personal injury cases was actually quite as seamy. Companies sent agents to homes and hospitals to sign releases for cheap settlements. Railroad legal departments bribed witnesses or sent them out of town to defeat lawsuits. Meanwhile, corporate lawyers solicited clients on golf courses and in downtown city clubs. But high-end lawyers almost entirely escaped the notice of disciplinary committees, whose mission seemed increasingly to scapegoat low-end lawyers for the ethical failings of the profession.

As bar associations gradually became less gentlemen's clubs and more inclusive and heterogeneous, the bar's disciplinary machinery, never very effective, decayed into insignificance; by the 1970s, more than 90 percent of complaints were dismissed with little or no investigation, and aberrant lawyers were usually reprimanded, but rarely disbarred or suspended except if convicted of a felony or the outright theft of client funds. Bar committees virtually never went after major law firms or their partners, even after egregious public scandals. By 1980, as will be seen, outside agencies were playing more important roles than the bar in policing misbehavior.

Compared to other nations' legal professions, the American legal profession has always stressed lawyers' duties to their clients over duties to the courts, legal system, third parties or the public interest. As late as the 1980s, lawyers' rhetoric continued to celebrate the contrasting ideal of the lawyer as a high-minded independent counselor as well as an adversary advocate or hired gun who steers his client in the paths of legality and warns of adverse consequences if the client strays. Yet as a practical matter the bar's ethics rules and informal norms aligned lawyers' interests almost entirely with those of clients and – most of all – other lawyers. Successive versions of the bar's ethics codes, such as the ABA's Model Code of 1969 and Model Rules of 1983, made fidelity to clients mandatory; lawyers should keep quiet even if the client were about to commit crime or fraud, unless they believed the criminal act was "likely to result in imminent death or substantial bodily harm."[6] Duties to the courts remained vague and mostly unenforced; duties to the public were hortatory and optional.

[5] Thomas M. Cooley, "The Contingent Fee Business," *Albany Law Journal* 24 (1881), 26.
[6] ABA Model Rules of Professional Conduct, Rule 1.6 (1983).

Judges and Prosecutors

Since their inception the bar associations sought to play a key role in the selection of judges, going against political party machines that preferred to keep judgeships as patronage rewards for loyal party service. Appointment or (as in most state systems) election to judgeships remained a reward for the politically well connected. Bar associations pervasively tried to insert themselves as official filters or endorsers of candidates in state and federal procedures for nominating judges. In some states, starting with California in 1934 and Missouri in 1940, they were able to get "merit" selection systems adopted: a special commission would nominate a list of candidates for judicial vacancies and the governor (or a commission) would make short-term appointments from the list, after which the judge was subject to a retention election. This system basically supplemented party politics with bar politics, a contest among lawyers representing different client interest groups. Whether appointed or elected, partisan, non-partisan or "merit," state court judges tended to stay in office for long terms. The ABA was formally consulted on nominations for federal judgeships from 1952 until 2001, when President George W. Bush discontinued the practice. The bar's influence tended to be conservative – prosecutors and corporate lawyers, for example, rather than criminal defense, plaintiffs' personal injury, or labor lawyers were consistently favored for federal judgeships – but with probably generally positive effects on competence and honesty.

But the bar's influence was limited. In Chicago it was estimated that from 1900 to 1950 more than 60 percent of the party nominees for municipal courts were not endorsed by the city bar associations. Anyway, bar association lawyers also needed the favor of sitting judges and could not be too critical. Since the 1980s segments of the bar – usually trial lawyers representing plaintiffs on one side, and lawyers representing corporate defendants and insurers on the other – have turned some state judicial electoral contests into the rawest kind of interest group politics, funneling campaign contributions to candidates to purge the bench of judges who issue rulings unfavorable to their clients and causes.

In the criminal process the important state official was not the judge, but the public prosecutor. In cities run by political machines, the machine picked the district attorneys and his assistants as well as the judges. A caustic 1929 study of the office found that prosecutors tended to be very young men (in Missouri, between 25 and 29 years old) who took the job for a few years to get the publicity, contacts, and experience to prepare them for careers in private practice or politics. All lawyer members of Congress in 1914, 1920, and 1926 and all lawyer governors in 1920 and 1924 were former prosecutors. "The office itself is unprofitable and to remain in it long is to create the unpleasant impression that the incumbent is unable to make a living at the practice of law."[7]

Despite this unpromising process of selection for his office, the prosecutor exercised enormous power. He had the discretion whether to accept the results of police work, whether to charge arrested suspects, and with what crimes to charge them. Grand juries, originally a check on the prosecutor's power to indict, had become his creatures. Since nearly all cases ended in plea bargains, neither trial nor appellate judges reviewed his conduct. Temptations were irresistible to use the discretion for political ends, to come down hard on suspects when the crowd was clamoring for their blood and to punish political enemies, but to go easy on the well connected. Some big-city district attorneys, however, like Frank Hogan of New York, took advantage of their long-term political favor to build professional prosecutors' offices with career bureaucracies, relatively insulated from immediate pressures of public opinion. The prosecutor's office continued for the rest of the century to be one of the best springboards into public office, as the careers of Thomas E. Dewey and Rudolph Giuliani attest, as well as into judgeships.

Market Control

Skeptics about professions claim that they are primarily economic cartels, designed to create and protect a guild monopoly. The organized bar of the twentieth century certainly did its share to prove those skeptics right. State bars put in place an impressive array of arrangements that restricted competition among lawyers and between lawyers and other professions. Proponents invariably argued that such arrangements, like statutes forbidding the "practice of law" by corporations or rules forbidding lawyers to advertise their services or solicit clients, were needed to preserve law as a high-minded profession against commercial money-grubbers who would turn it into a mere business. Starting in the 1920s, "unauthorized practice of law" committees fought fierce turf battles with encroaching neighbors – accountants giving tax advice, "administrative" specialists handling cases before agencies, collection agencies, trust companies writing wills and administering trusts, title insurers and real estate brokers handling property sale closings, unions and automobile clubs offering group legal services, and most recently paralegals offering help in preparing legal documents. Like the bar's efforts to restrict access, these fights met with uneven success. Aside from signing pleadings and appearing in court, there was never any agreement on what constituted the "practice of law" that lawyers were entitled to monopolize. Turf battles often led to treaties marking off boundaries of

---

[7] Raymond Moley, *Politics and Criminal Prosecution* (New York, 1929), 80.

practice or allowing peaceful coexistence. The bar enjoined or prosecuted competition from lay providers of such services as divorce advice, even in markets that lawyers did not serve. But court decisions favorable to civil rights legal organizations and threats of antitrust enforcement persuaded the bar to end its hostility to group legal service plans with "closed" panels of lawyers (the legal equivalent to Health Maintenance Organizations).

Access to Legal Services

In theory justice is a universal public good: equality before the law requires access to the law, which in turn requires access to lawyers. Another public good, health care, began to move away from direct patient financing in the 1930s: hospital services were provided through non-profit charitable hospitals and doctors' services paid by employer-sponsored health insurance, and the federal government subsidized a growing share of total medical costs (more than 50 percent by 2000) of veterans, the elderly, and the poor and of medical research and education. Yet lawyers in the United States were and still are mostly paid out of pocket by clients. The non-profit sector has always been tiny and the government contribution (to criminal public defender programs and civil legal services) negligible (less than 1 percent of legal fees). From the late nineteenth century, lawyers for plaintiffs with personal injury claims worked on contingency, financing the costs of suit themselves, taking 30 to 40 percent of damage awards if they won the case and nothing if they lost. For a few types of lawsuits, statutes awarded attorney's fees to successful parties. For most the usual rule was the "American Rule" that parties pay their own fees and costs. Most people could not afford much of a lawyer's time, and poor people, who were often in the worst trouble with the legal system, could not afford any. For most of the century extending access to legal services relied on the sporadic efforts of a few maverick reformers such as the Boston lawyer Reginald Heber Smith, whose pioneering *Justice for the Poor* (1919) became the Bible of the legal aid movement. The organized bar fiercely resisted alternatives to delivery of legal services through means other than fee for services or charity, and the great mass of lawyers was indifferent.

Before the revolution in rights pioneered by Warren Court decisions of the 1960s, the ordinary mass of people suspected, accused, and convicted of crimes either pawned what possessions they had to buy a plea bargaining agent or, if too poor (as most were) even for that, were made objects of casual charity or simply became invisible to the legal profession altogether. Throughout the century some states assigned court-appointed counsel to criminal defense or to brief and argue appeals *in forma pauperis*; but except in the rare localities where a professional service was created to handle these cases, such assignments tended to fall on the most marginal courthouse loiterers, unable to attract clients by other means. Free lawyers for felony defendants were not required at all in many states until the Supreme Court's decision in *Gideon v. Wainwright* (1963), and even after that criminal defender programs were funded stingily out of the fear that suspects would manipulate the system to escape just punishment. In some states defense lawyers would earn derisory fees even in capital cases. Severely underfunded and overburdened, too busy to investigate cases or take them to trial, defenders were reduced to high-volume plea bargaining. Though the quality of representation was often abysmal, courts would not reverse convictions for "ineffective assistance of counsel" even if the defense lawyer was visibly incompetent, drunk, drugged, or even fast asleep for most of the trial.

As with criminal, so with civil practice for the poor. Elite lawyers in major cities founded legal aid societies in the early part of the century with the usual Progressive mixture of philanthropic and social-control motives: to help give access to justice to the poor, to discourage disfavored claims, and to displace immigrant legal aid societies that were considered over-aggressive in bringing personal injury suits. Legal aid programs traditionally refused to take divorces, bankruptcies, or personal injury accident cases and insisted on conciliatory approaches to eviction and debt collection. Yet while pursuing cooperative instead of confrontational approaches to their clients' cases, legal aid leaders maintained their identities as lawyers – as distinct from social workers or social reformers – addressing the strictly legal problems of one client at a time, rather than the family and work situations or structural conditions that had caused them.

Most lawyers simply took no interest in establishing or contributing to legal aid. In 1950, only 9 percent of legal aid funding came from lawyers; in 1963 only about 400 legal aid lawyers were available nationwide. Bar regulations contributed to the problem of unequal access. The upper bar resisted the contingent fee (still not allowed in criminal cases and divorces) and, for most of the century, group legal services. As we have seen, the bar prevented entry into markets monopolized by lawyers – even markets they left unserved – by lay providers or paraprofessionals.

Other industrial societies by mid-century had enacted state-funded systems of legal aid for indigent clients. Britain led with the Legal Aid and Advice Act of 1949; by the 1970s, more than half of all British barristers' income came from state-funded legal aid. In the United States, by contrast, organized law, like organized medicine, battled fiercely against government-funded services (fearing the controls that would come with them) until 1965, when the ABA and local bars switched to strong and effective support for the federally funded legal service programs initiated as part of President Lyndon Johnson's War on Poverty.

The profession did little better representing unpopular clienteles. Lawyers' livings depended on cultivating good business relations with clients and collegial relations with judges, regulators, and court personnel; in small communities especially, lawyers could not afford to offend the local power structure. Such dependencies set severe limits on accepting even paying clients if their causes were unpopular or their interests adverse to regular clienteles. Railroads would give free passes or pay retainers to all the able lawyers in towns along their lines to inhibit representation of clients injured in railroad accidents; they would insist on loyalty not only to a particular railroad client but also to railroad interests generally. In most of the Jim Crow South a white lawyer would only be available to represent an African American criminal defendant if appointed by a court. Even then, if the crime charged had a white victim, and especially if it were rape, his defense had to be perfunctory. Southern white lawyers could not take on civil rights cases for African Americans without risking the loss of all their clients. During the Red Scare of the 1950s, several bar associations passed resolutions discouraging or even forbidding members to represent communists. Other associations affirmed the principle that every person, however vile, deserved representation, but in practice did nothing to ensure lawyers would be provided for communists; usually they were not.

Practitioners, Scholars, and Legal Science[8]

The year 1870 was an annus mirabilis for new professional institutions – it was the birth year of the revitalized law school and of new bar organizations. Legal professions have always sought to justify their privileges, monopolies, and aspirations to high social standing on the ground that law is a learned mystery. In America elite lawyers from the Revolution forward sought to persuade their fellow lawyers and the public that law was a "science" demanding special training and lifetime study. Antebellum legal science was a medley of humanistic learning in the classics and ancient and modern history, technical learning in the common law reports and treatises (especially the law of property and pleading), and – to train lawyer-statesmen as well as attorneys – constitutional, comparative, and international law and political science. After the Civil War the spectacular successes of natural science, like the public health discoveries applied to eradicate age-old

---

[8] Chapter 2 in this volume tells the history of modern legal education. My narrower concern here is with the schools' relation to the bar and its professionalization projects.

diseases, gave lawyers along with many other occupations the platform to argue that scientific practice required university-based training. In 1870 President Charles W. Eliot of Harvard appointed Christopher C. Langdell as dean of Harvard Law School to carry out a program of scientific legal education. Langdell was a refugee from New York City practice who had conceived a "hearty disgust for the means and methods by which business, place and reputation are . . . gained" in New York City.[9] He retreated to the higher ground of a New England university to institute a program of long-term reformation of his fallen vocation.

Langdell's idea of legal science was more up to date in some ways, but also more narrow and parochial than the antebellum version. The mass of Anglo-American law could be generalized into a system of harmonious principles. "[L]aw is a science, and . . . all the materials of that science are contained in printed books," the common law reports of appellate cases.[10] This was an exclusively private law curriculum: it expelled from the law school both the humanistic liberal arts and the public law and lawyer-statesman components of the old learning; it taught nothing of legislative policy. Students would learn how to induce the principles by means of the "case method," a Socratic dialogue between teacher and students primed with the close reading of cases. Under Langdell and his successor James Barr Ames, Harvard instituted a three-year sequenced curriculum, progressively stricter pre-legal education for admission (a B.A. by 1895, well before any other law school), regular examinations, and a high flunk-out rate for those who failed them. Langdell imagined the school would prepare graduates for careers as "counselors," something like the English barrister class, an elite corps of lawyers specializing in appellate advocacy. Harvard's idea of the law professor's job, however, looked to Germany rather than England. English law teachers of that period had to struggle against an insular, ingrown, intellectually conservative profession of judges and lawyers who put no value on a scientific training in law. In the United States, the emerging bar groups were too weak to dictate to the schoolmen, whose model was the German full-time professoriate. Freed from the time demands and client pressures of practice, Americans could do original research to uncover the true principles underlying unruly masses of case law, produce monumental commentaries, serve as authoritative advisers to judges and legislatures, draft model codes, and gradually produce a truly national and even transatlantic common law.

Parts of this program succeeded beyond its founders' wildest dreams, though in oddly mutant forms. The idea of teaching law as a science of

---

[9] James Coolidge Carter, letter to Charles W. Eliot, Dec. 20, 1869 (C. W. Eliot Papers, Harvard University).

[10] C. C. Langdell, "Harvard Celebration Speeches," *Law Quarterly Review* 3 (1887), 124.

principles was abandoned quickly and casually, but the case method itself flourished, now advertised as a practical method of teaching "how to think like a lawyer." Raising admissions requirements at first caused Harvard's enrollments to dive, but they recovered, and other schools (Pennsylvania in 1916 and Stanford, Yale, Columbia, and Western Reserve in 1921) followed suit. The Harvard template – increasing pre-legal educational requirements, the three-year private law curriculum, the case method and the full-time law-professor – spread to other elite schools from 1895–1925 and eventually to virtually every full-time university-based law school in the country.

Yet, the cadres of "counselors" the new law schools were supposed to train never materialized. As the Harvard model was gaining ground, few graduates of elite schools tried or argued cases; they worked in the new corporate law firms on complex deals such as mergers and reorganizations and kept clients out of court. Law schools openly competed to attract students who would be hired by these firms – not by teaching anything of direct relevance to the new practice, but by certifying their graduates as culturally suitable products of liberal arts colleges and survivors of a rigorous boot camp of Socratic inquiry, class ranking by exam grades, high attrition rates, and, beginning in the 1880s, the capacity for sustained attention to tiny points of detail as editors of law reviews. Law firm partners responded by subsidizing the schools and by hiring their graduates (at least the white Protestant ones) as associates.

The schoolmen's program and the bar's largely converged in the first decades (1870–1920), though rifts gradually opened between them. They shared an interest in raising the profession's intellectual standards and exclusiveness by credentialing requirements and enhancing the social status and cultural authority of the upper bar by alliance with university-based science. The schools fought to maintain the diploma privilege, the bar to end it; the bar mostly prevailed. The Association of American Law Schools, founded in 1900, fought side by side with the ABA to require college plus law school for admission to the bar. Law professors never achieved the authority of German professors as lawgivers and jurisconsults, but they took the leading role in technical law reform, drafting uniform codes and other model legislation like the Uniform Sales Act (1906; Samuel Williston of Harvard, chief reporter), the Federal Rules of Civil Procedure (1938; Charles E. Clark, Yale), the Uniform Commercial Code (1958–; Karl Llewellyn, Columbia), and the Model Penal Code (1952; Herbert Wechsler, Columbia). The great academic treatises – Williston on Contracts (1920), Wigmore on Evidence (1923), and Scott on Trusts (1939) – and law review articles were marketed to the bar in a deal whose implicit terms were that the writers would collect all the cases and arrange them in helpful categories, and the lawyers and judges in turn would rely on and propagate their interpretations. The West Publishing Company's *National Reporter System* originating in 1876–87, with its digests and organization of case law doctrines into law-finding categories tagged with keywords such as "Saws, Cutters and Grinders," performed similar functions in more intellectually modest ways.

The high-water mark of academic-practitioner collaboration on private law science came with the founding of the American Law Institute in 1923, an association of elite law professors, judges, and practitioners, with the goal to reduce unnecessary "uncertainty" and "complexity" in the law. Uncertainty resulted from lawyers' lack of agreement on the fundamental principles of the common law, "lack of precision in the use of legal terms," "conflicting and badly drawn statutory provisions," "the great volume of recorded decisions," and "the number and nature of novel legal questions." Complexity resulted from the "lack of systematic development" of legal science and variations among the many jurisdictions of the United States.[11] The ALI's mission was to promote the creation of a national private law through Restatements of the main common law fields – contracts, agency, trusts, torts, and so forth – distilling cases from every jurisdiction into propositions embodying the "best" views of law, in the hope that state courts would use them to direct the future of the law. For generations crowds of dark-suited lawyers gathered in the Mayflower Hotel in Washington to debate such questions as whether, if Uncle promised Johnny $5,000, and Johnny spent $1,000 in reliance on the promise, Johnny could sue Uncle for the full $5,000 or only the $1,000.

The school-bar alliances were always somewhat precarious, because as each sector evolved their ideas and interests often diverged. Harvard and its epigones might try to expel public law from their purview, because legislation and policy were not readily taught from casebooks by the case method. However, judges, bar leaders, and government lawyers could not ignore it. They were confronted with a rapidly growing volume of state and federal regulation, administrative agencies to implement it, and constitutional law challenging such regulation under state and federal (Fourteenth Amendment) Due Process Clauses, and the federal Commerce Clause. Indeed many elite business lawyers from the 1880s to the 1930s found an important source of cultural capital and professional identity by identifying with the conservative majority of the U.S. Supreme Court and the body of "classical" constitutional law it had developed and relying on that body of law as their chief bulwark against the New Deal's revolution in government.

---

[11] Report of the Committee on the Establishment of a Permanent Organization for the Improvement of the Law Proposing the Establishment of an American Law Institute (1923).

By the 1920s, however, most of the legal scholars interested in public law and policy were drifting leftward of their profession. Affiliated with various Progressive movements, they were developing alternatives to the classical vision, such as the "sociological jurisprudence" of Roscoe Pound and the "legal realism" and "legal-economic institutionalism" of scholars concentrated at Columbia and Yale. These movements were highly critical of classical legal science, both the private law doctrinal science of Harvard-influenced schoolmen and the public law science of the conservative bench and bar. The Progressives argued that legal science failed to describe how courts actually decided cases, concealed an implicit and often reactionary policy agenda, and ignored the effects and results of legal decisions ("law in action" as opposed to "law on the books"). They recommended that lawyers and legal scholars invest heavily in social science, the better to understand the legal system and to formulate policy. Their influence reached a peak in the New Deal, when Progressive scholars like Felix Frankfurter, James M. Landis, Jerome Frank, William O. Douglas, and Thurman Arnold were recruited en masse to draft new legislation and head federal agencies. Veterans of the New Deal repopulated law faculties after the war, ensuring that the legal academy remained somewhat more liberal than the business bar that it continued to supply with graduates and relied on for financial support.

The interests of academics and practitioners diverged still further in the 1970s, when legal scholars again moved away from purely doctrinal scholarship, incorporating theories and literatures from other disciplines, such as economics, history, philosophy, political science, and literary and cultural studies into their work. They also hired a few – but very conspicuous – teachers who were sharply critical of the legal and social status quo. Ironically one of these disciplinary turns paved the way for a partial rapprochement of law schools and the conservative bar in the 1980s. A striking exception to the general liberalism of the major law schools, the lawyer-economists at the University of Chicago Law School had preached since the 1930s the gospels of unregulated markets and libertarian freedoms. President Reagan's election in 1980 brought them out of the wilderness and into positions of power and influence. Several became federal judges, and others were appointed to high administrative posts. Free-market foundations like John M. Olin and Bradley subsidized teaching Chicago-brand economic theories of law in law schools and, through summer seminars, for law professors and judges. In some fields such as antitrust and regulated industries, their theories became government policy. The Federalist Society, an association of conservative judges, officials, practitioners, law teachers, and students, founded in 1982, rapidly evolved from a debating society to a powerful national network, with 25,000 members in 2000. In President

George W. Bush's administration it effectively displaced the ABA's role as expert advisor in the selection of federal judges.

The revival of the late nineteenth century had sought to base the legal profession's power, prestige, and privileges on its association with legal science, on the analogy of the medical profession's alliance with natural science. The ideal proved elusive. Law had no equivalent cognitive basis, certainly none with the requisite claim to objectivity. Doctrinal legal science had achieved real progress in imposing some rational order on legal fields, but it was savagely mocked as sterile, abstract, indeterminate. and politically biased by generations of Progressive-realist critics. The Progressives had similar ambitions for making social sciences such as statistics and institutional economics into the basis of law practice and administrative expertise. However, the social sciences proved to be just as dispute riddled, politically contentious, and uncertain in their prescriptions. By the 1970s legal economists were hoping to make their science the new cognitive basis of the profession. They did succeed in securing its adoption as the lingua franca of policy analysis in the regulatory bureaucracies and even to a limited extent in the federal courts. But most practitioners and judges resisted legal economics' attempt to displace the traditional, eclectic, multivalued discourses of legal argument. Law in every field of practice in the late twentieth century became more technical, more specialized, and more demanding of sustained investment in learning. But it was never plausibly any kind of science. Indeed, by the 1970s, as we shall see, the entire project of professionalization as the founding generation had conceived of it was under severe pressure, as the material and ideological foundations of the project eroded beyond recall.

II. LAWYERS AT WORK: 1870–1930

The history of lawyers is of course much more than the history of their guilds and professional projects. Four major new developments dominated this period: the founding of big-city law firms to service the nation's large corporations, the rise of a plaintiff's personal injury bar, the bar's increasing specialization and segmentation by clienteles as well as by subject matter, and the emergence of public interest lawyering.

The Corporate Elite: Organization, Law Jobs, and Social Tasks

Before 1900 the lawyers ranked by the public and their peers at the top of their profession were rarely exclusively or full-time "corporate lawyers." Certainly, a successful lawyer had important business clients: railroads, financial institutions, insurance companies and industrial firms. However,

he was also a courtroom lawyer who tried murders, divorces, and will contests as well as commercial cases; who argued appeals before the highest
federal and state courts; and who took time off from practice to serve in
high elective or appointive office. Typically he practiced in a small partnership, outside the management hierarchies of his principal clients.

The first exceptions to the pattern were a few men who rose to prominence
as full-time general counsel for emerging giant corporations, beginning
with the railroads. These jobs held enough prestige and pay to persuade
even distinguished judges like William Joseph Robertson of the Virginia
Supreme Court and federal judge G. W. McCrary to leave the bench to
become railroad counsel. Railroad counsel in turn sometimes rose to become
presidents of their roads, as did Chauncey Depew of the New York Central,
who was also a U.S. Senator; Frederick Billings of the Northern Pacific; and
George H. Watrous of the New Haven. General counsel directed the efforts
of the hundreds of local lawyers retained by the railroad in the towns along
its lines, who searched real estate titles, obtained rights of way, and fought
off or settled suits for grade-crossing accidents or damage to livestock. He
was foreign minister and war minister for his client, negotiating deals with
smaller or competing lines to build consolidated systems and taking them
over if they resisted. He directed strategy against striking unions, obtaining
injunctions and hiring deputies to enforce them. He was active in the state
and federal capitals, arguing before utilities commissioners to set high rates
and before courts to reverse the commissions, and as a lobbyist for liberalized
corporation laws and special favors.

By 1900, however, the pinnacle of success at the bar was being redefined
as partnership in an independent multispecialty firm that served exclusively
corporate clients. Paul Cravath's New York City firm pioneered the model of
the new firms as meritocratic (though largely restricted to white Protestant
males) career hierarchies of associates recruited from high-ranking graduates
of elite law schools, who were paid a salary and competed with one another
for partnership and as partners formed a lifetime membership with the firm.
Most new firms were in New York; but the model spread to other cities. By
1915 the five largest American cities had 29 firms with 7 or more lawyers;
by 1924 they had 101.

The big law firm, and with it the modern career of corporate lawyer, was
born of the Big Deals, Big Cases, and increasingly Big State of the industrial
era. The agreements to build giant consolidated enterprises, first railroads
and then other sectors such as oil and steel, required both highly skilled
and specialized legal work and massive bundles of routine tasks, such as
searching titles for oil leases and complying with the securities laws of all
the separate states. So too did the defense of such enterprises against lawsuits challenging their very existence, like suits for patent infringements

and antitrust violations. Alongside big business arose the administrative agencies of the modern state to regulate it, starting with regulation of the railroads and public utilities. All of this created technical, specialized work for lawyers and a demand for law offices with the numbers and expertise to staff a railroad merger or bankruptcy organization, defense of a massive antitrust action, or public utility rate-making hearing, as well as the voluminous miscellaneous business of large industrial and financial clients. Over the century, law firms experienced their biggest expansions during merger movements producing Big Deals, rises in litigation (especially with other corporations and against the government), and above all, with expansions of the regulatory state. Most of this work was done in offices and boardrooms, rather than in courts. The most prestigious and lucrative law firm work of 1900–40, for example, was in representing committees of bondholders and stockholders to draft and negotiate plans for the reorganization of bankrupt corporations.

Business lawyers did much more than furnish distinctively "legal" services, such as representing clients in courts, predicting judicial decisions, interpreting statutes and regulations, and drafting and planning to obtain favorable and avoid unpleasant legal consequences. They were also brokers and fixers. Lawyers served as the crucial intermediaries between finance capital and entrepreneurs. They traveled the world on behalf of businesses looking to sell bonds and shares in new American ventures and of American investors such as investment banks looking for profitable foreign ventures. A law firm usually had a bank for its anchor client: it would steer its manufacturing or transport clients to the bank, and the bank to those clients. In New York, law firms brokered deals between the great European and American merchant and investment banking houses and expanding business combines. In regional centers lawyers played the same role, linking local banking and manufacturing clients with national networks of investors and investments. Lawyers leveraged their positions as executors and trustees and as directors of client companies, banks, and insurance companies to steer capital into favored ventures. When lawyers finished brokering deals, they did the legal work of putting them on paper.

They also leveraged their contacts with state officials. Business lawyers liked to strike libertarian attitudes, comparing their jobs with the heroic role of the criminal defense lawyer who protects the liberty of the individual against the overreaching state. But in fact what most business clients wanted lawyers to get from the state were favors: concessions, franchises, tax exemptions, subsidies, regulatory loopholes, monopoly rights, and public works contracts. Lawyers were natural intermediaries between clients and the state, because they had the contacts. They had often held office themselves or knew brothers at the bar in the legislature or administration; they were more cosmopolitan than business managers who had spent their lives inside an enterprise. They were among the few Americans of the period who were widely traveled and spoke foreign languages. William Nelson Cromwell, co-founder of the Sullivan & Cromwell firm of New York, on behalf of his client, the (originally French) New Panama Canal Company, intrigued in the U.S. Senate to defeat the rival Nicaraguan canal route in favor of Panama; he then helped instigate Panama's revolution from Colombia in 1903 and the new republic's transfer of control of the canal to the United States.

Ad hoc deal-making expanded over time into the work of building stable contractual structures among business entities and between them and the state. The new giant enterprises made long-term investments in constructing railroad lines or huge plants for assembly-line mass production. Facing high fixed costs, they sought to stabilize their operating environments by securing predictable relations with creditors, shareholders, suppliers, distributors, customers, their labor forces, and governments. The function of lawyers was to help design, negotiate, and craft the legal instruments to minimize the risks of instability. Much of this was done through private contracts that adapted old legal forms such as the real estate trust and mortgage to securing corporate debt, giving managers the authority to spend borrowed money flexibly and lenders the legal resources to monitor them. Law firms were developers and the curators of the lengthy form documents that together made up a large body of private legislation.

Similarly, lawyers sought long-term stable relations for their clients with the state. As agents of a major structural transformation of the economy, they were now concerned to redesign the basic legal framework to accommodate the new forms of industrial and financial enterprise. This redesign was less a matter of negotiating specific concessions for particular clients, though of course that still continued, as of changing the general law so as to legalize consolidations (as by legislation permitting holding companies), and securing narrow executive and judicial interpretations of the antitrust laws and antitrust exemptions for entire industries. Lawyers like the legendary James B. Dill of New Jersey got corporate law changed to facilitate centralize control in management; for example, by reducing common law directors' and officers' liabilities, liberalizing standard state law charter provisions to relax restrictions on corporate powers and capitalization, and authorizing managers to exercise "business judgment" without fear of shareholder suits. Lawyers enlisted the state to help suppress militant labor by pressing the courts to recognize new forms of corporate "property" in economic relations protectible by injunction and to validate use of the antitrust laws to prosecute labor conspiracies.

As ad hoc deal-making expanded into stable structure-building, so structure-building expanded into statesmanship. At the urging of or through the medium of their lawyers, leading business firms often pursued a corporatist politics. They pressed for (or acquiesced in) regulatory schemes that would satiate populist clamor against monopoly while also enforcing their price-fixing agreements and raising costs of entry and operation to their small competitors. They sought cooperative relations with antitrust enforcers who would grant prior clearance to merger plans and with public utilities commissions that would prove captive and friendly regulators while staving off pressure for public ownership of power companies and streetcar companies. They supported Progressive measures like national labor standards (outlawing child labor, setting minimum wages and maximum hours) that would remove advantages of competing firms in anti-labor states, for social wages financed out of general tax revenues that would improve labor relations without their having to pay for it, and for workers' compensation plans that would quiet labor agitation over safety at acceptable cost. They instituted cooperative accords with labor unions or set up company unions that could help maintain discipline and contain militancy in return for job security and high wages and benefits.

Lawyers played a critical part in both designing and staffing such institutional arrangements, not only in their roles as counsel for particular firms or trade associations or business policy groups but also as members of civic associations such as the National Civic Federation, which brought together business executives and conservative labor leaders, and as lawyers on leave from practice as officials in city, state, and federal governments. In many respects their roles in office were their private roles writ large – making the state, nation, and world a congenial environment for American capitalism. Eastern corporate lawyers – Elihu Root, Charles Evans Hughes, James Coolidge Carter, Henry Stimson, Russell Leffingwell, William J. Donovan, Dean Acheson, and John Foster Dulles – dominated high foreign policy posts in the first half of the twentieth century. The policies of such men generally reflected the interests of their business clienteles: a peaceful, prosperous, and economically reconstructed Europe; the use of military and diplomatic power to promote stable governments reliably committed to promoting and protecting foreign direct investment and payment of foreign debts; and a system of international treaties and arbitration to enforce transnational contracts and settle international disputes. To be sure, such lawyer-statesmen were much more than tools for clients: their vision was often broader, more cosmopolitan, and more farsighted in anticipating that compromises would have to be made for the sake of industrial peace. They differed sharply among themselves about policy directions, however.

How did it come about that *lawyers* performed these state-building functions? In Britain, Continental Europe, and Japan, state bureaucrats negotiated the design and enforcement of regulations directly with corporate managers, rather than through lawyers; private lawyers were rarely conspicuous public intellectuals compared to economists, journalists, academics, and literary figures; and they rarely became senior ministers of state. Even in Germany, where law-trained officials dominated the bureaucracy, they were lawyers who entered public careers, not "advocates," who in Europe tended to be confined to the narrow role of representing clients in court. In the United States by contrast, the central state apparatus developed late, only after (and partly as a response to) the emergence of giant corporations. From the Revolution forward, suspicion and devaluation of public careers had inhibited the development of an elite corps of civil servants with high prestige, whereas Congressional government favored patronage appointees and part-time amateurs in government agencies. By default, private corporate lawyers did much of the design of the legal forms of state-business relations that in Europe was done by central bureaucracies, in part because so many of such relations were administered through courts, where lawyers held the monopoly of practice. Basic private law was court-made common law; and the highest law was court-declared constitutional law. Lay advocates competed with lawyers for representation before administrative agencies, but ultimately all important administrative actions were reviewed in courts. Courts administered the general body of corporate law and had to ratify and enforce contracts between corporate shareholders, managers, and creditors; courts in their equity jurisdiction managed bankrupt corporations – which at one time included nearly every American railroad – as receivers and approved or disapproved consolidations; courts even oversaw much of the regulation of monopoly through the (awkward) forms of criminal and civil antitrust lawsuits; and they governed labor-capital conflicts through labor injunctions. Constitutional law – a familiar resource of business lawyers because of its uses for challenging regulations – supplied the basic public language for arguing about the distribution of government and private, federal, and state power and the appropriate limits on government action; in speaking this discourse, lawyers held the advantage over rival professions.

This elite took on another major project: building an ideological framework of legal order, a set of overall structuring, ordering principles (rationalizations, justifications, inspirational guiding norms) of the legal system. Lawyers contributed to this project as public intellectuals – judges, officeholders, law reformers, civic activists, treatise-writers, and bar leaders – from a variety of public pulpits.

There were actually at least two rival projects or visions of ideal legal order. The older was the "classical" ideal being perfected as a legal science of private law principles in the law schools and their articles and treatises and in decisions of the courts. The private law principles called for strict enforcement of all contracts, even the most one-sided, such as employment contracts; tended to limit the liability of companies for industrial accidents; and were hostile to most collective tactics of organized labor such as strikes and boycotts. Classical public law, developed out of Due Process Clauses in state constitutions and the federal Fourteenth Amendment, produced a rich jurisprudence of constitutional limitations on legislators' and administrators' powers to change the ground rules of economic life, which inspired courts to strike down some "Progressive" social legislation, such as minimum wage, maximum hours, and federal anti-child labor laws; laws creating worker's compensation commissions to replace jury trials at common law; and laws favoring union organizing.

The challenge to the classical vision came from the Progressive ideal that began to emerge in the 1890s; was developed by Progressive reformers and intellectuals; secured beachheads in legislatures, on regulatory commissions, and even with some influential judges (Oliver Wendell Holmes, Jr., Louis Brandeis, Benjamin Cardozo, Learned Hand, and Julian Mack among others); and achieved its institutional triumphs first at the state and local levels and then at the federal level in the New Deal. The Progressives criticized classical law as biased and inadequate to deal with social problems; they proposed to substitute social-science-based expertise applied by administrative commissions. Relatively older and more conservative lawyers of the 1890–1940 era, men like James Beck, John W. Davis, and William D. Guthrie, favored the classical vision, as it gave them a basis in constitutional principle for fighting legislation and regulation that disfavored their clients and the sympathetic and conveniently final forum of the judiciary to make their arguments. But as many leading lawyers denounced the famous Supreme Court *Lochner* (1905) decision invalidating state maximum hours laws for bakers and the New York *Ives* (1911) decision invalidating state workers' compensation laws as applauded them. As we have seen, business interests and their lawyers were among the driving forces behind much of the administrative state-building efforts of the early part of the century. Business lawyers tended to switch back and forth between classical and Progressive visions as political contexts and client interests changed.

Rise of the Tort Plaintiffs' Bar

The most dramatic development in the legal practice sector serving individuals, and certainly the one with the broadest and most controversial social effects, was the rise and transformation of personal injury tort practice.

Tort practice hardly existed in the United States before the 1880s and 1890s. Injured persons rarely sued. The wounded soldiers of industry were compensated, if at all, by small payments from mutual benefit societies or paternalistic employers. The routine expectation of "total justice," that someone else could be blamed and should have to pay for accidental injuries, was not yet widely embedded in the culture. Plaintiffs who did sue usually either lost or recovered tiny damage awards. Corporate defendants, and employers in particular, had many effective defenses such as rules denying compensation to workers injured by fellow employees or who could be alleged to have "assumed the risk" of injury by taking on a dangerous job or contributed to the injury by their own negligence. The sudden rise in tort claims was a response both to the enormous carnage of death and injury caused by industrial technology – railroads, factory machinery and mining operations, streetcars, and eventually automobiles – to workers, passengers and bystanders and to a mostly immigrant urban bar of attorneys, working for contingent fees of 30 to 50 percent of the amounts recovered, willing to take on cases for the injured.

Personal injury practice was never for the ethically fastidious. Plaintiffs' lawyers chased ambulances, hung around hospital rooms and funeral parlors, hired "runners" and policemen and doctors to refer business, and bribed witnesses. As we have seen, elite lawyers used their control of bar associations to discipline the plaintiffs' bar for "solicitation" and tried to limit contingent fees and keep out of the profession graduates of the night schools where (until mid-century) most plaintiffs' lawyers were trained. Company lawyers also developed tricks of their own. They sent agents into hospitals to get injured plaintiffs to sign releases of liability in return for low settlements, smuggled inconvenient witnesses out of town, and deployed a vast and versatile arsenal of procedural weapons to delay cases, exhaust adversaries, and move cases into more sympathetic legal forums than state jury trials: the appellate courts and the federal courts.

Where accidents were common, the mutual interest of injurers and injured in quick and predictable settlement resulted – after much conflict and dissent – in the routinizing of claims processes. For industrial injuries to workers, the tort system was displaced, in part through political compromises negotiated between big businesses and unions and embraced by Progressive reformers, by an administrative no-fault non-judicial system – worker's compensation, which spread to almost all states between 1910 and 1920. (This system was supposed to do away with the need for lawyers as well as courts, but lawyers soon came back in to represent injured workers, if only to argue about whether the injury was suffered on or off the job.) Auto accidents, eventually by far the biggest class of injuries – in 1930 more than 30,000 Americans died in auto accidents – remained in the tort system; however, the great majority of cases were disposed of without suit by insurance company claims adjusters and the rest by stables of specialist defense lawyers working in-house or on retainer for insurance companies.

Segmentation by Clienteles

As late as the 1870s, even the lawyers who appeared most often for railroad clients in appellate cases appeared almost as often for individuals suing railroads. Clarence Darrow was still general counsel for the Chicago and Northwestern Railway while trying to get pardons for the Chicago Haymarket defendants; he resigned from the railroad job to represent Eugene Debs in his legal battles with the Pullman Company and the nation's railroads, but continued to do legal work for his railroad client part-time. But by the 1880s lawyers for railroads no longer appeared for adverse interests. Those who tried to retain their independence were overwhelmed by the railroads' insistence on an exclusive loyalty. If they wanted any railroad work, they had to agree to represent the railroad exclusively. Often the most able lawyers in towns along the line were paid retainers, not for actual legal work, but to prevent them from appearing for anyone on the other side, not just of the client but of any anti-railroading interest. Railroad legal departments organized lawyers as political as well as legal agents; they formed trade associations, lobbied and paid for friendly legislation and friendly commissions, and financed campaigns of friendly politicians. By 1900, a lawyer who had railroads among his clients was expected to support and be a spokesman for railroad interests generally. Some carried their loyalties into public office. Richard Olney remained general counsel for the Boston & Maine and Chicago, Burlington & Quincy Railroads while, as Cleveland's Attorney General, he was seeking and enforcing injunctions against Eugene Debs's strikes against railroad associations, including his clients.

Fatefully, the bar had begun to specialize careers by clienteles – one specialty for tort defense against personal injury suits with another bar, usually immigrant in origins and ethnically distinct, for plaintiffs; and in labor disputes eventually a bar for management and a bar for labor, whose members almost never crossed over the line to represent the other side. To the great distress of some lawyers – but, it must be said, to the apparent satisfaction and enrichment of most – the most reputable segment of the bar had become a dependency of business empires, and often very unpopular empires at that. In 1910, the same Richard Olney who broke the Pullman strike painted a vivid contrast between the private and public views of lawyering. He deplored the new image of the lawyer who was represented

only as one variety of businessman; as an adjunct to business and its adventures with functions as much a part of its routine as those of its wage earners and day laborers; as using his "legal acumen and agility," so far as he remains a lawyer at all, in advising how nearly the extreme limits of the law can be approached without being overstepped; as influencing legislation in favor of his clients' interests; and as dexterously manipulating the issue and sale of corporate securities. . . . [L]awyers as members of a community absorbed in money-making, are themselves more or less infected, so that it is not surprising that many, consciously or unconsciously, come to regard money-making as the real aim and object of their career.[12]

These alliances sometimes proved embarrassing to lawyers who sought political office or judgeships; and several notable lawyers severed their ties with clienteles altogether to support Progressive reform causes that regulated them.

Rise of Public Interest Lawyering

Progressive lawyers invented a new institutional form, the job of legal counsel for the public interest group claiming to represent an amorphous and diffuse constituency – Citizens for Good Government, or Public Franchise League, or Committee of One Hundred for the Improvement of Education. As representative of such an abstract "client," the public interest lawyer naturally had a good deal of discretion about how to deploy his influence. The master of this form of public interest practice was the Boston lawyer Louis Brandeis, a successful corporate lawyer. Brandeis represented public interest causes without fee and reimbursed his partnership for the diversion of his time. In a famous address of 1905, Brandeis said that the public standing of lawyers had declined because "[i]nstead of holding a position of independence, between the wealthy and the people, prepared to curb the excesses of either, able lawyers have . . . allowed themselves to become adjuncts of great corporations. . . . We hear much of the 'corporation lawyer' and far too little of the 'people's lawyer.'"[13]

Progressive policy entrepreneurs' ultimate goal was usually to set up an expert commission. They were experts at creating publicity. After a scandal revealing some social horror – exploited child labor, tainted meat, railroad bribery of legislators or kickbacks to preferred customers, prostitution rings, or insurance fraud – reformers in collaboration with the muckraking press would persuade legislatures to establish commissions with the power to investigate, hold hearings, and make recommendations. These commissions were mostly staffed by part-time amateur volunteers, usually lawyers. Sometimes they turned into permanent administrative agencies. The reformers also brought test-case litigation, not to get courts to declare rights, but to refrain from interfering with Progressive legislation. Brandeis and the lawyer-reformers Florence Kelley and Felix Frankfurter brought

---

[12] Richard Olney, "To Uphold the Honor of the Profession of the Law," *Yale Law Journal* 19 (1910), 341–44.

[13] Louis D. Brandeis, "The Opportunity in the Law," in *Business – A Profession* (Boston, 1927), 333–34.

test cases on behalf of the National Consumers League (which supported maximum hours and minimum wage legislation) and also testified before legislatures in favor of legislative reforms and intervened in administrative agency proceedings. After being appointed to the Supreme Court in 1916, Brandeis continued to direct public interest crusades from behind the scenes through Frankfurter, his agent and disciple.

The more traditional model of cause lawyering, dating back to the legal tactics of the anti-slavery societies of the antebellum period, was to bring test cases in constitutional courts to extend rights of liberty and equality to new constituencies. The American Civil Liberties Union (ACLU) was founded in the Red Scare of World War I, when several thousand people, most of them connected to militant labor organizations, were prosecuted by the federal government for impeding the war effort or deported as undesirable aliens. Supported largely by membership subscriptions and the volunteered time of lawyers, the ACLU built an impressive record of using the federal courts to prevent persecution of political and religious dissenters by providing them with free legal representation; in the process it helped produce the United States' extraordinarily libertarian (by world standards) regime of judicial protection for free speech. The most amazing and dramatic use of the model was by the National Association for the Advancement of Colored People (NAACP) and its legal arm, the Legal Defense Fund. The NAACP brought and won an important test case in its early years, *Buchanan v. Warley* (1917), in which the Supreme Court struck down a racial zoning ordinance in Louisville that forbade homeowners in white neighborhoods to sell to African Americans. The Legal Defense Fund's epic journey began in 1930 with a small foundation grant to study the conditions of educational inequality in the South and culminated in 1954 with the Supreme Court's decision striking down legally mandated segregation.

The reformers who led these early rights-activist crusades were an interesting alliance of establishment and marginal lawyers. Some were patricians, like the Boston corporate lawyer Moorfield Storey who headed the first NAACP legal committees. Others were highly educated professionals confined to the margins of their profession by prejudice: Jewish, African American, and women lawyers such as Morris Ernst, Osmond Fraenkel, Crystal Eastman, Carol Weiss King, Pauli Murray and Ruth Bader Ginsburg (mainstays of the ACLU); and Charles Hamilton Houston, Thurgood Marshall, Constance Motley, Robert Carter and Jack Greenberg of the NAACP Legal Defense Fund. Cause lawyering was hardly the pathway to economic success for marginals: it paid very badly and able lawyers made severe financial sacrifices to undertake it. But it was a path upward in other ways, to respect and status. The courtroom, especially in a high-profile case, was one of the few places where an African American could appear on a plane of equality with white Protestant males and where courtroom decorum would ensure they would be treated with respect.

The noted African American lawyer Raymond Pace Alexander of Philadelphia, though a Harvard Law School graduate, could not get a job with any law firm or be admitted to any bar association except the association for African American lawyers. In his early years of practice, even well-off African American clients and businesses would not hire him, thinking they would fare better in a white court system with a white lawyer. He had to get by on a smattering of small clients and criminal cases. He could not rent office space downtown or, when in a Southern city like Washington, D.C., eat at the restaurant across from the courthouse or hang out at the bar with the other trial lawyers. But in court, he was called Mr. Alexander and treated by the judge and court personnel as equal to the white lawyer on the other side; he could cross-examine white witnesses, display his talents, and win cases. Thurgood Marshall was denied admission to the University of Maryland Law School in 1930 because he was African American. In 1936, soon after graduating from Howard, he had the satisfaction of winning the case that desegregated the school that rejected him.[14]

Women similarly found a practice niche in supporting the causes and concerns of women and other social underdogs. Leaders of the women's rights movements like Belva Lockwood of Washington, D.C., and Myra Bradwell of Illinois also led the fights for admission of women to the bar. Once admitted, and facing strenuous resistance to their presence in the courtroom and in business law firms, many women lawyers played up their comparative advantage as members of the gentler sex devoted to charity and reform. One of the most impressive pioneers, Clara Shortridge Foltz of California, took on poor as well as paying clients, and led the movement to create the first state public defender system, though she also hard-headedly commented that if a woman lawyer "prefers to engage in child welfare work, takes up legal aid work, runs here, there and everywhere at the whim of every ambitious clubwoman, omitting to charge for her services, she cannot hope to win while her eyes are bright."[15] The pattern held for the rest of the century. Women lawyers were prominent among the leaders of Progressive reform, civil liberties, labor, and civil rights movements. By 2000, though admitted to the bar in numbers almost equal to those of men, they were under-represented relative to their proportion in the profession in private law firm partnerships but over-represented in legal services, public defenders, public interest firms, NGOs, and in government.

---

[14] *Pearson v. Murray*, 169 Md. 478, 182 A. 590 (1936).
[15] Bureau of Vocational Information questionnaire 180, March 9, 1920 (BVI Records, Schlesinger Library, Radcliffe College).

III. NEW DEAL, POSTWAR STABILITY, AND THE RIGHTS REVOLUTION: 1930–1975

The Depression of the 1930s was as hard on lawyers as on other occupations. The median income of lawyers fell by 8 percent between 1929 and 1933. Younger lawyers suffered worst: in New Jersey, beginning lawyers' income fell 67 percent (1925–37) and those with fifteen years in practice by 53 percent (1928–38). Michigan lawyers reported to a 1940 survey that 38 percent of them had been unable to make a living in at least one year between 1929 and 1934.

The New Deal and Postwar Order

The New Deal set in motion a revolution in government that would ultimately yield substantial business for lawyers and a variety of new specialties and functions. The New Deal itself was a vast employment program for lawyers – by 1939 there were 5,368 lawyers in federal service – and not just for government lawyers but lawyers for client groups and constituencies needing to deal with the new government agencies. The New Deal's hiring policies mostly expanded – but also in some ways limited – social mobility for marginals. A huge number of new positions opened up. New Deal agencies managed to hire most lawyers outside civil service requirements (which gave strong preferences for veterans and for geographical distribution) and to bypass Congressional patronage for non-civil service appointments. For the top positions, the New Dealers used much the same meritocratic criteria as big firms, except that they discriminated much less against Jews, Catholics, women, (occasional) African Americans, and lawyers with overtly left-wing political views. The best record for a job applicant was a high-grade average from an elite Northeastern law school and the recommendation of a law professor, preferably Felix Frankfurter. This was a great system for marginals who had somehow made it to Harvard, Columbia or Yale, but would never be hired by a Wall Street firm. It was not so good for lawyers without elite credentials, protégés of Congressmen, most graduates of Washington, D.C., area law schools, graduates with only a year or two of college and with law degrees from unaccredited law schools, and for women law graduates who had often been admitted to civil service in non-legal positions such as stenographers but were eligible to rise through the ranks.

For many lawyers and perhaps most, however, the main reason for joining the government was not employment opportunities: it was the challenge of the cause. About half of the leading lawyers of the New Deal came out of corporate practice, taking a big pay cut to do so and often risking their relationships with anti-New Deal business clients. Some of them were law professors who had already left, or shunned, corporate practice. The New Deal offered a chance to do something important, glamorous, and in tune with political convictions. Many of these lawyers thought they were severing their ties with the world of private business lawyering by crossing over to the government side. But of course as the federal government's functions and agencies expanded, they created large new domains of practice for lawyers – tax, antitrust, regulation of securities, public utilities, power, and labor relations, among others. The New Deal lawyers found they had acquired professional capital that they could convert back into to private practice. After the war, some of the principal New Deal lawyers, "young men with their hair ablaze" like Tommy Corcoran and James Rowe, Thurman Arnold, and Abe Fortas, become founders of Washington D.C. firms, representing corporate clients before agencies such as the SEC, created by legislation they had written and that they had originally staffed.

Business lawyers were ambivalent about the New Deal. Even those who were classical conservatives swallowed their doubts about the most constitutionally dubious of the New Deal's experiments, the National Industrial Recovery Act, because their major clients initially supported it. They then celebrated its invalidation by the Supreme Court after their clients had turned against it. Many represented business clients who bitterly opposed arrangements such as the New Deal's schemes of securities, public utilities, and especially labor regulation, or they supported them as long as they thought they could control the regulators and went into opposition only when they could not. Some lawyers were themselves by ideological conviction ferociously opposed to any large federal or government role in the regulation of business. In the 1930s, two thousand lawyers headed by such luminaries as John W. Davis, a former presidential candidate; James M. Beck, former Solicitor General; and George W. Wickersham, former Attorney General, formed the National Lawyer's Committee of the American Liberty League. The League counseled its industrial clients to civil disobedience of the orders of the New Deal's new Labor Board, in the certain (and ultimately mistaken) conviction that the Supreme Court would invalidate the National Labor Relations Act. With allies in the ABA, led by the increasingly conservative Roscoe Pound, they led the struggle, embodied in the Walter-Logan Act of 1940 vetoed by President Roosevelt, to burden the administrative process with so much trial-type due process as to bring it to a total halt. But other business lawyers, such as those who signed the New York City Bar Association's report opposing Walter-Logan, did not wish to hamstring the administrative process, but to keep it informal and flexible and negotiate cooperative deals with it on behalf of their clients. By the 1950s most of the New Deal's innovations had settled cozily into the familiar pattern of tripartite deals between industries, their friends in Congress, and regulatory agencies. Leading firms viewed them as an at least tolerable and often very useful revised framework for a capitalist economy.

Certainly, the New Deal was good for the law business. By virtue of the federalization of regulation, all big-city law firms became specialists in national law able to compete with the New York firms. Baker & Botts of Houston is a good example. The Public Utility Holding Company Act of 1935, which broke up the nation's utility systems, first gave the firm the job of fighting the act; then, when the fight was lost, the firm took on the business of reorganizing all its utility clients to comply with the act, which in turn brought valuable contacts with New York financial houses and experience working with government agencies. The Railway Labor Act of 1926 and Wagner Act of 1935 delivered the business of helping defend hundreds of labor cases before the new labor boards. A partner at the firm, looking back on the era, commented, "Of course lawyers were as vociferous as their clients in complaining about the New Deal legislation, but in retrospect one may wonder how lawyers would have survived without the legislation."[16]

The relative stability of large corporations in 1945–65 – oligopolies within a legal-regulatory framework of business-friendly corporatism – extended to their lawyers, who helped administer the framework from both the private side and the public side. Younger lawyers often started their careers with a brief term in government to learn the system from the inside. Older firm lawyers were appointed to senior positions in the agencies. Large-firm corporate practice became still more technical and specialized, much less a matter of negotiating new conventions with the state than of administering existing ones. Lawyers continued to cultivate relations with the bureaucracy, but their main stock-in-trade became their expertise, rather than their contacts. Business firms turned over their political action work to specialists in lobbying and government relations. Practice conditions were stabilized as well. Law firms were locked into long-term relations with major corporate clients and handled all but the most routine of those clients' business. Younger lawyers entered the firm hoping to stay with it for life. Companies rarely switched firms; partners rarely left them.

Labor Lawyers and Radicals

The New Deal also fostered the creation of a labor bar, something that previously had scarcely existed. Through the 1930s the American Federation of Labor, the umbrella organization of craft unions and dominant spokesmen

---

[16] "Memorandum Prepared by John T. McCullough as Basis for Remarks . . . on November 27, 1979," Baker & Botts Historical Collection.

of labor, pursued the goal of "voluntarism" (collective laissez-faire); its only legal aim was negative – defense of its members against employers' legal campaigns against them. Unions still needed lawyers to fight court injunctions, criminal contempt proceedings for defying injunctions, and antitrust suits. They found them among left-leaning general practice and business lawyers willing to suffer the stigma of association with organized labor. Some of those lawyers, such as Clarence Darrow, Felix Frankfurter, Donald Richberg, David Lilienthal, and Harold Ickes, went on to serve in high posts in the New Deal. More radical lawyers of the period, mostly from socialist immigrant Jewish households, were drawn to the growing industrial union movement, like Maurice Sugar, general counsel of the United Automobile Workers (1939–47) and Lee Pressman, general counsel of the Congress of Industrial Organizations (1933–48).

After World War II, lawyers with commitments to social reform continued to go into labor law, often after a stint on the National Labor Relations Board staff in Washington. But labor law gradually lost some of its appeal for reformers. Union officials, often Catholic blue-collar workers, tended to be hostile to the Jewish intellectuals who did their legal work, however much they needed them. The New Deal's labor regime stabilized labor relations by embedding them in legal procedures: this created a steady demand for labor lawyers, but also routinized the work of representing unions and deprived it of the romance of a cause. The labor movement lost some of its most intensely committed lawyers when the Taft-Hartley Act (1947) required a purge of Communists. Incorporated, albeit grudgingly, as a regular partner with business in the postwar economic order, most unions grew more conservative in their aims and ideology, more interested in bread-and-butter bargaining gains than social transformation, and (in many locals) actively hostile to the new claims of African Americans and women for jobs in union-controlled workplaces. Others, like the Jewish labor lawyers, stayed with the cause and went from the government National Labor Relations Board into jobs representing labor in unions or labor-side law firms. But even these relatively self-denying cause lawyers were propelled into professional prominence as their cause of organized labor flourished in the 1950s and 60s, when union general counsel had the status of foreign ministers negotiating general policies affecting wage rates and working conditions in vast industries, were routinely invited to join boards and commissions setting national government policies, and in liberal administrations were appointed to Cabinet posts and even (in the case of the labor lawyer Arthur J. Goldberg) to the Supreme Court.

Some radicals (like Pressman) also joined the Communist Party. Most joined the National Lawyers' Guild, founded in 1937 as a broad coalition organization of liberal and radical labor, civil rights, and civil liberties lawyers aspiring to be more inclusive than the major bar associations (it admitted Jews, women and African Americans) and to function as an organized counterweight to the conservative politics of the ABA. The Guild split apart and lost most of its non-Communist center-left members when it rejected their pleas to expel Communists. Although harried by the Justice Department and House Committee on Un-American Activities, Guild lawyers continued to represent those involved in unpopular radical causes and were sometimes the only lawyers that some radicals such as Communists could rely on. The most radical lawyers joined the Communist-affiliated International Labor Defense (ILD), whose most famous cause had been its defense of the Scottsboro Boys, nine African American teenagers charged with the gang rape of two white girls in 1931. ILD lawyers fought fiercely to obtain legal victories in their cases, though their primary and sometimes conflicting aim was to publicize and dramatize the injustice of capitalist society.

Lawyers and the Rights Revolution

Beginning in the 1930s, the NAACP's Legal Defense Fund, with a tiny staff of low-paid lawyers headed by Charles Hamilton Houston and Thurgood Marshall, embarked on a twenty-five-year campaign of test-case litigation in the federal courts to try to establish, by gradual degrees, the principle that state-mandated separation of the races in public institutions and places violated the constitutional requirement that states give all persons the "equal protection of the laws" and by so doing to dismantle the system of legally established racial apartheid in the South. That campaign climaxed in 1954 with a moral triumph – the Supreme Court's declaration in *Brown v. Board of Education* that state-mandated segregation of the races in public schooling (and by implication in other public settings as well) was unconstitutional. It would, however, take many more years of protest movements, legal challenges, and federal legislative and executive action before much was done to implement the principle.

The spectacular victory of civil rights lawyers in *Brown* inspired more and more groups to follow the strategy of the civil rights movement. In the 1960s and 1970s these strategies met with astonishing success. The reformers found surprisingly receptive allies in the – as often as not, Republican-appointed – judges of the U.S. Supreme Court, under the leadership of Chief Justice Earl Warren and Justice William J. Brennan, and of the lower federal courts: middle-class men who could be provoked to outrage by what test-case litigation revealed of the treatment of marginal and outcast groups in American society. Federal judges embarrassed by the racism and backwardness of the old South, for example, were so revolted by the conditions exposed in Southern prisons – long run on the feudal model of slave plantations and characterized by ferocious levels of filth, torture, and coerced labor – that they stretched their legal authority to construct far-reaching remedial orders that placed entire institutions for years under professional reform administrators. Other judges were provoked to sweeping remedial action by the obstruction and resistance of local authorities to court orders, especially orders to compel school integration. Every act of defiance created more judicial sympathy for rights activists, who now appeared as champions of the rule of law against the lawlessness of regularly constituted authorities. Client groups asserting rights to be free from arbitrary or contemptuous treatment by government also found judges receptive to this traditional libertarian strain. Rights litigators were sometimes able to recruit allies in elite law firms to help their causes.

Rights activism was not radical in principle. It aimed simply to extend accepted legal principles of equality and fair procedural treatment to groups of persons who had been excluded from their coverage; it did not challenge the principle, only the operation in practice, of distribution of social goods by capitalist markets; and it wished only to open the chance to compete on equal terms. This might seem a centrist or even conservative program, but taken seriously and given elite judicial and political backing, it profoundly disrupted existing patterns of hierarchy, authority, and inequality. Suits brought to achieve declarations of new rights were rapidly followed by more suits for judicial remedial orders and by lobbying for legislation and executive action to enforce them. Claims of rights to equal opportunity and fair treatment rapidly turned into claims for major redistribution of resources – admission of women, African Americans, and other minorities to professions and crafts; equalization of public school finances among rich and poor districts; and drastic overhauling of institutions like schools, prisons, and mental asylums and welfare administration. Such actions energized a major political backlash against the rights revolution. The Republican Party engineered a major electoral realignment based in large part on recruiting voters angered by Warren Court and Democratic administration support for black civil rights, especially school integration orders involving busing and affirmative action plans designed to remedy employment discrimination, the feminist campaign for equal rights for women and the constitutionalization of the right to abortion, and expanded protections for criminal defendants. A succession of Republican administrations under Presidents Nixon, Reagan, and Bush gradually replaced the generation of liberal reform-minded federal judges with conservatives committed to reversing, or at least not extending, the proliferation and aggressive enforcement of rights. By the 1990s, liberal lawyers who thirty years earlier had fought to get their cases into federal courts now fought to stay out of them.

In some ways, rights activism was an elite reform strategy high above the fray of ordinary politics. For some rights-activist lawyers the important goal was more to vindicate a principle or implement a policy than to advance the interests of a concrete group. Some lawyers seeking judicial recognition of the rights of religious dissenters or people accused of crimes neither identified with nor even met actual clients. This was not invariably so. To build their test cases, Legal Defense Fund lawyers had to do the arduous and dangerous work of recruiting plaintiffs and organizing suits in the rural South. And though rights activists were often criticized for over-investing in judicial rule change and paying too little attention to political mobilization and bureaucratic implementation, in fact they rarely relied on litigation alone to achieve their aims. Litigation was always one strategy among many others, including lobbying, supporting candidates for elections, conducting voting drives, mobilizing allies such as labor organizations, dramatizing causes to the media, doing grassroots organizing, and staffing and monitoring enforcement bureaucracies. For example, once a grassroots civil rights movement had started, the LDF lawyers switched a large part of their efforts from test-case litigation to advancing the goals of the movement and keeping its members out of jail. Still, the natural home of rights-activist lawyers was the courts, especially the upper federal courts.

An entirely new field of endeavor, poverty law, was opened up in the mid-1960s. President Lyndon Johnson created a federally funded Legal Services Program in the Office of Economic Opportunity (OEO) as part of his War on Poverty. In 1965 the combined budgets of all legal aid societies in the United States totaled $5,375,890, and their combined staffs numbered 400 full-time lawyers. By 1968 OEO Legal Services had an annual budget of $40 million and had added 2,000 lawyers; by 1980 (before President Reagan cut it by a third) the budget was $321 million, supporting 6,000 lawyers. OEO Legal Services also funded "backup centers" in fields such as health and employment discrimination to serve as research centers and information clearinghouses for poverty lawyers in the field. In the early 1970s foundations led by the Ford Foundation began making grants to "public interest firms," about half of which identified the poor as their principal clientele; by 1975 foundation grants contributed 42 percent of public interest law firm budgets.

The new poverty lawyers were a very mixed lot. Like labor, civil rights, and civil liberties lawyers, some came from left-of-center families and backgrounds in social activism. In its early years poverty law practice also attracted high-ranking graduates of elite schools, many of them paid for by OEO "Reggie" (Reginald Heber Smith) Fellowships. But just as often, poverty lawyers came from solo practice or other low-paid "legal rights" jobs like legal aid or public defender practice. Though turnover in Legal Services was always high – few stayed more than four or five years – even lawyers who left kept up their activist commitments in other jobs.

The poverty lawyers often disagreed about what their objectives should be. Traditional legal aid lawyers and their supporters in the organized bar thought the main mission was a service function, taking care of clients' individual needs and not antagonizing local political or commercial power structures. Others favored a model closer to the Progressive settlement house of "storefront" services located in poor neighborhoods, combining legal with other social work services that were focused on enabling families to move up and out of poverty. Most of the new lawyers had a more ambitious vision of law as a means of broader social reform, which would work major structural changes in the situation of the poor. An important group favored test-case litigation directed at reforming the indifferent and repressive bureaucracies that served the poor. Others saw litigation as one component of a strategy directed at helping communities of poor people mobilize politically to articulate their own needs and demands and to participate in making and applying policies of the new anti-poverty agencies in the cities.

Poverty lawyers involved in reforming the welfare system (1965–73) tried combining all of these strategies. They brought test cases to force welfare bureaucracies to apply their own rules faithfully and fairly and eliminate arbitrary paternalist regulations; then they helped organize a movement (the National Welfare Rights Organization) of welfare recipients to insist on their rights, in hopes that such claims would overwhelm the bureaucracy and move the government toward a system of unconditional grants. They also sought to repeat the successes of the civil rights movement: to define the poor as a pariah group subject to unconstitutional discrimination, and to constitutionalize a general substantive right to a guaranteed minimum income. After initial successes on all fronts of its strategy, the movement for welfare rights backfired. As welfare rolls burgeoned – partly because of the lawyers' successes in enrolling eligible families – state and federal governments began to cut back on welfare spending and to impose new requirements. The courts had granted procedural rights to fair hearings, but refused to create substantive rights to welfare. The nascent political organizations collapsed.

The poverty lawyers stirred up a hornets' nest. Established legal aid programs, local bar associations, charitable organizations, and local political machines saw them as threats to their own turf and patronage relations and tried to close them down and restrict their operations to routine individual services. Several governors tried to abolish the programs in their states, after Legal Services sued the states for violating their own laws and policies. President Reagan tried to abolish the federal program and succeeded in crippling it; it limped onward under many restrictions on its systemic reform activities. The bar associations, however, switched sides and after 1975 became staunch supporters of Legal Services, in part because the programs created jobs for lawyers, in part because the bar wanted the profession to look good, and lawyers instinctively resisted attempts to restrict whom they may represent and by what means.

The Progressive model of lawyer as policy entrepreneur acting on behalf of diffuse and unorganized constituencies was reinvented in this period. In the late 1960s and early 1970s the model was developed into the role of public interest representative in administrative proceedings. The muckraker and consumer lawyer Ralph Nader, who organized cadres of college and law student volunteers to investigate government programs and their failures, became the best known and one of the most effective. The mission of the public interest lawyers was to repair glaring defects in political pluralism – to open up the administrative agencies that the Progressives and New Dealers had created to the broad constituencies that they were supposed to serve. Until the late 1960s, administrative agency decision procedures – such as hearings on the construction of energy projects like nuclear power plants or the granting or renewal of radio or TV licenses – were usually dominated by representatives of industries they regulated. The new public interest lawyers claimed that other, more diffuse constituencies – TV viewers, lovers of wilderness and the environment, consumers, future generations – also had interests in the decision. The lawyers claimed to represent those interests. With the help of the federal courts, public interest lawyers were increasingly permitted to intervene in agency proceedings and to challenge agency decisions on judicial review. They established a regular place at the table in administrative decision-making processes. In politically congenial administrations, such as President Jimmy Carter's, they were brought in to staff important government posts.

The most successful public interest representatives turned their abstract constituencies into real ones. The environmental movement, for example, began as a few vanguard activists. However, it used its activism to create a mass middle-class movement, aroused, well financed, and able to mobilize politically around major initiatives or perceived threats to its core interests. Other examples may be found in the movements for women's rights, disability rights, gay and lesbian rights, and animal rights. Many public interest constituencies, however, limited their involvement to writing checks to keep the movements alive: real decision-making power remained with their representatives.

IV. EXPANSION AND UPHEAVAL: 1970–2000

A century after the founding of its major modern institutions, the legal profession began to undergo momentous changes in virtually all sectors of practice.

Size and Composition of the Profession

The bar's project to limit admissions by raising pre-legal and legal educational requirements and lowering bar exam pass rates – combined with the collapse of part-time night schools in the Depression – had kept the proportion of lawyers to the population reasonably stable since 1900. But after 1970 the volume of new entrants soared. The number of approved law schools increased and their student bodies increased rapidly (from 22,000 law students in 1950 to 132,500 in 1990), particularly after the arrival of the baby boomers in the cohort of college graduates and the opening of the profession to women. The total number of lawyers rose from 355,000 in 1970 to 542,000 in 1980 and by the end of the century had doubled again to over a million: just over 3 lawyers per thousand of population. By effectively handing over admission to the profession to the law schools, the bar had surrendered its role as gatekeeper.

Beginning in the late 1960s, anti-discrimination laws and affirmative action combined to produce a substantial increase in African American enrollments in law schools, from 2,000 in 1969 to 6,000 in 1985. Thereafter, however there was a slight decline; and African American lawyers remained strikingly underrepresented in law firms, making up 3.3 percent of associates in 1996 and only 1.7 percent of partners. In 2000 4.2 percent of all lawyers were African American. The biggest change was in the profession's acceptance of women. Between 1967 and 1983, enrollment of women at ABA-approved law schools rose 1,650 percent, from 4.5 to 37.7 percent of the total; at the end of the century it had stabilized at almost 50 percent. In 1980 only 8 percent of lawyers were women; by 2000, 27 percent were women. However, some combination of continuing discrimination and the brutal time demands of corporate practice continued to keep law firm partner ranks predominantly male – around 85 percent or more in most firms. By 2000 women were much better represented (around 25 percent) in prosecutors, government, and house counsel offices and among law teachers; they were often the majority in legal aid offices and public interest firms. Hispanic-Americans in the profession rose slightly from 2.5 percent in 1980 to 3.4 percent in 2000, Asian Americans from 1.4 to 2.2 percent.

As striking as the higher numbers were the shifts in jobs among sectors. The proportion of lawyers in private practice declined significantly in the post-World War II years, from 89.2 percent in 1948 to about 68.3 percent in 1988. In 2000, however, it was back up to 74 percent. In that category the biggest decline was in solo practice, from 61.2 to 48 percent. Where did the private practitioners go? Primarily to private employment, as in-house employees of business – up from 3.2 percent in 1948 to 8 per in 2000 – and to governments. Federal government employment of lawyers, as a proportion of all lawyers, fell from 5.6 percent in the 1950s and 60s to 3.5 percent in 2000, but state government employment of lawyers increased (from 1.8 percent in 1950 to 6.7 percent in 2000). All government lawyers in 2000 accounted for 10.3 percent of the total; all legal aid and public defenders, for 1 percent (down from 2 percent in 1980). A few more became law teachers, up from 0.6 percent in 1951 to 1 percent in 2000.

Within private practice the big reallocation was from individual to corporate practice. A study of Chicago lawyers found that in 1975 the share of lawyers' efforts going to corporate matters was 53 percent versus 21 percent going to individual "personal plight" clients. In 1995 the share of effort going to corporate clients increased to 61%, whereas effort to personal plight clients was down to 16 percent.

The Corporate Sector

The most explosive transformations were in the corporate practice sector. The demand for corporate lawyers multiplied with client demands for lawyers to staff an exploding increase in transactions, government regulations, and litigation. The main origins of the new phase were in the severe shocks to the settled corporate-legal order delivered by international competition, the new mobility of capital, and the new volatility of the market for corporate control. The federal government lifted regulatory controls on some industries (airlines, trucking, communications, banking) in the 1970s and 80s, but created whole new fields of regulation to take their place – bans on employment discrimination against African Americans, women, the disabled, and the old; environmental controls on polluting, land use, drilling, and grazing; consumer protection, toxic substance, and occupational safety regulation – as well as several major changes in the federal tax code.

In response, big business firms switched strategies. Instead of negotiating cooperative compacts with government agencies and labor unions, companies began to aggressively challenge regulation and labor agreements they once accepted as the price of stability. Meanwhile they became more prone to mergers or takeovers as targets or raiders and driven to constant restructuring – acquiring new divisions, shedding or spinning off old ones, and rearranging profits, losses, and debts on paper – to manage financial appearances to the capital markets and taxing authorities. Before the 1970s companies rarely sued for breach of contract; by the end of the century, corporate contract suits accounted for the largest share of new lawsuits filed in federal courts. Suits against companies rose as well, notably for mass torts such as toxic waste emissions and defective products. Whole new industries emerged such as the high-tech ventures of the Silicon Valley, whose products called for invention of new fields of law. As deals with new trading partners around the world replaced informal ties of businesses in long-term continuing relationships, lawyers were called in to craft contracts covering performance terms and reducing the business and legal risks of new ventures. All this work required platoons of lawyers in many different specialties: to manage major lawsuits with their warehouses full of documents sought in discovery; to avoid, work around, resist, or simply comply with complex regulations, taxes, and disclosure and reporting requirements in many different states and foreign countries; to staff transactions such as mergers or takeovers or initial public offerings of new companies; and to do the paperwork for deals. As businesses expanded globally, firms hired lawyers from many jurisdictions and nationalities to join the teams.

The most visible effect of these demands for more lawyers was a sharp rise in the number, size, and geographic reach of law firms. In 1900 a "large firm" – so large that contemporaries called it a "law factory" – was eleven lawyers. Around 1960 only thirty-eight firms had more than fifty lawyers; half of them were in New York City. In 1978, 15 firms had over 200 lawyers; by 1987, there were 105. By 2005, 17 firms had over 1,000 lawyers, 30 over 800, 70 over 500, 196 over 200, and 405 over 100. Firms with more than 100 lawyers made up only 1 percent of American firms, but employed 14 percent of all lawyers in private practice and a tenth of the entire profession: 107,472 lawyers.

Some firms grew internally, others by merger. In the 1980s and 90s, firms extended their reach by opening both domestic and foreign branch offices. A sample of ten of the largest firms showed them operating between one and six domestic branch offices and one to six foreign offices in 1983. In 1999 those firms had doubled their domestic branch offices and almost tripled their foreign offices. Houston's Vinson & Elkins was typical. Like other big firms, Vinson & Elkins expanded geometrically in the boom legal market of the 1970s and 80s. By the late 1970s the firm had 286 lawyers; by 1999, more than 500; by 2002, 862 in eighty different practice specialties. More and more business came in from increasing state and federal regulation, and Vinson & Elkins lawyers began to specialize in energy, environmental, patent, admiralty, and municipal bond law; in antitrust, securities, and mass tort litigation; as well as its old fields of oil, gas, banking, and insurance. It opened branch offices in Dallas, Austin, Washington, New York, London, Moscow, Tokyo, Beijing, and Dubai.

As they expanded, firms transformed the nature of legal practice by competing aggressively with one another to attract clients and to hire senior lawyers and associates. Confronted with escalating legal costs, companies tried to keep these costs down by severing long-term ties with outside firms and bringing substantial pieces of legal work in-house. The job of in-house general counsel to a business, once a resting place for lawyers who had failed to make partner in law firms, became newly prestigious and powerful and – like railroads in the 1870s – attracted lawyers at the top of their profession. The general counsel's job was purchasing and managing all the legal services for his or her company, auctioning off fragments of specialized work – especially complex litigation – to many different outside firms. The result was a whole new style of corporate practice – ruthlessly competitive, powered pretty nearly exclusively by the drive for profits, so demanding as to leave no time or energy for other commitments, and mostly indifferent to social responsibility and public values.

The practice was very lucrative for lawyers and firms who succeeded but also highly stressful because the specter of failure hovered so close by. Huge firms, some new, some long established – Finley, Kumble and Lord Day & Lord of New York; Gaston Snow and Hill & Barlow of Boston; Brobeck, Phleger of San Francisco; and many others – collapsed from over-expansion or over-caution.

The old stable institutional order of law firm practice dissolved. Lawyers no longer expected a lifetime career in a single firm, but moved among firms who bid for their services and from firms to house counsel's offices, investment banks, accounting firms, and business consulting services. Firms raised associates' salaries from 1986 onward to compete with pay in alternative careers newly open to law graduates – by 2004, beginning lawyers earned $125,000 or more. However, with more pay also came longer hours of work (eighty hours or more a week in some firms) and much lower chances of making partner or of obtaining secure tenure even after partnership. Clients around the world wanted service night and day from their lawyers. Compensation was tied to the ability to attract clients: "You eat what you kill." With the rise of the new practice, the old ethnic barriers fell. Blue-chip white-shoe firms eagerly sought after the Jewish and Catholic lawyers who had staffed formerly degraded specialties such as litigation and had expertise in mergers and acquisitions. Firms also hired African American and women lawyers, but were less likely to retain and promote them. Both groups were less likely to have the business contacts to recruit the clients necessary for survival in firms. Women still had the double shift at home, which limited both their capacity and desire to spend every waking hour at work or travel for weeks out of town to prepare a big case or close a big deal.

Meanwhile, American firms and the American style of corporate law practice spread to foreign countries, especially Europe. They encountered many competitors: English solicitors' firms, multinational accounting firms, and new European multidisciplinary consortia. In 1999 only ten of the largest twenty international firms (with between 700 and 2,500 lawyers each) were American law firms. Six were firms of English (and one of Australian) solicitors. The rest were giant accounting firms. Accounting firms dominated legal services in Europe and even in the United States employed more than 5,000 lawyers who gave advice on tax shelters and bankruptcy reorganizations. American lawyers were also competing fiercely for a share of the increasingly lucrative business of international arbitration, formerly dominated by Europeans, and promising to bring the dubious blessing of American-style litigation practice to the rest of the world. In competition with European solicitors and accountants, American lawyers were building the new legal frameworks for the transaction of international commerce.

Practice for Individual Clients

The profession's individual practice sector also experienced seismic shocks. In 1900 solo and small-firm lawyers serving individuals and small business encompassed the entire profession save for a few big-city big-business firms. In 2000 individual practice was still numerically the largest segment of the private bar, but accounted for a rapidly diminishing share, relative to corporate practice, of total lawyers' effort and earnings. Over the century it had included some very wealthy and famous members, such as tort plaintiffs' lawyers who were richer than all but a few top corporate lawyers, and celebrity trial lawyers, like Max Steuer, Louis Nizer, F. Lee Bailey, and Edward Bennett Williams, who took on high-profile clients and cases. Its staple business throughout the century remained much the same: claims for simple debt and collections, personal injury suits, criminal defense, divorce and other family work, real estate closings, wills and trusts, bankruptcies and foreclosures, and miscellaneous problems of small businesses.

Specialization carved out large segments of general office practice. The leaders of the bar in 1900 were still mostly generalists. Elihu Root and Joseph Hodges Choate made their mark as trial lawyers who tried a medley of civil and criminal cases, such as wills, divorces, libels, murders, and as constitutional lawyers argued before the Supreme Court, as well as serving as general business advisers. The growth of the regulatory state with its arcana of complex technical administrative rules doomed the generalist in corporate practice: a lawyer could spend a lifetime mastering a few sections of the corporate tax code or securities laws and keeping up with new amendments and regulations. Fields such as prosecution and patents were already specialized by 1900; labor, tax, patents, antitrust, oil and gas, and securities were highly specialized by mid-century. In the late 1970s, 22 percent of Chicago lawyers worked in only one field, and by the late 1980s, that figure had risen to 32 percent. Criminal defense and personal injury had become specialty fields. But many solo and small practitioners still engaged in a general family practice.

At the bottom were solo and small-firm practitioners making a precarious living on the cliff's edge of unemployment. They were the most vulnerable to business cycle downturns; to competition (since their staple work was real estate work, wills, debt collection, auto accidents, and divorces) from non-lawyer organizations, such as trust departments, title insurance companies, and accounting firms; to reforms reducing the need for lawyers, such as no-fault auto accident and no-fault divorce laws; and to do-it-yourself forms, manuals, and software programs. Incomes of partners and associate in corporate practice rose sharply after 1970; those of solo practitioners declined by 30 percent between 1970 and 1985, while their numbers were increasing (by 34 percent from 1980–88). One response to these precarious market conditions was the organization of franchised law firms, which attempted to realize scale efficiencies and product standardization through consolidation and rationalization of legal work for middle-class individuals.

Personal Injury Practice

The most dramatic development in the individual practice sector, certainly the one with the broadest and most controversial social effects, was the rise of a mass-tort class action specialty within the personal injury bar.

The first mass-tort cases – involving large numbers of victims injured by the same cause – were cases arising from accidents: fires, floods from bursting dams, sinkings of boats. Litigation of such disaster claims had unpromising beginnings. Victims were often poor, hired local counsel to fight experienced company lawyers, and faced daunting jurisdictional requirements, procedural obstacles, and hostile courts. Only one civil suit was brought in the wake of the 1911 Triangle Shirtwaist Fire caused by unsafe tenement conditions, in which 145 New York sweatshop laborers died. Plaintiffs rested their case after only one day and lost it; the remaining civil suits settled for $75 each. Few lawyers could risk the costs of taking on such suits, given the risks of loss and low settlements.

The tort bar began to organize itself after World War II. An association of workers' compensation lawyers founded in 1946 added tort practitioners in the 1960s and eventually became the Association of Trial Lawyers of America (ATLA). In 1951 it had 2,000 members; by 1971 it had 25,000 and had become a clearinghouse for information, a means for recruiting cadres of lawyers to take on and coordinate mass-tort litigation, and a powerful political interest group with a massive war chest for lobbying legislatures and influencing judicial elections.

As the tort bar organized, it developed specialties. The first was airplane accident law, a desultory practice area before the 1940s. Stuart Speiser pioneered the role of coordinator and general contractor of teams of plaintiffs' attorneys who represented families of air accident victims from different jurisdictions, helping the lawyers consolidate cases and prepare a common litigation strategy. In the 1960s, 288 lawyers, representing all about 75 percent of the 1,500 plaintiffs who sued the Merrill Company for harmful side effects caused by its anti-cholesterol drug MER/29, combined into a group that drastically cut the costs of litigation by centralizing research and document discovery, deposing witnesses, and finding and preparing scientific experts.

Meanwhile changes in substantive law and procedure transformed the landscape of tort disputes. The courts opened the door to "strict products liability" claims against manufacturers of products alleged to have caused plaintiffs' injuries, which did not require proof that the company was negligent, only that the product was "defective." The "asbestos era" of the federal court system began in 1973, when a federal appeals court ruled that asbestos manufacturers were strictly liable (*Borel v. Fibreboard*). By 1987, around 50,000 asbestos claims were pending in the nation's courts; by 1992 there were 200,000 claims; and 6,000 to 9,000 new claims were being filed annually. In 1986 the federal courts began to allow the aggregation of asbestos claims as class actions (*Jenkins v. Raymark*). Patterns established in asbestos litigation rapidly spread to other mass torts litigation, such as DES, Bendectin, the Dalkon Shield, Agent Orange, breast implants, and most recently and profitably, tobacco.

Mass-tort practice as it evolved gravitated to an increasingly smaller number of specialized firms headed by celebrity "Kings of Torts," such as the Peter Angelos firm of Baltimore, which in the 1990s represented more than 10,000 asbestos plaintiffs. In 1995 a Forbes list of the twenty-five trial lawyers with the highest incomes listed nine who specialized in mass-tort products or accident cases. The mass-tort lawyers' successes in court and their growing wealth and political influence made them very controversial. Manufacturers anxious to limit exposure to products liability verdicts and conservative politicians eager to deprive Democrats of a reliable funding base led "tort reform" movements to induce legislatures and judges to make product liability suits harder to bring and to win and to limit damage awards and attorneys' fees. Tort reformers accused plaintiffs' lawyers of growing fat on the fees of an out-of-control "litigation explosion" of groundless claims based on "junk science," brought only to induce settlements and, by making companies fearful of huge punitive damages awards, tending to stifle innovation and cripple the American economy. From the 1980s onward conservative politicians made tort reform and the crusade against plaintiffs' lawyers a centerpiece of their campaigns. In riposte, friends and allies of the plaintiffs' bar portrayed plaintiffs' lawyers as populist heroes willing to fight the system of callous corporate wrongdoing on behalf of little guys, who needed the occasional big verdict to cover the high risks of litigation and "send corporate America a message."

More disinterested observers told a less Manichean but just as troubling story. The most serious defect of the tort system was not that it encouraged too many meritless claims, but too few meritorious ones. Most injured parties simply absorbed their losses without complaint; of those who consulted lawyers, many were turned away because their case was not worth enough to generate a substantial contingent fee. Punitive damages were rarely awarded; when awarded they were usually a low multiple of compensatory damages and, if high, were invariably reduced on appeal. Evidence that fear of product liability had bad macroeconomic effects was weak to non-existent. Clearly some mass-tort claims (like the Bendectin and, more disputably, the Agent Orange and breast implant cases) were indeed based on dubious science. In others (like tobacco) the bad science was generated by the corporate defendants.

The biggest problem with mass-tort actions turned out to be that some of them ill served not corporations, but the victims themselves. Corporate lawyers came to welcome class actions as a means to consolidate and dispose of all the claims against their clients. Plaintiffs' lawyers acquired a strong interest in colluding with their opponents to settle cases quickly for low total damage figures, so they could earn extravagant fees for themselves without having to do much work. Trial judges went along with the collusion and with plans to prevent individual plaintiffs from "opting out" of class actions and bringing suits on their own, because such arrangements made cases manageable and reduced pressures on dockets. The administrative costs, including lawyers' fees, of adversary procedure in tort cases were always distressingly high, likely to consume at least half and often more of the total recovery. This fact alone kept most small individual claims out of the tort system, because lawyers could not afford to litigate them. Yet for all its high costs, the personal injury lawyer working for a contingent fee remained the only practical means by which an ordinary individual could confront a powerful corporate entity and effectively seek redress for injuries. Such a person, however, increasingly needed protection from abuse by some of his champions as well as his injurer.

Cause and Public Interest Lawyering

In the 1970s conservative public interest law groups emerged as rivals to longer established liberal and left-wing groups. The Virginia lawyer Lewis

F. Powell, Jr. wrote a famous manifesto to the Chamber of Commerce in 1971, just before his appointment to the U.S. Supreme Court, complaining that leftist opinions hostile to the capitalist system dominated the academy, the press and, by means of public interest litigation, the courts. He urged business to finance a counter-offensive. Out of this project eventually flowed the tidal wave of conservative foundations, think tanks, John M. Olin Foundation scholarships, programs, research funding, professorships in Law and Economics in the law schools, and a new generation of public interest law firms. In the view of firms like the Washington Legal Foundation and Pacific Legal Foundation, what the public interest required was dismantling inefficient regulation, especially anti-discrimination law and health, safety, and environmental regulation, and a return to free-market principles that would genuinely serve consumers and create wealth. Well funded by business interests, such firms borrowed all the techniques of the liberal groups, from intervention in agency proceedings to seeking judicial review of agency action to challenging economic regulation as violating the Commerce and Takings Clauses and the First Amendment; they scored victories as conservatives increasingly occupied the judiciary and (for most of 1968–2004) the executive.

Liberal public interest law groups also continued to proliferate, though their financial support was always uncertain. In the 1980s a new specialty attracted lawyers' organizations, in response to the growing influence of international human rights laws and treaties and both public and non-governmental bodies reporting on violations (Helsinki Watch and Charter 77, Amnesty International, Human Rights Watch, the State Department's human rights reports) and organizations to sanction them (the European and Inter-American Courts on Human Rights, the International Criminal Court, the South African Truth and Reconciliation Commission, various special UN Tribunals for the former Yugoslavia, Rwanda, etc.). As many Communist and military dictatorships collapsed in the 1980s, the United States funded programs to bring the blessings not only of Western-style democracy but of the rule of law to the ex-Communist and developing world; these programs were well funded by the World Bank, U.S. Aid for International Development, and the ABA. Lawyers signed up by the hundreds to join such programs.

Professionalism Imperiled, 1970–2000

Professionalism as a strategy for organizing occupations and justifying occupational privileges reached its high tide from 1880 to 1960. Recall how promoters of the professions had framed the goals of their projects: basing practice standards on scientific learning; raising standards of education and admission to practice; regulating ethics, competence, and discipline; seeking primary rewards in recognition among peers for learning, craft, and quality of client service and disdaining commercialism; maintaining independence from non-professional outside controls over the quality, conduct, and conditions of work; and finally, promoting public goods – in the legal profession's case the integrity of the framework of laws and procedures, the improvement of the legal system, and universal access to justice. By the 1960s, the professional ideal – and the attendant privileges and authority – were under attack from the right, the left, and within the professions' own ranks. Left-wing cultural critics attacked the professions as elitist conspiracies to exclude, dominate, exploit, and paternalistically control social inferiors by mystifying professional knowledge. Right-wing critics and economists attacked them as cartels designed to restrict entry and fix prices. Lawyers were especially vulnerable to such critiques. Their moral standing had always been somewhat dubious because one of their jobs had been to put the best face on even unattractive clients and causes and because they were suspected of overselling their competence to profit from the misery of others. Valid or not, the critiques had a corrosive effect on attempts to defend professional values, good as well as bad, in terms of civic virtue or social trusteeship. The left-wing solution was lay empowerment of consumers, entry of lay providers, and redistribution of social and economic power. The right-wing solution, which generally prevailed, was deregulation, increasing competition, and faith in market forces. On balance, lawyers' own behavior undermined more effectively the plausibility of some of their professional claims than any outside critics could have done.

The legal profession did succeed in raising admissions standards, at some cost to the promise of law as an avenue of upward mobility. Its self-regulatory enforcement record – lax, unresponsive, self-protective, and never directed against the upper bar – was a conspicuous failure. Under pressure of scandals, bar associations came increasingly to share control of discipline with external regulators: judges, new full-time disciplinary bureaucracies, regulatory agencies such as the Internal Revenue Service and Securities and Exchange Commission (which regulated by conditioning the right to practice before them), new legislative controls such as consumer protection laws requiring standardized contract terms and disclosure to clients, malpractice actions, and insurers against malpractice and other risks trying to reduce the risks of lawyers' incompetence and misconduct. Malpractice claims doubled in the seven years between 1979 and 1986, and the average settlement increased from $3,000 to $45,000. The practice of law, almost completely unregulated in 1900, was in 2000 hedged about by thickets of rules, some with effective sanctions behind them.

As with collective self-regulation, so with control over work. After the 1970s many types of lawyers, like doctors, lost much of their residual discretion to determine the terms, pace, and quality of their work, as they were reclassified as subordinates within bureaucratic hierarchies. An especially harried group were insurance defense lawyers who now had to process their cases according to rigid standardized protocols dictated by their employers or were governed by detailed contract terms imposed by clients or insurers. Even lawyers at the top of the hierarchy, partners in large firms, had to submit to close monitoring by clients. Time billing, introduced in the 1940s as an internal accounting device for allocating costs among cases and clients, had become a Taylorist instrument for monitoring and increasing lawyer work output within the firm; as a result, associates padded hourly billings to increase their chances of partnership, and firms padded billings to clients. In response clients began to impose budget caps and to dictate instructions on how to travel (coach, increasingly), and how many and which associates they might use on a case. In turn inside corporate lawyers who hired firms had to justify their legal budgets to their chief financial officers. But even in the lower tiers of practice, cost-cutting franchised law offices crowded many lawyers out of practice and imposed a strict work discipline on those who remained by standardizing forms, transactions, and caseloads and enforcing strict time accounting.

Another casualty of the period was the professional ideal of independence from clienteles. The reformers of the 1870s and after looked to professional organizations and norms to open some distance between themselves and the more corrupt and unscrupulous tactics of their own business clients, by defining their jobs so as to strengthen their independence from illegitimate client demands. While lawyers were supposed to be zealous advocates of legitimate client claims, they also aspired to be objective independent counselors, discouraging clients from actions that were legally or morally dubious and that might invite retribution from popular or political backlash. They also tried to preserve their capacity to argue for general legal reforms and changes that clients might not support.[17] In its most grandiose moments, the bar leadership aspired to be independent guardians of constitutional and common law principle and statesmen guiding legal and legislative reform in the public interest, rising above party and faction and the local and particular interests of clienteles. For reasons explored earlier in this chapter, the emerging material bases of lawyers' practices precluded most of them from

[17] Lawyers in the New York State Bar Association's tax section, for example, consistently promoted legislation to close tax loopholes that benefited the reformers' clients, and municipal bond lawyers in the City's bar association ensured the adoption of an ethics rule prohibiting "pay to play" contributions to politicians who could be clients.

taking up these exalted roles. But the ideal of independence persisted in professional rhetoric and sporadically in lawyers' actions. As late as 1960, a study of Wall Street lawyers confirmed that the bar's elite still gave at least lip service to the ideal of the independent counselor and lawyer-statesman. Even this rhetorical commitment, however, mostly vanished in the intense competition for clients in the 1980s. The last thing most lawyers wanted to advertise was their superior scruples as monitors of client conduct or as proponents of legal reforms their clients might not welcome. Ironically, lawyers in the most lucrative and prestigious specialties had less autonomy from client controls than general practitioners at the bottom.

Lawyers also undercut their traditional claims to pursue criteria of craft and service above those of the marketplace. Some of the bar's more dubious rules for expressing anti-commercial values, its bans on advertising and minimum fee schedules, were struck down by the Supreme Court as violations of the antitrust laws and the First Amendment,[18] though the rules against direct solicitation of clients survived challenge. More important, lawyers began openly to flaunt purely commercial criteria of success. A new legal press, led by *The American Lawyer* (1979–) and *National Law Journal* (1978–), broke down law firms' long-standing genteel reluctance to discuss salaries and fees in public and with the firms' eager connivance began to rank them by profits-per-partner. Firms hired business consultants to improve their profitability and market consultants to market services to clients; they began to reward rain-makers (partners who pulled in new business) rather than highly skilled advocates or specialists with the largest shares of profits. While Paul Cravath's firm had forbidden its partners to invest in clients or sit on their boards, lest their objectivity be impaired, the new firms eagerly bought stock in their clients in exchange for services.

When the older rhetoric of professionalism resurfaced in this period, it was usually to repel threats of competing professions and lay "unauthorized" providers. By the 1990s, the most formidable challenges to American corporate lawyers' practice turf came from accounting firms employing lawyers and giving tax and business consulting advice, foreign law firms such as vast English solicitors' offices, and proposals to permit "multidisciplinary practices" (combines of lawyers, accountants, financial consultants, and others.) In the individual practice sector, the flow of lay services in the form of advice books, do-it-yourself manuals, form books, and computer software programs became a deluge that no bar group could stop. In the face of such encroachments, lawyers appealed to a morality above mere commerce to justify their monopolies of practice fields. But in the wake of their unabashed

---

[18] *Goldfarb v. Virginia State Bar*, 421 U.S. 773 (1975), *Bates v. State Bar of Arizona*, 433 U.S. 350 (1977).

embrace of business criteria of success the appeals rang hollow. Lawyers have never ranked high in public opinion surveys of occupations. In the 1980s and 90s their reputation sank still further.[19]

CONCLUSION

The century began with ambitious efforts to establish the legal profession as a distinct and powerful institutional force in American society, to increase lawyers' prestige and cultural authority, and by augmenting their influence to promote the rule of law – a legalist vision of governance enforced through neutral principles, rules, and expert systems by cadres of professionals specially trained and experienced in legal and administrative sciences and the procedures to make them effective.

In some respects the project was stunningly successful. The spheres of governance through law and legal procedures, and those where legal expertise was required or useful, expanded and multiplied. American-style models of transactional planning and lawyering, dispute settlement, legally mediated regulation, and even rights-seeking and rights-protecting public interest law were spreading through the globe. But these very successes created backlashes and doubts about the professional project. Lawyer's law was expensive and thus priced out of the reach of almost all but wealthy users. Litigation was perceived by almost everyone as a colossally wasteful mode of dispute settlement. Legal-rights-seeking as a means of producing social justice was questioned as ineffective or counterproductive for its beneficiaries. Proliferating regulation provoked widespread business and libertarian revolts. Professionalism and professional ideals were perceived on both right and left as camouflage for a narrow economic self-interest. Business lawyers scrambled to join the ranks of financial services businesses, and now, without a distinctive product to sell, faced intensifying competition from non-lawyers in similar trades and regulation from outside agencies. Since the elites consistently put self-interest and loyalty to primary clienteles over maintaining their profession's independence and serving the Republic, nobody took seriously their aspirations to be spokesmen for a vision of the rule of law above politics and faction; by the 1980s private lawyers had mostly ceased to pay those aspirations even lip service.

[19] To a poll question, "Please tell me how you would rate the honesty and ethical standards of people in these different fields," 26 percent of respondents rated lawyers "Very High" or "High" in 1977. This number slid to 13 percent in 1999 and then rose slightly to 18 percent in 2001. Meanwhile the public standing of the other traditional professions was rising (physicians, from 51 to 66 percent; college teachers, from 46 to 58 percent; engineers, from 46 to 60 percent), except for bankers (from 39 to 34 percent) and journalists (from 33 to 29 percent). CNN/USA Today Gallup Poll, Nov. 26–27, 2001.

The plaintiffs' bar began its career as the populist champion of the injured weak, but at its apex grew wealthy and powerful at the expenses of its own clienteles. The traditional general practice solo practitioner, like the family doctor, was threatened with obsolescence.

Traces of the older ideals survived and continued to attract some students, if only a small minority, to the profession of law, having migrated from elite business lawyers to public interest and international human rights lawyers and non-governmental organizations. The dream of a universal rule of law, a world blanketed by legal controls on war, genocide, corruption, environmental damage, ethnic strife, and racial and gender hierarchies, had never had so many lawyers and institutions working energetically toward its practical achievement, even as every day's headlines testified to the huge obstacles to its realization and to new horrors and injustices to overcome.

4

THE COURTS, FEDERALISM, AND THE FEDERAL CONSTITUTION, 1920–2000

EDWARD A. PURCELL, JR.

The history of American federalism in the twentieth century falls into three distinct periods. The era of post-Reconstruction federalism, which began in the late nineteenth century, ended in the years after 1929 when a shattering series of domestic and international crises combined with the innovative presidency of Franklin D. Roosevelt to reorient the nation's laws, politics, and institutions. The resulting "New Deal Order" lasted for almost five decades before crumbling in the century's last quarter when massive social, cultural, economic, and political changes combined with the dramatizing presidency of Ronald Reagan to begin reorienting the system once again. At century's end, the nature and course of that emerging era remained unsettled.

I. THE NATURE AND DYNAMICS OF AMERICAN FEDERALISM

With a de facto default rule favoring decentralization, American federalism is a governmental system based on the existence of independent political power at both state and national levels. Its essence lies, first, in the institutional tensions that the Constitution structured between the two levels of government, and second, in the complex processes of decision making that the Constitution established to maintain satisfactory relations between the two levels. Those processes were complex because they involved, on the national side, three distinct and counterpoised branches of government and, on the state side, a growing multitude of equal, independent, and often conflicting governing units. In theory, and sometimes in practice, national power served to foster economic integration and efficiency, facilitate the development and enforcement of desirable uniform standards, enable the people to deal effectively with problems national and international in scope, protect the security and general welfare of the nation as a whole, and safeguard liberty by checking the potential tyranny of local majorities. Conversely, also in theory and sometimes in practice, state power

served to foster economic innovation and efficiency, nourish social and cultural diversity, encourage democratic participation, facilitate the adoption
of narrow solutions tailored to special local problems, and safeguard liberty
by checking the potential tyranny of national majorities.

As a matter of historical development, American federalism gave rise to
a dynamic and fluid political system in which competing groups and coalitions struggled for control of the nation's diverse centers of governmental
power and used constitutional arguments to place decision-making authority over contested issues in the level and branch of government that seemed,
at any given time, most likely to support their values, interests, and aspirations. The claim of "state sovereignty," for example, which limited or denied
the authority of the national government, served a variety of diverse groups
over the centuries: Jeffersonian Democrats in the 1790s, New England
Federalists during the War of 1812, South Carolina nullifiers in the1830s,
Northern anti-slavery civil libertarians before the Civil War, and then from
Reconstruction to the late twentieth century those who defended racial
segregation and disenfranchisement. The pressures generated by successive waves of such diverse groups and coalitions – themselves the products
of relentless social and economic change – drove the system's evolution.
Certain widely shared cultural commitments – to republican government,
the common law, religious freedom, private property, and individual liberty – combined with the idea of a written Constitution and the reality
of institutionally divided powers to constrain and channel that evolution.
But the system's operations and assumptions continued to shift as changing cultural values, social conditions, economic innovations, institutional
practices, legal theories, judicial decisions, and constitutional amendments
blurred or redrew the lines of state and federal authority.

In that long and complex historical process, one issue repeatedly emerged
as pivotal: what institutions or procedures existed to settle disputes over the
respective spheres of state and federal authority? Americans debated that
issue vigorously for eight decades and then, in the Civil War and its three
constitutional amendments, settled it in part. The national government,
not the states, held dispositive authority. Neither the war nor its resulting constitutional amendments, however, answered two further questions:
which branch or branches of the federal government held that authority?
And how was the authority to be exercised? Much of the history of American
federalism after the Civil War revolved around the contested answers given
to those two questions, as the three federal branches – each responding to
the values and interests that dominated it at any given time – adopted
diverse and sometimes conflicting policies that led them to defer to state
prerogatives on some occasions and trump them on others.

Indeed, as American life became increasingly centralized and homogenized in the late nineteenth and twentieth centuries, many of the distinctive and authentically "local" values and interests that had originally given the federal system its embedded social meaning withered or became suspect. Some blended into emerging and widely shared national values and interests; others grew attenuated or disappeared entirely; a few – most obviously, those involving racial oppression – were explicitly repudiated by new national majorities and constitutional amendments. The result was that the ingrained cultural understandings of the late eighteenth and early nineteenth centuries gradually disintegrated, the lived social meaning of American federalism grew more amorphous and contestable, and the distinctively local values and interests that the system protected increasingly appeared either narrow and parochial or vague and abstract. Over the course of the twentieth century the idea of American federalism as a normative concept – that the Constitution set out clear lines that defined and distinguished state and federal powers – grew ever more amorphous and manipulable.

Thus, the history of American federalism cannot be understood by focusing solely on constitutional provisions or theories of federalism. The Constitution provided a sound framework of government and a shrewd system of institutionalized checks and balances, but it did not draw bright or generally determinative lines of authority between state and federal power nor specify any particular "balance" between them. Similarly, theories of federalism provided a range of normative baselines, but their specific injunctions were invariably construed diversely and contested sharply. Indeed, conflicting views of federalism existed from the nation's beginning, and the passing years produced a smorgasbord of new variations, each inspired by and suffused with the emerging values, interests, expectations, and preconceptions of its advocates. The federal structure helped sustain the nation's commitment to limited government, cultural diversity, and individual liberty, but its history can be understood fully only by examining how and why its practical operations evolved, its political significance shifted, its social consequences unfolded, and its ideological contours periodically eroded and reformed.

Since the early decades of the nineteenth century, the prevailing theory held that the Constitution established a system of "dual federalism." The principles attributed to the system were few. The national government was one of limited and delegated powers only; the states were independent sovereigns with exclusive authority over local matters reserved to them by the Tenth Amendment; and the powers of the two governments were limited to "separate spheres" and intended to serve as checks on one another.

Although the actual practice of American federalism was always more complicated than the theory of dual federalism implied, during the late nineteenth and early twentieth century five accelerating developments substantially reshaped the system. First, spectacular revolutions in transportation and communications together with the ongoing processes of industrialization, urbanization, westward expansion, and economic centralization remade American society. What in 1789 had been a collection of geographically rooted, locally oriented, and culturally diverse island communities had by 1920 become an increasingly mobile, nationally oriented, and economically and culturally integrated nation. Ever widening areas of life were coming to have national significance, and Americans from coast to coast increasingly faced similar problems that flooded beyond the ability of individual states to remedy.

Second, the powerful nineteenth-century belief that the primary function of government was to protect private property and economic freedom was weakening. Since the Civil War governments at all levels had become increasingly active in attempting to deal with the massive social disruptions that came with urbanization and industrialization. Repeatedly the states increased taxes and expanded their activities, legislating over a widening variety of social and economic problems and establishing administrative agencies to regulate railroads, insurance companies, and many other types of business. They raised their funding for local governments, for example, from barely $50 million in 1902 to almost $600 million by 1927.

Third, the federal government was growing at an even more accelerated rate. Although the states still employed several times as many workers and spent more than twice as much money as the federal government, the balance of power between the two was shifting. As economic and cultural centralization proceeded, the political consensus that had tilted strongly toward decentralization in the early nineteenth century was moving by century's end toward support of more and broader government action at the national level. In 1887 the federal government began to use its authority over interstate commerce to regulate the new national economy, and by the second decade of the twentieth century it had asserted extensive national control over interstate transportation and communications while subjecting other interstate businesses to an expanding variety of new federal regulations.

Fourth, running against that nationalizing current, a vehement reaction against Reconstruction among white Americans had severely constrained the power of the federal government to protect the rights of African Americans. Notwithstanding the Civil War amendments, an informal national settlement in the century's last decades had successfully redefined most matters involving black civil and political rights as local issues that properly fell within the exclusive authority of the states. Increasingly, the cries of "states' rights," "state sovereignty," and the "principles of federalism" were identified with the establishment and preservation of racial segregation and disenfranchisement.

Finally, the power of the federal judiciary was growing relative to that of both Congress and the states, and by the early twentieth century the U.S. Supreme Court had emerged as the ultimate – if still sharply contested – authority on the law of both American federalism and the new national economy. The nation's commitment to law and the ideal of limited constitutional government had led Americans gradually to embrace the Court – "*the* Court" as they came to call it – and its umpiring role, while the structure of the federal judiciary – like that of the executive branch but unlike that of Congress – allowed the Court to act relatively quickly and decisively. The Court determined the extent to which any government could regulate business and property as well as the particular level of government that could regulate them. On the former issue, it held that a narrow range of economic activities "affected with a public interest" were subject to extensive regulation, but that most business and property remained "private" and subject only to minimal regulation. On the latter issue, it held that specific economic activities found to be "closely" or "directly" related to interstate commerce were national in scope and hence subject to federal control under the Commerce Clause but that the bulk of such activities remained local and subject to regulation only by the states. As a general matter, the Court's rulings gradually extended the powers of the federal government while restricting the power of the states to intrude into the workings of the burgeoning national market. To enforce its mandate, the Court reshaped the jurisdiction of the lower federal courts to make them more effective instruments of national judicial authority, turning them from disputes between private parties over issues of local law to suits that challenged government action or raised issues of national law. Increasingly, too, the Court exercised its burgeoning power. In seventy-one years up to 1860 it had held only 2 federal and 60 state statutes unconstitutional, but in a mere thirty-nine years from 1898 to 1937 it voided 50 federal and 400 state laws.

II. NATIONALIZATION AND THE DECLINE OF POST-RECONSTRUCTION FEDERALISM: FROM WORLD WAR TO THE GREAT DEPRESSION

When 1920 dawned, American federalism seemed on the verge of even more substantial change. Pre-war Progressivism had focused American politics on the national level, and constitutional amendments authorizing a federal income tax and the popular election of senators had expanded federal power enormously while curtailing the power of state legislatures. Both amendments gave the American people a new and direct involvement in their national government, while the income tax provision allowed the federal government to raise virtually unlimited amounts of money, paving the way for explosive growth in the future. The Supreme Court, too, had seemed willing to approve some widening assertions of national power by stretching the limiting categories of business "affected with a public interest" and activities "closely" related to interstate commerce.

Most dramatic were the changes that followed American entry into World War I. Relying principally on their war powers, Congress and Democratic President Woodrow Wilson exercised unparalleled authority. They established national conscription, took control of the nation's transportation and communications systems, imposed tight restrictions on the distribution of food and fuel, asserted authority over relations between labor and management, and expanded the federal income tax system drastically. In addition, through the Espionage and Sedition Acts they prohibited a variety of activities – including speech critical of the government – that might interfere with the war effort. They criminalized, for example, "disloyal, profane, scurrilous, or abusive language" directed at the Constitution, the armed forces, the government, or the flag.[1] Perhaps most arresting, by statute and then by constitutional amendment Congress and the states prohibited the manufacture, sale, and transportation of alcoholic beverages in the United States. Ratified in 1919, the Eighteenth Amendment conferred on the federal government authority to enforce nationwide Prohibition and expanded its power into areas that had previously been considered both local and private.

The war challenged the structure of post-Reconstruction federalism in other ways as well. Politically, it led to the adoption of yet another nationalizing constitutional amendment, the Nineteenth, which prohibited the states from denying the vote to women and conferred on Congress the power to enforce its mandate. Institutionally, the war induced the Supreme Court to back away from its umpiring role and watch passively as Congress and the president exercised sweeping war powers. Socially, the war's proclaimed goal of making "the world safe for democracy" even hinted at the possibility of change in the nation's racial status quo.

Although post-Reconstruction federalism trembled, it did not crumble. The end of the war brought a series of bitter labor strikes, a brief but virulent Red Scare, repeated outbreaks of anti-black violence, rapidly rising prices followed by a short depression, and spreading resentment at the administration's continued use and abuse of its war powers. Those events destroyed

[1] Act of May 16, 1918, ch. 75, 40 Stat. 553.

wartime unity, fragmented Progressivism, and generated a powerful desire for a return to a more stable and tranquil order. In 1920 the reaction gave the Republicans control of both Congress and the presidency. With the help of returning prosperity, the Republicans maintained that hold for a decade, ensuring a government of order, conservatism, business domination, and minimal economic regulation. Under their rule, Republicans announced, America was entering a "New Era" of sustained economic progress and prosperity. For almost a decade their promise seemed golden.

The national turnaround in 1920 induced the Court to reassert its authority. In cautious dicta it began to suggest judicially enforceable limits on federal war powers, and in 1921 it invalidated on vagueness grounds the statute that had authorized federal control over food during and after the war. Then, within two years, Warren Harding, the new Republican president, appointed four new justices – including ex-President William Howard Taft as Chief Justice – who were more conservative and property conscious than their predecessors. The stage was set for a period of conservative judicial activism.

The new Taft Court moved quickly to ensure social stability, impose judicial limitations on both state and federal governments, and protect business, property, and the expanding national market. In less than a decade it invalidated legislation – in most cases measures passed by the states – in approximately 140 decisions, a rate far higher than that of any previous Court. Its efforts were unwittingly enhanced by a seemingly technical jurisdictional statute enacted in 1925. The so-called Judges' Bill made the Court's appellate jurisdiction almost wholly discretionary, thereby enabling it to decide freely not just how, but when and where, it would assert its authority. After 1925 the Court's role in American government continued to expand, and its efforts became more purposeful, as shifting coalitions of justices learned to use the Court's new jurisdictional discretion to set their own agendas.

Three of the Taft Court's early decisions revealed its determination to impose limits on government. *Pennsylvania Coal Co. v. Mahon* (1922) limited both state and federal power over private property by holding that regulatory actions that went "too far" constituted "takings" that, absent compensation, were invalid under the Fifth and Fourteenth Amendments.[2] Similarly, *Adkins v. Children's Hospital* (1923) invalidated a minimum wage law, a type of statute the Court's conservative justices considered especially obnoxious. *Adkins* proclaimed freedom of contract "the general rule" and government regulation an "exception" confined to a few narrow categories of specially "public" matters."[3] As much as the two cases demonstrated the

---

[2] 260 U.S. 393, 415.   [3] 261 U.S. 525, 546.

Court's determination to limit government regulation, however, they also suggested the difficulty the justices faced in their task. In each, the Court acknowledged that the limiting categories it used were incapable of precise delineation, a confession that highlighted the extent to which the lines it drew were the product, not simply of the Constitution, but of the dominant attitudes of the era and the specific values of the justices themselves.

The third decision, *Bailey v. Drexel Furniture Co.* (1922), was directed solely at the federal government and sought to infuse new life into the idea of dual federalism. Only four years earlier the Court had struck down the first federal Child Labor Law, ruling in *Hammer v. Dagenhart* (1918) that the commerce power did not allow Congress to ban the products of child labor from interstate commerce. Though seemingly inconsistent with prior decisions, *Hammer* voided the child labor statute on the ground that it was not a true effort to regulate interstate commerce, but rather a disguised attempt to intrude into a "local" activity – the production of goods – that the Tenth Amendment reserved to the states. Amid a popular outcry against the decision, Congress responded with the Child Labor Tax Act, relying on the federal taxing power to impose special charges on employers who used child labor. *Drexel Furniture* declared the second federal child labor act another subterfuge, one intended not to raise revenue but to regulate a local matter. Following *Hammer*, it held the act invalid as a violation of the Tenth Amendment. It was "the high duty of this court" to protect "local self-government" from "national power" and to preserve the federal system that, the justices declared, was "the ark of our covenant." If it failed to block the Child Labor Tax Law, *Drexel Furniture* warned, Congress could use its taxing power "to take over to its control any one of the great number of subjects of public interest" that the Constitution reserved to the states.[4]

Like earlier Courts, however, the Taft Court shaded its federalism decisions to fit its social values. It ignored *Hammer* when Congress passed a statute prohibiting the movement of stolen vehicles in interstate commerce, avoided *Drexel Furniture* when Congress used its taxing power to control narcotics, and construed the commerce power with exceptional breadth when business invoked the federal antitrust laws to break a small union's boycott of local employers. The Court stretched national power in the first case to protect private property, in the second to allow government to control what the justices viewed as a moral and social evil, and in the third to check a potentially powerful weapon of organized labor.

The particular social values that the Taft Court protected quickly generated political controversy. Provoking strong opposition from Progressives and organized labor, its decisions sparked a variety of proposals for "curbing"

---

[4] 259 U.S. 20, 37–38.

the Court by restricting its jurisdiction or requiring a supermajority vote of six or seven justices to invalidate legislation. In 1924 Republican Senator Robert M. LaFollette of Wisconsin helped organize a new Progressive Party and ran for president on a platform that indicted the Court as an anti-progressive and pro-business partisan. He proposed a constitutional amend-ment that would authorize Congress to override any decision invalidating one of its statutes. Rising to the Court's defense, most Republicans and Democrats castigated the proposal as a radical and destructive assault on the foundations of American federalism. In the election LaFollette did well for a third-party candidate, but he was overwhelmed in a Republican land-slide. While the election revealed widespread hostility to the Taft Court, it also suggested that the great majority of Americans supported the Court's institutional role, even if many of them disliked some of its individual decisions.

Responding to LaFollette and other critics, Charles Warren, the nation's preeminent historian of the Supreme Court, seemed to speak for most Amer-icans – even many Progressives – when he praised the Court for playing an essential institutional role in the federal system. The "existence of the American form of government – a federal republic with limited national powers – implies and requires for its preservation the existence of a Supreme Court," he declared. "The retention of such a republic is inseparably bound up with the retention of a Court having authority to enforce the limitation of national powers." Warren articulated a belief that had been spreading since the mid-nineteenth century and that had become sacred writ among conservatives by the early twentieth: the Supreme Court was the anchor of American government, the paramount bulwark protecting the American people and their liberties from the dangers posed by an otherwise uncon-trollable and centralizing national government. "It is, of course, possible to have a republic without a Supreme Court," Warren explained; "but it will be a republic with a consolidated and autocratic government, a government in which the States and the citizens will possess no right or power save such as Congress, in its absolute discretion, sees fit to leave to them."[5]

Although Taft and a majority of his Court shared both Warren's suspi-cions of Congress and his conclusions about the Court's essential role, they nevertheless sought to accommodate what they considered the reasonable demands for more active government that flowed from the continuing cen-tralization of American social and economic life. Cautiously, they continued the process of expanding federal power under the Commerce Clause and, in a more innovative move, approved a broadened use of federal taxing and spending powers. In *Massachusetts v. Mellon* (1923) the Court upheld

---

[5] Charles Warren, *Congress, the Constitution, and the Supreme Court* (Boston, 1925), 4, 5.

a statute that provided federal funds for state infant and maternity care programs. The decision in effect sanctioned the federal government's power to offer monetary grants to states conditioned on their acceptance of federal use restrictions, and it thereby allowed Congress to legislate – albeit indirectly – over matters that seemed entirely "local." In the 1920s such federal grants were few in number and small in scale, but during the next half-century they would expand dramatically.

The Taft Court also extended federal judicial power over the states by expanding the meaning of "liberty" in the Fourteenth Amendment. On one front it voided state statutes that restricted the educational opportunities of children. The Court held that the amendment protected certain personal and familial rights, including the right of parents to rear and educate their children as they wished. On a second front the Court began to consider the claim that the First Amendment right of free speech also constrained the states. Successful prosecutions under the Sedition and Espionage Acts had provoked powerful dissents from Justices Oliver Wendell Holmes, Jr. and Louis D. Brandeis; and, after the postwar hysteria had dissipated, many Americans came to believe that governmental power to punish speech should be limited more tightly. In *Gitlow v. New York* (1925) the Court announced that the right of free speech recognized by the First Amendment was part of the "liberty" protected by the Fourteenth Amendment and, consequently, was binding on the states as well as the federal government. Although the Court's decisions in these areas were few, they created a rich seedbed for the future.

Conversely, considering the rights of African Americans, the Taft Court left post-Reconstruction federalism essentially unchanged. Refusing to question racial segregation and disenfranchisement, it protected African American rights only in the most outrageous and exceptional cases. In one, where it granted habeas corpus relief to an African American sentenced to death in a Southern state court, it could not ignore the fact that the defendant had been convicted on unsubstantiated charges by an all-white jury that had been surrounded and intimidated by an angry white mob. In another, where it invalidated an "all-white" Texas primary election system, it could not deny the explicitly racial nature of the legal discrimination or its negation of the fundamental constitutional right of all citizens to vote. In each case, however, the Court stressed the narrowness of its decision. Federal habeas corpus was rarely available, it declared, and criminal matters were ordinarily local issues for the states alone to resolve. Similarly, the all-white primary was unconstitutional solely because its racially discriminatory nature was explicitly written into state law. Indeed, a decade later the Court unanimously approved a slightly more indirect version of the all-white state primary, one that was equally effective in maintaining black disenfranchisement but more cleverly designed as a matter of reigning constitutional law.

For their part, the states in the 1920s continued to set policy not only in matters concerning race but also in most other areas that affected daily life, and they continued as well to provide most of the government services that Americans received. During the 1920s the states accounted for almost three-quarters of all public spending and two-thirds of the taxes collected. While a few sought to sustain the tradition of pre-war reform, most conformed to the conservative national mood that underwrote the Republicans' New Era. Largely abandoning efforts to regulate business and enact progressive social legislation, they sought to trim government regulation and concentrated much of their spending on highway construction to meet the exploding demands created by the automobile. Indicative of the political mood, the states raised most of their highway money through regressive gasoline taxes, which by 1929 accounted for 25 percent of their total tax receipts. Indeed, while thirteen states had enacted mildly progressive income tax laws in the decade after 1911, during the New Era only one state, New Hampshire, adopted such a tax. As a general matter, the governments of both states and nation seemed in accord on the basic issues of social and economic policy. Both seemed content, for the most part, to keep a low profile and give business its head.

III. FROM THE GREAT ECONOMIC TO THE GREAT PSYCHOLOGICAL DEPRESSION: NATIONALIZING AND RECONCEPTUALIZING LIBERTY AND EQUALITY, 1930s–1970s

The year 1929 witnessed the onset of the decade-long and world-wide Great Depression. Causing massive disruptions and hardships, the Depression challenged the capacities of democratic governments throughout the world. The resulting turmoil paved the way for Adolph Hitler to seize power in Germany, energized the forces of international Communism, and ultimately helped bring on a second and far more destructive world war. In the United States it gave birth to the New Deal and, together with the war and Cold War that followed, transformed American federalism.

The Great Depression and the Foundations of the New Deal Order

The ravages of unemployment, bankruptcies, foreclosures, bank failures, lost savings, and crushed hopes savaged all classes and regions. Those identified with the roseate New Era of the 1920s – primarily business, the Republican Party, and the federal judiciary – quickly became objects of anger and distrust. Governments at all levels tried to respond to the emergency. State and local agencies, however, could provide neither the relief nor the structural reforms that seemed necessary. By 1931 their resources were exhausted, and the national and international scope of the ever-deepening crisis was undeniable. The federal government under Republican President Herbert Hoover became increasingly active, but it furnished far too little in the way of either money or leadership. The experience taught Americans two fundamental lessons: that a massive governmental response was necessary and that only national action could possibly be adequate.

From 1930 to 1936 four successive elections repudiated the Republicans, and after 1932 the Democrats firmly controlled both the legislative and executive branches of the federal government. President Franklin D. Roosevelt's New Deal initiated a wide range of efforts to provide emergency relief, restructure and stimulate the economy, and reform the nation's financial institutions. Although the administration worked closely with state and local governments, political power shifted decisively to the federal level. The National Industrial Recovery Act (NIRA) and the Agricultural Adjustment Act (AAA), for example, the New Deal's major initial efforts to reorganize and revive the economy, imposed sweeping federal controls and reached extensively into matters of industrial and agricultural production that hitherto had seemed both local and private.

While the conservative orientation of the federal judiciary clouded the future, it seemed possible that the New Deal might proceed without encountering fatal constitutional obstacles. The Taft Court had been split between six conservatives and three progressives, but that lineup had changed in 1930 when Taft and one of his conservative colleagues died. Charles Evans Hughes, a relatively progressive Republican, became Chief Justice, and the moderate Republican, Owen J. Roberts, filled the second opening. In the early 1930s the two new justices voted with the three progressives in a number of critical cases, and they seemed to have tipped the judicial balance. The Court applied the Fourteenth Amendment to safeguard freedom of speech and provide some protection for African Americans in Southern state courts, and it gave broad constructions to both the commerce power and the category of business "affected with a public interest." Further, in two sharply divided 5–4 decisions – with both Hughes and Roberts joining the Court's three progressives – it recognized the need for both state and federal governments to have emergency powers to combat the depression.

If the Hughes Court was different from the Taft Court, however, it nonetheless remained committed to enforcing limits on economic regulation by both the states and the federal government. In early 1935 it invalidated a part of the NIRA and then began a series of rulings – with Roberts and sometimes Hughes joining the four conservatives – that checked state and federal regulatory power and, in the process, declared both the AAA and the remainder of the NIRA unconstitutional. Invoking the Tenth Amendment to invalidate another New Deal measure, Roberts and the four conservatives emphasized that "every addition to the national legislative power to some extent detracts from or invades the power of the states."[6]

While the anti-New Deal majority invoked the idea of federalism, the dissenters often did the same. Illustrating the intrinsically double-edged nature of the concept, Justice Brandeis, the Court's leading progressive, deployed it to undermine the conservative majority. Excessive centralization could flow not only from Congress, he warned in 1932, but from the federal judiciary as well. In voiding the reasonable social and economic regulations that the states attempted, Brandeis declared, the Court was not exercising "the function of judicial review, but the function of a super-legislature." Its anti-progressive decisions unwisely restricted the states and improperly centralized American government. Moreover, he charged, the Court's decisions negated a signal virtue of American federalism. "It is one of the happy incidents of the federal system that a single courageous State may, if its citizens choose, serve as a laboratory," Brandeis explained, "and try novel social and economic experiments without risk to the rest of the country." Confronted by "an emergency more serious than war," Americans had the right to experiment with a variety of possible remedies, and the nation's federal system was designed to allow such diverse and creative efforts.[7] Turning the tables on the conservative majority, Brandeis used his progressive theory of "experimentalist" federalism to indict the Court itself as a centralizing force that was obstructing the federal system's proper operation.

Not surprisingly, the double-edged nature of American federalism provided the Court's anti-progressive majority with a ready response. The states could "indulge in experimental legislation," Justice George Sutherland replied for the conservative majority, but they could not "transcend the limitations imposed upon them by the federal Constitution." National limits existed and controlled, and the Court itself was the institution that identified and applied those limits. "The principle is embedded in our constitutional system," he declared, "that there are certain essentials of liberty with which the state is not entitled to dispense in the interest of experiments."[8] Thus, the Supreme Court – the ostensible bulwark of federalism – once

---

[6] *Carter v. Carter Coal Co.*, 298 U.S. 238, 294–95 (1936).

[7] *New State Ice Co. v. Liebmann*, 285 U.S. 262, 280, 300, 306, 311 (1932) (Brandeis, J., dissenting, joined by Stone, J.). Justice Cardozo, the third "progressive," did not participate in the decision.

[8] *New State Ice Co.*, 279, 280 (1932) (Sutherland, J.).

again served not as the defender of state autonomy but as an agent of
national power.

The Court's anti-New Deal decisions set up one of the most famous
episodes in its history, the "Constitutional Revolution of 1937." The standard tale is familiar and the storyline dramatic. Overwhelmingly reelected
with crushing Democratic majorities in both Houses of Congress, Roosevelt
stunned the nation with his proposal to "pack" the Supreme Court by adding
one new justice, up to a total of six, for every member of the Court over
the age of seventy. Then, while Congress and the nation debated the plan,
the Court suddenly seemed to change its position. In a series of 5–4 decisions – Hughes and Roberts joining the three progressives – it discarded
the doctrine of liberty of contract and drastically broadened federal power.
Over the next few years the Court's four conservatives resigned, and the
president replaced them with loyal New Dealers who extended the changes
the Court had begun in the spring of 1937.

The traditional story over-inflates the role of the Court-packing plan and
oversimplifies the processes of constitutional change. The label "revolution,"
moreover, obscures complexities. There was continuity as well as change
in the Court's decisions, and many of the innovations that occurred had
roots in earlier periods and witnessed their full flowering only in later
ones. In spite of the qualifications necessary, however, the traditional story
highlights a fundamental fact: the New Deal years brought fundamental
and far-reaching changes to the federal system.

First, the New Deal altered the way the system functioned. Centralizing many areas of American life, a dozen path-breaking measures asserted
new or expanded federal authority over the nation's economy and financial
system. The National Labor Relations Act, for example, which the Court
upheld under a broadened commerce power, extended federal regulatory
authority to the employment relationship and guaranteed labor the right
to organize and bargain collectively. The result was the centralization of
government labor policy, the preemption of many state laws considered
hostile to workers, and the transformation of organized labor into a newly
powerful and nationalizing force in American politics. Similarly, the Social
Security Act, which the Court upheld under a broad construction of the
spending and taxing powers, established the institutional foundations for a
limited national welfare state. The act placed special taxes on workers and
employers, created a variety of federal social support programs, and used
conditional grants to enlist state participation and impose federal standards
on their operation.

In addition, the New Deal moved the federal government into a widening range of previously local areas. It established agencies to insure individual home mortgages and private bank accounts, for example, and it

funded a series of massive projects to construct local public facilities and provide employment for millions. Using its power to tax and spend, it provided grants to states for a variety of new programs and raised the amounts involved into the billions of dollars. The grants extended federal involvement into such previously local areas as employment counseling, health care, public housing, conservation, slum clearance, social welfare, and child care programs.

Numbers told much of the story. In 1913 state and local governments had spent more than twice as much as the federal government, but by 1942 their spending amounted to barely a quarter of the national total. Federal expenditures skyrocketed from less than 30 percent to almost 80 percent of total government spending in the United States. Similarly, in 1929 federal grants to state and local agencies had stood at less than $100 million, but after 1935 they averaged more than a billion dollars a year.

Further, the New Deal altered the functioning relationship between federal and state governments. As growing federal financing made national direction seem increasingly appropriate, the federal government began to expand its administrative capacities and enforce tighter and more detailed controls over its grants. Some of the conditions it imposed began to regulate not just spending but also the operations of the state and local government agencies that administered the grant programs. Further, the rapid expansion of federal-state grant programs began to alter the politics of intergovernmental relations. It nourished larger bureaucracies at all levels of government; intermixed the operations and interests of the federal, state, and local officials who administered them; and began to create new interest groups made up of program beneficiaries and their varied political supporters. Still embryonic in the late 1930s, those institutional changes would accelerate in the coming decades and increasingly reshape the de facto operations of American federalism.

The New Deal, moreover, tipped the balance of the federal system even more by expanding the institutional authority of the national executive. Roosevelt broadened the power of the presidency by providing a charismatic image of national leadership, assuming a major role in initiating and securing passage of legislation, and by boldly exercising his authority to issue executive orders. He also strengthened the institutional resources of the presidency. Although Congress refused to adopt his sweeping plan to reorganize the executive branch, in 1939 it established the Executive Office of the President, providing an expanded staff and other resources that allowed the president to exert greater control over the executive branch and to project his policy decisions more effectively.

The second major change that the New Deal brought was to inspire substantial changes in constitutional law that allowed governments at all levels to assert expanded regulatory powers. Most obvious, the post-1937 Court stretched federal legislative power far beyond its prior limits. In *United States v. Darby* (1941) it overruled *Hammer v. Dagenhart* and renounced the idea that the Tenth Amendment created a substantive barrier against national power. The Tenth Amendment, it declared, could never block an action that was otherwise within the constitutional powers of the national government. Further, the Court broadened the commerce power to allow far-reaching regulation of economic activities. In the late nineteenth century it had held that the "production" of goods was not "commerce" but a local activity immune from Congressional reach, and in the early decades of the twentieth century it had maintained that distinction while expanding the types of local activities that were sufficiently "close" to interstate commerce to come within Congressional power. After 1937 it found an ever wider range of activities falling within that power, and in 1942 it discarded both the close relationship test and the distinction between "production" and "commerce." In *Wickard v. Filburn* (1942) the Court held that Congress could regulate any activity that – as part of the aggregate of all such activity – was likely to have some practical effect on interstate commerce. Under that construction the commerce power seemed capable of reaching almost anything. Finally, going beyond *Massachusetts v. Mellon*, the Court construed the Taxing, Spending, and General Welfare Clauses with exceptional breadth. It held that they constituted independent grants of power, authorized taxing and spending for the broadest purposes of national welfare, and allowed the federal government to make grants to the states contingent on the states' acceptance of federal conditions and limitations. Such restrictions, the Court ruled, neither coerced the states nor invaded any of their reserved rights.

Similarly, as the international situation grew ominous in the late 1930s and Roosevelt moved toward a more activist foreign policy, the Court enhanced the powers of the president over the nation's foreign affairs. It ruled that the nation's "powers of external sovereignty"[9] lay in the executive branch, existed independent of the Constitution, and operated free of restriction from any reserved rights of the states. In a striking decision in 1937 it held that the president had authority to make "executive agreements" without Senate approval and that such agreements trumped otherwise valid state laws. Thus, as foreign policy emerged as a newly dominant concern in the late 1930s, the expansion of presidential power accelerated even more rapidly, bringing larger areas of American life under federal authority and, in an increasingly vital area of national concern, edging the states toward the periphery.

---

[9] *United States v. Curtis-Wright Export Corp.*, 299 U.S. 304, 318 (1936).

While constitutional changes during the New Deal years substantially expanded federal power, they also broadened state regulatory authority. The Court narrowed its use of both federal preemption and the negative Commerce Clause to allow states an expanded role in regulating economic activities, made state rather then federal common law controlling in the national courts on issues of state-created rights, and in a variety of cases instructed the lower federal courts to defer to the proceedings of state courts and administrative agencies. Further, when it abolished the doctrines of substantive due process and liberty of contract, the Court freed state as well as federal legislative power. In *West Coast Hotel Co. v. Parrish* (1937) it overruled *Adkins v. Children's Hospital* and upheld the authority of states to enact minimum wage statutes for women, substantially enlarging their general police powers. The states were not shy about using their new powers, moreover, extending their regulatory, service, and welfare activities substantially. In 1913 state and local governments had raised and spent approximately $1.8 billion, but by the early 1940s the comparable number was five times that amount. In addition, one of the most striking, if indirect, results of the New Deal was the adoption in 1933 of the Twenty-First Amendment, which repealed the Prohibition amendment, thereby eliminating a major grant of federal authority and restoring power to the states.

The third major change that the New Deal brought was the transformation of the federal judiciary. Roosevelt restaffed the lower courts with appointees sympathetic to his policies, and between 1937 and 1943 he reoriented the Supreme Court by filling seven of its seats with administration loyalists. The new judges, in turn, began to reshape federal law in line with the goals and values of the New Deal. Some maintained that they were merely casting off crabbed doctrinal accretions from the late nineteenth century and restoring the expansive constitutional principles that the Founders had originally intended. Others began to articulate a new attitude toward constitutional law. They advanced the idea that the Constitution was a flexible, practical, and even "living" instrument. The Founders had used broad and adaptive terms, they argued, so that Americans would be able to respond effectively to future problems as the changing demands of their well-being required.

Drawing on those ideas and their New Deal sympathies, federal judges began to infuse new meanings into the constitutional ideals of liberty and equality. They began to give increased protection to the kinds of "personal" liberties that they believed all individuals should enjoy in a democratic society while downgrading the economic liberties that accrued, as a practical matter, primarily to the benefit of large corporations and the economically powerful. Further, they sought to move beyond mere formal legal equality and nourish a greater practical equality by showing, often though surely

not invariably, a special solicitude to individuals and groups that were weak
or disadvantaged – African Americans, workers, consumers, labor unions,
political dissenters, victims of industrial injury, and unpopular ethnic and
religious minorities.

Haltingly and somewhat erratically, the post-1937 Court floated a variety
of constitutional theories to justify its shifting social orientation, including
the idea that the Constitution required it to provide special protection for
rights that were "vital to the maintenance of democratic institutions" or
that were so "fundamental" as to be "implicit in the concept of ordered liberty."[10] Although the Court did not consistently apply any single theory,
one of those it suggested would – decades later and in the wake of the Warren
Court – become particularly influential. When normal democratic political
processes were working and citizens had fair opportunities to influence their
governments, five justices declared in *United States v. Carolene Products Co.*
(1938), the Court should defer to decisions of the political branches. Conversely, when normal democratic processes were blocked or when they led
to systemic abuses against helpless minorities, the Court should intervene
to remedy the situation. Translating theory into doctrine, *Carolene Products*
suggested that judicial review should operate on two tracks. When the
Court reviewed ordinary economic regulations that resulted from normal
political competition and compromise, it would apply a "rational basis"
test, upholding government action if the action bore a reasonable relation
to some legitimate government end. When, however, it reviewed cases
involving the denial of fundamental non-economic rights or discrimination against "discrete and insular minorities" – situations in which ordinary
democratic processes had failed to work properly – the Court would apply
a "stricter scrutiny," an inquiry that would validate government actions
only on a showing that the actions were narrowly tailored and essential to
achieve a compelling governmental goal.[11]

Regardless of its varied justifications and sometimes contradictory rulings, the post-1937 Court was proposing itself as the protector of abused
individuals and minorities, and, in so doing, it was also turning away
from its earlier role as umpire of the federal system. On the ground that fair
democratic politics should ordinarily prevail and that the legislative branch
represented the states as well as the people, it accepted the principle that
Congress was ordinarily the proper institution to determine whether and to
what extent federal power should be exercised. Similarly, on the ground that
the president had vast authority and discretion in the conduct of foreign

[10] *Schneider v. Irvington*, 308 U.S. 147, 161 (1939); *Palko v. Connecticut*, 302 U.S. 319, 325
(1938).
[11] 304 U.S. 144, 152 n.4, at 152–53.

relations, it increasingly deferred to executive decisions that implicated foreign policy concerns. The altered role the Court sketched would help define the triple tracks of governmental centralization that marked the years after 1937. In economic matters Congress would exercise sweeping national legislative authority; in foreign policy matters the president would exercise an ever-growing and often unchecked executive discretion; and in certain areas involving non-economic social and political rights the Court would come to assert an expanding national judicial authority.

War, Cold War, and Civil Rights: The High Years of the New Deal Order

World War II and the dominating events that followed – the birth of the nuclear age, the onset of the Cold War, and the emergence of the United States as the undisputed leader of "the free world" – reinforced the nationalizing trend that the Depression, the New Deal, and the nation's long-accelerating economic and cultural centralization had forged. The war led to massive expansions in the federal bureaucracy, sweeping national controls over the domestic economy, and the induction of more than 16 million men and women into the armed forces. The Cold War that followed sustained the national mobilization, generated a pervasive anti-Communism that further homogenized and centralized political debate, and provided a national security justification for growing federal intrusions into areas previously left to the states. Turning the nation from its traditional and relatively aloof foreign policy, the war and Cold War transformed the United States into a global military and economic superpower at least potentially interested in even the smallest and most distant regions of the world. The power and activities of the federal government grew apace, and the role of the presidency, in particular, continued to swell. The National Security Act of 1947 established both the National Security Council and the Central Intelligence Agency as powerful and well-funded agencies of the executive branch, and the White House staff, which numbered 64 people at the end of World War II, jumped to 399 by 1957 and then to 485 only six year later. All extended the president's ability to control and enforce national policy and to shape the contours of the nation's domestic political debates. The escalating foreign policy challenges, moreover, induced the Court to adopt a highly deferential attitude toward both Congress and the president, temporarily checking its proclaimed new commitment to protect civil liberties. During the war the Court refused to challenge the army's decision to place more than a hundred thousand Japanese-Americans in concentration camps, and into the 1950s it failed to protect the civil liberties of many of those who ran afoul of the second Red Scare that erupted in the early years of the Cold War.

Although postwar politics grew more conservative, the major achievements of the New Deal remained largely in place. Harsh memories of the Great Depression, the unprecedented efforts of the Roosevelt administration to alleviate the nation's ills, and the stunning and sustained economic boom that followed wartime mobilization combined to inspire a broad new consensus. Americans had come to believe that many of the pressing difficulties they faced were "social" in nature, not "individual," and that government could and should take a more active role in resolving them. Indeed, their acceptance of the idea that a newly muscular federal government was necessary to protect national security in the Cold War strengthened their belief that the same national government could also act as an effective instrument of rational, democratic problem solving at home. Increasingly, they looked to government at all levels for an expanding variety of services. Most immediately, they had come to believe that anything affecting the American economy was properly a national issue for which the federal government should take responsibility. Sustaining economic growth and ensuring full employment became domestic goals of the highest priority, and Americans assumed that one of the primary duties of the federal government was to underwrite the nation's continuing economic welfare. Accordingly, government at all levels grew, and the federal government expanded most rapidly. With its unparalleled capacity for raising funds through the national income tax, and the distinct advantages its members realized from dispensing public money, Congress proved increasingly ready to finance new programs and expand old ones. Funds allocated to regular domestic grant programs, for example, doubled in only the first two years after the war.

Although the Republicans controlled of one or both Houses of Congress as well as the presidency for much of the period from 1946 to 1960, they gradually acceded to most New Deal reforms and even joined in expanding the activities of the federal government. Congress passed new public housing, urban redevelopment, and minimum wage legislation, and it expanded federal spending programs to enlarge Social Security, guarantee opportunities for returning veterans, and provide funding for education, conservation, hospital construction, scientific research, and rural electrification. During the presidency of Republican Dwight D. Eisenhower from 1953 to 1961, federal aid to states on a per capita basis more than doubled. The system of "dual federalism" had passed away, replaced by one of "cooperative federalism" in which governments at all levels participated in a widening variety of joint programs and dealt with national problems by blending federal funding and direction with state and local administration. Illustrating both the spread of cooperative federalism and the ways in which Cold War national defense concerns fostered the expansion of the national government, Republicans and Democrats joined forces in 1956 to pass the

Interstate Highway Act. The measure provided massive federal funding for the construction of a 40,000-mile interstate highway system that promised to benefit a wide range of groups and interests across the nation. The states supported it enthusiastically, and Congress easily justified it as necessary for national defense.

Indeed, the extent to which the federal system, and normative theories about it, had evolved became apparent rather quickly. Between 1947 and 1959 Republicans and other supporters of states'-rights ideas initiated four major efforts to study the federal system and find ways to check and reverse the trend toward centralization. None had a noticeable impact. During his presidency, Eisenhower sponsored two such efforts. In 1957, for example, he urged the creation of a special government task force designed "to designate functions which the States are ready and willing to assume and finance that are now performed or financed wholly or in part by the Federal Government."[12] To accomplish that end, he cooperated with the National Governors Conference in establishing a Joint Federal-State Action Committee composed of officials from the highest ranks of state and federal government. After an elaborate and well-financed study, the committee was able to identify only two programs – vocational education and municipal waste treatment – that should be transferred from federal to state control. Together, the two programs accounted for a barely noticeable 2 percent of total federal grants to state and local governments. While a variety of political and economic factors conspired to trivialize the committee's conclusions, its much-heralded effort revealed one overpowering fact. By the 1950s a complex system of nationally directed and funded cooperative federalism had been firmly established and was becoming widely accepted in both theory and practice.

While some conservatives still hoped to restore a more decentralized system, liberals worked to shape the operations of the new order to their purposes. If national power had been drastically expanded and federalism transformed into a "cooperative" system, they reasoned, then the Supreme Court required a new institutional role adapted to those new conditions. The horrifying brutalities of Nazi and Soviet totalitarianism inspired an intensified commitment to the idea of the rule of law, and the tumultuous Cold War campaigns against Communism heightened their belief that the nation needed a strong judiciary to protect individual liberties. Further, the growing conservatism of the states in economic matters, their enthusiasm for fighting Communism by restricting civil liberties, and – most

---

[12] Dwight D. Eisenhower, "Excessive Concentration of Power in Government Is Dangerous: Power and Responsibilities of State Government Must Be Preserved," *Vital Speeches of the Day* 23 (July 15, 1957), 578, 580.

crucially – the adamant determination of those in the South to preserve racial segregation combined to cast a new and unflattering light on the idea that the states were democratic laboratories that should be free to conduct social experiments. Indeed, in the postwar years the very term "social experiment" raised images not of beneficent progressive reforms but of Nazi death chambers and Stalinist labor camps. Increasingly, Democrats and liberals turned to the reoriented post-New Deal federal judiciary as the government institution most likely to enforce national rules that would serve their new values, interests, and aspirations.

One of the most thoughtful, and eventually influential, formulations of those liberal attitudes came from Herbert Wechsler, a prominent legal scholar and old New Dealer. The normative constitutional problem that postwar liberals faced, Wechsler explained, was to find a principled way to "defend a judicial veto" when used to protect "personal freedom," but to "condemn it" when used to block government actions "necessary for the decent humanization of American capitalism."[13] In 1954 Wechsler suggested an elegant solution. The Constitution itself guaranteed state sovereignty by providing the states "a role of great importance in the composition and selection of the central government." Those "political safeguards of federalism" included equal state representation in the Senate, control over many aspects of voting and districting for the House, and a key role in electing the president through the system of electoral votes. Thus, the very structure of the Constitution meant that Congress and the president would "be responsive to local values that have large support within the states." Consequently, there was no need for the Court to protect the states or to serve as the umpire of federalism. Instead, the constitutional structure suggested that the Court should focus its efforts elsewhere. First, because the federal government had no part in composing the state governments, it was the federal government, not the states, that needed the Court's protection. Thus, the Court should ensure "the maintenance of national supremacy against nullification or usurpation by the individual states." Second, because the Constitution's majoritarian "political processes" would not remedy popular and democratic abuses against disfavored minorities, the Court should enforce "those constitutional restraints on Congress or the states that are designed to safeguard individuals."[14] Thus, post-New Deal liberalism began to develop the idea that *Carolene Products* had voiced:

[13] Norman Silber and Geoffrey Miller, "Toward 'Neutral Principles' in the Law: Selections from the Oral History of Herbert Wechsler," *Columbia Law Review* 93 (1993), 854, 924.

[14] Herbert Wechsler, "The Political Safeguards of Federalism: The Role of the States in the Composition and Selection of the National Government," *Columbia Law Review* 54 (1954), 543, 554, 559, 560, n. 59.

the Constitution underwrote the principle that the Court should protect abused individuals and helpless minorities, not the already powerful states or the well-entrenched federal system.

In the postwar years the most systematically disadvantaged minority in the United States was African Americans, and a variety of factors pushed the Court to take action on their behalf. Some were internal: a few useful precedents, the spread of post-New Deal liberal values, the justification provided by the *Carolene Products* idea, and key changes in the Court's personnel – especially the appointment in 1953 of Earl Warren as Chief Justice. Others were external. The African American community had been leaving the South, developing a strong middle class, increasing in organization and militancy, and gaining political influence in the North. Further, the atrocities of Nazi Germany had discredited racist ideas, and the Cold War made repudiation of racism necessary to counter Soviet efforts to undermine American influence in the Third World. The Democratic Party, too, had been transformed since the New Deal. Increasingly urban, northern, liberal, and reliant on African American votes, it was ready to support meaningful efforts to end racial oppression. Finally, the National Association for the Advancement of Colored People was pressing a methodical legal campaign against racial segregation, and its efforts presented a series of well-designed constitutional challenges that allowed the Court to chip away at legalized racial segregation. Together, the changes highlighted the discordant nature of Southern racial practices, led increasing numbers of Americans to reject them, and helped install in the federal courts judges sympathetic to the cause of racial equality.

The judicial turning point came in 1954 when the Court ruled in *Brown v. Board of Education* (1954) that racial segregation in the public schools violated the Equal Protection Clause and then, over the next few years, extended its ruling to a variety of other public institutions and facilities. Exemplifying and dramatizing the idea of the federal judiciary as the protector of both fundamental non-economic rights and "discrete and insular minorities," the decisions asserted national authority over the states in a crucial area of social policy, one that had been labeled "local" since the end of Reconstruction. When Southern state governments and private citizens' groups pledged massive resistance to *Brown*, the Court responded in 1958 with an extraordinary assertion of national judicial supremacy signed by all nine justices. "[T]he federal judiciary is supreme in the exposition of the law of the Constitution," they proclaimed in *Cooper v. Aaron*, and "the interpretation of the Fourteenth Amendment enunciated by this Court in the *Brown* case is the supreme law of the land."[15] The decisions strengthened

---

[15] *Cooper v. Aaron*, 358 U.S. 1, 18.

a galvanizing civil rights movement, but they also provoked bitter and
sometimes violent opposition. By themselves they were unable to end
racial segregation in the South. That had to await events of the following
decade.

Brown and the civil rights struggle helped fire the tumultuous era known
as "the sixties," a politico-cultural phenomenon that began sometime after
1957, became self-conscious in the early 1960s, peaked between 1965 and
1972, and expired rapidly after 1974. Underlying social developments – a
sustained economic boom, rapid expansion and luxurious federal support
of higher education, the emergence of experimental "youth cultures" and
radical "liberation" movements, and the popularization of social theories
that challenged traditional ideas across the board – combined to spur major
changes in American attitudes and values. Melding with escalating and
disruptive protests against an ever widening and seemingly futile war in
Vietnam, the changes generated a volatile era of turmoil and transformation,
of vaulting hopes and intensifying hates.

With respect to the federal system, the sixties initially accelerated
the trend toward centralization. Democratic President John F. Kennedy
inspired a new enthusiasm for liberal activism after his election in 1960,
and his successor Lyndon B. Johnson strove to build a "Great Society," one in
which the federal government would achieve the social and economic goals
of the New Deal and ensure that all Americans shared in their benefits. The
Supreme Court became increasingly active in imposing liberal national
standards on the states, and after an overwhelming Democratic victory in
1964, Congress responded with a series of major domestic reforms. Further,
between 1961 to 1971 the nation ratified four constitutional amendments,
three of which protected the right of Americans to vote, limiting state
authority and giving Congress power to enforce their mandates.

Of most enduring importance, the federal government as a whole finally
committed itself to the cause of black civil rights. Kennedy and Johnson
increasingly embraced the issue, and between 1964 and 1968 Congress
passed three monumental civil rights acts. Two broadly prohibited racial
and other types of discrimination in housing, education, employment, and
"public accommodations." The third negated a wide range of legal and practical obstacles that Southern states deployed to deny African Americans the
franchise. Equally important, the statutes created effective remedies for violations and made the federal government an active and continuous agent of
enforcement. Illustrating the relatively consistent purpose that animated
the entire federal government in the late 1960s, the executive branch immediately initiated or expanded a variety of programs to enforce the new civil
rights statutes, while the Supreme Court quickly upheld their constitutionality. It approved the sharply challenged public accommodations provision

by applying the sweeping interpretation of the Commerce Clause advanced in *Wickard v. Filburn*, and it validated federal control over voting rights on the ground that Section 5 of the Fourteenth Amendment gave Congress the broadest possible power necessary to enforce the amendment's rights. By the end of the 1960s legalized segregation was crumbling, and the constitutional pillar of post-Reconstruction federalism that had survived the New Deal – the principle that racial matters were local – had been obliterated.

Congress expanded federal authority in other areas as well. Johnson's Great Society reached into the backwaters of American life, identifying the very existence of poverty and inequality as problems of national importance. Like the theory of *Carolene Products* and the concerted attack on racial discrimination, his War on Poverty sought to assist the nation's poorest groups and remedy fundamental structural inequalities. Congress authorized ever more generous grants to state and local governments for a seemingly limitless variety of "categorical" purposes, including welfare, housing, child care, mass transit, job training, education, urban renewal, medical insurance, and legal services for the poor. Similarly, the federal government began a concerted effort to deal with issues of environmental pollution and the conservation of natural resources. Increasingly, moreover, the new programs were intended not merely to help state and local governments deal with their problems but to implement national policies designed to achieve national objectives.

A report of the federal Advisory Commission on Intergovernmental Relations published in 1967 charted the steady and accelerating expansion of federal funding programs. Before 1930 the national government offered funding to state and local governments in only ten areas of activity. The New Deal brought federal funding to seventeen more areas, and the early postwar years added another twenty-nine to the list. The period from 1961 to 1966, however, witnessed the most explosive growth. New programs extended federal funding to another thirty-nine areas of state and local government activity – an increase of almost 70 percent in only six years. Thus, by 1967 the federal government was funding state and local government activities in 95 areas and doing so through 379 separate categorical grant programs. In a decade, total federal aid to state and local governments tripled, rising from $4.9 billion in 1958 to $15.2 billion in 1967.

The political momentum carried into the next decade. Even under Republican President Richard M. Nixon, who talked about a "new federalism" that would return power to the states, national activism continued. Indeed, in the first two years of his administration federal funding to state and local governments jumped by more than a third, reaching $25 billion in 1970. Through a variety of changes within the executive branch, Nixon enhanced presidential power to manage both the federal bureaucracy and

the distribution of funds to the states. He sought not so much to limit
federal power and government activism as to make all government agencies
more streamlined and efficient. Moreover, stressing the problem of "crime
in the streets" and the need for "law and order," he accelerated the use of the
national government to fight crime, particularly "organized" crime and narcotics trafficking. New legislation expanded the scope of the federal criminal
law, turned a multiplying number of state-law crimes into federal violations,
and in the Racketeer Influenced and Corrupt Organizations Act (1970) gave
the national government muscular new tools to investigate and prosecute transgressors. Similarly, the decade brought major federal initiatives
aimed at protecting the environment and expanding government welfare services. Although some social programs, particularly those involving
Johnson's War on Poverty, were crimped or terminated, many others took
their place. During the decade total federal spending on welfare programs
more than doubled. By 1979 Congress had established more than five hundred grant programs that accounted for a third of the federal budget and
furnished state and local governments with approximately 30 percent of
their total revenue. Moreover, although Republicans criticized many aspects
of the civil rights movement, especially school busing, affirmative action,
and some aspects of anti-discrimination law, the party – or at least its Northern wing – accepted many of the changes the movement had brought.

As federal funding gushed forth, the national government's control over
its programs continued to tighten. Although Nixon sought to minimize federal restrictions through unconditional "revenue sharing" and less restrictive
"block grants," his efforts were only minimally successful. Federal agencies
swelled in number and responsibilities, while the scope and complexity of
their regulations multiplied geometrically. Expanding and reorganizing the
federal bureaucracy, for example, Congress established the Departments of
Housing and Urban Development (1965), Transportation (1966), Energy
(1977), and Education (1979), as well as the Environmental Protection
Agency (1970), to help administer some of its new programs. The agencies spawned a growing body of regulations that ranged from detailed
rules controlling individual categorical programs to broad across-the-board
rules covering many or all grant programs. Increasingly, moreover, federal
regulations sought to serve a variety of national policies – ending discrimination, protecting the environment, expanding opportunities for the
disadvantaged – unrelated to specific grant programs themselves. During
the 1970s the total number of federal regulations more than doubled, and
Congress and the federal bureaucracy were increasingly regulating not just
the distribution of funds but the policies and operations of state and local
governments themselves.

The continued growth of federal activism was driven in large part by three fundamental changes in the political system. One was the increasing centralization that marked all areas of American public life and transformed ever larger numbers of issues into matters of national concern. The accelerating nationalization and internationalization of economic enterprise, the dramatic and unifying power of ever more pervasive mass media, the growing ease and speed of travel, and the frequency with which Americans moved their homes from state to state and region to region combined to homogenize American life and culture, and the attitudinal changes that resulted increasingly made most problems seem national in scope and resolvable only with national solutions. Moreover, the ever-tightening tyranny of money in the political process magnified the influence of those private organizations – almost always national in operation and concern – that were capable of providing the huge campaign donations that the political parties required. Those organizations – corporations, labor unions, industrial and professional associations, and swelling varieties of ideological advocacy groups – almost invariably sought, in return for their support, national policy decisions that would provide them with advantages national in scope.

The second change lay in the new and stronger sets of interlocking local, state, and national interests that resulted from the massive federal spending programs of the prior decades. The programs were attractive to members of Congress who found them ideal ways to shape policy while assisting their favored interest groups, funneling money to their districts, and improving their chances of reelection. Further, the programs developed their own powerful constituencies: grant recipients and the interest groups who supported them; professionals who designed and administered the programs; and innumerable officials at all levels of government who for reasons of public policy, bureaucratic influence, and personal advancement found the programs highly desirable. As federal spending grew, so did the power of those interlocking interests, and they continued to drive expanded federal spending in the 1970s even as the animating values of post-New Deal liberalism were withering.

The third change was rooted in the altered role of the presidency in an age of mass communications and cultural centralization. Dominating national politics and the public agenda, presidents – and all serious candidates for the office – found it essential to propose national solutions for almost every problem that drew national attention. By the late twentieth century American presidents were expected to act not only as chief executives and commanders-in-chief but also as legislative leaders and all-purpose national problem solvers. The nation's seemingly limitless demands on the office magnified its irresistibly centripetal force.

While Congress, the executive, and concentrating social pressures were extending federal power, the Supreme Court was doing the same. Beginning in the early 1960s, the Warren Court launched a new and broader phase of liberal activism. Shifted leftward by the retirement of two conservatives – including Justice Felix Frankfurter, the Court's leading advocate of "judicial restraint" and deference to the states – and galvanized by the reformist nationalism of Warren and Justice William J. Brennan, a new majority coalesced in almost perfect harmony with the decade's vibrant liberal politics. Between 1962 and 1969 the Court expanded its efforts far beyond civil rights and announced a breathtaking series of decisions that imposed federal limitations on the states in a variety of areas. Perhaps of greatest institutional importance, the Court asserted national authority over the districting and apportionment of state and local legislative bodies. Rejecting earlier decisions, it ruled that the Equal Protection Clause required that electoral districts have closely comparable populations based on the egalitarian standard of "one person, one vote."[16]

Similarly, the Court substantially expanded the reach of the First Amendment. Construing the amendment's religion clauses, it prohibited a variety of government-sponsored religious practices, ruling that states could not require officeholders to declare their belief in God, sponsor Bible reading as part of the public school curriculum, or compel schoolchildren to recite compulsory prayers. Construing the Free Speech Clause, it ruled that the states could punish advocacy only if a person's words were specifically calculated to incite imminent unlawful actions, and it held that the right of free speech created a qualified privilege against state defamation suits, a decision that not only limited state law but opened the way for particularly vigorous criticism of state and local officials. Perhaps most innovative, in *Griswold v. Connecticut* (1965) it held that the First Amendment, in conjunction with other amendments, created a constitutional right of privacy that barred states from prohibiting residents from using or conveying information about contraceptives.

Equally controversial, the Warren Court applied most of the rest of the Bill of Rights to the states. Again reversing prior doctrine, it held that the central provisions of the Fourth, Fifth, Sixth, and Eighth Amendments were "incorporated" in the Due Process Clause of the Fourteenth Amendment. Moreover, it repeatedly broadened the protections that the clauses offered. In what was probably its most controversial decision in the area, *Miranda v. Arizona* (1966), it required law enforcement agents to inform arrestees about their constitutional rights and to respect their decision to exercise those rights. To enforce its rulings, the Court expanded the availability of

---

[16] *Gray v. Sanders*, 372 U.S. 368, 381 (1963).

federal habeas corpus for state prisoners, enabling the lower federal judiciary to review state court criminal convictions more frequently. The decisions created, in effect, an expanding federal code of criminal procedure that bound the states, restrained police behavior across the nation, and provoked bitter and widespread criticism.

As Congressional activism continued into the 1970s, so did the Court's. Although Chief Justice Warren resigned in 1969 and Nixon appointed four new justices, including the new chief justice, Warren E. Burger, the Court changed less than many expected. Indeed, in several areas it continued to extend federal power, making the early Burger Court seem almost a third, if somewhat ambivalent, phase of the Warren Court. During the 1970s the Burger Court gave constitutional sanction to some types of affirmative action, confirmed the broad power of Congress under the Fourteenth Amendment, and upheld a substantial, if limited, remedial authority in the federal courts to order local officials to integrate previously segregated public school districts. In addition, it provided due process protections for welfare recipients faced with termination of benefits and continued the Warren Court's efforts to expand the relief that injured individuals could obtain under a variety of federal regulatory statutes.

In three areas the Burger Court's decisions seemed particularly liberal, activist, and nationalist. First, it held that the Equal Protection Clause applied to gender classifications. Congress had begun to address gender inequality in the 1960s, and in 1971 the Court ruled in *Reed v. Reed* that a state statute disfavoring women violated the Constitution. Second, reaffirming and broadening the constitutional right of privacy that the Warren Court had pioneered in *Griswold*, it held that the right barred states from prohibiting the sale of contraceptives to unmarried persons and, far more innovative and controversial, announced in *Roe v. Wade* (1973) that it guaranteed women the right to an abortion. The Burger Court thus confirmed that a new and vibrant "public/private" distinction had entered American constitutional law. Unlike the pre-New Deal Court, which had used the distinction to protect property and economic liberty from government regulation, however, the Warren and Burger Courts infused new meaning into the dichotomy, using it to protect intimate matters involving sex and procreation from such interference. Finally, the Burger Court extended the reach of the Eighth Amendment, mandating minimum federal standards on both capital punishment and prison conditions. Its rulings prevented the states from executing hundreds of condemned prisoners, forced them to make substantial revisions in their criminal laws, and compelled them to institute a variety of reforms in the administration of their corrections systems. By the 1980s more than 200 state prisons and 450 local jails in forty-three states were operating under federal court orders.

The growing control that the federal courts exercised over the nation's prisons was only one of the more visible areas in which federal judicial supervision cabined the power of state and local officials. After *Brown* the federal courts had gradually taken over hundreds of schools in their efforts to ensure that the Court's mandate was enforced. Inspired by their role in combating racial segregation and energized by a burgeoning faith in the judiciary's power to redress social wrongs, the federal courts grew increasingly willing to take on broader and more complex social problems. Moreover, the explosion of Congressional legislation compelled them in the same direction. Numerous statutes created new and sometimes vague rights under many of the cooperative programs that the federal government funded, and those provisions spurred a rapidly expanding range of suits in the national courts against state and local governments. Increasingly, federal judges became active managers of ongoing litigations that sought to reform the structures and procedures of those governments, and they often issued detailed orders establishing federal rules over many areas that Congressional funding had brought within the indirect, but nevertheless effective, control of the national government.

Although national law and national standards had become pervasive by the 1970s, the states nevertheless remained vital centers of power. For the most part, their laws still controlled many of the most basic areas of American life: marriage, family, education, criminal justice, commercial transactions, zoning and land usage, estate planning and inheritance, the use of automobiles and the highways, and most of the broad common law fields of tort, contract, and property. Indeed, in lawsuits where state law properly controlled, federal constitutional law continued to bind the national courts to follow and apply it. State and local governments, moreover, were heavily involved in providing most services in such basic areas as education, transportation, social welfare, police and public protection, housing and developmental planning, natural resource conservation and usage, and labor relations and employment practices. While from 1950 to 1975 the number of federal civilian employees edged up from 2.1 to 2.9 million, the number of state and local government employees jumped from 4.2 to 12 million, almost 60 percent of whom were concentrated in the fields of education and health services.

Further, stimulated by the federal government's expanded activism, local reformers pushed to modernize state governments and enhance their administrative capacities. Liberals sought to strengthen their ability to provide greater ranges of social services, while many conservatives hoped that stronger state governments would help check the increasing nationalization that marked the post-New Deal decades. From the 1940s through the 1970s the states increased their use of professional administrators and drafted expert commissions to frame constitutional amendments and other structural reforms that would strengthen the institutions of state government. In 1962 only twenty states held annual legislative sessions, for example, but by the mid 1970s forty-two did so. Influenced by the growing emphasis on executive leadership that marked the national model, sixteen states extended gubernatorial terms to four years, and a dozen eliminated long-established restrictions to allow their governors to serve a second successive term. Further, nineteen states restructured their entire executive branches, expanding gubernatorial powers over a variety of budgetary matters and giving their governors greater administrative control over a wide range of state and local agencies. Moreover, state employment, revenues, and expenditures generally expanded relative to those of local government entities, and most states centralized their administrations by imposing a growing number of requirements and restrictions on local government institutions.

Finally, states and localities were able to protect their positions in the federal system by exerting persistent and effective pressures on the national government. They marshaled their power by establishing a variety of organizations – including the National Governors' Association, the National Conference of State Legislatures, the National League of Cities, the U.S. Conference of Mayors, and the National Association of Counties – to influence federal policy and ensure that national programs were tailored to local needs and interests. Further, by administering many cooperative state-federal programs, they were able to help shape their operations and impact. The states, too, retained substantial independence in their actions because their officials continued to be elected directly by their citizens and derived neither office nor authority from the national government. While the states helped elect federal officials, the federal government had no such role in state electoral processes.

IV. RESHAPING FEDERALISM IN AN AGE OF FRAGMENTATION AND REALIGNMENT: VECTORS OF AN UNFOLDING ERA, 1970s–2000

The 1960s ended badly for post-New Deal liberalism. Escalating militancy in the civil rights and antiwar movements brought mass protests and civil disobedience to the center of American politics, while the appearance of communes, youth cultures, feminism, sexual freedom, gay liberation, black nationalism, and varieties of political radicalism fueled a growing backlash among older and more conservative Americans. Three stunning political assassinations – President Kennedy; his brother, Robert, a senator and Democratic presidential candidate; and Dr. Martin Luther King, Jr., the revered and despised leader of the civil rights movement – compounded a growing sense of turmoil, division, and crisis.

The events fragmented post-New Deal liberalism. On the level of ideas, the fundamental assumptions that underwrote the regulatory state – faith in science, expertise, and administrative neutrality – seemed increasingly dubious and misconceived. On the level of politics, the war in Vietnam pitted Johnson's Great Society against a rising tide of antiwar sentiment that increasingly enlisted the support of women, students, liberals, intellectuals, and racial minorities. Those core elements of the Democratic coalition came to view the war as a political betrayal, and an outspoken radical minority transformed the very word "liberal" into a term of derision. At the same time, other key elements of the coalition veered off in the opposite direction. Many white Americans, including urban workers and ethnic Catholics, grew increasingly angry at civil rights advances, antiwar activism, and what they regarded as the social and cultural outrages that exploded in the decade's second half. To make matters worse, organized labor, a central pillar of the Democratic coalition, began shrinking in both membership and influence.

The result was rupture and defeat. In 1968 the anti-war movement drove Johnson from office, and disaffected Democrats – some by voting Republican and others by abstaining in protest – helped elect Nixon president. Campaigning against crime, radicalism, affirmative action, and the Warren Court itself, Nixon joined leftist radicals in blaming liberalism for the nation's problems. Although the election was close, it marked the beginning of the end of the New Deal order.

If the 1960s had been strife-torn but optimistic, the 1970s were strife-torn and pessimistic. Dominated by the party's left wing, the Democrats lost disastrously in 1972, and the Republicans suffered an equally humiliating blow two years later when the Watergate scandal forced Nixon into the first presidential resignation in the nation's history. The civil rights movement fragmented over both goals and tactics, while white resentments stoked a burning opposition that focused on school busing and affirmative action. The war in Vietnam, moreover, came to an excruciating end when the United States withdrew its forces in 1973 and then watched as the Communist North conquered the South, the fanatic Khmer Rouge seized control of neighboring Cambodia, and literally millions of Southeast Asians – many of whom had loyally supported the United States during the war – were murdered, starved to death, or drowned trying to escape. Further, *Roe v. Wade* began to unite moral traditionalists, Evangelical Protestants, and the Catholic Church in a passionate anti-abortion movement that widened what seemed an unbridgeable moral divide among Americans. At the same time the Yom Kippur War in the Mideast triggered an Arab oil embargo and drastic price increases that created a severe energy crisis. The result was a steep recession and a debilitating inflation that lingered into the 1980s. Fundamental economic problems – severe inflation, sharply rising interest rates, high levels of unemployment, and persistent economic stagnation – compounded the national downswing. Increasingly, American industry lost out to foreign competition, and in 1971 the nation witnessed its first trade deficit in almost a century, a deficit that multiplied more than tenfold by 1981. Finally, a grisly national humiliation capped the decade. Iran, a critical Cold War ally, fell to a violently anti-American Islamic movement that seized the United States embassy and held seventy-six Americans as hostages. Daily television coverage carried anti-American denunciations across the world; and, when a rescue mission failed in early 1980, the nation watched in horror as Iranian radicals gloated over the burnt remains of dead American soldiers and their crashed helicopters.

Those events combined to destroy the New Deal order, but they failed to generate a successor regime that was equally stable and well defined. The economic depression of the 1930s had confronted the nation with a single and overwhelming challenge, one that focused attention and interests on a national effort to revive and reform the economy. In contrast, the psychological depression of the 1970s enveloped the nation in a web of amorphous anxieties and multi-cornered conflicts. If the earlier depression had pitted business and the wealthy against the unemployed and the middle class, the later one tended to divide Americans into a splintered multitude of groups identified not only by economic and class position but also by race, age, region, gender, religion, ethnicity, sexual orientation, and political ideology. The *Carolene Products* idea of "discrete and insular minorities" seemed to have become the "big bang" of a new and fragmenting politico-cultural universe.

One result was that both liberals and conservatives showed a chastened sense of limits. Liberals enjoyed their major successes in opposing the war and cultivating a growing concern with the environment. The former was premised on the limits of American power and the latter on the limits of industrial society. Conservatives enjoyed their greatest triumphs in bringing traditional religious ideas and neo-classic economic thinking into the political mainstream. The former was based on the mandate of a transcendent God and the latter on the iron laws of the market. All reflected a declining faith in the power of reason, science, and government to bend the future to the nation's wishes.

While the psychological depression deepened, other forces were beginning to nudge Americans in new directions. One was a complex but profound set of attitudinal changes: escalating distrust of government, resentment against minorities, hostility toward welfare programs, rejection of "liberalism" and its regulatory tradition, and a festering anger directed against challenges to traditional religious and moral ideas – particularly feminism, abortion rights, and gay liberation. A second factor was a long-brewing revitalization of market economics. Together with the general assault on government and scientific expertise, the spreading market ideology helped turn the nation toward deregulation, privatization, and a renewed faith in the power of private enterprise and the virtue of becoming rich. A third factor was the formation of what appeared to be a new Republican majority based on the merger of the party's traditional supporters – especially business, the well-to-do, rural America, and the old Anglo-Saxon middle class – with new social groups, such as Catholics, ethnic whites, disaffected members of the working class, the culturally conservative "solid South," and the growing forces of Evangelical Protestantism.

Drawing the new Republican coalition together was a cultural synthesis that implicitly reversed the values of *Carolene Products* and post-New Deal liberalism. Disillusioned intellectuals began to articulate a new conservative ideology that called for a return to "authority" and to a social order build solely on "merit." Market theorists developed the idea that politicians responded only to organized interest groups that sought to use government to gain special favors contrary to the common good – "rent seeking," as they called it. Traditional conservatives and Evangelical groups maintained that secular liberalism and the welfare state were undermining the nation's moral fiber, family values, and religious foundations. Business interests sought to minimize their legal liabilities and avoid regulatory requirements by claiming that their productivity was at the mercy of "frivolous" lawsuits brought by dishonest or deluded claimants seeking undeserved windfalls. Property owners and other groups, squeezed by recession and angered at government spending on social welfare programs, organized "taxpayer revolts" designed to secure substantial reductions in local, state, and national taxation. Finally, those who harbored resentments against racial and ethnic minorities were angered by the "preferential treatment" that the civil rights laws gave to those whom they considered unable to succeed on their own. Subtly and only half-consciously, those varied attitudes blended into a new social persuasion, one that saw the weak, disadvantaged, non-conformist, and ill treated as morally unworthy and judged their attempts to secure governmental assistance as trickery and exploitation. Simply put, the ideology of the new Republican coalition transmuted "discrete and insular minorities" into "rent-seeking interest groups," the systemically disadvantaged into the morally unworthy. Conversely, the ideology elevated business and the economically successful into exemplars of merit and paladins of the common good. Those groups were not special interests but pillars of economic growth, national might, and moral rectitude. Thus, it was appropriate for government to foster business with deregulation and favor the prosperous with tax cuts.

As New Deal liberalism had done, the new conservatism generated and popularized its own supporting constitutional theories. Rejecting what they considered unlimited Congressional power over the economy and improper judicial activism by the Warren Court, conservative thinkers sought to discredit the former with revived ideas of state sovereignty and the latter with restrictive ideas about separation of powers. Although they advanced a variety of arguments, often supported by reasoning drawn from market economics, they rallied around the unifying claim that post-New Deal liberalism had distorted the Constitution and abandoned its "original" meaning. Rejecting the idea of a "living" Constitution, they maintained that the document's meaning was fixed and unchanging. Those not biased by liberal nationalism, they charged, could identify the Constitution's authentic meaning by focusing on its text, the "original intent" or "understanding" of its drafters and ratifiers, and the social and moral context that surrounded its adoption.

Edwin Meese III, who served as attorney general under Republican President Ronald Reagan in the 1980s, emerged as the most prominent national proponent of the new conservative constitutional theory. The federal judiciary was designed to protect federalism and limited government, Meese insisted, and "the literal provisions of the Constitution" and "the original intentions of those who framed it" provided the clear and correct "judicial standard" for interpreting its meaning. Castigating the "radical egalitarianism and expansive civil libertarianism of the Warren Court," he charged that liberal judicial decisions were "ad hoc" and even "bizarre," often "more policy choices than articulations of constitutional principle." To preserve limited constitutional government and construe the Constitution properly, the Court must return to the original intentions of the Founders, "the only reliable guide for judgment." Such a return, Meese promised, "would produce defensible principles of government that would not be tainted by ideological predilection." Thus, he announced, it "has been and will continue to be the policy of this administration to press for a Jurisprudence of Original Intention."[17]

Although the idea of "original intent" was an old one and, like the theory of *Carolene Products*, had some merit, it suddenly began to command attention and inspire devotion because it was – again like *Carolene Products* – a highly serviceable tool of constitutional politics. For the new conservatives,

---

[17] Edwin Meese III, address to the American Bar Association, July 9, 1985, reprinted in The Federalist Society, *The Great Debate: Interpreting Our Written Constitution* (Washington, DC, 1986), 1, 9, 10.

the idea of original intent provided theoretical grounds for discrediting much of the constitutional law of the preceding half-century, and it justified both attacks on the Warren Court and the demand for justices who would overturn its decisions and restore the "authentic" Constitution. Indeed, the concept of a normative original intent was inherently an instrument of doctrinal disruption and change. Asserting the existence of a "true" constitutional meaning established in a distant past, the idea provided theoretical justification for casting off constitutional interpretations that had evolved over the subsequent centuries and for rejecting judicial decisions rendered in more recent periods. Equally important, by making eighteenth- and nineteenth-century attitudes the touchstone of constitutional meaning, the idea promised to strengthen the legal and historical arguments that conservatives advanced against the political adversaries they opposed most intensely – those supporting gay rights, abortion, gun control, affirmative action, restrictions on the death penalty, more expansive tort liability, rigid separation of church and state, institutional reform litigation, and broad federal anti-discrimination laws.

Influenced by Nixon's four appointees, the Burger Court began to reflect those spreading attitudes. Trumpeting a new concern with what it called "Our Federalism," it increasingly sought to counter liberal nationalism by limiting the reach of federal law into the operations of state and local government. It expanded the immunity of government officials from civil rights suits, curtailed remedies for those injured by violations of federal statutes, and narrowed the scope of the Fourteenth Amendment. Similarly, it cabined many of the Warren Court's criminal law decisions, narrowing both the Fourth Amendment exclusionary rule and the Fifth Amendment right to counsel. Although it did not overrule *Miranda v. Arizona*, it repeatedly found ways to shrink its reach. Most commonly, the Court targeted the institutional power of the lower federal courts, developing a variety of procedural restrictions to limit their opportunities for liberal activism. It required them to abstain more frequently in favor of state forums, limited their power to issues writs of habeas corpus to state officials and to order remedies in school desegregation suits, and used the Eleventh Amendment to deny them jurisdiction over suits against states for money damages.

Although it employed the rhetoric of federalism, the Burger Court seemed increasingly committed to a substantively conservative political agenda, especially after the appointment of Justice Sandra Day O'Connor in 1981. Its decisions, for example, commonly deployed the rhetoric of federalism to close the federal courts to groups that the new Republican coalition had targeted – tort plaintiffs, civil rights claimants, and state criminal defendants. Indeed, when deference to the states led to unpalatable results, the Court often balked. In *Michigan v. Long* (1983), for example, deference to state decision making would have meant upholding the constitutional claim of a criminal defendant. The Court's majority would allow no such result. Instead, it broadened its own jurisdiction to review decisions of state courts and thereby extended the reach of federal authority to overturn state court rulings.

Most fundamental to the federal system, in a 5–4 decision in *National League of Cities v. Usery* (1976) the Burger Court sought to strike directly at the New Deal legacy by reviving the Tenth Amendment. Overruling a decision of the Warren Court, it held that the Fair Labor Standards Act of 1938 (FLSA) could not be applied to state employees and, for the first time since 1937, voided a Congressional statute enacted under the commerce power. Citing the Tenth Amendment, *National League* declared that there were "definite limits upon the authority of Congress to regulate the activities of the States as States by means of the commerce power."[18] The Court, *National League* reasserted, was responsible for protecting the states from national legislative power. For three liberal dissenters, Brennan rejected the majority's holding and invoked the post-New Deal theory of the "political safeguards of federalism." The "fundamental tenet of our federalism," he insisted, is "that the extent of federal intervention into the States' affairs" was properly determined not by the Court but "by the States' exercise of political power through their representatives in Congress."[19]

Indicative of its transitional nature as both a third Warren Court and the ur-Rehnquist Court, the Burger Court – actually, a single justice – changed its mind nine years later. Overruling *National League* in another 5–4 decision, *Garcia v. San Antonio Metropolitan Transit Authority* (1985), it upheld an application of the FLSA to a municipal transit system on two closely related constitutional grounds. One was that the Constitution offered "no guidance about where the frontier between state and federal power lies" and, hence, gave the justices "no license to employ freestanding conceptions of state sovereignty when measuring congressional authority under the Commerce Clause." The other ground was a liberal version of original intent, a broad theory of the Framers' design: "the principal means chosen by the Framers to ensure the role of the States in the federal system lies in the structure of the Federal government itself."[20] In explicit terms the Court adopted the reigning liberal theory that the federal system was properly protected not by the Court but by the "political safeguards" that the Framers had built into the constitutional system.

[18] 426 U.S. 833, 852.
[19] 426 U.S. at 876–77 (Brennan, J., dissenting).
[20] 469 U.S. 528, 550.

Reviving the pre-New Deal views of William Howard Taft and Charles Warren, four Republican appointees dissented vigorously. Justice Lewis F. Powell rejected the "political safeguards" theory as both functionally inadequate and constitutionally unfounded, and he insisted that "judicial enforcement of the Tenth Amendment is essential to maintaining the federal system." Casting a hopeful eye to the future, Justice William H. Rehnquist, Nixon's last appointee and the author of *National League*, agreed. The principle of state sovereignty, he declared defiantly, "will, I am confident, in time again command the support of a majority of this Court."[21] Little more than a year later Ronald Reagan appointed Rehnquist Chief Justice.

Elected president in 1980, Reagan did far more than that. He helped reorient American politics, lead the nation out of the psychological depression of the 1970s, and inspire a crystallizing Republican majority in its drive for national dominance. That coalition reelected Reagan in 1984, put two other Republicans – George Bush in 1988 and George W. Bush in 2000 – in the presidency, and forced Democrat Bill Clinton to move his party substantially to the right in order to scratch together two presidential victories in the 1990s. Equally important, the new Republican coalition steadily increased the party's strength in Congress, which the Democrats had dominated since the Great Depression. After 1980 the Republicans frequently controlled the Senate, and in 1994 they won control of the House, a position they retained to century's end.

Reagan established both the rhetoric and direction of the new era. "[G]overnment is not the solution to our problem," he announced. "Government *is* the problem."[22] His greatest success came in reshaping the parameters of public debate and establishing the values of the new Republican coalition – religious traditionalism, suspicion of government, faith in business and the free market, and opposition to welfare, abortion, homosexuality, and affirmative action – at the center of American politics. His administration pursued four principal policies: business deregulation, tax cuts weighed in favor of the wealthy, heavy increases in military spending, and a balanced budget. In large part it delivered on the first three and, likely by design, failed on the fourth – a result that led to skyrocketing federal deficits and, consequently, to intensifying pressures to cut federal domestic spending on welfare and other social programs. Further, Reagan, who had opposed both the Civil Rights Act of 1964 and the Voting Rights Act of 1965, altered the position of the federal government on civil rights issues. His administration opposed affirmative action and school busing, and it

---

[21] 469 U.S. 570 (Powell, J., dissenting); id. at 580 (Rehnquist, J., dissenting).
[22] Ronald Reagan, "Inaugural Address," Jan. 20, 1981, in *Public Papers of the Presidents of the United States, 1981* (Washington, DC, 1982), 1.

slackened substantially federal efforts to enforce the national civil rights laws.

Proclaiming another "New Federalism," Reagan sought to restructure the system far more substantially than Nixon had attempted. Nixon's "new federalism" had embraced the idea of active government. Accepting the need for massive federal spending it had attempted to make government more responsive and efficient by decentralizing management. Its primary method was to abandon highly restrictive categorical grants in favor of block grants and general revenue sharing, thereby maintaining the flow of funds to state and local governments but with far fewer federal use restrictions. In contrast, Reagan rejected revenue sharing and, more important, sought to minimize or terminate federal financing and supervision in as many areas as possible. His goal was to shrink government at all levels. Although his most ambitious federalism proposals failed, he succeeded in ending revenue sharing and reducing federal grants to state and local governments. During the 1980s funding for welfare programs fell, and federal grants to state and local government dropped by 25 percent. Along similar lines, Reagan substantially reduced federal supervision over state and local governments. His administration adopted administrative procedures to slow the growth of federal rule making and altered many existing regulations to allow the states greater discretion and to relieve them of costly reporting requirements. It consolidated seventy-seven categorical programs into nine broad block grants, for example, condensing and simplifying a wide range of rules and restrictions. In social terms, the weak and disadvantaged, both the working and non-working poor, bore the hardships and deprivations of his federalism reforms.

In spite of its commitment to decentralization, however, the Reagan administration readily embraced federal power when necessary to advance its political objectives. While in most cases – welfare spending and civil rights enforcement, for example – curtailing federal activism served its social purposes, there were exceptions. When business interests advocated both uniform national standards to open more miles of highway to larger trucks and a national product liability law restricting consumer rights, Reagan supported the proposals in spite of the fact that they required federal preemption of state laws in areas of traditional state control. Similarly, his administration readily advocated national standards in its effort to impose workfare requirements on state welfare programs, extend federal criminal law to fight a variety of social evils, and defeat the affirmative action programs that dozens of state and local governments had established.

Indeed, although Republican administrations from Nixon to the second George Bush formally upheld the banner of federalism, all contributed to the further centralization of American government. In domestic matters

they joined Democrats in expanding national involvement in such traditional state areas as education and family relations, and they pushed –
against determined Democratic opposition – to nationalize elements of tort
law in order to restrict suits against business and government. Further, they
helped federalize ever larger realms of the criminal law. Indeed, by 1996
more than 40 percent of all federal criminal statutes had been enacted since
Nixon's election in 1968. Similarly, the Republicans steadily reinforced
the expansion of presidential power and the prioritization of military and
foreign policy concerns. That persistent emphasis impinged on the states
by centralizing issues of paramount public concern, expanding the de facto
scope of federal authority, and diverting resources from domestic programs
that the states helped control to the military and national security institutions that operated under exclusive federal authority. Ironically, the end of
the Cold War between 1989 and 1991 seemed to lead only to rapid international destabilization, further magnification of foreign policy anxieties,
and an ever greater concentration of power and discretion in the federal
executive.

By the end of the 1980s the successive achievements of post-New Deal
liberalism and the decentralization efforts that began after 1969 had combined to alter and in some ways strengthen the nation's federal system.
The former accomplished three critical results. First, compelling the states
to redistrict their legislatures, post-New Deal liberalism increased urban
representation in many states and helped create new legislative coalitions
that began to address the pressing problems that earlier rural-dominated
legislatures had ignored. Second, it brought the franchise to African Americans in the South and forced broad non-discrimination policies on all
states. The result was to ensure fairer treatment for minority groups and to
begin mitigating abuses that had long tarnished the claim of states' rights.
Third, federal matching grants stimulated new social programs and spurred
many states to modernize and professionalize their governmental structures.
Between 1965 and 1980, for example, twenty-two states redesigned their
executive branches; the number of state employees who worked under merit
systems rose from 50 to 75 percent. Similarly, thirty-four states reorganized
and expanded their court systems, and all fifty established offices of court
administration to address caseload burdens and increase judicial efficiency.

Those achievements substantially enhanced the ability of the states to
handle the consequences of the new decentralization that began in the
1970s. On one level, the decentralization effort made the national government more responsive to state complaints about bureaucratic waste and
unnecessary administrative burdens. The result was the elimination or sim-
plification of many federal regulatory procedures and a greater flexibility
at the state and local levels in shaping government programs. On a second

level, decentralization allowed states to take greater control over the programs they administered and encouraged them to modernize their administrative structures and use their enhanced capacities to initiate new programs and approaches of their own. Beginning in the 1970s the states embarked on a range of new initiatives to expand social services, improve financial capabilities, attract outside investment, develop energy and conservation programs, and reform their public education and criminal justice systems. On a third level, the decentralization movement revived the idea of the states as laboratories that could attempt valuable social experiments. The states began to look to one another – rather than to the federal government – for new ideas and techniques, and with increasing frequency they borrowed from the approaches that their sister states had tried and found effective.

Wisconsin exemplified both the era's new state activism and its growing social conservatism. In the century's early decades Wisconsin had pioneered many progressive social measures, and in the 1990s it emerged once more as an innovative force, this time in developing restrictive "workfare" programs designed to reduce taxes, curtail welfare coverage and benefits, and compel recipients quickly to find private employment. Its approach encouraged conservative attacks on the federal welfare system and not only influenced other states but also had an impact at the national level. In 1996 Wisconsin again stood as a paragon of laboratory federalism when the federal government invoked its experience in substantially revamping the nation's welfare law. A monumental federal welfare reform act encouraged the wider use of workfare requirements, eliminated some national programs, expanded the use of block grants, and allowed the states greater leeway in shaping their own systems.

In spite of the decentralization efforts, however, governmental power at the national level remained decisive. That fact was nowhere more apparent than in the movement to replace welfare with workfare. Although Wisconsin illustrated a renewed vitality in state governments, the welfare reform law that Congress enacted in 1996 demonstrated that the federal government remained the paramount force in establishing national welfare policy. The act not only required the adoption of workfare policies, but it also compelled the states to comply with a number of other rigorous federal mandates, including the imposition of time limits on eligibility, reduction or withholding of benefits for certain classes of recipients, reporting procedures involving the paternity and immigration status of underage beneficiaries, and the development of various centralized procedures for administering key elements of state welfare programs.

Contemporaneous developments in the state courts suggested similar conclusions about the continuing dominance of national standards. Those courts had authority to construe their own state constitutions, and they were

free in most cases to establish broader individual rights and liberties than
the U.S. Supreme Court recognized under the Federal Constitution. Not
surprisingly, then, in the 1970s liberals reacted to the narrowing constitutional decisions of the Burger Court by urging the state courts to use their
independent authority to counteract its decisions by expanding individual
rights under their separate state constitutions. Some responded, and a number of state judges invoked their authority to establish rights broader than
those recognized in federal law. The liberal appeal to state judicial power,
however, brought only limited and scattered results. For the most part state
courts spurned their opportunities and in the overwhelming majority of
relevant cases chose either to rely on federal constitutional law directly or
to conform state constitutional law to the contours of federal law. Indeed,
when the courts of California and Florida refused to follow decisions of the
Burger Court, they were abruptly reigned in. Both states responded with
constitutional amendments that required their state courts to bring their
interpretations of certain state constitutional provisions into conformity
with the decisions of the U.S. Supreme Court.

The relatively conformist behavior of the state courts suggested several
interrelated conclusions about American federalism in the late twentieth
century. One was that underlying social, cultural, and economic forces were
continuing relentlessly to centralize national affairs. In spite of the swelling
paeans to federalism, Americans were ever more commonly advancing their
values and policies as properly "national" in scope. Although they frequently
and sometimes bitterly disputed the nature of the values that were proper,
they nevertheless insisted ever more stridently that their own values –
whatever they were – be given national recognition. The second conclusion was that the U.S. Supreme Court was playing an ever more prominent
and important role in public affairs. To a growing number of Americans it
was the truly "supreme" authority that could and should rule on all major
issues that faced the nation. Americans were beginning to view the Court,
in other words, as they had come to view the presidency – as an institution
that should address not only problems that were properly "national" in
some antecedent and technical constitutional sense but also all issues that
had become, as a practical fact of everyday life, important to the nation as a
whole. A third conclusion was that the concept of "federalism" had lost most
of its substantive meaning as an independent normative guide to the distribution of governmental powers. While theories of federalism continued
to proliferate and activists of all stripes persisted in invoking the concept's
authority, little remained of the idea that could not readily be turned to
partisan use by able and designing hands. The fourth and last conclusion
was that a politically conservative and socially ungenerous mood had come
to pervade political attitudes across the nation. The state courts properly

followed the U.S. Supreme Court, many Americans seemed to believe, not just because it was the authoritative voice of the national Constitution but also because it was – with a few glaring exceptions – moving that law, for the time at least, in the general directions they considered desirable.

Although the Court increasingly reflected the values of the new Republican coalition, Reagan and his successors failed to transform the Supreme Court as quickly or completely as the New Deal had done. Between 1933 and 1969 the Democrats had controlled the presidency for twenty-eight of thirty-six years, the Senate for all but four of those years, and both together for twenty-four years. Conversely, in the decades after 1968 the Republicans controlled both the presidency and the Senate simultaneously for only six years, 1981 through 1987, a period in which only two vacancies occurred. Thus, Republican nominations were commonly subject to Democratic check. Then, further diluting their drive for control, during the 1990s Clinton was able to add two moderate liberals to the Court.

Even though Republican presidents were responsible for ten of the twelve justices placed on the Court after 1968, their new appointees failed to form a consistently united bloc. Indeed, only three of them pushed aggressively and relentlessly to implement the values of the new Republican coalition. In contrast, three others edged into the Court's moderate-to-liberal wing, and the remaining four were often cautious and respectful of precedent, rather than ideological and ardent for change. As both conservatives and opponents of judicial activism, the moderate four may have felt themselves bound to honor the principle of *stare decisis* and to remain for the most part within existing constitutional channels. Thus, a combination of external checks, internal barriers of role and doctrine, and differing jurisprudential orientations prevented abrupt change in many areas.

Although a variety of obstacles slowed Republican efforts to remake the federal judiciary, the party's determined drive nevertheless began to bring increasingly substantial results by the late 1980s. Methodically appointing ideologically sympathetic judges, Reagan and Bush increasingly turned the lower federal judiciary toward the values of the new Republican coalition. Far more visibly, they did the same to the Supreme Court. Reagan markedly changed its direction when he elevated Rehnquist to the center chair in 1986 and then added conservative Justices Antonin Scalia and Anthony Kennedy to the bench. Then, when Bush replaced liberal Justice Thurgood Marshall, the last survivor of the Warren Court, with the rigidly conservative Justice Clarence Thomas in 1991, he established a relatively firm five-justice conservative bloc that began to act with increasing boldness.

In the name of federalism the new majority took particular aim at the powers of Congress, and in the century's last eight years it voided at least ten Congressional statutes on federalism grounds. In *United States v. Lopez*

(1995), the five-justice bloc voided the Gun-Free School Zones Act, which made it a crime knowingly to possess a gun near a school. The decision seemed to limit the Commerce Clause to formally "economic" activities that Congress could show were directly related to interstate commerce. Five years later in *United States v. Morrison* (2000) the same five justices relied on *Lopez* to void a provision of the Violence Against Women Act that created a federal remedy for victims of gender-motivated violence. Such violence, the Court explained, was "not, in any sense of the phrase, economic activity."[23] Similarly, the Court deployed the judicially created doctrine of standing to trump Congressional power to enforce federal environmental laws through private lawsuits, and it even suggested doctrinal grounds for possible future use in enforcing limits on the spending power.

More pointedly, reacting against national regulation of state and local governments, the Court severely constrained federal power over the states themselves. First, in 1996 it held that the Eleventh Amendment barred Congress from using its commerce power to create claims against states, and three years later it extended that holding to all of Congress's Article I powers. Second, it narrowed the Fourteenth Amendment for the same purpose. Although the Court did not challenge the principle that Congress could abrogate state sovereign immunity when legislating under Section 5 of the Fourteenth Amendment, it created severe limitations on the power and invalidated a series of Congressional statutes that imposed liabilities on states for violating federal civil rights statutes. Finally, the Court further insulated the states from federal power by developing an "anti-commandeering" principle that forbad Congress from requiring states or their officials to assist in implementing federal regulatory programs.

Although the Rehnquist Court revived the Tenth Amendment, it did not use it to remove a broad category of "local" activities from federal authority as the Taft Court had done in *Drexel Furniture*. Rather, in the spirit of *National League*, it employed the amendment more narrowly and seemed primarily interested in protecting the operations and institutions of the state governments themselves. Its decisions restricting the lower federal judiciary paralleled its decisions limiting Congressional power. The Rehnquist Court curtailed federal habeas corpus, shrank remedial authority over institutional reform suits, and narrowed substantive liabilities under federal statutory and constitutional provisions in order to minimize federal judicial intervention in the operations of state and local governments.

Beyond insulating state governments, the Rehnquist Court's decisions limiting Congressional power seemed targeted primarily at civil rights legislation. Its Commerce Clause decisions limited Congressional authority

[23] 529 U.S. 598, 613.

to activities that were primarily "economic;" its Section 5 decisions struck directly at the principal Congressional power specifically designed to protect disadvantaged social groups. Politically, then, the Court's efforts to constrain Congress seemed to reflect the social and cultural strains of the new Republican coalition more than its free market and business-oriented aspects.

The Rehnquist Court's lack of sympathy with the federal civil rights laws was apparent. Immediately after the last Reagan appointee took his seat in 1988, it issued a stunning series of decisions that methodically narrowed the civil rights laws and restricted the remedies available for their violation. Its decisions struck most ruthlessly at affirmative action programs and employment discrimination law. Revealingly, when the Court dealt with affirmative action, it readily set aside its goal of insulating the states and imposed federal constitutional restrictions on their power to establish such programs.

The political significance of the Court's civil rights decisions was clear. Since 1968 Republicans had deployed the language of federalism to shape a "Southern strategy" that sought white votes by opposing civil rights activism and, in particular, affirmative action programs. The Reagan administration had followed the same course, intensifying the rhetoric, limiting enforcement of the civil rights laws, and – for the first time since *Brown* – bringing the federal government into court to oppose civil rights claims. Then, in 1988 Reagan's vice president, George Bush, was elected president after a campaign that promised "law and order" and featured a notorious television advertisement that was widely perceived to be racist. When the Democratic Congress attempted to pass legislation to counter the Rehnquist Court's civil rights decisions, Bush vetoed one bill and then compelled Congress to weaken another before signing it. The Rehnquist Court's civil rights decisions fit snugly with the Republican program.

Not surprisingly, the Rehnquist Court also followed the Reagan and Bush administrations in asserting national authority to enforce other values of the Republican coalition. Joining the effort to restrict tort claims against business, it readily displaced state law when federal rules served the purpose. Similarly, it expanded federal power under the Due Process and Takings Clauses, limited state power to enforce environmental regulations, and applied a broad First Amendment right of association to allow large private organizations to exclude homosexuals. Indeed, in decisions protecting private property, it again set state authority aside by imposing a federal constitutional duty on states to provide tax refunds in certain cases and, further, suggested that the Takings Clause might override state sovereign immunity and allow federal courts to order states to pay just compensation for certain regulatory actions.

Equally revealing, however, the Rehnquist Court also asserted federal authority for other purposes as well. It enforced First Amendment limits on governments at all levels, and it used the negative Commerce Clause and the doctrine of implied preemption to displace state law and expand the reach of much federal legislation. Indeed, during the last decade of the twentieth century the Rehnquist Court voided actions taken by states in 54.7 percent of the relevant cases it decided (111 of 203), an invalidation rate that was slightly higher than the Warren Court's rate of 53.6 percent in such cases during its sixteen years of existence (128 of 239). Most arresting, on occasion it even asserted national power in ways that conflicted with the values of the Republican coalition – though only over scathing dissents from the justices most fervently committed to those values. A slim, moderate majority, for example, preserved the federal constitutional right to an abortion and used the Fourteenth Amendment on occasion to protect both women and homosexuals.

Thus, in spite of its rhetoric, the Rehnquist Court did not simply defer to the states or check national power in all areas. Nor, of course, did it invariably honor the values of the Republican coalition. Rather, it did what its predecessors had done: it enforced its own peculiar version of federalism as determined by shifting coalitions among its justices, each of whom sought to meet the new and unexpected challenges that were generated by a changing and dynamic society. Like the liberal Courts that followed the New Deal, it reflected the variations and inconsistencies of its nine justices as well as the characteristic values that marked the shared jurisprudential ideas of its generally dominant majority. Indeed, as its frequent willingness to assert a muscular federal judicial power evidenced, the Rehnquist Court seemed driven as much by three substantive social goals as by any principled concern for the states. It sought to limit government regulatory authority, particularly in the areas of civil rights and environmental protection; it sought to restrict lawsuits against both business and governments; and it sought to shrink the rights of criminal defendants and prison inmates.

Beyond the specific social policies it served, the Rehnquist Court stood at century's end on three fundamental propositions about American federalism. One was that the power of Congress had become all encompassing and that limited constitutional government required the imposition of some kind of effective limits. The second was that the power of the national government over the states themselves had to be circumscribed severely. The last was that the "political safeguards" of federalism, whatever their efficacy in prior times, were no longer adequate to check federal power and protect state independence. All three propositions pointed to the same conclusion: the Court itself must enforce limits on national power.

However sound the Court's premises and conclusion, at century's end the fundamental – and operational – questions remained as they had been ever since 1789: What specific vision of federalism should be adopted? What specific limits should be enforced? Which governments – and which branches of government – should be subject to federalism's limitations? For what purposes, and in whose interests?

CONCLUSION: AMERICAN FEDERALISM AT CENTURY'S END

The twentieth century ended, almost literally, with *Bush v. Gore* (2000). There, the five-justice Rehnquist majority asserted a questionable jurisdiction to determine who would win the presidential election of 2000 and then, on sharply contested grounds, ruled in favor of Republican George W. Bush.

In the most dramatic manner possible the decision revealed two fundamental characteristics of American federalism. First, it demonstrated the extent to which the Supreme Court had moved to a position of institutional centrality in American government. In troubled elections in 1800 and 1824 the House of Representatives had followed constitutional provisions in determining who would be the next president. In the bitterly disputed election of 1876 a special extra-constitutional commission composed of five representatives each from the Senate, House, and Supreme Court had convened to resolve the same issue. Notwithstanding prior practice, constitutional clauses, and statutory provisions that suggested Congress or the state legislature as the authoritative institution, the Court stepped into the disputed election of 2000 and decided the outcome. Alone. No branch of Congress sought to intervene or participate, and no branch of state government moved to oppose. Deeply and closely divided, the nation accepted the Court's decisive role as practically necessary and constitutionally proper.

Bush v. Gore capped the Rehnquist Court's basic institutional achievement: confirming the evolution of the role and authority of the federal judiciary – and, particularly, the Supreme Court itself – that had occurred over the previous century or longer. That evolution had elevated the Court, with the lower judiciary as its wide-reaching arms, to a position of sweeping institutional authority. Repeatedly, the Rehnquist Court insisted that it was the final arbiter of the Constitution, and it brought new vitality to the Warren Court's pronouncement of judicial authority in *Cooper v. Aaron*. "It is the responsibility of this Court, not Congress, to define the substance of constitutional guarantees,"[24] it declared in shrinking Congressional power

---

[24] *Board of Trustees of the University of Alabama v. Garrett*, 531 U.S. 356, 365 (2001).

and asserting its own primacy under the Fourteenth Amendment. Not surprisingly, the Rehnquist Court exceeded the Warren Court in the rate at which it held federal as well as state actions unconstitutional.

Second, *Bush v. Gore* exemplified the shifting, contested, and instrumentalist nature of American federalism. Although some of the legal issues were novel, the decisive constitutional issue was stark: did authority to settle the matter reside at the state or national level? Unlike the many cases in which the ideology of the new Republican coalition coincided with deference to the states, in *Bush v. Gore* the two conflicted. The five-justice majority bloc rushed to trump state sovereignty with national power. "[T]he federal government is not bad but good," one of the majority justices had told a conservative audience some two decades earlier before ascending to the Court. "The trick is to use it wisely."[25] As the twentieth century ended, *Bush v. Gore* stood as a monument to the dynamics of American federalism, the system's paradigmatic case.

Thus, in spite of the many changes that reshaped the system and restructured its operations, American federalism closed the twentieth century much as it had begun it, as a somewhat disjointed and malleable, but nevertheless stable and democratic, system of government with the capacity to confront new problems and adapt to new conditions. A variety of social and cultural factors sustained its working order: a strikingly diverse population that enjoyed prosperity, education, and freedom; a variety of formal and informal checks that helped counter concentrated power; the ingrained social values, cultural habits, and institutional practices that constituted the nation's vital, if inherently human, rule of law; and a sustaining popular faith that the nation was committed, ultimately if quite imperfectly, to the lofty ideals it formally proclaimed. American federalism maintained itself in the twentieth century not because the Constitution set forth bright lines that defined state and federal power or because the Court articulated its own consistent and unchanging rules but because the system's complex operations were shaped and constrained by that social, cultural, and institutional base.

[25] Antonin Scalia, "The Two Faces of Federalism," *Harvard Journal of Law and Public Policy* 6 (1982), 19, 22.

5

THE LITIGATION REVOLUTION

LAWRENCE M. FRIEDMAN

This chapter examines myths and realities in the recent history of litigation in the United States. It looks at the actual figures – how many people are suing, and where are they suing; and are they suing more or suing less than they did in the past? It looks at the differences between federal and state litigation. It looks at litigation qualitatively as well as quantitatively: are the *kinds* of lawsuit changing, and in what ways? It examines the disputed question of the impact of litigation on society. It also examines alternatives to litigation and their popularity.

Litigation is controversial and has been controversial for more than a century. To say that a person or a society is "litigious" is not complimentary. This is true not only in this society, but in other societies as well. It is an interesting question why this should be the case. After all, the right to a "day in court" is one of the hallmarks of an open, democratic society. Modern societies insist that people must have access to justice (though they often fall far short of this ideal); why then is it considered bad if people take advantage of this right?

There is no easy answer. Lawsuits, however, are costly, take time, and exact a toll. They may be inefficient and overly technical. Charles Dickens' notorious description of a lawsuit in equity – the fictional *Jarndyce v. Jarndyce* in *Bleak House* – was an exaggeration, but it tapped into widespread feelings of dismay at the pathologies of litigation. On the whole, litigation is procedural and rule-bound, and the lay public has trouble grasping the reasons for some of the rules. In litigation, too, there are winners and losers, and the losers usually feel they have been wronged. Also, as we shall see, litigation has the capacity to upset powerful interests, and they can retaliate, and do retaliate, with influence and propaganda. For the last few decades of the twentieth century, a resourceful anti-litigation movement has been gathering strength, and it has achieved a measure of success.

Here are some of the main points of this chapter. First: Because Americans are accused of litigating too much, it is important to know the facts: how

175

much litigation *is* there? But litigation rates are extremely difficult to measure. This is so in part because it is hard to define litigation in a way that can command general agreement. But surely "litigation" implies some sort of dispute that is settled in court. If we take this as a rough definition, then – despite what many people think, including lawyers and judges – there is little hard evidence that litigation rates are rising or that people in the United States are more litigious than they have been at various periods in the past.

Second: There are many different types of lawsuits. Some types are more common than they were, and sometimes it is easy to see why. Without civil rights laws, for example, there would be little or no civil rights litigation; there would be little or no environmental litigation without environmental law. Yet at the same time, some types of litigation are, in fact, diminishing – debt collection, for example. There are probably more massive, giant lawsuits than before – huge antitrust cases or humongous clusters of lawsuits against asbestos companies – and this is part of what gives the impression of an "explosion" of litigation. And, in fact, the amount of money that businesses and individuals spend on legal services, including litigation, has risen quite sharply in the late twentieth century.

Third: Though evidence of a "litigation explosion" is slim, there is plenty of evidence of what we might call a "liability explosion," particularly in tort law. Old doctrinal barriers to lawsuits against doctors and hospitals, against manufacturers and municipalities, broke down in the twentieth century. Clearly, too, in such fields as civil rights and environmental law, as we have just noted, new legislation and new doctrines allowed or even encouraged litigation.

Fourth: Businesses – but not only businesses – have resented the liability explosion and have poured money into campaigns to curb what they consider excesses. Much of the population, as we have said, finds litigation odious. Some scholars have argued that litigation is hurting the country, economically and otherwise – although this is in fact a difficult case to prove. Politicians, particularly on the right, campaign against the "plague" of lawsuits. Many states have passed laws to try to curb litigation or to put a ceiling on the amounts plaintiffs can collect. And judges, scholars, and policymakers have led a search for detours around the court system. ADR (alternative dispute resolution) has flourished in the late twentieth century. The idea is to save time and money and to avoid litigation. Whether that has been the result, however, is unclear.

I. THE SO-CALLED LITIGATION EXPLOSION

One of those "facts" that the general public seems very sure about is that there is an explosion of litigation in this country. Americans love to sue, it is said, and they are suing each other in droves. What this would mean, first of all, is that in absolute terms there is a great deal of litigation, perhaps too much litigation, although there is no easy way to decide how much is too much. More specifically, to talk about an "explosion" implies change, and dramatic change at that: a vast increase in the number of lawsuits filed, in proportion to the population. The hypothesis would be, therefore, that in some period – the last half of the twentieth century, for example – litigation climbed at a very striking rate, compared to earlier times.

In fact, evidence for such an explosion is rather hard to come by. There are two basic problems. The first is the definition of "litigation." The second is counting the cases – figuring out the actual numbers. As to the first: not all the cases filed in court are necessarily litigation, if by litigation we mean actual disputes between two or more parties. Thousands and thousands of cases filed in court are not disputes at all. Petitions to change a name, to adopt a child, to open an estate, to end a marriage, to collect a debt, or to evict a tenant usually do not involve a dispute at all. To be sure, any of these situations can generate a dispute: a bitter custody battle, a contested will; a tenant can fight back against a landlord, a debtor against a creditor, a birth mother can oppose an adoption. But these are exceptions. So although a huge increase in uncontested divorces can give the *appearance* of a rise in litigation rates, if the bulk of the increase is in uncontested divorces, matters where no one disagrees and which never result in a trial, it would be misleading to count these cases as evidence for an explosion of lawsuits.

Gathering national data, that is, data for all the states, is particularly difficult. What courts should we measure? Do we include traffic courts? Small claims courts? If we restrict ourselves to trial courts above the level of traffic courts, small claims courts and the like – that is, to courts of general jurisdiction – there are issues of comparability: each state defines jurisdiction rather differently. There is, of course, no doubt that courts are heavily used in the United States (though, as we have said, not necessarily for litigation). The actual number of cases filed in all courts is impressive. There is little evidence, however, for any *recent* increase. In the state courts, according to one count, filings in 1984 totaled 85,796,447; in 2000 the total was 91,954,001. This represents an increase on the order of 7 percent, which, in the light of population growth, is hardly an increase at all. The bulk of these cases were traffic cases (no fewer than 55,742,240 in 2000). "Domestic" cases (mostly uncontested divorces) rose from 2,890,546 in 1984 to more than 5,000,000 in 2000. Other civil cases showed no growth at all. According to figures provided by the National Center for State Courts there were just over 15,000,000 filings in 1991 and just under 15,000,000 in 2000.

If we try to look at a broader time span, we run into serious data problems. Nationally, historical statistics hardly exist. Research even on individual jurisdictions is rather thin. Robert Percival and I studied two trial courts in California between 1870 and 1970, one rural (San Benito County), and one urban (Alameda County); we found no evidence for a litigation explosion, at least up to 1970. Both counties had higher rates of filing in 1970 compared to 1890, but the Alameda rate was in fact higher in 1910 than in 1970, and the rate in San Benito County actually declined between 1950 and 1970. Marc Galanter, reviewing the literature on litigation rates up to the early 1980s, came to the same general conclusion; so did Wayne McIntosh, who studied St. Louis data. John Stookey's analysis of the flow of litigation in Arizona in the twentieth century found great fluctuations, which were associated with the business cycle.

Figures from some states do suggest that civil court filings have risen in absolute numbers over various time periods. In Texas, for example, some 65,000 filings in 1938 in the basic trial courts had grown to about 235,000 in 1971. Of these, some 86,000 were divorce cases. In the year ending August 31, 1996, 373,000 civil cases were filed; 118,000 of these were divorce cases, and 90,000 were "other family law matters." In the twenty-five-year period from 1971 to 1996 tort claims had more than doubled, from about 17,000 to 43,000. On the other hand, some categories had declined (workers' compensation, for example), either absolutely or in proportion to the population, and on the whole the evidence from state courts is mixed. Moreover, there have clearly been periods in American history in which citizens resorted to the courts more often than they do today. In the colonial period, courts were cheap and ubiquitous and handled a wide variety of matters – administrative as well as judicial. The names of most adult citizens in a locality would appear in its court records each year for one reason or another – something that is certainly not true today. In rural areas in the nineteenth century, too, there is reason to think that courts were more generally used than they are today.

Of course, use is not the same as litigation. The hypothesis is not just a quantitative hypothesis; it also assumes an attitude, an aspect of legal culture, a psychological bent toward claims consciousness. It also assumes that institutions and doctrines exist that foster and stimulate this culture of suing. These qualitative matters, of course, are almost impossible to document and to test.

Some facts about American litigation are beyond dispute. For example, the *distribution* of litigation, between state and federal courts, changed over the course of the twentieth century. It remained true in 2000, as in 1900, that the overwhelming majority of lawsuits were filed in state courts. But the federal courts have grown in importance in the last hundred years. Their caseload spiraled upward steadily in the course of the twentieth century. In 1900, 12,230 cases were filed in federal district (trial) courts; in

1941, there were 38,477 such cases. By 1970, this number had grown to 87,321. Since then, the rise has been even more dramatic. Between 1950 and 1986, the increase in civil filings in federal court was up by 367 percent. In 1992, 224,747 cases were filed in the district courts; in 2001, 254,523. The increase is much greater than the increase in the number of people in the United States.

The figures on federal litigation should come as no surprise. The federal courts have always had jurisdiction over certain cases – for example, admiralty (maritime) cases – and they have always been open to certain "diversity" cases as well (cases in which, for example, a resident of Wyoming sues a resident of Maine). But most of the matters that concern the state courts – ordinary contract cases, tort cases, divorce, and family cases – were largely absent from federal courts, except in diversity situations. In the twentieth century, however, the federal government grew exponentially. It did more, regulated more, and monitored more behavior than ever before. Consider, for example, the increase in civil (and criminal) litigation due to the income tax law, which came into being by act of Congress in 1913. The Prohibition Amendment jammed federal courts and federal jails in the 1920s; the drug laws did the same later in the century. The New Deal of the 1930s added a whole host of regulatory statutes – for example, the Securities and Exchange Act and the National Labor Relations Act – all of which added somewhat to the stock of litigation. The great Civil Rights Law of 1964 and then the Voting Rights Law (1965) produced a rich harvest of lawsuits in federal court about sex and race discrimination. Before these laws, there were only a handful of civil rights cases. In 1971, however, 4,621 cases under these laws were filed, and in 1986, 17,776; by the end of the twentieth century, victims or alleged victims of age discrimination and discrimination against the handicapped added their numbers to the roster of plaintiffs in civil rights cases.

Bankruptcy filings are a special instance of growth. The Constitution gave Congress specific power to enact bankruptcy laws. At times, in the nineteenth century, Congress did so, but those laws were short-lived. Bankruptcy law really dates from a law of 1898 – frequently amended, added to, and tinkered with ever since (very notably in 2005, for example). In the first decade of the twentieth century, there were about 20,000 petitions for bankruptcy. During the depths of the Depression, the numbers rose greatly to more than 60,000, but World War II and prosperity drove the numbers down dramatically: there were 12,862 petitions in the year ending June 30, 1945. Then the figures started climbing again. By 1990, there were well over a million bankruptcy petitions. Of course, these range from little people over their heads in credit card debt to giant corporations that collapse like beached whales. All of them have to go through some sort of process in federal court, but few of these proceedings qualify as litigation in the sense that there are two sides or three sides or many sides at legal war with each other. Bankruptcy figures tell us something about the economy and, even more so, about legal culture. Clearly, bankruptcy (like divorce) has lost a great deal of stigma. It is also an index of a vigorous entrepreneurial culture, and a consumer culture in which deferring gratification plays little or no part.

One of the most striking aspects of modern American litigation is the use of the *class action*: a lawsuit brought on behalf of a whole group or class of people. The legal basis of the class action, in the federal courts, is Rule 23 of the Federal Rules of Civil Procedure, which in turn rested on an earlier Equity Rule (Rule 38). However, Rule 23 is much broader and more powerful than the older rule. The Federal Rules were adopted in 1938, and many of the states either swallowed them whole or revamped their own rules along similar lines. Amendments in 1966 to the Federal Rules strengthened the class action; and the class action has become more and more important since then. Its utility in certain types of case is obvious. If an airline overcharges a million customers $1 each, obviously none of them will bring a lawsuit; but a class action, aggregating all their claims, is another matter. The giant tort cases – for example, against asbestos companies – are sometimes aggregated as class actions. Some important civil rights cases are also pursued as class actions, such as the claim that some huge corporation discriminated against women. While federal cases are over-represented among class action suits, the majority of such cases (almost 60 percent) appear to be filed in state courts. There is also some evidence that the number of such cases has been growing in recent years.

Class actions are hard cases legally and are also hard to manage and decide. First, there is the issue of defining the class. Then there is the issue of keeping the members or potential members informed. People have to have the right to opt in or opt out. For the lawyers who have learned how to try these cases, they can be a gold mine. The members of the class might collect a few dollars each or some sort of certificate entitling them to a discount on the defendant's products, but the lawyers, who get a cut of the proceeds, can reap a succulent fee that might run into the millions. In some cases, the lawyers received more, in fees and expenses, than all of the members of the class put together. Businesses, on the whole, detest class actions and feel that many of them are scraped together by unscrupulous lawyers. The lawyers surely play an important role, and many class actions would be unthinkable without lawyer-entrepreneurs, who put the class together and run the show. But the lawyers are in many ways simply taking advantage of claims-conscious aspects of contemporary society.

The term "litigation" conjures up, in most peoples' minds, the image of a trial: a judge and jury, a courtroom with an American flag, rows of seats crowded with onlookers. Above all, it conveys the idea of a trial – a procedure in court. In fact, trials went into a steep decline in the late twentieth century, so much so, that Marc Galanter and other scholars began to talk about the "vanishing trial." Federal civil cases filed in 1962 ended up as actual trials in only 11.5 percent of the cases – which seems like very little; yet by 2002, the portion that ended up in an actual trial was astonishingly low – 1.8 percent. The same decline seems to be taking place in state courts.

Most cases, then, do not fit the popular image of the trial. The trial, in fact, has been vanishing for a long time. Jury trials have been declining for more than 150 years. Certain categories of case never went before a jury – cases involving family trusts, for example, or maritime cases – and even where there is a right to a jury, the parties can, if they wish, choose to waive a jury and let a judge handle the case by herself. Moreover, it would surprise people to know how little time litigation lawyers actually spend in a courtroom arguing a case. Mainly this is because, as we shall see, most cases settle, so that what litigation lawyers do has been described as "litigotion," that is, a process of bargaining and dickering, outside of court.

But it is also because the center of gravity in trials, even those that do not settle, has shifted dramatically to the pre-trial phase. Many of the witnesses are "deposed"; that is, their testimony is taken and recorded in a kind of mini-trial outside the courtroom. Also important is the rise of "discovery." Under Rule 34 of the Federal Rules, either side, for "good cause," can get a court order to "discover" any "documents, papers, books, accounts, letters, photographs, objects" from the other side, if they "constitute or contain evidence." Discovery, at its worst, permits wild and expensive fishing expeditions; at its best, it makes for more efficient trials, avoiding surprises and wasted energy. All of this pre-trial activity, however, by now perhaps outweighs the actual trial as an element in the life-course of litigation.

II. ADVERSARIAL LEGALISM

In the last section, we learned that there is little or no evidence of an explosion in litigation *rates*. Since the 1950s, however, the amount of money spent on litigation has probably ratcheted upward. At any rate, the amounts spent for legal services have grown tremendously – from 7 billion dollars in 1970, to 46 billion in 1985, to 82 billion in 1990, and 125 billion in 1999. Of course, the dollar has fallen in value, but in constant dollars current expenditures are about four times as great as they were in 1970. "Legal services" is a term far broader than litigation, but there is no doubt that litigation has shared in this harvest of expense.

Americans may not be litigious, on the whole, but no doubt there are some Americans who actually *are* litigious; and there are undoubtedly areas in which a fair number of Americans do not feel inhibited in the least from filing a lawsuit. The role of litigation in society may be more crucial than the naked figures suggest. Robert A. Kagan, for example, claims that there is something quite distinctive about the American way of law, which he calls "adversarial legalism." He defines this to mean a system of "policymaking, policy implementation, and dispute resolution by means of lawyer-dominated litigation." The United States, he claims, relies much more on adversarial legalism than other developed countries; other countries lean more heavily on "bureaucratic administration, or on discretionary judgment by experts or political authority." Moreover, litigation in the United States is different from litigation in most other societies; it is not "judge-dominated," but "lawyer-dominated."

Kagan is particularly harsh on the ways in which litigation can make a shambles of the administrative process. Litigation can make building an airport, or dredging a harbor, or constructing *any* major public work slow, costly, and sometimes perhaps even impossible. In some countries, administrative agencies have practically unfettered discretion. They make their decision, and that's the end of it. But American law grants much less discretion to the agencies. Partly because their discretion is limited, the agencies tend to rely much more on formal rules than their counterparts overseas. Also, the law allows private litigants, in a wide range of cases, to go to court in opposition to the work of the agencies. They can attack particular administrative decisions or the agency's rules themselves. The good news is that American regulatory law is more open to the public and more responsive to all sorts of interests than it is in other countries. The bad news is that it is often proceeds at a snail's pace and is often tangled in endless webs of litigation.

III. THE LIABILITY EXPLOSION

In many ways, the *subject matter* of litigation has altered quite dramatically in the course of the twentieth century. There is much more evidence of a liability explosion than of a litigation explosion. The most obvious case is in the law of torts. Tort law is a ragbag of causes of action for damages ("civil wrongs"), including such things as trespass to real estate, libel and slander, and invasion of privacy. But what has exploded is that segment of tort law that deals with personal injuries. Personal injuries – and personal injury law – first became a significant social and legal problem with the dawn of the Industrial Revolution. It takes machines, factories, locomotives, and the like to wreck the human body on a wholesale scale. In nineteenth-century tort law, however, a cluster of doctrines tended to protect "tortfeasors" (mostly corporations) from liability in whole classes of case. Most notorious was the so-called fellow servant rule. A worker could not recover for an injury on the job if the injury was due to the carelessness of a fellow worker. This rule effectively prevented most workers from collecting *any* damages for work accidents. Moreover, well into the twentieth century, juries were stingy with awards in tort cases (despite mythology to the contrary). Randolph Bergstrom's study of New York City in 1910 showed that plaintiffs won less than half of their personal injury cases and they collected, on the average, only $958.

The twentieth century proceeded to dismantle the restrictive rules of the nineteenth century, one by one. It opened the door to a huge expansion of liability for personal injuries. *Products liability* is itself largely a product of the twentieth century. A key case was *MacPherson v. Buick*, decided by the New York Court of Appeals in 1916. Benjamin Cardozo wrote the majority opinion. The plaintiff bought a Buick car; a wooden wheel crumbled while he was driving, and MacPherson was injured. He sued the Buick Motor Company. What stood in his way was an old doctrine, the doctrine of "privity," which insisted that a plaintiff generally had to sue whoever sold him the product, not the ultimate manufacturer. Cardozo's opinion undermined the rule totally – though he never said so directly – and MacPherson won his case. Clearly, the privity doctrine made no sense in the age of mass-produced, advertised goods. Hence, it is no surprise that other courts followed Cardozo's lead and buried the privity doctrine once and for all.

The fellow servant rule also came to an inglorious end. The Federal Employers' Liability Act (1906) got rid of it for railroad workers. The Supreme Court struck down this statute, but Congress passed a new version in 1908, and this one the Court upheld. In 1920, maritime workers got the same protection. In the states, however, what replaced the fellow servant rule was the system of *workers' compensation*. Basically, the compensation laws abolished virtually *all* tort actions for industrial accidents and replaced them with a guaranteed (but limited) scheme of payment. Fault, negligence, and other considerations were brushed aside. If you were injured on the job, if you had an accident at work, you had the right to claim compensation. By 1920, almost all of the states had a workers' compensation law; the last straggler, Mississippi, joined the other states in 1948. The fifty state statutes cover the overwhelming majority of the working people of the country.

Workers' compensation laws were supposed to get rid of the massive amount of litigation over industrial accidents. They were supposed to change the orientation of tort law dramatically, from concern with individual fault to a more social theory of causation and, in the process, to create a more efficient and fairer system. Beyond a doubt, the laws were successful in getting rid of at least *some* potential litigation. But this branch of the law has had its own version of the liability explosion. The typical workers' compensation law purports to cover accidents and injuries "arising out of

and in the course of employment" (these words were borrowed from an earlier British statute of 1897). The core meaning of the phrase seems obvious:
the injury has to be something that happened during work hours and has
to be connected somehow with the job. But the courts have expanded the
meaning of these terms enormously. Behind the passage of the statutes was
a concrete, specific social problem, the classic industrial accident: thousands
of lives were sacrificed on the altar of production every year, and the harvest
of broken bones, lost limbs, blinded eyes, and wrecked lives ran into the
tens of thousands every year. The underlying image was the factory, railroad yard, or mine; the loud noise of heavy machinery; and dangerous, dirty
work in dirty and dangerous environments. Indeed, the original Oklahoma
compensation law (enacted in 1915) was confined to workers in "hazardous
occupations"; the law specifically excluded white collar workers, among
others. And most statutes, at first, were about *accidents* quite literally: if the
job made the worker sick, or exposed her to harmful chemicals, or if she
simply wore out over the years because of work, there was no claim and no
coverage.

Courts and legislatures moved hand in hand to expand the scope of the
compensation laws. Recovery for occupational diseases was added to most
statutes; New Jersey, for example, in 1949, amended its law to include
"diseases" that "are due to causes and conditions . . . characteristic of . . . a
particular trade, occupation, process, or employment." Workers' compensation litigation did its part. Thus, a secretary who slipped and fell in the
company restroom or its cafeteria, a worker injured at a company picnic, a
traveling salesmen burned in a fire at a motel – courts held that plaintiffs of
this sort were entitled to recover. Dozens of cases wrestled with the issue of
heart attacks on the job. Then came an epidemic of psychological claims –
claims that the job had thrown A into deep depression, or had driven B
crazy, or that getting fired pushed C's mental condition over the brink.
These claims, toward the end of the twentieth century, became so numerous and costly that businesses panicked and demanded relief. A number of
states, including California, passed laws radically cutting back on psychological claims. Under the new California statute, no worker could recover for
"psychiatric injury" if it was caused by a "lawful, nondiscriminatory, good
faith personnel action." The statute seemed to make a difference. Workers'
compensation, which cost $11 billion in California in 1993, dropped to
$8 billion two years later. But "reform" of workers' compensation was still
on the agenda at the beginning of the twenty-first century in California. It
was still considered too lenient, too worker-friendly, too hostile to business.
Labor of course disagreed.

The courts and the legislatures have modified other doctrines that stood
in the way of tort claims. In the nineteenth century, one of the most powerful was the doctrine of contributory negligence. The plaintiff not only had

to prove the defendant was negligent; she also had to be totally free of negligence herself. If she had displayed even the tiniest degree of carelessness, there could be no recovery at all. In 1908, the Federal Employers' Liability Act abolished the doctrine for railroad workers. A jury was entitled to "diminish" damages "in proportion to the amount of [the worker's] negligence," but the claim remained valid. This was essentially what came to be called comparative negligence. The idea made its way slowly in the states; it was still a minority view in the 1960s, but by the end of the century, almost all of the states had some version or other of this new rule. In some, a plaintiff who is, say, 80 percent at fault can still sue a negligent defendant, collecting 20 percent of the damages. In other states, the plaintiff wins if he was not *as* negligent as the defendant. In either case, the traditional rule has lost most of its bite.

The main engine of the liability explosion, doctrinally speaking, was through expansion of the *concept* of negligence. "Strict" liability – that is, holding a defendant liable without the necessity of showing fault – has struggled for a place in the doctrinal world. It is most clearly recognized for "abnormally dangerous activities," like storing or using dynamite or other explosives in residential areas. But on the operating level, in the course of ordinary litigation, the basic change that expanded the law of torts was less a change in doctrine than a change in attitudes. Judges and juries seemed more willing to listen sympathetically to the stories plaintiffs (and their lawyers) told. The law reflected, as usual, popular ideas of right and wrong, and these were (apparently) changing. The law also reflected the growth of insurance and the feeling of judges and juries that, in most cases, the insurance company would actually do the paying, not the nominal defendant. This was particularly important in cases of automobile accidents. After all, jurors and judges were drivers themselves and knew or thought they knew that almost everybody carried accident insurance.

Medical malpractice was another growth area in tort law. It had, of course, always been the case that a doctor (like anybody else) was liable for his acts of negligence. But malpractice cases were never common in the nineteenth century or well into the twentieth century. In Randolph Bergstrom's study of New York courts in 1910, only about 1 percent of the tort cases were cases of malpractice. After 1950, the number of such cases grew rather strikingly: in San Francisco County, between 1959 and 1980, they amounted to 7 percent of all the civil trials. Most plaintiffs lost their cases. Neil Vidmar's study of malpractice cases in North Carolina in the 1980s found that half the malpractice cases were settled, another 40 percent were dropped or otherwise terminated, and doctors won about 80 percent of the cases. In some places plaintiffs did better, but in the nation as a whole, the win rate for plaintiffs in malpractice cases was less than three cases in ten.

Nevertheless, enough plaintiffs won and there was enough bad publicity to frighten the country's doctors half to death. Doctors claimed the plague of lawsuits forced them to practice "defensive medicine" (or drove them, through higher insurance premiums, out of the business altogether). The doctrine of "informed consent," which dates from the late 1950s, made matters worse (for the doctors). If a doctor did not tell the patient enough about the risks and side effects of some medical procedure, then the patient had not really given her "informed consent" to the procedure and could sue the doctor if something went wrong, or if the risk or side effect turned up.

A small but exceedingly important group of lawsuits have arisen out of what has been called mass toxic torts. In the typical auto accident cases there are one, or two, or a handful of victims. Even train wrecks and plane crashes have limited numbers of victims. But there are incidents and situations in which the number of victims can run into the thousands, or millions. This has been the case with asbestos litigation. The first case against the asbestos companies was decided in the early 1970s. By the middle 1980s, there were more than 30,000 claims, brought by men and women who had sickened or died after exposure to asbestos. The number of claims soon rose to over 100,000 and even higher, and the amounts involved were so great that the asbestos industry essentially ceased to exist.

Some of these mass toxic torts cases were class actions, and they were exceedingly complex, factually, legally, and procedurally. In some of them, there was a serious question whether the companies should have been liable at all. Agent Orange was a herbicide sprayed over Vietnam to clear the jungle. Vietnam veterans by the thousands blamed Agent Orange for birth defects in their children, cancer, and many other harms. The scientific evidence was, to say the least, cloudy. Lawsuits against the A. H. Robins Company, which manufactured an intrauterine device, the Dalkon Shield, drove that company into the sheltering arms of the bankruptcy court. Tobacco and firearms companies are recent objects of mega-lawsuits, so far with indifferent success, but the potential impact is enormous. Fast-food restaurants that sell junk food may be next in line.

A liability explosion, of course, is not the same as a litigation explosion; the older studies found little evidence, as we have seen, for a litigation explosion, including the law of torts; and this continues to be the case. In a study of ten states published in 2001, Jeff Yates and associates found a modest growth between 1975 and 1995 in tort filings; but in three of the states there had actually been a decline. Nor have all forms of litigation shared in the explosion of liability. Some issues of family law have become, apparently, more common and more heavily contested. "No-fault" removed the *issue* of divorce (and the argument over grounds for divorce) from the scene, but custody and property disputes remain. They are probably more common sources of litigation than earlier in the twentieth century. As we noted, civil rights litigation has been a growth area. All of the great civil rights laws of the last half of the twentieth century allow private citizens, under certain circumstances, to bring lawsuits. The numbers are fairly large, as we have seen, but, as in the case of tort law, it is not the quantity but the subject matter and the scale and scope of the cases that have been controversial. Civil rights laws have put new burdens on business and branches of government, have required more red tape and record-keeping, and have, in many cases, engendered a fair amount of resentment. This is also true of some environmental litigation. The number of lawsuits during the year that try to use environmental protection laws to fight plans or policies is not large, but these can be very significant cases. Some of them are attempts to scuttle major projects; some raise issues that are politically and economically sensitive. Filing a lawsuit to stop a huge dam on behalf of some tiny fish, or a lawsuit that puts the jobs of lumberjacks at risk, for the sake of an endangered owl, is asking for trouble and for headlines, passion, and countermoves.

In fact, there are many kinds of litigation that have not shared at all in the richness of the twentieth-century docket. Some, such as disputes over title to real estate, have been in deep decline in the twentieth century. Debt collection cases that in the nineteenth century made up an appreciable percentage of filed cases in trial courts, have also lost ground in the twentieth century, as Robert Kagan has shown. In the St. Louis Circuit Court, such cases at one time in the nineteenth century were a large part of the docket, but by 1970, they amounted to less than 5 percent. Kagan feels that the dominant position of "large, bureaucratized, legal sophisticated institutions," such as banks and department stores, helps account for the decline. Title to land is now regularized and governed by title insurance companies; there are fewer reasons to fight over land titles. In the nineteenth century, when banks and money supplies were wobbly and unreliable, people often paid their debts with personal instruments, and they tried to get wealthy or reputable people to endorse these instruments and guarantee their credit. These endorsements produced a lot of lawsuits when endorsers tried to wriggle out of payment, but this kind of case is now exceedingly rare. No-fault divorce put an end to contested divorces (though not, of course, to disputes over children and property). The docket, in short, shifts over the years, as old problems move off the stage and new ones come forward.

IV. THE CULTURE OF LITIGATION

It is widely believed that Americans are litigious. They are supposed to be "claims-conscious" or perhaps even quarrelsome. This may be a matter of structure – Robert Kagan's adversarial legalism depends heavily on such structural features as federalism, decentralization, and the common law tradition. But it is also felt to be a statement about culture or personality. This kind of idea is very hard to examine rigorously. It is true, though, that people *think* of Americans as litigious. And the *perceived* litigation rates are perhaps almost as important as the (unknown) real rates. There is only weak evidence of an explosion in litigation rates, as we have said, but most people are unaware of the facts. Millions of people – including lawyers and judges – are firmly convinced that Americans sue at the drop of a hat and that our society is incurably addicted to lawsuits. This belief is fed by the urban legends and newspaper horror stories that describe, in gory detail, the excesses of litigation and the hunger of litigants for money they do not deserve. This belief has consequences. It has fueled a political and legal backlash that I describe shortly. The "victims" of litigation – doctors, big businesses, municipalities – are only too willing to take advantage of a popular mood for reform. To be sure, some debates and disputes about litigation are technical and professional; the public hardly knows anything about the pathologies, such as they are, of class action cases or the assumed need to control "fishing expeditions" (abuse of the discovery process) that cost litigants money and time. But public opinion does seem to provide *general* support for the movement to curb or control litigation.

In fact, the vast majority of Americans have not sued anybody and have no plans to do so. Many Americans agree that litigation is messy and undesirable. Many Americans think badly of people who do litigate – this was even the case before the tort reform movement. David Engel, for example, studied attitudes in a rural county in Illinois. He found that many people resented tort litigants. The people in this county considered tort plaintiffs greedy and dishonest, people who wanted something for nothing. Shrill newspaper accounts of wild, irrational lawsuits are taken as evidence that Americans really are litigious. One famous example was the old woman who spilled hot coffee on herself and sued the living daylights out of McDonald's; she collected an enormous sum of money because of what most readers assumed was her own careless behavior. Another bogeyman was the (fictional) burglar who supposedly had the gall to sue after he suffered an injury during the course of his burgling. In fact, these horror stories are evidence of something that is almost the opposite of litigiousness: a pervasive American belief that litigation is sometimes or often a racket.

"Litigious," if it means anything, must mean that Americans are claims-conscious or prone to litigate, not in absolute terms but comparatively: either compared to the past or compared to other countries and cultures. But it is very difficult to make these comparisons. The historical comparisons are especially troublesome, because the figures are simply not available.

Undoubtedly, however, there have been cultural changes that do have an impact on litigation. In the nineteenth century, there was no welfare state, very little insurance against liability except for marine insurance and (business) fire insurance, and life was precarious in terms of both health and finances. In the twentieth century, modern medicine, the welfare state, and widespread use of insurance may have led to what I have called a culture of "total justice." This is the expectation that compensation is due and by rights ought to come from some source or other, when calamity occurs. If other sources fail, there is always litigation.

There is no question that litigation is an important social phenomenon in the United States, quite apart from whether people are or are not litigious. Whether or not *rates* of litigation rise, it may well be that the cases that *are* litigated are more important or that a small subset of lawsuits have enormous social or economic importance. In fact, more and more money is spent in the United States on lawyers and lawyering; businesses, governments, and large institutions shell out billions of dollars, and a good deal of this goes into litigation. Corporations are more and more the main litigators, and they tend to win their cases.

The litigation habit, whether myth or reality, has in any event been the target of enormous criticism. Litigation has been accused of many sins. One of them is harming the economy, and this accusation has particularly fueled the reform campaign against tort litigation. But the true impact of litigation on American society is almost impossible to measure. Economists have attempted to assess the costs of litigation – not only the amounts spent on lawyers and lawsuits, but the net loss to the economy from "excess" litigation. The benefit side is much more difficult to measure. Nobody would choose, in a Utopian society, to use litigation as a tool for social reform. But under certain circumstances, there is no alternative. Consider, for example, the civil rights movement. African Americans were effectively shut out of political power in the Southern states. They did not vote, hold office, or serve on juries; there were no African American sheriffs, police, or judges and almost no African American lawyers. Southern senators were all powerful in the Senate and blocked any hope of even the mildest civil rights legislation. The federal courts came to seem like the only hope. The NAACP and other civil rights organizations, therefore, pursued a litigation strategy – and the strategy seemed to pay off.

This is by no means the only example in which litigation seemed to produce social change, although the actual impact is often problematic and can be (and is) debated. On the surface, the case seems sometimes fairly clear. To take one example, lawsuits in the federal courts accused some states of running archaic and brutal prison systems; some of these lawsuits ended up with strong court orders, telling the states to produce reforms. Lawsuits shook up the world of school finance. Lawsuits have blocked or delayed or killed many projects or proposals, from airports to dams to logging operations. Litigation is a way to probe weaknesses in the structure and scale of the welfare-regulatory state. Litigation is like a siege engine, which exploits soft spots in a wall of resistance. Kagan, who is unsparing in his criticism of some aspects of "adversarial legalism," is quite explicit that the system does produce some benefits.

Also, there are places where litigation seems to be badly needed. Kagan points out that, in the 1970s and 1980s, Dutch workers had five to ten times the rate of asbestos-related diseases as the United States. But fewer than *ten* lawsuits were filed in the Netherlands. By 1991 the number of lawsuits filed in the United States for asbestos-based torts, was, as we have seen, incomparably greater – perhaps almost 200,000. Why the difference? Because, Kagan argues, disabled Dutch workers will receive medical care and generous benefits for life. Welfare laws already provided for the Dutch a level of care that only a lawsuit could accomplish in the United States. The Dutch system was clearly more efficient than the American non-system. In the United States, the tort system filled the gap; but it was painfully slow and incredibly wasteful. Each lawsuit reached its own idiosyncratic result. The results of class action cases varied legally and financially. And up to two-thirds of the money recovered – in settlements and trials – ended up in the hands of lawyers and other professionals, rather than in the hands of victims and their families.

For all the reasons mentioned – because the results of tort litigation were chaotic, wasteful, and inconsistent and because they seemed so damaging to important interests – a strong campaign emerged, particularly in the last third of the twentieth century, to put limits on litigation. It was directed mostly against tort litigation.

There had been earlier campaigns. In the first part of the twentieth century, there were campaigns against "ambulance chasers": personal injury lawyers and their "runners," who, it was said, raced to the scene of an accident, or the hospital, or the home of the victim to sign the victim up as a client. In 1928, there was a major investigation of ambulance chasing in New York City. Jury trials for tort cases had risen dramatically; and the increase was blamed on the personal injury lawyers. The investigation made headlines and ended up recommending disciplinary proceedings against some seventy-four lawyers who were guilty of turning legal practice into a dirty and disreputable business. Nothing was said about the fact that businesses also chased ambulances; that is, they sent claims adjusters out in a race with the lawyers, trying to induce victims to sign releases in exchange for small settlements. In the end, only a few lawyers were disciplined.

Filings, however, dropped dramatically in New York, though probably less because of the investigation than because of a huge increase in filing fees.

In the 1970s, businesses, stung by fears and threats of litigation, mustered as much political muscle as they could in the battle to limit tort lawsuits. (Another focus has been on stockholder suits against corporations). The anti-tort campaign has made its mark on legislation. The Republican Party, in particular, made tort reform one of its promises. Litigation, especially tort litigation, was supposed to be damaging the economy. Japan and Europe – it was said – were getting an edge over the United States. Lawyers were parasites and trouble-makers whose activities were sapping the strength of the country, costing money and jobs.

In the 1970s, doctors were important figures in the movement to do some-thing about the "flood" of litigation. Many doctors faced sharply increased rates for insurance against malpractice. This created a sense of crisis in the profession. Many in the profession put the blame squarely on tort litigation. From 1975 to 1978 there was a wave of legislation aimed at alleviating the malpractice "crisis" and other problems thought to come from tort liti-gation. No fewer than twenty states put limits on contingent fees; some fourteen states put caps on money damages. In the mid-1980s, a new wave of reform – also stimulated by increases in liability insurance – led to caps in sixteen states on "pain and suffering"; more than half the states also put limits on punitive damages. Almost every state, in fact, passed some sort of legislation with the aim of reform tort litigation and curbing the assumed avalanche of lawsuits.

What has been the impact of this wave of reform? Litigation rates, in tort suits, do seem to be dropping. Is this because of the new laws against tort cases? To a degree, perhaps. More powerful, according to some studies, has been the *indirect* impact. The powerful campaign against tort litigation has had an impact on the general public. It has affected, in other words, the pool of people from which juries are chosen. And if juries become tougher, then insurance companies also get tough in bargaining and negotiation because they are less fearful of what juries might do if the case were to go to trial. And personal injury lawyers, whose income is on the line, will take fewer marginal cases and settle other cases for much less money than before in this kind of litigation climate. Stephen Daniels and Joanne Martin examined the evidence for Texas and found this to be the case. Tort filings in Texas trial courts dropped by almost 25 percent between 1995 and 2000: tougher juries led to tougher insurance companies, leading in turn to changes in the behavior of the lawyers. And the income of at least some litigation lawyers had also been in decline.

V. ALTERNATIVE DISPUTE RESOLUTION

No study of litigation would be complete or realistic without attention to some of the alternatives to litigation. Litigation is obviously a last resort. Of the thousands and thousands of problems that *might* give rise to a lawsuit, only a tiny fraction actually do. Lawsuits are expensive and troublesome. Individuals and businesses, for the most part, try to avoid them.

There have been a few attempts to investigate the actual life-cycle of disputes. The most notable has been the Wisconsin study of civil litigation carried out in the 1970s. An accident occurs; a woman slips on the sidewalk and breaks a bone. The woman might, for example, blame only herself. For those cases where she blames somebody else, in only a fraction of occurrences does the blame turn into a *claim*. And many claims – most claims – never go very far; they are dropped or settled. Few of these claims turn into a *dispute*, and fewer still of these disputes turn into lawsuits. The process can be pictured as a kind of pyramid: incidents are at the base, and the pyramid gets narrower and narrower toward the top; the surviving claims that end up in court are relatively rare events. For the population sampled, only fifty court filings resulted from every one thousand grievances. There was, however, considerable variation, depending on the type of case: only 38 of every 1,000 tort grievances and a tiny 8 of 1,000 discrimination grievances resulted in the filing of a lawsuit; but "post-divorce" grievances (disputes over child custody or over the question of dividing up property) were much more litigation-prone: almost half of them went the whole route and ended up in court. A study of aviation accident litigation showed an even more dramatic recourse to courts. In 1970–76, 64 percent of the claims arising out of aviation accidents (and a claim was filed for virtually every victim) turned into a lawsuit, and for fatal cases between 1979 and 1982, an astonishing 84 percent went to court.

It is more common to settle a case out of court than to pursue it to the bitter end. Most settlements are informal, arranged by the parties or their lawyers. *Mediation* is a more formal method of settling a dispute. A mediator is a third party who works with the parties in dispute and tries to help them find a way to settle it. The mediator has no power to impose a solution; if the parties decide to give some third party that power – the authority to make an actual decision and to make it stick – we call that third party an *arbitrator*. Arbitration and mediation are old substitutes for litigation, and they continued to be very popular in the twentieth century and into the twenty-first. With regard to arbitration, there are many legal questions: what, for example, is the legal impact of an arbitrator's decision? Under what conditions is it absolutely binding? Must a court follow it, if the losing party tries to shift the dispute into the courtroom? More and more contracts contain an arbitration clause – the parties promise to arbitrate and not to go to court. Is such a promise enforceable? These clauses are not politically and economically neutral; they are favorites of the business community, but not so popular with individuals, especially workers.

There has also been a movement, some of it coming from within the legal profession itself, to develop methods and procedures of alternative dispute resolution (ADR). As a movement, ADR rose to prominence in the 1970s. A conference in St. Paul, Minnesota, in 1976, focused on "Popular Dissatisfaction with the Administration of Justice" (echoing the title of a famous talk given by Roscoe Pound seventy years earlier). The conference promoted the idea of quicker, more efficient, "alternative" justice. The Civil Justice Reform Act of 1990 put a kind of federal stamp of approval on ADR; this law asked all federal district courts to adopt a "civil justice expense and delay reduction plan," including methods of ADR. The Administrative Dispute Resolution Act, passed by Congress in 1996, was intended to encourage ADR in the handling of administrative disputes. The Act begins with certain "findings": that "administrative proceedings" were too "formal, costly, and lengthy" and that ADR could offer a "prompt, expert, and inexpensive means of resolving disputes as an alternative to litigation." The act applies to all federal agencies; and it imposes on these agencies the duty to "adopt a policy that addresses the use of alternative means of dispute resolution and case management." There have been parallel developments in the various states.

The ADR idea, like arbitration, is quite attractive. Nobody likes the *idea* of litigation, except for the people (trial lawyers, mostly) who make their living out of litigation. For almost everybody else, it is undesirable – sometimes a necessary evil, sometimes very beneficial to society, but still it is regrettable if litigation is the only way to achieve some desirable goal. Business people find litigation particularly obnoxious for all sorts of reasons – cost and disruption among them. Business people appreciate procedures that are quick, simple, and private. A fair number of private companies are geared up to provide ADR, for a price. In California, under a program nicknamed "Rent-A-Judge," parties can choose to have their own, private trial, with a private "judge," who often is (in fact) a retired judge.

Roughly, formal alternatives fall into four categories – mediation, arbitration, private ADR, and court-annexed ADR; that is ADR run and managed by the regular courts. Whether all of these ADR methods have the virtues claimed for them is another story. There is some evidence that at least some of these methods save very little in the way of time and effort.

Litigation, even when replaced by alternatives, is never totally irrelevant. Bargaining and negotiation often turn on how litigation would turn out – or, at any rate, on the way in which lawyers and potential litigators assess the probabilities and how they read the law. This is what Robert Mnookin and Lewis Kornhauser have called "bargaining in the shadow of the law." They coined this phrase in the course of an article about negotiation in divorce cases. Somewhat earlier, H. Laurence Ross had described the same process in his study of settlements in auto accident cases. Litigation no doubt casts a long shadow. But, as Ross makes clear, the "shadow" of the law is often a distorted one. The law itself is complex and subtle and the outcome of litigation never quite predictable. Negotiation, then, often proceeds on the bases of guesses or hopes, leavened by social norms that may or may not coincide with the operating norms of the legal system. Moreover, it is not really the shadow of the law that concerns the parties so much as the shadow of adjudication – the costs and troubles of going to court.

CONCLUSION

This chapter has examined the ebb and flow of litigation in the twentieth century. Reality is complex and, in a way, almost contradictory. The country spends a lot more time and money on legal services, including litigation, than at the beginning of the century. But it appears that the actual rate of litigation has not exploded the way most people think. Nor is there strong evidence that Americans are, by nature, litigious.

But the clouds of smoke that pour out of the debates over lawsuits do suggest that somewhere, somehow, there is a fire. Indeed, in the world of litigation, there have been important *qualitative* changes. New forms of action have arisen. Liability in tort law has indeed exploded, so much so as to generate a backlash. "Adversarial legalism" is a reality in administrative law. Courts are powerful and exercise their power when they wish to and when litigants press them to. The early twentieth century never dreamed of so-called mass toxic torts.

Litigation does not mean, necessarily, trials, which have, on the whole, decreased in the latter part of the twentieth century. More and more of the work of settling disputes gets done outside of court – in the settlement process, in the back- and-forth dance of discovery and other forms of pre-trial process, and through diversion to the various forms of ADR. Litigation will never disappear, but it will continue, no doubt, to evolve.

6

CRIMINAL JUSTICE IN THE UNITED STATES

MICHAEL WILLRICH

Anyone vaguely familiar with the career of American criminal justice in the twentieth century knows this story does not have a happy ending. A liberal democracy that incarcerates more of its people per capita than any other nation on the planet cannot take pride in its crime policies; nor have those policies, like a revolver in the nightstand, made Americans feel particularly secure. Criminal justice – like crime itself – is often assumed to be an intractable social problem, timeless and impervious to reform. Who among us can imagine modern society without the prison? But criminal justice is inescapably the product of history. The historical trajectory of American criminal justice no longer seems as certain or progressive as it once did. When American criminology was still in its infancy as a scientific discipline, around the turn of the twentieth century, practitioners told the story of punishment in uniformly whiggish terms: a steady march toward ever more humane, modern methods. The past century in criminal justice now looks far otherwise: a record of abrupt shifts, stark continuities, and stunning reversals.

The twentieth century opened with a dramatic transformation in the ideas and institutions of American criminal justice. The United States was in the throes of industrial expansion, an era of rapid urbanization and mass immigration that had already turned a predominantly agrarian country into the world's most productive industrial economy. To regulate the harshest human consequences of industrial capitalism, social reformers, lawmakers, and innovative government officials began to put together the pieces of an administrative-welfare state. They built this "modern" interventionist state from old and new materials, assuring that long-established criminal justice institutions – codes, police, courts, jails, prisons – would not be displaced by the new-fangled administrative agencies and welfare bureaus. In fact, criminal justice reform was at the cutting edge of institutional change. In the industrial cities, which seemed overrun with poverty and crime, a broad cross-section of people – social activists, social scientists,

legal academics, lawyers, lawmakers, judges, and criminologists – strove
to redefine criminal justice. They rejected traditional retributivism and to
some degree punishment itself, as barbaric, and they regarded the whole
notion of individual responsibility with a distinctly modern skepticism.

For these thinkers and reformers, the rising social science disciplines
confirmed what right-thinking Americans already knew from experience:
in an urban industrial nation, the traditional concept of the individual as a
"moral free agent" no longer made much sense. Crime had its causal origins
not in the moral free will of the autonomous individual, but in "social"
conditions that determined human behavior: bad heredity, poverty, broken
homes, and the urban environment. The reformers sought to remake criminal justice institutions into instruments for the therapeutic treatment of
criminals, the production of useful social knowledge, and the governance
of society as a whole. The new social conception of crime inspired institutional innovations – the juvenile court, the indeterminate sentence and
parole, probation, even eugenics-inspired laws to sterilize "mental defec-
tives." All of these experiments aimed to prevent crime and to reduce the
centrality of the prison to the American way of justice.

A century later, those Progressive era ideas and institutions were being
deemed a failure and slated for destruction. The last quarter of the twentieth century brought domestic deindustrialization, sharply rising economic
inequality, and sustained political attacks on the welfare state. Retributivism and a rhetoric of "personal responsibility" returned. Politicians
declared a "war on crime." Lawmakers enacted mandatory minimum sentencing laws that reined in judicial discretion and ensured that convicts
spent much more time behind bars. The prison system, whose future seemed
uncertain a century before, experienced a population explosion, surging
from the 500,000 prisoners in the system on any given day in 1980 to
1.8 million prisoners in 2000. (The entire European Union had some
300,000 people behind bars that year.) In many American states, spending
on corrections grew faster than any other item in the budget, and private
corporations won lucrative contracts to build and run prisons. Progressive
era reformers and 1960s liberals had viewed criminal justice institutions
as means for rehabilitating offenders of all nationalities and races. At the
end of the century that optimism had withered. In 1996 African Americans
were incarcerated at a rate *eight times* that for whites.[1]

In this chapter I offer an interpretive history of American criminal justice
since 1920. Two central themes run though it. First, in criminal justice, as
in other areas of American political development, institutions and political

[1] Figures are from John Irwin et al., "America's One Million Nonviolent Prisoners," *Social Justice* 27 (2000), 135–47.

structures matter a great deal more than historians usually give them credit for. The distinctive institutional complexity and decentralized constitutional structure of the American polity are crucial to the story of criminal justice. In fact, to a significant degree, they *are* the story. Second, criminal justice institutions, which occupy little more than a sidebar in most U.S. history textbooks, belong at the center of American historical analysis. Defending society from crime and bringing criminals to justice – vast enterprises in their own right – are not the full measure of criminal justice. Criminal justice is an extremely complex and far-reaching field of political ideas and governmental practices that has profoundly affected the development of law, constitutionalism, liberalism, and the modern state. To be sure, the historical development of criminal justice institutions has *reflected* broader social, cultural, and political changes. But it has also *shaped* them.

A few preliminary words about each of these themes. Compared to those in other Western nations, criminal justice institutions in the United States are sprawling and decentralized. They constitute a system only in a tenuous sense. The widespread usage of that familiar term – "criminal justice system" – was one of the achievements of 1960s liberals, who supported the efforts of the U.S. Supreme Court to impose greater national uniformity in procedural rights and advocated a greater role for the federal government in crime prevention. In reality, the United States has nothing to compare with Great Britain's Home Office – a central authority charged with setting crime policy and overseeing criminal justice institutions for the entire nation. In America, the public institutions of lawmaking bodies, police forces, prosecutors offices, courts, jails, and prisons operate at the local, state, and federal levels. The shifting boundaries of federalism – rooted in the Constitution, legislation, and judicial rulings – determine the scope of authority and power in each domain. This distinctively American lack of centralized policy coordination has important consequences. It leaves the nation's criminal justice institutions exceptionally vulnerable to the influences of partisan politics, reform movements, local customs and norms, and policymaking through litigation. These institutional arrangements help explain the contradictory trends in criminal justice that have confused students of history and frustrated Americans on both the political left and right. During the 1970s, for example, litigation in the federal courts greatly expanded the rights of prisoners, even as the pressure of popular partisan politics spurred lawmakers to enact new "tough on crime" policies. All of this institutional complexity makes telling the story of criminal justice in modern America a daunting task. But without an appreciation of institutional arrangements that story is incomprehensible.

Throughout the twentieth century, criminal justice was a central – at times, *the* central – problem of liberal governance in the United States.

Its historical trajectory shaped and was shaped by the critical issues of liberal politics and state formation: the growth of the administrative-welfare state, the changing conceptions of individual freedom and responsibility that redefined liberalism, the related struggles over the legitimate scope of government intervention, and the politics of social and cultural pluralism. Conceiving of criminal justice in these explicitly political terms puts criminal justice institutions at the heart of central issues in twentieth-century history. Changing conceptions of criminal responsibility informed public perceptions of what the state could and should do to alleviate poverty and inequality. Criminal justice institutions such as juvenile courts were proving grounds for emerging techniques of bureaucratic governance. Since 1920, criminal justice, traditionally the province of state and local authority, has exemplified the increasing centralization of economic, cultural, and governmental power in America. Even after the recent decades of devolution of public authority back to the states – particularly in the area of social welfare programs – criminal justice's status as an issue of national concern and governance continues to grow. Despite these significant trends, the history of criminal justice since 1920 has been marked by continuities and retreats as well as change: the persistence of localism, the survival and revival of old ideas of individual responsibility and deterrence, and the recent decline of the venerable Enlightenment idea that criminal justice must have a rational purpose beyond punishing individual offenders.

The chapter is organized into three chronological sections. Part I examines the decades between the world wars when Americans grappled with the progressive legacy of "socialized" criminal justice in an era of political conservatism and "crime wave" scares. With Prohibition and the growth of the Federal Bureau of Investigation, the nation took its first serious (but tentative) steps toward nationalizing crime policy, and in a new reckoning of racial and economic inequalities in the administration of local criminal justice, the U.S. Supreme Court tried to impose uniform procedural standards on local courts.

Part II traces the trends in the post-World War II era that culminated in the liberal moment of criminal justice policy in the 1960s. The Model Penal Code, a distinctive product of Cold War legal culture, promoted an unprecedented level of uniformity in the substantive criminal law for the states and attempted to resolve long-standing tensions between sociological and legal understandings of criminal responsibility. Under Chief Justice Earl Warren, the U.S. Supreme Court launched a "due process revolution" that established new procedural rights for accused criminals and empowered federal courts to police state and local criminal justice institutions. In the 1960s crime became a litmus-test issue in national politics, signaled by the 1967 release of a report commissioned by President Lyndon Johnson,

The Challenge of Crime in a Free Society. In retrospect, the report's publication was the high-water mark of liberal crime policy in America.

Finally, Part III examines the "severity revolution" that transformed American criminal justice in the last quarter of the century. In an era of rising political conservatism, lawmakers enacted "get tough" crime measures and drug laws that flooded prisons and had their greatest impact on urban minority communities. With the collapse of the progressive tradition in American liberalism, the social problems of poverty and inequality lost much of their moral claim on the state. The notion that society bore some collective responsibility for crime was perhaps the most battered legacy of the old tradition.

I. CRIMINAL JUSTICE BETWEEN THE WARS

Historical memory of American criminal justice between the world wars is dominated by a single, failed experiment in social control: national Prohibition. By any rough quantitative measure – institutions built, policies introduced, hearts and minds won – the decades following ratification of the Eighteenth Amendment in 1919 would seem fallow compared to the Progressive era. After all, it was during those two previous decades of institutional reform that the modern criminal justice system took shape. Urban police administration, long the prize of political factions, began to resemble a profession. The defining beliefs of progressive criminology – that crime had social causes and criminals could be rehabilitated by a therapeutic regime of individual treatment – won many converts and enjoyed institutional success. Rehabilitative practices took root in state and local criminal justice institutions: indeterminate sentences and parole for felons; court-monitored probation for juvenile delinquents and first-time adult offenders; and "socialized" criminal courts, staffed with social workers and psychological experts, for juvenile delinquents, bad parents, and prostitutes. Progressive ideas reached even into the deteriorating corridors of jails and prisons, where wardens classified and sorted convicts according to the latest scientific behavioral categories and penological experts ministered to the souls of convicts, like the jailhouse chaplains of the past. Nothing that happened in the 1920s and 1930s could quite match that earlier era of experimentation and reform. And yet, the interwar years were consequential ones, marked by ideological controversies, new crime-fighting initiatives, an unprecedented expansion of federal power, and the first critical academic surveys to take stock of the vast American archipelago of criminal justice institutions as a national system.

For American criminal justice, the Twenties began in 1919. The year that the war in Europe ended was an exceptionally terrifying one in the United

States, punctuated by huge general strikes, deadly urban race riots, a string
of anarchist bomb plots, and a nationwide crackdown on political crime.
America's first Red Scare, which peaked in the winter of 1919–20, was in
one sense the last act of World War I – a shockingly repressive crackdown
triggered by fears of revolutionary insurgencies abroad and immigrant and
worker radicalism at home. But the brief nationwide campaign to round
up and, in the cases of many immigrants, forcibly deport suspected radicals
also foretold a long-term build-up in the domestic surveillance capacities
of the federal government.

In the Red Scare's most famous episode, the Palmer Raids of January
1920, more than five thousand alleged radicals, mostly members of left-
wing immigrant groups or labor organizations, were arrested in thirty-three
American cities. The U.S. Department of Justice, under Attorney General
A. Mitchell Palmer, directed the round-up. The administrative capacities
to carry out such an action had been built up during the late war, when
Congress enacted three statutes – the Espionage Act (1917), the Sedition
Act (1918), and the Immigration Act (1918) – that gave the federal government new authority to police or deport individuals who aimed to impede
the war effort or advocated violent overthrow of the government. After the
war, the Bureau of Investigation, which had been established in 1908 to
help the Department of Justice enforce antitrust laws, closely monitored
suspected radicals. Under the zealous young J. Edgar Hoover, the Bureau's
General Intelligence Division amassed files on civil rights leaders, pacifists,
and other radical individuals and organizations. The federal government had
no monopoly on anti-radical activities. Thirty-two states enacted their own
sedition and criminal syndicalism laws to check subversive activities, and
local police departments created Bomb Squads and Red Squads. Local and
federal authorities ignored procedural niceties. Suspects were arrested without warrants, hundreds were summarily deported, and many were detained
for long periods without access to lawyers.

The growth of government surveillance mobilized an emerging network of civil liberties activists and lawyers. As the Red Scare subsided,
they developed a formidable constitutional defense of political speech. The
group included former Progressives who had applauded the expansion of
federal power during the war, but had grown concerned about the government's readiness to trample fundamental rights in the name of security. The
American Civil Liberties Union, established in 1920, soon won important
legal victories (and half-victories) that laid a foundation for civil rights and
civil liberties cases of the 1930s and beyond. In *Gitlow v. New York* (1925),
the ACLU represented a Communist party leader convicted under New
York's Criminal Anarchy Act of 1902 for publishing a pamphlet called
The Left-Wing Manifesto. The U.S. Supreme Court upheld the New York

statute and affirmed Benjamin Gitlow's conviction. But Justice Edward T. Sanford's majority opinion created a crucial precedent for First Amendment rights. Sanford initiated the long process, realized in the next four decades, of "incorporating" the Bill of Rights into the Fourteenth Amendment's Due Process Clause – that is, using the clause to apply the Bill's provisions against the states. Sanford wrote that "for the present purposes we may and do assume that freedom of speech and of the press – which are protected by the First Amendment from abridgment by Congress – are among the fundamental personal rights and 'liberties' protected by the due process clause of the Fourteenth Amendment from impairment by the states."[2] Though of little immediate aid to Gitlow, this language held great promise for civil liberties, particularly in the field of criminal justice. If the Due Process Clause carried the First Amendment to the states, why couldn't it do the same for the Fourth through Eighth Amendments, which protected the rights of suspects, defendants, and convicts? For the time being, though, the Court was in no hurry to impose national standards on the local realm of criminal justice.

Since the creation of the republic, criminal justice had been almost exclusively a local affair, an expression of those broad police powers reserved for the states by the Tenth Amendment. In the aftermath of Reconstruction, the 1878 Posse Comitatus Act threw an additional harness around the federal government by forbidding the use of federal troops in civil law enforcement. Until the 1890s, the federal government did not even have its own prison system; state penitentiaries housed federal prisoners (in exchange for boarding fees and the right to seek a return from the prisoners' labor). As the population of federal prisoners rose in the 1880s and 1890s, and the prevailing leasing system of state penitentiary labor fell under political assault from the labor movement, Congress authorized the creation of the first federal prisons (in Leavenworth, Kansas; Atlanta, Georgia; and McNeil Island, Washington). By 1930, the federal government owned seven prisons. The federal criminal code, which covered mostly interstate crimes and conspiracies, remained a shadow of the state codes. But as early as the Comstock Law of 1873, which made it a federal crime to send "obscene" materials through the mails, Congress had proved willing to throw federal power behind morality crusades. In 1910, at the height of the progressive legal assault on prostitution, Congress enacted the Mann (White Slave) Act, which made it a federal crime to transport a woman across state lines for "immoral" purposes. Still, nothing quite prepared the federal government – or the American public – for the extraordinary expansion of federal authority required to put into force the commands of the Eighteenth Amendment.

---

[2] *Gitlow v. New York*, 268 U.S. 652, 666 (1925).

Local alcohol regulations dated back to the colonial era. In a burst of temperance reform between 1851 and 1855, twelve of the thirty-one states followed Maine's example and enacted statewide laws outlawing the manufacture and sale of liquor. With the notable exception of New York's 1855 prohibition statute, which was struck down by that state's highest court in an early enunciation of substantive due process doctrine, most of these state measures survived constitutional challenge. By the 1880s and 1890s, as the American economy grew ever more national in scope, federalism had become a major source of frustration for prohibitionists. Interstate commerce doctrines, promulgated in the federal courts, made it legal for liquor dealers based in wet states to import their goods into dry states. The federal liquor excise tax conferred a measure of legitimacy on the liquor industry and, by making a stream of federal revenue dependent on the free flow of liquor, made prohibition reform less politically appealing. By 1900, only five states (three of them in New England) retained statutory or constitutional prohibition.

The passage of national prohibition just nineteen years later was a remarkable achievement that revealed the changing character of American politics, particularly the growing power of interest groups and the centralization of government authority. With the founding of the Anti-Saloon League in 1895, temperance advocates boasted a national coalition with a strong base in Protestant congregations. Like the most effective women's political organizations of the day, the League organized across the federal system. The prohibition crusade illustrates how effectively early twentieth-century activists linked criminal justice issues – in this case, the control of drinking – to pressing social and political issues: family dependency, woman's suffrage, the corruption of government by business interests. The League took advantage of the era's reforms of political procedure. The direct primary laws enabled it to press both parties to put forward dry candidates. Dry state legislatures submitted the saloon question on referenda to the voters. By 1916, twenty-one states banned saloons.

The national elections of that year produced a Congress ready to make prohibition federal law. In 1917 Congress submitted the prohibition amendment to the states. *National* Prohibition so threatened the tradition of federalism that even many temperance advocates initially opposed the idea. But American entry into World War I eased the passage of federal prohibition laws, justified as war measures to conserve both grain and the morals of American servicemen. With the ratification of the Eighteenth Amendment in 1919, the Constitution now permanently banned the "manufacture, sale, or transportation of intoxicating liquors." Enacted over President Woodrow Wilson's veto, the 1920 National Prohibition Enforcement Act (the "Volstead Act") outlawed beverages that contained more than 0.5 percent alcohol by volume, set fines and prison terms for violations, and entrusted enforcement authority to the Bureau of Internal Revenue, a branch of the Treasury Department.

From a law enforcement perspective, national Prohibition had a belt-and-suspenders redundancy built into it. Like many other social policies adopted by the federal government during the 1920s and 1930s (including child labor controls and public assistance to single mothers), Prohibition effectively nationalized existing state policies. Since the state prohibition laws did not fall off the books, Prohibition had the virtues and account-ability problems of concurrent state and federal enforcement. Concurrent jurisdiction diffused responsibility for enforcement and emboldened states to attach their own standards to the controversial law. The 0.5 percent alco-hol standard, adopted from an older Bureau of Internal Revenue standard for taxable alcoholic beverages, was much scorned in some states. In 1920, Massachusetts, New Jersey, and New York enacted laws authorizing the manufacture and sale of low-alcohol beer and wine above the federal limit. That same year, the U.S. Supreme Court forced the states into line with federal law.

For national Prohibition to work, the U.S. government needed to marshal vast political will and financial resources to the cause. But fiscal conservatism ruled in the 1920s. With little encouragement from the Republican admin-istrations of Presidents Warren Harding and Calvin Coolidge, Congress never gave the Treasury Department a budget large enough to fund an effec-tive nationwide enforcement effort. A great rural-urban enforcement gap revealed that no single constitutional amendment could easily overcome the resilient localism of American legal cultures. Many rural communities had little need for national Prohibition, having voted themselves dry early in the twentieth century. But in urban centers like Chicago, Prohibition opened an enormously profitable field of enterprise to urban ethnic entrepreneurs, including Al Capone, who turned the illicit manufacture, distribution, and sale of alcoholic beverages into a big business. Wet mayors, like New York's Jimmy Walker and Chicago's William Hale Thompson, strengthened their political bases by openly flaunting the dry laws. Mayor William Dever of Chicago (1923–27), motivated by a sense of personal duty and the many letters of petition he received from poor immigrant women, actually tried to enforce the law, ordering his police to shutter hundreds of businesses. His actions triggered a deadly run of gangland violence in which more than 115 people died. Dever was voted out of office after only one term. In contrast to the dramatic clashes of Treasury Department officials and bootleggers memorialized by Hollywood, much of the actual resistance to Prohibition enforcement was decidedly mundane. Local criminal courts were overrun with Prohibition cases. Lacking funds to hire more clerks and judges for the job, many courts instituted docket-clearing "bargain days," inviting masses of defendants to barter guilty pleas for light fines.

It took awhile for Americans to get around to the unprecedented act of repealing an amendment to the U.S. Constitution. In the 1928 presidential election, the voters passed over the wet Democratic candidate Al Smith for the dry Republican Herbert Hoover, who called Prohibition "a great social and economic experiment, noble in motive and far-reaching in purpose." As president, Hoover authorized construction of six new federal prisons. But many Americans already favored modifying the Volstead Act to legalize light wines and beers. During the Depression, the Association Against the Prohibition Amendment, a group led by manufacturing interests, claimed that repeal would lift the economy by creating jobs and restoring federal tax revenues. Repeal also had the support of the Women's Organization for National Prohibition Reform, which argued that Prohibition violated women's individual freedom. The bold public arguments of these wealthy women for repeal attested to the dramatic cultural transformation in morals and manners that had occurred during the 1920s. Most urban ethnic voters, whose communities bore the brunt of dry law enforcement, readily supported repeal. When the Democratic Party persuaded Franklin Roosevelt to run as a wet in 1932, the end of Prohibition was assured. The Democratic landslide returned an overwhelmingly wet Congress. The Congress got around the state legislatures, many of which were still controlled by the drys, by submitting the Twenty-first Amendment directly to state ratifying conventions. The strategy worked. National Prohibition was repealed in 1933, returning control of liquor regulation to the states.

For all of its limitations, Prohibition had a large impact on American society, culture, and politics. The day-to-day criminal justice functions of the federal government expanded; by 1930 the federal prison system held more than 12,000 inmates, more than one-third of them convicted under the Volstead Act. Prohibition was also apparently effective in curbing the consumption of alcohol, particularly among wage earners, who were hardest hit by the steep cost of bootleg booze and beer. Arrests for public drunkenness dropped. Medical treatments for some alcohol-related diseases declined. Per capita consumption of alcohol in America did not return to pre-Prohibition levels until 1970.

But it was in its failures – actual and perceived – that Prohibition had its greatest impact on the public life of criminal justice. By the mid-1920s, the violence and lawlessness associated with the bootlegging industry aroused public fears that a "crime wave" had overtaken America. A rage for crime control dominated the politics of criminal justice for the next decade, as self-appointed urban crime commissions, county prosecutors, and state lawmakers launched, in the words of the editor of the *New York Times*, the

nation's first "country-wide war on crime."[3] In 1926, the New York legislature enacted crime-fighting measures collectively known as the "Baumes
laws" (after their sponsor, Republican State Senator Caleb Baumes). The
laws introduced new criminal offenses, narrowed the procedural rights of
accused criminals, and mandated that anyone convicted of a fourth felony be
sentenced to life in prison. The Baumes laws (which anticipated the "three
strikes and you're out" laws of the 1990s) served as a model for similar legislation in California, Michigan, and West Virginia. But they wreaked havoc
on New York's own sentencing and parole system, helped trigger prison
riots, and added fuel to a prison population boom that caused Governor
Franklin Roosevelt to launch construction of five new state penitentiaries
(including the ill-fated Attica).

Prohibition and the war on crime were both context and cause for an
extended public debate over the progressive legacy of socialized criminal
justice. At the heart of the progressive reforms was the protean concept of
social responsibility for crime: since social conditions had a large hand in
causing criminal behavior, society bore collective responsibility for alleviating those conditions and rehabilitating the individuals driven to commit crime. A burst of interest in criminal jurisprudence, criminology, and
criminal justice administration during the 1920s strengthened the hold of
progressive ideas in the professional disciplines of law and social science. As
one social scientist observed in the *American Bar Association Journal*, "The
traditional views of human nature and conduct in which all of the older and
most of the younger men in the legal profession were brought up have been
seriously challenged for the past thirty years and all but demolished during
the past decade."[4] Lawmakers and crime-fighters, however, were operating under an entirely different set of premises: individual responsibility,
deterrence, and social defense.

In popular culture, a traditional moral view of crime prevailed. This view
was evident in national magazines, in the unfavorable public response to the
psychiatric testimony put into evidence by Clarence Darrow in the 1924
trial of the teen murderers Leopold and Loeb, and, most conspicuously,
in the figure of the public enemy. A product of urban culture – ripped,
as Hollywood script writers liked to say, from the headlines of the big-
city newspapers – the celluloid gangsters in movies like *Scarface* seemed
to mock the whole notion of social responsibility. Having triumphed over
their own humble beginnings as urban immigrants, the public enemies,

---

[3] Quoted in Rebecca McLennan, "Punishment's 'Square Deal': Prisoners and Their Keepers
in 1920s New York," *Journal of Urban History* 29 (2003), 609.
[4] Nathaniel Cantor, "Law and the Social Sciences," *American Bar Association Journal* 16
(1930), 387.

like the crime commissioners their real-life counterparts often foiled, were successful businessmen.

The riddle of responsibility was not merely theoretical. Many judges in criminal trial courts felt compelled to address the tension between the deterministic implications of social science knowledge, which by the 1920s was a staple of higher education and intellectual discourse, and the formal assumptions of individual freedom and responsibility that lay at the foundation of the criminal law. For those who took this problem seriously, this was an immensely complicated question. The institutional logic of American judicial administration provided some answers.

Judicial recognition of social causation had made its greatest inroads in the handling of the great mass of criminal offenses below the grade of felony – cases that did not involve life-threatening violence or substantial amounts of property. Social responsibility was also most plausible with regard to certain classes of offenders who were assumed, even in the best of circumstances, to lack the reason and strength of adult men. Since the creation of the first juvenile courts in Cook County (Chicago) and Colorado in 1899, socialized criminal justice techniques had been adopted most widely in criminal courts that handled misdemeanor offenses or crimes involving women or children (juvenile offenses, prostitution, desertion, and non-support). Following the model of the Municipal Court of Chicago, the first bureaucratic big-city court system, many local communities had created special "socialized courts" – staffed with social workers, psychologists, nurses, and probation officers – to handle such cases. Judges used the personal data gathered by the court's experts to devise individual treatments for each offender, ranging from probation to eugenical sterilization, designed to remove, cure, or incapacitate the root causes of their deviant behavior.

In the administration of felony cases, which were typically committed by adult men, social responsibility and individual treatment were a harder sell. By the 1920s, judges had established a kind of working compromise in dealing with felonies. The compromise enabled them to maintain the formal legal concepts of individual political liberty and free will (and the related criminal law concepts of intent and culpability) while extending some recognition to the social and personal factors that impinged on individual choice. Again, the compromise was derived in practice from the institutional structure in which judges worked. During the guilt-assessment phase – the trial itself – the old common law presumptions of free will and responsibility would remain undiluted. In the sentencing phase, judges could legitimately take notice of mitigating social facts, tailoring the sentence to their own subjective calculus of social versus individual responsibility in the case at hand. The compromise did not put the matter to rest, of course. By the 1960s, whether to reckon crime as a social or individual problem had become one of the defining domestic issues in American politics.

The rhetoric of the urban businessmen, criminal justice officials, and other reformers who led the crime-control movement of the 1920s and early 1930s may have rejected the behavioral premises that underlay much modern social science. But the reformers were eager to harness the cultural authority and explanatory power of social science to their purpose of producing a more efficient system for preventing crime and punishing criminals. The well-funded crime commissions established in major American cities and states during the period styled themselves as non-partisan, scientific bodies that would investigate and reform the administration of criminal justice. In a series of well-publicized local and state "crime surveys," the crime commissions produced thickly documented analyses of working criminal justice systems. The national model was the Cleveland Crime Survey of 1922. Funded by the Cleveland Foundation, directed by professor Felix Frankfurter and Dean Roscoe Pound of Harvard Law School, and based on research conducted by thirty-five legal experts and social scientists, the survey was the first scientific investigation of an entire criminal justice system. Urban criminal justice reformers had long suspected that urban criminal justice was corrupted by political influence and unwarranted official discretion. But surveys revealed the extraordinary discretion and hidden administrative strategies that prosecutors and judges used to cut through overwhelming caseloads. The major discovery of the Cleveland Survey, for example, was the prevalence of botched cases and plea bargaining. The surveyors learned that almost 60 percent of felony cases were either discharged or reduced to less serious charges. The Cleveland Survey was followed by similarly thorough and damning investigations of the entire state systems in Missouri (1926) and Illinois (1929). Funded largely by private business interests or community foundations, the social scientific studies discounted social conditions and highlighted political influence and systemic efficiencies in the policing, prosecution, and punishment of crime.

In 1931, the crime survey went national, signaling one of Prohibition's most enduring legacies: the consolidation of crime and law enforcement as plausible subjects of national politics and federal policy. In 1929 President Hoover had appointed a National Commission on Law Observance and Enforcement to report to him on the problems facing law enforcement under the "noble experiment." Headed by former Attorney General George W. Wickersham and comprised of prominent lawyers and legal academics, including Pound, the Commission did confirm, as expected, that Prohibition was widely flaunted and inadequately enforced. Even so, the Wickersham Commission argued against repeal. The Commission did much more than study Prohibition, however. In fourteen thick reports, published in 1931, the Commission produced the first systematic national study of American criminal justice.

Although the Great Depression diminished their public impact, the Wickersham Commission reports added up to a powerful indictment. Edith Abbott, dean of the Graduate School of Social Service Administration at the University of Chicago, contributed an exhaustive report on crime and the foreign-born. It plainly refuted the popular belief, which had been exploited by the eugenicist supporters of federal immigration exclusion legislation in the early 1920s, that immigrants caused much of the nation's crime problem. Abbott's data showed that the foreign-born constituted a disproportionately *small* share of criminals in America. A Commission report on prisons and parole revealed the authors' frustration with the dramatic local variation among the nation's penal institutions – "an unwieldy, unorganized, hit-or-miss system" of more than three thousand jails, prisons, reformatories, farms, workhouses, and chain gangs.[5]

The Commission's most shocking report documented the pervasive brutality of local police forces – the frontline troops of the era's crime war. The provocatively titled *Report on Lawlessness in Law Enforcement* was written by three civil liberties advocates recommended to the Commission by the ACLU: Zechariah Chafee, Jr., of the Harvard Law School, and New York lawyers Walter H. Pollak and Carl S. Stern. Copiously documented from local investigations and the records of sixty-seven appellate court cases, the report concluded from the "naked, ugly facts" that "the third degree – that is, the use of physical brutality or other forms of cruelty to obtain involuntary confessions or admissions – is widespread." The interrogation tactics of the New York police included "[p]unching in the face, especially with a hard slap on the jaw; hitting with a billy; whipping with a rubber hose; kicking in the abdomen; tightening the necktie almost up to the choking point; squeezing the testicles." In Chicago, police clubbed interrogation subjects with the city phonebook, heavy enough to "stun a man without leaving a mark." The report teemed with examples of Southern police beating confessions out of African Americans. In one Birmingham case, "a confession of miscegenation was extorted by a city detective from an aged Negro at the point of a pistol."[6] Samuel Walker wrote in his history of the ACLU that the report "created a national sensation." "[T]he ACLU drafted a model statute requiring the immediate arraignment of all arrested persons, detention by an agency other than the police, and the right of all

---

[5] U.S. National Commission on Law Observance and Enforcement, *Report on Penal Institutions, Probation, and Parole* (Washington, 1931), 5.

[6] *Report on Lawlessness in Law Enforcement* (Washington, 1931), 6, 4, 92, 126, 70.

suspects to consult a lawyer. Eventually, the courts embraced most of these ideas."

The contention that the local administration of criminal justice must answer to national constitutional standards – an issue of special importance to African Americans in the South – was beginning to have its day in court. During the early 1930s, the U.S. Supreme Court took steps toward making local justice institutions heed the Bill of Rights. The first two cases arose from the Scottsboro Cases, a cause célèbre of the American left. In 1931, nine poor black boys were falsely accused of raping two white girls. In a single day, all nine defendants were convicted in a rural Alabama court and sentenced to death. In *Powell v. Alabama* (1932), the Supreme Court ruled that an indigent defendant charged with a capital crime had the right, protected by the Due Process Clause of the Fourteenth Amendment, to have an attorney appointed by the state at his trial. In *Norris v. Alabama* (1935), the Court held that systematic exclusion of African Americans from jury service violated the amendment's Equal Protection Clause. One year later, in *Brown v. Mississippi*, the Court overturned the convictions of three African American men who had confessed to murder after being brutally whipped. Extracting confessions by torture – the "third degree" that the Wickersham Commission had found to be such an entrenched part of local law enforcement – now clearly violated national standards of due process.

The rulings were a significant step in the Supreme Court's jurisprudence, toward the more general incorporation of Bill of Rights protections achieved by the Warren Court. But the 1930s cases had little immediate impact. According to Michael Klarman, "[S]outhern blacks continued to experience nearly universal exclusion from juries, to endure beatings aimed at coercing them into confessing crimes, and to suffer convictions for capital offenses after sham trials in which court-appointed lawyers barely went through the motions of providing a defense." The limits of federal protections for Southern African Americans were evident, too, in the NAACP's failed campaigns for anti-lynching legislation. The House of Representatives passed anti-lynching bills three times – in 1922, 1937, and 1940 – but actual or threatened filibusters by Southern Democrats killed the legislation in the Senate. President Roosevelt, who needed Southern support for his New Deal programs, refused to publicly support anti-lynching legislation.

The Roosevelt administration is best remembered for its economic regulations and welfare programs; in criminal justice, the administration is credited with laying national Prohibition to rest. Indeed, New Deal liberalism has long been praised for stripping away, once and for all, the moral excess of the progressive political tradition. The historical record, however, contradicts this conventional wisdom. Even as the New Dealers helped end Prohibition, their policies greatly expanded federal criminal justice authority in other areas, and Congress continued to legislate morality.

It is a little-noted fact, for example, that the New Deal economic regulations, such as the codes promulgated by the National Industrial Recovery Administration, carried criminal penalties and were enforced in federal trial courts. Roosevelt had established respectable crime-fighting credentials as governor of New York, when he called for a massive program of prison construction. As president he demanded "immediate suppression" of crime in his 1934 State of the Union Address. His attorney general called crime "a war that threatens the safety of our country."[7] The same New Deal Congresses that built the modern administrative state created a passel of new federal crimes and appropriated funds for a burgeoning federal law enforcement bureaucracy. In 1932, following the sensational kidnapping and murder of the son of Anne and Charles Lindbergh, Congress made kidnapping a federal crime. Amidst heightened public fascination with rural gangsters, Congress passed a series of laws that authorized the use of federal law enforcement where local and state enforcement efforts consistently came up short. The Fugitive Felon Law made it a federal crime to flee prosecution by crossing state lines. The Interstate Theft Act gave federal authorities jurisdiction over stolen goods worth more than $5,000 transported between states. In 1934, with Roosevelt's support, Congress enacted the National Firearms Act, the first major piece of federal gun control legislation. The statute imposed high taxes and background checks on purchases of saw-off shotguns, silencers, and other hardware associated with the crime war. In 1937, Congress responded to a moral panic over marijuana (a panic colored by racist perceptions of Mexican migrant workers and urban African Americans) by passing the Marijuana Tax Act, which set stiff penalties for the possession or sale of marijuana.

Collectively, these statutes greatly increased the criminal jurisdiction of the federal government and especially the Bureau of Investigation, which was officially renamed the Federal Bureau of Investigation in 1934. Beginning in the early 1930s, FBI director J. Edgar Hoover took control of the federal fingerprint network and the Uniform Crime Reports system, under which all American law enforcement agencies were required to submit data on major crimes to the bureau. Hoover put pressure on Hollywood to make films that glamorized the bureau's work. The expansion and bureaucratization of federal crime fighting extended to corrections. The 1930 Bureau of Prisons Act gave the Federal Bureau of Prisons centralized administrative control over federal penitentiaries, which previously were run according to

---

[7] Quotes are from Samuel Walker, *Popular Justice: A History of American Criminal Justice* (2nd ed., New York, 1998), 160.

the procedures set by their local wardens. In 1934, the Bureau opened the island prison of Alcatraz, a maximum security facility to house criminals of the "vicious and irredeemable type."

The federal government never seriously threatened to seize control of criminal justice from the state and local governments. Even in the 1990s, when federal drug policies and sentencing guidelines greatly increased the federal prison population, local and state governments outspent the national government on criminal justice functions by nearly six to one. In the year 2000, state felony convictions totaled roughly fourteen times the federal count.[8] Given the American constitutional framework of federalism and the persistent distrust of centralized power, the federal government is unlikely to eclipse the local and state role in law enforcement any time soon. But the interwar period of the 1920s and 1930s – the era of the Red Scare, Prohibition, the birth of the modern FBI, and New Deal crime policies – did represent a historic departure of lasting significance. New policies, measures, and institutions modified the long tradition of localism in American law enforcement and launched the federal government into the business of fighting crime. And the actions of the U.S. Supreme Court, however tentative and ineffectual in the short term, laid important groundwork for the creation of viable national procedural standards in American criminal justice.

II. CRIMINAL JUSTICE IN POSTWAR AMERICA: THE LIBERAL MOMENT

The 1960s marked the high tide of liberal optimism in American criminal justice. Not since the Progressive era had there been such a sustained surge of public concern, academic interest, political debate, and calls for government action to prevent crime and reform criminal justice institutions. The liberal agenda, which had been in the making for a decade or more, drew on old and new sources. In its expansive social rhetoric and its concrete proposals for penal reform, criminal justice liberalism owed a large debt to the progressive tradition of scientism, social responsibility, and individual treatment. In its decidedly national orientation and its aim to create a more unified criminal justice system, the agenda built on the foundation of federal social intervention laid during the New Deal and expanded in President Johnson's Great Society programs. And in its heightened concern for civil liberties and civil rights, anticipated by the Supreme Court decisions of the 1920s and 1930s, criminal justice liberalism bent to both the grassroots

---

[8] U.S. Department of Justice, Bureau of Justice Statistics (hereafter BJS), "Key Crime and Justice Facts at a Glance," http://www.ojp.usdoj.gov/bjs/glance.htm, accessed 8/18/2004.

mobilizations of the civil rights movement and the Cold War imperative of fortifying America's international image as a beacon of liberty and equality before the law.

Three clusters of events – an influential private reform initiative, a wave of federal court decisions, and political skirmishes on the national stage – defined the postwar decades in American criminal justice. The Model Penal Code, a lawyers' reform project launched in 1952, aimed to clarify and unify the substantive criminal law by proposing a template for revising the fifty state criminal codes. A landmark in criminal law theory, the Code strived to reconcile the progressive tenets of scientism, determinism, and treatment with a renewed concern for the formal legal principles of culpability and deterrence. During the 1960s, the Warren Court handed down a series of decisions that strengthened the procedural rights of accused persons, defendants, and prisoners. This "due process revolution" imposed a new level of constitutional uniformity on local and state criminal justice institutions. With less fanfare, lower federal courts brought state prisons under federal judicial oversight. In the mid-1960s rising crime rates became a pressing subject of national politics. President Johnson appointed a blue-ribbon commission and charged it to "deepen our understanding of the causes of crime and of how society should respond to the challenge of the present levels of crime."[9] The commission's report was an eye-opening analysis of American criminal justice and the definitive liberal statement on the causes and cure for crime.

The Model Penal Code was commissioned by the American Law Institute, a Philadelphia-based organization founded in 1923. The ALI project was to get the nation's best legal minds together and produce authoritative "restatements" of common law principles, in areas such as torts and contracts, and in this way to make American law more unified, rational, and scientific. In criminal law, the ALI lawyers concluded, a restatement was not enough. For all of the progressive innovations in the administration of justice, there had been little effort to reform the substantive criminal law: the hodge-podge principles of criminal liability, the catalogues of crimes and penalties, and the rules of punishment contained in the copious state codes and common law precedents. Under the direction of Herbert Wechsler, a Columbia University law professor, an ALI committee labored on the Model Penal Code from 1952 to 1962, producing thirteen drafts for review and comment. The final result resembled an actual criminal code: its articles, sections, and subsections glossed penal principles, defined crimes, outlined the proper organization of a correctional system, and specified how

---

[9] President's Commission on Law Enforcement and Administration of Justice, *The Challenge of Crime in a Free Society* (Washington, DC, 1967), 2.

convicted criminals must be treated. But the Code was deceptive both in name and appearance. Much more than a prototype for state reform, the Code was the most important American treatise on the criminal law since the nineteenth century.

The Code bore the unmistakable impress of the 1950s and that decade's distinctive postwar legal culture. The horrors of totalitarianism – whether in its fascist, Nazi, or Stalinist guise – reverberated throughout American intellectual life. In diverse academic disciplines, scholars turned from inherently political questions of substance and value to matters of form, technique, and process. Law scholars associated with the ascendant "legal process" school drew categorical distinctions between law and politics, procedural versus substantive justice. The legal realists of the 1920s and 1930s had challenged those old formal dualisms with devastating intellectual force. But times had changed. In a world visibly threatened by absolutist regimes, legal process scholars insisted, official discretion must be restrained through an almost religious adherence to the constitutional processes and institutional arrangements – the neutral rules of the game – that made the American rule of law exceptional. Herbert Wechsler, who had served as a legal adviser at the Nuremberg trials, took this argument to its logical extreme in his infamous critique of the Warren Court's decisions banning state policies of racial discrimination. The decisions, he argued, rested on political or moral judgments, rather than "neutral principles." Though this position was controversial, Wechsler's legal faith fit the times. For many Americans (including many civil rights activists) the concept of a rule of law, founded on formal equality and individual justice, distinguished the United States from the USSR as the powers vied for the allegiance of nations around the globe.

In this Cold War context, it seemed more important than ever to ensure that American criminal justice rested on time-honored legal principles, rather than political fiat or administrative discretion. This concern permeates the 1952 *Harvard Law Review* article in which Wechsler made his case to America's legal elite for a model penal code. Given its immense importance – its power to protect and to destroy – the criminal law was in a disgraceful condition. Criminal law was a poor relation in the legal academy and profession. State codes were mindlessly imitative and full of uncertainty. Wechsler was especially concerned by the widening range of criminal offenses in which the courts applied a standard of strict liability: proving the act itself, without clear evidence of a guilty mind (*mens rea*), was sufficient for penal sanction. The vagueness and harshness of state codes encouraged judges and prosecutors to cut plea bargains with defendants. Wechsler worried that such informal administrative techniques had "so largely come to dominate the field," eclipsing traditional legal concerns like *mens rea*. Echoing Roscoe Pound's famous condemnation of the growth of the administrative process during the New Deal, Wechsler warned that "to a large extent we have, in this important sense, abandoned law – and this within an area where our fundamental teaching calls most strongly for its vigorous supremacy."[10]

In criminal justice institutions, the procedural problem of administrative discretion was closely tied to the substantive riddle of criminal responsibility. The prospect of "abandoning" the law had first been raised by Pound's Progressive generation, as they struggled to bring jurisprudence and the administration of justice into line with the new scientific knowledge of society. Central to this first encounter between law and the social and behavioral sciences was the problem of culpability. The criminal law presumed that people were moral free agents, and for a criminal code to deter potential criminals one had to assume that people were rational actors, capable of choosing to obey the law. But from the perspective of disciplines like psychology and psychiatry, such unfettered individual free will was an indefensible concept; human behavior, including criminal acts, was largely determined by socioeconomic circumstances, heredity, and mental disorders. As these disciplines rose in cultural authority, the tension between the new common sense of educated Americans and the old common sense presumed by the criminal law grew ever more acute. By the 1950s, the consensus in the social and behavioral sciences was, as Wechsler put it, "that the penal law is ineffective, inhumane, and thoroughly unscientific." Free will was a fiction, the penal law's actual function "nothing more than vengeance in disguise." Wechsler was sympathetic to these complaints, which came, he said, from "important groups seeking to further public interest." So he made it a central purpose of the code project "to explore the merits of such criticism in the context of a reconsideration of the law."[11]

The institutional challenge was how to make criminal law run in accord with the recognition that the individual will was neither the sole cause of crime nor the sole object of penal control, without abandoning the law for an entirely administrative penal regime. For Pound's Progressive generation, the solution had been to "socialize" the criminal courts: bring in the social experts, and make the courts run more like bureaucracies, without entirely loosening the old common law restraints on discretion. By the 1950s, techniques of individual treatment such as juvenile courts, probation, and parole, were almost universal in the judicial and correctional systems of the states. Still, in the eyes of many social and behavioral

[10] Herbert Wechsler, "The Challenge of a Model Penal Code," *Harvard Law Review* 65 (1952), 1102.
[11] Wechsler, "Model Penal Code," 1103.

scientists of the era, the treatment programs remained a thin veneer for a system founded on retribution. For Wechsler, the challenge was to synthesize the scientists' renewed calls for therapeutic treatment of offenders with a more traditional commitment to culpability and deterrence.

The Model Penal Code appeared in 1962; official commentary filling six volumes came out by 1985. The drafters did much to clarify state law. They created an integrated law of theft to replace the long menu of crimes – embezzlement, larceny, false pretenses, larceny by trick, and so forth – that state codes had imported from the common law. The Code's central theme, though, was its reaffirmation of *mens rea*. In place of the confusing array of terms that the common law used to define *mens rea*, the Code specified "four modes of acting with respect to the material elements of offenses – purposely, knowingly, recklessly, and negligently." One of these had to be present to establish criminal liability. The Code took a modest stand against strict liability crimes, which in the regulatory environment of twentieth-century America had grown to cover acts ranging from traffic violations to statutory rape to felony murder. The Code insisted that penal law properly dealt only with blameworthy behavior. Minor strict liability offenses were not called crimes at all; they were redefined as violations, punishable by fines only.

The eminent postwar criminal law scholar Herbert L. Packer praised the Code as a triumph of "principled pragmatism"; the drafters had shrewdly accommodated their reform principles to "existing institutions."[12] In fact, it was the existing institutions that held the whole enterprise together, making it possible for the Code drafters to reconcile their own contradictory principles: legal authority and scientific knowledge, individual responsibility and therapeutic treatment.

Wechsler and his colleagues assumed that there was a definite societal consensus about the proper purpose of the penal law: to prevent culpable behavior that harmed the interests of society. They enshrined this principle in the Code's emphasis on individual culpability and deterrence (which implied the moral free agency and rationality of criminals). But when it came to dealing with convicted criminals, the Code emphasized therapeutic treatment (which implied that offenders were abnormal individuals who should be restored to society only after undergoing treatment to rehabilitate the curable and incapacitate those beyond cure). This was no small contradiction. After all, correctional treatment programs like parole and psychiatric confinement involved the sort of broad administrative discretion that postwar legal academics professed to abhor. Like criminal court

---

[12] Herbert L. Packer, "The Model Penal Code and Beyond," *Columbia Law Review* 63 (1963), 594.

judges in the 1920s, the Code drafters found a solution to this problem in *the legal process*. At the front end of the criminal justice system – in the definition of specific offenses, in the judicial determinations that proved a defendant's guilt or innocence – the neutral standards of *mens rea* and individual culpability reigned supreme. But at the back end of the system – in the handling of convicted criminals – treatment of deviant personalities, rather than simple retribution or punishment, best served the end of crime control. Accordingly, the Code set generous sentencing ranges. These gave correctional officials wide authority to determine the actual time served according to their assessment of the offender's personal history, character, or mental condition. Such vast discretion was safely granted, the logic of the Code implied, because treatment was reserved for people who had demonstrated a high level of legal culpability.

During the next two decades thirty-four states revised their criminal codes in ways that reflected the Model Penal Code's influence. The Code also sparked interest in reforming federal criminal law, which, Charles McClain has noted, "was in a sorrier condition than that of most states." For many years after its publication, the Code had a strong (some would say stultifying) influence on legal scholarship and education. Above all, the Code helped judges, lawyers, lawmakers, and perhaps the public envision American criminal justice as a system, founded on unified, consensual principles that could reasonably unify purposes of deterrence and treatment within a framework of protecting society from blameworthy conduct.

Compared to the progressive reform discourse on criminal justice, however, the Code articulated a narrowly procedural notion of justice. Even as it reaffirmed the Progressives' commitment to rehabilitation, the Code said little about society's responsibility to address structural inequalities that caused crime. In this sense, too, the Code was a product of the postwar years, when a moderately liberal law professor like Herbert Wechsler could profess to find no "neutral principles" on which white racial discrimination against blacks could be legitimately condemned by the courts. The quest for substantive justice – racial or economic – was too political to have a place in the neutral legal process.

All the while the legal process was changing. As the ALI Code authors circulated their drafts, the U.S. Supreme Court, under Chief Justice Earl Warren, embarked on one of the most consequential eras in its history. In one landmark decision after another, the Court remapped the boundaries of governmental power and individual rights in America. Collectively, the Court's decisions greatly enhanced the power of the federal government (including the Court itself) as the guarantor of civil liberties and civil rights. Although history has shown that these decisions were not enough to guarantee economic, racial, or gender justice, this train of decisions gave the phrase "equality before the law" a substance it had never before possessed in American history.

The roots of the due process revolution reached back to the post-World War I First Amendment decisions and extended through the 1920s and 1930s, when the Court, for the first time since Reconstruction, acted to restrain the practices that made due process apply for whites only in Southern courts. In 1938, the Court gave notice, in Justice Harlan Fiske Stone's famous *Carolene Products* footnote, that henceforward the Court would apply a higher level of scrutiny to state laws that interfered with civil liberties or civil rights. Despite these important precursors, the due process revolution was clearly a product of the post-World War II era. The urgency came from many sources: the recent global experiences with totalitarianism, African Americans' struggle for civil rights, and the Cold War imperative to square the American creed of liberty and equality with the realities of racism and police violence. It is no surprise that one leading edge of this revolution in rights was the constitutional law governing criminal justice institutions, for it was there that the coercive power of the state to destroy human liberty was most explicit. Long-tolerated local practices like the third-degree suddenly carried global implications.

The Supreme Court's actions defied the long tradition of localism in criminal justice, a tradition in which Earl Warren himself was exceptionally well versed. From 1926 to 1938 he served as the crime-fighting district attorney of Alameda County (Oakland), California. He prosecuted suspected radicals under the state's criminal syndicalism statute. During his subsequent tenure as California attorney general, prosecutors working under him were known to build cases on warrantless wiretaps and coerced testimony. In the decades before President Dwight Eisenhower appointed him to the Supreme Court, a local or state law enforcement officer like Warren could rest assured that there were virtually no federal constitutional restraints on how he went about enforcing the state law and very little risk that any conviction he won would be undone by a federal court. The protections that the Bill of Rights extended to the accused – freedom from unreasonable search and seizure, the right to an attorney, freedom from self-incrimination, freedom from cruel and unusual punishment – were understood (correctly or not) to restrain only the federal government. There were important precedents arising from the Scottsboro cases in the 1930s. Even so, the Warren Court's decisions were virtually unprecedented. And for many Americans, there was something undemocratic about nine appointed federal judges, tenured for life, striking down laws enacted by elected state lawmakers and telling local communities how to fight crime.

Thanks partly to the journalist Anthony Lewis's 1964 best-seller, *Gideon's Trumpet*, which explained and celebrated the achievements of legal liberalism for a national audience, the Warren Court's criminal justice decisions are among the most familiar in American constitutional history. The Warren Court effected a wholesale constitutional transformation of criminal procedure by using the Fourteenth Amendment's Equal Protection and Due Process Clauses as a textual basis to "incorporate" the Bill of Rights protections and apply them against the states. In *Mapp v. Ohio* (1961), the Court applied the exclusionary rule, established in 1914 for federal cases, against the states. No longer would evidence turned up using faulty warrants be admissible in state cases. The Court recognized that the Fourth Amendment's protection against unreasonable search and seizure was virtually meaningless if prosecutors could introduce evidence gathered by such means. In *Gideon v. Wainwright* (1963), the Court applied the Sixth Amendment's guarantee of counsel in felony cases to the states. In *Cooper v. Pate* (1964), the Court declared that state prisoners (in this case, a black Muslim in Illinois's Stateville prison) had a First Amendment right to free exercise of religion. In *Miranda v. Arizona* (1966), the Court required local and state police to alert criminal suspects, before interrogation, to their Fifth Amendment right not to incriminate themselves. The Court struck against the procedural informality of progressive criminal justice in the case *In Re Gault* (1967), ruling that juvenile defendants must have at least partial procedural rights, including the rights to counsel and to confront one's accusers. In *Furman v. Georgia* (1972), the Court ruled that the death penalty, as applied in Georgia, was arbitrary and thus violated the Eighth Amendment's ban on cruel and unusual punishments.

Many of the rights newly guaranteed by the Court in cases like *Mapp* and *Gideon* were in fact already protected by the statutes or constitutions of many states – but not all. That was what made the cases significant. Together they imposed an unprecedented level of national constitutional uniformity on the practices of local and state police, criminal courts, prisons, and jails. As with many Supreme Court decisions, the Court's decisions protecting the rights of defendants and the accused depended to a large degree on the willingness of public officials to abide by them – and such cooperation was often refused. But there is no question that the cases opened up new protections for individuals and imposed a new level of constitutional uniformity on the states. Like the Model Penal Code, the due process revolution helped turn American criminal justice institutions into something more closely resembling a national system.

The lower federal courts were also taking action to impose new norms of liberal constitutionalism on state and local criminal justice institutions. Before 1965, no federal court had ever presumed to tell a state prison or local jail to reform its practices or improve its conditions. The "hands-off doctrine" prevailed. As one federal appeals court put it, "The Government of the United States is not concerned with, nor has it power to control or regulate the internal discipline of the penal institutions of its constituent states."[13] Meddling by a federal court in the internal affairs of a state prison, judges had long reasoned, would be tantamount to making prison policy, violating long-settled principles of federalism, separation of powers, and the rule of law itself.

The old constitutional restraints began to unravel in 1965. The U.S. District Court for the Eastern District of Arkansas ruled that conditions at the Cummins Farm State Prison violated the Eighth Amendment's prohibition on cruel and unusual punishment. With that decision, the federal district courts and appellate courts asserted jurisdiction over state prisons and local jails. Individual prisoners and prisoner's rights organizations filed a steady stream of suits. The ensuing train of federal prison cases far outlasted the Warren Court. By 1995, write Malcolm Feeley and Edward Rubin in their exhaustive study, "The ACLU estimated that prisons in a total of forty-one states, as well as the District of Columbia, Puerto Rico, and the Virgin Islands, had at one time or another been under comprehensive court orders, as had the entire correctional systems of at least ten states." Federal courts told state officials how large cells must be, how often a prisoner must be allowed to shower, even what nutritional value prison meals must have.

This thirty-year wave of "judicial policymaking," as Feeley and Rubin have shown, reflected a broader transformation in the fabric of American governance during the late twentieth century. The hundreds of individual federal judges who participated in these discrete prison decisions were not radicals; they were "middle-of-the-road, upper-middle-class Americans, largely white and male, appointed by Republican and Democratic presidents." Their decisions were not guided from above by the Supreme Court. Their institutional base – federal courts – spanned the nation. Decades of institutional and intellectual change had made federal judges willing to lay the hands-off doctrine to rest. The growth and apparent permanence of the administrative state had eroded the "conceptual power" of the formal legal doctrines – dual federalism, separation of powers, and the rule of law ideal – that had once justified the hands-off doctrine.

In retrospect, federal judges and liberal Democratic politicians picked a tough time to pursue sweeping institutional reforms and policies that critics could plausibly denounce as soft on crime. By the mid-1960s, the nation was in the throes of an extended, historically exceptional surge in reported

---

[13] *Siegel v. Ragen*, 180 F.2d 785, 788 (1950).

crimes. As early as the 1964 presidential election, the Republican candidate, Senator Barry Goldwater, issued a stern warning about escalating "violence in our streets."[14] Goldwater cited the FBI's *Uniform Crime Reports*, data-rich publications whose very existence invited Americans to think of crime as a national problem that Congress and the president must address. Reported crimes in the United States rose from 1,861,000 in 1960 to 2,780,000 in 1965 to 5,568,000 in 1970. By 1975, that figure doubled again. In popular culture, the crime fears of the moment crystallized in the racial stereotype of the young black male "mugger." Goldwater's speech was a turning point. Explaining the crime epidemic and identifying the true culprits were now major issues in national politics, for liberals and conservatives alike.

Even if Goldwater had not raised the issue during the 1964 campaign, it seems unlikely that President Johnson could have avoided addressing the surging crime rates or the race riots – typically triggered by an incident with the police – that took place in more than forty cities between 1964 and 1967. Still, Johnson went much further than he had to. In 1965, he became the first president to address Congress on crime, announcing, "Crime is no longer merely a local problem." Like Hoover before him, Johnson created a crime commission, the President's Commission on Law Enforcement and the Administration of Justice. Chaired by Attorney General Nicholas Katzenbach and directed by Harvard law professor James Vorenberg, it conducted the most extensive survey of American criminal justice since the Wickersham Commission. The sixty-three-member staff included police officers, sociologists, correctional personnel, prosecutors, lawyers, and psychologists. They took ride-alongs with city police, visited courtrooms, and toured urban slums. The Commission's 1967 report, *The Challenge of Crime in a Free Society*, was a powerful statement of Great Society liberalism. It called for a massive federal government effort to reform criminal justice institutions and to fight crime by reducing poverty and racial discrimination.

It says something about how far American politics has traveled in the past three and a half decades that the report's language now sounds so radical:

America must translate its well-founded alarm about crime into social action that will prevent crime. [The Commission] has no doubt whatever that the most significant action that can be taken against crime is action designed to eliminate slums and ghettos, to improve education, to provide jobs, to make sure that every American is given the opportunities and the freedoms that will enable him to assume his responsibilities.[15]

[14] Barry Goldwater's Acceptance Speech at the Twenty-Eighth Republican National Convention, 1964, at http://www.washingtonpost.com, accessed 7/29/03.

[15] President's Commission, *Challenge of Crime*, 15.

The report attributed the escalating crime rates to urban poverty, institutional racism, and the economic process of deindustrialization, which drained industrial jobs from the cities just as the baby boomer generation entered their late teen years. Bristling with more than two hundred recommendations, the report called for an extensive federal effort to finance and coordinate local and state law enforcement. The commission urged that prisons be reserved for the most dangerous offenders; the rest should receive treatment in the community. At least for its supporters, the report served as a powerful argument for expanding the Great Society's poverty programs.

In February 1967, shortly after the report's release, Johnson sent Congress legislation to provide major federal funding in direct grants to the cities and states to start implementing the commission's recommendations. Congress debated the act in 1968. It was a year of riots, demonstrations against Johnson's faltering war in Vietnam, and a presidential campaign in which George Wallace and Richard Nixon appealed to voters with promises of "law and order." Congress eventually passed an Omnibus Crime Control and Safe Streets Act, which Johnson signed with serious misgivings. The law contained several provisions offensive to the administration: it gave law enforcement officials enlarged powers to engage in wiretapping and other provisions aimed to limit the reach of the Warren Court's due process decisions. The statute also required that federal monies be distributed to the states in block grants – rather than direct grants – giving states wide discretion over how the money would be spent. But the statute also launched the Law Enforcement Assistance Administration (LEAA), an agency within the Justice Department that would administer federal grants to state and local law enforcement agencies, educational institutions, and private organizations.

Weakened by Vietnam, Johnson did not seek his party's nomination in 1968. The Republican Platform repudiated the Crime Commission report: "We must re-establish the principle that men are accountable for what they do, that criminals are responsible for their crimes, that while the youth's environment may help to explain the man's crime, it does not excuse that crime." Nixon appealed to die-hard Republicans and white working-class voters with his demands for "law and order," and he denounced the Supreme Court's due process decisions for handcuffing the police.

Johnson and Nixon had one thing in common, though. Both invited rising public expectations that the federal government must fight crime. During Nixon's first term, the federal law enforcement budget tripled; aid to the states exploded from $60 million to nearly $700 million. Since 1968 crime has become a seemingly permanent addition to national political discourse, and American criminal justice has become increasingly punitive. Yet, liberalism survived as an institutional influence in American criminal justice long after 1968. Rehabilitation programs and the community-based services expanded. From 1965 to 1975, the number of adults on probation rose from 144,000 to 923,000; the parole population grew from 63,000 to 156,000. The new Law Enforcement Assistance Administration also sustained a liberal perspective on crime causation by bankrolling social science research. Liberalism survived in criminal justice because legal activists, politicians, and litigants helped keep it alive. It persisted also because many of the achievements of liberal reform – the nationalization of criminal justice, the constitutionalization of criminal procedure, federal judicial oversight of prisons – were grounded in broader changes in American governance. On the flip side, America's second "war on crime," just getting underway during Nixon's presidency, would have been unthinkable before the 1960s, when crime became a national issue. Unfortunately, this unintended legacy of the liberal moment outlived many of its other achievements. America's second war on crime made the first look like a schoolyard scuffle.

III. THE SEVERITY REVOLUTION

Whether we ought to reckon crime as a matter of personal choice or social conditions may be an ultimately irresolvable question. But criminal justice is decidedly the product of human political decisions. In a representative democracy, the people share responsibility with their political leaders for how crimes are defined, communities policed, and criminals punished. This is especially true in the United States. The nation's exceptionally decentralized government institutions and fiercely competitive party politics render criminal justice policymaking at the local, state, and federal levels particularly vulnerable to popular pressure, media representations, interest group demands, and the demagoguery of ambitious politicians.

In the last quarter of the twentieth century, as a rising tide of conservatism transformed American politics, government officials responded aggressively to rising public concerns about crime. Collectively, their innumerable policy choices, made in the nation's thousands of legislative, judicial, and administrative arenas, launched what Albert Alschuler called a "severity revolution" in criminal justice. As lawmakers rolled out "get tough" measures – stiff mandatory sentences for drug offenders, huge appropriations for prison construction, and a revival of chain gangs and public shaming – the widening color gap behind bars demonstrated the enduring significance of racial inequality in a nation premised on equal justice for all. The number of people of color, particularly young African American men, under state restraint and police surveillance vastly exceeded their proportion of the general population. By century's end, the world's most powerful liberal democracy incarcerated nearly two million of its members in the West's harshest penal regime. The vast U.S. penal system – the last in the industrialized West to retain capital punishment – drew uncomfortable (and, by some measures, unfavorable) comparisons to apartheid-era South Africa, Communist China, and Taliban-ruled Afghanistan. A headline in the British *Economist* expressed the growing disapproval of America's Western allies: "Crime in America: violent and irrational – and that's just the policy."[16]

America's severity revolution reflected and reinforced the dramatic social, economic, and political changes underway in the nation from 1970 to 2000. The historic achievements of the civil rights movement were undermined by widening economic inequalities and new forms of racial politics. Deindustrialization of the Northern cities – the movement of manufacturing jobs from old industrial centers like Detroit to suburbs, the Sunbelt, and increasingly offshore – tightened urban job markets. African Americans, who migrated to Northern manufacturing centers by the tens of thousands during and after World War II, disproportionately suffered as the industrial job base in those communities shrunk. The suburbanization of America during the postwar decades encouraged a political realignment in the nation. Predominantly white suburbanites of both parties rallied to protect their property values and children from all threats, especially crime and the perceived threat of state-enforced school integration. The shifting suburban political base fostered the rise of a new conservatism in American politics that gave the Reagan and Bush Republicans control of Washington during the 1980s. Conservatism transformed Democratic politics too, culminating in the election of "New Democrat" Bill Clinton on campaign promises of free trade, welfare reform, and tough crime policies. For many Americans, the collapse of the USSR provided powerful confirmation for a set of assumptions widely shared on both sides of the political aisle by Clinton's election. "Big government" welfare programs and regulatory policies must be scaled back. Many of the government's social functions could be better managed by private firms and charitable associations. The old "liberal" ethics of social responsibility needed to be updated or discarded altogether.

Born of a political movement against big government, America's second war on crime triggered the greatest build-up in the coercive power of the state in the nation's history. During the last quarter of the twentieth century a population explosion of Malthusian proportions took place in America. It happened behind bars. According to data compiled by the Bureau of Justice Statistics, a branch of the U.S. Department of Justice, in 1980, the total population of jails and prisons in the United States stood at 504,000 persons. By 1990, that population more than doubled, reaching 1,149,000.

[16] *Economist*, June 8, 1996, 23–25.

By 2000, it had climbed to 1,937,000.[17] By contrast, in 2000 the European Union – which had a population of some 370 million, compared with 274 million Americans – incarcerated about 300,000 people.[18] The raw numbers cannot fail to impress: Imagine if the general population doubled every decade! But a more meaningful measure is the incarceration *rate*: how the swelling ranks of the incarcerated tracked with the nation's overall population growth. For this the Bureau of Justice Statistics offers up a different indicator: the number of "sentenced inmates under State and Federal jurisdiction" per 100,000 U.S. residents. That indicator climbed sharply from 139 in 1980 to 297 in 1990 to 478 in 2000, when the incarceration rate showed signs of leveling off.[19] "America's per capita incarceration is now the highest in the world," James Whitman noted in 2003, "approaching, and in some regions exceeding, ten times the rate in Western Europe."

Plummeting crime rates failed to slow the severity revolution. From 1991 to 2000, America's homicide rate fell 44 percent, burglaries dropped 42 percent, and robberies declined 47 percent. Criminologists called it "the Crime Drop." Politicians and law enforcement officials rushed to take credit for the good news; surely tougher policing and stiff sentences had deterred or incapacitated criminals. Criminologists were not so sure. Their hypotheses revealed how complex and divisive the study of crime causation had become. Some experts attributed the Crime Drop to the aging of the population, others to law enforcement strategies such as community policing initiatives and crackdowns on "lifestyle" offenses, others to the decade's economic boom, and still others to the decline of the "crack" cocaine trade. The most controversial theory (because of its eugenicist implications) chalked it up to *Roe v. Wade*. The availability of legal abortion, researchers suggested, prevented the births of thousands of unwanted, impoverished children, whose diminished life chances would have put them at risk for careers of crime. In the midst of all of this speculation, a few experts conceded that perhaps the mystery of the Great American Crime Drop could not be solved.

How could the incarceration rate continue to rise if reported crime was falling?

A simple answer: Convicts were spending more time in prison. At the heart of the severity revolution was a legislative movement for longer, determinate sentences. From the beginning this movement was tightly linked to the War on Drugs, which started in the waning years of the Vietnam War.

---

[17] BJS, "Correctional Populations," http://www.ojp.usdoj.gov/, accessed June 7, 2004.
[18] Irwin et al., "Nonviolent Prisoners."
[19] BJS, "Incarceration Rate, 1980–2002," http://www.ojp.usdoj.gov/, accessed June 7, 2004.

In 1973, Governor Nelson Rockefeller of New York pushed through his famous anti-narcotics law, which curtailed judicial discretion and imposed hefty mandatory sentences for even relatively small offenses. In the 1980s, federal and state lawmakers bound judges to mandatory minimum sentences for an ever-widening range of offenses. As crime levels dropped during the 1990s, Congress and many state legislatures further flexed their muscles, mandating "enhanced" sentences for drug dealing, use of a firearm during a crime, and, most notoriously, for a third felony conviction (under the "three strikes and you're out" laws).

Drug offenses accounted for much of the rising prisoner head count. Consider another Bureau of Justice Statistics indicator: the number of persons in the custody of state correctional systems, classified by the most serious offense they committed. By this measure, in 1980 the states had custody of 19,000 drug offenders; in 1990, that figure hit 148,600; and by 2000, it reached 251,100 – more than thirteen times the 1980 figure. By comparison, during the same twenty-year period the number of violent offenders in state custody grew from 173,300 to 589,100 (3.4 times); the number of property offenders rose from 89,300 to 238,500 (2.7 times); and the number of public order offenders climbed from 12,400 to 124,600 (10 times).[20] The rising tide of drug and public order offenders behind bars has had a curious cumulative effect. As a recent report observed, while the public worries most about violent crime, "[m]ost of the growth in America's prisons since 1978 is accounted for by nonviolent offenders."[21]

America's severity revolution hit hardest in metropolitan minority communities. Nearly half of all people incarcerated in the 1990s were African American, though blacks comprised only 13 percent of the population.[22] On any given day, nearly a quarter of all African American men in their twenties were "under some form of criminal restraint – prison, jail, probation or parole." Although American criminal justice has a long, violent history of racism, the glaring racial disparity in the nation's prison systems intensified during the twentieth century. In the 1930s, when the FBI first began compiling *Uniform Crime Reports*, 75 percent of the people sentenced to state and federal prisons were white, in rough proportion to the demographic composition of the United States. By 2000, racial minorities accounted for 70 percent of new prison admissions and more than half of all American prisoners. The contrast in per capita prison admissions by population group was stark. In 1996, American prisons held 193 white

---

[20] BJS, "Number of Persons in Custody of State Correctional Authorities by Most Serious Offense, 1980–2000," http://www.ojp.usdoj.gov/, accessed June 8, 2004.

[21] Irwin et al., "Nonviolent Prisoners," 135.

[22] "More Than Any Other Democracy," *Economist*, March 20, 1999, 30–31.

Americans per 100,000 whites, 688 Hispanics per 100,000 Hispanics, and 1,571 African Americans per 100,000 African Americans. The glaring eight-to-one disparity between rates of incarceration for blacks and whites was to a great extent due to the war on drugs.[23]

In an era of fiscal conservatism, America's severity revolution has been enormously expensive. In 1982, local, state, and federal governments spent a total of $35.9 billion on criminal justice functions. By 1990, that figure had more than doubled. By 1999, Americans were spending $146.6 billion per year in their war on crime.[24]

Politicians had good reason to conclude this was the sort of criminal justice regime Americans wanted. Since 1985, the Bureau of Justice Statistics has been tracking American attitudes about crime and criminal justice. As the criminal justice system got tougher and tougher during the next decade, roughly 85 percent of Americans interviewed told pollsters that their local courts treated criminals "not harshly enough." Party affiliation made little difference in how Americans graded the courts' severity; neither did race. As to capital punishment, the same polling data indicated how far public opinion has moved since the 1960s. In 1965, only 38 percent of Americans said they "believe[d] in" the death penalty, compared to 47 percent who were opposed. (The remaining 15 percent were "not sure" or "refused" to answer.) By 1976, 67 percent of Americans were believers, with 25 percent opposed (and 8 percent not sure/refused). Support continued to climb. By 1997, 75 percent of Americans supported the death penalty, against only 22 percent opposed (with only 3 percent not taking a position).[25]

All of which helps explain why the sort of liberal concern for social root causes associated with President Johnson's Crime Commission's 1967 report all but vanished from the political discourse of either of the nation's two major parties. A telling example was the way Democratic presidential candidate William Clinton, then governor of Arkansas, established his tough-on-crime credentials during the 1992 campaign. In a well-publicized move, Clinton returned to Arkansas shortly before the New Hampshire primary to affirm the execution of Ricky Ray Rector, an African American man convicted of murdering a police officer. The Rector case was controversial because Rector was severely brain damaged; in an attempted suicide

[23] Irwin et al., "Nonviolent Prisoners."

[24] BJS, "Direct Expenditure by Level of Government, 1982–2001," http://www.ojp.usdoj.gov/, accessed June 8, 2004.

[25] In 1994, for example, 88 percent of Republican respondents, compared with 85 percent of Democrats, said the courts weren't harsh enough. See BJS, *Sourcebook of Criminal Justice Statistics 2002*, pages 140, 141, 143, http://www.albany.edu/sourcebook, accessed June 7, 2004.

following his crime, he had shot himself in the head. After Rector's last meal, a guard asked him why he had not eaten his dessert. Rector reportedly answered that he was saving it for later. He appeared to have no idea that he was headed to his own execution. Had Clinton halted Rector's execution he might have appeared soft on crime – a potentially fatal reputation for any ambitious politician to have in late twentieth-century America.

The severity revolution also registered in a profound ideological shift. Public concern about the social causes of crime did not vanish, but there was rapidly diminishing support for a criminal justice system that aimed to recognize and rehabilitate offenders as distinct individuals. Both the treatmentist consensus expressed in the Model Penal Code and the liberal, sociological perspective on crime reflected in the 1967 Crime Commission Report lost their currency in political discourse and public action. Emphasis shifted from treating the criminal to punishing the crime; as rehabilitation declined, retributivism and deterrence came back with a, well, vengeance. These developments had support from the political right, but also from civil liberties advocates on the left, who had long argued that the progressive ideal of individual treatment had too little regard for either the autonomy of the individual or due process of law.

The retreat from rehabilitation transformed criminal justice. After 1970, the states imposed new limits on (or, in some cases abolished altogether) the institutions of probation, the indeterminate sentence, and parole. When lawmakers established mandatory minimum sentences for specific crimes, they aimed both to deter crime with the threat of more severe penalties and to eliminate judges' discretion to consider offenders' personal background (other than criminal record). (In the process, the new sentencing statutes effectively shifted much of the old sentencing discretion to plea-bargaining prosecutors.) Prison rehabilitation programs, including prisoner education, suffered from declining resources and support. Between 1984 and 1997 nearly thirty states built "supermax" prisons, in which inmates typically spend 23 hours a day alone in their cells, and there was little pretense of reforming anybody.

The juvenile court was the greatest institutional casualty in this backlash. The idea that malleable young offenders were entitled to judicial paternalism and therapeutic intervention in a court of their own, rather than an adversarial trial and punishment as fully competent adults, was one of the most successful products of the Progressive era emphasis on social responsibility for crime. Since the 1960s the institution had weathered criticism from the right (for being too lenient on young criminals) and the left (for subjecting vulnerable young offenders to the arbitrary discretion of judges). But the most serious assault on juvenile justice did not occur until the late 1980s and early 1990s. America was hit by a wave of juvenile violent crime.

Between 1985 and 1991, homicides committed by boys aged fifteen to nineteen jumped 154 percent. As criminologists warned of a rising generation
of young male "superpredators," the states "got tough." Most states enacted
automatic transfer laws. Juveniles charged with any one of a growing list
of felonies – ranging from murder to car-jacking to dealing drugs near a
school – were transferred automatically to an adult criminal court. When
advocates marked the hundredth anniversary of the Cook County Juvenile
Court in 1999, the institution there and across the nation had lost much of
its public support and many of its young wards.

   Other innovations in criminal justice heralded a new penal communita-
rianism: "victims' rights" laws, the revival of public shaming punishments
in local communities, and sex offender notification laws. The notification
legislation was called "Megan's Law," in memory of a seven-year-old New
Jersey girl raped and murdered in 1994 by "a twice-convicted sex offender
who lived across the street." A model notification statute was enacted by
Congress in 1996 and then adopted, with modifications, by all fifty states.
The statutes required sex offenders to register with the police, who then noti-
fied the public. The requirements affected some 386,000 past offenders –
46,000 in California alone. Many states extended their registration requirements to people convicted before the notification laws took effect, and many
states posted their sex offender registries on the Internet. Despite their popularity, Megan's laws were a nightmare for civil libertarians, who insisted
that applying such a law to people convicted before its passage violated
constitutional protections against double jeopardy and ex post facto laws.
But the U.S. Supreme Court upheld the Alaska's notification law against
such challenges, declaring that the statute's registration and community
notification requirements created a "civil, nonpunitive regime." The Court
used similar reasoning to uphold other controversial practices, including
the seizure of drug dealers' property. The Court insisted that such measures constituted civil remedies, not criminal penalties, and were therefore
immune from ex post facto and double jeopardy claims.[26]

   Criminal justice cases contributed to the rise of conservative constitutionalism in late twentieth-century America. The U.S. Supreme Court took
steps to scale back the due process revolution. In *Gregg v. Georgia* (1976),
the Supreme Court cleared the constitutional hurdles to the death penalty,
leading to its reinstatement and rapid spread in the states. By 1999, ninety-
eight people were executed in the United States, the largest number since
1951; as of the year 2000, 3,601 Americans awaited the ultimate penalty

<hr/>

[26] *Smith v. Doe*, 538 U.S. 84, 96 (2004). Linda Greenhouse, "Justices Reject Challenges to
Megan's Laws," *New York Times*, March 6, 2003, 29.

on death row.[27] In numerous other decisions, the Court proved a major player in the severity revolution, mostly by restricting individual rights. The Court created new exceptions to the exclusionary rule and the Miranda warning requirement,[28] upheld the constitutionality of preventive detention laws ("tough" statutes that gave judges greater authority to refuse bail to defendants believed to be dangerous),[29] upheld California's model "Three Strikes and You're Out" law,[30] and handed down many opinions limiting death row appeals. The Warren Court had given federal district court judges wide authority to reform state institutions, including criminal justice institutions, in order to protect civil rights. The Rehnquist Court scaled back that authority. In 1996, Congress acted to curtail the prisoner litigation that had placed so many state prison systems and local jails under the effective control of federal judges. In two separate statutes, Congress curtailed prisoners' habeas corpus suits and limited the authority of federal district courts to interfere with the operations of state prison systems. The actions of the Court and the Congress seemed in synch with popular attitudes toward prisoners' constitutional rights during a period when states passed or strengthened laws to disenfranchise convicted felons.

Few artifacts reveal so much about the changing character of American liberalism at the twilight of the twentieth century as the private prison. The idea that a liberal regime might contract out its monopoly on the legitimate exercise of violence to profit-seeking manufacturing firms dates back at least to Jeremy Bentham's eighteenth-century penological manifesto, "Panopticon." But in America the late nineteenth-century labor movement had fought, with great success, for the curtailment of convict leasing and other forms of private convict labor. And from the Progressive era through the New Deal and beyond, the sphere of governmental action had expanded to include many areas of social life once largely left to the market or to private initiative. The rising conservatism of the late twentieth century aimed to roll back the sphere of public action and social responsibility, and a whole host of public functions and responsibilities were dismantled or contracted out to private firms.

Private corporations entered the field of prison and jail management during the 1980s, as lawmakers lauded the superior efficiency of private enterprise and the prison population explosion placed enormous stress on

---

[27] BJS, "Prisoners on Death Row," http://www.ojp.usdoj.gov, accessed June 11, 2004. BJS, "Executions," http://www.ojp.usdoj.gov, accessed June 11, 2004.

[28] *U.S. v. Leon*, 468 U.S. 897 (1984). *New York v. Quarles*, 467 U.S. 649 (1984).

[29] *U.S. v. Salerno*, 481 U.S. 739 (1987).

[30] *Ewing v. California*, 538 U.S. 11 (2003). *Lockyer v. Andrade*, 538 U.S. 63 (2003).

the penal infrastructure. By 2000, private detention facilities held more than 87,000 state and federal prisoners – more than 6 percent of the total. Shares of prison corporation stock traded freely on Wall Street. For critics not wholly persuaded by the neo-liberal promise of market efficiencies, there was something deeply disturbing and, perhaps unconstitutional, about statutes that delegated such vital government functions to profit-seeking firms. But others argued that private prisons offered a cheaper alternative to state-owned prisons. Moreover, private prison operators had to answer to stock-holders as well as the governments with which they contracted, and they were liable for torts and civil rights violations.

Privatization of the power to punish has not been limited to the ownership and management of prisons. The private market in prison labor has been reinvented for a post-industrial, globalizing economy. In 1979, Congress opened the gates when it effectively repealed its 1929 ban on interstate commerce in goods manufactured in prisons. More than thirty states have since passed laws authorizing private businesses to employ convict laborers, who now do everything from telemarketing to making computer parts. To date, private firms have gained control over only a small portion of the American prison system. But like welfare reform, prison privatization speaks to a broader theme in recent American history: the diminishing sense of public responsibility for the nation's most marginalized populations.

One area of policy innovation in criminal justice seemed to push back against the severity trend. In 1989, the first American "drug court" – a therapeutic court for drug offenders – was established in Dade County, Florida. America had reached a stalemate in the drug war. Narcotics cases put enormous pressure on criminal court dockets. Judges chafed under the statutory regimes that gave them little sentencing discretion. And recidivism rates indicated it was time for fresh thinking about drug policy. Blending judicial paternalism with therapeutic intervention, the new specialized tribunals resembled the "socialized" criminal courts of the early twentieth century. To become a "client" of a drug court and avoid a normal criminal trial, narcotics offenders had to accept the basic contract of the institution. In exchange for participating in an intensive regimen of court-supervised treatment – drug treatment, counseling, twelve-step programs, urinalysis testing, and regular appearances in court – the offender stayed out of jail and might eventually have his or her charges dismissed. Backsliding or noncompliance triggered sanctions, including short periods in jail. Supported by $40 million in Clinton Administration seed money, the institution spread rapidly. By 2003, nearly eleven hundred drug courts were up and running with four hundred more in the pipeline. The institutional success of the drug courts have provided a model for the creation of other specialized "problem-solving courts" at the local level to deal with domestic violence cases, mental health cases, and other cases where judges seek the assistance of social service workers and therapeutic experts to end a cycle of crime or violence.

At first glance, the drug courts and other problem-solving courts seem a curious liberal throwback in a conservative age. In fact, the tribunals appear to have spread so rapidly because there is something for everyone in the drug court model. Conservatives find merit in the courts' stern emphasis on personal responsibility. Liberals applaud the courts' basic recognition that drug addiction is not only a criminal act but a disease with social and personal root causes. For all of their limitations, these powerful new courts have created a space that had been lacking in the late twentieth-century American criminal justice system: a space where policymakers, judges, and the public can seriously consider alternatives to the relentless incarceration of the past quarter-century.

CONCLUSION

Nothing about the current prison crisis in the United States was foreordained. What politics wrought, politics might undo. At the turn of the twenty-first century, after several years of declining crime rates, many Americans seemed ready to rethink the wisdom of mass incarceration. Proliferating drug courts and other "problem-solving" criminal courts even had some hallmarks of a progressive-liberal revival. It seemed a promising way to launch a revival – through a practical rethinking of the purpose and practices of criminal justice institutions. Unfortunately, just as these reforms were getting underway, world events launched a new, largely unprecedented phase of American crime control. The "war against terror," whose history is just now unfolding, has already raised a host of new questions about national security, federalism, and civil liberties in the world's most powerful – and, in many respects, its most punitive – nation.

During the course of the twentieth century, Americans had a remarkable series of conversations about the changing nature of criminal responsibility, the purposes of criminal justice, and the related problem of social inequality in a liberal democracy. If in the twenty-first century the United States is to arrive at a more just and effective system for defining crime and dealing with offenders, those conversations must continue. And they must be, to a very large extent, conversations about history.

7

LAW AND MEDICINE

LESLIE J. REAGAN

Both law and medicine possess considerable social significance and power. The two professions and their institutions, practices, and ethics speak to and engage each other continuously. Interestingly, however, "law and medicine" is an underdeveloped field of history. No doubt the relative inattention that law and medicine have received from historians is related to the way in which the fields of legal history and medical history initially developed. Both grew out of the professions themselves and within law and medical schools, each producing an emphasis on a single profession, its interests, activities, and heroes. Medical jurisprudence, a specialized product of two professions with specialized knowledge and practitioners, provided a point of intersection. The history of medical jurisprudence includes the intellectual relationship between the legal and medical professions around specific scientific and medical questions that arose in the legal arena, as well as the professional relationship between physicians and attorneys (especially regarding malpractice). Yet, the traditional subjects of medical jurisprudence are only part of the history of medicine, law, and society.

Here, rather than sticking to a narrow formulation of the legal history of medicine focused on medical jurisprudence, I expand the definition of the field and recast it to include public health, health-related legislation, and the regulatory apparatuses of administrative law. An enlarged field of analysis allows us to examine public health and its relationship to the state and to criminal law and then to take those insights and look again at individual medical practices. Analysis across areas of law and medicine typically thought of as separate makes visible links that are otherwise concealed and presumed nonexistent. In particular, the ways in which medicine has become a key component of state systems of surveillance in the twentieth century, as well as the ways in which that role has been contested, become apparent. What became customary practices in public health were transferred to individual clinical practices and hospital policy in order to assist the state in its criminal justice investigations. As the police powers of public health moved into the clinical arena and assisted in criminal investigations, the questions of civil liberties and constitutional rights that public health traditionally raised became more widespread and acute.

When we bring medical jurisprudence and public health law together, it becomes evident that the public's use of private litigation to resist the power and practices of heath authorities and medical practitioners is not a recent phenomenon but a continuation of enduring individual and collective struggles for recognition of bodily integrity, patient autonomy, and due process rights. When social movements were lacking or legislative concern weak, the courts were the only system available for regulating medical and public health power and practices; at various moments, private litigation won improvements in medical practice, public health, and safety. This use of the legal system underlines the ways in which ordinary Americans insisted on rights as individual patients and citizens (often with the support of their peers on juries). Those individual cases provided the path for later "consumer" rights as patients in hospitals and clinics.

Although jokes and cocktail conversation suggest an enmity between the legal and medical professions, in fact, they enjoy a long history of mutual respect. Historically, the judiciary and lawmakers granted the medical profession a great deal of autonomy and deferred to physicians' judgment and rights in medico-legal matters. For most of the nineteenth century, the American medical professions were free of licensing requirements. Although elite, highly educated medical men resented this state of affairs – the American Medical Association (AMA), formed in 1847, sought state regulation of medical practice in order to delegitimate its competitors – these physicians nonetheless retained the respect of powerful men in law and politics. In the twentieth century, battles over national health insurance programs and malpractice took place in public courtrooms and political spaces, yet the alliance between medicine and the law strengthened in the less visible venues of hospitals, immigration checkpoints, and police stations.

Both the state and the medical profession have enhanced their power through their mutual alliance. The results for ordinary people could be quite intrusive; as law and medicine reinforced one another they appeared to be overpowering social forces. Under the police powers intrinsic to state-level governance, public health officials could arrest, hold, and treat individuals. And though Americans regularly protested – both violently and in court – the police and the judiciary alike generally upheld the powers of state health officials. With habeas corpus suspended for reasons of public health, citizens found there was little they could do to challenge the actions of health officials.

Over the twentieth century, medicine was drawn into an increasingly close relationship with the law and its agents as physicians and hospital staff became accustomed to collecting information and data for law enforcement and other state officials. All too often, medical abuses became "normal," bureaucratized, and invisible to those in power. It was left to outsiders and people below – lone individuals, the subordinated, the "deviant" poor – to bring the abuse of patients and citizens to light and into public consciousness. Eventually, the medical profession came itself to understand the medical misuse of power and mistreatment of patients, and began to learn respect for patient rights from those it had marginalized.

Because medicine is intimately involved with life and death and involves, by definition, touching and invading the body, it has been a primary area in which battles over individual civil liberties, autonomy, and bodily integrity have taken place. The struggles over an array of medico-legal issues were not confined to the pages of professional journals or courtrooms, but have claimed popular and political attention as well. Indeed, medicine and law is an especially useful arena for investigating the development and workings of power. Analysis of the actions of ordinary Americans, as well as of elites in hospitals, police stations, courtrooms, and public health offices, is important for understanding the frameworks of law and medicine that people negotiated, used, challenged, and remade. Here, too, we can examine how law and medicine (together and sometimes in opposition) create, enforce, or dismantle class, race, gender, sexualities, hierarchical medical arrangements, and corporate power.

The state's long-standing interest in controlling reproduction and sexuality is perhaps the most revealing prism through which the law-medicine nexus may be viewed. The definitions of citizenship in the nation, the inheritance of enslaved status (based on biological reproduction through the mother), the laws regarding marriage and child custody, and the legal interest in and state intervention in pregnancy and even childbirth itself all point to the significance of reproduction to the state. This history too indicates both the power of specialization and the ongoing struggles to guarantee legal and social deference to experts. Indeed, the medical profession's struggles to gain social and legal authority were often launched by focusing on reproduction and sexuality. For physicians, writing their will into law was achieved earliest and most easily in the reproductive arena. Reproduction and sexuality, then, have never been peripheral, but have mattered enormously in the construction of American law, medicine, society, and the state. Historical shifts in state surveillance and legal recognition of the autonomy of pregnant women have great relevance for patients in general. Changes in the relationships among medicine, law, and patient-citizens have often developed in this arena first.

In this chapter I have adopted a chronological and thematic framework to highlight the ways in which traditional medico-legal issues, public health, and criminal law come together. Starting with medical jurisprudence in the nineteenth century, the chapter moves to the turn-of-the-twentieth-century courtroom where the jousting of medical experts became public spectacle. From popular interest in cases centered on insanity and the female body, I turn to analysis of the nation's historical legal interest in reproduction and sexuality as expressed through legislation, law enforcement, and regulation of individual medical practices. The chapter then shifts to a focus on public health and the growing importance of administrative law. Through litigation and social movements, Americans demanded that the government act and provide services and that it protect the rights of individual citizens and patients. Public expectations of services, protection, and rights contributed to the development and reach of numerous federal agencies that worked to protect and improve the public's health.

Finally, I return to analyses of medico-legal issues. As we will see, the focus of jurisprudence at the turn of the twenty-first century shifted from medical expertise in the courtroom to decision making and procedures in the hospital. In addition to the medico-legal questions regarding end-of-life decisions, patient rights, and privacy that became a focus of law school textbooks in the late twentieth century, I consider the incorporation of the medical system into the state's policing systems over the century as a whole. Policing practices reliant on medical cooperation and expertise that began in public health – often as part of patrolling the borders between citizens and strangers – have, I suggest, increasingly merged with criminal law and increasingly take place in the hospital. These policing practices tend to focus first and most on stigmatized populations and to divide the "good" citizen-patient from the "the bad," usually marked by color and class. Yet, the habit of policing has expanded so that everyone is now subject to state surveillance through medicine.

I. MEDICAL JURISPRUDENCE IN NINETEENTH-CENTURY AMERICA

In the nation's earliest years, educated, elite leaders of the regular medical profession enjoyed a great deal of respect from the upper echelons of the legal profession and lawmakers. In matters of medical and scientific expertise, legal leaders deferred to the knowledge of elite physicians. An excellent example is the New York state legislature, which, in the mid-1820s, decided to address its mish-mash of common law, colonial law, and state law by rewriting and codifying the state's law. The three-man drafting committee invited John B. Beck, the foremost international expert in the field of medical jurisprudence, to write codes relevant to medicine and public health. This pattern persisted across the new nation as it created its own American legal culture. Despite the apparent hostility, derision, and division that developed between the professions later, lawyerly deference to professional medical knowledge continued into the twentieth century. Lawyers and doctors saw each other as professionals who had special knowledge, who served the public good, and who should be trusted to make decisions and judgments on behalf of the public. When the American Law Institute (founded in 1923) envisioned the reform and standardization of American law, it solicited, listened to, and followed the advice of the corresponding elite leaders of medicine.

Medical jurisprudence as a field of medicine originated in Scotland and France. The early-nineteenth-century American men who took up medical jurisprudence dreamed that a system of state medicine like that in France, with its system of medical police and close ties between physicians and the state, would be created in the United States. From the 1820s–1840s in the United States, medical jurisprudence gained a growing reputation, journals developed, and medical schools all offered training in the field. The physicians saw their medico-legal expertise and work – of determining insanity, performing autopsies at inquests, distinguishing between infanticide and stillbirth or between murder by poison and death by natural causes – as public services. As important as their knowledge was, however, physicians received little respect and no payment for these services. Medico-legal experts hoped to change this situation.

That some of the earliest medical researchers worked to answer questions that had no diagnostic or therapeutic relevance but were of legal significance indicates the desire among the medical elite to enhance their own status by making medicine useful to the law. The emphasis in the medical-legal relationship was on how medicine might serve the medical needs of the state in criminal cases, public health, and the protection of property rights.

Equally telling, the actual research questions pursued underscores the centrality of reproduction and family to both medicine and law. Many addressed paternity and inheritance. For instance, was the widow's newborn really that of her deceased spouse? The scientific answer to this question could determine the distribution of inherited wealth. Embedded in such medico-legal problems were gendered norms regarding sexual behavior, marriage, monogamy, and patriarchal control and possession of women and children. Physicians investigated the length of human gestation in order to answer questions about posthumous births as well as false claims of pregnancy. This research contributed to new scientific understandings of pregnancy and helped erode traditional ideas about the importance and meaning of quickening – when the pregnant woman felt fetal movement, at approximately the fourth or fifth month – at least among (some) regular (educated, orthodox) physicians, if not among the general public. Beck himself focused on infanticide and investigated birth weight and the processes of suffocation in an effort to determine whether an infant's death was due to natural or criminal causes. Others, knowing the battles that too often ensued when wills surprised expectant heirs, investigated the precise definition of insanity as death approached and claimed that physicians should determine whether the deceased had been clearheaded or demented when he authored his will.

Just as the field of medical jurisprudence was booming in the medical schools, a sudden rise in malpractice cases in the 1840s and 1850s produced a new hostility between lawyers and doctors. Historians explain the rise in suits as a result of regular physicians' growing expertise, the development of a medical literature that set standards, and rising public expectations fueled by physicians' claims. For instance, regular doctors' new ability to set bones in compound fractures was an improvement over the old method of amputation; yet, the limbs were often crooked and imperfect. Those crooked arms and legs were a disappointment that led to suits; juries sympathized more with the deformed than the doctor. Medical-legal experts campaigned to eliminate the emerging system that treated medical knowledge as a debate between opposing experts and urged the criminal justice system to create a board of medical experts to advise judges in medical matters. With such a board in place, the judge in each case would listen to a panel of experts and act on their careful and reasoned expertise rather than leaving medical knowledge, diagnosis, and appropriate therapeutics to be decided by a laymen's jury on the basis of conflicting testimony.

Close analysis of the testimony and complaints brought by ordinary people and their families in malpractice and injury suits, as well as juries' decisions in tort cases, offers insights into the world of law and medicine. In these venues, ordinary Americans expressed their sense of rights and expectations. Through official briefs and transcripts we can learn of popular beliefs and "unwritten laws" about the body, sickness and health, life and death, and social responsibility in the face of disease, death, or tragedy. In the thousands of suits brought by injured travelers against railroad and streetcar companies in the nineteenth century, it is clear that Americans – as injured travelers and as jurors – believed they had the right to expect that corporations would take care to prevent injury and death and that they had the right to damages when accidents occurred. Furthermore, they expected the state to act as a mediator and resolve the damages to bodily integrity, both in the courts and through state regulation of industry. Although the courts upheld the idea of the free man who was responsible for himself and who could be found negligent (and thus denied financial compensation), under the onslaught of suits, they also legitimated the payment of damages to injured white women – and even, when pressured by findings of repeated juries, to an African American man injured when forced to jump from a moving train. Similarly, a series of suits brought against physicians whose performance of illegal abortion injured or killed their patients indicates that American families expected physicians to perform safe procedures (regardless of their legality) and, if and when there were injuries, to take responsibility for their mistakes by providing medical services and by paying for emergency medical care, hospitalization, and even funeral costs. Juries agreed. So did half of the state supreme courts that ruled on the question.

In the early years of the Republic, elite educated physicians had won licensing requirements through state legislatures. In the 1830s and 1840s, however, the legal recognition and protection secured by the medical profession disappeared in the face of anti-elitist and democratic impulses. Instead of recognizing the aspirations of physicians and ensuring that medical practice was the exclusive right of an exclusive profession, the nation chose to protect the rights of all citizens to practice various forms of medicine and to choose among competing practitioners. State licensing of practitioners was quickly dismantled, not to be reinstated until the end of the nineteenth century. The lack of licensure laws and the laissez-faire attitude toward the education of doctors produced a diverse and competitive medical climate. The sick and injured could purchase guides and medications to practice their own medicine at home or seek out midwives, specialists in water cure, homeopathic doctors, or regular physicians. To the chagrin of the highly educated, more socially conservative regular physicians, all could claim the title "doctor," and all were equal in the eyes of the law and the eyes of many Americans.

With the failure of licensing and the proliferation of practitioners, elite physicians looked for other ways to constitute their authority and to form ties with the state. Regular physicians staked their claim to social authority and medical expertise not only on their expert knowledge but also on their claim to moral superiority. The creation of new criminal abortion laws in every state is an important example of regular medicine's drive for social power. The laws were rewritten according to the perspective of an elite group of specialists in obstetrics, a specific procedure was preserved to doctors only, and the process cultivated a respectful association between the state and the leaders of the regular medical profession. Under common law, early abortion had been permitted; only abortion *after* quickening was illegal. The AMA-led campaign of the 1860s and 1870s to criminalize abortion in early pregnancy dramatically changed the law governing pregnancy. In rewriting the law, regular physicians marked themselves off from the irregulars and midwives whom they blamed for abortion and also proclaimed their own purity in contrast to the Protestant ministry, which accepted quickening and did not join in the anti-abortion campaign. In securing laws that simultaneously criminalized early abortion and granted doctors the authority to make exceptions when they determined abortion to be medically necessary, regular physicians won exclusive power to determine the morality, medical necessity, and legality of abortion in specific cases.

Regular medicine's social power also rose in tandem with the great scientific discoveries in bacteriology in the late nineteenth century. The bacteriological discoveries of Robert Koch and Louis Pasteur in the 1870s and 1880s and the ensuing development of vaccines impressed journalists who glorified these men and their stories. Modern science and its achievements became part of the newspaper-reading public's daily fare. The discoveries of the laboratory and the decline in infectious diseases that were attributed wholesale to the germ theory (the effects of improving nutrition and public health measures attracted much less notice) made it seem that disease could be conquered decisively. Science became sacred, and medicine claimed the power of bacteriology. By the 1890s, medical students sat in front of microscopes and physicians donned white lab coats.

II. THE NEWSPAPERS, MEDICINE, AND THE COURTROOM

The horrors of medicine also captured press and popular attention. Such stories could be found in the courtroom. The press looked for, publicized, and helped produce these stories for public consumption. The identification, treatment, and punishment of the insane were of great interest at the turn of the century, as were the female body, sexuality, and gynecological surgery. Newspapers, courtrooms, and medical specialties – particularly psychiatry, surgery, and gynecology – worked together and against each other to develop narratives, to sell papers, to protect and destroy reputations, as well as to address and create social differentiation, norms, and deviance. Social hostilities and dilemmas around gender, class, race, and sexuality got worked out in the intertwined arenas of the courtroom and the newspaper.

While the legal system's adversarial format may have helped determine the guilt or innocence of the accused, negligence or not, for the practitioners of medicine the attorneys' battle to find "the truth" by questioning and undermining all opinions that did not fit their argument did not clarify the truth of medical diagnosis, therapeutics, theory, or practice. Instead, the questioning of expert witnesses degraded the reputation of the entire profession. When divergent medical testimony reached the newspapers, the problems within medicine were deepened and broadcast widely. Many cases required graphic descriptions of the body, surgical instruments, and techniques, and actual body parts were often passed around the courtroom.

Tumors, uteri, and other body parts preserved in jars were displayed by attorneys, identified by witnesses, and seen and handled by jurors. The medical profession would have preferred that matters medical – in both senses of the phrase – be contained within professional discourse and spaces.

As the medical diagnosis of insanity entered the courtroom, its causation, diagnosis, and definition moved out of medical control to become an object of contention among attorneys and expert witnesses and decided by judges, juries, and journalists. Because defendants could be found innocent by reason of insanity, the insanity defense was especially attractive to those accused of murder. In insanity cases, the "M'Naghten Rule," the rigid rule followed since the mid-nineteenth century, held that if a defendant knew that his or her act was forbidden by law, then he or she was legally sane, regardless of other behaviors. If the person did not realize at the time of the act that it was wrong, then the person was deemed insane and not responsible. The 1881 assassination of President James Garfield and the subsequent prosecution of his killer, Charles Guiteau, provided an extended moment during which the public, the psychiatric profession, and the legal system observed, debated, and judged insanity and sanity. Arguing that Guiteau was insane, his attorney brought in new German-trained neurologists who testified to the hereditary nature of the condition. The prosecution argued that Guiteau was sane and presented insane asylum superintendents as expert witnesses. The trial gave the public the treat of observing the assassin defend himself by insisting that he followed God's orders. To the cheers of the attending crowds, the jury found Guiteau sane and guilty. The M'Naghten Rule and the public's desire for a hanging won out over the new scientific understanding of insanity, which emphasized heredity. The spectacle of Guiteau continued as the dead man's body was autopsied and scrutinized. On finding lesions, medical men and medical journals changed their view and declared Guiteau had been insane after all.

Ten years later, another murder and the question of insanity gripped the nation's attention; this case found its way into the definitions of psychiatry and sexology. The murderer was a woman, as was her victim. Alice Mitchell, a white, middle-class daughter of Memphis, slashed the neck of the girl she intended to marry. Mitchell avoided a murder prosecution by agreeing to a lunacy inquisition. If the defendant was found insane, execution could be avoided, but lifetime incarceration was virtually guaranteed. The evidence of insanity in Mitchell's case was, as in Guiteau's, composed of both evidence of hereditary insanity and a lifetime of strange and inappropriate behavior. The odd behavior and the marks on the body that the defense offered as proof of insanity were defined by the norms of gender and heterosexuality. The behavior to which family and friends testified began with Alice's interest in boys' games as a child and her refusal to dance with young men and ended with her special friendship with Freda Ward. Alice was determined to marry her and had given Freda an engraved gold band. For the psychiatric experts, Alice Mitchell's desire to marry a beloved woman proved her delusional state. Same-sex desire was understood as sickness; gender-bending was proof of insanity.

The Alice Mitchell case was one of a series of turn-of-the-century cases that brought together medicine, crime, and sex and captured the imagination of the press, the public, and the courts. All of them – Alice Mitchell's crime, the contemporaneous investigation of Chicago's abortion business, the "Jack the Ripper" murders in London (which invoked evil gynecological surgeons), and the trials of Brooklyn gynecologist, Dr. Mary Dixon Jones – underline the importance of female sexuality and medical matters to the New Journalism of the 1880s and 1890s. The front-page newspaper coverage of Brooklyn gynecologist Dr. Mary Dixon Jones's questionable surgical practices and subsequent manslaughter and libel trials in 1888– 89 and 1892 spotlighted the gendered expectations of medical demeanor and courtroom deportment. The Dixon Jones trials, like the contemporaneous insanity trials, served as a lightning rod for divergent views about the direction of medicine. Dixon Jones violated the expectations of the female physician. Instead of being wary of surgery and science like most women in the profession, she embraced both; instead of displaying personal modesty, she was ambitious. Instead of feminine sympathy, she coerced women into gynecological surgery. Although prominent physicians and sixty patients testified on her behalf, fifty other women testified to their discomfort with Dixon Jones, of her insistent demands for money, and of surgeries they never agreed to. Although Dixon Jones was acquitted of manslaughter and homicide charges, she lost her libel case and her hospital license was revoked.

III. FROM DRAMATIC CASES TO THE TRIALS OF DAILY LIFE: REPRODUCTION AND THE LAW

Big cases, like those of Dixon-Jones, Mitchell, or Guiteau, which captured the attention of the press and the public, offer the historian opportunities to analyze legal precedents and medical theory, as well as American values, anxieties, social relations, and social structures. Smaller, less visible cases rarely reported in legal treatises or newspapers offer similar and other opportunities: the ability to see how the most ordinary investigations and trials were conducted on a daily basis and to analyze the more typical treatment of working-class witnesses and defendants. Even the most routine, most trivial of interactions from the perspective of police or attorneys were important moments for the men and women caught in them. Those routine questions, investigations, and processes taught people the power of the law, the operations of justice, and the law's capacity to punish. Enforcement of the states' criminal abortion laws provides an example.

Raids and trials of accused abortionists sometimes dominated the newspapers, but relying on press reports alone would distort our understanding of the law in practice because newspapers emphasized the unusual – abortion-related deaths of unmarried women – and produced a terrifying picture of a deadly, criminal underworld. The widespread availability of abortion services and the relatively small number of convictions for criminal abortion may suggest the failure of the criminal abortion laws, but to conclude that the laws mattered little would also be incorrect. Data on prosecution and incarceration do not tell the true story of the state's ability to punish. To see how law worked in practice requires analysis of the routines of enforcement. Local police regularly investigated criminal abortion, collected evidence, interrogated witnesses, and arrested suspected abortion providers. Because juries often refused to convict in abortion cases, prosecutors learned to concentrate on cases where a woman died. As important, the state's police officers and prosecutors did not enforce the laws alone, but relied on the assistance of private entities, particularly the medical profession.

The process of collecting evidence against accused abortionists punished women for their efforts to end a pregnancy. To obtain dying declarations, police and physicians questioned women on their deathbeds, threatened to withhold medical care, and required them to identify their abortionists and sign documents stating their belief that they were about to die. In the process, women, their lovers, husband, relatives, and friends learned first-hand that the law condemned them and their actions. For unknown thousands of women, these were the final events of their lives. For many others who survived their abortions as well as those who were questioned relentlessly after a miscarriage, it was a humiliating, frightening, and punitive experience. Women did not need to be arrested, prosecuted, or incarcerated to feel punished. The use of the hospital to identify crimes and the interrogation of vulnerable patients were standard components of the state's criminal investigation practices and continued until the decriminalization of abortion nationwide in 1973.

The state's reliance on medical policing of patients in abortion cases began at the turn of the century. A few physicians urged their colleagues to help coroners and police in the repression of abortion, but many doctors resisted. The state needed medical cooperation, however, and obtained it by threatening to prosecute physicians or damage their reputations. Coerced, physicians learned to comply; notifying the police and interrogating women became standard hospital routine. In the post-World War II period, physicians themselves developed new methods, namely therapeutic abortion review committees of physicians, to monitor their colleagues' abortion practices, to define legal and illegal, and to restrict access to (legal, therapeutic) abortions in hospitals. The intentions of these committees were not clear-cut; they both limited abortion and legitimated abortions in order to allow physicians to provide them. Overall, however, the committees reduced the number of abortions performed in hospitals by dissuading physicians and patients from seeking committee-endorsed, therapeutic abortions and thus pushed many into the world of illegal abortion. There, despite the law and organized medicine's opposition to abortion, however, the medical profession was always heavily involved in providing illegal abortions. And in the late 1950s, a small group of physicians who found the profession's review processes and the injury to women intolerable and unjust initiated the earliest efforts to reform the nation's criminal abortion laws. By the late 1960s a few brave physicians broke the laws openly in order to challenge and, they hoped, change them.

The legal history and practice of contraception and abortion have long been connected. The 1860s and 1870s saw a frenzy of lawmaking to criminalize the avoidance of childbearing; to prosecute practitioners, pharmacists, and others who provided contraceptives and abortions; and to censor discussion of sexuality, pregnancy, contraception, and abortion. Congress enacted the Comstock Law in 1873, which banned publication about and the provision of contraceptives and abortion and equated both with "obscenity." The Comstock Law and the criminalization of early abortion underlined the nation's interest in controlling sexuality and reproduction, enforced maternity as a marital duty, indicated support for censorship, and re-entrenched the notion that sexuality was shameful. In the 1870s YMCA anti-vice activist Anthony Comstock advanced his career with an attack on free lover and feminist, Victoria Woodhull; appointed Special Agent of the U.S. Post Office, he revived his reputation at the end of his life when he seized Margaret Sanger's publication, *The Woman Rebel* in 1914, and shut down one of the first birth control clinics in New York City two years later.

Comstock's activities energized an emerging new pro-sex movement that demanded the legalization of contraception. Sanger and her socialist supporters used Comstock's raids to develop a new movement for freedom of speech and a movement willing to open birth control clinics in defiance of the law. Sanger turned to winning legislation granting physicians the legal right to prescribe contraceptives, but the AMA continued to strenuously oppose both birth control and abortion. During the Depression, birth control and abortion boomed as families found it essential to prevent the birth of children. In the 1930s a series of federal cases – *Young's Rubber Co. vs. C. I. Lee and Co.* (1930), *Davis v. The United States* (1933), *United States v. One Package of Japanese Pessaries* (1936) – found that contraceptives were not necessarily "obscene" and that physicians could legitimately purchase and prescribe contraceptives. By the late 1930s, the American Birth Control Association sponsored more than 300 birth control clinics; mail-order firms, pharmacies, and door-to-door saleswomen sold contraceptive devices and medications to the general public. Police raided and shut down birth control clinics in the 1910s and 1920s when clinics first opened as a political project and were publicly advertised; abortion clinics were similarly raided as they became open and visible during the Depression. Both remained criminal until the 1960s and early 1970s though both contraception and abortion were widely practiced by ordinary Americans.

The federal government quietly provided funds for contraceptives beginning in the Depression years, but it was not until 1965 that the U.S. Supreme Court recognized the right of married couples to use contraceptives. *Griswold v. Connecticut* (1965) recognized that a "zone of privacy" existed in which the married couple in their private home had the essential right to make decisions about procreation and family. In 1972, *Eisenstadt v. Baird* found the same right existed for unmarried heterosexual couples (again recognizing reality). In this period, a dozen states reformed their abortion laws, and several states legalized abortion, most importantly New York in 1970. In *Roe v. Wade* and *Doe v. Bolton* (1973) the Supreme Court overturned the nation's criminal abortion laws in recognition of the right of women to make decisions about their bodies and reproduction and, at least as important, in recognition of physicians' rights to carry out their medical judgment without interference.

The poor women who died – many of them African American and Latina – and the thousands of women injured every year as a consequence of the criminalization of contraception and abortion should not be overlooked. Nor should the benefits of legalization. Maternal mortality fell in half following the legalization of abortion. In countries where abortion is still illegal, by comparison, the procedure accounts for 25 to 50 percent of all maternal mortality. Legalization of contraception and abortion significantly improved women's health and life chances and recognized their rights as citizens to bodily integrity and self-determination. After *Roe v. Wade*, the pro-life movement's strenuous work to undermine the legality and availability of medically provided abortions gained it significant media attention. Less noticed was the anti-abortion movement's effort to suppress the legitimacy and use of contraceptives – and not just in America but worldwide.

The state's emerging reliance on medical experts in criminal law was not unique to abortion at the turn of the century. It was an innovative feature of Progressive era judicial efforts to address crime in general as a product of larger social problems. The Municipal Court of Chicago led the nation in the new strategy of "socialization" of the law, creating new courts for special areas – a family court, a morals court, a boys court – and new agencies to investigate the underlying social causes for criminal violations. The courts then tailored their response to the particular individual's pathology.

In the 1910s and 1920s, eugenics strongly influenced the criminal justice system. Elite eugenic theory converged with intellectual and popular anxiety about crime and colored the criminal justice system's actions. The crime problem, in eugenic thinking, was a problem of reproduction. The propensity to crime, deviance, hypersexuality, and more was inherited: the criminal classes (re)produced criminals, and the "feeble-minded" prostitute gave birth to feeble-minded criminals. As Progressive era judges, social workers, and reformers adopted these views, often alongside environmental beliefs that poverty produced criminal behavior, many concluded that crime control required preventing crime before it occurred, both by holding the "mentally defective" preemptively and by preventing the reproduction of the feeble-minded and criminal. The Chicago Municipal Court system included its own Psychopathic Laboratory to which local judges sent criminal defendants and others for IQ and psychological testing. What began as a way to sensitize the law to an individual's social circumstances and to help defendants' reform themselves quickly became a method for identifying potential criminals to be ordered to institutions for the feeble-minded and held indefinitely. This individualized assessment system tested and incarcerated thousands of working-class citizens annually – in mental institutions, not prisons, and without due process. Across the country, many of the inmates of these institutions were also subjected to surgery as part of the state's crime control program.

The history of sterilization reveals how medicine and law collaborated in the past to control specific populations, to shape society in their own image through involuntary and undemocratic means, and to reinforce and maintain historical inequalities and hierarchies. The targets of involuntary sterilization changed with the historical context and the changing sense of who threatened the social order and the public good. The law did not take the lead; rather, it followed medical practice by authorizing the practice of involuntary sterilization through statutes endorsed in the notorious U.S. Supreme Court decision, *Buck v. Bell* (1927).

Systematic, involuntary sterilization began as a private program of sterilizing male prisoners, a program initiated by Dr. Harry Sharp at the Indiana State Reformatory. Dr. Sharp soon advertised his success; by 1909 he reported he had sterilized more than 200 male inmates. Eugenicists and physicians endorsed the program, and the states soon officially sanctioned the involuntary sterilization of the "feeble-minded," "defective," "delinquent," "criminal," and infected. By 1913, twelve states had passed such legislation. Individuals and civil rights organizations fought these involuntary procedures and often won, but ultimately the U.S. Supreme Court endorsed the practice. *Buck v. Bell* showed legal deference to accepted medical and scientific practice and thought. It also indicated how the practice of sterilization had changed; the person to be sterilized was not a "defective" or "criminal" man, but a young white woman in Virginia who, along with her mother and infant daughter, was thought to be "feebleminded." Sterilization had shifted to women, the sex that literally produced the next generation.

The state did not officially approve every sterilization or require informed consent or review procedures, but instead assumed that social policy and public morals were in good hands when entrusted to physicians. As mass sterilization became standardized in the states and tens of thousands were sterilized through official state programs, private hospitals and private physicians also carried out their own sterilization policies for their vision of the public good. By the 1950s and 1960s, abusive sterilization practices were widespread and routine. Individual physicians and hospital committees regularly pushed or insisted on female sterilization in exchange for prenatal care, obstetrical services, or therapeutic abortions. If patients did not cooperate, some physicians threatened to have state officials cut off welfare payments or take away their children. Still others neither asked nor threatened, but simply performed sterilization procedures during delivery without the knowledge or permission of the woman. The belief of some individual physicians in their right to act as judges who punished and issued edicts is remarkable. It must also be said, however, that some physicians never subscribed to such ideas, broke their profession's rules by providing reproductive services requested by women, advocated reproductive rights, and bravely sought to end patient abuse by bringing abuses to professional, public, and media attention.

By the 1950s and 1960s involuntary sterilization was increasingly used to punish single women and single mothers of every race and class for their sexual activity. Low-income women of color, however, were especially vulnerable to compulsory sterilization. In the Southwest, Mexican and Mexican-American women were targeted by physicians in public hospitals (who used Spanish language as an indicator of welfare abuse, illegal immigration, and overpopulation to justify coercive sterilization practices). In the South and in Northern industrial cities, individual physicians and state programs targeted low-income African American women, represented as unwed mothers and resented by whites for their claims on public funds through AFDC (Aid to Families with Dependent Children). The women coerced into "consenting" to a sterilization procedure in order to obtain a safe, legal therapeutic abortion performed in a hospital were likely to be unmarried white women of the middle class. Sexually active single women, pregnant or mothers already, bore the brunt of anger at the changes in heterosexuality, social mores, and gender then taking place. In a fervently pro-natalist period, these women would have their ability to reproduce permanently taken away. Although the majority of the involuntarily sterilized were apparently single, neither married women nor men were protected. In Puerto Rico and in Los Angeles, married Latinas were pressed to agree to sterilization as part of population programs or simply sterilized without being told. In California, one judge pressured a Latino father into "agreeing" to sterilization in order to avoid imprisonment. Federal programs promoted and paid for sterilization procedures on American Indian reservations. At the same time, patients who wanted sterilization procedures were routinely refused. Affluent whites, married couples, and African Americans all ran into road blocks and denial when they requested sterilization.

Sterilization abuse reached a crescendo in the 1960s, yet in-depth studies of specific regions complicate generalizations about the ability of eugenicists to exert control. For instance, in the face of racist policies in North Carolina, some poor African American women obtained sterilizations they wanted for their own reasons through the system designed to prevent the birth of "undesirables." Collective efforts could change the law. Even when suits brought against physicians and hospitals for sterilization abuse failed (as in Los Angeles), organizers could still win. Chicana feminists, with allied physicians, attorneys and media attention, won protections against sterilization abuse in the Los Angeles County Medical Center and wrote California's state regulations. In 1978, the federal government (through the Department of Health, Education and Welfare) adopted guidelines called for by reproductive and civil rights activists. Protections included waiting periods, informed consent, prohibition of threats regarding welfare services, and the availability of Spanish-language materials. As feminist health and civil rights groups learned, however, new laws and rules designed to protect poor and minority women would be ignored without continuous monitoring.

IV. PUBLIC HEALTH

The myriad local, state, and federal institutions and regulatory agencies that acted to protect public health and safety or provide health care all deserve attention as sites of law and medicine and as sites of legal conflict. The police powers wielded by local municipalities and the states that undergirded public health measures in the eighteenth and nineteenth centuries gave way to a greater emphasis on administrative law by the turn of the twentieth century together with a growing emphasis on federal responsibility for the health of the nation. After the turn of the century, the powers granted bureaucratic agencies worried many; administrative law did not follow standard judicial practices regarding habeas corpus, due process, or evidence and was generally not subject to judicial oversight and review. Congress and the courts tempered agency powers by mid-century, but certain arenas – notably immigration – continued to be exempt from adhering to due process procedures. Areas of public health law were also treated as inherently in the public interest and left significantly free from judicial review. For well over a half-century, for example, Americans had been discovering through personal suits that there were few restraints on health authorities' powers over the public or over "inmates" of state-sponsored health institutions. Indeed, health authorities' commonplace usage of the term *inmates* rather than *patients* or *citizens* implicitly equated disease with crime, and institutionalization with incarceration.

The power and public funds granted health-related institutions and agencies indicate that government action on behalf of health is a long-held American value. The legal powers enjoyed by health authorities, however, were predicated not only on a commitment to health but also on social stigma and inequality. Social support for controlling undesirable and subordinated groups, racism, nativism, and sexism made up the foundation on which the power of health officials stood. The common association of infectious diseases with downtrodden groups – whether foreign-born, non-white, poor, criminal, sexually deviant, or alcoholic – lent a hand in enabling the state to enforce quarantines. The diseased were blamed for their diseases; the public tended to be more concerned about keeping away from the sick than caring for them. Diseases often provided the occasion to create racial and class difference, to discriminate, and to exclude those whom the majority feared, whether Chinese bachelors in San Francisco blamed for bubonic plague, African American domestic workers in Atlanta identified as the spreaders of tuberculosis, or Mexican, Asian, or European immigrants at the nation's borders who were searched for trachoma, tuberculosis, and a host of other diseases and disabilities.

Boards of health benefited from epidemics: in fear of disease, the public, lawmakers, and the courts granted them greater powers. Fear of epidemics prompted quarantine, official surveillance, and civic action; much more common causes of death – tuberculosis and childbirth – produced little panic or action. In the face of a global cholera epidemic in 1866, for instance, New York City health officers assisted by city police inspected businesses and private residences and issued orders requiring premises to be cleaned, basements drained, privies emptied and pigs moved. Public health requirements overrode property rights claims: some businesses were ordered to cease operation altogether. Following New York City's success in avoiding a deadly epidemic, cities around the country established boards of health.

Although the state has long had the legal power to quarantine, businesses and individuals often challenged that power and health departments sometimes lost it. Worried about lost profits, businesses involved in trade or tourism disputed the quarantine of ships, sailors, travelers, and products. Involuntary quarantine and/or treatment sometimes provoked violent protest. In 1894, Milwaukee saw rock throwing and death threats in response to the traditional public health measures taken during a developing smallpox epidemic. City health officials had quarantined the sick at home, isolated others at the city hospital, and offered vaccinations to the public. When health officials attempted to forcibly remove children from parents to take them to the hospital (where immigrant mothers were sure their children would die), the individual agony of mothers turned into a neighborhood riot. Battles broke out among the German immigrant population, health officers, and police as the health commissioner insisted he was simply enforcing the law. The health commissioner's insensitivity to Milwaukee's German population produced a public health failure: smallpox became widespread in German neighborhoods, and the city council revoked the commissioner's legal authority to quarantine without consent. Public health authorities learned that seeking cooperation through public education and the encouragement of civic-mindedness were better strategies than coercion.

State-mandated vaccination to protect the public from smallpox also raised constitutional questions. When cities or states required vaccination, some people objected and took their cases to court on the grounds of personal liberty and religious freedom. In the face of a smallpox epidemic in Cambridge, Massachusetts, the board of health "ordered, that all inhabitants of the city be vaccinated." When Henning Jacobsen refused to be vaccinated, he was arrested and fined. He took his case all the way to the U.S. Supreme Court, arguing that the compulsory vaccination law was arbitrary and that the free citizen had the right to make decisions about his own health. In *Jacobson v. Massachusetts* (1905), the Supreme Court upheld local and state laws that mandated vaccination for the good of the larger public's health and at the same time allowed individuals to reject vaccination. The state could not forcibly vaccinate, but it could fine or incarcerate those who refused vaccination and could require vaccination of those wishing to attend school.

The late nineteenth century and early twentieth century saw a marked shift in the reach of police powers to protect the public's health as health authorities increasingly focused on individuals. The transformation in scientific knowledge of disease undergirded the expansion of administrative law in health matters. As scientists and health officials embraced germ theory, public health authorities focused on infectious disease and insisted that

monitoring and correcting individual behavior were the keys to protecting the public's health. In this new context, the contributions of poverty,
ill health, malnutrition, environmental toxins, and the like tended to be
absolved. Health officials pinned blame for the spread of deadly infectious
disease on individuals (and entire groups); they often regarded the diseased
as akin to criminals.

The treatment of one early-twentieth-century New York City woman,
Mary Mallon, who became known as "Typhoid Mary," exemplifies these
changes and the importance of social stigma. Bacteriologists had theorized
the notion of a "healthy carrier," an individual who showed no symptoms
of disease, yet was contagious. Mallon was the first person in the United
States to be identified as a healthy carrier of typhoid fever. Although it
was not clear that city health authorities had the legal authority to isolate
a healthy individual, in March 1907 New York City Health Department
officials and police officers seized Mallon and took her to the city's hospital
for contagious cases where her feces and urine were collected and analyzed
against her will. She was soon placed in isolation. Not until two years later
did a court hear her case in a habeas corpus hearing.

As public health focused its force on individuals, it increasingly provoked
individual lawsuits over civil rights. In Mallon's case, despite the ambiguity of the law, conflicting laboratory evidence, and the clear possibility that
hundreds of healthy citizens could be held by the state without recourse (as
Mallon's attorney pointed out), the court allowed the health department
to isolate Mallon. The court's willingness to overlook the unequal application of health regulations underlines the convergence of public health and
administrative processes. That is, as was true of federal immigration law in
the early twentieth century, local courts granted public health officials enormous authority to apply health regulations and exempted administrative
decision making from the usual due process standards. Health authorities
well knew that thousands of healthy typhoid carriers walked freely in the
city, but few were pursued. Indeed, in keeping with a socialized and highly
gendered view of the law, officials helped healthy male carriers of typhoid
who had families to support, instead of holding these men in quarantine.
For Mallon alone the health department required isolation and continuous
collection and examination of her bodily wastes for evidence of infection.
The complex historical record suggests that Mallon's unique status as the
first healthy carrier along with her demeaned social status as a single, Irish,
working woman all conspired to make her an example of the state's power
over uncooperative citizens. If New York health authorities had tried to
isolate the thousands of other healthy typhoid carriers – most of whom
would have been hard-working, respectable citizens – it is likely that the

authorities would have faced substantial resistance from the public and politicians.

Yet, there were instances when health authorities did hold thousands of women and men in order to prevent the spread of infectious diseases without generating public disapproval. The people held did not come from all classes nor were they perceived as respectable. Instead, they came from stigmatized groups – namely, female sex workers and male alcoholics – whom the respectable majority already disliked and wanted off the streets, In pursuing specific categories of people, that is, public health punished the socially and sexually deviant. Few were concerned about their rights in disease-control efforts. The judiciary's hands-off attitude toward public health law further isolated these stigmatized people and left them without legal means to challenge their treatment by authorities. The criminalization of health law bred distrust of both public health and the law; vulnerable citizens who feared health authorities' links to police and prison avoided health officials, physicians, and medical institutions.

Venereal Diseases

Federal policy toward the spread of sexually transmitted infectious diseases, or venereal diseases in the language of the time, first developed in the military. During the Civil and Spanish-American Wars, the military assumed that soldiers would visit prostitutes and so officially regulated brothels, regularly examined women, and required soldiers to undergo chemical treatments to prevent disease or be disciplined. By World War I, the British battle over the Contagious Disease Acts and a new sexual politics informed American policies. Now allied with social purity forces, the military took a different approach to the spread of venereal diseases among the troops. Within the ranks, the military stressed sexual purity and attempted to replace sexual activity with sports, movies, and books. Outside, meanwhile, it enforced "pure zones" of at least five miles radius around military bases. Military and local officials emptied these zones of all women believed to be prostitutes. *Prostitute* was defined broadly to include all women suspected of being such, including women who walked alone on city streets, women out at night, and young women who dated military men or had sexual relationships with them, as well as women who worked in brothels and exchanged sex for money.

The local and federal policies pursued during World War I against venereal diseases treated disease as a crime and sexually suspect women as criminals. Only one sex and only one type of person, the prostitute, was seen as infectious and responsible for venereal diseases. Suspicious women were arrested, subjected to forcible gynecological examination, and held by local boards of health until declared free of disease. Men were exempted. The U.S. Attorney General promoted the detention and compulsory examination of women by declaring it "the constitutional right of the community" to hold those suspected of disease in order to prevent its spread. With the encouragement of the Attorney General and the military, cities and states passed legislation requiring the examination, isolation, and treatment of women suspected of having venereal diseases. When women complained of violations of habeas corpus for being held without charges or trials and without any end in sight for their incarceration, their cases were dismissed. The federal government financed the construction of eighteen institutions to hold the detained women, and between 1918 and 1920, more than 35,000 women were arrested and more than 18,000 incarcerated, in many cases for a year or longer. Chicago's Morals Court had pioneered the method of requiring physical examination of prostitutes for syphilis and then "offering" them free medical care instead of fines. With the federal government endorsing the incarceration of prostitutes as part of the war effort, Chicago's Morals Court changed its methods. It refused bail to all women brought in, required them to undergo a police-enforced mandatory medical examination for venereal disease, then ordered them held under quarantine until non-infectious, often for months. Due process did not apply to public health law.

The women trapped in this punitive system suffered violation of their bodily integrity and their civil rights and were blamed for harming the troops and the nation. They had few places to turn for protection. The full impact of this history on working-class women, primarily in the South where the army camps were located as well as in cities like Chicago, has yet to be unraveled. The founder of the American Civil Liberties Union (ACLU) later called the tens of thousands of incarcerated American women "prisoners of war."[1] The policies of this period perpetuated the sexual double standard and showed that blame for infectious diseases could easily be shifted to women. Working-class women learned of the power of public health officials and learned to associate them with the military and the police. As health departments turned to other efforts to improve the public's health (prenatal care or tuberculosis programs, for example), those with personal experience may have resisted all measures, knowing how easily public health could turn into prison.

At the end of the twentieth century in the face of another stigmatized epidemic, HIV/AIDS, some politicians drew on the same historical

---

[1] Quotation of Roger Baldwin in David J. Pivar, *Purity and Hygiene: Women, Prostitution, and the "American Plan," 1900–1930* (Westport, CT, 2002), 217.

assumptions and practices to write laws requiring that suspected or convicted prostitutes be tested for HIV/AIDS (again, female sex workers were identified as the criminal source of fatal disease, not as its potential victims). Public health professionals generally opposed mandated testing and quarantine for HIV, knowing that such programs would drive people away from public health and enlarge the epidemic.

Tuberculosis

The difficulty of protecting the rights of stigmatized and sick populations in the mid-twentieth century can be seen in the example of Seattle's Firland, one of the nation's largest tuberculosis sanatorium. The state identified the typical tubercular, infectious person as a homeless alcoholic man living on the streets; its handling of the disease was correspondingly coercive, restraining tuberculosis patients in isolation against their will. Patients, including the down-and-out alcoholics of Seattle's Skid Road, questioned the fairness and constitutionality of the state's policies, but winning attention to patient complaints was an arduous task. In the mid-1950s patients pointed to practices they considered particularly egregious violations of their civil rights and of the rules governing quarantine: holding patients for long periods of time and in the "lockdown ward" without hearings or opportunities for appeal, treating patients identified as alcoholics differently from other tuberculosis patients, and using institutionalization and isolation as punishment for behavior. A handful of patients and one unusual former health worker of the institution wrote numerous letters to successive governors of Washington State, to health officials, and to newspapers. Most of these letters were dismissed or returned to the head of the institution, who promptly censored the mail.

The former staff member finally caught the attention of the Washington State ACLU when he produced a 51-page report of complaints. Although the ACLU confirmed that the public tuberculosis sanatorium was violating the civil liberties of its patients, public health officials refused to make any changes and the ACLU dropped the matter. The lack of progress in this case points to the power of public health. The state gave police powers to public health officials with few restrictions and then trusted them. Once the sick were placed in the hands of public health officials in order to protect the health of others, they had little redress. The sick were not convicted criminals, but with the adoption of locked wards and mandatory institutionalization and treatment for months, they could be treated as such. In the early 1960s, in light of growing legal and social concern for the rights and treatment of inmates in prisons and health institutions, Firland created a hearings process headed by a local judge. Yet, the judge continued to allow the use of isolation for punishment (for drinking or escaping the institution) and permitted patients who were not infectious – and thus not a threat to the public's health and not valid for quarantine – to be held against their will. Furthermore, the differential treatment of alcoholics, who were held for a full year rather than the 3–6 months needed to make a patient non-infectious, persisted.

Like the history of the public response to sexually transmitted diseases, the Firland case demonstrates that public health law and criminal law were not distinct but intertwined. As alcoholism came to be understood as a disease, Washington State judges sent men brought in for public drunkenness to the TB sanatorium rather than jail. In other states, these men were still sent to jail, and their quarantine and treatment for tuberculosis occurred there. The Firland institution itself was a mixture of hospital and prison: the institution was located in a former naval hospital, and the new locked ward was the old navy brig. Originally built for punishment, the locked ward was used that way again as the staff turned to it to manage a large and sometimes difficult and argumentative population. State law guaranteed health officials' right to quarantine people with tuberculosis without providing the due process rights required in criminal law.

V. FEDERAL AGENCIES AND THE HEALTH OF AMERICANS

At the beginning of the twenty-first century, the United States, unlike the rest of the industrialized Western world, does not have a national health care system. Yet, lawmakers from small towns up to the federal level constantly pass health-related laws, form agencies with their own administrative laws and systems, and spend significant shares of tax monies on health and medicine. The U.S. system is deliberately piecemeal because it has been constructed against the idea of a universal health care system and in the name of the idea of a private physician-patient relationship. It is a system sensitive to political clout. Instead of a universal system, U.S. government-supported health services are awarded to a narrow set of those deemed ideologically "worthy."

The new political power of the AMA in the twentieth century can be seen in its influence on federal health legislation. The AMA vigorously fought early-twentieth-century reform efforts to win universal health insurance as achieved in Europe. Attacks on all things German during World War I and the rise of hysteria over socialism and the "Communist menace" after the war ensured that universal health care was defeated. Instead, Congress awarded health benefits to specific groups of deserving citizens: mothers and soldiers. In 1920, under the threat of losing office as a result of the new voting bloc of women created by the Nineteenth Amendment, Congress passed and President Wilson signed the Sheppard-Towner Act for maternal and infant health. The Sheppard-Towner Act was a major, early act of federal social welfare legislation. With shared funding from the federal government and the states, it was intended to reduce maternal and infant mortality (a source of national shame as the highest rate in the industrialized, "civilized," world) through the education of mothers, midwives, and doctors. As much as this was a victory for the women's suffrage and health reform movements, the AMA limited the act's reach. The AMA succeeded in ensuring, first, that the Children's Bureau focused on education, not on the provision of needed medical services, and, second, that all educational messages urged pregnant women and mothers to see private doctors, preferably specialists in obstetrics. Nonetheless, the AMA led the fight that ended the program in 1929 by associating the Sheppard-Towner Act with "socialized medicine" and "mannish" women. As to soldiers, in 1921 Congress appropriated more than $18 million to build Veterans Administration Hospitals around the country to provide care to veterans exclusively.

When President Harry Truman endorsed universal health insurance legislation in the wake of World War II, the AMA again shot it down by charging Communism. Postwar federal funding went instead to biomedical research and to the construction of hospitals to provide space in which private physicians could practice. Both contributed to the increasingly technological and expensive approach of American medicine. Congressional legislation to finance care for specific patient populations – such as those needing dialysis – or to support specific research agendas – such as cancer – passed in response to the lobbying efforts of voluntary organizations, patients, and their families. Not until 1965 did federal funding for patient care through a compulsory insurance program finally pass, but, again, for specific groups rather than for the entire citizenry: Medicaid for the poor and Medicare for the elderly. At the start of the twenty-first century, Medicare continues to be funded (even if threatened regularly by anti-welfare administrations) because senior citizens act as a voting bloc. In contrast, ever since the demise of President Lyndon B. Johnson's War on Poverty, health services for the poor – known to be unlikely to flex their muscle as voters and represented as undeserving, criminal, cheating, and African American (thus playing into and sustaining racism) – have been perpetually subject to cuts. At the start of the new century, approximately one-third of all Americans lacked health insurance.

During the course of the twentieth century, the U.S. Public Health Service (USPHS), which originated in the need to provide for the care of sailors at the end of the eighteenth century, came to encompass most of the federal agencies with public health or medical responsibilities. One infamous early-twentieth-century Public Health Service program became the impetus for new regulations to protect patients and research subjects. In the Tuskegee Syphilis Study, the health service tracked venereal diseases not in order to treat or quarantine infectious individuals, but in order to *not* treat them. Although this study and the deception and abuse of poor African American men for which it is remembered never went to trial and never resulted in a court opinion, the class action suit to which it gave rise nonetheless raised awareness about the medical rights of patients, highlighted the need for regulation to protect patients and human subjects, and contributed to changing the laws under which biomedical research could be conducted. The Tuskegee Syphilis Study observed "untreated syphilis in the Negro male" for forty years, from 1932 to 1972. The "study" was based on an assumption of biological racial differences and was intended to prove it through pathology. Several hundred African American men from Macon County, Alabama, all extremely poor sharecroppers and tenant farmers, were recruited for a study of "bad blood." They were lured by the seeming provision of health care and with promises that their funerals would be paid for by the government. No explanations of the experiment were ever offered nor informed consents obtained despite the medical understanding since at least the nineteenth century that research on human subjects required their consent. The economic and medical poverty of the men, the "ignorance" attributed to them, and racism all justified the Public Health Service's failure to provide care.

In 1972, the Associated Press exposed the project, thanks to the continuing efforts of a young, low-level employee in the health service who pressed his superiors to see the wrongs committed and to treat the men. In the context of powerful civil rights and health movements as well as contemporaneous scandals that revealed the paternalistic and racist attitudes toward and abuse of patients in both public health and medical settings (such as sterilization abuse and the dangers of the pill and IUDs), news of the Tuskegee Study quickly generated national attention. When the subjects themselves learned from the national news of their use in a racist experiment, they turned to the most prominent African American attorney in Alabama. Fred Gray had represented Rosa Parks during the Montgomery Bus Boycott, and on behalf of the study's subjects, Gray filed a class action suit against the Public Health Service and the state of Alabama for failing to obtain informed consent. The federal government finally agreed to pay $10 million to the subjects or their survivors, to provide free health care to the subjects and their families, and to provide the long-promised burials. Exposure of the Tuskegee study resulted in the writing of new federal guidelines to prevent future abuses of human subjects in biomedical research. All federally funded research on human subjects was made subject to approval by cross-disciplinary Institutional Review Boards (IRB). Despite the new regulations, concern remained that IRBs might be inadequate for the detection of abuses, especially of patients and subjects who are poor, immigrants, non-English speaking and/or non-white.

By the late twentieth century, myriad federal agencies had responsibilities for American health and welfare; each developed its own regulations and administrative law processes. Such federal agencies included the Food and Drug Administration (FDA), the U.S. Department of Agriculture (USDA), the Office for Occupational Health and Safety (OSHA), the Environmental Protection Agency (EPA), the Indian Health Service (IHS), the National Institutes of Health (NIH), the Centers for Disease Control (CDC), and the Department of Health and Human Services (HHS), among many others. The enormous number of agencies and their accompanying administrative law machinery indicate the continuing interest in public responsibility for medical and health matters; their number also points to the difficulty of reaching any unified policy, priority, or program. Furthermore, the work of federal agencies was always vulnerable to legislative de-funding or other forms of political interference from Congress, the President, or outside business or political interests.

At times, industry practices so blatantly threatened the public's health that reformers succeeded in translating public outrage and fear into greater power for regulatory agencies. The FDA was formed in 1907 in reaction to Upton Sinclair's exposé of the meat industry. In 1938, Congress granted the FDA expanded powers to regulate drugs before they reached the market after more than a hundred people died due to poisoning by a sulfa drug mixed with toxic sweetener. In 1962, Congress and President Kennedy again expanded the FDA's powers following the thalidomide tragedy, which damaged thousands of newborn children worldwide. The EPA (formed in 1970) has banned a number of chemicals because of the threat they pose to human health. When the EPA attempted to take pesticides off the market, however, the chemical industry challenged administrative law and hit the agency with grinding, lengthy, and expensive suits. As a result, regulators learned to choose cases that would be most successful in the courtroom and in Congress.

In 1990, people long regarded as patients or potential criminals, institutionalized because of diminished intellectual capacity or physical disability, won recognition as rights-bearing citizens with the passage of the Americans with Disabilities Act (ADA). The ADA forbade discrimination against people with disabilities; mandated that workplaces, schools, city streets and public services accommodate the disabled; and required the Equal Employment Opportunity Commission to issue guidelines and pursue complaints. The ADA showed the power of an organized social movement to win legislation; the subsequent erosion of the ADA indicates the larger power of business interests.

VI. PATIENT AUTONOMY, PRIVACY, AND SURVEILLANCE

In the last thirty years of the twentieth century, the intersections of law and medicine within the United States proliferated endlessly, particularly around questions of patient autonomy, privacy, and civil liberties. Over the same period, the impact of U.S. funding, regulation, and involvement in health policies, services, and biomedical research was increasingly felt around the world. The growing intersections between law and medicine in both domestic and international contexts require considerable research; the historical global reach and power of American medical foreign policy and regulation in particular have not been studied or integrated sufficiently into U.S. legal and medical history.

Here my analysis concentrates on just two areas of controversy that illuminate the developments of the later twentieth century: decisions at the end of life, and decisions around reproduction. In both cases, American rights to "privacy," whether we mean privacy of information, decisions about medical treatment or non-treatment, or the privacy of reproductive and sexual practices, have increased due to the advocacy of social movements. Backlash movements with highly organized legal and political arms have also eroded those rights.

End of Life

Since the 1970s, the legal system has been directly involved in scrutinizing medical practices at the end of life. Standard interpretation finds that the law intruded into medical practice and the relationship between physician and patient, but in fact the judiciary was invited in by physicians and hospitals who imagined their vulnerability to prosecution. As death and dying moved out of the home and into the hospital and as new technologies extended the process of dying through artificial ventilation and feeding systems, growing numbers of Americans began to fear the process of death and the prospect of "turning into a vegetable" who spent years in a hospital or nursing home bed. In unknown numbers of instances, physicians and families decided together to turn off the machines that kept the dying breathing, but did not cure or bring the person back to an active, conscious life. They allowed people to die. (No doubt in most of these cases the families tended to be privileged with medical insurance and a relationship with physicians rooted in a common racial or class background. For others, the problem was not discontinuing unwanted treatments, but obtaining adequate medical care in the first place.) In other cases, physicians or hospital administrators refused and some families sued. In 1975, press and television coverage of the case of Karen Ann Quinlan, a 21-year-old New Jersey woman who was comatose, in a persistent vegetative state, and attached to a respirator first brought these problems to national attention and debate. For reasons that were unclear, Quinlan had stopped breathing and lapsed into a coma; after several months of daily visiting and hope for improvement, Quinlan's family met with her doctors and asked that the ventilator be removed so that she could return to her "natural state" and be allowed to die. (Interestingly, the Catholic family had turned to their priest for comfort and had been assured that allowing a natural death did not violate Catholic teachings.) The doctors and hospital agreed; Quinlan's father signed paperwork to protect the medical professionals. The next day the doctor refused to carry out the family's wishes. When the case eventually went to court, the doctor and hospital opposed allowing the father to serve as Karen Quinlan's guardian, argued that removing a ventilator violated medical standards, and equated doing so with homicide. The New Jersey Supreme Court, *In the Matter of Quinlan* (1976), affirmed Joseph Quinlan's appointment as Karen Quinlan's guardian and also affirmed that removing a ventilator and feeding tube – when she could not be cured or returned to cognitive life and the treatments were only "prolong[ing] her inevitable, slow deterioration and death" – was constitutional under the right of privacy found in *Griswold* and other cases. On request of the patient's family and guardian and with the agreement of a hospital ethics committee that Quinlan could not emerge from her comatose state, physicians and hospital could withdraw life support without fear of civil or criminal penalties. After further delay and resistance, the hospital finally removed the ventilator after "weaning" Quinlan from the system. She survived unassisted. According to her mother's account, Karen Quinlan and her family suffered another ten years until her eventual death.

The physician and hospital in the Quinlan case feared being held criminally liable if they acted on the Quinlan family's request; in their fear, they provoked a suit. The hospital and doctors wanted advance approval from prosecutors to do what physicians and hospitals had long done outside the legal eye. Fearing legal trouble, medicine brought greater legal scrutiny on itself. *Quinlan* established that a trusted family member or guardian could make decisions in the best interest of the patient and that, for medical professionals, there was a difference between "curing the ill and comforting and easing the dying." The case also prompted other legal/medical reforms. Living wills in which people explicitly declared their wish to avoid life support systems if they were in a persistent vegetative state and registered "do not resuscitate" orders were developed in order to produce a clear record of the testator's wishes in advance of these difficult situations. In light of the New Jersey court's expectation that hospitals would have ethics committees for consultation, hospitals set up such committees.

A Missouri case rigidified the requirements permitting the withdrawal of life support. In a case similar to *Quinlan*, the parents of Nancy Beth Cruzan, who remained in a persistent vegetative state after a 1983 car accident and resuscitation by paramedics, asked the hospital to end artificial feeding. When the hospital refused, the parents went to court and won a ruling to the effect that a person in Nancy Cruzan's state had a constitutional right to refuse or end "death prolonging procedures." On appeal, however, the Missouri Supreme Court reversed the decision, a reversal affirmed by the U.S. Supreme Court in *Cruzan v. Missouri Dept. of Health* (1990). The divided U.S. Supreme Court held that the state had passed legislation requiring that "the incompetent's wishes as to the withdrawal of treatment be proved by clear and convincing evidence" and that this was constitutional. In the Cruzan case, the majority of the court found that a "serious" conversation with a friend was insufficient to establish a patient's values and wishes on which a guardian could act. The state, *Cruzan* declared, could "decline to make judgments about the 'quality' of life . . . and simply assert an unqualified interest in the preservation of human life." The burden of proof on those seeking to withdraw life support was greater. The dissenting justices pointed to the rights of privacy, the rights of individuals to assert their wishes to avoid medical care, and their right to expect that those wishes would be respected, all of which were undermined by the decision. The family's battle continued in Missouri courts, where they finally convinced the court with additional witnesses of their daughter's expressed preferences, and after several years of legal battles, "life support" systems were removed. Cruzan died in 1990.

Cruzan undermined people's ability to avoid a prolonged dying, but the case also inspired Congress and the states to provide legal mechanisms to ensure that such cases need not occur. The federal government required hospitals to inform patients of their right to make advance directives; states passed medical proxy laws so that people could choose who would make decisions for them if incapacitated and permitted living wills. As a consequence of the *Cruzan* case, those who feared prolonged dying were strongly encouraged to sign living wills and appoint health care powers of attorney. Yet only a tiny minority of Americans have taken such steps (approximately 10 percent have living wills).

When advance directives are lacking, guardianship for making decisions about medical care goes first to the spouse, then adult children, and then parents. The political effort to prevent people from refusing artificial life support in order to die continued dramatically in the fall of 2003 in Florida.

The Florida legislature and Governor Jeb Bush undermined the end-of-life decision-making process and the legal processes of adjudication when families disagreed by intervening in the hotly contested case of Theresa Marie "Terri" Schiavo. In 1990, Terri Schiavo suffered respiratory and cardiac failure leading to severe brain damage and dependence upon a feeding tube. After Schiavo had spent ten years in a persistent vegetative state, the Pinellas County (Florida) Circuit Court ordered the removal of the feeding tube in response to the petition of her husband Michael, and according to her verbally expressed wish. Schiavo's parents and the right-to-life movement fought these decisions, demonstrated, and prayed. Republican legislators passed a law allowing Governor Bush to overturn court orders and require physicians to reinstall the feeding tube into Schiavo's body. The orders, and the President's endorsement, were widely perceived to be part of President George W. Bush's re-election strategy. In the spring of 2005, after the Florida Supreme Court struck down "Terri's law" and state and federal appeals courts upheld the previous decision to remove the feeding tube, President Bush and Congress intervened to pass legislation giving a federal court jurisdiction over this one special case with the opportunity to overrule the decisions of numerous courts. The diagnosis of Schiavo's condition by politicians in Washington, D.C., and the refusal to accept the legal system's decisions revealed a disregard for medical privacy, patient rights, and professional ethics, as well as the rule of law and the separation of powers. Every court that considered the case, however, including the U.S. Supreme Court on repeated occasions, rejected these political and religious efforts to evade the legal process and returned the case to the original county court that had reviewed all of the evidence. That court again ordered the removal of the feeding tube as requested by Michael Schiavo, and on March 31, 2005, Terri Schiavo died. Many Americans found the Schiavo case riveting and upsetting. Many also, conservatives and liberals both, were deeply concerned at the manipulation of family grief and division at a time of severe medical crisis for political purposes and to undermine the Constitution. Congress and the President trampled not only on the rule of law but also on the founding idea that American democracy included and respected people of different values and religions. The long-term repercussions of the Schiavo case are yet to be seen.

A related problem for many patients not only at the end of life but also following accidents that produce long-term disability is the medico-legal assumptions about who should make decisions with doctors on behalf of an incapacitated patient. The immediate assumption when patients are incapacitated and unable to voice their own decisions is that either a spouse or a parent is in charge, but for many adults this is inappropriate. Unmarried individuals – notably gay women and men whose relationships are legally unrecognized and often resented by homophobic family members, hospital staff, and/or judges – have had their most intimate and trusted partners excluded from hospital rooms and overruled by hospitals and/or the courts. A prominent example is the Sharon Kowalski case. From the time of a car accident in 1983 and over the next ten years, Kowalski of Minnesota and her partner, Karen Thompson, struggled in the courts and through public protest to gain recognition of Kowalski's right to have her lesbian partner visit and act as her medical advocate and Kowalski's own right to make decisions for herself as a disabled woman, even if she could not speak. When Kowalski's father was made her legal guardian, he prohibited visits by Thompson. Five years after the accident, the courts recognized that Kowalski could speak her mind by typing, but it was several more years before legal guardianship for her care was granted to her partner. Civil rights, gay and lesbian rights, and disability rights groups all celebrated the Kowalski-Thompson case for securing recognition of the rights of the disabled and lesbian or gay couples in the medical arena. A health care power of attorney in advance of unexpected accidents, comas, and major medical decisions would ensure that, when people suddenly become incapacitated patients, their self-selected entrusted advocates will be listened to by the medical system. Most people, however, have not completed such legal documents. When they do, cases like Kowalski's suggest they will still need social movements and attorneys to back up their wishes.

It is striking that the most highly publicized cases of intense struggles among parents, partners, hospitals, and the courts over decision-making power all involve young, injured white women. One may speculate whether American culture is peculiarly attached to young white women whom it imagines as "sleeping beauties" – a phrase used repeatedly in the Quinlan media coverage – princesses, and daughters whose lives are threatened and who need to be rescued.

The formal commitment to patient rights of autonomy and privacy strengthened in the last thirty years of the twentieth century. In exercise, however, the rights were highly contested. Posters on hospital walls announced patient rights (and responsibilities), patients signed detailed informed consent forms repeatedly, and federal laws assured patient privacy. In response to public anxiety about insurance companies' information sharing and denial of coverage, the U.S. Department of Health and Human Services developed privacy protections as part of HIPAA (Health Insurance Portability and Accountability Act, 1996). But here, in fact, is an example of administrative law with enormous and unanticipated effects. In effect as of April 2003, federal privacy standards promised to prevent unknown individuals, insurance companies, or other businesses from gaining unauthorized access to patients' personal medical records. However, unclear about the precise intentions and requirements of the new standards, hospitals cited federal privacy standards in refusing to allow visitors or to send medical information to third parties as specifically requested by patients. Such actions revealed the medical system's commitment to hospital control of patient information and distrust of patients' desires and decisions about their own medical care and medical information. (For instance, the domestic adoption process has been one site for information obstructions of this nature, both when adoptive parents attempt to provide medical information to agencies and when birth mothers seek to give adoptive-parents-to-be their own and their child's medical information in order to provide appropriate pediatric care).

HIPAA also restricts access to archival and historical records. In the name of patient privacy, medical materials and information are being removed and made inaccessible and may be suppressed depending on individual archivists' and legal departments' interpretation of the law, commitment to historical inquiry, and the funding and political support (or distrust) of the archive. HIPAA may make it difficult for historians to research many of the issues discussed in this essay. It is at least debatable whether the "privacy" being protected in some cases is that of patients or of powerful institutions and state agencies against the interests of patients and citizens.

Less than a year after HIPAA went into effect, the nation saw unprecedented federal intrusion into physician practices and patient privacy. Attorney General John Ashcroft issued demands for patient records from Planned Parenthood Clinics, hospitals, and physicians for investigation into possible violations of the new "partial-birth abortion" ban. In 2003, Congress and the President of the United States had taken the unprecedented step of prohibiting a specific medical procedure, an action that overturned the long history of respect for medical autonomy in diagnosis and therapeutics. That this federal involvement in medical practice occurred in the arena of reproductive rights is both in keeping with a long history of state interest in reproduction and a product of a thirty-year-old backlash against feminism, patients' rights, and the recognition of constitutional rights to privacy in sexuality and reproduction.

Reproduction

Attorney General Ashcroft's 2004 demands for patient records capped years of legal intrusions in clinical practice and the surveillance of patients, especially in the reproductive arena. Since the 1980s, hospital personnel and policies have played a central role in criminalizing patients and in inserting criminal law into the medical system. Physicians and hospitals have gone to court to force patients to comply with medical advice or have initiated state investigation of the patients in their care. Medical, prosecutorial, and judicial actions have revealed the degree to which many medical and legal professionals distrust pregnant women and regard them as malevolent adversaries to the infants to whom they give birth. Individual doctors, nurses, judges, and police officers have appointed themselves child protectors in disregard of the pregnant woman/mother's rights to bodily integrity and due process and in denial of the truth that mothers – even the most destitute or addicted – attempt to improve their own health and behaviors on behalf of their future children.

The women who have been most subject to medical policing during pregnancy in the late twentieth century tend to be African American, poor, and drug-addicted – or suspected of illegal drug use because of their color. No woman, however, has been immune, once she deviates from medical expectations; even the most elite, white women with education, money, and health insurance have been threatened with investigation by child protective services when they rejected recommended tests, examinations, and procedures for either themselves or their newborns. Most have given in. The legal power granted public health authorities to protect the public's health has been extended to and claimed by individual physicians in clinical practice; doctors may call in police or agency officials when pregnant women, mothers, and families attempt to overrule the dominant medical system.

Doctors have shocked pregnant women and their families by turning to the law to transform medical advice into court orders. Obstetricians have won court orders to force pregnant women to undergo cesarean sections against their wishes. In cases like these, the physician's belief that the baby's life is threatened and the tradition of judicial respect for medical judgment have overruled the woman's decisions about her body and her pregnancy. (In several cases women fled and delivered healthy babies elsewhere; in others, surgery was forcibly performed and both the woman and baby died). The American College of Obstetricians has officially rejected the turn to court-ordered surgeries, yet threats and court orders have persisted. Despite the medical profession's complaints about patients' propensity to sue and the law's intrusion into their practices, physicians have often been the ones to call the law in against their patients. In doing so, physicians and hospitals have insisted on their power to make decisions for patients and point to potential malpractice suits while betraying their lack of anxiety about patients suing for assault or for violations of their autonomy and bodily integrity.

Beginning in the 1980s, state and federal prosecutors forged new ground as they prosecuted pregnant women for their behaviors and decisions during pregnancy. Pregnant women who refused a recommended cesarean section and then delivered a stillborn child have been prosecuted for manslaughter; others who use alcohol and drugs have been prosecuted for the "delivery" of illegal narcotics to an "unborn child." Male reproductive and societal contributions to ill health, low birth weight, and infant death are denied and obscured by the focus on the supposed wrongs committed by poor pregnant women. The most systematic effort to capture and punish pregnant women occurred in South Carolina at the behest of medical institutions. The hospital of the Medical University of South Carolina in Charleston contacted a local prosecutor about what it might do to "assist" in the prosecution of mothers who used cocaine. In 1989, prosecutors, police, and hospital staff devised a plan to test pregnant women who entered the hospital for the presence of illegal drugs in their urine; the hospital would report positive tests to the prosecutor, and the woman would be arrested for delivery of an illegal substance to a minor and for child neglect. During delivery, patients were handcuffed to their beds as criminal suspects and afterward taken away in chains. All of the women were low-income and all but one of those arrested were African American. The collection of information did not occur in a legal setting nor was it done by police or other state officials. Instead, lab tests presumably for the patient's health were collected by health care providers as evidence. The state then used that evidence to threaten, arrest, incarcerate, and prosecute pregnant women and to terminate their parental rights. All told, more than two hundred women tested positive, thirty were arrested, and two were sentenced to prison. Statewide, seventy to eighty pregnant women were arrested on these grounds.

The Charleston case may be the most egregious example of the criminalization of pregnant women and the ways in which legal and medical authorities together have created racist policies that do not attend to the health needs of women or children, but instead demean, discriminate, criminalize, and punish. In 1993, attorneys Lynn Paltrow and Susan Dunn with the ACLU filed suits on behalf of ten women who had been arrested. The lower courts upheld the policy and found that it was not discriminatory in application, but in 2001 the U.S. Supreme Court found it unconstitutional because it violated the Fourth Amendment's protections against illegal search and seizure.

CONCLUSION

The historical relationship between law and medicine in the United States has been both collaborative and combative. By the opening of the twenty-first century, the medical profession had achieved a form of the close relationship with the state that its early-nineteenth-century forerunners had desired. The police power that authorized public health measures ultimately contributed to a refashioning of the relationship between doctors and the law. Through the nineteenth century, much public health regulation had focused on business practices, property maintenance, or the construction of public works for sanitation and clean water; individuals became the objects of scrutiny and quarantine only sporadically during epidemics. From the late nineteenth century on, as local and federal public health officers increasingly focused on the individual, individual physicians and medical institutions were increasingly involved in enforcing public health measures and identifying those viewed as a danger to the public's health.

The criminal justice system's use of the hospital as a site for locating and identifying suspects and its vision of the body as a source of evidence of criminal activity simultaneously created a new medico-legal relationship that put medicine into the service of the criminal justice system, rather than in the service of the public and their patients. The state's reliance on the medical profession and its institutions for the collection of evidence, information gathering, and investigation for public health and criminal justice purposes brought both power and problems. The medical profession enjoyed great political and economic clout, but also saw its own autonomy undermined and the trust of patients eroded. As medicine became enmeshed within a state system of medical policing, it become subject to policing itself.

Medical professionals in their practices often stand at the intersection of constitutional rights. Because medicine is a site of great personal significance where the body is invaded and where life and death hang in the balance, and because the hospital has been used by the public health and criminal justice systems, the hospital and clinical practices are intimately tied up with constitutional rights regarding confidentiality, privacy, bodily integrity, equality, and due process. Understandably, most physicians and other health care workers do not see themselves as defenders of civil liberties and patient rights for those are the responsibilities of attorneys and courts or activists and social movements. The job of health care providers is to practice medicine and make people well. Yet, contests over civil liberties issues cannot be escaped in the medical arena; health care professionals are not innocent bystanders in the struggles for justice. Unfortunately, some assume a policing attitude toward their patients as part of their practice of medicine.

The field of law and medicine deserves our attention for an array of theoretical reasons – it provides rich avenues for critical analysis of how the law works in practice and for examination of the complex development and deployment of power in many guises. The problems and oppressions that many have experienced at the hands of public health officers or in hospitals and other health institutions have also been the source of major achievements in civil liberties. In moments of crisis and pain, ordinary people have pushed to change the law and the practices of medicine, public health, and crime control and have articulated the rights of patients to autonomy and self-determination. They have done so through collective protests, law breaking, political campaigns, and social movements as well as individual private suits. As we have seen, litigation has often been the only path that has brought recognition of the damage done by medical and health authorities to the rights of patients. The late twentieth century has seen organized medicine and some elected officials campaign to impose limits on the rights of patients and citizens to litigate. In the light of historical evidence underlining the importance of litigation in securing patients' rights, their success would clearly place severe limitations on the public's capacity to restrain the abuse of power and to force changes in medical and state practices.

The historical efforts to recognize the rights of patients and citizens in medical and public health systems and to bring medicine into line with democratic and egalitarian ideas often included principled and independent bureaucrats, students, attorneys, physicians, low-level workers, and others who worked within the institutions and professions of medicine and law. More research on the people who recognized abuse, discrimination, and inequality and acted on behalf of civil liberties and patient rights in conjunction with their work on behalf of health is needed. They provide examples of medicine and law at their best.

8

THE GREAT DEPRESSION AND THE NEW DEAL

BARRY CUSHMAN

The New Deal era was the principal watershed in twentieth-century American constitutional development. The profound economic crisis that gripped the nation during the Great Depression inspired a period of extraordinary legislative ferment, generating a series of strikingly wide-ranging and far-reaching changes in the American legal and constitutional order. On the eve of World War II, Congress would wield an unprecedented degree of authority over the nation's peacetime economy. The national legislature underwrote a voluminous array of spending programs to relieve distress and to stimulate economic growth, while at the same time it enacted a remarkable succession of regulatory programs designed to restore health to the economy. The administration of these new programs called for the creation of new federal agencies and the significant expansion of existing ones, resulting in an explosive growth in the size and power of the federal bureaucracy and the full flowering of the administrative state.

At the apex of this burgeoning fiscal and administrative apparatus stood the office of the presidency, supported by a significantly expanded staff and invested with enhanced authority over agencies within the executive branch. Just as the chief executive emerged from the Depression with greater authority over the administration of domestic affairs, so the commander-in-chief would enter World War II with greater discretion over the conduct of American foreign policy. Meanwhile, the federal judiciary receded from its traditional role as the umpire of the federal system and the guardian of vested rights, but would become increasingly assertive in the vindication of civil rights and civil liberties, such as freedom of speech and rights of the accused. In upholding new programs of redistributive and protective legislation that might once have been condemned as "special" or "partial" legislation, the Supreme Court's evolving jurisprudence cleared the way for a style of national politics frankly centered on a model of interest-group pluralism.

The signature transformation of the New Deal era was the dramatic growth in the size, power, and responsibility of the federal government. A deepening conviction that only the national government could effectively ameliorate the protracted distress provided a powerful impetus to the centripetal forces of regulatory and fiscal centralization. President Franklin Roosevelt's New Deal embodied a striking expansion of both the scope of federal authority and the ambition of its exercise. Federal spending programs would undertake to provide economic security for all citizens; Congress would extend its regulatory influence over areas previously controlled principally, when at all, by state governments. Banking, securities markets, agriculture, energy, industrial labor relations, and much more would fall under the authority of federal officers.

Though the preemption of state regulation in such critical areas significantly reduced the formal authority of state governments, the states were by no means subsumed into a unitary national state. Local officials were often granted substantial discretion in the administration of federal grants-in-aid, while states retained most of their traditional authority over the content of vast domains of law regulating such subjects as property, contracts and commercial transactions, business associations, torts, crime, and the family. Similarly, the Supreme Court lifted long-standing impediments to state regulation as it retired economic substantive due process and relaxed restraints imposed by the Contract and Dormant Commerce Clauses of the Federal Constitution.

Nevertheless, the concentration of an unprecedented degree of authority and responsibility in a national regulatory and welfare state constituted a revolution in the American federal system. The breathtakingly novel reach of federal economic regulation, its effect on vested property rights, and the scope of discretionary authority confided to the executive branch in its administration each stretched established understandings of constitutional limitation, sometimes to the breaking point. To be sure, existing constitutional doctrine provided a comfortable foundation for the many New Deal spending programs designed to relieve poverty. Yet a number of Congressional measures rested on understandings of federal regulatory powers that were unprecedented in their breadth, while several state and federal statutes curtailed private economic rights in a manner raising serious constitutional questions under the Contract Clause and the Due Process Clauses of the Fifth and Fourteenth Amendments. The fate of state and federal legislation addressed to the economic havoc wrought by the Depression accordingly turned on two critical variables: the capacity of lawmakers to accommodate transformative statutory initiatives within the structure of contemporary doctrine and the inclination of Supreme Court justices to relax or abandon constitutional constraints on federal and state regulatory power.

The mechanisms through which the New Deal order ultimately secured the Court's constitutional sanction are readily discernible. The conditions of the Great Depression and the inadequacy of Republican efforts to deal with them cemented the electoral influence of a political coalition that would entrust the presidency and both Houses of Congress to the Democratic Party from 1933 forward. The sustained dominance of that coalition ensured that the demand for national action to grapple with the crisis would be both powerful and persistent. That persistence would in turn have two important ramifications. First, in those instances in which the justices held that an initial legislative attempt to address a particular problem did not pass constitutional muster, the New Deal Congress would have the opportunity to reformulate the program to achieve the desired end through means consistent with prevailing constitutional doctrine. Throughout the 1930s, New Dealers would repeatedly employ this adaptive strategy with remarkable success.

The second consequence grew out of Franklin Roosevelt's repeated reelection to the presidency. Facing a federal judiciary bearing the imprint of twelve years of Republican ascendancy in presidential politics, throughout his tenure Roosevelt steadily filled lower court vacancies with loyal Democrats. Yet, neither death nor resignation provided a frustrated Roosevelt with an opportunity to appoint a Supreme Court justice during his first term. Though President Hoover's three appointments to the Court had created a majority seemingly more receptive to government regulation than the Taft Court had been, that majority was fragile and by no means fully committed to the constitutional views of the administration. Between 1937 and 1941, however, President Roosevelt would elevate seven New Dealers to life tenure on the nation's highest court. Fully reflecting the constitutional sensibilities undergirding the New Deal vision of government, these appointees would in turn transform the nation's constitutional law to accommodate regulatory innovations that their judicial predecessors could not have approved. The continued electoral success of Democrats even after Roosevelt's death would enable the party further to entrench its position in the federal judiciary, so that New Deal constitutionalism would remain a powerful orthodoxy even as its sponsoring political coalition began to fray.

The balance of this chapter consists of five topical parts and a conclusion. Part I describes the economic conditions of the Great Depression and details the executive and legislative responses produced under the Hoover and Roosevelt administrations. Part II examines contemporary controversies over the growth of federal executive authority and the elaboration of the administrative state. Part III documents the relaxation of constraints on economic regulation imposed by the Fifth and Fourteenth Amendments and the Contract Clause. Part IV analyzes various manifestations of the revolution in constitutional federalism. Part V explores the growth of protections for civil rights, civil liberties, and democratic processes.

I. THE GREAT DEPRESSION: CONDITIONS AND RESPONSES

At the close of a decade celebrated for its prosperity, the American economy underwent a profound contraction whose baleful effects were remarkable both for their duration and their intensity. Though the Depression would linger throughout the 1930s until dispatched by the stimulus of wartime production, the precipitous economic decline of its first four years was particularly staggering. Between 1929 and 1933 national income was cut in half. Manufacturing output, retail sales volume, and wholesale and commodity prices all suffered devastating reductions. In 1930 alone a record 26,355 businesses failed, while 1931 recorded some 65,000 cases in bankruptcy. Between September 1929 and March 1933 the aggregate value of all domestic stocks listed on the New York Stock exchange declined by 80 percent, from approximately $80 billion to about $16 billion. During the same period, farm values declined by a third, and foreign trade was dramatically curtailed, with both exports and imports decreasing by nearly 70 percent. By 1933 the ranks of the unemployed had increased to nearly thirteen million workers, leaving one-quarter of the American workforce idle. Even those who survived the epidemic of layoffs saw their wages decline and their working hours reduced. At the same time more than 5,000 banks collapsed – nearly 2,300 in 1931 alone – decimating more than nine million savings accounts. Though the business cycle had produced recurrent periods of boom and bust throughout American history, such punishing economic collapse was unprecedented.

The Hoover administration was not entirely inert in the face of this crisis. Throughout the 1920s Congress had grappled unsuccessfully with the seemingly intractable problem of depressed prices resulting from the overproduction of farm commodities. Early in his term President Hoover called Congress into special session to enact the Agricultural Marketing Act of 1929. This statute established a Federal Farm Board, which was authorized to make loans from a $500 million revolving fund to farmer-owned commodity stabilization corporations and agricultural marketing associations. It was hoped that, by using the funds to purchase and store surplus farm produce and to regulate its flow to terminal markets, these private entities might increase the demand for agricultural commodities and thereby raise the prices at which they traded. Similarly, Hoover oversaw the creation of the federal Reconstruction Finance Corporation, a temporary agency authorized to extend billions of dollars in loans to prevent the economic collapse of railroads, insurance companies, banks, and other financial institutions.

Yet, Hoover's valorization of individual initiative, his preference for economic solutions grounded in voluntary cooperation in the private sector rather than government regulation, and his aversion to concentrations of political and economic power led him to resist far-reaching proposals for federal intervention of the sort embraced by his successor. For example, his program contained no proposal for legislative reform of the national securities markets. He opposed the delegation of government power to private interests, rejecting proposals from business interests calling for a suspension of antitrust laws that would enable them to establish federally administered cartels. In 1931, Hoover vetoed a bill that would have authorized government-owned electricity and nitrogen plants built at Muscle Shoals during World War I to sell power and fertilizer in competition with privately owned concerns. And although he supported such initiatives as the expansion of credit, tax relief, and modest appropriations to support public works, President Hoover was reluctant to heed requests for federal relief expenditures to aid the millions of the unemployed.

Hoover's limited and ineffectual responses to the crisis left him vulnerable to his Democratic challenger in 1932, the affable governor of New York. Franklin Roosevelt's platform did call for greater federal relief to the unemployed, but in most other respects it differed little from the economic policy espoused in its Republican counterpart. Though one may in retrospect detect germinal hints of portions of the New Deal in some of Roosevelt's campaign speeches, for the most part he was content to rely on vague references to the need for bold experimentation, "imaginative and purposeful planning," and greater solicitude for "the forgotten man." In November Roosevelt and the Democrats coasted to victory in a landslide.

Shortly following his inauguration in March 1933, campaign generalities began to take shape as specific policy proposals. By the time Roosevelt assumed the presidency, officials in thirty-eight states had closed their banks in the face of a growing spate of bank failures; banking operations had been curtailed in the remaining ten states. Meanwhile, the monetary system was increasingly roiled by nervous hoarding of gold and currency and a troubling flight of gold to foreign markets. The president immediately initiated a series of emergency measures to staunch the hemorrhaging, proclaiming a nationwide "bank holiday" and proscribing further exports of gold. At the same time Roosevelt called into special session the new Congress, which quickly ratified his actions with the Emergency Banking Act of 1933. The statute provided for the reopening of solvent banks under executive supervision, confirmed presidential control over transactions in gold, and required that those holding gold bullion, gold coin, and gold certificates surrender them to the Treasury in exchange for new Federal Reserve notes. Once federal control over the nation's gold supply had been rendered more secure, Roosevelt would undertake to arrest the deflationary spiral by significantly reducing the gold content of the dollar.

Having eased the banking crisis, the Roosevelt administration next placed before the Congress an ambitious program of prescriptions for relief, recovery, and reform. Relief measures took a variety of forms. The Federal Emergency Relief Administration distributed direct public assistance through state and local agencies. Other federal programs – such as the short-lived Civil Works Administration and later the Works Progress Administration and the Public Works Administration – employed the jobless in a variety of public works and improvement projects. Similarly, the Civilian Conservation Corps put unemployed youth to work on reforestation projects in the national forests. Meanwhile, the Farm Security Administration offered low-interest loans to distressed tenant farmers and sharecroppers, just as the Farm Credit Administration and the Home Owner's Loan Corporation underwrote a massive refinancing of defaulting farm and home mortgages. The swelling federal budget tells the story of this remarkable proliferation of federal programs and grants-in-aid to support relief and public employment: between 1929 and 1939 federal expenditures mushroomed from $2.6 billion to $9 billion. The relief of persistent poverty by the federal government proved enormously popular with the voters and contributed in no small part to the remarkable electoral successes of the New Deal coalition.

Roosevelt's recovery program could not lay claim to comparable laurels. Its two principal pillars were the Agricultural Adjustment Act (AAA) of 1933 and the National Industrial Recovery Act (NIRA). The AAA sought to raise farm prices not by purchasing the agricultural surplus and either storing it or dumping it abroad, but instead by decreasing production. It imposed a tax on the processors of specified agricultural commodities, the proceeds of which were used to pay farmers who contracted with the Department of Agriculture to reduce their production of those commodities. The NIRA similarly sought to stabilize plummeting prices by limiting industrial output. Suspending enforcement of the antitrust laws, the program provided for an unprecedented degree of industrial self-regulation. Acting under the sanction of the newly created National Recovery Administration (NRA), business representatives were authorized to promulgate elaborate and legally enforceable "codes of fair competition" to govern their respective industries, including the prescription of minimum wages and maximum working hours. Section 7(a) of the NIRA guaranteed the rights of workers to organize and bargain collectively with their employers. Dogged by vocal criticism and widespread unpopularity, each of these short-lived programs would be declared unconstitutional before Roosevelt's first term was finished.

More enduring were the New Deal's contributions to economic reform. Restoration of confidence in the nation's troubled financial sector ranked high among the Roosevelt administration's priorities. The Glass-Steagall Banking Act of 1933 mandated the separation of commercial banking from investment banking, thereby preventing bankers from using ordinary deposits to underwrite securities issues or to speculate in securities markets. This act also created the Federal Deposit Insurance Corporation, which helped revive flagging faith in the banking system by providing insurance on small bank accounts. The Securities Act of 1933 required that all new securities offered to the public through either the facilities of interstate commerce or the postal service first be registered with the Federal Trade Commission (FTC). All registration statements were required to disclose detailed financial information concerning the securities and to be certified by an independent accountant. Those failing truthfully to disclose the required information were subjected to civil and criminal penalties, and the FTC was granted considerable regulatory authority over the issuance of new securities. The Securities Exchange Act of 1934 created the Securities and Exchange Commission (SEC) and transferred to the SEC the authority confided to the FTC under the 1933 Act. The 1934 act extended the disclosure requirements of the 1933 act to all companies listing securities on a national exchange, requiring them to file detailed annual financial reports with the SEC. The 1934 act further authorized the SEC to regulate the stock exchanges, to police abuses such as stock market manipulation, and to prohibit fraud in connection with secondary market transactions. Finally, the Public Utility Holding Company Act of 1935 required such companies conducting interstate business to register with the SEC and subjected the utilities to the agency's supervision in matters pertaining to corporate structure and dissolution. The Federal Power Commission was authorized to regulate the rates and business practices of such companies.

The Social Security Act of 1935 brought two major innovations in social insurance. One title of the act created a federal program of compulsory, contributory old age and survivors insurance financed by payroll taxes levied on employers and employees, with the first benefits payable in 1942. A second title established a cooperative federal-state system of unemployment insurance: employers paying into a qualifying state unemployment compensation fund would receive a credit against a tax otherwise payable to a comparable federal fund. By mid-1937 every state and territory had adopted a qualifying statute. Other provisions of the act authorized federal grants-in-aid to states for aid to the blind and disabled, to dependent children, and to those among the needy aged – such as domestic and agricultural workers – who were ineligible to participate in the old age insurance program. The Social Security Act further authorized grants to state programs for the promotion of public health, for maternal and child health and welfare, and for vocational rehabilitation. A Social Security Board was vested with authority to administer these programs.

The New Deal similarly produced two enduring reforms in the field of labor relations. The National Labor Relations Act of 1935 (NLRA) sought to prevent or resolve labor disputes threatening to disrupt interstate commerce. It guaranteed to selected industrial workers the rights to organize and to bargain collectively with their employers through their elected representatives and prohibited employer interference with those rights. A National Labor Relations Board modeled on the Federal Trade Commission was created to administer the act's organization and representation provisions; it was empowered to issue orders enforceable in federal court to cease and desist in the commission of "unfair labor practices," such as cultivating employer-sponsored "company unions" and discouraging union membership through discrimination in hiring, discharge, or terms of employment. Three years later, the Fair Labor Standards Act of 1938 prohibited the interstate shipment of selected goods manufactured by children or by workers employed at wages below or for hours exceeding federally prescribed standards.

The reform efforts of the New Deal Congress did not stop there. Legislation establishing the Tennessee Valley Authority, for example, went well beyond the earlier Muscle Shoals bills envisioning government manufacture and sale of electricity and fertilizer. The act further authorized a massive regional development project involving the construction of new dams and public power plants, as well as programs for flood control, reforestation, and the prevention of soil erosion. By 1941 the Rural Electrification Administration had increased from ten to forty the percentage of American farms with electric power. The U.S. Housing Authority and the Federal Housing Administration underwrote the construction and rehabilitation of low- and middle-income housing. The year 1938 saw significant revisions to existing federal legislation concerning both bankruptcy and food and drug regulation. And under the leadership of Commissioner of Indian Affairs John Collier, the Roosevelt administration inaugurated an "Indian New Deal" for Native Americans. Collier discontinued existing federal policies restricting enjoyment of civil liberties, such as the freedoms of speech and religion and the right to travel, and extended criminal procedure protections of the Bill of Rights to proceedings in Courts of Indian Offenses. In 1934 Collier persuaded Congress to enact the Indian Reorganization Act, which abolished the policy of land allotment, authorized a substantial measure of tribal self-government, and established funds to support the education of Native Americans and to promote economic development on Indian reservations.

The New Deal was thus breathtaking in scope and freewheeling in style. The product of pressure from disparate elements within the Democratic coalition, the Roosevelt administration's program was grounded in no single coherent or systemic theory. Roosevelt himself was a pragmatist who once elusively described his ideological commitments as those of "a Christian and a Democrat," and his administration produced policies that occasionally conflicted in their objectives and effects. Whereas the relief program sought to alleviate widespread conditions of want, for example, the AAA aimed to raise the price of food through enforced scarcity. Similarly, the administration's recovery efforts chafed against the Social Security Act's withdrawal of capital from the economy through payroll taxes. Yet, Democratic control of the White House and both houses of Congress offered a much-anticipated chance to implement a long-frustrated progressive agenda for reform, while the exigencies of the moment nurtured an experimental temperament congenial to young lawyers reared on sociological jurisprudence and legal realism at institutions like Harvard, Yale, and Columbia.

Those young lawyers would be central to significant developments in the practice of law and in the composition of the American bar. Although the economic contraction reduced the demand for lawyers engaged in private practice, the New Deal offered fresh and exciting possibilities for public service in Washington. Many graduates of elite law schools who might earlier have heeded the call of Wall Street were now drawn to the nation's capital by the appeal of Roosevelt's crusade and the attractions of power and a steady paycheck. Jewish and Catholic lawyers facing discrimination in private employment were particular beneficiaries of the expanded legal opportunities centered in the Justice Department and the alphabet agencies. At the same time the profuse generation of new federal law created significant new opportunities for private sector specialization in burgeoning areas, such as administrative law and labor law – opportunities of which many New Deal lawyers would soon avail themselves.

Several of the New Deal's legal innovations presented serious issues concerning the scope of federal power, the separation of powers, and constitutional protections for property rights. Although many New Deal initiatives would never face judicial review, challenges to some of the central features of the programs for recovery and reform would produce landmark decisions in the Supreme Court. Several of these decisions were unanimous in upholding or invalidating Congressional or executive action. Other important cases were decided by a closely divided Court. It is always hazardous to offer general characterizations of a justice's jurisprudence, as the complexity of a jurist's record so often confounds stereotypic assessments. Yet, of the Taft Court veterans the justices most likely to regard elements of the New Deal as constitutionally problematic were the so-called conservative Four Horsemen: Willis Van Devanter, James Clark McReynolds, George Sutherland, and Pierce Butler. Their more liberal Taft Court colleagues – Oliver Wendell Holmes, Louis Brandeis, and Harlan Fiske Stone – by contrast, had shown somewhat greater receptivity to state and federal economic regulation.

Between 1930 and 1932 President Hoover appointed three justices to the Court. In 1932 he replaced Holmes with Benjamin Cardozo, who shared many of the jurisprudential views of his predecessor. The outcomes in several closely divided cases would therefore be determined by the votes of Hoover's 1930 appointments of Charles Evans Hughes to replace Taft and Owen Roberts to take the seat previously occupied by Edward Terry Sanford. When New Dealers could draft statutes, select test cases, and craft arguments securing the support of these two constitutional moderates, they were virtually certain of victory. It would take some time and bitter experience, however, before reformers in Congress and the administration were able to formulate and execute consistently successful legal strategies.

II. EXECUTIVE AUTHORITY AND THE ADMINISTRATIVE STATE

The persistent economic crisis besetting the country in the 1930s consolidated the popular conviction that an unregulated free market guided solely by the invisible hand of private interest could lead only to grief. The Roosevelt administration insisted that the countervailing power of government, administered by disinterested expert regulators, was necessary to discipline the market and stabilize an economy that "economic royalists" had left in tatters. The result was a stunning expansion of administrative authority both within and independent of the executive branch.

Agency government was by no means a novelty in 1933. Congress had established the Interstate Commerce Commission (ICC) in 1887, and during the half-century that followed the federal legislature had enacted a series of regulatory statutes authorizing administrative bodies to superintend a variety of activities and enterprises. Some of these statutes were administered by independent regulatory agencies; others had delegated new responsibilities to specific cabinet departments. The explosion of federal administrative authority inaugurated by the Roosevelt administration and the New Deal Congress was nevertheless unprecedented both for the number of agencies created and the scope of regulatory authority conferred. The Depression decade witnessed the creation of several new independent commissions: the Securities and Exchange Commission, the Federal Communications Commission, the National Labor Relations Board, the U.S. Maritime Commission, and the Civil Aeronautics Authority (transferred in 1940 to the Department of Commerce). To regulate prices and trade practices in the troubled coal industry, statutes enacted in 1935 and 1937 each created a National Bituminous Coal Commission, whose brief and turbulent life ended in 1939 when an executive order assigned its functions to the Department of the Interior. Still other existing commissions saw their jurisdictions enlarged or their powers enhanced. The Federal Power Commission, which had been reorganized in 1930, was given expanded responsibilities under the Federal Power Act of 1935 and the Natural Gas Act of 1938. The

Motor Carrier Act of 1935 gave the ICC regulatory authority over the interstate trucking industry. The New Deal created a vast new federal bureaucracy with extensive administrative authority over a multitude of activities
that had previously been regulated by state and local government or not
at all.

This dramatic expansion of federal administrative authority promised
to raise numerous constitutional controversies centered on questions of
due process, federalism, and the separation of powers. With respect to the
last of these issues, agency authority received a warmer reception from
the justices than many might have anticipated. In 1937 the President's
Committee on Administrative Management, also known as the Brownlow
Committee, would denounce independent federal commissions as comprising "a headless 'fourth branch' of the Government, a haphazard deposit of
irresponsible agencies and uncoordinated powers" doing "violence to the
basic theory of the American Constitution that there should be three major
branches of the Government and only three."[1] By contrast, advocates for
the administrative state such as former SEC Chairman and Harvard Law
School Dean James Landis valorized the specialized expertise and political independence of agency officials, dismissing "the traditional tripartite
theory of government organization" as talismanic "political conceptual-
ism."[2] Yet on the eve of the New Deal the Court had fortuitously secured
the constitutional footing of the administrative state with its decision in
Crowell v. Benson (1932). In upholding the Congressional delegation to
a deputy commissioner of authority to adjudicate workers' compensation
claims filed by maritime employees, the Court approved conferral of broad
fact-finding and adjudicative authority on administrative agencies as consistent with the requirements of both due process and the separation of
powers. Administrative agencies, the Hughes Court justices recognized,
were necessitated "by the increasing complexities of our modern business
and political affairs."[3] Though judicial review of agency action remained
essential to preserve constitutional limitations and to safeguard constitutional liberties, ordinary administrative findings would enjoy the deference
traditionally accorded to jury verdicts. And although a narrow majority of
the Court would continue to insist that Congress could not make agency
findings of "jurisdictional" facts final, Justice Van Devanter's retirement at
the conclusion of the 1936 term would herald the triumph of the minority's
more deferential position.

[1] President's Committee on Administrative Management, *Administrative Management in the Government of the United States* (Washington, DC, 1937), 36.
[2] James M. Landis, *The Administrative Process* (New Haven, CT, 1938), 12.
[3] *Jones v. Securities & Exchange Commission*, 298 U.S. 1, 24 (1936).

Perhaps the most significant safeguard of the political independence of the regulatory commissions came in an opinion that was widely perceived as a reproach to the president. In *Humphrey's Executor v. United States* (1935), President Roosevelt had removed a Hoover appointee to the FTC without cause, notwithstanding provisions of the Federal Trade Commission Act limiting presidential removal of commissioners to instances of inefficiency, neglect of duty, or malfeasance in office. The Court affirmed the view announced in *Myers v. United States* (1926) that the president enjoyed sole and illimitable power to remove "purely executive officers" such as postmasters. Yet notwithstanding obiter dicta in *Myers* that appeared to suggest the contrary, a unanimous Court held, that with respect to independent agencies exercising legislative and judicial functions, Congress might constitutionally restrict the president's removal power as it had in the Federal Trade Commission Act.

At the same time, however, particular exercises of agency authority could still provoke strong judicial reactions. While sustaining the registration requirements imposed by the Securities Act of 1933 and the Public Utilities Holding Company Act of 1935, for example, the Court nevertheless denounced the SEC's refusal to permit withdrawal of a registration statement allegedly containing material misrepresentations and quashed its subpoena of the withdrawing registrant's testimony and business records. The majority castigated the Commission for unauthorized appropriation and arbitrary, autocratic exercise of power, encroaching on fundamental liberties in a manner reminiscent of "the intolerable abuses of the Star Chamber." The three dissenting justices, who found "hyperbole in the sanguinary simile," maintained that the majority's ruling would "invite the cunning and unscrupulous to gamble with detection," knowing that they could evade investigation and punishment by the simple expedient of a timely withdrawal. Thus, wrote Justice Cardozo, might the act and its sanctions "become the sport of clever knaves."[4]

The Court was by no means alone in its anxiety over excessive agency discretion. The American Bar Association's Special Committee on Administrative Law, chaired by former Harvard Law dean Roscoe Pound, was a persistent critic of what Pound viewed as growing "administrative absolutism."[5] The 1938 Pound Report's allusion to the looming totalitarian threat across the Atlantic found a receptive ear in Congress, which the following year took up a bill to promulgate a uniform code of procedure for federal agencies, formalizing their internal processes; separating their

[4] 298 U.S. 1, at 28, 32–33.
[5] *Report of the Special Committee on Administrative Law*, 1938 A.B.A. Annual Report 331, 343 (1938).

legislative, prosecutorial, and adjudicative functions; and expanding judicial review of their decisions. Though passed by both houses of Congress
in 1940, the Walter-Logan Bill was vetoed by President Roosevelt. Yet the
bill's ambition to constrain administrative discretion would persist. It was
embraced in moderated form in the "minority bill" proposed in 1941 by
the Attorney General's Committee on Administrative Procedure, which in
turn provided the blueprint for the Administrative Procedure Act of 1946.

Though members of Congress were anxious to see federal agencies subjected to greater control, they were uncomfortable entrusting that task
to the president. Roosevelt's veto of the Walter-Logan Bill followed on
the heels of a bruising political battle over his proposal to reorganize the
executive department. In 1937 Roosevelt requested that Congress embody
in legislation the Brownlow Committee's recommendation that the president be granted authority to bring under greater presidential control more
than one hundred federal administrative bodies, including independent
regulatory commissions, by consolidating and merging them into existing executive departments. Roosevelt publicly denied charges of attempted
executive aggrandizement, asserting that the measure was necessary for
effective management and coordination of the activities of bodies charged
by Congress with the administration of federal law. This admonition went
unheeded in the House, which rebuffed the President's request in 1938.
Congress did enact an executive reorganization bill granting the president
much weaker authority in 1939, but at the same time sought to restrain
the power of the executive branch by restricting the political activities of
its employees. Concerns among Republicans and conservative Democrats
that federal relief officials had improperly used their positions to influence
voting behavior prompted Congress to enact the Hatch Act of 1939, which
prohibited lower level executive employees from taking an active part in
any political campaign.

The central separation-of-powers issues confronting the Hughes Court
concerned the scope of Congressional power to delegate legislative authority. Previous decisions had identified limits on the authority of Congress
to confer legislative power on the executive branch, but never before had
the Court held that a statute failed to satisfy those limiting criteria. That
would change in early 1935, when two oil companies challenged the constitutionality of section 9(c) of the National Industrial Recovery Act in
Panama Refining Co. v. Ryan (1935). In response to price destabilization in
the petroleum industry brought on by a frenzy of wildcat drilling in the
East Texas oil fields, Congress had authorized the president to prohibit the
interstate shipment of "contraband" or "hot" oil produced in violation of
quotas imposed by the state of production. The president had announced
such a prohibition by executive order, delegated to the Secretary of Interior
authority to promulgate appropriate rules and regulations, and approved

a Code of Fair Competition for the petroleum industry. An 8-1 majority found that section 9(c) transgressed previously latent limitations on Congressional delegation. That section, objected Chief Justice Hughes, offered the president no guidance concerning the circumstances under which he was to prohibit interstate transportation of hot oil. Rather than establishing a policy or standard to govern the president's course, Congress had instead conferred on him an unlimited legislative authority.

The *Panama Refining* decision cast a pall of doubt over the constitutionality of the broader recovery program, and the Court let the other shoe drop in *Schechter Poultry Corp. v. United States* (1935), the famous "sick chicken" case. *Schechter* involved the conviction of a kosher slaughtering concern in Brooklyn for violation of various provisions of the Live Poultry Code promulgated pursuant to section 3 of the NIRA. That section authorized the president to prescribe codes of fair competition to govern various trades and industries and to approve codes proposed by trade and industry representatives. The president was further authorized to provide exceptions and exemptions from the provisions of the codes where in his sole discretion he deemed it necessary to accomplish the policy of promoting industrial recovery.

A unanimous Court condemned this unprecedented delegation of legislative authority to the executive. Section 3, wrote Chief Justice Hughes, prescribed neither rules of conduct nor any meaningful standard to guide the exercise of the president's "virtually unfettered" discretion to prescribe and approve codes. Congress might authorize the executive branch to promulgate subordinate legal rules, so long as the legislation established standards sufficient to guide and confine the discretion of the executive in carrying out the declared legislative policy. But Congress could not alienate the essential legislative functions with which it was vested. Even Justice Cardozo, who had dissented alone in *Panama Refining*, would not defend section 3. Its delegation of legislative power, he observed, was "not canalized within banks that keep it from overflowing. It is unconfined and vagrant." The president had been granted "a roving commission to inquire into evils and upon discovery correct them." This, Cardozo exclaimed, was "delegation running riot."[6]

Following the *Schechter* decision Congress enacted the Bituminous Coal Conservation Act of 1935, also known as the Guffey Coal Act. Seeking to impose order on a chaotic industry plagued by cutthroat competition, the act created a National Bituminous Coal Commission, which it authorized to regulate the price at which bituminous coal moved in interstate commerce. A further provision created a labor board to adjudicate labor disputes in the industry, and it safeguarded the right of coal company employees to organize

[6] 295 U.S. 495, at 542, 551, 553.

and bargain collectively. This act provoked numerous constitutional objections, among them that one of its provisions unlawfully delegated to a majority of coal producers the power to fix the hours and wages of the employees of other coal producers. In *Carter v. Carter Coal Co.* (1936) the Court held that this delegation of legislative power, not to a government official, but to private parties having interests possibly and often actually adverse to the competitors over whom they would wield such power, was "clearly arbitrary" and thus a denial of the rights safeguarded by the Fifth Amendment's Due Process Clause.

The practical significance of these decisions should not be overestimated. Few mourned the death of the NIRA, which had been greeted with widespread noncompliance and weak enforcement. Consumer prices and unemployment had risen during its tenure, while workers' wages (especially those of African American workers) had remained low, as employers flouted with impunity the wage, hour, and collective bargaining regulations of the codes. The code-making authorities had been dominated by the representatives of larger business enterprises, whose efforts to reduce competition and to restrict production ill served their smaller competitors. The NIRA's two-year charter was set to expire within three weeks of the *Schechter* decision, and difficulties with the unpopular statute's administration had already made any extension doubtful. Moreover, Congress had no difficulty placing its oil and coal programs on a sound constitutional footing. Within six weeks of the *Panama Refining* decision Congress enacted the Connally Act, which solved the delegation problem by simply prohibiting the interstate shipment of hot oil. The statute was uniformly sustained in the lower courts and unanimously upheld by the Court in 1939. Similarly, Congress enacted a revised Bituminous Coal Conservation Act in early 1937, stripping out the provisions that had not withstood constitutional scrutiny. With the objectionable delegation to private producers now removed, the Court had no difficulty upholding the revised act in 1940. In two cases decided in 1939 the Agricultural Marketing Agreement Act would again provoke Roberts, Butler, and McReynolds to press delegation objections. By the late 1930s, however, a series of Roosevelt appointments to the Court had consigned the delegation views of these justices to the minority. The non-delegation doctrine was never a serious obstacle to the accomplishment of the administration's domestic policy objectives.

Nor did scruples over legislative delegation impede the president's conduct of foreign affairs. In 1934 Congress passed a joint resolution authorizing the president to prohibit arms sales to Paraguay and Bolivia, except under such limitations and exceptions as the president might prescribe, should he find that such a prohibition might contribute to the cessation of ongoing hostilities between those neighboring countries. Had the resolution pertained to the internal, domestic affairs of the nation rather than to international relations, one might have expected the Court to brand it an unconstitutional delegation of legislative of authority insufficiently confined by a standard. Yet in *United States v. Curtiss-Wright Export Corp.* (1936), only Justice McReynolds dissented from Justice Sutherland's opinion upholding the president's action under the resolution. The federal government's power to conduct foreign relations, the Court held, was an inherent feature of sovereignty rather than an enumerated grant. The president was the sole representative of the nation in the field of international relations, and the requirements for the successful conduct of those complicated and delicate relations justified Congress in conferring on the chief executive a degree of discretion that would be impermissible in the domestic context.

The implications of *Curtiss-Wright* were elaborated the following year in *United States v. Belmont* (1937). The case involved the validity of an assignment to the United States of Soviet claims against American nationals by the so-called Litvinov Agreement, a bilateral compact entered into coincident with the establishment of diplomatic relations between the two countries in 1933. The Litvinov Agreement took the form of an executive agreement rather than a treaty and was accordingly never presented to the Senate for its advice and consent. The Court confirmed that entry into the Litvinov Agreement was within the competence of the president and that the agreement, like a treaty, was entitled to the dignity accorded the supreme law of the land. The principles established in *Curtiss-Wright* and *Belmont* would soon underwrite an array of Congressional authorizations and executive measures undertaken following the outbreak of hostilities in Europe. As the continental powers lurched toward global conflict, the Court's decisions consolidated the triumph of executive discretion in the conduct of American foreign relations.

It is perhaps not surprising that Congressional delegation to the judicial branch received a warm reception at the Supreme Court. Throughout the nineteenth and early twentieth centuries, legal actions in the federal trial courts had been governed by the Process and Conformity Acts, which instructed federal judges to follow the forms of civil procedure employed by the courts of the state in which the federal court sat. The federal courts also continued to employ the traditionally distinct forms of procedure for actions at law and cases in equity, long after many states had merged the two into a single system. The bar's growing dissatisfaction with the resulting lack of uniformity in federal procedure provoked Congress to enact the Rules Enabling Act of 1934, authorizing the Supreme Court to prescribe uniform rules of pleading, practice, and procedure for civil actions in the federal trial courts. The act further authorized the Court to unify the procedure for actions at law and cases in equity brought in the federal courts by establishing a single set of rules to govern both. The Court in turn appointed an Advisory Committee to draft the rules and, after modification of the draft in response to comment from the legal profession, approved the new Federal Rules of Civil Procedure in 1938. As approved, the rules merged law and equity, simplified and relaxed rules of pleading, and expanded procedures for pre-trial discovery. In *Sibbach v. Wilson* (1941), the justices treated the delegation of legislative authority under which they had promulgated the Rules as constitutionally unproblematic. At the decade's close it appeared that, if any constitutional limitations on the power of Congress to delegate legislative authority still remained, it would require an effort to transgress them.

III. THE REVOLUTION IN DUE PROCESS JURISPRUDENCE

Liberty of Contract, Rate Regulation, and the Minimum Wage

The idea that the Due Process Clause of the Fourteenth Amendment might limit the power of state and local governments to regulate prices had emerged before Reconstruction's close. In *Munn v. Illinois* (1877), the Court had held that prices charged could be fixed by law only if the business in question were "affected with a public interest."[7] "Private" businesses were not amenable to such regulation. Over the course of the next half-century, the Court upheld price regulation of such "public" enterprises as railroads, grain elevators, water utilities, and public stockyards, yet forbade regulation of prices charged by theater ticket brokers, employment agencies, and, in early 1929, by the Standard Oil Company for gasoline. Decisions concerning price regulation in the District of Columbia revealed that federal regulatory power was similarly constrained by the Due Process Clause of the Fifth Amendment. On the eve of the Great Depression, governmental authority to regulate prices was tightly circumscribed.

This distinction between public and private enterprise similarly informed the Court's views on wage regulation. In *Adkins v. Children's Hospital* (1923), the Court invalidated a Congressional statute authorizing the prescription of minimum wages for women working in the District of Columbia. Analogizing wage regulation to price regulation, the Court observed that such legislation could be constitutionally applied to those engaged in public employment and to those working in businesses affected with a public interest. As applied to those employed in a private business, however, wage regulation was not an appropriate exercise of the police power. It

---

[7] 94 U.S. 113, 126.

deprived the parties of their "liberty of contract" and took the property of the employer without due process of law.

Adkins' declaration that wages might be regulated in businesses affected with a public interest was reaffirmed in 1930 when a unanimous Court upheld federal regulation of fees charged by commission men on sales of livestock in major stockyards and again in 1931 when a narrowly divided Court sustained a New Jersey statute regulating commissions paid to agents selling fire insurance. Yet, prospects for more systemic wage regulation, and for the minimum wage in particular, remained dim so long as the category of businesses affected with a public interest remained narrowly defined. That constitutional obstacle was removed in 1934, when a sharply divided Court upheld state regulation of minimum retail milk prices in *Nebbia v. New York* (1934). Rejecting as impertinent the contention that the milk business was not "affected with a public interest," the majority opinion insisted that the guarantee of due process required "only that the law shall not be unreasonable, arbitrary, or capricious, and that the means shall have a real and substantial relation to the object sought to be attained." "There is no closed class or category of business affected with a public interest," wrote Justice Roberts. The term meant "no more than that an industry, for adequate reason, is subject to control for the public good."[8]

The dissenting Four Horsemen were not alone in recognizing that the principles advanced in the majority opinion "would support general prescription of prices for . . . labor, when some legislature finds and declares such action advisable and for the public good."[9] (Shortly after the decision was announced, Justice McReynolds wrote his old friend, former Solicitor General James Beck, lamenting "the end of the constitution as you and I regarded it. An alien influence has prevailed."[10]) Commentators arrayed across the political spectrum recognized that *Nebbia* could underwrite the constitutionality of ambitious programs of state and federal price regulation and virtually guaranteed the demise of *Adkins*. This latter promise was fulfilled in *West Coast Hotel v. Parrish* (1937), in which the justices comprising the *Nebbia* majority narrowly upheld Washington state's minimum wage statute for women, thereby pronouncing last rites for what Justice Holmes had once called "the dogma, Liberty of Contract."[11]

[8] 291 U.S. 502, 511, 515, 516.
[9] *Nebbia v. New York*, 291 U.S. at 523 (McReynolds, J., dissenting).
[10] J. C. McReynolds to James M. Beck, April 10, 1934, quoted in Morton Keller, *In Defense of Yesterday: James M. Beck and the Politics of Conservatism, 1861–1936* (New York, 1958), 254.
[11] *Adkins v. Children's Hospital*, 261 U.S. 525, 568 (1923) (Holmes, J., dissenting).

The preceding year, however, Justice Roberts had confounded observers by joining the majority in a 5–4 decision invalidating a comparable New York statute on the authority of *Adkins*. This has prompted speculation concerning the cause of Justice Roberts' contrasting performance in *Parrish*. Some wags have described it as "the switch in time that saved the Nine," suggesting that Roberts was capitulating to the pressure brought to bear by the president's scheme to "pack" the Court. Yet this cannot be the case. Roosevelt's proposal to add a new justice to the Court for each justice who had not retired within six months following his seventieth birthday was introduced on February 5, 1937. The vote to uphold the Washington minimum wage statute was taken in conference on December 19, 1936, more than six weeks before the plan, known only to a handful of the president's most intimate advisors, was unveiled. Others have speculated that Roberts might have been responding to Roosevelt's landslide victory in the November 1936 elections, yet this hypothesis is also problematic. The New Deal had won an enormous vote of confidence with the Congressional Democrats' historic triumphs in the 1934 mid-term elections. Yet Justice Roberts and his colleagues had appeared completely unfazed by this popular endorsement, proceeding over the next two years to invalidate a bevy of major federal programs for recovery and reform. Moreover, the results of the 1936 presidential election could convey no independent information concerning popular support for the minimum wage, as both the Republican platform and party standard-bearer Alf Landon explicitly endorsed such legislation.

On his retirement in 1945, Roberts acceded to Felix Frankfurter's request that he prepare a memorandum explaining his behavior in the minimum wage cases. In that memorandum Roberts recalled that counsel for the state of New York had not requested that *Adkins* be overruled, but had instead sought to distinguish the statute from the law invalidated in *Adkins*. Roberts had been unable to see any constitutionally significant distinction and had accordingly been unwilling to rest a decision upholding the statute on that ground. Justices Brandeis, Stone, and Cardozo had been willing to overrule *Adkins*, but Chief Justice Hughes had written separately insisting that the New York statute could be upheld without impairing the authority of *Adkins*. In both *Schechter Poultry* and *Carter Coal Co.* (two cases decided after *Nebbia* but before the 1936 minimum wage case), the Court had declined to invoke liberty of contract as a rationale for invalidating federal regulation of wages – presumably because Roberts, the author of *Nebbia*, had refused to join the Four Horsemen to make a majority for this view. Although it is possible that better communication among the justices might have altered the result, it appears that Roberts' unwillingness to uphold the New York statute unless at least four of his colleagues were prepared to confront and overrule *Adkins*, combined with Hughes's insistence that the precedent be distinguished rather than overruled, conspired to produce the anomalous 1936 minimum wage decision. In *Parrish*, by contrast, where Hughes was prepared to confront and overrule *Adkins*, Roberts would join him to form a new majority to sustain the minimum wage.

Decisions in the early 1940s solidified this revolution in due process jurisprudence. *United States v. Darby Lumber Co.* (1941) confirmed that the minimum wage provisions of the Fair Labor Standards Act of 1938 did not violate the Fifth Amendment. *Olsen v. Nebraska* (1941) reaffirmed *Nebbia's* abandonment of the "affected with a public interest" limitation in upholding state regulation of fees charged by employment agencies. Contemporaneous decisions receded from decades of precedent under which the Court had rigorously scrutinized public utility rate regulation to ensure a fair return to investors. Governmental powers to regulate wages and prices had emerged from the Great Depression virtually unconstrained by the Constitution's Due Process Clauses.

Liberty of Contract and Collective Bargaining

When the United States entered World War II in 1941, the rights of American workers to organize and bargain collectively were more robust than at any time in the past. This was made possible by the eradication of due process constraints that had previously limited legislative efforts to secure those rights. In *Adair v. United States* (1908), the Court had invalidated provisions of the 1898 Erdman Act prohibiting interstate carriers from discharging or discriminating against any worker because of his membership in a labor union or requiring him to agree as a condition of his employment not to join a union. Similarly, in 1915 the ruling in *Coppage v. Kansas* had invalidated a Kansas statute outlawing such "yellow dog" contracts. In each instance, the Court had held that such legislation deprived the employer of his liberty of contract. Legal support for efforts to organize had reached its nadir on the eve of the nation's engagement in World War I in Europe. In the 1917 case of *Hitchman Coal & Coke Co. v. Mitchell*, the Court had enjoined an effort by the United Mine Workers to organize a non-union mine as an unlawful attempt to induce the company's employees to breach their yellow dog employment contracts.

All of this was to change over the ensuing two decades. In 1926, Congress enacted the Railway Labor Act, which safeguarded railroad workers' rights of organization and collective bargaining from employer interference. A unanimous Court upheld the act in *Texas & N. O. R. Co. v. Brotherhood of Railway and Steamships Clerks* (1930). Emphasizing employee rights of association and downplaying the employer's claimed injury to its liberty of contract, the Court affirmed the order of a lower court requiring the

railroad to reinstate employees it had discharged for engaging in lawful
union activities. This decision inspired Congress to insert into the Norris-
LaGuardia Act a provision declaring yellow dog contracts contrary to public
policy and unenforceable in federal courts. Finally, the 1934 amendments
to the Railway Labor Act requiring carriers to negotiate exclusively and in
good faith with the selected representatives of their employees were upheld
by a unanimous Court in March of 1937.

This set the stage for the Court's decision the following month upholding
the NLRA. The National Labor Relations Board initiated a series of test cases
in which employers had fired employees for engaging in activity protected
under the statute. The Court unanimously sustained the act as applied to
an interstate bus company that, as a common carrier, was a classic business
affected with a public interest. The justices narrowly divided on the due
process issue in the three cases involving manufacturing concerns, however.
For the majority, the issue had been effectively settled in the 1930 decision
upholding the Railway Labor Act's protection of the "fundamental right"
of self-organization. In the view of the dissenting Four Horsemen, however,
that principle applied only to businesses affected with a public interest, not
to "private" enterprises. Here again, the issue that divided the justices was
the one that a fractured Court had settled three years earlier in *Nebbia*.

Subsequent construction of the statute would make clear that the justices had not abandoned all solicitude for employers' rights of property and
contract. For example, the Court read the act to authorize struck employers
to hire permanent replacement workers, but not to protect from discharge
aggrieved employees staging sit-down strikes. By the spring of 1941, however, with each of the Four Horsemen having retired, there was no one left
to dissent from the assertion that "the course of decisions in this Court since
Adair v. United States and *Coppage v. Kansas* have completely sapped those
cases of their authority."[12] The Court had consolidated the constitutional
revolution in labor law.

The Contract Clause and Due Process: Debt Relief

In the early 1930s, widespread unemployment, a wave of bank failures, and
a powerful deflationary spiral placed profound stress on relations between
debtors and their creditors. Prices and wages fell nearly 25 percent between
1929 and 1933, and millions of workers lost their jobs and remained chronically unemployed. However, although the contraction of the money supply
diminished the prices and wages that businessmen, farmers, workers, and
other debtors could command in the marketplace, it did not alter the face

---

[12] *Phelps Dodge Corp. v. NLRB*, 313 U.S. 177, 187 (1941).

amount of obligations undertaken before the economic collapse had so devastated their earning capacity. In the winter of 1932–33, frustration over the inability to service mortgage debt boiled over into riots protesting the epidemic of residential and farm foreclosures in several Midwestern states. A number of state legislatures responded by enacting various forms of debtor relief legislation.

In Minnesota, where more than half of the owner-operated farms were mortgaged, the state legislature passed a mortgage moratorium law in April 1933. The statute empowered the state courts to extend the period of redemption up to two years beyond the one year provided by prior law, provided the defaulting mortgagor in possession paid the reasonable rental value of the mortgaged property during the extended period. Though much of the existing precedent suggested that such a legislative modification of the debtor's obligation would violate the Contract Clause, a sharply divided Court upheld the law as a valid and reasonable exercise of the state's police power in *Home Bldg. & Loan Assn. v. Blaisdell* (1934). Under such conditions of economic emergency, wrote Chief Justice Hughes, the statute's temporary, conditional, and limited alteration of the mortgagor's undertaking did not impair the underlying obligation of the contract.

At the federal level, the government sought to ease the debt crisis by reinflating the currency. A critical feature of the administration's monetary plan depended on the power of the federal government to abrogate a provision routinely inserted in long-term debt contracts. This so-called gold clause required the obligor to repay in gold coin of a specified weight and fineness or in an equivalent amount of paper money as measured by the gold content of the dollar on the date of the contract. Congress had therefore enacted a joint resolution declaring all gold clauses against public policy and forbidding their enforcement even with respect to existing contractual obligations. The constitutionality of this prohibition was contested in the *Gold Clause Cases*.

In *Norman v. B. & O. R. R. Co.* (1935), the Court upheld the abrogation of the gold clause in private contracts by a vote of 5–4. Such action, wrote Chief Justice Hughes for the majority, was a necessary and proper means of exercising Congress's power to establish and regulate the value of a uniform national currency. The administration, fearing an avalanche of bankruptcies were the nation's debtors required to repay obligations at $1.69 on the newly devalued dollar, breathed an enormous sigh of relief. The opinion in *Perry v. United States* (1935), by contrast, held unconstitutional the abrogation of the gold clause in federal government bonds. Yet, the administration's expectation that the rise in the price of gold resulting from government purchase and its devaluation of the dollar would be accompanied by an immediate general increase in domestic prices had not been realized. Chief Justice Hughes accordingly maintained for the majority that payment to Perry in the uniform devalued currency had left him with no less purchasing power than he would have enjoyed had no devaluation occurred. Accordingly, he had suffered no injury and was entitled to no relief. Congress subsequently withdrew the government's consent to suit on monetary claims as of January 1, 1936, thereby depriving bondholders of the opportunity to show actual damages.

Both *Blaisdell* and the *Gold Clause Cases* provoked impassioned dissents from the Four Horsemen. "Fewer questions of greater moment than that just decided have been submitted for judicial inquiry during this generation," wrote Justice Sutherland dissenting in *Blaisdell*. "He simply closes his eyes to the necessary implications of the decision who fails to see in it the potentiality of . . . serious and dangerous inroads upon the limitations of the Constitution which are almost certain to ensue."[13] Justice McReynolds condemned the monetary program as embracing "a debased standard, adopted with the definite purpose to destroy obligations." Such "arbitrary and oppressive action" violated the Fifth Amendment. "Just men regard repudiation and spoliation of citizens by their sovereign with abhorrence," he remonstrated. "Loss of reputation for honorable dealing will bring us unending humiliation; the impending legal and moral chaos is appalling."[14] When delivering his dissent from the bench, he extemporaneously gave voice to sentiments he had earlier expressed privately over *Nebbia* and *Blaisdell*. "This is Nero at his worst," he thundered. "The Constitution is gone."[15]

These reports of the Constitution's demise turned out to be greatly exaggerated. In the twenty-five months following the announcement of the *Blaisdell* decision, the Court heard three cases involving challenges to state debtor relief legislation under the Contract Clause. In each case, the Court invalidated the legislation by a unanimous vote. *W. B. Worthen Co. v. Thomas* (1934) struck down an Arkansas statute absolutely and retroactively exempting the proceeds of certain insurance policies from liability for debts and seizure under judicial process. *W. B. Worthen Co. v. Kavanaugh* (1935) disapproved another Arkansas debtor-relief package as "an oppressive and unnecessary destruction of nearly all the incidents that give attractiveness and value to collateral security." "With studied indifference to the interests of the mortgagee or to his appropriate protection," wrote Justice Cardozo, the legislature had "taken from the mortgagee the quality of an acceptable

---

[13] 290 U.S. 398, 448 (Sutherland, J., dissenting).
[14] *Perry v. United States*, 294 U.S. 330, 372, 362, 381 (McReynolds, J., dissenting).
[15] Elliott Thurston, "Biggest Barrier to U.S. Monetary Program is Removed," *Washington Post*, Feb. 19, 1935, at 1.

investment for a rational investor."[16] And in *Treigle v. Acme Homestead Assn.* (1936), the justices found that a Louisiana statute diminishing the rights of withdrawing members of building and loan associations was neither temporary nor conditional, but instead arbitrary and oppressive. Nor did the celebrated events of 1937 mark the end of judicial enforcement of the Contract Clause. Over the objection of some Roosevelt appointees, the Court would find fault with statutes impairing the obligation of contract in 1938 and again in 1941.[17] Though the Contract Clause would slumber for more than three decades after Hughes retired in the summer of 1941, throughout his tenure as Chief Justice context-specific judgments of reasonableness continued to constrain state legislative regulation of contractual obligations.

The same was true at the federal level. The Frazier-Lemke Farm Debt Relief Act of 1934 permitted distressed farmers to stay foreclosure proceedings for a period of five years, during which time they could take title to the mortgaged property free and clear by paying its appraised value rather than the amount of the debt. In *Louisville Joint Stock & Bank Co. v. Radford* (1935), the Court unanimously held that the act unconstitutionally impaired the vested rights of mortgage creditors. Yet, Justice Brandeis's opinion for the Court offered Congress guidance on how the statute might be reformulated so as to conform to the requirements of the Fifth Amendment. Congress accepted the advice and quickly redrafted the measure accordingly. When the inevitable challenge came before the Court in *Wright v. Vinton Branch Bank* (1937), the opinion upholding the revised statute was again unanimous. It was not a change in constitutional doctrine, but instead a change in legislative means that enabled Congress to attain its desired objective.

The Persistence of the Old School and the Significance of the Roosevelt Appointments

The Court upheld state and federal regulatory legislation more frequently in the late 1930s than it had earlier in the decade. This was due in no small part to greater efforts by legislative draftsmen, such as those who rewrote the Frazier-Lemke Act, to comply with constraints imposed by contemporary constitutional doctrine. At the same time, a good deal of this increased success resulted from transformations in constitutional doctrine brought about by changes in Court personnel. Just as decisions such as *Nebbia* and its progeny were the result of Hoover's appointments of Hughes, Roberts, and Cardozo, later decisions relaxing the restraints of the Fifth and Fourteenth Amendments on federal and state regulatory power were the consequence

---

[16] 295 U.S. 56, 60, 62.

[17] *Indiana ex rel. Anderson v. Brand*, 303 U.S. 95 (1938); *Wood v. Lovett*, 313 U.S. 362 (1941).

of Roosevelt's nominations from 1937 to 1943, which placed Hugo Black, Stanley Reed, Felix Frankfurter, William O. Douglas, Frank Murphy, James F. Byrnes, Robert H. Jackson, and Wiley Rutledge on the Court. The voting patterns of Hughes and especially Roberts in cases decided between 1938 and 1940 belie the notion that they "switched" in 1937 to the view that those amendments did not constrain governmental regulatory authority. In fact, the decisions illustrate the remarkable persistence of these centrist justices' moderate constitutional views.

In the 1935 case of *Railroad Retirement Board v. Alton*, Justice Roberts wrote for a narrowly divided Court that the Railroad Retirement Act of 1934 was unconstitutional, first because several of its provisions violated the Due Process Clause of the Fifth Amendment, and second because the establishment of a pension system for railroad workers exceeded Congress's power to regulate interstate commerce. Though *Alton* marked no retreat from *Nebbia's* dramatic abandonment of the "affected with a public interest" limitation, it did indicate that *Nebbia's* requirement that regulatory legislation "not be unreasonable, arbitrary, or capricious" was not entirely toothless. Chief Justice Hughes, whose opinion for the four dissenters agreed that one of the statute's provisions violated due process, was one among many observers who believed that the Commerce Clause holding doomed any comparable pension legislation, even if redrafted to address the Court's due process objections. Yet, astute members of Congress realized that such a pension program funded from general revenue rather than from an earmarked source might be immunized from constitutional attack under the taxpayer standing doctrine announced in *Frothingham v. Mellon* (1923). The pension payments could be made directly from the general treasury rather than from a segregated fund, with the necessary revenue derived from a special tax on interstate carriers. President Roosevelt persuaded representatives of the major railway unions and railway companies to join Congress and the administration in hammering out the details of such a program, which were then set forth in the Railroad Retirement and Carrier Taxing Acts of 1937. Representatives of the unions and the companies also kept their promises not to challenge the program's constitutionality, and their pension system, with some modifications, remains in place to this day.

Though this turn of events precluded relitigation of the precise issues that had been before the Court in *Alton*, Roberts' subsequent treatment of the precedent testifies that his views had not changed. In the 1938 decision *United States v. Carolene Products Co.*, Justice Stone famously declared that "regulatory legislation affecting ordinary commercial transactions is not to be pronounced unconstitutional unless in light of the facts made known or generally assumed it is of such a character as to preclude the assumption that it rests upon some rational basis within the knowledge and experience of the legislators."[18] Yet, New Dealer Justice Black refused to join this portion of the opinion, for Stone then proceeded to qualify that pronouncement in a passage citing Roberts' *Alton* opinion as authority. As every other justice joining that portion of Stone's opinion had dissented in *Alton*, the citation is explicable only as an accommodation to Roberts. Roberts again expressed his conviction that his 1935 decision had been correct when *United States v. Lowden* (1939) effectively overruled *Alton*. The reconstituted "Roosevelt Court's" decision was unanimous, but only because Roberts suppressed the dissenting vote he had cast in conference.

Still other decisions from the mid- and late 1930s illustrate how *Nebbia* and *West Coast Hotel* could coexist with a rationality standard that stopped short of complete deference to the legislature. For example, in 1935 Hughes and Roberts joined the 6–3 decision in *Colgate v. Harvey* holding that a provision of a Vermont tax violated the Equal Protection and Privileges or Immunities Clauses of the Fourteenth Amendment. *Colgate* would be overruled in *Madden v. Kentucky* in 1940, but only over the dissent of Justice Roberts. Similarly, in the 1932 case of *New State Ice v. Liebmann*, Hughes and Roberts had joined the opinion holding unconstitutional an Oklahoma statute designed to exclude aspiring entrants to the ice business. In the 1936 decision of *Mayflower Farms, Inc. v. Ten Eyck*, these justices again voted with the majority, this time to strike down a New York milk industry regulation that operated to freeze out potential market entrants. And in *United States v. Rock Royal Cooperative* (1939), this time in dissent, Hughes and Roberts voted to invalidate a federal milk regulation they believed placed smaller milk dealers at an unconstitutional disadvantage in the competition with their larger rivals. Hughes and Roberts continued throughout their careers to maintain that the Constitution safeguarded the right to pursue a lawful calling on terms of legal equality with all others. These features of constitutional doctrine changed not because Hughes and Roberts revised their long-standing views, but because President Roosevelt repopulated the Court with justices harboring different commitments.

When Justice Roberts retired in 1945, then-Chief Justice Stone prepared a draft of the customary farewell letter from the remaining members of the Court. Stone's draft contained the encomium, "You have made fidelity to principle your guide to decision."[19] Justices Black and Douglas, partisans of the "switch-in-time" narrative, refused to sign any letter containing such an assertion, while Justices Frankfurter and Jackson refused to join any

---

[18] 304 U.S. 144, 152.
[19] "Memorandum for the Court," from Harlan Fiske Stone (undated), Frankfurter Papers, Harvard, Series III, Reel 4.

letter from which the sentence was omitted. This impasse resulted in no letter being sent. Yet it now appears that Stone, Frankfurter, and Jackson had come correctly to see in Roberts' jurisprudence a principled character that Black, Douglas, and many others could not or would not recognize.

IV. THE REVOLUTION IN FEDERALISM JURISPRUDENCE

The Commerce Power

In 1929, the power of the national government to regulate the economy was qualified not only by the restraints of the Due Process Clause but also by those of constitutional federalism. By the end of 1942, both of those limitations had dissolved, and federal regulatory power over economic matters was virtually plenary. The principal means through which Congress exerted control over "ordinary commercial transactions" was through exercises of its power to regulate commerce among the several states.

Since 1895, Commerce Clause jurisprudence had been organized around two fundamental distinctions. Each of those distinctions was drawn from the Court's Dormant Commerce Clause jurisprudence, a branch of constitutional doctrine that articulated implied limitations on the power of state and local governments to tax or regulate interstate commerce. Those distinctions were between production and commerce and between direct and indirect effects on commerce. The Court recognized broad federal authority to regulate interstate transportation and interstate sales. Yet, a series of cases involving the Sherman Antitrust Act had established the principle that the power to regulate commerce did not as a general matter include the power to regulate activities of production, such as agriculture, mining, and manufacturing. The Sherman Act might reach such "local" activities as corporate mergers and labor strikes were it shown that they were *intended* to restrain interstate commerce. In such instances commerce was affected "directly." Without proof of such intent, however, the effect on commerce – irrespective of its magnitude – was merely "indirect" or "incidental," leaving the activity in question beyond the reach of federal authority.

One of the principal qualifications to this general framework found expression in the "stream of commerce" doctrine. A series of Fuller and Taft Court decisions had held that the activities of a "local" enterprise might nevertheless be subjected to federal regulation if they occurred in a "current" or "flow" of interstate commerce that began outside the state and later continued beyond its borders. In *Stafford v. Wallace* (1922), for example, the Court upheld federal regulation of "local" transactions in the Chicago stockyards. The livestock came from the western states to Chicago, where they were housed, fed, watered, sold, and often slaughtered. They then continued their interstate journeys to other states in the Midwest or East for ultimate consumption. The stockyards were the "throat" through which this current of interstate commerce flowed, the transactions therein being essential to its interstate movement.

The scope of the stream of commerce doctrine was constrained, however, by the due process requirement that the "local" business regulated be affected with a public interest. Only these businesses had the capacity to exact exorbitant charges and thereby affect the flow of interstate commerce "directly." So long as that category of business remained small and select, the stream of commerce promised to cut a narrow channel. With *Nebbia's* abandonment of the public interest limitation in due process jurisprudence, however, the potential range of application of the stream of commerce doctrine was enlarged dramatically. Now any business located in a current of interstate commerce was amenable to federal regulation.

Yet it remained necessary that the local activity be situated within the current of interstate commerce, rather than at one of its terminals. Just as the Court's Dormant Commerce Clause decisions continued to maintain that activities that took place before interstate commerce had begun or after it had ceased remained subject to state and local powers to tax and regulate, so the Court's affirmative Commerce Clause jurisprudence adhered to the view that such activities lay outside federal regulatory competence. Thus, the stream of commerce doctrine was inapposite in *Schechter Poultry Corp. v. United States.* The chickens butchered at the Schechters' slaughterhouse had "come to a permanent rest"[20] in New York and were sold locally rather than in interstate trade. Because interstate commerce in the poultry had come to an end, the NIRA's Live Poultry Code regulated local activity that affected interstate commerce only indirectly. Such activity was subject to exclusive state jurisdiction. Though President Roosevelt denounced the decision as adopting a "horse and buggy"[21] era conception of interstate commerce, the judgment was unanimous. Indeed, Justice Department lawyers and other Roosevelt advisors had regarded *Schechter* as an extraordinarily weak case for the government and had tried to prepare the president for an adverse outcome.

Administration lawyers similarly were convinced that the provisions of the Guffey Coal bill regulating labor relations at the mine were unconstitutional in view of the Court's opinion in *Schechter*, and Attorney General Cummings refused to offer to a subcommittee of the House Ways and Means Committee an opinion on the bill's constitutionality. Instead, he urged the

[20] 295 U.S. 495, 543.
[21] Samuel I. Rosenman, ed., *The Public Papers and Addresses of Franklin D. Roosevelt*, 4 (New York, 1938), 200, 221.

representatives to "push it through and leave the question to the courts."[22]
President Roosevelt similarly cajoled the subcommittee's chairman, Sam
B. Hill, not to "permit doubts as to constitutionality, however reasonable,"
to block the bill's enactment.[23] Majorities of both the subcommittee and
the full committee considered the bill unconstitutional, and it was only
through such vigorous prodding from the administration and the resulting
abstention of dissenting Democrats that the bill was even reported to the
House floor. Though Democrats vastly outnumbered Republicans in both
the House and the Senate, the bill was passed in each by uncharacteristically
narrow margins.

The constitutional doubts of the bill's critics were vindicated in *Carter v.
Carter Coal Co.* Justice Sutherland's majority opinion echoed what Congressional opponents had pointed out: the stream of commerce doctrine could
have no application where the interstate flow had not yet begun. The Guffey
Coal Act presented the same difficulty the Court identified in *Schechter*,
though from the opposite end of the stream. The coal mine in question lay
at the source rather than amid the flow of the current of commerce. The
act therefore regulated labor relations in the local activity of production,
which affected interstate commerce only indirectly. The majority accordingly invalidated the Guffey Coal Act's labor provisions. Moreover, despite
the act's severability clause, the majority held that the labor provisions were
inseparable from its price regulation provisions, thereby vitiating the entire
statute. Chief Justice Hughes wrote separately, agreeing with the majority
that the labor provisions were unconstitutional. Yet, Hughes maintained
that those provisions were separable from the price regulation provisions,
which were constitutional in light of *Nebbia*. In dissent, Justices Cardozo,
Brandeis, and Stone insisted that the price regulation provisions were constitutional, that they were separable from the labor provisions, and that
the constitutional challenge to the labor provisions was premature. Significantly, none of the justices contended that the labor provisions were within
the scope of the Commerce Power.

A number of observers read the *Schechter* and *Carter* decisions as casting
doubt on the constitutionality of the NLRA. Government lawyers preparing cases to test the act's constitutionality before the Court disagreed. In
selecting those test cases they had shrewdly pursued instances involving
labor disputes at steel, trailer, and clothing plants that imported raw materials from other states and then shipped their products across state lines for

---

[22] *New York Times*, July 6, 1935, p. 2, quoted in Ralph Baker, *The National Bituminous Coal
Commission* (Baltimore, 1941) 50.
[23] Franklin D. Roosevelt to Samuel B. Hill, July 5, 1935, reprinted at 79 Cong. Rec. 13449
(74–1).

subsequent purchase. Labor Board lawyers contended that these factories, like the Chicago stockyards in *Stafford v. Wallace*, were located in a stream of interstate commerce whose flow would be disrupted by work stoppages produced by labor strife. The power to enact regulations designed to prevent or curtail such disruptions was therefore comprehended by Congress's power to regulate interstate commerce. The Court upheld application of the NLRA to such manufacturing enterprises in the *Labor Board Cases*,[24] with Justices Brandeis, Stone, Roberts, and Cardozo joining Chief Justice Hughes' opinions for the majority. Hughes maintained that it was unnecessary to decide whether the factories in question lay in a stream of interstate commerce, for that doctrine was merely one illustration of a principle also immanent in the Court's Sherman Act and railroad regulation precedents: any activity whose "close and substantial relation" to interstate commerce made its regulation necessary to protect such commerce from burdens and obstructions was subject to appropriate Congressional control.[25] Hughes cautioned readers against interpreting this formulation too broadly, and both the dissenting opinion of the Four Horsemen and subsequent remarks by Justice Roberts strongly suggested, as many contemporary observers recognized, that the government's stream of commerce analogy had in fact provided the basis for Roberts' crucial fifth vote to sustain the Act.

Others, however, have suggested that Roberts' behavior – and that of Hughes as well – was prompted by entirely different considerations. President Roosevelt's proposed Judicial Reorganization Act – known colloquially as the "Court-packing plan" – remained pending in Congress even as the justices were deciding and announcing the result in the *Labor Board Cases*. Because six of the sitting justices had already celebrated their seventieth birthdays, the bill would have empowered Roosevelt to expand the personnel of the Court from nine to fifteen immediately. Roosevelt claimed that the measure was necessary because the aged justices – the "Nine Old Men," as a popular book of the day[26] called them – were unable to keep pace with the demands of the Court's docket. Yet, it was generally understood, as Roosevelt essentially admitted in a fireside chat in early March, that the bill's objective was to secure a Court majority sympathetic to the New Deal.

Though neither house of Congress would approve the president's proposal, there has long been speculation that Hughes and Roberts voted to uphold the NLRA in order to blunt Roosevelt's attack on the Court and thereby defeat the Court-packing plan. The question of motivation cannot

[24] *NLRB v. Friedman-Harry Marks Clothing Co.*, 301 U.S. 58 (1937); *NLRB v. Fruehauf Trailer Co.*, 301 U.S. 49 (1937); *NLRB v. Jones & Laughlin Steel Co.*, 301 U.S. 1 (1937).
[25] *NLRB v. Jones & Laughlin Steel Co.*, 37.
[26] Drew Pearson & Robert S. Allen, *The Nine Old Men* (New York, 1936).

be resolved with absolute certainty, but there are reasons to be skeptical of this view. Although acknowledging the strain the justices felt during the crisis, both Hughes and Roberts denied that the pending bill had affected their votes. One would of course not expect a contrary admission, but there is abundant evidence to corroborate their claims. First, the justices had ample reason to doubt that Congress would enact the president's proposal. The bill provoked vigorous opposition from the moment it was introduced, from powerful forces both inside and outside Congress. It was denounced in the press, by leaders in higher education, and by a variety of civic organizations including the American Bar Association. It was conspicuously criticized by prominent liberals and former members of Roosevelt's own administration. While organized labor offered the proposal only faint praise, farm organizations launched public campaigns of opposition. Congressmen found that constituent correspondence ran heavily against the Plan, and contemporary public opinion polls registered both consistent opposition to Court packing and a steady decline in Roosevelt's popularity.

The signals from Congress were similarly ominous. The president's failure to consult with Congressional leaders before unveiling his proposal created hard feelings on Capitol Hill. Hatton Sumners, chair of the House Judiciary Committee, responded with two measures. First, he quickly pushed a judicial retirement bill through Congress with the aim of persuading his colleagues that the problem of judicial opposition to the New Deal could be solved simply by offering elderly conservative justices a financial incentive to leave the bench. In this Sumners was successful. Two of the justices were anxious to retire, and had remained on the Court only because the Economy Bill of 1933 had left the provisions for retired federal judges at unacceptably parsimonious levels. Justice Van Devanter would announce his retirement within two months of the retirement act's passage; Justice Sutherland would step down the following January, and but for the pendency of the Court-packing bill would have retired with Van Devanter the previous spring. Second, Sumners lined up a comfortable majority of his committee against the president's plan, assuring the opposition control of the hearings and the power to bottle the bill up in committee for an indefinite period.

Because of the opposition of Sumners and his colleagues on the House committee, the administration took the unusual step of introducing the bill instead in the Senate. There as well, however, the plan faced stiff resistance. All of the Senate Republicans and many Senate Democrats, led by liberal Burton Wheeler of Montana, announced their opposition. By mid-February Henry Morgenthau, Roosevelt's Secretary of the Treasury, assessed the bill's chances as even at best. Two events later in March prompted observers to revise this estimate downward. On March 29, the Court took wind out of the plan's sails when it announced its decision upholding the minimum wage in *West Coast Hotel v. Parrish.* A week earlier, on March 22, Senator Wheeler had read before the Senate Judiciary Committee a letter he had solicited from Chief Justice Hughes with the approval of Justices Brandeis and Van Devanter. The letter rebutted point by point each of the president's allegations concerning the Court's efficiency. Hughes insisted that the Court was fully abreast of its calendar, was granting all meritorious petitions for review, and that the addition of new justices would frustrate rather than enhance the Court's efficient operation. The impact of Wheeler's recitation prompted Vice-President Garner to telephone Roosevelt to tell him, "We're licked."[27]

At least two weeks earlier, it had become clear that the opposition intended to filibuster the bill on the floor of the Senate and appeared to have at least enough votes to prevent cloture, if not to defeat the bill in an up-or-down vote. Even had the bill's proponents succeeded in cutting off debate in the Senate, however, the obstacles raised by Sumners and his colleagues remained looming in the House. Yet the continuing deterioration of the bill's fortunes throughout the spring prevented it from getting even that far. By early May the opposition held a clear majority in the Senate; at mid-month the Senate Judiciary Committee issued its adverse report on the bill. In early June Roosevelt finally relented to Democratic leaders and agreed to support a compromise measure that would have permitted him to appoint a smaller number of additional justices over a longer period of time. Efforts to revive the plan again foundered in the Senate, however, and the bill was recommitted with instructions to excise its Court-packing provisions.

Moreover, the voting patterns of the justices are difficult to reconcile with the claim that they were influenced by the president's proposal. Several Congressional bills to constrain the Court had been introduced in 1935 and 1936, yet none of them appeared to have any effect on its decisions. The Court upheld New York's unemployment compensation statute over due process objections ten weeks before the announcement of the plan; *West Coast Hotel* was decided in conference six weeks before the justices could have known of the president's intentions, and the Social Security Act was upheld after it appeared that the plan was doomed. Moreover, Hughes and Roberts continued to vote to uphold state and federal regulatory statutes – and occasionally to invalidate them – long after the Court-packing plan was dead and buried. And while some or all of the Four Horsemen occasionally voted to uphold such programs after 1936, their votes to invalidate important New Deal measures in the spring of 1937 demonstrate the failure of Roosevelt's effort to pressure them into compliance. Improvements in Congressional

---

[27] Burton Wheeler, *Yankee from the West* (Garden City, NY, 1962), 333.

draftsmanship and administration lawyering, rather than raw power politics, best account for the Court's greater receptivity to the NLRA and other New Deal initiatives.

Subsequent NLRA decisions underscored the continuity in doctrinal development. *Santa Cruz Fruit Packing Co. v. NLRB* (1938) upheld the application of the NLRA to employees engaged not in production, but in the initial stages of interstate transportation. *Consolidated Edison Co. v. NLRB* (1938) concerned a company whose activities were indispensable to the operation of a vast network of interstate communication and transportation, and it upheld NLRB jurisdiction only on this narrow ground. *NLRB v. Fainblatt* (1939) involved a clothing manufacturer situated in a stream of interstate commerce, receiving raw materials from outside the state and shipping its products across state lines.

Nor did contemporaneous decisions upholding federal regulation of the coal industry and agriculture push back the frontiers of Commerce Clause jurisprudence. In a series of statutes enacted between 1935 and 1938, Congress had revised its strategy for stabilizing prices in these troubled sectors of the economy. Rather than controlling the conditions or quantities of local *production* in these enterprises, Congress now regulated the interstate *marketing* of their products. This price stabilization was to be accomplished either directly, through price regulation, or indirectly, through limitation of the amount of the item that could be marketed in interstate commerce. Before *Nebbia*, the Fifth Amendment's Due Process Clause would have prohibited price regulation with respect to such ordinary commodities; after *Nebbia*, federal regulation of the price at which goods moved in interstate commerce was constitutionally unproblematic. Yet, members of Congress recognized that coal and agricultural produce sold in intrastate commerce competed with such items sold in interstate commerce. If price stabilization in interstate commerce were to be effective, these intrastate transactions would have to be comprehended within the federal regulatory scheme.

Congressional sponsors found authority for such intrastate regulation in the 1914 *Shreveport Rate Cases* (1914). There the Court had held that Congress could regulate the intrastate rates charged by interstate carriers where necessary to make federal regulation of rates for competing interstate carriage effective. This authority to regulate intrastate rates was thus derivative of Congress's authority to regulate interstate rates. Before *Nebbia*, the Due Process Clause had confined that authority to businesses affected with a public interest. Indeed, before 1934, every decision following the *Shreveport* doctrine had involved regulation of that paradigmatic business affected with a public interest, rail carriage. After *Nebbia*, however, the potential application of the *Shreveport* doctrine expanded dramatically. Now Congress could regulate the price at which coal and agricultural commodities were sold in interstate commerce, and as intrastate sales of coal and agricultural commodities competed with interstate sales of these items, *Shreveport* authorized federal price regulation of these local transactions as well.

Thus the Bituminous Coal Conservation Act of 1937, unlike its predecessor struck down in *Carter Coal*, did not purport to regulate labor relations and conditions in the coal industry. Instead, its sponsors invoked *Nebbia* and *Shreveport* in support of the act's regulation of the price at which coal was sold in both interstate and intrastate commerce. In *Sunshine Anthracite Coal Co. v. Adkins* (1940) the Court upheld the act over the lone dissent of Justice McReynolds, the sole remaining *Nebbia* dissenter. The Agricultural Adjustment Act (AAA) of 1938 similarly did not seek to prescribe the amount of specified commodities that farmers could produce. Its proponents instead again pointed to *Shreveport* in support of the act's restrictions on the quantities of such commodities producers could market in either interstate or intrastate commerce. Justice Roberts, joined by Chief Justice Hughes, wrote the opinion upholding the act in *Mulford v. Smith* (1939). The sponsors of what became the Agricultural Marketing Agreement Act of 1937 maintained that *Nebbia* and *Shreveport* supported the act's provisions authorizing the Secretary of Agriculture to set minimum prices for interstate and intrastate sales of certain agricultural commodities. The Court accepted this contention, upholding the act in a series of decisions between 1939 and 1942. By regulating marketing rather than production, Congress could address the problems that had plagued the energy and agricultural sectors with programs that could withstand judicial scrutiny, and all of this could be accomplished, as Justice Cardozo put it, "within rulings the most orthodox."[28]

Thus, although *Nebbia's* transformation of due process doctrine allowed existing Commerce Clause precedents far greater scope than they had previously enjoyed, developments in Commerce Clause doctrine itself remained relatively modest in the late 1930s. This helps to explain Justice Brandeis's landmark 1938 opinion in *Erie Railroad Co. v. Tompkins*. Ever since the decision of *Swift v. Tyson*[29] in 1842, the Court had interpreted section 34 of the Judiciary Act of 1789 to require federal courts sitting in diversity to apply the statutory but not the common law of the states in cases coming before them. Where the relevant state legislature had enacted no statute covering the issue in question, the federal courts were to apply the "general common law," the content of which many came to criticize as unduly favoring corporate litigants. In *Erie*, the Court held that this long-standing interpretation of section 34 was not only incorrect but also unconstitutional. Federal

---

[28] *Carter v. Carter Coal*, 298 U.S. at 329.   [29] 41 U.S. 1 (1842).

courts henceforth would be required to apply state common law rules as
rules of decision in diversity cases. "There is no federal general common
law," declared Justice Brandeis. "Congress has no power to declare substantive rules of common law applicable in a State whether they be local in their
nature or 'general,' be they commercial law or part of the law of torts."[30]
The federal courts had no power to declare general rules of commercial and
tort law for the states, Brandeis maintained, in part because Congress had
no power to do so. As Chief Justice Hughes had written in the *Labor Board
Cases*, the reach of the Commerce Power "must be considered in light of our
dual system of government and may not be extended so as to embrace effects
upon interstate commerce so indirect and remote that to embrace them, in
view of our complex society, would effectually obliterate the distinction
between what is national and what is local and create a completely centralized government."[31] The justices made it clear throughout the 1930s that
the Commerce Power remained subject to judicially enforceable constraints
of constitutional federalism.

That would change in the early 1940s. By February of 1941 all but three
of the sitting justices were Roosevelt appointees. None of the remaining justices had participated in the notorious case of *Hammer v. Dagenhart* (1918),
in which a 5–4 majority had invalidated the Keating-Owen Child Labor
Act's prohibition of interstate shipment of goods made by child labor. The
statute, the majority had held, was a pretextual use of the Commerce Power
to regulate manufacturing, a matter reserved to the states. *Hammer* and a
subsequent decision invalidating an excise tax on firms employing child
workers had inspired a movement to amend the Constitution to empower
Congress to regulate the practice. The Child Labor Amendment received
the requisite endorsement of Congress in 1924, but fell eight states short of
ratification. In 1938, however, Congress again asserted its authority under
the Commerce Power to regulate employment of children, as well as the
wages and hours of adult employees, in the Fair Labor Standards Act. In
United States v. Darby (1941), the Roosevelt Court unanimously overruled
Hammer in upholding provisions of the act prohibiting interstate shipment
of goods made by employees working under substandard labor conditions.
The Court also unanimously sustained provisions of the Fair Labor Standards Act prohibiting employment of workers engaged in "production for
interstate commerce" at substandard wages or for excessive hours, though
internal Court records reveal that Chief Justice Hughes was deeply troubled
by this latter extension of the Commerce Power. Although in cases following
Hughes's retirement the Roosevelt appointees would find that Congress had

[30] *Erie Railroad Co. v. Tompkins*, 304 U.S. 64, at 77–78.
[31] 301 U.S. 1, at 37.

not intended by this language to include every employee working for firms engaged in production for interstate commerce, only Roberts would insist that Congress was powerless to reach "purely local" activities.

Wickard v. Filburn (1942) cast grave doubt on whether there were any activities left in that category. The Secretary of Agriculture had penalized Roscoe Filburn for growing wheat in excess of his annual allotment under the amended AAA of 1938. Filburn maintained that the surplus wheat was intended solely for personal use and for consumption rather than for sale and that its production was therefore a purely local activity beyond the reach of federal authority. This extension of the Commerce Power sought by the government troubled many of the justices, including several Roosevelt appointees, and when the case was initially argued in the spring of 1942 there was not a majority to uphold it. After reargument in the fall, however, the Court unanimously sustained the penalty. In an opinion that did not even cite the *Labor Board Cases*, Justice Jackson reasoned that if many farmers satisfied their own needs by growing for personal use, they would reduce the total demand for the crops marketed and thus the price at which those crops were sold in interstate commerce. The aggregate effect of such activity on interstate commerce might be "substantial." Congress's regulation of such activity was therefore a necessary and proper means of regulating the interstate price of agricultural commodities.

Roberts' opinion in *Mulford* had taken pains to demonstrate that the AAA of 1938 regulated "marketing" rather than "production." At the *Darby* conference, Chief Justice Hughes had voiced concern over the Fair Labor Standards Act's regulation of all "production for commerce." These justices had regarded "production" as presumptively immune from federal regulation. In NLRA decisions such as *Santa Cruz Fruit* and *Consolidated Edison*, moreover, Hughes had continued to employ the older vocabulary of "direct" and "indirect" effects. The *Wickard* opinion, by contrast, expressly repudiated the notion that such nomenclature was even useful, much less controlling. Though initially expressing doubts about the government's position in just such traditional terms, Jackson had come to believe that the Court never had succeeded – and never could succeed – in developing a workable legal standard for determining which economic effects made federal regulation appropriate and which did not. Neither the direct/indirect test nor the "close and substantial" test provided an adequate legal criterion for judicial evaluation of Congressional policy judgments. Indeed, Jackson could no longer conceive of an activity whose relation to commerce was so attenuated as to make its regulation by Congress inappropriate. He consequently despaired of the enterprise and turned instead to a conceptualization of Commerce Power issues as presenting political rather than judicial questions. The national political process would allocate regulatory authority between the state and federal governments, and the Court would defer to those political judgments. Whereas Hughes and Roberts had insisted that the Court was responsible for policing the line beyond which exercises of the Commerce Power usurped state regulatory authority, the *Wickard* Court concluded that "effective restraints" on the power's exercise "must proceed from political rather than from judicial processes."[32]

The Dormant Commerce Clause

Just as political process theory helped to rationalize the Court's withdrawal from enforcing federalism limitations on Congressional exercises of the Commerce Power, so it also explained the persistence of judicial enforcement of the Dormant Commerce Clause. State interests were theoretically represented in the national Congress, but as Justice Stone observed in *South Carolina Highway Department v. Barnwell Bros.* (1938), out-of-state interests were often not adequately represented in state legislatures. "[W]hen the regulation is of such a character that its burden falls principally upon those without the state," Stone explained, "legislative action is not likely to be subjected to those political constraints which are normally exerted on legislation where it affects adversely some interests within the state."[33] So, for example, in 1941 the Court invalidated a California statute that prohibited transporting into the state indigent non-residents, as the excluded persons were "deprived of the opportunity to exert political pressure upon the California legislature in order to obtain a change in policy."[34]

Yet, this persistence of enforcement was accompanied by significant doctrinal change. Since the 1870s, Dormant Commerce Clause doctrine had been organized around the same categories that had structured affirmative Commerce Clause jurisprudence. State or local regulation that affected interstate commerce "directly" was forbidden; regulation that affected such commerce only "incidentally or indirectly" was permitted. In the late 1930s the Court continued to employ these categories in analyzing questions of both state and federal power. With their abandonment in *Wickard*, however, their persistence in Dormant Commerce Clause doctrine became anomalous. Adjectives inadequate for describing the effects of activities on interstate commerce were surely equally inadequate to describe the effect of state and local regulations on such commerce. Moreover, understood through the older vocabulary, *Wickard* suggested that virtually every local activity affected interstate commerce sufficiently "directly" to warrant its federal regulation. If it now followed that state and local regulation of those local

[32] *Wickard v. Filburn*, 317 U.S. 111, at 120.   [33] 303 U.S. 177, 184–5, n.2.
[34] *Edwards v. California*, 314 U.S. 160, 174 (1941).

activities now also affected interstate commerce "directly," then all such regulation would violate the Dormant Commerce Clause. The expansion of federal power thus threatened to destroy traditional state and local regulatory authority by implication. The Court's solution to this difficulty, adopted in *Parker v. Brown* (1943) later in the same term that *Wickard* was decided, was to decouple Dormant Commerce Clause doctrine from its affirmative counterpart, to abandon the categories each had shared, and to treat regulatory authority over local activities as presumptively concurrent. Henceforth, in the absence of Congressional preemption, non-discriminatory state and local regulation would be evaluated by "comparing the relative weights of the conflicting local and national interests involved."[35]

In one area of the law, the uncertainties created by this doctrinal reorientation were sufficient to provoke Congressional intervention. Since 1869 the Court had consistently maintained that the business of writing contracts of insurance was not itself interstate commerce and that state regulation of the insurance industry therefore did not violate the Dormant Commerce Clause. In view of the prevailing symmetrical relationship between affirmative and Dormant Commerce Clause doctrine, each of the branches of the federal government had treated the regulation of insurance as a matter for the states rather than the federal government. The Court disrupted this understanding in 1944, however, holding in two cases that the activities of certain insurance companies bore sufficient relation to interstate commerce to bring them within the reach of the Sherman Act and the NLRA. These decisions created anxiety over how much state insurance regulation would now be treated as implicitly preempted by federal statute or the Dormant Commerce Clause. Congress quickly responded by enacting the McCarran-Ferguson Act of 1945, providing that neither Congressional silence nor federal legislation should be construed to displace such state regulation by implication. Only statutes specifically relating to the business of insurance would trump state law.

Taxing and Spending

This expansion of the realm of concurrent jurisdiction in Commerce Clause jurisprudence found its complement in the erosion of intergovernmental tax immunities. In 1939, *Graves v. New York ex rel. O'Keefe* overruled *Collector v. Day* (1871) and its more recent progeny in announcing that the salaries of federal officers and employees would no longer enjoy constitutional immunity from state taxation, nor would the compensation of state officials be exempted from the federal income tax. Similarly, in *United States v. Bekins*

---

[35] *Parker v. Brown*, 317 U.S. 341, at 367.

(1938) the reconstituted Court upheld a federal municipal bankruptcy act comparable to one narrowly invalidated two years before under related principles of intergovernmental immunity. Moreover, while "essential" functions and instrumentalities of the national and state governments would retain their traditional implied immunity from taxation by the other sovereign, that category came to be understood more narrowly than it had been previously. Nevertheless, the doctrine continued to be complicated by lines of distinction that Justice Jackson would later characterize as "drawn by an unsteady hand."[36]

The Court's Tenth Amendment jurisprudence similarly constrained Congressional power to impose regulatory taxes on activities whose control had been reserved to the states. In early decisions such as *McCray v. United States* (1904) and *United States v. Doremus* (1919), the majority opinions for divided benches had come near to suggesting that Congress enjoyed unfettered authority to levy substantial excises on disfavored activities. Yet, the Court had corrected that impression in *Bailey v. Drexel Furniture Co* (1922). There Chief Justice Taft wrote for an 8–1 majority including Justices Holmes and Brandeis that an excise on 10 percent of the net profits of companies employing child labor was a penalty rather than a tax. As the penalty was imposed only on mines and manufacturing establishments failing to comply with the statute's prescribed regime of employment relations, it transcended the limitations of the Tenth Amendment.

The Hughes Court's regulatory taxation decisions suggested some differences among the justices concerning these Tenth Amendment limitations on Congressional power, but did not openly question the underlying structure of the doctrine. In fact, the divisions among the justices concerning the Congressional authority to regulate through the use of fiscal powers emerged most openly in a case involving the Spending Power. *United States v. Butler* (1936) involved a constitutional challenge to the AAA of 1933. A food processor challenged the tax by which the acreage-reduction benefit was funded as a step in a federal scheme to regulate the local activity of agricultural production and thus a usurpation of the powers reserved to the states by the Tenth Amendment. By a vote of 6–3, the Court invalidated the act.

The differences between the majority justices and the dissenters boiled down to a question of the perspective from which the benefit payment should be viewed. Assuming non-compliance with the federal scheme and thus non-receipt of the benefit payment as the baseline, the dissenters saw payment of the benefit as a reward for compliance with the terms of a contract the farmer was free to reject. "Threat of loss, not hope of gain, is

---

[36] *United States v. Allegheny County*, 322 U.S. 174, 176 (1944).

the essence of economic coercion," wrote Justice Stone.[37] By contrast, the majority justices assumed compliance with the scheme and thus receipt of the payment as the baseline – and, indeed, the vast majority of American farmers did comply and receive the payment – and therefore regarded the withholding of the benefit as a regulatory tax on non-compliance. In *Bailey*, a manufacturer remained free to employ child labor, but only by paying a tax that would presumably place him at a competitive disadvantage with competitors who complied with the federal regulation. Similarly, in *Butler*, a farmer remained free to produce in excess of the Secretary's target quota for his farm, but only at the cost of forgoing a benefit payment that his compliant competitors were receiving. In each instance, an enumerated fiscal power was employed to induce compliance with a federal effort to regulate local production.

The *Butler* Court did not, however, adopt the Madisonian understanding of the spending power. While that power might not be employed to usurp regulatory prerogatives confided to the states by the Tenth Amendment, it was not limited to carrying into effect exercises of other powers enumerated in Article I, section 8. Instead, and for the first time, the Court explicitly endorsed the Hamiltonian view of the power to spend as an independent grant of power not so limited. This commitment provided the foundation for Justice Cardozo's 1937 opinions for the Court upholding the old age pension and unemployment compensation titles of the Social Security Act in *Helvering v. Davis* and *Steward Machine Co. v. Davis*. The vote in *Helvering* was 7–2, with Justices Van Devanter and Sutherland joining the majority. The vote in *Steward Machine* was 5–4, but Van Devanter and Sutherland's dissent voiced general approval of the statute, objecting only to certain easily correctable administrative provisions. Similarly, when the Court upheld the Alabama state unemployment compensation law in *Carmichael Southern Coal & Coke Co. v. Alabama* (1937), Van Devanter, Sutherland, and Butler agreed that the statute's objective was constitutional and took issue only with the particular means selected by the state legislature. Their dissent detailed how the statute might be revised so as to pass constitutional muster, pointing to the Wisconsin statute as an exemplar of constitutionality. Even at the height of the Court-packing struggle, these conservative justices had set a face of flint to minimum wage legislation and federal regulation of local employment relations. Yet, they clearly shared the majority's view that no constitutional revolution was necessary to sustain state and federal programs of social security.

Even the significance of the Court's embrace of the Hamiltonian understanding of the spending power should not be overestimated. Though the

[37] *United States v. Butler*, 297 U.S. 1, at 81.

proper understanding of that power's scope had long been the subject of controversy in Congress and elsewhere, *Frothingham v. Mellon's* 1923 taxpayer standing doctrine had operated to confine the debate to extra-judicial fora. The taxpayer standing doctrine so thoroughly insulated federal expenditures from judicial review that the constitutionality of a wide array of New Deal spending initiatives financed from general revenue was never challenged. Among these were the Civilian Conservation Corps, the Farm Credit Act, the Reconstruction Finance Corporation, the Rural Electrification Administration, and the Emergency Relief Appropriation Act of 1936. Moreover, the Supreme Court and the lower federal courts repeatedly invoked the *Mellon* doctrine in rejecting constitutional challenges to loans and grants made by the Public Works Administration.

Indeed, the taxpayer standing doctrine played a central role in the subsequent history of the administration's farm program. After the *Butler* decision invalidated the AAA's tax on food processors, the government continued to pay the benefits payments it had promised to individual farmers, but now in unchallengeable fashion from general revenue. Within two months of the decision, Congress had replaced the AAA with the Soil Conservation and Domestic Allotment Act of 1936. This act authorized the Secretary of Agriculture to pay farmers to shift acreage from overproduced "soil-depleting" crops to "soil-conserving" crops. The bill's sponsors refused to support a companion taxing measure designed to produce the revenue necessary to finance these expenditures and thereby successfully inoculated the measure against constitutional attack.

While instances involving the taxpayer standing doctrine were the most important examples of the manner in which justiciability doctrine shielded the New Deal from judicial review, they were not alone. A series of lower court decisions refused to consider constitutional challenges to various New Deal initiatives on the ground that the plaintiff had not suffered a legally cognizable injury, and it was on this basis that the justices rebuffed constitutional attacks on the Tennessee Valley Authority. Throughout the 1930s, the "passive virtues" served as a significant, self-imposed restraint on judicial superintendence of the political branches.

V. THE EMERGENCE OF MODERN CIVIL RIGHTS

At the same time that the justices were sustaining state and federal economic reforms designed to secure "positive" liberties for working men and women, the Court's decisions also increasingly evinced heightened concern for certain "negative" liberties of American citizens. With one eye on the alarming rise of repressive totalitarian states in Europe, the Hughes Court affirmed and elaborated American constitutional commitments to civil rights, civil liberties, and democratic processes at a time when many Western intellectuals were questioning the future of democracy. In *Carolene Products*, the Court had declared that legislation regulating "ordinary commercial transactions" would enjoy a robust "presumption of constitutionality." But if constitutional law had become increasingly agnostic on matters of economic policy, it nevertheless remained and would become more strongly committed to certain core political values. In the famous "Footnote Four" of his *Carolene Products* opinion, Justice Stone identified three types of statutes that would be subjected to "more exacting judicial scrutiny": legislation appearing to conflict with "a specific prohibition of the Constitution, such as those of the first ten amendments"; "legislation which restricts those political processes which can ordinarily be expected to bring about repeal of undesirable legislation"; and statutes directed at "discrete and insular" "religious, national, or racial minorities," prejudice against whom tended "seriously to curtail the operation of those political processes ordinarily to be relied upon to protect minorities."[38] There was often considerable overlap among these categories: a law directed at a discrete and insular minority might itself restrict the political process or implicate a provision of the Bill of Rights, and a law implicating the Bill of Rights might itself restrict the political process. Nonetheless, the categories provide a useful heuristic. And though subsequent decisions would both enlarge the scope and strengthen the content of these three categories of prohibition, none of them was without recent precedent in the Court's jurisprudence.

For decades since Reconstruction the Court had rejected contentions that the Fourteenth Amendment incorporated various of the criminal procedure protections of the Bill of Rights. In the 1937 case of *Palko v. Connecticut* Justice Cardozo's opinion unanimously reaffirmed these precedents, holding that the protection against double jeopardy was not so "implicit in the concept of ordered liberty" that its observance was a requirement of due process. Only principles of justice "so rooted in the traditions and conscience of our people as to be ranked as fundamental," those "fundamental principles of liberty and justice which lie at the base of all our civil and political institutions," were so comprehended.[39] Yet, two significant Hughes Court decisions, although they did not incorporate the corresponding provision of the Bill of Rights, read the Due Process Clause to afford criminal defendants comparable protections. In *Brown v. Mississippi*, decided in 1936, the Court overturned the murder conviction of an African American man who had denied commission of the offense until subjected to a

[38] *United States v. Carolene Products Co.*, 304 U.S. 144, at 152, 153.
[39] 302 U.S. 319, 325, 328.

severe beating by police. The unanimous Court held that the brutal extortion of this confession, which constituted the principal basis for the conviction, was "revolting to the sense of justice." The states were not bound by the Fifth Amendment's prohibition against compulsory self-incrimination, wrote Chief Justice Hughes, but "[t]he rack and torture chamber may not be substituted for the witness stand."[40] In 1940 *Chambers v. Florida* would extend this principle, unanimously overturning murder convictions secured on the basis on confessions elicited from four African American defendants through the sorts of third-degree methods of interrogation condemned by former Attorney General George W. Wickersham's Committee on Official Lawlessness nearly a decade earlier.

The decade similarly witnessed significant development of the right to counsel in criminal cases. *Powell v. Alabama* (1932) involved the first trial of the "Scottsboro Boys," nine African Americans charged with raping two white girls. There the Court overturned the capital convictions due to the failure of the trial court either to provide the illiterate defendants adequate opportunity to secure counsel or to appoint effective counsel to act on their behalf. Effective assistance of counsel in a capital case was a necessary component of the hearing to which a defendant was entitled as a matter of due process. *Powell* found a more expansive federal counterpart in *Johnson v. Zerbst* (1938), decided the same term as *Carolene Products*. There the Court held for the first time that in federal criminal prosecutions the Sixth Amendment did not merely overturn the older English rule severely limiting the assistance felony defendants could receive from their counsel. Instead, the right to assistance of counsel ensured by the Amendment imposed an affirmative obligation to provide an attorney to federal defendants who were unable to obtain representation. Not for another quarter-century, however, would the Court fully guarantee this right to defendants in state criminal prosecutions.

Enforcement of national Prohibition by federal authorities had also presented the Court with a series of cases implicating the search and seizure provisions of the Fourth Amendment. Though the Eighteenth Amendment and the Volstead Act were successful in reducing the consumption of alcohol in the United States, by the late 1920s they had come to be regarded with widespread public disaffection and even disregard. As public enthusiasm for the "Noble Experiment" waned, the Court routinely excluded evidence obtained by warrantless searches without probable cause, evidence obtained by searches beyond the scope authorized by the warrant,

---

[40] *Brown v. Mississippi*, 297 U.S. at 285–86.

and evidence obtained illegally by state officials cooperating with federal officials. Powered by demands to stimulate legitimate job growth and to redirect the resources of federal law enforcement, by the desire for the excise revenue that legalization could afford, and by Congressional reapportionment that enhanced the clout of more urban, ethnic constituencies, the Democrat-led movement for repeal sailed to victory in 1933 with the ratification of the Twenty-First Amendment. The first constitutional amendment ever to repeal another was also the only amendment for which Congress has required ratification by popularly elected ratifying conventions rather than by state legislatures.

Though many of the decade's leading criminal procedure decisions involved the discrete and insular minority of African American defendants, the Court's opposition to racial bias in the administration of criminal justice emerged most explicitly in cases involving discriminatory practices in the selection of grand and petit juries. The Hughes Court consistently overturned such convictions, two of which involved subsequent trials of the Scottsboro Boys. Meanwhile, the Court fired its opening salvo in support of the NAACP's incipient campaign to desegregate public education in the 1938 case of *Missouri ex rel. Gaines v. Canada.* Rather than admitting blacks to its state law school or providing separate legal education to its black citizens within the state, Missouri officials paid the tuition of black Missourians admitted to law schools in adjacent states. The Court held that furnishing legal education within the state to whites while not doing so for its black citizens denied them equal protection. Missouri must either admit its qualified African American residents to its existing state law school or establish within the state "substantially equal" facilities for their legal education.[41]

By 1938 the justices could also claim to have invalidated numerous statutes restricting the operation of political processes. Critical to the proper functioning of that process was the freedom of the press. In the 1931 case of *Near v. Minnesota*, the Court struck down a statute authorizing the imposition of prior restraints on publication of any malicious, scandalous, or defamatory matter, even if true. Such a restriction on the power of the press to report and criticize the actions of public officials, wrote Chief Justice Hughes, was "the essence of censorship."[42]

While the White and Taft Courts had developed the modern "clear and present danger" framework for analyzing questions of free speech, it was

---

[41] *Missouri ex rel. Gaines v. Canada*, 305 U.S. 337, at 351.
[42] *Near v. Minnesota*, 283 U.S. 697, at 713. See also *Grosjean v. American Press Co*, 297 U.S. 233 (1936).

the Hughes Court that deployed the doctrine to shield political dissenters
from prosecution. Though the Court upheld denial of citizenship to foreign
pacifists – two of them women – for refusing to pledge armed defense of
the United States, the justices repeatedly vindicated the speech and assembly rights of leftist citizens. In *Stromberg v. California*, decided in 1931,
the Court overturned the conviction of a summer camp counselor for violating a California statute prohibiting the display of a red flag "as a sign,
symbol or emblem of opposition to organized government." Stromberg had
supervised campers in a daily ceremony in which the children raised a reproduction of the flag of the Communist Party of the United States. During
the ceremony the children stood, saluted, and recited a pledge of allegiance
"to the workers' red flag, and to the cause for which it stands; one aim
throughout our lives, freedom for the working class." "The maintenance of
the opportunity for free political discussion to the end that government may
be responsive to the will of the people and that changes may be obtained
by lawful means," wrote Chief Justice Hughes, "is a fundamental principle of our constitutional system." Insofar as the statute was "so vague and
indefinite" that it might be construed to punish protected expressions of
"peaceful and orderly opposition to government by legal means and within
constitutional limitations," the Court held, it offended this fundamental
principle.[43]

In 1937 the Court again invoked this fundamental principle, unanimously reversing Dirk De Jonge's conviction under Oregon's criminal syndicalism statute for his participation in a peaceable assembly of the Communist Party at which no unlawful conduct was advocated. "[P]eaceable
assembly for lawful discussion cannot be made a crime," Hughes insisted.
"The holding of meetings for peaceable political action cannot be proscribed."[44] Later that year the Court again vindicated this fundamental
principle. Angelo Herndon, an African American and a paid organizer for
the American Communist Party, had been convicted for violating a Georgia
statute prohibiting any attempt, "by persuasion or otherwise, to induce others to join in any combined resistance to the lawful authority of the State."
Herndon had held meetings seeking to recruit members for the Party and
was found in possession of Party literature advocating mass action and revolutionary struggle against the ruling white bourgeoisie. But there was no
evidence that Herndon had read or distributed any of the literature, nor that
he had himself advocated or incited the forcible subversion of governmental authority. A divided Court held that to construe the statute to prohibit
Herndon's actions deprived him of his rights of free speech and peaceable
assembly. Unlike the power of the state to regulate ordinary commercial

---

[43] 283 U.S. 359, at 361, 362, 369.   [44] *De Jonge v. Oregon*, 299 U.S. 356, 365.

transactions, the power to abridge freedom of speech and assembly was "the exception rather than the rule" and "must find its justification in a reasonable apprehension of danger to organized government."[45]

Among the chief beneficiaries of this New Deal for free speech was organized labor. In *Hague v. CIO*, decided in 1939, the Court held that the Fourteenth Amendment protected the freedom of labor organizers to assemble peaceably to disseminate and discuss information concerning the provisions of the NLRA. A municipal ordinance prohibiting exercise of those rights on public streets and in public parks unless authorized by municipal officials enjoying unfettered discretion was accordingly facially void, as was an ordinance absolutely prohibiting distribution of handbills. The following year, in *Thornhill v. Alabama* (1940), the justices relied explicitly on Footnote Four to make clear that peaceful labor picketing was also protected speech. Exercise of the right to picket was subject to reasonable regulation to preserve order, and acts of violent intimidation and defamation lay outside the scope of constitutional immunity. But state statutes and common law policies prohibiting peaceable persuasion and communication of grievances impaired "those opportunities for public education that are essential to effective exercise of the power of correcting error through the processes of popular government."[46]

The Court's solicitude for rights of expression ran to religious speech as well. In the late 1930s and early 1940s the Jehovah's Witnesses, often assisted by the American Civil Liberties Union, conducted a vigorous and remarkably successful litigation campaign to vindicate the rights of their members to proselytize for their faith. Between 1938 and 1940 the Court invalidated several ordinances prohibiting the distribution of literature on public streets. During this time the justices similarly struck down as prior restraints on expression ordinances punishing the distribution of literature and solicitation of contributions on the public streets or door-to-door without first obtaining a permit that might be conferred or withheld in the discretion of local authorities. Such regulations, the Court maintained, restricted "appropriate means through which, in a free society, the processes of popular rule may effectively function."[47] This string of victories under the Free Speech and Free Exercise Clauses was brought to an abrupt if temporary halt in *Minersville School District v. Gobitis* (1940), in which the Court upheld a state regulation requiring public school students to participate in a daily ceremony saluting the flag and reciting the Pledge of Allegiance. Rendered in the midst of Hitler's devastating conquests in

[45] *Herndon v. Lowry*, 301 U.S. 243, 258 (1937).
[46] *Thornhill v. Alabama*, 310 U.S. 88, 95.
[47] *Minersville School District v. Gobitis*, 310 U.S. 586, 599 n.6 (1940).

Western Europe in the spring of 1940, the decision held that the scriptural injunction against bowing down before graven images must yield to the public interest in promoting sentiments of patriotism and national unity. The Free Exercise Clause did not exempt individuals from the commands of generally applicable laws that did not target the religious commitments of particular sects. Justice Stone, dissenting alone, affirmed the values and elaborated the theory he had articulated in Footnote Four. Asserting that the Constitution required more than "that democratic processes must be preserved at all costs," Stone maintained that the free exercise rights of "this small and helpless" "discrete and insular minority," which were "admittedly within the scope of the protection of the Bill of Rights," must be secured through a more "searching judicial inquiry into legislative judgment" than that afforded by the majority.[48] A properly functioning democracy afforded protection of such minority rights.

Stone's position would command a majority within three years. In *Jones v. Opelika* (1942), the Court upheld the application of non-discriminatory municipal license taxes on itinerant sales agents to Jehovah's Witnesses selling religious literature. Stone again dissented, insisting that the freedoms of speech and religion – two of the "Four Freedoms" identified by President Roosevelt in his 1941 State of the Union address – occupied "a preferred position."[49] Those freedoms could thus be afforded no less protection from burdensome taxation than the Court had given ordinary commercial transactions in interstate commerce. This time, however, Stone was joined in dissent by three members of the *Gobitis* majority – Justices Black, Douglas, and Murphy. Apparently influenced in part by the outpouring of unfavorable commentary on the decision and reports of widespread and often violent private and official persecution of Witnesses that followed in its wake, these justices took the extraordinary step of confessing error in voting to uphold the compulsory flag salute. By the following term this dissenting bloc had become the core of a new majority to renounce both *Jones* and *Gobitis*. Now non-discriminatory license taxes could not be imposed on the privilege of selling religious literature, the door-to-door distribution of such literature could not be prohibited, nor could the flag salute be made compulsory. "If there is any fixed star in our constitutional constellation," wrote Justice Jackson overruling *Gobitis* in *West Virginia Board of Education v. Barnette* (1943), "it is that no official, high or petty, can prescribe what shall be orthodox in politics, nationalism, religion, or other matters of opinion.... Authority here is to be controlled by public opinion, not public opinion by authority." Alluding to "the fast failing efforts of our present totalitarian enemies," Jackson cautioned that "[t]hose

[48] 310 U.S. 586, at 606–07.   [49] *Jones v. Opelika*, 316 U.S. 584, 608.

who begin coercive elimination of dissent soon find themselves eliminating dissenters. Compulsory unification of opinion achieves only the unanimity of the graveyard."[50]

Cases involving voting rights illustrated both concern for the proper functioning of the political process and the doctrinal limitations on that commitment. In the 1915 decision of *Guinn v. United States*, the Court had unanimously invalidated an Oklahoma suffrage regulation exempting from its literacy requirement anyone lineally descended from a person qualified to vote in 1866. This "grandfather clause," obviously designed to exempt whites but not blacks from the literacy test, violated the Fifteenth Amendment's prohibition against racial discrimination regarding the right to vote. A special session of the state legislature had responded by enacting a new election law bestowing permanent registration status on anyone who had voted in 1914 under the now-invalidated election law, and granted all other qualified electors only twelve days within which to register or be permanently disfranchised. The effect of this transparent attempt to prolong the discriminatory impact of the grandfather clause was not as great as one might surmise: African Americans were permitted to register and vote in most counties despite the statute. When an Oklahoma citizen disfranchised under the statute brought a constitutional challenge in the 1939 case of *Lane v. Wilson*, he won the support of a unanimous Court.

In other voting rights cases, the results were mixed. In *Nixon v. Herndon*, decided in 1927, a unanimous Court had held that a Texas statute excluding its black citizens from participation in the primary elections of the Democratic Party denied them equal protection. The Texas legislature had responded by repealing this statute and enacting another simply authorizing the Executive Committee of each of the state's political parties to prescribe qualifications for membership and participation in its primary elections. The Executive Committee of the state Democratic Party had in turn adopted a resolution excluding blacks from voting in its primaries. In *Nixon v. Condon*, handed down in 1932, a narrowly divided Court held that, as the authority to prescribe the qualification was derived from the statute, the action of the Executive Committee constituted impermissible discriminatory state action. Three weeks after the decision in *Condon*, the state Democratic convention adopted a resolution limiting membership in the party to white voters. This time, however, a unanimous Court invoked the state action limitation in rejecting the black petitioner's equal protection challenge. In 1935 *Grovey v. Townsend* held that the Texas Democratic Party was a voluntary, private association, unconstrained by the requirements of the Fourteenth Amendment. And in *Breedlove v. Suttles*, rendered

[50] 319 U.S. 624, 641–42.

in 1937, a unanimous Court upheld a provision of the Georgia constitution treating payment of a poll tax as a prerequisite to exercise of the elective franchise. Though proposed constitutional amendments to abolish payment of poll taxes as a prerequisite to voting in federal elections would be introduced in Congress regularly over the next twenty-five years, it was not until 1964 that the goal was achieved through ratification of the Twenty-Fourth Amendment, nor until 1966 that the Court would invalidate poll taxes for state elections as well.

The white primary's lease on life would prove short by comparison. As the culminating step in a more general reorganization of the Justice Department in the 1930s, Attorney General Frank Murphy created the Civil Liberties Unit (later renamed the Civil Rights Section) of the Criminal Division in early 1939. Encouraged by the success of prosecutions under federal statutes prohibiting peonage and involuntary servitude in the mid- and late-1930s, the Unit initiated a series of actions under Reconstruction-era civil rights statutes in cases involving both official and private infringements of civil rights and liberties. Among these was the 1941 case of *United States v. Classic*, in which the justices sustained convictions under the Enforcement Act of 1870 of Louisiana Commissioners of Elections who had fraudulently tabulated the results of a Congressional Democratic primary election. Qualified voters had the right to participate in Congressional primary elections that were either integral to the selection process or that effectively determined the ultimate electoral outcome, and Congress could protect that right by appropriate legislation. Three years later, in *Smith v. Allwright* (1944), the Court relied on *Classic* in overruling *Grovey v. Townsend*. Because a series of state actions had made the Democratic primary integral to the electoral process, party determinations of eligibility to participate constituted state action within the meaning of the Fifteenth Amendment. The invalidation of the white primary, bolstered by shifting white attitudes and the enforcement efforts of the NAACP and the Justice Department, contributed to a dramatic increase in Southern black voter registration: from 3 percent in 1940 to 20 percent in 1952.

Despite the obvious significance of these decisions as articulations of official constitutional ideology, their actual impact on law and social practice should not be overstated. Poverty and lack of access to adequate legal services conspired with improvised strategies of official evasion and private intimidation to diminish the significance of incipient constitutional protections for those accused of crime, and the Warren Court revolution in criminal procedure doctrine still lay two decades in the future. Widespread disfranchisement of Southern blacks would persist until enactment of the Voting Rights Act of 1965. The Court would soon sustain the administration's disgraceful wartime treatment of Japanese Americans, the Cold War's severe challenge to civil liberties lay just around the corner, and much of American society would continue to be legally segregated by race. Nevertheless, by the time the war effort had begun inexorably to rouse the American economy from its long Depression nightmare, it had become apparent that protection of civil rights, civil liberties, and democratic processes was emerging as a central preoccupation of the nation's highest court.

CONCLUSION

Americans surveying the legal and constitutional landscape from the vantage of World War II could hardly have mistaken the transformation that had occurred. Congress and the federal administrative state now exercised virtually unlimited authority over the nation's economy. Constitutional dual federalism had been supplanted by fiscal cooperative federalism, as the ballooning federal budget bore witness to the national government's commitment to guaranteeing economic security, promoting public works, and placating powerful constituencies. Substantive due process and related doctrines no longer posed a threat to state and federal regulatory programs, yet the federal judiciary increasingly invalidated government restrictions on the exercise of non-economic civil rights and civil liberties. A great deal had happened in a relatively short time.

Yet, despite the seemingly frenetic pace and panoramic quality of these developments during the Great Depression, one must not underestimate the importance of the groundwork laid in preceding decades. The New Deal constitutional order did not emerge overnight. It instead marked the culmination of a long, slow, tortuous, and occasionally painful process. For more than a generation, progressive reformers at the state and federal levels had persistently sought to realize their policy objectives within the structure of contemporary constitutional law and, where that was not possible, to persuade the Court to alter its doctrine. In some instances, social experience or convincing argumentation had prompted justices to reevaluate and revise doctrinal premises that no longer appeared to suffice as persuasive descriptions of social reality. In others, changes in Court personnel had been the principal agent of doctrinal change. Yet while some periods witnessed more significant developments than did others, the dialectic of the American constitutional system ensured that doctrine was always in motion, never fully at rest. Doctrinal formulations were persistently expanded, qualified, elaborated, and reshaped. This process of constitutional evolution regularly revealed channels of new legislative opportunity to creative and sophisticated reformers alert to possibilities latent in the doctrine.

These persistent pressures of statutory innovation and efforts at accommodation, dramatically accelerated by the New Deal but by no means begun there, thus steadily worked to reshape both the legal system on the ground and the constitutional terrain confronting subsequent reformers. By the time Franklin Roosevelt first took the oath of office, the Court had already sanctioned a vast array of state police power statutes, including wage and payment regulations, workers' compensation statutes, regulation of working hours and child labor, blue sky laws, and utility and price regulations. Similarly, the Court had upheld extensive regulation of interstate business practices, approving initiatives ranging from federal antitrust laws and the Federal Trade Commission to the Pure Food and Drugs Act. The Court had sustained extensive federal regulation of the railroad industry as well, upholding a series of acts creating and conferring authority on the Interstate Commerce Commission, as well as the Federal Employer Liability Act, the Safety Appliance Act, and the Railway Labor Act. The *Shreveport* and stream of commerce doctrines further permitted federal regulation of "local" activities having a sufficient nexus with interstate commerce, while the taxpayer standing doctrine offered a recipe for unfettered federal spending and grants-in-aid. For decades preceding Franklin Roosevelt's inauguration, the Court had repeatedly though by no means uniformly acquiesced in the growth and elaboration of a nascent regulatory and welfare state. At the same time, the justices had already begun to render significant decisions protecting the civil rights and civil liberties of ethnic, racial, and religious minorities, political dissenters, and those accused of crime.

By 1933, then, antecedent doctrinal development had already brought American constitutional law to the point at which significant elements of the New Deal order could be envisioned as within the realm of constitutional possibility. Those aspirations for reform would become realized, however, only through the concentrated and innovative legal efforts of New Deal reformers and jurists, who together expanded dramatically the repertoire of the American legal imagination and left a remarkably durable imprint on American law.

9

LABOR'S WELFARE STATE: DEFINING WORKERS,
CONSTRUCTING CITIZENS

EILEEN BORIS

This chapter analyzes the emergence of labor law as a distinct field. It examines the discursive and political struggles that gave birth to state regulation of collective bargaining, the passage of employment standards legislation, and the growth of social provision during the first half of the twentieth century. Definitions of work and worker, embedded in legislation and upheld by courts, proved crucial not only for civil rights on the job but also for citizenship rights in the developing welfare state. These rights, whether to old age insurance and unemployment or to minimum wages and union representation, depended on an individual's social as well as occupational position and, for those programs subject to discretionary implementation in the states, even geographical location. By equating work with wage labor, excluding motherwork and other forms of caregiving, law and social policy privileged the adult man in his prime as the ideal worker. The needs and experiences of the industrial worker, predominantly white men, constituted the norm; the woman, pregnant, immigrant, disabled, older, child, and African American worker was considered a special type, requiring protection when not prohibited from the workforce or relegated to lower paid and intermittent labor.

The standard story told by generations of historians since the 1940s celebrates the New Deal and the labor law regime that nourished and was made possible by the rise of industrial unionism, especially the Congress of Industrial Organizations (CIO). But this veneration of collective bargaining and mass organization of basic industry obscures the larger contours of welfare state development for which constructions of work and worker were fundamental. Constrained by Supreme Court precedents to rely on the Interstate Commerce Clause of the Constitution rather than Thirteenth Amendment protections against involuntary servitude or the police power of the state, New Deal policymakers generated a maze of procedural and substantive rules that curbed the ability of unions to organize and shaped their institutional development. Regulations privileged mass production

over agriculture and service industries, the CIO over the American Federation of Labor (AFL), and blue collars over pink, white, or no collars. The
labor lawyer emerged as a key figure whose expertise navigated arbitration
and interpreted the fruits of collective bargaining.

Here we discuss key New Deal measures – the National Recovery Administration (NRA), the National Labor Relation Board (NLRB), the Fair Labor
Standards Act (FLSA), and Social Security – central to the standard story.
But we also assess expanded state intervention into the employment contract in light of how state action both reflected and reinforced race, gender,
nationality, and other markers of social inequality. To be sure, a wide range
of factors – including the power of business, the practice of states' rights
and traditions of limited government, and ideologies of individualism –
generated the particularly American public-private regime of social provision, so that the state offered a limited safety net to those without family
or other private resources but stopped short of entitlements to health care,
housing, education, fulsome pensions, and social services that in European
welfare states offered protection from the vagaries of the market. The chapter highlights legal and policy definitions that, in designating what work
was and who was a worker, restricted social citizenship.

A full understanding of labor law in U.S. welfare state development
requires a turn back from the New Deal to the Progressive era and forward to World War II and the early postwar years until Title VII of the
Civil Rights Act of 1964 opened another chapter in labor's relation to the
state. This chronology expands the cast of historical actors beyond lawyers,
judges, government officials, and trade unionists to include women reformers, who were predominantly white, and African American activists, who
were usually male. We must also pay attention to workers disadvantaged
by the law, sometimes for being outside of its protections, other times for
being denied the status of worker in the first place because they labored at
home or in the fields or were mothers, servants, disabled, or supervisors.
And we must consider the double meaning of the right to work, a demand
for inclusion by African Americans and then by additional excluded groups,
and an assertion of employer prerogatives by anti-union firms.

Who became covered in law and social policy was a political question:
that the occupations dominated by men and women of color as well as
by white women were omitted from major initiatives furthered inequality
within the welfare state. The New Deal only partially fulfilled its promise
to incorporate economic and social rights into a new welfare constitution
because access to those rights remained limited. This shortcoming was
historically contingent, partially dependent on an obstinate occupational
segregation by race and sex, which union practices did not initiate but could
exacerbate. It further derived from the inability of progressives inside and

out of the Democratic Party to extend the New Deal in the wake of the Cold War and a recalcitrant Dixiecrat hold on Congress. Health, retirement, and other benefits became contingent on one's employer as well as on identity factors, like racialized gender, with larger corporations and manufacturers providing private sector plans that undermined political pressure to enhance Social Security.

This analysis makes three assumptions about law. First, while lawyers and judges search for legal precedents, lawmaking is a historical discipline in that it is also a product of history. Rather than a self-contained system, law is subject to social, ideological, economic, and political forces, including racial, gendered, and class assumptions. It is a product of its time. Second, and simultaneously, law creates categories and identities through which groups and individuals become known and know themselves. Finally, standpoint matters. By pivoting the angle of vision, by considering legal and policy developments from the position of those outside of the dominant models, we gain a more critical interpretation of the past and thus the ability to understand fissures and disruptions as well as continuities. In short, an intersectional analysis in which race, gender, national status, and other social factors appear not as additions but as integral to understanding power, class, and authority permits connection of policy arenas – the workplace, family, and polity – too often seen as separate, thus illuminating the shape of the welfare state developed out of the New Deal.

I. THE STANDARD STORY MODIFIED

The industrial worker stood at both the symbolic and policy center of the welfare state that emerged out of the struggles of working people during the Great Depression. Protected by collective bargaining and employment standards, his labor brought social rights to the family, including pensions, health insurance, and other forms of income maintenance. In this sense, trade unionism served as the Americanizing agent for a generation of European immigrant men, who gained economic citizenship sometimes prior to naturalization. The 1935 Social Security Act solidified this model of the citizen-worker by creating an unequal system that linked the most generous benefits to employment, but excluded agricultural and service occupations dominated by white women and men and women of color. The 1938 labor standards act similarly limited its coverage to smokestack America, whereas collective bargaining, guaranteed by the National Labor Relations or Wagner Act of 1935, required additional measures to bring fair representation to minority workers.

A political response to economic breakdown, the New Deal promised security: the right to a job, housing, education, and other components of a decent standard of living associated with the welfare state. The right to live meant the right to earn, which government perhaps for the first time embraced as its duty by assuring that men could work and work would pay. This right was also an obligation. After addressing a near collapse of the nation's financial, productive, and distributional systems, the Roosevelt administration concentrated on the immediate needs of the unemployed – 15 million were out of work in 1933 – through a variety of work relief programs, such as the Civilian Conservation Corps (CCC), the National Youth Administration (NYA), and the Works Progress Administration (WPA). Participants in these programs received cash for labor, maintaining the link between individual self-worth and the work ethic that Roosevelt feared would be undermined by the dole. As he announced in the first inaugural address: "Our greatest primary task is to put people to work."[1] Work meant independence and stood in opposition to dependency, a condition associated with the helpless and derelict, the young and the old, and the wife and mother.

The disabled found themselves in a quandary. Discriminated against by employers, those able to support themselves too often were relegated to sheltered workshops, usually run by private agencies, where the goal was rehabilitation rather than living wages. The president was a polio survivor unable to walk unsupported, but his administration conflated employable with able bodied. Executive Order 7046 (1935) prohibited work project placement of anyone "whose age or physical condition is such as to make his employment dangerous to his health or safety, or to the health and safety of others," yet it permitted "the employment of physically handicapped persons, otherwise employable, where such persons may be safely assigned to work which they can ably perform."[2] This ambiguity opened WPA jobs to some deaf and otherwise disabled individuals, though not to recipients of Aid to the Blind. Activists still had to fight against segregation into special projects. Considered less than real workers, the disabled would be among the first laid off during cutbacks in work relief.

Only after relieving destitution did the New Deal attempt structural reforms. Realizing the individual's right to work required rebalancing the power between employers and employees, made possible through enhanced state capacity. Rather than eliminating liberty of contract, the doctrine enshrined in post-Reconstruction interpretations of the Fourteenth Amendment, the New Deal transformed its contours. Policymakers would curb

---

[1] Samuel I. Rosenman, ed., *Public Papers and Addresses of Franklin D. Roosevelt,* 2 (New York, 1938), 13.
[2] Executive Order No. 7046 (1935) in *Presidential Executive Orders, Numbers 1-7403* (1854–June 1936) (Microfilm, 11 reels, Trans-Media Publications, 1983), reel 11.

the ability of workers to disrupt the economy by recognizing their right to choose their own bargaining agents; they pushed for national labor standards as a tool to stabilize industry. To increase the purchasing power of workers, as advocated by the British economist John Maynard Keynes, was to stimulate the economy. Guiding New Deal labor policy, and thus welfare state development, was the notion that good citizenship required good wages. But the New Deal also equated economic success with industrial efficiency. Since ending unemployment and raising purchasing power did not necessarily promote business efficiency, policy initiatives would vacillate between divergent political imperatives.

For trade unionists, the New Deal provided an emancipation proclamation – as the United Mine Workers (UMW) President John L. Lewis named the National Industrial Recovery Act (NIRA) of 1933 – of their own. (African American newspapers, in contrast, referred to the National Recovery Administration [NRA], the agency created by the act, as "Negroes Ruined Again"[3] because provisions indirectly excluded them.) While employers gained freedom from antitrust prosecution, the NIRA recognized the right of employees to organize and bargain collectively with employers through representatives of their own choosing. Section 7(a) mandated labor standards – minimum wages and maximum hours – in codes of fair competition to be established and monitored by tripartite boards representing industry, labor, and government. The Supreme Court would overturn the NRA in *Schechter Poultry Co. v. U.S.* (1935) for an inappropriate delegation of power and unconstitutional application of the Interstate Commerce Clause beyond activities directly involved with the "flow" of commerce. By that time, the NRA had approved more than a thousand codes.

The New Deal's initial attempt to raise production, end unemployment, and stabilize industry, the NRA contained two streams: collective bargaining and labor standards. These strands delineated workers' rights in the liberal welfare state. Its definitions of work and worker carried over into subsequent, more permanent manifestations of these streams, the NLRB and the FLSA. Employment standards derived from earlier campaigns to protect women industrial workers through floors on their wages and ceilings on their hours. The right to organize and bargain encouraged democracy for those already employed, a status controlled by employers in unorganized workplaces. But when unions moved from voluntary organizations to public institutions, racial exclusivity, tolerated in private clubs, became a discriminatory practice. Differentiation by gender, in contrast, remained acceptable, based on what still appeared as natural distinctions. Women of

[3] John P. Davis, "Blue Eagles and Black Workers," *The New Republic* 81 (November 14, 1934), 9

color experienced a double discrimination of their own. Access to collective
bargaining became crucial not only for private pension and health insurance but also for recognition as a worker and thus for full citizenship in the
welfare state.

Collective Bargaining

Before Title 7(a), unions were ensnarled in a legal contradiction: liable for
their actions under injunctions issued by courts on behalf of employers but
without legal personality. In *Loewe v. Lawlor* (1908), the Danbury Hatter's
Case that outlawed the secondary boycott, the Supreme Court held strikers accountable under the 1890 Sherman Antitrust Act for conspiracy in
restraint of trade, implicitly recognizing the collective nature of a union. But
courts would not enforce trade agreements with employers because unions
were voluntary associations, not persons under the law. Only individuals
could contract, a proposition that led the Supreme Court to uphold "yellow
dog" contracts that forbid an employee from joining a union in *Adair v. U.S.*
(1908) and *Coppage v. Kansas* (1915). To maintain a collective agreement,
each individual would have to assent, and then only those eligible could
sue in the breach. Unions lacked the authority to bind their members to an
agreement; thus employers could not hold the union responsible for member actions, which made trade agreements unenforceable under the law of
contracts.

United Mine Workers of America v. Coronado Coal Company (1922) threatened
the viability of trade unions by allowing companies the right to sue unions
for damages, but in this case the Supreme Court laid the legal foundation for
the doctrine of "responsible unionism." Progressive reformers long sought
to inscribe unions with agency, that is, the ability to enter into contracts,
so to enforce trade agreements. This was a procedural guarantee rather than
a substantive one, expanding rather than challenging the private ordering
of employment by incorporating unions into the process. Into the 1930s,
the Supreme Court continued to reject statutory protections offering labor
"special privileges" as class legislation that by definition vitiated the equal
rights of employers, as enunciated in *Truax v. Corrigan* (1921). No equivalent
understanding of class legislation that violated worker rights existed.

After World War I, "responsible unionism" guided the reconstruction
of labor relations, beginning with the railroads, which had provided the
template for Wilsonian corporatism. That solutions to the labor question
on the railroads generated the dominant paradigm for industrial relations
was not surprising, given their crucial role in national economic exchange.
The workforce was predominantly male, subjected to occupational segregation by race and embroiled in racial conflict over job classifications; this

would have a complex influence on both the expansion of social provision and the struggle against employment discrimination. The National War Labor Board supported collective bargaining and the right to union membership. It extended to other war industries the 1916 Adamson Act, which guaranteed labor standards on the rails. The Railroad Administration imposed labor standards more successfully. It bypassed recalcitrant employers by entering into national railroad labor agreements, thus facilitating an unprecedented unionization, especially in the shop crafts and among the less skilled.

After the war, newly ascendant Republicans upheld state oversight of the railroads through quasi-judicial agencies, with the goal of safeguarding the public. The 1920 Railroad Labor Board encouraged collective bargaining through worker representatives, but interpreted representation to include company unions, thus allowing the open shop to flourish. By maintaining the private contours of industrial relations and emphasizing the rights of individual workers rather than organized labor, state supervision favored employers, who retained the freedom to dismiss unionizing employees or refuse to accept their demands. Shopmen came to this knowledge the hard way during their 1922 strike, a response to decisions by the Railroad Labor Board that abrogated national agreements and decreased wages. The Harding administration resorted to settlement by injunction, weakening the union and setting in motion a political resolution in the form of a new board with greater powers of mediation. The 1926 Railroad Labor Act, upheld two years later by the Supreme Court, established workers' right to representation and imposed on both employers and workers the duty to negotiate trade agreements. Disputes over such agreements were subject to arbitration under presidential compulsion. "Responsible unionism" translated into collective bargaining without strikes. In essence, the state propped up the private system of contract.

With the Depression, Congress instituted greater stability on the rails with major amendments to the Railroad Labor Act in 1934. These amendments created a National Mediation Board with compulsory powers to certify union representation and a National Railroad Adjustment Board under joint union-management control with the charge to interpret conflicts over contracts. But in insisting on majority representation, the amendments inadvertently ratified the unholy alliance of carriers and the white Railroad Brotherhoods that pushed black operatives out of the industry. Through secret agreements as well as negotiated contracts, the Brotherhoods – which under majority rule represented African Americans despite denying them union membership – negated black seniority. The outlawing of company unions undermined whatever leverage independent black unions, whose grievances the white-controlled boards rejected, had found in employer paternalism. In this context, government directives, as for dieselization, further decimated the black workforce because the Brotherhoods grabbed control of new jobs. Railroad labor law, upheld by the Supreme Court, turned the black railworker into "an industrial fugitive," charged Willard Townsend of the CIO's Red Caps Union.[4]

The Railroad Act's emphasis on conduct also shaped the 1932 Norris-LaGuardia Anti-Injunction Act. This law outlawed the notorious yellow dog contract by ending prohibitions on third parties, such as unions, that ignored such agreements. For the previous quarter-century, the AFL had sought legislative remedies to the injunction that would immunize it from antitrust prosecution. But the Supreme Court had rejected this line of reasoning, refusing to accept the 1914 Clayton Antitrust Act's exemption of unions from restraint of trade and other prohibited practices. Thus Norris-LaGuardia framed its curbing of injunctions in labor disputes around expanding freedom of contract for unorganized workers, who could call on a union to bargain for them. It also limited accountability for unauthorized actions taken by members, placing unions more squarely within agency law. Protections given to railwaymen extended to other industrial workers.

The NRA guaranteed more fully the right to join a union, even though large employers and trade associations dominated the codes regulating their industries. Codes advanced the interests of larger firms over smaller, more marginal ones. They contained blatant wage discriminations based on factors outside of the work process itself. Northern textile mills paid higher wages than Southern ones; "learners" (new hires) and industrial homeworkers earned less than others for the same task; and gaps between men and women, black or Mexican and white remained, only partially explained by skill differentials.

Despite controlling code authorities, employers failed to reckon with the powerful utopian promise of Section 7(a). The story circulating among miners that President Roosevelt wanted them to join the UMW was probably apocryphal, given his lukewarm support of unionization. But in California's San Joaquin Valley, the site of bloody confrontations between growers and cotton pickers, Mexican women and men affirmed faith in the NRA through placards on the picket line. So did Pennsylvania farm workers, Massachusetts cranberry harvesters, and Florida citrus pickers – all unaware of the exclusion of agriculture under the Presidential Re-employment Agreement. Demanding minimum wages mandated by the NRA, an organizer from the Cannery and Agricultural Workers Union expressed the feelings of entitlement that were engendered even among the uncovered: "we're behind the president

---

[4] Willard S. Townsend, "One American Problem and a Possible Solution," in Rayford Logan, ed., *What the Negro Wants* (Chapel Hill, NC, 1944), 1801.

when he says that concerns unable to pay a living wage to their employees should go out of business."[5]

Under the sign of the Blue Eagle, the emblematic indicator of business compliance with the codes, labor-management cooperation proved elusive. The NRA emboldened worker organizing. After its passage in 1933, the AFL granted 340 new charters; the next year that number expanded to more than 1,000. In July 1933 alone, 125,000 workers engaged in more than 200 strikes. Massive picketing erupted among Toledo autoworkers, Minneapolis truckers, and West Coast longshoremen and seamen in 1934 as numerous groups of white men sought to enforce 7(a) rights through direct action. The UMW and International Ladies Garment Workers Union (ILGWU) recovered membership lost to Depression layoffs, whereas the Amalgamated Clothing Workers of America (ACWA) tripled its size. Collective bargaining flourished in highly competitive sectors, such as garment making, that combined immigrant and female workforces with male union leadership. By 1935, nearly a hundred agricultural locals had formed. But organizing drives hit mass production industries with mixed results: auto companies resisted weak unions, which failed to gain exclusive bargaining rights during the code-making process.

For bituminous coal miners, the NRA code followed collective agreements, retaining regional and other preexisting differentials for an industry in which employers insisted on local over national standards. It was unable to rationalize the wage structure or stabilize the industry, but neither could subsequent Congressional measures. The 1937 Guffey-Vinson Coal Conservation Act passed constitutional muster by removing previously imposed labor provisions that the Supreme Court rejected as beyond the regulation of interstate commerce in *Carter v. Carter Coal Co.* (1936). According to the Court, the relation between the parties was local. The labor relations of firms engaged in production, it argued, at best produced an indirect impact that lay outside of Congressional jurisdiction. The Commerce Clause did not extend to manufacturing. While the miners won increased benefits during the next decade, only improvements in efficiency halted the decline of this once dominant industry.

Captive to cutthroat competition, Southern textile employers welcomed the NRA as an opportunity to level the playing field. Coming from states governed by white elites that disenfranchised white as well as black working people, employers had greater access in Washington, DC, and their trade association, the Cotton Textile Institute, dominated the subsequent code authority. However, textile magnates negated their own agreed-on

---

[5] Quoted in Devra Weber, *Dark Sweat, White Gold: California Farm Workers, Cotton, and the New Deal* (Berkeley, 1994), 82.

provisions by running mills full blast and then adding machinery, increasing workloads, and cutting jobs, a common response to NRA mandates. Wages remained stagnant except for unskilled women, whose compensation grew by 25 percent. Complaints by workers, sent to the code authority, circulated back to employers, generating reprisal against the complainants. Bureaucratic delay further stymied implementation, with only 96 of more than 1,700 charges of wage and hour violations investigated. Meanwhile, the code authority manipulated statistics to paint a glowing portrait of employer compliance.

Textile workers – mostly white, U.S.-born men, women, and children – especially embraced the NRA promise, but were sadly disappointed. Throughout the twenties, laborers had contested with episodic success the stretch-out, or increase in customary workloads gained through either new technology or additional spindles per worker. They viewed the economic crisis in terms of unemployment, pushing with other AFL unions for a shorter workweek to generate more jobs. The textile labor mediation board facilitated the growth of a wider union movement by forcing workers to create state councils to use its mechanisms. The national leadership of the Textile Workers Union (TWU) lobbied for a seat on the code authority. It gained only a position on the ineffectual mediation board, with the charge to police its own members. Meanwhile, a militant Southern rank and file launched the 1934 General Strike not against the government, as opponents later portrayed their walkout, but as an attempt to put the New Deal into practice. By early September, half of the workforce went out. Flying squadrons, including women, shut down plants, whereas private guards and state militia kept non-union strongholds open. Georgia's governor declared martial law.

To cope with this unrest, Roosevelt enhanced the NRA by creating the National Labor Board (NLB) to investigate and settle disputes. (The textile industry, however, kept its own, more pro-business board formed before the NLB went into effect.) This short-lived agency had greater impact than its lack of recognizable enforcement powers foretold: though reliant on the voluntary cooperation of labor and business, it enunciated principles of labor relations, a "common law," that would guide the future NLRB. These principles included defending workers from employer coercion, which essentially outlawed company unions; safeguarding secret balloting for employee representation elections; and demanding employer recognition of the workers' chosen representative. By early 1934, the board no longer attempted merely to mediate the question of representation, but it supported majority representation, or the presence of an exclusive worker agent in collective bargaining. This involvement profoundly shaped collective bargaining because a quasi-judicial board would determine the contours of the bargaining unit, specifying voter eligibility among a myriad of other "rules of law." But employers either refused to hold representation elections or manipulated the slates. Roosevelt's establishment of separate boards for the automobile and steel industries undermined compliance. The creation in June 1934 of a new, but equally weak, National Labor Relations Board with three public members faced similar employer intransigence.

The textile strike of 1934 exposed the gap between the people's New Deal and the judicial apparatus forged by the NRA. A presidential task force brokered an agreement with the battered TWU, but this resolution – a new textile board, non-discriminatory rehiring, and an investigation into the stretch-out – evaporated when mill owners retaliated against strikers in the months that followed. Employers ignored the new, more impartial, board out of the belief that it lacked legal authority. An agreed-on inquiry into the stretch-out actually legitimized the practice, whereas the code authority continued to mask company violations of labor standards. Textile workers had depended on a government that did not and could not speak for them; they would remain skeptical when the new CIO Textile Workers Organizing Committee asked them in 1936 to put their faith in the Wagner Act, proclaimed as "Labor's Magna Charta."

In finally establishing an independent agency with the ability to enforce its decisions, Congress decisively altered the relationship of trade unions to the state. The Wagner Act sought to enhance worker freedoms, increase their purchasing power, and end industrial unrest. However, the framework required to pass constitutional muster hampered its radical potential even before conflicts between employers and unions and between the AFL and CIO limited its substance. A language of contracts and interstate commerce, forged by lawyers from the old NLRB and Wagner's staff, replaced an earlier rationale – "to ensure a wise distribution of wealth between management and labor."[6] To encourage "the free flow of commerce," the preamble to the National Labor Relations Act declared, public interest required mitigating "inequality of bargaining power between employees who do not possess full freedom of association or actual liberty of contract" and their employers. Supportive briefs emphasized Congress's power to suppress strikes rather than labor's right to strike or freedom from employer coercion. Rather than establishing a jurisprudence of economic justice, New Deal lawyers expanded the state's power to regulate economic freedom.

Lawyers constructed the new NLRB on the basis of their own professional understandings. Hearings took the form of trials reliant on legal discourse and rules of evidence. The Board's legal division developed a

---

[6] National Labor Relations Board, *Legislative History of the National Labor Relations Act, 1935*, 2 vols. (Washington, DC, 1949), 15.

bureaucracy and procedures for handling cases. The NLRB, not workers and managers, would determine an unfair practice. It would constitute the shape of bargaining units, which would define who had rights and who did not, and manage the representation election, certifying results. From 1935 through 1939, through 2,500 elections and more than 25,000 cases, these expert – theoretically non-partisan – administrators regulated the terms and conditions of collective bargaining. Findings of fact took precedence over preexisting union jurisdictions, so that no union had an a priori right to certification. The old AFL craft unions, whose cooperation with employers appeared out of step with the law, lost control of the process. Early decisions favored the CIO, whose dynamic growth coincided with – even as it was facilitated by – the NLRB. Radicals, Communists, and industrial union partisans initially staffed the Board, belying the neutral patina of expertise that pro-business appointments later would rely on to justify their decisions. By the late 1930s, in response to both Congressional investigation and internal power struggles, the NLRB began to emphasize institutional stability, rather than impose new jurisdictional structures. It crafted an administrative law of its own.

The Supreme Court sustained the Wagner Act in *National Labor Relations Board v. Jones & Laughlin Steel Corp.* (1937) by expanding its definition of interstate commerce to include manufacturing and other forms of production. But for eighteen months prior to that decision, employers defied the NRLB as just another interference with their freedom of contract. CIO victories at General Motors and United States Steel in 1937 derived not from the law but from the power of mass mobilization. State and local officials responded to popular pressure when allowing sit-down strikers to occupy private property. As one organizer quipped following *Jones & Laughlin,* "the Supreme Court has simply ratified a right which American workers have long possessed theoretically, but which it took the CIO to establish in actuality."[7] Thus, labor law was made not only through administrative and legal precedents but also through the self-activity of industrial workers, abetted by wives and daughters who ran soup kitchens, diverted police attention, and protested for greater purchasing power.

Roosevelt's overwhelming victory in 1936 provided the larger context in which the employment relation gained a modicum of stability in law and social policy. The Supreme Court named collective bargaining "a fundamental right,"[8] though it limited worker militancy over the next decade. In *NLRB v. Mackay Radio and Telegraph Company* (1938), the Court affirmed the employer's right to bring in replacement workers except during a strike

[7] Len De Caux, "A Right That Had To Be Won," *Union News Service* (April 17, 1937), 1.
[8] *NLRB v. Jones & Laughlin,* 301 US 1, 33 (1937).

involving unfair practices. Still, strikers remained employees, and employers could not refuse to rehire on the basis of strike participation. More significant at the time, in *NLRB v. Fansteel Metallurgical Company* (1939) the Court defanged the sit-down tactic by permitting the firing of such strikers, whom it condemned as engaging in violent, illegal takeovers of private property.

This new labor contractualism most benefited those in covered workplaces poised to take advantage of the law. For wives, daughters, and sisters whose community activities and union support work contributed to labor's mid-decade upsurge, but whose own labor force participation often proved intermittent, the codification of collective bargaining brought gains on the basis of familial or household relationships. Women in mass production industries, as well as larger numbers in the garment trades, certainly won for themselves greater economic security, but they were a minority. NLRB procedural advances did even less to upset existing racial hierarchies. Like the NRA, the NLRB excluded agricultural and domestic labor. Also outside the law were public and non-profit employees; that is, the majority of educational, health, and protective service workers, like fire and policemen. Such lacunae eliminated about two-thirds of all African Americans, most Mexican Americans, and vast numbers of white women who labored in offices, schools, and homes. White workers, especially organized skilled men, retained an income advantage over everyone else, an inequality that collective bargaining as established by the NLRB could not dislodge.

Labor Standards

Wage and hour standards constructed the meaning of work under the welfare state as surely as did the procedural guarantees of the Wagner Act. These regulations were to protect those without collective bargaining against the vagaries of the market. Before the NRA, protective laws existed on the state level and applied mostly to women or children, groups considered incapable of freely contracting their labor and thus proper subjects for the police power of the state. Women predominated in industries, like garments and laundry, characterized by low wages, long hours, homework, and poor working conditions, including seasonality, improper ventilation and health hazards, sexual harassment, and arbitrary fining and treatment. Organizing these industries with their abundant labor supply proved difficult despite the tenacious militancy of women in New York and Chicago during the 1910s that gave birth to the ILGWU and the ACWA.

The cross-class Women's Trade Union League fought against poor circumstances under slogans – "The Eight Hour Day," "A Living Wage," and

"To Guard the Home"[9] – that expressed no contradiction between women's rights and domesticity. Led by the National Consumers' League (NCL), under the indomitable foe of the sweatshop Florence Kelley, women from more prosperous classes spearheaded the political and legal drive for labor standards with the aid of future Supreme Court justices Louis Brandeis and Felix Frankfurter. Though they deployed the language of protection, of suffering motherhood and victimized childhood, maternalist is too narrow a label for women reformers who emphasized industrial equality. They would reward women's work for its skill, rather than basing wages on familial position, and thus improve the larger social welfare. They promoted measures like a 1912 hazardous occupations referendum in Ohio, which protected men as well as women, but always had one eye on constitutionality. With the minimum wage challenged in the courts, lawyers gained control of strategy, and they did not necessarily share the feminist goals of reformers.

In *Lochner v. New York* (1905), the Supreme Court struck down a maximum hour law for male workers as a violation of substantive due process under the Fourteenth Amendment. But it upheld such a ceiling for women in *Muller v. Oregon* (1908), on the basis of social responsibility for women's potential or actual motherhood. Such conditions as poor health from standing for long hours, which reformers documented to justify state intervention, were translated by the justices as indicators of fundamental gender difference. Over the next decades, laws for the woman worker generated the template for standards for all workers, shifting the discourse from the regulation of dangerous work to the protection of needy workers. Conceptions of gender, particularly notions of women's biological and social disadvantages, fueled both discussions about and the development of sociological jurisprudence, the documentation of social conditions to argue for legal changes. This emphasis on the state's responsibility to counter economic oppression derived from women's dual position at home and in the marketplace. The Great Depression would provide a contextual argument for those searching to end exploitation of male workers as well.

Between 1908 and World War I, seventeen states stipulated the circumstances under which women and children could labor. Laws prohibited child labor and restricted the jobs for which youths could obtain work permits. They prohibited employment in some occupations, like foundries, deemed dangerous for childbearing and/or actual pregnancy and set minimum wages and maximum hours to alleviate "sweating." Such measures, some hoped, might save young women from lives of prostitution, even though wages

---

[9] "Emblem of the National Women's Trade Union League," 1903. Margaret Dreier Robins Papers, Rare Books and Manuscript Library, University of Florida.

were too low for self-support. Night work bans also promised to protect morals along with health. But they barred women from lucrative jobs in trades like printing and bartending dominated by men, whereas entertainments dependent on the allure of female bodies remained outside the law. Such "protective" labor laws left out part-time and home labor; employers reorganized work to take advantage of such lacunae.

Although wage and hour regulation improved conditions in female-dominated manufacturing, they encouraged the concentration of women in jobs unwanted by men. Beset by lower wages, many young women saw marriage as an escape from bad jobs. But men could not always support families, leading mothers to return to a sex- and race-segmented labor market where women earned fewer rewards and women of color who were concentrated in agricultural and personal service occupations had no legal recourse against poor conditions and low pay.

In *Adkins v. Children's Hospital* (1923), the Supreme Court pulled the plug from minimum wage boards that calculated wages on the basis of women's needs rather than on the rate for the job. Drawing on a brief submitted by the National Women's Party (NWP), Justice Sutherland determined that "revolutionary . . . changes . . . in the contractual, political and civil status of women, culminating in the nineteenth amendment" superseded the reasoning of *Muller*.[10] However, equality concerns would not trump cultural anxiety over women's welfare when women threatened men's work. The same court upheld restrictions on night work in *Radice v. New York* (1924). The Women's Bureau, in contrast, championed women's labor legislation against the similar-treatment paradigm of the NWP. Still, from its origins as a wartime agency, it advocated equal pay for equal work. By 1925, it viewed a woman's wage as both an individual expression of worth and reflective of familial responsibilities.

Adkins ruled that wage setting, unlike hour ceilings, went to the heart of the labor contract, violating substantive due process. Kelley proposed a constitutional amendment to permit federal and state wage statutes, but Frankfurter offered another direction. He suggested manipulating Justice Sutherland's defense of the fair wage, one related to "the value of the service rendered" rather than the standard of living. To reinterpret due process, NCL advisors recast the minimum wage: the financial health of industry, rather than the physical health of women, would determine a fair wage.

This linguistic shift from minimum to fair wage generated both unease among reformers and proved ineffectual in the courts. New York NCL leader Molly Dewson feared that any fair wage law would reach only women earning below a subsistence level, neglecting others who lacked just recompense.

---

[10] 261 U.S. 525, 553 (1923).

Industrial relations pioneer John R. Commons predicted that the fair wage
would circumscribe collective bargaining by emphasizing individual performance over union representation, indirectly weakening male craft unions.
Following his lead, Wisconsin amended its women's minimum wage to
prohibit an oppressive rather than mandate a fair wage. Its commission
retained rates based on the cost of living rather than deploy the impossibly
vague standard of fairness.

New York's 1933 minimum wage included all proposed standards –
living, fair, and oppressive wages, as well as protection of health. This
cacophony of wrongs and remedies gave courts multiple points to object.
In *Morehead v. New York ex rel Tipaldo* (1936), the Supreme Court relied on
Adkins to dismiss the New York law, adhering to the right to contract and
equating the fair wage with the minimum one. But within two years, perhaps in reaction to Roosevelt's reelection and Court-packing threat against
its institutional power, the Court upheld Washington State's nearly identical 1913 minimum wage law and overturned *Adkins*. Its decision, *West
Coast Hotel v. Parrish* (1937), sustained the legislature's discretionary use
of the police power. It affirmed the state's right to enact measures to mitigate women's disadvantages in the labor market on the basis "that they
are in the class receiving the least pay, that their bargaining power is relatively weak, and that they are the ready victims of those who would take
advantage of their necessitous circumstances." Arguing that the community
need not "provide what is in effect a subsidy for unconscionable employers,"
Chief Justice Hughes promoted the general welfare over contractual rights,
especially in cases where the relation between the parties was unequal.[11]
Such reasoning maintained women as a different kind of worker, disadvantaged when it came to collective bargaining and requiring state protection.
Nonetheless, this move toward a structural analysis of the position of workers further opened the way for labor standards to include men by way of the
Commerce Clause. The Court concluded that, although Washington State
protected only women, extension of its laws to men would be a valid legislative act. In asserting that the relationship between employer and employee
was public, not private, *West Coast Hotel* blurred the boundaries between
state and market.

In federalizing previous wage and hour laws, FLSA represented a gender-
neutral culmination of a fifty-year struggle against sweated labor, an attempt
to provide "the minimum standard of living necessary for health, efficiency,
and general well-being of workers."[12] It set minimum wages, required
time–and-a-half overtime after the forty-hour week, and restricted child

---

[11] 300 US 379, 398 (1937).
[12] *Fair Labor Standards Act, Statutes at Large*, 52, sec. 2 (a), 1060.

labor. Prior federal attempts to regulate child labor had failed to pass constitutional muster: In *Hammer v. Dagenhart* (1918) and *Bailey v. Drexel Furniture Company* (1922), the Supreme had Court declared Congress in violation of the Commerce and Due Process Clauses. Blocked from a constitutional amendment, reformers incorporated child labor into FLSA. Three years after the demise of the NRA, private enterprises finally came under federal labor standards, joining holders of government contracts subject to the 1936 Walsh-Healey Public Contracts Act.

Industrial boards, remnants from the initial bill, set wages and hours, industry by industry. FLSA also created the Wage and Hour Division in the Department of Labor under a single administrator who held compliance powers. Beginning wage rates of 25 cents were to rise within seven years to 40 cents an hour, but industry boards quickened this process. Like the Wagner Act, FLSA claimed to free the flow of goods from the burdens of labor disputes, unfair competition, and unfair labor conditions. In sustaining the FLSA, *United States v. Darby* (1941) firmly established the principle of state regulation of the labor market.

Loopholes reflected political and cultural power relations. Southerners gained low thresholds for minimum wages, as well as exclusions of occupations in which African Americans predominated. The "Shirley Temple Clause" exempted child actors, and farm parents could employ their own children during loosely defined school recess. Nothing kept industries, like pecan shelling in Texas, from mechanizing rather than raising the wages of Mexican migrants. Administrative boards determined standards for homeworkers, prohibiting the practice only for seven garment-related industries; otherwise, homework fell under general wage and hour regulations.

Legal definitions also shaped coverage. Unsure whether *Jones & Laughlin* completely overturned *Schechter*, Ben Cohen – Frankfurter protégée and the law's main drafter – included manufacturing but not distribution processes (like retailing) that occurred after items traveled through interstate commerce. Sales clerks, laundry operatives, beauticians, government employees (including teachers), non-profit workers, and a host of other women's labors belonged to intrastate commerce and thus remained uncovered. Except for those working in agriculture (22.8 percent of the workforce in 1940), most uncovered men received more than the minimum wage. Women, especially African American, were at least twice as likely to be exempt from FLSA. A law originating in women's quest for economic justice actually reinforced gender inequality because much of women's work, other than garments and textiles, stood apart from its mandate. Initially fewer than two million workers benefited.

For some Congressional supporters, FLSA promised to restore the family wage. It would allow men who earned less to come closer to the standards already won by skilled workers, who made above its initial minimum. However, men of color found their jobs uncovered by the law. In this respect, labor standards legislation, even though the AFL offered lukewarm support, helped reinforce a hegemonic white working-class masculinity that associated manhood with the solidaristic power of free men. Despite clinging to the notion that real men engage in collective bargaining, with the Depression, the AFL moved away from its philosophy of voluntarism to support extending wage and hour standards to men when necessary to maintain their status as providers. But AFL leaders retained the association of collective bargaining with freedom, and wage boards with indentured servitude. They reluctantly accepted legislated floors on wages not because they thought that the resulting wage would enable a man to support his family. Rather they sought to hamper low-wage competition – the reasoning behind organized labor's backing of equal pay as well. When Congress finally passed an equal pay act in 1963, it placed it under FLSA, subjecting equal pay to the same coverage restrictions as wages and hours.

Social Security

More than any other welfare state measure, the Social Security Act (SSA) embodied racialized gendered understandings of work and dependency. With Wisconsin economist Edwin Witte as chair, the President's Committee on Economic Security (CES) formulated the act to protect industrial workers from unemployment. For such workers, it was assumed, unemployment derived from economic dislocation, rather than from individual flaws. They were eligible to participate in contributory social insurance – old age insurance (commonly called social security) and unemployment insurance. These programs contrasted with the less generous and punitive requirements of relief, including forced work or acceptance of any job, whether or not related to a recipient's training or below customary pay scales. By basing security on the employment relation, CES relegated those with irregular work histories, part-time hours, or jobs in marginal sectors of the economy to means-tested social assistance – old age assistance and Aid to Dependent Children (ADC). It subjected non-workers to personal scrutiny, disparaging them as less deserving than those who qualified for benefits through paycheck deductions, touted as individual contributions, or taxes on employer payrolls. Evoking the general welfare as ample justification, the Supreme Court upheld unemployment insurance in *Steward v. Davis* (1937) and old age assistance in *Helvering v. Davis* (1937). Freedom from want had replaced freedom to contract as the Court shunted aside old doctrines to bolster the citizenship rights of former and current industrial workers.

Social Security emerged in response to more radical calls for a social wage. CES crafted old age pensions to deflect the popular Townsend Movement, which demanded a generous monthly pension of $200 for all over 60 who were non-employed and without criminal records, provided that they spend the money within thirty days. This plan included women equally with men; it recognized the labors of housewives and mothers as work. But it would have ended all other federal relief to the destitute or unemployed and would have relied on a regressive sales tax for financing, features that may have harmed the vast majority of the poor.

A more potent legislative challenge came from the Workers' or Lundeen Bill introduced in 1934 and 1935 by Minnesota's Farmer-Laborite Congressman Ernest Lundeen. This act for unemployment, old age, and social insurance originated with the Communist-dominated Unemployed Councils in the early 1930s. Russell Sage social investigator Mary Van Kleeck drafted its various versions. As she explained in 1935, "The needs created by involuntary mass unemployment are also 'mass needs' reflected in lowered standards of living both for the individual and the community."[13] The Lundeen Bill offered an alternative to Social Security's individual categories of need, each with its own operating mechanism.

A comprehensive stand against discrimination – on the basis of race, sex, age, or political belief and including farm, domestic, and professional as well as industrial labor – earned the Lundeen Bill wide support among all types of progressives, including T. Arnold Hill of the Urban League. However, the bill excluded immigrant non-citizens from its "universal" provisions. Early drafts granted unemployment assistance to those who refused work under unfair labor practices (such as striker replacement), beneath union standards, or at unreasonable distances from home. Other provisions included maternity disability payments for fourteen weeks that further recognized women as workers and childbearing as labor; benefits equal to the average of local wages that privileged the standard of living of workers over employment stability; financing from current taxation rather than payrolls and paychecks; and administration by worker councils to encourage democratic control by those affected.

In contrast, Social Security had a quasi-independent administrative board run by appointed experts. Despite this centralized administration, its various programs were hardly uniform in their rules or structures. The states

---

[13] Mary Van Kleeck, "An Outline of Principles," *Unemployment Insurance Review* 4 (1935), quoted in Kenneth M. Casebeer, "Unemployment Insurance: American Social Wage, Labor Organization and Legal Ideology," *Boston College Law Review*, 35 (March 1994), 300–01.

had greater control over old age assistance (OAA) and ADC, programs that served women; they could establish level of benefits and eligibility without attention to "reasonable subsistence compatible with decency and health,"[14] the criteria that Congress removed during enactment. The percentage of federal financing also varied, with states receiving fewer monies for ADC than for unemployment insurance. Old age insurance (OAI) alone had national standards and existed as a right of all qualified wage earners and, after 1939, their survivors. But it excluded those employed by charitable and religious organizations as well as professional, domestic, and agricultural labor.

Technically, OAI was not insurance because it relied on a "pay-as-you-go formula." Over the next decades, this formula necessitated expansion to new groups of workers – including non-profit, employed professional, and regularly employed farm and domestic workers in the1950s – turning Social Security into the most universal component of America's truncated welfare state. But by basing benefits on earnings, old age insurance rewarded those with higher wages. On the eve of its first disbursements, about a fourth of those covered had earned too little to receive any. A decade after enactment, only half of all contributors qualified to collect benefits; others had not stayed in covered occupations long enough, such as nearly half of 2.8 million agricultural laborers who additionally had worked in a qualifying job at some point during the year. Those with the least stable employment, disproportionately people of color, in essence subsidized the rest. As NAACP lawyer Charles Hamilton Houston predicted in 1935, Social Security acted "like a sieve with holes just big enough for the majority of Negroes to fall through."[15]

Unemployment insurance sought to regulate the economy and maintain a skilled workforce, but it also left implementation to the states. Based on state unemployment reserve funds, it reduced the payroll tax on large firms that maintained employment levels. By including only businesses with at least eight employees, however, it excluded the most vulnerable workers: 98 percent of farm workers, 90 percent of household workers, and 46 percent of trade and wholesale employees. Like the other provisions of the Social Security Act, occupational exemptions removed about half of black laborers but only a third of white ones. Unemployment insurance became a program to sustain virile white manhood during a temporary crisis; those who lost jobs earned benefits as a right of prior employment.

[14] House Ways and Means Committee, *Hearings on the Economic Security Act*, H.R. 4120, 74th Cong., 1st Sess., February 6, 1935, 975.
[15] U.S. Congress, Senate, *Economic Security Act*, 74th Cong., 1st Sess., 1935, 641.

By the 1940s, what began as a protection from unemployment would turn into an income-replacement strategy for the most favored workers.

Those qualifying had to pass a threshold of earnings and hours. That they had to search actively for new work separated recipients from the disabled and ill. Unemployment had to result from employer actions, not laziness or quitting without "good cause." The vagueness of these criteria allowed arbitrary personalism or race and sex discrimination to creep into eligibility evaluations. By 1950, workers were required to take any suitable work even if incommensurate with their training or pay level. Thus, administrators would reject benefits for those who refused jobs with hours incompatible with family schedules.

Among part-time, seasonal, and casual laborers targeted for exclusion were, according to economist Congressmen Paul H. Douglas, "those who have more than one leg in the home."[16] CES rejected the inclusion of housewives as well as women temporarily out of work due to maternity. Pregnant workers, women without child care, and those quitting jobs to move with their husband or fulfill other marital obligations by definition became unavailable for labor, rather than unemployed. Women with employment profiles like men's might gain unemployment, but their generally lower wages meant fewer benefits. States inadvertently exacerbated this gap by increasing maximum but not minimum benefits. Such were the gendered consequences of gender-neutral policy.

The 1939 amendments to the Social Security Act responded to the problem of female dependency. The housewife gained her own Social Security, equal to half her husband's. She could draw from her own "contribution" if a larger benefit would result. During a time when a majority of wives lacked sustained labor force participation, this amendment both subsidized female domesticity and provided some women with real material gains. Assuming that women would follow older husbands into retirement, the 1956 amendments lowered the pension eligibility age for women to 62, but also reduced the amount received. This change increased the overall income of couples, but did little for single women who often could not afford early retirement. In essence, old age insurance privileged marriage. Divorce could strip a non-wage-earning woman of Social Security earned during her earlier marriage until a 1979 amendment restored a percentage of spousal benefits to those whose marriages had lasted at least ten years.

The 1939 amendments also required that state-administrated OAA go only to indigent elderly who failed to qualify for OAI, which was for

---

[16] Paul H. Douglas, *Standards of Unemployment Insurance* (Chicago, 1933), 50.

"retired" workers. Although there was no right to social assistance, all states but Virginia offered OAA by 1938. Discriminatory administration, however, plagued Southern and Southwestern states, where African, Asian, Mexican, and Native Americans were kept off the rolls or received less. Nonetheless, during the late 1930s, OAA's relatively generous administration became a political problem for OAI, which was accumulating a surplus from taxes on employers and employees began in 1937. However, OAI was not scheduled to pay benefits – which would be on the average less than those under OAA – until 1942. By advancing payment to 1940, the 1939 amendments furthered political support of OAI.

Under the concept of "equity for covered men," the amendments also directed survivors insurance to children of deceased fathers. Widows with children under eighteen received three-fourths of the pension coming to their late husbands, unless they remarried or entered the workforce. The amendments thus removed the widowed, deserving because her deceased husband could have qualified for social insurance, from the divorced or never married, considered undeserving because no man mediated her relation to the state. The divorced and never married were left to the more arbitrary and state-run ADC program, thereby differentiating citizenship rights among women on the basis of marriage and wealth.

The ADC program represented a semi-takeover of previously state-run mothers' pensions. Enacted during the teens and twenties, mothers' pensions reached 1,600 counties in forty-five states before the Depression undermined the ability of local governments to provide aid. States were required to offer the Aid to Dependent Children program in all jurisdictions as a condition for receiving federal funds. But lack of federal oversight meant that the states actually controlled eligibility; they could impose residency and citizenship requirements, limit eligibility by marital status, and force employment outside the home. Children and their caregivers would not receive the same assistance throughout the nation.

During the 1930s, when government sought to remove those judged less efficient from the labor force to lessen unemployment, the U.S. Children's Bureau preferred to see the mother remain at home. It considered motherhood an occupation deserving recompense. Dependency among adult men who received relief was demoralizing, but children by definition were dependents. Despite valuing the work of mothering, the Bureau was willing to ignore Social Security's separation of mothers from other workers and classification as unemployable when needed to pass legislation. The designation "non-worker" obscured the labor that mothers performed for their families. As unemployables, mothers also became ineligible for the WPA and other work relief, an exclusion with a disproportionate impact on poor single mothers.

Sentimentalized gender norms never fully inured even "worthy" widows from the expectation of earning something toward their upkeep. With monies covering only children until 1950, ADC lacked a caregiver's grant, and thus mothers had to obtain additional funds to make ends meet. From the start, Southern states assumed that black women would go out to service or into the fields. "Ability to earn" turned into a mechanism to deny aid; only a third of those eligible received any by 1940. When the referent for mother became non-white, states beginning with Louisiana in 1943 adopted "employable mother" rules to compel would-be recipients into the labor market if any form of employment was available. Georgia's 1952 rule kicked in for mothers with children as young as three. By 1960, thirty-three states limited access to ADC in this manner. But migration to the North led to greater numbers of black women qualifying for ADC.

Suitable home and "man in the house" rules linked ADC eligibility to morals tests. The dependent child was one without breadwinner support being cared for by a mother or other specified relative. That ADC made no mention of marital status allowed half of the states to transfer illegitimacy rules from their old mothers' pension programs. Five Southern states denied aid to the never married, with birth status as a proxy for race. With more privileged widows eligible to receive OAI, ADC during the 1940s included greater numbers of the never married (from 2 percent in 1938 to 14.1 percent in 1948). At best their child care work went unrecognized; at worst, it was disparaged and stigmatized. As a consequence, poor single mothers experienced a lesser citizenship. Law circumscribed their reproductive as well as economic rights in ways that only would be temporarily alleviated during the rights revolution of the 1960s when the Supreme Court upheld the fair hearing, ended residency barriers, and struck down "man in the house" rules.

As with collective bargaining, the railroads had their own social security system. In 1946, amendments to the Railroad Retirement and Railroad Unemployment Insurance Acts of 1938 launched a comprehensive social insurance program that would protect workers and their families against old age, disability, death, unemployment, and sickness. The strong seniority system on the rails meant that older men experienced not unemployment but sickness and disability, leading the Railroad Brotherhoods to demand the opening of unemployment reserves to combat other factors that led to economic insecurity. They would determine insurance on the needs of the worker and his family, rather than the actuarial concept of fault, which had come to guide workers' compensation. Based on employer contributions alone, the 1946 amendments generated fierce opposition for bringing socialism to one industry. Republicans failed to repeal them in 1947, but neither did they generate a model for other industries.

A recognized innovation of those amendments was the inclusion of sickness, accident, and maternity benefits that opponents classified as a stealth insertion of health insurance. This social democratic vision incorporated the premise of the National Resources Planning Board that "the health of the individual is the concern not only of the individual himself but of society as a whole,"[17] that productivity, efficiency, and national planning required health and accident insurance. The coverage of maternity leave for women employees, mostly clerical workers, developed as an administrative convenience rather than as a commitment to gender equity. But, when pressed, defenders of the act insisted that employment earned even pregnant workers the right to benefits. As the only federal health care program until Medicare, the Railroad Retirement System remained an anomaly in a postwar welfare state bent on using tax incentives for private pensions. Only those employed by the carriers, predominantly white men, and their families had access to this system, further underscoring the racialized link between work and welfare.

II. PERSISTENT FAMILIALISM

Work associated with home and family, presumably distinguished by relations of intimacy or familialism within the household, stood outside of the labor law. In *North Whittier Heights Citrus Association v. NLRB* (1940), the Ninth Circuit Court asked, "Why is 'any individual employed by his parent or spouse' exempted?" It answered, "Because . . . there never would be a great number suffering under the difficulty of negotiating with the actual employer and there would be no need for collective bargaining and conditions leading to strikes would not obtain. The same holds good as to 'domestic service', and . . . 'agricultural laborer.' . . . Enlarge the meaning of any of these terms beyond their common usage and confusion results."[18] Thus, women's labor in the home, paid as well as unpaid, remained underrecognized. This separation of the home, which included idealized visions of the farm, from other workplaces, even when manufacturing took place there, excluded women from social benefits. By refusing to recognize such locations of labor as worksites, the law reinforced social hierarchy as much as it did by classifying mothers as unemployables under unemployment insurance and Aid to Dependent Children.

---

[17] *Railroad Retirement*, Hearings Before the Committee on Interstate and Foreign Commerce House of Representatives, 79th Cong., 1st Sess. On H.R. 1362 (Washington, DC, 1945), 77.
[18] *North Whittier Heights Citrus Association v. NLRB*, 109 F. 2d. 76, 80 (1940).

The Home as Workplace: Industrial Homework, Domestic Service, and Babysitting

Gendered constructions of the home had shaped the debate over industrial homework since the late nineteenth century. According to detractors, manufacturing in the home transformed a place of nurturance into a site of production, undermining motherhood, childhood, and family life in the process. State regulation would restore the separation between home and work. Defenders of homework embraced the same association of the home with the private sphere when attacking regulation as interfering with a man's privacy as well as his freedom of contract.

Ordinances restricting tenement production were difficult to enforce, requiring an inspector in front of each door. Thus, reformers sought to curb homework through general labor standards, which in turn would be strengthened through outright prohibitions. With the aid of the garment unions and unionized employers, the New Deal network of women won bans on homework in more than a hundred NRA codes. Rather than gain better conditions, homeworkers lost their advantage of cheapness and, thus, their jobs. But those who sent work into the home thwarted regulation through stays of code provisions and definitional wrangles. Especially in Appalachia and Puerto Rico, they sought to classify homework as crafts work, as art rather than industry. They courted public opinion by claiming that the New Deal kept mothers from feeding their children.

The FLSA prohibited homework in seven garment-related trades, but employers again attempted to circumvent the law. They classified homeworkers as independent contractors under the common law understanding of the master-servant relationship that held that "employees" labored at the employer's premises. Most courts rejected this subterfuge. In *McComb v. Wagner* (1950), for example, a New York federal district court upheld Wage and Hour Division criteria for independent contractors that emphasized control over the labor, opportunity to profit, degree of initiative, permanency of relationship, and extent of investment. That rural women sandwiched their homework labor in between farm chores and household duties did not exempt them from the law.

The extension of women's work for the family into the market created an ambiguous space, easily cordoned off as impossible to regulate. Who labored in the home – disproportionately women of color and immigrants – further linked domestic work with low wages. So too did the isolated conditions of the labor, its often intermittent and irregular hours, and non-standard routines. Associated with unpaid family labor, skills necessary for cleaning, cooking, laundry, child care, nursing, and other tasks lacked value. Finally, the mistress-maid relationship continued to mystify the employer-employee one, subjecting domestic service to arbitrary personalism. Asked whether FLSA would "force" Southern housewives to "pay your negro [sic.] girl eleven dollars a week," President Roosevelt replied that no wage and hour bill would "apply to domestic help."[19]

Although the CES staff felt that administrative problems precluded inclusion of domestics under Social Security, no powerful advocate emerged to argue otherwise. Professional women with a vested interest in a cheap supply of servants and housewives never viewed themselves as employers. Women reformers, through the YWCA-backed National Committee on Household Employment, attempted to upgrade the occupation through training classes and model contracts. This voluntarist approach reinforced the feeling that household labor was different, that individual negotiation – rather than social regulation – was more appropriate. Only in 1951 did domestics who worked for one employer at least twice a week and earned at least $50 in a calendar quarter receive coverage under Social Security; not until 1974 did household workers come under FLSA. Then a coalition of civil rights and feminist groups succeeded in having Congress amend the law to account for the transformed understandings of housework as work.

What constituted domestic service generated debate, the outcome of which determined a worker's relation to the labor law. Nurse-companions and other in-home care workers hired directly by clients became defined as domestic servants. So too were babysitters. A 1953 survey of state departments of labor or child welfare discovered that child labor laws exempted domestic service, and thus babysitters neither required work permits nor fell under wage and hour laws. Some states exempted them as casual laborers. Though sections of its child labor law covered babysitters, the New York State Department of Labor explained, "It is very difficult to do anything about enforcing the Labor Law inasmuch as it would involve going into homes and we would have no idea where to go."[20] During the 1974 revisions of FLSA, Congress actually eliminated casual babysitters and elder companions from the definition of domestic; in 2007, the Supreme Court upheld the decision of the Department of Labor to classify home care workers employed by for-profit firms as elder companions, and thus placed some 1.4 million workers in one of the fasting growing occupations outside the law.

[19] Franklin D. Roosevelt, "April 8, 1938," *The Complete Presidential Press Conferences of Franklin D. Roosevelt*, 9 (New York, 1972), 297.
[20] Emily S. Marconnier to Selma M. Borchardt, July 21, 1953, Borchardt Collection, Box 99, folder 11, Wayne State University Archives.

Agricultural Labor

Secretary of Labor Frances Perkins recalled, "Farmers were farmers with helpers, some of whom were their relatives, some of whom were their partners, and others of whom they hired. In the old farm pattern the hired man was a temporary member of the family."[21] Romantic images aside, by the 1930s agricultural laborers toiled without recognition in labor law. Seasonal employment and small contributions justified their exclusion from unemployment insurance and old age insurance, though lack of political will rather than technical impediments caused their removal. A stamp book system could have resolved record keeping, as in Europe. Although the New Deal sought to shore up agricultural production, it feared that increased wages would raise consumer prices and fuel overall wage demands. The National Farm Bureau and other organized agricultural interests had the political clout to eliminate their labor force from collective bargaining and social insurance. That more than one-quarter of such workers were nonwhite complicated the levels of discrimination faced by those who toiled in the fields. Coercive laws that criminalized debt or quitting maintained the Southern plantation system, despite recognition of such acts as violations of the Thirteenth Amendment in *Bailey v. Alabama* (1911). Falling outside of the law also disadvantaged workers struggling against growers in California orchards and New Jersey truck farms. They could collect relief, but lacked the status of worker.

Migrants especially found themselves in a definitional vise disconnected to their lives. The unemployed among them could move to one of 190 camps in forty-four states established for transients under the Federal Emergency Relief Act (FERA) of 1933, where they could obtain various necessities, including health care, and work relief. (Later the Farm Security Administration established more than ninety "permanent" migrant camps that provided welfare services until World War II, when their purpose shifted to greater production.) However, the category "transient" omitted migratory or other poverty wage earners. FERA ruled that states and employers were responsible for such migrants. Some farm owners relied on government relief programs to carry over hirelings until the next season, though local elites discriminated against blacks and Mexicans in providing relief. Fears that paying more for work relief would raise expectations proved true; relief set an unofficial minimum wage, providing California's cotton hands,

[21] Frances Perkins, "The Reminiscences of Frances Perkins: Book IV, US Department of Labor and the First Year of the New Deal," Interview with Dean Albertson, December 3, 1955, Oral History Research Office, Columbia University, n.p.

for example, with leverage in negotiating working conditions. After 1935, residency requirements restricted eligibility, as did the manner in which states administrated federal funds. "Work or starve" framed relief policy.

Farm labor initially came under the more conservative Agricultural Adjustment Administration (AAA), which the Supreme Court struck down as an overextension of federal powers in 1936. Collective bargaining only included those who processed or prepared farm products for sale and were located beyond "the area of production" – a description that left the status of packers and canners at the point of harvest in limbo. The cotton ginning industry reacted by removing its employees from NRA codes. The NLRB also distinguished between field and processing workers, covering only the latter. Unionizing farm workers could hold crops hostage but, without legal protection, could not force growers to live up to contracts. The bloody 1935 battle between workers and police at Seabrook Farms in New Jersey derived from such employer intransigence. The U.S. Department of Labor's Conciliation Service ended the strike, raising wages but refusing union recognition. State paternalism substituted for worker empowerment.

Removal of thousands of Southern sharecroppers from the land represented the most profound impact of New Deal policies. Acreage-reduction programs attempted to raise the price of cotton and other basic commodities by mandating farmers to plow back a quarter of their crop in return for cash subsidies. Payments went to large growers, who in turn evicted tenants rather than share government checks with these black, Mexican, and poor Anglo families. Here too definitions mattered: since cash renters and "managing share tenants" were to receive AAA funds, landlords manipulated the classification of tenant. Social policy distinguished tenants by amount of supervision, which local oversight committees, controlled by white landowners, interpreted in such a way as to deny the independence of even those who managed their own shares. Sharecroppers thus became hired laborers for subsidy purposes. Landlords also replaced Anglo white tenants with African Americans and Mexicans, whom they forced to sign away payments as a condition of employment. Such labor practices not only intensified the racialization of farm labor and lowered standards of living but also further increased anti-immigration and anti-black sentiments among Anglo workers in the South and Southwest. The Southern Tenants Farmers' Union organized the displaced into roadside encampments, but failed to reverse the evictions. Mechanization of Southern agriculture followed, further encouraged by a renewed Great Migration north in response to wartime labor shortages.

To meet such needs, in 1942 the Farm Security Administration initiated the labor importation or *Bracero* Program to transport Mexican nationals to California, Arizona, and Southwestern fields and Caribbean migrants to East Coast ones. Within a year, Congress turned the arrangement over to the War Food Administration and ended the promotion of labor standards and collective bargaining except when required by contracts with foreign governments. It essentially gutted the housing of U.S. citizens in federal migrant camps for what became a foreign guest worker program. The importation program served to curb militancy and keep wages in line by ending labor shortages. After reauthorization in 1947, Congress sold the federal labor camps, cutting import labor off from social assistance and state protection by privatizing their living arrangements. By the time that a coalition of liberals and labor ended the *Bracero* Program in 1964, during a period of farm worker militancy and civil rights protest, farms appeared not as homes but as factories in the fields. Only in 1966 did agricultural workers gain coverage under the Fair Labor Standards Act.

By creating the "illegal alien," immigration law during these years facilitated the growth of a low-wage, racialized transnational labor force. The 1924 National Origins Act cut off the supply of Japanese farm workers. But, as colonial subjects, Filipino men had unrestricted entry and, along with Mexicans, provided a new workforce. During the 1920s and 1930s, their labor militancy in West Coast agriculture and canneries fed a more generalized anti-Asian sentiment that feared Asian competition for "white" jobs and "white" women. Independence for the Philippines transformed foreign nationals into "aliens," with a quota that essentially eliminated immigration. Mexican border crossers also became "illegal aliens" during this period. The "wetback" was the bracero without contract, vulnerable to deportation for speaking up, striking, or malingering on the job. When skipping out of a contract, braceros themselves lost the protection of Mexican consuls. These officials served as their bargaining agents until 1954 amendments to the Migrant Labor Agreement undercut any Mexican control over labor supply and, hence, working conditions.

During the war, West Indians had replaced African Americans in Florida's sugar cane "slave camps" as growers attempted to deflect government investigation into peonage-like working conditions. Equal protection was a weak reed for agricultural laborers and others, like domestics, forced into forms of involuntary servitude. The Justice Department's Civil Rights Section, formed in 1939, turned to the Thirteenth Amendment to defend "free labor" in the process of fighting such physical and economic coercion. This group of progressive lawyers understood labor rights as civil rights. With the Thirteenth Amendment, they maneuvered the shoals of federalism and restrictions on private actions. In *Pollock v. Williams* (1944), the Supreme Court broadly defended labor mobility, calling into question not only contract labor statutes but also vagrancy, "work-or-fight," and "enticing labor" statutes. Workers themselves protested transferring debt through employer selling of the labor of employees, substandard living conditions, and lack of pay among domestics. Into the 1950s, the NAACP continued to expose cases of involuntary servitude, investigating the practices of New York employment agencies that lured Southern women to household positions where employers confined them against their will. A new assumption reigned: even those with the most fragile status as workers would not choose to labor under substandard conditions. This turn to the Thirteenth Amendment attempted to extend the rule of (labor) law to agricultural and domestic laborers excluded by the politics of the New Deal.

III. WHOSE RIGHT TO WORK? FAIRNESS DEFINED AND REDEFINED

While civil rights organizations, notably the National Urban League and the NAACP, argued for federal administration of assistance and universal coverage for Social Security, African American workers sought fair employment and fair representation to make collective bargaining apply to them. A. Philip Randolph of the Brotherhood of Sleeping Car Porters launched the March on Washington Movement in 1941, the same year that he formed the Provisional Committee to Organize Colored Locomotive Firemen that challenged the hegemony of the white Brotherhoods through the courts. Black demands for "the right to work," understood as a fundamental right, insisted on federal action against employers who refused to hire or promote on the basis of race. But for labor's political opponents, "right to work" took on a more sinister meaning: the right of employers to run a non-union or open shop embodied in the 1947 Taft-Hartley law, condemned by unionists as a "slave labor act." As organized labor sought to maintain its institutionalized power, African Americans sought to take advantage of the opening that World War II offered for incorporation into the New Deal order. They sought union – as much as management or government – accountability. Fair employment and fair representation facilitated social citizenship; in the early postwar years, before deindustrialization, greater numbers of black men and women would become eligible for Social Security because of increased employment in jobs covered by the law.

Fair employment became official government policy during World War II with Executive Order 8802 in June 1941. Roosevelt established the Fair Employment Practice Committee (FEPC) to contain protest as much as to address discrimination in employment related to the war effort. Without enforcement powers, FEPC was an embattled agency, attacked by both Southern segregationists and Northern defenders of the free market. Without sufficient resources, the agency suffered from a hostile Congress that curtailed its funds in 1944 and refused to make the agency permanent with the war's end. Although it was able to hold hearings, publicize abuses, and jawbone employers, it usually relied on individual complaint rather than patterns of abuse. Its 1943 hearings on the railroad industry, for example, publicized widespread discrimination. But when the carriers refused to abide by its directives and President Roosevelt established another fact-finding committee rather than revoke contracts or seize the rails, the FEPC could do nothing. Despite such limits, its integrated staff of militant liberals worked with local race advancement organizations to negotiate 5,000 cases and stop 40 strikes within three years. It legitimized black protest, as a few thousand filed complaints. Title VII of the Civil Rights Act of 1964 saw the FEPC reconstituted as the Equal Employment Opportunities Commission (EEOC), with discrimination on the basis of sex as well as race, color, religion, and nationality prohibited.

Banning sex discrimination in employment was available to those who formulated the FEPC. Black New Dealer Robert Weaver, the National Defense Advisory Commission official who developed the first wartime non-discrimination policies, included sex in his clause for defense training under the U.S. Office of Education. A 1940 job training act also prohibited discrimination on the basis of sex as well as race. That year, NAACP lawyers analogized from sex to race in making a Fourteenth Amendment claim for equal pay for black schoolteachers, a separate but equal victory that the Supreme Court sustained in *School Board of Norfolk v. Alston* (1940).

The wartime increase in women wage earners, especially whites in the industrial workforce, led the most progressive trade unions – notably the United Automobile Workers and United Electrical Workers – to include "sex" in contract non-discrimination clauses, though unequal pay, dismissal of married women, and sex-typed work persisted into the postwar period. These conditions sparked a new feminism within the labor movement, which in the next decades pushed for maternity and parental leave, the equal pay act, and work and family policies to accommodate women's disadvantages in the marketplace. But the association of equality with the opponents of protective labor legislation and a National Women's Party dominated by white business and professional woman discredited the attempt in the 1940s and 50s to include sex in employment discrimination law. Not until the 1970s would feminism significantly challenge social and legal understandings of work to account for the sexual division of labor within the home and other sites of labor.

When fair employment directives failed, activist African American workers turned to the courts. *James v. Marinship Corporation* (1944) – a case heard in the California Supreme Court against the International Brotherhood of Boilermakers, Iron Ship Builders, and Helpers of America (AFL) – reaffirmed that the right to earn a living was fundamental. The Boilermakers had exclusive jurisdiction over West Coast shipyards, but offered African Americans only segregated auxiliary lodges without equal membership rights or benefits. Militant black ship workers demanded equal membership, not the end to the closed shop, claiming, "The MEN and WOMEN who build the ships are the unions," that "true unionism" demands "an end to discrimination."[22] The next year the Supreme Court ruled in *Wallace Corporation v. NLRB* (1945) that employers could not rely on a closed-shop contract to discriminate. This went beyond the duty of fair representation that the Court interpreted the Railway Labor Act as imposing on an exclusive bargaining agent in *Steele v. Louisville & Nashville Railroad Company et al.* (1944) and *Tom Tunstall v. BLFE et al.* (1944). But these decisions failed to address the closed membership that poisoned the collective bargaining process, but was essential to union power. While the Brotherhood of Locomotive Firemen and Enginemen (BLFE) had to bargain for all workers in the industry without discrimination, it sought to maneuver around this equal protection dictate. In the late 1940s, the BLFE embraced equality by forcing all engineers to meet the same promotion requirements or be dismissed, a strategy that denied fairness to black firemen by removing them from their current jobs because they could not qualify for others. Subsequent litigation enjoined this provision. By the early 1950s black firemen retained equal rights to jobs that soon would disappear.

Opponents of fair employment linked freedom of association, which they presumed permitted segregation, with freedom of contract. They insisted that a permanent FEPC meant the nationalization of business; federal bureaucratization would extend its arm from economic to intimate relations. This notion of freedom dovetailed with Taft-Hartley's "right to work," which under the guise of protecting the rights of anti-union employees, strengthened management by outlawing secondary boycotts, allowing state bans on the closed shop, sanctioning employer "free speech" during NLRB elections, and implementing other measures that increased union liability. Taft-Hartley also empowered the president to interfere in strikes deemed disruptive of the national welfare by ordering a cooling-off period and state mediation.

For the most part, Taft-Harley codified the direction of NLRB rulings. In shrinking the definition of worker, however, it profoundly impeded the organizing of the white collar and business service sectors that would come to dominate the economy during the last decades of the twentieth century. Section I excluded foremen and other supervisors from NLRB coverage,

---

[22] "Plaintiff's Memorandum in Support of Order for Issuance of Injunction," 2, Reel 108F, "Boilermakers' Local 6," Papers of the President's Committee on Fair Employment Practice (FEPC), microfilm edition of RG228, National Archives.

reversing a 1945 ruling that defined "the man in the middle" as an employee because he did not set policy. This was an ideological victory for corporate America as much as a fatal blow for foreman unionization. According to the legislative history of the Taft-Hartley Act, "it is wrong, to subject people . . . who have demonstrated their initiative, their ambition, and their ability to get ahead, to the leveling process of seniority, uniformity and standardization."[23] Consequently huge numbers in engineering, finance, health care, law, and education, including professors at private universities, fell outside of NLRB as well as FLSA jurisdiction. By the 1980s, an electorate that distanced itself from the label "worker" lacked the ideological ammunition to defend the American welfare state version of the workingman's paradise, once encoded in the New Deal.

IV. FROM THE SOCIAL DEMOCRATIC PROMISE TO THE DEMISE OF THE NEW DEAL ORDER

Surveying the domestic landscape in the early 1940s, liberal defenders of the New Deal optimistically envisioned a panoply of rights: rights to wages, agricultural parity, social security, public housing, soldiers' reemployment, and fair employment. Before the Republican capture of Congress with the 1946 elections, many believed that a cradle-to-grave welfare state was within grasp: national health insurance would pass, full employment would be mandated, and education access expanded. The National Resources Planning Board proclaimed the right to work as essential to the general welfare. Greater opportunity would usher in a new era of prosperity.

Work remained the gatekeeper for social citizenship and herein lay the problem. The 1944 Servicemen's Readjustment Act (known as the GI Bill) rewarded the labor of military service with veteran's benefits, which included unemployment insurance, job training, low-interest loans, educational payments, and civil service preference. With their service defined as work, veterans – unless disqualified by the less than honorable discharge handed to homosexuals and more often to African Americans than whites – gained economic advantages over other citizens. Most were men; the few women who qualified found themselves directed by government job counselors to lower paid, female-dominated occupations. Veteran preferences would persist, with the Supreme Court finding even in 1979, after more than a decade of measures against sex discrimination, that they did not violate women's Fourteen Amendment equal protection claims. Indeed, despite women's wartime labors, their right to a job was conditional. The 1945 House version of the Full Employment Act made that clear when it claimed that "all

---

[23] H.R. Rep. No. 245, 80th Cong., 1st Sess., 16–17 (1947).

Americans able to work and seeking work have the right to useful, remunerative, regular, and full-time employment," but excluded those who had "full-time housekeeping responsibilities."[24] The Full Employment Act that passed replaced the right to a job with a presidential responsibility to report to Congress on the state of the economy and to promote national economic health.

After 1945, some white men gained further economic security when corporations, under pressure from strong trade unions and encouraged by favorable tax measures, initiated their own, more extensive, systems of social insurance. The resulting public/private regime contained an undeveloped state sector with limited provisions that provided goods and services mostly to those for whom the market and/or family failed, those labeled as dependents, not workers. In the context of a hostile Congress, dominated by states' rights Southern Democrats and pro-business Republicans, the promise of a welfare constitution faded, or more accurately, shifted from public duty to private responsibility encouraged through public incentives. This was particularly the case with health care, where tax breaks encouraged employment-based benefits run by the Blues, Blue Cross and Blue Shield, or private for-profit insurance companies.

During the final decades of the twentieth century, structural and ideological shifts, including deindustrialization, deregulation, and faith-based conservatism, threatened the gains that industrial workers had won against corporate capitalism. Whereas the number of manufacturing jobs had grown by four million in the decade 1958–68, three million were lost between 1978 and 1983 alone. Republican presidents transformed the NLRB into a defender of employers, further restricting the kinds of workers under their jurisdiction: teaching assistants in private universities, charge nurses, and disabled people in sheltered workshops, were some of those excluded from the collective bargaining law. Not only did employers use procedural delays to avoid collective bargaining, but NLRB decisions on who belonged to a bargaining unit and related questions made it ever more difficult to even have a certification election.

What happened at Duke Medical Center typified the difficult terrain that unions had to navigate by the mid-1970s. Though the NLRB had extended collective bargaining rights to private, non-profit hospital workers in 1974, a year later it included clerical and technical workers in the unit at Duke, turning an organizing drive by women cooks, laundresses, and other auxiliary laborers, part of the growing civil rights unionism of black

[24] U.S. Congress, *Hearings before a Subcommittee of the Committee on Banking and Currency on Full Employment Act of 1945*, S.380, 79th Cong., 1st Sess., July 30-September 1 (Washington, DC, 1945), 6.

municipal and service workers, into a more difficult struggle, which was ultimately lost. President Ronald Reagan's firing of the air traffic controllers for violating a no-strike pledge in 1981 gave employers permission to undermine unions through replacement workers and engage in aggressive anti-union propaganda without consequences, especially since the AFL-CIO failed to pass labor law reform.

The whittling away of the New Deal undermined the very economic and social security that workers thought they had secured. But this process took decades and occurred only after some significant expansion of rights to groups previously excluded, as with the adding of agricultural, hotel/motel, restaurant, laundry, and hospital labor in 1966 and domestics in 1974 to the Fair Labor Standards Act, and the extension of worker protection, as with the 1970 Occupational Safety and Health Act and the 1974 Employee Retirement Income Security Act. Public sector unionism flourished and accounted for growth in an era of union decline. Inclusion came about because of the civil rights movement, which opened up the nation's workplaces and governance not only to African Americans and then to other racial/ethnic minority groups but also to women as a legal class and later to the middle aged through the 1968 Age Discrimination in Employment Act and to disabled people through the 1990 Americans with Disability Act. Title VII of the 1964 Civil Rights Act generated thousands of complaints, first to the EEOC and then to the courts, against both business and trade unions. By 1981, the federal courts had acted on more than 5,000 such suits, at least one-third of them class actions. By 1973, as one measure of impact, some 13,000 women and 2,000 minority men were eligible for back pay from the precedent-setting consent decree involving AT&T, then one of the nation's largest employers. Two years earlier, the Supreme Court in *Griggs v. Duke Power Company* (1971) struck down hiring requirements, like exams and degrees, that eliminated minority workers, but were not essential to perform the work. Of equal significance, in *United Steelworkers of America v. Weber* (1979), the Court upheld a voluntary "affirmative action" program that reserved half of the training slots for skilled jobs to African Americans. Employers took notice, especially as white-, blue-, and pink-collared workers, emboldened by the promises of Title VII, challenged the notion of "employment at will."

Title VII transformed the face of industry, no more effectively than in Southern textiles. The Office of Contract Compliance, sustained through Presidential executive orders since Eisenhower, targeted these mills for model programs of what later came to be known as affirmative action. Black and white women found jobs and black men gained better ones. As one woman explained, "The best thing that has ever happened to black women in the South in my lifetime is a chance to become full-fledged citizens.... And that comes from their work."[25] But such advancement was short-lived, as foreign competition was setting the stage for textile's steep decline.

Throughout manufacturing, blacks and other minorities entered just as global outsourcing curtailed employment within the United States. Thus, in the fourteen years after the 1974 landmark consent degree that opened up basic steel to African Americans, their numbers actually dropped from 38,000 to under 10,000 in that once core industry. Black men, in particular, came into decent-paying blue-collar labor just as such work disappeared; whereas about half of black young men were in semi-skilled jobs in 1974, only a quarter were in 1986. Resistance by white tradesmen made construction, still a high-wage sector, a battleground, which in turn led the Nixon administration to the Philadelphia Plan with its goals and timetables to avoid racial quotas. The recession in the mid-1970s led to layoffs and stimulated an employer offense that decimated the ranks of the construction unions. For women, as well as African American and other minority men, the percentages employed in these skilled crafts hardly expanded over the next twenty years, even with President Carter's executive order in 1978 to increase the numbers of women in the trades, which amounted only to 2 percent by 1983. Even many eligible for compensation arising from the AT&T settlement never received what they were owed, as the corporation drastically reduced its workforce in the 1980s. However, better paying jobs in construction and elsewhere did have an impact on individual lives and families, lifting thousands of women of color out of poverty.

Title VII had provided employers with a loophole in the form of the "Bona Fide Occupational Qualification" exception (BFOQ), but courts ruled that fundamental rights took precedence over business necessity.[26] What constituted such a right was not always clear; different circuits concluded that cultural expressions like braids or Afros, for example, were or were not proxies for race, and thus removal of employees for such hairdos was or was not a violation of the law. Flight attendants won legal protests against age and marriage restrictions, but found that employer-imposed weight limits stood as long as men came under similar rules.

Women's responsibility for childbirth and child care long offered an excuse to discriminate against them in the workplace. The Supreme Court in *Geduldig v. Aiello* (1974), a case brought under the Equal Protection Clause, found no sex discrimination present when employers denied maternity

---

[25] Victoria Byerley, "Corine Lytle Cannon," oral history in *Hard Times Cotton Mill Girls: Personal Histories of Womanhood and Poverty in the South* (Ithaca, NY, 1986), 160.

[26] This legal provision allows employers to justify bypassing non-discrimination provisions on the basis of needs fundamental to the nature of the employment.

leave, because the relevant distinction at hand was not men and women, but pregnant and not pregnant workers. But after the Court similarly ruled in *General Electric v. Gilbert* (1976), in which plaintiffs relied on Title VII, a feminist coalition won from Congress the Pregnancy Discrimination Act of 1978. Other decisions recognized that discrimination against women came from sex plus another factor; in *Phillips v. Martin Marietta Corp.* (1971), the justices labeled unlawful employer denial of jobs to women with small children. During the last third of the twentieth century, the Court more often than not upheld equal gendered rights in the workplace, making employers liable for sexual harassment on the job in *Meritor Savings Bank FSB v. Vinson* (1986), striking down factory policies that restricted the jobs open to fertile women in *International Union, UAW v. Johnson Controls* (1991), and upholding the inclusion of state workers in the Family and Medical Leave Act in *Nevada Department of Human Resources v. Hibbs* (2003), which relied on a male plaintiff in crafting its case.

By the early 1980s, definitions of class in class action suits, especially the use of statistical means rather than individual plaintiffs to show group harm, had become more limited. Backlash against affirmative action in employment intensified in the 1980s and expanded in the 1990s. Cases like *Firefighters v. Stotts* (1984), which upheld union-negotiated seniority systems, also highlighted the tension between trade unions, which had evolved in milieus of racial and gender segregation, and the civil rights goal of workplace equity. The Court both defended individuals against union rules, as when supporting the right of workers to resign union membership without retaliation or penalty, and maintained the principle of majority representation, as when defending the union against unauthorized actions by minority caucuses. Responding to *Emporium Capwell Co. v. Western Addition Community Org.* (1975), New Left historian-turned-lawyer Staughton Lynd charged that the entire purpose of labor law now was to "get the workers off the streets, or the shop, and into the chambers of some purportedly neutral umpire"; that is, to squash any return to the power of rank-and-file militancy lost with the NLRB's rule of law.[27] That this case involved black activists fired for an unauthorized wildcat strike further reflected the difficulties that unions had with adjusting to the needs of workers subject to multiple harms, a problem found in sexual harassment cases as well.

Though the last decades of the twentieth century witnessed a shriveling in the union idea, work remained central to the definition of American citizenship. With the decline of the family wage, however, a majority of mothers even of small children were in the labor force, albeit on a part-time

---

[27] Staughton Lynd, "The Right to Engage in Concerted Activity After Union Recognition: A Study of Legislative History," *Indiana Law Journal* 50 (1974–75), 720.

basis, and tolerance for poor solo mothers on public assistance, increasingly a racialized group, waned. Aid to Families with Dependent Children (AFDC) recipients benefited from the rights revolution of the 1960s, with the Court establishing the right to a fair hearing. The Court reinforced the criteria of need, upheld the mobility of recipients, and sustained the privacy of poor women, but the right to live without employment was another matter. Beginning with 1956 amendments to the Social Security Act through various workfare schemes from the late 1960s into the 1990s and culminating in the Personal Responsibility and Work Opportunity Act of 1996, the ending of poor women's dependency through work became national policy.

But the kinds of jobs under workfare, like picking up garbage or caring for other recipients' children, rarely led to employment at livable wages. They competed with public employees and denigrated the motherwork of poor women. When these laborers demanded job protections, minimum wages, and other worker rights, municipalities questioned their status as workers under the FLSA. Indeed, other poor women of color and immigrants, like home health care aides, also found themselves struggling during the 1990s for recognition as workers under labor law. As with the Justice for Janitors campaign, the development of sweatshop workers' centers in Los Angeles and El Paso, and the unionization of California's home care workers, immigrant laborers – now predominantly from Asia and the Americas – again won a kind of citizenship through organization.

As many low-wage workers gained entrance into the law and even unions, professional workers, some like doctors and professors who sought to join labor's ranks, found themselves excluded by the law. A widening gap between who was a worker and which work counted as work promised to divide wage earners from each other. President George W. Bush hoped to take advantage of generational, racial, gender, and occupational divisions by encouraging some workers to buy into an "ownership society," in which Social Security would be replaced by individual retirement accounts vulnerable to the fortunes of the stock market and individual employees would be saved from union misappropriation of their dues by "paycheck protection."

CONCLUSION

During the twentieth century and into the twenty-first, the expansion of the welfare state around a citizen's relation to employment defined the meaning of citizenship itself. This process, we have seen, was interactive, but had differential paths and histories. Though excluded from the letter of the law, African Americans embraced the promise of citizenship on the job to push for an expanded welfare state. As part of the Roosevelt coalition, they experienced the possibility of having their needs addressed by a government from which previously they had expected little. That happened during World War II when they fought a Double V campaign against fascism abroad and Jim Crow at home. The wartime FEPC was a civil rights remedy that also belonged to a series of measures limiting the actions of employers against the public welfare. Fair employment – like child labor restrictions and the aptly named "Fair" Labor Standards Act – restricted freedom of action, one notion behind freedom of contract. It represented a renewed interest in the Due Process Clause of the Fourteenth Amendment, also apparent in the black quest for equal pay and fair representation by trade unions. Meanwhile Justice Department lawyers and NAACP staff deployed the Thirteenth Amendment to fight persistent agricultural peonage and domestic servitude among African American and Caribbean migrants.

While a New Deal network of women had promoted maternal and infant health and economic security, in contrast to black protest, no unified feminist movement marched in the streets to extend women's rights during the 1930s. Only with the growth of women's industrial participation during World War II would a new generation of labor feminists demand union contracts and state policies to remedy workplace disadvantages on account of sex. Most continued to accept protective labor laws for women, the results of early-twentieth-century campaigns by women reformers. While equal rights feminists condemned women-only minimum wages and night work bans as reinforcing occupational segregation and contributing to women's inequality, social justice feminists and maternalist reformers alike had demanded that the state take account of female difference, the double burden of breadwinning and breadgiving endemic to working-class motherhood. Women reformers and unionists, especially in the garment industry, engaged in a dialectic of strikes and standards, an interplay between shop-floor action and government regulation. The Fair Labor Standards Act was their triumph for presumably universalizing the concept of fairness and establishing wage, hour, child labor, and homework standards.

But breadwinner ideology and tensions from the equal treatment/special treatment conundrum persisted. That the Social Security Act of 1935 privileged certain forms of work over others reflected social norms even as it intensified the devaluing of carework, whether done for the family or for wages. The welfare state also was a heterosexual state, reinforcing the marriage relation and discriminating against homosexual conduct through job dismissals and GI Bill regulations, which had economic consequences. Women received benefits more often on the basis of family connection to a man, for being a wife or daughter, than on account of their own wage record. These women were more likely to be white, married, and U.S. born. Like minority men, who disproportionately suffered from underemployment and unemployment, women went in and out of the labor market, worked part time, and concentrated in workplaces uncovered by either law or union contract.

This system doubly disadvantaged the vast majority of African American, Mexican American, and immigrant women whose own labor histories and those of their men left them uncovered by private or public benefits. Public assistance for the poor, stigmatized as welfare, was unavailable or inadequate and subject to arbitrary determination by local authorities. Aid to non-citizens was difficult to come by; laws both restricted citizenship, especially among migrants from Asia, and curtailed immigration itself. To the extent that resource mobilization by white men through both the Democratic party and trade unions sought to maintain the white male breadwinner as the ideal worker and thus welfare state citizen, then this liberal state reinforced a racialized gendered order that devalued the motherwork of racial minority women and denied breadwinner status to minority men, often forcing the former into the low-wage labor force and the latter out of the labor force altogether.

Before deindustrialization and the ascendancy of a service workforce, industrial unions – whose mobilization helped make the New Deal possible and who in turn were shaped by resulting law and policies – struggled not only for their own members but also for a larger social wage. Emerging victorious from World War II, these unions fought for national health insurance, full employment, anti-discrimination, higher wages, and more social security. Containing multiple strands of political ideologies, the unions suffered from the purge of Communists and the morphing of a social democratic vision into a form of labor liberalism, whose fortunes depended on those of a Democratic Party that was itself internally divided. The civil rights movement and mid-century feminism particularly challenged workplace exclusion. But few questioned the association of worker with the citizen, even though immigrant advocates sought to reward the labor of the undocumented. Even those who would roll back worker gains idealized the work ethic. But in the twenty-first century, whether social supports based on employment would continue remained uncertain, as employers sought reduced costs in a new global economy and the federal government sought to disinvest itself of responsibility. Instabilities in both the public and private components of the welfare sate called for creative solutions, which could emerge from mobilization by workers from below as much as from imposition by elites from above.

I O

POVERTY LAW AND INCOME SUPPORT: FROM THE PROGRESSIVE ERA TO THE WAR ON WELFARE

GWENDOLYN MINK, WITH SAMANTHA ANN MAJIC
AND LEANDRA ZARNOW

The roots of poverty law stretch back to the late nineteenth century, when privately funded organizations arose to provide legal assistance to poor immigrants. Legal aid offered services to people who could not afford to pay for them, often helping them secure money that was owed when deserting husbands failed to pay child support or when unscrupulous employers failed to meet the terms of the wage contract. But although legal aid did often secure funds owed to indigent clients, the purpose and focus of assistance were to open access to the justice system, not to assure poor people an income.

Poverty law can be distinguished from ordinary legal aid in that the heart of poverty law is advocacy for poor people's access to resources. A political practice as much as it is a legal analysis, poverty law emerged as a coherent body of law and legal advocacy during the 1960s, when the civil rights movement, the War on Poverty, the introduction of public legal services for poor people, and grassroots welfare activism combined in an ambitious legal and political movement to secure rights for economically disfranchised people. Poverty lawyers challenged the differential legal treatment of low-income individuals, especially those who needed government assistance. They also developed affirmative claims for income support as part of an overall strategy to increase resources for poor people and win rights for welfare recipients.

Although poverty lawyers sought to establish firm bases for income claims through new and aggressive constitutional arguments, their legal work for income assistance was confined by well-established policy frameworks largely to the world of welfare. By the 1970s, poverty law included the principle that families eligible for public assistance were entitled to receive benefits, and it guaranteed basic rights to recipients. But despite the efforts of welfare rights activists and lawyers, poverty law never

359

established that individuals were entitled to an income, or a "right to live."[1]

Beginning in the 1960s, poverty lawyers assisted poor people – especially poor mothers and children – in their individual encounters with governmental income programs and related services, such as housing. Poverty lawyers also assisted the movement made up of poor mothers – the welfare rights movement – as it demanded access and fair treatment for families that needed Aid to Families with Dependent Children, the income program for poor children and their caregivers in families without breadwinners. Navigating the welfare system while challenging it to democratize its relationship to poor families, poverty lawyers had to take on powerful policy precedents, as well as the ideological legacies and institutional arrangements from which they were born.

First in the Progressive era and then in the New Deal, anti-poverty reformers promoted policies to mitigate income insecurity. These policies at once improved the material circumstances of some families while channeling those most in need into separate and subordinate relationships with government. At the heart of poverty policies confronted by poverty lawyers in the 1960s were inequalities imbricated in the social policies of the 1910s and 1930s. Despite the radical interventions of poverty lawyers during the 1960s, many of these inequalities still exacerbate the injuries of poverty today.

I. REGULATING THE POOR IN THE PROGRESSIVE ERA

The first income program for the poor was what we now call "welfare." It arose in the name of domesticity from the nexus of capitalism with nativism and patriarchy to provide support to "worthy" mothers who were raising children without the help of a male breadwinner. That a public income program arose at all was something of a feat, for the idea that poverty is as much the fault of the poor as it is of economic conditions runs deep in American political thinking. That welfare benefited domestic women rather than employable men eased its embrace by state legislatures. Even so, the welfare policies widely adopted by states during the Progressive era followed the teaching of Josephine Shaw Lowell, the leading nineteenth-century theorist of charity and public assistance, to make aid to poor mothers a means of regulating them.[2]

---

[1] A. Delafield Smith explained the claim to a "right to live" in his seminal article "Public Assistance as a Social Obligation," *Harvard Law Review* 63 (1949), 266–88.

[2] Josephine Shaw Lowell, *Public Relief and Private Charity* (New York, 1884).

Known as mothers' pensions, Progressive era welfare policies were adopted by states and administered by counties without interference from the national government. Protected by nineteenth-century conceptions of federalism, which celebrated the authority and discretion of states, Progressive era policies maximized the power of local governments to differentiate among the needy and then to discriminate in favor of those deemed "worthy."

The core of federalism resides in the Tenth Amendment, which delegates to states all powers not specifically allocated to the national government. During the nineteenth century, this arrangement invested states with considerable discretionary "police" authority to regulate communities in the name of promoting public morals and welfare. Before the 1930s, when the Supreme Court began the slow process of holding states accountable to the national Bill of Rights, states were not limited in the exercise of their police powers by provisions of the U.S. Constitution guaranteeing individuals protection from unwarranted search and seizure and other personal liberties. Although the Fourteenth Amendment, ratified in 1868, promised individuals due process and equal protection in relations with state governments, these guarantees were not enforced before the 1940s, and then only incrementally.

Until the New Deal, states alone created and controlled policies toward the poor. State-level policies served the regulatory goals of states and localities, goals that included: enforcing the "less eligible" concept so that no person would receive a relief benefit that was higher than the lowest wage; disciplining the "undeserving" poor; and maintaining the race and gender order through policies that policed, excluded, and punished poor people differentially based on ascribed social station. When states did offer income assistance to poor individuals, such assistance was understood as temporary "relief" and a "gratuity" – a benevolent gesture from state or local governments to which relief agencies could attach various social controls.

Although the New Deal welfare state extended income assistance to the non-poor as an earned entitlement, not a gratuity, the status of the poor in the welfare state has been governed by Progressive era practices that regulated the poor. Whereas the template for the regulation of the male poor was the capitalist market, the template for the female poor was the patriarchal family. The intellectual and ideological foundations of the welfare state were drawn in the late nineteenth and early twentieth centuries by political and economic concepts of morality and personal responsibility that sharply demarcated home from market, assigning moral men the responsibility of breadwinning while confining worthy women to the domestic sphere. Labor laws backed up this demarcation by limiting women's employment.

Working for free in married families, worthy women were expected to sustain the home as a moral haven.

This model met many women's material needs but, by entrenching dependency on a male breadwinner, left many women resourceless if their husband lost his job or if they lost their husband. In response to the dilemma of the resourceless but worthy widow with young children, during the 1910s states began to devise income assistance programs for deserving families. This assistance followed in the relief tradition, providing a contingent and conditional gratuity, but it deviated from ordinary public relief in two major respects. First, assistance went only to recipients who were presumed to deserve their benefits. And second, assistance was not tied to an expectation of employment; in fact, ideal pensioners were expected to devote themselves to full-time caregiving for their children.

Still, like public relief (and "scientific" charity), mothers' pension policies also assumed that recipients needed to be policed and reformed. Although a mother could not receive a pension unless her worthiness first established her eligibility, state and local welfare workers insisted that recipient mothers be monitored to assure their continuing worthiness.

In most states, marriage was the threshold for worthiness. Only two states explicitly permitted unmarried mothers to receive mothers' pensions, and a few states limited eligibility to widows only. Several states deemed deserted mothers eligible for benefits, but in practice such mothers typically were directed to domestic courts to secure income from deserting husbands. Meanwhile, local agencies favored worthy widows even when authorizing statutes did not require them to do so. In general, then, the "worthy" mothers reached by the program were overwhelmingly widows.

They also were overwhelmingly white, for a companion threshold for worthiness was whiteness: of the families receiving mothers' pensions in 1930, 82 percent were the families of widows; 96 percent of them were white.[3] In many states before the New Deal, mothers' pensions were not made available to African American mothers. Some states directed Black mothers into work relief, rather than into mothers' pension programs. In the South, where 90 percent of the adult African American female population lived in 1920, four states did not mount pension programs at all. Elsewhere, policy administrators made it impossible for Black mothers to establish eligibility. In the West, similar exclusionary practices made mothers' pensions inaccessible for Mexican immigrant mothers. In Los Angeles, county officials adopted a policy of refusing pensions to Mexican widows on the grounds that their "feudal background" made it unlikely that they

---

[3] U.S. Children's Bureau, *Mothers' Aid, 1931*. Children's Bureau Publication No. 220 (Washington, DC, 1933), 11–13.

could "understand and not abuse the principle of a regular grant of money from the state."[4]

Unlike Mexican or Asian immigrants, the immanent whiteness of immigrants from southern and eastern Europe gained them access to mothers' pension programs. However, stereotypes about them – about their living arrangements, child-raising practices, and the food they ate – produced the requirement that such immigrant mothers assimilate Anglo-American norms in exchange for benefits.

Anglo-Americanization, in fact, was a primary social control imposed on "worthy" mothers enrolled in mothers' pension programs, especially in the urban and industrial Midwest and Northeast. "Americanization" required unlearning immigrant cultural practices ranging from diet and cuisine to the allocation of family work across generations in a household. It also required adopting moralistic prescriptions attached to mothers' pension policies or to casework, including teetotalism, church attendance, and celibacy. Mothers' pensioners demonstrated their continuing eligibility by surrendering to surveillance and instruction from visiting nurses, social workers, and dieticians who enforced "American" standards.

Although mothers' pension advocates prescribed Americanized domestic motherhood for worthy beneficiaries, pension programs were perhaps more successful at promoting assimilation than at ensuring domesticity. States simply did not offer benefits in amounts sufficient to sustain single-mother families. Benefits were meager and even so were available only to a select group of mothers. Nevertheless, mothers' pensions transformed poverty assistance for eligible mothers and their children, providing support that was less meager and less arbitrary than ordinary relief and doing so outside of almshouses and orphanages. The first public cash assistance program aimed at the structurally impoverished – mothers without income from a husband's wage – mothers' pensions established a conceptual foundation for public income transfers to the poor.

II. SEGREGATING THE POOR IN THE NEW DEAL

Responding to the income and employment effects of the Great Depression, the New Deal administration of President Franklin Roosevelt embraced the mothers' pension concept by including federal financial support for state-run mothers' pension programs in the Social Security Act of 1935. Title IV of the act created the federal Aid to Dependent Children program, which guaranteed funds to states that offered benefits to children without

---

[4] Mary Odem, "Single Mothers, Delinquent Daughters, and the Juvenile Court in Early-20th Century Los Angeles," *Journal of Social History* 25 (1991), 27, 29.

a breadwinning parent. Although many federal ADC officials aspired to uniformity and non-discrimination across jurisdictions, in practice states were allowed to transpose their disciplinary and discriminatory mothers' pension practices onto their ADC programs.

The decentralized structure of ADC, along with the state-level discretion that decentralization implied, took on new significance after passage of amendments to the Social Security Act in 1939. The 1939 amendments created the Survivors Insurance program, which at the time provided benefits to elderly widows as well as to widowed mothers and their minor children. Marriage was one threshold criterion under this program, as mothers had to be widows for themselves and their children to qualify. The other threshold was socially insured employment; that is, the deceased father had to have worked in a job covered by the Social Security Act. The Social Security Act itself, along with the Fair Labor Standards Act, excluded from coverage occupations in which people of color tended to be employed – agriculture, for example. Consequently, beneficiaries under the Survivors Insurance program were not only by definition married but also were disproportionately white.

The Survivors Insurance program split off from ADC those single mothers who were a priori worthy because they had been married to their lost breadwinner. With this innovation, ADC became the income program for a priori "unworthy" mothers – those who had never married, were divorced, or had been married to the wrong (that is, not socially insured) men. Beginning in the 1940s and increasingly over the next two decades, mothers of color came to be disproportionately represented in the new universe of ADC. With this change, state ADC agencies stepped up surveillance practices – not to enforce worthiness through uplift, as did mothers' pension programs, but to chase mothers from the rolls. Southern states were especially famous for their punitive, exclusionary provisions, such as "employable mother," "suitable home," and "man in the house" rules. But Southern states were by no means alone in stigmatizing, demeaning, and rejecting mothers of color who needed welfare.

Worthy widows who were admitted to the Survivors Insurance system enjoyed a significant improvement in the form and amount of income support they received. First, the Survivors Insurance system overcame the pitfalls of federalism – state-level discretion over eligibility and benefit levels and state-determined rules for program participation. Built onto the old age insurance program of the Social Security Act, the Survivors Insurance system awarded benefits based on a deceased marital father's participation in the Social Security payroll tax and on predictable and automatic criteria (socially insured father-worker dies; mother of his children gets a monthly income, unless she earns too much; and in any case the children get a monthly benefit until age 18). An entitlement through marriage, survivors benefits could not be conditioned on a mother's behavior or culture. Nor, because the benefit was centrally administered and automatically disbursed, could a mother be monitored for the quality of her motherhood.

The distinctions between single-mother populations created by Survivors Insurance, then, also created distinctions in citizenship. Widowed mothers became social citizens – albeit through marriage – with income provided as an earned (and deserved) unconditional social protection. Nonmarital mothers, by contrast, were required to surrender basic rights to privacy and intimate liberty as a condition of receiving welfare. Barred from claiming a right to an income under the decentralized and discretionary ADC program, non-marital mothers were also deprived basic constitutional protections.

During the 1950s and into the early 1960s, states devised increasingly restrictive eligibility rules aimed at excluding disdained families from the ADC program. While the federal ADC program grew in the 1950s with the addition of a caregiver's benefit (under the 1935 measure, grants had been awarded for children only) states also devised schemes to limit growth in participation rates among families of color. And while the federal ADC program was renamed the Aid to Families with Dependent Children (AFDC) program and it expanded to include a social services component in the early 1960s, states found ways to deter participation by mothers of color or to punish those who managed to enroll in it.

In addition to the means test for program participation were multiple morals tests that targeted African American non-marital mothers and children in particular. Some states promulgated the "illegitimacy" bar, which defined the home of a non-marital mother as "unsuitable," and the family therefore ineligible for ADC benefits. Some states also adopted "substitute father" rules that disqualified poor non-marital mothers with boyfriends from ADC. These sorts of rules were enforced through midnight raids and other forms of surveillance. Their enforcement and impact were racially skewed: for example, Louisiana's illegitimacy restriction purged 23,000 mostly African American children from the welfare rolls in the summer of 1960; only 5 percent of affected families were white.

Compared to the treatment of worthy widows in the national welfare state erected by the Social Security Act, the treatment of non-marital mothers in the ADC/AFDC system mirrored the dual system of family law exposed by Jacobus tenBroek's ground-breaking analysis of welfare in the states.[5] In this work tenBroek laid the foundations for welfare rights law more than a decade before it was seen as a field of legal research and activism.

[5] Jacobus tenBroek, "The Impact of Welfare Law on the Family," *Stanford Law Review* 42 (1954), 458–85.

In his analysis, tenBroek focused on the state of California to show how the welfare systems in the states created dual systems of aid to the poor, which, in turn, also created dual systems of family law. Arguing that even as the Great Depression challenged the United States to develop comprehensive national social provision, what emerged in the New Deal as income policy for the poor borrowed heavily from preexisting policies and practices. According to tenBroek, legislators embraced preexisting legal doctrines with respect to spousal support, residency, income, adoptions, and other family issues – and built the welfare system around them.

In this jerry-built system, the law of domestic relations (family law) yielded to welfare law, putting poor people on a different legal footing in mediating relations within families and families' relations to government. One example of the legal differentiation of welfare families arose in the treatment of stepfather obligations. Under the California Civil Code, the stepfather was defined as the person married to the mother of the children. As the male head of household in a married family, the stepfather was liable for the family's support. In the absence of a legal marriage, however, the male householder would not be liable to support his partner's children. In contrast, under the Welfare and Institutions Code, the male partner of a mother with children was defined as a stepfather whether he was married to the mother or in a common law relationship with her. Thus, any man living with a mother receiving welfare became obligated to support her children, and his income became a measure of the mother's need for welfare.

Another example of the different legal status of welfare families arose from a comparison of the dispute resolution processes for welfare and non-welfare families. Whereas family law matters under the Civil Code were to be settled by judges in courts of law, disputes under the Welfare and Institutions code were to be settled through extra-judicial administrative rules and rulings. As a result, according to tenBroek, when it came to welfare laws, judges were stripped of their decisional role and instead became reviewers of administrative decisions. Given these examples, tenBroek concluded that family law under the California Civil Code was far more comprehensive and general, reaching rich and poor alike, whereas welfare laws tracked poor families into a separate system that modified and contradicted the code.

This dual system of family law sorted the "deserving" from "undeserving" poor and rights-bearing from non-rights-bearing families. In his address to the San Diego Urban league in 1961, tenBroek traced this differentiation to the distinction between social insurance and welfare. According to ten-Broek, both the public and government viewed social insurance (e.g., old age insurance, survivors insurance, and unemployment insurance) as an earned benefit, whereas public assistance became "a kind of national dump for the disposal of unsolved social ills."[6] Far from "earned" in the public imagination, welfare was seen as charity, its availability always contingent and revocable.

According to tenBroek, the view of welfare recipients as a social problem justified the contingency of welfare benefits and exposed recipients to the penal code and other sanctions to help "solve" their poverty. In San Diego in 1961, for example, the district attorney acquired sweeping powers over welfare, including the power to determine eligibility. The DA and the local police eclipsed the welfare director, investigating welfare recipients and applicants and subjecting them to the penal code for infractions of welfare rules. The use of the police to deal with welfare recipients in San Diego provided a telling illustration of how the poor were assumed to be deviant and defiant, their poverty a sign of moral failure rather than the consequence of social and economic arrangements and inequalities.

The central figure in the dualities illuminated by tenBroek – in the separate and unequal arenas of income support – was the non-marital mother raising her own children. Yet when poverty law emerged during the 1960s to advocate income rights for the poor, it based few claims on the fact that the single parent in most low-income families that needed welfare was usually a mother. As a result, the inequality between Survivors Insurance mothers and welfare mothers was never broached, nor were welfare recipients' rights as women and mothers directly joined as legal issues.

III. LEGAL ADVOCACY FOR THE RIGHTS OF THE POOR

Beginning in the mid-1960s, the welfare rights movement nourished the development of poverty law. Composed of low-income mothers, the welfare rights movement made claims as mothers and as women, exposing how disdain for unmarried poor women's childbearing and motherwork ran to the core of welfare rules and restrictions. Linked nationally through the National Welfare Rights Organization, grassroots activists mobilized locally to challenge welfare agency practices that injured dignity and to claim public policy changes to achieve economic equality.

Welfare rights activism arose at the grassroots to protest unfair treatment, but also engaged law reform. Although the interracial movement of low-income mothers expressed an acute consciousness of the gendered basis and experience of their poverty, the law reforms accomplished for these mothers generally focused on essential but ungendered principles, such as

---

[6] Jacobus tenBroek, "Social Security: Today's Challenge to Public Welfare" (Speech to the Seventh Annual San Diego Urban League, February 26, 1961). *Vital Speeches of the Day*, 27 (13) (1961), 411–16.

due process, property rights, and the prerogatives of states in the shared federalism of welfare law.

These principles formed the core of the bill of rights proposed for welfare participants in 1965 by Edward Sparer, one of the seminal welfare rights lawyers. Inspired by the work of Jacobus tenBroek, Sparer set out a bill of rights for welfare recipients that he hoped could be won via strategic litigation. The four tenets of this bill of rights claimed for recipients the right to privacy and protection from illegal searches, the freedom to travel and change residence, the right to fix one's own standard of morality, and the right to refuse work relief without suffering penal or other improper consequences.[7] The overriding goal of litigation to secure these rights was to establish a constitutional right to live – namely, the right to welfare or at least a minimum guaranteed income.

Eventually known as the "father of welfare law," Sparer brought a lifetime of social activism to his war on poverty. After leaving the City University of New York, where he led a student strike against racism and anti-Semitism among the faculty, Sparer joined the Communist Party and worked to promote it at the General Electric Plant in Schenectady, New York.[8] When he learned of Stalin's slaughters, Sparer left the party, returned to New York City, and enrolled in Brooklyn Law School.

After a stint doing legal work for the International Ladies' Garment Workers' Union, in 1963 Sparer began work in poverty law when he joined the new Mobilization for Youth (MFY) project. Based on the theory of Lloyd Ohlin and Richard Cloward, the MFY project confronted poverty comprehensively with the goal of reducing juvenile delinquency by increasing opportunities for young people.

Situated on the Lower East Side of Manhattan, the MFY project saturated the community with counselors and other staff, as well as with legal workers. Sparer headed up the legal unit, where he pursued direct litigation to change the institutional arrangements that created and sustained poverty. Following the methods of groups such as the NAACP and the ACLU, Sparer dedicated the MFY legal unit to ending inequality and empowering the poor. Sparer trained social workers and other MFY affiliates to address the legal needs of their clients and worked toward a day when poor people would act as their own advocates.

Through his tireless work for the MFY legal project, Sparer came to realize that routine legal services provided by the neighborhood legal offices

---

[7] Edward Sparer, "The Role of the Welfare Client's Lawyer," *UCLA Law Review* 12 (1965), 380.

[8] Ed Sparer, "Critical Legal Studies Symposium: Fundamental Human Rights, Legal Entitlements, and Social Struggle – A Friendly Critique of the Critical Legal Studies Movement," *Stanford Law Review* 36 (1984), 509.

would not accomplish the necessary strategic work he envisioned for comprehensive social change. To strengthen the capacity of poverty lawyering to engage in strategic litigation, in 1965 Sparer obtained support from the Ford and Stern Family Foundations to set up a legal center dedicated to litigation to secure rights for welfare recipients. At the Center on Social Welfare Policy and Law, nine lawyers coordinated nationwide welfare litigation to bring the confusing half-federal, half-state welfare system set up by the 1935 Social Security Act under coherent federal control. If successful, this litigation would preserve state administrative control over welfare programs, but would win national rights for recipients to assure their constitutional protection across jurisdictions.

Sparer sought to discover a constitutional right to live, an affirmative right that could only be guaranteed by governmental provision of income support to those in need. Against many critics who disputed his constitutional reasoning, Sparer held fast to his ideas, claiming that since the government already guaranteed income for many groups (for example, by providing subsidies for farmers who were not producing crops) it therefore should guarantee the subsidy of life to those who were resource-poor. Claiming that the constitutional guarantee of equal protection meant that poor Americans deserved rights, including subsistence rights, Sparer urged the courts to deploy the Constitution in the war on poverty.

In tandem with Sparer's constitutional claims, in 1964 and 1965 law professor Charles Reich posited the concept of "new property" to describe the government benefits made available to individuals by the New Deal welfare state, including welfare. Reich developed the concept to establish a constitutional claim to due process protection for recipients of welfare, much as was enjoyed by other governmental beneficiaries. He began to develop his ideas while clerking for Supreme Court Justice Hugo Black. As Black's clerk, Reich worked on *Barsky v. Board of Regents* (1954), which involved a doctor whose medical license was suspended when he refused to submit to a subpoena by the House Un-American Activities Committee. Justice Black's dissenting opinion, developed by Reich, argued that Dr. Barsky's medical license should be seen as a type of property, not a mere gratuity from the state, and thus should be protected by the Fourteenth Amendment.

After his clerkship, Reich worked as a lawyer in Washington, D.C., and then went to teach law at Yale. There, he continued to develop his ideas on new forms of property. In his course on property law he chose to focus on the meaning and function of property itself and not just the arcane legal rules governing its use. Reich was asked by a group to comment on the legality of raids on welfare recipients' homes by local welfare agencies, and his work soon came to be informed by his ideas on welfare as a form of property.

Working closely with many poverty lawyers and social welfare scholars and activists, Reich began to see that his views on property could be applied to improve the conditions of welfare recipients.

Reich concluded that the raids violated recipients' right to privacy and were used to coerce certain behavior. He argued that recipients' very need for welfare to survive made them vulnerable to welfare administrators when they tried to coerce personal behaviors and choices in exchange for benefits. Overall, Reich maintained that the lower one's class status the fewer rights one had and the harsher the treatment by government. To Reich, this violated the principle of equality.

Reich's insights into property culminated in his seminal *Yale Law Review* article, "The New Property."[9] Concerned that receipt of government benefits was often accompanied by a loss of liberty, especially for the very poor, Reich developed the claim that benefits are a new form of property to which constitutional protections applicable to more traditional property must apply. Reich argued that the New Deal created various forms of governmental largess that became a source of wealth for many. Such government largess included government jobs, occupational licenses, franchises, contracts, subsidies, and public services, as well as categorical income supports.

Reich also reasoned that personal property was a form of largess as well, for individual property was protected by government and subject to certain governmental conditions. In other words, *all property* is a form of public largess: "Once property is seen not as a natural right but as a construction designed to serve certain functions, its origin ceases to be decisive in determining how much regulation should be imposed. The conditions that can be attached to receipt, ownership, and use depend not on where property comes from, but on what job it should be expected to perform."[10]

Reich believed that all recipients of largess fell under the government's power; however, he also found that the subjugation by governmental power is especially pronounced for persons on public assistance. Reiterating an argument he first made when asked to comment on welfare raids, Reich explained that because persons on public assistance fear the loss of subsistence, they cannot easily assert rights against governmental power. As a result, welfare officials impose conditions on recipients that deeply invade their individual freedoms and impair procedural guarantees.

Arguing that recipients should not be forced to "choose between their means of support and one of their constitutional rights,"[11] Reich enumerated limits on the kinds of conditions that government could attach

---

[9] Charles Reich, "The New Property," *Yale Law Review* 73 (1964), 733–87.
[10] Reich, "The New Property," 779.   [11] Reich, "The New Property," 762.

to benefits as well as on delegation and discretion. First, the government should not have the power to buy up constitutional rights by imposing conditions on some beneficiaries of government largess that would be invalid if imposed on others. Second, the power of legislatures to regulate or police beneficiaries should be limited to legitimate and relevant actions. Third, the "grant, denial, revocation and administration of government largess should be governed by fair procedures."[12] By this Reich meant that there should be no denial of benefits for undisclosed reasons, and even higher standards of procedural fairness should be mandated when administrative action has the effects of a penal sanction. Moreover, Reich maintained that governmental administrators must not undertake adjudications of fact that normally are made by a court of law.

In addition to articulating rights-based restrictions on government's regulation and coercion of recipients, Reich also insisted that government benefits should be viewed as a right. As a right – the source of livelihood and sustenance for most Americans – government largess should be governed by a system of regulatory, civil, and criminal sanctions, rather than by a discretionary system of suspension, denial, and revocation. Further, under Reich's framework the confiscation of largess would be viewed as a last resort, rather than as a commonly used and convenient penalty.

The welfare rights principles developed by tenBroek, Sparer, and Reich won judicial recognition and enforcement of an entitlement to AFDC benefits for families who met the economic criteria of the program. In the first of three watershed decisions, the Supreme Court in *King v. Smith* (1968) struck down Alabama's substitute father rule, which had disqualified some 16,000 children – 90 percent of them African American – when the rule was first promulgated. Finding the Alabama regulation in conflict with the federal AFDC statute's "paramount goal" of providing economic protection to children, the Court prohibited states from denying "AFDC assistance to dependent children on the basis of their mothers' alleged immorality or to discourage illegitimate births."[13] Striking at states' discretion over welfare programs, the Court suggested that state AFDC programs could not deny aid to any mothers and children eligible by need unless the federal law specifically authorized them to do so.

In two key decisions following *King*, the Court further reduced states' discretion over welfare programs. In *Shapiro v. Thompson* (1969) state residency requirements fell as the Court asserted that the fundamental right to travel belongs to families that need welfare as it does to everyone else. In *Goldberg v. Kelly* (1970) state or local summary termination of public assistance benefits fell to due process requirements of a fair hearing. Nodding

---

[12] Reich, "The New Property," 783.   [13] 392 U.S. 309, at 324.

to Reich's theory of the "new property," Justice Brennan wrote for the majority that "it may be realistic today to regard welfare entitlements as more like 'property' than a 'gratuity.'" Quoting Reich, Brennan continued:

Society today is built around entitlement. . . . Many of the most important of these entitlements now flow from government: subsidies to farmers and businessmen; routes for airlines and channels for television stations; long term contracts for defense, space, and education; social security pensions for individuals. Such sources of security, whether private or public, are no longer regarded as luxuries or gratuities; to the recipients they are essentials, fully deserved, and in no sense a form of charity.[14]

King, *Shapiro*, and *Goldberg* improved poor families' access to welfare and the reliability of benefits. Enforcement of the federal welfare entitlement diminished the discretion of states to impose moral conditions on benefits; to abridge poor people's right to travel, including across state lines; or to deprive eligible families of their benefits without due process protections, especially a fair hearing. But the new welfare entitlement did not include a "right to live" and hence did not require states to provide income support in the amount necessary to sustain families. In *Dandridge v. Williams* (1970), the Court validated Maryland's maximum family grant limitation and with it states' claim that they may provide aid only "as far as practicable under the conditions in such State."[15] Even while upholding federal jurisdiction over the standards of welfare administration, the Court in *Rosado v. Wyman* (1970) observed, "While participating States must comply with the terms of the federal legislation, *see King v. Smith, supra*, the program is basically voluntary, and States have traditionally been at liberty to pay as little or as much as they choose, and there are, in fact, striking differences in the degree of aid provided among the States."[16]

Although the statutory and constitutional protections ushered in by *King, Shapiro* and *Goldberg* bore fruit in additional Court rulings – striking down California's "man in the house" rule (*Lewis v. Martin*, 1970), New Jersey's rule limiting AFDC benefits to families in which parents were legally married (*New Jersey Welfare Rights Organization v. Cahill*, 1973), and New York's requirement that lodgers help with AFDC family rents (*Van Lare v. Hurley*, 1975) – the Court simultaneously undermined some of these protections. For example, in *Wyman v. James* (1971), the Supreme Court upheld New York City's mandatory home inspection rule against a privacy claim on the grounds that welfare was a gratuity – charity – and that states have a right to monitor how their charitable funds are spent.

[14] 397 U.S. 254, at 295.   [15] 397 U.S. 471, at 478.
[16] 397 U.S. 397, at 408.

Other protections were eroded by federal statutory innovations designed to accomplish the moral regulation and punishment that states, under *King v. Smith*, could no longer do.

IV. THE WAR ON WELFARE RIGHTS

The welfare rights movement and poverty lawyers accomplished legal victories for recipients at the same time that political hostility against welfare recipients flared. The persistently disproportionate presence of mothers and children of color on the welfare rolls and a rise in caseloads made necessary by racialized poverty and made possible by successful welfare rights litigation inflamed anti-welfare politics. The central figure in the anti-welfare narrative was the poor mother of color who was variously described as a "brood mare," a "cheat," "lazy," and, by the mid-1970s, as a "welfare queen."[17]

These epithets summoned old hatreds, resentments, and bigotry to the new, national welfare context. The long-standing racism that had quarantined poor mothers of color from local mothers' pension programs defined African American mothers as workers primarily and mothers only incidentally. Their increasing participation in an income program once intended to honor mothers was seen as a blight on the social order. Not accidentally, even as welfare rights litigation made gains for recipients, federal and state welfare policies introduced the idea that recipients should work outside the home rather than care for their own children. It would take thirty years for this idea to take root in coercive national welfare policy provisions, but by the early 1960s most states had some form of work requirement and in 1962 and 1967 the federal government gestured its support for work programs.

Equally important, new thinking focused the public gaze on the African American family. Blaming the Black "matriarch" for the causes and consequences of racialized poverty, social scientists and policy designers maintained that unmarried, poor, African American mothers and the structure of their families were agents of a "culture of poverty." This argument had been anticipated in scholarship of the 1940s and 1950s, but the proposition that mother-of-color-headed families were "pathological" only received widespread attention in the mid-1960s with the release of Daniel Patrick Moynihan's *The Negro Family: A Case for National Action*.

Moynihan argued that the structure of the mother-headed African American family held the key to poverty in the Black community – both to

---

[17] Gwendolyn Mink and Ricki Solinger chart the elaboration of the anti-welfare narrative through primary documents in *Welfare: A Documentary History of Welfare Policy and Politics* (New York, 2003).

explaining it and to correcting it. Single motherhood signaled family disorganization, according to this view, leading single mothers' sons to delinquency, school failure, and adult dysfunction, which perpetuated single motherhood in the next generation. One remedy suggested by Moynihan's analysis was public investment in cultivating economic opportunities for Black men to make them marriageable and restore them to family headship. Consistent with this strategy, many of the War on Poverty programs, especially those aimed at employment training, focused on men. But Moynihan also called for a focus on the African American single-mother family itself, which he saw as a self-perpetuating pathology measurable in "welfare dependency." Improvements in Black men's employment and income would help in "the establishment of a stable Negro family structure," but would not alone extinguish the "pathology" of single motherhood among Black women.

Moynihan's assessment fed anti-welfare nostrums. Over the course of the 1960s, a public discourse gained traction that linked AFDC, single motherhood, and poverty in an inexorable causal web. Poverty law's march to secure income rights for poor single-parent families ran headlong into calls to use welfare policy to pressure welfare mothers to adopt heteronuclear patriarchal family norms. These calls for "welfare reform" produced legislative changes to the AFDC statute in 1967, changes designed to "make papa pay" and thus to tie paternal child support to the welfare policy scheme. Where mothers' pensions and ADC had provided benefits *because* single-mother families were deprived of paternal support, AFDC after 1967 slowly shifted into a program that provided benefits *only if* biological fathers could be identified and tracked down for child support. It would take thirty years for this change to be fully accomplished, but even in the late 1960s the idea had taken root that welfare should undermine single motherhood, not support it with an income.

During the 1960s and 1970s, poverty law was ill equipped to head off policy assaults that abridged women's right to form families on their own terms, to forego marriage, or to divorce – in short, to live independently of men. Poverty law lacked its own analysis of welfare recipients' rights as women and mothers. Moreover, it could not borrow such an analysis from feminist legal advocacy, for at the time feminist law reform did not offer theories or strategies for securing equality for caregiving women, for poor women, for women of color – or for women who inhabited all three axes of subordination. Poverty lawyers did challenge some of the paternity establishment requirements imposed on welfare mothers, winning fifteen lower court lower court rulings against state paternity rules between 1969 and 1973. But when courts limited the scope of the requirement they generally did so in the name of children, not their mothers (*Doe v. Shapiro*, 1969). The gendered conditions of welfare participation – sexual surveillance, paternity establishment, pressure to enter a father-mother financial dyad – did not enjoy much attention in welfare rights litigation during poverty law's heyday.

Later in the century, feminist poverty lawyers would challenge certain welfare rules and practices that injure recipients' rights as women – reproductive rights impaired by the child exclusion (family cap), for example, as well as the right to be free from sex discrimination in workfare programs. But they were unable to thwart the racialized, gendered juggernaut of "welfare reform" that in 1996 withdrew the welfare entitlement and undermined welfare rights to punish recipients for being single mothers.

CONCLUSION

From the mothers' pensions of the Progressive era to the welfare system set up by the New Deal, income policy for poor families drew lines between women based on race and marriage. During the Progressive era, on one side of the line stood seemingly "assimilable" southern and eastern European immigrants and upliftable poor Anglo-Americans, both deemed worthy enough to receive mothers' pensions if they had been married. On the other side of the divide fell women of color, whether or not they had been married, and those white women who failed the moral means test for welfare eligibility. Beginning in the New Deal, on one side of the line stood worthy widows with minor children – in the survivors insurance system – mothers whose marriages to socially insured men assured them an income until their children were raised. On the other side – in the welfare system – fell unmarried mothers and widows of low-wage workers whose jobs were not covered by social insurance. Increasingly, this side of the line became identified with women of color, just as poverty law began to secure procedural guarantees for participants in welfare.

The advances in the rights of welfare recipients emerged from a legal framework drawn by the civil rights movement. A key aspect of that framework shifted the locus of citizenship toward the national government, chiefly by nationalizing and universalizing certain constitutional rights – for example, the right to personal security from illegal searches, the right to marry, and the right to travel – and holding states accountable to them. An equally pivotal aspect of the civil rights framework was the successful claim that the Fourteenth Amendment's Equal Protection Clause forbade government, state and federal, from treating individuals or groups differently based on race. Poverty lawyers hoped to win a similar claim for the poor, thereby laying the basis for challenges to the unequal treatment of the poor such as tenBroek described. But in *San Antonio School District v. Rodriguez* (1973) and then again in *Harris v. McRae* (1980), the Supreme Court refused to treat poverty as a suspect classification deserving of stringent judicial scrutiny. As applied in these cases, this precedent protected economic inequalities in children's access to public educational resources and in women's access to abortion services.

Judicially imposed constitutional hurdles to interrogating the unequal treatment of poor people by the welfare state limited the potential of poverty law. Political and intellectual hurdles to recognizing the intersecting vectors of subordination in poor mothers' treatment by the welfare state further limited poverty law's ambition. While the rights won for poor mothers in litigation were undeniably important, they did not establish strong claims to income support nor did they equalize the terms and degree of income assistance for all participants in the welfare state. They did not disturb differentiation in rights and provisions for married and unmarried mothers, labor market workers and caregivers, and people who "need" income assistance and those who have "earned" it. The existence of a welfare state has made it possible for poor people to claim resources, but its structure is an intractable deterrent to income security and social equality.

I I

THE RIGHTS REVOLUTION IN
THE TWENTIETH CENTURY

MARK TUSHNET

Americans have always framed claims of injustice in the language of rights, but the late twentieth century saw a large expansion of the domain in which the language of rights played a major part in political and legal contestation. This "rights revolution" in the twentieth century also transferred large parts of that contestation from purely political arenas to administrative and judicial forums.

Rights consciousness has been an important component of the way in which ordinary Americans have seen their place in the social world. Americans have translated their claims about what they wanted and needed for fulfillment in life – claims about their interests – into claims about their rights as human beings. The American Revolution was in part fueled by the widespread belief that the British Parliament was denying Americans their rights as Englishmen. Economic development produced conflicts over land and the use of public space that Americans framed as conflicts about their rights to property.

For most of U.S. history Americans sought to vindicate their rights through legislative action. The rights revolution of the twentieth century expanded the number and nature of the claims that could be presented as claims about rights and added the courts to legislatures as important venues for appeals to rights. The rights revolution was indeed revolutionary, but that revolution had significant conservative elements. Claims about rights were typically appeals to *existing* values that were not adequately realized in current practices, rather than appeals for some basic reorientation of American values. In presenting rights claims to courts, participants in the rights revolution called on judges to draw on traditions and doctrines that the advocates and the judges could find already in place.

Some of the conditions for appeal to rights were long-standing features of U.S. constitutional and institutional life. U.S. constitutionalism contained important elements of a general ideology of liberal individualism, which fostered the framing of political and legal appeals in the language of rights, rather than that of social duties or the responsibilities of the claimant's opponents. Federalism, and more generally the institutional dispersion of authority, including the absence of a centralized party system, made the courts a natural locus in which people could seek to establish policy that was to some degree uniform. Other conditions for the rights revolution were created in the late nineteenth and early twentieth centuries. The Progressive movement of the early twentieth century endorsed the use of expertise in making and enforcing social policy and supported the creation and elaboration of administrative agencies. As those agencies developed, they became venues in which people could present claims that agency decision makers had violated their statutory or constitutional rights. Rights, for Progressives and their heirs in the Democratic Party were a social practice itself subject to the expertise of lawyers, and early Progressives created institutions staffed by lawyers dedicated to ensuring that courts and agencies enforced the rights the lawyers pressed on those bodies. Further, the Progressives and Democrats became committed to a substantive or programmatic liberalism, which entailed government action in the service of substantive goals of equality and liberty. Appeals to rights naturally accompanied programmatic liberalism.

By the last third of the century, the institutions for enforcing rights had expanded dynamically, breaking the bounds of programmatic liberalism in two ways: programmatic liberalism generated a theory of rights that departed from classical liberal individualism, and rights claims became asserted by *opponents* of programmatic liberalism, who asserted rights based in the older form of liberalism that Progressives had transcended.

This chapter takes up the institutions of the rights revolution first, because those institutions were the preconditions for creating and, perhaps more important, for sustaining a rights revolution concerned with substance. But, of course, those institutions were inserted into a political and intellectual universe with its own features. The second part of this chapter addresses a tension that became more apparent as the rights revolution advanced – the tension between individualist and collectivist understandings of rights.

I. THE INSTITUTIONS OF THE RIGHTS REVOLUTION

In the late nineteenth century, women, African Americans, and business interests organized litigation that was self-consciously designed to seek the vindication of constitutional rights. They brought cases designed to test the constitutionality of laws they believed violated their rights. Advocates of women's suffrage challenged the exclusion of women from the franchise as a violation of the Fourteenth Amendment. Susan B. Anthony, for example, invited a criminal prosecution for her attempt to vote in 1872. She used her trial to put forward the argument that the Fourteenth Amendment, adopted only four years earlier, had made woman suffrage a constitutional requirement. Only after the courts rejected these and similar arguments did the suffrage movement turn to other forms of political action. African Americans designed and supported litigation against newly enacted segregation statutes and never abandoned attempts to secure their rights through judicial action. For example, African Americans in New Orleans organized *Plessy v. Ferguson* (1896) as a test of Louisiana's law requiring segregation in railcars, and they hired the celebrated lawyer and novelist Albion Tourgée to present their case. Late in the nineteenth century and into the twentieth century, lawyers for businesses coordinated their challenges to Progressive era labor legislation and their defenses of common law injunctions against labor unions.

Sometimes rights that had staying power emerged almost incidentally from litigation that was merely defensive and uncoordinated. In the aftermath of World War I, for example, some state legislatures adopted jingoist legislation aimed at suppressing forms of education – in private schools and in foreign languages – they regarded as un-American. Schools and teachers threatened with sanctions, and sometimes prosecuted for violating these laws, successfully challenged them in the Supreme Court (*Meyer v. Nebraska*, 1923; *Pierce v. Society of Sisters*, 1925).

The first sustained and national organization taking its charge to be the enforcement of constitutional rights was the National Association for the Advancement of Colored People, created in 1909 by an interracial group of progressive professionals, including academics, social workers, and lawyers. The NAACP engaged in campaigns of public education and lobbying. From the beginning, the NAACP accepted the earlier "test-case" litigation approach, paying particular attention to Supreme Court litigation, largely because one of the NAACP's founders and early presidents, Moorfield Storey, was a prominent Boston lawyer. The NAACP filed an amicus brief in *Quinn v. Oklahoma* (1915), the Department of Justice's challenge to an Oklahoma law disfranchising African Americans, and supported litigation brought by a local NAACP activist that successfully challenged a Louisville ordinance requiring residential segregation (*Buchanan v. Warley*, 1917).

The American Civil Liberties Union joined the NAACP in providing sustained institutional support for rights claims. The ACLU was the successor to the National Civil Liberties Bureau, which was founded in 1917 to support conscientious objectors during World War I. Roger Baldwin, the ACLU's most prominent voice in its early years, was a social worker dismayed with what he saw as the ravages of capitalism. Baldwin saw civil liberties litigation as essential in the defense of political radicals, but not as the vindication of any deep principles to which he thought the organization should be committed.

The ACLU and the NAACP offered two competing institutional models for rights-based litigation. The ACLU continued the test-case approach and was primarily defensive, relying heavily on affiliated attorneys scattered throughout the nation to alert the national organization to civil liberties problems experienced locally. A generation later Jehovah's Witnesses pursued a similar defensive strategy aimed at establishing nationwide precedents, but they coordinated the constitutional strategy somewhat more closely because of the religious organization's tighter control from the center.

The NAACP also relied on cooperating attorneys and, particularly in criminal cases arising out of threatened lynchings, had a substantial docket of reactive or defensive cases. But, the NAACP attempted to provide greater coordination from its central office in New York, in large part because the lawyers it relied on – Charles Hamilton Houston and Thurgood Marshall – were major leaders of the national African American community, in contrast to the dispersed leadership of the radical community that the early ACLU served.

During the 1920s the differences between the ACLU's defensive posture and the NAACP's grew as the NAACP began to develop a proposal for a sustained litigation challenge to segregation. James Weldon Johnson, the NAACP's executive secretary who had been trained as a lawyer before turning to poetry and organizing, applied to a left-wing foundation, the American Fund for Public Service (usually called the Garland Fund after the person who endowed it), for a grant to support litigation against segregation. The proposal, later elaborated by Nathan Margold, a protégé of Harvard Law professor Felix Frankfurter, described litigation that could be brought against segregated education, transportation, and housing. Baldwin, who ran the Garland Fund, was extremely skeptical about the sort of affirmative litigation strategy the NAACP proposed, but in the end he was outvoted, and the NAACP received a grant to plan and then implement the litigation strategy.

The Garland Fund never came through with all the money it promised. The NAACP's proposed litigation strategy proved impossible to implement anyway, because it would have required a degree of coordination and resources, particularly in the form of plaintiffs willing to bring lawsuits and lawyers able to pursue them, that were beyond the NAACP's capacity. Nonetheless, the vision of a strategic plan to achieve rights persisted. That vision had several elements. First, select constitutional arguments that reach the broadest desired goals by increments small enough that no single step will seem overly threatening to courts assumed to be unsympathetic to large-scale change. Second, identify factual scenarios in which the injustice of the rules being challenged is most apparent. Finally, to the extent possible locate a sympathetic plaintiff, who can be presented to the courts and public as someone obviously entitled to what he or she is seeking.

The NAACP implemented this vision in a series of lawsuits against segregated education. One group of cases sought to equalize the salaries of white and African American teachers, whereas the other aimed at desegregating Southern universities. The litigation in both groups extended over a decade and was only partly successful. Salaries for teachers in large urban districts were equalized, but the NAACP could not persuade courts to adopt legal theories that would equalize salaries on a statewide basis.

The university cases were more successful as part of a strategic plan. The incremental theory the NAACP adopted began by accepting as settled law the proposition that schools could be segregated if they were equal and challenged the facilities available to African Americans as unequal to those provided whites. By stages the NAACP expanded the criteria by which equality was to be measured, finally emphasizing the intangible aspects of education at Texas's public law school (*Sweatt v. Painter*, 1950). With a victory in that case in hand, the NAACP's lawyers were then in a position to challenge segregation itself. Still, few litigants were willing to suspend their life plans while long-term litigation over universities took place. Nonetheless, the NAACP and its lawyers took the lesson of their litigation efforts to be that carefully calculated strategic litigation could achieve substantial changes in the law. The NAACP's dedication to strategic litigation culminated in five reasonably well-coordinated lawsuits challenging segregation in elementary and secondary schools. The strategic model of litigation was widely taken to be vindicated by the U.S. Supreme Court's decisions in *Brown v. Board of Education* (1954, 1955) holding school segregation unconstitutional.

Considerations of race affected the Supreme Court's expansion of the rights of criminal defendants in the 1960s as well. The justices were concerned that decisions by police and prosecutors were too often affected by racial bias. Providing criminal defendants with more constitutional protections, the justices believed, would reduce race-influenced exercises of discretion in the administration of justice. The NAACP itself engaged in a litigation campaign against the death penalty, during which capital punishment was suspended. Though the NAACP's campaign did not succeed in permanently eliminating the death penalty in the United States, the attack on capital punishment did lead to a substantial restructuring of the law, and, probably, to a reduction in the numbers of defendants executed.

The ACLU also experienced a significant number of successes, sometimes when its affiliated attorneys represented defendants and sometimes when the ACLU filed *amicus* briefs in major Supreme Court cases. The distinction between ACLU-style defensive litigation and NAACP-style affirmative or strategic litigation narrowed in the second half of the twentieth century, largely because of procedural innovations supported by progressive lawyers and endorsed by a Supreme Court reshaped by Franklin Roosevelt. The federal Declaratory Judgment Act (1934) allowed litigants to anticipate lawsuits against them, giving civil liberties lawyers the opportunity to take the initiative to challenge statutes before the statutes were actually enforced. For several decades the Supreme Court placed restrictions on these anticipatory challenges and was particularly skeptical about using declaratory judgment proceedings to attack state criminal statutes. Cases arising out of the civil rights movement of the 1950s and 1960s led the Court to rethink its position, however. Seeing Southern lawmakers and prosecutors engaging in what the justices regarded as blatant injustice, the Court relaxed its doctrines of federalism, standing, and ripeness to allow litigants to bring lawsuits against criminal investigations and newly enacted statutes. The Court returned to a more restrictive posture in the 1970s and after, but by the end of the century it still remained relatively easy for civil liberties lawyers to obtain judicial review of newly enacted statutes. What had been defensive litigation on the ACLU model had been transformed into a version of strategic litigation on the NAACP model.

Other developments in procedural law promoted rights-based litigation. In traditional litigation, winning litigants could benefit themselves and others through the precedential effects of the court rulings, but those rulings would not formally require the losing defendant to change its general mode of operating unless the decision came in a class action. Until 1966 the law regarding when a litigant could bring a lawsuit in the federal courts on behalf of a class was quite technical and fairly restrictive. Critics of the narrowness of the class action rules argued that class actions could be an important vehicle for vindicating the rights of large numbers of people, each of whom was harmed but not to a large enough extent to make it sensible for individuals to bring lawsuits. Responding to this concern and specifically mentioning the experience with civil rights litigation as well, the drafters of the federal rules of procedure proposed a major restructuring of the class action rules, which went into effect in 1966. Class actions became available for widespread harms to workers and consumers, broadening the reach of rights consciousness beyond the traditional civil rights and civil liberties communities. Entrepreneurial private lawyers began to identify targets for class actions that would generate substantial recoveries and attorneys' fees awards and thus provide the lawyers with substantial incomes and finance additional litigation. In 1976 Congress enacted a statute making routine the payment of attorneys' fees in successful constitutional litigation.

The federal government contributed another institutional support for rights-based litigation when Congress expanded statutory rights in the service of substantive liberalism and committed enforcement of those statutory rights to administrative agencies with staffs that were to be run by experts who would nonetheless be responsive to political concerns. The tension between expertise and political responsibility led Congress to provide for judicial review of agency decisions to ensure that agency expertise would not override individual rights nor agency political responsiveness undermine the substantive goals Congress sought to achieve. The interest groups that paid attention to agency decision making developed litigation centers to support presentations to the agencies, to be followed if necessary by judicial review. In the 1940s the Supreme Court tended to limit the rights of individuals and groups to participate in agency decision making and to appeal decisions with which they disagreed. But, in the 1960s the Supreme Court held that those arguably within the zone of interests Congress sought to protect could appeal adverse agency decisions. Interest groups could then participate in agencies' decision-making processes and seek judicial review with few restrictions.

By the late 1960s these legal and institutional developments converged to generate an explosion in rights-based litigation in a wide range of areas. The federal Legal Services Corporation, created in 1967 as part of the War on Poverty, provided lawyers to poor people seeking the benefits provided by federal anti-poverty statutes. In addition to doing work on behalf of individual clients, poverty lawyers drew on the NAACP model of strategic litigation to develop what they called "impact litigation." This litigation challenged state rules restricting benefits, for example by denying assistance to poor children if their mother had a "man in the house," as inconsistent with federal statutes and, sometimes, as unconstitutional. Impact litigation based on statutory claims was often successful, that based on the Constitution much less so.

The ACLU created a women's rights project, headed by Ruth Bader Ginsburg, that similarly pursued strategic litigation on the NAACP model. Ginsburg proceeded incrementally, carefully identifying what she thought were statutes that were the most constitutionally problematic for her first challenges. Notably, the ACLU's litigation generally targeted laws discriminating against men, believing not only that they reflected the kinds of gender stereotyping that the Constitution should be interpreted to prohibit but also that laws discriminating against men were the best vehicles for persuading courts staffed primarily by men of the unfairness of gender-based discrimination.

The environmental movement took on a rights-based orientation in the 1970s. Many environmentalists at the turn of the twentieth century were

Progressive technocrats, seeking to manage public resources to preserve a natural domain. As they did with many other issues, they treated the environment as an issue that ought to transcend politics. By mid-century, an increase in environmental consciousness, probably fueled by the nation's increasing wealth, began to place environmental questions on the national political agenda. Lobbying groups supported by individuals and foundations persuaded Congress to enact new environmental statutes and, increasingly, to provide for court enforcement. Environmental litigation groups challenged both executive agencies' decisions about the environment and, equally important, judicial decisions defining who could sue and when. Their successes took advantage of looser standards for judicial review and pushed the courts to relax the standards even more.

A disabilities rights movement took shape in the 1970s and 1980s and achieved its major success with the enactment of the Americans with Disabilities Act (1990), a statute that prohibited discrimination against the disabled and required public agencies and private employers to accommodate their programs to the needs of the disabled. Like the environmental movement, the disabilities rights movement succeeded largely because of its middle-class character; in the debates over the Americans with Disabilities Act, members of Congress routinely invoked the problems faced by friends and members of their families with disabilities. Later, advocates of gay and lesbian rights struggled, much less successfully, to use the courts to eliminate laws prohibiting sodomy and to protect gays and lesbians against discrimination in employment. Largely because of the state of the "culture wars" in the late twentieth century, the movement for gay rights had little traction until the century's final decades, but then made quite rapid progress. Even after the U.S. Supreme Court rejected a constitutional attack on prohibitions on sodomy, for example, many state courts found that their own state's similar statutes violated their state's constitution. The U.S. Supreme Court also invalidated a widely noticed Colorado initiative that would have prohibited state and local governments from adopting ordinances barring discrimination against gays and lesbians (*Romer v. Evans*, 1996).

The NAACP's strategic litigation had another effect on litigation in the second half of the century, achieved through the courts' response to desegregation. In 1955 the Supreme Court ordered that schools desegregate "with all deliberate speed." School systems in the Deep South were recalcitrant and offered desegregation plans that, even if implemented fully, would not have resulted in large numbers of white and African American students attending the same schools. After a decade of resistance, the Supreme Court required school systems to develop plans that promised to "work," as the Court put it (*Green v. New Kent County*, 1968). Lower courts understood this ruling to mean that they had the power to require school systems to make extensive changes in school district boundaries and student assignment policies, including ordering that schools transport students from one part of the district to another.

The structural remedies in school desegregation cases became a model for litigation over other claimed violations of constitutional and statutory rights. The legal services impact litigation aimed at changing the rules implemented by social service bureaucracies. Structural litigation, in contrast, aimed at changing the bureaucracies themselves. The ACLU again pioneered in extending the model of structural litigation through its National Prison Project. The Prison Project's lawyers developed a substantive constitutional theory, that the conditions prevailing in an institution might in the aggregate subject prisoners to cruel and unusual punishment in violation of the Eighth Amendment. Remedying those conditions meant changing the institution from top to bottom. Prisons could be required to abandon systems by which some prisoners had charge of others, to eliminate overcrowding in individual cells or "dormitories," or to provide substantially improved medical care.

Courts imposed structural remedies most often in cases involving race discrimination and prisons, although such remedies occasionally were used in cases challenging police practices and the provision of social welfare services. Unlike remedies in individual cases, which might sometimes involve only overturning the conviction of one or a handful of defendants, structural remedies could have large impacts on public programs and, particularly, on public budgets.

Politics and Legal Theory in the Rights Revolution

Progressive lawyers capitalized on the courts' receptiveness to rights claims compatible with the substantive liberal commitments of the New Deal and the Great Society. As the federal courts became more conservative after 1968, conservative lawyers learned from their progressive counterparts how they might use the courts for strategic litigation as well. Foundation-supported organizations of conservative lawyers, such as the Pacific Legal Foundation, provided the institutional base for conservative rights claims. These lawyers developed strategic plans to limit the power of state and local government to regulate land uses by persuading the courts that land use regulation could amount to an unconstitutional taking of property without compensation. The Institute for Justice sought out attractive plaintiffs to challenge affirmative action programs in universities and for public contracts. In short, conservative litigating groups appropriated the models developed by progressive lawyers and turned rights-based litigation to conservative ends.

The progressive lawyers had succeeded to the degree that their rights-based claims fit comfortably with the substantive liberalism to which the courts were committed; the conservatives' rights-claims succeeded for parallel reasons as the courts' substantive commitments changed.

The changing political composition of the federal courts and the rise of conservative rights-based strategic litigation made clear the nature of rights litigation in the late twentieth century. From the beginning the NAACP had understood its litigation as only one component of a larger political strategy to eliminate racial discrimination. The organization lobbied Congress to enact anti-lynching legislation and distributed information to shape public opinion. Restrictions in the tax laws, which barred political activity by organizations that received tax-exempt contributions, led the NAACP to separate its legal operations from the larger organization in a limited way in 1939, and more extensively in the 1950s when the Association faced a sustained attack by Southern politicians who promoted an investigation of it by the Internal Revenue Service.

The division of the NAACP into one branch oriented to public education and political activity and another oriented to litigation had some real effects on coordinating civil rights work generally. Litigation remained one component of a larger strategy, albeit one less well integrated into that strategy than had been the case in the early stages of the NAACP's strategic litigation. Similarly, rights-based litigation by other groups was loosely coordinated with political activity. Conservative rights-based litigation drew on think tanks funded by conservative foundations. Trial lawyers who brought consumer class actions became large contributors to the Democratic party, and their organization, the Association of Trial Lawyers of America, became an important lobbyist opposing restrictions on consumers' rights to sue.

The political dimensions of rights-based litigation became apparent only as such litigation became an important feature of political life. In the early years of the NAACP and the ACLU, their lawyers treated the specific rights claims they presented as analytically neutral derivations from agreed-on general rights: All agreed, they argued, that the Constitution protected equality and free expression, leaving open only interesting, important, and clearly controversial questions about the proper interpretation and application of those constitutional rights. The lawyers were too sophisticated to believe that they sought interpretations that were neutral in some transcendent sense, but for psychological reasons they had to present their claims as if they were indeed asking only for neutral interpretations.

The rise of legal realism in legal theory and the regular interactions between the lawyers conducting litigation and advocates seeking redress through legislation and executive action eventually made it apparent that rights-based litigation was political action in a different forum. The role of litigation in the civil rights movement of the 1960s made the connection between rights-based litigation and political action apparent. Much of that litigation took the form of defenses against prosecutions for public order offenses during demonstrations. The demonstrations were designed to place public pressure on lawmakers to repeal segregation laws and enact anti-discrimination statutes. The defensive litigation was primarily designed to ensure that civil rights protestors could continue to engage in such demonstrations and only secondarily to vindicate fundamental claims about rights; indeed, the lawyers grasped for any legal theory on which to overturn their clients' convictions, whether it went to fundamental constitutional questions or was purely technical.

The transformation of rights-based litigation into a form of interest group politics made rights claims vulnerable to ordinary political reactions. The largest reaction was provoked by the expansion of criminal justice rights, as Republicans ran as law-and-order candidates charging that the Supreme Court had contributed to the significant rise in crime during the 1960s. Statutory litigation about social welfare rights had been more successful than constitutional litigation, but new statutes could overrule statutory decisions. Various welfare statutes, culminating in the welfare reforms of the Personal Responsibility and Work Opportunity Reconciliation Act (1996), undid much of what the poverty lawyers had achieved. Congress restricted government-supported lawyers for the poor essentially to representing individuals, not allowing them to bring impact litigation that would challenge the systems of law that placed individuals in poverty.

Not surprisingly, some state officials mounted substantial challenges to structural remedies. The Supreme Court placed some restrictions on what lower courts could order in prison cases, and the Prison Litigation Reform Act (1996) substantially reduced the possibility of successful structural litigation over prison conditions. The Supreme Court also placed some modest limits on class actions, and Congressional efforts to reduce the influence of consumer-oriented trial attorneys culminated in a relatively mild cutback, the Private Securities Litigation Reform Act (1995). The Supreme Court also interpreted the civil rights attorneys' fee statute in ways that reduced the payments that would have to be made when constitutional challenges succeeded.

Still, there was no true rights counterrevolution on the institutional level. Public officials sometimes actually favored structural litigation, as a way of increasing the importance of a particular bureaucracy's claims on the overall budget. Structural litigation persisted, therefore, although it occupied a less prominent place at the end of the century than it had a few decades earlier. The class action rules remained in place, and judges persisted in using class actions to manage large-scale litigation with substantial public effects. Interest groups on the right and the left continued to provide funds for litigation challenges. In the 1990s, a new set of actors, transnational nongovernmental organizations, began to advance the idea that U.S. law had to change to recognize international human rights.

By the end of the twentieth century, the rights revolution had transformed rights-based litigation: Beginning as an effort to vindicate fundamental rights, such litigation had become simply another form of the interest group politics that characterized the wider political system.

II. THE CONCEPTUAL UNDERPINNINGS OF THE RIGHTS REVOLUTION

At the turn of the twentieth century constitutional rights were primarily property rights. The Constitution protected individuals and corporations against state laws that changed contractual obligations and required states to compensate property owners for taking their property. Late in the century the Court held that the Fourteenth Amendment's Due Process Clause protected the liberty of contract (*Allgeyer v. Louisiana*, 1895), a holding that spawned significant litigation challenging Progressive era legislation. Many such challenges failed, the courts finding that public health and safety justified infringements on the liberty of contract. When the courts concluded that the statutes were simply efforts to change the balance of bargaining power between business and labor – what the Supreme Court called labor laws "pure and simple" – they struck them down as violations of due process. A law limiting the hours bakers could agree to work, for example, fell to constitutional challenge (*Lochner v. New York*, 1905). These economic due process cases rested on a conception of constitutional rights that was deeply individualistic, combining contemporary libertarian ideas with an older tradition hostile to "class legislation" that benefited only segments of the wider society rather than advancing a community-wide public good.

After the New Deal constitutional crisis of 1937, the Supreme Court began to articulate a somewhat different rationale for judicially enforced constitutional rights. Rejecting an economic due process challenge to a statute prohibiting the shipment of "filled milk," a cheaper substitute for whole milk, the Court noted that it might be more aggressive in finding constitutional violations when statutes were challenged as interfering with the democratic process or when statutes imposed disadvantages on "discrete and insular minorities" (*United States v. Carolene Products*, 1938). The *Carolene Products* argument, sometimes called the "footnote four" argument after the note in which Justice Harlan Fiske Stone articulated the theory, became the foundation for a vigorous law of civil liberties and civil rights in the succeeding decades. Yet, footnote four arguments retained the individualistic focus of prior constitutional doctrine: The Constitution protected *individual* rights, and hostile legislation aimed at minorities was a close cousin of the class legislation at which constitutional concern had been directed in the prior generation.

Footnote four arguments supported three distinct branches of constitutional doctrine, dealing with voting rights, free expression, and discrimination. The Supreme Court understood that footnote four helped explain and justify its decisions overturning state laws and practices excluding African Americans from effective participation in Southern elections. It was initially more reluctant to develop a law dealing more broadly with apportionment, calling the area a "political thicket" (*Colegrove v. Green*, 1946), but by the 1960s and after what the justices regarded as their successful interventions in other fields, the Court adopted the "one person, one vote" standard for apportionments and enforced it with increasing rigor.

Free speech claims by union organizers led the Court in the early 1940s to start to develop a robust law of free expression, limiting local efforts to regulate picketing and other organizing techniques. The Court extended these precedents in the 1940s when presented with claims by Jehovah's Witnesses, whose door-to-door proselytizing and anti-Catholic rhetoric provoked sometimes violent reactions. The development of free speech law was affected as well by the Cold War, as the Court sporadically endorsed efforts to regulate the activities of members of the U.S. Communist party. As the perceived threat of domestic Communism receded, the Court pushed the bounds of free speech law even farther outward, protecting not only political expression but also explicitly sexual material and eventually commercial advertising. The early stages in the expansion of free speech protection fit comfortably within a footnote four theory, for restrictions on political speech clearly limited the public's ability to direct the development of public policy in legislation. As the boundaries of free speech expanded, the connection between protecting expression and promoting political liberty became increasingly attenuated.

African Americans formed the paradigmatic discrete and insular minority, and civil rights was a natural domain for footnote four jurisprudence. The cases the Court faced after the New Deal seemed conceptually easy. Statutes that explicitly used racial categories and singled out African Americans for disadvantageous treatment could easily be understood as aimed at a discrete and insular minority. Only slightly more troubling during the height of the civil rights movement were statutes that, while not identifying African Americans as such, clearly had a disproportionate adverse impact on them. The Court had not developed a mature jurisprudence of disparate treatment by the time Congress stepped in and in the Civil Rights Act of 1964 and later statutes made practices with a disparate racial impact *statutory* violations.

Successful litigation on behalf of African Americans generated similar efforts on behalf of other groups that could be characterized as minorities in some sense. Non-citizens living in the United States faced a number of legal disabilities in the provision of social welfare services and in limiting employment opportunities. Lacking the right to vote, non-citizens were readily brought into the domain of a footnote four jurisprudence, although the Supreme Court did allow governments to deny non-citizens access to jobs that, the Court believed, were closely bound up with the nation's definition of itself.

Women were not a statistical minority and had, since the Nineteenth Amendment, been fully enfranchised. Even so, women's rights groups took advantage of the footnote four jurisprudence. They identified statutes that reflected hostility to women's role in a modern nation through the adoption of stereotypes about the roles men and women should play in the workplace and, especially, in the family. In subjecting to close and skeptical examination laws classifying on the basis of gender, the Supreme Court drew the analogy between women and African Americans as historical targets of laws that improperly generalized about an individual's capacities and responsibilities.

Footnote four jurisprudence rested on the idea that the Supreme Court's role was to protect the institutions of democratic self-government against degradation by self-serving politicians. Initially a tool for liberal reformers, footnote four jurisprudence could be turned to more conservative ends through the concepts developed in the economic literature on public choice. Public choice scholars agreed that democratic political institutions could function badly, but they were more concerned with malfunctions arising because dispersed interests – like those of consumers – could mobilize less political power than concentrated special interest groups. They turned the rhetoric of democratic self-government against the interest group pluralism that was the characteristic form of liberal government from the New Deal through the Great Society years.

It was possible to cast some constitutional developments in the last quarter of the century in footnote four terms. Affirmative action programs, which came under close constitutional examination, could be described as resulting from a political bargain struck between racial minorities and upper- and middle-class whites, to the disadvantage of white members of the working class who were unable to protect themselves through ordinary political means. When the courts invoked the First Amendment to protect the interests of commercial advertisers and donors of large amounts of money to political campaigns, footnote four ideas could be brought to bear in arguing that the challenged statutes resulted from a legislative process distorted by the power of narrow special interest groups. These footnote four explanations, however, were strained. The better account of the changes referred more simply to the way in which specific construals of existing constitutional doctrine had become more compelling to judges, as the courts drifted from their commitment to the programmatic liberalism associated with the New Deal and the Great Society in the direction of a corporate-oriented conservatism associated with the presidency of Ronald Reagan.

Another constitutional jurisprudence competed with footnote four and gained increasing strength in the 1960s. This was a more purely individualistic and morally grounded account of constitutional rights. According to this account, free expression was important not simply because it was the means by which voters in a democracy became informed about public issues, but because self-expression was an important dimension of individual value. The moral reading of the Constitution made more sense of cases involving sexually explicit expression than did footnote four jurisprudence. However, its real power came in explaining the Court's development of a law of constitutional privacy and autonomous decision making in cases striking down laws restricting the distribution of contraceptives and, more important, in the Court's decisions invalidating laws restricting the availability of abortions.

Liberals interested in defending the Warren Court's rights-based jurisprudence were the initial proponents of the moral reading of the Constitution, but libertarian-minded conservatives also turned the moral reading against progressive reforms. These conservatives agreed that the Court's privacy decisions rested on the value of individual choice about important matters, but they argued that free choice in the market for ordinary goods was just as important to most people as choice with respect to reproduction was to women seeking abortions.

Liberals and libertarians could sometimes find common ground in moral readings. The most prominent example is the gay rights movement, which capitalized on liberal precedents protecting privacy against unwarranted government intrusion and on the individualistic ideology shared by libertarians and some liberals. The rights revolution had achieved much before the gay rights movement was able to advance, but proponents of gay rights built on the cultural transformation in gender roles that accompanied the rights revolution and on the revolution's conceptual underpinnings.

The moral reading and footnote four jurisprudence were the most prominent of several competing efforts to develop a conceptual apparatus that would explain and justify the Supreme Court's rights-based decisions in the second half of the twentieth century and that would also lay the groundwork for later developments. Each apparatus was available for use by political liberals and political conservatives, and yet each rested on widely shared individualist premises. As the rights revolution proceeded, problems arose that placed strains on the individualist conceptualization of constitutional rights, but no alternative, group-based conception took hold. Decisions and arguments for new constitutional protections that were explained more easily in group-based terms were vulnerable to displacement and dismissal. Three areas – race discrimination and affirmative action, social welfare rights, and what came to be known as third-generation rights, involving environmental and cultural rights – provide useful case studies of the way in which the law in the late twentieth century addressed the tension between a preferred individualist understanding of rights and a subordinate collectivist understanding.

Race Discrimination and Affirmative Action

Conceptual tensions arose first in connection with race discrimination. The first stages of desegregation were readily understood as vindicating individual rights. Indeed Thurgood Marshall argued against implementing desegregation with "all deliberate speed" precisely because courts justified delay on the ground that step-by-step implementation would integrate the schools more effectively in the long run, but acknowledged that delay meant that the rights of individual schoolchildren would be sacrificed in the interim. The focus shifted from individuals to groups when the Supreme Court got impatient with the pace of desegregation and demanded that schools implement plans that "worked." A plan that worked could only be understood as one that achieved some desired degree of actual integration, to be measured by examining how many whites and African Americans attended each school.

Beyond the law of desegregation, other aspects of race discrimination pushed the law toward acknowledging concern for the rights of African Americans taken as a group. The courts readily rejected laws that classified explicitly on the basis of race, as in segregation statutes and laws prohibiting racial intermarriage. The civil rights revolution made it clear, however, that the disadvantages suffered by African Americans resulted at least as much from laws that were not drawn in racial terms but that imposed disproportionate disadvantages on African Americans. In *Griggs v. Duke Power Co.* (1971), the Supreme Court agreed that the federal statute prohibiting racial discrimination in employment barred employers from using tests that had a disparate racial impact, such as a requirement that unskilled workers have a high-school degree. Advocates persuaded the courts that other anti-discrimination statutes should similarly be interpreted to bar practices with a disparate impact on minorities.

Legal theories, whether statutory or constitutional, that found practices unlawful because of their disparate impact were necessarily group oriented. Claims that a job applicant or employee had been discriminated against by being treated differently from other applicants or employees – known as disparate treatment claims – were clearly focused on individual claimants. Courts could identify the disparate impact of practices, though, only by looking at the effects of those practices in the aggregate, on the relevant groups.

The disparate impact theory had the potential to alter the status quo quite extensively; when confronted with constitutional challenges to statutes on the ground that they had a racially disparate impact, the Supreme Court rejected the claims. Justice Byron White observed accurately that holding statutes with a racially disparate impact unconstitutional "would raise serious questions about . . . a whole range of tax, welfare, public service, regulatory, and licensing statutes that may be more burdensome to the poor and to the average black than to the more affluent white" (*Washington v. Davis*, 1976). In the statutory context, claims of disparate impact remained available, although courts gradually became less receptive to them.

Affirmative action programs posed the most serious and sustained challenge to conceptions of rights cast in individualist terms. The earliest affirmative action programs, which consisted of self-conscious searches by employers for minority employees who could satisfy existing employment requirements, were easily understood in individualist terms: The guiding principle was to assure consideration of individual applicants for jobs on their individual merits, without race playing a role either in excluding the applicant from the job or, more important, in structuring the process by which individual applicants came to the employer's attention. President Lyndon B. Johnson, in a celebrated speech at Howard University, defended affirmative action programs in individualist terms, saying, "You do not take a person who, for years, has been hobbled by chains and liberate him, bring him up to the starting line of a race and then say, 'you are free to compete with all the others,' and still justly believe that you have been completely fair." Fairness to individuals was the hallmark of affirmative action.

As in the school desegregation context, however, government officials became impatient when they observed that these outreach efforts had little effect on the composition of employers' workforces or, as affirmative action programs expanded beyond employment to education, on the composition of university classes. As the courts had done earlier, government officials administering public programs began to demand affirmative action programs that "worked." Employers and university administrators began to set targets for their workforces and classes, seeking to ensure that racial minorities formed an appropriate proportion of their employees and students. Although the law rarely required numerical quotas, employers and universities found it easier to allay enforcement officials' concerns by demonstrating that the numbers matched some ideal target than by showing that low levels of minority employment or enrollment resulted from nondiscriminatory practices.

A conceptual elaboration accompanied the administrative transformation of affirmative action from an individual to a group focus. Affirmative action plans with implicit or explicit targets did not require that any individual who obtained a position demonstrate that he or she had personally been discriminated against by the employer or university or even by any identifiable wrongdoer. Understanding these programs as responses to discrimination, then, required looking to institutions rather than individuals for an account of discrimination. Proponents of affirmative action looked to a history of discrimination against African Americans, women, and other minorities. More generally, they argued that affirmative action was justified by what they called societal discrimination, which referred in large measure to the institutions and practices at which the law of disparate impact had been directed already.

Affirmative action rapidly became controversial politically. To the extent that its defenders relied on collectivist arguments, it was vulnerable to conceptual challenge in a society in which individualist accounts of rights had pride of place. Critics repeatedly emphasized that specific beneficiaries of affirmative action programs might not have been discriminated against in any conventional understanding of the term *discrimination*, that the costs of affirmative action were sometimes placed on people who could not be said to have participated in historic practices of discrimination, and that the concept of societal discrimination swept far too broadly to justify programs that spoke specifically in racial terms. Supreme Court justices referred to affirmative action programs as a form of *apartheid* and criticized the racial dimension of such programs. Concurring with the Court's decision in *Adarand Constructors, Inc. v. Pena* (1995), Justice Antonin Scalia wrote, "In the eyes of government, we are just one race here. It is American."

By the end of the twentieth century, the collectivist conceptual basis of affirmative action programs had been weakened severely, and no adequate individualist alternative had been developed. Still, the institutional pressures favoring affirmative action programs were strong enough that they persisted in only slightly diminished form in universities and public and private employment programs.

Social Welfare Rights

Social welfare rights – or entitlements, as they came to be called in the late twentieth century – had a significant place in the rights revolution. The United States never had as strong a welfare state as existed in Europe. Progressive reformers of the early twentieth century, particularly social workers and those they influenced, constructed some modest social welfare institutions, ordinarily targeted at what the reformers described as the "deserving" poor. The Great Depression substantially increased the numbers of people whose poverty was self-evidently not the result of their own choices. President Franklin Roosevelt's New Deal, in which Progressive lawyers and social workers played a large role, expanded social welfare institutions by creating programs of assistance to the needy and, more important, by establishing the Social Security system, a program of social provision for the elderly.

Building on these initial steps toward a large social welfare state, President Roosevelt in 1944 proposed that the United States commit itself to a "Second Bill of Rights," which would supplement the established guarantees of civil rights and civil liberties with new guarantees of social welfare rights, including "the right to a useful and remunerative job," "the right of every family to a decent home," and "the right to adequate medical care and the opportunity to achieve and enjoy good health." Roosevelt and his successor made little progress toward actually implementing this Second Bill of Rights. A proposal for guaranteed jobs was watered down in the Employment Act of 1946, which ended up merely as an exhortation to policymakers to seek full employment, and President Harry Truman's proposal for universal health care went down to defeat after a sustained campaign against it by the medical profession.

However, the New Deal had made some degree of social provision politically unassailable, and proponents of expanding the social welfare state continued to press their case. Their major victory came in the adoption of Medicare, a health insurance program for the elderly, and Medicaid, a similar program for the poor, during the administration of Lyndon Johnson. Advocates for the poor, implementing a strategy developed by sociologists Richard Cloward and Frances Fox Piven, organized their clients to demand the rights nominally already available in the law. Through the 1960s and into the 1970s, social welfare budgets, particularly those devoted to health and to the poor, increased substantially.

Some doctrine suggested that social welfare rights could become constitutionally protected. The doctrines were awkward because they had to fit what were essentially claims to collective rights into the strongly individualist framework of existing constitutional doctrine. Welfare advocates' major constitutional victory was *Goldberg v. Kelly* (1970), which, consistent with the Court's individualist focus, held that each person had a right to a hearing focusing on his or her individual circumstances before the government terminated a public assistance grant. Although the Supreme Court held that the Constitution required that the poor be provided with some minor benefits, mostly associated with participation in the criminal process, a robust constitutional doctrine guaranteeing social welfare rights never developed. The Court decisively rejected arguments that there was a constitutional right to housing or to employment. Nonetheless, the idea that social provision was an entitlement persisted.

Entitlements were subject to ready political attack because they were merely statutory. Increasing welfare budgets placed fiscal strain on state and local governments, and conservative Republicans found in public assistance programs a powerful metaphor for their general hostility to government programs. Entitlement reform, meaning reduction in social provision, became an important theme in American politics in the 1980s and 1990s. William Clinton, running as a "New Democrat," pledged to "end welfare as we know it" and, over the opposition of more traditional Democrats, signed welfare reform legislation in 1996 that ended public assistance as a permanent entitlement.

As president, Clinton still remained interested in social provision. His major social welfare initiative revived earlier proposals for universal health insurance. His proposal sought to rely on existing insurance mechanisms and used employers as the major conduit for providing health care insurance, which resulted in an extremely awkward design. By the 1990s physicians chafing under restrictions on medical practice imposed by insurance companies were significantly more enthusiastic about a federal health insurance program than they had been when Truman and Johnson sought to expand the federal role. But insurance companies mounted a fierce public relations campaign against Clinton's plan, which led to its defeat and to Republican victories in the 1994 elections.

President Clinton proposed coupling welfare reform with provision of subsidized child care and transportation to work for the poor, which would have eased the transition from welfare as an entitlement to welfare as temporary support. His weak political position forced him to accept welfare reform without these supplements. The individualist strain in U.S. social welfare policy was captured in the use of the term *personal responsibility* in the title of the 1996 welfare reforms. Poverty was not a condition attributable to the organization of the society and the economy; rather, it resulted from failures of personal responsibility, and social policy should target those failures rather than attempt to change social arrangements.

The idea of social provision remained important, however, albeit in a somewhat disguised form. The disabilities rights movement clearly originated in individualist concerns, that people with disabilities were being denied opportunities as a class because of prejudice and stereotypes that were not accurate as to particular individuals. Building on earlier statutes that addressed the concerns of religious adherents by requiring employers to accommodate the religious person's requirements by making reasonable alterations in work schedules and the like, the Americans with Disabilities Act (1990) required not simply non-discrimination, but reasonable accommodation for the disabled. These accommodations were responses to problems of disparate impact and in that respect were forms of social provision, imposed on public agencies as they designed their programs and on private employers in staffing their operations.

Third-Generation Rights: The Environment and Identity Politics

Conventionally, scholars describe traditional civil and political rights as first-generation rights and social welfare rights as second-generation rights. The third generation of rights is defined in part negatively, as rights that cannot be reduced to individual rights without losing important insights, and in part by an enumeration that identifies rights to environmental quality – or the rights "of" the environment – and rights of cultural minorities to preservation of their culture's distinctive practices such as language.

The environmental consciousness of the 1970s produced a new, non-individualistic right. An individualistic framework could encompass statutory guarantees of clean air and water and requirements that agencies take environmental considerations into account when they made their decisions – by saying, for example, that each person in the United States had a personal right to breathe clean air. But it was far easier to describe these rights as ones that inhered in the people collectively or even, to some environmentalists, in "the land" or in "nature" understood as something quite independent of human agency. The backlash at the end of the twentieth century against expansive interpretations of rights had a far less substantial effect in the environmental area than elsewhere, largely because the environment had become an issue with wide and deep support among the middle and upper classes. Critics could take aim at particular regulations as excessive and sometimes succeeded in scaling back environmental initiatives. But, the persistence of environmentalism showed that sometimes the usually subordinated collectivist conceptualization of rights could come to dominate the individualistic conceptualization.

Third-generation rights involving claims about the distinctive interests of cultural communities such as racial minorities were, in contrast, highly contentious, in large measure because they were in dramatic tension with the traditional understandings of civil rights. During the 1950s, historian Kenneth Stampp's major book on slavery, *The Peculiar Institution*, stated a common assumption of the time, that "innately Negroes *are*, after all, only white men with black skins, nothing more, nothing less." The civil rights and civil liberties traditions took rights to be universal, inherent in humans simply on the ground of their humanity. Racial discrimination was wrong, in the universalist view, because racial characteristics were irrelevant to anything that the law properly took as its subject. Defenses of race discrimination in the early twentieth century sometimes denied the universalist claim and argued that racial characteristics were themselves relevant to social decision making. By the 1960s if not before, that defense collapsed, and defenders of segregation were reduced to arguing against abrupt social transformations without challenging the need for change.

The mid-century women's movement raised more serious questions about universalism. The argument for women's suffrage combined an element that asserted that women were entitled to the vote as a civil right because they were just like men with one that asserted that women's distinctive culture and sensibilities could improve the quality of politics. Questions about the precise meaning of equal treatment for women persisted after Congress enacted laws prohibiting discrimination on the basis of sex and the Supreme Court began to invalidate statutes that reflected stereotypes about women's place in the economy and the home. Within legal circles, these questions – often described as a conflict between a "sameness" feminism that insisted that women should be treated exactly as men were and a "difference" feminism that insisted that equal treatment for women required accommodating what was distinctive about women – crystallized in debates over whether laws requiring employers to grant medical leaves for their pregnant employees violated the norm against sex-based discrimination. Those debates were resolved in practical terms by two federal statutes, one overturning a contrary Supreme Court decision, stating that discrimination based on pregnancy *was* discrimination based on sex, and the other subsuming pregnancy leaves into a broader class of parental and caregiving leave. Both statutes tended to support the "sameness" feminist position, but to the extent that each required somewhat greater accommodation to the distinctive needs of women, they provided some support for "difference" feminism as well.

The testing cases for third-generation cultural rights arose when some women's rights advocates and some minority legal scholars proposed that universities, cities, and states prohibit hate speech. The proposals varied in detail, but their common thrust was to make it an offense to use in public forums terms that were widely understood as disparaging racial minorities or women, generally when those terms were targeted at individual women or members of racial minorities in face-to-face confrontations but sometimes when the terms were used in a more general way. The hate-speech proposals did not themselves protect cultural characteristics directly, as other third-generation rights might, but they did rest on the proposition that language had a cultural context and to that extent were compatible with the premises of third-generation rights. These proposals, which were adopted by a significant number of universities and some legislatures, also reflected the increasing political power of women and racial minorities.

The hate-speech regulations were one form of identity politics and to that extent too reflected third-generation interests in the legal status of communities as distinct from their individual members. The courts, implementing traditional first-generation constitutional theories, concluded that regulation directed solely at hate speech was rarely permissible, but allowed criminal punishment to be increased when an already existing offense was motivated by group-based animosity (compare *R.A.V. v. St. Paul*, 1992, with *Wisconsin v. Mitchell*, 1993). Once again the legal system reached an uneasy compromise in which individualist conceptions of rights predominated but collectivist ones retained some purchase.

Another major arena of contest between individualist and collectivist versions of rights was language policy. The Civil Rights Act of 1964 prohibited discrimination on the basis of race and national origin. In *Lau v. Nichols* (1974) the Supreme Court held that schools denied equal opportunity, and therefore violated the 1964 Act, if they did not provide classes that enabled non-English-speaking students to learn English and other subjects. This decision produced a substantial constituency for bilingual education, both for a transition to full instruction in English and for significant substantive instruction in languages other than English. The largest group receiving bilingual instruction was Spanish speakers.

Here too a conservative backlash developed among people concerned about the demographic transformation of the United States in the late twentieth century. Focusing in part on unauthorized immigration, conservatives promoted "English-only" policies that insisted bilingual education be implemented only as a short-term policy to aid students in the transition from their home languages to full instruction in English. Some members of non-English-language communities supported reducing the scope of bilingual education as well, believing that their children should rapidly become fluent in English. Still, the nation's new demographics gave bilingual education an important enough constituency that the programs could be reduced but not eliminated.

The bilingual education controversy, and its association with questions of immigration policy, brought to light the deepest tensions within the dominant universalist discourse of rights. The universalist conception turned out not to be quite universal, because rights would be guaranteed to all *citizens*, not to every human being. A system of rights predicated on citizenship was inevitably a system predicated on recognizing the importance of at least one specific group, citizens of the United States. Legal doctrine struggled to resolve the tension by recurrently reducing the differences between the system's treatment of citizens and lawful resident aliens and by increasing the legal protections available even to those alleged to be present unlawfully in the United States.

III. THE CHALLENGE TO THE RIGHTS REVOLUTION

In each of its aspects the rights revolution faced significant opposition. Claims of rights were also claims about the allocation of political power, and successful claims necessarily altered power relations to someone's detriment. Sometimes opponents of rights claims responded with their own claims of rights. Property owners claimed that environmental regulations took their property without just compensation. Whites asserted that race-based affirmative action programs violated their right to protection against race-based discrimination. As rights claims came to be understood as interventions in pluralist politics, political backlash against expansive rights claims was common, forcing the retrenchment of previously achieved advances even though the rights themselves received the legal system's endorsement in concept.

By the late 1980s critics of the rights revolution had begun to develop a conceptual counterattack as well. Some critics styled themselves communitarians and drew on what they described as a republican, community-oriented tradition in political theory; others invoked the social teaching of the Catholic Church. In conventional political terms, these critics found themselves positioned to the right of both the more aggressive proponents of traditional civil rights and civil liberties and the advocates for third-generation rights, although some of the critics regarded themselves as working within a social democratic tradition that respected first-generation rights and sought to implement second-generation social welfare rights. Critics of the rights revolution in the social democratic tradition believed that second-generation rights could best be defended and advanced by developing collectivist conceptions of rights to counter the excessive individualism they saw in the rights revolution and, importantly, in capitalism itself.

The critics' common theme was that individualist conceptions of rights failed to take adequate account of the necessarily social nature and the social implications of legal rights. Recognizing "too many" rights, they argued, impaired the community's ability to constitute itself as a community, which required that members share values rather than treat themselves as wholly autonomous individuals as the rights revolution encouraged them to do.

Programmatically, some of these critics urged that community values be taken more into account when courts considered whether a law enforcement program violated individual rights, thereby working within established doctrines that called for balancing individual and social interests. For example, they supported efforts, rejected by the Supreme Court in *City of Chicago v. Morales* (1999), to allow local police to stop gang members from congregating at street corners. Harvard law professor Mary Ann Glendon argued that the excessive focus on individual rights that accompanied the rights revolution had had the effect of disparaging the deeply held views of many people who regarded collective values as equally important, and she sought to reconceptualize rights in a way that would express respect even in the course of rejecting those positions.

The critics of the rights revolution developed few institutions to support their initiatives, acting more as critics of the ACLU and other advocates of individual rights than as participants in directly legal struggles. The themes they sounded, however, resonated with aspects of the political opposition to the rights revolution, notably political calls for individuals to show greater responsibility in exercising rights they were conceded to possess.

CONCLUSION

The rights revolution occurred because institutional elements combined with ideological trends. The existence of numerous venues for the assertion of rights claims made rights-based arguments particularly attractive, for losses in one venue need not preclude victories elsewhere. Rights-oriented litigation organizations emerged as lawyers and other technocrats began to play a large role in structuring public policy. Moving from purely defensive to affirmative litigation, these groups prodded the courts to develop remedial measures that subjected government bureaucracies to greater oversight by the courts, the public, and other government bureaucracies. Initial successes for rights-oriented claimants gave other groups models for their own organizations. Rights claims spread from the left to the right, a move aided by the individualism that pervaded most rights-based claims and that was readily accommodated to some elements of conservative political thought. Perhaps most important, by the end of the century, rights-based claims had lost whatever special weight they gained from appealing to something transcendent about the U.S. Constitution and became arguments of the usual sort in pluralist politics.

The rights revolution of the twentieth century faced substantial challenges at the century's end, but the institutions and concepts that fueled it remained powerful. Because assertions of rights had become typical elements in the characteristically pluralist politics of the United States, the institutions of the rights revolution – innovations in procedural law as well as in the organization of groups to support litigation – had support from the political beneficiaries of rights claims. As with most pluralist bargaining, pluralist politics over the institutions of the rights revolution produced modest changes as the political fortunes of those beneficiaries waned. But, because the beneficiaries retained significant political power, the changes were only incremental. The wide scope of possible rights claims gave groups across the political spectrum an interest in preserving large parts of the modern institutions on which the rights revolution had relied.

The deep individualism of the rights revolution flowed from, and supported, fundamental cultural and therefore legal commitments among the American people. Always vulnerable to challenge from alternative, more community-oriented commitments, individualist conceptions of rights retained their predominant place in legal discourse, sometimes straightforwardly defeating collectivist conceptions but more often relegating those conceptions to a distinctly subordinate position in legal discourse.

12

RACE AND RIGHTS

MICHAEL J. KLARMAN

Profound changes in American racial attitudes and practices occurred during the second half of the twentieth century. The U.S. Supreme Court often receives substantial credit for initiating those changes. In this chapter I examine the social and political conditions that enabled the modern civil rights revolution and situate the Court's racial rulings in their historical context. As we shall see, the Court's decisions reflected, more than they created, changing racial mores and practices. Even *Brown v. Board of Education*, so often portrayed as the progenitor of the civil rights movement, was rendered possible only by sweeping social and political forces that emanated mainly from World War II.

I. BETWEEN THE WORLD WARS

As World War I ended in 1918, few would have predicted that the U.S. Supreme Court would one day become a defender of the rights of racial minorities or that its rulings would have a significant impact on the struggle of blacks for racial equality. Late in the nineteenth century, the Court in *Plessy v. Ferguson* (1896) had declared state-imposed racial segregation consistent with the Equal Protection Clause of the Fourteenth Amendment; in *Williams v. Mississippi* (1898) the justices had rejected constitutional challenges to state measures that disfranchised blacks. Court rulings such as these led a black newspaper in the North to opine in 1913 that "the Supreme Court has never but once decided anything in favor of the 10,000,000 Afro-Americans in this country"; the recently formed National Association for the Advancement of Colored People (NAACP) concluded in 1915 that the Court "has virtually declared that the colored man has no rights." Even when the Court in the second decade of the twentieth century invalidated local ordinances mandating racial segregation in housing and so-called grandfather clauses (which immunized illiterate whites from the disfranchising effect of literacy tests), those decisions had no discernible effect on residential segregation or black disfranchisement.

Yet, it was around this time that the social and political conditions that would foster transformative racial change were beginning to develop. The Great Migration of blacks from the rural South to the urban North, which began in response to wartime labor shortages in Northern industry, enhanced black political power: hundreds of thousands of blacks relocated from a region of pervasive disfranchisement to one that extended the suffrage without racial restriction. The rising economic status of blacks in the North eventually facilitated social protest, as blacks acquired a measure of economic independence from whites and the resources necessary to finance collective protest. More flexible racial mores in the North permitted blacks to challenge the racial status quo in ways that would not have been tolerated in the South.

As some Southern blacks migrated north, others moved from farms to cities within the South. Better economic opportunities in urban areas fostered a black middle class, which capitalized on the segregated economy to develop the wealth, leisure time, and economic independence from whites necessary for participation in social protest. Urban blacks were better educated, which proved important for organizing civil rights movements. Because racial etiquette in the cities was somewhat less oppressive, urban blacks were freer to participate in politics and other forms of protest activity. Urbanization also reduced the collective-action barriers to establishing a social movement. Urban blacks lived closer to one another, enjoyed better communication and transportation, and shared social networks – such as black colleges and churches – that helped overcome the organizational obstacles that confront any social-reform movement.

World War I also had more immediate implications for race relations, including the ideological ramifications of a "war to make the world safe for democracy." Blacks who had set aside their special grievances to close ranks with whites, borne arms for their country, and faced death on the battlefield were not hesitant about asserting their rights. Returning black soldiers demanded access to the ballot. Heightened black militancy proved an enormous boon to the NAACP, whose national membership increased ninefold between 1917 and 1919.

Such developments eventually enabled civil rights protest, yet in the 1920s the immediate prospects for American blacks were bleak. Black migration fed the racial prejudice of Northern whites, who resisted the movement of blacks into their neighborhoods with racially restrictive covenants, hostile neighborhood associations, economic pressure, and violence. Segregation in Northern housing increased dramatically in the 1920s and translated directly into increased school segregation. The influx of *white*

Southerners to Northern cities further exacerbated racial tensions and contributed to the postwar political successes of the Ku Klux Klan in many Northern and Western states.

Southern blacks had it much worse than their Northern counterparts. Many Southern counties with large black populations did not provide high schools for blacks until the 1930s. With regard to parks, playgrounds, and beaches, separate-but-equal frequently meant that blacks got nothing. Fearful that returning black soldiers would launch a social revolution, Southern whites had prepared for a race war. Black soldiers were assaulted, forced to shed their uniforms, and sometimes lynched. In Orange County, Florida, thirty blacks were burned to death in 1920 because one black man had attempted to vote. In 1919, when the NAACP's national secretary, John Shillady, traveled to Austin, Texas, to defend a beleaguered branch from state legal harassment, a white mob beat him nearly into unconsciousness.

The outlook for blacks was little better at the national level. The racial policies of national administrations in the 1920s were abysmal. After Southern Democrats in 1922 filibustered an anti-lynching bill passed by the House, Republicans dropped the measure for the remainder of the decade. Republican administrations did not curtail segregation and discrimination in the federal civil service, they did not appoint blacks to patronage positions from which the Southern-sympathizing President Woodrow Wilson had removed them, and they did not support black factions in struggles for control of Southern Republican parties. The NAACP told its followers in the mid-1920s that Republican presidents were no better than Democrats, "and Democratic presidents are little better than nothing."

The Great Depression of the 1930s left blacks in worse condition economically than ever before, and race discrimination pervaded early New Deal programs. Yet, the New Deal proved to be a turning point in American race relations. Its objective was helping poor people – and blacks, as the poorest of the poor, benefited disproportionately. Perhaps more important was its racial symbolism. However discriminatory its administration, the New Deal at least included blacks within its pool of beneficiaries – a development sufficient to raise black hopes and expectations after decades of malign neglect from Washington. President Franklin D. Roosevelt appointed a "black cabinet" of advisors within departments. Eleanor Roosevelt, another important symbol of progressive racial change, served as an intermediary between black leaders and the administration and also wrote newspaper columns criticizing discrimination.

Roosevelt quickly became the most popular president among blacks since Abraham Lincoln. With the New Deal making some Northern states electorally competitive for the first time in a generation, and blacks no longer dependably voting Republican, both parties had renewed incentives to appeal for black votes. An unprecedented thirty black delegates attended the Democratic national convention in 1936; a black minister gave the invocation and a black Congressman the welcoming address. Republicans also bid for black votes with a more progressive civil rights platform.

By the second half of the 1930s, racial attitudes and practices in the South were becoming slightly more progressive. Black voter registration increased, and in a few cities blacks ran for local office for the first time in generations. Defunct branches of the NAACP came back to life. Racial disparities in education funding slowly declined outside the Deep South. Opinion polls revealed that the majority of white Southerners supported federal anti-lynching legislation.

Incipient racial progress was also occurring in the North. The New Deal inspired Northern blacks to register to vote in record numbers. Increased political power produced more black officeholders and stronger public accommodations laws. Some Northern churches began criticizing racial segregation, and Catholic schools started admitting blacks.

By 1940 blacks had greater reason for optimism than at any time since Reconstruction; however, actual changes in racial policies had been minor. President Roosevelt continued to oppose civil rights bills, which still could not survive Senate filibusters. The disfranchisement of Southern blacks remained nearly universal outside of the largest cities, and school segregation remained deeply entrenched in the South and was spreading in the North.

Supreme Court rulings on race during the interwar period reflected these social and political conditions. The most striking civil rights triumphs came in four criminal cases that revealed Southern Jim Crow at its worst. *Moore v. Dempsey* (1923) involved six blacks sentenced to death for a murder allegedly committed during an infamous race riot in Phillips County, Arkansas. The justices reversed these convictions on the ground that trials dominated by the influence of a lynch mob violate the Due Process Clause. *Powell v. Alabama* (1932) and *Norris v. Alabama* (1935) involved the infamous Scottsboro Boys episode. Nine black youths, aged thirteen to twenty – impoverished, illiterate, and transient – were charged with raping two white women on a freight train in northern Alabama in 1931. They were tried in a mob-dominated atmosphere, and eight of the nine received death sentences. The Supreme Court twice reversed their convictions – the first time because the right to counsel had been abridged and the second time because of race discrimination in jury selection. *Brown v. Mississippi* (1936) reversed the death sentences of three black sharecroppers convicted of murdering their white landlord. The confessions of the defendants constituted the principal evidence of guilt, and these had been extracted through torture. The Court ruled that such convictions violate due process.

These four cases arose from three similar episodes. Southern blacks were charged with serious crimes against whites – rape or murder. Mobs consisting of thousands of whites surrounded the courthouses and demanded that the defendants be turned over for execution. Lynchings were barely avoided. The defendants' guilt was in serious doubt. Several of the defendants were tortured into confessing. Defense lawyers were appointed at most a day before the trials, which lasted at most a few hours. Juries, from which blacks were intentionally excluded, deliberated only a few minutes before imposing death sentences.

Not one of these defendants was plainly guilty; it is entirely possible that all of them were innocent. Yet, guilt or innocence was often beside the point when Southern blacks were accused of killing white men or sexually assaulting white women. The defendants in these four Court cases would possibly have been lynched before World War I. However, by the interwar period, the annual number of lynchings had declined dramatically. That decline had many causes, including the ability of Southern states to replace lynchings with quick trials that dependably produced guilty verdicts, death sentences, and swift executions. Prosecutors in such cases often urged juries to convict in order to reward mobs for good behavior.

State-imposed death sentences in such cases were little more than formalizations of the lynching process. Such farcical proceedings invited intervention by Supreme Court justices who believed that criminal trials were supposed to determine guilt, not simply prevent lynchings. Had the injustices been less obvious, the Court might have been reluctant to interfere. Federal courts were restrained from supervising state criminal trials by a long tradition grounded in federalism concerns. Yet, even justices who showed little solicitude for the interests of blacks were offended by trials that amounted to legal lynchings.

Between the world wars the Court also considered several constitutional challenges to "white primaries." Because the Democratic Party dominated Southern politics after the 1890s, excluding blacks from primary elections effectively nullified their political influence. But in *Nixon v. Herndon* (1927), the Court invalidated a Texas statute that barred blacks from primary elections. *Herndon* was unanimous, commanding support even from those justices who were least sympathetic to the rights of blacks. Only one state, Texas, had seen fit to bar blacks from primary elections by statute; in other states, a similar result was accomplished by party rule.

In subsequent white-primary cases, the justices confronted the intractable question of state action: for which discriminatory behavior of private actors is the state constitutionally accountable? After *Herndon*, the Texas legislature immediately passed a law that empowered party executive committees to prescribe membership qualifications, and the Democratic Party executive then quickly passed a resolution excluding blacks. By a 5–4 vote, the justices in *Nixon v. Condon* (1932) found the state constitutionally responsible for the exclusion on the ground that the Texas legislature, not the state Democratic Party, had empowered the executive committee to prescribe membership qualifications.

Condon's only effect was to defer for three years the more fundamental state-action question: did the Constitution permit a political party to bar blacks from membership? Three weeks after *Condon*, the annual convention of the Texas Democratic Party resolved to exclude blacks. *Grovey v. Townsend* (1935) unanimously declined to find state action under these circumstances.

Grovey is a confusing opinion. Justice Owen Roberts conceded the ways Texas regulated primaries – for example, requiring that they be held and that voter qualifications be the same as in general elections. He found two differences between primary and general elections dispositive on the issue of state action: in primary elections, Texas did not cover the expenses, nor did it furnish or count the ballots. Even so, Roberts failed to explain why certain forms of state involvement in primaries, but not others, constituted state action.

The Court's failure to find state action in *Grovey* reveals in two ways how little the racial attitudes of the justices had changed by 1935. First, general conceptions of the appropriate spheres of public and private authority underwent dramatic change in the 1930s. The Great Depression and the New Deal led many Americans to deem the state responsible for economic arrangements that previously were considered private; when markets generally produced desirable results, government failure to regulate them had seemed to warrant less accountability. The Court's non-racial jurisprudence reflected such shifting perceptions of state responsibility. In 1934 the justices obliterated the public/private distinction in cases of economic regulation and enabled legislatures to intervene in areas that had previously been deemed private and thus beyond legislative purview. This shift should have had implications for state action under the Fourteenth Amendment: if the "private" sphere was no longer constitutionally immune from government regulation, then the state could more easily be held accountable for its choice not to regulate it. That the justices failed to integrate changing conceptions of government responsibility into their equal protection jurisprudence says something about their racial attitudes.

Second, the justices could have found state action in *Grovey* without ruling that inaction was tantamount to action. The more heavily a state regulated political parties, the less difficult it would be to ascribe to it responsibility for areas not regulated. Texas regulated political parties in many ways. Indeed, Texas even restricted party membership decisions. For Texas to tell state Democrats that they could not exclude persons based on membership in social clubs, but (implicitly) that they could exclude them based on race, made the state seem much more responsible for the party's exclusion of blacks than if the state had not regulated membership at all.

Thus, the justices' determination that the exclusion of blacks by the Texas Democratic Party was not state action indicates a relative indifference toward race discrimination in the political process. Indeed, public opinion regarding black suffrage in the South probably had not changed much since 1900 when blacks had been largely disfranchised. Through the 1920s, prominent Republicans continued to lament the Fifteenth Amendment as a great mistake. And through the mid-1930s, the national Democratic Party and the Roosevelt Justice Department showed no interest in interfering with Southern white primaries.

During the interwar years the Court also declined to intervene against "private" actions that produced housing segregation. In *Corrigan v. Buckley* (1926), the justices unanimously rejected a constitutional challenge to racially restrictive covenants on land, dismissing as patently insubstantial the claim that the private covenants were themselves state action. Although the opinion observed that the appeal did not challenge *judicial enforcement* of the covenants, the justices indicated that such a claim would also have been insubstantial. Yet, judicial enforcement of such covenants was plainly a kind of state action; precedent had clearly established that judicial decrees, like executive orders or legislation, could constitute the state action necessary for a constitutional violation. The real question in *Corrigan* was not whether the state had acted when enforcing these covenants but whether its action amounted to unconstitutional discrimination. If courts enforced all private contracts regardless of their terms, then the enforcement of racially restrictive covenants would seem less like discrimination and more like neutral support for a regime of private contractual freedom. But in the 1920s courts did not enforce a regime of universal contractual liberty. Although all state courts enforced restrictions on the use or occupancy of land, their response to restraints on sale varied, depending on the length of the restriction and the number of parties covered. If courts were unwilling to enforce certain restrictive covenants, then it could be argued that the choice to enforce others was one for which the state should be held accountable.

The social and political context of race relations may explain why the justices found permissible the judicial enforcement of racially restrictive covenants. The Great Migration spawned by World War I transformed residential segregation from a Southern issue to a national one. Northern blacks endured bombings, cross burnings, and mob assaults as they sought to escape ghettos by purchasing homes in white neighborhoods. By the 1930s, the Federal Housing Agency explicitly promoted restrictive covenants, and the U.S. Housing Authority selected public housing projects with an eye toward preserving segregated housing patterns. With the political branches of the national government legitimizing restrictive covenants and residential segregation, the justices were disinclined to interfere.

Nor do the justices of this era appear to have been troubled by state-mandated racial segregation in public schools. In *Gong Lum v. Rice* (1927) the Court rejected a Chinese American's challenge to Mississippi's decision to send her to a black school rather than a white one. Technically, Gong Lum did not challenge school segregation. Her principal argument was that Mississippi denied equal privileges to the Chinese by combining them with blacks while whites enjoyed separate schools. Chief Justice William Howard Taft's opinion for a unanimous Court failed to address that argument. Instead, he interpreted the case to pose the question that lower court precedent had laid to rest – the constitutionality of public school segregation – and dismissed that challenge almost out of hand.

In 1927 school segregation was as securely grounded as ever. Many Northern cities that had enjoyed integrated schools before World War I experienced increased segregation afterward. Northern black communities were divided over whether to challenge such segregation, which usually ensured jobs for black teachers and enabled black students to avoid the hostility and insults that they often endured in integrated schools. Southern blacks knew better than to challenge an aspect of Jim Crow that was so dear to whites. NAACP policy in the interwar period was to contest the spread of school segregation in the North but not in the South, where it was so entrenched that a legal challenge would have been fruitless and possibly suicidal. The *Gong Lum* case was brought by Mississippi Chinese, not the NAACP. And because Gong Lum herself did not contest segregation and because Mississippi Chinese were not blacks, a prestigious local law firm took the case, and a respected trial judge granted relief, without alienating local opinion. Blacks who challenged school segregation in the South would have received very different treatment.

Only toward the end of this era did the Court give some hint of the role it would soon play in race cases. *Missouri ex rel. Gaines v. Canada* (1938) challenged out-of-state tuition grants to blacks who sought graduate and professional education denied to them in Missouri. Court decisions interpreting the Fourteenth Amendment had long established that separate must be equal to be constitutional. Yet in *Gaines*, Missouri purported to extend equal treatment, offering to subsidize blacks' law school tuition, just as it did for whites. To be sure, blacks had to pursue their education outside of the state, though whites did not. Yet, segregated education inevitably offered different opportunities to blacks and whites. Courts applying separate-but-equal principles had ruled that the Constitution required only "substantial equality."

Gaines was a case of first impression, requiring clarification of the equality prong of separate-but-equal. The Court concluded that out-of-state travel was substantial inequality, but did not explain why. The justices expressly disavowed reliance on obvious inequalities, such as Missouri's failure to subsidize travel and other living expenses. Instead, they observed that "[t]he basic consideration is not as to what sort of opportunities other States provide . . . but as to what opportunities Missouri itself furnishes." Yet it was Missouri, not some other state, that provided resident blacks with tuition grants.

In light of the Court's unconvincing rationale, the *Gaines* result suggests that the justices had simply become more solicitous of civil rights claims. By 1938, with black professionals playing unprecedented roles in federal administrative agencies, the justices may have found incongruous the wholesale exclusion of blacks from higher education in the South. Ten years earlier, *Gaines* would not have been argued by a black lawyer such as Charles Hamilton Houston, who demonstrated through his Harvard legal pedigree and his forensic skills what blacks could achieve if afforded equal educational opportunities. Moreover, by 1938 several justices were becoming more attentive to the interests of racial and religious minorities – partly as a reaction against the oppressive practices of foreign totalitarian regimes.

By the late 1930s the NAACP was detecting "a new South . . . in the making." Several thousand blacks had registered to vote in large Southern cities, and racial disparities in educational funding were starting to narrow. By 1939 the number of blacks lynched annually had fallen to three. During the 1930s the NAACP's national membership grew by more than 150 percent. Southern branches obliterated by the white supremacist backlash that had followed World War I showed new signs of life.

Such changes, though significant, must be kept in perspective. In Congress, the era ended much as it began – with a Senate filibuster of the most rudimentary civil rights legislation, the anti-lynching bill. Despite the liberalism of the Roosevelt administration, the president felt too politically beholden to the South to endorse anti-lynching or anti-poll tax legislation. In 1940, blacks in the rural South remained almost completely disfranchised and excluded from jury service.

The Supreme Court's rulings on race during this era conformed to this social and political context. As the racial attitudes of the nation began to change, so did those of the justices. Criminal procedure rulings imposed constitutional constraints on Southern lynch law at practically the same moment Congress was deliberating on – and might have passed, were it not for the anti-majoritarian filibuster rules of the Senate – laws against lynching. Yet, changes in the constitutional jurisprudence of race were not dramatic in the 1920s and 1930s. Public school segregation remained as secure at the end of this era as it had at the beginning. Nor did this Court question the constitutionality of most Southern methods for disfranchising blacks. It would have been nearly as hard to predict at the start of World War II as it had been at the conclusion of World War I that the Supreme Court would ever play a prominent role in the liberation of black Americans.

II. WORLD WAR II AND ITS AFTERMATH

World War II was a watershed in the history of American race relations. The ideology of the war was anti-fascist and pro-democratic. Blacks realized the paradox in America's fighting against world fascism with a segregated army, and they added a second front to the war, making it a fight against fascism at home as well as abroad. Many blacks reasoned that if they were good enough to fight, they were also good enough to vote.

If the cognitive dissonance created by a Jim Crow army fighting Aryan supremacists was insufficient to induce most Americans to reconsider their racial practices, Axis propagandists' exploitation of American racial hypocrisy supplied more concrete incentives. Within forty-eight hours of the lynching of Cleo Wright – a black man – in Sikeston, Missouri, in 1942, Axis radio transmitted the details around the world. The federal government had previously disclaimed jurisdiction over lynchings by private citizens. Now, however, Attorney General Francis Biddle explained that lynchings had acquired international significance and thus came under federal control.

During the war, blacks began more forcefully demanding their citizenship rights. Southern blacks registered to vote in record numbers and demanded admission to Democratic primaries. Weary of Jim Crow indignities, many Southern blacks refused to be segregated any longer on streetcars and buses, stood their ground when challenged, and thus provoked almost daily racial altercations. Hundreds of thousands of blacks channeled their militancy into NAACP membership, which increased ninefold during the war. A. Philip Randolph, the head of the Brotherhood of Sleeping Car Porters, threatened to mobilize one hundred thousand blacks to march on the nation's capital in 1941 to protest racial discrimination in the military and defense industries. Desperate to avoid such a spectacle, Roosevelt issued an executive order that banned employment discrimination in defense industries and in the federal government and established a Fair Employment Practices Commission (FEPC) to monitor compliance.

Black political clout increased during the war. The strategic importance of black voters in the North inspired the House to pass anti-poll-tax bills every two years in the 1940s. Fear of alienating Northern blacks helped convince Democratic leaders to reject South Carolinian Jimmy Byrnes, formerly a white supremacist senator from South Carolina, as a vice-presidential candidate in 1944. Harry S Truman, who received that nomination, had voted for anti-lynching and anti-poll-tax bills in the Senate. After the war, partly as a result of growing black political influence, Truman became a civil rights enthusiast. In 1948 he proposed sweeping civil rights legislation and issued executive orders desegregating the military and the federal civil service. In the fall, Truman won a stunning reelection; the support of black voters in the North was critical to his victory.

The Cold War, together with America's postwar emergence as an international superpower, also aided progressive racial change. As Americans and the Soviets competed for the allegiance of a predominantly non-white Third World, American race relations acquired greater international significance. In the ideological contest with Communism, American democracy was on trial, and Southern white supremacy was its greatest vulnerability. One State Department expert estimated that nearly half of all Soviet propaganda directed against the United States involved racial issues.

Actions undertaken by the national government show that the social and political context of race had shifted dramatically by the late 1940s. The Justice Department vigorously prosecuted lynchings and submitted briefs in civil rights cases, anti-lynching and anti-poll-tax bills were passed by the House, and President Truman pursued various civil rights initiatives. Outside of government, one development of great symbolic significance was the desegregation of professional baseball, which began in 1946–47. By the late 1940s, church leaders of most denominations were condemning racial segregation, and Hollywood movies for the first time confronted such issues as interracial marriage and lynching.

In the South, the commitment of whites to Jim Crow was less intense than it had been before, thus paving the way for gradual racial reform. Black voter registration increased fourfold in the 1940s. Protection against police brutality was a top priority for many blacks, and many Southern cities hired their first black police officers after the war. Southern cities also began providing black communities with better public services and recreational facilities, and states increased their spending on black education. Cracks began to appear in the walls of segregation. Many cities, including some in the Deep South, desegregated their minor league baseball teams, and in the peripheral South some blacks began playing football for formerly white colleges. In many border-state cities, Catholic parochial schools admitted their first black students, and public swimming pools, theaters, and some lunch counters in department stores and drugstores desegregated.

In the North, hundreds of organizations devoted to improving race relations and promoting civil rights reform were established in the late 1940s. Northern states and cities passed a barrage of civil rights legislation after the war, including novel fair employment measures and stringent mechanisms for enforcing bans on school segregation.

Shifts in the broader racial environment profoundly influenced the Court's racial jurisprudence. In *Smith v. Allwright* (1944), the justices voted 8–1 to overrule *Grovey* (1935) and invalidate the white primary. This was a stunning reversal, within only nine years, of the unanimous *Grovey* decision. The timing of *Smith* is probably not accidental: the justices cannot have missed the contradiction between black soldiers dying in a war purportedly being fought for democratic ends and the pervasive disfranchisement of Southern blacks. Almost simultaneously with *Smith*, Congress was debating a bill to repeal poll taxes in federal elections as well as a more limited suspension of poll taxes for members of the armed services. The same democratic ideology that inspired Congress to consider these measures probably influenced judicial thinking about the white primary.

One further variation on the white primary remained for the justices' consideration. In Fort Bend County, Texas, the Jaybird Democratic Association, whose membership consisted of all whites residing in the county, selected candidates who then invariably became Democratic nominees and were elected to office. At the conference discussion of *Terry v. Adams* (1953), the justices expressed concern that approving the Jaybirds' scheme would practically overturn *Smith*. However, finding state action here risked eliminating protection for private political association – protection that several of the justices believed that the First Amendment guaranteed. An initial vote at conference revealed that the justices were split 5–4 in favor of *rejecting* the constitutional challenge. Eventually, however, they overcame their doubts and by an 8–1 vote invalidated the Jaybirds' scheme.

After World War II, the Court also decided cases involving segregation in higher education. When Heman Sweatt demanded admission to the all-white University of Texas School of Law, the state set up a separate black law school. In 1950 the Court ruled it inadequate and ordered Sweatt's admission to the white law school. In addition to noting the tangible features of the black school that were obviously inferior, such as the size of the faculty and the number of books in the library, the justices emphasized intangible differences between the two schools, such as the reputation of the faculty and the stature and influence of the alumni. Most commentators believed that *Sweatt* had nullified segregation in higher education.

The same day as the decision in *Sweatt* was announced, the Court in *McLaurin v. Oklahoma* ordered the graduate education school of the University of Oklahoma to cease segregating – in classrooms, the library, and the cafeteria – a black man it had admitted pursuant to federal court order. George McLaurin was receiving a tangibly equal education, but the justices apparently would no longer accept segregation *within* an institution of higher education. *Sweatt* had proscribed segregation in *separate* institutions. The two decisions, in combination, seemed to leave nowhere for segregation to go.

These rulings were not as easy for the justices to decide as the unanimous outcomes might suggest. At the conference in *Sweatt*, Chief Justice Fred M. Vinson noted a long list of precedents that had sustained separate-but-equal education. He also stated that the Fourteenth Amendment had not been directed at segregated education – a view with which Justices Stanley Reed and Robert Jackson indicated agreement.

The *Sweatt* and *McLaurin* rulings, which were in tension with the legal sources to which these justices generally looked for guidance – precedent and original intent – are best explained in terms of social and political change. By 1950 major league baseball had been desegregated for several years, and the military services were undergoing gradual desegregation. The administration intervened in these 1950 cases to urge that *Plessy* be overruled, invoking the Cold War imperative for racial change. The Court's first black law clerk, William T. Coleman, had served two terms earlier and authored a memo to Justice Felix Frankfurter endorsing the same view. Coleman's very presence at the Court demonstrated that segregated legal education could no longer be defended on the basis of supposed black inferiority. Moreover, several justices noted at conference that segregation in Southern higher education was already eroding, and thus their rulings were unlikely to generate much resistance.

The postwar Court also considered challenges to residential segregation. The dearth of new housing construction during the Great Depression and World War II, combined with the massive increases in urban populations resulting from internal migration, led to severe housing shortages. The problem was especially acute for blacks because in some Northern cities a huge percentage of housing stock was covered by racially restrictive covenants. *Shelley v. Kraemer* (1948) was an injunction suit to keep a black family from taking possession of property covered by such a covenant. The defendant argued that judicial enforcement would violate the Equal Protection Clause. Precedent on this issue was about as clear as it ever gets. Not only had dicta in *Corrigan* (1926) denied that judicial enforcement of racially restrictive covenants was unconstitutional, but all nineteen state courts that had considered the issue had reached the same conclusion.

Precedent notwithstanding, *Shelley* barred the use of injunctions to enforce racially restrictive covenants. Vinson's opinion explained that judicial orders, like legislation and executive action, can qualify as state action – a point that nobody had disputed. Indeed, the Court had ruled many times that judges discriminating in jury selection or devising common law rules, such as restrictions on union picketing, were state actors bound by the

Constitution. Yet Vinson's rationale, if taken seriously, threatened to obliterate the private sphere, as *all* behavior occurs against a backdrop of state-
created common law rules. Vinson missed the real issue in *Shelley*: was
judicial enforcement of private housing covenants – both those that discriminated based on race and those that did not – the sort of discrimination
that was proscribed by the Constitution?

By 1948 public attitudes toward race discrimination specifically and
state responsibility for private wrongs generally had changed enough to
enable the justices to decide *Shelley* as they did. The Great Depression and
the New Deal altered conceptions of government responsibility for conduct
occurring in the private sphere. The Four Freedoms articulated in President
Roosevelt's famous 1941 inaugural address included freedom "from want"
and "from fear" – not typical negative liberties protected against government interference, but affirmative rights to government protection from
privately inflicted harms. A principal function of the Justice Department's
civil liberties unit, which was created in 1939, was to protect citizens from
private interferences with their rights. During and after World War II, the
justices responded to such changed understandings of government responsibility by expanding the state-action concept in both racial and non-racial
contexts.

Perhaps even more important to the outcome in *Shelley* were changes
in racial attitudes. *Shelley* was decided the same year that a national civil
rights consciousness crystallized. Earlier in 1948 Truman had endorsed
landmark civil rights legislation, and the issue of civil rights played a significant role in the presidential election that year. Truman's civil rights
committee had specifically recommended legislation to prohibit racially
restrictive covenants, and it successfully urged the administration to intervene in litigation challenging their judicial enforcement. Moreover, restrictive covenants, unlike many racial issues, directly affected other minority
groups – Jews, Asians, Latinos, Native Americans – whose collective interests were likely to command the attention of New Deal justices.

In the years during and after the war, the Court also decided several cases
involving discrimination and segregation in transportation. These issues
had generated legal rulings from as far back as the late nineteenth century.
Soon after the enactment of the Interstate Commerce Act in 1887, the
Interstate Commerce Commission (ICC) interpreted the statutory ban on
"undue or unreasonable prejudice or disadvantage" to forbid racial inequality but not segregation. By the early 1900s, the ICC had become lax in
enforcing the equality prong of separate-but-equal. Yet *McCabe v. Atchison,
Topeka & Santa Fe Railway Co.* (1914), which construed the Equal Protection
Clause rather than the Interstate Commerce Act, denied that blacks could
be excluded from luxury accommodations merely because of their lower

per capita racial demand. *McCabe* arose under the Constitution because Oklahoma *law* authorized the exclusion of blacks. In *Mitchell v. United States* (1941) the same issue arose under the Interstate Commerce Act, because it was railroad policy, not state law, that authorized the discrimination. Yet, the Court had long applied the same substantive standards under these different legal regimes, and the railroad's justification for excluding Mitchell from Pullman accommodations was the same one that had been rejected in *McCabe*. Thus, *Mitchell* was not difficult for the justices, who unanimously invalidated the exclusionary policy.

Even without *McCabe* on the books, the Court in 1941 might easily have invented its rationale. Though not yet ready to invalidate segregation, the Court would no longer turn a blind eye toward blatant racial inequality. *Gaines* (1938) had suggested as much. By 1941 the federal government had made several concessions to black political power, and that year Roosevelt issued the first executive order on race since the Emancipation Proclamation, creating the Fair Employment Practices Commission. Moreover, Arthur W. Mitchell was a U.S. Congressman. The justices cannot have been eager to permit a Southern railroad to exclude a black Congressman from accommodations available to whites as the nation became embroiled in a world conflict that would redefine the meaning of democracy. Even white newspapers in the South generally endorsed *Mitchell*.

Henderson v. United States (1950) raised a similar issue. By the time this case reached the Supreme Court, the policy of the Southern Railway was to allocate exclusively to blacks one table, located behind a wood partition, out of eleven tables in the dining car. The ICC upheld this practice on the ground that blacks, though generating less than 5 percent of dining car demand, were receiving 9 percent of seating space. The Supreme Court unanimously reversed this ruling. Several High Court precedents had insisted that equal protection rights are "personal" – that is, they belong to individuals, not groups. Thus, the relevant question in *Henderson* was not whether blacks received the same *average* benefits as whites, but whether particular blacks received the *same* benefits as particular whites. The answer was clearly not. A black person who entered the dining car when the "black" table was full would be denied service, whereas a white person arriving simultaneously might be served. This was racial inequality, as the justices had previously defined it. Yet, as in *Sweatt*, the justices in *Henderson* were still not ready to explicitly bar segregation under the Equal Protection Clause.

The Court actually did condemn segregation in transportation, but under the Dormant Commerce Clause, which forbids certain state laws that threaten to disrupt interstate commerce. *Morgan v. Virginia* (1946) invalidated a state law that required segregation on common carriers, as applied to an interstate bus passenger. In one sense, that result was completely unexceptionable: The Court had made clear since the 1870s that state laws that regulated the seating of interstate passengers on steamboats or railroads – whether they compelled or forbade segregation – violated the Dormant Commerce Clause. Yet, beginning about a decade before *Morgan*, the Court had begun to transform doctrine in this area to permit the states significantly greater regulatory leeway. *Morgan* was difficult to reconcile with such rulings.

The justices' growing solicitude for civil rights probably explains this doctrinal disjuncture. A Gallup poll conducted in the late 1940s revealed that national opinion opposed racial segregation in interstate transportation by 49 percent to 43 percent. Perhaps more important, the justices realized that Southern whites would be less resistant to ending segregation in interstate transportation than in public education. Interracial contact on buses was transitory, impersonal, and generally involved adults, not children – all features distinguishing it from grade-school education. The availability of a non-racial doctrine such as the Dormant Commerce Clause to achieve a result that the justices found personally congenial may have proved irresistible. This rationale forbade segregation only in interstate travel and thus did not directly threaten other forms of segregation – an important limitation, given that Justice Frankfurter later observed that he would not have supported a school segregation challenge in the mid-1940s.

While the Court during this era was invalidating the white primary, segregation in higher education and in interstate transportation, and judicial enforcement of racially restrictive covenants, Congress remained unable to pass a single civil rights bill. Every two years in the 1940s, the House passed anti-poll-tax measures, which then failed in the Senate. In 1950 a bill mandating fair employment practices also failed to survive a Senate filibuster. The drafters of the Fourteenth Amendment had anticipated that Congress, not the Court, would be its primary enforcer. This assumption was vindicated in the 1870s, but was belied during and after World War II. What accounts for the postwar Court being so much more racially progressive than Congress?

Anti-majoritarian features of the Senate are the strongest explanation. The House surely reflected majority national opinion when it passed anti-poll-tax bills in the 1940s. But the Senate is not majoritarian. Under then-governing procedural rules, a two-thirds vote was necessary to cut off a filibuster. Moreover, committee chairs exercised inordinate influence over legislation. When Democrats controlled Congress, as they usually did during this period, Southerners tended to control committee chairmanships by virtue of their greater seniority.

The Court's relative progressiveness on civil rights may have another explanation as well. Though the constitutional interpretations of the justices generally reflect their times and culture, these individuals occupy an elite subculture, characterized by greater education and higher economic status. On many policy issues that become constitutional disputes, opinion correlates strongly with socioeconomic status, with elites holding more liberal views on social and cultural issues (though not on economic ones). Early in the twenty-first century, such issues include gay rights, abortion, and school prayer; in the postwar period, racial segregation and discrimination were such issues.

III. *BROWN* AND ITS AFTERMATH

On May 17, 1954, the Court in *Brown v. Board of Education* unanimously invalidated racial segregation in public schools. The Court emphasized the importance of public education in modern life and refused to be bound by the intentions of the drafters of the Fourteenth Amendment, most of whom had held more benign views of segregation. Segregated public schools were, according to the Court, "inherently unequal" and thus violated the Equal Protection Clause.

Brown's unanimity can be misleading. When the school segregation cases were first argued in the fall of 1952, the outcome was uncertain. Initially, only four justices – Hugo Black, William O. Douglas, Harold H. Burton, and Sherman Minton – were clearly prepared to invalidate school segregation. Two others – Chief Justice Fred Vinson and Justice Stanley F. Reed – were inclined to sustain it. Three – Felix Frankfurter, Robert H. Jackson, and Tom C. Clark – appeared undecided.

For several of the justices, *Brown* was difficult because it posed a conflict between the law, as they perceived it, and their personal preferences. Frankfurter and Jackson may have been the most conflicted in this regard. Both abhorred racial segregation. In a 1950 letter, Jackson, who had earlier left the Court for a year to prosecute Nazis at Nuremberg, wrote to a friend: "You and I have seen the terrible consequences of racial hatred in Germany. We can have no sympathy with racial conceits which underlie segregation policies." Yet, both justices were committed to maintaining the distinction between law and the personal values of judges. The problem for them (and perhaps to a lesser extent, for the other justices) was that the traditional legal sources to which they looked for guidance – text, original intent, precedent, and custom – pointed more toward reaffirming than overruling *Plessy*.

Jackson explained his dilemma in a draft opinion that he ultimately decided not to publish: "Decision of these cases would be simple if our personal opinion that school segregation is morally, economically or politically indefensible made it legally so." When he turned to the question of whether existing law condemned segregation, however, Jackson had difficulty answering in the affirmative. He saw no explicit prohibition of segregated schools in the text of the Fourteenth Amendment. With regard to its legislative history, he concluded, "It is hard to find an indication that any influential body of the movement that carried the Civil War Amendments had reached the point of thinking about either segregation or education of the Negro as a current problem, and harder still to find that the amendments were designed to be a solution." As for precedent, Jackson noted, "Almost a century of decisional law rendered by judges, many of whom risked their lives for the cause that produced these Amendments, is almost unanimous in the view that the Amendment tolerated segregation by state action." Unable to "justify the abolition of segregation as a judicial act," Jackson agreed to "go along with it" as "a political decision."

Fearing irreconcilable differences among themselves, the justices decided in June 1953 to set the school segregation cases for reargument the following term. Then, in September, Chief Justice Vinson died suddenly of a heart attack – Frankfurter recorded his death as "the first indication I have ever had that there is a God" – and President Eisenhower appointed Governor Earl Warren of California to replace him. At the justices' conference after the reargument, the new Chief Justice opened the discussion by announcing that "[the] 13th, 14th and 15th Amendments were intended to make equal those who once were slaves." Warren could not "see how segregation can be justified in this day and age." Anyone counting heads – and all of the justices were – would have immediately recognized that the outcome in *Brown* was no longer in doubt.

With the result settled, two factors encouraged unanimity. First, the justices understood that white Southerners would receive *Brown* belligerently and perhaps violently. Resisters would be sure to exploit any hint of internal Court dissension. Justices who disagreed with the outcome thus felt pressure to suppress their convictions for the good of the institution. Second, after December 1953 ambivalent justices such as Frankfurter and Jackson were irrelevant to the outcome, whereas a year earlier they had controlled it. Perhaps they would have allowed their constitutional views to trump their personal predilections if it affected the outcome, but not for the sake of a dissent.

For justices to reject a result so clearly indicated by the conventional legal sources suggests that they had very strong personal preferences to the contrary. Why were these justices so repulsed by segregation at a time when national opinion was divided roughly down the middle? One possibility is chance: integrationists just happened to dominate the Court in 1954. A more satisfying explanation emphasizes the culturally elite biases of Supreme Court justices. In 1954, 73 percent of college graduates approved of *Brown*, in contrast to only 45 percent of high-school dropouts. Racial attitudes and practices were changing rapidly in postwar America. As members of the cultural elite, the justices were among the first to be influenced.

As they deliberated over *Brown*, the justices expressed astonishment at the extent of the recent changes. In his draft opinion, Jackson observed that "Negro progress under segregation has been spectacular and, tested by the pace of history, his rise is one of the swiftest and most dramatic advances in the annals of man." Frankfurter similarly noted "the great changes in the relations between white and colored people since the first World War," and he remarked that "the pace of progress has surprised even those most eager in its promotion." These justices understood that their ruling in *Brown* would be working with, not against, the current of history.

Brown struck down public school segregation, but imposed no immediate remedy, deferring that issue to the following term. In *Brown II*, decided on May 31, 1955, the justices opted for a vague and gradualist remedy. They remanded the cases to district courts to issue decrees in accordance with "local conditions." They required a "prompt and reasonable start toward full compliance," with additional time allowed if "consistent with good faith compliance at the earliest practicable date." District courts were to order the parties admitted to public schools on a non-discriminatory basis "with all deliberate speed."

Several factors may account for this temporizing result. An informal deal had enabled the Court to be unanimous in *Brown I*; several justices had insisted on gradualism as their price for voting to invalidate segregation. The justices also strongly opposed issuing unenforceable orders, which could injure the Court. Justice Minton, for example, urged that the Court not "reveal its own weakness" with a "futile" decree. The unlikelihood that Congress or the president would support immediate desegregation heightened this concern. Furthermore, the justices feared that immediate desegregation would cause violence and school closures. Sympathy toward the plight of white Southerners may also have inclined the justices toward gradualism: They felt guilty about undermining the expectations of those who had assumed the legitimacy of the separate-but-equal doctrine based on prior Court rulings. Finally, several justices believed that they could defuse resistance among Southern whites by appearing sympathetic and accommodating.

Southern politicians and newspapers lauded *Brown II* as a distinct victory for the South: the Court had approved gradualism, imposed no deadlines for beginning or completing desegregation, issued vague guidelines, and entrusted (Southern) district judges with broad discretion. The justices had conceived of gradualism partly as a peace offering to white Southerners – an invitation to moderates to meet them halfway. Some Southern politicians understood this and applauded the Court for its moderate and reasonable decision. Yet, others perceived *Brown II* as judicial weakness or backtracking and concluded that threats of school closures and violence had intimidated the justices. Some expressed hope that further pressure might persuade the Court to abandon *Brown* altogether, just as Northern whites had abandoned Southern blacks during Reconstruction.

The justices backed off after *Brown II*. With the notable exception of the Little Rock case, *Cooper v. Aaron* (1958), they distanced themselves from school desegregation for the next eight years. The justices apparently had decided to say no more on the subject until they had received some signal of support from the political branches. That signal was not immediately forthcoming. President Dwight Eisenhower repeatedly refused to say whether he endorsed *Brown*. Asked by reporters for a message to youngsters on desegregation, he repeated the mantra of Southern whites that "it is difficult through law and through force to change a man's heart." Congress did not support the Court either. Throughout the 1950s, liberal Congressmen failed even in their efforts to pass symbolic statements affirming that *Brown* was the law of the land. Congress did finally pass weak civil rights legislation in 1957, but a proposal to empower the Attorney General to bring desegregation suits was eliminated, with the president's assent, from the final bill. The tepid commitment of politicians to the enforcement of *Brown* was mirrored by that of their constituents: polls revealed that national majorities of nearly four to one preferred gradualism to immediate action.

The Court briefly reentered the fray during the Little Rock crisis. In September 1957, after Governor Orval Faubus of Arkansas used the state militia to block enforcement of a court desegregation order, President Eisenhower sent in the army's 101st Airborne Division to implement the decree. Several blacks attended Central High under military guard during the 1957–58 school year. The situation was chaotic. Hundreds of white students were suspended for harassing blacks, and there were more than twenty bomb threats. Early in 1958 the Little Rock school board petitioned the federal district judge for a reprieve of two and a half years to allow community resistance to subside. He granted it. The court of appeals reversed him, and the justices then convened in special session that summer to determine whether a district judge could delay school desegregation, once it had begun, owing to community resistance.

Cooper v. Aaron was not difficult for the justices, who understood that rewarding violent resistance in Little Rock by postponing desegregation would encourage similar behavior elsewhere. *Cooper* was a forceful opinion, and one might have inferred from it that the justices would now aggressively monitor the desegregation process. But the apparent boldness of the interventions by the president and the Court was misleading. Eisenhower had used federal troops only after a governor's blatant defiance of a desegregation order. The justices had acted primarily to support the president. Neither party had abandoned gradualism.

IV. *BROWN*'S IMPACT

What were the consequences of *Brown*? Large cities in border states, such as Baltimore and St. Louis, desegregated almost immediately (although, in practice, formal compliance with *Brown* did not usually translate into substantial race mixing). *Brown* pushed against an open door in these cities, where rapidly changing racial attitudes smoothed the way for peaceful school desegregation. The eleven states of the former Confederacy responded to *Brown* very differently than did the border states. Other than in a relatively few districts in Tennessee, Arkansas, and Texas, no desegregation at all occurred until 1957. On *Brown*'s sixth anniversary in 1960, 98 of Arkansas's 104,000 black school students attended desegregated schools, 34 of North Carolina's 302,000, 169 of Tennessee's 146,000, and 103 of Virginia's 203,000. In the five Deep South states, not one of the 1.4 million black schoolchildren attended a racially mixed school until the fall of 1960. As late as 1963, only 1.06 percent of Southern black students attended desegregated schools.

How could *Brown* have been so inefficacious for so long outside of the border states? The answer lies partly in the incentives of Southern school boards and federal judges for non-compliance and partly in the constraints faced by Southern blacks and the NAACP. The burden of implementing *Brown II* initially lay with school board members. Most of them undoubtedly thought that *Brown* was wrongheaded, as did most white Southerners, so their inclinations were to delay and evade as much as possible. Board members had additional incentives to avoid compliance with *Brown*: Those responsible for desegregating schools received hate mail, had crosses burnt on their lawns, suffered economic reprisals, and even endured physical violence. They faced little pressure from the opposite direction. Until local litigation produced a desegregation order, they ran no risk of contempt sanctions. Criminal prosecution and civil damages actions were also unlikely, as defendants in such suits have a right to a jury trial, and white jurors – blacks remained almost entirely absent from juries in the South until the 1960s – were unlikely to convict public officials for resisting desegregation. Given these lopsided incentives, few school boards desegregated until courts ordered it or at least until blacks threatened to litigate.

Accordingly, the implementation of *Brown* depended on the ability of black parents to bring suits and on the willingness of federal judges to order desegregation. Neither condition was easily satisfied. *Brown* technically bound only school board defendants in five cases. Thus, litigation was necessary in every Southern school district – of which there were thousands – in which resistant boards declined to desegregate voluntarily. Because few blacks could afford to litigate, virtually all desegregation litigation involved the NAACP. Comprehending this situation, Southern whites declared war on the association. States passed laws seeking access to NAACP membership lists, the disclosure of which would have exposed members to economic and physical reprisals. Private segregationist organizations known as white citizens' councils ensured that known NAACP members lost their jobs, credit, and suppliers. More than one lawyer representing the association in school desegregation litigation had his home bombed.

Even when the NAACP financed litigation, individual blacks still had to enlist as plaintiffs. The association desperately solicited litigants, but in the Deep South few blacks volunteered. Hundreds of blacks who signed school desegregation petitions in Deep South cities in 1954–55 suffered swift and severe retribution, which clearly deterred prospective litigants. Not a single black in Mississippi sued for grade school desegregation until 1963. In Georgia the first desegregation suit outside of Atlanta was not filed until 1962. In Alabama the first suit outside of Birmingham was not filed until 1963. Ironically, suits proliferated where desegregation was already farthest along.

Litigation could only bring the issue before a judge, who would have to determine whether, when, and how schools would desegregate. In 1954 all Southern federal judges were white, the vast majority had been born and raised in the South, and their views on school desegregation did not deviate far from those of most white Southerners. Many of them were openly disdainful of *Brown*, and almost none endorsed it publicly. The view expressed by Judge George Bell Timmerman of South Carolina was typical: whites "still have the right to choose their own companions and associates, and to preserve the integrity of the race with which God Almighty has endowed them," and "[t]he judicial power of the United States ... does not extend to the enforcement of Marxist socialism as interpreted by Myrdal, the Swedish Socialist." Even those judges who were less viscerally hostile to *Brown* were subject to influence by the disapprobation of friends and colleagues and by the threats of vigilantes. Judges who issued desegregation orders endured hate mail, harassing midnight phone calls, and cross burnings outside of their homes.

Even when judges eventually ordered desegregation, most of them endorsed gradualism and tokenism. Pupil placement laws, which were adopted by all Southern states, authorized administrators to place students according to a long list of racially neutral factors, such as psychological fitness, scholastic aptitude, and the availability of space and transportation.

Although race was not an enumerated criterion, the purpose and effect of these plans were to enable administrators to maintain segregation, yet insulate the system from legal challenge because of the difficulty of proving that a multifactor decision was racially motivated. Refusing to presume discriminatory administration, lower courts generally declined to invalidate pupil placement plans on their face, and the Supreme Court concurred. School districts that eschewed pupil placement in favor of neighborhood schools generally offered liberal transfer options that curtailed desegregation. The vast majority of both whites and blacks exercised their prerogative to leave desegregated schools to which they had been assigned. Courts sustained such plans well into the 1960s. When Congress passed the 1964 Civil Rights Act, still only one or two black children in a hundred attended a racially mixed school in the South. The federal judiciary, acting without significant support from either Congress or the president, had proved powerless to accomplish more.

Even so, Supreme Court rulings can direct public attention to previously ignored issues, and *Brown* surely had this intangible consequence. *Brown* forced many people to take a position on school segregation. Before *Brown*, desegregation of the military and of major league baseball had been salient issues; school segregation was not. In 1952 neither the Democratic nor the Republican national party took a position on school segregation, but in 1956 both of them did, and so did all major presidential candidates.

That *Brown* forced people to take a position on school segregation is not to say that it influenced the position they took. Some endorsed it and others condemned it. Southern politicians, forced to confront an issue that many of them would have preferred to avoid, overwhelmingly denounced *Brown*. By contrast, Northern liberals, who may not have had much prior occasion to consider school segregation, now condemned it as a moral evil. In the mid-1950s any serious Democratic presidential candidate also had to endorse *Brown*, as did most national religious organizations.

But being forced to take a position in favor of *Brown* did not equate to being strongly committed to implementing the ruling. One could endorse *Brown* without supporting the use of federal troops to enforce it or the termination of federal education funds for districts that defied it. According to 1956 Gallup polls, more than 70 percent of whites outside of the South thought that *Brown* was right, but less than 6 percent considered civil rights the nation's most important issue. In the South, where more than 40 percent thought that civil rights was the leading issue, only 16 percent of whites agreed with *Brown*. In the mid-1950s those whites with the strongest feelings about *Brown* generally disagreed with it the most vehemently.

Conventional wisdom holds that one of *Brown*'s most important consequences was to educate white Americans to condemn racial segregation. Yet,

Americans generally feel free to disagree with the Supreme Court and to make up their own minds about moral controversies. Rather than educating people to oppose the death penalty, *Furman v. Georgia* (1972), which ruled capital punishment unconstitutional under certain circumstances, seems to have mobilized support for it. Polls suggest that *Roe v. Wade* (1973), which invalidated most statutes criminalizing abortion, has not changed many minds on that subject. If landmark decisions such as these educated few people to agree with the Court, why should *Brown* have?

Indeed, opinion poll data suggest that *Brown* did not educate many Southern whites. A 1959 Gallup poll showed that only 8 percent of them supported *Brown*, *down* from 16 percent in earlier polls. Rather than persuading Southern whites to support desegregation, *Brown* inspired them to ridicule the Court and to recommend impeaching its members or at least investigating them for Communist influence. Southern whites were not educated by a decision that they believed ignored precedent, repudiated original intent, and infringed on the reserved rights of states. The Southern newspaper editor James J. Kilpatrick stated a typical view: "In May of 1954, that inept fraternity of politicians and professors known as the United States Supreme Court chose to throw away the established law. These nine men repudiated the Constitution, sp[a]t upon the tenth amendment, and rewrote the fundamental law of this land to suit their own gauzy concepts of sociology."

Most Northern whites did not ridicule *Brown*, and many of them strongly endorsed it, but they were not necessarily educated by it. Powerful social and political forces impelled Americans toward more egalitarian racial views, quite independently of the Court's pronouncements. Moreover, poll data reveal no large shift in Northern attitudes toward school segregation in the years after *Brown*, as one might have expected if the ruling were truly educational.

Brown was, of course, not needed to educate *blacks* about the evils of segregation. Yet the decision unquestionably motivated them to challenge the practice. After *Brown*, blacks petitioned school boards for immediate desegregation on threat of litigation in hundreds of Southern localities, including in the Deep South, where race relations had hitherto been least affected by impulses for racial change. One might have predicted that a campaign for racial reform in this region would have begun with voting rights or the equalization of black schools, not with school desegregation, which was hardly the top priority of most blacks and was more likely to incite violent white resistance. *Brown* plainly shifted the focus of Southern blacks to school desegregation.

Brown motivated litigation, but did it inspire direct-action protest, such as the Montgomery bus boycott in 1955–56, or the sit-ins, Freedom Rides, and street demonstrations of the early 1960s? There is no denying *Brown*'s symbolic importance to blacks. Many black newspapers treated *Brown* as the greatest victory for civil rights since the Emancipation Proclamation, and they reported that the ruling had blacks literally dancing in the streets. Because a principal obstacle confronting any social reform movement is convincing potential participants that success is feasible, *Brown* certainly facilitated the mobilization of civil rights protest.

Yet neither the symbolism of *Brown* nor the hopefulness it inspired were tantamount to putting black demonstrators on the streets. The Montgomery bus boycott was an epic event in the civil rights movement, but if *Brown* directly inspired the boycott, it is puzzling that protestors for the first two months did not include integration among their demands. Rather, they mainly sought an end to the insulting behavior of white bus drivers and the adoption of a seating policy that would fill buses on a first-come, first-served basis – whites from the front and blacks from the rear. At the outset of the boycott, black leaders repeatedly stressed that they were not seeking an end to segregation, which would have been the logical goal had *Brown* been their primary inspiration. Moreover, a similar bus boycott had occurred the year before *Brown* in Baton Rouge, Louisiana, proving that direct-action protest did not require the inspiration of the Court.

After Montgomery, little direct-action protest took place in the South until 1960, when the region exploded with such activity: sit-ins, Freedom Rides, and street demonstrations. The nearly six-year gap between *Brown* and the landmark sit-in demonstrations in Greensboro, North Carolina, in February 1960 suggests that any connection between the events is indirect and convoluted. The outbreak of direct-action protest can be explained independently of *Brown*: background forces created conditions that were ripe for racial protest. As Southern blacks moved from farms to cities, they organized more easily as a result of superior urban communication and transportation facilities and the growth of black institutions that provided a framework for social protest. The rising economic status of Southern blacks enabled the financing of protest activities as well as boycotts to leverage social change. Better education for blacks created leaders who could direct social protest. A better educated white population meant that there were fewer diehard segregationists. Greater restraints on violence also facilitated direct-action protest. The increasing political power of Northern blacks made the national government more supportive of the civil rights protests of Southern blacks. The growing political power of Southern blacks made local officeholders more responsive to the concerns of the black community. The explosive growth of national media, especially television, ensured that news of black protest spread quickly to other Southern communities, where it could be duplicated, and to the North, where sympathetic audiences

rallied in support of its goals. The ideology of racial equality that suffused
World War II left fewer white Americans empathetic with Jim Crow. Black
soldiers who served during and after the war were not easily intimidated
by the threats of white supremacists, and they often found intolerable the
incongruity between their role as soldiers for democracy and their racially
subordinate social status.

Conditions for a mass racial protest movement were ripe, but that does
not explain why the explosion came in 1960 rather than, say, five years
earlier. Two factors may help explain the precise timing of the modern civil
rights movement. First, in the 1950s, with a dire threat of nuclear holocaust
and Americans in a frenzy over McCarthyite charges of rampant domestic
subversion, the time was inopportune for social reform movements, which
were vulnerable to charges of being Communist-inspired. Liberal organizations such as the NAACP devoted considerable energy in the early 1950s to
purging left-wingers. By 1960, fear of domestic subversion had subsided,
and the threat of nuclear holocaust had receded, if only slightly. According
to this view, the civil rights revolution of the 1960s had little to do with
Brown and much to do with the demise of McCarthyism and the slight
easing of Cold War tensions, which had proven temporary impediments to
a protest movement mainly spawned by World War II.

Second, the decolonization of Africa may also help explain why direct-
action protest broke out in 1960 rather than a few years earlier. American
civil rights leaders identified the African freedom movements as an important motivation for their own. The successful efforts of African colonies
to win independence beginning in the late 1950s demonstrated to American blacks the feasibility of racial change through collective action while
heightening their frustration with the domestic status quo. As black author
James Baldwin famously put it, "all of Africa will be free before we can get
a lousy cup of coffee." The decolonization of Africa may have provided the
spark that was necessary to detonate a social protest movement that was
already set to explode.

It is possible that *Brown discouraged* direct-action racial protest more than
it inspired it. The NAACP's enormous Court victory encouraged blacks
to litigate, not to protest in the streets. *Brown* also elevated the stature
of the NAACP among blacks, and the association favored litigation and
lobbying, not direct-action protest. Though speculative, this claim about
Brown's influence has the virtue of explaining the relative absence of direct-
action protest in the middle to late 1950s. Before World War II, sit-ins
and street demonstrations were probably impractical in most of the South,
because they would have elicited violent suppression. The Montgomery bus
boycott demonstrated that conditions had changed by the mid-1950s. Yet,
even after Montgomery, little direct action occurred until 1960.

Despite Montgomery, the NAACP leadership remained committed to the same litigation tactics of the last half-century and rejected pleas from some branches in the late 1950s to support direct action. The association had a vested interest in discouraging alternative strategies of protest that it could not monopolize, and it was composed of lawyers, who by nature were disinclined to march in the streets. In 1960 and 1961, association leaders initially opposed the sit-in demonstrations and the Freedom Rides. Only after such protests proved enormously popular and successful did the NAACP change tack and emphasize its involvement in such activities from the very beginning. Yet even then, association leaders continued to misunderstand the significance of direct action. While Martin Luther King, Jr. was urging student demonstrators to go to jail to arouse the nation's conscience, the NAACP was telling them to take bail, and it was trying to convert the sit-ins into test cases for challenging the constitutionality of laws that protected the right of shopkeepers to racially segregate their customers.

The NAACP's predominant focus on litigation was myopic, given the limited capacity of litigation to transform race relations. Litigation did not foster black agency – the belief among individual blacks that they could meaningfully contribute to racial change. Rather, it taught the lesson that blacks should sit back and allow elite lawyers and white judges to transform race relations for them. Litigation could not involve large numbers of blacks in the same way that boycotts, sit-ins, and street demonstrations could. Moreover, litigation was limited in its capacity to generate conflict and violence – conditions that proved indispensable to transforming Northern opinion on race. By contrast, white supremacist vigilantes and law enforcement officers had difficulty restraining themselves when confronted with black street demonstrators.

In the short term, *Brown* may have delayed direct action by encouraging litigation. But this consequence of the decision was self-correcting: Within a few years, it became clear that litigation without a social movement to support it could not produce significant social change. Over the long term, *Brown* may have encouraged direct action by raising hopes and expectations, which litigation then proved incapable of fulfilling. Alternative forms of protest arose to fill the gap. One cannot precisely measure the connection between black frustration over the pace of court-ordered desegregation and the explosion of direct-action protest, but many contemporaries explicitly identified such a linkage.

Brown contributed to direct-action protest in another way as well. Before *Brown*, most white Southerners had grudgingly tolerated the NAACP, but afterward the association became an object of consuming hatred for them. Southern whites proved enormously creative at translating this animosity into legal and extra-legal mechanisms for attacking the organization. Alabama shut down NAACP operations for eight years (1956–64), and Louisiana and Texas for briefer periods. The association's Southern membership fell from 128,000 in 1955 to 80,000 in 1957, and nearly 250 branches shut down.

With the NAACP under assault, Southern blacks had no choice but to support alternative protest organizations. Black ministers, many of whom held prominent positions in NAACP branches, formed new organizations, such as the Southern Christian Leadership Conference (SCLC). Such groups used the NAACP's base of supporters, but they deployed their resources differently. Thus, by inciting massive retaliation against the NAACP, *Brown* ironically fostered new organizations that lacked the association's institutional and philosophical biases against direct action.

Brown had another, possibly more important consequence: It generated white-on-black violence, often in settings where it was broadcast to national television audiences. Virtually every year after *Brown*, school desegregation resulted in violent resistance somewhere in the South. These episodes tarnished the national image of white Southerners. Most Americans believed that judicial rulings should be obeyed, even by those who strongly disagreed with them; the alternative was anarchy. For individuals to violate court orders was bad enough, but mob resistance was even worse. In addition, violent confrontations over school desegregation tended to reveal blacks at their best and whites at their worst. The few blacks who had been handpicked as desegregation pioneers were almost always middle class, bright, well mannered, and nonviolent. The mobs that sought to exclude them from white schools tended to be lower class, vicious, profane, and unruly.

Brown also crystallized Southern whites' resistance to racial change, radicalized Southern politics, and increased the likelihood that direct-action protest, once it erupted, would incite a violent response. Civil rights demonstrators of the early 1960s often sought racial reforms that were less controversial than school desegregation – voting rights for blacks, desegregated lunch counters, and access to better jobs. If not for the fanaticism that *Brown* inspired in Southern politics, such demands might have been received sympathetically or at least with less violence.

Brown may have directly fostered white vigilante violence against blacks. Polls revealed that 15 to 25 percent of Southern whites favored violence, if necessary, to resist desegregation. Most Southern politicians avoided explicit exhortations to violence, and many affirmatively discouraged it. But the extremist rhetoric they used to condemn *Brown* probably encouraged violence. A speech by Congressman James Davis of Georgia was typical: He insisted that "[t]here is no place for violence or lawless acts," but only after he had called *Brown* "a monumental fraud which is shocking, outrageous

and reprehensible," warned against "meekly accept[ing] this brazen usurpation of power," and denied any obligation on "the people to bow the neck
to this new form of tyranny."

The linkage between particular public officials who benefited from the
post-*Brown* political backlash in the South and the brutality that inspired
civil rights legislation is compelling. T. Eugene ("Bull") Connor, Birmingham's fiery Commissioner of Public Safety since 1937, had been run out of
politics in the early 1950s by local business and civic leaders who considered his racial extremism harmful to the city's image. After Connor's ouster,
racial progress rapidly ensued, including the establishment of the first hospital for blacks, desegregation of elevators in downtown office buildings,
and serious efforts to desegregate the police force. After *Brown*, Birmingham's racial progress ground to a halt, and Connor resurrected his political
career. In 1957 he regained his seat on the city commission by defeating an
incumbent he attacked as weak on segregation. In the late 1950s, a powerful Klan element wreaked havoc in Birmingham by launching a wave of
unsolved bombings and other brutality. The police, under Connor's control,
declined to interfere. Standing for reelection in 1961, Connor cultivated
extremists by offering the Klan fifteen minutes of "open season" on the
Freedom Riders as they rolled into town. Connor won a landslide victory
at the polls.

In 1963 the SCLC, looking to conduct demonstrations in a city with
a police chief who was likely to respond with violence, selected Birmingham partly because of Connor's presence there. The strategy worked
brilliantly: Connor unleashed police dogs and fire hoses against demonstrators, many of whom were children. Television and newspapers featured
images of police dogs attacking unresisting demonstrators, including one
that President John F. Kennedy reported made him sick. Newspaper edi-
torials condemned the violence as a national disgrace. Citizens voiced their
outrage and demanded legislative action to curb such savagery. The Birmingham demonstrations dramatically altered Northern opinion on race and
enabled passage of the 1964 Civil Rights Act.

Perhaps more than any other individual, George Wallace personified the
post-*Brown* racial fanaticism of Southern politics. Early in his postwar political career, Wallace had been criticized as "soft" on segregation. Soon after
Brown, however, he felt the changing political winds, broke with Alabama's
racially moderate governor, Big Jim Folsom, and cultivated conflict with
federal authorities over race issues in his capacity as circuit judge. In 1958
Wallace's principal opponent in the Alabama governor's race was the state
attorney general, John Patterson, who bragged of shutting down NAACP
operations in the state. The Klan endorsed Patterson, whom Wallace criticized for not repudiating the endorsement. Patterson won easily, leaving

Wallace to ruminate that he would never be "outniggered" again. Wallace made good on that promise in 1962, winning the governorship on a campaign promise of standing in the schoolhouse door to defy federal integration orders.

In June 1963, Wallace fulfilled that pledge by physically blocking the admission of blacks to the University of Alabama – before, in a carefully planned charade, stepping aside in the face of superior federal force. Wallace continued, however, to promise a forceful stand against grade-school desegregation, which federal courts had ordered in Alabama for the fall. In September Wallace used state troops to block school desegregation in several cities, and he encouraged extremist groups to wage a boisterous campaign against desegregation in Birmingham, which they did, leading to a minor race riot. Threatened with judicial contempt citations, Wallace eventually relented. The schools desegregated, but within a week tragedy had struck, as Birmingham Klansmen dynamited the Sixteenth Street Baptist Church, killing four black schoolgirls. Most of the nation was appalled by the murder of innocents, and Wallace received much of the blame. One week after the bombing, tens of thousands across America participated in memorial services and marches. Northern Congressmen, reflecting their constituents' anger, introduced amendments to strengthen the administration's pending civil rights bill.

Early in 1965, the SCLC brought its voter registration campaign to Selma, Alabama, a site chosen partly because of the presence there of a law enforcement officer of Bull Connor-like proclivities, Dallas County sheriff Jim Clark. The result was another resounding success (albeit a tragic one). Clark's brutalization of unresisting demonstrators culminated in Bloody Sunday, March 7, 1965, when law enforcement officers viciously assaulted marchers as they crossed the Edmund Pettus Bridge on the way to Montgomery. Governor Wallace had promised that the march would be broken up by whatever measures were necessary, and his chief law enforcement lieutenant later insisted that the governor himself had given the order to attack. That evening, the national television networks broadcast lengthy film reports of peaceful demonstrators being assailed by stampeding horses, flailing clubs, and tear gas. Most of the nation was repulsed, and over the following week, sympathy demonstrations took place across America. Citizens demanded remedial action from their Congressional representatives, scores of whom condemned the violence and endorsed voting rights legislation. On March 15, 1965, President Lyndon B. Johnson proposed such legislation before a joint session of Congress. Seventy million Americans watched on television as the president beseeched them to "overcome this crippling legacy of bigotry and injustice" and declared his faith that "we shall overcome."

Brown played a role both in generating direct action and in shaping the response it received from white Southerners. The ruling made Jim Crow seem more vulnerable, and it raised the hopes and expectations of black Americans, which were then largely dashed by massive resistance, revealing the limited capacity of litigation alone to produce meaningful social change. *Brown* also inspired Southern whites to try to destroy the NAACP, with some temporary success in the Deep South, which unintentionally forced blacks to support alternative protest organizations that embraced philosophies more sympathetic to direct action. Finally, the Southern white backlash ignited by *Brown* increased the chances that, once civil rights demonstrators appeared on the streets, they would be greeted with violence rather than gradualist concessions. In the end, it was the beating of peaceful black demonstrators by Southern white law enforcement officers that repulsed national opinion and led directly to the passage of landmark civil rights legislation.

V. POST-CIVIL RIGHTS MOVEMENT

As the civil rights movement peaked in the 1960s, so did the Court's activism on race. In school desegregation cases, the justices declared that the time for "all deliberate speed" had expired. They strongly hinted that federal courts had the power to order the reopening of schools that had been closed to avoid desegregation decrees, and they invalidated freedom-of-choice plans that had failed to produce meaningful desegregation. In several decisions, the Court manufactured novel constitutional law to protect the NAACP from the legal harassment of Southern states. In another series of rulings, the justices turned doctrinal somersaults to overturn the criminal convictions of sit-in demonstrators. Several decisions in the 1960s expanded the concept of state action, enabling the justices to strike at instances of race discrimination that previously were thought beyond the reach of the Fourteenth Amendment. The Court also began to revolutionize First Amendment doctrine, criminal procedure, the law of federal courts, and habeas corpus rules, based largely on the justices' conviction that Southern states could not be trusted to deal fairly with matters involving race.

Changing social and political circumstances halted civil rights progress just as the movement reached its zenith. Opinion polls ranked civil rights foremost on the nation's political agenda from the summer of 1963 through the spring of 1965, but the war in Vietnam displaced it. Moreover, as civil rights leaders shifted their focus to the North and broadened their objectives to include economic redistribution, many previously sympathetic whites became alienated from the movement. Less than six weeks after President Johnson signed the Voting Rights Act into law in the summer of 1965, a devastating race riot swept through the Watts neighborhood of Los Angeles, killing thirty-four; it proved to be the harbinger of dozens of other race riots in that decade. By the mid-to-late 1960s, black nationalism, which eschewed racial integration as a goal and non-violence as a tactic, was sowing divisions within civil rights organizations and souring many white Americans on racial reform. "We shall overcome" proved to be a more appealing message than "burn, baby, burn" to most whites. In 1964 the Republican Party nominated for president Senator Barry Goldwater, a vocal opponent of the Civil Rights Act.

Goldwater's nomination accelerated a national political realignment, as five Deep South states voted Republican for the first time since Reconstruction. By 1966, a racial backlash among whites was also evident in the North, as urban race riots, proposals for fair housing legislation, and black demands for economic empowerment sundered the civil rights coalition. In 1968 Republican candidate Richard M. Nixon won the presidency on a platform emphasizing law and order, a relaxed pace for school desegregation in the South, and neighborhood schools (i.e., no busing) in the North; 97 percent of blacks voted for Democrat Hubert Humphrey that year, but only 35 percent of whites. The 14 percent of voters who supported George Wallace's third-party bid for the presidency encouraged the Republican Party to move even further right on race issues in the future. Nixon's victory at the polls directly translated into changes in the Court's racial jurisprudence: He appointed four new justices during his first term.

The race rulings of the Burger Court (1969–86), named for Chief Justice Warren Burger, proved to be a halfway house between that of the Warren Court (1953–69) and that of the Rehnquist Court (1986–2005). In its early years, the Burger Court aggressively pushed school desegregation. The justices sustained the busing of pupils as a remedy for segregation, and they approved the imposition of sweeping desegregation orders on proof of fairly minimal constitutional violations. Yet, this Court drew the line at a school district's boundaries. In *Milliken v. Bradley* (1974), probably the most important school desegregation ruling since *Brown*, a slim majority of the justices refused to countenance the inclusion of largely white suburbs within an urban desegregation decree, absent proof that district lines had been drawn with discriminatory intent or effect. As a consequence, federal courts could not effect meaningful school desegregation in most cities.

The Burger Court followed a similarly modulated approach with regard to affirmative action – the use of racial preferences to advantage traditionally disfavored racial minorities. A narrow majority of the Court approved the use of such preferences but only under certain conditions. Inflexible quotas were disapproved, as were concentrated burdens on "innocent" whites. Because the Burger Court was so closely divided, the fate of particular affirmative action plans depended mainly on the predispositions of Justice Lewis F. Powell, Jr.

On perhaps the most important racial issue of its tenure, the Burger Court ruled in *Washington v. Davis* (1976) that laws making no racial classification would receive heightened judicial scrutiny only if they were illicitly *motivated*; showing that a law simply had a disproportionately burdensome *impact* on racial minorities was deemed insufficient. Yet, this stringent interpretation of the Constitution was partially offset by more generous interpretations of federal civil rights statutes. Most important, *Griggs v. Duke Power Co.* (1971) interpreted the ban on race discrimination in employment contained in the 1964 Civil Rights Act to forbid such disparate impact.

The racial jurisprudence of the Burger Court has been interpreted several ways. Some have argued that it confronted more difficult racial issues than the Warren Court. In other words, it is supposedly easier to determine the constitutionality of de jure racial segregation and discrimination than of laws that do not classify according to race but nonetheless have a disparate racial impact. To invalidate all such legislation would require government officials to constantly consider race, and it would wreak havoc on the plethora of laws that especially burden the poor, given the strong correlation in America between minority racial status and poverty. Yet, to validate such laws is to allow government to compound the disadvantages of historically oppressed racial minorities for no substantial reason and to permit much legislation that was invidiously motivated to pass constitutional muster, given the difficulty of proving intentional racial discrimination. On this view, affirmative action also poses a more vexing constitutional issue than did the public school segregation that the Court invalidated in *Brown*. Even those most committed to progressive racial reform generally concede that minority racial preferences risk stigmatizing the intended beneficiaries, inflaming racial tensions, and contradicting the ultimate goal of treating all people as individuals regardless of their race.

One can also interpret the Burger Court's race rulings as reflections of a more conservative social climate. Public hostility toward school desegregation – especially once the litigation migrated North – was reflected in numerous Congressional proposals to curb busing in the early 1970s. *Milliken* reflected national opinion better than an opposite ruling would have. Still, the role of individual justices – and thus the vagaries of the Supreme Court appointments process – cannot be ignored in accounting for these less progressive outcomes. The vote in *Milliken* was 5–4; all four of the recent Nixon appointees were in the majority. The Warren Court almost certainly would have decided differently the issue of inter-district busing orders. Whether it could have made such a ruling stick in light of hostile public opinion is another question.

The Rehnquist Court sounded a more consistent note: the cause of progressive racial reform lost nearly across the board. The Court sounded the death knell for court-ordered school desegregation. In two decisions from the early 1990s, *Dowell v. Board of Education* and *Freeman v. Pitts*, a conservative majority emphasized that judicial desegregation orders were not intended to last forever and that most of the remaining racial imbalances in public schools resulted from housing segregation, for which the state was not legally responsible. *Missouri v. Jenkins* (1995) indicated for the first time a limited judicial tolerance for remedial alternatives to busing. There, the conservative majority forbade the use of magnet schools to entice suburban whites back into racially integrated urban schools and rejected judicially ordered increases in educational funding that were not tied closely to remedying the initial constitutional violations.

On two other important race issues, the Rehnquist Court used the Fourteenth Amendment (ironically) to invalidate legislative measures that were designed to benefit racial minorities. With regard to affirmative action, a bare conservative majority agreed that all racial classifications – whether their intent was benign or malign – had to be subjected to the same exacting judicial scrutiny. These justices insisted on specific proof of the past discrimination that affirmative action policies purported to remedy. They also required that minority racial preferences be narrowly tailored to avoid benefiting those who had not themselves been victims of discrimination and to avoid burdening "innocent" whites. These decisions implied that most affirmative action plans were unconstitutional, and many lower federal courts so interpreted them. In another series of 5–4 rulings, the Court invalidated several Congressional districts that had been gerrymandered to enhance the prospects of minority racial groups electing representatives of their own race. The conservative justices ruled that the Fourteenth Amendment generally bars such districts when the predominant motive behind their creation was racial. Both the affirmative action and the minority voting district rulings were difficult to reconcile with the original understanding of the Fourteenth Amendment, which had not forbidden the use of all racial classifications.

Perhaps most disturbing, the Rehnquist Court proved fairly indifferent to race discrimination in the criminal justice system. In *McCleskey v. Kemp* (1987), the conservative justices narrowly rejected an equal protection challenge to the discriminatory administration of the death penalty in Georgia. Specifically, according to a study that the justices stipulated to be valid for purposes of the case, defendants who murdered whites were 4.3 times more likely to receive the death penalty than were those who murdered blacks. Rejecting the challenge, the Court observed that racial discrimination could not be eliminated entirely from the administration of the death penalty so long as actors integral to the system – such as prosecutors and jurors – exercised significant discretion. The majority also noted that similar racial disparities existed throughout the criminal justice system, which meant that vindicating McCleskey's claim would have had potentially enormous consequences.

Similarly, in *United States v. Armstrong* (1996), the Court imposed a virtually insurmountable hurdle for defendants who alleged racially selective prosecution. Before black defendants could gain discovery – access to the prosecutor's files – on such claims, they had to demonstrate that similarly situated whites had not been prosecuted. Yet, this was the very point on which discovery was sought. Although the justices in cases that challenged the constitutionality of minority voting districts had frowned on the assumption that blacks and whites generally have different political preferences (which might warrant creating majority-black districts), *Armstrong* rejected the lower court's assumption that all crimes are equally likely to be committed by members of all races. The particular U.S. Attorney's office in question had prosecuted in the preceding year twenty-four blacks and not a single white for crack distribution, but according to the Court this did not establish the prima facie case of selective prosecution that was necessary to justify an order for discovery. The vote in *Armstrong* was 8–1, which suggests that even the Rehnquist Court's liberal justices were less sensitive to racial discrimination in the criminal justice system than were their predecessors on the Warren Court.

The Rehnquist Court's racial jurisprudence ended on a somewhat ironic note. Because most of its important race decisions were 5–4, the shift of a single vote – that of Justice Sandra Day O'Connor – had the potential to dramatically transform outcomes. At the beginning of the twenty-first century, O'Connor voted with the liberal justices in two important race decisions. In *Easley v. Cromartie* (2001), she joined an opinion that sustained a racially gerrymandered Congressional district that was not easily distinguishable from those previously invalidated by the Court. And in *Grutter v. Bollinger* (2003), O'Connor wrote the majority opinion that sustained the race-based affirmative action plan of the University of Michigan Law School. Based on her earlier opinions and votes, one might have predicted that O'Connor would invalidate that admissions policy on the grounds that it relied on the impermissible stereotype that race correlates with diversity of perspective and that it failed to adequately consider non-racial alternatives for securing a diverse student body.

O'Connor's votes in *Cromartie* and *Grutter* may be explicable on similar grounds: O'Connor was a classic conservative, who valued preservation of the status quo. By the early twenty-first century, multiculturalism and multiracialism had become entrenched features of American life. Predicting such a development twenty years earlier would have been difficult. But probably in response to the growing racial and ethnic diversity of the nation, and possibly in response to the forces of globalization as well, most Americans had come to accept that important social, political, and economic institutions should "look like America." Friend-of-the-court briefs filed in the University of Michigan case symbolized the extent to which even relatively conservative American institutions such as Fortune 500 companies and the U.S. military had embraced this multiracial vision. These briefs warned the justices that America's economic success and military strength depended on the continued use of affirmative action. In *Cromartie*, O'Connor refused to obliterate the Congressional black caucus, and in *Grutter* she declined to put the nation's elite universities at risk of becoming lily white.

LESSONS

What can be learned from this history? First, it is not clear whether the Supreme Court, over the course of American history, has been more of a help or a hindrance to the cause of black liberation. Pre-twentieth-century Courts invalidated the personal liberty laws of Northern states that were designed to protect free blacks from kidnapping by slave catchers, voided Congress's effort to restrict the spread of slavery into federal territories while denying that even free blacks possessed any rights "which the white man was bound to respect," and struck down the provision in the 1875 Civil Rights Act that guaranteed blacks equal access to public accommodations. In the twentieth century, on the same side of the ledger, the justices legitimized racial segregation and black disfranchisement for several decades; more recently, they invalidated numerous affirmative action plans and minority voting districts that were designed to benefit racial minorities. On the other hand, beginning in the 1920s the Court curbed the legal lynching of black criminal defendants, gradually chipped away at Southern state mechanisms for disfranchising blacks, and eventually invalidated racial segregation in housing, transportation, and public education. It is by no means certain how one should evaluate this balance sheet. At a minimum, the Court has plainly not been the unvarnished defender of racial minorities it is sometimes portrayed to be.

That anyone should have believed otherwise is probably attributable to *Brown*, which is often credited for inspiring the modern civil rights movement. Yet that ruling was the product of a particular historical moment in which social and political circumstances were turning public opinion – especially that of the cultural elite – against white supremacy. *Brown* was also a product of fortuity: in 1954 the Supreme Court happened to consist almost entirely of liberal New Dealers and not at all of dyed-in-the-wool

Southern racists. There is no systemic reason to expect Supreme Court justices over time to favor the interests of racial minorities over those of competing claimants. In the antebellum period, when white Southerners constituted a majority of the Court, its rulings favored the interests of slave owners. Had there been five Justice Reeds in 1954, *Brown* would likely have come out the other way.

Nor can the Court's strong support for civil rights in the middle third of the twentieth century be ascribed to the clarity of constitutional law on race issues. Most civil rights victories did not reflect determinate law so much as the justices' personal preferences, which generally tracked dominant public opinion. The justices themselves admitted that the legal case for *Brown* was weak. Hard as it is to accept today, *Plessy v. Ferguson* was not a ridiculous decision, if judged by the conventional sources of constitutional law: text, original intent, precedent, and tradition.

This survey of the Court's twentieth-century racial jurisprudence also suggests that even those rulings favorable to civil rights claimants had limited impact on actual racial practices. There are several reasons for this. Lower court judges are the principal interpreters of Supreme Court rulings, and in the South, few of them supported racial equality. Those officials charged with the initial enforcement of the civil rights of Southern blacks – law enforcement officers, school board members, voter registrars – were generally even less supportive of the Court's rulings. Given the constitutional right of trial by jury and the continued exclusion of blacks from Southern juries well into the 1960s, such officials ran little risk of incurring civil or criminal sanctions for violating the civil rights of blacks. Another reason why litigation victories had limited consequences for racial equality before World War II is that few black lawyers practiced in the South, most white lawyers would not take civil rights cases, and the NAACP was absent from much of the region. Last, constitutional rights are worth little when asserting them is likely to get one beaten or killed. Not until the second half of the twentieth century did Southern blacks enjoy sufficient physical security to aggressively assert their rights, and even then blacks in the Deep South risked economic reprisals and physical violence by doing so.

Such factors help explain why *Brown* was so difficult to enforce. Most power holders in an entire region, including the actors initially responsible for enforcement, thought the decision was wrong and mobilized against it. Congress and the president were unenthusiastic about implementing the decision. The effective monopolization of enforcement resources by the NAACP created a situation in which opposition forces could effectively nullify the ruling simply by shutting down a single organization. A multitude of techniques for evading the right were available, and sanctions against violators were mostly unobtainable. Only when Congress became involved in the school desegregation process, empowering the U.S. Attorney General to bring desegregation suits and threatening to cut off federal education funds to defiant school districts, did most parts of the South begin to experience meaningful school desegregation.

Perhaps the most important lesson to draw from this history is that the Supreme Court generally reflects the social mores of its time, with only slight deviations. This is not to say that Court decisions do not matter, only that they reflect social attitudes and practices more than they create them. The justices who participated in *Brown* understood this, commenting on the "spectacular" advances and the "constant progress" being made in race relations. In the absence of such changes, *Brown* would have been decided differently.

Because social and political context plays a substantial role in the justices' constitutional decision making, the romantic vision of the Court as a heroic savior of oppressed minorities is misguided. The justices reflect dominant public opinion too much for them to protect truly oppressed groups. The Court failed to intervene against slavery before the Civil War, and it validated the internment of Japanese Americans during World War II and the persecution of political leftists during the McCarthy era. In the heyday of Jim Crow, the justices approved racial segregation and black disfranchisement.

The justices seem to possess neither the inclination nor the capacity to impose racial justice on a society that is not voluntarily committed to it (which may be a good thing, if one believes that judicial conceptions of racial justice are no more likely to be correct than are those that emerge from the political process). *Brown* was a strong statement – qualified by the weak remedial decree in *Brown II* – condemning formal white supremacy in the South. The ruling reflected a consensus on race that was then emerging outside the South. But there is little evidence that a majority of the nation was ever committed to undoing the full legacy of Jim Crow and achieving substantive racial equality. The same year that Congress, through the 1964 Civil Rights Act, commanded an end to formal white supremacy in the South, legislatures and voters in many Northern states were rejecting fair housing laws to govern their own jurisdictions. Also in 1964, George Wallace, the most rabidly segregationist of the post-*Brown* Southern governors, won astonishingly high percentages of the vote (30 to 45 percent) in the Democratic Party's presidential primaries in Indiana, Wisconsin, and Maryland. As soon as the Court hinted that it might impose a serious remedy for school segregation in the North as well as the South – in the 1973 *Keyes* decision – a backlash against busing erupted in Congress, and the justices retreated the following year in *Milliken*. The Court did not seriously challenge race discrimination in housing – which one could argue is the root cause of most of the nation's other racial problems – until it was too late to do anything about it (beginning in the late 1960s). The Court has never – not at the peak of the civil rights movement and certainly not today – been willing to confront the most vexing issues of racial discrimination in the criminal justice system. Nor have the justices been willing, except during a few years in the late 1960s and early 1970s, to treat issues of economic inequality, the resolution of which is critical to the aspirations of racial minorities, as raising serious constitutional concerns.

In the end, with regard to race or any other issue, the Court has limited power to make the nation better than it is inclined to be. To paraphrase the great jurist Learned Hand, a nation that is genuinely committed to racial justice does not need the help of a Supreme Court. A nation lacking in that commitment cannot be saved by such a Court.

13

HETEROSEXUALITY AS A LEGAL REGIME

MARGOT CANADAY

In the late 1990s, an American serviceman was tried for an unusual crime of larceny: the court ruled that the serviceman had entered into a sham heterosexual marriage in order to obtain government benefits for himself and his male partner. Specifically, the U.S. Court of Appeals for the Armed Forces asserted that the serviceman had married a lesbian and then applied for a military allowance to live off-barracks with his "dependent" in Makakilo, Hawaii. But, in reality, the serviceman's wife lived in her apartment in Honolulu while the serviceman used the allowance to support a household with his male lover. In his testimony, the serviceman admitted to homosexual conduct, but denied that his infidelity had any bearing on the legitimacy of his marriage. He told the court that while his wife's job kept her in Honolulu, he put her name on the lease because he expected her to move in with him in the future. In the meantime, he said, they spent weekends together whenever his schedule permitted. But the prosecution responded with evidence from the serviceman's friends who admitted that the soldier "got married to live off base, that it was a business deal." The wife got the privileges of the military's "dependent ID card," these soldiers told the court, and "there was nothing more to it than that."[1]

The court defined the central issue in the case as whether the serviceman and his wife were married "for the purpose of obtaining government benefits, or whether they intended to establish a life together and assume certain duties and obligations." The judges read the serviceman's sexual relationship with his male housemate as evidence that the soldier was solely engaged in the pursuit of state resources, but denied that homosexuality was key to its decision. "The relevance of the evidence flows not from the homosexual nature of the relationships," the court argued, "but rather from the fact that those relationships existed before and continued after the marriage."

---

[1] 52 M.J. 268; 2000 CAAF Lexis 221; 55 Fed. R. Evid. Serv. (Callaghan) 785, United States Court of Appeals for the Armed Forces.

But homosexuality was, of course, critical. The court asserted that the man had married either because he was committed to making a life with his spouse or because he intended to claim government benefits. But for married couples whose heterosexuality was presumed, the two were not seen as mutually exclusive – one of the purposes of marriage was to secure benefits, to greater or lesser degree. One judge explicitly conceded the point when he asserted that "the timing of marriage and the nature of marital living arrangements may be heavily influenced by such unromantic factors as tax laws, occupational benefits, and professional opportunities." Indeed, it was not that the serviceman had seen marriage as a vehicle for state benefits that so confounded the court. Rather, it was that he had sought such benefits (in the court's view) as a gay man married to a lesbian.

At first blush, this case clearly belongs to the late 1990s and beyond, resonating as it does with the campaign to legalize gay marriage then underway in Hawaii and soon to erupt in other states. But I open with it less because it anticipates the early twenty-first century than because of the way it may help draw the previous century to a conclusion. This is a case through which to look backward in time, in other words, for embedded within it are the fundamental principles that guided state regulation of gender and sexuality for most of the twentieth century. Those principles – simply put, to encourage marriage and to discourage homosexuality – were advanced through the intensification of legal penalties for homosexuality and the simultaneous expansion of state economic subsidies for marriage. These two elements (which we might think of as carrot and stick) were obviously intertwined in the serviceman's case – his claim for benefits as a married man was hopelessly tangled up with his larceny conviction, as well as the likelihood that he would eventually be separated from the service as a homosexual.

What seems unusual about this case also reveals what is typical to the point of being systemic: while rarely so meshed in one individual life, the state's impetus both to punish homosexuality and reward marriage was part of a common regulatory project, one that I call the *legal regime of heterosexuality*. The emergence, expansion, and consolidation of this regime is one of the major stories we can tell about sex, gender, and law in the twentieth century. I employ the concept of a regime to evoke heterosexuality not as a behavior, a set of attributes, or an identity, but as a regulatory system. I use heterosexuality, moreover, to designate the regime not because I want to privilege the term but to suggest the way that state regulation privileged it, making heterosexuality a legally persuasive institution in part by burdening homosexuality with stigma and penalty. Excavating the history of this regime will require looking at the administrative arena as well as the courts; at local, state, and especially federal levels of governance; and across doctrinal areas that legal scholars usually consider separately.

It will also require bringing legal historians and historians of sexuality
into the same room – a beneficial gathering, I believe, for all parties. Legal
historians can take away from such a gathering all of the following: new ways
of conceptualizing family law, regulation, state formation, and citizenship;
a fuller understanding of the law's place in intimate realms of identity and
experience; and more evidence of the law's vast power to give what may be
legally constituted the veneer of the natural. For their part, historians of
sexuality are no strangers to the law – they have long trolled about in legal
sources for evidence regarding sexual practices, identities, and communities
in the past. But this has usually entailed reading legal sources "against the
grain" – pulling social history, in other words, out of legal sources. Reading
with the grain, by contrast, would mean looking for the ways that sexuality
may be deeply embedded in legal categories and legal institutions and
examining how state authorities respond to and, in turn, help produce
sexual difference.

A close encounter with legal history is valuable for historians of sexuality
for another reason. Law can serve as a bridge that joins the subfields of
women's history and gay and lesbian history. Readers who are unfamiliar
with these two subfields may question the extent of separation between
them, perhaps due to a general acceptance in the broader culture of the
notion that gender and sexuality have a privileged relationship to one
another. But what seems to be common sense on the streets has been problematic within the academy: "It is essential to separate gender and sexuality
analytically," the influential anthropologist Gayle Rubin wrote in the early
1980s (with growing skepticism toward feminism), "to more accurately
reflect their separate social existence." Whether Rubin was merely chronicling a development already well underway or prophesizing the future,
her statement accurately captures the way that queer studies and feminist
studies then cleaved across the disciplines. For historians, that separation
meant that scholars focused on women's lives did not share many of the
questions or frameworks of historians who had written about the gay past;
the result (despite substantial growth in both subfields) was a diminished
understanding of heterosexuality as a historical system. We have, on the one
hand, an incredibly rich historiography on marriage and the family, heterosexual dating and courtship, reproduction and its limitation, and prostitution. On the other hand, we know the rhythms and contours of early
gay worlds in increasingly textured ways. But only rarely have we explored
these topics in a way that brings them together into a coherent whole.
Looking for that coherent whole in law – mapping the evolution of heterosexuality's legal regime, elaborating its central characteristics – reveals
that state initiatives to support heterosexuality during the past century

were rarely gender neutral and that the legal project of maintaining het-erosexuality has also maintained male privilege. Gender and sexuality were not autonomous in law and policy, but tethered together – even when the policing of homosexuality has targeted men – by the oppression of women.

We can also see this by looking even further backward in time and con-necting the legal regime of heterosexuality to the legal regime that preceded it – coverture or the law of marital status. Coverture belongs more to the nineteenth century, but many of the legal arrangements that subsumed a wife's identity to her husband's lingered on well into the twentieth century.[2] Historians document two major points of rupture for coverture in the twen-tieth century. First, by the 1930s not only had the passage of the Nineteenth Amendment recast women's relationship to the political arena as one that was no longer derivative, but legal reforms made it possible for a woman living in any state in the nation to own, inherit, and will property; to enter into contracts; and to sue in court. Coverture was diminished even more in the 1970s, as part of a broader feminist revolution in law that further weakened the principle that a husband owned a wife's labor (including her person). No-fault divorce became the norm; marriage laws were redrafted in gender-neutral language.

The timing is important: in the feminist legal doldrums between the 1930s and the 1970s, the legal regime of heterosexuality arose and took shape. Mid-century can be identified most clearly as its foundational moment. The regime of coverture and the regime of heterosexuality thus move along opposite arcs: as the first was coming undone, the second was rising in its stead. This was a ragged and uneven transition – one whose periodization is difficult to capture with exact precision – in part because the old regime left a sediment on the new. It would perhaps be overly instru-mental to suggest that coverture could finally fade because another system had taken over many of its functions, but it is certainly safe to say that the legal regime of heterosexuality diminished the impact of coverture's wane. It is not that the feminist revolution in law has meant so little, but rather that it should have meant so much more: a profound legal transformation was blunted by the way that coverture and the legal regime of heterosexual-ity were aligned. The two systems did not operate in identical ways or even necessarily on the same stage (the legal regime of heterosexuality played out, for example, more on the federal level than coverture had). But despite differences, the new regulatory schema did not erase and in fact continued coverture's main purpose, which was the legal subordination of women. A feminist and queer legal history can begin with this same point of origin.

---

[2] On coverture in nineteenth-century America, see Chapter 8 in Volume II.

I. ANTECEDENTS

Hendrik Hartog has described the history of coverture as one that belongs to the "very long" nineteenth century, a century that spills well over the chronological boundaries that demarcate its beginning and end. We might similarly conceive of the legal regime of heterosexuality as belonging to a "foreshortened" twentieth century, a time period that roughly encapsulates the period from the 1930s to the end of the century. Over those years, the state created the administrative structure to direct substantial resources toward married couples. It also created a massive state-federal apparatus that policed homosexuality. Sometimes the legal instruments for achieving these two distinct but interrelated aims were located in remote corners of the government's legal architecture. At other points, as we shall see, both were accomplished through a single piece of legislation or program. But whatever the particular venue, policing homosexuality and rewarding marriage had a few antecedents earlier in the century.

The earliest large-scale government attempts to regulate sexuality were in fact visible some years before the New Deal, arising with the emergence of major government bureaucracies. But notably, these initial efforts to police sexuality were directed mostly at heterosexual deviance (primarily in women), rather than at gender inversion or same-sex erotic behavior. George Chauncey has described a 1928 incident, for example, in which vice investigators discovered 5,000 people at a "Fag Masquerade Ball" in Harlem, but quickly left the scene because they "could learn nothing" there about female prostitution. Measures to suppress prostitution, then, vigorously involved the state in the policing of sexuality, especially during the Progressive era. A local-state-federal anti-prostitution campaign was concentrated during these years around the Bureau of Immigration. Indeed, the very first federal law to limit immigration (the 1875 Page Act) was enacted to prevent prostitutes from coming into the country (lawmakers were especially concerned about Chinese women). The 1903 Immigration Act forbade importing women for the purpose of prostitution, and the 1907 Immigration Act barred from entry women or girls who had entered the country for prostitution or "any other immoral purpose." The same law provided for the deportation of alien prostitutes within three years of their arrival and made it a felony to harbor, maintain, or otherwise control alien women for the purposes of prostitution.

Three years later, in the midst of hysteria about female aliens being forced into prostitution, Congress passed the White Slave Traffic Act. Also known as the Mann Act, the legislation prohibited the transportation of women or girls across state lines for immoral purposes. Under the Mann Act, both men and women were prosecuted for prostitution. Most prosecutions under the law ended up being for cases of consensual prostitution; some were for adultery or fornication or other forms of heterosexual vice, among native-born as well as immigrant populations. (One of the law's greater ironies was its use to prosecute the son of the Commissioner-General of Immigration, Anthony Caminetti.) Enforcement was carried out by the fledgling Bureau of Investigation – vigorously enough that the Mann Act ended up being a major factor in the transformation of the Federal Bureau of Investigation into an enormous agency that wielded power in most large cities and every state and region across the country.

The Mann Act and the Bureau of Immigration increasingly drew federal officials into the business of regulating morality, but in ways that relied on local police and vice commissions and thus created a partnership across various levels of governance. The same was true with the military's attempt to control prostitution and venereal disease around its bases during World War I. During the war, thirty-two states enacted laws providing for the incarceration of any woman suspected of carrying venereal disease; at least 18,000 women were so detained. And, in 1917, Secretary of War Newton Baker created the quasi-public Commission on Training Camp Activities (CTCA) to keep "moral zones" around military camps free of alcohol and prostitution. The Commission not only kept an eye on conditions surrounding military facilities but also ordered local vice investigators into urban red light districts to identify potential threats to troop morals.

Those agents – focused on heterosexual deviance and especially on prostitution – got an eyeful on such trips. "From 9th Street at the Post Office Building to Juniper Street, the corners contain from one to five male perverts or 'fairies,' waiting for the street cars coming with their loads of sailors from the Navy yard," reported one Commission investigator in Philadelphia. "These degenerates take the sailors into the alleyways . . . also into the lavatories of the cheap saloons, and occasionally into their own rooms." Another report from Providence – "as wide open a town as there is" – warned that intoxicated soldiers shared the streets and saloons with perverts of both sexes. Immigration officials as well became aware of perversion in their attempts to monitor and suppress prostitution. The immigrant inspector Marcus Braun warned the Commissioner-General of Immigration in 1909, for example, about a "new species of undesirable immigrant" after having encountered "pederasts" while investigating white slavery in Berlin, London, Vienna, and Rome. A 1910 Congressional report on the importation of immoral women made mention of a similar "traffic in boys and men."

In their pursuit of prostitutes and other loose women, then, government officials were introduced to "sodomites" and "pederasts," to use the terminology of the era. Such discoveries did not lead to an immediate shift of regulatory priorities; government officials were in fact rather sluggish in their response to homosexual deviance during these years. (My own research has uncovered, for example, only thirty cases of aliens who were deported for perversion in the years before immigration restriction.) But the fact that local police, vice commissioners, FBI agents, and military and immigration officials often became aware of perversion on their forays into brothels and cabarets makes it unsurprising that the same legal instruments would be used to target heterosexual, homosexual, and/or gender deviance during the early twentieth century. Disorderly conduct, public lewdness, vagrancy, solicitation, as well as state sodomy laws were used not only against female prostitutes, in other words, but also against a much broader assortment of sex/gender non-conformists. Moreover, while aliens were not deported for perversion in huge numbers, when they were it was generally as "public charges" – a provision of immigration law commonly used against single women and prostitutes. Heterosexual deviance garnered far more attention than homosexual deviance, but both were part of what Ariela Dubler has called the same "genus" of immoral sex.

If the early comings and goings of the Bureau of Immigration thus provide hints as to what would later evolve into highly systemized and aggressive state policing of homosexual deviance, the same institution similarly foreshadows the channeling of substantial economic resources toward marriage. (It also suggests the way that both elements of the legal regime would grow up in tandem with the federal bureaucracy.) Pensions for Civil War veterans, workmen's compensation, and mothers'/widows' aid were other early experiments with social provision, but because immigration as well entailed access to state resources, immigration (as a threshold for residence) can also be thought of as a benefit. (Federal officials certainly made this link when they began to deport aliens on public relief during the Depression.) And it was one – like Civil War pensions or benefits for the wife of a wounded or dead "industrial soldier" – that also flowed through marriage. The literacy test that was incorporated into immigration law in 1917, for example, required a male immigrant over age 16 to be literate, but did not require his immediate family members to be able to read. Such legislation, as Nancy Cott has argued, was based on the assumption that to be accompanied by one's wife and child (literate or not) was a prerogative of manhood in America. The principle that men could bestow not only entry but also citizenship upon their wives was part of this same marital paradigm. With such benefits at stake, immigration officials were suspicious of single men and women, and they worried that pimps, procurers, prostitutes, and other unworthies would try to improve their legal standing through "marriage fraud." Here then – with marriage emerging as a repository of state goods and sexuality as one way to differentiate legitimate recipients from the undeserving – are the inchoate beginnings of what by mid-century would evolve into the more sharply demarcated legal regime of heterosexuality.

Before that evolution got fully underway, the state would retrain its eye on homosexual rather than heterosexual deviance. To be clear, this does not mean that the state stopped policing prostitution and other forms of heterosexual vice. It meant that the system's primary regulatory animus was redirected toward gender inversion and same-sex erotic behavior. A more liberal legal environment for heterosexual expression was evidenced during the 1930s by several high-profile court cases. In its 1934 opinion in *Hansen v. Haff*, the Supreme Court overturned the deportation under the immoral purposes provision of a female alien who had engaged in sexual relations with a man to whom she was not married. Sex outside of marriage was, in the Court's estimation, not immoral by definition. In the same year, the Court of Appeals for the Second Circuit ruled that James Joyce's *Ulysses* was not obscene, a decision that dovetailed a more general narrowing of the state regulation of obscenity. And in the landmark 1936 *U.S. v. One Package*, the Supreme Court overturned the 1873 Comstock law's prohibition on contraception by allowing doctors to prescribe birth control. The increasing availability of birth control (not including abortion) was one of the most fundamental differences separating a woman born in the twentieth century from her nineteenth-century forbearers. The Depression years even made birth control somewhat respectable. But the "loosening of sexual taboos" that occurred during these years was, as Linda Gordon remarks, "specifically heterosexual."

II. EMERGENCE

The legal regime of heterosexuality emerged and took shape most dramatically in the years between 1930 and 1960. During these years – as coverture continued to lose force – the federal government would come to be involved in both punishing homosexual deviance and rewarding heterosexual marriage in previously unprecedented ways. Such processes would be especially visible in federal employment (including the military), Social Security, taxation, immigration, and benefits policy. But while increasingly federal in nature, the regime was always spread across multiple layers of governance. Indeed, state laws providing for the incarceration of "sexual psychopaths" were one of the earlier harbingers of the shift of regulatory energy from female to male (and heterosexual to homosexual) deviance. Prompted by well-publicized assaults on children, these laws were passed in waves from the mid-1930s on during sex crime panics. Despite their association with sexual violence, the sexual psychopath laws did not distinguish between violent and non-violent offenses or between consensual and forcible behavior; frequently, men suspected of homosexuality were the ones who were rounded up and detained. Michigan pioneered with a statute that provided for indeterminate incarceration in state mental institutions for offenders determined to be sexual psychopaths. Those institutionalized – in Michigan and elsewhere – might be subject to lobotomies, electric shock treatment, injection of male hormones, and even castration. The sexual psychopath statutes drew a new boundary that, Estelle Freedman has argued, Americans used to "renegotiate . . . the definitions of sexual normality." They reflected the extent to which an increasing comfort level with female desire meant that "female purity [had] lost its symbolic power to regulate sexual behavior."

Not so with male perversion: it would be hard to overstate the force of the law's weight upon sex and gender non-conforming men as mid-century approached. Local vice squads regularly raided drag balls and later gay bars (whose licenses were frequently revoked by state liquor authorities). Undercover police officers entrapped unsuspecting men in public toilets and baths. The state of California, which in 1950 made loitering around a public toilet a new offense, required registration of loiterers and other lewd vagrants. Police throughout the country, in fact, routinized, systematized, and expanded their surveillance of sexual deviants, with homosexuality increasingly becoming the primary focus of any given department's vice squad. Between 1923 and 1967, some 50,000 men were arrested on loitering charges in New York City alone; sodomy convictions reached record numbers as well (and not just in New York) in the years between 1946 and 1961. William Eskridge speculates that a socially active gay man at mid-century was likely to end up doing time in jail. The consequences of such arrests could ripple outward. One might leave jail to find himself not only shunned by family and community but perhaps without a job as well.

The increased regulation of male sexual deviance was evidenced too at the federal level and by some of the same institutions that had earlier in the century targeted female prostitutes. By 1937, for example, Hoover's FBI had already begun to compile information about homosexuality among certain high-profile subjects. During World War II, the military turned what had been a seldom enforced set of induction standards into a massive and routinized method for screening incoming recruits for signs of perversion or "sexual psychopathy." During these years the military also implemented a new policy for handling the discharge of soldiers suspected of homosexuality. Until World War II, the military had court-martialed soldiers who engaged in sodomy; during and after the war, soldiers were undesirably discharged for being homosexual (for having a status rather than for committing an act). While seemingly less draconian than an exclusive reliance on the court-martial, the new policy vastly expanded the number of persons affected – hundreds had been court-martialed, thousands would be discharged. And whereas trial by court-martial involved the procedural protections of criminal law, a soldier could be discharged for being homosexual almost without recourse to evidence. By 1949, the military had completely eliminated a provision that had made it possible to retain soldiers who committed homosexual acts or who had homosexual "tendencies," but who had been determined by military psychiatrists to be reclaimable for the service.

Federal-level repression intensified after the war, in part because the charge of homosexuality (like Communism) could be used to political advantage. When a Republican Senator from Nebraska claimed in 1947 that the Truman administration was honeycombed with perverts, the administration conducted checks for perversion among nearly two hundred government employees (and later many more). The Civil Service Commission began routinely to cross-reference FBI files to ensure that job candidates with arrest records for sex perversion were not hired. (The FBI itself became a huge clearinghouse for information on homosexuality compiled by the military, vice squads, the Post Office, and its own surveillance.) In 1950, a widespread Congressional investigation concluded that the federal bureaucracy was overrun by homosexuals, raised the issue of potential blackmail, and warned that even "one homosexual could pollute an entire government office." The *Lavender* Scare actually outpaced the *Red* Scare: more civil servants were fired for homosexuality than for Communism.

In 1953, President Dwight D. Eisenhower issued an executive order barring homosexuals from civilian or military government employment under the federal loyalty security program. Critically, Eisenhower's industrial security program – which made sex perverts ineligible for security clearances whether they were public or private employees – took the Lavender Scare into the private sector (especially into the defense industry). The culture within the federal civil service also spread in other directions: back to the military, which intensified its purge, and also to state and municipal governments, which conducted their own witch hunts. At the state level, regulatory agencies revoked licenses on morals grounds for a variety of professions, including doctors, dentists, and lawyers. Teachers were especially vulnerable. In Florida, the Johns Committee targeted high-school teachers and university professors in a vigorous campaign that lasted into the mid-1960s. By that time, so extreme were government harassment and surveillance that the United States stood apart from other Western democracies. The United States was "the only major power in the world" that excluded homosexuals from its armed services and from government employment, the sociologist Donald Webster Cory concluded in 1965, noting that "the homosexual is the only individual who is punished in this manner, not only for any activities that may be indulged in, but for harboring the desire to perform such activities."[3]

In the legal regime of heterosexuality, then, homosexual activity (or being perceived as homosexual) exposed one to considerable economic vulnerability as well as the threat of criminal sanction. As sex and gender nonconformity were becoming economically risky, however, heterosexual marriage was becoming more economically secure. The U.S. government was not only exceptional, that is, for its homophobia. In contrast to the way that other industrialized democracies made welfare benefits a right available to citizens as individuals, in the United States social provision was channeled through marriage. More precisely, the way that the labor market and the marriage market were tied together meant that, as the welfare state expanded and grew, so did the costs of remaining single, especially for women. And if this was the legal regime's gentler side, it was still extremely coercive.

Women's access to the welfare state was disproportionately through marriage to male workers. Welfare benefits were distributed, to be more precise, not exactly through marriage but through the kinds of jobs that men were most likely to hold. The 1935 Social Security Act, which established that old age and unemployment insurance would be financed by employers and through a payroll tax, excluded many of the industries in which women were employed in high numbers. Moreover, the right to work was, as Alice Kessler Harris has shown, a *male* right. As women began in the early years of the twentieth century to seek paid work outside the home in greater numbers, the law sanctioned discrimination in the labor market. Even as protective labor legislation was intended to improve conditions for women at work, it kept women from competing with men for jobs. So too did cultural sanctions: "The woman who worked in or trained for the atypical trade signaled she was deviant," writes the economic historian Claudia Goldin. "To challenge the norms of the marketplace was often to place at risk other social relationships, such as marriage."

The already considerable gender bias of the labor market was thus reinforced by New Deal policy and not only by distributing social insurance through traditionally male occupations. The 1932 Economy Act mandated that when a husband and a wife both worked for the government the latter should be the first laid off in any staff reduction. The policy actually affected only a small number of women, but it suggested that the luxury of having federal employment during labor scarcity was a male prerogative. A similar philosophy shaped work relief. Jobs on the Works Progress Administration

[3] Donald Webster Cory, *The Lesbian in America* (New York, 1965), 221.

were regularly reserved for men, designed as one contemporary put it, to put a "brake on women's eagerness to be the family breadwinner." Even relief that was unconnected to work was biased toward men, as if hunger felt different in a male stomach. Facilities for the Depression's most destitute, for example – federal camps for the hundreds of thousands of transients who wandered the country in search of jobs and food – were reserved for men rather than women. And Social Security's other "track" – public assistance for single mothers – was deliberately miserly in order to make it difficult for women to live outside of marriage. Ironically, female (and feminist) reformers played a critical role in the creation of public assistance (as well as the equally skimpy mothers' aid programs from which public assistance descended). Whether crafted by women or men, that such policies were effective is suggested at least in part by rates of non-marriage, which were extraordinarily low throughout this period relative to Europe.

The American welfare state thus encouraged marriage by limiting women's direct access to all sorts of benefits – relief programs, social insurance, government jobs. It also did so by awarding supplemental benefits to men who married. The 1939 amendments to the Social Security Act, intended to spend down ballooning reserves, made matrimony especially lucrative. The amendments did not extend coverage to the excluded occupations, but rather enhanced benefits to men who were already covered by offering survivors benefits for their widows when they reached 65. (The gender bias of survivors benefits built on the precedent on workmen's compensation laws, so named because widows but not widowers could collect under them.) At that same age, wives had the option of collecting Social Security based on their own contributions or taking 50 percent of their husbands' benefits. Because of the disparity between men's and women's wages, as well as the way Social Security penalized workers who had gaps in their employment history, most women collected Social Security as dependents rather than as workers. The additional benefit was never intended for the wife, as historian Nancy Cott has observed. It was provided to the husband (as breadwinner) and meant to acknowledge him, not her.

Social Security was thus a tax that redistributed income in two ways: from the unmarried to the married, and from marriages with two relatively equal earners to traditional marriages, in which wages were either heavily skewed or wives did not work at all. This redistribution was intentional. Policymakers saw this tax on all single people and on working wives as encouraging men to become fathers and husbands, Cott argues, and women stay-at-home wives and mothers. That the law encouraged women to forego paid employment made its provisions in the case of divorce – which forbade women from collecting retirement benefits based on their ex-husbands' contributions – especially cruel.

As divorce became easier to obtain and somewhat more common toward mid-century, Alice Kessler-Harris has explained, legislators made marriage even more rewarding. They did so in 1956 by reducing to 62 the age at which women were eligible to collect benefits under Social Security; in 1965, that number was lowered to 60. And as the age of eligibility was declining for wives and widows, benefits for the latter steadily increased until the widow's entitlement was 100 percent of what the couples' combined benefit would have been had the husband survived. In the 1960s, the law was also amended to allow men and children to collect on their wives' accounts, but only if they could prove financial dependency. (The wife's dependency was assumed.) Congress's continuing reluctance to help establish women as primary breadwinners meant that a wife got less out of her Social Security taxes than her husband did. Social Security's benefits to married couples, then, did not flow to both spouses evenly. Men were thus doubly rewarded for marrying: they avoided the economic penalties of remaining single, *and* they collected marital benefits in a way that positioned their wives as subordinate to them. The deal for women who married was only half as good. Women, it should be clear, did stand to profit economically from marriage. Yet while marriage put a woman under the umbrella of state benefits, it simultaneously put her under male authority.

The other major public policy innovation at mid-century – the rise of the mass income tax – performed similar work in heterosexuality's legal regime by shoring up marriage while subordinating women to their husbands. The federal income tax was brought into being by constitutional amendment in 1913, but it was not until after World War II that most Americans paid taxes. At that time, lawmakers were confronted by a lack of equity among states. In the handful of community property states, spouses were able to pool their incomes and pay taxes as though each had earned half of the family's total income. In common law states, by contrast, spouses could not pool incomes and had to pay taxes on what each spouse actually earned. Because the tax structure was progressive – higher incomes were taxed at higher marginal rates as income moved up the tax bracket – not being able to split incomes meant that a household in a common law state paid far more tax than a household with the same income in a community property state. The only circumstance in which taxpayers in community property states were not advantaged was when a husband and a wife earned equally; this was, of course, rare at mid-century.

In addressing this inequity (and in response to the fact that some states were changing to community property systems in order to reap tax benefits), lawmakers not only brought common law states into sync with community property states but they also brought tax policy more generally into sync with Social Security. They were acting on what Alice Kessler-Harris calls a common sense of gender, which increasingly made marriage and not the individual the basic unit for social policy. Here again, America would split company with other industrialized nations, most of which taxed individuals rather than couples. In 1948, Congress rewrote the tax code to provide for income splitting between married couples so as to allow spouses everywhere to have the same benefit as those in community property states without actually having to share property between spouses. Indeed, some of the states that had converted to community property to take advantage of the tax break before 1948 quickly reversed course after the joint tax return became available. Similarly, wealthy men in common law states who had in prior years passed ownership of stocks and bonds to their wives to avoid paying taxes on them no longer had to do so.

Women's groups objected to joint filing, and not only because it seemed a symbolic step back toward coverture and away from the principle of women's legal autonomy. Joint filing, as the legal scholar Edward McCaffrey has shown, encouraged taxpayers to think in terms of a primary and secondary earner and then to "place an extra burden on the secondary worker because her wages come on top of the primary earner's." Income splitting actually reduced the husband's tax burden while increasing the wife's liability. Like Social Security, the new tax structure reflected and exacerbated the gender bias that already existed in the labor market; high marginal rates on the secondary earner diminished the social and economic value of women's contributions to the household and sometimes took away the incentive for women to work at all. Once again, state policies that supported marriage did not necessarily support the women inside those marriages. For tax purposes, the only thing worse than being a wife was being single. Income splitting was enormously punitive to singles, who (having no one with whom to split incomes) paid at the highest marginal rates. But when policymakers began in the early 1960s to wonder if the tax structure was in fact *too* hard on the unmarried, it was mainly widows and widowers they had in mind. "Bachelors and spinsters'" who "'shirk[ed] the responsibilities which families shoulder,'" opined experts at a 1963 Brookings Institute conference on tax reform, should "not [expect] much sympathy."[4]

III. TWO CASES: VETERANS BENEFITS AND IMMIGRATION POLICY

At mid-century, then, a homo/heterosexual binary was being inscribed in government policy. It was generally male homosexuality that was penalized

---

[4] Harold Groves, *Federal Tax Treatment of the Family* (Washington, DC, 1963), cited in Edward J. McCaffery, *Taxing Women* (Chicago, 1997), 60.

most heavily, and it was male heterosexuality that was rewarded most generously. But whether men were being sent benefit checks or to jail, policies that centered on men also subordinated women through marriage. In heterosexuality's legal regime – as with coverture during the prior century – women were thus a repressed and hidden, but also a core term. The coherence of the regulatory project can only be seen by placing disparate initiatives side by side– tax benefits and bar raids, dependents' allowances and the civil service purge, the male right to work and sexual psychopath laws – and looking at how they complemented each other. It is also evident in two of the specific policy arenas in which policing homosexuality and provisioning heterosexuality were tightly fused at mid-century: veterans benefits and immigration policy.

With the passage of the 1944 G.I. Bill, veterans became the recipients of state largesse on a scale not seen before. Expenditures for the program – which provided home and business loans, educational grants, unemployment benefits, and employment services – comprised 15 percent of the federal budget by 1948. Except for Social Security, veterans benefits at mid-century thus accounted for the largest portion of welfare state expenditure. But the program resembled Social Security in more than just its size; the benefits of the G.I. Bill, even more than Social Security, flowed toward men because women's participation in the armed services was capped by law at 2 percent. And the tiny percentage of women who *were* eligible for the program found, like women who paid Social Security taxes, that their benefits were not worth as much as men's. Women veterans could not collect an unemployment allowance until they demonstrated that they were not receiving support from a male wage earner. Moreover, the provisions that allowed male soldiers to collect dependency allowances and survivors benefits for their wives were not equally available to women soldiers who were married. Married women veterans were likewise discriminated against when the Veterans Administration (VA) assessed their credit risk for loans. (Low-interest government-backed FHA loans were not generally available to women whether or not they were vets; neither was the mortgage interest deduction.) The G.I. Bill thus envisioned marriage to a male veteran as the primary point of access for women to the benefits stream, and it rewarded men who did marry with more generous benefits than were designated for those who remained single. Profoundly domesticating legislation, the G.I. Bill was intended to help soldiers make the transition from the homosocial (and homoerotic) environment of wartime to marriage and family in peacetime. It tamed male soldiers into husbands.

But not all men got to make the leap. In response to the vaguely worded text of the G.I. Bill, the VA Administrator in 1945 issued instructions that barred from benefits any soldier undesirably discharged for reason of homosexuality. Significantly, while the military awarded the undesirable discharge for a variety of traits and behaviors, only the discharge for homosexuality led to a separate policy statement from the VA. This first explicit exclusion of homosexuals from the benefits of the welfare state came from an official who had long worried that the social insurance and work relief programs of the New Deal were having a degenerative effect on the "moral fiber" of the American people. Congress intended veterans benefits to be distributed as broadly as possible and issued a 1946 report challenging the VA policy. But as state homophobia spread, Congress changed position and tacitly endorsed the use of sexual identity to separate veterans who deserved benefits from veterans who did not.

So to the FBI, the vice squad, the Civil Service Commission, the military, and the Post Office, another instrument can be added to the state's anti-homosexual apparatus at mid-century, this one tucked inside the welfare bureaucracy. VA offices could be extraordinarily aggressive in going after undesirably discharged soldiers who attempted to use the G.I. Bill. In one such instance, for example, the VA not only demanded that a man who obtained his college degree after being discharged for homosexuality repay the government but also threatened him with a civil suit and imprisonment for receiving money under false pretenses. "What am I to do?" another veteran discharged for homosexuality asked in a letter to the VA Administrator. "Starve?" Yet however draconian the intentions of the VA, only some of those who experienced or acted on homosexual desire were prevented from collecting benefits. "You know as well as I that there have been many 'homosexuals' in the army and the navy," one soldier frankly told Secretary of the Navy James Forrestal, and "that many have been discharged 'under honorable conditions' because they were undiscovered." These soldiers were able to collect benefits in exchange for remaining hidden while in the service. As in the case of wives, there was a big payoff for conforming (or even appearing to conform) to the heterosexual and familial imperatives of postwar America.

Aliens who wanted access to what Nancy Cott calls the "circle of entitlement" through immigration also had to conform to these same imperatives. The consequences of being arrested in a washroom for loitering or other forms of disorderly conduct were never without significance for aliens, but the stakes grew higher at mid-century (as did the overall likelihood of being arrested in a public bathroom or park). In the 1952 McCarran Walter Act, Congress greatly enhanced the power of the Immigration Service to deport aliens for immorality by adding a provision to the immigration law that provided for the removal of aliens considered to be "psychopathic personalities." In contrast to the moral turpitude provision (in existence since the turn of the century), the psychopathic personality clause was not bound up with criminal law (or with evidence regarding actual acts), but instead vetted the homosexual alien as a class of person. Despite the potentially broad application of the term, Congress specifically stated its intention to use the psychopathic personality provision to target homosexuals (against whom it appears to have been used almost exclusively). It is difficult to say how many aliens were deported as psychopathic personalities in the 1950s and 1960s. The existence of at least thirteen federal court cases (which represent the tip of an iceberg in immigration regulation) in which aliens sued to prevent their deportation during those years suggests that the total number is probably substantial.

As with veterans benefits, mid-century immigration policy not only penalized homosexuality but also heaped rewards on heterosexuality. Besides adding the psychopathic personality to the list of excluded classes, the McCarran Walter Act permitted husbands and wives quota-free entrance for the first time. Just as the psychopathic personality provision intensified but did not inaugurate attempts by immigration officials to screen for sex/gender non-conformity, so too did this instance of marital preference have roots in earlier provisions of the immigration law. Eileen Boris notes, for example, the way that immigration policy had since the turn of the century "incorporated notions of ideal families and proper homes," citing the 1910 Dillingham Commission's conclusion that those who migrated with families "'exhibit[ed] a stronger tendency towards advancement.'" Marriage could also be a shelter against deportation for aliens suspected of immorality, as we have already seen. And at the end of World War II, the War Brides Act and GI Fiancées Act allowed for the admission of foreign wives and fiancées of American soldiers. But the McCarran Walter Act more sharply inscribed the homo/heterosexual binary into federal immigration law. Several years later, the 1965 Hart-Cellar Act did so in ways that were even more pronounced. That law made family reunification one of the guiding tenets of postwar immigration policy – yet another marital perk that was most likely to be distributed through men, thereby reinforcing gendered power within the family. And, in response to concerns that the psychopathic personality provision might be "void for vagueness," the Congress simultaneously included more precise language barring "sex deviates" from the country. This was a ratcheting up on both sides of the line.

IV. KEY ATTRIBUTES

By the 1960s, then, the legal regime of heterosexuality was well established. So far, we have mapped out the most important of the arenas in which it took hold in roughly the middle third of the twentieth century: in vice and criminal law, public employment, Social Security, taxation, benefits policy, and immigration law. What can they now tell us about the regime's primary characteristics?

First, this was a *gendered regime*, meaning not only that it affected men and women in different ways but also that gender difference was central to the operation of the whole system. The regime was laid on top of an economic structure in which men had far better alternatives than women. Protective and restrictive labor legislation reinforced female dependency throughout much of the twentieth century; bias in the labor market, in other words, made marriage much more of an economic imperative for women. But female disadvantage in the labor market was also male advantage, such that men enjoyed greater freedom *not* to marry. Male autonomy was thus potentially more destabilizing than female autonomy, and many of the laws that formed heterosexuality as a legal institution were written and enforced with men in mind as much or more than women. Historians have tended to see the coercive impact of laws governing marriage, for example, as falling primarily on women. But such laws also served to rein men in – beckoning them to matrimony in the first instance and then issuing ultimatums that they meet their obligations as providers as well. Welfare policy could be directly punitive to unmarried men, as when single men were swept off WPA rolls. And married men who deserted or otherwise failed to support their wives could also find themselves ensnared by municipal and state courts. Such "breadwinner regulation" was motivated by the specter of abandoned wives and children living off the public purse. It forced men's participation in the traditional nuclear family in order to staunch the redistribution of state resources toward poor mothers.

The weight of the law was more on making men want to be husbands than on managing how they actually performed their roles. But providing incentives to men to marry was not a gender-neutral initiative. It meant re-inscribing through public policy a male head-of-household who had just been, Nancy Cott has shown, written out of the common law. Setting up men as the conduit for the family's benefit package ensured men's access to women (their labor, their reproduction, and their bodies), and it guaranteed gendered power inside the family as coverture was losing some of its capacity to do so. Women could vote, they could own their own property, and they did not lose their citizenship when they married foreign men. But economic security was still channeled through husbands. Securing male privilege within marriage while coverture was, in fact, waning required the state to offer not minor credits but huge subsidies to married men.

It was not only the rewards that were substantial. The way that the state simultaneously penalized men who engaged in homosexual behavior also operated on what Gayle Rubin has called a "misplaced scale" where "the penalties for violating sex statutes [were] universally out of proportion to any

social or individual harm." So a Cuban immigrant was ordered deported in a
1959 case not for committing a homosexual act, but merely for loitering in
a public restroom for twenty minutes. In some states, the crime of sodomy
carried a twenty-year sentence. William Eskridge documents an episode
in which a gay man was incarcerated as a sexual psychopath for writing
a bad check. The way that sexual acts were "burdened with an excess of
significance," according to Rubin, meant that even when the laws did not vet
large numbers, they had the power to shape behavior. "Fear of homosexuality
kept heterosexual men in line as husbands and breadwinners," Barbara
Ehrenreich writes in her study of postwar masculinity. "The ultimate reason
why a man would not just 'walk out the door' was the taint of homosexuality
which was likely to follow him."

Throughout most of the years during which heterosexuality's legal regime
was being constructed, the state was thus relatively indifferent to homosexuality in women. This was a point that Alfred Kinsey made explicitly
in his 1953 volume on female sexuality, and he explained the phenomenon
in terms of women's lack of proximity to social, cultural, and economic
power. Even at mid-century, when the state's crackdown on sexual dissidents was most extreme, women were rarely the primary focus of state
policing. Sexual psychopath laws (and the sex crime panics out of which
they emerged) ignored women. Lesbians might be rounded up in bar raids
and arrested, but far less commonly than men. Women were occasionally
fired but still underrepresented in the civil service's "lavender" purge. Even
the Florida Johns Committee – which targeted teachers – included but, as
Stacy Braukman concludes, "subsumed" lesbians.

Only the case of the Cold War military provides a powerful exception to
the principle of state indifference – military officials reported that homosexuality was more disruptive and more prevalent among female than male soldiers, and efforts to remove homosexuals from the service targeted women
especially. But the Cold War military is also the exception that proves
Kinsey's rule. The crackdown on lesbians in the service dovetailed the
permanent integration of women into the regular military establishment.
Policing women may have been a way of maintaining gender subordination
among a population that was entering into a new relationship with state
power, and that, in choosing a military career, simultaneously rejected the
career of marriage. These were women, after all, who had better options for
remaining single than many of their peers at mid-century.

The legal regime of heterosexuality was not only a gendered regime
but it was also a *racialized regime*, such that the same legal apparatus that
channeled generous resources toward married men also directed them away
from African Americans and other racial minorities. Eileen Boris has noted
how the emergence of the welfare state coincided with the construction of

legalized segregation. Subsequently, the federal government collaborated with Southern states in blocking the access of African Americans to all kinds of benefits. Most fundamentally, occupational categories that were disproportionately black and/or Latino were excluded from coverage under the Social Security Act. African American veterans also had a hard time enjoying the plenitude of the G.I. Bill because the program was administered in racially discriminatory ways; VA officials were sometimes hostile to black soldiers, colleges refused them admission, and banks denied them housing loans. Lawmakers acknowledged that family reunification in immigration law was a way to maintain an immigrant pool that was largely European. Theirs was an ironic statement, Siobhan Somerville concludes, as it denied "the state's own history" of destroying "structures of kinship [among slaves] that might directly tie the United States to Africa." And miscegenation laws – which still existed in thirty states in 1950 – further prevented benefits from making their way into the black community through interracial marriage.

Something of a "catch-22" was thus at work by mid-century: state benefits rewarded men for marrying, but African American men, who were less firmly attached to social provision through Social Security, the G.I. Bill, or tax relief, had less economic incentive to marry. And all of this was compounded by social class in a welfare state that tended to direct the most generous resources to those who were already relatively well off. It was, specifically, their poverty (and thus their tenuous attachment to the kinds of jobs through which benefits flowed) that meant most African American men were less likely to tap into social insurance programs for themselves or their wives. Likewise, poverty meant that the benefits of filing joint income tax tended to bypass black families.

If the American system of social provision provided fewer reasons for black couples to marry, it also did little to help black families as they actually were. African American women, although far more likely than white women to be heads of household, were generally not able to claim state support on that basis, even in the temporary work relief jobs of the Depression era. Alice Kessler-Harris estimates that approximately 85 percent of wage-earning black women were ineligible for Social Security benefits.

Indeed, black women experienced the other side of the welfare bureaucracy – the side that was stingy and punitive and that policed not white homosexuality but black reproduction. State-supported birth control services emerged first in Southern states where they were (ironically) tied to anxieties about black population growth. That North Carolina welfare officials petitioned for sterilization operations for their clients suggests an inverse relationship between social provision and reproductive autonomy. And while some women may have seen in North Carolina's coercive reproductive policies a means to control their own fertility, the limited range of choices available to poor black women set them apart. (Even during the 1950s crackdown on abortion, white middle- and upper-class women who were married had a reasonable likelihood of being able to obtain a legal abortion.) North Carolina, moreover, was a leader in state-funded sterilization, though certainly not unique. Some of the worst abuses were committed in state institutions (both prisons and hospitals) where institutionalized blacks, according to Dorothy Roberts, had by World War II, taken "the place of poor whites as the main target for the eugenicist's scalpel." By the time the federal government issued a moratorium on forced sterilization in the 1970s, it was estimated that the government was funding between 100,000 and 200,000 operations per year. More than a quarter of Native American and Puerto Rican women of childbearing age were believed to have been sterilized. This was a very different investment of state dollars than the one that the government was simultaneously making in white heterosexuality.

Third, this was a *federalized and bureaucratized regime* that systematized what had been haphazard local and state initiatives into a federal partnership. In the late 1920s, before the regime had really emerged, the government of Denmark sent a letter to the U.S. State Department asking what the American government did about the problem of degeneracy. The State Department told Denmark that it did not know how the U.S. government handled degeneracy and then sent a letter to every governor asking how each of the states dealt with degenerates.[5] By the 1950s, this kind of a response would have been unimaginable: at mid-century, the federal government *knew* how degeneracy was handled in the country, and it would not have needed to consult with state governors. True, federal officials never took all responsibility away from local and state authorities, but they assumed more control for policing homosexuality as time went on, and by mid-century, it was the federal government that set the pace. In the last few years of the twentieth century, when some states and localities began to reverse patterns of government homophobia somewhat, it was the feds that held out.

Federal authorities also reached across to the other side of the homo/heterosexual binary as well. Legislators, jurists, and legal scholars have most often depicted anything pertaining to family law/marriage as a state or local concern. Legal historians such as Jill Hasday, Reva Siegel, and Nancy Cott have instead shown that in a myriad of ways the family and marriage were matters of federal law in the twentieth century. Some examples of arenas of federal law that have also encompassed family law include federal tax law,

---

[5] File # 811.115/53, Box 7449, Central Files 1910–1929, Records of the State Department, RG 59, National Archives and Records Administration (College Park, MD).

Social Security law, military law, and immigration law. Judith Resnick has argued that the idea that family law was not part of federal law reflected a devaluation of women and a related refusal to see them "as legitimate participants in the national world," as well as a belief that issues pertaining to family are not issues that merit federal attention.[6] A similar logic may have earned "gaylaw" its association with local and state law, even though defining who has qualified as a family for the purposes of federal tax, Social Security, military benefits, or immigration status has also brought issues of sex and gender non-conformity to federal law, as have exclusionary military and immigration policies that are based on homosexuality. "What constitutes a crime involving moral turpitude is a Federal question," one court asserted in one such deportation matter, "and is not dependent on the manner in which the State law classifies the violation."[7]

The legal apparatus that policed homosexuality and the legal apparatus that supported marriage were both federalized during these same years, in other words, and federalization led toward further uniformity, toward a more carefully elaborated and more universally followed set of rules about which kinds of people got to occupy the various positions in the legal regime. Expanding benefits, more than anything else, increased the definitional stakes. States became less likely to recognize common law marriage as the welfare state emerged and took form. "If common law marriage functioned as a privatized system of female support," Ariela Dubler has concluded, "the rise of alternative public sources of support [Aid to Dependent Children, for example] likely diminished the critical role that the doctrine played in the socio-legal order."

But it was not only that the welfare state may have made common law marriage less necessary, as Dubler suggests; distributing the most generous benefits through marriage put a premium on conforming to the precise legal form. Marriage was becoming, that is, something of an all-or-nothing proposition, such that murkiness was problematic. This was as true when one was exiting as when one was entering the institution. In the 1940s, the Supreme Court thus applied the "full faith and credit" clause of the U.S. Constitution to divorce, meaning that a resident of one state could travel to another state with a more liberal divorce law and have that divorce recognized at home. By 1969, when the Court struck down miscegenation laws in its landmark *Loving v. Virginia* decision, the nation was most of the way toward a marital paradigm in which, as Hendrik Hartog has put it,

---

[6] Judith Resnick, "'Naturally' Without Gender: Women, Jurisdiction, and the Federal Courts," *New York Law Review* 66 (1991), 1749–50, 1766, quoted in Jill Elaine Hasday, "Federalism and the Family Reconstructed," *UCLA Law Review* 45 (1998), 1399.

[7] *Wyngaard v. Roberts*, 187 F. Supp 527 (D.C. District Court 1960).

"marriages anywhere were about the same as marriages everywhere in the United States."

Increasing bureaucratization of the regime – especially the bureaucrat's compulsion to sort, screen, and classify – meant that government officials also pushed toward a common definition of homosexuality. Ironically, during the years in which Ariela Dubler argues that lawmakers were driving a wedge between marital performance (acting married, as in common law arrangements) and marital identity, state authorities (including courts) were increasingly collapsing homosexual performance and homosexual identity. This process was clearly visible by the late 1940s, when military officials generally dismissed the wartime notion of casual or situational homosexuality; it was articulated even more sharply in postwar immigration policy in which both immigration officials and the courts rejected more nuanced psychiatric definitions and defined homosexuality as a *legal* category in which a homosexual act connoted homosexual status. Immigrants at mid-century were not able to reverse the terms: even if they could claim to have participated in heterosexual sex (and many of them did make that claim), such behavior did not make them heterosexual in the eyes of the law.

If the state's rules defining homosexuality made the status increasingly easy to achieve at mid-century, heterosexuality was less so. What secured heterosexual status as homosexuality became more culturally salient during these years was marriage. And marriage was an especially easy shelter; not only was it the template for an increasing array of public and even private benefits, but once ensconced in it one could pretty well expect to be left alone. Indeed, as government agents across the country set up informants and stakeouts, opened mail, and performed polygraphs to drag consensual homosexual encounters into the public eye, the Supreme Court confirmed the zone of privacy around marriage in its 1965 *Griswold* decision. Privacy could thus be added to the list of benefits that the state doled out on matrimony. Like all the other perks, of course, privacy did not benefit husbands and wives equally; it could actually insulate the family from state intervention in cases of domestic violence. The revolution in equal protection law that was to come in the 1970s did little to change this. Coverture's ebb would leave the legal regime of heterosexuality largely intact.

V. STASIS OR CHANGE?

Assessing the last quarter of the twentieth century – what those years meant in terms of gender, sexuality, and law – is somewhat difficult. Not only does the boundary between past and present begin to soften and blur, but the closing years of the twentieth century seem to have been a period of both change and stasis. On one hand, coverture unraveled with accelerating speed. On the other, the legal regime of heterosexuality remained firmly planted, in some instances sinking even deeper roots into the law. Women's legal subordination through marriage altered in character, but was maintained in fact across the two regimes. The persistence of that principle hints that coverture's demise may have been less a clear death than a hand-off, a baton-pass, a kicking-up of the ways of governing women from primarily state to predominantly federal actors that dovetailed the federal government's own steady rise as the chief locus of state action.

If this line of argument seems tilted toward stasis, however, it should not diminish the magnitude of what happened in the 1970s with regard to women's position under the law. Feminism's second wave was characterized by "years of an extraordinary legal transformation," Linda Kerber has written, during which "the principle that discrimination on the basis of sex was a burden, not a privilege, challenged law and custom in virtually every sector of American life." The ground for that transformation was laid by the Civil Rights Act of 1964, in which Congress unexpectedly barred discrimination in employment based on sex alongside race and established the Equal Employment Opportunity Commission (EEOC) to enforce the law. While it would take the Commission some years to treat sex discrimination seriously, a conceptual shift was underway by the early 1970s. Federal affirmative action plans were expanded to include women as well as racial minorities, the EEOC was given standing to sue in court, and, as Alice Kessler-Harris notes, "the Labor Department yielded to the notion that sex was not an appropriate classification."

Soon after, the courts began to treat arbitrary sex classification as a violation of constitutional guarantees of equal protection in areas far beyond employment. The Supreme Court's landmark 1971 opinion in *Reed v. Reed* ruled that an Idaho law that automatically preferred men over women as administrators of an estate made an irrational distinction on the basis of sex. It was the first of a flurry of similar rulings. In *Frontiero v. Richardson* (1973) – a case in which a female soldier sought a dependency allowance for her husband – the Court came close to calling for the same test of "strict scrutiny" for sex that it used for race. Instead, in the 1976 *Craig v. Boren* case it arrived at the "intermediate scrutiny" standard that has guided the law of sex discrimination ever since. Under that standard, courts would not require evidence of a compelling government interest to uphold a law that classified on the basis of sex. Rather, to pass constitutional muster, "classifications by gender must serve important government objectives and be substantially related to these objectives." The passage of the Equal Rights Amendment in both houses of Congress (although never ratified by the states) and the decision in *Roe v. Wade* (1973) were other major feminist legal victories during these years.

The application of equal protection law to marital relations finally eviscerated the law of coverture. *Frontiero's* dismantling of the presumption of female rather than male dependency was followed by *Orr v. Orr* (1979) in the late seventies, which made men as well as women eligible for alimony. Shortly thereafter, the Court ruled in *Kirchberg v. Feenstra* (1981) that a law giving a husband exclusive control over his wife's property was unconstitutional. Married women gained autonomous access to credit (under the Equal Credit Opportunity Act of 1974) and the ability to sue third parties for a husband's loss of companionship. The obligation of a husband to support a wife became the obligation of one spouse to support another. Across the country, state legislatures removed gendered terminology from marriage laws. Eventually, even state laws that exempted men from prosecution for raping their wives were rewritten in gender-neutral language. Some states eliminated the marital rape exemption altogether.

Yet, as classification by sex was pulled out of various statutes, penalizing sex and gender non-conformity may have become even more important. Heterosexuality's legal regime did not fall along with coverture. Rather, as Peggy Pascoe has shrewdly demonstrated, reforms to make marriage laws gender neutral simultaneously inscribed the previously unarticulated assumption that marriage was an opposite-sex institution into the law. (Colorado's revised marriage law, by illustration, no longer referred to marriage as a contract between two "parties," but to a legal relationship between a "man" and a "woman.") If this instance somewhat complicates an overly sanguine narrative of coverture's decline, so too does looking beyond the arena of state law. As Jill Hasday has pointed out in her critique of what she calls the "canon" of family law, the emphasis on state law in legal scholarship on women overstates the change that has occurred in women's lives over the past century. Hasday redirects the attention of legal historians instead to the federal arena, where the picture is less rosy. Crucially, this is also a move that shifts attention back to many of the institutions that I have identified as part of the legal regime of heterosexuality, a regime that straddled multiple layers of governance, but was increasingly federal in nature as the twentieth century progressed.

Federal support for heterosexual marriage – support that was punishing not only to the unmarried, but still, in some aspects, to wives – was unabated in the last quarter of the twentieth century. This was true even as central components of the regime ostensibly became more gender neutral. Such was the case when the Supreme Court held in 1975 that the denial of a widower's claim to his dead wife's Social Security benefits was unconstitutional. (Asymmetrical benefits for husbands and wives under workmen's compensation statutes were similarly rejected by the Court during these same years.) This decision meant that the contribution of either a husband or a wife bought more insurance than that of a single person of either sex. Making Social Security fairer for wives, in other words, made it even less fair for the unmarried (with or without partners). But even for married women, the principle of fairness did not translate into actual equality.

Most late-twentieth-century wives continued to collect Social Security through their husbands, while the government increasingly offered incentives to private corporations to provide health care and retirement pensions. Like Social Security programs more generally, these private benefits were also channeled through marriage, covering not only an employee but an employee's dependents. Because male workers were more likely to hold jobs that carried such benefits, the private welfare state mirrored its public twin in making marriage nearly essential for many women and enhancing male authority in the family. But the government has not only subsidized corporations that provide these benefits to workers and their families. The 1974 Employment Retirement Income Security Act (ERISA) protected spouses from losing private retirement benefits, but not unmarried partners. Similarly, married but not unmarried partners were eligible to purchase health care for spouses after a layoff through the 1986 Consolidated Budget Reconciliation Act or COBRA.

Tax rates were altered in 1969 to ease the penalty on singles, but a reform that made the tax structure less lucrative for equally earning married couples continued to provide an enormous subsidy to traditional families with a primary breadwinner. "We expect all persons to make all decisions in life in light of their tax effect," read a 1978 Court of Claims opinion, *Paul A. Mapes and Jane A. Bryson v. The United States*, rejecting one couple's challenge to the new tax rates. The court further acknowledged that the tax code added to the "attractiveness of a prospective spouse without taxable income." Tax reform has done nothing, moreover, to address the bias against secondary earners (almost entirely working wives) – a much more serious equity issue than the marriage "penalty" or "bonus." (Gender discrimination on this basis was one of the main claims of the plaintiffs in *Mapes and Bryson v. U.S.*) And the whole discourse surrounding the "marriage penalty" failed to account for numerous other benefits built into the tax code – for example, the way that the IRS decided in 1970 that it would only provide tax-exempt status to organizations that did not have the word "gay" in their names or promote homosexuality in any way, or the way that married but not unmarried couples were shielded from estate and inheritance taxes. More recently, as corporations have begun to provide private domestic partner benefits to same-sex couples, those benefits have been taxed as income while private spousal benefits have not been so taxed. Likewise, access to veterans benefits

continued to turn on marital status, and most immigrants entered the
country through family reunification policies at century's end.[8]

Direct sanctions for homosexuality were also maintained and even intensified in some arenas. Some such penalties continued to target men more
forcefully than women, perhaps as a way of maintaining men's incentive
to marry as coverture's demise blunted (even if it did not eliminate) male
privilege within marriage. Sodomy laws were rewritten to explicitly target same-sex couples during these years, and in 1986, the Supreme Court
upheld the enforcement of Georgia's sodomy law against two men engaged
in sex in their own home. The *Bowers* decision affirmed the criminalization
of homosexual status, and the existence of state sodomy laws continued to
justify other exclusions, especially in law enforcement and military employment. Federal legislation prohibiting discrimination based on sexual orientation has never been enacted. (Such legislation has been introduced in
every Congress since the early 1970s, but hearings were not even held until
the 1990s.) The Civil Service Commission lifted its ban on the employment
of gay and lesbian employees in 1975, but continued to deny security clearances to those who had homosexual "tendencies" until the mid-1990s. In
1990, homosexuality was removed from the list of excluded classes under
federal immigration law, but a new provision barring aliens with HIV was
adopted, and provisions allowing for the entry of aliens married to U.S. citizens were not extended to same-sex couples. In 1994, the military adopted
the Don't Ask/Don't Tell policy, which actually led to an increase in the
number of personnel being purged for homosexuality. And, as had so often
been the case throughout the century, a new penalty on homosexual status was accompanied by a sweetening of the pot for heterosexual marriage
with the passage of the Family Medical Leave Act (FMLA). That law protected the jobs of workers who took up to twelve weeks off to care for
sick family members, defined to include parents, children, and spouses, but
not unmarried partners. Finally, in 1996 Congress passed two laws once
more confirming that, while not unaltered, heterosexuality's legal regime
remained viable as the century drew to a close: The Defense of Marriage Act
defined marriage in federal law as limited to opposite-sex couples; simultaneously, a major overhaul of the welfare system (the Personal Responsibility
and Work Opportunity Reconciliation Act) pointed to marriage as the way
out of poverty.

That same year, the Supreme Court issued its first major sex discrimination opinion in years, ruling that women could not be prevented from
attending the Virginia Military Institute. The proximity of the ruling to

[8] *Paul A. Mapes and Jane A. Bryson v. The United States*, 576 F.2d 896 (United States Court
of Claims 1978).

the Defense of Marriage Act suggests that the state's continuing opposition to homosexuality was not only a reaction to notions of the family in crisis (pervasive since the 1970s) or to gay liberation but to equal protection law as well. Indeed, when opponents of the ERA such as Phyllis Schlafly and Sam Ervin argued more than two decades before that equal rights for women would lead to homosexual marriage, they foresaw the way that the position of women and the position of gays would remain conjoined in the law during the post-Stonewall era. An examination of the earliest gay marriage litigation leads to a similar conclusion: when Jack Baker and Michael McConnell sued for the right to marry in Minneapolis in 1970, they were asked "who's going to be the wife?" It was not a silly question, concludes legal scholar Mary Anne Case, but rather one that "had serious legal consequences at a time when legally enforced sex-role differentiation in marriage was firmly entrenched in law and not yet seen as constitutionally problematic."

Less than three years later, when sex role differentiation *was* seen as constitutionally problematic, it was an obvious move for gay rights advocates pursuing same-sex marriage to make the law of sex discrimination central to their litigation strategy. That argument (that prohibiting same-sex marriage was sex discrimination because, as Peggy Pascoe explains, George could marry Sally but Linda could not) was put forth in the state of Washington's 1974 *Singer* case. Despite the fact that Washington had a state equal rights amendment, judges on the Washington State Court of Appeals denied the claim. Advocates of the national ERA (the amendment had by then been sent to the states for ratification) breathed a sigh of relief. The decision – while murky – provided a legal precedent that would be used to deny gay marriage cases for the next two decades. During these same years, the gay rights movement itself abandoned the argument that anti-gay discrimination was discrimination based on sex. In part this was a reaction to the way that gender conservatives (Phyllis Schlafly, Sam Ervin, and Anita Bryant, among others) had explicitly articulated the linkage between women's rights and gay rights. But it was also a result of the Court's ultimate refusal to grant strict scrutiny to distinctions based on sex. "Attaching themselves to emerging theories that distinguished sexuality from both sex and gender," Peggy Pascoe writes, lesbian and gay plaintiffs "began to argue that 'homosexuality' itself should be seen as a 'suspect' legal category and/or protected as part of a constitutional right to privacy."

This was the argument, in fact, that plaintiffs made before the Hawaii Supreme Court in the 1993 *Baehr* case. The decision was remanded back to a lower court, which ruled in 1997 that the state's marriage law was a violation of the state's equal rights amendment. Reluctant to connect "gay rights issues to categorization by sex," Pascoe concludes, the sex discrimination argument in the *Baehr* case "came as a surprise" to many in the gay community. While the legal drive for same-sex marriage in Hawaii ended in failure (when state residents enacted a constitutional amendment defining marriage as an opposite-sex institution), gay marriage campaigns in other states such as Vermont subsequently replayed the sex discrimination strategy. Finally, in Massachusetts, the state's Supreme Judicial Court ruled in *Goodridge v. Department of Public Health* (2003) that there was no rational basis for the state's ban on the marriage of same-sex couples. In May of 2004, the state began issuing marriage licenses. (Two years later Massachusetts became the first state to offer near-universal health insurance, suggesting the state's willingness to rethink marriage as the primary conduit for social provision.) Equal protection law had indeed paved the way for gay marriage, as conservatives had once warned that it would.

The recent campaigns for gay marriage have revealed how gender and sexuality are in fact still tightly conjoined in state policy. So did the Supreme Court's landmark 2001 decision (*Lawrence v. Texas*) decriminalizing state sodomy laws, which also relied on the sex discrimination argument. Nevertheless, Nan Hunter has argued that as yet "there is no clarity as to what relationship exists between sex equality law and sexual orientation claims."

Clarity, I have suggested here, can be found by looking to the history of the past century. For most of the century, the legal structures that have benefited heterosexuality have also hurt women's chances to be autonomous and fully actualized human beings. This has been true even when women have benefited economically from their status as wives; it has been true as well even when state policies have foregrounded men.

Of course there is at least the possibility that the story of the twenty-first century might be different: the significance of gay marriage may lie not only in its bringing back into view the ways that gender and sexuality are, in fact, interwoven in law and policy, but also in unraveling those ties by "short-circuit[ing]," in Peggy Pascoe's terms, the process by which marriage connects men and women to "social power differentials." So *Goodridge* threatens, on the one hand, to undercut the primary device that the state has used to reward heterosexuality for the past century. On the other, the Supreme Court's *Lawrence* decision may signal the state's waning desire to penalize homosexuality. Are we witnessing the end of marriage as an instrument to channel state benefits to heterosexuality as well as the demise of state penalties for homosexuality? Do we see here the emergence of a new regime for a new century that treats any consensual adult dyad as an acceptable unit for governance purposes? If this model portends something less than universal social provision (which would channel resources to individuals rather than couples, same-sex or otherwise), it would at least take the state out of the business of maintaining gender subordination via marriage.

Yet, to be skeptical that this is actually what the future holds is only to keep an eye on the past, looking back at the way that gendered power steadily re-inscribed itself as coverture gradually dissolved across the last century. If the twentieth century teaches us anything, it is that gender subordination and heterosexual privilege in law are not only intertwined, but incredibly tenacious.

14

LAW AND THE ENVIRONMENT

BETSY MENDELSOHN

At first glance, "environmental law" might seem, from its name, a phenomenon of the late twentieth century, growing out of the 1960s environmental movement and taking off with the National Environmental Policy Act of 1969. In fact, environmental law cannot be understood apart from the long-established debates and tensions that define the traditions of American law as a whole: individual rights and the extent of state power, the authority of law and its means of implementation. Long before the mid-twentieth century, American law was fully engaged with such matters as, for example, the private use of common resources, such as wildlife and rivers; private activity that injured public health and welfare, such as the emission of industrial wastes; and the municipal assumption of administrative power to build networked sanitary infrastructure. Courts had accepted science-based rationales to authorize law that limited private rights. Governments had engaged in interstate responses to environmental problems that crossed jurisdictional boundaries.

Two essential categories of environmental law and litigation, nuisance and natural resources, are ancient and capacious: they have occupied courts, legislatures, and other governmental authority for centuries. To resolve problems that, today, we call "environmental," Anglo-Americans have continuously developed or recognized new kinds of nuisances – from the wastes of medieval "noxious trades" to the invisible and odorless ozone created by twenty-first-century motor vehicle engines. In like manner, they have vastly broadened the category of natural resources, extending it far beyond substantial objects like fish to, for example, the stratospheric ozone layer, observable only by experts using esoteric instruments and conservable only by many nations acting in collaboration. Yet notwithstanding the transformation of these categories, all the nuisances and natural resources we encounter in this chapter do have one crucial characteristic in common: they are all public goods, to which all individuals have access, from which none may be excluded and through which, therefore, the consequences of one individual's acts are visited on all other users.

Since the turn of the twentieth century environmental law has been based largely on non-legal, fact-based disciplinary inquiry into the environment and society's usage of common resources. For example, economics theorizes the sustainable harvesting of fish and models human use of the environment, including the incentives that conserve fish in private waters and over-exploit fish in international waters. "Hard" sciences model the use of resources such as minerals, air, water and wildlife, estimating their reserves, their augmentation through natural activity, and their diminishment by human extraction or damage. Statistics has developed essential mathematical tools for making sense of the many, repeated measurements that comprise the empirical models generated by these and other disciplines. Disciplinary knowledge useful to understanding the environment gelled in the nineteenth and early twentieth centuries. Its appearance was a necessary antecedent of our modern notion of "the environment" of common resources managed by environmental law. The state has always acted to shape resource use and nuisance, but only in the twentieth century did a class of experts emerge to manage resources on a scientific basis and to assist in constructing and implementing the law. With their appearance, the role of the law changed dramatically. Legal venues ceased to dictate action as such. Disputes were reframed as conflicts between scientific information about the world on one hand and established principles of private right and state practice on the other.

The reordering of state administration in response to empirical knowledge that began in the early twentieth century occurred after hundreds of years of legal action affecting nuisance and natural resources. Justice Oliver Wendell Holmes Jr. recognized the consequences for the law of the massive importation of science fact and theory into legal venues when rendering his opinion in *Missouri v. Illinois* (1906). Bacteriologists had stated in evidence that the presence of microscopic bacteria in water samples caused typhoid fever, even though the water in question tasted and looked clean. Holmes noted that the admission of such modern, science-based evidence required that the law accept extra-legal knowledge that made an "inference of the unseen" because there was "nothing which can be detected by the unassisted senses."[1] In this and a multitude of similar cases, science and technology shifted the rules of evidence by revealing previously undetected processes through which individuals injured each other. This change greatly affected the tradition of nuisance and natural resources jurisprudence. Once the use of scientific knowledge and practices in nuisance and natural resource

---

[1] *Missouri v. Illinois*, 200 U.S. 496, 522 (1906).

disputes became common, consequential or remote injuries could be linked more firmly to a defendant's actions. Legal venues furnished opportunities for opposed interests to criticize each other's science-based methods for generating information and conclusions, but environmental lawmaking per se inexorably incorporated more and more science. In a nutshell, the development of the field during the twentieth century can be characterized as the repeated refitting of revised scientific knowledge into a system of lawmaking. Here the executive branch's incessantly expanding administrative agencies are key, where corps of experts actually implemented the laws under circumstances that also expressed the politics and economics of private rights and public powers.

Passage of the National Environmental Policy Act (1969) meant that federal courts and Congress became fully engaged with the problem of making the behavior of individuals and firms conform to science-based models of proper environmental actions. Especially challenging in this important task was dealing legally with what Ann Vileisis has pithily called the "commons component" of private property, its existence in a flux of physical and biological resource flows in time and space that communicate the consequences of private actions among all users of shared resources.[2] English and colonial American law had recognized overlapping estates in property; the modern state has substituted a set of administrative encumbrances that harness, or constrain, individual uses of property to serve the public welfare.

The economic and legal rationales for state involvement in shaping resource use are based on historical conclusions that the aggregated behavior of millions of autonomous individuals could not spontaneously generate sustainable or utilitarian employment of common resources. For example, an individual could not know the full environmental consequences of an action on private land, such as the filling of a wetland. The benefit to the individual of building a house on that land might be obvious, but the full cost to its "commons component" – the public's interest in the wetland – is not. That cost might include the eradication of stopover habitat for migratory birds or the displacement of flood waters to an already taxed watershed. These are impacts that an ornithologist or hydrologist could determine handily, but that an economist might monetize only with difficulty and that the private landowner could well discount utterly.

Environmental law tackles problems far more complex than the filling of a wetland for a house lot. But because the commons component is a universal characteristic of property ownership, this simple example illustrates a universal problem that those who shape environmental law

---

[2] Ann Vileisis, *Discovering the Unknown Landscape: A History of America's Wetlands* (Washington, DC, 1997), 6.

confront – that modeling impacts on the commons component can produce radically different outcomes according to the interests and expertise of those debating the matter. In actions involving environmental questions, contenders can be clumped roughly into two groups according to their approach to the commons component: (1) those who, relatively speaking, are willing to discount it and hence call for property rights with fewer administrative encumbrances and (2) those less willing or unwilling to discount it and hence propose to temper property rights with individual rights to access a healthy environment.

These are the themes that inform this chapter, pursued across three distinct eras of U.S. history. Through the mid-nineteenth century, natural resource laws were exercised positively to serve public welfare; as the definition of public welfare shifted, however, lawmakers both in the individual states and new nation emphasized economic growth more than public health. Nuisance law development was more varied. Cities exercised their police powers to promote public health and welfare; meanwhile, rural neighbors turned wilderness into settled land by spending natural resources to make wealth.

The Civil War proved to be a watershed because the war affirmed the effectiveness of central state power. Between the Civil War and World War II, the state and federal governments grew immensely both in budget and in expert-advised administrative capacity, and they redefined public welfare, extending public ownership over, and even expropriating, natural resources. As we have seen, nuisance law was transformed by the turn to science-based evidence, increasing the range of opportunities to show legally how people were doing injury to each other and also to public resources, such as water and wildlife.

Immediately after World War II, and in reaction to the growth of administrative state authority during the New Deal and then the headlong rush to mobilize for wartime production, Congress moved to require greater transparency in administrative procedure by passing the Administrative Procedure Act (1946). Congress also legislated particular controls on industrial pollution. Nuisance would provide an avenue for advocates of a clean environment to link pollution with public health.

The forces driving changes in environmental law have shifted over time. In the first era, widely held social ambitions for population increase and economic growth shaped political decisions and therefore legal developments. In the second era, government began to assert power over common resources as a way to influence their use and counteract the negative consequences of private development by millions of autonomous individuals and firms. It also may be true that government at both the state, and, notably, at the federal levels, experienced institutional imperatives to perpetuate and increase their bureaucracies by identifying new areas of public life to control. The third (modern) era continued the trends of the second, but moderated by the novel interjection of a popular voice into the implementation of law by expert-staffed government agencies, safeguarded by the Administrative Procedure Act. An additional marker of modern environmental law is its prospective consideration of alternative plans for government-funded projects, an administrative step established by the National Environmental Policy Act in 1969, that injects some creativity and flexibility into agency rulemaking. During this most recent era, the role of environmental advocacy in lawmaking has been broadened as a growing proportion of local, state, federal, and even international policymaking is framed using environmental rationales. The commons component reflects not only the mutual dependence of individuals and peoples on shared resources but also provides the rationale for government management of that interdependence.

I. THE COLONIAL AND ANTEBELLUM ERA: USING RESOURCES FOR PUBLIC WELFARE

The state's power to shape private actions respecting public nuisances and natural resources was imported to the colonies. Neighborly disputes over nuisances, meanwhile, were resolved at common law. In general, English law promoted resource conservation and avoidance of nuisance, but in the new landscape of abundant resources and living space, American law incrementally abandoned the English approach. American society and politics encouraged economic and population growth and spent the continent's natural wealth to achieve these ends.

The material stuff of the landscape – wildlife, soil, water, timber, and stone – was valued primarily for its utility in attracting population and fueling economic growth. In the 1960s, intellectual historians such as Roderick Nash documented the cultural bias of New England settlers against the natural American landscape, linking it to a Protestant religious understanding of "wilderness" as a place of individual and communitarian moral trial. American courts overturned the English notion of "waste" in an American context that celebrated deforestation as a great step taken to civilize the wilderness. On the way to making a pastoral landscape, colonial town governments coerced private landowners to develop their property – for example, by requiring that a mill be put in operation at a good waterpower site on pain of forfeit of title to that piece of ground.

Community oversight did not vanish from the legal landscape at the end of the colonial period, for the police power endured, but the political meaning of the Revolution, as written into the early national period's land law, liberalized the ownership of land. Several legal scholars have shown that Americans transformed private law in the nineteenth century to ease entrepreneurial uses of natural resources associated with landed property by, for example, allowing waterpower dams to overflow private land with impunity. Resources were used actively to fuel an economic pump: in the antebellum period, law operated on the premise that what was good for the entrepreneurial landowner was good for the community. American life became resource intensive, with dispersed agriculture, high per capita wood and water consumption, and an ideological bias in favor of independent, autonomous land ownership. Thus, federal law favored dispersed household landholdings over nucleated town settlements. European visitors reported the Americans' "wasty ways," but Americans identified deforestation and the consumption of resources as steps toward civilizing the landscape.

The colonies had been established by the Tudor-Stuart monarchy as enterprises integral to a mercantilist empire. Based on trade between the wealthy central state and the resource-rich peripheral colonies, the mercantilist trade scheme established the extraction of barely processed resources as the primary economic practice of the colonies. Fish, furs, timber products, and agricultural products flowed into transatlantic trade. England established its right over particular resources by blazing trees significant for shipbuilding. England and France chartered companies that built extensive networks of fur extraction relationships among native peoples affiliated with one or another empire. These networks played political roles by establishing alliances, through trade, among the peoples that populated the interior of North America. The vessels that carried these resources to England were the targets of piracy, though the wealth they carried was puny compared to the Spanish vessels filled with silver from South America. In return, ships brought people and manufactured goods to the New World. Machines to fabricate useful and desirable things, and the skilled people to operate them, resided in Europe.

The Beginnings of Environmental Law

Two stories from this first period of legal development, typically interpreted for their importance to property law, hold central interpretive sway for the beginnings of environmental law. One is the story of the eighteenth-century mill acts, which Morton Horwitz analyzed so fruitfully to document a liberalization of property rights. Later scholars have expanded the list of interested parties in this story to add to the competition between mill owners and farmers with grazing land along riparian property that caught Horwitz's attention. A more highly contested interaction between customary and entrepreneurial users of rivers is revealed in lawsuits between dam owners and their neighbors, the one seeking to operate water-powered mills, the other to catch migrating fish. These conflicts arose not over the flooding of a neighbor's private property, but over the customary easement asserted by the public to catch fish in rivers navigable "in fact" by vessels used in the area (a wider definition of navigability than customary common law definitions). The mill acts might suggest that over the course of the eighteenth century the legal definition of rivers reduced them to mere sources of water power, but the law as experienced argues for a much messier course of development: Some rivers, such as the Merrimack, became entirely dominated by textile mills. Elsewhere, however, the public easement question remained a live issue. Courts would revisit the matter throughout the nineteenth century, some confining their inquiry to navigation or fishing, others taking a broader approach to include harvesting ice and digging gravel. Thus, while some rivers became dominated by industry, others retained their public easement. This would serve as the kernel for the state's assertion of power over rivers in the late nineteenth century.

A second story about property law arises from the typical interpretation of a New York case, *Pierson v. Post* (1805). In this case, Pierson (a "saucy intruder") encountered and appropriated a fox pursued by one Lodowick Post. The court supported Pierson's right to the fox against Post's claim to have created a property interest in the "noxious beast" by means of chasing the fox using dogs. After consulting many traditional European authorities, Judge Daniel D. Tompkins held that a piece of land or an animal becomes property when it is marked as such by an artifact, such as a fence surrounding land or a decoy floating by a wild duck, or of course by the act of someone taking it into possession. The case clearly defined the moment of creating property in a fox and provided dicta about asserting ownership over other animals. For environmental law purposes, however, the case both confirmed the contemporary belief that foxes were vermin or nuisances that should be killed and also found that – had it wished to exercise it – the state's police power extended to fox hunting. The colonies and young states enacted bounty laws on wolves, bears, and bobcats to shape their rural ecology by eliminating predators and perhaps simply to reduce the threatening nature of the wilderness that surrounded them. Modern jurists interpret *Pierson* for its importance to property, yet it also serves to underline contemporary assumptions of the state's legitimate police power to regulate the taking of wildlife and its ultimate control over that wildlife's fate. When social movements to conserve wildlife arose in the 1870s (at the beginning of the second period in the history of environmental law), they tapped this latent authority.

Police Powers

Just as colony and state governments exercised police power to shape the use of public resources like rivers and to eradicate predators, urban places also exercised police power to ameliorate urban environments that spread disease through land, air, and water contaminated by human and animal wastes. Towns used quarantine and inspection powers and also passed special laws that responded to nuisances in particular geographic areas, such as those on the fringe of urban areas experiencing land use pressures.

In the mid-seventeenth century, New York City had supported an outlying area of farms; one hundred years later merchants rebuilt the area with country estates. The Collect Pond, a seventy-acre, seventy-foot-deep water body, had provided fresh water in the colonial period; it had a drinking water pump at its eastern outlet. Soon after independence, however, the Collect Pond had been turned over to support industries characteristic of the pre-industrial city, such as tanneries, breweries, stockyards, and slaughterhouses. Wastes fouled its waters, and the urban population divided along lines of wealth into those who bought water from vendors who trucked it in from the countryside and the poor who used shallow wells around town. From old travel accounts, it appears that Americans tolerated a higher degree of odor, inconvenience, and rubbish than their European visitors, an urban counterpart of the "wasty ways" apparent in the inefficiency of rural husbandry. Like other colonial American cities, however, New York City used its police power to define nuisance activity and public nuisances, to require owners to clean up around these nuisance industries and other urban features like privies and stables, and to determine their waste disposal practices. At times, cities banished the nuisance trades from city limits, requiring them to relocate on the urban fringe, away from residences; this in part explains why industries clustered on the urban fringe at the Collect Pond. Without zoning or planning, however, the growing city crept up to and around the nuisances in their polluted neighborhoods, inspiring lawsuits and ordinances that drove nuisance trades farther from residential areas.

Colonial cities grew into the countryside, but were anchored by their orientation to water for commercial transportation. Their ports sustained the economy, yet the flow of people through ports threatened urban public health by bringing diseased people from elsewhere. The colonial city therefore exercised the power of inspection and quarantine to protect its people and markets from communicable disease. Ordinances to abate nuisances could not prevent the epidemics of yellow fever that decimated port cities in the 1740s and 1790s, however. It took more than the exercise of power to promote public health and welfare; effective action required accurate information about the causes of disease, information that was lacking until the late nineteenth century.

The Significance of the Federal Constitution

The American Revolution created a legal break with the predominantly English law tendencies of the colonial era. Three provisions in the subsequent Federal Constitution created the foundations for new and distinctive federal powers that would prove of major importance to natural resource conservation and pollution. These were the regulation of interstate commerce, federal adjudication of interstate conflicts, and constitutional provision for compensation for property takings. The Constitution also enumerated the power of the states to inspect goods imported into their limits. Finally, repeating the broad terms of the Preamble, Article 1, section 8 granted Congress power to provide for the "general Welfare," an umbrella term that has authorized, by analogy and the addition of detail, many environmental laws. At first, the impact of these provisions was essentially negative: they limited the extent to which the states might compete with each other and thus preserved important degrees of cooperation among them. In the second and third periods of environmental legal development, however, these provisions would become the basis on which the federal government began itself to act positively to conserve natural resources and reduce pollution.

The Federal Constitution lodged power to regulate commerce among the states in the national government. Article 1, section 10, however, reserved to the states the power of inspecting goods brought into a state (although this action could not create a revenue stream beyond the cost of inspection). The power of inspection enabled the states to use their police powers to establish and enforce laws that conserved the health of domestic animals and plants from insect and disease threats that emerged in other states. The Commerce Clause also provided a basis for Congressional authority to conserve wild game animal populations; subsequent laws expanded the federal power to regulate the taking of species that crossed state lines, a special police power that no one state could implement effectively.

Within the terms of the Constitution, one may detect a rationale for removing environmental conflicts from the states – the traditional arena of police regulation – to the federal government. Article 3, section 2 gave the federal courts authority to adjudicate conflicts in several situations that would prove strategic in the development of environmental law, among them conflicts between states and conflicts between a party and the federal government. As described earlier, science theory and practice fueled the emergence of evidence of harms among distant neighbors and neighboring states, breeding new types of nuisance and enabling parties to litigate about new kinds of problems. In the early twentieth century, when interstate conflicts about water-borne and air-borne pollution raised the legal question of the federal government's responsibility to intervene in interstate conflicts, these constitutional provisions turned the federal courts into venues of environmental conflict resolution.

Coincidentally, the legislative and executive branches, especially during the administration of Theodore Roosevelt, became preoccupied with conserving the quality of common resources – water, land, and wildlife – in the public interest. Whereas in the nineteenth century constitutional provisions enabled neighboring states to call on federal courts to resolve conflicts about shared boundaries on watercourses, in 1900 they sought federal injunctions against the continued pollution of one state's natural resources by another. Combined with Roosevelt's activism for resource conservation and Congress's legislation to enlarge the scope of administrative agency action, the federal courts' review of interstate conflicts meant an enormous acceleration in the activity of the federal government in resource management, and also – to a lesser extent – in pollution control.

A final provision of the Constitution set the stage for the modern movement against the "regulatory takings" that characterize the implementation of modern environmental legislation. The Fifth Amendment, ratified in December 1791, required that owners be compensated justly if the government took their property for public use. Not all states adopted this provision for the construction of state infrastructure and state-chartered transportation companies. The states and federal government subsequently compensated owners for taking private land or for removing valuable materials from it to build highway, canal, harbor, drainage, water supply, irrigation, flood control, soil conservation, waterpower, and railroad infrastructure and to consolidate lands preserved as national forests and parks. In the modern period of federal environmental statutes, the government has adopted a strategy long used by cities: shaping the private development of land, wetlands, and water. This exercise of police power has earned the modern label of "regulatory takings" – the use of law to take not the value of the land as it has been improved by the owner, but, by foreclosing the owner's developmental options, to "take" potential future market value. These provisions of the Constitution were not used by states or the federal government to promote environmental law in the antebellum period, but became important late in the century and continue to frame environmental law today.

Treaties

Early federal treaties also served as a vehicle for forms of environmental regulation, establishing, for example, legal precedents for a national interest in the conservation of wild animal populations. The natural resource of fish was specifically noted in Article Three of the Treaty of Paris (1783), by which Great Britain undertook not to harass American vessels fishing at the Grand Banks near Newfoundland. Access to wildlife carried national security implications. Scores of treaties between the United States and native peoples excluded the latter from ranging through ceded territory to hunt. This expressed in treaty form the colonial practice of using land sales contracts to limit access by native peoples to natural resources. Natural resources typically did not themselves form the object of law, but laws and policies affected access to natural resources to such a degree that there were political consequences. For example, in the 1790s, when he was Secretary of State, Thomas Jefferson found that British and French tariffs on whale oil, intended to protect their own domestic whalers, injured American profits and kept ships in port, thereby luring experienced sailors from the United States at a time of diplomatic uncertainty with those nations.

The Environment in Antebellum Legal Development

Though limited in the scope of its power, the antebellum federal government acted through its responsibilities for defense and the public domain to modify the environment. On the frontier, the Army negotiated treaties with the Indians for cessions of strategic nodes and corridors, and its Topographical Bureau improved some of these areas into harbors and navigable rivers. These strategic concerns differed from the many later schemes forwarded by Western settlements to draw federal money to their area to build better communication with the East. Despite the many petitions from Western cities and states, few transportation proposals won subsidies from a Congress divided over the sectional controversy of Western internal improvements. The Army also assessed the Western lands and published reports of its explorations that described and illustrated the West's topography, travel routes, residents, and natural resources. The acquisition and publication of this wealth of detail informed laws regarding Indians, emigration, timber, coal, water, and land ownership. The primary military and land stewardship concern of the period was to settle the land, binding it to the political and economic systems of the East Coast.

Of similar environmental impact were administrative procedures promulgated by the Treasury Department's General Land Office. This agency surveyed the public domain, assessing its value qualitatively by describing vegetation, topography, and mineral resources and quantitatively by measuring the extent of land and water and the boundaries between them. The Land Office departed from the nucleated, town-controlled settlement and property ownership patterns established by the English in the East and the Spanish in the Southwest and the clustered agricultural settlements created by the French in the Mississippi Valley. Its deputy surveyors generated thousands of plats that became the "legal description" of land by which the Treasury Department sold title according to a mile-square grid to individuals.

By instructing surveyors how to measure water and dry land, the Commissioner of the Land Office forced all varieties of land into one of these two categories, a legal fiction examined and tinkered with over subsequent decades by courts that sought to quiet title to contested areas that fell between the two, wetlands and small bodies of water. Only at the turn of the twentieth century did federal courts resolve the problems of lakebed and marsh ownership generated by the Land Office's simplistic initial categories. In selling the public domain to individuals, the federal government also eschewed all but the most simple, initial planning of which land to sell when failing to consider the utility of matching settlement types to its environmental resources and geographic location. Whereas settlement of the colonies proceeded after assessing local resources, settlement of Ohio and parts west proceeded quickly and atomistically in a climate of economic speculation. The abstractly square parcels of land offered at a land office were selected based on the location of a particular tract and its land characteristics. To pursue advantages that cut across several tracts, such as a spring and river, an owner had to purchase all of them, creating a tract tessellated from several parts. The administration of land measurement and sale obeyed a political judgment that favored quick sales over orderly settlement.

The states formed during the antebellum period retained broad powers over landed property, exclusive of those enumerated for the federal government. They acted to transform their natural landscapes by improving rivers for navigation, building roads and canals, outlawing timber trespass on private or public lands, and placing bounties on pest species such as the wolf. In Illinois, profits from developing salt deposits funded road improvements, indicating both the intimate relationship between two landscape change activities, resource exploitation and infrastructure development, and the co-creative relationship between resource extraction and state power. State laws, such as one enacted by Illinois in 1829, also promoted particular land use practices that recognized the legitimacy of shared management in the registration and enclosure of common fields. By setting out rules for neighbors to manage common fields, Illinois established a legal process that drainage districts would use to powerful effect during the 1860s and later to increase the productivity of the region's heavy clay soils.

Environment and Continental Expansion

To the end of reorienting natural resource policy toward building a nation and increasing domestic settlement and commerce, the original states had relinquished their claim to Western lands, so that the public domain became a bank of natural resource wealth. Congress sold these lands to settle the frontier, but also to raise money for the cost of running the government. In addition, between 1789 and 1861 the United States acquired vast additional domains of land, by purchase, treaty, and war. As its population center shifted westward, cities arose where once there had been colonial trading posts, and state and federal governments subsidized railroads, canals, harbors, roads, and river improvements that would bring agricultural products and natural resources into the economy. Typically, federal investments in infrastructure developed sites selected by the War Department in its treaties with native peoples in the 1790s and later; therefore, they flowed along lines that military planners considered strategic to consolidating the frontier in an era of water-based transportation. Despite this hint at an organized system, most laws shaped the American landscape by transferring the public domain into the hands of millions of individual landowners. In terms of governance, the transfer of title to individuals in the public domain states diffused settlement to the degree that counties, not towns, became the administrative units that implemented state laws and collected taxes. Except for brief periods of direct taxation before 1802 and during 1812–17, in the antebellum period federal land sales and customs duties funded most of the national government's expenditures. The government's desire for revenue and the prevailing cornucopian vision of wilderness meant that Americans conceived of the natural environment as having value only when taken from nature, turned into property, and used.

Given the cultural value of civilizing the wilderness and the lack of ecology and earth sciences, there was no conception of planning land use by watersheds or any other regional characteristic. The Treasury Department's system of severing national title to the public domain and vesting it in millions of households implemented an utterly decentralized plan that departed from colonial systems of creating title in land. In another way that remained in keeping with colonial practice, however, antebellum law continued to depart from English precedent by equating deforestation with progress, rather than with the traditional notion of waste. Whereas in settled and cultivated England, law managed overlapping estates in land conservatively to sustain the land's productive value, American land and resource law existed in conditions of abundance. There were fewer over-lapping interests, there was a bias against wilderness, and people valued clear-cutting a tract for timber cash rather than maintaining it for a constant stream of firewood by cutting branches carefully. The countervailing timber trespass acts of the early nineteenth century merely sought to protect the state's title to timber as an economic asset. The doctrine of waste, which in England had permitted one owner to prevent another owner from changing the productive use of land radically, stopped curbing land use changes by the early nineteenth century. In the antebellum period, state after state rejected waste and adopted a rationale of good husbandry to authorize clearing or deforestation as an improvement to land. State courts, therefore, changed the law to fit American conditions by legitimating the destruction of forests that physically impeded the goals of political and economic growth held by an agricultural nation.

The system of property ownership, land titles, and recordation also changed in the United States from English precedent. Beginning in the colonial era, title to land was not customary or based on long use, but rather recorded in order to be observed by the community; this practice was adopted by the Land Office through a system of plats and patents recorded in the national capital. Private transactions, such as signing over a deed or patent, signing a quitclaim, or creating a right of dower for particular tracts, became legally defensible only when recorded in the county court. Because of the great degree of speculation in Western lands, owners often did not possess land or improve it, opening the door for squatters to earn title to land through adverse possession. Squatters could gain title to another's land by using it openly for many years; the emergent American law therefore preferred resident land users rather than absentee landowners. In trial court proceedings about adverse possession, neighbors testified about the activi-ties of claimants, describing when they cleared land of trees and brush, when they planted fruit or shade trees, when they fenced, when they plowed or cultivated, when they built a structure, and when they resided there. By favoring land users, courts placed a burden on absentee landowners to survey periodically the land they owned and eject squatters in order to interrupt their continuous possession of the land and thus prevent them from seeking title to it. The American standards for adverse possession favored use over non-use of land and therefore favored environmental change in the form of landscape transformation from a natural to a cultivated state.

Apart from the natural resources located on individual property, courts and legislatures recognized some broader, landscape-scale environmental features. Most significantly, they recognized rivers for the public interest of navigation in them. In the antebellum period, Congress acted on the lan-guage of the Northwest Ordinance (1787) that labeled navigable tributaries

of the St. Lawrence and Mississippi Rivers as "common highways and forever free" (Article 3) by giving to the Corps of Engineers responsibility for
improving major rivers for navigation by creating harbors, reducing shoals,
maintaining channel depths, and removing snags. Their work linked East to
West along the Ohio River and Great Lakes, and North to South along the
Mississippi River. These civil engineering works complemented the Army's
frontier activities of surveying strategic routes to the West and consolidating the frontier; skills for both were taught at West Point, established under
President Jefferson in 1802 as an officer training school.

To extend these national improvements to tributaries, states authorized
counties to assess taxes to fund the removal of snags in rivers that the
legislature considered to be public highways. These laws and their means
of financing and execution mirrored the creation and maintenance of state
highways and concomitant drainage ditches and bridges. There were no
standardized technical practices for doing any of this work; it was left to
the will of, typically, three residents of good judgment, who served as
highway commissioners and also assessed payments and awarded damages
to neighbors of the road or navigable route whose lands were affected.
Whereas the route of an improvement might be set in the state house, its
execution and financing were determined by commissioners who resided in
the counties.

Environment and Improvement

The nineteenth-century Mississippi River and its floodplain were objects
of early federal efforts at infrastructure improvement. The vast valley presented an asset for navigation and a potential asset for agriculture; its history
traces changes in science, technology, and law that permitted its management to occur not at a local but at a regional scale. To be useful to the
new steamboats, snags had to be removed and channels marked, and to be
useful for agriculture, floods had to be blocked by levees. In 1824, Congress
authorized the Corps of Engineers to do snag and channel work, but work on
land, building levees, remained in the hands of local landowners with occasional intervention by states. Individuals in the Mississippi Valley bought
sections of dry ground from the public domain, but usually not wetlands,
leaving millions of soggy acres in the hands of a distant federal government. Because these swamp lands often bordered navigable waters, their
potential value for agriculture and ports was high, and the Swamp Lands
Act of 1851 transferred these leftovers from federal to state ownership so
that states could divest them and promote their drainage. This act affirmed
the states' broad right to manage land in the public interest, and Mississippi River states responded in the 1850s by authorizing levee districts that

enabled neighbors to collaborate on flood control. Only with the Mississippi hydrology study in the late 1850s did the Corps of Engineers measure and model the hydrology of this enormous watershed and create good information on which to base a catchment-wide system of flood control; thereafter the Corps operated not simply in the river, but also on land to build levees and stabilize banks using steam-powered technology. In 1888, the Corps was authorized to extend its administrative authority to any obstruction of a defined navigable channel, and in 1899 Congress required the Corps to issue permits for obstructions to navigable channels. Today, the Corps is present in all water management, and because surface waters are the major component of ecosystems, its activities implement environmental law on the ground.

Just as the prevailing atomistic, market-based conception of land ownership denied the value of land-use planning, antebellum American law – as reflected in *Pierson v. Post* – also viewed animals and plants as free and available for the taking. States sought to eradicate unwanted animals and plants through the police power to regulate public nuisance. Illinois placed bounties on wolf scalps in the 1840s, but even earlier, in 1819, criminalized timber trespass with the high penalty of $8 per tree. Canada Thistle (an aggressive, creeping perennial weed that infested crops, pastures, and rangeland) was to be grubbed out by owners, or a neighbor could do so and require the county clerk to collect the cost from the negligent landowner. By the 1850s, natural historians in Illinois and Wisconsin noted that three decades of agriculture had "driven out, by the hand of improvement" many if not most earlier plant and animal species. This naturalist's observation recognized the destruction of habitat by agricultural cultivation and town-building, and the disruption of species by habitat fragmentation, but it did not mobilize any type of conservation law. On occasion, state legislatures used their police powers to enact statutes that limited hunting or fishing, but these often applied only to particular counties; they were intended to protect the rights of county residents from competition by strangers who traveled to counties on the migration routes of game birds to hunt. Antebellum conservation laws therefore expressed the state's property interest in natural resources, protected the public welfare as understood at the time, and favored local interests.

Antebellum Urban Environments

Cities confronted environmental problems from their inception because dense populations impose incompatible activities on shared, common resources, such as surface waters, air, and common lands. Long before industrialization, nuisances of soot, vibration, noise, odor, filth, drainage, and fire

jostled unavoidably in cramped town spaces with the necessary resources of
clean water and air, peace, orderliness, and public health and safety. Municipal law had a long and strong tradition of recognizing a public interest in
common resources and resolving conflicts among incompatible users. Once
categorized as public nuisances, stables and privies could be inspected to
see whether their upkeep had deteriorated to such a degree that their stench
was more than an inconvenience and constituted an actual public nuisance.
In addition, city governments enforced the cutting of weeds and other activities intended to reduce miasmas – foul air from rotting organic matter –
that were thought to cause disease. Inspectors could require the owners
to abate these nuisances, or they could remedy them and bill the owners
for costs. Public health, therefore, provided an avenue by which public
authorities used nuisance law to change the environmental conditions of
cities. Although science did not explain accurately how sanitation problems caused disease, many of the steps taken by city governments, based
on miasma theory rather than the modern germ theory, effectively reduced
illness. The marked growth of state and city government in the antebellum
period seemed to promise modern civil society – its economy based in food
production, natural resource extraction, urban commerce, and industry –
an active and beneficent state to police private action in these areas.

When Thomas Cooley wrote his *Treatise on the Constitutional Limitations
Which Rest Upon the Legislative Power of the States of the Union* in 1868, he
acknowledged the beneficent power of city ordinances, as authorized by
states, even as he noted new challenges presented by emerging technologies. The financing of public improvements, such as drainage and street
paving, progressed block by block as groups of neighbors agreed to bear the
cost, even if construction plans were determined in city hall. This privatism
led to the building of infrastructure in segments, as neighbors demanded it,
reflecting closely held beliefs about the relation of neighbors to the city as a
whole. Many cities adopted bureaucratic government and general taxation
as they provided networked infrastructure to supply clean water and drain
away wastes, thereby protecting the health and welfare of their residents
through new types of technology. Some of these municipal activities, such as
banning wood construction and spending general taxes on local segments of
networked public drainage, were challenged in the courts by private owners. Urban residences in the antebellum city were more self-reliant, which
helps explain their privatism. Thousands of individually managed, fenced
yards received sewage, household and workshop wastes, and some produced
food such as vegetables, milk, and meat. Only later, at the time of Cooley's
treatise, would urban populations begin to acknowledge their shared destiny, despite differences in ethnicity and income. That acknowledgment

created for the first time the political will to authorize general taxes to pay for city-wide infrastructure.

The antebellum period also witnessed a broadening of manufacturing from its exclusive location at waterfall sites in the countryside to coal-fired steam-powered factories in cities. Cities based on water-borne commerce, such as New York, Boston, Philadelphia, Baltimore, Chicago, Cincinnati, St. Louis, and New Orleans, developed an overlay of rail transportation infrastructure that ended at wharves, and they also saw the establishment of rail-oriented manufacturing suburbs on the urban fringe where land was cheaper and parcels larger. This shift in commercial and factory geography shaped perceptions of nuisance in the antebellum "walking city," in which stables, residences, slaughterhouses, markets, and coal-fired steam-powered factories existed in close proximity.

Before coal-fired steam-powered factories arose in cities, however, the rotting organic wastes from markets, stables, stockyards, and slaughterhouses formed nuisances, and the last two assumed a large scale in many cities. The consequences for law included a growth of public nuisances defined by ordinances and a growth of permanent city employees who policed violations; cities also built the administrative capacity to construct drainage systems that removed fluid organic wastes from densely populated areas. Like their colonial antecedents, antebellum cities on occasion required "noxious" trades to relocate to the edge of town, thereby creating separate manufacturing districts that concentrated pollution and normalized its presence. Courts recognized the rights of plaintiffs against traditional nuisance industries more readily than against new types of polluters, not because the former caused more severe pollution but rather because, culturally, they were perceived more readily as engaged in polluting activity. The power that cities exerted in the public interest should, similarly, be distinguished from the effectiveness of that power, since physical chains of evidence between cause and effect – for example between drinking sewage-laden water and getting sick – were established by science only late in the nineteenth century. As historians have detailed, the realities of American political culture meant that citizens of each city had to empower their local governments to solve systemic sanitation problems by enacting ordinances that shaped behavior and authorized bricks-and-mortar solutions.

Underneath the politics of cities, whether expressed in privacy, boosterism, segmentation, or bureaucracy, is the physical material of transportation, buildings, people, markets, resources, and wastes that creates the urban environment. For most post-Civil War cities, that physical conglomeration grew rapidly, encroaching on land dedicated to other uses and absorbing it into its structure. The internal geography of cities also increased in diversity as commercial entrepôts acquired manufacturers, transportation grafted a layer of railroads onto navigation, and public transportation permitted residential neighborhoods to exist far from workplaces. In the 1880s, with the advent of steel-frame construction, cities gained in density and wealth as buildings became taller. Giving up their previous reliance on privacy, assessments, and segmentation to provide public services to urban localities, by the mid-nineteenth century cities had begun to turn to what would become a more modern form of bureaucratic government. State constitutions, however, limited the power of local governments to raise taxes and own infrastructure. When states enlarged the power of municipal corporations in response to urban lobbyists, cities were able to build the sanitary infrastructure that compensated for the poor environmental quality generated by hundreds or thousands of human organisms and their animal helpmates living in a dense urban settlement. This money paid for the installation of networked water supply, drainage, transportation, and sometimes other utility technologies that supported the same, old goals of clean water and air, peace, public health and safety, and orderliness.

Managing Antebellum Environments

Scholarship on nuisance has examined urban places where coal-fired steam power manufacturers generated smoke, smells, vibrations, and noise at levels new to cities. The fuel shift from water to coal-steam generated a shift in location; factories no longer had to be located at river falls, but rather could be located wherever bulk coal could be carried by water or railroad, even near their labor force in cities. Urban boosters celebrated these new manufacturers, but others complained that factories prevented neighbors from enjoying their own private property. Neighbors filed private nuisance suits to enjoin manufacturers from casting ashes and other annoyances, and they sought damages to compensate for particular harms. In the densely populated, unzoned walking city, private nuisance suits and public nuisance ordinances and enforcement interacted. Emergent industries based on coal-fired steam power, such as iron foundries, rolling mills, sawmills, railroad shops, and machine tool mills, received the brunt of case law attention, and they clustered themselves with like neighbors and on the edge of town, a practice that reduced drawing neighborly lawsuits. Traditional nuisances, such as tanneries, breweries, slaughterhouses, and stables, also attracted regulatory attention, earning the legal label of public nuisances that had to be located in certain places or operated in certain ways. An increase in administrative power in municipal government was approved by state legislatures in the decades before and after the Civil War to manage the infrastructure that enabled thousands of people and their animals and waste to coexist.

State and federal management of landed resources became more pronounced with time, but certain features of the national landscape enjoyed an early, high level of attention because of their economic or political importance to the nation's economic growth. Significantly, the Mississippi River experienced a shift from local to national management. The states used the concept of public nuisance to provide incentives to shape the species composition of the countryside. Cities used their broad police powers to promote public welfare among a dense population of incompatible users of land, air, and water. To provide effective networked infrastructure supported by general taxation, however, cities had to wait until their populations realized that rich and poor shared a common interest in public health and welfare.

II. GILDED AGE THROUGH WORLD WAR II: CREATING GOVERNMENT ADMINISTRATION

The Civil War and two world wars shaped American perceptions of nuisance by inuring neighbors to new levels of manufacturing pollution that were associated with productivity, prosperity, and the war effort. Once the impediment of Southern obstructionists had seceded from the nation, a united Congress authorized contracts for a northern route of the transcontinental railroad and authorized the Department of Agriculture and new Western land policies in the 1860s. In the decades after the war, highly capitalized railroad corporations, subsidized by grants of land from the public domain, opened the West to wheat agriculture and mining. Government also grew, as it retained some of the controlling practices created for the war effort. To build the transportation system and the infrastructure desired by growing cities, industry created ingenious devices to compensate for environmental conditions. Coal-fired steam-powered machines moved earth to make levees for flood control, dredge channels for navigation and sanitation drainage, build dams for reservoirs, and dredge low areas or level hills to fill marshes. Steel manufacturers stamped out pipes to carry water from one watershed so that a city might prosper in another, and iron works cast the pipe that hooked up millions of urban residents with networked sewerage. In a mutually beneficial interaction, ship manufacturers built vessels with deeper drafts, and the Corps of Engineers annually requested greater appropriations to fund the dredging of deeper harbors and channels to accommodate them. This iron and fossil fuel technological system spread through the landscape with changes to law that are better documented for their impacts on liability and economic growth than for environmental quality and the growth of municipal power. Big, new technology offered possibilities for environmental transformation that David E. Nye calls an "American technological sublime" or human-made perfection of landscape.[3]

Governing the Environment

Even as firms grew in the Gilded Age, state governments also grew, and they asserted and extended their authority into those areas of the environment in which the law did not recognize private property. In *Pierson v. Post* the court had concluded that wildlife existed *res naturae*, in a state of nature, and its taking and ultimate fate were determined by state law. The police power reserved to the states by the Constitution became the vehicle by which states enacted hunting and fishing laws and created state and county park systems. State legislatures authorized enlarged powers for municipal corporations to tax residents to build, operate, and own the massive infrastructure that enabled urban populations to prosper with some semblance of public health. The legislatures also created agricultural standards and inspection regimens that favored entrepreneurial commercial horticulture and agriculture over older methods of rural production.

The Progressive era legislation that often is seen as the point of origin for modern conservation law also can be understood as a particular strategy by which the states and the federal government chose to control access to resources: by physically sequestering areas rather than by enforcing rules about hunting, lumbering, irrigation, or other types of resource use on private lands. President Theodore Roosevelt established the proprietary nature of federal resource stewardship during his administration in 1901–09 by creating the U.S. Forest Service within the Department of Agriculture and stocking it with more than 200 million acres of trees. In grasping for the sublime, the Department of Interior used the power of the Newlands Act (1902) to initiate dam-irrigation projects to reclaim arid lands in the West. During the New Deal, the government continued to manage natural resources through proprietorship, for example by pursuing the Tennessee Valley Authority as a pilot project for expert-determined rural land use and by acquiring large wetland refuges that were significant to migratory game birds. Generally welcomed during the Depression, this public power was in place when the country geared up to manufacture vehicles, arms, and other material for World War II.

During the period from the Civil War to World War II, the state exercised more power over territory, a kind of national zoning for landscape conservation, than over private activities. Administrative bureaucracies established

[3] David E. Nye, *American Technological Sublime* (Cambridge, MA, 1994).

ways of controlling private economic activity by permitting private firms to enter public lands and take timber or water according to a scientifically determined management schedule. In that tributary of the Progressive era known as the efficiency movement, some engineers and other specialists focused on wasted common resources, such as the waste of rivers flowing wild to the sea without generating one kilowatt of electricity or the waste of a flood plain that lay idle because every spring it was inundated by twenty feet of water. President Franklin Roosevelt's executive actions and the laws enacted by Congress during his administrations redressed these types of waste by employing big technology to build dams and levees, making the irrigated desert and the drained marsh produce commodities. Similarly, the federal government sought to increase efficiency by killing predators thought to damage species beneficial to a managed environment. A parallel citizen's movement promoting wild bird conservation likewise divided wildlife into good and bad species, reflecting a non-ecological understanding of wildlife interrelationships. Beginning in the 1890s the science of ecology generated several new theories of species interactions, including interactions with the physical environment, which re-informed both federal wildlife policy and popular understanding.

Finally, in the years immediately following World War II, two important transitions occurred: government began to identify polluted water bodies and halt pollution through the Federal Water Pollution Control Act (1948), and Congress put in place limits on the discretion of administrative agencies through the Administrative Procedure Act (1946). The transition to hands-on regulation and oversight of the regulatory process established the legal setting for the modern environmental law movement that culminated in NEPA in 1969.

The Civil War affected environmental law indirectly by permitting a newly unified Congress to create national institutions like the Department of Agriculture and to initiate infrastructure projects like the transcontinental railroad. The absence of Corps of Engineers officers and maintenance budgets for commercially oriented improvements during the war required cities to become capable of maintaining their navigation improvements, including dredging their own wastes out of harbors. The national government also increased its tax base by raising excise taxes and began to serve a larger population of veterans with land bounties and pensions. By enlarging responsibilities, income, and indebtedness, the war established a greater role for the federal government that Americans sustained after the war as they expected to continue receiving these services.

Cities demonstrated greater energy during the war as the entrepôts that supplied the armies; urban merchants, carriers, and manufacturers were successful at acquiring, transforming, and trans-shipping arms, food, animals,

clothing, and other materials. The fitful response to epidemics that characterized antebellum city governments was transformed in the 1860s, as
residents linked health with economic prosperity and began to expect city
government, backed by business leaders, to protect public health. Their
demands were fueled by experiences like that of New Orleans in 1862,
where after decades of denying the endemic yellow fever that decimated
its population, the city began enforcing the sanitation ordinances that had
languished on its books and promptly enjoyed four straight years without an epidemic. This enforcement flowed directly from the occupying
Union Army. The U.S. Sanitary Commission sought to preserve the health
of fighting men, despite the staggering losses from contagious disease, and
its influence prompted cities to shift from quarantine methods, or isolat-
ing sick people, to a far greater emphasis on sustained environmental, or
sanitary, methods of improving public health. In the late 1860s and 1870s,
cities authorized permanent, rather than ad hoc, boards of health, created
park systems, and improved water supplies and drainage by assuming debt
to build new infrastructure. The reduction in per capita mortality that
resulted demonstrated the value of using municipal power to build and
maintain a public health infrastructure.

One constitutional outcome of the war, the Fourteenth Amendment ratified in 1868, also affected the development of environmental law. As
interpreted by Justice Samuel Miller in his majority opinion in *Slaughterhouse Cases* (1873), the Fourteenth Amendment did not shape or reduce
the police power, or regulatory power, of the states. From the perspective
of one thread of legal history, Miller's conservative interpretation of the
amendment enabled states to pass laws that undermined its goal of protecting the rights of newly emancipated citizens. From the perspective of
environmental history, however, his decision affirmed the authority of states
to exercise their police power by regulating privately owned but socially
significant business activity (in this case, slaughterhouses) in the public
interest. Although the federal government promoted environmental conservation by sequestering landed resources in reserves, cities could use their
state-derived police power to control firms defined as public nuisances. For
instance, during the Progressive era, urban officials would use this police
power to respond to popular campaigns against coal smoke by enacting
anti-pollution ordinances.

In the wake of the Civil War, both the state governments and the federal
government grew immensely, as legislative bodies created the administrative capacity to survey natural resources and plan their development. While
most of this state activity focused on bringing natural resources into the
economy, some legislation sought to protect species and natural areas that
were important to sportsmen or nature tourists. As technology grew in

scale with the implementation of powerful coal-fired steam engines and steel machines, Americans conceived of grander ways to alter natural and built landscapes to fit their desires. This was evident not only in extractive industries like coal and timber but also in ranching and wheat agriculture. The growth of technological systems was especially evident in places devoted to human habitation or areas of the environment that intersected most intimately with public health, taking the form, notably, of sewerage and other sanitary infrastructure.

The presence of large-scale technology and its concomitant private and public administrative organizations affected environmental law profoundly. No longer did private rights and lay knowledge determine the limits of state power to shape private action, but rather experts and professionals ensconced in businesses and bureaucracies implemented the policies that shaped private activities. Building sewers, water treatment facilities, and water supply networks required centralized municipal systems of taxation, debt-based financing, and construction and maintenance expertise. After the Civil War, states typically amended their constitutions to provide enlarged powers for municipal corporations, and this enabled cities to build the infrastructure that compensated for environmental problems.

Environmental Diplomacy

An example of wildlife diplomacy in international waters occurred when the United States began managing the harvest of fur seals after acquiring the Pribiloff Islands in 1867 as part of Alaska. In the 1880s Congress asserted the right to control access to fur seals in the Bering Sea to prevent boats from taking the pregnant females that were especially vulnerable as they swam near the breeding islands. In consequence, Customs Service revenue cutters seized several British boats that were sealing in open water, and federal courts condemned them. The two nations agreed to arbitration, during which the United States argued the ecological basis for protecting seals in the water; it also claimed that because the United States managed seals like domestic animals, it had a right of property in the animals themselves though they ranged in international waters. Arbitrators rejected these novel arguments in 1893, and sealing increased, causing populations to plummet until sealing nations bound themselves to controls in a 1911 treaty. The arbitration and subsequent treaty demonstrate how a management style, the "open access" of international marine resources, has resisted the extension of property rights as a means of preventing the over-harvesting of commercial species. Subsequent treaties about marine resources have established permanent scientific review and policy commissions to tailor the harvests of the parties to fit within the health of wild populations. Despite these benefits, treaties present a problem in managing sustained yields because they cannot be enforced against non-signing nations that take animals. It is common, for example, to hear complaints from treaty signatories that factory-style fishing ships operated by non-signing nations behave in wasteful and lawless ways.

Concern over natural resources became a diplomatic issue in 1908. Congress refused to ratify the Inland Fisheries Treaty negotiated with Canada that year because of vocal opposition from fishermen. Subsequently, Canada and the United States ratified the Boundary Waters Treaty of 1909, which created an International Joint Commission (IJC) to resolve conflicts about Great Lakes fishing and water use. Interested parties desirous of influencing policy now had to do so through public comment and other administrative means stewarded by the Commission. From its beginning, the IJC confronted the multiple uses of the Great Lakes – as an international body of water provided with customs offices, as a regionally significant fishery, as a navigable route for valuable commercial shipping, as a repository of industrial and sewage wastes, as a generator of electricity at Niagara Falls, and as a source of drinking water for millions of inhabitants living in seven states and provinces. Established in Theodore Roosevelt's first administration, the International Joint Commission remains a lasting contribution to negotiated, collaborative, and iterative resolutions to shared resource problems.

Gilded Age Resource Management

During the early Progressive era, America symbolically yielded up its frontier. As historians like Frederick Jackson Turner wrote a "national" history, Americans began to notice resource scarcity for the first time. The animal extinctions recorded in this period injected urgency and larger geographic scope into the earlier, hunting-based conservation laws; economically dangerous outbreaks of crop and livestock disease in industrialized agriculture prompted state inspections and the public destruction of privately owned plants and animals. As Congress found new outlets for its authority over interstate commerce, it established ways to control the treatment of animals and plants that migrated across state and national lines, whether as property or in the wild. Land speculators in Western cities admitted that land development operated within the constraints of water distribution, and they acted powerfully to effect transfers of water from distant sources. They also lobbied to make water scarcity not a local, but rather a federal problem, and were able to embed environmental planning in a rapidly growing, technocratic federal bureaucracy; for example, through the enactment of the Newlands Act (1902), which funded the construction of big dams through public land sales. As large-scale business organizations emerged that were regional or national, public and private, Americans busted trusts and regulated interstate commerce even while becoming increasingly dependent on the large-scale organizations and technological systems that mediated access to the natural resources – food and energy – on which they relied.

In the 1880s, after state-employed scientists had established that valuable fish bred in river wetlands, which usually were privately owned, state policy shifted. In addition to passing hunting and fishing laws, states began to assert a proprietary interest in the beds of navigable waters. This extension of state ownership was successful in Illinois, based on a line of legal reasoning that ownership of river and lake beds passed to the states when the U.S. government transferred the upland to patentees earlier in the nineteenth century. State courts, and eventually federal courts, reviewed many cases brought by owners of the wetlands and lakeshores who insisted that they owned the beds; they eventually sorted out ownership in 1903 in favor of the states. In some cases, patentees had paid county taxes on lakebed acreage, but this did not matter: Illinois assumed ownership of many lakebeds throughout the state in the name of the public interest in fish and its superior proprietary claim. Thus in *Parker v. People* (1884), arguments for state ownership of lakebeds included reference to the importance of fish as food for the poor, the activities of the state in sponsoring scientific investigation of fish and in propagating them through hatcheries and stocking, and in general the public interest of the state in wild fish and their breeding habitat. In other words, legal arguments about prior ownership stood side by side with pragmatic arguments about new science and the state's interest in wild fish. At the same time that states criminalized traditional ways of taking game and fish for subsistence by enacting laws that set technology and daily bag limits, they inserted themselves as the guardian of the public's interest in these foodstuffs.

The federal Geological Survey and Department of Agriculture pioneered the institutional practices of gathering and publishing data and recommendations about natural resources and their use. In particular, the Morrill Act (1862) that provided the states with small appropriations to establish agricultural experiment stations generated a vast amount of state-based knowledge about natural resources, including soils and insects. This movement to fund public knowledge about resources culminated in the Hatch Act (1887) that granted $15,000 to establish agricultural colleges and in the Rivers and Harbors Act (1888) that authorized the Corps of Engineers to manage rivers navigable in fact, meaning a vast network of waterways far from the coasts. Groups of citizens also created state and national organizations to promote the conservation of game fish and animals, and scientists organized themselves in 1886 to protect non-game birds. These efforts in

agriculture, navigable waters, and game identified problems in the prevailing practices of permitting individual, private actions to determine public
access to natural resources. Rivers became obstructed by the wharves and
jetties of private companies without a federal standard-setting and permitting body. Farms and agriculture investors suffered massive losses from pests
and diseases in their single-species fields, and they funded scientists who
sought their cases and prevention. The state became the creator of trustworthy scientific knowledge about the interaction between private economic
activity and the public resources on which it relied.

Extinctions that occurred during this period included two famous species,
the passenger pigeon and Carolina Parakeet, and of course the wild breeding
population of bison. All died because agriculture severely fragmented and
reduced the forest canopies or prairies that supported huge, foraging groups
of birds and animals. In addition, predators such as bears, coyotes, and
wolves had been hunted out of many states, and were shot on sight as
vermin in many others. In 1886, ornithologists noticed declining numbers
of birds in agricultural and suburban areas and proposed a "model law"
that states could pass to prevent the non-scientific collecting of inedible
or non-game birds. This strategy followed the earlier success of sportsmen
who had begun the practice of lobbying for model laws in the 1870s to
conserve waterfowl such as ducks and rails. In this period before federal
action to conserve wildlife (except for the fur seal), model laws became the
primary tactic to create uniform conservation or hunting law among the
states.

The ornithologists gained an immense boost when the premier sporting
journal, *Forest and Stream*, advocated that the wives and sons of sportsmen join an "Audubon Society" by pledging not to injure wild birds for
fancy hats or amusement. This club lasted only a few years, but was consciously imitated a few years later by ornithologists and wealthy women
who formed the Massachusetts Audubon Society in 1895. The monthly
journal, *Bird-Lore*, began publication in 1898 to serve about twenty independent Audubon societies, most of them state based, that arose in the
interim. States responded to the lobbying of Audubon societies by passing
bird protection laws and creating facilities for nature study supervised by
their departments of education. This movement was organized and effective, harnessing elite interest in conservation to the passage of environmental law and using education to cultivate a moral bias for conservation in
children.

Theodore Roosevelt was a friend of the *Forest and Stream* publisher who
advocated for hunting laws. In this early Progressive period, the elite
in America had a cultural passion for hunting, fishing, gardening, and

traveling to remote natural places such as Yosemite or the Adirondacks. As the frontier passed, weekly and monthly literary magazines featured the romantic, yet scientifically informed essays of John Burroughs and John Muir. The pre-presidential Roosevelt, authors like Ernest Thompson Seton, and artists like Frederick Remington brought the frontier to life for settled readers through their essays and illustrations. Just as Turner lamented that immigrants no longer would become Americanized by exposure to the frontier, elites created conservation laws that protected the nation's heritage in land and resources to ensure that the masses would have some access to the natural world.

As millions of acres were set aside in forests and parks and protected by law, however, a new goal of preservation was grafted onto the familiar state goal of managing resources in the public interest, or conservation. Preservation protected by law the non-utilitarian value of a landscape, such as its unique beauty. John Muir was the spokesperson for the preservation of natural landscapes in their own right, as sublime or reflecting the awesome creative power of God on earth. Muir's moral outrage about the taming of beautiful valleys in the Sierra Nevada mountain range has echoed throughout the intervening 100 years, in the creation of The Wilderness Society in the 1930s and the establishment by Congress of wilderness areas in the 1960s. It persists as a counterpoint to science-based arguments for conserving landscapes, species, and resources.

This period of legal development witnessed the rise of federal activities to conserve landscapes by sequestering them and by controlling access to their resources. These resources were brought into urban markets by an expanding system of navigation and railroad transportation. In the decade between the Rivers and Harbors Acts of 1888 and 1899, cities became enormous, ringed by manufacturing along their waterways where railroads entered. The federal interest in improving waterways for large-scale navigation meant that the Corps of Engineers acted in all major ports, including inland ports like Chicago and along inland rivers, to support this commerce. Whereas finished products might travel to market by railroad, raw materials for production, such as corn, wheat, cotton, limestone, timber, iron ore, and coal, traveled by barge and ship. Congress responded to this intense growth of manufacturing-oriented navigation by enlarging the powers of the Corps in the Rivers and Harbors Act of 1888; they required the Corps to standardize inland navigation by dredging channel depths and harbors and by setting and enforcing harbor lines or limits to the length of docks and piers.

In this period, manufacturers and cities dumped into streams, and the solids in these effluents shoaled navigation. Congress first authorized, then in 1899 required, the Corps to review and regulate dumping, and district engineers immediately began confronting city governments about these practices. Beginning in 1888, Chicago and the Corps's district engineer battled in private correspondence and meetings, but rarely in published annual reports, about dumping in the river, dumping barges of waste into Lake Michigan, and the private dumping of manufacturers. These battles had a new urgency because of the 1888 law, though local district engineer records as early as the 1830s noted the injury that Chicago's wastes posed to navigation. Beginning from this narrow focus on navigation and its obstructions, Congress developed the Corps's oversight over surface waters so that it grew profoundly in the late twentieth century.

Progressive Era Scientific Management

The 1890s witnessed the ascent of science-based explanations for injuries, and thereby the public acceptance of a germ theory of disease that profoundly changed the rationale for ameliorating water pollution. Pre-Civil War city councils charged aldermen to smell neighborhoods for dangerous odors in the belief that miasmas caused disease. In contrast, in the 1880s they hired consulting engineers to keep drainage water away from drinking water supplies. In the 1870s, the foremost public health advocate in the country, John Rauch, correlated the length of sewage pipes to disease rates to argue for the improvement of infrastructure in poor neighborhoods, not just in rich neighborhoods that could pay for street paving after the pipes were laid. Despite the statistics on wind, weather, lengths of sewage pipes, and disease outbreaks that he had collected over the years, however, Rauch could not demonstrate the link between drainage and mortality. In the 1890s, the Chicago Department of Health began to examine water samples for bacteria, but their collection scheme was not designed to show disease vectors, and therefore their statistics did not correlate dirty water with disease. By 1900, federal courts accepted scientific information of bacterial presence as evidence, even though experts could not substantiate claims that bacteria in water caused epidemics in cities beyond reasonable doubt. In 1906 Justice Holmes remarked that scientific instruments and data permitted people to make inferences about causation that the unassisted senses could not. The twentieth century witnessed how the law changed in keeping with Holmes's observation: legal systems integrated scientific data that documented new harms among people arising from environmental sources, such as foul air and water and diseased wildlife.

Jurists recognized that the technological systems of clean water and drainage that enabled modern urban life defied private controls and required public management. In the 1870s and 1880s, therefore, public officials began to levy general taxes to support the construction of city-wide infrastructure that previously had been built in segments by moneyed neighbors. Municipalities assumed responsibility for water quality as a responsible exercise of their police power, effectively removing it from the sphere of private action and reducing the inequitable access to clean water. By spreading the cost, a public system delivered water more widely and with less expense than thousands of private systems; the transition is analogous to the growth of insurance in the nineteenth century as a concomitant to interconnected modern life. In a pooled system, whether of public infrastructure or private insurance, sharing one's occasional risk of dirty water and catastrophic property loss also meant sharing typically clean water and the security of an economic safety net. To pursue this analogy, an urban resident who eschewed municipal water for backyard well water became as foolishly antiquarian as James Ryan, the 1854 homeowner who did not buy insurance and did not recover the value of his incinerated home from the railroad company that caused the fire. The New York Court of Appeals, in 1866, stated, "In a commercial country, each man, to some extent, runs the hazard of his neighbor's conduct, and each, by insurance against such hazards, is enabled to obtain a reasonable security against loss."[4] As the state called on science to establish the breadth of environmental resource flows on which private activities depended, it established authority to manage the use of public good resources.

Cities acted before states or the federal government in resolving environmental resource problems, but as new transportation moved animals, plants, and commodities to markets and populations grew denser, environmental problems were experienced over larger areas. Jurists tangled with the implications of the geographic and jurisdictional "scaling up" of the municipal model of environmental problem solving when adjudicating interstate pollution conflicts at the turn of the twentieth century. Take the example of drinking water: municipal governments began to resolve the technical problem of effluent contaminating drinking water before the Civil War, and state governments resolved conflicts between cities on the same river at the end of the nineteenth century. In the absence of a federal agency charged with defining water purity, should the federal courts then resolve interstate water quality conflicts? Justice Holmes, in his *Missouri* (1906) decision, noted that the original jurisdiction responsibility of the High Court to adjudicate conflicts between states was not the municipal power writ large. However, the outcome of a particular water quality contest, *Wisconsin v. Illinois*, was on the Supreme Court docket thirty-six times between 1922 and 1980, a level of judicial oversight that does not seem efficient. Is it

---

[4] *Ryan v. New York Central Railroad*, 35 N.Y. 210 (1866), 217.

possible that this perpetual struggle over Chicago's extraction of water from Lake Michigan has no legislative or executive solution? The example is intended to illustrate the messy nature of environmental law's origins and implementation.

The law has promoted both exploitation and conservation of resources in the public interest, but as science advanced in the late nineteenth century, judges and legislators heeded science-based links between one person's action and its impacts on others. Theories of science and phenomena measured by increasingly sophisticated instruments revealed what occurred within public goods media, yet were not detected by the senses. Given the proliferation of measuring instruments and scientists around 1900, it is not peculiar that courts ruled various ways about whether the flood of new data embodied evidence or opinion. Environmental law paralleled similar trends toward empiricism in other areas of law, and law's incremental adoption of science culminated in the 1923 *Frye* rule that distinguished between "experimental" science or technique and the data that resulted, and "demonstrable" science of evidentiary quality. In his opinion, Judge Josiah Van Orsdel conceived of a "twilight zone" of emergent scientific techniques, in which only those that had gained "general acceptance" among practitioners generated evidence-quality findings of fact.[5] *Frye* may have expressed the law's best understanding of how to deal with scientific information in 1923. It also implicitly recognized the authority of disciplines outside of the law and the integrity of their autonomous professional standards for vetting practitioners, legitimating techniques, and finding facts. It remained for the judge to decide whether an expert's technique or underlying principle had earned general acceptance among disciplinary practitioners. The *Frye* opinion glossed over the problem of legitimate disagreements among experts in the interpretation of scientific information.

The Growing Role of the National Government

When President Theodore Roosevelt and Secretary of Interior Gifford Pinchot reserved portions of the public domain for National Forests in 1909, they replicated on a federal level what the states had begun. Today, any road map shows the great extent and variety of state and federal park, forest, conservation, sanctuary, reclamation, and wilderness lands; these categories of public lands have distinct origins and changing purposes. The mandates of their custodial agencies have shifted as legislators responded to public opinion, emergent ecological information, and new technologies. Crucial policies for these agencies and lands were set during the administrations of

[5] *Frye v. United States*, 54 App. D.C. 46 (1923).

the Roosevelt cousins (1901–09 and 1932–45). The forty years between 1905 and 1945 witnessed immense changes in American society, importantly the growth of manufacturing to service a wartime military, automobility, electrification, the commodification of food, and suburbanization. The federal government managed resource exploitation and conservation during both world wars and the New Deal, establishing patterns of interaction with industry that would continue during the Cold War. At the end of the era, after the country emerged from World War II and retooled for peacetime prosperity, Congress recognized the excessive pollution generated by American manufacturing technology and passed the Federal Water Pollution Control Act (1948).

In this period, Congress asserted federal authority over species of animals and plants that crossed state lines as living wildlife or as property. Its authorization resided at first in the constitutional power to regulate interstate commerce and then was buttressed by the public trust principle, as elevated to a doctrine. Congress passed the Lacey Act of 1900 to support the relatively stronger state conservation laws by declaring it illegal to sell wildlife during a state's closed (no hunting) season. Subsequent litigation established the power of state market inspectors to destroy wares and fine vendors for selling game that had been obtained legally in another state, but offered for sale during the closed season of the state where it was marketed. In effect, this prevented poachers in Iowa, Indiana, and New Jersey from selling birds in the big game markets of Chicago and New York City. In 1913, the Weeks-McLean Act declared migratory birds "in the custody of the United States," rather than in state control, opening the door to federal regulations for hunting that would displace more than a century of state law. The rationale for this shift was established by science and concerned the life habits of the birds: by migrating, they crossed state lines, and only the federal government could manage an interstate good. Finally, in 1917, the transboundary problem of wild birds was recognized to such an extent that President Woodrow Wilson signed a treaty with Great Britain forbidding the hunting of migratory wildfowl that ranged between the United States and Canada, except as regulated by the Secretary of Interior. As ratified by Congress in 1918, the Migratory Bird Treaty Act also forbade the commercial sale of feathers, nests, and eggs. So certain and enforceable was this law that in 1991 the U.S. Department of Justice successfully sought a $1 billion fine from Exxon Corporation after its agent, the captain of the oil tanker *Valdez*, "took" migratory birds without a hunting license. Subsequent laws have broadened the federal government's regulatory authority over wild animals to include amphibians, mammals, reptiles, and even plants whose populations are threatened by extinction. The federal power over all of these things began with the interstate, roaming habits of birds and then shifted rationale to replicate the state's interest in wildlife as a public trust.

The colonies had regulated the taking of wildlife, but more to eradicate vermin than to protect wild species. Bounty systems provided incentives to kill animals by permitting property owners to offset a portion of their taxes by paying them in the scalps of wolves or foxes or the heads of English Sparrows. In 1889 the new federal Bureau of Economic Ornithology and Mammalogy, located in the Department of Agriculture, began publishing information about the dietary habits of animals to help state officers distinguish good (insect- or vermin-eating) from bad (fruit- or grain-eating) species. The Bureau published this information so that farmers would know which animals to kill and which to spare. By 1909, the federal government turned to more active steps in its management of wildlife on federal lands stewarded by the Department of the Interior. This action paralleled increased federal scrutiny by the Department of Agriculture into the diseases and pests that afflicted the increasingly massive shipments of animals, plants, and produce to urban markets and the interstate shipment of saplings for nursery stock.

Large-scale, industrialized agriculture could convey commodities long distances to market, and these journeys affected ecological and environmental health on their routes and at their destinations. Stockmen's associations noted that herds of cattle walking to Midwestern slaughtering centers caused disease in herds they encountered; in response, counties and states took steps, under the police power, to reroute cattle drives, and stockyards required new droves to walk through tick-killing baths before they accepted the animals. State horticultural associations noted similar, significant ecological disruptions from industrial plan agriculture. In the 1890s state legislatures in the East instituted strict inspection laws that required the destruction of nursery stock infected by the San Jose scale, an Asian insect imported to California in 1870 and thence across the country. These inspectors of nurseries were located in Crop Pest Commissions or Horticultural Departments established by Virginia and Maryland in 1896, by Pennsylvania in 1900, and by West Virginia in 1901. From this beginning forms of inspection, the state legislatures extended their oversight to crops and trees not merely on the railroad siding or at the commercial nursery but also to those growing in private orchards. As ecological information grew, so did the state's authorization for power to inspect, control, and destroy privately owned property that threatened others' private property. Virginia, and subsequently a score of states, enacted laws requiring the destruction of healthy trees on private land because they hosted a fungus that injured some varieties of commercially valuable apple trees. The growth of this type of legislation in the Progressive era echoed colonial ordinances for grubbing out domestic shrubs that hosted fungi that attacked white pines and wheat.

The growth of state power after the Civil War impressed itself on the landscape in several ways. States authorized drainage districts made up of neighbors and private companies with the power of eminent domain to aggregate rights of way and obtain building materials for transportation infrastructure. The goals of drainage districts and subsidized railroads were twofold: to create transportation inexpensive enough to bring timber to market and to prepare the countryside for agricultural settlement. In the 1860s, Iowa and Illinois focused on increasing agricultural productivity through drainage, overturning the doctrine of *sic utere tuo* that prevented one farmer from draining fields by throwing water onto a neighbor's fields. In *Livingston v. McDonald* (1866), Judge John F. Dillon of the Iowa court adopted the civil law rule that erected agricultural land drainage over other land uses. In *Gormley v. Sanford* (1869) the Illinois court proclaimed that "nature has ordained such drainage," thereby infusing the upper land with a natural easement of flowage over the lower land.[6]

Even as states like Wisconsin and others sought to build wealth and population, some observers linked deforestation to eventual economic and political decline. George Perkins Marsh, for example, is credited with creating a forceful, well-documented rationale for establishing state power to manage forests. Marsh's *Man and Nature* (1864) inspired the Wisconsin legislature to seek forest conservation, although its policies enabled the eventual clear cutting of the state. At the turn of the century, several states, and even counties, pursued the public ownership of forested land to be managed specifically as forests. Some states realized this goal at the turn of the century, as in New York's protection of the forests around its central lakes in the Adirondacks. The Cook County Forest Preserve District, around Chicago, was established by the county commissioners in 1914 only after the state enacted general enabling legislation for all counties. The District experienced legal challenges to its implementation of eminent domain, which it exercised to remove private landowners as it assembled preserves. For example, Mary Wing filed suit in Cook County court with an argument that the value of her land so condemned should reflect the potential development value of the suburbs then encroaching on it, not the history of recent sales of lands similar to her annually flooded tract. She lost the suit in 1922, but its cause, regulatory takings, endures as a central tension in the enforcement of environmental law because of its tendency to reduce the possible uses of land.

---

[6] *Gormley v. Sanford*, 52 Ill. 158, 162 (1869).

III. SCIENCE IN THE SERVICE OF BEAUTY, HEALTH, AND PERMANENCE

Law has continued to mediate among individual rights, state power, environmental quality, and competing models of actions and injuries that occur through environmental media. After World War II, Congress enacted laws that shifted away from the Progressive era policy of conserving natural resources through public ownership and technocratic management of forests, and the transformation of landscapes through dam-irrigation infrastructure. The new laws concerned common resources, with the terms water, pollution, air, solid waste, and endangered species in their titles, and therefore had an explicitly environmental focus. These material parts of the environment were those that could not be stewarded by sequestering them in the bounded National Forests, National Parks and Reclamation Districts. Government could further shape private behavior only by regulating use, the activities of individuals and firms that affected the "commons component" of private property. Of these more diffuse environmental qualities, water pollution received the first attention with the Federal Water Pollution Control Act of 1948. As people shifted from wartime production to postwar prosperity they began to value environmental quality, a shift that embodied what Samuel Hays has called modern America's desire for "beauty, health and permanence."[7] Today, this succinct list of goals should include a fourth term, justice, or the distribution of these qualities among Americans, and a fifth term, wealth, for most Americans want consumer goods and convenience. Because state-employed administrators or experts or enforcers have acted at the interface of private rights and public power, environmental law is mixed inextricably with administrative law that shapes public power and its correct exercise. The Administrative Procedure Act of 1946 is a watershed in environmental law because it helped initiate a postwar citizen and consumer movement that sought to influence how regulations are made and implemented in the modern regulatory state.

Environmental Law and Administrative Procedures

The Administrative Procedure Act compensated for some excesses of the New Deal by requiring agency administrators to publish proposed plans for public comment and, in response to these comments, to revise their plans before finalizing them. The Federal Register, which began to appear

---

[7] Samuel P. Hays, *Beauty, Health, and Permanence: Environmental Politics in the United States, 1955–1985* (Cambridge, 1987).

in 1936, became the periodical publication by which the executive branch communicated its proposals and final rules to citizens. The excesses of the New Deal included many of the measures taken to alter fundamentally the use of privately owned landscapes, such as the use of eminent domain to remove farmers in Tennessee from hillsides and valleys and of state power to build dams whose electricity was sold at prices lower than those charged by preexisting private hydropower companies. After World War II, criticism of these actions – without effect during the Depression – reappeared. In response, the Administrative Procedure Act required the federal government to publicize federal activities, and the scope of material published by agencies in the Federal Register expanded.

Excluded from this sunshine activity were the many security classified projects pursued during the Cold War, including the processing of critical materials and the development of weapons. The Critical Materials Program began during the war and expanded in the 1950s; it created partnerships between the government and many firms that had the capital and facilities to refine and process minerals. Many of the facilities that stockpiled or processed, for example, uranium, lead, or cadmium, created areas of polluted land, riverbeds, and ground water that are being remediated today under federal programs; for the legacy of historic pollution, see the discussion below of the Comprehensive Environmental Recovery, Compensation and Liability Act (CERCLA). Military sites were exempt from the sunshine requirements, and military organizations typically developed similar, internal policies to safely dispose of dangerous wastes many years after Congress required these of civilian and federal agency activities. Charles Francis Adams demonstrated in the 1870s that sunshine laws helped regulators manage the interests of powerful actors to serve public welfare; conversely, the necessary secrecy of military projects may enhance national security, but it risks camouflaging threats to the public health of neighborhoods living near military sites.

Historians identify a shift in public concern about pollution around 1960 arising from two exposés – the detection of fallout from nuclear weapons testing in milk, published by *Consumer Reports* in 1959, and the impact of the pesticide DDT on wildlife ecology, publicized by Rachel Carson in her 1962 book, *Silent Spring*. Together, these publications sharply increased the public's awareness of the presence of toxins in air, water, and food undetectable to the senses. Substances such as DDT had been used as effective parasite controls for soldiers in tropical areas, and after World War II manufacturers marketed them for use in commercial agriculture and in backyards. The argument of Carson's book was based on wildlife ecology studies that measured the unintended effects of pesticide use; for example, its incidental killing of beneficial insects and predatory birds like hawks, owls, ospreys, and eagles. Any homeowner reading the book, however, connected this wildlife mortality to the presence of DDT insecticide under the kitchen sink or in the garage. In the 1950s and 1960s, the Administrative Procedure Act empowered citizens to express their opinions by challenging federal regulators, while the growing wealth of consumers enabled them to put producers on notice by directing their purchases among a wide array of consumer products.

The decimation of birds of prey by DDT may have catalyzed the public's romantic turn toward nature preservation that resulted in the Wilderness Act (1964), a law that sought to preserve large areas of the public lands without roads. This preservationist impulse coincided with the 1967 publication by Roderick Nash of his enduringly popular book on the intellectual roots of the American conception of "wilderness."[8] Bob Marshall and others had created The Wilderness Society in the 1930s to promote roadless areas as an antidote to the automobility of modern life and the federal government's ecological tinkering with natural landscapes. However, wilderness appreciation did not become popular until the 1960s, when the preservation of animals and ecosystems for their intrinsic value, as opposed to their use value, emerged to anchor one segment of the environmental movement.

The success of citizens in lobbying federal policymakers helped the movement gel in the 1960s. In the seventeen-year conflict known as *Scenic Hudson*, a local citizens' group, the Scenic Hudson Preservation Conference, challenged the plan of the local electricity utility, Consolidated Edison (ConEd), to build a reservoir to generate hydroelectric power. ConEd sited the facility in a place known for its recreational hiking, for its prominence in the paintings of the nineteenth-century Hudson River School, and the attractiveness of its hill along the Hudson River. The citizens testified before the Federal Power Commission (FPC), the agency charged with licensing such facilities, and in 1965 filed an appeal from the FPC's license in the Second Circuit Court of Appeals. That December, the court set aside the Commission's license and issued an opinion significant to subsequent environmental policymaking and litigation. The ruling, which the Supreme Court subsequently refused to review, required federal administrators to "include as a basic concern the preservation of natural beauty and national historic sites, keeping in mind that in our affluent society, the cost of a project is only one of several factors to be considered."[9] For the next fifteen years, ConEd persistently sought licenses for modified versions of the project, and Scenic Hudson and its allies used litigation creatively to criticize the FPC

[8] Roderick Nash, *Wilderness and the American Mind* (New Haven, CT, 1967).
[9] *Scenic Hudson Preservation Conference v. Federal Power Commission*, 354 F.2d 608, 624 (1965).

for failing to require the utility to address additional facets of the project, among them downstream fish kills, discharge of heated wastewater, dumping spoil into the Hudson River without a Corps of Engineers permit, and economic impacts on local communities. In 1980, ConEd withdrew its application for a license, demonstrating the power of well-organized, well-educated, and well-connected activists to make environmental law contrary to the expertise of agency administrators.

Post-World War II environmental advocacy has been identified by several historians as a suburban phenomenon sustained by the new economic security of suburbia's working residents, their desire for environmental quality, and their sensitivity to pollution. This non-elite basis for environmentalism has older middle- and working-class roots in Progressive era urban environmental reform. Whereas in the first half of the twentieth century, rural people and immigrants moved to cities to work in factories, after the war urban residents moved out of cities to suburbia as part of a vast housing boom characterized by extensive, car-oriented tract housing. They also vacationed in National Parks and state parks, using the facilities built by the Civilian Conservation Corps during the Depression and expanded in the decade after the war. Prewar conservation was a matter of expert-defined, technocratically managed use of public resources. Postwar conservation concerned individual access to the environment through private nature recreation. Despite this rising affection for nature and concern for environmental quality, historians have shown that the levels of pollution actually accepted as normal in the middle twentieth century would have been found a half-century later. Even after the Federal Water Pollution Control Act (1948), Americans tolerated visible air and land pollution as a normal accompaniment of industrial activity. At mid-day in Gary, Indiana, and Donora, Pennsylvania, to name two prominent examples, cars drove with their headlights on and residents stayed indoors when smog descended to street level.

Smog was a new and widely experienced phenomenon in car-oriented cities, although particular industrial locations had experienced smog for decades. Comprised typically of auto exhaust, it is a fog that keeps ozone, sulfur oxides, carbon particulates, and other pollutants at ground level where people breathe them, damaging lungs and causing breathlessness and pain. The smog in Donora, Pennsylvania, came from a zinc smelter. In 1948 it killed twenty people in a few days and injured the health of hundreds. But neither that industrial fog nor the smog in Los Angeles, Gary, or elsewhere provoked any immediate and effective legal solution. Congress enacted an Air Pollution Control Act in 1955 and began appropriating $5 million annually for several years to fund air pollution research by the Public Health Service. This first clean air law and its amended version in 1960 located the environmental concern of air quality within the ambit of public health and prioritized research about health effects over other environmental effects; it also gathered information about the problem, aiming to create a scientific description of it, rather than prescribing solutions based on political or economic rationales. Air quality research has continued in its early focus on public health, perhaps because the air is generally perceived as a common resource and because the stress that air pollution places on breathing is immediate and obvious.

Having funded the study of air pollution's impact on public health, the federal government turned to a variety of regulatory approaches to the problem. The Clean Air Act of 1963 recognized the trans-state boundary problem of pollution from coal-fired electricity generation plants. In response, engineers devised scrubbers to remove sulfur oxides from smokestacks and precipitators to capture fly ash, which contains heavy metals and radioactive particles. Before the devices were installed, smokestacks had generated visible downwind plumes that spread pollutants over land and surface waters. After their installation, pollutants were captured at the plant and dumped nearby, typically on the land of the power plant. The Clean Air Act (CAA) of 1970 added a new type of regulation to air quality law by promulgating general standards for air quality and by compelling the states to regulate motor vehicles and factories to attain those standards. The 1970 Clean Air Act also required pollution-control technology to be installed in pollution generators, such as by installing scrubbers, precipitators, and catalytic converters, thereby preventing the dispersal of pollution by containing it in concentrated form within the device.

Managing Waste

An insight that Americans had after the war was that nothing could be thrown "away," even though the consumer culture proliferated objects that were soon obsolete or discarded. The quantity of refuse generated per capita grew immensely and with it a new awareness that wastes not only moved from one place to another but also could be transformed from a nuisance to a toxic substance. Fly ash collected from precipitators required landfills, and other industrial waste products required special disposal procedures; the simple collection of wastes could transform benign substances into dangerously concentrated toxins.

Landfills were typically low-lying ground that in the previous twenty years had received not merely organic trash and garbage but also synthetic chemicals. Airports built and enlarged in the postwar period often were built on fill land from dredged harbor sediments and other urban wastes.

Manufacturers in industrial suburbs and rural areas had used the margins of their extensive tracts to dump production wastes, sometimes filling wetlands and water bodies with slag and liquid wastes that raised the ground more than ten feet over many acres. Geographer Craig Colten has described the years 1875–1950 as an era of uncontrolled dumping of manufacturing wastes, and the next twenty-five years as the time when government and the public began to seek to reform pollution practices by shifting the immediate costs from the public to pollution-generating private firms.

The sanitary landfill, a dump that had little groundwater leaching and a daily "cap" of soil, became one innovation in waste disposal in the postwar era. The Public Health Service researched and publicized techniques for operating sanitary landfills to reduce the problems of hazardous leachate, gas buildup, and flies and vermin. The desirability of sanitary landfills for solid waste disposal became encoded in law with the Solid Waste Disposal Act of 1965, but the Public Health Service had no power to enforce the substitution of sanitary landfills for older forms of dumps operated by thousands of local governments nationwide. Only in 1976, in the Resource Conservation and Recovery Act (RCRA), did Congress require the Environmental Protection Agency to generate criteria for handling a broad array of hazardous and non-hazardous wastes. The 1984 Hazardous and Solid Waste Amendments to the Resource Conservation and Recovery Act empowered the EPA to generate criteria for landfills and require their enforcement by local governments. Solid wastes, especially the municipal solid wastes disposed of in landfills, continue to be the object of locally controlled environmental enforcement.

Another category of waste was scrap metals, comprised mainly of old cars and collected at salvage yards and kept out of landfills by the metal industry's demand for them. Scrap recycling of metals and rags had been part of the colonial economy and had attracted Progressive era municipal regulation as a nuisance trade. Although the thousands of dealers and workers collecting junk and industrial scrap turned wastes into resources, they were marginalized in the emerging environmental movement because the activities necessary to resource recovery were unaesthetically dirty, smelly, and noisy. In 1965, for example, the Highway Beautification Act required salvage yards to be walled off from public view. The aluminum and steel industries had sought scrap as inputs into generating new ingots since the turn of the century, and they enjoyed a high resource recovery rate using market mechanisms.

Only in 1972 did states seek to include consumers, when Oregon enacted its first "bottle bill" to create an incentive for individual scavengers and potential litterbugs to earn cash for trash. Ten states enacted similar legislation by 1987, but this regulatory solution turned in a new direction as thousands of places began to implement curbside recycling as a municipal service. These laws removed benign metal wastes from the environment, but an additional raft of laws enacted after 1970s targeted the recovery and disposal of hazardous and toxic substances. Laws that affected wastes included regulations determining disposal practices; the publication of information about releases of toxics to the land, air, or water; and laws paying for the remediation of lands polluted long ago.

The EPA Era

In 1969, Congress passed the National Environmental Protection Act (NEPA) that aggregated environmental responsibilities scattered throughout federal agencies to a new home within the new Environmental Protection Agency (EPA). The act required administrators to anticipate the environmental consequences of federally funded projects by researching and writing environmental impact statements (EISs). The implementation of subsequent federal laws about air, water, endangered species, solid waste, pollution, and legacy pollution have generated numerous environmental impact statements. The impact statement requirement directed regulation away from reacting to problems and toward their anticipation and avoidance, following a "precautionary principle" that required administrators to plan several implementations of a government-financed project and to plot their costs and benefits to health and public resources. Because of Administrative Procedure Act requirements, these alternatives were published, which means that in the conceptualization and implementation of projects as diverse as highways, National Parks, and Superfund cleanup sites, alternatives elicited comments from interested parties and the public. Lynton Caldwell, the primary author of NEPA, celebrates this procedural requirement of the impact statement as a gift from environmental law to all administrative policymaking.

The environmental impact statement poses a challenge to administrators by requiring transparency in complex judgments about projects. For example, the act requires that a highway designed by traffic engineers also be assessed by ecologists, economists, and public health experts. An impact statement could, for example, assess several qualities of a proposed park, among them the value of tourist dollars to local business and the health costs of the air pollution that tourist cars generate. Economists have become prominent in environmental policymaking in part because they have developed ways to quantify previously unmeasurable qualities, such as devising a contingent valuation method to capture the public's willingness to pay to visit a proposed park. By creating metrics for many types of information used by several disciplines and reducing them to dollars, economists have emerged to provide the *lingua franca* of modern policymaking, a trading language for the many types of experts who sit around the table. Ecological economists have developed ways of monetizing an array of "ecosystem services" provided by environments, such as the flood control of a wetland or the noise muffling of trees, both of which provide economic value to the neighborhood. In a similar response to these policymaking opportunities, ecologists have shifted from an exclusive focus on pristine ecosystems to spawn subdisciplines of conservation biology and restoration ecology that examine disturbed environments and include humans and their devices as parts of the natural world. In response to the law's demand for interdisciplinary evaluation, these and other experts developed observation techniques and analytical methods that have become increasingly useful to public policymaking.

NEPA also has proven its value as a tool that, by requiring the assessment of alternative development scenarios, enables departures from institutionalized conventional wisdom or the solutions that agencies habitually implement. One example is embodied in strategies for flood control. In 1995, when the Corps proposed a flood control strategy for the Napa River, Napa County residents used the public comment process to lobby for changes to the plan. Property damage had increased with flood plain development, and residents had no confidence that the Corps solution of a wider channel and higher levees would contain the river. Napa voters proposed to "live *with* the river, instead of trying fruitlessly to rein it in," having chosen a flood control and watershed management plan that did not require them to "choose between their economy and their environment."[10] In March 1998, Napa County residents approved a sales tax increase that funded the local partial payment of a revised Corps flood control plan, thereby creating a blueprint that only the Environmental Protection Act could have facilitated: a new type of flood control that reflected the merits of enrolling local participation into expert agency decision making. The Napa plan fulfilled the promise of the Administrative Procedure Act and proved that, by requiring alternative plans, NEPA serve as a robust mechanism for successful policymaking.

The EPA itself was created by the 1969 legislation, and it provided science-based recommendations about pollution limits, oversaw state compliance programs, reduced conflicts and regulatory differences among states, and enforced the pollution limits. Actions that state and local governments had taken previously to regulate emissions to the commons of land, air, water, and ecology yielded to federal rules. However, a variety of federal agencies continued to implement programs that were not aggregated into

---

[10] Kathleen A. McGinty, "Statement from the Chair," *Council on Environmental Quality 1996 Report* (Washington, DC, 1996), ix.

the new EPA, notable examples being the Army Corps of Engineers, the Department of Interior, and the Department of Agriculture. The consequence is the perpetuation of institutional cultures in these agencies that seem ill coordinated with the EPA's focus on improving environmental quality. The missions of these agencies are based on the efficient use of natural resources, with a focus on use and the extraction of utility from natural areas. Those missions shifted in the 1980s and 1990s, however; for example, adopting environmental restoration as an area of river development expertise, multiple use as a strategy for managing forests, and integrated pest management as an economically efficient way to control agricultural pests. In addition to aligning the actions of other federal agencies with the environmental policies it is charged to enforce, the EPA also oversees the implementation by states of plans intended to increase water, air, and ecological quality and to conform waste disposal practices to federal standards.

In the years after the passage of the Environmental Protection Act, Americans learned that foreign wars challenged the affluent and energy-intensive lifestyle that had been characteristic of the postwar period. After the Oil Producing and Exporting Countries (OPEC) oil embargo that began in October 1973 and the second constriction of oil imports in 1978–80 resulting from the revolution in Iran, the federal government promoted oil exploration domestically, in offshore waters and in Alaska. The Department of Energy began to promote the domestic exploitation of other fuels, such as cleaner coal and natural gas, and also promoted the implementation of alternative energy sources. The EPA required fuel-efficient technologies to be incorporated into cars and began to "get the lead out" of gasoline for the public health benefit of cleaner air. State regulation began to use incentives such as tax credits to favor more fuel-efficient cars and energy-efficient technologies for homes. In the 1970s technological changes mandated by environmental law and regulation created demand for a new environmental service sector of the economy, which monitored effluent, manufactured pollution abatement devices, and marketed industrial processes as environmentally desirable.

On the consumer side, individuals retreated from the use of household and garden chemicals and demanded fruits and vegetables with lower amounts of pesticide and herbicide residues. Citizens also organized locally to inquire into and protest against the location of polluting facilities, including dumps and power plants that generated benefits like employment and tax income. The popular use of the term "Not In My Back Yard (NIMBY)" to characterize localities that resisted development began in around 1980, and the rise of these groups was facilitated by the Administrative Procedure Act process of public comment on agency plans to license these facilities.

If salvage yards fit uncomfortably within the environmental movement, NIMBY groups likewise play an important but challenging role. The central insight of NIMBY groups is that particular localities provide services to much broader regions of people by receiving, for example, the risks flowing from waste disposal or energy generation while their distant neighbors receive only the benefits. Critics of NIMBY groups deride them as intent on excluding people who might come to the neighborhood, such as when one such group blocked a municipal low-income housing project to exclude poor people. NIMBY has been an effective tool for protecting particular areas from development, but because development is driven by demand, this form of activism may merely shift development geographically to a place that is less organized, less wealthy, and less connected.

A countervailing use of NIMBY activism, begun in the mid-1980s, served to require the EPA to recognize the geographic nature of pollution in association with the residential clustering of populations by income and race. This countervailing activism has a different name, "environmental justice," which sheds the NIMBY acronym that typically is used as a derogatory label by critics. Environmental justice has a complicated history, but was recognized in July 1990 when the EPA created a working group that responded to criticism by the Congressional Black Caucus that white communities and wealthy communities received far greater benefits from agency enforcement activities than poor communities and non-white communities. In 1992, the agency altered its administrative structure to create an Office of Environmental Equity in response to the working group's report (changed in 1994 to Office of Environmental Justice). The agency's focus on redressing the historic, disproportionate experience of pollution by non-white communities and by poor communities was buttressed by President Bill Clinton's 1994 executive order requiring all federal agencies to create environmental justice strategies; notably, the Department of Justice promulgated its strategy one month later by identifying criteria for redressing environmental justice problems. The environmental justice movement can be noted for its success in bringing environmental enforcement to densely populated urban places, poor communities, and non-white communities. It reminds legislators that people experience pollution in the form of bad public health and degraded environmental quality in the geographic areas they traverse as they pursue their daily lives: where they live, work, and play.

In amending the first generation of federal environmental laws, Congress responded to criticism in two ways. It acknowledged the geographic dimension of regulation as experienced in communities, and it injected economics, not just public health, as a metric agencies use to choose one policy over another. The federal courts assisted in this transition by reviewing challenges to the implementation of these acts that were brought by private landowners, natural resource extractors, developers, and firms that polluted.

During these same years, amendments to the Endangered Species Act (ESA) elevated the importance of critical habitat conservation as a prerequisite for saving particular species. Clean Air Act amendments addressed the geographic concentration of numerous, varied pollution sources in cities that existing technology standards for particular sources, such as tailpipes and smokestacks, could not redress. Cities sought to meet the clean air standards by seeking more federal subsidies for public transportation, controlling car access to downtowns, and collaborating with metropolitan counties to reduce car commuting. In this period, a backlash against centralized regulatory control challenged all manner of state and federal attempts to regulate private property use; while some of the challenges have improved environmental quality, other aspects have advanced an anti-scientific agenda that places private economic behavior above public welfare. At the same time, a key element of environmental law in the modern era has been the effort to deal with the polluted lands, damaged ecosystems, and dangerously built human communities that are the legacy of past inadequate environmental law. So, for example, we see that the National Laboratories that heralded the era of nuclear weapons testing and power generation have become experimental areas for environmental remediation. Similarly, the Corps of Engineers that had subordinated all other water uses to navigation and flood control remade itself in the 1990s into an environmental agency. Similarly the Forest Service, which had optimized its management for "timber on the stump," began to incorporate ecosystem services and multiple uses into its implementation of environmental law on the ground. In the mid-1990s, the growing use of Internet commentary, safeguarded by the Administrative Procedure Act, incorporated public comments more prominently into agency rulemaking.

In the last quarter of the twentieth century, government confronted the legacy of a century of accumulated wastes, including those left by military research and weapons development at the National Laboratories first established during World War II. Rocky Flats National Laboratory near Denver, for example, shifted its mandate from creating nuclear weapons to creating the science to clean up its own irradiated and toxic site. The Department of Defense took on management of the cleanup of hundreds of decommissioned Army, Navy, and Air Force facilities, some of which, like the Spring Valley site in Washington, D.C., contained unusual substances, such as waste from chemical weapons development in the 1910s.

On the civilian side, Congress enacted the Comprehensive Environmental Recovery, Compensation and Liability Act (CERCLA) in 1980 to create a trust fund that helps pay for the cleanup of toxic sites for which a responsible party is unable to pay. Environmental economists recognize that, when pollution injures the public and the polluting firm is not required to pay compensation, the future cost of cleanup might also fall to the public rather than to the party that benefited from this shifting of cost. The Superfund established by the 1980 legislation taxes today's polluters to help defray the cost of cleaning up the legacy of past polluters. Congress amended the act in 1986 to create the Defense Environmental Restoration Program (DERP), which oversees the remediation of polluted military sites. The modern generation, therefore, pays for the cleanup of air, water, and land contaminated by our predecessors.

Economists drew on theoretical literature to interpret the sometimes counter-intuitive consequences of implementing particular environmental laws and especially to examine the social problem of laws that required insolvent polluters to pay compensation to the injured or the cost of cleaning up. The Comprehensive Environmental Recovery, Compensation and Liability Act made all parties associated with a polluted site "jointly and severally" liable, so that the EPA could recover the costs of cleaning up from the operators of the site, the waste producers, and the transporters of waste. This strict liability, regardless of whether parties acted legally, drew a great amount of ire and prompted defensive litigation that now is the typical response to the environmental recovery act and adds an enormous amount to the cost of remediating polluted sites. Because polluted sites could be manufacturing sites that had been in operation for more than a century, the EPA's implementation of the act drew on the research skills of historians to document past activities at the site. The similar Defense Environmental Restoration Program has sought to clean up polluted military sites, which exist wherever there were bases, depots, camps, airfields, dumps, testing ranges, or other fixed facilities. Paying for the remediation of long-lived polluted sites is, by its nature, ex post and does not prevent future pollution.

Cleaning up polluted sites has generated litigation, government research into the mechanisms for cleanup, and new businesses that conduct cleanups of legacy pollution, measure contaminants, and monitor and maintain sites. Other regulations have altered the ways that wastes are processed by firms, farms, and cities before being released to the environment. Yet, manufacturing, agriculture, and urban public works continue to generate annoying and hazardous wastes that must be handled and disposed of. The sanitary landfill takes domestic wastes, but beginning in 1965, federal law required special handling in the Solid Waste Disposal Act, updated in the 1970 Resource Recovery Act and currently active in the form of the Resource Conservation and Recovery Act (RCRA) passed in 1976. The conservation and recovery act requires licensing of waste operators and a paperwork trail for the generation, handling, containment, and disposal of listed hazardous wastes, including the maintenance of underground storage tanks. Congress's intent in passing the act, amended in 1984, was to create processes that would prevent the uncontrolled disposal of wastes that might enter the commons to injure the quality of water and air, and ultimately of ecological and public health.

An important buttress to the act was the Toxics Release Inventory (TRI), created in 1986 by the Emergency Planning and Community Right-to-Know Act. The inventory publishes information about firms that regularly emit hazardous wastes to the environment. As implied by its title, the law seeks to harness citizen interest to the tasks of monitoring the activities of firms and the enforcement of pollution control by local government. In passing the law, Congress responded to the deaths and hospitalizations that resulted from the release of a chlorine-based gas in Bhopal, India, and Institute, West Virginia, by plants operated by the same company. The resulting database is searchable by zip code, and although it does not list every polluter in a neighborhood, it is one place a resident can find information of the NIMBY variety.

In addition to pollution, the federal government responded to other hazardous conditions in the American landscape. Several years of enormous Western wildfires in the 1990s provoked new criticism of the public land management policies of federal agencies such as the Bureau of Land Management and Forest Service. A century of fire-suppression practices yielded to new research about the efficacy of periodic fires for reducing dead branches and trees on the forest floor, the very tinder that transforms a wildfire into a scorching inferno. The timber summits held in the early 1990s during the Clinton administration aired a variety of arguments against then-prevailing forest management policy, including the claim that it promoted the infestation of forests by parasites such as bark beetles. Timber salvage provisions were incorporated by Congress into general appropriation laws to permit logging companies to remove fallen timber to prevent these infestations, incidentally building logging roads into removal areas. It became widely known that the U.S. Forest Service managed more miles of roads than any other government entity, as the Sierra Club and other environmental non-profits publicized the ecological impacts of clear-cutting and road building on woodland species and fish whose streams were damaged by erosion-caused sedimentation.

The crisis in forests came to a head around the plans to designate critical habitat for the northern spotted owl, a species whose favored hangouts were very tall, large, old trees standing in a state of semi-decay. The owl population became a proxy for forest ecological health, and its preservation seemed well within the authority of the Endangered Species Act. Large classes of people in the Pacific Northwest, however, believed that not only logging jobs but a regional culture was being sacrificed for an insignificant bird solely because suburban environmentalists newly removed from California had turned state policies against natural resource extraction. In the 1980s, America, which had witnessed the evacuation of the steel industry from the Midwest to Asia, watched as the timber industry moved to Canada, South America, and Asia. The negotiations about the North American Free Trade Agreement (NAFTA) and the General Agreement on Tariffs and Trade (GATT) likewise contributed to a sense of job loss among laboring people, even as the "haves" who worked in cities profited from speculation in a growing stock market emerging from its 1988 low. Strong popular movements for the removal of federal proprietary management of lands have emerged in Western states, especially those with extensive federal land holdings – Nevada, Utah, New Mexico, Oregon, Wyoming, and Idaho. Popular movements articulate an ideology that those who live on the land will manage shared use of its resources more effectively than Washington regulators who impose values from outside.

Economists have made their discipline important to environmental litigation, notably over pollution, by helping quantify injuries that people experience. Using survey and contingent valuation methods, some economists have analyzed spending behavior, for example, to capture the impact of foregone recreation on a town that suffered an event that degraded environmental quality. In a 2001 study, David J. Chapman and W. Michael Hanemann described in great detail the disagreements among economists who sought to monetize the injury of a 1990 oil spill to beach visitors and towns near Los Angeles. They interviewed lifeguards and surfers, hired surveyors to count visitors throughout the day, and took aerial photographs. *People of the State of California v. BP America Inc.* ended in 1997 with a jury damage award of about $18 million; on appeal, the defendant and California agreed to a settlement of $16 million the following year. The economists' goal was not to observe these people in order to model their economic behavior regarding recreation, but rather to come up with a dollar figure for the loss of money spent on recreation and the pleasure they derived from visiting the beach.

CONCLUSION

Environmental law in America has shifted in several ways from its origins in private property law and police powers of the colonial era to the present proliferation of explicitly environmental laws, and yet there are undeniable continuities. The legal category of public nuisance has persisted as the primary route of state involvement in coordinating private activity to preserve the public welfare. The state has exercised its power to preserve the public interest in natural resources, though definitions of the public interest have shifted and those of natural resources have broadened. Colonial and state governments used their police power to address private behavior that polluted air, land, and water. They also acted positively to shape rural ecology by promoting the eradication of species that preyed on domestic animals or harbored disease threats to agriculture. The site of power for exercising environmental law has since shifted from the locality to the nation and even the globe. That said, the federal government did little to limit private use of common resources before the Civil War, but its land policy shaped the first 100 years of unplanned, private exploitation of land, water and wildlife. Between the Civil War and World War II, the federal government adopted a strategy of controlling private access to land-based resources by creating a proprietary interest in certain landscapes. These included parks of exceptional beauty, but more importantly featured the National Forests, water reclamation districts, other public lands managed for grazing, and wildlife refuges. The states also implemented a proprietary strategy of controlling the private use of common resources, especially of rivers and their floodplains. Right about 1900 conflicts appeared in federal court about water and air pollution that heralded the influx of scientific data as evidence for resolving environmental conflicts. Two generations of technocratic managers populated an array of federal agencies that increased in scale and scope during the New Deal, exercising immense federal powers to relocate entire communities into more appropriate environments.

In the late nineteenth century, city government grew in response to the demands of an ever denser population that officials protect the public health by providing shared resources and infrastructure. As municipal law extended the financial and police power of cities, states and courts observed its beneficial results for the public health and economic growth of urban places. Thus, albeit decades later, states and the federal government exercised similar powers to build, own, and manage infrastructure, including proprietary conservation areas, such as wildlife refuges, reservoirs, dams, and irrigation districts. The federal government, in particular, affirmed the constitutional basis for state action even as it seized on the transboundary nature of environmental problems as a rationale for its own expanded scope of action. Over the course of the twentieth century, the custodial responsibilities of the federal government grew from bounded forests and tracts of land to ranging wildlife and the healthfulness of air and water. Post-World War II environmental laws have turned away from conserving natural resources for their use by the public and toward preserving environmental qualities that safeguard the public health. The modern American values beauty, health, permanence, and justice in environmental policy and seeks to have these things while spending great amounts of wealth on consumer goods.

Twenty-first-century environmental law may strengthen a republican vision of a healthy, wealthy society in which individuals pursue their interests without injuring the collective reliance on common resources. This future will require experts, ensconced in federal agencies, who have mastered disciplinary knowledge and also know how to collaborate with those trained in other disciplines, who can model environmental complexity and perceive the ramified consequences of millions of private actions. The impact of Hurricane Katrina on New Orleans (2005) exemplifies the complexity of environmental behavior and human responses. Many people, including even public executives, did not heed the warning of meteorologists to evacuate. In the storm's aftermath, the romance of property rights was so strong that the federal government put in place programs to enable city residents to rebuild, despite rising sea levels downstream and the ever-increasing sedimentation from agriculture and other development upstream. Sediment drawn downstream by one of the biggest rivers in the world is a constant feature of the Mississippi ecosystem. The very levees put in place to protect New Orleans from floods themselves contribute to the risk of disastrous flooding, for they force sediment to accumulate in the river channel, simultaneously raising the riverbed and starving the delta of the sediment that roots the mangrove swamps that dampen the storm surge. American law continues to deny the environmental context of places like New Orleans by favoring local development over regional or national planning. And yet, without local knowledge, federal plans can uproot communities as they did during the New Deal.

15

AGRICULTURE AND THE STATE, 1789–2000

VICTORIA SAKER WOESTE

Legal history is full of stories about agriculture, but few of them are told as such. This becomes all the more surprising when one pauses to consider that many of the legal historians who revolutionized the field after 1950 did so by studying phenomena that were in fact central to the history of agriculture in the United States. In the work of James Willard Hurst, for example, land policy, commodities trading, and the rise of modern markets and transportation networks were hallmarks of the new socioeconomic mode of legal history. Yet, even as Hurst and others pioneered the move away from doctrinal and constitutional analysis toward the real-world problems of economy and society, they generally failed to notice that the economy from which the problems that fascinated them arose was in large part distinctively agricultural. The successor generation of historians who expanded Hurst's economic focus to include race, ethnicity, and gender likewise paid scant attention to the overwhelmingly rural character of American society during most of the nation's history, except to note a perhaps oversimplified progression away from agricultural and rural to industrial and urban. To generalize, the new legal historians' commitment to law "in context" was, it turns out, quite selective in the contexts it chose to consider of importance. "Economy and society" were important, but apparently did not vary much according to where they were situated.

Hurst's magnum opus, *Law and Economic Growth* (1964), illustrates the irony of selectivity. A comprehensive history of Wisconsin's lumber industry, the book charts the story of lumber companies driven by capitalistic incentives to mine the state's forests for every last stand of logs as quickly as possible, leaving lands denuded and wildlife habitats destroyed. Saddened by an outcome he attributed to a lack of regulatory oversight, Hurst nonetheless admired the lumber industry as an achievement of sorts: it demonstrated the power of entrepreneurial energy that a creative application of the doctrines of private (judge-made) law had unleashed. Hurst saw private law as a liberating and enabling device that both freed and

directed the energies that Americans poured into nineteenth-century economic development: "[I]t does not exaggerate the role of law to see that
its procedures and compulsions were inextricably involved in the growth
of our market economy. By providing authoritative forms of dealing and
by enforcing valid agreements, we loaned the organized force of the community to private planners."[1] Intent on calling attention to the profound
consequences that resulted from the instrumentalist use of law by private
actors, Hurst located the overwhelming power of the nineteenth-century
state, which he defined by its role in enabling market exchange, in the
private, judge-made law documented in trial and appellate court records.

The problem is, the Wisconsin story of an energetic private law that Hurst
found so striking was embedded in legal, political, and spatial circumstances
that owed their existence to the constitutive effects of American public law
and policy's prior commitments to building a distinctive kind of political
economy. What enabled citizens and settlers to move to Wisconsin in the
first place, to stake claims to lands there and in other new territories, and,
most critically, to convert natural resources into wealth by conveying them
to markets was a body of state and federal law that consciously sought
to permit, promote, and regulate such activities. Hurst's Wisconsin story
would not have been there to be written were it not for that prior *public*
impetus to the creation of a vast, viable, *agricultural* economy.

To write the legal history of American farmers is to correct two anomalies
in American legal history. First, and most simple, it is to build into legal
history an awareness of where most American social and economic activity
took place throughout most of the two centuries following the creation of
the Republic and, in so doing, to recognize one more way in which context
in legal history is important: "society" and "economy" are not generic, but
rather are situated terms. For most of American history their situation has
been agrarian. Second, and more important, it is to correct the tendency to
treat private and public law as separable phenomena. The legal history of
farmers is proof positive that a private law methodology of close readings
of court cases and statutes must be combined with the broader perspective of
public law and its continuous construction of all the conditions of economic
life. Such an integrated perspective enables us to understand the course of
American legal history in general.

The fact that the U.S. economy was an *agricultural* economy for most of
its first two centuries affected the course of American law. But law was also
of the first importance to the course of agriculture. Here we can begin by
returning to Hurst. Although seemingly unaware of agriculture as such,

---

[1] J. Willard Hurst, *Law and the Conditions of Freedom in the Nineteenth-Century United States*
(Madison, WI, 1956), 11.

Hurst still made an important contribution to its legal history by emphasizing the importance of law in constituting economic institutions, such
as farms, and enabling commercial enterprise, such as agriculture. Though
legal historians have yet to mine the fruits of that insight, others have displayed sensitivity to law's role in shaping rural life. In an essay published in
2001, for example, Richard L. Bushman drew attention to the importance
of the relation between farmers and courts in eighteenth-century North
Carolina and suggested that the relationship might be fruitfully explored
in other periods of American agricultural history. His work shows the profound interpenetration of state authority into the forms of everyday land-
based activity. Meditating on how the very existence of farms depended on
legal provisions and mechanisms, on how the state and financial interests
could regulate the activities and livelihoods of even remote and disconnected rural Americans, Bushman demonstrates one way of bringing the
law into the history of agriculture and putting agriculture into the history of
American law.

As Bushman points out, even in the period before the Revolution, farmers
constantly resorted to legal institutions and legal authority to determine
the fundamental issues of their livelihoods and lives. The ownership of
real and personal property, the settlement of debts, and the distribution
of estates to heirs and legatees after death all required judicial intervention and adjudication. Farmers, Bushman argues, routinely relied on legal
rules and processes, even when they grew mistrustful of the persons who
dispensed justice. Legal institutions and the decisions that they made "constructed both farms and farmers in the largest sense of producing identities
and formulating imagined worlds in which farmers lived portions of their
lives."[2]

Although Bushman shares Hurst's preoccupation with judge-made law
and his empirical focus on trial courts, their common emphasis on the
constitutive role of law in agriculture suggests its applicability in other
times and places. "The entire farm enterprise," as Bushman put it, did indeed
rest on how agents of the state defined property, set out its legal qualities, and
limited its use. Each farmer had to be concerned with how the state decided
such issues. Each farmer had to attend to such issues "as conscientiously
as he worked his land."[3] Thus, even before the start of formal nationhood,
farmers were as closely bound up in the American state's institutional and
legal powers as any group of economic actors.

[2] Richard Lyman Bushman, "Farmers in Court: Orange County, North Carolina, 1750–
1776," in Christopher L. Tomlins and Bruce H. Mann, eds., *The Many Legalities of Early
America* (Chapel Hill, NC, 2001), 389.
[3] Bushman, "Farmers in Court," 389.

Bushman's observations on the role of law in colonial era agriculture invite legal historians to take up where he left off and examine the mutually constitutive relationship between law and farms after independence. I have already indicated that the best approach is one that incorporates the histories of both public and private law, so as to reveal how the state acknowledged, accommodated, and regulated various agricultural interests after the Founding. What would such a history have to say, specifically, about the development of public law and its influence on agricultural history?

Insights from the history of public land law, slavery, labor, and transportation place farmers and agriculture on the side of historians arguing for an activist state. From the Founding, whether through legislative intervention or judicial validation of changing balances of economic power, the state variously protected, promoted, and distressed farmers – sometimes all three. Ultimately, I suggest, public law, more than common law, shaped the legal history of agriculture in the nineteenth century. The essentially complete and apparently permanent federal administration of agricultural markets established during the 1930s cemented the bonds between farmers and public law.

The public law perspective reveals an essential, persistent tension in the legal history of agriculture between market capitalism and small-scale self-sufficiency. American government consistently encouraged the former while proclaiming the virtues of the latter. Although plant cultivation and animal husbandry usually required little legal intervention or recognition, land transactions required considerable legal infrastructure, and markets required public sanction and governance. Farmers needed markets not only to sell what they produced but also to purchase goods and labor. Markets changed in scale and scope over time, but from the very beginning, the state constituted and policed the legal relationships that arose in commercial transactions. Soon after the Founding, the commercial implications of agricultural development became explicitly linked to national economic prosperity, and this linkage endured through civil war, industrialization, depression, and world wars. Throughout, the state's indulgent promotion of and deliberate indifference to the constitution of markets and market relations were essential to the growth of American agriculture.

In this chapter I relate a broad survey of American agricultural development to trenchant and formative moments of legal change. During the period before the Civil War, markets were primarily local and regional in scope, and as a result, the states and not the federal government assumed primary responsibility for preserving and expanding agricultural economic exchange. Federal land policy represented the major substantive area of Congressional intervention in matters affecting the livelihoods of farmers; tariffs were another. Important regional differences became apparent during this period as well. Southerners relied on a cash crop economy, principally cotton and tobacco, and exported these commodities to the North and Europe to pay for everything else they needed. In the North, a much more diverse agricultural economy developed; there, too, a fairly stable manufacturing base was established early in the nation's history. During and after the Civil War, the federal government paid greater attention to the physical and legal expansion of markets, transportation networks, and agricultural production. A period of intense and increasing centralization of market power ensued, during which railroads served as one of the principal agents driving both the realignment of individual producers within the marketplace and the increasing distance between physical production and eventual consumption.

As national markets expanded in the latter part of the nineteenth century, farmers increased production, invested more heavily in farm technologies and mechanization, and increased their reliance on third parties to sell and speculate in agricultural commodities. The continuing expansion of agricultural productive capacity nationwide generated long-term economic instability and contributed significantly to the conditions that produced the Great Depression. The federal government's response to the crisis in agriculture was to federalize the administration of markets on an unprecedented scale. The explicit management of surpluses and price controls cemented the marriage of agriculture and the modern federal administrative state. This administrative shift has governed federal farm policy ever since.

I. FROM THE FOUNDING TO THE CIVIL WAR

From the first days of colonial settlement, agriculture was so fundamentally and obviously the bedrock of economic development that no one ever stopped to question it. The Founding Fathers were also the founding farmers; men of property and profession, they owned and in many cases worked farms of considerable size and diversity. Nearly everyone living in eighteenth-century America was dependent on land for survival; most saw land as the font of wealth as well. In just about every measurable way, agriculture dominated the national profile. The nation's population in 1790 was 3.9 million, of which all but 200,000 lived in rural places. As Douglass North points out, the Constitution made no guarantees about the nation's prospects. Physical barriers, including the slowness of and lack of access to overland transportation, limited commercial exchange within and among the states; foreign trade likewise was slow to become established. The United States was at a decidedly pre-industrial state of development at the time of its founding. Capital and labor were expensive, impeding the growth of manufactures. Agriculture and agricultural-based trade enabled most people to feed themselves, their growing families, and a steady stream of newcomers.

The indisputability of agriculture's economic significance did not mean that law protected farmers from adversity in all its forms. Important developments, such as the rise of canals, railroads, and other forms of transportation that invaded the rights of landowners, competed with owners' plans for the use of their land. The gradual diversification of economic activity led to conflicts between farmers and mill owners over riparian water rights, between farmers and railroads over the collateral damages caused by the dangers of train operations, and among farmers over property boundaries and noxious uses. State legislatures and courts had to decide these conflicts. The various jurisdictions generated differing precedents and unpredictable results, often adding to the economic pressures that drove farmers further west. Before the Civil War, the federal government's primary mechanism for encouraging agriculture was its land policy, by which it transferred the vast public domain into private hands.

Federal Land Policy

Initially, the goal of federal land policy was simple: to raise revenue for the cash-strapped central government while encouraging settlers to farm and farmers to settle. Two ordinances passed by the Confederation Congress during the 1780s provided for the surveying and subdivision of Western lands according to a plan Thomas Jefferson originally suggested. To help increase sales, the Confederation Congress offered the equivalent of owner financing; nevertheless, settlement lagged far behind federal expectations. The very abundance of land meant that would-be settlers could find other sellers; the states sold off public lands of their own during this time, and private land companies that rushed into the business drew profits away from public sales. Squatters who flouted the law's already benign requirements only increased the pressure on the government to make the public land programs gainful. The Northwest Ordinance of 1787, the most influential federal land statute, was framed on the assumption that territorial governments would eventually grow into fully fledged states, permanently and equally joined to their older siblings. Likewise, citizens of the original states would carry their constitutional rights with them when they crossed state and territorial lines. Interestingly, in a nod to the idea that land monopoly was antithetical to representative democracy, the law prohibited the establishment of large estates, though it also required anyone wishing to serve as territorial representative to own at least 200 acres in his district.

The federal government's divestment of the public domain to individuals, including farmers and speculators alike, performed an enabling and distributive function in which the federal government acted as an agent in the massive transfer of property from public to private ownership. But though the Ordinance of 1787 embraced a Jeffersonian model of economic self-sufficiency and republican government, it said nothing about requiring people to farm the lands they obtained under the law. Nor did it require them to live on the land; instead, the government relied on the attractiveness of agriculture as both a way to make a living and a way of life to entice people to farm in the Northwest Territories. To speed settlement further, and to ease credit and cash flow restrictions in tight times, the federal government raised land prices in 1800 and periodically thereafter, made credit more easily obtainable, and delayed the onset of interest accrual. But as a matter of course, most of those who purchased lands under antebellum statutes were speculators who took advantage of favorable prices and then gorged on the profits they made on resale.

By the 1840s, the calls for free homesteading as a solution to speculation and monopoly had spread from settlers in Illinois, Indiana, and Missouri, among other Western states, to land reform proponents in the East. Stressing the ills of the cities – unemployment, poverty, general deprivation – these reformers called for free homesteading in Jeffersonian terms, arguing that economic self-sufficiency went hand in hand with virtuous political citizenship. The Preemption Act of 1841 granted squatters the opportunity to purchase their lands at affordable prices, but this discount failed to silence homesteading proponents. Indeed, the issue fueled the formation and influence of the Free Soil party a few years later. The issue's political traction was such that Congress was obliged to consider free homesteading bills in nearly every session during the 1850s; the South's fight to introduce slavery into new territories meant that the constitutional and regulatory issues raised by free homesteading bled into the sectional struggles that dominated the decade. Southerners wanted federal land policy to maintain order in the new territories without undercutting the rights of slaveholders.

The South had its own troubles with agricultural instability. At the time of the Revolution, the region's initial crops of choice – tobacco, rice, and indigo – were significant money losers. Though farm labor continued to be in short supply, demand for slaves actually declined in the late eighteenth century because those labor-intensive cash crops were becoming less profitable to produce, transport, and sell. The invention of the cotton gin in 1793 changed everything; not only did the South now have a profitable crop to market but it also had an abundant pool of forced labor with which to produce it. The gin's inventor, Eli Whitney, proudly informed his father that "my machinery . . . is likely to succeed beyond our expectations. My greatest apprehensions at present are, that we shall not be able to get machines made as fast as we shall want them."[4] His joy at the utility of his invention was chilled by the attempts of several state governments to reduce or forfeit on royalty payments owed to him. Still, as he predicted, his machine transformed Southern agriculture.

It is perhaps an exaggeration, but not much of one, to say that what cotton was to the South, wheat was to the North. Here too the advent of new technologies accomplished efficiencies in harvesting that helped compensate for the lack of labor. By mid-century, the United States was producing nearly as much wheat as Great Britain, and in the 1860s the great wheat ranches of California extended the country's output still further. The country's output in wheat and dozens of other commodities created a total agricultural economy of immense value and capacity. Official government reports boasted of the new profits gained from new commodities and new methods for producing and processing old ones. Roads, canals, and railroads pushed the reach of markets further westward into more remote territories while also imposing high social costs in accidental injuries and deaths.

Transportation and Markets

More than any other form of transportation, railroads benefited from government grants and secured the redistribution of publicly owned land into private hands on a massive scale. Unlike canals and turnpikes, which were owned by the states, railroads remained in private ownership; they took land grants from Congress directly or through the states as intermediaries. Railroad building began in 1830 and drew settlers westward with it; new population centers popped up in Indiana, Illinois, and Missouri. By 1850, New England's railway system was essentially completed; the network across the rest of the Atlantic seaboard was not far behind. In the Midwest, railroads needed more help connecting far-flung cities, towns, and settlements, and an 1850 law sponsored by such influential figures as Illinois Senator Stephen Douglas secured land for the railroads on favorable terms. Eastern interests were pacified with the promise of branch lines that would eventually link Chicago to the Atlantic via the Great Lakes, Southerners likewise with a provision extending the lines to Alabama and Mississippi. By giving something to everyone in these early railroad grant laws, Congress not only eased regional tensions and resentments but also ensured that the railroad network would encompass nationally significant routes. In promoting railroad construction not "as a sovereign state, but on its prerogatives as a landed

---

[4] Eli Whitney to Eli Whitney Sr., Aug. 17, 1794, in Matthew Brown Hammond, ed., "Correspondence of Eli Whitney relative to the Invention of the Cotton Gin," *American Historical Review* 3 (1897), 90–127, 101.

proprietor," Congress overcame much of the constitutional opposition to direct governmental involvement in transportation.

In sum, during the first half of the nineteenth century, the federal government's land policies accomplished the significant transfer of public lands to land speculators and transportation companies. Farmers came a distant third in total land grants received. How the land was used after the terms of the grants had been executed was largely left to entrepreneurs and owners to determine. The land laws did little to specify in explicit or positive ways whether agriculture was to be the first and best use for these lands, though by giving away large plots for very little or, under the terms of the Homestead Act of 1862, nothing at all, Congress seemingly meant to attract people of small means who would farm manageable plots as fee simple owners. Yet, it did little to ensure that this result would actually come to pass.

What the public land laws did accomplish is obvious in hindsight: they rapidly put white Americans across the continent. The native peoples already there were obliged to make way, either through military force or negotiated relocation. By 1860, the nation's physical territory had expanded to nearly four times its size at the time of the Revolution. Though much of this land remained unsettled and undeveloped, farmers had succeeded in putting substantial acreages to the plow, and merchants, craftsmen, and tradespeople built towns and cities that helped interrupt the physical isolation of the countryside. In 1850, the first year for which the census collected data on agricultural holdings and output, the United States boasted nearly 1.5 million farms containing nearly three million total acres, of which about one-third was improved (i.e., being farmed, pastured, or used in other ways). That year, the United States produced about 2.5 million bales of cotton, 100 million bushels of wheat, and 150 million bushels of oats. Production of each of these crops increased exponentially over the next ten years, suggesting that before the economic disruption of war the country had established a vibrant agricultural sector that had maintained a fairly steady pace of growth despite recurrent recession, internal conflict over slavery, and relatively little direct government promotion of commodity production or marketing. Even the significant debt that piled up with land purchases, credit shortages, and periodic recessions did not slow this process much.[5]

These accomplishments in agricultural productivity and the physical expansion of farming would not have been possible without the concomitant

---

[5] Donald B. Dodd, compiler, *Historical Statistics of the United States: Two Centuries of the Census, 1790–1990* (Westport, CT, 1993), 309–10. In 1850, the nation's population totaled 23,191,876, distributed over 2,940,042 square miles; the comparable figures for 1790 were 3,929,214 people and 864,746 square miles. George Thomas Kurian, ed., *Datapedia of the United States, 1790–2005: America, Year by Year* (Lanham, MD, 2001), 6.

development of markets, meaning both the physical spaces at which exchanges took place and the networks that linked production regions to consumers. Eighteenth-century farmers, particularly those living inland, had only limited access to urban colonial markets; the advances in land settlement and transportation opened up new markets in what once were hinterlands. The market revolution of the Jacksonian period, according to Charles Sellers, was a wide-ranging transformation of the cultural and political institutions on which producers and consumers relied. Sellers joins Oscar and Mary Handlin, Louis Hartz, and others of the so-called Commonwealth school who reject the model of the nineteenth-century market as autonomous and self-regulating. Instead, they describe state governments in the early national and Jacksonian periods as actively involved in debates over land use and transportation projects because they recognized the relationship between market capitalism and commercial agriculture. The emergence of local, regional, and interstate markets helped push innovations in transportation and maintained the pressure on state governments to invest in public works.

Thus, as historians of the "transportation revolution" have described, the key to the gradual creation of markets in places where they had not previously existed was the progression from roads to turnpikes to canals to railroads. Intrastate and sectional tensions indelibly shaped policy decisions about transportation at each step. In Pennsylvania, for example, farmers living nearer Eastern urban centers opposed transportation development. According to Louis Hartz, they feared that "the construction of an east-west canal would flood the Philadelphia market with products from the west" and cause their higher land values to collapse. East Coast states worried about what they saw as the diversion of public resources and money to far distant territories, where social change and the different, larger scale of production and exchange made Jefferson's vision of virtuous, self-sufficient producers seem an unlikely prospect. The Erie Canal, an engineering feat as inspiring in its day as the Panama Canal a century later, drew opposition from farmers and other vested interests, such as turnpike owners, wagoners, and innkeepers. Funded entirely by New York State, the Erie Canal stood as a rare example of a successful state-level public works program; building it also served to train nearly every engineer working in the antebellum West.

In short, transportation construction and westward settlement were inseparable phenomena. Through the 1820s, few people seriously denied "the legitimacy of transportation ownership as a function of the state."[6]

---

[6] Louis Hartz, *Economic Policy and Democratic Thought: Pennsylvania, 1776–1860* (Chicago, 1968), 135.

While demand for transportation increased sharply, private investment capital was too scarce to underwrite it. Local opposition to bridges, ferries, canals, and roads ultimately collapsed for the same reason that state-based opposition to interstate commerce could not last: it was impractical and entirely at odds with the pro-development impulse of early-nineteenth-century mercantile capitalism. Proponents of state support for and public ownership of transportation projects argued that farmers in established areas would not suffer if their Western counterparts prospered as a result of access to Eastern markets. Not everyone bought this "rising tide floats all boats" theory of promotion; state subsidies to farming as well as transportation were responsible for mounting public debts during the 1820s and 1830s, and the tide abruptly lowered for all after the panic of 1837. Moreover, with rivers of public money spilling so abundantly, private corruption was pervasive, and the states and federal government lacked the regulatory structures and practices needed to supervise the expenditure of so many millions of dollars, the construction of increasingly complex transportation technologies, and the appropriation of so many millions of acres in so short a time.

II. FROM THE CIVIL WAR TO THE NEW DEAL

The Civil War brought a new kind and degree of federal involvement in agriculture, particularly in areas where Congress had previously paid little attention or where the "shrewd politics" of Southern lawmakers had long thwarted legislative action.[7] After the South vacated both Congress and the executive branch, the federal government swiftly enacted the Homestead Act, the Pacific Railroad Act, the National Bank Act, and the Morrill Land Grant Act. With the necessity of slavery-driven political compromise removed, Northern, Midwestern, and Western representatives imbued these laws with more liberal provisions than would otherwise have been possible. Free homesteading, favorable terms for railroads to lay track across the continent, and larger grants for the agricultural colleges were part of the bonanza that agriculture gained as a direct result of the war. Once the slaveholding interests decamped from Washington, the political dynamics surrounding these issues changed entirely.

The bellwether event was the establishment of the Department of Agriculture in 1862. Before then, agricultural matters had been handled by the office of Commissioner of Patents. A Jackson appointee, Henry Ellsworth, had boldly diverted revenue from inventors' fees to help agriculture in imaginative ways. An Indiana farmer, landowner, and "pioneer protagonist

[7] Paul Wallace Gates, *Agriculture and the Civil War* (New York, 1965), 264.

of prairie agriculture," Ellsworth had used his office to provide free seed and cuttings to producers, to collect and publish agricultural statistics, and to publish annual reports containing all manner of information about crops, weather, diseases, exports, the importation of new species of plants, and farm machinery. By the time of the Buchanan administration, politics and regional tensions had pervaded the work of the Patent Commissioner's office. Having become attached to the free seed program, which distributed 1.2 million packets of seeds in one year alone, farmers were generally inclined to demand more direct aid from the federal government.

Chances for the passage of the law creating a separate executive-level department for agriculture greatly improved after Abraham Lincoln endorsed the idea in his first message to Congress. Still, conservatives, some from agricultural states in the Northeast, managed to impose significant limits on the new department; in specifying a low salary for the new Commissioner of Agriculture, they ensured that the first several appointments went to undistinguished candidates. In material respects, the responsibilities and obligations of the infant U.S. Department of Agriculture (USDA) were no different from those of the agricultural bureau in the Patent Office. There were immediate problems to confront, and at least one was of the government's own making: the free seed program introduced new and destructive diseases and pests into the country. Still, the popularity of the annual reports, which gathered valuable scientific and practical information in one place, ensured the USDA at least a modest claim on the nation's purse. The department's first annual report displayed the bureaucrat's skill for self-preservation and positive spin: "[N]otwithstanding our early difficulties in planting an empire in the wilderness, our wars, our want of a market, our vast territory, sparse population, cheap land, and ruinous system of exhausting a virgin soil, yet great and manifold progress has been made in agriculture."[8]

The agricultural college law also expanded the federal government's administrative responsibilities in agriculture. The Morrill Land Grant Act, signed in 1862 after having been vetoed in 1859, set out the terms by which states would receive grants from the public lands for the construction of institutions of higher education. Each state would receive 30,000 acres for each member of Congress, and the Eastern states that contained no available federal lands received scrip to sell to homesteaders and other private individuals, who could then claim unoccupied lands in the new states for $1.25 an acre. The South's objection to the original bill was a not unreasonable fear that the scrip would end up in the hands of speculators who would then gobble up the best quality lands in the new states. The

---

[8] *Report of the Commissioner of Agriculture, 1862* (Washington, DC, 1863), 4–25.

newer states had their own problems with the plan; fearing the "evil effects of land speculation and absentee landlordism," they attached amendments limiting the acreage that could be acquired with scrip and requiring a one-year waiting period before such transactions could be executed. The money generated from land sales under the Morrill Act then funded the construction and operation of agricultural colleges in every state of the Union. Fears of concentrated ownership were realized as well. Three states – California, Nevada, and Wisconsin – each contained more than a million acres of scrip lands by 1903. Together, the agricultural colleges and the USDA would greatly expand public support of scientific advances in farming and spread the idea of scientific farming among landowners.

The scrip program's numbers are remarkable considering that it had to compete with the other major plank of Civil War-era land policy, the Homestead Act of 1862. That law represented the culmination of decades of pressure for free land for settlers in the West, which was fueled by the Jeffersonian insistence on small farms, the long-standing practice of giving land grants as payment for military service, and, most tellingly, the repeated claims that the lands belonged, after all, to the people. As Free Soil Democrats proclaimed in 1852, "The right of all men to the soil is as sacred as their right to life itself," a position their rivals, the Republicans, co-opted in 1860.[9] By the time war arrived, free homesteading had become synonymous with anti-slavery; or, perhaps more accurately, by opposing anti-slavery provisions in the territories, Southerners had positioned themselves as opponents of free homesteads. In fact, Southerners and Northern Democrats shared objections to free lands that had nothing to do with slavery; for example, the losses in federal revenue that homesteading would cause. Against the backdrop of the burgeoning constitutional crisis, the free lands bill, vetoed by President Buchanan in 1859, became an important issue in the 1860 presidential campaign. The Republicans redeemed their promise to the homesteaders and railroads with a bill Lincoln signed in May 1862. The law enabled settlers to claim up to 160 acres free, aside from a small filing fee, and to secure title after five years' residency. In Paul Gates' classic expression, the Homestead Act "was grafted . . . upon a land system to which it was ill-fitted and incongruous."[10]

In the ensuing sixty years, more than two hundred million acres would be claimed under the law. Most of that acreage would never be divided into small tracts for farming, and much of it went undeveloped for decades. Under the terms of the Homestead Act, free settlers could convert their lands

[9] S. M. Booth, "Land Reform Plank of the Free-Soil Party," *Chicago Daily Tribune*, November 19, 1887, p. 14.
[10] Gates, *Agriculture and the Civil War*, 287.

to preemption by paying $1.25 or $2.50 per acre. This provision enabled landowners to escape the 160-acre limit of the Homestead Act and to amass hundreds, even thousands of acres in the West. Even more acreage than that patented by homesteaders was never made available for free settlement. Much of the better quality land was held back for the railroads, state grants, and Indian reservations. The drumbeat of political pressure before the war in favor of free homesteading meant that Congress took little time to consider whether conditions west of the hundredth meridian would support small-scale farming. Aridity made vast stretches of the plains unsuited to the production of anything but field crops on a large scale.

During the period between the Civil War and World War I, Congress continually attempted to address the conflicts caused by the superimposition of systems of husbandry designed for a temperate climate onto an arid environment. Most significant were the various laws that subsidized the construction of irrigation works, at great environmental cost. The forests of the West were made subject to the Homestead Act, which opened them to the rapacious operations of lumber companies. Mining, grasslands, water, and other resources called for special handling to preserve the public interest and ownership in them; Congress would still be legislating on these subjects at the time of World War I. As developments during the postbellum period would reveal, the signal legislative accomplishments of the Civil War Congress would open up more problems and challenges for agriculture and the state than they solved. For the moment, as Heather Richardson has pointed out, the agricultural legislation that Northern Republicans enacted during the Civil War "involved the national government actively and innovatively in the economy."[11]

The Growth of National Markets After the Civil War

Wartime patterns of involvement and regulation made necessary a decidedly interventionist system of government-business relations in the postwar period. That expanded role would call for greater attention to the sustained problems raised by a national market and the increasingly interstate nature of agricultural production and consumption after the war ended. The federal government increased in size, mostly due to the war, and the costs of running a larger administrative institution rose as well. Lands policy now no longer treated the public domain as a tangible asset of the government; in addition to tariffs, taxes would now supply the basis for federal revenues. For taxes and tariffs to generate sufficient income to support the government,

[11] Heather Cox Richardson, *The Greatest Nation of the Earth: Republican Economic Policies During the Civil War* (Cambridge, MA, 1997), 149.

the nation had to prosper. The fates of the government and the economy were now inseparable. Nowhere was this relationship more evident than in the marketing of agricultural commodities.

The federal government's involvement in directly encouraging agricultural production and monitoring commodity prices during the Civil War set an important precedent for later incursions of federal regulatory power into the market. After the war, agriculture boomed, particularly in the Midwest and Far West, but not because of the large-scale success of small-scale, self-sufficient farmers. Rather, the exigencies of wartime had pushed American agriculture so far from the Jeffersonian vision that there was no longer any realistic chance of recapturing it. Instead, what began to emerge was a system of production in which farmers were caught up in a marketing system that often as not failed to reward them adequately. As Richardson writes, "The war, with its railroad boom and need to move crops in large amounts, had tied farmers directly to a national economy and promoted commercial farming at the expense of the old system of subsistence farming supplemented by surplus cash crops."[12]

This process of economic nationalization transformed both production and marketing in two ways. First, production and processing became more specialized, more industrialized, and divorced from concerns for consumer health or worker safety. After the Civil War, farms in the South returned to the commercial production of cotton or tobacco. In the Great Plains, large landowners planted field crops and raised large herds of livestock. Far Western states such as California, Oregon, and Washington began producing horticultural commodities and wheat on an industrial scale. In the Northeast, where distance was less of a factor and the transportation infrastructure extended to most towns, a more diverse productive economy did continue to flourish. However, even small farms, which tend to be linked with productive diversification and self-sufficiency, began to focus on selling one or two crops commercially. The large farms of the Midwest and West and the sheer volume of their agricultural productivity tied those regions to major selling hubs in Chicago and St. Louis and, after the completion of the transcontinental railroad in 1869, San Francisco and Los Angeles. Chicago in particular became the nexus for the physical transfer of commodities such as beef and wheat as well as for the sale of commodities futures. The meat-packing industry generated huge profits and disgusting byproducts that posed serious hazards to public and environmental health. It took reformers decades to obtain meaningful regulatory oversight. The packinghouse industry in Chicago operated on an industrial scale and strove for efficiency at every turn; the big meatpackers' processing practices, famously captured

---

[12] Richardson, *Greatest Nation of the Earth*, 168.

by Upton Sinclair, "turned waste into profit whatever the noneconomic cost."[13]

Second, the scale and scope of marketing changed. New mechanisms of exchange arose after the Civil War that interposed new economic actors and institutions between producers and consumers. Facilitated by the railroads, the nation's population gravitated toward urban places, creating concentrated markets of people who had to rely on others for food, clothing, and other consumables. Agricultural goods such as fruit, cheese, or meat that were sold close to home required little preservation, preparation, storage, or handling, but goods sold to distant markets required all of these things. Farmers seeking to capture a share of distant markets had to rely on the services provided by transportation companies, processors, grain warehouses, distributors, and retailers. The increasing interdependence of farmers and middlemen shifted the rules of the market. Farmers became less self-sufficient, and as agricultural exchange became more impersonal and volume-oriented, their individual and collective bargaining power declined. The rise of corporate control over buying and selling diminished farmers' economic status within the market and led to the first sustained political protest movement with farmers at the center.

The Farm Protest Movements of the Late Nineteenth Century

These changing circumstances prompted farmers as a group to mobilize on an unprecedented scale and to seek political intervention to restructure market relationships. Their first target was the railroads. In the second half of the nineteenth century, railroad lines expanded at a stunning rate, increasing from 30,000 miles of track in 1860 to 240,000 by 1910. The railroads set low rates for long-haul routes and high rates for short distances, sending farmers into a collective rage that united them in novel ways. As the first integrated interstate carriers, the railroads held everyone's fortunes in their hands. During the 1870s, a decade marked by panic and depression, the swift emergence of a nationwide monopoly in transportation frightened farmers and other groups whose political power had hitherto been predominantly local in nature.

The National Grange of the Patrons of Husbandry, better known as the Grange, spearheaded the movement to obtain legislative relief from monopolies in transportation, grain storage, and distribution. During the 1870s, the Grange built local organizations in Illinois, Iowa, Minnesota, and other Midwestern states, and these locals pressured legislators for relief. State legislatures readily responded to farmers' complaints about unfair rate

---

[13] William Cronon, *Nature's Metropolis: Chicago and the Great West* (New York, 1991), 253.

structures, but could do little to control the railroads. Instead of directly subsidizing the growth of the railroads, however, as states had done before the war, legislatures began to constrain industries and corporations in an attempt to "humanize ... industrial society," in the words of Richard Hofstadter.[14] Reluctant to cross the constitutional Maginot Line and regulate prices directly, legislatures opted for commissions with stronger oversight authority and even, in a few cases, with the power to set maximum rates. Massachusetts led the way in 1869, and state watchdog commissions became fairly common, though essentially toothless. In addition, many states, responding to hard times, pulled back on their direct grants to railroads and other private transportation projects. The strongest attempts to constrain the railroads were made in the Midwest, where grassroots political movements fueled by agrarian discontent emboldened legislators and resulted in some of the period's most significant clashes between statutory authority and judicial oversight.

In response to new regulations that directly affected rates, the railroads hauled the Illinois state commission into court, challenging the state laws as an interference with the substantive due process rights of private entrepreneurs. Earlier in the decade, the U.S. Supreme Court had handed down landmark decisions curtailing state regulatory authority, among them a ruling striking down a Louisiana law erecting a monopoly in the slaughterhouse business because it obstructed the rights of others to enter the industry. In the Illinois railroad case, the Court tacked differently, upholding the state's authority to set maximum rates but hinting ominously that substantive due process yet lived. The farmers' fight to tame the railroads continued in the legislatures, where many Grangers held office.

The Grangers also attempted to reform agricultural marketing. Their ambitious platform aimed to give farmers more control over everything that took place after crops left the farm. Here, in contrast to their tangles with the railroads, the farm movement focused on self-help methods that farmers could implement without the aid of regulatory legislation. In the early 1870s, state and regional Granges in the Midwest, Plains, and South set up cooperative purchasing agencies and consumer stores to deal in farm equipment. As the Grange grew, the locals expanded into distance marketing as well, especially for grain, cotton, livestock, tobacco, and wool. Most Granger cooperatives were unincorporated and delegated transactions to local agents. They were also utterly unspecialized, selling "nearly everything their members produced, from green onions to dressed beef."[15] This

[14] Richard Hofstadter, *The Age of Reform: From Bryan to F.D.R.* (New York, 1955), 242.
[15] Herman Steen, *Cooperative Marketing: The Golden Rule in Agriculture* (Garden City, NY, 1923), 5.

over-inclusive approach, coupled with a preference for informal organizational structures, took its toll on Granger cooperatives. By 1875, most had failed entirely; others were converted to purely commercial operations. Farmers impatient for help became disillusioned and left the Grange in droves.

The Farmers' Alliance, which began to emerge in the late 1870s, inherited and vastly expanded on the Grangers' legacy of legislative regulation to reform the market. Like the Grangers, the Alliance became a national political movement that was directly involved in electoral politics. In a forthright attack on monopolies in processing and transportation, the Alliance argued that the unequal bargaining power between farmers and distributors provided a legitimate rationale for state intervention on behalf of farmers.

While it lasted, the Populists' ride was a fascinating one. The Alliance originated in northeastern Texas, scored some impressive successes in organizing cooperatives there, and soon strung a network of cooperatives across the South and Midwest. The Alliance copied the Grangers' organizational structure, organizing local cooperative stores, grain elevators, and cotton sales yards. This second farmers' movement became even more overtly political, challenging the two-party system in local, state, and federal elections through the Populist Party. The Populists broadened the agrarian agenda to include the interests of workers and even some small businesses while appeasing racist Southerners by holding separate rallies for black and white farmers. The Populists' anti-monopoly critique gained steam during the late 1880s and 1890s, bolstered by a radical attack on the banking system, silver currency, and a credit crunch that was derived from defaults on Civil War-era bonds.

The very breadth of the Populists' attack on the financial system made it difficult to sustain, particularly in the competitive atmosphere of presidential elections. By 1896, as Daniel Rodgers has noted, sympathetic reformers such as Henry D. Lloyd were "shaken by the degeneration of Populism into mere free-silver politics."[16] Populist candidates never polled more than 10 percent in a U.S. presidential race. Late-nineteenth-century state and federal judges resisted many Populist-inspired reforms of corporate capitalism, including state laws to regulate the wages and hours of industrial workers. The courts largely – but not without exception – sided with corporations that challenged federal regulation of industrial prices on interstate commerce grounds and assailed state regulations of hours and wages on due process grounds. In particularly hazardous employments such as mining, the courts agreed that considerations of public health justified limitations

---

[16] Daniel T. Rodgers, *Atlantic Crossings: Social Politics in a Progressive Age* (Cambridge, MA, 1998), 67.

on hours. In common, ordinary occupations, the courts preserved what they called the contractual freedom of workers to bargain for the conditions of their employment. Agriculture, as one of the most ordinary of common occupations, merited no such special treatment; attempts to exempt farmers from state antitrust laws failed repeatedly in both the state and federal courts. Around the turn of the century, the judiciary was generally inclined to think that farmers were no different from any other business entrepreneur.

What was the Populist movement's long-term influence on law and politics? It produced a lingering strain of economic liberalism, focused on the interests of the small-scale producer. Cross-threaded within it were demands that corporate capitalism be made more orderly and fair and that the state take responsibility for fiscal and regulatory policies that maintained the power of corporate capitalism on the one hand while undermining democratic politics on the other. Populism was principally a movement of farmers that called for certain kinds of governmental protection against the social and economic forces that seemed responsible for widening gaps between the rich and poor, owners and labor, and country and city. Though the farm protests of the late nineteenth century were predicated on the perception that agriculture was losing ground to industry, at certain times it was the industrial sector that "had trouble competing for resources with a vibrant, competitive, and rapidly expanding agricultural sector."[17] The agrarian protest movements dominated national politics from the 1870s until 1900 by, in part, emphasizing the perception that the rapidly industrializing economy put agriculture at a disadvantage.

Progressive Era Administrative Expansion

The Populist movement marked farmers' emergence as a powerful national interest group at the time when the country was exchanging a predominantly rural society for a predominantly urban one. The battles that farmers waged, both during the Populist era and afterward, marked the beginning of their long and successful quest for positive federal protection and promotion of agriculture. The sense of marginalization that farmers felt after the demise of Populism fueled their claims for federal assistance and relief, particularly as cities and their growing social and economic problems commanded the spotlight. This relief took the form of collecting and disseminating information to make markets work more efficiently. Rural credit, agricultural

---

[17] Alan L. Olmstead and Paul W. Rhode, "The Transformation of Northern Agriculture," in Stanley L. Engerman and Robert E. Gallman, eds., *The Cambridge Economic History of the United States: Volume III: The Twentieth Century* (Cambridge, 2000), 693–742, 695.

extension and experiment stations, and market data collection and analysis became part of federal support of agriculture after 1900.

During the Progressive era, agriculture's productivity continued its mete-oric rise. Corn production rose from 1.1 billion bushels in 1870 to 2.6 billion in 1900; during this period, wheat rose from 254 million to 599 million bushels and cotton from 4.3 billion to 10.1 billion bales. Increased produc-tion prompted processors and manufacturers to expand capacity accordingly. During that same thirty-year period, crop prices went into free fall. Wheat growers who had received $1.53 per bushel in 1865 got only $.62 in 1900; cotton, a less valuable crop to begin with, dropped from $.32 per pound to $.09. Corn held its value somewhat better, going from $.47 to $.36 per bushel. At the same time, regional discrimination in freight rates contin-ued unabated, with the result that farmers in the West and South faced higher per-mile costs in shipping their crops east than producers nearer to the coast.

When the Progressives turned their attention to farmers' grievances, mar-keting supplied a convenient catch-all category for the sorts of issues that government could legitimately address while leaving matters of produc-tion for individuals to decide. It was a division of labor that was compatible with both the constitutional limits on the administrative reach of govern-ment and the Progressives' fascination with science, technology, expertise, and information. The idea that furnishing producers and corporate proces-sors with accurate information about the movement of commodities across space and over time would improve market efficiency led to the widespread establishment of state bureaus of agricultural marketing after 1900. These agencies were not much different from their counterparts that watched railroads; they could not do anything that affected prices directly, but the very practice of aggregating such data as the price differentials between raw and finished commodities empowered farmers seeking to strike more profitable deals with processors and distributors. The federal Office of Mar-kets, established within the USDA in 1913 and raised to bureau status after World War I, was little more than an information conduit. Primarily, it served the agricultural colleges and, later, federal county extension agents who provided scientific expertise and information on market conditions to farmers under the Weeks Act of 1914. Its impact on market exchanges was mostly indirect. It was hardly likely that the USDA could do more; the department remained a second-tier executive branch agency with limited administrative capacity and even less clout on Capitol Hill.

State marketing agencies gathered and disseminated information on mar-kets and market activity, including commodity prices, transportation costs, and distribution sector margins. Intended to help farmers without interfer-ing with actual transactions, public marketing agencies sometimes became controversial. For example, in 1916 the California State Market Commission secured legislation compelling all wholesale sellers of fish to participate in the State Fish Exchange, which set prices and suspended many state and local fishing regulations. Consumers, fishers, and the California Fish and Game Commission mobilized public opinion against the Market Commission. A statewide strike of sardine fishers in 1919 forced the removal of price controls and the dissolution of the Market Commission. Such responses indicate that, according to those being regulated, public marketing agencies were intended to help farmers but not constrain their behavior.

An area in which the USDA excelled was the development of cooperative programs in education, research, and extension. Beginning with the Hatch Act of 1887, which established the agricultural experiment station system, the USDA built structures for federal-state cooperation that piggybacked on the land grant colleges established under the Morrill Act. In the first decades of the twentieth century, the USDA's budget for scientific research tripled, and the department used this money to create "specialized scientific research bureaus" and build research programs that coordinated with state experiment stations. The Smith-Lever Act of 1914 deepened the USDA's administrative capacity for research; it authorized the agricultural cooperative extension service, through which government agents transmitted scientific information developed at universities to farmers for use in the field.

After 1900, producers continued their attack on the food distribution system by attributing depressed crop prices to the high or increasing costs of retailing. Since the states were generally disinclined to police trusts and corporate combinations, farmers began to mimic the business practices of corporations and monopolies in order to prosper like them. Using an updated form of traditional cooperation, California fruit growers achieved what many people thought was beyond the power of far-flung farmers: they organized industry-wide corporations that took control of the entire crop from the moment of harvest through retail sales. In economic terms, these cooperatives were integrated horizontally and vertically, enabling them to monopolize supply and to control production and retail prices. The California model worked well for commodities for which production was fairly contained geographically; in other regions of the country, where staple crop production spread across eight or ten states, achieving a high degree of control over an entire crop proved difficult.

Although farmers were the foremost proponents of state-level regulation of trusts in the Progressive era, many of them were practiced in the art of monopoly. In 1913 and 1914, for example, farmers were working with organized labor to prod Congress to exempt unions and farmers' bargaining associations from the original federal antitrust law, the Sherman Act of

1890. At the same time, agricultural cooperatives were themselves fighting to keep from being prosecuted under state and federal antitrust laws. The Clayton Act of 1914 was intended to close some of the loopholes that corporations had exploited in the Sherman Act by specifically prohibiting practices that restrained trade. Certain forms of holding companies and interlocking directorates were outlawed, as were discriminating freight agreements and the distribution of sales territories among so-called natural competitors. The new law specifically exempted laborers and farmers' cooperatives with no capital stock from federal prohibitions on anti-competitive behavior.

Oddly, prosecution of farmers under federal antitrust laws accelerated after passage of the Clayton Act, while the courts quickly neutralized the provisions least friendly to corporate combinations. In agriculture's case, the political traction of Jeffersonian agrarianism eventually trumped the waning public distrust of economic combination. The highest profile federal prosecution of farmers under the Sherman Act involved California's highly monopolistic raisin cooperative. The suit was effectively scuttled in 1922 by a new federal law that expanded the Clayton Act exemption for cooperatives and placed regulatory oversight powers in the friendly hands of the Secretary of Agriculture. Farmers may not have succeeded in taming industrial combinations, but they proved sufficiently adept at the strategic use of the image of the yeoman agrarian to secure protective legislation for themselves.

By the time war broke out in Europe in 1914, it had become broadly accepted that "governmental power was to be used to encourage farmers to build credit systems, accept scientific research, control the marketing of their commodities, and plan what crops and livestock to raise."[18] Other important regulatory accomplishments of the Progressive era resulted from expanded federal oversight of processing industries under such laws as the Federal Trade Commission Act and the Grain Futures Act. In its early years, the Federal Trade Commission conducted path-breaking investigations of meatpacking and the grain trade that resulted in landmark remedial legislation. In some cases, the laws survived constitutional attack. The Supreme Court upheld the Packers and Stockyards Act of 1921 against an interstate commerce challenge, holding that the nation was entitled to a clean meat supply. The Cotton Act of 1914 imposed excise taxes on all sales for future delivery and taxed participation in cotton futures exchanges and boards of trade. In 1916, the first federal Farm Loan Act was enacted, creating cooperative national farm loan associations and joint-stock land banks.

---

[18] David E. Hamilton, *From New Day to New Deal: American Farm Policy from Hoover to Roosevelt, 1928–1933* (Chapel Hill, NC, 1991), 6.

During World War I, the states and federal government continued to expand their involvement in scientific experimentation and innovation through the agricultural colleges and, after the early 1920s, the administrative agencies themselves. New varieties of plants and seeds were bred, new techniques for planting and harvesting were developed, and farmers were encouraged to pay attention to such important problems as soil exhaustion and crop rotation. The states funneled appropriations from the cooperative extension program and the information it generated to farmers, and the federal government continued to expand its investigative, scientific, and marketing studies within the USDA. Among other things, the USDA began to study pests such as the boll weevil as well as the consequences of the chemical insecticides and fungicides used to eradicate them. Federal legislation establishing the first controls on these chemicals was passed in 1910; its object was not to reduce harms to humans from the heavy metals they contained but to limit adulterated and diluted forms of popular formulas. The U.S. Forest Service, which was transferred from the Department of Interior to the Department of Agriculture in 1910, began to focus on sustainable harvest of small woodlots and the use of trees to prevent soil erosion. Quality control, inspection, and post-harvest handling all became objects of federal regulation in the years before and after the war.

The Post-World War I "Farm Crisis"

These trends represented a substantive expansion of public administrative authority into previously unregulated areas of the agricultural economy. Still, many farmers believed that government's inattention to the causes of the "farm crisis" that followed World War I helped bring it about. The farm crisis was rooted in three distinct phenomena. First, around the turn of the twentieth century, the stream of farmers from the country to the city in every region except the Far West became a torrent. Second, the evident decline in farm population reinforced farmers' worries about the lack of labor available to them. Finally, farm leaders believed that after 1900 the farm movement had lost considerable steam. A 1913 USDA report noted proudly the leadership of regional organizations all claiming the legacy of the Grange, but it overlooked the fact that national leadership was lacking and that farmers needed "a permanent body to give consistency to the movement."[19] Though farmers had benefited substantially from the expansion of federal support for agriculture, they expected an immediate public response at the onset of bad times.

[19] T. N. Carver, "The Organization of Rural Interests," in *U.S. Department of Agriculture Yearbook* (Washington, DC, 1913), 239–58.

Despite the expanded administrative capacities of the national state, the USDA and its sub-agencies worked under considerable political and legal constraints during the Progressive era. In an assessment of the related political mobilizations of farmers and labor, Elizabeth Sanders argues that by 1917 farmers were more successful at obtaining the legislation they wanted, but not by much. Though farmers obtained legislation to tame futures markets and deter fraud in marketing, their signal achievement also undercut their claims to additional help. The agricultural cooperative extension service, established by the Smith-Lever Act of 1914, essentially supplanted the Farmers' Union and what was left of the Grange by funneling information and assistance to farmers through the states. It took the extraordinary conditions of wartime to bring federal administration to the farm through price and marketing controls and to override, at least temporarily, constitutional scruples regarding government interference in private exchange.

The war – and government's responses to it – changed economic conditions in unexpected ways. It closed lucrative export markets to U.S. farmers, who responded by producing less. Staple crop production leveled off after 1914, leading to sporadic shortages. The resulting price inflation triggered an unusual exercise of federal emergency powers. In 1917, Congress passed one law to encourage food production, an entreaty laced with patriotic appeals, and another to create the U.S. Food Administration. Headed by Herbert Hoover, the Food Administration was given unprecedented authority to fix maximum prices, control inflation, and supervise marketing throughout the country. The lid on prices meant that agricultural profits were sacrificed in the short term, which generated resentment, but farmers as well as processors and distributors recognized that wartime sacrifice should be shared. After the Armistice, the limits were swiftly rescinded, and the resulting market chaos threw the country into a deep recession. To reverse this downturn, agricultural interests deployed the sympathetic image of the farmer in distress to build on the imaginative hybrid of promotion and regulation that had begun under Wilson. By this time, it was apparent that agriculture needed no political alliances with labor or anyone else to make its case before Congress.

The consequences of a narrow emphasis on achieving annual increases in yield and in total crop size came crashing down on American farmers after the war. Having been urged to expand production in wartime for the good of the nation, American farmers were then stuck with the excess capacity; when they increased prices after the war, they were tagged as profiteers. As one farmer put it, "Many of us in the coming year, in spite of slogans such as 'Food Wins the War'... will merely try to feed the farmer."[20]

---

[20] Ralph H. Gabriel, "The Farmer in the Commonwealth," *North American Review* 213 (May 1921), 577–86, at 577.

Having become accustomed to federally mandated low prices, consumers revolted when the controls were lifted and prices surged. For a time, serious consideration was given to the idea of prolonging federal price controls.

Reinvigorated by the economic crisis, the farm movement reemerged during the 1920s. The relative disunity of the postwar farm lobby, however, reflected the increasingly complex social and economic landscape of American agriculture. The American Farm Bureau Federation was organized in 1920; conservative and dedicated to preserving producers' economic prerogatives, the Farm Bureau opposed public controls on production and favored stronger regulation of commodities futures trading, better rural credit, and a strong endorsement of cooperative marketing. Other less influential groups wanted more direct public supervision of trading and processors. Congressional Republicans from strong farm states pushed for direct surplus abatement. Their proposed legislation, known as the McNary-Haugen bills, would have dumped surpluses abroad at steeply discounted prices. The idea was widely popular in agricultural circles, but President Coolidge, catering to isolationist and laissez-faire sentiments, vetoed it twice. Spurred by Secretary of Commerce Herbert Hoover, Presidents Harding and Coolidge signed several other bills on the Farm Bureau's agenda. The Capper-Volstead Act of 1922 broadened the federal antitrust exemption for cooperatives. The Agricultural Credit Act of 1923 set up federal credit banks to deal in notes issued by cooperatives on favorable terms. The Cooperative Marketing Act of 1926 created a Bureau of Cooperative Marketing to help farmers organize and exempted all cooperatives from the income tax. For a long time, many scholars regarded these measures as signs of the success of Herbert Hoover's Progressive-inspired "associationalist" model of government-business relations, which envisioned government as focused on maintaining institutional fairness while leaving business free to compete or combine.

Associationalism did not, however, solve the broader "farm problem," as people commonly understood it during the first three decades of the twentieth century. The farm problem was not merely persistent low prices and large supplies. It was the development, in more or less permanent form, of a new level of structural inequality between farmers and the non-agricultural economy. The spread of mechanized processes of production sharpened the race to harvest and put farmers under constant pressure to mechanize further and to carry huge debt loads to do so. Overproduction did more than depress prices; it increased regional competition for national and international markets, especially in staple crops such as corn and wheat.

Recovering pre-war price levels for these commodities proved difficult. Overproduction and the turn to monoculture on many farms increased agriculture's dependence on an unstable business economy. Tenants and laborers worked on small farms where soil depletion and erosion made it difficult to earn a decent living. Rural poverty became more widespread during the 1920s, and these marginal classes were hit hardest when the bottom dropped out for everyone in 1929. Commercial farmers were better off, individually, but collectively they faced increasingly competitive market conditions both domestically and abroad. As a group, farmers could do little to protect their investments in land and capital under such conditions.

Struggling farmers demanded interventionist responses from government. Throughout the 1920s, conservatives in Congress kept at bay controls on production that would have maintained surpluses at manageable levels. More tolerance of combination and monopoly in such industries as grain harvesting, steel, and the railroads marked the important antitrust decisions of the decade. Even the cooperative movement, which many conservatives and moderates had hoped would provide needed corrections in the market, failed to live up to its promise. Cooperatives collapsed by the dozens after 1924, even as the courts upheld the legality of their marketing arrangements and membership contracts. As Morton Keller concluded, "[T]he regulatory system of the 1920s was more committed to the competitive individualistic past than to a corporative future."[21] Even so, farm prices and incomes rebounded somewhat, and after losing population and farms between 1900 and 1920, the agricultural sector held constant, more or less, over the postwar decade.

When the stock market crashed in 1929, agriculture had not yet fully recovered from the self-perpetuating cycle of overproduction and low prices that had marked the postwar years. Herbert Hoover spent his first months as president planning for a "new day in agriculture." The Agricultural Marketing Act of 1929 established the Federal Farm Board and declared it federal policy to put "agriculture on a basis of economic equality with industry." Agriculture's chronic distress may have made it seem ripe for more direct public regulation, but its own traditions of localism, dependency, and decentralized decision making placed it at odds with the acute interest group politics of 1920s farm policy. As David Hamilton has observed, "The tensions inherent in state-building were acutely evident when it came to agriculture."[22] What Hoover faced when he took office were the battle scars resulting from the ongoing clash between agriculture's interest group goals, which put farmers in conflict with labor and industry, and the associationalist approach many of them thought the cooperative movement

---

[21] Morton Keller, "The Pluralist State: American Economic Regulation in Comparative Perspective, 1900–1930," in Thomas P. McCraw, ed., *Regulation in Perspective: Historical Essays* (Cambridge, MA, 1981), 56–94, at 85.

[22] Hamilton, *From New Day to New Deal*, 5.

exemplified. The discouraging record of cooperatives had weakened but not destroyed the associationalist model. Indeed, the Progressives under Wilson had worked elements of both aspects of agricultural state-building – interest group politics and associationalism – into their public policy on agriculture. After 1929, the major regulatory and political question for agriculture was which approach would prevail.

At the time and for decades afterward, Hoover was criticized for failing to respond to the economic crisis adequately. It is perhaps more accurate to say that his responses were measured and limited, proving insufficiently flexible as the crisis deepened. Markets and institutions failed to improve under the limited relief measures that his administration offered. The workings of the Farm Board offer a case in point. It was created in June 1929, several months before the crash, and its initial objective was to speed a boggy recovery, not to remedy the enormous structural collapse that followed Black Tuesday. The Farm Board's mandate was "to promote the effective merchandising of agricultural commodities in interstate and foreign commerce."[23] To this end, it administered a revolving fund of $500 million, which it loaned to cooperatives to finance marketing plans, make advance payments to growers, and construct processing facilities. Stabilization corporations were set up to hold cotton and wheat surpluses temporarily until prices rose. Instead, prices continued to drop. Cooperatives and their traditional opponents could not agree on marketing plans and stabilization terms, and their inability to work together further hampered recovery. The Farm Board did take some extraordinary steps: it created government-owned corporations to buy surplus crops, launched voluntary programs to limit production, underwrote the sale of commodities to foreign governments, exchanged surplus wheat for surplus coffee, distributed government-owned stocks to relief organizations, and paid some fruit growers to destroy their crops. Even these measures were not enough.

Despite the desperate conditions of the Depression, the Farm Board could only advocate but not require that farmers reduce production. Never a believer in governmental price controls, Hoover was unwilling to authorize the Farm Board to intervene further. In its final report in 1932, the Board explicitly defined the political and constitutional obstacle in the way of recovery: "No government measure for improving farm prices, aside from increasing consumer demand, could be effective unless it included a more definite control over production."[24] The interdependency of the rural and urban economies made farm recovery impossible without a more general return to prosperity. The key economic problem for agriculture during the

---

[23] Hamilton, *From New Day to New Deal*, 46.
[24] U.S. Federal Farm Board, *Third Annual Report* (Washington, DC, 1932), 1.

1920s and early 1930s was that farmers were too productive for existing urban and international markets. The key policy problem, both before and after the Depression, was "how to limit production and increase farm prices and incomes to preserve the family farm."[25] The major difference before and after 1933 lay in the legal mechanisms the federal government was willing to adopt to meet changing circumstances.

III. FROM THE NEW DEAL TO THE PRESENT

The election of Franklin Roosevelt and the enactment of the Agricultural Adjustment Act (AAA) of 1933 "mark[ed] the demise of a discredited farm program and the start of a 'new deal' for American farmers."[26] But there were more continuities between Hoover and Roosevelt than this characterization admits. Hoover's farm policy was more activist and Roosevelt's more conservative than is generally acknowledged. Roosevelt's agricultural recovery program displayed a greater propensity to use formal legislative power and to build statist bureaucracies to manage the agricultural economy, but these changes were more of degree than of kind. The New Deal relied on farmers' cooperative and voluntary action just as heavily as the Farm Board had, but it also compelled processors to participate. The AAA institutionalized the authority to restrict production and control prices in a formal legal structure governed by public power rather than private prerogative.

The New Deal federal agricultural programs supplied the piece missing from the 1920s regulatory regime: they imposed limits on production. The AAA levied taxes on agricultural processors and used the revenues to fund rental or benefit payments to farmers – in effect, offering them a wage for not producing. The law also empowered the secretary of agriculture to enter into agreements with groups of producers, associations, processors, and others to provide for the orderly marketing of commodities; the secretary had the power to issue licenses to anyone seeking to market crops in interstate commerce. Overall, the purpose of the act was to reduce commodity surpluses while increasing the purchasing power of farmers.

Certainly Roosevelt's foot soldiers in the agricultural new deal – Secretary of Agriculture Henry A. Wallace and his deputies, Mordecai Ezekiel, M. L. Wilson, and Jerome Frank, among others – were adept at claiming to uphold traditional agrarian democracy even as they expanded the reach of federal power over economic decisions made on individual farms. In 1933, Wallace described the local wheat adjustment committees of the AAA

---

[25] Olmstead and Rhode, "Transformation of Northern Agriculture," 695–96.
[26] Hamilton, *From New Day to New Deal*, 237.

as "a modern re-expression of real Jeffersonian democracy – decentralized responsibility, local decision, local control."[27] The AAA's opponents, who included farmers as well as processors and distributors, hotly disputed that claim, but there was a grain of truth to the idea. AAA licenses and marketing agreements could only proceed with the approval of a supermajority of producers in the regulated commodity. Sometimes, as in the case of specialty crops such as dried fruit, growers and processors refused to agree to the license, so that no price or marketing regulation could be implemented. When prices improved, processors often sold more than they were permitted under the marketing agreements. The AAA's benefits did not penetrate all local economies. Agricultural sectors heavily populated by tenants remained unprofitable, even with strong control mechanisms in place. Wheat, hog, and cotton tenant farmers who had never had much power in local affairs were systematically shut out of the local program committees set up under the AAA and denied the benefits to which they were entitled by law.

The AAA had many shortcomings. It was poorly drafted. It did not address the demands of distributors who had long profited by manipulating the supply and price at which surplus commodities were sold. By alienating these agents, the AAA created powerful enemies. In fact, the distributors of such staple crops as milk, tobacco, and fruit had vested interests in the continuation of surpluses. The AAA tried to attack the surplus problem by destroying commodities before they left the farm. The law's opponents seized on such actions as Wallace's order of the slaughter of thousands of baby pigs to ridicule the administration.

Milking the administration's public relations disasters was one of the many strategies of the New Deal's conservative opponents. Another was to challenge the legislation in court. Anticipating this move, the alphabet agencies looked for favorable test cases they could bring first, thereby preempting the opposition. The AAA's attorneys, however, had trouble finding a case with a favorable set of facts. In 1935, the U.S. Supreme Court struck down the production control provisions in *Schechter Poultry Co. v. US*, declaring them an unconstitutional delegation of legislative power to the executive branch. Attempting to maintain more or less consistent boundaries between public and private governance and between state and federal authority, the Court struck down the AAA's tax on processors in 1936 as an unconstitutional restraint on local commerce. The AAA was born again after the 1936 reelection of Roosevelt, rechristened as the Agricultural Marketing Agreement Act of 1937 and upheld by the Court later that year as part of the watershed group of decisions ratifying the New Deal.

---

[27] Sherman Ellsworth Johnson, *Wheat Under the Agricultural Adjustment Act* (Washington, DC, 1934), 33.

Congress always intended for the states to supply complementary regulatory programs to help stabilize agriculture. Many of them complied, with mixed results. Farmers in staple and specialty crops across the country pressured state legislatures to impose direct price controls during the first years of the Depression. In New York, for example, dairy farmers staged milk strikes to protest the low prices offered by the Borden Company, the region's largest dairy purchaser. Borden colluded with the Dairymen's League, a cooperative, to divert milk to less valuable uses such as cheese, butter, and cream. The state legislature enacted price control laws in 1933 to bring economic stability to the dairy industry and to calm outbreaks of violence in the dairy regions. The milk dealers swiftly brought suit, harboring every confidence of prevailing. Instead, the U.S. Supreme Court held in *Nebbia v. New York* (1934) that the state's mandatory minimum price rule was a valid exercise of its emergency powers. What the Supreme Court gave in one decision, however, it limited in another, ruling in 1935 that states could not regulate the price of milk sold outside their borders. Interstate compacts to regulate milk sales in New England foundered for lack of support. New York finally repealed its price-fixing regulations in 1937.

The story of the New York dairy industry contrasts sharply with the outcome in California's specialized fruit crops, where state control programs took effect only after 75 percent of growers and processors agreed to terms. The California state courts upheld these price and production controls, as did the U.S. Supreme Court. In contrast to the sharp divisions between dairy farmers and their corporate customers, horticultural producers and processors agreed to divert surpluses from the market. The political battles ignited by these state-level regulatory programs died away when prices improved after the outbreak of a new war in Europe and domestic foodstuffs were allocated to the Lend-Lease foreign aid program.

Notwithstanding the change from Hoover to Roosevelt, farm policy after 1929 pursued the same essential goal as it had before the crash, which was "to create the institutions needed for a more rational and efficient national economy."[28] Emergency relief was a means to that end, but was not intended to remake government permanently. Unfortunately, the government's interest in rationalizing and regulating agriculture was an ambition that most commercial producers and farm interest groups viewed suspiciously. The New Deal reinforced the interest group politics of the modern corporatist state while giving greater authority to national bureaucratic power. It facilitated a modest recovery for farmers by reducing the risks of an unstable business economy, by stabilizing prices and credit, and by establishing production controls that depended significantly on local decision making.

[28] Hamilton, *From New Day to New Deal*, 247.

However, New Deal administrative management programs did not succeed in instilling long-term planning and rational economic coordination in federal agricultural policy.

As the remainder of this chapter suggests, many of the economic issues and trends in American agriculture that first surfaced in the 1930s and 1940s – subsidy programs, farm credit, and antitrust – continued to influence policy debates throughout the twentieth century and into the twenty-first. Other issues – environmental harm and deregulation – arose for the first time in the 1960s and 1970s, as policymakers, lobbyists, and interest groups sought to diagnose and solve agriculture's continuing problems.

Federal Subsidy Programs and the Growth of Agribusiness

The New Deal's state-centered regulatory programs of subsidies, publicly sponsored credit, and land conservation remained in place after World War II ended the Depression. Farmers continued to maximize production, maintaining downward pressure on prices and undermining the economic status and prospects of everyone whose livelihoods depended on farming. After World War II, despite the robust economy, farm profits did not keep pace with the value of the capital that farmers invested in their businesses, with the prices of non-farm goods, or with non-farm wages. At times, domestic demand stagnated, and exports could not always take up the slack. To address this problem, in 1954 Congress passed a modified version of the 1920s-era McNary-Haugen plan, which would have permitted farmers to dump surpluses abroad. This law generously subsidized the export of surplus commodities as part of a humanitarian food aid program. It encouraged American farmers to overproduce, rewarding them for planting from fence line to stream's edge, and the foreign export program "increased many nations' dependency on food imports by undercutting indigenous producers." As the debate continued over "the wisdom and need for commodity programs" and crop subsidies, the government experimented with different kinds of loan, price support, and diversion programs.[29]

The emergence of full-blown agribusiness, a phenomenon of the post-World War II period, resulted partly from these artificial measures. The government's reliance on heavy subsidies to maintain agricultural income in the face of rising surpluses increased dramatically in the postwar period. Rural electrification, mechanization, the development of new breeds of plants and animals, and the invention of new chemicals to control pests and weeds all contributed to the revolution in productivity. Meanwhile,

---

[29] David Danbom, *Born in the Country: A History of Rural America* (Baltimore, 1995), 240; Olmstead and Rhode, "Transformation of Northern Agriculture," 735.

the family labor that had sustained many farms became more valuable elsewhere. Many commodities remained profitable only because they relied on the importation of cheap migrant labor for essential seasonal work. Individual farms grew larger, but there were fewer of them in each census. In 1950, there were 5.3 million farms in the United States; by 1990, that number had dropped to 2.1 million. In 2000 the occupational category of farmer dropped out of the census entirely, because fewer than 1 million people lived on the farms they worked. The social effects of this "great migration" continue to affect not just the rural society that farmers abandoned but also the urban communities that they joined. Monopolization and combination pervaded every aspect of agricultural production, processing, and distribution. Food costs remained low relative to inflation rates and the prices of other necessities. Finally, the strong national economy that flourished between 1950 and 1973 enabled many Americans to remain oblivious as industrial farming and agribusiness generated new and more widespread environmental harms.

Toward the end of this period of economic growth, Congress attempted to reform the marketing and subsidy programs. When it became known that some farmers were receiving as much as $1 million annually from the government, the Agricultural Act of 1970 capped payments made directly to producers of feed grains, wheat, and cotton. By dividing up their holdings on paper, however, large-scale producers could easily circumvent the cap. They had ample incentive to do so, because, thanks to political pressure from agricultural lobbies, Congress maintained high support prices and favorable loan rates during the 1970s. Another attempt to cut production in 1983 produced the largest decrease in acreage under production since the New Deal, but at $78 billion it was also the most expensive in history. The idling of so much land adversely affected farm suppliers and laborers, hurting many participants in the rural economy. By this time, the nation's farm programs "cost domestic consumers and taxpayers about $1.53 for every dollar received by farmers."[30] The skill with which large-scale farmers and corporate producers subverted statutory limits on payments became a subject of outrage. The rich prospered on government funding, whereas those on the margins abandoned farming.

The Farm Credit Crisis of the 1980s

The political inviolability of farming, which rested on the continuing belief that land and individual independence went hand in hand, shaped federal policy on farm credit throughout the twentieth century. The Farm Credit

[30] Olmstead and Rhode, "Transformation of Northern Agriculture," 737.

Administration (FCA), created in 1916 to make credit more available to farmers, greatly expanded its loan programs over time. During the 1970s, a prosperous decade for agriculture, FCA lending quadrupled, spurred by low interest rates, a sharp rise in farmland values, and over-capitalization by financially aggressive farmers. Indeed, farmland values rose by 278 percent between 1970 and 1980, compared to a 104 percent rise in the GNP. Total farm debt also skyrocketed, even as expanded subsidies increased farm income.

The increase in lending and indebtedness during the stable 1970s primed agriculture for disaster. When inflation and interest rates soared in 1982 as a result of tightened monetary policies, farmland values collapsed, and the federal lending agencies were left with millions of dollars in bad loans. Congress passed remedial legislation in 1985 and 1986, but the emblematic image of the decade was the foreclosure and sale of thousands of family farms in Iowa, Nebraska, Illinois, and other Corn Belt states. One study put nearly 20 percent of all U.S. farms in financial distress in 1985.

The crisis also endangered many agricultural banks and severely strained government lending agencies. Delinquency rates at the Farmers Home Administration rose from 17 percent of all loans in 1980 to 37 percent six years later. Local federal land banks failed in numbers not seen since the Depression, causing ripple effects in the rural towns they served. Worst of all, the widespread liquidation of mortgaged farms failed to raise sufficient cash to cover the loans, and the FCA teetered on the verge of default. The agricultural crisis elicited two conflicting public reactions. One was the criticism that welfare for farmers needed to come to an end, a view that gained currency during the Reagan years. The other was that the family farm needed to be preserved, an enduring conviction in American culture that at this time equated the farmer with economic actors in the developing world: "Today . . . farmers are lumped with starving Africans as objects for benefit performances by popular musicians."[31]

As with subsidy programs, proposals for saving family farms and keeping federal farm banks open tended to obscure the fact that not everyone in the agricultural sector was hurting. While the financial crisis was both real and deep for some farmers, many maintained "relatively manageable debt loads" throughout the decade. Small farms, which were generally perceived to be most in danger of disappearing, were actually most likely to rely on high proportions of non-farm income. The Federal Deposit Insurance Corporation protected most rural banking customers from catastrophic

---

[31] Thomas F. Hady, "Is There a Farm Crisis," *Journal of Economic Education* 18 (1987), 409–20, at 409.

loss, lessening the impact of bank closures on rural communities. The most important fact about American agriculture in the 1980s, however, undercut farmers' claims that massive bailouts were needed. As economists Alan Olmstead and Paul Rhode put it, "It is understandable how 25 percent of the population, many suffering extreme financial distress in the 1930s, might convince the federal government to grant them economic relief. It is less obvious how the 2 percent of the population remaining on farms [in the 1980s] continues to receive such special treatment."[32] By that time, corporate farms, which produced much of the nation's food, relied too heavily on subsidies for the government to discontinue or cut back those programs. In 1987, Congress bailed out the Farm Credit Administration by authorizing a $4 billion bond.

Antitrust

The subsidy programs did not preserve family-owned farms. Rather, they rewarded the corporate entities that increasingly controlled agricultural production, processing, and distribution. During the 1960s and 1970s, some corporations grew to such size and attained such market dominance that public outcry forced the government to try to take corrective measures. In 1977, the Federal Trade Commission instituted Sherman Antitrust Act proceedings against Sunkist, the citrus growers' cooperative, after Sunkist acquired processing facilities in two states and a market share estimated at between 50 and 80 percent of the crop. The Sunkist case raised many of the same issues as earlier antitrust controversies involving farmers. No less a friend of business than the *Wall Street Journal* described Sunkist as "the OPEC of the citrus industry."[33] As a cooperative with an open membership policy and short-term (one-year) contracts with its members, Sunkist argued that it could never build a lasting monopoly. The government agreed, ordering no meaningful change in Sunkist's business operations. Today, farmers' cooperatives retain the statutory and political immunity from antitrust prosecution that Congress granted in 1922, despite unrelenting pressure to change the law.

Purely corporate agricultural businesses have fared less well. Concentration and monopoly in the processing sector became the object of renewed regulatory attention in the 1990s. In the grain and meat-processing industries, for example, ConAgra and Archer Daniels Midland were hit with

---

[32] Olmstead and Rhode, "Transformation of Northern Agriculture," 737.

[33] Richard T. Rogers, "Sunkist Case Study: A Discussion," *The Wall Street Journal*, March 18, 1993, p. A2.

separate antitrust suits when they sought to acquire other companies. Archer Daniels Midland "set up international price-fixing cartels to rig world markets in three commodities," one of which was high fructose corn syrup, used to sweeten sodas and many processed foods. The company pled guilty to criminal antitrust charges and paid a fine of $100 million in 1996; its top officers went to jail for fraud, money laundering, and tax evasion.

The impulse to police combinations in agribusiness did not last, however. Some of the same companies that had been accused of antitrust violations in the nineties were later permitted to consummate mergers that increased their market control. In 2002, the federal government approved a merger between Archer Daniels Midland and another large corn syrup producer, despite objections from other processors that the merger would increase prices and decrease competition. Similar combinations took place in soybeans, ethanol, beef, and poultry. Cargill, the nation's largest grain processor, acquired the next largest in 1999; the giant corporation also ranks among the top five processors of beef, pork, turkey, and animal feed.

Agriculture and the Environment

Many of the forces that drove corporate farmers to maximize production have also induced them to adopt environmentally destructive practices, whereas practices that husband resources and promote sustainability have fallen away. The crop diversification so necessary to keeping soil arable came to be seen as prohibitively expensive; farmers turned more and more to chemical additives and other artificial aids to produce an unvarying harvest of staple crops. When environmentalism began to form as a coherent political and social movement during the 1960s, one of its first targets was industrial agriculture. Rachel Carson's exposé of the effects of DDT, a widely used pesticide, helped bring about a nationwide ban and called attention to the harmful effects of a chemically dependent industrial mode of production. Toxic streams of runoff into municipal water supplies spurred the passage of clean water legislation in the early 1970s; sweeping pesticide and herbicide controls soon followed. The appalling conditions under which migrant farm workers labored went largely unnoticed until Cesar Chavez began a unionization movement in the 1960s. One of its principal claims was that the state was failing to protect the health and safety of agricultural workers, who were exposed to particularly concentrated levels of chemicals.

Since then, state and federal enforcement of environmental protection laws has been spotty. Agribusiness has fought enforcement directly while seeking to lessen its reliance on chemicals by backing the breeding of disease- and pest-resistant plants and animals. Genetic manipulation, the use of growth hormones and antibiotics, and other scientific innovations are coming to present regulatory challenges every bit as complex as those generated by mass production. Public awareness of the health risks of chemical use and consumers' resistance to commodities produced with the aid of genetically modified organisms and growth hormones have increased friction between farmers and consumers since 1970. In response to an outbreak of mad cow disease in England and Canada in the late 1990s, the U.S. government ordered a ban on beef imports from those countries. After the disease was found in American herds, the domestic beef industry fought proposals calling for more vigorous testing and the exclusion of "downed" or sick cows from the food supply.

Deregulation

What farmers and the Department of Agriculture saw as the attainment of the "good farmer" ideal – the triumph of planning, efficiency, rationalization, and industrial methodologies in production and processing – has led to a kind of modern agriculture that cannot achieve long-term sustainability in its present form. The anti-regulatory impulse of the late twentieth century, which "free[d] airlines, cable television, telecommunications and other core industries from oversight of market structure, pricing, and anticompetitive tactics," reached the farm sector in 1996. The Federal Agricultural Improvement and Reform Act, also known as the Freedom to Farm Act, sought to roll back the massive subsidies permanently. It ended many marketing agreement programs by limiting the total number of marketing orders allowed in any given industry (ten to fifteen in milk, for example). The law also eliminated the mandatory set-aside program, established in 1963, which required farmers to idle a percentage of their total acreage in order to be eligible for price-support payments. At its peak in the mid-1980s, this policy had taken nearly 75 million acres out of production, but politicians and supply-side economists argued that prices did not improve significantly enough to warrant keeping the program. In fact, because other countries increased their production of staple crops to make up for the decline in world supplies, prices fell.

The drop in domestic farm prices that followed implementation of the Freedom to Farm Act drew a predictable response from Congress, which authorized emergency assistance payments to growers in 1998, 1999, and 2000. These payments exceeded the subsidies paid out in all previous years save one. In 1999, Congress repealed the restriction on milk marketing agreements. These actions showed the extent to which American agriculture had become dependent on the federal state. The farm sector's development since the 1930s has been shaped so completely by the federal government that it is unclear whether agriculture could survive in an unmediated relationship with the market. The Freedom to Farm Act's attempt to reinstitute a model of disaggregated market decisions – to let farmers decide what the market would bear – failed for reasons having to do as much with the new, integrated global marketplace as with faulty assumptions about agricultural stabilization embodied in the law.

Persistent rural poverty throughout the twentieth century attests to the difficulty of creating and preserving an economically stable rural sector. Episodic recessions only exacerbate the marginality of traditional rural life; what's worse, they make it clear that law and regulation have not altered the long-term instability of American agriculture. Despite the super-sizing of the national appetite, domestic markets cannot absorb the fruits of the production revolution. The capital-intensive nature of modern cultivation makes over-reliance on credit both essential and inherently risky. Farmers are beginning to recognize that science and technology are mixed blessings that can backfire as well as produce the next boom.

At the same time, evidence points to the emergence of countervailing trends. Alternative methods of cultivation, particularly organic farming, have begun to catch on. Consumer awareness that commercial agriculture relies heavily on chemicals and entails long-term depletion of non-renewable resources has given rise to an increasingly significant market for organic goods of all kinds. Seeking to obtain a share in this market, mainstream agriculture has tried to weaken strict designation requirements for organic food. Urban families making a new trek "back to the land" view organic and truck farming as economically viable and philosophically appealing. In particular, women have rediscovered farming; they own and operate many of the farms created since 2000. To capture more of the American food dollar, farmers are integrating vertically, organizing cooperatives and corporations that manufacture and market cheese, pasta, and specialty foods from their own crops. Diversification is wending its way back on to farms of all sizes. Huge grain operations are turning to livestock as a buffer against instability. In Detroit, a city plagued by urban and industrial blight, sizeable plots of land have been abandoned. In what may be an unintentional nod to the Jeffersonian agrarian ideal, some officials have suggested giving those plots to people who agree to farm them. Forced to buy Monsanto's genetically modified seed, Nebraska wheat farmers organized, networked globally with farmers, and ousted state legislators who voted for a Monsanto-backed ban on the use of saved wheat seed. Although it may be premature to conclude that a systemic restructuring of agriculture is underway, recent developments indicate that agriculture is experiencing important shifts and reorganizations, with consequences for future policy decisions.

CONCLUSION

For decades, historians have viewed agriculture as a prime example of the federal government's limited involvement in the economy prior to the Civil War. As the federal agricultural commissioner Henry Ellsworth proudly noted in 1838, "Husbandry seemed to be viewed as a natural blessing that needs no aid from legislation."[34] Yet, a legal history of agriculture that combines the private law focus of traditional legal history with an appreciation of the structural contributions that public law made to economic development points to a different interpretation. From the Founding, public authority and private initiative functioned interdependently to frame the physical and legal conditions in which American farmers were free to flourish and fail. The twentieth-century record of increasing centralization of private agricultural wealth and public authority over markets represents more a continuation of developments that first manifested themselves in the nineteenth century than a radical break from them.

Agriculture played a fundamental role in shaping American society and economy. In the early national period, farming was thought to be closely connected with political virtue and economic self-sufficiency. It conferred a connection to land that held out the promise of wealth, and in a society that equated property ownership with legal personhood for white men, few could afford consciously to gamble on something else. Agricultural prosperity was not possible without the creation of markets, and this process of creation was both physical and legal. Markets developed as a consequence of the spatial expansion of the nation, which brought with it a physical transformation of the landscape through new transportation systems. As the result of public land and transportation policy decisions, conflicts arose over access to markets, and these conflicts mirrored the regional divide over slavery in the pre-Civil War period.

Regional differences defined the American agricultural experience in other ways. The kinds of crops farmers produced, the levels of productivity and mechanization, and the demand for labor all varied across region and over time. The monoculture of cotton in the nineteenth-century South contrasted sharply with the more diversified agricultural economy in the North and, later, the Plains states. During the decades before the Civil War, the railroads opened the lands of the old Northwest Territories to settlers and farmers, again reinforcing the relationship between spatial expansion and agricultural commerce. Connecting new states to Eastern markets was

---

[34] Commissioner of Patents, *Report*, Senate Doc., 25th Congress, 2d session, vol. II, no. 105 (Washington, DC, 1838), 4.

the primary effect of transportation policy before the Civil War, and it also set an important precedent for postwar priorities.

The Civil War brought a sea change in federal administration and policy regarding agriculture. In adopting a policy of free homesteading, the federal government abandoned the notion that the public lands of the nation should be used to raise revenue. Instead, land was distributed to individuals, whether farmers or speculators, for the purpose of populating new territories and building viable local economies. The creation of the U.S. Department of Agriculture and the land grant university system in the early 1860s tied the public lands distribution system to new administrative structures that were designed to promote agricultural research and funnel the fruits of that scientific inquiry directly to farmers.

The growth of national markets was the single most important structural development of the period from 1865 to 1920. National markets opened up lucrative, if risky, systems of exchange that encouraged farmers to maximize the production of cash crops. The increasingly national scale and scope of agricultural production and exchange discouraged crop diversity on farms and made self-sufficient farming difficult to sustain over time. The advent of commodities trading added new layers of speculation and risk to those occurring in nature. By the 1870s, the rise of monopolistic control in railroads, grain elevators, meatpacking, and other important points of exchange created a surge of discontent that translated into a sustained movement of political protest. The Grangers and then the Populists expressed farmers' economic grievances in attacks on what they saw as government's connivance with monopolies. In failing to check the growth of large corporations, the Populists claimed, government was acquiescing in the maldistribution of economic power to the detriment of the individual producer. The Populists' critique of market capitalism contributed an important and lasting ideological strain to American politics, but it produced only middling reforms. The interpenetration of public governance into agriculture, which had become an industry in its own right, had progressed to the point where even the Populists' stinging critique could make little political headway.

The Progressive era saw the expansion of the administrative state, which had as its purpose to bring rationality and predictability to agricultural markets. A renewed focus on antitrust enforcement – and the granting of a limited exemption for farmers in federal antitrust law – scored some victories for Populist interests over corporate power, but nothing of much permanence resulted from the reforms adopted between 1900 and 1920. More than any particular policy, war served to spur the process of administrative centralization and coordination; the adoption of emergency measures to control prices and maintain the food supply led, at least for a while, to the elimination of wide swings in the business cycle. But with the end of war came the end to such extraordinary intrusions into the market proper, and the repeal of World War I era emergency price and supply controls led to a stark and sudden collapse for agriculture in 1919. Agricultural interests and lobbying groups used that turn of misfortune to extract a series of important concessions for farmers during the 1920s, including tax and antitrust exemptions, but they were unable to procure what they wanted most: a publicly subsidized scheme to "dump" surpluses abroad and shore up domestic prices.

The Depression essentially mooted this dispute. Global markets were just as affected as U.S. exchanges by the economic crash in 1929. American governments at all levels struggled to implement reforms that would cure the Depression without making too steep an incursion into private economic rights. The election of Franklin D. Roosevelt as president and the New Deal he instituted essentially adopted many of the tools of wartime emergency legislation to get the country through the worst of the economic disaster. Although Roosevelt's solutions were never as socialist-leaning as his critics argued, the New Deal did lead to the most lasting realignment of public and private economic power in the nation's history. In agriculture, the New Deal created a state-centered program of administered markets, the economic incentives of which led to an unprecedented concentration of ownership in farmland, agricultural production, processing, and marketing in the ensuing half-century.

The nineteenth-century agriculturalist Henry Ellsworth was wrong. Agriculture has always accepted "aid from legislation." The question facing future generations is not whether the state shall continue to regulate and stabilize agriculture, but what form that legal intervention will take. How that intervention will be understood depends on whether future scholars take the step of mapping an appreciation of public sector economic ordering onto the more familiar geography of private law doctrinal change. This move requires a merger of two perspectives: Richard Bushman's insight that public law constructs the economic identity of farmers, on the one hand, and J. Willard Hurst's enduring contribution that private doctrinal innovation fostered economic change, on the other. When seen in this light, the twentieth-century record of increasing centralization of private agricultural wealth and public authority over markets represents more a continuation of nineteenth-century innovation and unfettered development than a radical break from it.

To be sure, the constitutive function of the federal government in agriculture remains contested. The economist Bruce Gardner has observed, "The main job of government in agriculture is not to be its CEO but to reconcile conflicting views and interests."[35] The legal history of American agriculture reveals that the federal government may not be a good CEO, but it is even worse at arbitrating among conflicting interests. Localism and federalism, agricultural mechanization and innovation, and democratic politics and interest group pressures will all factor in the processes of reconciliation and mediation that state governance of agriculture entails.

[35] Bruce L. Gardner, *American Agriculture in the Twentieth Century: How It Flourished and What It Cost* (Cambridge, MA, 2002), 353.

16

LAW AND ECONOMIC CHANGE DURING THE SHORT TWENTIETH CENTURY

JOHN HENRY SCHLEGEL

At the beginning of the short twentieth century heavy, blue-collar industry dominated the physical economy. Railroads were the dominant form of continental transportation; the ocean liner (for passengers) and the freighter (for cargo) the only available form of intercontinental transportation. Radio was the new, wonderful, transformative industry, and national consumer brands were beginning their domination of the grocery store's growing cornucopia.

At the end of the century, service industries dominate the economy. Were there any notion of the physical economy, it would probably focus on multiple kinds of imported consumer goods. Continental transportation of goods is dominated by interstate trucking; that of passengers, by airplanes. The ocean liner has changed into a floating hotel called the cruise ship; intercontinental passengers travel by air and goods in large steel boxes on truly ungainly looking, specially designed container ships. The Internet qualifies as the new, wonderful, transformative industry, and produce from Latin America has begun to dominate the grocery store's still expanding bounty.

Looked at in a more schematic way, the story is the same. During years that witnessed an amazing growth in the administrative apparatus of all levels of government, there simultaneously occurred three large-scale changes, three of those developments that somehow define eras. First, the middle class expanded to include a portion of the working class as part of a dominating consumer culture. Second, the imperial Northeastern manufacturing economy, the colonial Southern agricultural economy, and the colonial Western agricultural and natural resources economy all declined while simultaneously a lighter manufacturing economy in the South and West grew, as did a service economy throughout the country. And third, the American island economy that followed World War II declined as a significantly more international economy of manufacturing, finance, and, to a lesser extent, agriculture and natural resources took shape.

Surely then, these years have seen profound economic change. Yet in some ways, a concomitant change in the way that the economy is experienced, structured, thought of is equally important. At the beginning of the short twentieth century the model of a good economy was one in which groups of manufacturers or retailers believed that, by associating together with the objective of treating each other fairly, a high-price, high- wage economy could deliver prosperity for all. And during the Depression the federal government put into place a legal framework that could support such an associationalist economy. But by the end of that century, such a model was of interest only to historians. Its obliteration was so complete that many advocates of unionized labor had little understanding of how their language of fairness tied into a lost economic model dependent on local and regional oligopolistic conduct. In place of that model we now have a new one, based on atomized and decentralized production tied together with round-the-clock instantaneous communication and with financial structures favoring very short time horizons, that has for its hallmark a collective obsession with speedy flexibility.

What significance can we ascribe to law – by which I mean *the many and variable actions undertaken by lawyers and other governmental officials, the formal and effective norms originating from the practices of these individuals, and the systematic presuppositions shared among them* – in the extraordinary story of economic change that is the short twentieth century? I wish to argue that, properly understood, the answer to this question is "very little," though a not unimportant "very little." In so arguing, I am not to be understood as embracing either of the following perspectives on the general relationship of law and economy. First, law is not simply a prisoner of the market forces of a time and place. Nor, second, is it irrelevant except to the extent that it unwisely attempts to constrain market actors from pursuing their self-interest. Rather, the pervasiveness of law in structuring the economy of this and any other set of years is or ought to be obvious to all but the most unreflective Marxist or vulgar free marketeer. Indeed, I would go so far as to assert that, at any given time and place, price – the efficient market solution to a question of demand and supply – is fully determined by law, seen as a set of legal entitlements, together with the set of resource endowments distributed among economic actors at that time and place. Moreover, any significant alteration in those legal entitlements will cause an alteration in that efficient market solution. However, questions about such, almost static equilibriums are not my concern here. Instead, I wish to talk about change, about movement from one economy to another.

Then what do I mean by "an economy?" *An economy, a persistent market structure, is the fusion of an understanding of economic life with the patterns of behavior within the economic, political, and social institutions that enact that understanding*. Law contributes pervasively to any such understanding; it affirms, structures or restructures, and so, in an obviously separable sense, enacts, the relevant institutions that economic actors use when buying and selling, working and investing, as part of their daily life. But questions of economic change are not answered by summing all of the activities, including legal change, that make up daily economic life. Economic change is the shift from one enacted (in both senses) understanding of economic life to another – in the case of the short twentieth century, from an associationalist economy to what I call an impatient economy. In this chapter I hope first to explicate this economic change, and then to interrogate it in order to understand the role of law in its occurrence.[1]

I. THE TWENTIES AND THIRTIES: AN ASSOCIATIONALIST IDEAL

At the end of World War I, the United States, which had just completed an extraordinary period of industrial expansion followed by one of industrial concentration, was the largest national economy in the world. Its greatest strength, aside from a substantial natural resource base, was its enormous domestic market tied together by a strong railroad network that allowed the country to be a relatively insolated, self-sufficient economic entity. This is not to say that the United States did not participate in international trade and finance. It was a key player in both areas. Rather, the size of the domestic market and its relative affluence meant that most manufacturers and many retailers had a market so large that they could grow to an enormous size based on transactions within the domestic economy alone, protected, of course, from foreign competition by relatively high trade barriers.

Given these obvious advantages, the economy's overall performance in the following two decades was surprisingly erratic, but overall disastrously weak. A sharp postwar inflationary spurt was followed first by an equally

---

[1] A word about periodization is in order. I take the twenties to extend from the end of the postwar demobilization – about 1919 – until the stock market crash in 1929. The thirties is a long period continuing until 1941 when, with the adoption of Lend-Lease, the U.S. economy was placed on a wartime footing. The forties extend only to 1947, the end of the post-war inflation. Then came the fifties. The sixties begin late – in 1962 – and end with the rise in oil prices that accompanied the Yom Kippur War in 1973. The seventies continue until the onset of the Reagan administration in 1981 or maybe until inflation finally turns down in the wake of the terrible recession of 1982. The eighties begin thereafter or possibly in 1979 when the Federal Reserve Board moved to contract the money supply sharply, and last until the end of the recession just before the start of the Clinton administration, that is the nineties. These are, I must emphasize, economic periods; I would identify social periods quite differently.

sharp recession and then by a somewhat frenetic period of genuine growth. Thereafter, a general recession that began just slightly before the famous stock market crash of October 1929 terminated a classic market bubble turned serious – turned into the Depression. Four years later, when the economy bottomed out, the unemployment rate was about 25 percent; prices, particularly of farm products, had declined significantly; mortgage foreclosures had hit record levels, as had bank failures; and not surprisingly, industrial production had plummeted as well. For the balance of the decade the economy grew slowly, interrupted only by a decline in 1937, though not to the level of its pre-Depression high.

If one factors out the substantial amount of noise in the economic record of these years, several significant changes stand out. The most obvious is the growth of an extensive consumer electric (though surely not electronic) appliance industry led by radios, irons, vacuum cleaners, and to a much lesser extent refrigerators, as electrical service was extended to most urban and increasing numbers of rural households. Equally noticeable was the great expansion in automobile ownership, though here the impact of this growth was more significant in rural areas, where auto ownership provided a significant opportunity to reduce isolation, than in urban ones, where existing transit networks and shops within walking distance made the cost of ownership seem more of a barrier to purchase.

More invisible, but in the long run equally significant, were two changes. The first was the slow development of the commercial aircraft industry whose major success with the DC-3 began the increase in air travel in the late thirties. The second was the expansion of consumer services, especially in the twenties, both in the financial area, with the growth of installment purchase of autos and appliances, and in retail trades of all kinds. Nevertheless, the economy of the Northeast still was dominated by heavy industrial production, such as steel, autos, and electrical machinery, and by rail transport, all of which employed enormous numbers of blue-collar, variously skilled workers, pretty much in accordance with late-nineteenth-century industrial norms. The South was still largely an agricultural economy and the West an agricultural and mining economy. Both thus provided low-value goods to feed Northeastern factories and mouths. The whole was stitched together with a railroad system that had reached its peak size just before the Great War and had begun to shrink in size thereafter.

With immigration cut off, the ethnic makeup of the population was largely settled; immigrants and their families from Eastern and Southern Europe provided much of the workforce in the large industrial plants. This was the backbone of the working class. Northern Europeans provided much of the white-collar workforce, staff and line, that ran the predominantly dispersed, divisional structure of large industrial corporations. These individuals were the dominant element in the middle and lower middle class that had come numerically to overwhelm the upper middle class of professionals and local owners of shops and small factories. At the same time, the growth of line functions in large industrial corporations and of service industries brought an increase in female, particularly unmarried female, waged labor, beyond the traditional work in textiles and apparel.

Such a structure to the economy was not wholly surprising, given the persistence of the remains of the large turn-of-the-century industry-specific mergers designed to create effective product monopolies. The surviving firms had, as a result of effective antitrust intervention during the Taft and Wilson administrations, devolved into relatively stable oligopolies that tended both to maintain their production processes and to grow vertically so as to control supplies and distribution. At the same time, "discounters" or "chain stores" – national retail organizations such as the Great Atlantic & Pacific Tea Company (the A & P), Sears, Roebuck & Co., or Montgomery, Ward & Company – began to establish branches in order to infiltrate local retailing markets that previously were effectively insulated from competition by the still significant difficulties of greater than local passenger transportation. The simultaneous growth of distribution through nationally controlled, locally franchised retailing organizations caused much consternation to local elites unused to more than incidental competition at the retail level. As a result, these local elites began to utter the same variety of complaints about ruinous or destructive competition and predatory pricing that had been voiced by those large manufacturers who sought refuge in the great merger movement twenty-five years earlier. These complaints, which continued to be heard from producers in such more competitive industrial segments such as lumber, coal, and cement, coalesced in a movement that is commonly called associationalism.

Many economic theorists who supported associationalism in the twenties and thirties believed that economic instability was the result of excess production of goods and services coupled with relentless downward pressure on producer prices caused by "chiselers" who reduced prices and otherwise "cut corners" for temporary personal advantage. These economists argued that downward pressure on prices could be resisted if producers banded together into groups that would work both to "coordinate" production (i.e., manage reduction and expansion) and to isolate and vilify chiselers, so as to enforce good – and thereby suppress "unfair" – trade practices. This theory also held that insufficient demand in poor times could be remedied by increasing employment and by providing Social Security and unemployment insurance so that the disposable income of wage earners, and thus demand, could be maintained: a Keynesian prescription before John Maynard Keynes produced his famous volume.

Associationalism was essentially a Main Street, though not therefore a small town, theory. It hoped to maintain high wages through the high prices that would support the small, local retail or wholesale businesses that were being undercut by the growth of large regional or national retailers, as well as the more competitive sectors of the producer economy. This design was for an economy of uniform, high prices, such as that found in more oligopolistic markets or as was enshrined in the steel industry's basing-point price system whereby all steel prices were quoted as if the product were being shipped from Pittsburgh. It denied distant local producers locational monopoly pricing ability, but at the same time allowed them to make up in freight charges collected, but not incurred, the costs associated with their smaller scale, and so higher cost, production processes.

Not laissez-faire in a different guise, associationalism assumed some level of governmental involvement in the economy, as befits a theory whose public champion was Herbert Hoover, first as Secretary of Commerce under both Harding and Coolidge and then as president. Supported by the Federal Trade Commission, the theory received and required a crabbed construction of the antitrust laws so as to permit associations to perform their regulatory and disciplinary functions, as well as some legal support for suppressing unfair trade practices. It also seemed to require high trade protection for American industries, and indeed, these ideas are popularly associated with the Smoot-Hawley Tariff of 1930. When reduced to legislation, associationalism regularly echoed Progressive concerns about the protection of small producers and ordinary workers, as can be seen in the "first" New Deal of the Roosevelt administration, in which associationalism spawned the National Recovery Act and the Agricultural Adjustment Act, as well as such seemingly unrelated legislation as the Social Security Act, the Wagner Act, the Fair Labor Standards Act, the Federal Housing Act, and the Robinson-Patman Act. The prevalence of agricultural marketing cooperatives and state retail price maintenance statutes are of a piece. Surviving bits of the self-regulatory norm inherent in the theory still can be found in the New York Stock Exchange, the National Association of Securities Dealers, and the numerous bodies setting industry standards that exist in fields such as plumbing and electrical equipment. The theory can even be seen in Karl Llewellyn's early plans for the sales article of the Uniform Commercial Code.

The accuracy of the associationalist diagnosis of the problems of business in the twenties and thirties is, for present purposes, unimportant. Accurate or not, the managed, associationalist market was a prominent economic ideal in the years between the wars. However, that ideal had another side to it. Stabilization of prices at high levels and control over the introduction of innovation protected the market position of large producers as well as small retailers. For such producers, the theory could be seen as justifying classic cartel behavior, behavior that in Europe led to collusion with large trades' unions and to industry-wide bargaining, still epitomized by the metalworkers union in Germany. In the United States this variation on the cartel model supported the relatively static competitive position of participants in the more oligopolistic markets. Under oligopolistic competition, leading firms in effect negotiated price publicly and then strove to avoid undercutting that price. Simultaneously, they used their research staffs and advertising to generate product differentiation that might alter market share in their favor, always dreading the possibility that a competitor would develop a "breakthrough" product that could remake current, reasonably stable relationships in unforeseen ways.

Although associationalism as a theory clearly preferred the private organization of markets implicit in the ideal of an association, it just as clearly recognized that stable economic relationships that yielded high prices, high wages, and continuous profits could be established by governmental regulation. Thus, it could support a regulatory response to the widely felt sense that a weak and speculative financial system was a contributor to the Depression. The extension of speculative credit, especially in the real property and securities markets, was viewed as "unfair," as were widespread self-dealing, manipulation, and even fraud in bank lending practices and in the underwriting of securities issues and their trading in the stock market. The response at the federal level was the creation of significant federal legislation directed at boosting confidence in the financial system. The Glass-Steagall Act (Banking Act of 1933), requiring a separation of commercial from investment banking, and the legislation establishing the Federal Deposit Insurance Corporation, Federal Savings and Loan Insurance Corporation, Federal Home Loan Bank Board, and the Federal Farm Credit Administration were each designed to increase the soundness of the banking system by creating the stable, profitable relationships among the providers of a major source of credit for the economy that were favored by associationalism's theorists. The legislation establishing the Securities Exchange Commission and securing for it the means for regulating the securities markets based on a principle of disclosure and of penalties for non-disclosure, including the Securities Act of 1933, the Securities Exchange Act of 1934, the Investment Company Act, and the Trust Indenture Act, was structured similarly. Together such legislation was designed to strengthen those institutions essential for the credit and investment expansion that would undergird recovery, and, not incidentally, honestly finance both oligopolistic producers and Main Street merchants.

Law and Economic Change: An Initial Interrogation

This brief recounting of the American economy in the twenties and thirties raises obvious questions about law and economic change. As one lists even a small part of the New Deal's legislation, one can quickly identify the response of law to economic dislocation. Local relief efforts were supplemented with funds supplied by federal programs mounted by the Works Progress Administration and the Civilian Conservation Corps, programs that are largely lost in any brief telling of the story of the economy in these years, but crucial for those whose hunger they reduced and shelter they supported. The great structural statutes in agriculture, banking, communications, labor, securities, and transportation that survived Supreme Court challenge, as well as those that did not – the National Recovery Act (NRA) and Agricultural Adjustment Act (AAA) – also exemplify the way that law is regularly mobilized in times of trouble. All were significant changes in the doctrinal matrix that is the law at a time and place. They can even be seen to have significantly aided the creation of the administrative state. But that said, the role that these statutes played in economic change remains unclear.

Each changed the efficient market solution to a problem of supply and demand; that much is clear. Consider only two modest changes – the Fair Labor Standards Act and the Trust Indenture Act. Both were classic associationalist pieces of legislation based on its diagnosis of under-consumption as the root of economic weakness and its penchant for picking up on unfinished Progressive causes. The first created the rule requiring time-and-a-half for overtime for certain groups of workers. After adoption it could be expected that such a rule would, at the margin, make employers respond to the opportunity to increase production by relying less on extending the hours of existing workers and more on increasing total employment. At the same time, the Fair Labor Standards Act's adoption of a firm rule worked toward minimizing the old problem of whether employers unfairly coerced employees to work long hours. The Trust Indenture Act yoked old problems even more directly to new objectives by establishing rules dictating "fairer" terms in the indentures that governed bond issues with respect to trustee selection, notice to bondholders, and their consent to the restructuring of bond obligations. Such statutory provisions were expected, again at the margin, to increase the willingness of investors to purchase bonds because they knew that their interests were better protected. However, the change in the efficient market solution to a problem of supply and demand at a hypothetical margin is like a tree falling in the forest unheard. Unless that margin is reached, legal change changes nothing in the economy. What passage of the law means is that a set of structures have been put into place that may or may not become relevant under future economic conditions, dependent as they are on future political, technological, even demographic occurrences.

But to notice the structural element in such legislation is to bring to the forefront the matter of the degree to which the New Deal statutory reforms enacted the associationalist economy. Here the answer is a resolute negative. The creation of potentially efficacious institutional structures is not enough to "enact" an economy. Consider the possibility that, contrary to fact, World War II had ended with a long-term truce among four or five countries whose manufacturing capacity remained in good shape and so whose economies competed vigorously. There is little reason to believe that in such circumstances, circumstances in which relative insulation from the world economy would decrease as air and ocean transportation improved, the margin where any of these statutes would bite would ever be reached. These laws might well have been of antiquarian interest, but little else. Indeed, their notoriety today is a function of the fact that at some point action within the institutions that they created actually took place, that the economic relations that they made possible came to pass.

Note, however, that even though a change of behavior at the margin may never take place, a change in legal entitlements may easily work a change in the distribution of economic resources. The Fair Labor Standards Act immediately made some employees wealthier, those whose wage gains were less than the cost of hiring additional employees, especially where slack demand or capacity constraints effectively turned the choice to hire additional employees into the choice to begin a second shift. And this increase in disposable income of individual workers may well have been enough to alter, as always at the margin, the efficient market solution to other questions of supply and demand, most obviously those of clothing, food, and housing. But such an alteration is no more a change in an economy than would be the modest change in the market for legal services brought on by adoption of the Trust Indenture Act. Law changes lots of things in the details of economic life for the participants without bringing about a transformation of the economy from one enacted understanding of economic life to another.

II. THE FORTIES AND FIFTIES: ASSOCIATIONALISM AT WORK

Wartime mobilization and then production pulled the economy out of the Depression in ways that all the thinking and writing of economists and all the action of politicians could not manage. By taxing some, borrowing much, and spending it all to win the war, the United States adopted a Keynesian solution to its economic problems, but out of necessity, not out of theoretical understanding, for such a theoretical solution was still rejected by most economists, as it had been during the Depression.

Total war meant that there were jobs for virtually everyone not actively engaged in the armed forces. However, the rationing and price controlling of most consumer products, combined with the termination of production of other products, meant that wartime wages were, by default, largely saved. The technological innovations that the war spawned were notable – synthetic rubber, radar, sonar, separation of uranium isotopes using the hexafluoride compound, and the vacuum-tube-dependent ENIAC computer – but changed the lives of Americans very little during those years. Much more significant was the wartime spread of military installations and, to a lesser extent, war production plants, in the South and West that over time began to break the agriculturally based colonial economy of the former and the natural resources and agriculture based colonial economy of the latter.

Wartime economic practice continued to support the associationalist bent of the economic/legal understanding of the period that preceded it. Given the inflationary pressures that came with a sharp growth in total wages and the wartime price control mechanism that was designed to deal with those pressures, the existing structure of commercial relations was, if anything, reinforced. Not only did the large, established firms that secured the greatest portion of war-related contracts prosper, but also firm prices on rationed goods meant that small units of production and distribution prospered as well. The war may not have been won on Main Street, but Main Street prospered as much or more that it had in the very brief euphoria that was the economy of the twenties.

Labor also prospered. Though wage increases were drastically limited under the War Labor Board's fabled "Little Steel formula," at least union recognition and bargaining over working conditions were ensured. Strikes, like wages, were limited, at least in theory. In practice the incidence of strikes increased over the course of the war. However, out of the wartime experience both labor and management started down the road toward understanding that the country preferred industrial peace at a modest price. Acceptable were increased costs from modest wage increases, from the introduction of non-wage benefits, from the recognition of work rules that kept production expensive but labor less onerous (a covert form of a wage increase), and from the proliferation of by law guaranteed time-and-a-half overtime, the major source of increased prosperity for workers.

Overseas, American aircraft were attempting to destroy both European and Japanese industrial might while allied diplomats planned for a postwar international order, efforts that at Dumbarton Oaks led to the creation of the United Nations and at Bretton Woods to the outline of a new economic order. The Bretton Woods agreements reestablished the fixed rate regime for foreign exchange that Roosevelt had interred when he took the United States off the gold standard in 1933. Under the Bretton Woods gold exchange standard, the United States agreed to exchange dollars for gold, but only in transactions with foreign central banks, at a rate of $35 per ounce. The currencies of the other states that participated in the system were then tied to the dollar or gold at fixed rates, and states agreed to maintain their currency within a band (generally, 1 percent) of the fixed rate. The International Monetary Fund, also established at Bretton Woods, was designed to lend money to states that had insufficient gold or foreign currency reserves to keep the actual value of their currency at the agreed-on rate, usually because of an inability to cover their trade deficits.

At the end of the war, Europe, even victorious Great Britain, was prostrate with a combination of significant population loss, destruction or exhaustion of industrial plant and equipment, destruction of infrastructure, and removal of captive sources of raw materials. Indeed, the destruction had been so severe that economic conditions throughout the continent were worse in 1947 than they had been in 1945. Only with the Communist takeovers of countries in Eastern Europe did economic conditions begin to pick up when, in response, the United States began to pour into Western Europe economic aid under the Marshall Plan and military aid, always a prop to an economy, under NATO. Still, even with all this aid, Europe and comparatively less aided Japan were restarting their economies from a very low level.

In contrast, the United States had won all the marbles. As the only truly functioning major economy north of the equator, it held virtually all economic power in its hands and thought that it held all political power as well. Like Julius Caesar, it bestrode "the narrow world like a Colossus." The returning GIs cared little about such things, however; they needed jobs. Their needs brought about the replacement of women workers with men in many of the best paying jobs, though only a temporary decline in female participation in the waged workforce. The development of an ideology in support of this maneuver exalted the notion of the one-wage-earner family supported by a "family wage." Although the decline of overtime in the immediate post-war years initially made the notion of the family wage quite difficult to achieve, the GI Bill, for a time at least, served to sop up much potential unemployment, with its extension of benefits for servicemen who sought further education, particularly higher education, which the colleges were quick to supply.

Immediately after the war, the rise in consumer demand – fueled first by the simple absence of goods and services during the war, second by the disproportionately large savings that were accumulated in those years when high wages could find few goods to purchase, and finally by the developing baby boom – brought significant inflation. But by 1947 inflation subsided, with only a modest spurt in 1950 associated with the onset of the Korean War. Housing and autos then led the postwar economic expansion. In addition, the United States was exporting goods, including farm products, at a very high level. These exports earned large, if not wholly meaningful, trade surpluses; they were financed with aid or credit from the federal government, for there was little that European countries and Japan had to export.

America's military and economic spending in Europe, the same kind that drove the American economy during the war, was modestly helpful in supporting domestic postwar expansion. The reintroduction of wartime production that accompanied the Korean War meant that large-scale government stimulation of the economy returned for the better part of four years; it was accompanied by another dose of somewhat less generous GI Bill benefits. But Korea was not fought under conditions of "total war." This time consumption was not particularly squeezed as a result of war mobilization.

The economy grew strongly during these war years and continued its growth into its next decade. Purchasing power was reasonably stable after 1950; capital, reasonably plentiful; consumer goods, everywhere to be found; foreign sales, large. Only agriculture seemed to lag. Farm employment continued its wartime decline; farm size, its wartime increase; farm income, its relative stagnation. This is not to say that in urban areas the great postwar expansion was inexorably upward. Indeed, there were three modest recessions during the chronological fifties, the last coming at the end of the decade and contributing to the election of a Democratic administration in 1960. But these were rightly seen as good years by consumers, wage earners, and businessmen, fueled, as they were, by the insulation of the domestic economy from international competition originating in the still recovering European and Japanese economies and by the interaction of this insulation with the practices of the associationalist legal/economic model of a good economy.

The lack of international competition meant that American industry could raise wages and easily pay for such wage increases by raising prices modestly, relying on increases in demand to lower unit costs, and by deferring improvements in production processes, plant, and equipment. Nor was there any internal need to do otherwise. Industry-wide bargaining meant that competitors were seldom differentially disadvantaged by increases in wages, increases that to some extent may have reflected productivity gains. The prices of non-labor product inputs were reasonably steady, and domestic companies controlled access to most raw materials, particularly petroleum, at low world prices. And stockholders were a quiescent, dispersed lot, as

Adolph Berle and Gardiner Means had observed a generation earlier, who looked primarily for predictable dividends and less for capital appreciation. Disgruntled investors sold; they did not fight management.

The continued authority of the associationalist ideal of managed, rather than ruinous, competition seemingly protected retail business owners, though here the development of new national chains, such as McDonald's and Holiday Inn, and the expansion of discounting beyond groceries into hard goods ought to have given careful observers pause. And that ideal similarly protected members of the numerous oligopolistic industries by limiting them to "gloves on" competitive fights for market share. American industry had become big, cumbrous, comfortable, and more dependent for its prosperity on the gross level of demand derived from increases in total employment than on product improvement derived from capital investment.

In some ways the quiescent state of American industry in these years is somewhat counterintuitive. At the same time that producers were insulated from international competition to their products, capital costs were unusually low because the United States maintained a sheltered market in credit growing out of the structure that New Deal legislation left behind. Checking account demand deposits were largely limited to corporations and upper- or upper-middle-class families, and there were few equally liquid investments offered elsewhere. Securities were effectively purchased by a similarly limited group, due in part to high and fixed minimum brokerage commissions and in part to a lingering fear of the stock market that many middle-class people had learned from the Great Crash. Savings for most people were channeled into time deposit savings accounts, often at savings and loan associations that were statutorily limited to paying low rates of interest – 2 or 3 percent for most of these years – and similarly limited in their investment of these funds to home mortgages, often insured under the FHA or the GI bill. This segmentation of the national pool of savings provided support for the housing markets, as well as a pile of corporate bank balances available for lending to corporate borrowers at rates that were secure from serious competition from the long-term, debt-oriented securities markets.

One might have expected that the relatively low cost of credit would have brought forth a torrent of investment in new product development, old product innovation, and improvement of production processes to make up for the lack of such investment since 1929. But this did not happen on a grand scale. Innovation was obvious in the mass production of the primarily suburban, new housing modeled on Levittown and in air conditioning, television, and stereo. But the results of a lack of innovation were also already evident. In iron and steel, little significant investment in new processes was made after the Korean War. In rails, new investment was limited to replacing steam with diesel power. This obvious improvement in technology drew attention away from the continuing decline in demand, both in terms of passengers and freight, that the boom in heavy transport during World War II had obscured. Passenger rail travel declined with the proliferation of private autos and later with the growth of business air travel; freight declined with the increasing availability of truck transport, a circumstance obvious even before the war. Indeed, the plans for what became the Eisenhower Interstate Highway System in 1957 were first drafted in 1941. At that time the proposal was advanced on precisely the twin grounds successfully offered sixteen years later – national defense and highway congestion from increasing truck traffic.

The social consequence of what in retrospect was a hot-house economy, insulated from competition abroad and limited in competitive pressures at home, was a dramatic increase in the middle class, both white collar and blue. This larger middle class was built on three things: reasonably high wages; low housing costs, aided by the nationwide adoption of the fully amortizable, thirty-year mortgage (introduced on a mass scale by federal agencies during the Depression) available at interest rates intentionally kept low by the structure of banking regulation and effectively lowered even further by the tax deductibility of mortgage interest in a time of high marginal tax rates; and the extension of college education – more a matter of increasing status than improving skills – to groups that previously would never have been able to afford it. This was the "Quiet Generation," quiet because times were good and families needed building.

These new, middle-class Americans, still segregated by income, sought to leave their familiar urban neighborhoods for the suburbs. Their reasons for doing so were many and conflicting. They sought to escape the rising tide of black migration to Northern cities that had picked up during the war and further increased with changes in Southern agricultural practices, such as the introduction of the mechanical cotton picker, that made the sharecropper's or tenant farmer's already precarious livelihood even more fragile. They also sought to escape the family pressure that was omnipresent in old ethnic neighborhoods of multiple family dwellings wedged closely together. Especially, they hoped to fulfill that quintessential American dream, sold endlessly in the popular press as well as by producer advertising, of owning one's own home. In their separate suburban enclaves, often still as separated by ethnicity, as well as race, as were their old neighborhoods, these individuals created a middle class that was both different from that of the classic *bourgeois* shopkeeper or professional of nineteenth-century Europe and America or from that of the salaried middle management ubiquitous in corporate life since the latter part of that century, and far larger in scope than had ever been seen before. They were the first wage-earner middle class.

Meanwhile, the combination of Marshall Plan aid and NATO-related expenditures in Europe and similar economic aid and Korean-War-related expenditures in Japan, plus low domestic defense expenditures in both areas and incredibly high savings rates in Japan meant first slow, then explosive growth in the mid-fifties. As a result of this growth, the American balance of trade, the measure of current exports as against imports, which had regularly shown a surplus, began to decline. Consequently, given the continuation of governmental expenditures abroad, largely military after economic aid was ended in the early fifties, the declining positive balance of trade allowed the development of a negative balance of payments, the measure of total currency and gold outflows as against inflows.

Initially, that negative balance of payments was good for a world economy that was short of payment reserves. It allowed foreign countries to build up reserves, particularly of dollars, the reserve currency of choice. However, by the late fifties, what was once a good thing and remained so because an increase in reserves was essential for financing the continuing growth in international trade, given that a sufficient increase in the gold supply was not forthcoming, also came to be seen as troublesome. The first call on the American gold reserve was as fractional backing for the dollar as a domestic currency. The balance of the reserve was, under the gold exchange standard, held to guarantee the American pledge to redeem in gold the dollar holdings of foreign governments at the $35 per ounce ratio set by the Bretton Woods agreements. This guarantee of redemption was fine, so long as no foreign government sought to exercise the right to redeem its dollar holdings. Unfortunately, foreign governments did just that, and the gold reserve slowly was being depleted.

With outstanding dollar reserves exceeding the gold available to back them, the possibility that someone would be left without a chair when the music stopped began to worry foreign governments. These governments feared that the United States would devalue its currency, unilaterally increasing the price of gold and hence the amount of foreign dollar holdings required to be exchanged for a given amount of gold. At the same time, the U.S. government feared that devaluing the dollar would both spark domestic inflation and bring about an international economic crisis that could undermine the strength of the anti-Communist coalition that seemed essential for Western security. Thus began a period of intense official concern about the balance of trade, balance of payments, dollar outflow, current account, and other measures of a "problem" that most Americans couldn't understand, in part because the language used to describe the problem was so multifarious.

The first concrete and separable manifestation of that problem came in the early sixties. With the gradual opening of capital markets worldwide, European companies discovered that they could take advantage of a regulated American banking market that, because of the New Deal reforms, kept capital costs low in the United States, significantly lower than they were in Europe. These companies would borrow dollars in New York and use them to pay for capital investments abroad. Such a sensible business strategy had the obvious effect of increasing the supply of dollars abroad, a private outflow of capital on top of the governmental outflow for military and aid purposes, and so of increasing the balance of payments deficit and concomitant worries about the American gold reserve. In 1962, in an effort to reduce that outflow and the accompanying worries, the Kennedy administration introduced the interest equalization tax. This tax was designed to increase the effective interest rate on bonds denominated in dollars and sold in the United States by foreign borrowers to the interest rate that would have been paid on similar bonds had they been sold in foreign markets, and so to discourage the issuance of such bonds, by taxing American purchasers of the bonds.

The temporary success of this tax strategy is far less important to understanding the American economy in the immediate postwar period than two other things. First, the need to impose the tax serves to mark a significant change in that economy. For the first time in more than twenty years international economic activities were having a negative impact on management of the American economy. The interest equalization tax affirmed, though no one understood this at the time, that the United States was no longer an economic island. Domestic economic policies would thereafter have to be recognized as having international effects and foreign economic policies recognized as having domestic economic effects.

Second, although the imposition of the equalization tax largely ended the market for bonds denominated in dollars and sold in the United States by foreign borrowers, it did not dampen the demand of foreign corporations for dollar-denominated loans. Governments may have been worried about the American balance of payments, but borrowers were not. So, the market merely moved elsewhere – to the Eurodollar market, which is to say, really nowhere. That market, apparently born in the mid-fifties when the Russian government wanted a place to keep its dollar earnings where the American government could not confiscate them, lends dollars deposited in banks located in various countries in which the dollar is not the national currency. Somewhat unaccountably, such deposits are not subject to bank reserve requirements, which means that these lenders can offer lower interest rates than would be asked for loans in their various national currencies. Though such rates were not as low as American rates, the difference was still sufficient to be attractive to European borrowers, and so in time these deposits grew enormously. The growth of this market affirmed the dollar's central role in trade and investment worldwide, and, paradoxically, its role as an effective reserve currency, even as governments were worried about its "soundness." After all, the United States was still the largest economy in the world.

Law and Economic Change: A Second Interrogation

The most obvious indication that one is confronting an economy in full bloom, as it were, is that as one tries to tell its story there is almost nothing to talk about for there is almost nothing going on. The economic actors have settled into playing the economic roles that the economy seems to assume that they will play. Law is quite silent as well. Such is the case with the associationalist economy of the fifties.

After the adoption of the Taft-Hartley Act in 1947, there is but one significant piece of economic legislation in the succeeding fifteen years – the Interstate Highway Act of 1957. And that piece of legislation is more of a reflection of the impatience of the enlarged middle class with the limits on their ability to use their big cars and leisure time, their two weeks of paid vacation, than a reflection of any troubles that would cause those harmed to run to law for its uncertain succor. All of this is not to say that the organs of law shut down during these years. Rather, the legislative product – the expansion of the rice support program to two more counties in Arkansas where the existence of such support made it newly plausible to grow rice or the creation of a public authority to extend an airport or maintain a port – was so trivial as to beggar the mind.

The relative silence of law is, of course, misleading. Narrowly conceived as just the formal and effective norms originating from governmental entities, especially the law of property, contract and theft, of mine and thine, law is always there, the modest hum of a faithful dynamo. Looking at law more broadly conceived, as the many and variable actions undertaken by governmental actors, of discretionary action, as the traditional language of the law would have it, the matter is pretty much the same. Because in an enacted economy the formal and effective structures are pretty much in place, the work of the bureaucracy goes about its modest regulatory business constantly, but quietly. Yes, noise is always heard from narrowly interested parties and that noise bulks large in the business press, but when looked back on, tempests and teapots come readily to mind. This is the real significance of the interest equalization tax, buried as it was in an otherwise ordinary omnibus tax bill. Law was finally roused from its quiet work to attend to what in the longer run turned out to be a significant problem. The associationalist economy was in trouble.

III. THE SIXTIES AND SEVENTIES: A TROUBLED ECONOMY

For about the next twenty years, an increasingly troubled economy, centered in the production of consumer and heavy industrial goods, alternately slid and lurched down hill. How troubled? After the invasion of the Volkswagen Beetle, it took a flotilla of inexpensive Japanese imports to begin to knock the automobile industry out of denying that its market had changed. "Voluntary" export restraints entered into by Japanese manufacturers, designed to give the industry time to get back to its fighting weight, seemed not to help. Then there was the continuous decline of a steel industry that, once deprived of the stimulus provided by the Vietnam War and plagued with excess capacity devoted to an aged production process, ceded market after market to substantially cheaper imports and domestic upstarts, even while receiving trade protection. Similar stories might be told in the case of textiles (again despite significant trade protection), machine tools, clothing, footwear, and, of course, the television set, that quintessential product of the fifties life and economy. Most of the areas in which significant declines did not occur were industries where comprehensive federal or state regulation was in place, such as aviation, banking, communications, power, and securities. The only real growth industries in this period, other than entertainment, were real estate, plus the associated construction enterprises, and higher education, plus the associated spinoffs from the production of technological research conducted in medicine, electronics, and other science- and engineering-related fields.

How did this state of affairs come about? Initially, foreign manufactured products were attractive simply because they were cheaper. The associationalist model of a high-wage, high-price economy made it difficult for newly prosperous younger and lower-middle-class consumers, the expanded middle class that the fifties economy brought into being, to afford many things, especially small appliances and other electrical goods, or much of many things that were affordable only in small amounts, mainly soft goods. The discount stores that had begun to appear in the fifties – stores like E. J. Korvettes that sold American made hard goods at "discount" (i.e., less than the high "list" prices charged by the small Main Street retailers) – soon turned into specialty retailers, such as Pier 1, or into moderate-income department stores, such as K-Mart, Ames, or Hills, that sold many foreign-made goods, first soft goods, later small appliances, eventually electronics. Now, these families could have more clothes in their closets and small, inexpensive appliances in their kitchens; eventually they could have cheaper electronics in their family rooms.

Foreign products, especially soft goods, small appliances, and consumer electronics, often were cheaper simply because of wage rate disparities.

For other products such as steel and autos, lower wages combined with an unexpected advantage that derived from the wartime destruction of industrial capacity in Europe and Japan. Overseas, once capital could be assembled to revive these industries, capacity was built with the newest, most efficient technology and work processes – production methods in advance of those existing in the United States. The combination of better methods and lower wages was sufficient to offset the quite significant cost of ocean freight for heavy, often bulky goods. Transportation costs for soft goods, small appliances, and consumer electronics, when combined with loss or damage from trans-shipping to boats and from boats to trains or trucks, were a similarly significant expense. But, in time, transportation costs for these goods came down radically with the development of containerized shipping and of ships designed for containerization.

Eventually, foreign manufactured products were attractive because they were better. As foreign wages rose, first in Europe and then in Japan, producers there relied on technological advances that reduced costs or on mass production of new products – the Walkman stereo and the videocassette recorder are the best known – often actually invented in the United States. Faced with persistent consumer demand for low- priced or relatively inexpensive newly available products, American companies, used to oligopolistic competition, were not able, or at least not willing, to compete. Their response was to cede the low price market, as the steel industry had done, or to move production overseas. In either case, American companies eventually shrank domestic manufacturing capacity. Only later was "automation," the choice to substitute increasingly sophisticated machines (often manufactured abroad) for labor power, tried and then only sometimes successfully.

Explaining this pattern of manufacturer behavior is difficult. In some of the heavily unionized sectors such as steel and autos, management – fat, happy, and always inordinately concerned about its prerogatives; labor – a relatively immobile factor of production that can be expected to fight hard to preserve jobs; and especially poor labor-management relations, forged from the notion of quid pro quo, rather than the notion of joint problem solving, bear some share of the responsibility. In other unionized and in nonunionized sectors, family and management ties to declining enterprises, a sense of obligation toward local communities, possibly a sense of continuing obligation to workers derived from their status as veterans, and of course drift and default seem to have played a role. What is most significant, however, is that, in a surprisingly large number of cases, plant closure was avoided for as long as possible. Such was the strength of the associationalist model in the late sixties and seventies, long after it ceased its relevance to America's place in the world economy.

While the dysfunctional post-fifties American economy slid comfortably downhill, five developments silently continued to transform the country. The first was the malling of suburbia. This process largely destroyed the existing suburban versions of Main Street and continued the retail evacuation of the urban business core that had begun with the accelerated growth of the suburbs in the fifties, a development that only hastened the residential evacuation of those same cities.

The second development accompanied the completion of the interstate highway system. Initially, the existence of these highways magnified the evacuation of urban areas by their white, newly middle-class population. Then, in the same way that the new highway system had opened large tracts of land for residential development, it opened similar tracts for the development of light industrial and expanding service employment, particularly in banking, insurance, and health care, all within easy reach of this new suburban housing. Thereafter, jobs followed housing and housing jobs in a reinforcing cycle that created new suburban communities. Unlike the upper-middle-class suburbs of the twenties and thirties, these new suburbs were surprisingly independent of the urban areas that had initially spawned them.

The third development was the continuation of the evacuation of rural America, especially the Midwestern breadbasket. Though federal subsidies kept agriculture profitable, as farms increased in scale to pay for increasingly expensive hybrid seeds, chemical fertilizers, and equipment, the farm population declined. During these years, it was a real achievement for a rural community simply to maintain its population, even with recruited industrial employment, usually from firms attempting to escape a unionized work force, unless luck placed a growth industry – higher education was the most obvious one – in the area.

The fourth development was the growth of the South and West. In the South, the out-migration of blacks displaced by the mechanization of agriculture was offset by an even larger in-migration of Northerners escaping declining industries and chasing manufacturing jobs that were fleeing union labor contracts. In the West, aerospace and other military-related jobs were the draw. In both areas, the climate was made increasingly habitable by the perfection of air conditioning. And, as cities grew, construction and service jobs grew in tandem.

The fifth development was a significant change in the structure of the American industrial firm. Traditionally, industrial corporations, vertically integrated to a significant extent, made one major product and a few closely related ones. Such firms grew from the investment of retained earnings, either internally or by merger with other firms in the same industry. But in the sixties this type of growth by merger was stymied by the

Celler-Kefauver amendments to the antitrust acts. Apparently responding to this limit on growth, many American corporations began to use their retained earnings, in the form of new issues of common stock, to purchase strikingly diverse businesses, building what were called "conglomerates," the most famous being Harold Geneen's ITT and James Ling's LTV. This innovation unfortunately coincided with a steep decline in average annual increases in American productivity, from about 3 percent in the late fifties to nearly zero percent by the end of the seventies, and in corporate spending for research and development. For the time being, it seemed as if the traditional industrial corporation, already under siege by foreign competitors, would be succeeded by another form of industrial organization.

The slow slide of the American economy downhill that accompanied these social and economic changes was occasionally interrupted by less gentle lurches toward the bottom. The first such lurch followed from Lyndon Johnson's decision simultaneously to fight a land war in Asia, build a Great Society, and maintain the free importation of goods lest the American standard of living decline, but not to raise income taxes – a policy that Richard Nixon continued, though by diverting Great Society expenditures, and more than a few others, to the cause of Mars. Thus began a string of federal governmental deficits at a time when the economy was probably already operating at full capacity.

Unfortunately, during these years the Federal Reserve had adopted a policy of seeking regular growth in the money supply, further augmenting that supply during each recession under the Keynesian theory, by then generally accepted, that such action would lower interest rates and so expand employment. The result was the beginning of the Great Inflation, lasting close to a generation. By the time this event was over, it had reduced the value of the dollar by about two-thirds and the real value of wages by 20 percent. The newly broadened middle class was being seriously squeezed as interest rates increased significantly, especially on home mortgages; as the cost of common services, such as hair cuts and dry cleaning, not to mention more complex services such a medical care, began to accelerate; and as prices in the grocery and drug stores moved from a trot to a gallop.

The combination of inflation and a system of fixed exchange rates occasioned the second lurch downhill. Domestic inflation meant that, from the perspective of foreign buyers, American exports seemed more expensive; from the perception of American buyers, foreign imports seemed cheap. This disparity of perception led to a sharp deterioration in the American balance of trade as foreign buyers cut back on the purchase of American goods and American buyers clamored for more imported goods. Simultaneously, the further restrictions on the outflow of funds that were imposed soon after the interest equalization tax not only failed to solve the American balance of payments problems, but those problems were augmented by the increased overseas military spending occasioned by the Vietnam War. This augmentation compounded the effects of the deterioration in the balance of trade; foreign governments began quickly to convert their dollars into gold. In 1971, fearing that continuation of the outflow of gold threatened the "bankruptcy" of the country or, more properly, of the policy of guaranteeing the convertibility of dollars into gold at the fixed rate established by the Bretton Woods agreements, Richard Nixon, who had more than exacerbated the problem by intensifying the war in Southeast Asia, "temporarily" refused to honor the nation's commitment to exchange dollars for gold. Two years later, when circumstances had not improved, he abandoned the gold exchange standard entirely.

The demise of the gold exchange standard and its replacement with a system of "floating" exchange rates involving the major international currencies – rates determined in the market for foreign exchange and not by the willingness of governments to exchange currency at stated rates – was not the disaster for the world economy that many had feared it would be. Indeed, like the interest equalization tax, the adoption of a floating exchange rate may have been more a symbol of the continued decline of the American island economy that had made possible the realization of the associationalist ideal in the fifties than of much practical significance, given that the dollar continued to be freely accepted as a medium of foreign trade and indeed, as a reserve currency. But everyone expected that the short-term consequence for the economy would be a further increase in inflation.

Recognizing this expectation, when Nixon closed the gold window in 1971, he simultaneously took the unprecedented step of instituting wage and price controls in an allegedly peacetime economy. Such controls were anything but unwelcome to the American people, unused as they were to annual inflation rates of 6 or more percent. In addition to placing stress on family budgets, such inflation even decreased disposable inflated income, as wage increases were also eaten into by increases in marginal income tax rates as a result of moving to higher tax brackets. Controls, progressively weakened, were about as effective as could be expected, more so possibly because they were not in force long enough to spawn a fully developed black market.

Inflation, however, continued unabated. Indeed, next the economy experienced two more lurches toward the bottom, each accompanied by a significant increase in inflation. In 1973 came the Arab oil embargo that followed the Yom Kippur War, which when lifted was accompanied by the decision of the Organization of Petroleum Exporting Countries (OPEC) to quadruple the price of oil. The unemployment rate hit 8.5 percent. Then, in 1978 came a second shock, that from the loss of access to Iranian oil in the aftermath of the Iranian Revolution and from the further OPEC price rise that followed. Because the United States had become highly dependent on importing countless tankers of now very expensive oil, its balance of trade, already significantly negative, declined precipitously, and soon the world was awash with dollars.

Curiously, during these years, the most extraordinary – but usually unremarked – aspect of the American economy was the general inability of economists and policymakers to explain persuasively, much less to act effectively to alter, the cumulative slide in that economy. How it came to be that inflation did not bring economic growth, its traditional accompaniment, but instead allowed the continuance of a relatively stagnant economy – the dreaded "stagflation" – was a mystery. And not a pleasant one. The largest economy in the world was in real trouble.

Law and Economic Change: A Third Interrogation

Watching an economy come apart is not likely to be a pretty sight, and the disintegration of the associationalist economy during the sixties and seventies was no exception to this generalization. The bewildered, human pain that followed as solid expectations of future life were completely unraveled – labor, management, adolescents, and old people alike in their pain, though not in their loss – is perhaps the most characteristic aspect of these years. Gasoline wasn't supposed to cost a dollar a gallon; wages weren't supposed to lag behind inflation; imports weren't supposed to threaten established supports of community life. And this disorientation included public life; America wasn't supposed to be a pitiful, helpless giant suffering from economic malaise, as Jimmy Carter learned to his dismay.

That the experts could make no sense of these events is an understatement. Arthur Laffer could take a cocktail napkin, draw a curve on it that linked declining income tax rates with increasing tax collections, and it became a theory, somehow just as strong a theory as Milton Friedman's theory about changes in the growth of monetary aggregates and inflation, based as his was on years of research in monetary history. Ideas for taming inflation as sensible, but unprecedented, as Richard Nixon's embrace of peacetime price regulation and as silly as Gerald Ford's distribution of WIN (Whip Inflation Now) buttons were both worth a try because no one could understand what was going on anyway. Maybe a conglomeration of companies was a good idea if a group could be assembled so that the profits of its component parts experienced different temporal cycles, some always up when the others were down, so that the company as a whole always would be profitable. But then, maybe it was really dumb to assume that management by financial statement was better than management from the factory floor. Either was obviously arguable.

Law understood no more than the humans who used it. People felt pain, felt the times to be out of control, and so went to law in search of whatever nostrums seemed plausible at a given time and place. Trade protection made as much sense as did abandoning the gold standard as did reinvigorating antitrust enforcement as did price control as did price decontrol as did the strategic petroleum reserve as did airline price deregulation. As was the case during the Depression, people were hurting, and so law responded in such ways as the practical politics of the legislative process at that time and place allowed.

But to mention airline deregulation, a piece of the puzzle that only fit into *a, not the* pattern years later, is to bring to the fore something very important with respect to law and economic change. Although sensible people might have understood that the associationalist economy was coming apart and was not likely to be put together again, no one knew what kind of economy was in our future or even when a new economy might come together. No set of structures was put into place, intentionally or accidentally, that forged the next economy, except in the sense that lots of structures were tried that might or might not prove important depending on what happened next in economic life. The two nostrums that proved to be harbingers of things to come, the laughable Laffer curve and the deregulation of airline fares, do not bulk particularly large in any sensible story of these years. Indeed, it is hard to see exactly what the notion that raising the effective return on invested capital would aid the economy had to do with the notion that reducing price rigidity would have the same effect, except on the goofy theory, belied by the good years that were the fifties, that governmental regulation was somehow always and everywhere an economic mistake.

IV. THE EIGHTIES AND NINETIES: BUILDING AN IMPATIENT ECONOMY

One day in October 1979, Paul Volcker, newly chair of the Federal Reserve, decided that he had had it with inflation. He convinced the Fed to scrap the conventional wisdom; it would no longer increase the monetary supply in order to stimulate the economy and would let interest rates rise and fall as they pleased. Soon, interest rates hit sky-high levels, and in 1981 the country dropped into a deep recession that lasted for two years. The unemployment rate reached 10 percent. About the same time, Ronald Reagan both increased defense spending and cut taxes, producing enormous deficits in the federal budget. These actions helped pull the economy out of the recession that Volcker had created, once again proving that Keynes was most useful to those who did not believe in his prescriptions.

When the recession was over, the Great Inflation was over as well. Apparently, the precipitous rise in nominal interest rates in the early eighties interacted with a rise in real rates of return to boost the attractiveness of investment in capital assets and bring a decline in the actual rate of inflation. Such assets, especially those implementing newly developed technologies often related to computerization in both manufacturing and service industries, changed the structure of production. They tended either to increase the entry-level skills needed to operate production processes and so widened the gap between those skills, and the wages appropriate to them, and the remaining grunt jobs, or, as was particularly the case in the service sector, decreased the skill level and often the absolute number of entry-level jobs. In either case, the associationalist model of the economy was undercut.

A similar undercutting was felt in diverse segments of the economy. Among the ideas offered in the seventies to explain the dismal condition of the economy was the proposition that it was rooted in excessive regulation. Although the most heavily regulated sectors of the economy – communications, energy, and transportation – were few in number and generally entailed only modest direct costs for industrial producers, and the more lightly regulated sectors – banking and securities – arguably had been a crucial economic engine during the fifties by keeping capital costs low, numerous legislative programs of deregulation were adopted during these years. The effect of these programs was, however, mostly felt in the eighties.

Examples are numerous. In air travel, first came the disappearance of the single- price airfare, always and at any time the same, and the proliferation of cheap restricted fares, an event that helped airline traffic grow into a mass-market phenomenon in ways that it never had been before. Then came bankruptcies, consolidation, and the development of a hub-and-spoke route system that worked both to lower costs and to make new entry difficult, but allowed smaller niche players to emerge. A similar pattern developed in both truck and rail transport: lower costs, fewer, larger firms as a result of bankruptcy and merger, and small specialists. In all three areas a large, government-stabilized cartel was succeeded by a smaller oligopoly.

In communication and finance the sequence was different and the time frame longer, but the end point was much the same. First came lower prices – the decline in long-distance rates and the abolition of fixed commissions on stock trades – and then a great proliferation in new services: call waiting and cell phones, interest-bearing checking accounts, and automatic teller machines. Eventually came consolidation into seeming oligopolies, though in these cases less through bankruptcy and more through merger.

The effect on the economy from deregulation was not quite what the theory predicted. Prices did decline for most consumers, except for the road warriors of corporate sales departments who shifted from long boring rides in large comfortable cars ending at indifferent motel rooms to shorter cramped flights, boring waits in airports, and short drives in cramped rental cars ending at indifferent motel rooms. More significantly, however, in each deregulated industry the product or service seemed to change over time.

The simplest example is rail and truck transport where the transformation of industry structure combined with the potential of computerization to produce "just in time" manufacturing and retailing, a concept that significantly reduced inventory costs and eliminated dozens of local distributors. Trucks, rail cars, and ocean freight containers, always on the move, in effect became the inventory function, serving as rolling warehouses. Similarly, in communication first the fax machine, then the dial-up modem, and finally cable and wireless technology, again combined with the potential of computerization, transformed the humble phone call into something else – a document delivery service, an information-retrieval mechanism, a "real-time" financial transactions network. These changes transformed the phone into bandwidth to be used for purposes essentially unrelated to inviting neighbors over for dinner and a friendly game of cards. Likewise in banking and securities, the proliferation of products that are neither deposit taking nor lending nor the purchase and sale of debt or equity interests in business entities – bank cards, money market mutual funds, securitization, currency hedging, interest rate swaps – have created what can be seen as a new industry, rather grandiosely called financial services.

A significant portion of the economic growth in the late eighties and nineties came in these areas, though not without costs, often enormous, for the political process failed to realize that regulation creates patterns of investment, and so of personal commitment, that are upset when regulation is removed. In the securities industry predictable and promising careers ended and famous firms were swallowed whole, as competition created the need for new products and new skills. In railroads, the casualties were other industries that, and people who, had located in particular places and there depended on the existence of a particular mode of transportation that was no longer economical to maintain and so disappeared.

In bank regulation the matter was more complicated and ultimately expensive, but again had its roots in the seventies. The Great Inflation brought an enormous increase in unregulated interest rates. Soon there were complaints across the land that savings deposits were "eroding" because they were earning a regulated low return, a rate far below the rate of inflation. To make matters worse, the development of the money market mutual fund, a device that invested cash in short-term Treasury obligations and similar debt instruments of the most credit-worthy commercial borrowers – commercial paper – offered savers a heftier return than could savings accounts, because the rates on these investments were not regulated. In pursuit of such returns, savings poured out of deposit institutions. Savings and loans found that they lacked money for making new mortgages. Banks found that demand for corporate loans had declined as corporate treasurers issued the commercial paper that the money market funds craved, rather than visiting their local banker.

The initial governmental response to this problem was to allow commercial banks to offer interest on checking accounts and the savings and loan industry to offer higher rates on its deposits. The banks, left with a riskier portfolio of loans made to borrowers whose credit was not good enough for the commercial paper market, moved heavily into fee-generating business to pay for the now more expensive deposits. The savings and loans had a more embedded problem; the interest rates they were now paying for deposits were substantially higher than the interest rates on the portfolio of thirty-year mortgages they had made over time and still held. Thus, although these institutions had funds to loan, they were losing money with each transaction. Two changes followed.

The first was a great success, the invention of the collateralized mortgage obligation (CMO). Financial institutions would sell their mortgages to the New Deal's federal mortgage organizations – the Federal National Mortgage Association (Fannie Mae), the Federal Home Loan Mortgage Corporation (Freddie Mac), and the Government National Mortgage Association (Ginnie Mae). These organizations had long sold their own bonds to provide funds that could be lent to the providers of home mortgages. Now they began to issue similar securities, CMOs, with their own, extremely valuable guarantee and moreover collateralized by the newly purchased mortgages. This set of transactions allowed financial institutions to shift the risk of owning mortgages with fixed long-term rates to institutions with less sensitivity to interest-rate shifts, such as pension plans and insurance companies.

The other was anything but a success. In the name of maintaining fairness between different types of financial institutions, savings and loans were permitted to engage in lending other than home mortgages with the hope that they would earn the greater returns that those forms of lending provided. This decision was followed by the savings and loan crisis of the late eighties, as savings and loans around the country folded because of bad, occasionally even corrupt, investments or continuing "negative spreads" between deposit interest rates and mortgage portfolio returns, or both. The Treasury paid out billions on the claims presented by depositors who lost their savings in the process, an obligation that derived from the provision of deposit insurance, one of the little programs of the New Deal that had successfully enticed deposits back into a banking system that had imploded in the twenties and thirties.

Deregulation was, however, only a part of what was going on in the economy in the eighties and nineties. Much of the rest was the continued destruction of the economic model that had made the fifties economy such a spectacular thing, probably by accident, by being the right model for that particularly unforeseeable time. Increasingly, the associationalist model of high prices, high wages, and lifetime employment, at least for white-collar workers, came undone in a range of industries, whether trade protected or not. Copper, tires, textiles, clothing, shoes, televisions, stereos, dishes, glassware, cookware, watches, pens, and even telephones slowly became mostly imported products; autos, somewhat less. Manufacturers continued the process of first conceding the low-end products, then the oldest manufacturing facilities, and finally whole markets.

In some areas technological innovation or the development of new processes entirely – steel mini-mills using scrap for feedstock is a good example – kept parts of old industries alive. But more than occasionally, these were markets where manufacturing costs were not yet matched by foreign producers. In still other markets, a slimmed-down industry survived in niches – autos that are particularly designed for the odd tastes of the American consumer or specialty steels. What was left behind was a landscape surprisingly denuded of former industrial icons, except for a few long-term survivors. IBM, as well as Boeing and the rest of the aerospace industry, are the most obvious; General Motors and Ford, the most recurrently troubled. Even the conglomerate alternative to the fifties industrial behemoths passed from the scene, a victim of the eighties junk bond craze that facilitated busting up such entities for fun and profit.

As one examines this record of the decline of heavy industry, it becomes apparent that the broad increase in the standard of living that took place in the fifties and early sixties has been America's own version of the winner's curse. Although Americans have always searched for new markets and so have been alive to the world of international trade, free trade, and thus the idea of comparative national advantage, has been a more central part of the national consciousness since World War II. Free trade, really freer trade, was to be a way to avoid the recurrence of the Depression, to unite nations by means of growing mutual dependency, and to provide an object lesson for the Third World of the benefits of "open" economies, in contrast to the "closed" Communist economies in Eastern Europe and Asia. Foreign policy thus supported freer trade, though at times domestic considerations made freer trade look more like trade managed for strategic national advantage.

Freer trade interacted with the American standard of living in a crucial way. As the United States became less of an island, less capable of standing separately, maintaining the standard of living that was built in a high-wage, high-price economy became more difficult. In response to that difficulty, Americans, fighting to remain a part of the enlarged middle class, did many things. They drastically curbed saving. They supported tax reduction, borrowing from an uncertain future. They chose to try to stretch the dollar by working harder; the growth of the two wage-earner household during the seventies and eighties surely cushioned economic decline for families who found that local industrial jobs had disappeared. And they found it easy to continue to accept, indeed to increase their acceptance of, lower cost imports from an international arena with which they were familiar and in which they were comfortable, if not wholly dominant. That arena became the source for the goods that were necessary for membership in the lower middle class and above.

Of course, because of America's economic dependence on imported oil – environmental concerns, again a part of a middle-class standard of living, have kept coal and nuclear power from being winners – and because of American's addiction to computers and consumer electronics, there was really no other plausible choice than freer trade. Letting the dollar become a reserve currency, indeed even exulting in its becoming such, was, like the middle-class standard of living, a mixed blessing. It made trade easy, but it made investment easy as well. The interest equalization tax had a hidden lesson in it. Capital does seek its highest returns consistent with its tolerance for risk.

Once the value of major currencies was no longer tied to a stock of gold, numerous investment opportunities, denominated in various currencies, became real alternatives. Looked at critically, returns on investments denominated in dollars simply did not stand up to those available elsewhere. And so, those American firms that could move their funds around the world found that more promising investments in plant and equipment were to be had elsewhere. Often these investments were made simply in pursuit of lower labor costs. At other times, investments were in new production processes, especially those substituting lighter weight components for heavier, since the modest increase in the cost of production was less than the decrease in the cost of ocean freight and so the resulting product was still salable in the United States. Though investment in new plant and equipment was concentrated elsewhere, buying was still an available alternative for middle-class Americans addicted to their standard of living; increasingly, manufacturing was not.

There was, as often is the case, a counter-current. Ours was still the largest economy in the world, though the expanding European Union was trying to overtake us. Our addiction to a fifties standard of living maintained with imported goods meant that foreign producers rapidly acquired

great piles of dollars, for most the reserve currency of choice. Those earnings
had to go somewhere. Mattresses were implausible and conversion to foreign currencies would only result in a decrease in the value of the earnings.
So, many producers of imported goods used their dollars to make portfolio investments in New York, the largest and deepest securities market in
the world; to purchase tangible American assets, such as real estate, still
viable manufacturing companies, or almost any service business; or to dupli-
cate their existing, overseas plant and equipment in the States, thus saving
the transportation costs otherwise inherent in serving our market and simultaneously making their products more attractive to American customers.
Oddly, what seemed to many observers to be a dangerous tendency to live
well beyond our means proved to be not even a half-bad experience for many
Americans.

As the remnants of the fifties economy were being destroyed, a successor economy was growing, developed out of America's real economic
strength – higher education. Computers and their software, pharmaceuti-
cals, health care products, electronic technology spinoffs from defense industries, advanced engineering processes – all were high-growth, high-return
industries right here in America; all were significant sources of exports as
well. It seemed as if Americans were going to do the world's research and
development. Production was another matter. All major (and a surprising
percentage of minor) American corporations purveying consumer or industrial goods had built or acquired many international facilities capable of
producing goods for local markets and for export to the United States.
Production would increasingly be done elsewhere.

Another source of growth was in the continuing expansion of service
industries: banking, insurance, real estate, health care, "hospitality," travel,
and government. This was particularly true in the South and West, areas that
had already increased their light-manufacturing base and so could support
a similarly increased population. In Florida and in the Southwest, where the
natives had expanded water supplies through transport by canal, growing
numbers of retirees fueled still larger increases in the size of the service economy. In a real sense, service jobs too were a product of the American system of
education, though not necessarily one to be proud of, filled as they were by a
small number of college and professional degree holders and a large number
of others who at best held associates degrees and were paid accordingly.

These examples of growth were obvious in that other notable product
of the American educational system – the financial services industry. The
proliferation of new and modestly useful financial products coming out of
Wall Street's version of Hollywood's dream factories that took advantage
of the breadth and depth of the American capital markets and tapped into

international markets as well made many men (but few women) rich. In the process, the financial engineering that Wall Street delivered to the various "institutions" that increasingly came to dominate American financial markets – insurance companies, mutual funds, pension funds, the private foundations of the wealthy, university endowments and, let us not forget, hedge funds – transformed the financial landscape. Where once a solid dividend record was all that counted when measuring a stock's attractiveness, now institutions – many so large that they would find it very hard to sell their holdings in any given stock and others limited in their ability to do so by their choice to pursue indexing as an investment strategy – gave attractiveness an entirely new dimension, a dimension derived from the new high-growth, high-return industries. Total return, the sum of dividends received and stock appreciation, was now the measure of investment success, that and steady earnings growth. All one heard was the demand for "increasing shareholder value," a euphemism for raising a company's stock price.

So, at the end of the nineties the United States seemed to be left with an economy that consisted of the products of the American system of higher education; those things that were too heavy and too inexpensive to be effectively made and shipped from overseas; services that had to be delivered locally including construction; entertainment, always a viable industry for any cultural hegemon; autos, an industry kept alive by the growth of foreign manufacturers who, afraid of trade protection legislation, chose to use profits earned here to create plants producing for a market once served from abroad; and the sale of the myriad products that made up a middle-class lifestyle. While some argued that the industries reborn by deregulation had to be added to this list, it seemed more likely that, just as had proven to be the case with truck and rail transportation, unless the deregulated industries were tied to the products of the American system of higher education, their growth would prove to have represented one-time opportunities as, over time, the American preference for oligopolistic competition – a modest possibility of price control derived from branding and economies of scale, coupled with an endless fear of a competitor's "breakout" innovation – asserted itself.

To know something is to be able to name it. If the fifties instantiated an associationalist economy, what name properly describes the American economy at the end of the nineties? The decade did not see a return to the laissez-faire capitalism thought to have gripped the United States in the 1890s. For all the complaints about the costs of regulation, environmental, food and drug, labor relations, occupational safety, pension, product safety, securities, and wage and hour protections did not wholly disappear. Social

Security and Medicare, as well as unemployment, bank deposit, pension, and brokerage failure insurance survived as well. The economy did not emulate the Gilded Age financiers and break into an orgy of unrestrained, to-the-death competition. Nor is it likely that it will. Oligopoly is too much a part of the American and world experience now.

To understand the economy that emerged from the nineties, it is important to notice how, during the decade, financial markets became incredibly disciplining. Companies had to deliver ever higher total returns on capital based on steady, predictable earnings growth or face pressure to cut losses quickly. This was an unforgiving economy, an economy where people with the labor market skills of the hour were pampered as never before, but only for as long as their star shone brightest. No longer associationalist, the American economy had become an impatient economy.

The associationalist economy promised that economic growth would increase the availability of leisure; in response, some commentators even began to worry that so much leisure time would become a social problem. In the early twenty-first century all that is past; now there is no leisure time until retirement. The communications revolution means that the global stock market, which operates around the clock, can be checked at any time in the day or night while on safari in Africa. First, courier largely replaced real mail; in turn courier was replaced by fax; currently the on-time standards are email and text messaging, available essentially anywhere, anytime by mobile phone. Coast-to-coast and intercontinental flights are staples of commerce, where once the pace of train and ocean travel – both with real sleep caught on the way – was a break from the daily routine. Financial markets are driven, not by earnings trends, but by quarterly earnings, or even expectations about quarterly earnings; by expectations about the next Fed Open Market Committee meeting and not by the results of the meeting itself. The best production process is a "just in time" production process. Yes, in the early twenty-first century the American economy is an impatient economy.

V. EXAMINING A LOOSELY WOVEN FABRIC: SEEKING LAW IN ECONOMIC CHANGE

Whether one focuses on the details of economic life – dominant industries, modes of transportation, consumer products – or on larger scale phenomena – the expansion of the consumerist middle class, the shift in sectional economies, the decline of the American island economy – or on the highest level of generality – an economy as a whole, a persistent market structure that fuses an understanding of economic life with patterns of behavior within economic, political, and social institutions, an associationalist or impatient economy – the short twentieth century has been a time of significant economic change. As such it is plausible to examine the role of law in economic change, first at the highest level, then at lower levels, by focusing on these years.[2]

Forms of Law and Change from One Economy to Another

I hope that by now I have provided sufficient evidence for my initial assertion that the institution that is law (the many and variable actions undertaken by lawyers and other governmental officials, the formal and effective norms originating from the practices of these individuals, and the systematic presuppositions shared among them) did very little to bring about change from one economy to another. Though responding to distress when it wished, law mostly stood by and watched. Many changes happened; few might be traced from the actions, or back toward the reactions, of law. Capitalism as a form of economic organization seemingly went its merry way, complaining from time to time about law's particular intrusions, but generally too busy earning profits while profits could be earned, all the while coping with changes in markets, to be much influenced by law.

My assertion, contrary to so much of the received wisdom of law professors and legal historians alike, is not offered so much out of perversity, but in an attempt to get us beyond the legalism, the focus on the three forms of law enumerated above, that has infected the topic of law and economy for at least a century. That law in all three forms is important in the daily lives of humans is a proposition beyond question. That at times law attempts to have such an impact on lives is also true beyond peradventure. That it often fails of its intention is also reasonably clear. But great change, be it social, political, or economic, is not a matter for calculus – sum the impact of law on a large number of lives over the relevant range of years. Such change is not even a more irregular sum, but a qualitative experience that in retrospect is disjunctive, not additive, of this being a different time from some other, remembered or imaginatively recreated, time.

---

[2] Before doing so, it is important to note the futility of the task I undertake. Life is not lived in conventional academic boxes, even less the complex of lives that is a society at any time or times, place or places. Multivariate analysis makes sense only to the extent that all other things can be held constant, but they never manage to stay that way. More simplistic methods, such as mine, do not do the job of analysis any better, only differently. And so, as I attempt to separate "law" and "economy" in order to assess their respective roles in economic change, to separate the dancer from the music that together are the dance, I ask the reader to be tolerant of the intrusion of metaphor. It is, after all, a traditional way of capturing disparate elements into a readily, if only implicitly, understood whole.

To understand the way in which law mostly stands aside as economic change occurs, not for lack of trying, but because it is the creation of humans, cursed with memory and deficient in foresight, let us look sequentially at the role of the three forms of law as set forth in my story. Looking first at the systematic presuppositions of the law, it is clear that, as asserted many pages ago, the law of property, contract, and theft, of mine and thine, so structures capitalism that it is both impossible to notice and impossible to miss. The precise effect of this distinctive underpinning to economic life is, however, difficult to gauge when examining economic change.

All change takes place within a systematic structure of law and is modestly pushed in particular directions by the alternatives that law, thus understood, makes possible. It is unquestionably true that, in the United States in the short twentieth century, the systematic structure of law made it difficult to conceive of a social democratic or communitarian alternative to any one of a range of capitalisms, much less a state socialist alternative. However, to identify this aspect of law as central to an understanding of its role in economic change is to reduce the question of change to a tautological one that assumes that the change from, for instance, capitalism to socialism is the only important economic change possible. For humans the lived experience of less momentous changes may seem just as significant; in any case, it is a dubious practice to try to understand an institution by looking at its participation in, or response to, the most extreme change imaginable. Less extreme changes are difficult enough to understand all by themselves.

Although it is difficult to know what an agnostic scholar might conclude about the role of law in large-scale economic change under hypothetical capitalist alternatives or alternatives to capitalism, I rather doubt that he or she would conclude that law played a significant role in such change. The systematic structure of law is largely isomorphic with the particular political economy – capitalism, socialism, or whatever – in this or any other of the various countries of the North Atlantic world. To identify specific instances of law's action or reaction surely is to pull individual threads out of a loosely woven fabric held together in so many other ways. For this reason I believe it is best to treat the patient, silent work of law seen as systematic structure as it appears to most economic actors, as invisible.

Looking next at the second form of law – formal and effective norms – one can, of course, identify individual patches of law adopted for numerous reasons that turn out, often surprisingly, to be crucial supports for economic change, such as from an associationalist to an impatient economy. The expansion of the middle class was founded on the New Deal institutions that defined labor, housing, and finance in these years. The GI Bill and Cold War military expenditures did their part as well, as did the great growth of state university systems in the sixties. The shift in sectional economies was similarly founded on New Deal labor, agricultural, and industrial policies and on the concentration of new federal military and allied manufacturing resources in the South and West during World War II. The rise of the international economy of the last quarter of this century was founded on the multilateral financial and trade institutions established as part of the American strategy for an integrated postwar world, as well as on Marshall Plan aid.

However, no institution of law acted with even the vague intention of expanding the middle class as part of the development of a consumer society. Similarly, to the limited extent that wartime expenditures were designed to counteract the colonial nature of the Southern or Western economy, no one simultaneously wished to hasten the decline of heavy manufacturing in the Northeast, much less to shift the country as a whole toward a service economy. And, though the postwar financial and trade institutions and Marshall Plan aid were designed to foster international trade, the major point of that effort was to limit the possibility of renewed conflict in Europe, not to transform the international economy as a whole and American participation in it in particular. Thus, it is not wholly clear what to make of these more specific underpinnings for change beyond seeing them as examples of the law of unintended consequences. Probably they were reasonably essential to the particular large-scale changes identified and yet, there will always remain the nagging doubt as to whether the absence of one or more of these bits of law would have made much of a difference in the shape of such changes, any more than would a change in one or more threads alter a loosely woven fabric.

Looking finally at the third form of law – official action, the many and variable actions undertaken by lawyers and governmental actors – at least initially, this form seems more salient in the change from an associationalist to an impatient economy. Much of governmental effort directed toward managing economic life, both domestically and internationally, takes the form of, in the traditional language of the law, discretionary action. Lawyers worked endlessly to steer discretionary action and, when unable to do so, to avoid its objectives. This is the world of fiscal and monetary policy and international economic institutions, the world where economic historians argue about whether the Smoot-Hawley tariff really caused the Depression or whether Paul Volcker's actions to break the Great Inflation were effective in doing just that.

Clearly, Lord Keynes was right that such actions are of some causal significance. The question is how much and in what direction. The Kennedy tax cuts and Johnson's guns and butter (and no new taxes) policy clearly made a difference. But, it is not clear that they did more than provide very welcome life support for an economy built on an associationalism that was already facing problems with which it would be unable to cope. Similarly, twenty years of determined anti-inflationary policy, husbanded by both Paul Volcker and Alan Greenspan, made it easy for the United States to build its position as the broadest, deepest source of capital worldwide and, as the possessor of a reasonably solid currency available in large amounts, the effective central bank for the world. Still, it is not obvious that this tenacious policy preference did anything toward building a vital international economy other than speed up that process a smidgen by modestly lowering the cost of funds for the actors who were creating that economy, adding an occasional thread to, or adjusting an existing one in, the loosely woven fabric.

Gathered together, what all three forms of law – systemic presuppositions, formal and effective norms, and official action – seem to have done in the change from an associationalist to an impatient economy is to augment the prevailing winds, but modestly. Thus, the expansion of the middle class was aided by expenditures for schools and colleges, the development of urban road networks, permissive zoning for subdivisions and shopping areas, and the indexation of Social Security benefits. The shift in sectional economies was aided by the development of the interstate highway system, funding of the infrastructure necessary for expanded airline travel, toleration of sectional wage differentials, and the expansion of electrical capacity to support air conditioning in Sunbelt climates. And the rise of the international economy was aided by export incentives, policies favoring limited taxation of foreign income, support for the waterfront infrastructure necessary for containerized shipping, the relentless pursuit of tariff reduction, and support for the push by domestic banking and securities industries into foreign markets and for the creation of friendly domestic markets for foreign borrowers and investors. The contribution of the International Monetary Fund in attempting to stabilize currencies should not be underestimated either.

Now, none of these were trivial actions, and logically all could be inverted into a refusal to respond to claims for aid from those harmed by each of these actions. But all were at the time seen as "no big deal." Indeed, several of these actions taken by law do not even rate mention in any brief history of the American economy for these years. All might have been recognized as posing difficult problems at the time they were undertaken, but were not. Instead, they were seen as presenting no significant issues beyond the narrowly partisan ones. Their taken-for-grantedness is the key to understanding law's actions in these cases. What is taken for granted, what is merely a matter of course, is that which seems most natural, least controversial, in the eyes of the recognized participants in the "pointless bickering" about law and economy that always swirls throughout any governmental apparatus. And so, I believe it sensible to see such actions as no more than reinforcing large-scale change.

Why then is it that the best that law in its three forms can do in the face of the Schumpeterian "creative destruction" of capitalism is to augment the prevailing winds? Let me recapitulate. First, it is reasonably apparent that both economic and legal actors, to the extent that they may be more than formally distinguished, have at best a highly imperfect understanding of either economy or law at a given time and place. Second, this highly imperfect understanding is not the singular result of ideological blinkering, though, of course, all actors are both aided and limited in their vision as a result of shared or separate ideologies. Rather, both systems – economic and legal – are significantly more complicated than most actors are capable of understanding. At the same time, both systems are far more subject to perturbations that these same actors believe are external to the systems than most of them can conceive. Third, economy and law are also significantly more integrated than these actors realize, particularly with respect to the legal infrastructure, both doctrinal and institutional, that silently undergirds and channels economic activity and with respect to the durable patterns of economic life that are instantiated by the humans who are economic actors in all senses of that phrase – consumers, workers, manufacturers, retailers, financiers, and the like. Thus, the failure of law to direct or to respond to large-scale economic change is not a failure to act on the dictates of intellect or even a failure of will, as Willard Hurst may seem to argue, but a reflection of the limited ability of humans fully to understand these two complex systems, a reflection not of policy failure, but of human fallibility, as it were.

Three Attitudes Apparent in Law's Response to Smaller Scale Economic Change

That law can do little but add to the steady winds of large-scale economic change does not mean that it cannot and so does not act, occasionally significantly, at the level of smaller, more narrowly focused change. Here, where actors can see more clearly, where the impact on the lives of Americans is more obvious, law should be able to pay attention to the consequences that economic change brings. And consequences there are. Any significant change in an economy – expansion or contraction, domestic or international, technological innovation or climatic alteration – will benefit or harm identifiable, limited segments of that economy – producers, financial or commercial intermediaries, transporters, sellers, workers, consumers – in a systematic way. Those who are harmed by such change routinely respond by seeking support to maintain their present, or regain their previous, economic position from whatever piece of the modern state that seems to them likely to offer such assistance – administrative, executive, judicial, or legislative. Sometimes the support sought will be forthcoming, though not necessarily in the form requested, and at other times such support will not be forthcoming. Oddly, even when such support is forthcoming, the support provided will only sometimes have the anticipated effects, and when the support is denied, the absence of support will only sometimes bring forth the anticipated consequences. Such is the recurrent, less than wholly helpful, pattern experienced by those who would go to law.

Despite the essential indeterminacy of law's reaction to smaller scale economic change, a few underlying attitudes can be teased out. I can identify three of them – law's general attitude toward change, its attitude toward technological as opposed to cost-driven change, and its attitude toward system-wide change. First, with respect to law's general attitude toward smaller scale economic change, it is important to remember that there are three possible answers that law might regularly give when economic actors seek its aid – stonewall change, support it indiscriminately, or slow it down somewhat.

Consider stonewalling. Law might choose to stonewall change and so give complete support to existing, and so entrenched, potentially politically powerful, economic interests. It is actually hard to find examples of such a response of law in the short twentieth century. Most are reasonably obscure; none merits mention in my story. Some instances can be supplied, however, such as the refusal to eliminate the role of the liquor wholesaler after changes in transportation made it plausible for many large producers to do so or the surprisingly long refusal of law to respond to the demands of the railroads to countenance elimination of a fireman on a train after diesel engines had replaced coal fired engines, or of the brakeman after the airbrake replaced the hand brake.

Next consider indiscriminate support. Law's response to smaller scale economic change might be to choose to favor change essentially indiscriminately and so ignore entrenched economic interests. This response of law is less remarkably rather difficult to find. However, the continuing effort of the Supreme Court to see that out-of-state mail order retailers do not have to pay the same local corporate and sales taxes as in-state retailers is a conspicuous exception. Oddly, the record on atomic power might be seen to provide a double example of this response as law first ignored the objections of the owners of existing coal-fired plants and then, when the political winds changed, ignored the interests of the owners of the new atomic power plants.

Consider finally a modest slowing of smaller scale change. Law might choose to work to retard change somewhat, but not to block it. Such a course of action would allow entrenched interests to work down their investments over time – to avoid the economist's seemingly heartless notion that sunk costs are sunk and so everyone should move on. Instead, such interests might recover at least a further part of their investments in monetary or personal capital, though it should be remembered that the risks faced by monetary capital can in theory, and at times in practice, be diversified much easier than those faced by personal capital. Equally importantly, by allowing a work down of sunk costs, law might buy off those political interests that would most stridently oppose change and, in doing so, might indirectly facilitate such change. This is actually the response most often evident in my story.

The best examples are relatively recent. The entire panoply of trade protection legislation has the structure of providing short-term respites for industries suffering from the effects of foreign competition, which, though always defended as providing the industry a chance to get its house in order, are all but invariably followed by a decline in the size of the industry in question. Here steel, textiles, and apparel are the classic cases. The same is true of the negotiation of bi- or multilateral "voluntary export restraints," programs whereby foreign countries agree to hold their company's exports down to some level experienced at an earlier time for a certain period of years. Here autos, steel, and again textiles (the multi-fiber agreements) are equally classic cases, where on expiration of the agreement, again justified as allowing the industry to get back on its feet, somehow the industry is smaller.

A second attitude disclosed in law's response to smaller scale economic change, one that clearly overlaps with its more general response to such change, can be seen by separately considering technological change, usually domestic in origin, and cost-driven change, usually foreign in origin. Examples of the former within the short twentieth century would be the extension of electric power to more and more homes; the development of commercial radio, television, and the personal computer; and the building of an effective airline passenger transportation network. This kind of change alters the way that Americans as consumers can live their lives, spend their time, envision their world; for them the change is visible but unproblematic. Examples of the latter would be the growth of textile manufacturing in Asia and Central America, of export-oriented automobile manufacturing in Europe and Asia, of similarly oriented electronics manufacturing in Asia, of natural resources production in the South America and the Mideast, or of computer programming skills in South Asia, instances where foreign producers possess a comparative cost advantage. With this kind of change lives remain much the same for most American consumers; the change is almost invisible and almost equally unproblematic.

For domestic producers – both capital and labor[3] – of the same or of alternative goods or services, the matter is entirely different. It makes no difference to them whether change is technological or cost driven. These are the people identifiably harmed by change whatever its source; these are the people who will go to law for relief. The governmental response to the economic dislocations felt from both types of change might therefore be expected to be identical, given that the vast mass of consumers, the ostensible public of the public interest, is not obviously harmed by either. However, this turns out not to be so. Law will be more supportive of those whose lives are threatened by cost-driven change than of those who are threatened by technological change. Possibly, change in the way that Americans as consumers can live their lives, spend their time, envision their world makes it difficult to harness empathetic concern for those whose economic lives are harmed by this expansion in a consumer's surround. Definitely, the foreign invader is a more acceptable target than the domestic insurgent.

Good examples can be found of law's reaction to these two kinds of change. Consider first cost-driven change. In steel and autos, producers began by ignoring, then disparaging, the foreign-made goods, and finally ceding the lowest (and, on occasion, highest) margin products. When foreign producers were recognized as a real competitive threat to the investments of both capital and labor, a hue and cry went up to "save" the industry – in both cases an industry with complacent management and poor labor relations. Law repeatedly responded with temporary measures as the industry slowly shrank in size, though in autos, after foreign manufacturers established domestic plants, claims for assistance went largely unanswered.

Textiles and apparel, including shoes, provide an interesting contrast, as does consumer electronics. Here the initial pattern of management behavior was roughly the same as steel and autos; the response of law was not.

---

[3] It is perhaps foolish for me to use the classic nineteenth-century language of capital and labor when writing about owners and workers in the short twentieth century. Capital comes in many varieties. Portfolio investment of varying kinds and sizes; productive physical assets of bewildering types and ages, owned in diverse ways by people in quite diverse circumstances; a similarly diverse range of real estate investments; owner-occupied homes and their contents; and of course the varying types of human capital – might be considered a good start at a comprehensive listing, but nothing more. Similarly, labor ranges from the chronically unemployed through day laborers, union and non-union hourly workers in various settings, a similarly diverse group of salaried workers, to various freelance artisans and professionals who might be either workers or worker/owners. To attack this problem of understanding the contemporary structure of capital and labor would require an entirely separate article. As I am comfortable with the classic language because it ought to remind readers of significant questions of dependence and independence, I have chosen to maintain it.

Textiles received the most continuous support – perhaps a function of the concentration of the industry in the Southeast, where Congressmen tend to serve long and reach high positions in party leadership and maybe also a recognition of the continuous, significant investments in manufacturing technology made by the industry. In consumer electronics, television manufacturers received some support, but by the time the Walkman reinvented the radio, domestic manufacturers had moved their own production offshore, law's support ceased, and the market was quickly dominated by foreign products. In apparel, domestic producers were largely at the mercy of the branded apparel marketers, particularly in women's wear. Here, little effective opposition to foreign incursions was mounted and so law's response was weakest, for the marketers quickly outsourced manufacture to the very areas where the threatening off-brand goods were originating.

The strength of these examples can be seen by comparing them to similar, but domestic, changes in technology. As the computer replaced the business machine, the electric replaced the manual typewriter, and the Xerox machine replaced various duplication processes from carbon paper through stencils to thermofax, competitors either adapted or died. Mostly they died. As television replaced radio, radio struggled, gave up live entertainment, and finally reinvented itself as a purveyor of recorded music. Foreign, cost-based insurgencies brought forth a response when domestic, technologically driven ones did not. Capital is anything but xenophobic; this is not true of humans more generally.

A third attitude disclosed in law's response to smaller scale economic change, a pattern that again overlaps with the two previously considered, can be seen by examining a third type of economic change – system-wide change, boom or bust. Examples of this kind of change would be the great bust known as the Depression, the fifties and nineties booms and the Great Inflation. This kind of change tends to treat most, though never all, producers and consumers alike, as would the proverbial rising or falling tide. One might expect that the kind of economic change that is broadly felt would bring forth a similarly broad governmental response. However, system-wide change tends to bring forth governmental responses that are less uniform and broad based than narrow and targeted and are highly influenced by the political exigencies of the time.

The response of law to the Depression provides a well-known example. Although one can understand the New Deal's focus on agriculture and financial institutions, given the collapse in farm and stock prices and the raft of mortgage foreclosures and bank failures, other aspects of the Roosevelt administration's program are odd. Consider the relative exclusion of railroad aid. The high point of railroad domination of transportation was 1916. After that point the quantity of railroad trackage declined and competition from inter-city bus lines became serious. During the Depression a large percentage of trackage was in receivership. Yet more of law's attention was paid to civil aviation, marginal for both passenger and cargo transportation, and to trucking as well.

Natural resources industries were treated no more uniformly. Coal mining, incredibly depressed from the decline in industrial production and the slow increase in residential and commercial oil heating; dependent on the railroads, both as a customer and a transporter; and possessed of a strong, if troubled, union tradition was lavished attention as a "sick" industry, even receiving its own separate New Deal statute and so its own Supreme Court declaration of unconstitutionality. Oil, where state-supported pro-rationing of production still could not avert a price decline, was similarly supported with federal legislation, though oil field and refinery workers were not comparably powerful and the industry was substantially less essential to the national economy, even given the growth of auto transportation, than the railroads. Other mining industries, as well as timber, all a matter of natural resources, were mostly ignored once the NRA fell apart, only to be declared unconstitutional thereafter anyway.

Autos and steel were possibly not as depressed as coal, all things being relative anyway, but were just as crucial to the economy and shared an equally troubled history of labor relations. They received no special attention, nor did any other manufacturing industry. And even agriculture was treated spottily. Grains were lavished with law's attention, but meat, poultry, and fish production were largely ignored. Cotton got included in crop subsidies, but not wool. Beans were ignored, and potatoes too, but rice, another starch, though hardly a centerpiece of the northern European culture that shaped this nation, received support as did sugar.

Now, all of these seeming anomalies can be explained by a combination of political and economic analysis. But the need for such is precisely the point. Despite broad-based economic distress, broad-based legislative support for the economy was not forthcoming.

The Great Inflation of the sixties and seventies equally illustrates this proposition. That law paid enormous attention to oil and natural gas production and pricing during these years is again easy to understand; the two oil price shocks and one embargo gained the attention of an auto-dependent nation in nothing flat. Similarly, currency and balance of payments questions were of daily concern given the abandonment of the gold standard and the much increased price of imported oil. But in a virtual repeat of the Depression, banking, securities, and agriculture all received major attention from law, as did commercial aviation and trucking. The big shift in law's attention was the railroads, a clear response to the Penn-Central bankruptcy that led to the formation of Conrail and Amtrak. Yet, except for steel and autos, manufacturing was again largely ignored, as was most of agriculture, except for the historically favored crops. Consumer prices received attention with Nixon's price control plan in the early seventies, but before and after that event, ordinary Americans were basically left to lump it.

The similarity of the pattern of economic sectors attended to and ignored forty years apart suggests certain durable features to law's instantiation of the politics of the economy. The continued political attention paid to the economic interests dependent on law for the definition of their powers, such as banking and securities, or dependent on law for their current economic value, such as agriculture or natural resources, is not surprising. At the same time such interest does not translate into narrow attainment of economic desires, much less stability. The success of the savings and loan industry in securing law's ministrations led to the industry's demise. And the banking industry prospered, if not beyond, at least up to, its wildest dreams, through a period in which its greatest legislative desire – the repeal of the Glass-Steagall Act – was beyond its reach.

In some ways, more important than the durability of law's response to the politics of economy is the evidence that both the Depression and the Great Inflation provide of law's limited range of attention where matters of system-wide economic change are concerned. The production, distribution, and consumption of manufactured goods, whether industrial or consumer, seemingly the engine of economic life, were (except for the National Recovery Administration) largely ignored by law in cases of cyclical economic change. Perhaps these activities are too diffuse to bring politically organized attention; perhaps they are too far removed from law's regular concerns, except as a purchaser of military supplies or construction services; perhaps they are just too close to the heart of a capitalist economy.

Three Contexts for Law's Response to Smaller Scale Economic Change

In addition to the three discernible attitudes disclosed in law's response to smaller scale economic change, I can profitably examine three particular contexts for that response – infrastructural investment, regulatory investments, and social circumstances. Consider first infrastructural investments. One of the great, unheralded, and almost invisible legal inventions prominent in the short twentieth century is the public authority, an entity functionally similar to the eighteenth-century corporation. Originally it was nothing but a vehicle for evading state constitutional restrictions on state and local debt and still, of course, functions as such. A legal entity is formally established as separate from its parent governmental unit, given building and/or purchasing and, most importantly, bonding authority. It is then set on its way to pursue the public good. Under the fiction that, as it is separate from its parental authority, it is not bound by constitutional restrictions on the actions of the establishing entity, normally its objective is engaging in building or buying something using borrowed funds, the repayment of which is secured by some stream of revenue that the built or purchased asset is supposed to throw off.

The best known of such entities established by a state or local government is the Triborough Bridge and Tunnel Authority, the centerpiece of Robert Moses' New York empire. But such authorities also build and operate toll roads, canals, harbors, airports, transit systems, hospitals, dams and their power plants, convention centers, and sports arenas; they also build and then lease public housing, state universities and their dormitories, and defense plants. Creating such entities removes them somewhat from the rough and tumble of legislative and executive politics and even where debt restrictions are not constitutional, as is the case with the federal government, hides their debt a bit from public scrutiny.

Public authorities are regularly established for the purpose of providing infrastructure investment that it is hoped will bring positive economic results for the relevant community. They are thus classic examples of law working either to rehabilitate deteriorating facilities or to build new ones and thus either to retard or to facilitate change. Three federally established public authorities – Fannie Mae, Freddie Mac, and Ginnie Mae – figure reasonably large in my story; two others, the Tennessee Valley Authority and the Bonneville Power Authority, are also well known. All five were built to facilitate change; they and many others have served that objective remarkably well, if not exactly in the way initially envisioned.

In contrast, most attempts to use public authorities to retard change, for example by rehabilitating decayed canal or port structures with the objective of bringing traffic back to the area, have been notable failures. Buffalo provides a good, if obscure, example. In the early fifties Buffalo ceased to be an important place for the trans-shipment of grain for flour milling and export as the mills were moved closer to Midwestern grain markets and as barge transit down the Mississippi to the redeveloped port at New Orleans became an increasingly feasible alternative to the older route to East Coast ports via freighter through the Great Lakes and rail thereafter. An increasingly decrepit and inactive waterfront mirrored the decline of Buffalo's milling and trans-shipment activities, and so, a port authority was created to make the port more attractive. Soon thereafter the failure of the local surface transportation company brought the change of the port authority into a more general transportation authority that took over airport operations as well. Forty years later the result of these actions by law is instructive: a modest, but cheerful airport survives on landing fees; a surprisingly pleasant local transportation system limps along, despite significant grant-based investment, as ridership decline follows population decline; and the port is still sad to see. It can't possibly be rehabilitated because there is little reason for anyone to use it as lake freighter-dependent industry slowly disappears. So, almost no fee income is generated that might fund rehabilitation.

A second context for examining law's response to smaller scale economic change is in threats to regulatory investments, characteristically made as part of the legacy of various New Deal economic recovery programs. Tied to associationalism as they were, the New Deal economic programs tended to think of business relationships as static and so favored dividing markets in ways that, although they did not guarantee that profits would be made, did allow all existing participants to compete in gentlemanly ways within industry segments while keeping potential competitors happy with similarly protected hunks of the overall economic "turf." This policy is most obviously evident in the banking, insurance, and securities industries. It is also prominent in communications and transportation and can be seen in agricultural programs as well.

The associationalist assumptions underlying economic policies in areas such as these create particular problems when the affected industries find that economic change, sometimes technological, at other times cost driven, undermines the assumed static structure of competition. This is because over time this structure becomes built into the valuation of existing investments and leads to making further investments whose value is similarly dependent on the existing industry structure. How to unravel these investments fairly has bedeviled law for the past half-century. Two examples should suffice.

American agricultural policy, like the postwar agricultural policy of other major European and Asian industrial states, is an incredible mess. Here, the New Deal agricultural policy trio of ascertainably rational but practically ineffective production controls – predicated on acreage under cultivation rather than total yield, crop subsidies that sustained the most depressed segments of the increasingly irrelevant agricultural past, and modest soil conservation programs – has persisted despite generations of otherwise withering critique and through a period of extraordinary declines in the farm population and a technologically driven explosion in per acre productivity derived from increased use of expensive fertilizers, farm machinery, and hybrid crops. Although it is surely plausible that were the Senate elected in proportion to population, agricultural subsidies would be withdrawn, it seems to me that the continuing program less reflects the constitutional rule giving each state, regardless of population, two senators than it does the difficulty of withdrawing subsidies once they have been built into the fabric of economic assumptions that are farm valuation.

To withdraw subsidies imperils farm income, which imperils farm mortgages (and so ownership), which imperils farm mortgage lenders, a narrow, local branch of lending. Thus, what may be a rational economic plan for ending subsidies that in the long run may benefit agriculture and the entire national economy creates short-run problems that are extremely painful and threaten the owners of the existing farms, agricultural cooperatives, and financial institutions as well as farm communities, including not just farm implement dealers and feed, seed, and chemical sellers, but also auto dealers, grocers, schools, churches, and restaurants. Lacking the political will to buy existing beneficiaries out of their subsidies through a program of capital grants, and already having extended governmental guarantees under the program of mortgage insurance offered by Farmer Mac, the only politically palatable solution is hobbling along under an endlessly adjusted, obviously defective program.[4]

The tangled story of the transformation of the segmented worlds of banking, insurance, and securities provides a modest counterpoint to the difficulties with agricultural policy. The continuing breakdown of the segmented structure of these industries can be told either as a case of domestic insurgency, as each of these industries tried to escape from the straitjacket that was established during the Depression in the name of restoring confidence in the financial system, or as a case of a foreign insurgency, as the availability of more attractive foreign investments over times led to the unraveling of the New Deal financial order. And yet, rather than do nothing, as if the insurgent were domestic, or provide transitional support, as if the insurgent were foreign, law's response in almost all cases was to expand the powers of the institution whose separate protected sphere was threatened by financial innovation.[5]

Here again the long-standing set of economic controls created a set of investments whose value was significantly determined by the structure of regulation. Trying, though not necessarily succeeding, to maintain relative parity between industry segments was a response that served to protect the relative, though hardly the absolute, value of these regulatorily based investments. Thus, attempts to alter the income tax treatment of mutual as against stock insurance companies, where mutuals possessed a significant advantage, were never successful, but a change in the investment powers of one regularly led to a change in the investment powers of the other. Similarly, in the segmented world of banking, branching by commercial

---

[4] The recent case of tobacco acreage allotments is hardly an example to the contrary, for it took years of health concerns, unlikely to be reproduced elsewhere in agriculture, to overcome political opposition to such a "bailout."

[5] The case of the deregulation of interstate trucking under the Motor Carriers Act is to the contrary. I cannot explain why.

and by mutual savings banks grew approximately apace, though in the former case most often by merger and in the latter case because of the legal form, most often by building new offices. The same is true of change across industry segments. Banks became able to sell securities only when securities firms were able to offer bank-like services through money market "wrap" accounts that allowed check-writing privileges.

Of course, the most notorious examples of such attempts to maintain the relative value of regulatorily founded investments is the interaction between commercial banks and savings and loan associations – the savings and loan crisis, discussed previously. It began with the development of money market funds in the securities industry that drew deposits from a banking industry that was limited by law as to the interest it could pay on deposits. Eliminating these limits, the initial response, exposed the fact that the greater range of loans that commercial banks could enter into meant that they could earn more interest than could savings and loans that were limited to making residential mortgage loans. And so, these restrictions were lifted. An unpleasant cascade of events followed such well-intentioned actions.

A third context for examining law's response to smaller scale change can be identified by emphasizing certain social regularities in law's actions. Indeed, some would say that law nearly always allows the capitalists to win. This notion, coming largely out of labor relations where it has some real bite, is more difficult to support in circumstances where law confronts economic change more generally. In such circumstances capital and labor, employers and employees, stand on both sides of the issue that law faces – favor old capital and labor or new. Each has a claim to law's attention – the old, because of ties to the existing community; the new, because of its asserted but unprovable place in the economic future.

As is evident from my story of economic change and from the preceding analysis, at least in the short twentieth century, law has tended to favor new capital, and derivatively new labor, because dreams are easier to spin than realities are to dress up. At times law does this by providing some transitional support for the past while facilitating a seemingly brighter future. At other times, not even transitional support is provided. However, there is a regularity, an identifiable pattern of winners and losers among those whose lives and fortunes are altered by smaller scale economic change. Not surprisingly, most often law is more effective when offering transitional support to capital than to labor.

Examples are reasonably easy to identify. Consider, again, autos and steel. In both of these industries capital and labor received approximately the same protection from foreign competition. Indeed, labor arguably received more favorable treatment in that pension guarantee legislation extends protection to human capital that is unavailable to investment capital. Yet, there is no great record of poor, demoralized stockholders in either the auto or steel industries as there is of poor, demoralized employees in those industries who never made it to retirement before their jobs disappeared. The reason is simple. The time horizon of capital, especially financial capital, but also bricks and mortar capital, is shorter that that of labor. Moreover, capital can diversify more readily to reduce risk. A working life is forty to fifty years and retraining to build new human capital investments becomes increasingly difficult after fifteen to twenty of those years. In contrast, a long horizon for the recovery of a capital investment is surely those same fifteen and twenty years, at which point dis- and re-investment are substantially easier. And over the last twenty years of the short twentieth century, the mean time horizon for capital recovery has surely shortened. Of course, capital losses in the early years before recovery is had are common, indeed more common than long-term recovery. And everyone who studies industry carefully has discovered stories of capital loss after long- term recovery that are every bit as devastating to the individual entrepreneur as are similar job losses to individual laborers. But in many, perhaps, most cases, capital has more accumulated assets to fall back on, and so equal treatment of human capital is anything but.

VI. A MODEST CONCLUSION

How then might the complex relationship between law and economic change, the change from an associationalist to an impatient economy, in the short twentieth century be summarized? Although law contributes little to such large-scale change, again the great silent background of law that structures economic relations needs to be emphasized. Common assumptions about economic life under capitalism that are formalized as the rules of contract, tort, and property do their silent work. And as the winds of change blow and calm, so too do the institutions of law, including those that are commonly described as political, working as they do modestly to speed up change, to augment the prevailing winds.

What then of the more active work of law, work carried on with respect to smaller scale change? Description of law's response to the winds of change in terms of the great battle between laissez-faire and regulation that figures so prominently in the political rhetoric of both the left and the right in America is clearly inappropriate. In general, law favors neither position, but most commonly, but rather unsystematically, attempts to facilitate change by modestly retarding it. As it does so, it tends to be willing to respond more readily to economic harm suffered at the hands of foreign "invaders" of the allegedly national economic "turf" than of the domestic invaders of an individual industry's "turf." It pays more attention to segments of the economy whose powers, or the value of whose investments, are dependent on law. Overall, it is more solicitous of new capital and labor than old, but even here, more to the harms suffered by capital than by labor. None of this ought to be surprising. Law, like other human institutions, works most often by half-steps that affirm the past while moving cautiously into the present and hiding from the future. Americans, like most humans, are notoriously xenophobic, however much they love their imported DVD players. And the United States is a capitalist, though hardly a free market capitalist, and definitely not a social democratic, economy.

VII. CODA

Readers have asked that I explain more precisely what I mean by "law" and so its relationship to "society" and "the/an economy," as well as to flesh out the metaphor of the "loosely woven fabric." I can do none of these things, but my readers deserve an explanation for that fact.

Karl Llewellyn was fond of speaking of "law/government" as a way of eliding the separation of "law" from "politics," a separation that he believed to be unhelpful for analysis. I would be comfortable following his lead by eliding my definitional problems through the use of the cognates "law/society" and "law/economy," as I firmly believe that neither dichotomy is useful for understanding the subject I am trying to explicate (or any other subject either.) Unfortunately, I have learned that readers do not always accept such neologisms, as the soundless sinking of Llewellyn's makes clear. I am fully aware that his academic profile was far higher than mine. So, I have largely resisted doing what would be comfortable for me and have decided to work within the only language that I have, a language in which "law" by definition is neither "the/an economy" or "society," no matter how much I may wish them to be seen as deeply, inextricably intertwined.

In the vain attempt to avoid this aspect of "the prison-house of language," I have chosen to leave "law" and "an economy" but weakly demarcated (see italicized explanations offered at the outset of this chapter). I do not use "society" at all and leave "the economy" to a usage close to the rise and fall of the level of economic activity as well as the order and chaos experienced by participants in economic activity. In doing so, I have been able to focus on change in the form of, which is to say our understanding of, capitalism over time. By thus cabining usage I can present "law" and "an economy" as inseparable, except when analysis in the English language makes it impossible to avoid a usage that might imply to the contrary.

I have tried to bridge the gap between my understanding of the relationship between law and the/an economy and the usage available to me with a metaphor of the "loosely woven fabric." I like this metaphor because, if one pulls at too many threads in a loosely woven fabric, it rather quickly becomes a pile of thread and not a fabric at all. It is for this reason that I have not developed this metaphor extensively. Doing so would turn it into a pile of separate but entangled observations about "law" and "the/an economy" and it is just such a jumble that the metaphor is designed to avoid.

I hope that readers have been able to be patient with the locutions I have adopted. Until we have a language that allows for the suppression of dichotomies such as law and politics, law and society, law and economy, such is the best that this writer can do.

17

THE CORPORATE ECONOMY: IDEOLOGIES OF REGULATION AND ANTITRUST, 1920–2000

GREGORY A. MARK

At the end of World War I, the United States stood as the combatant state least bloodied, its economy not drained but stimulated by the conflict. It had become, and had become recognized, as an engine of production for the globe. Moreover, the requirements of mobilization for the war had given the federal government the opportunity, born of seeming necessity, to rationalize, or at least to organize, and thereby regulate, aspects of the economy it had not touched since the Civil War, if even then. The wartime actions seemed to consolidate a trend that had been in place since the last decade of the nineteenth century, a trend toward recognition of an integrated national economy embodied in the growth of the administrative state.

As events would turn out, the growth of America's administrative state, if relentless in retrospect, seemed at the time a great deal less certain – even to its most ardent advocates. The development of an integrated national economy was itself a phenomenon that was only dimly perceived. The tradition of state and local regulation of economic matters was deeply ingrained. The constitutional embodiment of the country's federal structure seemed to bar the creation of most national regulatory structures. The troubles of the integrated and continental economic empire seemed, in any case, only sporadically to call for national regulatory solutions. The very idea of national solutions seemed not just alien, but an idea with unwelcome foreign associations. Finally, the country's limited experience with national regulation was not such that it inspired automatic confidence.

Nevertheless, the seeds, at least, of the modern American regulatory state had long been planted. The absence of a centralized regulatory structure did not mean, as many scholars and political commentators have observed, that the country lacked regulation, that it was and had long been the province of commercial and industrial plunderers. Indeed, though the absence of centralized national power over the economy was part of the conceit that the U.S. government itself lacked the accoutrements of state authority, the American economy had long been subject to regulation. At least on the books, the country had a tradition of regulation that was not merely robust but pervasive. That tradition included regulation of the market. It did not disappear after the Civil War so much as it was overwhelmed by the novel difficulties of continental development.

The states had always chartered the country's businesses. Through those charters the states had attempted to limit their size and scope of operations. Augmenting the charters themselves was state and local regulation of business activities, whether conducted by chartered corporations or not. States and localities promulgated a myriad of licensing requirements. Their courts developed a thick common law governing institutional behavior. The statutory and common law schemes were sometimes clumsy, but were neither simple nor naive; they governed with a sophisticated array of incentives as well as punishments. Moreover, should the coaxing and cosseting of statutes, ordinances, and courts fail, the states retained not simply traditional common law antitrust powers, but also the ultimate power of *quo warranto*, the power to take back an institution's charter if the case could be made to a competent court. Finally, of course, market discipline itself limited the power of business to misbehave in some spheres while encouraging it in others. The commonly told tale of laissez-faire American capitalism in the late nineteenth century is, in short, both false and misleading and complicates any understanding of the twentieth-century development of the corporate economy and its regulatory state, however much it might accurately capture the lack of centralized authority.

From the end of World War I until the 1970s, the United States was forced to come to terms with its newly transcontinental and integrated economy, one largely beyond the power of any jurisdiction beneath the federal level to police by itself. Problems that had once seemed quintessentially local manifested themselves as cross-border difficulties. Sometimes the difficulties were obvious, as in the problems posed by air and water pollution. Other times the difficulties were subtler, involving products produced in one jurisdiction being sold in another – the problem that, for example, early announced itself in licentious literature to the consternation of local and later national authorities. Subtlest of all were the difficulties posed to a national economy by the simple existence of state regulation in a union that allowed free migration, not just of persons, but of businesses themselves, and not simply in their nominal location but in the actual location of plants and other facilities.

The multiplicity of jurisdictions once extolled by Justice Louis Brandeis for its capacity to create state-by-state laboratories of regulatory experimentalism soon seemed much less attractive to others, including most legal scholars. Multiplicity forced states to compete to retain businesses, giving away the regulatory store in a corrupt bargain to retain firms, their facilities, and their jobs and taxes. Only late in the century did some scholarly observers begin suggesting that this competition was largely salutary; others noted that it tended to ignore the potential of federal regulation. Should the competition become too pernicious, inflicting excessive damage on either the citizenry or the firms, the federal government could come to the aid of either the citizenry (the happy version of the story) or the firms (the less happy version, known as regulatory capture). What had developed, it appeared, was a system of overlapping and at times competing authority.

Sometimes a tug of war among the states and sometimes between states and the federal government, this system of overlapping authority also handed some states a kind of de facto national power. If attractive enough, a jurisdiction could become the nation's home for some aspect of the corporate economy, as Delaware did for incorporation or New York for insurance. If big enough on its own economic terms, a state could set a national standard simply because no firm could afford to ignore a large and lucrative market. By the last quarter of the century California exemplified this possibility, especially in its controls on auto emissions. Texas was not far behind, flexing its muscles to ensure that no publisher of school books ignore the Texan understanding of, for example, the manner in which American history should be taught to primary and secondary school students. In coming to terms with the corporate economy and its regulation, therefore, the famous argument of Willard Hurst that one should pay attention not simply to the controlling aspects of state action, but its facilitating and participating actions, rang at least as true in the twentieth as in the nineteenth century.

Hurst's telling insight requires that any retrospective understanding of the regulatory state in the twentieth century acknowledge the citizenry's fundamental ambivalence about an economy grown gargantuan, with concomitant private economic institutions, and the power necessary to control such an economy and its institutions. Americans, notwithstanding a not insignificant strand of thought concerned with the enervating and corrupting pursuit and obtaining of wealth, liked their prosperity and were loathe to risk it, certainly not to a self-aggrandizing state. Thus, as Hurst repeatedly noted, the American legal structure reflected a tension between law that regulated an economic institution's power to exploit and law that facilitated the entrepreneur's ambitions, sometimes through direct subsidy but more often by creating the pre-conditions for growth and then stepping back to leave the entrepreneur a relatively free hand. That tension defines the corporate economy of the twentieth century.

I. THE PREHISTORY OF THE CORPORATE ECONOMY
AND THE ADMINISTRATIVE STATE

The Civil War demonstrated that, however rich the United States was in aggregate, it was not a fully national economy, but really a set of cooperating regional economies among which capital, labor, and goods flowed – by comparison with the rest of the world – quite freely. The country's fleeting Hamiltonian experiment in national banking had long passed, yet there were no real restrictions other than the physical on the exchange of capital within the national borders. For many years after the war, however, only the country's railroad corporations hinted at the continental economy to come, and even the transcontinental railroad was the product of two cooperating, not one unified, enterprises. The postal service was the only truly national enterprise, and it was an arm of the government. But the mails served up the first hints of the difficulties a national and integrated economy would pose to the country's regulatory tradition. Before the war, when abolitionists mailed their literature throughout the country, it was the states that responded and attempted to squelch its spread. After the war, when publishers responded to local attempts to quash the production of and market for scurrilous and obscene publications by using the postal service to deliver their works across state lines, it became apparent that the states, although not powerless to regulate those acts, were just not very effective. Similarly, it was the postal service that facilitated the development of a national retail economy through the commercial vehicle of catalogs. Local merchants were, ultimately, powerless to thwart such competitors through local restrictions. But these harbingers of national enterprise had only limited impacts. They did not seem to challenge the regulatory preeminence of the states. They invaded the states' police powers over health, safety, and morals only at the edges.

By the end of the nineteenth century the edges were worn thin. The rapid consolidation of manufacturing enterprises, such as oil companies, the bankruptcy reorganization of the railroads by investment banking firms seeking to rationalize over-capacity, and the emergence of nationwide telephonic and telegraphic services and other corporate combinations transformed the American market economy. Monopolies and oligopolies, some shaky and others more robust, had replaced many small and local firms throughout the economy. The effects of production and manufacturing, once largely dispersed, became quite concentrated. The economy in many areas had become effectively national in scope. The combination of manufacturing and transportation efficiencies allowed the production of meat, for example, to be centralized in a few locations. Refrigeration and railcars meant that huge central stockyards and slaughterhouses replaced localized butchering. Work was de-skilled as precursors to the assembly line replaced individual labor, giving a worker a few simple tasks to be repeated rather than a more complicated process to be mastered.

Since the work took place at a great remove from ultimate consumers, its deleterious effects could more easily be masked and hidden. A cut of meat that produced sickness in a consumer was no longer a problem to be resolved locally, simply by switching butchers or complaining to the local magistrate about unhealthy products or conditions. In a mass market, simply switching products no longer guaranteed safety, for product branding and integrated production meant that finding out who or what was responsible was difficult. Even if one could find out that information, how could one avoid a producer with huge market share or a tainted process employed by most producers beyond the inspection of the consumer? Traditional legal remedies were of little use as one jurisdiction could not effectively exercise its authority beyond its own boundaries, even if it wanted to. Both market and law were compromised in the creation of the mass national economy.

And the economy had become mass. It was urban. As Frederick Jackson Turner famously noted, the frontier closed in the last decade of the nineteenth century, meaning that more people lived in areas denominated urban than rural by the census takers. Even if that definition was a bit rough, it was clear that the urban areas of the Atlantic coast – New York City, Boston, and Philadelphia – were being augmented by booming Midwestern and Western cities, such as Saint Louis, Cleveland, Chicago, and San Francisco. These population concentrations provided thick markets for mass-produced products. Just as concentration posed difficulties for a traditional system of law that relied on local authority to deal with problems of production and consumption, it equally posed problems of distribution. Opportunities for chicanery grew as dealing between producer and consumer became mediated by a growing number of wholesalers, jobbers, advertisers, financing agents, and retailers.

A mass national market also created a dynamic and innovative culture that bred demand for products never seen before. Although the expansion of the market economy of the late nineteenth century was centered in heavy industry, such as iron and steel mills supplying track for railroads, by the first quarter of the twentieth century the individual consumer had come to play a new role. If the railroads were the great consumer of industrial production in the nineteenth century, in the twentieth it was the individual. For example, an entirely new industry developed with the individual consumer as the ultimate purchaser: the automobile industry. No twentieth-century industry would play a larger role in changing the American legal landscape. What the railroads were to the nineteenth-century lawyer, automotive culture was to the lawyers of the twentieth. Problems of consumerism and managerialism created entire new legal worlds.

The emergence of a national market dominated by a limited number of large firms in the most important sectors of the economy also complicated the legal relations of individuals in ways that challenged the competence of traditional lawmaking bodies. Even if judges and lawyers could comprehend, for example, that a corporation had a separate legal existence from its managers and owners, how should they react when owners complained that managers took actions that harmed the corporation and ultimately their ownership interests? Owners no longer exercised much direct control in these enterprises. They supplied capital, but beyond that the traditional indicia of ownership seem to have evaporated. And what legal responsibility fell on those who did exercise the power traditionally exercised by owners? How could a legal community trained in the tenets of an individualistic law adapt its forms to these collective entities? What respect should be given to managerial decisions and why? Were the forms of an individualistic legal culture even appropriate to a type of ownership so disembodied and dispersed that a dissatisfied owner of a share of a corporation was almost always better off simply selling and then investing capital elsewhere than in exercising what legal rights to discipline managers he or she had?

If the courts lacked the competence to fashion legal tools sufficient to assist in controlling the new economy, what of the legislatures? The traditional tension between facilitating economic activity by chartering corporations and regulating their behavior to make the most of their economic and social utility was even more acute as the markets for securities became ever larger and more sophisticated in the twentieth century. If the point of a securities market was to channel capital into its best uses, how best to ensure that the market made the best uses apparent, especially because the more liquid the market the less individual equity owners had an incentive to control perverse managerial behavior rather than simply sell their shares?

In the three decades before the end of World War I, the states and the federal government did not sit idly by as the economy transformed itself. In the 1890s, New Jersey tipped the balance decidedly in favor of a corporate law that facilitated the growth of large enterprises through combination. In addition it enacted the first of what became known as enabling statutes, giving managers great freedom to deploy corporate resources. Although consolidating enterprises were slow at first to take up the New Jersey opportunity, corporate consolidation took place through other vehicles, such as the trust (hence the name antitrust given to the acts of consolidation's opponents). When those firms took up New Jersey's offer, largely after the marketing efforts of one enterprising lawyer named James B. Dill, the state quickly established itself as the nominal home to America's large corporations. That is, they incorporated in New Jersey to take advantage of its law governing the relationship among shareholders, managers, and the corporate entity, but continued to operate largely in other jurisdictions. Only when Woodrow Wilson, in a fit of political embarrassment, persuaded the New Jersey legislature to repeal much of the enabling code did the state relinquish its role as capital of corporate America. Delaware took immediate advantage of New Jersey's Wilsonian ethics and enticed many of the largest New Jersey corporations to abandon the state and reincorporate in Delaware. This they promptly did, never looking back. New Jersey, stung by the betrayal of its corporate subjects (and the loss of incorporation revenue), immediately tried to bring them back by reintroducing a facilitating code, but to no avail. Delaware was, however, a more trustworthy home: not only was its legislature willing to adapt its corporate code but it also possessed a court system (its Chancery Court) ready to keep its law predictable.

The sheer size of the entities formed in the early 1890s generated huge public concerns about their exercise of market power. Concern extended both to consumer welfare and, more inchoately, to the dangers to a way of life that an ever more relentless commodification of daily affairs threatened. Business managers, overwhelmingly economic rationalists, had merely sought stability – a stability born of market control best achieved by monopolization or cartelization. When states proved ineffective in controlling the size of entities (because they could simply change their legal form and their legal home – from Ohio trust to New Jersey corporation, for example), the federal government tried to step in. The Sherman Antitrust Act (1890) attempted to deploy national authority in such matters for the first time. The results were decidedly mixed, in part because of constitutional limits placed on the act by the federal courts. While the enterprises rarely succeeded for any length of time in achieving monopoly power – the markets were simply too fluid and dynamic, the barriers to entry too easy to surmount – they stayed huge. Though their effects on consumer welfare were blunted by their inability to exercise monopoly power in the long term, they nevertheless undermined the localism that the act was meant in part to protect. Even the advent of the antitrust authority of the Federal Trade Commission two decades later did little to blunt the trend toward large integrated firms with great market power.

The failure of state regulation to police some of the worst aspects of industrial development also seemed to create a momentum in favor of federal regulation. For example, the Food and Drug Act (1906), which had languished in Congress in one form or another for some time, was enacted and signed into law after the publication of Upton Sinclair's *The Jungle*. The novel's graphic descriptions of the unsanitary and dangerous production of meat catalyzed an otherwise lethargic federal government. Sinclair had, as his later political career as a socialist candidate for office in California suggests, loftier ambitions – he sought wholesale systemic change. These ambitions were, of course, unrealized. Moreover, his literary contemporaries, known as muckrakers, were far less successful than he in inspiring reformist legislation. Exposure in journalistic venues of the dark side of the corporate economy by Lincoln Steffens and Ida Tarbell, for example, fell far short of the successes achieved by Sinclair. Federal incorporation of large business entities was a topic much discussed, but nothing came of it. The use of antitrust actions waxed and waned. Save for the creation of the Federal Reserve, accomplished like the Bank some one hundred years earlier as an off-the-books entity closely connected to the federal government, the federal government created few new bodies that involved themselves in the day-to-day life of Americans.

World War I had the potential to change the country's view of the role of government. During the conflict the federal government mobilized industry in giant ship-building efforts, employed manufacturing entities to turn out the huge quantity of munitions needed to undergird the Allied war effort, and the like. Most dramatically and with the thinnest of legal authority, the president effectively nationalized the railroads and interstate water transportation systems in the name of rationalizing the systems of transportation to alleviate potential bottlenecks. These radical alterations in the normal pattern of the industrial and commercial economy might have had a legitimating effect on the role of the federal government's participation in the economy. They did not. To the contrary, the postwar era marked a reversion in the federal system to reliance on the states, at least in most economic matters.

II. THE ROARING TWENTIES

The end of World War I and Woodrow Wilson's exit from office were prelude to a decade in which the public imagination was subordinated to that of the private sphere. The American economy, undamaged by war and unencumbered by reparations, entered a lengthy period of growth. The automobile industry, which in the pre-war period was only beginning to lose the helter-skelter characteristics of a developing industry, became fully mature. Ford Motor Company, the dominant single factor in the industry and still under the control of its founder, faced the emerging power of General Motors. In 1923 General Motors came under the managerial control of Alfred P. Sloan. If Henry Ford is credited with actually putting into practice the machinery of assembly-line mass production, then it certainly is Sloan who deserves the credit for creating the consumer-market-controlling bureaucratic corporation. Sloan took the automobile conglomerate that was

General Motors and gave component companies responsibility for creating vehicles for overlapping market segments defined by income and wealth. He brought advertising, market analysis, and financing together in service to the producing sub-entities. If entrepreneurs and managers in the 1890s had sought to tame the market by eliminating competitors or by agreeing on how much to produce and sell, then Sloan sought to tame the market by analyzing it, breaking it down into its minute fragments, and creating niches and techniques that tied customers to the products of the corporation. By the early 1930s General Motors had surpassed Ford in the American market.

GM's strategies and processes seemed to create fewer problems, and thus called for less public scrutiny, than the seemingly crude tactics of the earlier decades. Perhaps, as Hurst has also trenchantly observed, so long as the corporate entity produces prosperity, its existence and actions are legitimated in a way that renders more direct public control illegitimate.

Consumerist prosperity characterized the decade. Suburban America, enabled by the automobile, took a central place in America between actual cities and the towns throughout the country. The telephone and radio created their own huge corporate bodies, the American Telephone and Telegraph Corporation succeeding in both rationalizing and monopolizing telephonic communication in private hands. Radio, too, remained in private hands, spawning giant broadcasting networks as well as independent stations throughout the country. From a trivially small number of stations at the beginning of the decade, radio stations multiplied rapidly so that they numbered in the hundreds by mid-decade. Whereas telephone service was rationalized in private hands and its rates subjected to the traditional regulation of natural monopolies, radio broadcasters threatened to invade each other's broadcasting bands at every turn. Ultimately the Federal Radio Commission was created in 1927 and given the task, among other things, of licensing broadcasting stations to bring some order to broadcasting.

Each form of regulation resulted in, as later decades were to make clear, consequences that the regulators never foresaw. Rate regulation of telephone service created, for example, a pattern of cross-subsidization that facilitated service to remote rural areas and made long-distance telephone service possible but kept local service relatively expensive. The method of broadcast licensing adopted in 1927 did not distinguish between densely populated urban areas, with their rich advertising markets, and sparsely populated rural areas, where advertising dollars were scarce and thus service more limited.

Markets for other goods and services remained largely unregulated, which meant that they were regulated only by extant market forces or remained regulated at the state or local level. Utilities, for example, were sometimes owned by private corporations, sometimes by localities. In either case their rates were controlled. Entire industries, such as motion pictures, largely escaped formal federal regulation. But local censors, and sometimes state censors, did act. Most of the new enterprises that catered to the consumer, however, were not regulated at all. If, for instance, radio broadcasters were licensed by the Radio Commission, the producers of radios were not. Creating no fears among the public, celebrated rather than suspect, the production of much of the corporate economy directed toward the ultimate consumer went largely untouched.

Had the antitrust statutes been construed more broadly or had public sentiment taken a different direction, a greater formal public role in the corporate economy could have been possible. The U.S. Supreme Court had earlier limited the reach of the Sherman Act in *Standard Oil v. United States* (1911). In that case the Court famously announced a "rule of reason," which meant that the Sherman Act could not be employed to attack corporations simply because they were big. However threatening size was by itself to the mores and attitudes of society, its habits and culture, or its values, the Sherman Act would apply only to corporations whose size and acts were "unreasonable." That is, it would apply when the actions of the corporation actually harmed or threatened to harm, and harm came to mean economic harm. In 1920, after the United States brought an action against the United States Steel Corporation, a leviathan of heavy industry and the product of years of amalgamation of lesser corporate entities, the Court applied the rule of reason and found that the corporation, though large, had not engaged in unreasonable behaviors. Whatever localist sentiment that had, at least in part, animated those who brought the act into being had been stripped from the law. The comparatively genteel General Motors and its kin were, for the time being, safe from antitrust scrutiny under the act.

If the Sherman Act represented a failed attempt to preserve localist American values through federal action, the preservation of those values tended to manifest itself in the postwar period in resistance to federal intervention in the economy generally. The country's attitude toward intervention was hardly historically uniform. Over time it had vacillated. Public action in the private sphere, at least at the federal level, even when facilitative, was often viewed suspiciously by the public at large or, at least, by large and vocal segments of the public. At one end of the spectrum lay federal actions in support of building the transcontinental railroad, which the public had celebrated (until its associated corruption became too evident). At the other lay the specter of the national bank, feared for its corrupting effects. Prosperity, of course, lowered demand for intervention generally. Finally, the existence of an alien ideology, threatening to a market economy in theory, had materialized in the shape of the Soviet Union. Opponents of state intervention seized every opportunity to align interventionists with the alien ideology. The confluence of these forces – embedded historical legacy, well-being, and the happenstance of a foreign socialist revolution – made federalizing even the traditional regulatory powers exercised at local levels exceedingly unlikely.

Formal state intervention was, however, not the only form of market control possible. Nor was it the only form of regulation possible. Private organizations could and did exercise public power. Sometimes the exercise of public power in private hands was done to ward off both the formal and informal exercise of public power. The motion picture industry banded together in an industry association in 1922 so that the studios might police themselves. Not exactly an act of cultural altruism, rather a response to scandal, the association was headed by Will Hays, who had previously headed Warren Harding's presidential campaign. He attempted to persuade the studios to curb some of the film industry's perceived excesses and to follow certain moral guidelines. The animating rationale was to avoid formal censorship. Although not successful in codifying a code of production until the following decade, the association's actions were representative of a clear pattern – self-policing allowed an industry to suggest that formal regulation was unnecessary. Of course, the movie industry also faced a far more powerful cultural regulator in the form of the Catholic Church. The Church was not, obviously, invested with formal authority. But, its reach and authority were formidable. Censorship by a board of duly empowered citizens in some small town was one thing, the potential loss of an audience of millions of Catholic filmgoers quite another. The industry's response to the exercise of local formal power as well as informal private power suggests a phenomenon of the corporate economy that has largely been unexplored by scholars of law, that of private rulemaking.

We should not assume that the phenomenon was a limited one. The 1920s are known, correctly, for the vast expansion of the country's securities markets. Equally known is that those markets were not regulated by the federal government. States traditionally regulated the relationship between investors and the entities they invested in through traditional common law mechanisms of fiduciary duty. States had, however, also begun to expand their regulatory roles through more direct avenues. Even before the 1920s expansion of the securities markets, for instance, Kansas enacted what became known as "Blue Sky Laws," requiring a corporation to file information about the corporation's operations before its shares could be sold in that state. Other states followed.

What is less known is the role that private organizations had in creating transparency in securities markets and directly regulating the market for securities. The New York Stock Exchange, for example, had for more than twenty years required its listed companies to file financial reports with the exchange. In the twenties it established an agency to deal with securities fraud. It tried to give shareholders a more effective voice by altering the shareholder voting portions of its listing rules. The question for students of regulatory history, of course, is why the listed corporations would ever have agreed to such rules since they impinged on the autonomy of the entity and managerial prerogatives within it. As with the motion picture industry, the motives were entirely mixed.

The exchange served several valuable functions for listed corporations. First and foremost, of course, it provided a location where those seeking to invest capital and the entities needing capital knew they could meet, reducing the cost of seeking one another out. The exchange itself, however, had an institutional rationale for attempting to ensure that the listing companies were honest and transparent – no capitalist would hand capital over to an entrepreneur in a market that was untrustworthy. Or, more appropriately, that reticence would be manifest in two other ways. First, those with capital would charge higher rates for the risk of dealing with the dishonest lurking among the honest; second, they would seek a market that helped ensure a higher degree of honesty; or third, they would do both. Listing companies, of course, sought the cheapest capital, hence an exchange with a good reputation. The listing companies, however, always were conflicted. The need to appear to be an attractive, that is, lucrative, place to invest warred with the need to be a place where one would not be cheated. An unsuccessful but honest company attracted few investors. The exchange also provided other services that made it a useful meeting ground and thus gave it some power to enforce its rules. For example, it created an efficient clearinghouse to facilitate transactions. Moreover, other institutions arose in the decade, institutions that had resources to investigate corporate strength and managerial honesty that were lacking in the vast majority of individual investors.

In 1924 the first mutual fund was chartered in Massachusetts. A mutual fund pools the capital of individual investors and places the investment decisions in the hands of investment professionals, individuals paid to know about corporations and their managers. Similarly, the Teachers Insurance and Annuity Association (TIAA), formed in 1918, began to attract professors from many institutions in the 1920s. Although its investment options were limited, TIAA gave the securities markets another set of eyes professionally paid to evaluate managers and corporations, though neither mutual funds nor TIAA became active critics of managerial or corporate acts. Along, however, with the traditional policemen of the capital markets, underwriters and creditors, such as banks, whose livelihood depended on assessing the risk of investments, these institutions served, at least theoretically, as checks on freebooting corporate managers.

As events were to demonstrate, however, private rulemaking had its limits, even when reinforced by powerful private institutions.

The twenties also were the decade in which Delaware consolidated its place as the legal home to America's corporations. At first glance it might seem as if the existence of dozens of jurisdictions would lead to an efflorescence of corporate laws, giving entrepreneurs a multitude of choices in business forms. In practice that did not happen. While the rush to reincorporate in Delaware has been exaggerated by many, it was true that Delaware eventually became home to the largest portion of the country's largest corporations. Elsewhere, convenience and the limited knowledge of the local bar meant that most small and medium-sized businesses adopted the business forms available in their local jurisdictions. Many states had begun to adopt the codification of partnership law created some years before and now urged on them by the bar's leading lights, but corporate law was where the action really was. And the corporate laws of different jurisdictions resembled each other more than they differed.

In some instances the resemblance was deliberate. West Virginia, for example, tried to out-Delaware Delaware, but to no avail. The phenomenon had less to do with the ambience of Wilmington as opposed to Charleston, though proximity to New York and Philadelphia, among other things, worked to Wilmington's advantage. Nor was it simply that Delaware's opportunism in the face of New Jersey's earlier actions created a unique second chance for a first-mover advantage. Delaware provided two things that, though rarely overtly acknowledged by players in the corporate economy, provided some assurance that incorporation in that state would provide predictability, something that other states could not easily provide. First, Delaware's comparative size worked to its advantage. Because it was a small state, incorporation fees provided a large part of the state's revenues, effectively shifting a large portion of the responsibility for paying for public services from the Delaware citizenry to the shareholders of Delaware corporations and the customers of those corporations, most of whom, obviously, were not residents of the Diamond State. That had also been true of New Jersey, of course, but that state's growth had made incorporation fees somewhat less important as a source of revenue than they had been earlier. Delaware's prospects for industrial and commercial growth, given its size and location, helped ensure that the state would be tied to incorporation fees as a source of revenue. It was in the state's interests, or, more explicitly, in the interests of the state's taxpayers and their elected representatives, not to upset the source of revenue.

Second, given the state's interests in remaining home to America's corporations, it adapted its institutions accordingly. Corporate law is a combination of statutes enabling the existence of corporate bodies and the judicial statements about those bodies, whether based on the statutes or on the common law. The common law of corporations is ensconced in the law of equity. It borrows its jurisprudence from the world of trust law, in which trustees are agents acting for the beneficiaries of the trust. A trustee's duties are policed in equity. In most jurisdictions courts of equity had long been merged with courts of law. New York led the way and other jurisdictions followed. Twentieth-century Delaware, however, had a separate Chancery Court – a great boon for the development of corporate law. Instead of having to appear before a random trial court judge whose docket might be packed with the regular assortment of civil and criminal cases, one could appear before the handful of Vice-chancellors or the Chancellor. Those few had a specialized docket. One could be assured of a relatively speedy hearing before a judiciary intimately familiar with the issues of corporate law. Moreover, as the Chancery Court heard its cases, and given the number of large corporations legally resident in Delaware that meant a large number of cases, the courts had the opportunity to develop a rich case law. A rich and detailed case law meant that corporate lawyers could better counsel their clients. Implicit, of course, and unchallenged until the 1970s, was that the corporations' lawyers would also receive a sympathetic hearing. Thus did Delaware seal its place as the font of law for the corporate economy.

What did that law look like? That is a matter of some controversy among contemporary scholars. For many years scholars and judicial critics characterized Delaware corporate law as the premier example of what happens when individual states compete with one another. These observers suggested that it was a "race to the bottom" and that Delaware won the dubious prize for coming in first. On this view the state and its judiciary abandoned any pretense of protecting shareholders from the depredations of corporate managers, who used the corporate vehicle as a tool for self-enrichment and aggrandizement at the expense of shareholders (and, in so doing, also harmed the public at large by diverting the corporation from its proper economic role). Since the middle of the 1970s, however, some scholars have taken issue with that characterization. The assumed depredations could not have been nearly as serious as claimed, they argue; in fact, the tale is not one of woe at all. Rather, they suggest, the legal organs of the state have continuously balanced the interests of shareholders, who seek to maximize their returns, with the interests of managers, who seek capital for the businesses they manage at the lowest cost, the better to remain at the corporate helm. Any shareholder who believed that the corporation was being managed by people who would steal from shareholders would put capital in the hands of those who were more trustworthy or in corporations chartered in states the laws of which did not enable managerial theft. That is a somewhat happier tale. In its turn, however, it too has been subject to criticism – a story too simple to be true and one, if not belied, at least limited, by the waves of managerial corruption that have regularly surfaced over the century.

Whatever the theoretical explanation for the path(s) of Delaware law, the route traveled is reasonably clear. In the 1920s the paths of Delaware corporate law became clear avenues. The derivative action, the suit in equity in which a shareholder can act in place of the corporation to sue its managers for actions that damage the corporation, was continually reaffirmed as the appropriate tool by which shareholders might police managerial misconduct. The outlines of what constituted misconduct were made much clearer. The Delaware judiciary sharpened the rules governing self-interested transactions, but in sharpening narrowed the definition of self-interest. That self-interest amounted only to a financial self-interest (or the interest of a close family member) unavailable to others became clear. Managerial incompetence, manifest in money-losing decisions, was not enough to ground a suit. Mere negligence was insufficient, though the courts did not focus on the substance of the negligent decision. Rather, they began the process of defining managerial incompetence as failure to adhere to an appropriate process of decision-making. Courts were reluctant to substitute their judgment, or even the judgment of shareholders, for the judgment of corporate managers. The economy needed businesses managed by individuals who could understand and exploit business opportunities, to take appropriate risks with shareholder capital. Corporate managers were risk-takers. Corporate managers were business experts. Judges were neither. Thus developed a rule of deference, in Delaware and elsewhere, that would become known as "the business judgment rule." In brief, it holds that courts will not impose liability on any corporate managers (either the shareholder's elected directors or the senior officers appointed by the directors) for decisions taken in "good faith," meaning after an appropriate process of information-gathering and deliberation, assuming, of course, the mangers did so without any self-interest. These doctrines, while not originating in the twenties, began to take their contemporary form, and the Delaware Chancery was a leader in developing the doctrines. Delaware law had become the nation's corporate law.

III. REBUILDING LEGITIMACY: DEPRESSION AND NEW DEAL

By mid-1929 the economy had begun to sputter. By the fall, calamity struck. Within a couple of years the country was in a deep economic depression along with most of the rest of the commercialized and industrial economies of the world. Active federal intervention in the economy was limited. Franklin Roosevelt, notwithstanding the class traitor rhetoric to which he was and would be subjected, had little interest in any ideological transformation of the country. He was not, however, blinkered in his views of federal power. The corporate economy, stripped of the protection of prosperity, could no longer countenance the fiction that state and local regulation was sufficient to police large enterprises and the markets in which they operated. Nonetheless, it took many years for the federal bureaucracy of the corporate economy to become legitimate. In part, of course, its legitimacy was subject to residual, albeit powerful, political opposition. The turn to national power was neither automatic nor wholesale. Perhaps as important, the activities of the federal government did not bring back the prosperity of the twenties immediately and in some spheres not at all. Thus, federal activity, including regulatory activity, though solidly supported by large Democratic majorities in the House and Senate throughout the 1930s – which in turn reflected solid support for Roosevelt's reformist agenda – was always subject to political and legal challenge from forces of tradition and reaction.

Indeed, when dealing with the corporate economy, and notwithstanding his willingness to indulge occasional populist political rhetoric, as when scourging the "malefactors of great wealth," the administration Roosevelt sat atop often moved as cautiously as it did boldly. Nowhere was this more true than in the administration's attitudes toward antitrust. It did move against large integrated utility holding companies in 1935 with the Public Utility Holding Company Act and also against integrated financial institutions in 1933 with the Glass-Steagall Act, which separated investment banking from commercial banking. But its antitrust activities under the Sherman Act in the early 1930s were neither extensive nor noteworthy. To the contrary, the National Industrial Recovery Act (NIRA) codified a form of cartelization by industry until the Supreme Court declared the act unconstitutional. In the last years of the decade the Temporary National Economic Commission (TNEC) was created to study the problems of the corporate economy. Not surprisingly it apportioned much blame on economic actors, especially the actors in the corporate economy: large businesses. The diagnosis, however, led to no real prescription – at least not one that was adopted.

The real innovation in antitrust policy in the administration, paradoxically, was to confirm the place of large entities within the economy, giving them implicit sanction. Roosevelt appointed Thurman Arnold to head the Antitrust Division of the Department of Justice in 1938, in the year after the TNEC was created. Arnold was an ironic appointee since he had pilloried trust-busting as a pointless, indeed counterproductive exercise, a "ritual" of the modern economy. He was more troubadour of the corporate economy than a confirmed localist. A man who dabbled in nearly every aspect of important twentieth-century lawyering – local politician (Wyoming), law dean (West Virginia), law professor (Yale), big firm insider lawyer (founder of what is now Arnold and Porter), judge (U.S. Court of Appeals for the D.C. Circuit), and more – he fully accepted, albeit with all their warts, that large corporations were a part of the economy and a salutary one at that, given their efficiencies of scale and scope. There is not a little irony, therefore in Arnold's reputation as a "trust buster." He was interested in curbing and channeling corporate behavior and only rarely saw any utility in atomizing corporate entities. His innovation was to threaten corporations with an antitrust action when they misbehaved. But instead of taking them to court and pressing the action, though his unit did so often enough to gain credibility, he would negotiate settlements that either caused a corporation to stop acting in a certain way or, on the other hand, to undertake to police itself in others. These settlements were embodied in consent decrees. The act of negotiating, of course, was not new, nor did consent decrees originate with Arnold's antitrust actions. What was novel was the attention to the remedy; what was legitimating, for the large corporation, was the construction of the remedy. Arnold's Antitrust Division negotiated treaties, not documents of surrender. From the man who understood the modern meaning of corporate personhood better than anyone else in law – he had devoted an edgy, almost satiric, chapter to the personification of the business corporation in one of his best-selling books – this was a powerful acknowledgment that corporations could not simply be acted on, but rather had to be dealt with, if not as entities equal to government, then at least as entities whose existence and legitimacy were beyond effective question.

While the corporatist streak of the New Deal was, perhaps, most evident in the NIRA and in Arnold's actions, none of the administration's forays into corporate law itself suggested any belief that corporations were somehow inherently illegitimate. Indeed, the acts that affected the capital markets most directly were conceived as vehicles to reinvigorate confidence in the institutions that had a role in those markets, not to delegitimate them. Where commercial financial institutions were concerned, for example, the government acted to restore confidence through the Federal Deposit Insurance Corporation (FDIC), established in 1933. The FDIC provided deposit insurance to federally chartered financial institutions, allowing depositors to know that their deposits were secure – up to a certain amount – whether the bank failed or not. The aim, of course, was to encourage individuals to keep their capital in banks, where it could play a part in a credit-based economy, rather than at home, where it would be sterile. Not immediately apparent, however, was the moral hazard presented by all insurance. In this case, the side effect would be to allow banks to lend to riskier borrowers than would otherwise be appropriate because the loss would be covered by insurance. Policing the moral hazard required other regulatory apparatuses within the federally chartered banking world.

More famously, though without touching as many lives as immediately as the actions of the FDIC, the federal government established oversight of securities markets, both equity and debt. Two acts, the Securities Act of 1933 and the Securities Exchange Act of 1934, were designed to help restore investor confidence in the capital markets. They were deliberately crafted to avoid trenching on the traditional equity jurisdiction of the state courts. They were not designed to use federal law to rewrite the relationships among corporate entities, their shareholders, and their managers. Instead, their purpose was to police the market for securities – a matter never properly addressed in traditional fiduciary law. Insider trading, for example, was a conundrum under traditional corporate law. If a corporate manager used proprietary knowledge to buy or sell securities, how had the manager injured the corporation? One could posit that such acts undermined the capacity of the business to raise money by issuing securities, but under existing law courts could not really indicate why that would be so. Investors might feel a palpable sense of unfairness at a manager exploiting information unavailable to the investing community, but what was the causal link between a mere sense of unfairness and unwillingness to buy the corporation's securities? Manipulating the securities markets to cause securities prices to rise or fall based on false or misleading information was one thing, though even that was difficult to assimilate within the prohibitions of fiduciary law. Simply taking advantage of untainted information was quite another. Because securities trades were mediated through the impersonal mechanism of the securities exchanges, the suggestion that an individual insider seller or buyer had somehow deceived the person at the other end of the transaction in violation of a duty owed to that person proved difficult to comprehend under laws of fiduciary conduct. *Caveat vendor* or *emptor*. The Securities Exchange Act was inserted into that breach, prohibiting insider trading in equity securities. (As we shall see, the provisions of the Securities Exchange Act that would eventually become the main weapon against insider trading were those proscribing market manipulation, an outcome made possible in the 1960s by artful judicial construction of the act.)

The 1933 and 1934 acts had separate aims. The 1933 act was, in essence, a full disclosure act. It required that securities sold through means of interstate commerce – any exchange counted automatically, among other vehicles – be subject to registration. The registration process involved disclosure of certain corporate information in a uniform fashion, allowing investors to judge for themselves whether and where to invest. Concomitantly, the act prohibited fraud or deception in the release of that information. Nonetheless, it did not require, indeed it did not allow, the government to offer any opinion on the quality of the corporation or its securities. In that sense it was unlike state Blue Sky laws, which allowed states to prohibit sale of securities based on riskiness. The 1934 act was, by contrast, fundamentally an anti-fraud act. Under it the government might regulate the conduct of those who dealt in interstate securities markets, such as broker-dealers. Later acts, such as the Trust Indenture Act of 1939, which dealt with the public sale of debt securities in more detail than either of the earlier acts; the Investment Company Act of 1940, which brought mutual funds and similar organizations within the ambit of federal regulation; and the Investment Advisers Act of 1940, which, true to its title, regulated those advising investors, all expanded the reach and depth of the federal market regulatory apparatus.

One specific aspect of the regulatory environment created by the New Deal bears mention. The statutes that regulated did not simply create law; they tended to create bureaucracies. The agencies created were not simply empowered to enforce the statute, but usually to create regulations that would give effect to the statute. While hardly novel – this is what being a bureaucratic state meant – the lawmaking bodies posed a question of legitimacy on a scale hitherto unknown at the federal level. The Securities and Exchange Commission (SEC), for example, was given wide-ranging authority to promulgate rules under the statutory authority of the 1933 and 1934 acts, as under the augmenting statutes that followed. The legitimacy of administrative law had long been established, but the degree of discretion accorded the agency under the statute was a far more delicate question. In the case of the SEC, at least, the Congressional (and other) authors tried to be careful, lest they hand political and legal opponents too easy a victory. The legitimacy of the different bureaucracies depended on creating structures that enjoyed sufficient authority actually to be effective, but were sufficiently constrained to run the gauntlet of both political and legal challenges.

As striking as these acts appear in retrospect and as disturbing as they were to the established order, very little of what they embodied was novel. Some of the problems they confronted, such as insider trading, had long been recognized; the inability of traditional mechanisms to resolve the issue was clear. Substantive attempts to regulate securities offerings, for example, had been proposed in Congress long before the Depression. In 1911, proposals had been advanced in Congress to require disclosure of financial information, but failed of enactment. Requirements for disclosure were not novel; they were already part and parcel of Blue Sky laws, as well as of the listing requirements for the New York Stock Exchange. What was new was that these requirements now had federal imprimatur. They could no longer be evaded by doing business in one jurisdiction rather than another. The federalization of the rules governing the capital markets meant a new seriousness, a new understanding that the markets were not playgrounds for speculators but were instruments of a wealth-creation policy sanctioned by the people. The rules now had the authority of the central government behind them, with all the awe and fear that went with it.

Federal securities laws also did not displace existing state law. That was a deliberate choice. In part because the authors of the acts had to contend with powerful questions of constitutionality, they were careful to specify the manner in which their creations dealt with interstate commerce. And then they collectively held their breath – to displace state law would ruffle too many political feathers, from Brandeisians concerned with the corporatist aspects of the New Deal to intransigent corporate managers comfortable with state law, to states with an interest in preserving their role (Delaware was not alone). Hence, the acts contained savings clauses that explicitly preserved a wide role for states, both state statutes and state common law. The specter of nationalizing the law of incorporation was too much, smacked too much of the statist agenda of the European powers, and seemed, moreover, unnecessary. If the academic distinction between regulating intra-corporate affairs, the traditional domain of fiduciary law, and regulating the market for securities, indisputably an interstate phenomenon, could be maintained and fostered in enacted law, then so much the better. The distinction took hold and, more or less, remains intact.

The clever and elegant distinctions wrought to carve out a place for the federal government in policing the market for securities are but one example of the manner in which the battalions of eager lawyers and others sought to create a space for federal action in the corporate economy. The New Deal served to legitimate the federal role in the corporate economy as a matter of politics. Its enactments and the creation of its administrative bodies were the legal embodiments that occupied the space so cleverly defined by the lawyers.

The constitutional legitimacy of the administrative state remained up for grabs for several years. Scholars have endlessly debated the nuances of Commerce Clause jurisprudence in the time between Roosevelt's first election and the country's entry into World War II. But whether a product of the death of old line justices and their replacement with Roosevelt appointees, or of a single switch in a justice's vote, or of the slow grinding of doctrinal adjustment, by the end of the 1930s it was evident that the Supreme Court had stopped – for the time being – tinkering with the economic legitimacy of federal law under the guise of its power to interpret the reach of the Commerce Clause. _Wickard v. Filburn_ (1942), simply confirmed what any good reader of judicial trends could have seen as more or less inevitable.

Interstate commerce was now read so broadly that the power of Congress to lay its collective hand on the economic activity of the country in even its minutest facets was now beyond question. In that case, an Ohio dairy farmer raised wheat in violation of his wheat-growing allotment. He sold none of the grain. Some he fed to his chickens, some he held in reserve for seeds, some of the rest was ground into flour for home consumption. How did his production fall within the power to regulate interstate commerce? Had he not raised the wheat he would have had to buy it; the market for wheat is an interstate market; since he did not have to buy it he decreased demand for wheat, at least by a tiny bit; controlling supply and demand of a product sold in interstate commerce was the aim of the allotments created under federal law; since his production of wheat altered the supply by altering demand, he was in violation of the law and the law itself was a legitimate exercise of the power to control an interstate market. The implications of the case for areas far beyond traditional markets awaited the imaginative exploitation of the legal community. But, within any traditional market – and the corporate economy was composed of nothing but traditional markets – the federal presence passed the constitutional litmus test.

IV. THE EFFECTS OF WAR

World War II, or, more accurately, the demand for goods prompted by the war, more than the reforms of the New Deal, lifted the United States out of the Depression and the insecurity left in its wake. The war that mobilized the entire country, as World War II surely did, had paradoxical effects on the corporate economy. The manufacturing capacity of the country had begun gearing up nearly two years before America's actual entry into the war. Its entry simply accelerated the pace. By war's end the American automobile industry was a colossus, turning out trucks, tanks, jeeps, and other vehicles at unprecedented rates; aircraft production reached into the tens of thousands; merchant ships were being constructed by what amounted to giant assembly lines; naval vessels were produced in such quantities that the American navy dwarfed the pre-war fleet of any combatant state. Moreover, industrial production and innovation went hand in hand. The America of September 1945 was vastly different from the America of September 1941. The country was not simply prosperous; it was overwhelmingly the dominant economic power on earth. Simultaneously, the federal government, which had presided over mobilization and victory, had proved its competence. Likewise, the corporations that had been the vehicles of wartime production had proved theirs. In tandem, government and corporations had organized and directed vast and sprawling empires of production. Both emerged from the war with great confidence in their capacities.

The mobilized state was one of bureaucratic control. The war helped legitimate both the corporations' bureaucracies and the government's. Was industrial, often oligopolistic, production that was characteristic of wartime enterprise a self-regulating model, or did it depend for its efficacy on the controlling hand of the federal government? How much should that hand relax its grip at war's end? The conclusion to that debate was largely foregone; indeed it was presaged by wartime attitudes. Wartime production called, first and foremost, for efficiencies. Any lingering desire to preserve small businesses at the expense of more efficient and larger ones was forgotten. Antitrust in wartime was largely moribund. Corporate misbehavior could be punished more directly. Production and prices were controlled directly, not indirectly through the market. Wartime price and wage controls were pervasive, and the mechanisms necessary to monitor their effect equally pervasive. The controls, however, did not completely eliminate market functions. They often simply drove them underground, often with lasting effects. For example, industry could not augment employees' wages in order to retain workers, but companies could and did create new benefits or greatly expand existing ones. The benefits had real value – employer-sponsored health insurance and pension plans are but two of the most obvious. Although not immediately apparent, of course, these developments would outlast the war and later engender regulatory structures to deal with the control of capital amassed in pension funds, the scope of insurance coverage, and more.

Mobilization also meant immediate regulatory control to ensure that the machinery of production remained active. The hard-won rights of organized labor were curtailed during the war. Job actions were especially limited. In the realm of consumption, meanwhile, where wage and price controls did not sufficient limit or direct behavior, rationing could. In some cases consumer goods were rendered scarce because factories were allocated for war materiel – tanks and planes, not cars, became the products of automobile manufactures. In other cases the rationing was regulatory. Gasoline consumption, for example, was limited, as was consumption of other commodities. The population did not like these most obvious of state controls, and they went by the board almost immediately at war's end, some even in anticipation of its end. But the structures of the New Deal that preceded the war, the ones designed to regulate the corporate economy, remained largely untouched. They survived intact, faced with the challenges of prosperity rather than those of a country trying to regain prosperity.

The SEC, the courts of the states, and the myriad bodies that monitored corporations did not disappear during the war, but their activities paled by comparison with the wartime bureaucracies. The capital markets simply took on a new form. Corporations got the capital they needed to expand for war production through contracts from the government. To the extent that they had to obtain capital on the market, it was available through the implicit guarantee of federal contracts. The SEC did not have to act to build confidence. After the battle at Midway (1942) and certainly before the Normandy landings (1944), confidence in the corporate capacity to produce a decent return on invested capital was apparent. Shareholders, largely secure in their corporation's profits, did little to alter the traditional landscape of fiduciary duty.

In short, notwithstanding complaints about shortages under rationing that manifested themselves in consumer black markets, the civilian population did not suffer during the war. To the contrary, as a matter of consumer economics, it grew in wealth. The bureaucracy of rationing may have contributed to popular resentment of the regulatory state, but it did not bring into question the legitimacy of the administrative state. At war's end, therefore, when American politics turned against state regulation the turn was fairly mild, manifesting itself mainly in areas that affected day-to-day life directly, such as rent control, rationing, price controls, and the like. The notable exception, of course, was in labor relations, but even in that field the administrative state was not dismantled. The Taft-Hartley Act imposed new restrictions on some of organized labor's practices, notably secondary boycotts, but the national Labor Relations Board remained. Of course, neither did the administrative state much extend itself at war's end, at least by way of interposing itself in the economy. Prosperity masked conditions that would otherwise have called for public solutions.

V. THE LONGEST DECADE

For purposes of periodization, the 1950s really began during the demobilization after World War II and did not end until the middle of the 1960s. Postwar recessions are expected. Working-age men flood back into the labor force, swamping available employment opportunities. Wartime demand is artificial, and civilian demand does not match it, at least for some time. Excess industrial capacity will therefore go unused, meaning that demand for goods for production, as opposed to consumption, will also remain slack. And, to be sure, some of the expected actually happened after the war. But several conditions forestalled the most dire predictions.

The great pre-war economies of Europe and Asia were destroyed or hugely damaged by the war. Germany and Japan, of course, were not simply ruined but became the subjects of debate whether they should even be restored as industrial powers. France, Italy, the Netherlands, and other continental economies had been hollowed out. The countries of Eastern Europe were removed, one by one, from the integrated global economy; they too had been rendered hollow. Great Britain, though never invaded, had been sorely taxed. Her empire in tatters, her role as entrepôt thereby cast into doubt, her manufacturing capacity clearly overwhelmed by that of the United States, Great Britain was in a weak position either to create or satisfy demand even had the country not elected a Labor government just before the end of the war that was committed to containing capital.

At the end of World War I, the United States had withdrawn from the world's diplomatic, though not its economic, stage. The carnage of that war, however, was dwarfed by the destructiveness of World War II. After that second war, the United States withdrew from nothing, at least not for very long. The Soviet Union, erstwhile ally, became foe, and rebuilding Western Europe became an act both of economic diplomacy and forward defense. Demand for America's products boomed. Domestic demand, unsatisfied during the war as resources shifted to military rather than civilian wants, shifted them back again. Civilian buying power was fat with years of unspent pay saved in war bonds and in other ways. Demand from abroad supplemented domestic demand. Heavy industry supplied the reemerging industries of Europe; for some time even European consumers were supplied in part from America's production.

Demobilization had been brief and never complete. The specter of hundreds of Red Army divisions poised to sweep into Western Europe meant that American military production soon resumed, though not reaching wartime proportions, as the nation's leaders chose to maintain a standing military of some size. Both the Korean War and the arms races fueled expansion of capital-intensive, technologically driven enterprises. These demands strained even the capacities of America's corporate economy.

Though jurisprudentially significant for other reasons, it is worth remembering in this context that President Harry S Truman ordered the seizure of the country's steel mills during the Korean War because he feared that labor unrest would deprive the economy of a key ingredient necessary for the production of war materiel. Even a casual reading of the opinions in *Youngstown Sheet & Tube Co. v. Sawyer* (1952) poignantly reveals that the conduct of corporate affairs had become completely interwoven with national security. The corporate economy had become thoroughly of a piece with the state, and that conjunction was reflected in many of the issues that animated even the simplest aspects of corporate law.

The twenty years following World War II include the highest points of judicial deference to managerial discretion in the history of corporate law. The slow accretion of case law suggests a strong tilt in this period in favor of managers and away from shareholders. In a reversal of the traditional rhetoric, shareholders and their lawyers became the real threats to the integrity of the corporation and thereby the well-being of the communities they inhabited. Corporate managers, by contrast, became the defenders of the enterprise against the rapacious and self-interested shareholder.

The derivative action, developed decades earlier, was the first target. It had been a target of the clients of the corporate bar for years, to be sure, but only after the war did it become clear how much the courts would countenance restrictions on such suits. Any form of litigation is open to abuse by cranks and opportunists. The derivative action, however, has been characterized as unusually prone to abuse. In a derivative action the shareholder acts on behalf of the corporation to obtain recompense from malfeasant managers who have wronged the corporation. Because, however, it is the corporation that suffers injury, it is the corporation that recovers whatever damages are awarded. The plaintiff shareholder, the one who brought suit, gets nothing directly and indirectly gains only in that the corporation is better off, presumably enhancing the value of the plaintiff's shares. But, of course, in a large corporation with many shares outstanding, that indirect increase in value may be – is likely to be – trivial. For the plaintiff shareholder, virtue is its own reward. Who, then, really profits from derivative actions? A plaintiff shareholder's lawyer who wins in court may be entitled to fees from the corporation for the victory on its behalf. More likely, however, given the vagaries of pursuing these actions, the plaintiff will settle the lawsuit on the condition that the lawyer gets paid. The allegation, therefore, is that the real party in interest (at least financially) is the plaintiff's lawyer. Thus, to complete the argument, the lawyer has an incentive to file a barely meritorious suit, or even one without merit, simply to garner a settlement – a nuisance suit in which the lawyer is paid to go away.

Although lucrative for the lawyer, of course, this state of affairs had less appeal to corporate managers who were the objects of the suits. Moreover, from the perspective of state legislators who valued productive corporations, managerial time would be better spent attending to the risk-taking for which their expertise has prepared them than spending time with counsel deciding which suits to settle (or yet worse, from both perspectives, than having managers spending time being cooped up in small offices while plaintiffs' lawyers pepper them with endless questions designed to harass and cause misstatements that lead to bigger settlements). Of course, one could reasonably observe that the threat of such lawsuits might have a powerful salutary deterrent effect, but that observation was largely lost as legislatures rushed to assist defendant managers. One solution arrived at by state legislatures, often prodded by bar committees peopled with members of the corporate bar, was to require the posting of bonds. That is, small shareholders had to post a bond subject to forfeit if the shareholder lost the suit. Since small shareholders had little to gain, since their proportional recovery was both indirect and small, requiring them to "put their money where their mouth is" would supposedly deter frivolous suits. By contrast, serious derivative actions would be filed by large shareholders, who would have more to gain from victory. They could escape being required to post bond.

This ingenious solution was enacted by many states (though not Delaware), among them New Jersey. As it turned out, New Jersey enacted its bond-posting statute in 1946 during the pendency of a major derivative action brought by a New Jersey citizen on behalf of a Delaware corporation against its managers. The suit was a diversity action – plaintiff and defendant from different states – so that it could be brought in federal court. The federal court upheld the right of the defendant to require the plaintiff to post a bond (curiously enough applying the New Jersey requirement in federal court against a New Jersey plaintiff on behalf of a Delaware defendant, even though Delaware had no such statute). The appeals made their way to the U.S. Supreme Court, which upheld the constitutional legitimacy of such a statute without so much as a raised eyebrow over its convoluted application and, of course, with full deference to the New Jersey legislature.

Some years later New Jersey's corporate jurisprudence once again reached center stage, this time through its courts, not its legislature. In a declaratory judgment action, *A. P. Smith Mfg. Co. v. Barlow* (1953), the New Jersey courts upheld the right of a corporation chartered in New Jersey to make charitable contributions. Corporate charitable giving had long been legitimated by statute, and this case arose only because the company had been chartered before the statute was enacted. What is striking is not the holding, but the judicial rhetoric, replete with heavy Cold War overtones. The opinion gives the broadest latitude to managers, on the thinnest of corporate rationales, to give away corporate funds to charities. That discretion was justified, not because the shareholders would actually benefit but because managers know what is good for the United States. Quoting testimony from the president of Princeton University (the object of this instance of corporate largesse) as well as the heads of United States Steel and other corporations, the opinion explicitly links the continued existence of free institutions of higher education to their private status and further insists that they will survive, and thus the country will survive, only if they are sustained by private giving – best exemplified by corporate contributions. (The opinion notes, but without exploring the meaning of the switch in charitable objects, that the corporation had previously given to a university in Newark.) What the owners might want (much less whether countenancing such contributions was sound governmental policy) was not even an issue. Business judgment was stretched to include the practice of corporate statesmanship.

Where more traditional business judgments were at issue, the courts were even more deferential. A little more than ten years after New Jersey's *Barlow* decision, the Delaware Supreme Court decided *Cheff v. Mathes* (1964). In that case the managers of Holland Furnace ran a company with, at best, questionable sales techniques – some of their salesmen would dismantle furnaces in winter and then suggest the need for a replacement. Sales were declining, as were profits. A shareholder wanted a managerial change to clear the way for termination of the sales force. The managers defended their business plan, arguing in part that they employed many men who would lose their jobs. The managers were allowed to buy out the insurgent shareholder at an above-market price for his shares to eliminate opposition to their business plan and preserve the enterprise. Within a couple of years the firm disappeared from the records.

The examples of such cases could be multiplied endlessly. The trend, however, was quite clear. Although any of these cases could have and might have been decided similarly before World War II or after the middle of the 1960s, on balance the expansive holdings would have been quite different. They would have been narrower. Certainly the rhetoric would have been different and would have served up a warning to managers to be more attentive to shareholders.

American business managers in this period were considered the best in the world; the view was not simply a domestic conceit. Given the belief that they had managed the most successful vehicles of the most successful economy of the modern era, the view was entirely justified. The American economy was indeed the most successful of its type. From the vantage point of forty or more years, however, managers had played an important though probably not a determinative role in America's economic dominance. Indeed, recent work in economic history suggests an understanding a bit more prosaic. America's success, while not inevitable, grew as much from lack of competition as anything else. Germany's "economic miracle" first had to satisfy the demand to rebuild before it could direct its attention to building wealth through exports. The same was true of Japan. When those countries turned to compete with American corporations, they succeeded admirably. Moreover, many American markets were protected, as in agriculture. In the industries that supplied the military, much of the research that fed innovations was secret. In related industries, notably aircraft production and computers, the implicit subsidies associated with production for the military fueled the success of civilian counterparts. Untangling the role of managers was, at a minimum, more complicated than simply crediting them with the economy's success and, as a result, deferring to their judgments.

One does not have to look directly at economic measures to understand that managers were not the giants so worthy of deference that state corporate law rhetoric might suggest. A simple glance at other areas of the law, such as torts, suggests that courts that deferred in corporate law asked hard questions elsewhere. One powerful example should suffice. In torts the postwar era is notable for developments in products liability. Although the New York case *MacPherson v. Buick* (1916) had cut through the privity requirements and opened up the possibility of such actions, it was not until the 1950s and 1960s, led by the California and New Jersey Supreme Courts, that manufacturers began to be held liable for bringing defective products to market. Although such tort actions did not implicate manufacturers directly, they did have the effect of undermining the sense of complacency associated with the corporate economy. If corporate managers were given credit for the successes of that economy, they would, ultimately, be held responsible for its failures.

Similarly, though it came only after products liability had become part of the legal landscape, the marriage of class actions to torts further called managerial competence and corporate noblesse oblige into question. If the defining quality of the corporate economy had been the capacity to produce quality goods for the vast bulk of the citizenry, what did it say about corporations and their managers when, through tiny but perceptible corner-cutting, they created profits at the expense of the consuming public? It would not be long before the lawyers who mastered the class action married it directly to anti-managerial claims, premised in both fiduciary duty and the securities laws.

The securities laws themselves underwent very subtle evolution in the years after the war. The 1933 and 1934 acts were not self-executing. Nor had they simply created authority in an extant arm of the government to employ them, as the Sherman Act had. Rather, the acts handed authority to a newly created agency, the SEC. The SEC, as with any organization, grew in stature as it grew in size and therefore generally sought to expand its mandate. The SEC, however, never had enough manpower to review and then actually investigate all the registration documents filed with it, much less to monitor all the actions and transactions under its jurisdiction. The courts recognized this limitation – indeed, so had the authors of the acts. In some aspects the acts provided for private actions – that is for civil liability in suits brought by private parties – not simply for liability in enforcement actions brought by the agency. The rationale, of course, was that private parties in the market would be both well situated to detect wrongdoing that harmed them and disposed to do something about it. Private parties could act to preserve the health of the securities markets, went the thinking, as well as governmental monitors, and could do so relatively cheaply and, best of all, without having to augment governmental resources. The deterrent effect would follow.

The provision that was to protect against insider trading was one such portion of the law; it dealt with "short-swing" profits. The provision provided that any insider – defined by the statute to include corporate directors, high-ranking managers, and large shareholders – would be prohibited from engaging in quick trades; that is, purchases and sales within a six-month window. The theory was that such trades were speculation, not investment, and therefore premised on information on which the trader could make a quick profit. Of course, the statute snared many innocent parties and missed many of those guilty of actual inside trading. For example, a corporate officer might well have legitimate reasons to both buy and sell within a six-month period. But reason was no excuse; liability was absolute. On the other side of the coin, the same officer might escape liability under this portion of the law, even if both purchase and sale were based on inside information, if the window was even one day longer than six months. The power to bring an action resided not with the SEC, but with the corporation whose shares were being traded. Any profits the trader made were to be returned to the company. The statute thus envisioned a place for private policing.

For a number of reasons the "short-swing" profit section of the 1934 Act proved to be of little value. The courts, at the behest of the SEC, fashioned a different action under an entirely different portion of the statute. The now-famous 10b-5 action grew out of the enforcement of Rule 10b-5, promulgated under the authority of Section 10(b) of the 1934 Act. Originally written to deal with those who defrauded or misled individuals or the market in the purchase or sale of securities, the rule was finally deployed against insider trading and upheld in the 1960s. The text of the rule and of its empowering law were artfully read – trading on inside information misled the market because insiders should not take advantage of information in their possession that was not also available to the public; that was unfair dealing and thus a form of manipulation. The SEC had begun its way down this path by the very early 1960s and never looked back. The authority that the SEC assumed under this broad interpretation of the law was enormous, all the more so since "security" was not a self-defining term and had been expansively read by the agency; the SEC had received judicial blessing for very expansive readings since the middle of the 1940s. If one recalls that the entire point of the acts was to restore confidence in the capital markets, then the agency's expansive interpretations were well warranted, since the capital markets were themselves both flexible and dynamic.

Notwithstanding the SEC's creeping expansion of its role in the capital markets, in most of the areas of the law traditionally given over to policing managerial behavior, such as the arenas covered by the states, the deference to managerialism reached its apogee in the postwar decades. It was in the 1950s, after all, that the Secretary of Defense uttered his famous line that "what was good for GM was good for the United States." Being a former GM executive, the Secretary presumably knew whereof he spoke. Antitrust actions at the federal level exemplify the attitude as well as any. The decade saw few prosecutions of note – the government brought some price-fixing cases – and little by way of theoretical development. Ironically, the most famous case of the decade forced DuPont to sell its share (nearly one-quarter) of General Motors. Brought by antitrust prosecutors under the Clayton Act in 1949, the government was upheld by the Supreme Court in 1957. Over the previous decades General Motors and DuPont had developed a close working relationship, sharing in product development. But their joint activities were a type of vertical integration, not the typical horizontal combination that the act had been written to attack. In other words, the statute was being applied to a relationship that did not try to monopolize an industry, but rather to tie together two entities, each of which catered to different markets. Nonetheless, the Court, over a vigorous dissent, upheld the novel application of the law. In such an integrated relationship, the Court held, the chance for anti-competitive behavior when supplying goods justified the novel application of the statute. And it was novel. Very few such actions were brought.

VI. THE DECLINE OF HEROIC MANAGERIALISM

The period from 1965 until 1975 fascinates. Few periods in American history contain such a rapid transformation of the culture. Bedrock institutions suffered challenges unimaginable even a few months before 1965 dawned. Among the most challenged were America's economic dominance in the world, the invincibility of its productive forces, and, ultimately, the very institutions of the corporate economy and their managers. In short, the corporate economy suffered a crisis of legitimacy, along with the crisis of legitimacy of many other American institutions.

The bases of the crisis were manifold. The American adventure in Vietnam proved to be vastly expensive. Unlike World War II, the Vietnam War brought not prosperity but strain. The inability to provide both guns and butter, in the vernacular, tested the economic patience of the population. American preeminence in every field of economic endeavor could no longer be taken for granted. Nothing better exemplified this challenge than the presence of the Volkswagen Beetle on American highways, a mobile affront to the Detroit-built automobile's claim to the centrality of American prosperity. It mattered little that within a few years Volkswagen was in its turn dethroned by the automobile producers of Japan. American hegemony in technological innovation was also challenged; the Boeing version of the Supersonic Transport was never built. Only the Concorde, an Anglo-French luxury jet, actually ended up shuttling passengers. By the middle of the 1970s the American economy's vulnerability to uncontrollable price shocks had been exposed when the country was subjected to an oil embargo. Faced with a world in which even their home market was insecure, America's corporations and their managers reacted slowly. They seemed determined to hold onto the illusion of dominance, rather than react to the competitive pressures of the now fully restored and powerful economies of the rest of the Western world.

At first the legal system deployed only the tools already in its bag, rather than create new ones to assist in restructuring the corporate economy in the face of competitive pressures. Nowhere was this approach clearer than in antitrust. In the late 1960s and early 1970s the federal government brought antitrust actions against some of the icons of American business. In a frontal challenge to the regulated telephone monopoly, the American Telephone and Telegraph Company, newly energized trust busters sought its dismemberment. After prolonged effort, the government won. The case was brought in the name of consumer welfare and innovation. The cross-subsidies of local and long-distance services disappeared, and new companies sprang up to offer telephone services. The huge and famous research facilities, the Bell Labs, home to both the most prosaic of applied research and Nobel prize-winners, were splintered. Whether scientific research won or lost is still debated. In the case brought against another icon, IBM, it was the corporation not the government that won the war. Infamous for the way it ground up young lawyers, the case lasted for well over a decade. After five years of preliminary inquiries, it was filed in January 1969. It was abandoned in the Reagan administration.

Curiously, antitrust actions were rarely brought, even under the Clayton Act theory upheld by the Court in 1957, against the newest form of corporate combination, the conglomerate. The conglomerate was a combination of widely disparate corporate enterprises, operating in often completely unrelated markets, under the aegis of a single holding company. The conceit of the conglomerate was that the superiority of managerial skills in the holding company, especially the skill of managers at allocating capital among the enterprises within the amalgamation, would be a superior way to conduct business, bringing the stability of diversification to a single unified enterprise. For example, one famous conglomerate, the Gulf and Western Corporation, came to own a sugar company (South Puerto Rico Sugar), a heavy equipment manufacturer (Allis Chalmers), a cigar company (Consolidated Cigar), and motion picture and television studios (Paramount, Desilu), among other enterprises.

Some of these enterprises were born of an anti-regulatory movement that took hold in the late 1960s. Where earlier generations had feared the power of monopolistic corporations and tamed their power through regulation, the generation coming into power in this era believed in markets and innovation, and their power to tame corporate misbehavior through market punishment rather than state action. Natural monopolies, utilities (like AT &T), and transportation companies had been the most heavily regulated. Limited to tending their own knitting, these entities were prohibited from expanding into related fields for fear that the market power in one sphere would allow domination in related spheres. In the late 1960s the regulators began to relax their grip. In one example, air freight companies were allowed to create holding companies, which owned operating companies, which actually flew the planes that transported the freight, whereas before only one entity existed, the air freight company. In the new structure the holding company could own not just the air freight company, but companies in entirely different industries as well as related industries. That, for example, was the fate of the legendary Flying Tiger Line. Reincorporated in 1969 as a holding company with an operating subsidiary, the corporation became a conglomerate, purchasing a railcar leasing business, a cement company, and other businesses. The deregulation movement gathered full force later, under both the Carter and Reagan administrations, but its origins lay in the desire to unleash the innovative strength of regulated entities.

This new faith in markets, as opposed to law, was no real friend of managerialism. It celebrated Schumpeterian creative destruction rather than the stability of the managed economy. Its heroes were inventors who made themselves rich rather than the manager who rose through the ranks. It was also a profoundly intellectual movement in some regards, its home in economics departments, with the beginnings of a toehold in law schools, and only the most theoretical corners of business schools. It ultimately revolutionized the law of the corporate economy. Curiously, it mixed the anti-statist sentiments of the late 1960s with an old-fashioned American triumphalism, suggesting that individual economic actors better knew their wants than managers, whether corporate or governmental. There were, of course, huge tensions in that vision, but they only surfaced later. Most profoundly, this vision sided with the shareholder over the manager, the market over the law, and, of course, enterprise over government.

It was in antitrust that the movement began its invasion of corporate law. Neo-classical economics scholars began by suggesting that monopolies and cartels are inherently hard to sustain. They suggested that the propensity to cheat regularly undermines cartels. They further suggested that innovation undermines the ability to control a market. Some kinds of antitrust activity, activity that resulted in regulated cartels or monopolies, had the net effect of buying a stability that led to stagnation because of stifled innovation. Hence, at a minimum, these scholars favored deregulation. But they also cast a jaundiced eye on traditional antitrust activities, largely because they appeared to be worthless. Why bother to bring in the state to smash corporate combinations when they would inevitably crumple under the pressure of competitive markets? General Motors would either innovate or lose its markets to Honda, BMW, and others. IBM might have a functional monopoly on mainframe computers, but so what? Digital Equipment with its minicomputers, then Sun with its work stations, and then Dell with its desktop and laptop personal computers would break up IBM's computing monopoly far more efficiently than the Justice Department with its lawyers.

What of the conglomerates? They would either succeed in their aims or not. Their power, so deftly satirized by the depiction of "Engulf and Devour" (presumable Gulf and Western) in Mel Brooks' *Silent Movie* (1976), was largely mythic, claimed the scholars. As it happened, the conglomerates were the first corporations to be dismembered in the merger movement of the early 1980s. Whether powerful or not, they were not particularly profitable.

Profits, of course, were the lifeblood of the corporate economy. The pressures on the economy from international competition and wartime spending cut into not simply the growth in profits that the corporate economy had come to take for granted under managerialism but also profitability itself. Undermining assumptions about the corporate economy led to certain paradoxes, many of which manifested themselves in corporate law. Charitable giving by corporations had long been sustained by the courts, encouraged by statute, and pursued by corporate managers out of a combination of altruism and the aggrandizement that comes with the gratitude one receives when one gives away another person's money. Charitable giving presumed the continuing profitability of the enterprise whose money was being given away. The new twist on charitable giving, however, was whose money was being given away. The mutual funds and pension funds, which had their origins in the 1920s, had become major players in the market for corporate securities. By the early 1970s they owned huge percentages of the largest corporations in the country. The law that had countenanced, and even encouraged, corporate charitable giving did not seem to notice that corporate wealth was really in large measure the collective retirement income of a large portion of the middle and working classes. Nor did it notice the legitimating effect that charitable giving had on other, less attractive aspects of corporate behavior.

The more progressive version of charitable giving, one which found a home in legal scholarship though not in law itself, was the corporate social responsibility movement. An aspect of the cultural transformation of the era, it, too, seemed to take for granted the profitability of the corporate enterprise at the very moment when the pressures on the corporate economy were casting stable profits into doubt. The movement contained a latent contradiction; it seemed to disdain the profit motive in favor of more socially acceptable actions while presuming that individual corporations would always be able to afford the actions called for (or that investors would not mind sub-par returns on investment). Corporations were asked to consider, among other things, the environmental impact and the social impact of their decisions outside of the regulatory mandates. Legal scholars opined about ways to import such responsibility into the fiduciary duty of managers as activists pressured consumers to boycott corporations that were not responsive. There were, of course, terrific contradictions in these countervailing pressures, and sometimes presumptive roles were turned upside down. For example, munitions makers defended unprofitable war production during Vietnam on grounds of public spirit as antiwar activists sought to use the tools of corporate law to force open corporate records and expose corporate machinations, only to be rebuffed by the courts when the activists (honestly) admitted that the welfare of the corporation was not their object.

It was not simply the normal tools of state law that gave corporate activists power. So did the securities laws. In particular the proxy solicitation rules – the rules governing the corporation's capacity to communicate with and solicit the votes of shareholders on matters on which a shareholder vote is called for – became a battleground of activists, both right and left, who variously sought precatory shareholder resolutions seeking objectives as disparate as the end of Vietnam war materiel production or the end of business contacts with the regimes of the Soviet bloc. This form of activism drove the SEC mad. Its staff was never able to reconcile the fundamental tenet of the proxy solicitation rules – that shareholder communication is a vital facet of corporate governance – with its knowledge that the proxy solicitation mechanism was being hijacked for extra-corporate political purposes.

This shareholder activism, however, was only the attention-grabbing part of shareholder concerns. Far more important for the corporate economy were the resolutions governing the structure of the enterprise, the proxy battles waged in contests for control of the corporation, and the general shareholder unrest those activities portended.

VII. TOWARD THE CLOSE OF THE CENTURY

The last quarter of the twentieth century witnessed a transformation of the corporate economy. Some observers dubbed it the liquefaction of the economy. Liquidity replaced stability as the economic ideal, and the legal structures of the economy abetted the change. Given intellectual backbone by the law and economics scholars, the Nobel Prize-winning market theorists in the new genre of finance, and a resurgent, though tiny, band of libertarians, the transformation was as rapid and thorough-going as any in American history.

At the state level, the law of fiduciary duty oscillated between managerial freedom and managerial duty, each, of course, with shareholder welfare as the ultimate end. Where it actually mattered, as in the law governing takeovers, the near-absolute judicial deference to the business plans of managers disappeared, held the Delaware courts, if the managers took actions against potential suitors that made it very unlikely that those plans could be realized. When that moment of improbability arrived, the corporate managers had to maximize the immediate return to shareholders. Judicial rhetoric took on a new cast; while rarely finding managers liable, the Chancery Court of Delaware seemed to take particular delight in scolding corporate managers for questionable activities. As institutional investors – the pension funds – began to initiate derivative actions, the actions themselves began to take on a new air of respectability. Not every twist, however, originated in respect for shareholders. States passed statutes that slowed the hostile takeover, usually at the urging of an unusual alliance of corporate managers and local labor. As scholars pointed out, however, it was usually labor, and not management, that was left saddened by victory. Managers survived and labor lost work anyway. In the end, however, a new market had entered the economic vocabulary, the market for corporate control.

Court interpretations, pushed by an aggressive SEC, expanded the reach of the securities laws. While the federal courts effectively resisted the attempts by the SEC to federalize violations of fiduciary duty by transforming every violation of fiduciary duty into a market manipulation, they did allow 10b-5 to expand in other ways. The courts expanded the implied right of action generally, creating actions for private plaintiffs where once only the agency could act. The courts understood, as they said regularly, that the SEC could not possibly police the markets by itself, and thus it was legitimate to deputize the investing community to police itself, each investor his or her own private attorney general. The courts gave a favorable nod toward expanding class actions and even imported the tools of market analysis created in the finance and economics departments to find ways to assist in certifying plaintiff shareholder classes.

The most dramatic example of the marriage of legal and financial analysis, however, was in the creation of entirely new securities, entirely new investment vehicles, and entirely new ways to control risk. Managerialism was, in essence, one generation's attempt to control risk. It married corporate law to an ethos of control to compensate for the vagaries of the market. In so doing it tamped out some of what markets do best: eliminate the inefficient. A new generation put its faith in markets, and it, too, married law to an ethos. The new generation, however, tried to control risk buy finding ways to chop it up and then to create a market for it, so that the risk-averse could buy protection and those with a taste for risk could buy more.

In 1973 the Chicago Board of Options Exchange was created. The Board took an ancient financial device, the option, and turned it from an artisanal product to a commodity. Options are vehicles that magnify or limit risk. They were but the first step in the creation of the market in derivatives, vehicles designed to deal with risk. From law the creator of a derivative borrows the insight that ownership is simply a bundle of rights. From finance the creator borrows the understanding that an investment is simply the acquisition of a right to a future income stream. A mortgage is, after all, a right to a stream of payments consisting of interest and principal payments. Why not unbundle them? Why shouldn't borrowers be allowed to pay to swap interest payment streams, one variable and the other fixed? In a world that both extols liquidity and seeks stability, the new vision of the corporate economy conceives ownership as a set of rights, each with independent value. One achieves stability by assembling the portfolio of rights best adjusted to one's need for stability.

In a fitting tribute to its origins, the new genuflection to the market profoundly announced itself in antitrust. While the telephone monopoly met its demise and its parts – the "Baby Bells" – were for some time forbidden to recombine, by the turn of the century the communications market was no longer simply a combination of two kinds of land lines, local and long distance. The entrepreneurialism sought in deregulation had been well realized. The corporations that had sprung up to lease long-distance lines from AT&T, under a judicial mandate to open its lines to others, had undercut the venerable but now constrained giant. The Baby Bells, at least the ones headed by managers with an entrepreneurial spirit, ventured into new fields, notably cellular telephone communication. Eventually cellular communication blurred almost completely the seemingly hoary distinction between local and long-distance lines. Consumer welfare, not localism, dominated antitrust thought, and the market seemed better able to provide for such welfare.

Once a thriving part of the practice of corporate law, by the 1980s antitrust was in many ways reduced to an obstacle to be overcome, a delaying tactic deployed by incumbent managers trying to fend off hostile takeovers in the market for corporate control. Nowhere was the new attitude more evident than in the odd attempt to revive a robust antitrust section of the Department of Justice by attacking Microsoft. Nary a word of the effort spoke to local concerns. Instead the attempt to dismantle the corporation was fought over engineering arcana: whether the software Microsoft had developed, the operating system that served as a platform for all other software applications, was a vehicle for a seemingly subtle form of monopolization, the more so since Microsoft required that hardware companies it contracted with load its operating system and accompanying (integrated) applications of the machines they sold. Only Microsoft software worked best (or at all) with its operating system because Microsoft refused to convey important parts of the software code that would make non-Microsoft software more compatible with the operating system. This refusal, since Microsoft supplied the operating system to the vast majority of computers, amounted to a competitive barrier.

In the end, the best that can be said of the government's victory is that it was a draw. Microsoft remained the dominant provider of operating system software; disclosing (reluctantly) information about its software did not stop it from creating application software compatible with its operating system, nor did it stop Microsoft from acquiring fledgling software companies. Software markets, meanwhile, in many ways began to outpace Microsoft.

What was true of the securities markets and securities regulation, corporate governance, and antitrust was true of the administrative state generally. Governmental regulation, while capable of passing constitutional muster, though even there rumblings of eventual limits on Commerce Clause jurisprudence were being felt, was presumptively a second-best solution. Areas as disparate as organized labor, occupational health and safety, public interest litigation, pension plans, and health care traditional structures, buttressed by law and federal funding, became vulnerable to actions that made them less relevant, undermined their legitimacy, subjected them to scathing intellectual scrutiny and political ridicule, and crippled their capacity to function.

Organized labor lost relevance as manufacturing became a less important part of the economy, power as the NLRB gradually came under the sway of members who lacked enthusiasm for aggressively entertaining labor's agenda, and authority as the entrepreneurial spirit and mobility supplanted lengthy or lifetime employment (not to mention, of course, the trauma early in the 1980s when America's air controllers struck, only to find an unyielding federal government, which not only struck back but did so with the apparent support of much of the population). Those who sought a safer and healthier working environment through regulation saw their efforts subjected to withering cost-benefit analysis accompanied by a large dollop of ridicule, as in stories about how rules proposed for agricultural work might require that multiple portable toilets be set up throughout farmers' fields.

Public interest litigation, once the province of the political left, saw the rise of counter-litigators, foundation- and industry-funded centers of legal activity whose function it was to challenge the rules of the administrative state as burdensome, beyond the authority granted by statute, or in some other sense legally illegitimate. The tools once deployed to stop construction of nuclear power plants, such as the requirements for extraordinarily detailed impact studies created in the most punctilious fashion, were appropriated by the anti-regulators, who deployed the same tools to slow or stop the creation of environmental regulations. Where traditional public interest litigation had been governmentally funded and wide ranging, the cry of "de-fund the left" arose, greatly curtailing enforcement expenditures, limiting funding of the Legal Services Corporation, and causing proposed limits on the kinds of actions that the lawyers might bring.

The traditional private retirement structure, the defined benefit plan, in which contributions of a company's workers were pooled and a definite payout provided for, all under the watchful eye of the Department of Labor, was gradually overborne by individual accounts, whether funded through paycheck deductions (largely the 401(k) and 403(b) accounts – names taken from provisions of the Internal Revenue Code) or Individual Retirement Accounts, where investment decisions were individualized (and harder to regulate) and the payout concomitantly irregular. The spectacular failure of the early Clinton administration's attempt to rationalize the provision and funding of health care through federal efforts neatly encapsulated the twentieth-century journey of the administrative state.

As with securities regulation, the seemingly inexorable trend of more than five decades in which federal regulations encroached on individual state actions and markets ended. The suggestions that the federal government itself act as insurer was never seriously entertained (the suggestion that the government act as provider was never even seriously suggested). What was most suggestive, however, was that no plan in which the federal government acted as insurer of last resort and market coordinator survived scrutiny. Regulation had lost the benefit of the doubt.

CONCLUSION: THE AMBIVALENT LEGACY OF POWER

The outraged reaction of the country's business elite to the reforms of the New Deal reflected an inappropriate certainty about the nature of the country's attitude toward powerful institutions. They felt, with some justification, that the depredations visited by nation-states on populations were iniquitous, and thus the extension of state power into the realm of the economy would be met with popular resentment, even when the private economy was in a deep fugue. They were wrong. A stronger popular sentiment called federal regulatory authority into action not to destroy the institutions that had been the vehicles for creating wealth, but rather in the hope that federal authority would revitalize those institutions while simultaneously redistributing some of the power they had accumulated. Wealth creation had not legitimated the many attempts to centralize private power, but had masked a widespread tolerance of those attempts; a truth laid bare when wealth creation shuddered.

The very federal agencies given the responsibility of redistributing power themselves became quite powerful. The elites who controlled the agencies developed a certainty about the country's attitude toward powerful institutions that also proved to be inappropriate. Wealth creation had legitimated public power, but had masked an ambivalence about the existence of that power in a manner that echoed sentiment expressed decades earlier. When prosperity was called into doubt in the Depression, public opinion had reacted negatively to existing centers of power. A similar sentiment arose in the 1970s when American economic dominance was once more cast into doubt and prosperity had an uncertain future. In that decade, however, public opinion turned against government and its controlling elites. Government had failed in its promise to continue prosperity; sentiment turned in favor of the private economy.

Each era bequeathed the nation institutions of lasting strength. Much of the growth of the administrative state has depended for its legitimacy on its claim simultaneously to support the wealth-creating aspects of the corporate economy while domesticating the corporate economy's expressions of power. State law governing the behavior of managers has deliberately tried to keep managers focused on wealth creation – other institutional expressions of authority belong not to corporations but to the state and civil society. Where wealth creation has swamped competing values, the antitrust laws have been deployed to limit the size – hence power – of corporations and, where those attempts failed, to use the threat of antitrust action to channel managerial acts to limit the expression of capital's power. Similarly, when the same institutions that charter the creatures of the corporate economy became ineffective in controlling the behaviors of the creations, then the federal government stepped in, albeit in fits and starts, to make the attempt. When, however, the very attempts at control threatened rather than enhanced the single aim for which corporations were chartered – the creation of wealth – control became itself suspect. In each era the institutions remain: In the early twenty-first century America still has corporations of gargantuan scale and scope, and the American administrative state has not withered away. But each era has generated powerful currents of doubt, reflected both in popular sentiment and high theory, and those currents of doubt have found legal expression in the creation and the criticism of legal institutions, the role of the institutions, and the expressions of their authority.

18

LAW AND COMMERCIAL POPULAR CULTURE IN THE
TWENTIETH-CENTURY UNITED STATES

NORMAN L. ROSENBERG

Over the course of the twentieth century, the commercial culture industry scanned nearly every nook and cranny of the U.S. legal system. Richard Sherwin spoke for many in the legal community when he complained, as the century ended, that law was in danger of going "pop." Others, however, saw a much longer term and less corrosive relationship between law and commercial popular culture. By the close of the century, both law professors and academics from other disciplines were launching a new research project that identified multiple links between commercial pop culture and the formal field of law.

I. THE BIRTH OF THE "LEXITAINMENT"
INDUSTRY, 1840–1960

The U.S. commercial culture industry, which emerged before the Civil War, quickly recognized the popular appeal of "things legal." The penny presses of the mid-nineteenth century eagerly gravitated toward "notorious cases" involving prominent figures, especially politicians and ministers, or salacious legal scenarios, particularly murder and seduction. By the 1880s, tabloid-style newspapers stories, stage plays, and pamphlets (including those that simply reprinted trial testimony and lawyers' arguments) entertained and informed a sizeable lay audience.

Writers of popular fiction also drew material from stories about a burgeoning criminal underworld. Early on, their work featured a theme that would repeatedly structure commercial representations of law: people looking at the legal system from the outside, it appeared, could invariably see issues, especially ones of guilt and morality, more clearly than the professionals who worked inside the machinery of the law. The pulp novels of George Lippard, such as *The Quaker City* (1845), portrayed a vast criminal underground in antebellum America that operated with legal impunity. Edgar Alan Poe's famous short stories, "Murders in the Rue Morgue" (1842) and "The Purloined Letter" (1845), introduced the character of the private detective, the sharp-eyed investigator who could locate clues and crucial evidence to which the public policing establishment remained blind. *The Octoroon* (1859) adapted this trope to the theatrical stage. Produced just as still photography was becoming a popular art form, this play depended on the claim that an accidentally produced photo could show the innocence of a murder defendant and the guilt of the primary accuser more clearly than the legal machinery.

Building on this base, a "lexitainment complex" steadily expanded during the following century. In 1906, one of the earliest in an ever-lengthening list of real-life "trials of the [twentieth] century," that of the wealthy socialite Harry K. Thaw, anticipated the wall-to-wall, 24/7 coverage of things legal that would eventually emerge. Authorities in New York City charged Thaw with murder after he fatally shot Stanford White, a well-known architect. Allegedly, the mercurial Thaw had become obsessed with White after learning of the architect's sexual history with the young Evelyn Nesbit before her marriage to Thaw. On trial for murder in 1907, Harry Thaw tapped his family's wealth to mount a vigorous defense.

Thaw-financed productions extended from the courthouse to the movie theater. A publicist supplied the press with handouts critical of White and supportive of Thaw. Going beyond the print-bound coverage that had surrounded late nineteenth-century legal spectacles, the Thaw family backed several stage plays and a motion picture about the case. The commercial press quickly took sides, with most newspapers condemning the deceased architect and sympathizing with Evelyn Nesbit Thaw. A writer for the New York *Evening Journal* denounced White as a "moral leper" and a "professional destroyer of innocence," and the paper's editors invited readers to answer a stark moral-legal question: "Was Thaw Justified in Killing Stanford White?" The sensationalized sexual innuendoes in some papers prompted President Theodore Roosevelt, who was following the Thaw case, to inquire if his Postmaster General could deny mailing privileges to publications whose coverage seemed to qualify as "obscene."

Harry Thaw's legal problems provided one of the twentieth century's earliest examples of commercial culture's attraction to – and its ability to help create – a succession of "trials of the century." A short list of these, extending into the 1950s, might include the initial prosecution and the numerous appeals involving the anarchists Sacco and Vanzetti during the 1920s; the Jazz-Age "Monkey case" in Dayton, Tennessee, which pitted Clarence Darrow against William Jennings Bryan in 1925; the trial of Bruno Hauptmann, convicted of kidnapping and murdering the infant son of Charles Lindbergh during the early 1930s; and the series of trials and hearings during the 1940s and 1950s involving members of the U.S. Communist Party, especially those that determined the fate of Ethel and Julius Rosenberg. According to one calculation, about 700 newspaper and media people, including more than 125 photographers and newsreel camera operators, descended on the Lindbergh kidnapping trial.

II. THE EXPANSION OF THE LEXITAINMENT INDUSTRY, 1960–2000

After about 1960, the intervals between these legal dramas shortened: one trial of the century threatened to blend into the next. By century's end, saturation-style television and Internet coverage regularly supplemented the array of print and visually mediated imagery that Harry Thaw's defense team had employed at its beginning. This multi-mediated theater of law, in Richard Sherwin's view, threatened to create a "jurisprudence of appearances," a legal landscape in which courtroom process was becoming inexorably infected by the imagery found in commercial culture.

Meanwhile, lexitainment's fictive side had grown apace. One of the earliest filmic narratives, *Falsely Accused* (1907), transferred the basic story line of *The Octoroon* to the silent screen. This movie featured a motion-picture camera, fortuitously running during the course of a brutal murder, which exonerated a falsely accused defendant and fingered the true villain. Private detectives – first in print and then on the screen and television – became increasingly "hard-boiled," using their brawn as well as their brain to uncover and thwart criminal schemes. Beginning during the 1920s, Dashiell Hammett's "private dicks" (including the "Continental Op," Sam Spade, and Nick Charles) sleuthed, brawled, and boozed their way through pulp magazines, popular novels, Hollywood movies, radio, comic books, and eventually into television.

The pop literary world, Hollywood, network radio, and television steadily expanded their fictive bars. Earle Stanley Gardner's "Perry Mason" practiced law in all of these media. After shedding an initially hard-boiled image, this super lawyer became a fixture in the staid *Saturday Evening Post* and on prime-time TV (from 1957 to 1966). Making a successful comeback during the 1980s, with Raymond Burr reprising his earlier television role until his 1993 death, the lawyer-detective worked his legal magic in twenty-five made-for-TV movies. Not surprisingly, in the mid-1990s, when pollsters asked people to name the best attorney in the United States, Perry Mason appeared near the top of the resulting list.

While Mason was relocating his lucrative law practice to television, at just about the mid-point of the twentieth century, two venerable commercial culture genres closely connected to things legal, the Western and the crime drama, continued to thrive. Updating imagery that could be found in the early-nineteenth-century novels of James Fenimore Cooper and the pulp fiction of the late Victorian era, Hollywood (and then television during the 1950s and early 1960s) constantly reinvented the Western genre. Movies and TV shows still celebrated the imaginary West's "outlaw heroes," pistol-packing knights in buckskin and denim who generally defined their values and actions against those of an overly complicated legal system. From the characters played by William S. Hart in silent epics such as *Hell's Hinges* (1915) to those portrayed by the nearly mute Clint Eastwood beginning in the 1960s, pop-Western gunfighters often appeared to see the world through a clearer moral lens than the law officers who harassed them. An analogous vision appeared in movie and TV crime dramas. *The Godfather* (1972), for instance, pushed its characterization of its outlaw-hero theme so aggressively as to portray its title character, mobster Vito Corleone (Marlon Brando), caring far more about justice than the judges and law officers he so easily bought off.

As the lexitainment industry expanded, the U.S. Supreme Court remained one of the few law-related institutions, real or fictive, without a prominent, ongoing role on the pop-cultural stage. At the end of the twentieth century the High Court still prohibited live visual coverage of its work, even of the public sessions in which it heard oral arguments. Its limited visibility seemed anomalous. Although not every other court allowed real-time video coverage, many did. TV cameras provided sufficient footage to sustain a flow of in-court imagery that almost matched the stream of pictures of law enforcement officers corralling suspected criminals featured on TV programs such as *Cops*. The nation's long-time Chief Justice William Rehnquist finally enjoyed a brief measure of fame for out-of-court activities: he wrote several popular commercial histories and served as the presiding officer in the televised 1999 impeachment trial of President William Jefferson Clinton.

Many legal figures did become popular personalities. Sometimes it seemed as if J. Edgar Hoover, who headed the Federal Bureau of Investigation from 1924 to 1972, had spent as much time cultivating his pop-cultural image as chasing subversives. Newspaper articles and books, a network radio program, and numerous motion pictures (such as 1957's *The FBI Story*) portrayed Hoover during his heyday, the years from the mid-1930s to the early 1960s, as a heroic crime fighter and gang buster. Even after Hoover's 1972 death, the persistence of his image in movies and TV programs allowed "the Director" to remain far better known, though now increasingly as a villainous or even comic figure, than any of his successors at the FBI.

Some judges also found the popular spotlight. Pollsters at the end of the century found many people struggling to identify the Chief Justice – or any other member – of the U.S. Supreme Court, but their sample public could easily recognize the jurists who presided over the nation's televisual tribunals. Beginning during the late 1980s, Judge (Joseph) Wapner, Judge Joe Brown, Judge Judy (Sheindlin), and their numerous colleagues conspicuously anchored the judicial branch – which one article dubbed the "syndi-court system" – of the lexitainment industry. The prolonged controversy over the 1991 nomination of Clarence Thomas to the U.S. Supreme Court could have been avoided, suggested one night-time comic, had President George H. W. Bush only asked Judge Wapner to move from TV's *People's Court* to the nation's Marble Palace.

The boom market in pop law gave ordinary consumers an ever fuller view of legal practice and principles – or at least an ever fuller view of how the commercial culture industry envisioned the legal process. Perhaps no other workplaces enjoyed the visibility that the culture industry lavished on the law office, the police station, and the courthouse.

Only toward the end of the twentieth century, however, did legal scholars begin to take serious notice of commercial culture's perspectives on things legal. Even as research agendas outside the field of law – in literary and cinema studies, for example – paid attention to law-related imagery in commercial products, legal scholarship, dominated by professors at the top-flight law schools, remained slow to acknowledge either this kind of academic work or the texts over which its practitioners labored. In 1950, when Hollywood released the twentieth century's only biopic about a Supreme Court justice, *The Magnificent Yankee* (which fictionalized the career of Oliver Wendell Holmes, Jr.), none of the legal academy's law reviews bothered to take note. Even twenty-five years later, during the 1970s, there was little in the legal-studies literature about the relationships among law, history, and commercial popular culture. By the century's end, in contrast, a law school site on the World Wide Web devoted to law and visual media ("Picturing Justice") immediately posted a law professor's favorable review of *First Monday*, a short-lived TV series about a fictive U.S. Supreme Court. About the same time, several schools began incorporating works of commercial popular culture into their offerings, and prestigious law reviews started accepting articles that critically analyzed various law-related works produced in non-legal realms.

As this kind of scholarship emerged, its critics in the legal establishment asked a series of questions. What useful legal knowledge could law students or attorneys ever hope to obtain from looking seriously at these commercial products? Were there any canonical, "landmark" popular texts, analogous to the judicial opinions that marked the familiar legal-constitutional histories? Were there "turning points" – as with the Court-packing episode of 1937 – that might provide temporal guideposts for commercial narratives about law and culture? How could a motion picture such as *The Magnificent Yankee* or a TV program such as *First Monday* be analyzed as if it were a "legal text"?

While students of "law and culture" began to address (or, more often, adroitly sidestep) questions such as these, they also tried to explain how the research traditions that had dominated twentieth-century scholarship, particularly legal classicism and legal realism, could have almost completely ignored the vast domain of popular culture.

III. LAW VERSUS COMMERCIAL CULTURE: THE CLASSICAL AND REALIST RESEARCH TRADITIONS

At the beginning of the twentieth century, the law school professors who were coming to dominate legal scholarship claimed to find no reason for considering the (mis)representations of law in commercial culture. The professoriate, and the leading judges whose opinions it evaluated, saw their own work grounded within a research tradition that viewed law through a tightly circumscribed aesthetic. A legal aesthetic, in the formulation of the law professor Pierre Schlag, "helps to constitute not only the way" those doing law think, "but also the law one encounters, the tasks at hand, and the already launched projects . . ."

The Classical Tradition

Adapting the research tradition of English common law scholarship, the early twentieth-century's professional legal writers carefully restricted their vision. "Law" meant practices, particularly litigation at the appellate level in state-created court systems, produced inside a largely autonomous "field of specialized practice." Law professors wrote learned articles for an emerging network of student-edited law reviews. The most distinguished of them, such as Harvard's Samuel Williston, wrote lengthy treatises solely for members of the legal profession. Both the articles and the magisterial treatises, such as Williston's *The Law of Contracts* (1920), claimed to bring internal order to the mass of individual rules and doctrines in a particular subfield of the law.

At the same time, these insiders also insisted that their professional training and legal expertise empowered them to assess social practices *outside* the specialized field of law in equally authoritative and systematic ways. To its celebrants, this classical vision offered a distinct way of seeing *both* the field of law and the broader social world. It thus purported to provide a privileged picture of the field of law and of the self-referential articles and treatises that surveyed and ostensibly systematized what this field itself produced. The classical vision also supposedly enabled the cognoscenti to discern threats, such as unwise social legislation and dangerous political trends, to the legal field's most important product, "the rule of law."

This classical view, which has retained considerable appeal into the twenty-first century, necessarily produced highly restricted pictures of relationships between the field of law and the other domains of daily life. First, it invariably envisioned a social world of free-willed individuals. These people inevitably clashed as they pursued what they saw as their best interests and most desirable goals. People could then invoke, or attract the attention of, institutions within the field of law for disputes that involved allegedly illegitimate acts. These included, to cite familiar examples, someone supposedly reneging on a private contractual agreement or matters that concerned governmental power, such as possible violations of a criminal law or an economic regulation.

Ultimately, the classical vision led to a focus on the coercive machinery of state-sanctioned law. Judges (and the legal commentators who later rejudged their work) confidently asserted that their own law-bound perspective, anchored by their own specialized social practice, gave them privileged insight into any real-world dispute and the social relationships that had generated it. Most importantly, the classical aesthetic envisioned that jurists could correctly resolve a specific dispute primarily by looking at legal rules, doctrines, and precedents that were part of the self-contained practice of law, only incidentally tapping the knowledge produced by other specialized practices such as economics or political science. As Pierre Schlag suggests, professionals working within this aesthetic tended to see the field of law – and its textual traces – through grid-like images of "bright-line rules, absolutist approaches, and categorical definitions" sufficient unto themselves.

Lochner v. New York (1905) illustrated how judges who viewed life and law in this way might articulate legal-social decisions. Here, a 5–4 majority of the U.S. Supreme Court ruled that legislation limiting the hours that bakers could work "necessarily interferes with the right of contract between employer and employees . . . " As the Court's majority saw the social world, bakers and bakery owners freely made contracts according to *pre-legal* calculations of their own best interests and desires. Judges should not interpose, after the fact, unnecessary restrictions and conditions on bargaining arrangements made outside the legal arena. The job of courts (and of subsequent legal commentators), in this classical view, involved identifying the "entitlements and preferences" that the law should legitimately affirm. Once they had developed their picture of these matters, as the law professors Guyora Binder and Robert Weisberg have argued, judges insisted they had also "fully represented society," at least for the purposes of making authoritative legal judgments. Throughout the twentieth century, the judges and commentators who embraced (and were ensnared by) this vision articulated what their critics saw as a narrow, formalistic view of legal inquiry.

Proponents of the classical gaze, however, steadfastly viewed the imagery generated from within the field of law as more scientific and sophisticated than any produced on the outside. Although advocates of a more "sociological jurisprudence" tried to bring research traditions from the social sciences into legal discourse, even they often assigned the work produced by professionals trained in non-legal disciplines to a second-class status. The field's leading judges and commentators firmly embraced the grid-dominated aesthetic long associated with their own profession. This classical vision purportedly enabled them to see beyond mundane matters and to grasp the grander ones that separated the field of law from less elevated realms, especially that of commercial popular culture.

The Legal-Realist Tradition

Always contested, this classical vision faced successive, increasingly more powerful challenges. During the late 1920s and early 1930s, an influential minority of law school academics (and a handful of judges) advanced what they hailed as a more "realistic" view of law. Rather than seeing law primarily as field-bound sets of rules, doctrines, and judicial precedents, a diverse group, ultimately lumped together as "legal realists," tilted against the classical perspective. Despite internal disagreements on precisely where their new research agendas might lead, people in the realist camp agreed on one issue: The classical view provided too restrictive a picture of both the legal field itself and its relationship to areas of life beyond its boundaries. In the realist aesthetic, law did more than settle disputes generated outside the legal field. Most realists saw the world outside as more interrelated and interconnected with the field of law than those who embraced the classical vision would allow.

The realist aesthetic, with its emphasis on law as a source of energy, stressed how decisions made within the field of law could affect the goals and desires of people in most of their social interactions. From this perspective, the labor contract in *Lochner* – which involved, in the classical vision, a freely negotiated bargain between two theoretically equal parties – could appear to be a coercive arrangement that shaped the expectations and behavior of entire social groups such as owners and workers, capital and labor. The property rights that the classical vision attributed to employers meant that workers, who lacked propertied wealth, must toil for wages under contractual conditions and terms that hardly resembled mutually negotiated agreements between people who possessed the liberty to enter the legal field on anything resembling equal terms.

Consequently, as the realist aesthetic took fuller shape, it seemed easier to imagine how expectations about the presence of law – or its absence – helped shape the behavior of people and institutions. Legal decisions made, and also *not* made, within the field of law, in short, seemed to affect the outside social ground on which people worked, lived, and played. Law could reach into daily life, writes Naomi Mezey, "in its absence as much as in its presence"; its impact might be "felt where it is least evident." From the realist perspective, then, law's reach could seem nearly ubiquitous.

Claiming to depict how law actually worked, or "the law in action," academics attracted to this vision constructed a multi-dimensional research tradition. Some eagerly embraced non-legal disciplines, particularly in the social sciences. Insights from psychology, political science, sociology, and economics seemed particularly useful in helping illuminate potential links between the field of law and social-political policymaking. In time, some of the realists left academe, for either full- or part-time work in Franklin Roosevelt's New Deal of the 1930s and in the regulatory agencies that guided the U.S. effort during World War II.

Possible relationships between the field of law and the domains of commercial culture also intrigued a few realist-oriented law professors. Thurman Arnold, who helped make Yale Law School a center for realist scholarship and teaching, wondered how legal practices and forms might interact with the powerful cultural symbolism circulating in the United States during the 1930s. Arnold later claimed that he was interested not only in judicial decisions but also in "*The Saturday Evening Post*, the movies, speeches by university professors, *The New Republic*, *The Nation*," and the larger "stream of current literature" that helped show the "attitudes of the time." Commercial culture, in this view, helped generate and circulate symbols that shaped how people saw, explained, and ultimately employed legal institutions and practices.

Looking beyond an academic audience, Arnold wrote *Symbols of Government* (1935) and *The Folklore of Capitalism* (1937). The first book argued, for instance, that the criminal trial system offered more than a field-bounded practice that determined the legal fate of litigants. Seen as a cultural ceremony, rather than simply as a narrowly legalistic enterprise, a trial involved ritualistic symbolism that could overshadow "all other ceremonies as a dramatization of the values of our spiritual government, representing the dignity of the state as an enforcer of law and, at the same time the dignity of the individual," even when she was an "avowed opponent of the State . . ." Without the "drama of the criminal trial," Arnold argued, "it is difficult to imagine on just what institution we would hang" conflicting notions of "public morality."

Although Arnold abandoned academic life, his colleague Fred Rodell remained at Yale, where he gained a reputation for highly eclectic, often bombastic popular writing. His critics thought titles such as *Woe Unto You, Lawyers* (1939), Rodell's caustic assault on nearly every aspect of the classical legal vision, more worthy of a popular gossip columnist than a law professor at Yale. (A British observer once called Rodell "the Walter Winchell of the law schools.") Undeterred, Rodell continued down his wayward path, and his law school course, designed to help non-lawyers write about things legal for a general readership, led some students to careers in legal journalism.

For much of the rest of the twentieth century, however, few legal professionals followed Arnold's or Rodell's turn toward commercial culture. The vast majority of lawyers, judges, and law professors showed far less interest looking at the symbolic dimension of the U.S. trial system than in seeing it in more traditional ways, especially in light of legal-constitutional doctrines, such as "due process" and the "right to counsel."

When the technologies of commercial culture entered the courtroom, legal insiders worried about the integrity of the judicial process. Litigants who sought to introduce imagery that included the kind of scripting and staging found in commercial motion pictures encountered especially strong opposition. In 1923, as Jennifer L. Mnookin and Nancy West have noted, a New York court refused to admit into evidence a filmed sequence intended to show how a one-legged performer had earned a living as a vaudeville dancer until injured in an automobile accident. It argued that the vaudevillian's "eccentric dancing, comic songs . . . had no place" in a court of law and that admitting filmic evidence of this kind "tended to make a farce of the trial."[1] About twenty years later, as Jessica M. Silbey has noted, a Wisconsin appellate tribunal overturned a lower court decision on the grounds, in part, that the trial judge had allowed the introduction of filmic evidence, thereby "permitting the plaintiff to convert the court into a 'movie' picture theater." The appellate decision complained that the filmed footage was likely "highly entertaining to the jury, but entertainment of the jury is no function of a trial."[2]

Most lawyers and judges took a similarly disdainful view of commercial culture's approach to cases that became notorious ones. In the wake of the Lindbergh kidnapping case, for example, the American Bar Association (ABA) moved to limit photographic and radio coverage. As one response to

---

[1] *Gibson v. Gunn* 202 N.Y.S. 19 (1923).

[2] *Hadrian et al v. Milwaukee Electric Railway & Transport Co.*, 1 N.W. 2d 755, 758 (Wis. 1942).

the ABA's initiative, Congress imposed a ban on photographs and broadcasts in all federal courtrooms. Several states, though, did permit the fledgling TV industry to place cameras in courtrooms during the 1950s. In 1965, a majority of the U.S. Supreme Court adopted a more traditional view when it held that TV coverage could violate a defendant's Sixth Amendment right to a fair trial. Critically reviewing TV coverage of a preliminary hearing in the much-watched case of Billy Sol Estes, an associate of Lyndon Johnson, the Court saw the media cameras depriving Estes of "that judicial serenity and calm" that the Constitution guaranteed any criminal defendant. Chief Justice Earl Warren's concurring opinion in *Estes* appended a series of photographs that purportedly showed video apparatus cluttering a courtroom and creating a media-created legal circus. Although subsequent Supreme Court decisions created space for cameras in some other tribunals, the High Court itself began the twenty-first century with its ban against visual media still in place.

Legal Realism and the Emergence of the "Law Ands"

Although the realist initiative moved to the fringes of the legal field during the 1940s, its core critique of the narrowly bounded vision of the classical approach persisted. Ultimately, this part of the realist aesthetic helped ground a number of academic projects that emerged during the last half of the twentieth century. All of the "law and" approaches, which reached beyond law schools into other areas of academic life, shared the earlier realist goal: trying to look beyond the formal texts produced within the legal field and toward images of things legal in other areas, including commercial popular culture.

A "law-and-society movement," focused on the social dimensions of legality, appeared around the mid-point of the twentieth century. It attracted both law professors and social scientists, especially those interested in criminal justice issues. Its growing visibility roughly coincided with the activism that found expression in Lyndon Johnson's Great Society and the U.S. Supreme Court under Chief Justice Earl Warren during the 1960s. To cite only one example, law-and-society research looked to social science expertise in hopes of better seeing how everyday practice eroded the practical value of the legal-constitutional guarantee of a fair trial. Criminal defendants who faced a possible prison sentence needed professional legal counsel, law-and-society studies maintained, and the state should provide effective legal assistance to those unable to employ their own lawyer.

At about the same time, a research tradition in "law and economics" also came into view, especially at the University of Chicago. Its adherents insisted, among their many other claims, that long-standing English common law doctrines of property and contract rested less on a uniquely legal gaze than on an economic vision of maximized efficiency. The law-and-economics framework helped reshape both legal practice and theory, particularly in antitrust and administrative law, during the last third of the twentieth century. Scholarly work within this framework, its proselytizers claimed, could transform law into a more precise instrument for making social-economic calculations, ones that invariably envisioned a more limited role for governmental action than studies in the equally instrumental law-and-society mode.

As the list of "law ands" expanded, a diverse agenda in "law and culture" took shape and eventually spawned several sub-initiatives. "Law and literature," the earliest of these, generally gravitated toward legal images and themes in canonized, "high-culture" texts, such as Mark Twain's *Huckleberry Finn* (1885) and Herman Melville's novella *Billy Budd* (discovered after the author's 1891 death but not published until 1921). Critics (including Richard Posner, a prolific exponent of law and economics) dismissed claims that the study of literary works could help legal professionals interpret and construct the specialized texts with which they worked. The study of literature, even when penned by Franz Kafka or Melville, could offer students of law virtually nothing, Posner insisted. Avowedly commercial popular culture – whether in the form of journalism, novels, motion pictures, or TV shows – seemed to provide even less promising materials.

Toward the end of the twentieth century, however, the scholarly case for exploring commercial culture's relationship to the legal field gained ground. A broadly based intellectual mood within parts of the academy, often called "the cultural turn," encouraged new styles of scholarship in the humanities and social sciences. Scholars familiar with TV, motion pictures, and other forms of commercial culture began to argue that their imagery be seen as part of the complex process by which people assigned meaning to every area of daily life, including those marked by the law. Commercial culture seemed to surround, perhaps even to "invade," the field of the law.

IV. THE LEGAL FIELD, COMMERCIAL CULTURE, AND THE CULTURAL TURN

Particularly during the 1960s, people both inside and outside academe passionately debated how commercial imagery helped frame public debate. In an age of ever more rapid communication and new forms of visual imagery, familiar ways of representing contested issues, from both the past and the present, no longer seemed adequate. People considered the challenge of a "new journalism," the products of a "new Hollywood cinema," and the "sensory bombardment" ricocheting through the "media matrix." In addition, of course, the nation's political culture seemed awash in pop iconography.

At the same time, visual images of possible connections between the judicial and the policing systems were flooding the "videosphere." People who wished to address the relationship between legal practice and crime, for example, needed to confront the representations on television. The turmoil surrounding the 1968 Democratic Convention provided one enduring emblem of the politics and theatrics of this cultural-legal process. Antiwar demonstrators, proclaiming "the whole world is watching," and the Chicago police officers who confronted them, became characters in a mass-mediated, pop-cultural spectacle that featured vivid, and highly contested, representations of the rule of law, the search for order, and the ideal of equal justice.

Similar dramas increasingly marked the last decades of the twentieth century. An idiosyncratic and incomplete list might include the following: the Chicago conspiracy trial of 1969; the 1974 shootout between the Los Angeles Police Department and the Symbionese Liberation Army, the televised Congressional inquiries of 1973–74 into Richard Nixon's administration, the Iran-Contra hearings, the "Rodney King case," the "White Bronco" chase that preceded O. J. Simpson's two trials, the murder prosecution of Eric and Lyle Menendez, the ongoing legal dramas of the Clinton presidency that culminated in his impeachment and trial, and the legal-constitutional maneuvering that followed the presidential election of 2000.

Initially, the television industry followed the practice of the 1950s and early 1960s and interrupted regular programming to cover at least a portion of all these spectacles. The news-saturated coverage of the late sixties and the subsequent arrival of 24/7 cable-TV operations such as CNN and Court TV, however, ensured an almost continual flow of legal imagery and commentary.

Making its debut during the early 1990s, Court TV seemed a logical outgrowth of a century of legal popularizing. Capitalizing on several notorious cases that other outlets, after the saturation coverage of O. J. Simpson's legal troubles, decided to ignore, Court TV solidified its base with coverage of the Menendez case in 1995–96. Initially the cable network specialized in real-time pictures of, and commentary about, subsequent court cases. Eventually, though, Court TV expanded its programming. It screened "mainstream" network dramas, such as *NYPD Blue* and *Cops*, which had moved into syndication; mounted its own documentary-style series such as *Forensic Files*; and ventured into feature-length movie-making. Court TV eventually would find a weekly spot for Dominick Dunne, once a successful Hollywood writer and producer, who had re-invented himself – through books, magazine pieces, and a column in *Vanity Fair* – as one of the nation's premier popular chroniclers of notorious criminal trials and lawsuits involving celebrities.

At roughly the same time, the Internet came to provide an arena for creating and circulating law-related imagery and commentary. Even the U.S. Supreme Court inaugurated its own Web site. In addition, law schools and law professors constructed sites that featured notorious trials from the past and reviews on law-related movies and TV. Ordinary people who sought legal advice could point their browsers to a variety of sites. Some provided authoritative reprints of "landmark" court decisions, others offered news and information on current legal issues, and some dispensed personal advice from anonymous "lawgivers." One of those advice sites attracted considerable attention when one of its experts turned out to be a teenager who derived his legal-sounding counsel from surfing other law-related spots on the Internet and from watching TV shows such as *The People's Court*.

Meanwhile, writers specializing in legal fiction replaced Perry Mason's creator, Earle Stanley Gardner, who had died in 1971. John Grisham, a lawyer-turned-author, published a steady stream of page turners, which sold in the millions and almost immediately provided the titles and templates for successful motion pictures: *The Firm* (book published 1991, movie released 1993), *The Pelican Brief* (both 1993), and *The Rainmaker* (1996, 1997). Large chain bookstores dedicated separate sections to entries in the burgeoning "True Crime" genre.

This cultural milieu helped a fledgling research tradition into law and commercial culture gain visibility. Although "culture" remained a difficult term to pin down, legal academics engaged in this new enterprise borrowed from other post-cultural turn areas of scholarship, especially in anthropology and cultural studies. They wanted to look at all the many places, including commercial popular culture, where people could be seen struggling to impute differing legalistic meanings to events of daily life. Culture in this frame encompassed the *processes*, simultaneously linguistic and material, through which people negotiated conflicting meanings and perceptions and then struggled to translate the results into social practice.

Sometimes, work in law and culture seemed to look so far beyond the traditional legal field that its critics could decry the absence of any "real" law in the accounts written within this aesthetic. Indeed, according to Naomi Mezey's study of culture's interrelationship with law, the legal-cultural dimension of daily life could justifiably include "*any* set of signifying practices" – shared, contradictory, and contested – "by which meaning is produced, performed, contested," or transformed." This wide-ranging vision emphasized, on the one hand, that activity within the formal legal field constituted "one of the signifying practices that constitute culture" and could never "be divorced from culture." On the other hand, it imagined that the images of commercial culture produced outside the formal legal field, such as those in an episode of TV's *Law and Order* or during a day's programming on Court TV, should surely interest students of things legal.

Scholars such as Mezey saw law-related imagery and activity, wherever produced and performed, helping "constitute" the variety of everyday roles that people might occupy when interacting with one another and with legal institutions. Drawing on research projects enabled by the cultural turn, law and culture scholarship, in contrast to that in both the classical and the realist traditions, saw a world neither of isolated individuals nor of coherent social groups. Instead, it envisioned socially and culturally constructed "subjectivities" and shifting "subject positions," terms increasingly familiar in late-twentieth-century academic discourse. The institutions of the law helped identify people, even if they were not actual litigants, as "legal subjects" – people who lived their everyday lives with the expectation that they might claim legal rights and enjoy access to legal institutions that might provide remedies for invasions of their rights. When someone asserted a law-related claim, such as a "right of free speech," they seemed to be calculating that other lay people and formal guardians of the law would acknowledge its potential legal power. When viewing themselves, in turn, as legal subjects, people could see their own "self," at least in part, as a "rights holder" and assess their full range of potential social options and roles, again in part, according to this legally constructed subject position or "identity." Conversely, of course, this view of law and subjectivity also suggested that people, particularly in light of their familiarity with the imagery of popular commercial culture, might also calculate that their assertion of a legal right would ultimately make very little difference either to their fellow citizens or to those credentialed professionals who manned the gates of access to the formal legal field.

This new research tradition gained additional traction because the people who were creating late-twentieth-century commercial culture seemed inclined to see themselves in light of legal, as well as cultural and economic, identities. Viewing their daily roles as involving more than the production of commodities for the marketplace, people in the commercial culture industry aggressively claimed legal rights that both protected and enabled their expression. Law could not only shield them, for example, from governmental regulation; it could protect the products of their imagination (and, often, their very image as well) under the legal rubric of "intellectual property." Take, for example, the pornography entrepreneur Larry Flynt. Flynt's ventures generated a highly celebrated legal trial, a successful appeal to the Supreme Court that would yield a much-discussed First-Amendment decision, and a Hollywood motion picture, *The People vs. Larry Flynt* (1996). This self-identified "sleazebag" thus translated his cultural activities into a starring role in moral-legal dramas that affected U.S. constitutional law, instructed other citizens – particularly those who worked within the commercial culture enterprise – in how to play their own roles, and generally entertained or enraged a popular audience in the millions.

V. LAW AS CULTURE, CULTURE AS LAW?

How has the growing attention to connections between the field of law and the sprawling domain of commercial culture begun to reshape the history of twentieth-century U.S. law? Two examples, one focusing on notorious cases and the other on imagery in Hollywood motion pictures and TV shows, can suggest some tentative answers.

Notorious Cases: The Courtroom Joins the Popular

Before the cultural turn, legal historians saw little of genuine interest in the first great trial of the twentieth century, the murder prosecution of Harry K. Thaw. Students of law and history traditionally drew a stark line between the imagery generated by mass-mediated spectacles such as the Thaw case and legal knowledge that appeared authentic, substantial, and professionally certified.

Recall, however, that the lead attorney in Thaw's 1907 trial largely ignored legal citations and criminal law precedents. Instead, his defense strategy rested on imagery drawn from commercial melodramas and from a pop psychological theory of the day called *dementia Americana*. Any husband who had come to know what Thaw eventually knew about his wife's sexual history, the defense insisted, could become afflicted by this culturally produced malady. According to this view of gender politics, "whoever stains the virtue" of a man's wife "has forfeited the protection of human laws and must look to the eternal justice and the mercy of God."

Legal scholars had once concluded that the media oriented theatrics of the Thaw case offered little useful evidence about the history of early-twentieth-century criminal law. Even the usually keen eye of the legal historian Lawrence Friedman saw a "carnival of scandal mixed with psychiatric mumbo-jumbo," all staged by Thaw's attorneys. This kind of "super sensation" reflected a fun-house-mirror reflection of what genuine law meant and of how the legal process normally worked.

Subsequent students of the Thaw case, employing a different view of law and culture and invoking gender-related scholarship, have filed dissenting opinions. Rather than seeing such notorious cases as examples of proper iegal forms corrupted by media hoopla and psychobabble, scholars such as Martha Merrill Umphrey have viewed spectacular trials as legitimate intersections between the discourses and imagery of official law and those that circulated outside the legal field.

The Thaw case, of course, featured a clash of competing narratives. It began with the prosecution's story – bolstered by kinds of formal written rules, doctrines, and precedents that the classical, and even the realist, aesthetic worked to highlight. Scripted by the official criminal law of New York, the fate of Harry Thaw seemed obvious. He had acted maliciously, or with an evil intent, in fatally shooting Stanford White before a room full of eyewitnesses. Thus, Thaw bore full legal responsibility for his actions.

The defense responded with a counter-narrative built on a popular view of law and spousal responsibility. Following the trajectory of several much-publicized trials during the late nineteenth century, which also turned on emotionally charged gender issues, its account drew from what students of law, particularly Susan S. Silbey and Patricia Ewick, now call "popular legal consciousness" or simply "popular legal culture" – the law-related images and stories, often drawn from the commercial media, that circulate outside the formal legal field. The term, "popular legal culture," does not imply a realm of law-related imagery that is simply "out there." Rather, the phrase signifies the embedding in everyday life of "meanings, sources of authority, and cultural practices that are commonly recognized as legal, regardless of who employs them or for what ends." In everyday life, people view things legal in ways that often differ from the formal legal scripts embraced by judges and commentators.

Popular legal imagery can exert a real impact on the field of law. It seemed to have shaped, for instance, some views of how the state's legal institutions should deal with an honor-avenging husband such as Harry Thaw. During the late nineteenth century, in fact, a few jurisdictions had already appeared to bow toward popular legal culture on the issue of *dementia Americana*. They had acknowledged that a sexually related physical attack or even a mere insult to a man's spouse or female relative might provoke a violent response that could, at least in some circumstances, deserve formal legal protection.

Throughout Thaw's first trial, then, his legal team detailed a struggle between good and evil. The Thaw case pitted innocent virtue – the youthful Evelyn Nesbit Thaw, who testified on her husband's behalf about her pre-marital sexual history with Stanford White – against absolute vice: the sexually libertine architect. Overcome by emotion, Harry Thaw had acted irrationally, but without any criminal intent, to redress both White's wicked attack on the youthful Evelyn and on *his own* honor as her red-blooded American husband. Continually invoking popular imagery, Thaw's defense team fleshed out a melodramatic story about their client's heroic, if rationally impaired, action. Moreover, the defense identified heroic avengers other than Harry Thaw – the twelve male jurors charged with deciding his case. The defense's story featured melodramatic evidence that seemed intended to position the jury – and the audience that consumed commercial accounts of the trial – as absent "witnesses," like Thaw himself, to White's sexual victimization of Evelyn. The defense encouraged the jurors to act heroically. These twelve men could themselves strike out at the now deceased villain by declaring his killer not guilty – on the basis of the popular, unwritten law of *dementia Americana*. Thaw's lawyers urged them to bring closure to a narrative that envisioned, as Martha Merrill Umphrey has put it, their client's act "as a triumph over evil, not an evil act in itself."

Appropriately, perhaps, in what proved to be only Thaw's initial trial, the jury seemed suspended between the official and defense narratives. It could not agree on a verdict. A second trial, in which the defense emphasized evidence of mental problems in Thaw's family history, resulted in a verdict of not guilty by reason of insanity.

Throughout the twentieth century, any number of notorious cases displayed the kind of legal-cultural interplay highlighted in the Thaw case. TV coverage eventually helped ordinary observers to render their own legal judgments on these cases *and* to anchor their verdicts in the wealth of evidence circulated by the media and dissected in numerous personal conversations. Did, for example, TV pictures of President William Jefferson Clinton's grand jury testimony – and endlessly recycled shots of the several public occasions when Monica Lewinsky was among the crowd greeting him – show a guilty man who had brazenly mocked the rule of law by committing perjury? Or did the weight of widely seen evidence point to an embattled president trying to evade ensnarement, on private matters, by zealous partisans who were wielding the legal process as a political weapon?

A decade earlier, Congressional hearings into the Iran-Contra operation of the Ronald Reagan era had graphically showed what could happen if lawyers failed to recognize the role of commercial popular culture. Approaching allegations of illegal activities by members of Reagan's administration through a familiar research tradition and legal aesthetic, Congressional lawyers meticulously compiled written documents and eye-witness testimony. They sought evidence to bolster a traditional case narrative and legal brief against several members of Reagan's national security team. In the case of Lieutenant Colonel Oliver North, this effort failed dramatically.

Although early accounts, recalling the initial view of the Thaw case, primarily talked about "Ollie Mania" and a media-created circus, a subsequent study by Michael Lynch and David Bogen detailed how North's defense team skillfully mobilized both legal and cultural resources. First, confronted by North's shredding and manipulation of documents, which North cheerfully claimed to have been part of his job description, the committee's staff struggled even to create a coherent narrative of events. Then, a media-savvy performance by North, carried live on day-time television, constructed a counter-narrative in which he played an outlaw hero trying to outwit rule-bound bureaucrats and overly legalistic second-guessers, whom he claimed underestimated the mendacity of foreign enemies. The nation's pop-cultural jury, after watching and listening to the Congressional case against North, overwhelmingly judged him to have broken only token rules and to have actually, in perilous times, protected the ideal of the rule of law. (Although a subsequent trial in federal court resulted in a conviction, it was overturned on appeal. North extended his Congressional performance into a lucrative media career.)

The most famous trial drama of the early 1990s, starring O. J. Simpson and a colorful cast of supporting players, perhaps best exemplified the inter-section of formal law and commercial popular culture. While authorities were gathering evidence with which to charge the former football star and media personality with the murders of Nicole Brown Simpson, his former spouse, and one of her friends, the lexitainment industry was assembling a mass audience. Subsequently, every stage of this multimedia production, from Simpson's pre-trial hearing through the jury verdict in his criminal trial, positioned viewers as both (second-hand) eye-witnesses and as jurors. The drama that unfolded within the field of law increasingly overlapped, and interacted with, the larger one that ran for more than a year in com-mercial media. In time, attorneys (such as Greta van Susteren) and former judges (such as Stan Goldman) who performed well in front of media cam-eras during the Simpson era found themselves fielding offers to become legal analysts for commercial television.

The Simpson case also recalled other legal dramas and their mass-mediated representations. Most obvious, it tapped into the earlier, racially charged 1992 trial of several Los Angeles police officers who had been indicted for allegedly assaulting Rodney King, an African American sus-pect. To some viewers, a repeatedly broadcast, home-made video of members of the LAPD trying to subdue and arrest King provided clear evidence of police brutality; to others, the same footage revealed a drugged-up suspect trying to attack the police officers. As in a number of other notorious cases, that of the LAPD officers produced multiple trials and differing, much-debated verdicts.

Racial prejudice and systematic police misconduct became only two of the issues in play at Simpson's trial. In addition, the case intersected with pop-legal narratives about how the criminal law dealt with spousal abuse and about how a defendant with substantial wealth could obtain a seemingly inexhaustible supply of legal expertise. Although the criminal jury's "not guilty" verdict kept Simpson out of prison, it marked just another act in a still unfolding, "larger-than-law" drama that extended into the next century.

The formal outcome of Simpson's criminal trial only accelerated the speed at which narratives about the wider OJ drama could travel. Long after the official verdict had come in, cable TV retried the case, with some law-soaked programs featuring "all OJ, all the time." As this post-trial phase of the criminal case proceeded, its viewer-jurors apparently agreed on only one thing: The legal process that had unfolded inside a Los Angeles courtroom failed to illuminate sufficiently – or was utterly blind to – what any clear-eyed observer of lexitainment should easily have seen. From one perspective, for example, the law had failed to bring the issue of spousal abuse, allegedly evidence of the defendant's history of violence toward women and emblematized by pictures of Nicole Brown Simpson's battered face, into sufficient view. From a very different angle, many of Simpson's defenders claimed that the prosecution team, even with an African American attorney in the forefront, had never appreciated that it lacked evidence against O. J. Simpson, except that which had been fabricated by racists within the LAPD. The relative blindness of the legal system, when compared to the keener eyes of commercial popular culture, thus remained a powerful trope in very different narratives about this and other trials of the century.

In short, the various trials of the century, such as those of Harry Thaw and O. J. Simpson, suggested the overlap between the formal legal field and the world of commercial popular culture. Official legal understandings, as research projects involving the interaction of law and culture have begun to argue, unfolded in complex conversations with discourses and imagery produced by the lexitainment industry.

Movie and TV Imagery and the Field of Law

The impact of commercial culture also seemed evident, outside the spotlight trained on notorious cases, in day-to-day operations within the legal field. As a result, some students of law turned toward a whole new set of "legal" texts produced by the culture industry. Drawing on academic studies of commercial culture, they often began by emphasizing how Hollywood motion pictures and television programs featured law-related imagery.

Especially after the arrival of sound films in 1927, Hollywood had turned out thousands of movies, and literally millions of images, about things legal. While doing so, the film factories themselves needed to negotiate a wide range of legalistic, political, and cultural forces. The industry promulgated its own, self-professed legal norms in the form of an industry-wide Production Code (the "Hays Code"), overseen after 1934 by an administrative body, the Production Code Administration (PCA), dominated by Catholic lay people. The Code ultimately decreed that the law, "natural or human, shall not be ridiculed, nor shall sympathy be created for its violation." It also conceded that crimes "against the law naturally occur in the course of film stories," but the Production Code Administration stood ready to intervene if movies portrayed law as if it were "wrong or ridiculous." It also scrutinized movies for any devils, such as corrupt police officers or judges, that might be hiding in the details of Hollywood's version of the law-in-action.

By doing the kind of private legal-cultural work for Hollywood that an analogous system of self-regulation performed for organized baseball, the PCA tried to deflect charges that the film studios fostered disrespect for the law. Prior to the PCA's creation, several controversial entries in the gangster genre, particularly *The Public Enemy* (1931) and *Scarface* (1931), had featured allegedly over-glamorous images of law-breaking by charismatic outlaw heroes. In response, the Production Code Administration and the Hollywood studios cooperated to reconstruct gangster movies. By first showing a mobster's dramatic challenge to legal authority and then by portraying his even more dramatic downfall, the industry could claim that crime dramas argued for the sanctity and ultimate solidity of the prevailing legal order. Similarly, movies that portrayed "shyster" lawyers as exciting, alluring figures embedded these images in story lines that showed the high-flying careers of these rogue attorneys heading downward, straight into the arms of law enforcement officials.

When this particular narrative structure, "transgression-followed-by-repression," failed to eliminate criticism, Hollywood adopted other strategies to defuse claims that the industry encouraged disrespect for both moral and legal norms. Hollywood filmmakers came to represent things legal within a narrative schema that students of cinema have called the "reconciliatory framework." Here, a filmic narrative would feature law-related disputes that, at first glance, seemed to lack any middle ground. A movie might initially pose a stark conflict between a fidelity to legal rules and the pursuit of justice. As the story line unfolded, however, it would try to show how this apparent conflict proved merely superficial and, ultimately, could become amenable to solutions that satisfied both goals – particularly when some heroic (male) figure assumed the initiative. Typically, the on-screen resolution involved showing how "bending" a few overly strict rules could achieve a just resolution without violating the spirit of the rule of law.

This reconciliatory frame, with law-related images typically at its center, appeared in many classical Hollywood genres including crime dramas, detective stories, and tales of the old West. It also structured a popular hybrid form that students of cinema later called the "disguised Western." Hollywood's most beloved disguised Western, *Casablanca* (1943), featured Humphrey Bogart playing Rick Blaine, a one-time left-leaning lawyer who manages to uphold the ideal of the rule of law in the worst of circumstances. Running an upscale gambling establishment in an isolated, frontier town, which happens to be in 1940s North Africa rather than in 1880s Montana, Rick seems hopelessly trapped between agents of an imperfect legal system and a cast of skilled law-breakers. As any (Hollywood) Western gunfighter might have done, he manipulates the town's corruptible law officer, Captain Renault (Claude Rains), and simply shoots down the movie's key "bad guy," a Nazi officer (Conrad Veidt) who is trampling through Vichy France's legal field for the benefit of the Third Reich. For good measure, Rick's actions help affirm other law-related norms. This outlaw hero, for example, respects the legally binding marriage of his former lover, Ilsa Lund (Ingrid Bergman) to the Resistance leader, Victor Lazlo (Paul Henreid). He also accepts the elaborate legal fiction of *Casablanca*'s famous "letters of transit," the documents that sustain the internal legal logic of the movie's narrative.

The PCA and the studios worked to devise another deflective strategy: offering moviegoers open-ended imagery of things legal that invited multiple interpretations. Rather than being straitjacketed by tightly closed narratives, Classical Hollywood's versions of law invariably featured contingent, ambiguous, and contradictory images that enabled a diverse audience to interpret them in different ways. The recent availability of shooting scripts, memos from the PCA, and deleted footage – once packed away in studio vaults and archives – has helped highlight the Production Code in action. In *Casablanca*, for example, the PCA encouraged the movie's producers to obfuscate the matter of "how far" Ilsa and Rick had "gone" while apparently trying to rekindle, in violation of her "sexual contract" with Victor, their earlier affair. The administrators also obtained what they considered crucial changes in set décor (eliminating any suggestions of a bed or couch in Rick's apartment) and in cinematic coding (substituting a simple dissolve for a supposedly more "suggestive" fade-out to conclude one sexually charged scene).

Hollywood, and later the television industry, also offered legal stories that appeared to parallel those structured by the Anglo-American trial process. It is easy, of course, to identify this resemblance in trial-structured movies, such as *They Won't Believe Me* (1947) and *To Kill a Mockingbird* (1962), or in an episode of TV's *Law and Order*. Both the initial setups and subsequent movement of the cameras in these kinds of texts seemingly work to position viewers as if they were jurors. Audiences are thus encouraged to imagine themselves hearing arguments, weighing divergent testimony, making tentative ongoing judgments of guilty or not guilty, and, ultimately rendering their own verdicts on an individual narrative's legal questions.

Similarly, as the literary scholar Carol J. Clover suggests, "trials are already movie-like to begin with and movies are already trial-like to begin with." Anglo-American jury trials have long inscribed a unique dramatic dimension, a "theater of justice," which contains a strong visual component that includes judicial robes, a raised bench, and a colorful cast of characters. Even a motion picture not organized around a trial sequence, Clover argues, might still be seen as one that "mimics the phases, the logic, and the narrative texture of a trial." *Casablanca*, for instance, "jurifies" its audience by presenting it with fragments of ambiguous evidence, conflicting witness-like testimony, and a series of emotionally charged encounters that resemble those found in real (and reel) courtrooms. Many of the most dramatic sequences in *Casablanca*, as already noted, involve law-related questions that its goal-oriented legal subjects must try to answer.

More recent Hollywood movies of the post-Classical era can seem to play, self-reflexively, with structural similarities between the theater of courtroom justice and forms commonly found in commercial culture. Again, these films need not, though they may, include sequences that depict a courtroom trial. Beginning its trial-like narrative with a brutal crime and concealing the identity of the perpetrator, for example, *Basic Instinct* (1992) seemingly hopes to jurify viewers by presenting them with a legal question on which to pass judgment. Then, it offers them contested information about possible suspects, motives, and alibis. *Basic Instinct* thus uses a cinematic structure that resembles how conflicting and rigorously cross-examined testimony and bits of evidence come out during a courtroom trial. Subsequent movies, such as *The Usual Suspects* (1995) and *Memento* (2000), confronted viewer-jurors with even more complex legal puzzles.

Some students of the law-as-culture framework have come to argue that Hollywood movies and TV programs can directly influence texts and activities within the formal legal field. Studies of real-world jury behavior, for example, have suggested that some jurors use the iconic, but entirely fictive, drama *12 Angry Men* (especially the 1957 movie version starring Henry Fonda) as a model. Some social science jury studies, it seems, molded their research design in light of images from this cultural product. Similarly, during the early 1990s, law school admissions officers claimed to find that their youthful applicants cited the influence of TV programs, particularly *L. A. Law* (1986–1994), as motivating them to pursue a legal career. In time, legal scholars would debate how CBS Television's popular crime drama *CSI* (Crime Scene Investigation) might impact the work of real-life prosecutors.

The following comparison of the lexitainment industry's images of criminal defense attorneys with the views of prominent lawyers and judges suggests yet another angle on the interrelationship between commercial legal culture and the formal legal field. During the 1930s, both state-empowered courts and Hollywood's fictive tribunals struggled over the role of defense attorneys in criminal proceedings. The U.S. Supreme Court confronted this issue in a series of cases involving the "Scottsboro boys," young African American men convicted in Alabama of having sexually assaulted two

Caucasian women. Beginning with the lengthy appeal process in these racially and politically charged cases, the U.S. Supreme Court expanded older views of when the Constitution demanded competent, professional representation for defendants. Ultimately, though, as the Court worked through the post-Scottsboro cases, it stopped short, in *Betts v. Brady* (1942), of requiring individual states to provide indigent defendants with attorneys in all non-capital, felony cases. The Constitution required states to furnish professional counsel to impoverished felony defendants *only* when courts found "special circumstances," such as a defendant's illiteracy or mental impairment, to be present.

The motion picture industry did much better by fictive defendants: it employed lawyers in virtually all of its cinematic trials. Many of the Silver Screen's leading men – including Henry Fonda, Gregory Peck, and Humphrey Bogart – stepped forward to defend persons accused of a crime and to uphold the rule of law. Television eventually provided a steady supply of its own attorneys eager to do pro bono work on behalf of indigent criminal defendants.

Commercial legal culture seemed incapable of representing a criminal trial, then, without casting a defense lawyer as a key player. In addition, whether the story portrayed its defense lawyer as heroic, venal, or ineffectual, motion pictures and TV shows invariably suggested how the U.S. legal system could overwhelm all but the most powerful defendants and suspects. Eventually, these popular tropes found their way into constitutional law.

In *Gideon v. Wainwright* (1963), the U.S. Supreme Court overruled *Betts v. Brady* and bridged the gulf between the formal legal field and that of commercial popular culture. It held that the Constitution required states to provide an attorney for all indigent felony defendants. From a law-and-culture perspective, *Gideon* nicely illustrated the convergence between the images in commercial productions and those in Supreme Court litigation.

First, of course, the person who initiated this case, a convict named Clarence Earl Gideon, hoped for a story line that more closely resembled those seen in theaters and on TV than the one scripted by the constitutional rule in *Betts*. Sitting in a Florida prison, after being convicted in a trial in which he had to represent himself because he lacked money for an attorney, Gideon imagined that he could revise the formal legal script by sending a handwritten appeal to the U.S. Supreme Court. Gideon viewed his own courtroom narrative, absent a defense attorney, as a substandard (as well as an "unconstitutional") legal drama.

Then, after the U.S. Supreme Court voted to hear Gideon's *in pauperis* petition, the Washington, D.C., law firm assigned to argue his appeal filed a brief that itself looked to commercial culture. It conspicuously contrasted the frequency of guilty pleas in the real-life legal system with images in commercial dramas. This discrepancy, according to the brief signed by Gideon's appointed attorney and future Supreme Court Justice Abe Fortas, suggested "that those who are arrested, particularly the penniless and persons who are members of minority groups, are more likely hopelessly to resign themselves to fate than aggressively to act like the defense counsel portrayed on television." When writing for the High Court in overturning *Betts*, Justice Hugo Black invoked similar cultural imagery. Since the state spends "vast sums of money to establish machinery to try defendants accused of crime," Justice Black's opinion argued, defense lawyers had become essential parts of the drama and not "luxuries."

Two years later, in *Miranda v. Arizona*, the Supreme Court extended the cultural images – as well as the legal citations – that had bolstered the *Gideon* ruling. In *Miranda*, a majority of the justices suggested the need at least to consider bringing lawyers into real-life legal dramas not simply during court trials but whenever police authorities were holding a criminal suspect for interrogation. Under what became popularly known as the "Miranda warning," a suspect "must be clearly informed that he has the right to consult with a lawyer and to have the lawyer with him during interrogation." Only such a rule, the Court held, could make the Fifth Amendment's right against self-incrimination truly meaningful. A suspect could still decline formal legal counsel, but this waiver needed to come after a warning about the right to professional assistance.

Images of the *Gideon* and *Miranda* decisions circulated through both commercial and professional legal cultures. The *Gideon* case, especially as recounted in a best-selling book (*Gideon's Trumpet*, 1964) by the journalist Anthony Lewis and in a movie starring Henry Fonda as Gideon, provided a celebratory legal drama about the importance of trained legal counsel to the protection of legally guaranteed rights. *Miranda* immediately gained even greater attention in the parallel worlds of constitutional theory, criminal law, and commercial culture. TV shows and movies began showing fictive police officers giving fictional suspects the Miranda warning. Seen in one powerful media frame, of course, this soon-familiar portrayal of police work simply displayed proper respect for the rule of law and for the rights of criminal suspects. From another perspective, however, the very same images could also suggest how much court rulings such as *Miranda* hindered law enforcement and coddled criminals.

Criticism of the Miranda warning quickly gained ground in the field of politics and, more slowly, in that of law. Beginning with the 1968 election, "law and order" politicians, most notably Richard Nixon and George Wallace, blamed *Miranda* for handcuffing police officers. Dissents against the Miranda warning circulated more slowly among legal professionals. In time, however, the decision's supporters within the legal field began complaining about how an increasingly conservative federal judiciary seemed to be dealing with *Miranda*-related cases. Court rulings during the 1990s, defenders of *Miranda* feared, were not only undercutting its practical value to criminal suspects but also were raising the possibility that the U.S. Supreme Court might eventually hold that the initial 1966 decision had only stated an evidentiary rule and not a fundamental constitutional requirement.

Meanwhile, images of *Miranda*'s supposed impact, even if tilted in a critical direction (as in Clint Eastwood's *"Dirty Harry"* motion picture series) remained a staple of commercial popular culture. The Miranda warning became so pervasive in the U.S.-dominated videosphere that many criminal suspects in Canada, whose legal system operated without a comparable process, expected to be read their Miranda rights. A U.S. scholar visiting a law school class in Spain claimed that students there, because of the ubiquity of Hollywood movies and U.S-made TV dramas, seemed to know more about the criminal law procedures of the United States than those of their own legal system.

Dickerson v. U.S. (2000), an end-of-the-century U.S. Supreme Court decision on the meaning of *Miranda*, dramatized the coupling of commercial popular legal culture and constitutional law. Here, a majority of the Court held *Miranda* to be a constitutional ruling and emphasized how the image of law enforcement officers reading suspects their Miranda rights "has become embedded in routine police practice to the point where the warnings have become part of our national culture." In other words, some of the justices voting to sustain *Miranda*, as the bitter dissent of Justice Antonin Scalia emphasized, appeared to see its survival as not so much required by the nation's formal Constitution as demanded by the representation of legal process people saw in movies and on TV. Commenting on the significance of *Dickerson* from a law-and-culture perspective, Naomi Mezey suggested that the case underscored how "law and culture are mutually constituted and legal and cultural meanings are produced precisely at the intersection of the two domains, which are themselves only fictionally distinct."

CONCLUSION

Building on developments in the nineteenth century, the imagery in twentieth-century commercial popular culture focused, ever more widely and intensively, on things legal. Over the same 100-year period, legal scholarship became more interested in the commercial culture industry and its place not only in notorious cases such as that of O. J. Simpson but in the daily life of the law. Taken together, the increasing popularization of things legal and the growing attention paid to popular legal images and practices by students of law began to reorient legal studies. The turn toward culture, including the images in commercially produced products such as movies and TV shows, helped make the case against research agendas that focused too narrowly on the formal legal field. A new research tradition began to suggest how the texts produced and the practices performed within the field of law interacted with broader domains, including that of commercial popular culture.

MAKING LAW, MAKING WAR, MAKING AMERICA

MARY L. DUDZIAK

At the close of the First World War, Woodrow Wilson embarked upon a utopian mission. It was not on American soil that armies had slaughtered each other, but Americans had been there in the carnage, and so in its aftermath an American president took up the task of ensuring that it would never happen again. Wilson hoped to create a world body, a League of Nations, and through it order for a lawless world. By such efforts, world leaders thought they might contain a force that had long structured and tortured human affairs and that had become, in their eyes, newly unthinkable due to the horrifying consequences of modern weaponry. The airplanes and submarines that took bloodshed across continents gave the world a new common goal: to end forever the specter of war.

The League is most famous, of course, for its failure, but in that utopian moment we can see an element that would not be lost on the rest of the twentieth century. Americans and others held on to the belief that somehow human action could stave off this most ancient form of politics. And they often turned to law as a means of holding back the forces of war.

War would not be contained by law, of course. Instead, war would be a defining feature of the twentieth century. This meant that war would play a central role in the history of American law.

Despite that reality, writing in American legal history touches rather infrequently on war. History is most often conceptualized as divided into time zones, wartime and peacetime; war is thought of as an exception to "normal" time. Unless the topic under consideration is the exception itself (war), war tends to disappear from the narrative. Writing that does focus directly on law and war shares the assumption that wartime is exceptional. The dominant metaphor is of a pendulum swinging back and forth between protection of rights during peacetime and protection of security during wartime. Switching from one time zone to another is thought to set the pendulum swinging in a new direction.

Zones of peace- and wartime serve a particular function in the law. They enable war to be seen as an exceptional state when, regrettably it is thought, the usual rules do not apply. In times of war, the saying goes, law is silent. Scholars debate the degree to which law really is, or should be, silent during wartime. But that debate does not disturb the underlying conception: that wartime is different from regular time and that wartime is preceded and followed by periods of normality. This way of thinking about law and war keeps us from seeing sustained impacts over time.

The time zone/pendulum conceptualization of law and war is, however, difficult to maintain in the twentieth century. First, Congress rarely officially declared war in the twentieth century, so formal legal markers of war cannot be employed to mark off the time zones. Second, military action in one form or another was more or less constant. According to federal government reports the United States was engaged in the use of military force overseas in all but ten of the years since the close of World War I.[1] When American troops went overseas, they took weapons and on occasion killed people. Out of all of this killing, only some made it into the pantheon of American "wars." Or perhaps it would be better to say it this way: of all the events experienced by humans on the ground as warfare, only some were treated by the nation as war. A bullet might have the same trajectory as it cuts through flesh, it might trigger the same nerve endings; what is different is its geopolitical rendering.

Whether military killing is a "war," then, depends less on the nature of the weapons deployed, and more on the narrative brought to bear on the action. Sometimes iconic events, like Pearl Harbor, signaled an unmistakable opening of war. But since, for Americans, twentieth-century military engagements defined as wars happened elsewhere, the moment that a war entered the American consciousness was usually some overseas crisis of murky dimensions: the sinking of the battleship *Maine*, the crossing of the 38th Parallel, the Gulf of Tonkin incident. Most often, the United States eased into war over time; beginnings and endings are difficult to see. Constructing events into a "war" on which American security depended required a narrative about who Americans were as a people and how the new enemy constituted a military threat to interests at home. Constructing some events as not-war helped maintain the idea that wartime was exceptional and that non-war military involvements were peripheral to the body politic.

---

[1] Richard F. Grimmett, Instances of Use of United States Armed Forces Abroad, 1798–2004, Washington DC: Congressional Research Service, Library of Congress, October 5, 2004. The tally does not include not-so-covert actions, like the 1961 Bay of Pigs invasion.

This chapter does not follow the traditional conceptualization in which times of peace and war are distinct states of being. Rather, it makes four central arguments. First, war and national security have cut through the twentieth-century history of American law. No temporal switch changes the legal terrain as the nation moves into a time of war. Instead, troops are deployed nearly always, although national engagement and mobilization vary over time. Even when soldiers are safe at home, the memory of war and the anticipation of the next conflagration are continuing aspects of law and legal thought. A central feature of national awareness and engagement with war is a narrative, the construction of a war, the way a conflict is understood and promoted.

Second, although rights are thought to ebb and flow, to be stronger in peacetime and weaker in wartime, rights do not track back and forth along a peace-war trajectory. Rights are at the heart of American identity; they are part of the way in which conceptions of the United States are expressed in law. What the nation is, what it stands for, what dangers it faces, are at stake in many individual rights cases. From this perspective, rights expand, contract, and are reconfigured in relation to conceptions of the nation and conceptions of its security needs. Who we are and what we fear affect rights more than what time it is.

Third, "war" is thought of as a natural category, existing outside the law. It is something to which law reacts. But here, as in other contexts, law helps bring into being the world that it then sets about regulating. There is no natural entity called "war" that exists outside human constructions of it. At times, law has been thought of as a way to stop war. Then, as the law of war was filled in, as humanitarian law defined wars outside the bounds of humanity, it constructed as well a vision of war within those bounds. Law does not turn war off and on, but law does tell us about how we understand war's character.

Fourth, just as the effect of war on rights has been constant rather than episodic, its impact on government power and state-building has been central and continuing. Just as nations are at times made by wars, war helped build the modern American state. Government programs and regulations created in wartime were often drawn on after war to serve new purposes. As national security came to be dependent on the development of weapons technology, a permanent armaments industry developed, drawing on increasing shares of government revenue. By the 1930s, the historian Michael Sherry has argued, militarization was a central feature of American life and war a central component of political rhetoric; the impact of war and militarization would only increase through the rest of the century.

In this chapter, I explore the different functions that law plays in relation to war: as a means to control war, as an aspect of war-related state-building, and as a way to manage American society during war.

After both the first and second world wars Americans thought law could be used as a mechanism to hold back war or to control its practice. In outlawing forms of warfare as inhumane, however, humanitarian law implicitly carves out forms of war that are right and noble. When it does so, law helps enable certain forms of warfare.

Perhaps ironically, alongside American hopes to eradicate war came an increasing focus on war in the U.S. economy and government. Programs, powers, and symbols of government originating in wartime were turned to "peacetime" uses; eventually "peacetime" came to be conceptualized not as a time of war's absence, but as a time of engagement in war prevention. Long before President Dwight D. Eisenhower warned of the dangers to democracy of a "military industrial complex," war had become a central feature of American political and economic life. War became both an engine of state-building and a logic of government.

Finally, law became a way to manage domestic matters that affected war and national security. The conventional narrative of law and war in American history highlights the relationship between civil liberties and executive power. The idea that there is a balance between liberty and security, and that during war the balance tips in favor of security, illustrates government use of law as a technology of national security: ratcheting back on rights is supposed to make the nation safer. But law has also been a tool of a different kind in what is often called the "war of ideas." Because American law is seen as a reflection of American democracy, at times the protection of legal rights, rather than their curtailment, has aided American war efforts, both by enhancing solidarity at home and by maintaining the image of the nation abroad. In these contexts, too, law is a tool of war.

The chapter ends with a discussion of war and law in the wake of the terrorist attacks of September 11, 2001. The attacks have been viewed as if they created a break from the past, a moment when "everything changed." Instead, the conception of war powers and American sovereignty that came into focus post-9/11 is an extension of developments in the twentieth century, rather than a departure from them. In this moment, fears expressed earlier in the century about the relationship between democracy and militarization became most stark. The era seems characterized by a retreat from law, as the United States took steps to shield its actions from scrutiny by domestic and international courts. But government action was predicated on another image of law – what Ruti Teitel has called the "sovereign police," at watch over the world, submitting to no lesser authority.[2] Although this image is powerful, the ultimate lesson of the 9/11 era may be that no sovereign power is without limits.

[2] Ruti G. Teitel, "Empire's Law: Foreign Relations by Presidential Fiat," in Mary L. Dudziak, ed., *September 11 in History: A Watershed Moment?* (Durham, NC, 2003), 198.

I. LAW AS AN END TO WAR

"It is not now possible to assess the consequences of this great consumma-
tion," Woodrow Wilson said to Congress, in announcing the Armistice on
November 11, 1918. "We know only that this tragical war, whose consuming flames swept from one nation to another until all the world was on fire, is
at an end and that it was the privilege of our own people to enter it at its most
critical juncture in such fashion and in such force as to contribute . . . to the
great result." Perhaps it is the inevitable fate of wars that they take on transcendent meanings. Perhaps there is a human need to ascribe such meanings
to wars, as a way to account, in retrospect, for the uncountable casualties. It
would be the ironic fate of this Great War to become the war to end all war. In
its wake, world leaders gathered in a hopeless quest to ensure that war itself
would not circle the earth again.

Ending War

The question of how peace would succeed war was a focus in the negotiations
that led to the Treaty of Versailles. Drafted at the Paris Peace Conference,
the treaty contemplated the creation of a League of Nations. The League
imagined legal process as a peaceful arena for conflict and an alternative
to war. Nations would agree to resolve disputes not by armed conflict, but
by arbitration and consultation. Nations that violated the pact would be
subjected to boycott by the League's members. Article 10, controversial
among American critics in the Senate, pledged signatories to aid any member attacked by another nation. President Wilson crossed the country in a
futile effort to raise sufficient American support to carry the treaty through
the Senate. In speeches, he urged that the League was the world's only hope
against war. Without the League to protect the peace, he warned, the alternative was a militarized nation with "secret agencies planted everywhere"
and a president transformed from a civil leader into "a commander in chief,
ready to fight the world." A mix of American isolationism and domestic
political conflict blocked Wilson's efforts. After a protracted debate, the
Senate rejected the treaty and, as Wilson famously put it, broke "the heart
of the world."

   If Americans could not prevent war through a League of Nations, perhaps
they could do it more directly, through law itself. On August 27, 1928,
fifteen nations signed a treaty, the Kellogg-Briand Pact, a solemn pledge
of peace. According to the pact, these nations' leaders were "[p]ersuaded
that the time has come when a frank renunciation of war as an instrument
of national policy should be made to the end that the peaceful and friendly
relations now existing between their peoples may be perpetuated." This

was a radical break from the past when national security was ensured by armaments rather than by agreements. But the consequences of war had been spelled out in the blood of their citizens, and for some, at least, it seemed too high a price to pay. Therefore the nations pledged to each other "that they condemn recourse to war for the solution of international controversies, and renounce it, as an instrument of national policy in their relations with one another." The power of Kellogg-Briand, however, lay only in its rhetoric. The pact had no means of enforcement. In ratifying it, the U.S. Senate made clear that the United States retained the right of self-defense and was not compelled to take action against a nation that broke the treaty. And so, powerful as the ideas behind this peace pact may have been, its words could not hold back the invasion of Manchuria by Japan only three years later, or Italy's invasion of Ethiopia in 1935, or the German march across Europe that began in 1938.

Once World War II had run its course, nations gathered for another conference, this time in San Francisco, hoping once again that they could create a world body and an international legal system that would replace warfare with a rule of law. After the carnage of the war their aim again seemed utopian, but so important was it that it is inscribed in the opening words of the founding document of the body they would create: the United Nations. The Preamble of the U.N. Charter announced that "WE THE PEOPLES OF THE UNITED NATIONS DETERMINED to save succeeding generations from the scourge of war, which twice in our lifetime has brought untold sorrow to mankind, . . . do hereby establish an international organization to be known as the United Nations." The Charter was ratified by the United States and, initially, forty-nine other nations, but the UN's effectiveness was quickly hampered by Cold War politics. Although it has played an important role in peacekeeping efforts at different times, its continued existence is perhaps the greatest testament to a lasting hope, if not belief, that law and global institutions can be an impediment to the forces of war.

Another step taken to end war through law after World War II was the prosecution of Nazi leaders at Nuremberg. The U.S. prosecution team was led by Supreme Court Justice Robert Jackson, on leave from the Court. The Nazis had engaged in the torture and slaughter of Jews and other innocent civilians, and a horrified world expected retribution. Many also believed that the Nazis had to be held responsible so that acts like theirs would never happen again. Nazi leaders were charged with conspiracy to wage aggressive war, waging aggressive war, and committing war crimes and crimes against humanity. The first two counts criminalized the very act of waging war. Evidence of the crime of aggressive war included Germany's violation of the Kellogg-Briand pact.

The most controversial aspect of the Nuremberg trials was that many of the charges lacked precedent in international law. Law was constructed after the fact and applied to the defendants, something that in the United States would be an unconstitutional ex post facto law. Debate raged about whether the tribunal was applying new international law retroactively and whether that was moral. In his opening statement, Robert Jackson defended the tribunal in this way:

The privilege of opening the first trial in history for crimes against the peace of the world imposes a grave responsibility. The wrongs which we seek to condemn and punish have been so calculated, so malignant, and so devastating, that civilization cannot tolerate their being ignored, because it cannot survive their being repeated. That four great nations, flushed with victory and stung with injury stay the hand of vengeance and voluntarily submit their captive enemies to the judgment of the law is one of the most significant tributes that Power has ever paid to Reason.

The prosecuting nations hoped to use international law "to meet the greatest menace of our times: aggressive war," he told the tribunal. "The common sense of mankind demands that law shall not stop with the punishment of petty crimes by little people. It must also reach men who possess themselves of great power and make deliberate and concerted use of it to set in motion evils which leave no home in the world untouched."

What is most interesting about this moment is the turn to formal legal process – as if the world itself had too much blood on its hands and could not bear the usual course of victor's justice: a bullet to the head. After a year-long trial, three of the twenty-four Nazi leaders were acquitted. Twelve were sentenced to death and seven to various prison terms. Two did not stand trial. The variety of outcomes – acquittals and varied sentences of imprisonment as well as executions – seemed in themselves a defense of the trials. It could be argued that they were not simply a long and bureaucratic means of execution. Yet, the Allies hoped to do more than to model lawfulness. Through the formalities of a trial, they hoped to display before the world, and embed in historical memory, evidence of the terrible crimes of the war and of the Holocaust. It was the trial process itself, not the imposition of the sentences, that was supposed to ensure that crimes like these would never happen again.

After World War II, the age of the "Great" and "Good" Wars had passed and the world slipped into a Cold War, seeming to teeter, at times, on the edges of self-annihilation. Law as a path to peace was supplanted by an arms race. The new way to guard against war was to have more nuclear weapons than your adversary. But a role for legal institutions would survive. Law became a tool of "peacekeepers" on more limited missions in various parts of the world. If law could no longer save the world from itself, it might still enable legal missionaries to act as saviors.

Making War

For the United States, one of the important innovations of the twentieth century was the creation of a new route toward officially sanctioned military actions. The founding of the United Nations created a new body to sanction war – the UN Security Council. The United States relied on this mechanism not long after it was created. On June 24, 1950, North Korean forces crossed the 38th parallel into South Korea, seriously escalating a civil war that had been simmering since the withdrawal of Japan after World War II left Korea without political leadership. Almost immediately, Korea became a Cold War battleground. President Truman ordered ground troops to Korea on June 30, without consulting Congress. He maintained that time was important and consultation unnecessary: "I just had to act as Commander-in-Chief, and I did." In the USSR's absence, the UN Security Council sanctioned the "police action" against North Korea's invasion, allowing Truman to justify foregoing Congressional approval.

In later years, presidents would act without formal UN Security Council authorization or a declaration of war, but often with some level of consultation with either Congress or the UN. In 1955, Dwight D. Eisenhower sought Congressional authorization to send troops into Taiwan to protect the government from the Communist Chinese. Eisenhower told Congress that his position as commander-in-chief gave him a certain amount of authority to act, but "a suitable congressional resolution would clearly and publicly establish" that such authority existed. Congress then ratified unilateral authority to deploy troops to protect against "international communism." Eisenhower relied on this Congressional resolution when he sent troops into Lebanon without Congressional approval in 1958.

President John F. Kennedy continued Truman's and Eisenhower's use of military power without Congressional approval. He dispatched air and naval transport for the ill-fated Bay of Pigs invasion intended to overthrow Cuban leader Fidel Castro, and he deployed troops in Vietnam without consulting Congress. Other armed conflicts involved the use of U.S. troops at the direction of the president alone: Laos in 1962, the Congo in 1964, and the Dominican Republic in 1965.

As the war in Vietnam escalated during Lyndon B. Johnson's presidency, Congress authorized military action, but not through a declaration of war. In circumstances that remain disputed, it was reported that a U.S. warship came under fire from the North Vietnamese in the Gulf of Tonkin. Although the veracity of these reports was questioned at the time, it was enough to motivate Congress to pass the Gulf of Tonkin Resolution, which gave Congressional support for "the determination of the President, as Commander in Chief, to take all necessary measures to repel any armed attack against the forces of the United States and to prevent further aggression."

Congress's failure to pass a declaration of war led to questions of the Vietnam War's legality. The State of Massachusetts filed suit against the Secretary of Defense, arguing that the war was unconstitutional without a formal declaration of war. The case was dismissed by the Supreme Court as non-justiciable, over a dissent by Justice William O. Douglas.[3] Meanwhile, Congress continued to pass appropriations bills, funding the war. Some have argued that this and other episodes eroding the use of Congress's formal constitutional role in declaring war cedes excessive war power to the president. For others, however, the power of the purse has become an alternative and more nuanced means through which Congress plays a role in the exercise of war powers.

Intending to reassert a Congressional role in warmaking, Congress passed the War Powers Act over President Richard Nixon's veto in 1973. This act requires the president to notify Congress within forty-eight hours of sending troops into hostilities. It requires that troops must be removed within sixty days if Congress does not declare war or authorize the use of force. Later presidents have challenged the constitutionality of the War Powers Act. The House Judiciary Committee also engaged in oversight of presidential war-related actions during the Nixon administration, investigating Nixon's order to bomb Cambodia without Congressional authorization in 1969.

The United States engaged in a number of overseas military engagements after Vietnam. For the most part, these engagements were limited in scope and duration, enabling the nation to maintain the self-conception of a nation at peace while at the same time sending troops into battle. Presidents drew on their commander-in-chief power and did not call on Congress for declarations of war. Some engagements were justified as extensions of the Cold War. For example, in 1983 President Ronald Reagan sent U.S. troops to the island nation of Grenada to put down a coup, based on false assumptions that Cuba's Communist government was supporting the coup. In 1985–86, rather than seek lawful authority for his actions, Reagan violated federal law in what became known as the "Iran/Contra Affair" by using Iranian arms sales to generate secret funds for the Contra forces seeking to oust the leftist Sandinista government of Nicaragua.

[3] *Massachusetts v. Laird*, 400 U.S. 886 (1970).

Law Makes War

War was also *made* in the law when war's contours were labeled and categorized. War since the beginning of recorded history has involved killing and destruction. But all killing and destruction is not the same in the law of war. The twentieth century saw the proliferation of categories of "war crimes" and also an increasingly complicated U.S. relationship to international law.

This aspect of the law of war is in part a reaction to the history of technology. New mechanisms of destruction led to new forms of atrocities. For example, the modern use of chemical weapons began in World War I. The Germans killed more than 5,000 Allied troops in just one chlorine gas attack on the Belgian village of Ypres on April 22, 1915. The British also used chemical weapons, and the United States developed chemical weapons capability. After the war, concerns about the horrendous and destructive nature of chemical weapons led to the signing of the 1925 Geneva Protocol on Chemical Weapons prohibiting their use (although not their production or stockpiling).

Spelling out unjust ways of waging war created as well an image of the good war. A lawless waging of war presumed the existence of lawful war. And so, just as human rights law carved out the categories of human rights violations, law enabled uses of war that could be seen as right, proper, and lawful.

It has been important to the American self-conception that American wars be perceived as the right kind of wars: lawful wars. One of the difficulties, of course, is that the history of warfare does not tend to play out in a tidy narrative. Some U.S. military efforts were conducted in secret, increasingly common after World War II but decreasingly secret in an age of high-tech media. And even in the nation's formally acknowledged wars, things could always go wrong. On the morning of March 16, 1968, for example, American forces were dispatched on a search-and-destroy mission against guerillas in the village of My Lai in South Vietnam. American forces had suffered heavy casualties at the hands of guerilla forces hiding among local villagers. Presuming that civilians would be away at market, U.S. troops entered My Lai expecting a firefight. Instead, they encountered elderly peasants, children, and unarmed women. Somehow their mission of killing continued in spite of the absence of its intended target or any enemy fire. The carnage is hard to imagine. The villagers were not just shot from afar, but bayoneted. At least one girl was raped before being murdered. Some were shot in the back of the head while praying. Others were ordered into a ditch and sprayed with machine-gun fire. Lieutenant William Calley, the only person charged in these events, was convicted of murder and sent

690 Mary L. Dudziak

to prison, but on orders of President Nixon was released after two days and his sentence commuted to home confinement. Calley's defense was that he was simply following the orders of his commander to kill everyone in the village. This defense, of course, had a chilling ring to it, since it had been heard before in the halls of Nuremberg.

How is it that the United States, a nation that saw itself as taking ideas of freedom and justice to other lands, had found itself implicated in the bullet-riddled bodies of children scattered in a Vietnamese rice field? There was no way to undo the horror of My Lai, of course, but there would have to be efforts to extricate America from it all. There would be two ways to do this. First, atrocities need not be seen as the acts of the nation, but only of rogue elements – abusive soldiers. That could be accomplished, perhaps feebly, through the prosecution of Calley. Second, in later years the United States would simply loosen itself from the bonds of international law.

In 1998, the Statute of Rome established the International Criminal Court, a permanent international body to prosecute human rights violations, a goal of the human rights movement for decades. The world now had a tribunal that could enforce human rights law – but not against the United States, for the United States refused to sign the treaty. The Clinton administration argued that it would subject American military personnel to politically motivated prosecutions. In defending this position in 2002, Under-Secretary of State John Bolton stressed that American troops overseas should be protected from prosecution in non-U.S. courts.[4]

The International Criminal Court decision coincided with a broader withdrawal from international law. The Clinton administration had signed the Kyoto environmental treaty in 1997, but President George W. Bush pulled the United States out of the treaty in 2001. By this time, the nation had retreated far from Woodrow Wilson's vision. The United States no longer sought to lead the world to peace through law. Instead, the law of the world now seemed dangerous, requiring a retreat behind the borders of American law.

II. WAR, STATE-BUILDING, AND GOVERNANCE

Franklin Delano Roosevelt is remembered as a great wartime president because he led the nation through World War II. But Roosevelt cloaked his presidency in the metaphor of war from its very beginnings. Delivering his first inaugural address in March 1933 in the face of unprecedented economic crisis, Roosevelt urged the nation to move forward "as a trained

---

[4] John R. Bolton, Under-Secretary for Arms Control and International Security, Remarks to the Federalist Society, Washington, DC, November 14, 2002.

and loyal army willing to sacrifice for the good of a common discipline."
Larger, national purposes would "bind upon us all as a sacred obligation with
a unity of duty hitherto evoked only in times of armed strife." Roosevelt
placed himself "unhesitatingly" at the head "of this great army of our people
dedicated to a disciplined attack upon our common problems." He promised
to recommend measures to Congress appropriate to a war-like emergency,
"that a stricken nation in the midst of a stricken world may require." If
Congress failed to respond, "I shall ask the Congress for the one remaining
instrument to meet the crisis – broad Executive power to wage a war against
the emergency, as great as the power that would be given to me if we were
in fact invaded by a foreign foe." The speech was celebrated, but Eleanor
Roosevelt admitted that it was "a little terrifying" that "when Franklin got
to that part of his speech when he said it might become necessary for him
to assume powers ordinarily granted to a President in wartime, he received
his biggest demonstration."[5]

Roosevelt would not need to go to Congress for war-like powers. They
remained in the president's office, left over from World War I. FDR's use
of war powers for domestic problems was just one example of a common
feature of twentieth-century governance. Sometimes, as for Roosevelt, war
powers could be used because the domestic problems were analogous to war.
Later, increasingly, domestic issues were seen as related to national security
and so germane to the war powers. In either case, war became a central
logic of twentieth-century American state-building. At the beginning of
the century, war had initiated a quintessential act of nation-building for the
United States: the acquisition of territory in the Caribbean and the Pacific.
From World War I onward, state-building instead took a different form –
new federal government regulatory powers.

War's Powers

American constitutional scholars tend to focus inward when examining
great debates about the scope of government power in the first decades of
the twentieth century, but global events, especially war, had an important
impact on the expansion of federal government power. Although no part of
the "Great War" was fought on American soil, many facets of American life
were affected by it. More than 50,000 U.S. soldiers were killed in combat,
and another 206,000 were wounded. U.S. allies depended heavily on billions
of dollars in American loans, and the United States had provided as much
as two-thirds of allied military supplies. The war was thought of as a new

---

[5] Arthur M. Schlesinger, Jr., *The Crisis of the Old Order: 1919–1933, The Age of Roosevelt*,
Vol. I (New York, 2003), 1.

kind of war, an unprecedented global conflict. Congress responded with new statutes giving the president power to raise armies by conscription, censor communications with foreign countries, regulate foreign-language press in the United States, and take control of rail, telephone, and telegraph systems.

A decade after World War I, emergency again would grip the nation. U.S. military uniforms were donned once more, this time by the "Bonus Marchers" of 1932, 20,000 veterans and others who traveled to the nation's capital to demand accelerated payment of military pensions, only to be violently dispersed by regular U.S. Army troops. Roosevelt's "trained and loyal army" took over Washington nine months later.

When the legal history of the era is told, the Great Depression that followed the Great War and intersected with the beginnings of World War II tends to appear as a domestic interlude between war periods. The three are better seen as continuous. World War I provided not merely starving veterans but also compelling precedents for the powers drawn on by both Herbert Hoover and FDR to address the economic crisis of the Depression. War was invoked as a metaphor to signal the need for national commitment and sacrifice. And the idea of war would, in this context, serve its conventional function: signaling a time of exception, reassuring the nation that an expansion of government power need not be feared. If conceptualized as war-related, it could be imagined as ephemeral.

It was not just the Bonus Marchers who cloaked themselves in wartime imagery during the Depression. "We all have been saying to each other the situation is quite like war," Secretary of State Henry Stimson wrote in 1931.[6] As Robert Higgs has written, Americans "looked back with nostalgia on Woodrow Wilson's quasi-dictatorial authority to mobilize resources during World War I. Proposals to revive the authoritative emergency programs of 1917–18 bloomed like wildflowers." As a presidential candidate, Franklin Delano Roosevelt had already argued that the nation was faced with "a more grave emergency than in 1917." Even before the election New Dealers were researching whether wartime grants of power could be used to allow Roosevelt to enact emergency measures. Once Roosevelt was elected, according to William Leuchtenburg, "There was scarcely a New Deal act or agency that did not owe something to the experience of World War I."

The new president turned immediately to wartime powers. Under the Trading with the Enemy Act of 1917, a World War I measure still on the books, he issued an executive order requiring banks nationwide to close for

[6] William E. Leuchtenburg, *The FDR Years: On Roosevelt and His Legacy* (New York, 1995), 36.

three days to curb a panic-driven outflow of capital. The president then sought retroactive approval from Congress in the quickly enacted Emergency Banking Act. Other wartime measures were revived with New Deal legislation, many in the famous first Hundred Days. Congress gave the president power to aid farming and industry with the Agricultural Adjustment Act (AAA) and the National Industrial Recovery Act (NIRA); Leuchtenburg argues that "the war spirit carried the Agricultural Adjustment Act through." Roosevelt named as the head of the Agricultural Adjustment Administration George Peek, who had served on the War Industries Board. The Tennessee Valley Authority, a New Deal experiment in regional planning, evolved from a wartime nitrate and electric power project. New Deal public housing projects also had their beginnings in the war. The Civilian Conservation Corps, formed to use civilians to help conserve natural resources, was purposely structured to be similar to the wartime mobilization of troops. Recruits gathered at Army recruiting stations, wore World War I uniforms, and slept in Army tents. These New Deal programs were defended in militaristic terms. Representative John Young Brown of Kentucky said to his fellow Democrats: "we are at war today. . . . I had as soon start a mutiny in the face of a foreign foe as start a mutiny today against the program of the President of the United States."

Rumors of mutiny were heard, however, in the courts. In 1935, the Supreme Court questioned the broad Congressional delegations of power to the executive to regulate commerce for the sake of economic recovery. In *Panama Refining Co. v. Ryan* (1935), the Court held one portion of the delegation of power in the National Industrial Recovery Act unconstitutional. The act allowed the president to prohibit the interstate shipment of oil in excess of state quotas, but the Court argued that there were not enough guidelines to support this delegation of legislative authority: "Congress left the matter to the President, without standard or rule, to be dealt with as he pleased."[7] *Panama Refining* had limited application, but it was soon clear that the case was the beginning of the unraveling of the New Deal. In *Schechter Poultry Corp. v. United States* (1935), the Court struck down Section 3 of the NIRA, which allowed the president to establish industry-wide regulations on wages, hours, and trade practices for the purpose of restoring economic stability. Wartime analogies would not move the Supreme Court, which found the statute to confer an unconstitutional delegation of government power. "Extraordinary conditions," the Court maintained, "do not create or enlarge constitutional power."[8] Concern for maintaining the constitutional balance of power also led the Court to strike down other

---

[7] *Panama Refining Co. v. Ryan*, 293 U.S. 388, 418 (1935).
[8] *United States v. A.L.A. Schechter Poultry Corp.*, 295 U.S. 495, 529 (1935).

New Deal measures, such as the Agricultural Adjustment Act in *United States v. Butler* (1936). This time the specter of totalitarian authority lurked behind the New Deal. Excessive federal power at the expense of the states would convert the United States "into a central government exercising uncontrolled police power in every state of the Union."[9]

By the end of 1936, federal judges had issued about 1,600 injunctions to prevent officials from enforcing acts of Congress. A conflict between the judiciary and the executive branch loomed, leading eventually to Roosevelt's infamous Court-packing plan. While the plan was pending, however, the Court handed down decisions that suggested the judiciary would be more supportive of New Deal goals. In *West Coast Hotel v. Parrish* (1937), the Court suddenly upheld minimum wage legislation that was almost exactly like legislation it had struck down a year before. In *NLRB v. Jones and Laughlin* (1937) it found the National Labor Relations Act to be constitutional, and appeared to embrace an analysis of the commerce power it had earlier rejected. Some suspected the Court's purpose was to avoid the Court-packing plan, but its apparent change of direction was already underway before the plan was even introduced. Others suggested the Court was simply bowing to Roosevelt's crushing reelection in 1936. More recently, historians have argued that the Court's jurisprudence shows a more gradual evolution, and later New Deal cases were based on more carefully drawn statutes.

Meanwhile, the Court-packing bill was defeated. Although the nation had rallied around the president as war leader in 1933, the rise of Adolph Hitler in Germany gave concentrations of power a more ominous ring. Letters to American newspapers ran strongly against the bill, claiming that FDR was engaging in a dictatorial power grab. Many also saw the courts as America's protection against the potential excesses of majority rule, in which an enflamed majority could harm a minority or support an overly powerful charismatic leader. The Senate Judiciary Committee's May 1937 report on the Court-packing bill invoked "the condition of the world abroad" and concluded that the Court plan was "a measure which should be so emphatically rejected that its parallel will never again be presented to the free representatives of the free people of America." But in other respects conditions abroad worked to the executive's advantage. Congress and the Court had already shown no hesitation in granting the president extraordinary powers when it came to war and foreign affairs. *Curtiss-Wright v. United States* (1936) confirmed apparently boundless presidential power in foreign relations by upholding a joint resolution of Congress delegating to the president power to embargo arms sales to warring Latin American

---

[9] *United States v. Butler*, 297 U.S. 1, 77 (1936).

countries at his discretion. The president's power in this area was not derived only from Congress, the Court declared. It was an aspect of the "plenary and exclusive power of the President as the sole organ of the federal government in the field of international relations."[10]

World War II Expansion of Powers

By that time Europe was haunted by the specter of another war. In 1935, Hitler violated the Treaty of Versailles by introducing military conscription and creating an air force. In 1936 German troops reoccupied the Rhineland, which was demilitarized in the Versailles Treaty. Hitler contemplated expanding Germany into Czechoslovakia and Austria. Civil war began in Spain in 1936, resulting three years later in the establishment of a fascist regime; in 1935–36 Italy, under fascist leader Mussolini, invaded and occupied Ethiopia. Japan, which had invaded and occupied Manchuria in 1931–32, invaded China in July 1937. Roosevelt called these developments an "epidemic of world lawlessness." Congress tried to use law to construct a buffer between the United States and the outbreak of war, passing the Neutrality Act of 1937, which forbade the shipment of weapons to nations at war. In 1938, in an effort to democratize war policymaking, Congress toyed with the idea of a constitutional amendment that would allow Congress to call a popular referendum to decide whether to declare or engage in war. Roosevelt argued strongly against it, privately saying that the proponents of the amendment had "no conception of what modern war . . . involves." The proposed amendment lost a test vote in the House and was not seriously pursued again.

In 1938, Hitler took Austria and Czechoslovakia, Japan captured the Spratly Islands southwest of Manila, Madrid was occupied by Franco, and Mussolini overran Albania. Roosevelt, alarmed by the speed with which fascism was spreading, began a rearmament campaign. Germany invaded Poland in 1939, leading Britain and France, who had pledged to help defend Poland, to declare war on Germany. By June 1940, Germany had taken Denmark, Norway, the Netherlands, Belgium, and France.

Stunned by the swiftness of Germany's conquest of Europe, Americans again looked to Roosevelt for leadership in the midst of crisis, yet their fears of Hitler had not yet coalesced into a national commitment to go to war. After six weeks of heated debate, the president convinced Congress to repeal the Neutrality Act, putting the United States in a position to aid Britain and France, and in September 1940, Congress authorized the first "peacetime" conscription. But the international context complicated

---

[10] *United States v. Curtiss-Wright Export Corp.*, 299 U.S. 304, 321 (1936).

domestic politics. The shifts of power involved in the New Deal's "war" on the Depression began to seem more menacing; it seemed that preparations for the war against the economic emergency could easily slide into preparations for involvement in the world war. It was unclear where one war ended and the other began. Roosevelt added to this ambiguity. In his January 1939 address to Congress, he said, "All about us rage undeclared wars – military and economic. All about us grow more deadly armaments – military and economic. All about us are threats of new aggression – military and economic." As Michael Sherry argues, preparations for World War II were "less a wholly new enterprise than a continuation of the earlier struggle on a different front, one with an identifiable enemy to replace the faceless fear of the Depression."

In May 1941, Roosevelt directly laid the basis for war-related expansion of federal power. He declared an unlimited national emergency, arguing that although war had not come to American soil, "indifference on the part of the United States to the increasing menace would be perilous," and therefore the nation "should pass from peacetime authorizations of military strength to such a basis as will enable us to cope instantly and decisively with any attempt at hostile encirclement of this hemisphere." The declaration allowed Roosevelt to use leftover World War I provisions as needs arose, and he used his authority to reinstate the Council of National Defense, create an Office of Emergency Management, call military reservists to active duty, regulate banking and foreign trade, and exercise control over such industries as munitions, power, transportation, and communications. The March 1941 Lend-Lease Act delegated authority to the president to sell, lend, or lease military materials to nations whose defense was deemed necessary to the United States and gave him broad discretionary power to regulate the armaments industry.

The expansion of war powers was not confined to sites of conflict or strategic resources, but touched the daily lives of average Americans. The War Powers Act of December 1941 gave Roosevelt the authority to redistribute war-related functions, duties, powers, and personnel among government agencies as he saw fit. It gave him broad control over international trade and foreign-owned property in the United States and allowed censorship of all communications between the United States and any foreign country. A Second War Powers Act soon followed, authorizing executive agencies to acquire any private property necessary for military purposes. It also gave the president the widest economic control ever granted to the executive, allowing him to "allocate ... materials or facilities in such manner, upon such conditions and to such extent as he shall deem necessary or appropriate in the public interest and to promote the national defense." Congress also passed the Emergency Price Control Act, establishing the Office of

Price Administration to control prices and rents. The income tax expanded from a "class tax" to a "mass tax," doing more than raising revenue needed at wartime: it provided individual citizens with an opportunity to participate in a wartime politics of sacrifice. The broad-based income tax would stay in place after the war, providing the mechanism for funding an expanded post-World War II state.

The Supreme Court added to the aggregation of federal power. The Court had adopted a more deferential posture in reviewing the constitutionality of acts of Congress in the late 1930s. During World War II the Court stepped back much further, sharply reducing the role of federalism as a limit on Congressional power. Compare the Court's decision in *NLRB v. Jones and Laughlin* (1937), which signaled its new approach to the commerce power, with *Wickard v. Filburn* (1942), which contemplated a much more extensive role for federal regulation of commerce. Jones and Laughlin was a major steel corporation with an indisputable presence in interstate commerce, its tentacles reaching throughout the nation. Roscoe C. Filburn was an Ohio farmer, who fed wheat grown on his farm to chickens raised on his farm. Unfortunately, Filburn's home-grown chickenfeed exceeded his wheat allotment under the Agricultural Adjustment Act, and he was fined. The Court upheld federal regulation of Filburn's chicken feed. Under the Court's "cumulative effects" test, Congress could regulate home-produced and consumed agricultural products. If an individual farmer's home-consumed wheat did not have a substantial effect on interstate commerce, it was still within Congress's regulatory power if, put together with others similarly situated, the cumulative effect of all the wheat was "far from trivial." The Court's holding seemed to decimate federalism as a limit on Congressional power. Why had the Court gone so far?

There is more to the wartime context of the decision in *Wickard* than its date. Secretary of Agriculture Claude Wickard had announced the wheat quotas at issue in a speech, "Wheat Farmers and the Battle for Democracy." He argued that federal control over wheat was crucial, so that the federal government would have a predictable supply. The United States needed to send wheat to England, a wheat-importing country, whose channels of supply had been disrupted by German U-boats. Wickard called on farmers to do their patriotic duty and comply with federal law because that would enable the U.S. government to use wheat supplies to help England fight the Nazis. The speech had confused Filburn about his wheat quota, so it was part of the record before the Court. It is important to the history of federalism to see the post-1937 expansion of federal power not as a defensive reaction to the Court-packing plan, but instead in the context of the importance of federal control over the economy during wartime. A stronger role for the states wilted in the face of wartime national security.

Endless War?

By the end of the war, the U.S. economy was booming, but Americans worried about the government's ability to maintain prosperity. Roosevelt's war analogies had treated the Depression and World War II as exceptional states requiring temporary solutions. Now permanent solutions were needed. Popular journalist John Gunther expressed Americans' "quarrelsome, anxious mood" after the war and inquired as to its meaning. Did the nation's lack of vision "show that, to become efficient, this country needs the stimulus of war?"[11]

In an effort to scale national control back to peacetime levels, President Harry S. Truman ordered government officials "to move as rapidly as possible without endangering the stability of the economy toward the removal of price, wage, production, and other controls toward the restoration of collective bargaining and the free market." Although most of the wartime control agencies were shut down by the end of 1945, government control was not surrendered. Some wartime agencies and programs became permanent, and many of the powers held by the dismantled agencies were transferred to permanent agencies. More than one hundred wartime executive orders and statutes were left in place after World War II, giving the president leeway in addressing the increasing tensions overseas. In 1946 Congress passed the Employment Act, basically imposing a duty on the federal government to use all available resources to maintain economic stability.

The Supreme Court signed on to an expansive use of the war power. To ease a postwar housing shortage, Congress passed the Housing and Rent Act of 1947, which restricted rents in "defense rental areas." Even though the act was passed after hostilities had formally ended, because the effects of war could be felt on the economy for years, the Court in *Woods v. Cloyd W. Miller* (1948) found the act to be a constitutional use of the war power.

During the Korean War, President Truman's exercise of broad power extended to the home front. Facing a threatened strike in the steel industry and concerned that it would disrupt production of war materiel, Truman issued an executive order seizing the steel mills. The controversy quickly made its way to the Supreme Court, and the Court put a break on the president's ability to define the scope of war-related executive powers. As Justice Black wrote for the Court majority, "Even though 'theater of war' be an expanding concept, we cannot with faithfulness to our constitutional system hold that the Commander in Chief of the Armed Forces has the

---

[11] Michael S. Sherry, *In the Shadow of War: The United States Since the 1930s* (New Haven, CT, 1995), 123.

ultimate power as such to take possession of private property in order to keep labor disputes from stopping production. This is a job for the Nation's lawmakers, not for its military authorities."[12] But in spite of the Court's efforts to pull back on federal government war-related powers, by mid-century war had become embedded in American governance in a way that no Court could undo.

The most important carryovers from World War II were not the bureau-cratic structures, the statutes, and the judicial precedents – the legal edifice of the war – important as they were. Instead, the most substantial impact on American politics and diplomacy, American culture and law, was the radiation that continued to fall across countrysides. What has often been mistakenly called the "postwar" era emerged under a nuclear cloud. Even to Americans, the destruction of Hiroshima and Nagasaki was ominous, for it was immediately clear that the awful power that had been unleashed upon the Japanese would someday find its way into the hands of American adversaries. And at mid-century, Americans lacked the utopianism of the World War I generation. They did not dare to hope that war would not come again; at the same time they came to believe that the next war would bring a nuclear holocaust and the end of human existence itself. And so at the end of the war, the nation's joyfulness was tinged with the unease we can feel in the words of Dwight Macdonald, as the story of Hiroshima and Nagasaki continued to unfold:

May we hope that the destructive possibilities are so staggering that, for simple self-preservation, [other nations] will agree to "outlaw" The Bomb? Or that they will foreswear war itself because an "atomic" war would probably mean the mutual ruin of all contestants? The same reasons were advanced before World War I to demonstrate its "impossibility"; also before World War II. The devastation of these wars was as terrible as had been predicted – yet they took place.[13]

When, a half-century later, the anniversary of the end of World War II was celebrated, historical memory embraced "bands of brothers," and not these dark elements. But it is important to remember that when soldiers returned home to kiss lovers and strangers, for many there was in the sweetness a bitter aftertaste.

The overwhelming threat of nuclear arms, and therefore the nation's dependence on nuclear technology, helps us see the logic underlying the post-World War II Red Scare, fueled by fears, real and fictional, of Ameri-can "atom spies." It also exposes a more enduring conundrum: the nation's very existence relied on advancement in military technology. Dwight D.

---

[12] *Youngstown Sheet & Tube Co. v. Sawyer*, 343 U.S. 579, 587 (1952).
[13] Dwight Macdonald, "The Bomb," *Politics* 2 (1945), 257–60.

Eisenhower addressed this latter issue in 1960, on the final day of his presidency. Eisenhower, himself a war hero, was swept into office in 1952 in the belief that he would lead the nation out of the muddled war in Korea. Eisenhower succeeded in negotiating a cease-fire that resulted in a stalemate: the permanent militarization of the border between North and South Korea. By the end of his second term this state of affairs served as a metaphor for America in the world. There was simply no escaping the militarization – not just of government and economy but of American life itself. Americans stocked their bomb shelters, children learned to "duck and cover" against a nuclear blast in school; military readiness was a part of daily living. Eisenhower left office warning the American people that peace itself now rested on a tie between the military and American industry. This "military-industrial complex" was both vital – supplying the armaments that would protect American security – and dangerous. As much as "we recognize the imperative need for this development," Eisenhower warned, "we must not fail to comprehend its grave implications." His concern was that the power residing in the alliance of industry and the military might undermine democracy itself. He urged, "We must never let the weight of this combination endanger our liberties or democratic processes." Ultimately American leadership and prestige rested "on how we use our power in the interests of world peace and human betterment." It was no longer possible to take war out of the project of American governance. The question, instead, was to what purpose the nation would put the tools of war.

III. LAW AS A TOOL OF WAR

Tanks and submarines are war materiel, but wars are fought also with other kinds of implements. Strategy is a weapon, information is a weapon. Another tool used in wartime, especially to manage the environment on the home front, is law. We can see this in the context of World War I civil liberties.

Managing Consent

"LONG LIVE THE CONSTITUTION OF THE UNITED STATES," a World War I circular seemed to shout to its readers. On the other side it began as emphatically: "ASSERT YOUR RIGHTS!" This antiwar circular would result in Charles Schenck being thrown in jail. It was, of course, not the document's quotations from the Constitution that would get Schenck and his Socialist Party compatriots into trouble. Instead it was the purpose of their arguments: to encourage opposition to the war and resistance to the draft. Drawing on the Thirteenth Amendment, the circular argued, "A conscript is little better than a convict. He is deprived of his liberty and of his right to think and act as a free man. . . . He is forced into involuntary servitude. . . . He is deprived of all freedom of conscience and forced to kill against his will."[14]

Schenck and other Socialist Party members mailed thousands of these circulars to men who had been called up for World War I military service. For this they were arrested for violating the Espionage Act of 1917, which made it a crime willfully to cause "insubordination, disloyalty, mutiny, or refusal of duty, in the military or naval forces of the United States."

The Supreme Court upheld Schenck's conviction, seeing his actions as an attempt to obstruct government enlistment efforts. As Justice Oliver Wendell Holmes wrote for the Court, "Of course the document would not have been sent unless it was intended to have some effect." In this context, the First Amendment would provide no protection. "We admit that in many places and in ordinary times the defendants in saying all that was said in the circular would have been within their constitutional rights. But the character of every act depends upon the circumstances in which it is done." Wartime was an exceptional context: "When a nation is at war many things that might be said in times of peace are such a hindrance to its effort that their utterance will not be endured so long as men fight and that no Court could regard them as protected by any Constitutional right." Holmes then invoked what would become a central First Amendment concept, even though in this case it seemed to have no teeth: "The question in every case is whether the words used are used in such circumstances and are of such a nature as to create a clear and present danger that they will bring about the substantive evils that Congress has a right to prevent."[15] In this case, even if Schenck's efforts were ineffective, it seemed enough that he was doing what he could to impede the draft. The Court upheld his conviction.

Schenck is a classic case in the traditional swinging pendulum analysis. It is taken as a prime example of the way in which the Court during wartime is less protective of rights and more protective of national security. But the swinging pendulum analysis is problematic, for in some contexts wartime has been the occasion for the expansion of rights. And the very fuzziness of what time is "wartime" makes movements of the pendulum hard to track.

Another way to view these cases would be to see the Court, like the executive branch, engaged in the project of wartime governance, managing rights – not along a narrow continuum but in a multifaceted way – in a manner that aided, or at least did not undermine, national security. Sometimes the differences on the Court are more about how national security is best enhanced than about the relative importance of rights and security.

---

[14] "Assert Your Rights," (1917), http://1stam.umn.edu/archive/primary/schenck.pdf.
[15] *Schenck v. United States*, 249 U.S. 47, 51–52 (1919).

In *Schenck* and other cases, the Court most often accorded the executive branch the powers it sought during wartime to raise an army, maintain wartime production, and protect national security. When courts loosened constitutional restraints on executive action during wartime, law functioned as a tool enabling wartime governance.

Civil liberties were restricted during World War I. An example is passage of the Sedition Act of 1918, which Geoffrey Stone has called "the most repressing legislation in American history." But even in this wartime context, some rights, such as voting rights, expanded, and in a landmark Sedition Act case, prospects of a broader vision of free speech could be seen. The Sedition Act criminalized the saying of things that were thought to endanger the war effort, including "disloyal, profane, scurrilous or abusive language about the form of the government, the Constitution, soldiers and sailors, flag or uniform of the armed forces," or to support the German war effort, or to engender opposition to the United States. The only Sedition Act case to reach the Supreme Court was *Abrams v. United States* (1919) involving Russian immigrants who protested the war by throwing leaflets off rooftops and out windows. The Supreme Court upheld their conviction. No matter how hapless their efforts, it was enough that the defendants intended to provoke opposition to the war.

In *Abrams*, Justice Holmes, joined by Justice Brandeis, began an important line of dissenting opinions. Government power was greater in wartime, Holmes argued, but "the principle of the right to free speech is always the same. It is only the present danger of immediate evil or an intent to bring it about that warrants Congress in setting a limit to the expression of opinion where private rights are not concerned." He found Abrams' flyers to be harmless and the prosecution to be unconstitutional. Holmes concluded with a vision of constitutionalism that would powerfully inform First Amendment jurisprudence:

Persecution for the expression of opinions seems to me perfectly logical.... But when men have realized that time has upset many fighting faiths, they may come to believe even more than they believe the very foundations of their own conduct that the ultimate good desired is better reached by free trade in ideas – that the best test of truth is the power of the thought to get itself accepted in the competition of the market, and that truth is the only ground upon which their wishes safely can be carried out. That at any rate is the theory of our Constitution.[16]

It may be that the power of Holmes's vision, carved in this wartime case, leads us to a paradoxical conclusion. This wartime suppression of rights, by leading to an expansive and influential vision of the First Amendment,

---

[16] *Abrams v. United States*, 250 U.S. 616, 628 (1919) (Holmes, J., *dissenting*).

albeit in a dissent, ultimately informed a broader vision of free speech rights in the long run.

The context of World War I infused American rights discourse, both where rights were denied and where they were extended. In the final years of the long campaign for woman suffrage, suffragists used wartime ideology to prove their point. In 1918, picketers from the National Women's Party surrounded the White House, holding banners with messages intended to embarrass the war effort. One banner read: "TO THE RUSSIAN ENVOYS... WE THE WOMEN OF AMERICA TELL YOU THAT AMERICA IS NOT A DEMOCRACY. TWENTY MILLION AMERICAN WOMEN ARE DENIED THE RIGHT TO VOTE."[17] President Wilson, who had resented the suffrage protesters, ultimately came to embrace woman suffrage as a war measure, arguing to Congress that it must consider "the unusual circumstances of a world war in which we stand and are judged not only by our own people and our own consciences but also in the view of all nations' and peoples'..." The president believed that the suffrage amendment "was vitally essential to the successful prosecution of the great war of humanity in which we are engaged." It was Wilson's "duty to win the war and to ask you to remove every obstacle to winning it." It was not just that the United States hoped to bring democracy to other lands, and in other lands democracy increasingly meant the inclusion of women in government. Also, the nation had made "partners of the women in this war," he continued: "shall we admit them only to a partnership of suffering and sacrifice and toil and not to a partnership of privilege and right?"[18] Once the Nineteenth Amendment was finally ratified in August 1920, some believed that women voters would support the League of Nations, in the interests of peace.[19]

Ideas about wartime rights – and obligations – informed a broad range of policies, even the constitutionality of forced sterilization. In *Buck v. Bell* (1927), Justice Holmes's majority opinion invoked the ultimate sacrifice in wartime to make the lesser sacrifice of sterilization seem, comparatively, inconsequential: "We have seen more than once that the public welfare may call upon the best citizens for their lives. It would be strange if it could not call upon those who already sap the strength of the State for these lesser sacrifices, often not felt to be such by those concerned, in order to prevent our being swamped with incompetence."[20] In eugenic theory, wartime took

[17] Sandra F. VanBurkleo, *Belonging to the World: Women's Rights and American Constitutional Culture* (New York, 2001), 196.

[18] *Wall Street Journal*, "President Urges Senate to Extend Suffrage," October 1, 1918.

[19] *New York Times*, "Cox Sees League Aid in Suffrage Victory," August 19, 1920.

[20] *Buck v. Bell*, 274 U.S. 200, 207 (1927).

too many of the best of the gene pool. Sterilization of the genetically inferior helped keep things in balance. In the mistaken science of the 1920s, a denial of rights to the "feeble minded" protected the nation against the genetic consequences of war. *Buck v. Bell* is an example of the way that ideas about war inform law during times we conceptualize as peacetime.

Rights in World War II

National security informed domestic policy during what is often called the "interwar years," but within the United States, December 7, 1941, was seen as ushering in a new era. In one sense, it is easy to tell when World War II began. December 7, as FDR would call it, was "the day that will live in infamy," the day of the Pearl Harbor attack. Congress declared war on Japan the following day, and on Germany and Italy soon after. But war had been fought in Asia since 1931 and in parts of Europe since 1936. The global military experience of World War II began in different places at different times. The domestic security environment within the United States had long been affected by these global events, even as the iconic moment of Pearl Harbor allowed America to experience entry into war as a sudden shock, as entry into a new world. It was Pearl Harbor that led Justice Felix Frankfurter to tell his law clerk: "Everything has changed, and I am going to war."[21] Pearl Harbor served as a catalytic point, the moment of most intense national mobilization. It led Justice Frank Murphy to become a lieutenant colonel in the Army on inactive status and to do literally what the rest of the Court did figuratively: during Court recesses, he put on a military uniform.

The Court, like the rest of the country, felt called into wartime service, though the justices would sometimes differ about how best to serve their country during war. They would have several opportunities to debate the matter.

Soon after Pearl Harbor, Japanese Americans became a target of wartime fears, especially once the West Coast began preparations for a possible attack, including air raid drills and blackouts. Roosevelt confirmed this nervousness in his radio address of December 9, saying, "The attack at Pearl Harbor can be repeated at any one of many points in both oceans and along both our coast lines and against all the rest of the hemisphere." Soon, public figures began to call for all persons of Japanese heritage to be confined to camps.

---

[21] Melvin I. Urofsky, "The Court at War, and the War at the Court," *Journal of Supreme Court History* (1996), 1–18.

On February 19, 1942, seventy-four days after the attack on Pearl Harbor, Roosevelt issued Executive Order 9066, which authorized the Secretary of War to prescribe certain areas of the country as military areas from which designated people might be excluded. On March 21, Congress passed a statute to enforce the terms of Executive Order 9066. This "exclusion order" was used to relocate people from their homes into internment camps in various places across the United States. Photographs of this relocation effort – of small Japanese American children tagged with numbers and under armed guard, and of families carrying children and household belongings as they left their homes – are some of the most powerful images of the impact of World War II at home. By the end of the war, thousands of people had been relocated.

Fred Korematsu would become the subject of perhaps the most iconic case about rights at wartime in the twentieth century. An American citizen born of Japanese immigrants, Korematsu had not intended to challenge the exclusion order; he was arrested while walking down a San Leandro, California, street with his girlfriend. He was convicted of being a person of Japanese descent present in an area covered by an exclusion order. In 1944, the Supreme Court upheld his conviction.

Justice Black insisted at the outset of his majority opinion that "all legal restrictions which curtail the civil rights of a single racial group are immediately suspect," and therefore "courts must subject them to the most rigid scrutiny." Still, the Court found the exclusion order to be justified under the circumstances. "Korematsu was not excluded from the Military Area because of hostility to him or his race," Black argued. "He *was* excluded because we are at war with the Japanese Empire, because the properly constituted military authorities feared an invasion of our West Coast and felt constrained to take proper security measures." The Court could not "– by availing ourselves of the calm perspective of hindsight – now say that at that time these actions were unjustified."[22]

Justice Roberts disagreed. *Korematsu* was a "case of convicting a citizen as a punishment for not submitting to imprisonment in a concentration camp, based on his ancestry, and solely because of his ancestry, without evidence or inquiry concerning his loyalty and good disposition towards the United States."[23] Justice Murphy also filed a dissent, arguing that the exclusion order "goes over 'the very brink of constitutional power' and falls into the ugly abyss of racism."[24] The most memorable opinion came from Justice

---

[22] *Korematsu v. United States*, 323 U.S. 214, 216, 223 (1944).

[23] *Korematsu*, 323 U.S. at 226 (Roberts, J., dissenting).

[24] *Korematsu*, 323 U.S. at 233 (Murphy, J., dissenting).

Jackson, who distinguished between executive and military actions during wartime, and the role of the courts. It was one thing for the military to distort the Constitution during wartime and entirely another for the courts to do so:

A military order, however unconstitutional, is not apt to last longer than the military emergency. . . . But once a judicial opinion rationalizes such an order to show that it conforms to the Constitution, or rather rationalizes the Constitution to show that the Constitution sanctions such an order, the Court for all time has validated the principle of racial discrimination in criminal procedure and of transplanting American citizens. The principle then lies about like a loaded weapon ready for the hand of any authority that can bring forward a plausible claim of an urgent need. Every repetition imbeds that principle more deeply in our law and thinking and expands it to new purposes. . . . There it has a generative power of its own, and all that it creates will be in its own image.[25]

Korematsu has been almost universally criticized in the decades since. Records indicate that actual subversive activities by persons of Japanese heritage were rare and quickly identified; detaining all people of Japanese descent – despite proof of citizenship, loyalty, or service to the United States – was an extreme reaction to a minuscule threat. Preexisting racism against Japanese on the West Coast counted heavily in the decision to exclude them from the area.

Like *Schenck*, the internment cases are often cited for the proposition that rights are restricted during wartime. The conventional assumption seems to hold – there is a trade-off between rights and security, and during wartime the pendulum naturally swings in the direction of security. But all rights cases were not decided in a fashion consistent with this assumption. In another important series of cases, the Court grappled with the question of whether the sacrifice of rights at wartime actually undermined security rather than enhanced it.

In *Minersville School District v. Gobitis* (1940), the Supreme Court took up the constitutionality of compulsory flag salute laws. The Court found that the expulsion of children from public school for refusing to salute the flag based on religious beliefs was not only acceptable but would also protect important national interests. According to Justice Felix Frankfurter, writing for the majority, the flag salute fostered unity, and "[n]ational unity is the basis of national security."[26] Just three years later, in *West Virginia State Board of Education v. Barnette* (1943), the Court reversed itself, striking down such a law. This time the Court viewed the liberty/security balance

---

[25] *Korematsu,* 323 U.S. at 246 (Jackson, J., dissenting).
[26] *Minersville School Dist. v. Gobitis,* 310 U.S. 586, 595 (1940).

differently. As Justice Jackson wrote for the Court, the "ultimate futility of such attempts to compel coherence is the lesson of . . . the fast failing efforts of our present totalitarian enemies."[27] According to Richard A. Primus, the reversal "was largely driven by the Court's desire to distinguish America from wartime Germany" where laws compelling salute of the national flag in the name of conformity of action and belief were the norm. It did not help that the West Virginia flag salute was reminiscent of the Nazi salute. Both cases invoked conceptions of national security. For Frankfurter, security required narrowing rights. For Jackson in *Barnette*, security was enhanced by expanding rights.

If rights expand or contract in the context of war, depending on their relation to constructions of national security, is there more to say about *Korematsu*? Conceptions of national identity and national security are framed in reference to perceived dangers. During the Cold War, the Soviet Union was the "other" against whom the United States defined itself and in terms of which the United States understood dangers in the world. During World War II, the United States often defined itself in egalitarian terms in contrast to Germany. However, as John Dower has shown, race permeated the war in the Pacific, which was framed as a battle against a treacherous race. This rhetoric crept into domestic policy and informed the idea that all "Japs" at home were security risks. Their seeming alienness decoupled even Japanese American citizens from basic citizenship rights. Viewed this way, the internment cases are an example of the way in which conceptions of national identity and national security, formed in reference to the perceived threats of an age, inform American law. This perspective helps us understand what otherwise would seem a paradox: equality rights both expanded and contracted during World War II.

The complicated relationship between rights and security during World War II and after can be seen in the civil rights of African Americans. African Americans participated in the war effort, but faced caps on enlistment and segregation within the armed services. Racial segregation was justified in part on the idea that integration would undermine the cohesion of military units, harming the nation's fighting strength. But the rest of the world noticed American race discrimination, and many came to wonder about the seeming contradiction that a war against Nazi racism was being fought by the segregated Army of a nation rife with racial discrimination. Gunnar Myrdal argued that discrimination harmed the war effort, and that "America, for its international prestige, power, and future security, needs to demonstrate to the world that American Negroes can be satisfactorily

---

[27] *West Virginia State Board of Education v. Barnette*, 319 U.S. 624, 641 (1943).

integrated into its democracy."[28] African American activists argued for a "Double V" during the war: victory abroad against fascism, victory at home against racism. Civil rights and labor leader A. Philip Randolph threatened a march on Washington to protest discrimination in defense industries. The threat of hundreds of thousands of African Americans marching on the nation's capital pressured President Roosevelt to issue an executive order banning race discrimination in defense industries. Also during the war, in *Smith v. Allwright* (1944), the Supreme Court struck down the "white primary," practices that had kept African Americans from voting in primaries, which in the heavily Democratic South usually selected the winning candidate. Thurgood Marshall, then a lawyer for the NAACP, would later call *Smith v. Allwright* the most important case he argued prior to *Brown v. Board of Education* (1954).[29] When internment is viewed in the context of the expansion of equality rights, rather than a swinging pendulum, we see a complex terrain of rights affected by conceptions of national identity and national security.

The best example of law as a "loaded weapon" that Justice Jackson warned of in *Korematsu* – the idea that a case of wartime necessity would become entrenched as legal precedent – was the Nazi saboteurs case, *In re Quirin* (1942). This case involved eight Nazi terrorists who landed under cover of night on East Coast beaches with the objective of slipping in unnoticed and committing acts that would terrorize civilians, such as blowing up department stores. But plans went off track rather quickly, and one of the Nazis who wanted to expose the plot ended up traveling to FBI headquarters and spilling a suitcase full of cash on the table when he was unable through other means to get agents to pay attention to his story. The saboteurs were rounded up and secluded. Once safely away from the press, a story of a supposedly successful FBI sting operation was released to the press with much fanfare. Roosevelt and his Justice Department quickly decided that the saboteurs must be tried by a military tribunal, not in civilian courts. But was this constitutional? The saboteurs' counsel filed a habeas corpus action that found its way quickly before the U.S. Supreme Court. On hearing of this action, the President told his Attorney General: "I want one thing clearly understood. . . . I won't give them up."[30] He wouldn't have to. The Court decided the case within twenty-four hours, issuing a short order

---

[28] Gunnar Myrdal, *An American Dilemma: The Negro Problem and Modern Democracy*, Vol. II (New York, 1944), 1016.

[29] "The Reminiscences of Thurgood Marshall" (Columbia Oral History Research Office, 1977), reprinted in Mark V. Tushnet, ed., *Thurgood Marshall: His Speeches, Writings, Arguments, Opinions, and Reminiscences* (Chicago, 2001), 426–28.

[30] David J. Danelski, "The Saboteur's Case," *Journal of Supreme Court History* (1996), 68.

upholding the tribunals. The Court's opinion itself would follow three months later. The tribunals themselves were concluded quickly, with guilty verdicts and death sentences for all. Five days later, FDR commuted two of the sentences to prison terms. The executions of the other six were carried out the same day.

Chief Justice Stone then had the unhappy task of writing an opinion justifying the constitutionality of a process that resulted in executions that had already been carried out. There were inherent difficulties in the arguments and conflicts among the justices' positions, rendering the writing, in Stone's words, "a mortification of the flesh."[31] An opinion was finally released, roundly criticized, and then seemed to drop into oblivion. But *Quirin* would experience a resurrection in the aftermath of the attacks on the United States on September 11, 2001. Again, foreign terrorists had come to the United States, intent on destabilizing American society. *Quirin* was dusted off and rehabilitated, a tool in a new "war on terror."

Cold War Rights

A Cold War national security environment would succeed World War II and soon affected domestic as well as international politics. To generate political support for foreign aid to non-communist governments, President Truman characterized the struggle between the United States and the Soviets as between two fundamentally different ways of life – one free, the other totalitarian. In a global zero-sum game, anything that undermined the United States was seen as aiding its adversary, the Soviet Union. This bipolar conceptualization of world politics, with the United States as the leading democracy, would continue to the end of the century, even after the collapse of what President Ronald Reagan called the "evil empire." In the name of the Cold War, the United States would sometimes support brutal, non-democratic regimes because they were anti-communist. And at home, for a time, Cold War domestic politics led to suppression of free speech and political rights, ironically undermining the practice of democracy in the nation held up as the democratic model.

If communist governments overseas were a threat, communists at home were feared as a "fifth column" that was ready to undermine American democracy from within. In an atmosphere of Cold War anxiety, a Wisconsin Senator seized the issue as a means of gaining political visibility. On February 9, 1950, in Wheeling, West Virginia, Joseph McCarthy claimed that he held in his hands a list of 205 employees of the State Department who were members of the Communist Party. He had no such list, but his

---

[31] Ibid., 72.

sensational claims that communists had infiltrated sensitive areas of the government helped fuel the witch hunts already underway.

Just as government and industry had banded together to fight a world war, they banded together to rout out communists. Much of the damage done in the name of anti-communism came not simply from the parading of witnesses before House and Senate committees, but from the private industry blacklists that followed. But the government's role was not only investigatory. Leaders of the American Communist Party were prosecuted for violating the Smith Act. By meeting to discuss Marx and Engels and by sharing a hope that someday a workers' revolution might overthrow capitalism, they were seen as conspiring to achieve violent overthrow of the U.S. government. The Supreme Court upheld their convictions in *Dennis v. United States* (1951). Although there was no evidence in the record of the harm to U.S. national security perpetrated by the defendants, Justice Frankfurter insisted in his concurrence that the Court could take judicial notice of the dangers of communism.

In the Cold War context, any political scuffle anywhere in the world seemed at best to affect the global balance between democracy and communism, and at worst a step toward global annihilation. In this context, the proportion of government activity devoted to defense was a reflection of the perceived size of the threat. A 1950 National Security Council report, NSC-68, warned that the USSR presented a threat like never before, because "the Soviet Union, unlike previous aspirants to hegemony, is animated by a new fanatic faith, antithetical to our own, and seeks to impose its absolute authority over the rest of the world. . . . With the development of increasingly terrifying weapons of mass destruction, every individual faces the ever-present possibility of annihilation should the conflict enter the phase of total war." The situation was not simply one of national security: "The issues that face us are momentous, involving the fulfillment or destruction not only of this Republic but of civilization itself."

Yet ultimately the battle to contain the Soviet empire would be one not only of weapons but also of ideology. As NSC-68 saw it, the conflict was between the freedom characterized by American democracy and the "slavery under the grim oligarchy of the Kremlin." One important way to fight the Cold War was to project a positive image of American democracy.

The United States, unfortunately, did not always project the image of the free, just society that NSC-68 had in mind. Racism and violence in the American South were making headlines around the world, and the Soviets used it to their advantage. For example, in 1946 Isaac Woodward, an African American veteran on his way home and still in uniform, was beaten and blinded in both eyes by police in South Carolina. The same year, George

Dorsey returned home to Georgia after serving five years in the U.S. Army only to be lynched by a mob of white men who shot Dorsey, his wife, and their two companions. These incidents were widely reported and caused particular outrage because the men were soldiers.

The widespread publication of stories like these reached beyond U.S. borders, undercutting the image of America the world was intended to see. The Dorsey story, for instance, was reported in a Soviet publication, which characterized it as an example of increasing violence toward African Americans in the United States. The Soviet press reported other lynchings and mob violence, and claimed that African Americans were deprived of economic rights, living in a state of semi-slavery, and often denied the right to vote. By 1949, the "Negro question" was a principal Soviet propaganda theme, and the U.S. government believed that racism at home was harming U.S. foreign relations. For this reason, civil rights reforms that aided the reconstruction of the global image of American democracy came to be seen as ways to enhance national security. Law became a tool in the Cold War through the protection of some civil rights.

The best example of this use of law was the line of school segregation cases leading up to *Brown v. Board of Education* (1954). The Justice Department filed *amicus curiae* briefs arguing that segregation damaged U.S. prestige around the world. The *Brown* brief quoted Secretary of State Dean Acheson, who argued that international attention given to American race discrimination was of increasing concern: "The hostile reaction among normally friendly peoples, many of whom are particularly sensitive in regard to the status of non-European races, is growing in alarming proportions. In such countries the view is expressed more and more vocally that the United States is hypocritical in claiming to be the champion of democracy while permitting practices of racial discrimination here in this country." School segregation was a particular focus of foreign criticism, said Acheson; "Other peoples cannot understand how such a practice can exist in a country which professes to be a staunch supporter of freedom, justice, and democracy." For these reasons, race discrimination was a "constant embarrassment" to the U.S. government and "jeopardizes the effective maintenance of our moral leadership of the free and democratic nations of the world."[32] When the Court ruled that school segregation was unconstitutional in *Brown*, the decision was covered extensively by the Voice of America and in State Department programming for other nations, and it was celebrated by the world press. The Court had finally addressed a matter that had been one

---

[32] Mary L. Dudziak, *Cold War Civil Rights: Race and the Image of American Democracy* (Princeton, NJ, 2000), 101.

of the Soviet Union's most successful propaganda themes since the Cold War began.

Although *Brown* greatly aided the U.S. image, American diplomats faced new challenges in the early 1960s as peaceful civil rights demonstrators were brutalized in the South. Images from Birmingham, Alabama, and elsewhere flooded the international press. Meanwhile, African diplomats from newly independent nations were refused service at restaurants, especially along a Maryland state highway, as they traveled from the United Nations in New York to Washington, D.C. Ultimately the Kennedy administration supported civil rights legislation, both for the nation and in the state of Maryland. President Kennedy said in an address to the nation, "We preach freedom around the world, and we mean it, and we cherish our freedom here at home, but are we to say to the world, and much more importantly, to each other that this is a land of the free except for the Negroes?" He then asked his Secretary of State to testify on behalf of the federal civil rights bill because the bill was needed to aid U.S. foreign affairs. A State Department staff member also testified in Maryland, urging the state legislators that the country needed them to pass a civil rights bill so that the nation could effectively wage the Cold War. In both jurisdictions – federal power to regulate civil rights and federal pressure regarding state civil rights laws – the national government pushed the boundaries of federalism to meet the needs of national security. Congress finally passed the Civil Rights Act in 1964. It would be celebrated around the world as evidence that the United States had moved down the road toward remedying its civil rights problems. The nation was coming closer to the vision of America that U.S. diplomats hoped to promote overseas.

Rights and security were also in play in several Vietnam War-era cases. In the "Pentagon Papers" case, *New York Times v. United States* (1971), the *New York Times* and the *Washington Post* published portions of a top-secret document disclosing government decision making regarding Vietnam. The government quickly sought to enjoin the newspapers from printing more of the document, arguing that the release of the confidential information was a threat to national security while the United States was at war. The case reached the U.S. Supreme Court in just eighteen days. Noting that "any system of prior restraints of expression comes to this Court bearing a heavy presumption against its constitutional validity," the Court held the government had not met its heavy burden of demonstrating that the potential harm from publication justified the suppression of publication. Quickly published as a paperback, *The Pentagon Papers* became an overnight best-seller.

In contrast to World War I, the Supreme Court also upheld the right to disagree publicly with the war, even when the "speech" involved wearing a jacket emblazoned with the words "Fuck the Draft."[33] Although the Court held that the First Amendment protected swearing as a legitimate expression of antiwar sentiment, its embrace of dissent was limited. In *United States v. O'Brien* (1968), for instance, the defendant argued that burning his draft card was constitutionally protected free speech. While noting that symbolic conduct was, in some contexts, protected by the First Amendment, the Court held that the ban on destroying draft cards was related to the important government interest of maintaining a military draft, even though the record seemed to indicate that Congress had banned draft card burning when it became a favorite form of antiwar protest.

The male-only draft came under scrutiny as well. With an expansion of women's rights through the Equal Protection Clause still on the horizon, a South Dakota district judge upheld the male-only draft in 1968. The judge found that Congress had properly "followed the teachings of history that if a nation is to survive, men must provide the first line of defense while women keep the home fires burning."[34] In 1980, another district judge found the male-only draft unconstitutional, but the Supreme Court overturned the ruling in *Rostker v. Goldberg* (1981). In *Personnel Administrator of Massachusetts v. Feeney* (1979), the Court also upheld a Massachusetts law that granted veterans absolute preference in employment despite the discriminatory impact on women.

Through the debates of the era, judges, legislators, litigants, and others often conceptualized rights in terms of national security. Rights could expand, contract, and change in ways that aided wartime governance or enhanced national security. Rather than a simple on/off switch triggered by wartime, in the jurisprudence of rights we find images of the nation and its fears.

IV. LAW, SOVEREIGNTY, AND THE SEPTEMBER 11 WORLD

September 11, 2001, brought massive destruction to American soil. Hijackers piloted two airliners into the towers of the World Trade Center in New York City and a third into the Pentagon building just outside Washington, D.C. A fourth airliner crashed into a field in Pennsylvania after its passengers, on hearing of the World Trade Center attacks, tried to overcome their assailants. For a moment, these events brought America and the world together, as peoples around the world made pilgrimages to American embassies with flowers and candles to express their grief. The strikes might have been characterized as a horrific crime. But President George W. Bush

---

[33] *Cohen v. California*, 403 U.S. 15, 26 (1971).
[34] *United States v. Sinclair*, 291 F. Supp. 122 (D.S.D. 1968).

soon announced that the nation was in "a new kind of war" that called for
a military response, rather than criminal prosecution and punishment.

This "new kind of war" was not against a nation, but against terrorism. As
Marilyn Young has argued, the United States has engaged in wars against
"isms" before, for example in Korea, when the nation portrayed itself as
fighting not Koreans but communists. Terrorists, like communists, were
not confined to a particular state, and so the nation could make war against
this new enemy wherever it seemed to reside. The new threat was cast
in apocalyptic terms reminiscent of the Cold War conceptualization of
the Soviet threat, so that survival of the nation and of civilization itself
seemed again at risk. The United States first set its sights on the Taliban in
Afghanistan, and then Iraq, with U.S. officials variously arguing that there
were ties between that nation and the Al Qaeda terrorist group and that Iraqi
President Saddam Hussein had weapons of mass destruction that threatened
American security, claims that it could never verify. Acting without UN
authorization, the U.S. war on Iraq would seem to be a lawless act, flouting
the idea of an international rule of law that had once been the promise of the
international organization. From another perspective, however, American
unilateralism contained a law-like logic. As Ruti Teitel has argued, the
United States saw itself as the world's superpower, the police power of the
world, the enforcer of law that could not itself be subject to the police
power. Acting in the face of disapproval of once close allies, the United
States easily toppled Hussein. That very act, however, was to threaten the
country's own legitimacy in the world community.

This new war had more dramatic effects domestically than had any military engagement since Vietnam. Congress passed the USA PATRIOT Act in
September 2001, giving the government broad powers to detain and deport
non-citizens and expanded investigatory power for law enforcement. Most
important, the president claimed sole authority to determine the scope of
executive power, and his administration tried to render its exercise of power
unreviewable. Administration officials justified their actions by asserting
that September 11 had "changed everything" and that the nation was in
a "new kind of war." Critics of administration policy were dismissed as
engaging in "September 10" thinking. And so September 11 inaugurated
yet another new time zone, a space of exception, a time when normal rules
must be suspended. While legal scholars fiercely debated what constraints
applied to an emergency, the administration acted to mold law in the service
of the new security regime.

Yet rather than a break with the past, the September 11 era illustrates
how embedded war had become in American law by the end of the twentieth
century. War had a way of uniting the nation. As would become clear with
the anemic national response to Hurricane Katrina, a national tragedy was

not a metaphor that would rally the nation or appeal to the electorate. And war brought with it the most expansive vision of government power. The most important power of the president, however, was simply the power to frame the September 11 attacks as a "war" in the first place. Calling it a "war" unleashed the war powers, and the president's continuing efforts to place the ensuing "war on terror" within a traditional American war narrative provided the administration's primary justification for maintaining those powers indefinitely.

In the name of the "war on terror," hundreds of prisoners taken in Afghanistan were not held as prisoners of war in that country and were not transported to the United States, but instead were taken to the U.S. military base at Guantánamo Bay, Cuba. The U.S. government claimed that Guantánamo lay beyond the jurisdiction of U.S. courts because it was not located on U.S. territory. The Geneva Conventions protecting prisoners of war did not apply either, the administration asserted, because the detainees were "unlawful combatants," rather than conventional military forces. Guantánamo therefore seemed to be a law-free zone. In both the domestic and international context, the administration claimed sole power to define the lawful scope of its own action. However, in *Hamdi v. Rumsfeld* (2004), the U.S. Supreme Court placed a limited restraint on the power of the executive to define the boundaries of its own power by holding that a U.S. citizen seized in Afghanistan could challenge his detention in U.S. courts. And in *Hamdan v. Rumsfeld* (2006), the Court rejected the government's plan to try detainees before military tribunals with fewer safeguards than those under U.S. military law. Still, the administration's vision of law was of the sovereign ruler as the embodiment of law itself. The administration justified such broad power as necessary to combat the threat of global terrorism. The difficulty with this vision was that the world was not inclined to follow along. The lessons of the Cold War, that American leadership rested in part on a belief that the nation hewed to its own moral principles, seemed long forgotten. The consequences of unreviewable power seemed evident not long after *Hamdi* was argued in the Supreme Court, as news broke of the torture of Iraqi prisoners by American soldiers. Images of naked, hooded prisoners flooded the international press, undermining American prestige throughout the world. It was clear that the United States had come far from the moment shortly after 9/11 when the world had grieved along with Americans. Now American power seemed tawdry and dangerous.

Prosecutions of soldiers involved in Abu Ghraib, it was hoped, would help distance the prisoner abuse from America itself by illustrating that the perpetrators had violated their nation's norms. But troublesome news from Iraq and Afghanistan continued to reverberate around the world. The image of America became linked, indissolubly, to its pursuit of the "war on terror."

The meaning of that engagement, like those that had preceded it, would be inscribed in the world's history books written far beyond the command of any American president. When America makes war, war makes America in the hearts and minds of all who are touched, and in ways beyond American control.

CONCLUSION

War has traditionally reconfigured sovereign power, with the ascendancy of the victor and the displacement of the defeated. At work in the twentieth century is anther kind of reconfiguration of sovereignty. War, through the century, has driven the expansion of the powers of American sovereignty. Where the ends of that power will lie is the question for the next age.

The great constitutional debates in the post-September 11 era often turned on the nature of a sovereign's war or emergency power and on whether the power to define the state of emergency and suspend the usual rule of law lies solely in the hands of the president. But the more enduring question was what the nation had become before the twin towers fell and how war had seeped into its center.

Early in the twentieth century, hopes flourished that global conflict might be avoided if only drafters of a convention could get the words right. Instead, law became embroiled in the project of demarcating those wars that crossed the bounds of humanity from those that did not. Law and war acquired an intimate familiarity with each other.

That familiarity welled up domestically too. Government powers did not ebb and flow with wartime. Government programs and regulations created during war did not go away, but were drawn on later to serve new purposes. The Supreme Court, like other branches of government, facilitated war-related state-building. While the beginnings of what is sometimes called the "New Deal revolution" on the Court happened before the United States entered the war, decisions during the conflict greatly extended federal power: what began in 1937 was consolidated and extended in a war-related context. War's impact on American legal history is not episodic, but central and continuing. Law is a vehicle through which war becomes embedded in American democracy over time.

Similarly, the twentieth-century story of individual rights has not been a simple one of a pendulum swinging between rights and security. Instead, security concerns often informed the Court's jurisprudence, but security might be advanced by contracting, expanding, or modifying rights, depending on the situation. *Korematsu* during World War II and *Dennis v. United States* during the Cold War are classic examples of decisions in which rights were restricted in the service of conceptions of national security. In

Brown v. Board of Education, by contrast, racial discrimination was recognized as an international embarrassment that undermined U.S. prestige. This led to an extension of individual rights. Individual rights cases help us see that conceptions of national identity are at stake in constitutional cases. Reflected across these cases is an image of the nation and its fears.

American national identity, reflected in American law, was not simply a domestic matter, as the story of *Brown* helps us realize. Projecting an image of American justice was central to maintaining a conception of American democracy – a story of America for the world. In the context of the Cold War, this mattered immensely to U.S. prestige and U.S. national security. More recently, the world's perceptions of American democracy have not weighed as heavily on American policymakers. Debates over the importance of the American image would again become a central issue after September 11, and especially after the exposure of abuses at the hands of Americans at Abu Ghraib. The United States seemed to retreat from international legal regulation of its actions, as if law itself was a threat to American security. The new world that many imagined had been created by September 11 required that the United States project power, rather than submit to the legal scrutiny of others. But bad news continued to filter out from Iraq, Afghanistan, and Guantánamo. As much as the United States tried to hold the reins of power, the story of the war and conceptions of its lawfulness informed the world's understandings of American identity in ways beyond any president's control.

Increasingly, the struggle within the United States has been preoccupied with the nature of constitutional limits on the power of a president who argues that any constraint on his authority threatens security. Domestic dissent over war has sometimes led to political realignment, and a change in direction. It is also the case that just as the forces of war come most often from outside a regime, limits to American sovereign power can come from outside U.S. borders. The rest of the world has long known it has a stake in the nature of American sovereignty. How it will realize that stake will surely be a central story of the twenty-first century.

LAW, LAWYERS, AND EMPIRE

YVES DEZALAY AND BRYANT G. GARTH

At the end of the twentieth century, scholars from many disciplines noted the rise of "norms" or even "legalization" in U.S. foreign policy and in the practice of international relations more generally. Legal debates about the rules for governing foreign relations and questions of how to enforce desirable laws such as those outlawing genocide or ethnic cleansing became central to international diplomacy. Even the debates for and against globalization came to feature lawyers, whereas trade debates focused on such issues as the legal standing of environmental groups in proceedings before the World Trade Organization (WTO).

For many scholars, these developments marked an important and desirable shift from the "realist" focus on struggles for power and influence toward greater cooperation and rule-oriented behavior. More than at any time in the past, ideas of how to build and improve laws and legal enforcement dominated the agenda of American foreign policy.

In this chapter we examine the process of legalization (and its celebration). By tracing current institutional developments to their geneses a century ago, we argue that the current situation in international relations reflects a relative success in "Americanization" abroad that also reinforces the power of lawyers and the clients they serve domestically. Law and lawyers have been central to what can be characterized as U.S. "imperial strategies" throughout the twentieth century, we show, but the role of law and lawyers in these strategies has changed over the course of that time. We examine in particular the process by which, during the first half of the twentieth century, the power of the so-called "foreign policy establishment" (FPE) was entrenched in the workings of the law. From the 1970s onward, power in international relations became more legalized and more autonomous, which meant that the *specific* power of the FPE declined.

Our approach in this chapter is historical and sociological. Since the sociological component may appear somewhat unorthodox, we highlight here at the outset some of the puzzles and paradoxes in the domain of internationalization and law that it helps explain. First, our analysis explains the combination of legal idealism and instrumental pragmatism that characterizes U.S. foreign policy (partly reflected in the never-ending debate between so-called realists and idealists). Second, it accounts for the way in which champions on each side often appear to change sides and why they receive help from unlikely partners, such as corporate speculators turned philanthropists (exemplified in the early twenty-first century by George Soros). Third, it explains why the acceleration of the process of legalization in the last decades of the twentieth century coincided with the relative demise of the legal elite that once enjoyed a quasi-monopoly over U.S. international politics.

Our analysis also highlights some odd combinations of continuities and discontinuities. For example, the field of human rights – to which we pay close attention – began deeply embedded in Cold War politics, was subsequently reinvented by critics of the Cold War, and then became institutionalized as a new orthodoxy. The legalization of trade disputes through the WTO was promoted at one and the same time by multinational companies such as Pfizer and by leading anti-globalists such as Lori Wallach, director of Global Trade Watch (a division of Ralph Nader's consumer advocacy group, Public Citizen). Even the war on terrorism, promoted by the neoconservatives behind George W. Bush, can be understood best not as the rejection of "multilateralism" and law as such but rather as an episode in the continuing series of battles that produce and globalize U.S. law.

More generally, our analysis explains why and how law could maintain throughout its central position as the battlefield for political and economic power in foreign relations. We recognize that the content of the laws that emerge from these battles is important. So are the contests (such as those between realists and idealists) that produce laws favoring one or another political position. And we also recognize that the law's growing autonomy and institutionalization from the 1970s onward have had major implications for the ability of individuals to enforce rights related to foreign policy domains. Nevertheless, our focus here is not on the content of laws or their enforceability but on the process through which a particular group of lawyers succeeded – and continues to succeed – in channeling successive waves of both realism and idealism, both progressive and conservative, into a foreign policy apparatus that empowers and allows them (despite various challenges) to manage the process in the overall interest of themselves and their large corporate clients.

To understand the international usages of American law, one must focus on how it is produced, by whom, and in what kind of social context. That is, to write the history of American law in the domain of foreign policy – or in any other domain for that matter – requires that one examine American law's mode of production. One must explore the identity of the legal elite, examine the means by which it influences the politics of law (how it controls the producers and dominates the mode of production of law), and survey the resources and strategies it employs. Our particular tool is individual and collective biography: this allows us to understand both the particular U.S. mode of production of law – and law firms – and how that mode has been transformed over the course of the twentieth century.

Transformation, as we shall see, took place both through external challenges to the legal elite, embodied in the FPE, and through challenges from within the legal field involving new entrants, increased competition, specialization, and a greater division of labor. Internal challenges pressured the old-style generalists who once could pretend to do a bit of everything – acting as the "wise men" for the state or business, as learned lawyers, and as idealistic visionaries. These internal challenges took place on the terrain of law, accelerated through the process by which battles in the field of state power are fought with the weapons of law.

Our starting point is a narrative of the FPE – its initial rise, relative decline, subsequent recovery, challenge, reconversion, and eventual institutionalization. In broad outline, the story is one of protracted and hardly inevitable Weberian movement from governance (in the sense of shaping and overseeing the government agenda) by the "charisma" of elite lawyers to the "routine" of bureaucratic institutions and a combination of "hard" and "soft" law. The broad outline, however, masks the details that determine the particulars of the early twenty-first century's contingent "rules of the game" for governance. In the United States "charisma" was situated in a recognizable group of individuals involved in contested struggles for power; "routine" emerged as a contested set of rules and approaches for the governance of foreign policy. In both cases, law and lawyers played their roles as part of a multi-polar field of "quasi" state power – a field of power without a core but structured around three main pillars: Ivy League campuses, Wall Street, and Washington, D.C.

U.S. law and U.S.-trained lawyers emerged from all this central to globalization and to America's relatively successful effort in the 1980s and 1990s to define and shape globalization to its specific ends – ends defined by the neo-liberal economists who became preeminent in the 1970s. The WTO's legal regime, as one prominent example, sought to lock in and legalize basic free-trade principles and approaches modeled on U.S. trade law. This mostly liberal trade regime complemented the somewhat earlier rise of a lex mercatoria and a system of international commercial arbitration that had moved U.S. (and English) contract law and U.S.-style litigation to the center of transnational business relations. As another example, during the last quarter of the twentieth century the international human rights movement succeeded in elevating the place of law and human rights – and of U.S.-based non-governmental organizations (NGOs) such as New York-based Human Rights Watch and foundations such as the Ford Foundation – in international relations.

Finally, combining human rights and business law into a recipe for legitimate governance, rule of law programs became central to the foreign aid policies of not only the United States but also the World Bank, the International Monetary Fund, and many European countries. These and parallel developments worked to promote globalization through states and economies reengineered to accommodate U.S. business and also the knowledge industry (especially legal service providers and the investment banking and business consulting industries modeled after corporate law firms) constructed to serve that business.

Legalization and globalization faced challenges both within the United States and abroad. The Bush-Cheney administration of 2000–08 questioned the WTO's trade regime by asserting protection for the steel industry (even though ultimately capitulating); it refused to adhere to treaties establishing an International Criminal Court, banning anti-ballistic missile systems, and seeking to regulate global warming; it used the war against terrorism to lower the profile and importance of human rights and activities directed toward the rule of law. The continuing vitality of the human rights regime remained quite evident, however, especially as seen in the response to the evidence of U.S. torture of detainees taken as part of the "war on terror." Indeed, the Bush-Cheney administration eventually grounded the second Gulf War largely on the theory that Saddam Hussein's human rights violations justified humanitarian intervention, and it devoted considerable resources to attempts to document Iraq war crimes. Although quite resistant to any legalization that threatens to constrain U.S. power, in other words, the Bush-Cheney administration was ready to take advantage of the persistent legitimacy of human rights considerations when it served administration purposes.

To ground our story of the position of law in international relations, we begin with the central figures of the FPE dominant for much of the century until its apotheosis in the 1960s. As we will see, their professional legal careers were the point of departure for the powerful positions they built in and around the U.S. state, but they relied at least as much on their capital of personal relationships, business connections, and social class. Legal authority was a key basis of their power, but their investment in the law itself was relatively light. We then move on to the demise of the Establishment amid the challenges of, especially, the Vietnam War and the protracted economic crises of the 1970s and 1980s. Here we address the issue of actual investment in law and "legalization." Though evident before World War I, legalization did not begin to gain any substantial importance, in the sense of actual institutionalization or autonomization, until well after the end of World War II.

I. FROM SERVANTS OF BIG BUSINESS TO LAWYER-STATESPERSONS: THE INVENTION OF THE FOREIGN POLICY ESTABLISHMENT AS A MEANS TO LEGITIMATE THAT SERVICE, MAKE IT MORE VALUABLE, AND PROTECT THE LONG-TERM INTERESTS OF THEMSELVES AND THEIR CLIENTS

The activities of the founders of the foreign policy establishment in the United States can only be understood in relation to the rise of the new industrial class in the late nineteenth century connected to the railroads, the banks, and the emerging oil industry – centered ultimately in New York City. The economic transformations presented both opportunities and risks to lawyers. One risk came from the way the so-called robber barons used legal hired guns instrumentally to defeat their competitors. Lawyers who served them became identified with and somewhat tainted by the businesses and business tactics they served. There was opposition within the more traditional, litigation-oriented bar to these alliances, which threatened the legitimacy of a profession beginning to organize and become more self-conscious. The continuing mode of production of U.S. law can be traced to the handling of this professional crisis of legitimacy.

The rising corporate bar in New York City adopted a variation on a traditional strategy of building a relative autonomy from their clients in order to make their expertise more valuable and their own roles more legitimate. They invested in regulatory law, including antitrust, and in the state through politics in the Progressive era and beyond. This investment took place at the local level, involving municipal justice and good government, but it was also found in the effort to build a legitimate but active foreign policy that would coincide with the interests of the corporate bar's clients in expanding their markets and maintaining their position as other powers expanded their empires. Elite lawyers became dominant in the FPE from early on. Simultaneously, the corporate lawyer as "lawyer-statesperson" came to embody the elite of the legal profession and to shape its norms and values.

The strategy of this group of lawyers serving business was a mix of professional and technical investment. It was also a learned strategy. The corporate law firms led by the Cravath firm (since 1944 Cravath, Swaine, and Moore) in New York City invested substantial resources in the law schools and in the science then being developed through the case method pioneered at Harvard. Those who excelled at the case method were invited to join the leading corporate law firms. The elite law firms valued and gained value from their close ties to leading law schools and their recruitment of the top graduates. Part of the state strategy for the law firms and their clients involved the mobilization of social capital to help civilize the robber barons into philanthropic patrons – led by the Carnegie and Rockefeller foundations. In this way the aspiring legal elite could use their clients to enhance the public arena, including foreign affairs. They could broker the interests of business and the state from positions of close proximity to both.

This ambitious strategy, which produced a unique group of elite corporate lawyers central to institutions of governance, required an initial accumulation of symbolic capital – combining social class, elite school ties, meritocratic criteria, political investment, law firm size, and entrepreneurship. The professional firms were able to combine the social capital of the well-bred cosmopolitan elite with the ambition and talent of meritocratic newcomers promised partnership if they could succeed as associates. Sullivan and Cromwell, founded in 1879 and still one of the most elite firms in the world, provided a perfect example: Sullivan brought ties to an old family; Cromwell was the driving entrepreneurial outsider. The pattern was repeated often, for example with the absorption much later of Irish and Jewish litigators into the corporate law firms.

The Wall Street law firm – often termed the Cravath model – became the institutionalization of this double agent strategy. Law firms served as buffers and crossroads between academia, business, and the state. This double agency can be seen as an institutionalized schizophrenia, according to which the lawyers would alternately seek to find ways for their clients to avoid state regulation and for the state to regulate their clients. The practical result was that it allowed the lawyers to construct rules to protect and rationalize the power of their clients, to build the need for their own professional services, and to gain some power in the state and economy.

The professional firms structured to serve corporate clients increasingly sought to cultivate the image of learned gentlemen of the law. Especially as they became older, they sought respect and recognition. The elite Wall Street firms balanced their profits with a certain amount of noblesse oblige. The top firms hardly ever competed with each other, their relations with clients were organized in an almost familial mode, and they were relatively few in number and socially homogeneous. Overall they comprised an exclusive cadre of old boys groomed and trained in elite institutions led by Harvard and Yale. Corporate law in this way became the core of the

Eastern establishment in the United States. Law in the United States became closely linked and identified with the reproduction of an establishment built around the state and a fraction of the corporate world closely linked to (and dependent on) state resources and patronage.

The links among lawyers, business, the academy, and the state were openly recognized and built into the system, and the system was cemented by other institutions such as the press and the philanthropic foundations. Well-connected and ambitious undergraduates easily came to the conclusion that, in the words of Kingman Brewster – direct descendent from the Mayflower, Harvard Law professor, and president of Yale – describing the 1940s, one went "on to law school, not to become a lawyer but because it seemed like the best way to move forward without burning any bridges." Such a "non-decision" assumed that one available base, source of financial security, if necessary, and network of like-minded friends was the elite corporate law firm. When Cyrus Vance, for example, left the Department of Defense in 1967, he went to Simpson, Thatcher because he "had five children approaching college age, and having depleted his savings after six and a half years in government service, 'I simply had to get back and earn some money.'" And the base in the corporate law firm facilitated service on various business and philanthropic boards, including oversight of the elite universities and law schools.

The career of Elihu Root, who became Secretary of War under President William McKinley in 1899 in the period of the Spanish-American War, shows how this mode of production of law and lawyers developed and how it led to investment in foreign affairs. Root at the time of his appointment was already quite prominent as a corporate lawyer. His clients included the infamous Sugar Trust, which he helped survive the threat embodied in antitrust legislation. He also made his name by investing in good government generally through the Republican Party in New York, including close ties to Theodore Roosevelt. As a generalist lawyer with cosmopolitan connections and a reputation for good judgment, Root made sense as a trouble-shooter for the new and problematic colonial ventures. A key task was to deal with the continued resistance in the Philippines to the U.S. occupation and colonization and, in the United States, to the idea of the United States as a colonizing power. Root brought the same approach to foreign affairs that he did to New York City – serving the general interests of his clients and seeking to build legitimacy for the world in which they operated.

Root had to work to overcome the traditional U.S. idea that colonialism was inconsistent with U.S. legal and moral values. McKinley and Root enlisted Judge William Howard Taft to help respond to the challenge. Taft, then the presiding judge of the Sixth Circuit Court of Appeals and dean of the law school of the University of Cincinnati, accepted the position in charge of the Philippines effort. The work to build a new government in the Philippines, he stated, was "a national obligation, indeed a 'sacred duty.'" He would "create a government adapted to the needs of the Filipinos, one that would help to develop them into a self-governing people." In line with Root's ideas, Taft led "the effort of the United States to transplant its values and institutions in the Philippines." According to Taft, "We hold the Philippines for the benefit of the Filipinos."

These lawyers sought to defend a U.S. brand of colonialism through this moral facade, both as a way to make it more legitimate, at home and abroad, than the more traditional Spanish colonialism that it replaced and to offer legal morality as a kind of civic religion to substitute for the conservative Catholicism that was a key component of the Spanish model of colonization. There were, of course, real economic interests and concerns underlying this U.S. assertiveness abroad, but the business concerns were combined with idealism that these corporate lawyers encouraged and expressed. Foreign involvement was an opportunity to transplant the universal U.S. values that they represented.

Some sense of this role of law can be garnered from testimony of one of the dominant "civilizers" in the Philippines. George Malcolm was a young law graduate of the University of Michigan who went to the Philippines to "see my country initiate a system of ever increasing self-government for the Philippines . . . [and] to take a stand in favor of resolute adherence to America's revolutionary anti-colonial policy."[1] Through entrepreneurial initiative, he helped establish the University of Philippines College of Law in 1911, and he became its first dean. His goal with the law school was "the training of leaders for the country. The students were not alone tutored in abstract law dogmas; they were inculcated with the principles of democracy." One of the graduates in 1913, who "established the reputation of the new school by topping all candidates in the Bar examination,"[2] was Manual Roxas, who became the first president of the Philippine Republic. The career of Roxas reflects the double strategy of the elite U.S. lawyers. One was to ally with – and even help produce – their counterparts in the Philippines. The second was to support a moral and legal front capable of aligning the colonial venture with U.S. values, including the idea of U.S. exceptionalism from the despised world of European colonialism.

The U.S. leaders used their Philippines experience, and its very high value on resumes at the time, to build their arguments for comparable approaches in U.S. foreign policy more generally. Expressing hostility to colonial

---

[1] George A. Malcolm, *American Colonial Careerist* (Boston, 1957), 23.
[2] Malcolm, *American Colonial Careerist*, 98.

empires, for example, Taft as president of the United States sought to open markets for U.S. business as an aspect of "dollar diplomacy" – designed to supplant military strategies while facilitating U.S. prosperity – through trade and investment rather than new colonial conquests. Dollar diplomacy led the way to the policies of Woodrow Wilson, who succeeded Taft as president. Those policies are often mistakenly characterized as policies of "idealism," when in fact they reflect the same mix of interest and ideals found in the legal elite's formula combining clients and civic service. The ideals were consistent with a worldview in which the lawyers and their clients would prosper.

Henry Stimson is another of the most prominent members of the FPE, and he too combined colonial service in the Philippines with corporate law and government service at home. After Andover, Yale, and Harvard Law School, Stimson in 1890 took advantage of a family friendship to secure a position working for Elihu Root. When Root became McKinley's Secretary of War in 1899, he turned over the law practice to his two partners, one of whom was Stimson. The law firm of Winthrop and Stimson thrived by representing the trusts and moving toward specialization in national and increasingly in international business. Stimson's personal ties and professional stature led him to be appointed Secretary of War by Taft in 1912.

When Stimson resumed the practice of law, he also resumed service on behalf of large corporate interests. He returned to the government as the Governor General of the Philippines in 1927; a year later he became Herbert Hoover's Secretary of State and still later Secretary of War for Franklin D. Roosevelt and Harry S. Truman (1940–45). Individuals close to Stimson, many of whom worked with him during World War II, including Dean Acheson, William and McGeorge Bundy, Cyrus Vance, and Elliot Richardson, were active well into the 1970s.

After World War I and the failure of the United States to join the League of Nations, a group of these elite lawyers and others formed the Council on Foreign Relations (CFR) to keep alive the case for active U.S. engagement with the international community. They worked closely with counterparts in Europe representing comparable mixes of social, legal, and state capital. As indicated by the early leadership of Elihu Root and John W. Davis, these activists were also leading corporate lawyers. Davis himself was J. P. Morgan's lawyer. He combined his representation of the J. P. Morgan interests with a strong internationalist portfolio including the Council on Foreign Relations, which he headed for twelve years, and service as Ambassador to the Court of St. James. John Foster Dulles, later Eisenhower's Secretary of State, fit the same mold. Dulles joined Sullivan and Cromwell before World War I, played a role as a young man in negotiations at Versailles, and went on to a career representing major corporations – including United Fruit – and supporting an internationalist foreign policy. He wrote one of the articles in the first issue of *Foreign Affairs*, the journal of the Council on Foreign Relations. Paul Cravath – the eponymous exemplar of the corporate law firm system – also became a director and vice president of the Council at the time it was established. In the era of so-called isolationism, the Council continued to promote interest in international relations: "To oppose isolationism had been the bedrock of the Establishment's policy during its years in the wilderness. . . . "

It took World War II, however, to bring the individuals associated with the Council to the pinnacle of power, and it took the Cold War to maintain and further build that position. Regional divisions in the United States between "American First nativism and pro-interdependence globalism" were put aside. As Leonard Silk and Mark Silk write, "Above all, there was the Communist threat. Resistance to the more humanitarian forms of foreign aid gave way before the ready argument that this was designed to hold off the Russians. Indeed, in many quarters this was the only argument that worked." John J. McCloy noted the importance of the Council in the 1950s: "Whenever we needed a man, . . . we thumbed through the roll of Council members and put through a call to New York."

McCloy, the emblematic figure of the FPE from the 1940s until the 1960s, merits elaboration. John Kenneth Galbraith designated McCloy the "chairman" of the establishment. According to Kai Bird, McCloy's biographer,

His story . . . encompasses the rise of a new national elite, composed largely of corporate lawyers and investment bankers, who became stewards of the American national-security state. Beginning in the 1920s, these men formed an identifiable Establishment, a class of individuals who shared the same social and political values and thought of themselves as keepers of the public trust. Unlike the British Establishment, from which the term is borrowed, the American Establishment was dedicated not to preserving the *status quo*, but to persuading America to shoulder its imperial responsibilities.

McCloy began his career at the Cravath firm just after World War I and eventually helped establish another "white shoe" firm, Milbank Tweed, which was the vehicle for his legal representation of the Rockefellers. His career included service as the High Commissioner to occupied Germany after World War II, the president of the World Bank, the chair of the Ford Foundation, and chair of the Council on Foreign Relations – but a few of his positions. He was also, in Bird's words, "legal counsel to all 'Seven Sister' oil companies, a board director for a dozen of America's top corporations, and a private, unofficial advisor to most of the presidents in the twentieth century."

The apotheosis of the FPE came in the Kennedy administration. The social profile, professional trajectories, and the political opinions of Kennedy's "action intellectuals" from Cambridge suggest their continuity with the establishment. Not all were corporate lawyers. Comparable careers could be made by circulation among the various institutions dominated by the legal elite, including the related career of investment banker. But the members of the establishment were all cut from the same mold. The central figure of the Kennedy administration, for example, was McGeorge Bundy, the principal organizer of Kennedy's elite group and later advisor to the president for foreign affairs. Bundy was a direct descendant from a traditional Eastern WASP family, a graduate of Yale, and the son-in-law of Dean Acheson – one of the famous "wise men" of the FPE. Bundy's cosmopolitan career also included service as a very young dean of the Harvard College of Arts and Sciences, the Council on Foreign Relations, National Security Advisor, and finally the leadership of the Ford Foundation, which he directed from 1967 to 1979. Unlike his father, Harvey Bundy, and brother, William Bundy, he did not attend law school, but he was close enough to law to be offered a Supreme Court clerkship by Felix Frankfurter. Bundy's generation and close circle of friends also included Cyrus Vance, then in his first government service with the Department of Defense (and whose father figure was his close relative, John W. Davis); Kingman Brewster, the president of Yale from 1963 to 1977; Eliot Richardson, Secretary of State and of Health Education and Welfare under Nixon; and John Lindsay, mayor of New York City.

This brief account of the names and influence of lawyers in the FPE attests to the importance afforded to lawyers and legal training in U.S. governance, especially after World War II. Yet, most general historical accounts of foreign policy during the Cold War pay almost no attention to law itself. The neglect is not an oversight. Neither the opening of markets and protection of investments, nor the attention to development in the Third World, nor the mobilization of foreign policy against Communism drew very much on law. The academic influences behind the policies were the realists represented by scholar/political activists, such as George Kennan, Hans Morgenthau, Reinhold Niebuhr, and Arthur Schlesinger, Jr., all of whom built their position by attacking remnants of "Wilsonian idealism" – characterized by Kennan as a "legalistic-moralistic approach" to foreign policy. They scoffed at the idea that international relations might be grounded in international law and legal institutions. Even as late as 1968, for example, Dean Acheson scolded an audience at the American Society of International Law for confusing what the law is with what they wanted it to be by invoking international human rights. The rhetorical posture against Wilsonian idealism, however, exaggerated the differences between these individuals and their predecessors in the FPE.

This relatively weak position of law over the entire period is not difficult to explain. Elite lawyers, it is true, were quite important as the embodiment of the establishment. Indeed, they had much in common with the law graduates who occupied similar positions in other countries. Prominent examples include the law graduates who dominated the state in Brazil or Chile. As in Latin America, in addition, legal elites also served as advisors to business, as business leaders themselves, and as intellectuals, professors, and reformers in and outside of the government. To be sure, the mode of production of law differed in key respects between Latin America and the United States, but in both cases a key source of the power of the legal elite was a relative lack of investment in pure law and legal institutions – or, put another way, a diverse portfolio of capital that could be drawn on at different times. These lawyers were at the top of the legal profession despite activities that relied relatively little on the formal law or legal institutions. And they were at the top of the social and political structure because of a combination of activities and connections that placed them above the mundane world of law. A relatively small number of people could occupy and rotate among a large number of power bases.

The FPE in the same way was able to dominate a number of related bases, including the elite campuses, exemplified by McGeorge Bundy's leading position at Harvard (despite only having a BA) and Kingman Brewster's presidency of Yale; the philanthropic foundations, including Ford and Rockefeller; the State Department; the media, especially the leading newspapers exemplified by the *New York Times*; and representation of the major U.S. corporations and financial institutions. All these individuals were generally united on the goals and tactics of the Cold War, which were of course quite consistent with their vision of the interests of the clients of the elite law firms that provided the glue that linked the other institutions. "Bipartisanship" in foreign policy safeguarded the power of the establishment and those they represented.

Bipartisanship was also consistent with a foreign policy built around collaboration with elites in the fight against Communism. The approach can be seen in the Cultural Cold War under the CIA and in the many related programs supported by the Ford Foundation and others. From the perspective of the Ford Foundation, for example, it almost did not matter what kind of economics it supported (as in Chile) as long as the programs made friends for the United States. Similarly, in the Philippines the policy was to build friendly leaders – largely from among the traditional Philippine elite – rather than truly reform the state or state policies. The "modernization" theory then fashionable on the campuses of the elite schools fit this mission perfectly, providing scholarly rationalization for the search for and support of "modernizing elites." That was also the strategy at home, where the FPE participated strongly in the reformist policies associated with a relatively activist state governed with a large dose of noblesse oblige.

Lawyers were not, of course, the only important group holding the elite together. Particularly after the Depression, economics became another important academic home. But mainstream economics was not inconsistent with the methods or approach of the lawyers. Within the Kennedy administration, for example, Walt Rostow's recipe for developmental assistance entitled "The Stages of Economic Growth: An Anti-Communist Manifesto" fit the Cold War strategy perfectly (and the politics of his lawyer-brother, Eugene Rostow, the Yale Law School dean before joining the government). One of Walt Rostow's collaborators at MIT, Max Millikan, also an economist, was a key leader of the CIA in the 1950s and later. The general consensus survived largely because the Cold War masked these and other tensions and conflicts. The legal establishment easily assimilated the challenges. Similarly, to the extent that the attack on Wilsonian idealism by non-lawyers was an attack on law in the name of a new field of international relations in the United States, it could also be absorbed and even used to bolster the position of the FPE *above* the law – and therefore relatively unrestrained in the tactics it could promote as part of the Cold War.

The general assumption is that after the 1960s the power of the establishment declined substantially in the United States and further that the lawyer-statespersons so important to that power were also on the road to extinction. By the early twenty-first century lawyers and law professors were issuing ever more frequent calls in one form or another for the return of such lawyer-statespersons. The number and weight of these panegyrics suggest that there was something to their analysis, even though it also served tactically to promote individual claims to embody the traditional virtues of the lawyer-statesperson. More importantly, however, the asserted decline notwithstanding, the legal project connected to the lawyer-statespersons had in many respects triumphed. Law and legal approaches had become far more important in foreign policy than they were in the past.

The apparent paradox can be explained by examining the challenges to the lawyer-statespersons and the FPE that took place in the 1960s and later. The effect of the challenges was to undermine the ability of lawyer-statespersons to occupy multiple positions while at the same time transforming and deepening institutional investment in the law – and the legal role as broker of choice for the Ivy League, New York, and Washington, D.C.

II. CHALLENGES AND RESPONSES: LEGALIZATION IN A NEW DIVISION OF LABOR OF DOMINATION AT HOME AND ABROAD

The Vietnam War and the civil rights revolution of the 1960s were the obvious manifestations of a profound challenge to the power of this legal establishment. By the end of the 1960s, the FPE was certainly on the defensive, leading to the rise of the new right, the presidencies of Richard Nixon and Ronald Reagan, and the two Presidents Bush. The establishment Republicans such as John Lindsay and Elliot Richardson lost their place in the Republican Party. More generally, as seen in all the presidential administrations, the relatively liberal and reformist-minded – or "progressive" – establishment gave way to a much more conservative social and economic orientation.

This change is often depicted as an ideological shift, an abandonment of the relatively progressive political agenda of the 1960s and 1970s. The ideological story is appealing, since it suggests that another ideological "change in direction" would bring a return to an age of social progressivism. However, the ideological story also distracts attention from the interests involved in the transformation and those who served them. The more complex story can be traced by using the FPE to focus on the field of political power. Challenges and continuities revealed through this analysis help explain the complex role of law in relation to corporate power and globalization.

The general sociological and historical approach here, based on Pierre Bourdieu's reflexive sociology, is to examine contending forms and amounts of capital doing battle within more or less autonomous fields, including especially the field of state power. The description of the leaders of the FPE over the course of the twentieth century is one of the reproduction of elites (with the addition of a relatively few meritocratic entrants, including for example McCloy) who attended the same prep schools and colleges, worked at the same law firms, represented the same clients, and knew each other and each other's families very well. They built a distance from their clients that in the United States allowed them to serve in the place of a European-style state. In the interests of winning the Cold War, preventing domestic turmoil, and protecting their own position, they worked on behalf of a reformist state through the institutions they controlled – including the state itself, the philanthropic institutions, and the elite universities. They embodied the realism of their clients' interests and the noblesse oblige/idealism that also served to define them as lawyer-statespersons.

One key element of the various challenges was built on a contradiction internal to the system that reproduced the FPE. The reformist policies of the Eastern establishment, accelerated by World War II and the GI Bill, contributed to an opening up of the elite educational institutions, which helped build the relative autonomy of the Ivy League and the enlargement (again in relative terms) of its social recruitment. This enlargement helped open the networks of power of the establishment to new arrivals, less disposed to accept the traditional hierarchies and orthodoxies. The demographic element underlies much of the pressure on the establishment that emerged over the 1960s and 1970s in the United States (and elsewhere in the world).

A second challenge included the escalation of the Cold War after Castro came to power in Cuba, the problems of that escalation represented by the Vietnam War, and then the consequences of failure in Vietnam. The war cut the FPE off from the campuses and the idealists who had helped bolster their role, and eventually the war divided the establishment itself. The bipartisan consensus that kept the establishment united failed to hold together, especially with the pressures that came with the demographics of the new set of actors. They new actors challenged the establishment for failing to adhere to its professed ideals and invested much more in the law itself, because they did not possess as much social capital as members of the establishment. New actors mounted political, academic, and other challenges, including "exposing" the FPE, the "power elite," and the connections between, for example, the CIA and a number of notable academics. Many of the protégés of the establishment split with their mentors and worked actively to defeat them.

A third challenge was economic. It became more difficult to combine Cold War expenditures, the social policies associated with liberal reform, and the Bretton Woods trade system then leading to huge U.S. deficits, especially with Japan. The oil crisis of 1973 was the last straw, leading to a fundamental challenge to the relatively activist state that had prevailed since the Depression of the 1930s. Expectations of reform had here too been exacerbated by the demographics of the 1960s, which accelerated the demands for reform and therefore the pressure on business to find a way to curb those demands. The literature from the right and the left at the time on the "crisis of the state" was consistent with this analysis. Within the "liberal establishment," Brewster at Yale, Bundy at the Ford Foundation, and Lindsay in New York all found their ideals thwarted to a large extent by the problem of shrinking resources. The perception of economic crisis helped shift attention and credibility away from Keynesian economics toward the emerging neo-liberalism associated with the University of Chicago. Nixon said "we are all Keynesians," but soon after, the orthodoxy changed through an alliance among Chicago economists, business leaders, and a supportive media led by the *Wall Street Journal*.

A fourth challenge, present in varying degrees throughout the twentieth century but exacerbated by the economic crises and the demographic transformations of the university, was to the generalist expertise of lawyer-statespersons. Challenges from political science and economics have already been mentioned. The most powerful of the academic and professional challenges, linked to economics, came from the business schools, which gradually gained power and credibility over the course of the century. They moved from low-status schools of commerce to high-prestige institutions producing a competing (but also complementary) elite group. Academic challenges from outside the law also became resources used by those investing more deeply in the law.

Each of these can be presented as an external challenge, but they were exacerbated by crises that can be conceptualized as internal to the mode of the production of the legal elite. The members of the FPE, as noted, invested in a variety of organizations that together supported and defined the establishment. They encouraged the idealism and scholarship connected to the law schools and the foundations, for example, and they supported efforts to make their leadership more legitimate by making more space for new and more meritocratic arrivals. After World War II, in fact, a group of establishment leaders – despite denunciations as traitors to their class – worked to open up and "modernize" the Ivy League and the foundations confronted by the antiwar and civil rights movements.

The leading individuals of the liberal establishment in these transformations comprised a small group with very privileged backgrounds and close personal ties, chronicled recently in Geoffrey Kabaservice's book on Kingman Brewster and his circle – McGeorge Bundy, John Lindsay, Paul Moore, Jr., Elliot Richardson, and Cyrus Vance. Four of the six were law-trained at Harvard or Yale, and all four worked at one time or another as corporate lawyers. As modernizers, they all to some extent participated in what Kabaservice describes as Brewster's project at Yale: "By reducing the weight of inheritance, wealth, and social standing in admissions, Brewster was helping to shrink the power of the WASP elite, even while he was gambling that its influence would be redistributed to other, rising groups." The modernizers sought to accommodate those who, lacking the social capital of the WASP elite, invested much more strongly in moral virtue, scholarly capital, and the law itself. They recognized the need to embrace and support the civil rights and feminist revolutions of the 1960s.

With the changing demographics, furthermore, these investments led to further growth, specialization, and the social diversification of recruitment. The new entrants pursued the professional strategies and investments pioneered by and controlled by individuals who had themselves invested only a little in a whole range of institutions. The new adversaries challenged each other by borrowing from (and therefore enriching) the same repertory of legal tools and moral arguments used to legitimate the FPE and its role. They also succeeded in deploying those tools to represent both the challengers and the defenders of the power and policies of the establishment. They made the legal battlefield central to the contest for power.

Finally, as described in more detail below, the establishment's efforts to accommodate the forces for change of the 1960s and 1970s faced not only an economic but also a social challenge that ultimately produced the New Right. The New Right, as we shall see, specifically challenged the "liberal elite" as out of touch with "Middle Americans" – as privileged elites fomenting social rebellion and permissiveness.

The story of the internationalization of American law thus shows both contrast and continuities between its genesis by pioneers and its further rationalization and autonomization by the later generations. By definition, law represented only one of the resources in the portfolio of the Founding Fathers; therefore it was only one of the objectives in their complex agenda of power. Yet, even if their investment in law was relatively limited, it had been successful enough to induce their followers to push it further and to work to channel competing social and economic interests toward confrontations in legal terms.

The multiplication and control of so many positions and institutions around the state, coupled with the claim of the "wise men" that they needed to be trusted to fight the Cold War, had given the FPE substantial autonomy in the implementation of policies on which they could generally agree. Every one of their sources of power – family, corporate-state alliances, academic legitimacy, philanthropic foundations, the state, and the Episcopal Church – was subjected to challenge.

The internal and external challenges led to some understandable defensive responses. One organizational embodiment of the perceived response was the Trilateral Commission, established in 1973. Led by David Rockefeller and funded appropriately by the Ford Foundation among others, the early documents provide a list of virtually all the factors we have mentioned. It sought to revive the establishment as an antidote to the "excesses" of democracy seen in the 1960s. Not without some successes, the Trilateral Commission became part of the story of transformation that we explore in this chapter.

The story of challenge and response could be traced in many spheres of domestic and foreign policy in the United States. Here we concentrate on the attacks and responses that help account for the details of the legal rules – and a more general legalization – that became characteristic of foreign policy in the 1980s and 1990s. We focus on three specific arenas: the accumulation of investment in international human rights, the development of a legalized trade regime, and finally the emergence of international commercial arbitration as a means to legalize business disputing globally. We also discuss the emergence of an industry promoting the rule of law as a means to institutionalize what was called the "Washington Consensus" and the movement that allowed other service providers – namely business consultants and investment bankers – to share and in part shape the field of business/legal advice.

International Human Rights

International human rights concerns and organizations played a very small role in the first two decades of the Cold War. Drawing on their own global networks and their access to a variety of domestic centers of power, the lawyer-statespersons of the FPE invested in human rights, but the activity came mainly in response to the Soviet support of the International Association of Democratic Jurists (IADJ), which had been very critical of McCarthyism in the early 1950s. John J. McCloy, then the High Commissioner for Germany, joined with a small group of political lawyers close to him – including Allen Dulles, then president of the Council on Foreign Relations and Deputy Director of the CIA – to respond to the Association. They feared it had "stolen the great words – Peace, Freedom, Justice." With funding and administrative support provided by the CIA, they created the International Commission of Jurists (ICJ), located it in Geneva, and entrusted it to the management of a group of notables in their own image: "The AFFJ (American Fund for Free Jurists) directors favored the Council on Foreign Relations approach – the organization of a highly exclusive elite, selected and governed by a small inner circle."

The Commission recruited well-known persons from the academic or diplomatic worlds to serve as secretaries-general. Those who served included Norman S. Marsh, barrister and fellow of University College, Oxford; Jean-Flavien Lalive, an eminent Swiss jurist who had held leading positions in the International Red Cross, the United Nations, and the Court of Justice at The Hague; Sir Leslie Munro, ambassador from New Zealand and president of the UN General Assembly; and, in 1963, Sean McBride. McBride, one of the founders of the Council of Europe and a signatory of the European Convention on Human Rights, was especially active until his dismissal in 1967 when the CIA's involvement was made public.

This human rights strategy was inseparable from the Cold War strategy linked to the FPE and implemented in all the major institutions in and around the U.S. state. There was little difference in this respect between the Ford Foundation and the CIA. Both were enlisted in a fight that was organized in part as a search for high-prestige friends who would fight

Communism (and reinforce the power of their counterparts back in the United States). Law was relatively unimportant in the struggle at the time. The International Commission of Jurists was reactive, created to provide a counterpoint to the International Association of Democratic Jurists. Despite the relative lack of importance of the law, except for the legitimacy and cover it might provide for politically motivated activities, the Commission did in fact develop legal expertise and a group of individuals schooled in human rights and willing to invest that learning and experience in other organizations where their expertise would be valued and where they could build their careers.

The move from the Commission (and related organizations) to a greater institutionalization of human rights came from a variety of investments and circumstances. First, there was the group of individuals who tried to take the ostensible ideals of the Commission more seriously. Several, for example, were active in the establishment of Amnesty International in 1961 in Great Britain. Seeking to remedy some of the Commission's perceived inadequacies, the founders of Amnesty International sought to gain more influence for human rights arguments (and their own expertise) through a mass organization financed exclusively by activists and characterized by a quasi-obsessive identification with neutrality. They sought systematically to focus the attention of the media on their campaigns and activities. They also gave priority to prisoners of conscience punished for the expression of their opinions, and they excluded those who had committed or encouraged acts of violence. The obsession with neutrality did not prevent many from thinking that Amnesty was a leftist organization, but it helped build legitimacy in the 1960s, particularly after the revelation of the Commission's links to the CIA put it on the defensive. The growing legitimacy helped put Amnesty and others who had increased their investment in human rights ideals into a position to take advantage of a series of events and crises that occurred in the late 1960s and early 1970s.

Although beneath the radar screen of the Cold War at the time, there was also some academic investment in a positive law of international human rights. The post-war quest to make law in this domain began with the Universal Declaration of Human Rights, adopted by the General Assembly of the United Nations in 1948 through work of a commission chaired by Eleanor Roosevelt. As the Cold War took shape, however, investment in this domain was quite small – relatively marginal to international law and to foreign policy in the United States. As part of the law schools' increasing emphasis on scholarship, a few scholars linked in one way or another to human rights issues began to invest in this domain.

The first U.S. casebook on international human rights was published in 1973. The authors were two scholars born in Europe, Louis Sohn and

Thomas Buergenthal, both somewhat out of the legal mainstream.[3] They drew extensively on European developments and quite self-consciously pulled together whatever might contribute to build law. The authors of the second casebook, Richard Lillich and Frank Newman,[4] followed the same strategy. These works of legal idealism and promotion began to gain some academic respectability in the 1970s, but the effort was not always easy. One of the early promoters of the field stated that the leaders of the American Society of International Law – still under the sway of the FPE – had argued that "human rights is not really law." Even worse, according to the leaders of the FPE, impractical idealism should not overstep the focus of the Society on the law as it is.

The circumstances surrounding the presidency of Richard Nixon reflected a challenge to the hegemony of the Eastern establishment. The challenge came from generational and other divisions about the war, symbolized by the Chicago Democratic Convention of 1968, which split the Democratic Party and made possible Nixon's election. The doves on one side of that division were crucial in responding with an increased investment in the field of human rights. The Congressional mandate to take human rights into account in foreign policy, in particular, was sponsored by Donald Fraser, a Minnesota Congressman who had earlier been a leading liberal protégé of Hubert Humphrey. Reacting to the revelations of the role of the CIA in the overthrow of Chilean President Salvador Allende, he and some activist members of Congress joined with the pioneer academics, including Frank Newman, to "put the country on the side of angels, by using human rights as the touchstone of US foreign policy."[5] Drawing extensively also on Amnesty International and the now-revitalized International Commission of Jurists, Congressional staffs produced a report on "Human Rights and the World Community" (1974), which led to legislation calling for the State Department to deny certain assistance to countries "committing serious violations of human rights."[6]

The key link between these idealists and the fights in the field of power was evidently Newman, the former dean at the University of California-Berkeley (and later California Supreme Court Justice). He came to this interest in human rights law through an acquaintance with the International Commission of Jurists in Geneva in the late 1960s (where he went for other

---

[3] Louis Sohn and Thomas Buergenthal, eds., *International Protection of Human Rights* (Indianapolis, 1973).

[4] Richard B. Lillich and Frank C. Newman, *International Human Rights: Problems of Law and Policy* (Boston, 1979).

[5] Interview with member of Congress at the time.

[6] Foreign Assistance Act of 1973, Section 32.

reasons). He worked on the Commission's case against Greece in the UN in the early 1970s, in the process developing materials that became central to the text that he and Lillich produced. Newman was reportedly the architect of the legislation enacted into law in 1975. The idealistic strategies of these scholars on the margin of international law thus played into U.S. palace wars, helping provide legitimacy for the liberal Democrats' attack on U.S. intervention in Chile.

Amnesty International's investment in neutrality similarly paid dividends after the coup that brought Pinochet to power in Chile – along with the military's "Dirty War" in Argentina. The process that produced this emphasis on human rights on both sides revealed the response to the attacks on the FPE and their counterparts. In Chile, the reformist elite removed from power and persecuted by Pinochet searched for legal arguments that would gain international support. They found that the invocation of international human rights gained credibility with the *New York Times* and others, including the Chilean representatives of the Ford Foundation, who had befriended and supported many of those persecuted by Pinochet.

The idealists in the Ford Foundation offices caught the attention of McGeorge Bundy, head of the Ford Foundation since 1966, and persuaded him that the public interest law he was supporting at home should also be implemented abroad. Ford proceeded to fund organizations in the United States and in many other countries to support this legalization, requiring the same kind of links to establishment boards and corporate law firms that Ford had required of the public interest law firms in the United States to ensure their respectability. The Ford Foundation became the leading provider of funds to human rights organizations, thus spreading the movement further.

Amnesty International's membership and activities grew substantially. In the 1960s, 900 prisoners were the focus of Amnesty campaigns, led by a staff of one full-time and one part-time salaried person. In 1976, the staff numbered about forty. Amnesty gained further credibility by winning the Nobel Peace Prize in 1977, based in large part on the report on Argentina published in March of that year. By 1981, Amnesty supported the campaigns of 4,000 prisoners, had 250,000 members, and drew on a budget of $2 million and a staff of 150 persons. The story of human rights is part of the attack on the FPE's authority – joined by a number of individuals who had been part of the consensus.

The attack on the establishment gained from the role of Humphrey Democrats (the "hawks"), including Jeanne Kirkpatrick and other neoconservatives who joined the camp of an emerging New Right organized at that time mainly around economic issues. A new and revived set of wellfunded think tanks – the American Enterprise Institute, Hoover Institute, Heritage Foundation, and Cato Institute – pushed this new economic and more aggressively anti-Communist agenda. They defended the authoritarian states of Latin America that showcased the neo-liberal economics centered at Chicago and promoted as the recipe to rebuild business power in the United States and circumscribe the regulatory state. The strategy of this counter-revolution, at the same time social and ideological, was to take on the "liberal monopoly on the intellectual marketplace" exemplified by the "liberal establishment" and the institutions they dominated. Politicians on the right noted quite clearly, for example, that it was the Eastern establishment – represented by Elliot Richardson and Archibald Cox – that made President Nixon submit to the legal authority that led to his resignation. While denouncing the networks of this "tight knit establishment," the new arrivals in politics – and others who felt marginalized in the field of power – followed the same set of tactics. As suggested above, the creation of a new generation of think tanks, such as the Heritage Foundation, sealed this new reactionary alliance that triumphed with the Reagan election, using the media in the process by playing on the double register of economic rationality and moral order.

The success of these new competitors nourished the development of a response that also changed the rules of the game. Each of the adversaries had to increase its investments in policy research while at the same time privileging the quest for media attention. The production of learning became less important than its packaging – designed to facilitate the task of journalists charged with organizing confrontations between experts as spectacles.

The new think tanks attracted one portion of the divided establishment, who entered into an alliance with conservative businesses and those disturbed by the various movements of the 1960s and the way the establishment related to them. However, their opponents drew on the full ensemble of the institutions – traditional foundations, professional associations, universities, churches, NGOs – where their positions remained very strong and the resources still formidable. These positions could be used to generate a counter attack against the ultra-conservative (and even populist) offensive.

The terrain of international human rights offered a number of tactical advantages to the individuals aligned against the emerging right. That is not to say that investment in human rights was simply a matter of opportunism. Again, we can best understand the dynamic by returning to the process of reinvestment in a professional movement in human rights. We can then examine how a very specific socio-political configuration contributed to shape the new structures around which the institutions for the protection of human rights were reconstructed.

President Jimmy Carter, fortified and guided by the Trilateral Commission, picked up the human rights mantle. He sought more generally, however, to reinvigorate the great design of an international alliance of notables. Compensating for the loss of the technocratic/reformist illusions behind the Alliance for Progress and the War on Poverty, he borrowed from the ideology of human rights. The appeal to morality was consistent with the rhetoric of the FPE, but the legalistic turn was also made more opportune by the perceptions of economic crisis. The various economic problems accumulating by the early 1970s had undermined the progressive reform ideals given voice in the 1960s. As stated cynically by Samuel Huntington, one of the key thinkers behind the Trilateral Commission, the conjuncture of crises seemed to require a limitation of the aspirations of subordinated groups toward more equality, even for more prosperity. Such aspirations, from this perspective, were rendering democracies ungovernable. The discourse in favor of human rights – limited generally to "political and civil rights" – offered a substitute ideology. It was not inconsistent with a new emphasis on the needs of business and a disqualification of social movements as "rent-seeking activity."

For the New Left encountering this aspect of the emphasis on human rights, the virtuous discourse was nothing more than the "moral mask on the face of trilateralism." This new tactic offered the advantage of turning the page on the failure in Vietnam and on the deeds of the military dictatorships while also allowing a counter offensive against the claims of the aggressive voices from the Third World who could also be pressured to conform to democratic dictates. In a parallel fashion and in a more classical manner, this human rights strategy could also put pressure, through the focus on the treatment of dissidents and Soviet Jews, on a Communist bloc weakened by the economic crisis. From a left perspective, therefore, this symbolic weapon continued the hegemonic enterprise in the name of the Cold War.

There was truth in the leftist critique of the human rights strategy. Yet the shifting of positions in the strategic game contradicts ex post this diagnosis. In particular, the later victory of the New Right and neo-liberal economics, embodied in the Reagan victory, transformed the nature of the human rights strategy. It became the center of a political fight between the new conservative holders of state power and a large coalition uniting the most liberal fraction of the establishment and a portion of the left coming from the civil rights movement (ACLU, NAACP).

This alliance gave birth to a third generation of the movements for the protection of human rights, with Human Rights Watch the leading example. Unlike Amnesty International, this third generation of actors and institutions was willing to accept more political ambitions and a more elitist profile. But it was not a matter of following a secret strategy among notables of the state, as had been the case ten years earlier. On the contrary, these professional notables decided to invest in the terrain of human rights to contest the orientations of a new ultraconservative right that was fighting against their institutional bases in the social state – in the name of an anti-Communist crusade. And in this combat, where the stakes were as much domestic as international, this potential new elite was quite prepared to mobilize its social capital of personal relations as well as the professional institutions that it controlled. The political configuration was in fact nearly the inverse of the International Commission of Jurists. The alliance was cemented by a common opposition to the hawks who supported the Vietnam War and similar interventions. Still, it also was the by now familiar mix of noblesse oblige and civic convictions that led them to mobilize in the service of the public interest. It was no longer the regime of the Soviets, however, that appeared to be the principal enemy. The target was now military dictatorships inherited from the Cold War and converted by the "Chicago boys" into a new religion of the market. The symbolic target was Jeanne Kirkpatrick and her rationale for the support of Pinochet and the Argentine generals – that they were authoritarians, as distinguished from Communist totalitarians.

In 1982, with funding from the Ford Foundation and others, Human Rights Watch, along with a new branch termed Americas Watch, became formally established. The director was Aryeh Neier, a prominent former leader of the ACLU, and the early board included establishment lawyers identified with opposition to the Vietnam War. As one of the individuals noted, the focus was on the state at home even though the investigations were conducted abroad: "we were oriented toward Washington, D.C. at the time."[7] This new elite of human rights – which flourished in institutions like Human Rights Watch – reinforced a strategy of "mediatization" (investing heavily in techniques of information circulation) designed to combat the tactics adopted by the New Right.

Professionalization and mediatization mutually reinforced each other. To gain the attention of the media in the new era of adversary politics, information not only had to be credible, but also "sexy." As NGOs multiplied in number, moreover, the competition increased in the media and in the domain of philanthropy. The competition intensified because the success of NGOs in gaining exposure in the media determined in large part their visibility, their capacity to recruit, and even finally their budget. The individual contributions made to these enterprises and, to a certain extent, their support from the foundations were closely connected to their notoriety. In this new context, the professionals that they recruited were anxious to operate with objectives and methods that appeared to be most effective pursuant to this media-oriented strategy.

[7] Interview with early leader of Human Rights Watch.

The new breed of activist NGOs were also dependent on the philanthropic foundations. Indeed, they owed their existence to the symbiotic relationship between the professionals of activism and the managers of philanthropy. The foundations made their decisions by consulting the judgment of peers, in this case the small network of professionals and intellectuals of philanthropic activism, both for the selection of projects and for their evaluation. The foundations also contributed to the education of new generations of professionals. Activities included the financing of seminars about human rights, courses on the elite campuses, and the granting of intern fellowships to young graduates who wanted an apprenticeship in an NGO – thus developing local paths for the development of leaders for the often related transnational NGOs. With the active support of the foundations, therefore, the human rights field was developed far more extensively.

Within the emerging field of international human rights, as in other domains, the competition permitted this space of practice to develop and to professionalize under the impulse of policy entrepreneurs. In many respects, as suggested by several journalistic accounts, the prosperity of the human rights field in the 1980s – and the conversion of the Reagan administration with respect to Chile – came from the widely reported debates among Reagan administration officials, especially Elliot Abrams, and human rights advocates, such as Aryeh Neier and Michael Posner. The media success on both sides of these debates ensured that, in the words of a *New York Times* editor, "the American public has made it fairly clear that it sees human rights as an absolute good – a universal aspiration to be pursued for its own sake . . . "[8] In addition, the debates forced the human rights movement to "balance" their reporting in terms of the countries that were looked at and to upgrade the quality of the work that was produced. Finally, and not insignificantly, the adversarial media campaign organized around human rights gave legitimacy and importance to law and to lawyers in debates around foreign policy. The legal expertise of the new generation of lawyers became central to the enterprise.

This return of the legal establishment was less about lawyer-statespersons and more about a set of connected organizations that produced and autonomized law in relation to the institutions that the FPE had controlled and served – the universities, the foundations, the law firms, and NGOs that drew on all these sources. International human rights law became central to U.S. foreign policy and closely defined in relation to U.S. politics. The international agenda depended on issues with credibility in the United

---

[8] Tamar Jacoby, "The Reagan Turnaround in Human Rights," *Foreign Affairs* 64 (1986), 1071–72.

States – violence against women, elections, a media free from government domination. These products of the alliance among elite campuses, the executive branch, and the U.S. media restored a provisional consensus in foreign policy that had been lost in the 1960s. They provided a justification for U.S. intervention in Kosovo and much of the eventual justification for the War in Iraq.

This return of the establishment in the form of a body of rules for foreign policy also reflected a new set of clients eager to move into the establishment. In particular, a new group of extremely wealthy business clients – the "Robber Barons" of the 1980s – sought both respectability and legitimacy in a new economic era of deregulation and lightning capital mobility. The new energy and body of resources helping sustain and revitalize the FPE were led and epitomized by George Soros, the leading funder of Human Rights Watch and creator of his own powerful Open Society Institute. But they could also be found in many of the activities of the foundations created by the technology boom of the 1990s. No longer able to dominate statecraft with lawyer-statespersons armed only with generalist knowledge, the establishment responded to the challenge of the 1970s and 1980s by drawing on its apparatus of institutions around the state to "legalize" a position consistent both with a strong role for law and lawyers and the global interests of their clients anxious to invest in places with legitimate governments to go with their newly privatized economies.

Trade and the World Trade Organization

One of the tenets of "dollar diplomacy" and Wilsonian idealism early in the twentieth century was a belief that free trade would lead to economic growth and world peace. The long-held U.S. hostility to a European-style empire was consistent with an opposition to systems of colonial exploitation that not incidentally closed markets to U.S. exports. This ideal was often expressed but faced difficulties in practice. High tariffs characterized U.S. policies throughout most of the first half of the century as the more particular interests of business overcame the general sentiments of the FPE.

The story revolves around the State Department – the establishment's traditional preserve in the executive branch – in the period after World War II. The State Department had long identified with free trade, and that position led to support after the war for the proposed International Trade Organization – one of the three proposed Bretton Woods institutions, along with the International Monetary Fund and the World Bank. Cold War tenets proclaimed by the establishment also tended to support more open trade policies as a way to open markets to U.S. goods and to build trading alliances against Communism, but there was no strong movement promoted either by businesses desiring more open markets or by the trade idealists at the State Department. As had happened in the past, the push for more open markets did not get top priority. Truman and Acheson were not willing to fight for it, and the trade idealists settled for the General Agreement on Trade and Tariffs (GATT) without the proposed organizational structure.

During the 1950s, in fact, the policies promoted by the Department of State were frequently at odds with business concerns. In part, the mismatch came from the social position asserted at the State Department. John Heinz, head of the Heinz food products company, reported that the department staff at a briefing "treated him as a sophomore, instead of the head of a great company with wide knowledge of world conditions in general, and trade in particular." The Cold War, in addition, provided a justification for the State Department to tolerate the "trade sins" of political allies. Neither the particular aims of businesses seeking broader markets nor the general commitment to free trade had a great impact in practice on the State Department. Free trade was just one of many positions supported in principle by the FPE, and it did not interfere with the practice of a more personal diplomacy linked to the Cold War and the alliance of notables.

The initiative on trade issues began especially during the Kennedy administration. Kennedy's Undersecretary of State for Trade was George Ball, a long-time pillar of the Cleary Gottlieb law firm; an advisor to Jean Monnet, the lawyer and lobbyist for the European Community; and later one of the founders of the Trilateral Commission. Fitting his position with the FPE, he had a strong belief in free trade as "a variation of the old nineteenth-century theology that free trade led to peace, updated for the Cold War world." In 1961, during the GATT tariff negotiations termed the Dillon Round, Ball persuaded Kennedy to allow the European Community to protect its markets from U.S. agriculture. From his perspective, once again, the relationships with the EC were more important than the details of trade issues. The Department of Commerce, much closer to business, complained of a lack of involvement in the decision and of the substance of the proposed policy, but Kennedy, as could be expected, proposed trade legislation close to Ball's policy orientation, kicking it off with speeches by Ball and others and strong media support by the *New York Times*. The bill ultimately passed in 1962, but growing business hostility to the State Department led Kennedy to make a key concession. He would appoint a Special Trade Representative who would be apart from the Department of State and who would negotiate further trade issues. Treating the concession as more symbolic than a mandate to move trade issues outside the establishment, Kennedy offered the position to John J. McCloy, but McCloy turned it down. After further consultations, Kennedy appointed Christian Herter to the position.

Herter had the classic profile of the elder statesman. He was the grandson of a German immigrant who had had a very successful career as an architect in New York. Born in Paris in 1895, both his parents were painters. He graduated from Harvard, entered into diplomatic service, and joined the State Department. His marriage to the granddaughter of an associate of John D. Rockefeller relieved financial concerns and permitted him to prolong his cosmopolitan apprenticeship, which was prestigious but poorly compensated. He became the assistant to Herbert Hoover for missions of aid to central Europe. After these "adventures of youth," he began a real career as a Massachusetts politician, where he was elected through the support of his Boston Brahmin friends. Valued by the reformist and internationalist elite, friendly with McCloy, he was named as Undersecretary and then Secretary of State by President Dwight D. Eisenhower. He was especially well prepared for the honorific functions of an elder statesman also by his experience in numerous quasi-governmental commissions of the Alliance for Progress and the Atlantic Alliance.

Despite the formal separation from the State Department, therefore, trade remained the province of the elite of the FPE. The close relationship between the Department of State and the trade representative continued after Johnson became President, although the trade representative began to take a stance more supportive of pressure on U.S. allies, especially the European Community (despite pressure from Acheson and McGeorge Bundy to ease up). Economic difficulties, the erosion of the power of the establishment, and a growing awareness of the imbalance in trade with the increasingly powerful Japanese economy, called into question the existing State-Department-oriented approach to trade issues. Nixon began to listen more carefully to business concerns and to increase the pressure on allies. The FPE – retooling in the Trilateral Commission in part in response to Nixon's seeming move toward protectionism – had continued to push for a liberalism akin to what the State Department had long fostered, and David Rockefeller, one of the key founders, had already began to lobby for stronger policies in favor of opening markets. However, it was the administration of Nixon, led by Treasury Secretary John Connally, that finally became more confrontational. Under the leadership of William Eberle, a Harvard JD-MBA and former business executive, the Office of the Trade Representative was retooled with the idea of actively promoting trade liberalization outside the United States, not simply promoting tariff reductions through new GATT rounds. The argument made by Eberle and Harold Malmgren, one of his deputies, was that economic and financial issues were "starting to replace traditional diplomatic issues as the main stuff of foreign policy."

The Trade Act of 1974, signed by Gerald Ford, ratified and reinforced this transformation in the position of the trade representative.

The Trade Act also provided the Section 301 remedy for U.S. businesses claiming that they are excluded unfairly from foreign markets. Now U.S. businesses could make their arguments without depending on the good graces of the executive branch. This and other more aggressive and pro-business positions on trade created opportunities for legal entrepreneurs to move away from a domain of negotiations among notables. As Steve Dryden notes in his study of the Office of the U.S. Trade Representative (USTR), "Many USTR graduates were finding steady employment through work for foreign governments and companies ... [a]s foreign trade began to play a larger role in the American economy in the 1970s and 1980s. . . . Starting with the Trade Act of 1974, representatives of American business were notably successful in engineering changes in the dumping laws and other trade regulations that virtually required foreign companies and govern-ments to hire small armies of Washington-based experts."

There were opportunities for both sides of the trade practice. Those who traditionally resisted opening U.S. markets to foreign competition could make a case through the doctrine of "anti-dumping," whereas the new generation of business – including the new financial services industries – aggressively seeking new markets and places to invest, could use Section 301. Adversarial trade practice began to flourish, helping sustain the tra-ditional FPE orientation toward more free trade, now bolstered by more demanding clients, but also giving legal doctrines that could be invoked by the more traditionally oriented businesses.

As noted by one of the long-time participants in trade law, the "trade bar was pretty small up through ... the middle 70s."[9] Steptoe and Johnson, a prominent Washington D.C. firm, appears to have been one of the pioneers, led by Monroe Leigh, a well-known figure in public international law, former legal advisor to the State Department, and a long-time teacher (until 1988) of trade law at the University of Virginia School of Law. Richard Cunningham, also at Steptoe, was another one of the deans of the practice field. Those who left the Office of the U.S. Trade Representative followed the pattern of the FPE in moving from government back to client service, but in this case they committed themselves to a specialized expertise: "at the end of the Tokyo Round [in the late 1970s, the USTR alumni] all made out really well. They got partnerships and the real boom, the boom really went up during the 80s. The early 80s was a great time to be in the trade

[9] Trade interview #1, p. 4 (unpublished transcript), interview conducted for the research project "International Strategies, Law, and the Reconstruction of Asian States," principal investigators Yves Dezalay and Bryant G. Garth.

practice because there was a drastic, you had a big expansion in imports, you had the high dollar policy of the . . . Reaganites."[10] Another participant put it this way:

I would view the major change in that as being the Tokyo round GATT negotiations, and the 1979 Trade Agreements Act. What that did was to greatly judicialize the practice. Ninety percent of the practice of trade law is dumping and countervail. . . . And so it went from being this wildly informal procedure where you never saw the other side's facts, and the files are literally this thick, to being everyone saw everyone else's facts. The files are now infinite. And I can actually quantify it for you. I was at Steptoe & Johnson. We had represented British Steel in 1978 in a series of 6 linked anti-dumping cases. And I was one of the junior lawyers. There were $3\frac{1}{2}$ lawyers working on it. And then . . . the cases were settled and the law was changed in '79. The same cases were brought in 1980. I mean literally identical, the identical cases, and it took $10\frac{1}{2}$ lawyers.[11]

Trade practice proceeded in two basic ways. One of the leaders of the trade bar in Washington, D.C., described them as "fairly separate. One is anti-dumping and countervailing duty litigation which is a kind of highly specialized form or administrative litigation which the law firms really got into in the 1980s when you had the dumping cases on steel. And so most of the big Washington, D.C. law firms will have an anti-dumping practice."[12] According to the same source, the other way was "sort of like trade policy," but with a strong legal aspect:

I think that trade law has always been unique because the GATT gave you a real legal system. There's always been this debate about . . . international rules or international norms [are] really law. And what happened in the GATT is you got a sanction in the dispute settlement process, it was built into GATT article 23 – the potential for getting compensation. . . . And then you see the process becoming much more elaborate and legal in the later 1980s. [T]he decisions become a lot longer, the effort to articulate doctrine becomes more elaborate. The process becomes more legalistic.[13]

Citing two U.S. professors, John Jackson and Robert Hudec, as influential in the process of legalization, the interviewee noted that GATT "was interpreted as a legal instrument rather than, you know, kind of a political/diplomatic instrument."[14] Advocacy, however, was somewhat muted: "The GATT has roots in diplomacy and for that reason is much more of

---

[10] Trade interview #1, p. 11.

[11] Trade interview #2 (unpublished transcript).

[12] Trade interview #3, p. 2 (unpublished transcript).

[13] Trade interview #4, p. 5 (unpublished transcript).

[14] Trade interview #4, p. 5.

a civil forum so . . . New York lawyers don't fit in real well."[15] This kind
of trade law, now focused on the World Trade Organization, also appeared
to be more prestigious. Rather than the strictly business efforts to limit
competition, the WTO partakes of "policy," "diplomacy," and the long
commitment of the Establishment to principles of free trade.

The WTO, established finally after the Uruguay Round and the support of the Clinton administration, protected the key elements of U.S.
trade practice, including anti-dumping, and provided a natural forum for
U.S. trade lawyers to push further in the direction of legalization. In addition, through the efforts of a coalition of U.S. businesses heavily invested
in the "knowledge industry" – drug companies, software companies, the
film industry – aggressive lobbyists succeeded first in making the Section
301 remedy available with respect to intellectual property protection and
then in moving the key forum for the protection of intellectual property
from the World Intellectual Property Organization to the WTO, thereby
entrenching and legalizing the rules that favor the United States and a
few other countries. One of the negotiators of the WTO agreement, more
generally, noted "there was general support for a more effective dispute resolution" that would eliminate the state veto process found in the GATT.[16]
And despite nearly universal opposition to U.S.-style anti-dumping laws,
long tainted as protectionist, the United States took the position that it
was politically impossible for negotiators to agree to any provision that
would restrict the scope of anti-dumping laws. The result was a further
increase in the legalization of U.S.-style free trade, which in turn provoked the other parties – including Europe and now even some developing
countries such as India and Brazil – to build up their own investment in legal
credibility and adversarial structure by taking advantage of the strategic
opportunities presented by the legal structure. Further, even the opponents
of globalization treated the WTO as a quasi-legal forum, criticizing it for
a lack of transparency, lack of independent appellate review, and above all
a lack of mechanisms to provide standing to environmental groups. As a
result, the international field of trade law acquired a very strong momentum
both to enforce rules that promote free trade, long part of the ideology of
the FPE, and to perpetuate U.S. approaches – built through U.S. politics –
defining how to enforce such policies and providing outlets for important
businesses harmed by international competition. By the early twenty-first
century an active body of panelists schooled in trade law and practice and
eager to continue to develop the field had emerged.

Economic challenges, the weakness of the establishment in the 1970s, a
stronger business commitment to opening markets abroad, a new generation

---

[15] Trade interview #4, p. 5.
[16] Trade interview #5, p. 13 (unpublished transcript).

of lawyers and academics investing in trade, and growing adversarial opportunities had again challenged the establishment and forced institutional responses. The responses legalized and provided some autonomy for what had been handled through the personal relations of notables. The province of generalists with multiple portfolios went mainly to what became a highly specialized bar. At the same time, the transformation kept and even enhanced the ability of law and lawyers to assert control over the domain of trade – even if the business concerns weighed very heavily on the rules that were put in place.

International Commercial Arbitration

Arbitration came of age with the international alliance of notables or statespersons. Elihu Root, the grandfather of the FPE in the United States, won the Nobel Peace Prize in part for his role in establishing The Hague Court of International Arbitration prior to World War I. After World War I, the same group of individuals behind the Council on Foreign Relations helped promote the International Chamber of Commerce (ICC), established in Paris in 1919 by business leaders from the allied countries to encourage trade and open markets. The ICC International Court of Arbitration was established right away, in 1923, to encourage the development of commercial arbitration to resolve transnational business disputes. International arbitration, quite simply, is based on the idea that, if other means fail to resolve a dispute, the dispute can be entrusted to the good judgment of wise statespersons known to the international community.

The business of arbitration began relatively slowly, consistent with a reliance on personal relations before entrusting the dispute to one or more of the notables acting as arbitrators. The ICC had some 3,000 requests for arbitration in the period from 1923 to 1976, and then the business rose dramatically, with the next 3,000 arbitrations coming in the following eleven years. The commercial arbitration was centered on French and Swiss professors, but there were important ties with the FPE in the United States. Two of the leading Swiss arbitrators in the period after World War II, for example, were Pierre Lalive and Jean-Flavian Lalive from Geneva; the latter was also one of the early heads of the International Commission of Jurists. The leading French figure in much of that period was Pierre Bellet, who also had close ties with the U.S. diplomatic community.

For the most part, however, international commercial arbitration was a relatively marginal – even if elite – activity until the 1980s. It was an activity of distinguished "amateurs" who were also involved in many other activities – as was true of the establishment. There was scholarly investment in the field, but it was the broad mix of intellectual and social capital that gave authority to the relatively small pool of arbitrators. At the same time, however, the prestige of arbitration – for state and business disputes – meant that arbitration clauses were placed in the various resource exploitation agreements that characterized the relationships between, for example, the Seven Sister oil companies and the countries where they operated their business.

Nevertheless, major multinational companies had little use for arbitration in practice, which is why the caseloads of the ICC and its few competitors remained quite small. Disputes were managed through personal relationships that extended over long periods of time. The lawyer for the Seven Sisters, for example, was John J. McCloy, and there is no evidence that McCloy played any role in handling disputes between companies and countries. He instead helped protect the Seven Sisters from antitrust trouble in the United States.

The oil nationalizations that occurred increasingly in the post-World War II period were resolved mainly through state pressure and personal relations, but they also provided an opportunity for the arbitration community to build its international business reputation and show its commitment to a private law – the so-called lex mercatoria – that would protect business investments against state action. This marketing in the developed world, coupled with a number of legal mavericks and entrepreneurs who helped convince Third World countries of the utility of legal investment, helped spread arbitration clauses, especially those naming the ICC as the presiding authority. The ICC also led the charge for the creation and adoption of the New York Convention of 1958, which made arbitration awards more enforceable than litigation in court.

The field of arbitration thrived as a small "club" of dilettantes under the umbrella of the ICC and the lex mercatoria in the 1960s. Disputes were resolved through a mix of social capital and legal capital, more like today's mediation than the litigation-like processes now associated with arbitration. The small world was shaken, however, by the establishment of OPEC, the petroleum crisis of 1973, and the subsequent recycling of petrodollars into large infrastructure projects, which meant a proliferation of arbitration clauses involving U.S. and other multinationals and Third World countries. Still, the proliferation of clauses did not mean that they necessarily would be used. There still were long-time personal relationships that could be used to moderate disputes and split differences when projects cost more than originally predicted.

The role of the lawyer-statesperson, as the activities of McCloy suggest, had been to give advice to company leaders, help them negotiate when appropriate with governmental entities, and use their company contacts to strengthen their own ability to hold numerous other positions in private and public life. Challenges mentioned earlier from within the United

States combined with the external changes to reshape the world of arbitration. Many have been listed, but they merit highlighting in relation to international commercial arbitration. First, business school graduates were gaining power in terms of business advice and in the management of corporations, and their training and relative lack of social capital led them to emphasize the specific terms of contracts and their performance over personal relationships. One of the reasons for an increase in arbitrations in the late 1970s and into the 1980s, therefore, was that a new generation of business leadership evaluated contractual and personal relationships differently than had predecessors, who had been confident that matters would work out to everybody's satisfaction. Another could be that "Third Worldism" in the developing countries also undermined some of the personal relationships between multinationals and elites in "host" countries.

The economic crisis and petrodollar abundance also meant that business school graduates could try out their financial tools and get involved in mergers and takeovers, which undermined the role of the lawyer advisor in two respects. One is that the lawyers lacked the financial tools to play a leading role, and the second is that a wave of mergers and acquisitions undermined longstanding lawyer-client relationships. The new situation also provided an opportunity for lawyers outside the elite to invent ways to make legal expertise serve business needs. Two firms in particular, Skadden Arps and Wachtell Lipton – now members of the New York elite – pioneered in aggressive litigation as part of a new business strategy both for general competition and for preventing or facilitating mergers and acquisitions. Soon the old "white shoe" firms of the FPE had to copy the strategy and boost the status of litigators long subservient to the elite of corporate advisors.

In the field of international commercial arbitration, the caseload started to expand dramatically in the 1980s. Finding themselves with a notable disadvantage using their own local legal resources, in addition, a number of Third World countries began to employ U.S. law firms, especially those located in Paris and socialized to the elite world of the ICC. Sonnetrach, the Algerian oil and gas company, for example, hired Shearman and Sterling for their arbitrations. As the field expanded and commercial litigation began to take off in the United States, litigators and their tactics began to be found in international commercial arbitration. Instead of gentlemanly proceedings conducted under the legal doctrine of the lex mercatoria, there were cross-examination, extended efforts at discovery, motions, and above all mountains of documents.

The "grand old men" of arbitration resisted this invasion, and they lamented the "proceduralization" and "bureaucratization" of arbitration that went with this increased caseload and adversarial approach. They continued to thrive because of their reputations and social capital, but a new group of self-conscious "technocrats" from the next generation led the transition away from the lex mercatoria and social capital (arbitration by the lawyer-statespersons according to the norms of the group) to "off-shore litigation," which replaced the vagueness of the lex mercatoria with the commercial law of New York or England. The U.S. law firms also helped multiply the number of arbitration centers, creating a competition and a pressure for all countries to join the international commercial arbitration mainstream. The field continues to thrive and bring the legitimacy of a full legal system to the norms that the statespersons had used to protect global business.

In relation to the other examples, we can see that the FPE thrived in a world of personal relations that informally guaranteed the rights of private property and the terms of investments and could, when necessary, draw on and work with their counterparts in Europe organized mainly around the ICC, which was itself a product of so-called Wilsonian idealism. The challenge of business school graduates, increased business activity, Third Worldism, and the related development of litigation – long subordinate to deal-making and business advice in the corporate firms – as a business weapon threatened the world of the grand old men while establishing an off-shore litigation that institutionalized in a specialized legal arena what had been handled informally by generalists cut from the same mold as the FPE. As with respect to trade, the move gave a more central place to business concerns and business power, but it also protected – even enhanced – the role of law and lawyers in presiding over the institutional arenas for handling business disputes.

A New Generation

Each of the three examples illustrates the decline of the FPE as a social group oriented around law, capable of occupying all the major positions in business, law, the academy, and the state. What replaced it was a multi-polar field of quasi-state power with a much more institutionalized division of roles. At the same time, however, there remained a fair amount of mobility and multi-positionality that could be tailored to fit the particular mixes of competencies and social capital available to the overlapping players in and around the law. Three examples of representatives of the generation that followed the establishment – one each from the three case studies – can illustrate the variation from the earlier generation.

Michael Posner joined Human Rights First (formerly the Lawyers Committee for Human Rights) in 1978. He received his JD degree from the University of California, Berkeley Law School (Boalt Hall) in 1975. While in law school, he became one of the "interns" of the International Commission of Jurists through his mentor, Dean Frank Newman of the University of California at Berkeley. (Newman, as we have seen, was one of the U.S. pioneers of human rights and later a justice of the California Supreme Court.) Since there were few if any legal jobs in the field of human rights at the time Posner graduated, he took a job with Sonnenschein, Nath & Rosenthal in Chicago. Luckily for him, the Lawyers Committee for Human Rights was formed and he became its executive director, after having been sponsored by Newman. As executive director, he lectured extensively at elite law schools, including Yale and Columbia. Posner is very well connected in the world of corporate law firms in New York; indeed they have been essential resources in the work of Human Rights First (HRF). The various boards and councils that support HRF represent the elite of the legal profession in the United States in the academy and in the large corporate law firms. During the Bush-Cheney administration, Human Rights First came to the forefront in coordinating an enlightened legal response to administration programs restricting civil liberties and limiting immigration in the name of national security.

Gary N. Horlick, a partner in the leading Washington, D.C., law firm of Wilmer, Cutler and Pickering, graduated from Dartmouth College (1968), Cambridge University (where he obtained a BA and Diploma in International Law, 1970), and the Yale Law School (1973). After graduation, he worked for the Ford Foundation in South America for several years and then moved into international work as an associate in Steptoe and Johnson in D.C. Through Monroe Leigh, a former Legal Advisor to the Department of State and one of the pioneers of trade law, which he taught at the University of Virginia, Steptoe was one of the first firms to do trade law. Horlick happened into some of the early trade cases and quickly became an expert, which then led to a position as International Trade Counsel for the U.S. Senate Committee on Finance. He followed that with a position as Deputy Assistant Secretary of Commerce for Import Administration, before leaving the government in 1983. Both positions focused heavily on the emerging field of trade law. Horlick has taught at Yale Law School and Georgetown Law Center, among other places, and has been on the Executive Council of the American Branch of the International Law Association. He is also a member of the Council on Foreign Relations. He frequently lectures on trade law and policy.

James Carter is a partner in New York with Sullivan and Cromwell. He attended Yale College, had a one-year Fulbright Scholarship, and then graduated from Yale Law School in 1969. He joined Sullivan and Cromwell because of his international interest. Working with his mentor John Stevenson, another former Legal Advisor to the Department of State, Carter became involved in several of the leading oil expropriation cases in the early 1970s. The oil arbitrations brought him into the world of international commercial arbitration, and he has been an arbitration specialist since then. He has been active in the American Bar Association, where among many other positions held he was the chair of the Section on International Law. He has been president of the American Society of International Law, chair of the executive committee of the American Arbitration Association, and a member of the Council on Foreign Relations.

All three of these leading international lawyers are active in the academy, the bar, and in practice. However, they are far more specialized than the previous generation and even than their own mentors – Frank Newman, Monroe Leigh, and John Stevenson – whose careers involved more positions and more interchange between government, the academy, and private practice. It is not that these leaders of the generation after the FPE neglect public service or the academy. They take advantage of and combine many activities, but each has a core specialization that is central to his professional career and practice. In addition, they reinforce the "hollow" field of power that allowed the establishment to prosper. Power comes from an interaction of New York representing business and finance; Washington, D.C, representing the state; and the Ivy League, representing legitimate and legitimating knowledge. Finally, in contrast to most of the members of the preceding generation of establishment notables, all appear to be from middle-class backgrounds and lack the prep school education so important to their predecessors.

CONCLUSION

External and internal challenges to the power of the FPE during and after its apotheosis in the Kennedy administration led in each case surveyed here – foreign policy, trade, and international commercial arbitration – to a weakening of the establishment's power. The cases are representative of developments in general. The legal and other capital behind the establishment allowed it generally to weather the storm in the governance of the state and the economy, but the price was the delegation of control to more specialized and legalized sets of institutions – a division of labor or bureaucratization in the terms of classical sociology.

The set of developments kept and indeed enhanced the role of law itself in all three areas, which now are embedded in mutually reinforcing institutions: in particular, the elite legal academy as source of talent and legitimating doctrine; leading corporate law firms in New York and Washington, D.C.; elite NGOs defending and attacking the various institutions and practices of, for example, U.S. foreign policy or the WTO; elite foundations bridging the worlds of law firms, the legal academy, and the NGOs; and sets of institutions including the World Bank, the International Monetary Fund, the WTO, and various centers of arbitration – all looking especially to the United States for legitimacy.

At the same time, despite the increasing division of labor, law schools continue to attract idealists socialized to expect that their career ought to start with a stint in a large corporate law firm. The rules that emerge from these sets of relationships, in addition, are bound to be ones that favor the interests and practices of the U.S. business establishment, incorporating now the 1980s versions of the nineteenth-century Robber Barons, and those who serve that establishment, including law firms. They are updated and legalized versions of the combination of client interests and lawyer ideals produced early in the life of the FPE and similarly promote law and lawyers, legitimating their role by investing and channeling noblesse oblige or legal idealism, and at the same time serving the general interests of their clients.

U.S. legal weapons – scorched earth litigation, playing the U.S. media – are of great importance in these settings. These sets of norms and practices provide the beginnings of a strong effort to legitimate U.S. domination in the global marketplace. The transnational legal fields that contain these practice areas are made up increasingly out of U.S. material. Along with the examples discussed, we can also point to the legal response to neo-liberal economics as a basis for foreign aid and the policies of the World Bank and IMF. Lawyers assimilated the attack and have succeeded in making the rule of law a key element of developmental assistance promoted by virtually all the actors in the field, including the investment banks and business consultants working equally hard to globalize a U.S.-friendly version of the rules of the game.

Our analysis reveals the contrasts and continuities between the grand notables of the FPE and the legal enterprises and technologies that they helped construct – from huge law firms to law schools competing to legitimate the law to legal specialties that serve as custodians of an area of practice and its orientation. Indeed, each of the case studies that comprise the second part of this chapter illustrates perfectly the process of institutionalization and autonomization. We see rather slow departures in frequently ambiguous contexts and dubious strategies (for instance, mobilizing the rhetoric of human rights in Cold War politics or bringing in lawyers for oil disputes) and then a sudden acceleration when social, political, or economic competition is channeled into these various legal arenas to contribute to their institutionalization. In the trade arena, for example, trade disputes become legalized and more "rule based" in dramatic contrast to an earlier period when trade issues were not considered as "real law." Indeed, the similarities among the three stories reveal the same process of professionalization occurring in new domains.

Another way to see the success of law is to reflect on the ability of lawyers to take external conflicts within and among the leading institutions of the state and manage them by translating them into law. In arbitration, trade, and human rights, the "take-off period" is the one during which contending groups use an emerging field as a battlefield, leading lawyers to prosper by selling their weaponry to both sides. The legal field succeeds by managing and facilitating exchange between the factions contending for the definition and control of the state. The institutions within each of the subfields manage to replicate and therefore "represent" the factions at war on the outside.

The price of legalization is some degree of autonomization, even if the rules and practices tend to favor the United States. Sometimes the United States will lose or be held accountable as a price for the legitimacy of the system. The Bush-Cheney administration's reaction in many arenas was that, as the most powerful nation, the United States ought not to lose. This explains its positions on global warming, the International Criminal Tribunal, the Anti-Ballistic Missile Treaty, and the initial but later reversed stand on steel and the WTO. The War in Iraq, similarly, could have been justified in some manner akin to the war in Kosovo, but the Bush administration elected to proceed with different rationales. The administration drew on human rights, and that proved the justification with the widest support. But the approach was very different from that of President Clinton. It is not surprising that in 2004 George Soros took a leading role in the campaign against George W. Bush's reelection, precisely because of Bush's undermining of the world capitalist system that Soros and others worked so hard to build and legitimate. The role of law and lawyers is therefore still contested by those who mounted the major challenge to the establishment from the right in the 1980s.

The transformations discussed in this chapter point to a survival and reinforcement of the position of law in the United States over the course of the century. The highest status in the legal profession still goes to those who embody the combination of major corporate clients and a noblesse oblige that helps create a legitimate playing field for those clients. The General Counsel for General Electric, for example, called for a reinforcement of the role of the lawyer-statesman, which he suggested might thrive best with in-house counsel rather than law firms.[17] The success in legalization,

---

[17] "Where's the Lawyer?" *The Economist*, March 18, 2004.

however, is also part of a pattern of circumscribing the power of the FPE. Serving almost as a relatively autonomous and reformist "state" in the period after World War II, thanks especially to the Cold War, the establishment survived attack but only by entrenching the law and losing some of their freedom to act – including some of their freedom to act "above the law."

BIBLIOGRAPHIC ESSAYS

CHAPTER 1: LAW AND THE STATE, 1920–2000

DANIEL R. ERNST

I borrow the concept of a political regime from Karen Orren and Stephen Skowronek, "Regimes and Regime Building in American Government," *Political Science Quarterly* 113 (1998–99), 689–702 and my understanding of state capacity and state autonomy from Daniel P. Carpenter, *The Forging of Bureaucratic Autonomy* (Princeton, NJ, 2001).

William J. Novak, *The People's Welfare* (Chapel Hill, NC, 1996); Morton Keller, *Affairs of State* (Cambridge, MA, 1977); and Stephen Skowronek, *Building a New American State* (New York, 1982) are essential readings on the nineteenth-century origins of administration in the United States. Thomas K. McCraw, "Regulation in America: A Review Essay," *Business History Review* 49 (1975), 159–83 and Robert L. Rabin, "Federal Regulation in Historical Perspective," *Stanford Law Review* 38 (1986): 1189–326 provide valuable overviews of command-and-control regulation in the late nineteenth and twentieth centuries.

Morton Keller's *Regulating a New Economy* (Cambridge, MA, 1990) and *Regulating a New Society* (Cambridge, MA, 1994) are indispensable guides to the American state from 1900 to 1933. Barry D. Karl, *The Uneasy State* (Chicago, 1983), an interpretive synthesis for the years 1915 to 1945, emphasizes the continuing force of localism in the twentieth-century state. John Teaford, *The Rise of the States* (Baltimore, 2002) is an excellent study of state governments from the 1890s through the 1980s.

Valuable studies of individual topics include James W. Ely, Jr., *Railroads and American Law* (Lawrence, KS, 2001); Theda Skocpol, *Protecting Soldiers and Mothers* (New York, 1992); W. Elliot Brownlee, *Federal Taxation in America* (New York, 1996); Lucy E. Salyer, *Laws Harsh as Tigers* (Chapel Hill, NC, 1995); Melvyn Dubofsky, *The State and Labor in Modern America* (Chapel Hill, NC, 1994); and Gail Radford, "From Municipal Socialism to Public Authorities," *Journal of American History* 90 (2003), 863–90.

Much of the development of the doctrines of administrative law can be gleaned from Kenneth Culp Davis, *Administrative Law* (St. Paul, MN, 1951), albeit from the perspective of a committed New Dealer. The *Annual Survey of American Law*, published by the New York University School of Law, provides yearly reports from 1942 on. The disparate treatment of the ICC and the FTC by the courts was noted by Gerard C. Henderson, *The Federal Trade Commission* (New Haven, CT, 1924). Valuable discussions of administrative law appear in Morton Horwitz, *The Transformation of American Law, 1870–1960* (Cambridge, MA, 1992), 213–46 and G. Edward White, *The Constitution and the New Deal* (Cambridge, MA, 2000), 94–127.

For a recent synthetic history of the United States during the Great Depression and World War II, see David M. Kennedy, *Freedom from Fear* (New York, 1999). Kenneth Finegold and Theda Skocpol, *State and Party in America's New Deal* (Madison, WI, 1995) explain why the AAA survived constitutional invalidation and the NRA did not. Jordan A. Schwarz argues for state capitalism as the greatest achievement of the New Deal in *The New Dealers* (New York, 1993). Other valuable studies of the New Deal years include Ellis W. Hawley, *The New Deal and the Problem of Monopoly* (Princeton, NJ, 1966); Michael E. Parrish, *Securities Regulation and the New Deal* (New Haven, 1970); Mae M. Ngai, *Impossible Subjects* (Princeton, NJ, 2004); Jennifer Klein, *For All These Rights* (Princeton, 2003); Suzanne Mettler, *Dividing Citizens* (Ithaca, NY, 1998); and Christopher L. Tomlins, *The State and the Unions* (New York, 1985).

For contrasting views of the origins and consequences of the Court-packing plan, compare William E. Leuchtenburg, *The Supreme Court Reborn* (New York, 1995) with Barry Cushman, *Rethinking the New Deal Court* (New York, 1998). On the ABA's campaign for the reform of administrative procedure, see Ronen Shamir, *Managing Legal Uncertainty* (Durham, NC, 1995) and George B. Shepherd, "Fierce Compromise," *Northwestern University Law Review* 90 (1996), 1557–683. On Landis, see Thomas K. McCraw, *Prophets of Regulation* (Cambridge, MA, 1984), 153–216 and Donald A. Ritchie, *James M. Landis* (Cambridge, MA, 1980).

Significant studies of World War II with important treatments of the state and politics include John Morton Blum, *V Was for Victory* (New York, 1976) and Bartholomew H. Sparrow, *From the Outside In* (Princeton, 1996). Other valuable studies of the wartime administrative state include Daniel Kryder, *Divided Arsenal* (New York, 2000); Paul D. Moreno, *From Direct Action to Affirmative Action* (Baton Rouge, LA, 1997); James F. Nagle, *A History of Government Contracting* (Washington, DC, 1992); and James B. Atleson, *Labor and the Wartime State* (Urbana, IL, 1998). Ellen Schrecker, *Age of McCarthyism* (2nd ed., Boston, 2002) provides a succinct introduction to anti-Communism.

An early and still influential constitutional history of the war is Edward S. Corwin, *Total War and the Constitution* (New York, 1947). Valuable studies of administrative procedure in the 1940s and 1950s include Reuel E. Schiller,

"Reining in the Administrative State," in *Total War and the Law*, ed. Daniel R. Ernst and Victor Jew (Westport, CT, 2002), 185–206; Peter Woll, "Informal Administrative Adjudication," *UCLA Law Review* 7 (1960), 436–61; Martin Shapiro, "APA: Past, Present, Future," *Virginia Law Review* 72 (1986), 447–92; and Bernard Schwartz, *The Professor and the Commissions* (New York, 1959). For competing views of Washington lawyers, compare Charles A. Horsky, *The Washington Lawyer* (1952, Westport, CT, 1952) with Joseph C. Goulden, *The Superlawyers* (New York, 1972).

On the Rights Revolution in general, see James T. Patterson, *Grand Expectations* (New York, 1996), 562–92, 637–77. On the welfare rights movement, see Martha F. Davis, *Brutal Need* (New Haven, CT, 1993). For an excellent overview of regulation in the 1960s and 1970s, see David Vogel, "The 'New' Social Regulation in Historical and Comparative Perspective," in *Regulation in Perspective*, ed. Thomas K. McCraw (Cambridge, MA, 1981), 155–85. Two articles by Reuel E. Schiller – "Enlarging the Administrative Polity," *Vanderbilt Law Review* 53 (2000), 1389–1453 and "Rulemaking's Promise," *Administrative Law Review* 53 (2001), 1139 – explain changes in administrative law doctrine and the rise of hybrid rulemaking.

For a compact but deeply informed summary of changes in federal administration since the Rights Revolution, see Richard B. Stewart, "Administrative Law in the Twenty-First Century," *New York University Law Review* 78 (2002), 437–60. My account of the deregulation movement follows Martha Derthick and Paul J. Quirk, *The Politics of Deregulation* (Washington, DC, 1985). For later developments, consult Richard D. Cudahy, "Whither Deregulation," *Annual Survey of American Law* 58 (2001), 155–86.

On rulemaking, its ossification under hard look review, and other recent developments in administrative law, consult Cornelius M. Kerwin, *Rulemaking* (Washington, DC, 1999); William S. Jordan, "Ossification Revisited," *Northwestern University Law Review* 94 (2000), 393–450; and Cary Coglianese, "Empirical Analysis and Administrative Law," *University of Illinois Law Review* (2002), 1131–36. Elena Kagan reviews presidential attempts to supervise the federal bureaucracy from Reagan through Clinton in "Presidential Administration," *Harvard Law Review* 114 (2001), 2245–385. On the spread of cost-benefit analysis in the federal government and the states, see Cass Sunstein, *Risk and Reason* (New York, 2002) and Robert W. Hahn, "State and Federal Regulatory Reform," *Journal of Legal Studies* 29 (2000), 873–912. For an account of experiments in market-based regulation, see Robert N. Stavins, "Market-Based Environmental Policies," in *Public Policies for Environmental Protection*, ed. Paul R. Portney and Robert N. Stavins (Washington, DC, 2000), 31–76. On privatization, see Jody Freeman, "The Contracting State," *Florida State University Law Review* 28 (2000), 155–214. Finally, on the anti-regulatory litigation of conservative legal groups, see Nancie G. Marzulla, "The Property Rights Movement," in *Land Rights*, ed. Bruce Yandle (Lanham, MD, 1995), 1–30.

CHAPTER 2: LEGAL THEORY AND LEGAL EDUCATION, 1920–2000

WILLIAM W. FISHER III

The literature exemplifying or commenting on American legal theory in the twentieth century is vast. Overviews of the subject, in which can be found bibliographies more extensive than can be offered here, include David Kennedy and William Fisher, *The Canon of American Legal Thought* (Princeton, NJ, 2006); Morton Horwitz, *The Transformation of American Law, 1870–1960* (New York, 1992); and Laura Kalman, *The Strange Career of Legal Liberalism* (New Haven, CT, 1996).

A selection of primary sources exemplifying the legal realist movement (defined broadly) might include the following: Thurman Arnold, "Institute Priests and Yale Observers – A Reply to Professor Goodrich," *University of Pennsylvania Law Review* 84 (1936), 811; Benjamin Cardozo, *The Nature of the Judicial Process* (New Haven, CT, 1921); Charles Clark, "The Restatement of the Law of Contracts," *Yale Law Journal* 42 (1933), 643; Felix Cohen, "Transcendental Nonsense and the Functional Approach," *Columbia Law Review* 35 (1935), 809; Morris Cohen, "Property and Sovereignty," *Cornell Law Quarterly* 13 (1927), 8; Walter Wheeler Cook, "Privileges of Labor Unions in the Struggle for Life," *Yale Law Journal* 27 (1918), 779; John Dewey, "Logical Method and Law," *Cornell Law Quarterly* 10 (1924), 17; Jerome Frank, *Law and the Modern Mind* (New York, 1949); Robert Lee Hale, "Coercion and Distribution in a Supposedly Non-Coercive State," *Political Science Quarterly* 38 (1923), 470; Karl Llewellyn, "Some Realism About Realism – Responding to Dean Pound," *Harvard Law Review* 44 (1931), 1222; Underhill Moore, "Rational Basis of Legal Institutions," *Columbia Law Review* 23 (1923), 609; Herman Oliphant, "Facts, Opinions, and Value-Judgments," *Texas Law Review* 10 (1932), 127; Max Radin, "The Theory of Judicial Decision: Or How Judges Think," *American Bar Association Journal* 11 (1925), 357; and Hessel Yntema, "The Rational Basis of Legal Science," *Columbia Law Review* 31 (1931), 925. Many of these materials are collected in William Fisher, Morton Horwitz, and Thomas Reed, *American Legal Realism* (New York, 1993).

The best secondary studies of the realist movement are the following: Grant Gilmore, "Legal Realism: Its Cause and Cure," *Yale Law Journal* 70 (1961), 1037; N. E. H. Hull, "Reconstructing the Origins of Realistic Jurisprudence: A Prequel to the Llewellyn-Pound Exchange over Legal Realism," *Duke Law Journal* (1989), 1302; Laura Kalman, *Legal Realism at Yale, 1927–1960* (Chapel Hill, NC, 1986); Edward Purcell, *The Crisis of Democratic Theory: Scientific Naturalism and the Problem of Value* (Lexington, KY, 1973); and John Henry Schlegel, "American Legal Realism and Empirical Social Science: From the Yale Experience," *Buffalo Law Review* 28 (1979), 459 and "American Legal Realism and Empirical Social Science: The Singular Case of Underhill Moore," *Buffalo Law Review* 29 (1980), 195.

Major works developing what came to be known as process theory include the following: Alexander Bickel and Harry Wellington, "Legislative Purpose and the Judicial Process: The Lincoln Mills Case," *Harvard Law Review* 71 (1957), 1; Felix Frankfurter, "Some Reflections on the Reading of Statutes," *Columbia Law Review* 47 (1947), 527; Lon Fuller, "Consideration and Form," *Columbia Law Review* 41 (1941) 799 and "The Forms and Limits of Adjudication," *Harvard Law Review* 92 (1978), 353; Erwin Griswold, "The Supreme Court, 1959 Term – Foreword: Of Time and Attitudes – Professor Hart and Judge Arnold," *Harvard Law Review* 74 (1960), 81; Henry Hart, "The Supreme Court, 1958 Term – Foreword: The Time Chart of the Justices," *Harvard Law Review* 73 (1959), 84; Henry Hart and Albert Sacks, *The Legal Process: Basic Problems in the Making and Application of Law*, tentative ed. (Cambridge, 1958); and Herbert Wechsler, "Toward Neutral Principles of Constitutional Law," *Harvard Law Review* 73 (1959), 1.

Excellent secondary studies of process theory in general or of individual works within the tradition include the following: Akhil Reed Amar, "Law Story," *Harvard Law Review* 102 (1989), 688; James Boyle, "Legal Realism and the Social Contract: Fuller's Public Jurisprudence of Form, Private Jurisprudence of Substance," *Cornell Law Review* 78 (1993), 371; Richard Fallon, "Reflections on the Hart and Wechsler Paradigm," *Vanderbilt Law Review* 47 (1994), 953; Kent Greenawalt, "The Enduring Significance of Neutral Principles," *Columbia Law Review* 78 (1978), 982; Duncan Kennedy, "From The Will Theory to the Principle of Private Autonomy: Lon Fuller's 'Consideration and Form,'" *Columbia Law Review* 100 (2000), 94; Henry Monaghan, "Hart and Wechsler's The Federal Courts and the Federal System," *Harvard Law Review* 87 (1974), 889; Gary Peller, "Neutral Principles in the 1950's," *University of Michigan Journal of Law Reform* 21 (1988), 561; Mark Tushnet, "Following the Rules Laid Down: A Critique of Interpretivism and Neutral Principles," *Harvard Law Review* 96 (1983), 781; and G. Edward White, "The Evolution of Reasoned Elaboration: Jurisprudential Criticism and Social Change," *Virginia Law Review* 59 (1973), 279.

The literature on law and economics is enormous. For a few of the major essays in this vein, see Gary Becker, "Crime and Punishment: An Economic Approach," *Journal of Political Economy* 76 (1968), 169; Guido Calabresi, *The Cost of Accidents: A Legal and Economic Analysis* (New Haven, CT, 1970); Guido Calabresi and A. Douglas Melamed, "Property Rules, Liability Rules, and Inalienability: One View of the Cathedral," *Harvard Law Review* 85 (1972), 1089; R. H. Coase, "The Problem of Social Cost," *Journal of Law and Economics* 3 (1960), 1; Robert Cooter and Thomas Ulen, *Law and Economics* (Glenview, IL, 1988); Robert Ellickson, "Alternatives to Zoning: Covenants, Nuisance Rules, and Fines as Land Use Controls," *University of Chicago Law Review* 40 (1973), 681; Christine Jolls, Cass Sunstein, and Richard Thaler, "A Behavioral Approach to Law and Economics," *Stanford Law Review* 50 (1998),

1471; William Landes and Richard Posner, *The Economic Structure of Tort Law* (Cambridge, MA, 1987); A. Mitchell Polinsky, *An Introduction to Law and Economics* (Boston, 1983); Richard Posner, *Economic Analysis of Law* (Boston, 1972); and Steven Shavell, *Economic Analysis of Accident Law* (Cambridge, MA, 1987).

Analyses and criticisms of the law and economics movement include C. Edwin Baker, "The Ideology of the Economic Analysis of Law," *Philosophy and Public Affairs* 5 (1975), 3; Jules Coleman, "Economics and the Law: A Critical Review of the Foundations of the Economic Approach to Law," *Ethics* 94 (1984), 649; Ronald Dworkin, "Is Wealth a Value?," *Journal of Legal Studies* 9 (1980), 191; Mark Kelman, "Consumption Theory, Production Theory, and Ideology in the Coase Theorem," *Southern California Law Review* 52 (1979), 669; Duncan Kennedy, "Cost-Benefit Analysis of Entitlements Problems: A Critique," *Stanford Law Review* 33 (1981), 387; and Anthony Kronman, "Wealth Maximization as a Normative Principle," *Journal of Legal Studies* 9 (1980), 227.

Leading works in the "law and society" tradition include the following: Donald Black, "The Social Organization of Arrest," *Stanford Law Review* 23 (1971), 1087; William Felstiner, Richard Abel, and Austin Sarat, "The Emergence and Transformation of Disputes: Naming, Blaming and Claiming," *Law and Society Review* 15 (1980), 631; Lawrence Friedman, *The Legal System: A Social Science Perspective* (New York, 1975); Marc Galanter, "Why the 'Haves' Come Out Ahead: Speculations on the Limits of Legal Change," *Law and Society Review* 9 (1974), 95; Joel Handler, "Controlling Official Behavior in Welfare Administration," *California Law Review* 54 (1966), 479; Herbert Jacob, *Justice in America: Courts, Lawyers and the Judicial Process* (Boston, 1965); Harry Kalven and Hans Zeisel, *The American Jury* (Boston, 1966); Robert Mnookin and Lewis Kornhauser, "Bargaining in the Shadow of the Law: The Case of Divorce," *Yale Law Journal* 88 (1979), 950; Frank Munger, "Introduction: Longitudinal Studies of Trial Courts," *Law and Society Review* 24 (1990), 227 and "Afterword: Studying Litigation and Social Change," *Law and Society Review* 24 (1990), 595; Phillip Selznick and Philippe Nonet, *Law and Society in Transition: Toward Responsive Law* (New York, 1978); and David Trubek et al., "The Costs of Ordinary Litigation," *UCLA Law Review* 31 (1983), 72. Major works of legal history written in a law-and-society vein are Lawrence Friedman, *A History of American Law* (New York, 1973) and James Willard Hurst, *Law and Economic Growth: The Legal History of the Lumber Industry in Wisconsin, 1836–1915* (Cambridge, MA, 1964); and *The Growth of American Law: The Law Makers* (Boston, 1950).

For good secondary studies or retrospective accounts of the law-and-society movement, see Richard Abel, "Redirecting Social Studies of Law," *Law and Society Review* 14 (1980), 805 and "Taking Stock," *Law and Society Review* 14 (1980), 429; Donald Black, "The Boundaries of Legal Sociology," *Yale Law Journal* 81 (1972), 1086; Bryant Garth and Joyce Sterling, "From Legal Realism to Law and Society: Reshaping Law for the Last Stages of the Social Activist State," *Law and Society Review* 32 (1998), 409; Frank Munger, "Mapping Law and Society," in Austin Sarat et al., eds., *Crossing Boundaries: Traditions and Transformations in Law and Society Research*, (Evanston, IL, 1998), 21; Felice Levine, "Goose Bumps and 'The Search for Signs of Intelligent Life' in Sociolegal Studies: After Twenty-Five Years," *Law and Society Review* 24 (1990), 7; Lee Teitelbaum, "An Overview of Law and Social Research," *Journal of Legal Education* 35 (1985), 465; and David Trubek, "Back to the Future: The Short, Happy Life of the Law and Society Movement," *Florida State University Law Review* 18 (1990), 4.

Essays drawing on the Kantian tradition in philosophy include Bruce Ackerman, *Social Justice in the Liberal State* (New Haven, CT, 1980); Ronald Dworkin, *Taking Rights Seriously* (Cambridge, MA, 1977); Charles Fried, *Right and Wrong* (Cambridge, MA, 1978) and *Contract as Promise: A Theory of Contractual Obligation* (Cambridge, MA, 1981); H. L. A. Hart, "Between Utility and Rights," *Columbia Law Review* 79 (1979), 828; Frank Michelman, "The Supreme Court, 1968 Term – Foreword: On Protecting the Poor Through the Fourteenth Amendment," *Harvard Law Review* 83 (1969), 7; and David Richards, *A Theory of Reasons for Action* (Oxford, 1971) and "Human Rights and Moral Ideals: An Essay on the Moral Theory of Liberalism," *Social Theory and Practice* 5 (1980), 461.

The quotation in the text from Michael Sandel is from *Liberalism and Its Critics* (Oxford, 1984), 9. The two essays discussed in the text applying classical republicanism to legal topics are Cass Sunstein, "Interest Groups in American Public Law," *Stanford Law Review* 38 (1985), 29 and Frank Michelman, "Law's Republic," *Yale Law Journal* 97 (1988), 1493. Among other articles invoking republicanism are Frank Michelman, "The Supreme Court, 1985 Term – Foreword: Traces of Self-Government," *Harvard Law Review* 100 (1986), 4; Suzanna Sherry, "Civic Virtue and the Feminine Voice in Constitutional Adjudication," *Virginia Law Review* 72 (1986), 543; Cass Sunstein, "Beyond the Republican Revival," *Yale Law Journal* 97 (1988), 1539; and Mark Tushnet, *Red, White, and Blue: A Critical Analysis of Constitutional Law* (Cambridge, MA, 1988). An excellent critical survey of this body of literature is Richard Fallon, "What Is Republicanism, and Is It Worth Reviving?," *Harvard Law Review* 102 (1989), 1695.

The essay by Duncan Kennedy discussed in the text is "Form and Substance in Private Law Litigation," *Harvard Law Review* 88 (1976), 1685. Other leading essays by authors associated with the Conference on Critical Legal Studies include Alan Freeman, "Truth and Mystification in Legal Scholarship," *Yale Law Journal* 90 (1981), 1229; Gerald Frug, "The Ideology of Bureaucracy in American Law," *Harvard Law Review* 97 (1984), 1276; Peter Gabel, "Intention and Structure in Contractual Conditions," *Minnesota Law Review* 61 (1977), 601, "Reification in Legal Reasoning," *Research in Law and Sociology* 3 (1980), 25, and "The Phenomenology of Rights-Consciousness and the Pact of the Withdrawn Selves," *Texas Law Review* 62 (1984), 1563; Mark Kelman, "Interpretive Construction in the Substantive Criminal Law," *Stanford Law Review* 33

(1981), 591; Duncan Kennedy, "The Structure of Blackstone's Commentaries," *Buffalo Law Review* 28 (1979), 205; Joseph William Singer, "The Player and the Cards: Nihilism and Legal Theory," *Yale Law Journal* 94 (1984), 1; Mark Tushnet, "Legal Scholarship: Its Causes and Cure," *Yale Law Journal* 90 (1981), 1205 and "An Essay on Rights," *Texas Law Review* 62 (1984), 1363; and Roberto Mangabeira Unger, *The Critical Legal Studies Movement* (Cambridge, MA, 1986). A good anthology of short papers in the field is David Kairys, ed., *The Politics of Law: A Progressive Critique* (New York, 1982). The best secondary study is Mark Kelman, *A Guide to Critical Legal Studies* (Cambridge, MA, 1987). An especially rich collection of articles – some explicating, others criticizing the movement – can be found in the January 1984 issue of the *Stanford Law Review*.

The two essays by Catharine MacKinnon quoted in the text are "Feminism, Marxism, Method, and the State: An Agenda for Theory," *Signs: Journal of Women in Culture and Society* 7 (1982), 515 and "Feminism, Marxism, Method, and the State: Toward Feminist Jurisprudence," *Signs: Journal of Women in Culture and Society* 8 (1983), 4. Revised versions of both, along with much additional material, may be found in *Feminism Unmodified: Discourses on Life and Law* (Cambridge, MA, 1997). The essay by Carrie Menkel-Meadow is "Portia in a Different Voice: Speculations on Women's Lawyering Process," *Berkeley Women's Law Journal* 1 (1985), 39. Other major works of feminist legal theory include Hilary Charlesworth, Christine Chinkin, and Shelley Wright, "Feminist Approaches to International Law," *American Journal of International Law* 85 (1991), 613; Ruth Colker, "Anti-Subordination Above All: Sex, Race and Equal Protection," *New York University Law Review* 61 (1986), 1003; Kimberlé Williams Crenshaw, "Demarginalizing the Intersection of Race and Sex: A Black Feminist Critique of Antidiscrimination Doctrine, Feminist Theory and Antiracist Politics," *University of Chicago Legal Forum* (1989), 139; Kathy Ferguson, *The Feminist Case Against Bureaucracy* (Philadelphia, 1984); Martha Fineman, "Challenging Law, Establishing Differences: The Future of Feminist Legal Scholarship," *Florida Law Review* 42 (1990), 25; Katherine Franke, "What's Wrong with Sexual Harassment?," *Stanford Law Review* 49 (1997), 691; Mary Joe Frug, *Postmodern Legal Feminism* (New York, 1992); Angela Harris, "Race and Essentialism in Feminist Legal Theory," *Stanford Law Review* 42 (1990), 581; Duncan Kennedy, "Sexual Abuse, Sexy Dressing and the Erotics of Domination," *New England Law Review* 26 (1992), 1309; Christine Littleton, "Reconstructing Sexual Equality," *California Law Review* 75 (1987), 1279; Martha Minow, "The Supreme Court, 1986 Term – Foreword: Justice Engendered," *Harvard Law Review* 101 (1987), 10; Frances Olsen, "The Family and the Market: A Study of Ideology and Legal Reform," *Harvard Law Review* 96 (1983), 1497, "Statutory Rape: A Feminist Critique of Rights Analysis," *Texas Law Review* 63 (1984), 387, and "From False Paternalism to False Equality: Judicial Assaults on Feminist Community, Illinois 1869–1895," *Michigan Law Review* 84 (1986), 1522; Ann Scales, "The Emergence of Feminist Jurisprudence: An Essay," *Yale Law Journal* 95 (1986),

1373; Elizabeth Schneider, "The Dialectic of Rights and Politics: Perspectives from the Women's Movement," *New York University Law Review* 61 (1986), 589; Vicki Schultz, "Telling Stories About Women and Work: Judicial Interpretations of Sex Segregation in the Workplace in Title VII Cases Raising the Lack of Interest Argument," *Harvard Law Review* 103 (1990), 1749; Reva Siegel, "Why Equal Protection No Longer Protects: The Evolving Forms of Status-Enforcing State Action," *Stanford Law Review* 49 (1996), 1111; Robin West, "The Difference in Women's Hedonic Lives: A Phenomenological Critique of Feminist Legal Theory," *Wisconsin Women's Law Journal* 3 (1987): 81 and "Jurisprudence and Gender," *University of Chicago Law Review* 55 (1988), 1; Joan Williams, "Deconstructing Gender," *Michigan Law Review* 87 (1989), 797 and "Feminism and Post-Structuralism," *Michigan Law Review* 88 (1990), 1776; and Patricia Williams, "Alchemical Notes: Reconstructing Ideals from Deconstructed Rights," *Harvard Civil Rights – Civil Liberties Law Review* 22 (1987), 401. A good anthology is Nancy Dowd and Michelle Jacobs, *Feminist Legal Theory: An Anti-Essentialist Reader* (New York, 2003).

The best and most comprehensive of the histories of American legal education – and the source of many of the facts set forth in Part II of this essay – is Robert Stevens, *Law School: Legal Education in America from the 1850s to the 1980s* (Chapel Hill, NC, 1983). An excellent set of primary and secondary materials, in which can be found many of the essays quoted here, is Steven Sheppard, ed., *The History of Legal Education in the United States: Commentaries and Primary Sources* (Pasadena, CA, 1999). A recent, comprehensive bibliography is Kathleen Carrick and Sally Walters, eds., *A Bibliography of United States Legal Education: From Litchfield to Lexis* (Buffalo, NY, 2003). An excellent overview of the changes in legal education over the course of the twentieth century, based largely on his own experiences in teaching at a wide variety of law schools, is Clark Byse, "Fifty Years of Legal Education," *Iowa Law Review* 71 (1986), 1063.

Among the contributions to the lively debate concerning the origins, character, and functions of the Harvard model of legal education are W. Burlette Carter, "Reconstructing Langdell," *Georgia Law Review* 32 (1997), 1; Anthony Chase, "The Birth of the Modern Law School," *American Journal of Legal History* 23 (1979), 329 and "Origins of Modern Professional Education: The Harvard Case Method Conceived as Clinical Instruction in Law," *Nova Law Journal* 5 (1981), 323; Bruce Kimball, "The Langdell Problem: Historicizing the Century of Historiography, 1906–2000s," *Law and History Review* 22 (2004), 277 and "'Warn Students That I Entertain Heretical Opinions, Which They Are Not to Take as Law': The Inception of Case Method Teaching in the Classrooms of the Early C. C. Langdell, 1870–1883," *Law and History Review* 17 (1999), 57; William LaPiana, "Just the Facts: The Field Code and the Case Method," *New York Law School Law Review* 36 (1991), 287 and *Logic and Experience: The Origin of Modern American Legal Education* (New York, 1994); Charles McManis, "The History of First Century American Legal Education: A Revisionist Perspective," *Washington University Law Quarterly* 59 (1981), 597; Andrew

Taslitz, "Exorcising Langdell's Ghost: Structuring a Criminal Procedure Casebook for How Lawyers Really Think," *Hastings Law Journal* 43 (1991), 143; and Christopher Tomlins, "Framing the Field of Law's Disciplinary Encounters: A Historical Narrative," *Law and Society Review* 34 (2000), 911.

Harry First's two essays tracing anti-competitive impulses in the development of American legal education are "Competition in the Legal Education Industry (I)," *New York University Law Review* 53 (1978), 311 and "Competition in the Legal Education Industry (II): An Antitrust Analysis," *New York University Law Review* 54 (1979), 1049.

Examples of the first round of criticisms of the Harvard model of legal education include George Chase, "A Comparison of the Use of Treatises and the Use of Case-Books in the Study of Law," *American Law School Review* 3 (1912), 81; Jerome Frank, "Why Not a Clinical Lawyer-School?," *University of Pennsylvania Law Review* 81 (1933), 907 and "A Plea for Lawyer Schools," *Yale Law Journal* 56 (1947), 1303; and Karl Llewellyn, "On What is Wrong with So-Called Legal Education," *Columbia Law Review* 35 (1935), 651.

Essays identifying ways in which modern legal education is inhospitable to women students include the following: Taunya Lovell Banks, "Gender Bias in the Classroom," *Journal of Legal Education* 38 (1988), 137; Mary Irene Coombs, "Crime in the Stacks, or A Tale of a Text: A Feminist Response to a Criminal Law Textbook," *Journal of Legal Education* 38 (1988), 117; Nancy Erickson, "Sex Bias in Law School Courses: Some Common Issues," *Journal of Legal Education* 38 (1988), 101; Mary Joe Frug, "Re-reading Contracts: A Feminist Analysis of a Contracts Casebook," *American University Law Review* 34 (1985), 1065; Catherine Hantzis, "Kingsfield and Kennedy: Reappraising the Male Models of Law School Teaching," *Journal of Legal Education* 38 (1988), 155; Cynthia Hill, "Sexual Bias in the Law School Classroom: One Student's Perspective," *Journal of Legal Education* 38 (1988), 603; Carrie Menkel-Meadow, "Feminist Legal Theory, Critical Legal Studies, and Legal Education or 'The Fem-Crits Go to Law School,'" *Journal of Legal Education* 38 (1988), 61; Faith Seidenberg, "A Neglected Minority – Women in Law School," *Nova Law Journal* 10 (1986), 843; Catherine Weiss and Louise Melling, "The Legal Education of Twenty Women," *Stanford Law Review* 40 (1988), 1299; Stephanie Wildman, "The Question of Silence: Techniques to Ensure Full Class Participation," *Journal of Legal Education* 38 (1988), 147; and K. C. Worden, "Overshooting the Target: A Feminist Deconstruction of Legal Education," *American University Law Review* 34 (1985), 1141. The study of gender differences at the University of Pennsylvania Law School quoted in the text is Lani Guinier et al., "Becoming Gentlemen: Women's Experience at One Ivy League Law School," *University of Pennsylvania Law Review* 143 (1994), 1, 5.

Major essays asserting that modern American legal scholarship and education neglect the voices of persons of color and offering ways to correct the problem are Frances Lee Ansley, "Race and the Core Curriculum in Legal Education,"

California Law Review 79 (1991), 1511; Milner Ball, "The Legal Academy and Minority Scholars," *Harvard Law Review* 103 (1990), 1855; Taunya Lovell Banks, "Teaching Laws with Flaws: Adopting a Pluralistic Approach to Torts," *Missouri Law Review* 57 (1992), 443; Derrick Bell, "Strangers in Academic Paradise: Law Teachers of Color in Still White Schools," *University of San Francisco Law Review* 20 (1986), 385; Kimberlé Williams Crenshaw, "Foreword: Toward a Race-Conscious Pedagogy in Legal Education," *National Black Law Journal* 11 (1988), 1; Jerome McCristal Culp, Jr., "Autobiography and Legal Scholarship and Teaching: Finding the Me in the Legal Academy," *Virginia Law Review* 77 (1991), 539; Richard Delgado, "The Imperial Scholar: Reflections on a Review of Civil Rights Literature," *University of Pennsylvania Law Review* 132 (1984), 561, "The Ethereal Scholar: Does Critical Legal Studies Have What Minorities Want?," *Harvard Civil Rights – Civil Liberties Law Review* 22 (1987), 301, "Storytelling for Oppositionists and Others: A Plea for Narrative," *Michigan Law Review* 87 (1989), 2411, "Minority Law Professors' Lives: The Bell-Delgado Survey," *Harvard Civil Rights – Civil Liberties Law Review* 24 (1989), 349, and "When a Story is Just a Story: Does Voice Really Matter?," *Virginia Law Review* 76 (1990), 95; Alex Johnson, "Racial Critiques of Legal Academia: A Reply in Favor of Context," *Stanford Law Review* 43 (1990), 137; Charles Lawrence, "The Word and the River: Pedagogy as Scholarship as Struggle," *Southern California Law Review* 65 (1992), 2231; and Mari Matsuda, "Affirmative Action and Legal Knowledge: Planting Seeds in Plowed-Up Ground," *Harvard Women's Law Journal* 11 (1988), 1. The two most influential responses to this body of literature – to which many of the articles just cited were rebuttals – were Stephen Carter, "Academic Tenure and 'White Male' Standards: Some Lessons from the Patent Law," *Yale Law Journal* 100 (1991), 2065 and Randall Kennedy, "Racial Critiques of Legal Academia," *Harvard Law Review* 102 (1989), 1745.

The essay by Duncan Kennedy mentioned in the text was published in several forms – as a law review article ("Legal Education and the Reproduction of Hierarchy," *Journal of Legal Education* 32 [1982], 591); as a free-standing pamphlet (Cambridge, MA, 1983); in a compressed form in David Kairys, ed., *The Politics of Law* (New York, 1982); and most recently in an expanded form, along with commentary by other scholars, by the New York University Press (2004). Other essays in the same vein are Gerald Lopez, "Training Future Lawyers to Work with the Politically and Socially Subordinated: Anti-Generic Legal Education," *West Virginia Law Review* 91 (1989), 305 and Gerald Torres, "Teaching and Writing: Curriculum Reform as an Exercise in Critical Education," *Nova Law Journal* 10 (1986), 867.

The question whether affirmative action is defensible – in general, as applied to law school admissions, or as applied to the hiring and promotion of law school faculty – has been addressed by legal scholars in many books and articles. In addition to several mentioned in the previous two paragraphs, the following have been influential: Carl Auerbach, "The Silent Opposition of Professors and Graduate Students to Preferential Affirmative Action Programs: 1969 and 1975," *Minnesota Law Review* 72 (1988), 1233; Derrick Bell, "Application of the 'Tipping Point' Principle to Law Faculty Hiring Policies," *Nova Law Journal* 10 (1986), 319 and "The Final Report: Harvard's Affirmative Action Allegory," *Michigan Law Review* 87 (1989), 2382; William Bowen and Derek Bok, *The Shape of the River: Long-Term Consequences of Considering Race in College and University Admissions* (Princeton, NJ, 1998); Paul Brest and Miranda Oshige, "Affirmative Action for Whom?," *Stanford Law Review* 47 (1995), 855; Robert Cooter, "Market Affirmative Action," *San Diego Law Review* 31 (1994), 133; Kimberlé Williams Crenshaw, "Race, Reform, and Retrenchment: Transformation and Legitimation in Antidiscrimination Law," *Harvard Law Review* 101 (1998), 1331; Richard Delgado, "Affirmative Action as a Majoritarian Device: Or, Do You Really Want to be a Role Model?," *Michigan Law Review* 89 (1991), 1222; Ronald Dworkin, *A Matter of Principle* (Cambridge, MA, 1985), 293–315; John Hart Ely, "The Constitutionality of Reverse Racial Discrimination," *University of Chicago Law Review* 41 (1974), 723; Kent Greenawalt, "Judicial Scrutiny of 'Benign' Racial Preference in Law School Admissions," *Columbia Law Review* 75 (1975), 559; Kenneth Karst and Harold Horowitz, "Affirmative Action and Equal Protection," *Virginia Law Review* 60 (1974), 955; Duncan Kennedy, "A Cultural Pluralist Case for Affirmative Action in Legal Academia," *Duke Law Journal* (1990), 705; Randall Kennedy, "Persuasion and Distrust: A Comment on the Affirmative Action Debate," *Harvard Law Review* 99 (1986), 1327; Charles Lawrence, "Minority Hiring in AALS Law Schools: The Need for Voluntary Quotas," *University of San Francisco Law Review* 20 (1986), 429; Sanford Levinson, "Diversity," *University of Pennsylvania Journal of Constitutional Law* 2 (2000), 573; José Moreno, *Affirmative Actions: The Educational Influence of Racial/Ethic Diversity on Law School Faculty* (Ed.D. thesis, Harvard Graduate School of Education, 2000); Robert O'Neil, "Preferential Admissions: Equalizing the Access of Minority Groups to Higher Education," *Yale Law Journal* 80 (1971), 699 and "Racial Preference and Higher Education: The Larger Context," *Virginia Law Review* 60 (1974), 925; Richard Posner, "The *DeFunis* Case and the Constitutionality of Preferential Treatment of Racial Minorities," *Supreme Court Review* (1974), 1 and "Comment: Duncan Kennedy on Affirmative Action," *Duke Law Journal* (1990), 1157; Martin Redish, "Preferential Law School Admissions and the Equal Protection Clause: An Analysis of the Competing Arguments," *UCLA Law Review* 22 (1974), 343; Jed Rubenfeld, "Affirmative Action," *Yale Law Journal* 107 (1997), 427; Terrance Sandalow, "Racial Preferences in Higher Education: Political Responsibility and the Judicial Role," *University of Chicago Law Review* 42 (1975), 653; Peter Schuck, "Affirmative Action: Past, Present, and Future," *Yale Law and Policy Review* 20 (2002), 1; Richard Seeburger, "A Heuristic Argument Against Preferential Admissions,"

University of Pittsburgh Law Review 39 (1977), 285; Kathleen Sullivan, "Sins of Discrimination: Last Term's Affirmative Action Cases," *Harvard Law Review* 100 (1986), 78; and Laurence Tribe, "Perspectives on *Bakke*: Equal Protection, Procedural Fairness, or Structural Justice?," *Harvard Law Review* 92 (1979), 864. The empirical study, discussed and quoted in the text, of the Michigan affirmative action admissions policies is Richard Lempert, et al., "Michigan's Minority Graduates in Practice: The River Runs Through Law School," *Law and Social Inquiry* 25 (2000), 395. The citations for the cases discussed in the text are *Regents of the University of California v. Bakke*, 438 U.S. 265 (1978), *Gratz v. Bollinger*, 539 U.S. 244 (2003), and *Grutter v. Bollinger*, 539 U.S. 306 (2003).

Helpful studies of the reemergence of clinical legal education include William P. Quigley, "Introduction to Clinical Teaching for the New Clinical Law Professor: A View from the First Floor," *Akron Law Review* 28 (1995), 463 and Philip Schrag and Michael Meltsner, reprinted in Schrag & Meltsner, *Reflections on Clinical Legal Education* (Boston, 1998). The citation for the MacCrate Report is Robert MacCrate, "Legal Education and Professional Development – An Educational Continuum," *American Bar Association Report of the Task Force on Law Schools and the Profession: Narrowing the Gap* (1992), 112. Essays setting the report in historical context are Brook Baker, "Beyond *MacCrate*: The Role of Context, Experience, Theory, and Reflection in Ecological Learning," *Arizona Law Review* 36 (1994), 287 and John Costonis, "The MacCrate Report: Of Loaves, Fishes, and the Future of American Legal Education," *Journal of Legal Education* 43 (1993), 157.

The best study of the emergence of student law reviews is Michael Swygert and Jon Bruce, "The Historical Origins, Founding, and Early Development of Student-Edited Law Reviews," *Hastings Law Journal* 36 (1985), 739.

CHAPTER 3: THE AMERICAN LEGAL PROFESSION, 1870–2000

ROBERT W. GORDON

General

There is no comprehensive general history of the American legal profession. A classic and still very useful overview is in James Willard Hurst, *The Growth of American Law: The Law Makers* (Boston, 1950), 249–375. Lawrence M. Friedman, *A History of American Law* (3rd. ed., New York, 2005), 483–500, 538–553 and *American Law in the Twentieth Century* (New Haven, CT, 2002), 29–43, 457–480 have good sections on lawyers. Jerold S. Auerbach, *Unequal Justice: Lawyers and Social Change in Modern America* (New York, 1976) is an important, highly critical, well-researched history of the bar's discriminatory practices and public projects. Richard L. Abel, *American Lawyers* (New York, 1989) is the definitive work on professional organizations and "projects."

Professional Projects, Organizations, and Offices: Associations, Admissions and
Exclusions, Market Control, Ethics and Discipline, and Public Offices
The concept of a "professional project" – the strategy of organized professions to develop and control a market for their distinctive services – is
theorized in Magali Sarfatti Larson, *The Rise of Professionalism: A Sociological
Analysis* (Berkeley, 1977) and systematically applied to the American legal
profession in Abel's *American Lawyers*. Abel's book is also now the indispensable source of comprehensive historical data on the legal profession,
conveniently summarized in tabular form in his appendices, 249–318. For
historical statistics on the legal profession, see also the excellent series of
Lawyer Statistical Reports (1956–) of the American Bar Foundation, edited
by Barbara Curran, Clara N. Carson et al. and the overviews in Terrence C.
Halliday, "Six Score Years and Ten: Demographic Transitions in the American Legal Profession, 1850–1980," *Law & Society Review* 20 (1986), 53–78
and Robert L. Nelson, "The Futures of American Lawyers: A Demographic
Profile of a Changing Profession in a Changing Society," *Case Western Reserve
Law Review* 44 (1994), 345–406.
   For an overview of the beginnings and growth of modern legal profes-
sional organizations, see Wayne K. Hobson, *The American Legal Profession
and the Organizational Society, 1890–1930* (New York, 1986). The New York
City bar's pioneering professional reform program is described in George
Martin, *Causes and Conflicts: The Centennial History of the Association of the Bar
of the City of New York* (Boston, 1970) and Michael J. Powell, *From Patrician to
Professional Elite: The Transformation of the New York City Bar Association* (New
York, 1988); this reform program is located in the larger context of political
reform movements in David C. Hammack, *Power and Society: Greater New
York at the Turn of the Century* (New York, 1982); Gerald W. McFarland,
"Partisan of Non-Partisanship: Dorman B. Eaton and the Genteel Reform
Tradition," *Journal of American History* 54 (1968), 806–22; and Robert W.
Gordon, "'The Ideal and the Actual in the Law': Fantasies and Practices of
New York City Lawyers, 1870–1910," in Gerard W. Gawalt, ed. *The New
High Priests: Lawyers in Post Civil War America* (Westport, CT, 1984), 51–
74. For the founding of the American Bar Association, see John A. Matzco,
"'The Best Men of the Bar': The Founding of the American Bar Associa-
tion," in Gawalt, *New High Priests*, 75–96. For the professional project of
the more broad-based Chicago Bar Association, see Terence Halliday, *Beyond
Monopoly: Lawyers, State Crises and Professional Empowerment* (Chicago, 1987).
The best accounts of the exclusionary and restrictionist projects of the bar
are Auerbach, *Unequal Justice* and Abel, *American Lawyers*. The Carnegie
Report of 1921 by Alfred Z. Reed, *Training for the Public Profession of the
Law* (New York, 1921) remains a useful guide to the early campaign to
raise educational and entry requirements.

On the entry and treatment of African Americans in the profession, see the encyclopedic J. Clay Smith, *Emancipation: The Making of the Black Lawyer, 1844–1944* (Philadelphia, 1993); on the early years of women lawyers, see Virginia Drachman, *Sisters in Law: Women Lawyers in Modern American History* (Cambridge, MA, 1998) and Karen Berger Morello, *The Invisible Bar: The Woman Lawyer in America, 1638 to the Present* (New York, 1986). There is no equivalently thorough study of Jewish lawyers, but for useful insights see Jerold S. Auerbach, *Unequal Justice* 102–29; Jerold S. Auerbach and Eugene Bardach, "Born to an Era of Insecurity: The Career Patterns of Law Review Editors, 1918–1941," *American Journal of Legal History* 17 (1973), 3–27; Jerold S. Auerbach, "From Rags to Robes: The Legal Profession, Social Mobility and the American Jewish Experience," *American Jewish Historical Quarterly* 66 (1976), 249–284; and Jerome Carlin, *Lawyers' Ethics: A Survey of the New York City Bar* (New York, 1966). Louis Anthes, *Lawyers and Immigrants, 1870–1940* (Levittown, PA, 2003) is helpful on the immigrant bar.

On ethics and discipline, Susan D. Carle, "Lawyers' Duty to do Justice: A New Look at the History of the 1908 Canons," *Law & Social Inquiry* 24 (1999), 1–44 and James M. Altman, "Considering the ABA's 1908 Canons of Ethics," *Fordham Law Review* 71 (2003), 2395–508 throw light on early arguments over lawyers' ethics codes. The ABA's trajectory from canons to codes to rules in ethics regulation can be traced through its *Canons of Professional Ethics* (Chicago, 1908), *Model Code of Professional Responsibility* (Chicago, 1970), and *Model Rules of Professional Conduct* (Chicago, 1983) and is summarized in Geoffrey Hazard, "The Future of Legal Ethics," *Yale Law Journal* 100 (1991), 1239–80. The ineffectuality of lawyer self-regulation is documented in Jerome Carlin's classic study, *Lawyers' Ethics*; the literature is summarized in Deborah Rhode, *In the Interests of Justice* (New York, 2000), 143–83; and a particularly good case study is William T. Gallagher, "Ideologies of Professionalism and the Politics of Self-Regulation in the California State Bar," *Pepperdine Law Review* 22 (1995), 485–628. The use of ethics committees to scapegoat lower status lawyers is detailed in Jerome Carlin, *Lawyers on Their Own: A Study of Individual Practitioners in Chicago* (New Brunswick, NJ, 1962) and *Lawyers Ethics: A Survey of the New York City Bar* (New York, 1966); Auerbach, *Unequal Justice*; and Anthes, *Lawyers and Immigrants*.

There is surprisingly little work on the selection and characteristics of judges other than justices of the U.S. Supreme Court and lower federal courts: on these see Henry J. Abraham, *Justices, Presidents, and Senators: A History of the U.S. Supreme Court Appointments from Washington to Clinton* (Lanham, MD: Rowman & Littlefield, 1999); Sheldon Goldman, *Picking Federal Judges: Lower Court Selection from Roosevelt Through Reagan* (New Haven, CT,

1997); and Lee Epstein and Jeffrey A. Siegel, *Advice and Consent: The Politics of Judicial Appointments* (New York, 2005). On state court judges, see Evan Haynes, *The Selection and Tenure of Judges* (Newark, NJ, 1944); Harry P. Stumpf and John H. Culver, *The Politics of State Courts* (White Plains, NY, 1992); and Charles H. Sheldon and Linda S. Maule, *Choosing Justice: The Recruitment of State and Federal Judges* (Pullman, WA, 1997); and for a good local study, see Albert Lepawsky, *The Judicial System of Metropolitan Chicago* (Chicago, 1931). Even more surprising, considering the importance of district attorneys offices as platforms for political careers and their dominance of criminal justice, is the absence of historical work on prosecutors. Raymond Moley, *Politics and Criminal Prosecution* (New York, 1929); the National Commission on Law Observance and Enforcement [Wickersham Commission] *Report on Prosecution* (Washington, DC, 1931); and James Eisenstein, *Counsel for the United States: U.S. Attorneys in the Political and Legal Systems* (Baltimore, 1978) are useful snapshots at different points in time; Mary M. Stolberg, *Fighting Organized Crime: Politics, Justice and the Legacy of Thomas E. Dewey* (Boston, 1995) is an illuminating biography of a famous district attorney.

The profession as an economic cartel is the primary subject of Abel's magisterial *American Lawyers*. An illuminating theory of professions as guardians of turf against other professions, with helpful historical examples, is Andrew Abbott, *The System of Professions* (Chicago, 1998). Bruce Green shows how New York lawyers excluded corporations as competitors in 1909 in "The Disciplinary Restrictions on Multidisciplinary Practice: Their Derivation, Their Development, and Some Implications for the Core Values Debate," *Minnesota Law Review* 84 (2000), 1115–58. The ABA compiled a compendium of state bar initiatives to police encroachments on lawyers' professional turf in Frederick C. Hicks and Elliott R. Katz, eds. *Unauthorized Practice of Law: A Handbook for Lawyers and Laymen* (Chicago, 1934). Modern treatments are Barlow F. Christensen, "The Unauthorized Practice of Law: Do Good Fences Really Make Good Neighbors – or Even Good Sense?," *American Bar Foundation Research Journal* (1980), 159–216 and Deborah L. Rhode, "Policing the Professional Monopoly: A Constitutional and Empirical Analysis of Unauthorized Practice Prohibitions," *Stanford Law Review* 34 (1981), 1–12.

On the early history of civil legal aid, see John A. Maguire, *The Lance of Justice: A Semi-Centennial History of the Legal Aid Society, 1876–1926* (Cambridge, MA, 1928) and especially Michael Grossberg, "The Politics of Professionalism: The Creation of Legal Aid and the Strains of Political Liberalism in America, 1900–1930," in Terrence C. Halliday and Lucien Karpik, ed., *Lawyers and the Rise of Western Political Liberalism* (Oxford, 1997), 305–47. On provision (or rather for most of the century the lack thereof) of counsel for indigent criminal defense, see the accounts of routine criminal court practice in Lawrence M. Friedman and Robert V. Percival, *The Roots of Justice: Crime and Punishment in Alameda County, California, 1870–1910* (Chapel Hill, NC, 1981); *Criminal Justice in Cleveland* [the Cleveland Crime Survey, directed and edited by Roscoe Pound and Felix Frankfurter] (Cleveland, 1922); and Raymond Moley, *Our Criminal Courts* (New York, 1930). Anthony Lewis, *Gideon's Trumpet* (New York, 1964) is the classic account of the Supreme Court's recognition of a constitutional right to free counsel for felony defendants.

Legal Education and Legal Science

The indispensable source on legal education is Robert B. Stevens, *Law School: Legal Education in America from the 1850s to the 1980s* (Chapel Hill, NC, 1983). On Langdell's Harvard, see also William LaPiana, *Logic and Experience: The Origin of Modern American Legal Education* (New York, 1994); on the ALI, see N. E. H. Hull, "Restatement and Reform: A New Perspective on the Origins of the American Law Institute," *Law & History Review* 8 (1990), 55–96. The law and economics movement still awaits its historian, though a good start is made in Neil Duxbury, *Patterns of American Jurisprudence* (New York, 1995), 301–419.

Lawyers at Work

Most biographies of individual lawyers focus on the public careers that made them famous, rather than their work in private practice. Some notable exceptions are William H. Harbaugh, *Lawyer's Lawyer: The Life of John W. Davis* (New York, 1973); Gerald Eggert, *Richard Olney* (University Park, PA, 1974); Laura Kalman, *Abe Fortas: A Biography* (New Haven, CT, 1990); George Martin, *The Life and Century of Charles C. Burlingham, 1858–1959* (New York, 2005); Elting E. Morison, *Turmoil and Tradition: A Study of the Life and Times of Henry L. Stimson* (Boston, 1960); and Clyde Spillenger, "Elusive Advocate: Reconsidering Brandeis as People's Lawyer," *Yale Law Journal* 105 (1996), 1445–535. Particularly well-researched and valuable biographies of lawyers at the margins of their profession are Barbara Allen Babcock, "Clara Shortridge Foltz: Constitution-Maker, *Indiana Law Journal* 66 (1991), 849–912; Kenneth W. Mack, "A Social History of Everyday Practice: Sadie T. M. Alexander and the Incorporation of Black Women into the American Legal Profession, 1925–1960," *Cornell Law Review* 87 (2002), 1405–74.

Law firm histories are generally an uninspiring genre of in-house commissioned coffee-table books chronicling firms' founders and expansions, but they contain valuable clues to the symbiosis of firms and business clienteles. A few are exceptionally informative on changes in corporate practice: Robert

T. Swaine, *The Cravath Firm and its Predecessors*, 3 vols. (New York, 1948); two histories of Houston firms by accomplished professional historians: Kenneth Lipartito and Joseph Pratt, *Baker & Botts in the Development of Modern Houston* (Austin, TX, 1991) and Harold M. Hyman, *Craftsmanship and Character: A History of the Vinson & Elkins Law Firm of Houston, 1917–1997* (Athens, GA, 1998); and a muckraking expose, Nancy Lisagor and Frank Lipsius, *A Law unto Itself: The Untold Story of the Law Firm of Sullivan & Cromwell* (New York, 1988). William G. Thomas, *Lawyering for the Railroad: Business, Law and Power in the New South* (Baton Rouge, LA, 1999) is a first-rate study of railroad lawyers in the 1880s and 90s.

On corporate lawyers as the core of the U.S. foreign policy elite, see Jonathan Zasloff, "Law and the Shaping of American Foreign Policy: From the Gilded Age to the New Era," *New York University Law Review* 78 (2003), 239–373 and "Law and the Shaping of American Foreign Policy: The Twenty Years' Crisis (1921–1933)," *Southern California Law Review*, 77 (2004), 583–682. For examples of lawyers as policy brokers between corporate clients and the state, see Charles D. Ameringer, "The Panama Canal Lobby of Bunau-Varilla and William Nelson Cromwell," *American Historical Review* 68 (1963), 346–363; Martin J. Sklar, *The Corporate Reconstruction of American Capitalism, 1890–1916: The Market, the Law and Politics* (New York, 1988); Louis Galambos, *Competition and Cooperation: The Emergence of a National Trade Association* (Baltimore, 1966); and Vicky Saker Woeste, *The Farmer's Benevolent Trust: Law and Agricultural Cooperation in Industrial America, 1865–1945* (Chapel Hill, NC, 1998). For data on and analysis of lawyers in legislatures, see Mark C. Miller, *The High Priests of American Politics: The Role of Lawyers in American Political Institutions* (Knoxville, TN, 1995).

The beginnings and development of a specialized personal injury plaintiff's bar are covered in Robert A. Silverman, *Law and Urban Growth: Civil Litigation in the Boston Trial Courts, 1880–1900* (Princeton, NJ, 1981); Edward A. Purcell Jr., *Litigation and Inequality: Federal Diversity Jurisdiction in Industrial America, 1870–1958* (New York, 1992); Randolph Bergstrom, *Courting Danger: Injury and Law in New York City, 1870–1910* (Ithaca, NY, 1992); and Lawrence M. Friedman, "Civil Wrongs: Personal Injury Law in the Late Nineteenth Century," *American Bar Foundation Research Journal* (1987), 351–77. On the increasing segmentation of the bar by clienteles, see Thomas, *Lawyering for the Railroad* and Frank W. Munger, "Social Change and Tort Litigation: Industrialization, Accidents and Trial Courts in Southern West Virginia, 1872–1940," *Buffalo Law Review* 36 (1987), 75–118 and "Miners and Lawyers: Law Practice and Class Conflict in Appalachia, 1872–1920," in Maureen Cain and Christine Harrington, ed., *Lawyers in a Postmodern World* (New York, 1994), 185–228.

Sources on the vast majority of lawyers in solo and small firm practice remain sparse. The most informative are contemporary sociological studies: Carlin, *Lawyers on their Own* and *Lawyers Ethics*; Joel Handler, *The Lawyer and His Community* (Madison WI, 1967); Carroll Seron, *The Business of Practicing Law: The Work Lives of Solo and Small-Firm Attorneys* (Philadelphia, 1996); and Douglas Rosenthal, *Lawyer and Client – Who's in Charge?* (New York, 1974).

For the early history of public interest lawyers, see, on the ACLU, Samuel Walker, *In Defense of American Liberties: A History of the ACLU* (Carbondale, IL, 1999) and Robert C. Cottrell, *Roger Nash Baldwin and the American Civil Liberties Union* (New York, 2000); and on the NAACP, Susan Carle, "Race, Class and Legal Ethics in the Early NAACP (1910–1920)," *Law & History Review* 20 (2002), 97–146 and Kenneth W. Mack, "Rethinking Civil Rights: Lawyering and Politics in the Era Before *Brown*," *Yale Law Journal* 115 (2005), 256–354. The model of public interest lawyering on behalf of "consumers" or "the people" pioneered by Louis Brandeis and Florence Kelley is described in Philippa Strum, *Louis D. Brandeis: Justice for the People* (New York, 1984) and Spillenger, "Elusive Advocate." Daniel Ernst tells the unusual story of a group of conservative public interest lawyers, the American Anti-Boycott Association, in *Lawyers Against Labor: From Individual Rights to Corporate Liberalism* (Urbana, IL, 1995).

New Deal and Postwar

Peter H. Irons, *The New Deal Lawyers* (Princeton, NJ, 1982) is the authoritative account of the lawyers who conducted the litigation to defend the constitutionality of New Deal legislation. Useful insiders' memoirs of their New Deal work are in Katie Louchheim, *The Making of the New Deal: The Insiders Speak* (Cambridge MA, 1983) and Thomas I. Emerson, *Young Lawyer for the New Deal* (Savage MD, 1991). Tracy Campbell, *Short of the Glory: The Fall and Redemption of Edward F. Prichard, Jr.* (Lexington, KY, 1998) and Kalman, *Abe Fortas*, 65–121, deal ably with New Deal lawyers as bureaucratic strategists. Daniel Ernst tells how elite recruiting agents such as Felix Frankfurter competed to staff the New Deal agencies with Congress and the civil service in "The Politics of Merit" in his *Washington Lawyers* (Cambridge MA, forthcoming). Ronen Shamir, *Managing Legal Uncertainty: Elite Lawyers in the New Deal* (Durham, NC, 1995) describes the shifting responses to New Deal policies among business lawyers; George Wolfskill, *The Revolt of the Conservatives: A History of the American Liberty League, 1934–1940* (Boston, 1962) describes the attacks of the policies' fiercest lawyer opponents.

Charles A. Horsky, *The Washington Lawyer* (Boston, 1952) and Kalman, *Abe Fortas*, 152–96 provide glimpses of the postwar practices of many ex-New Dealers. On corporate practice generally in the postwar period, see the law firm histories cited above, such as Lipartito and Pratt, *Baker & Botts* and Hyman, *Vinson & Elkins*; and Erwin O. Smigel, *The Wall Street Lawyer, Professional Organization Man?* (Bloomington IN, 1969). Useful material on the new labor law practice is in James A. Gross, *The Reshaping of the National Labor Relations Board* (Albany, 1981); Gilbert J. Gall, *Pursuing Justice: Lee Pressman, the New Deal, and the CIO* (Albany, 1999); Christopher H. Johnson, *Maurice Sugar: Law, Labor and the Left in Detroit, 1912–1950* (Detroit, 1988); and David Stebenne, *Arthur J. Goldberg: New Deal Liberal* (New York, 1996). A biography of the Washington labor lawyer Joseph L. Rauh, by Michael J. Parrish, is forthcoming.

The legal campaigns for black civil rights are well treated in Richard Kluger, *Simple Justice* (New York, 1975); Mark V. Tushnet, *Making Civil Rights Law: Thurgood Marshall and the Supreme Court, 1936–1961* (New York, 1994); Jack Greenberg, *Crusaders in the Courts* (New York, 1994); and Sarah Hart Brown, *Standing Against Dragons: Three Southern Lawyers in a Time of Fear* (Baton Rouge, LA, 1998), among many other sources. For radical lawyers, see Ann Fagan Ginger and Eugene Tobin, *The National Lawyers Guild: From Roosevelt Through Reagan* (Philadelphia, 1988), a collection of excerpts from primary records; John J. Abt, *Advocate and Activist: Memoirs of an American Communist Lawyer* (Urbana, IL, 1993); and David Langum, *William M. Kunstler, The Most Hated Lawyer in America* (New York, 1999).

The federal Legal Services (poverty law) program's rise and travails are covered in Earl Johnson, *Justice and Reform: The Formative Years of the American Legal Services Program* (New Brunswick, NJ, 1978) and Jack Katz, *Poor People's Lawyers in Transition* (New Brunswick, NJ, 1982). On other public interest law movements of the 1960s and 70s, see Martha Davis, *Brutal Need: Lawyers and the Welfare Rights Movement, 1960–1973* (New Haven, CT, 1993); David A. Vogel, "The Public Interest Movement and the American Reform Tradition," in *Kindred Strangers* (Princeton, NJ, 1996), 141–65; and Michael W. McCann, *Taking Reform Seriously: Perspectives on Public Interest Liberalism* (Ithaca, 1986).

Expansion and Upheaval, 1970–2000
The momentous demographic changes in the profession since 1970 may be tracked through the American Bar Foundation's (approximately quadrennial) *Lawyer Statistical Reports*. For an overview of the mass entry of women into law schools and law practices, see Epstein, *Women in Law*. The obstacle-strewn progress of new African Americans entrants to the profession is analyzed in Mitu Gulati and David B. Wilkins, "Why Are There

so Few Black Lawyers in Corporate Law Firms? An Institutional Analysis," *California Law Review* 84 (1996), 493–625. An exceptionally illuminating way to appreciate the major changes of the period, especially the reallocation of lawyers' services from individual "personal plight" to corporate clients, is to compare the first comprehensive study of the Chicago bar, John P. Heinz and Edward O. Laumann, *Chicago Lawyers: The Social Structure of the Bar* (New York, 1982) to the second study, John P. Heinz et al., *Urban Lawyers: The New Social Structure of the Bar* (Chicago, 2005).

The transformation of corporate practice is described and its causes analyzed in Marc Galanter and Thomas Palay, *Tournament of Lawyers: The Transformation of the Big Law Firm* (Chicago, 1991) and Robert L. Nelson, *Partners with Power: The Social Transformation of the Large Law Firm* (Berkeley, 1988). Accounts of particular firms that give the flavor of the new practice are Lincoln Caplan, *Skadden: Power, Money, and the Rise of a Legal Empire* (New York, 1993) and Kim Isaac Eisler, *Shark Tank: Greed, Politics, and the Collapse of Finley Kumble, one of America's Largest Law Firms* (New York, 1990). John P. Heinz, Edward O. Laumann, Robert L. Nelson, and Robert H. Salisbury, *The Hollow Core: Private Interests in National Policymaking* (Cambridge MA, 1993) describe changes in Washington practice.

On pressures on small firm and solo practice, see Seron, *The Business of Practicing Law*; Rosenthal, *Lawyer and Client*; and the Chicago Bar Studies. Sensitive studies of lawyers in particular practice settings are Michael J. Kelly, *Lives of Lawyers: Journeys in the Organization of Practice* (Ann Arbor, MI, 1994) and Lynn Mather, Craig A. McEwen, and Richard J. Maiman, *Divorce Lawyers at Work: Varieties of Professionalism in Practice* (New York, 2001). John Fabian Witt, "The King and the Dean: Melvin Belli, Roscoe Pound and the Common-Law Nation," in *Patriots and Cosmopolitans: Hidden Histories of American Law* (Cambridge, MA, 2007) 211-84 tells the story of the organization of the tort plaintiffs' bar and its successful lobbying to expand liability and increase damage awards. For overviews of the development of mass-tort practice, see Peter H. Schuck, "Mass Torts: An Institutional Evolutionist Perspective," in *The Limits of Law: Essays on Democratic Governance* (Boulder, CO, 2000), 345–91; Stuart M. Speiser, *Lawsuit* (New York, 1980); and John C. Coffee, Jr., "Class Wars: The Dilemma of the Mass Tort Class Action," *Columbia Law Review* 95 (1995), 1343–465.

Public interest or "cause lawyering" is viewed from a variety of perspectives in Austin Sarat and Stuart Scheingold, eds., *Cause Lawyering: Political Commitments and Professional Responsibilities* (New York, 1998). The rise of conservative public interest law organizations is treated in Ann Southworth, "Professional Identity and Political Commitment Among Lawyers for Conservative Causes," and Laura Hatcher, "Economic Libertarians, Property and Institutions: Linking Activism, Ideas and Identities Among Property Rights Advocates, in Austin Sarat and Stuart Scheingold, eds., *The Worlds Cause Lawyers Make: Structure and Agency in Legal Practice* (Stanford, 2005), 83–111 and 112–146, respectively; and at length in Steven M. Teles, *Parallel Paths: The Evolution of the Conservative Legal Movement* (Princeton, NJ, forthcoming).

On the increasing export of varieties of American law practice to other societies, see Yves Dezalay and Bryant G. Garth, *Dealing in Virtue: International Commercial Arbitration and the Construction of a Transnational Legal Order* (Chicago, 1996), on American styles of litigation and commercial arbitration; Robert A. Kagan, ed., *Regulatory Encounters: Multinational Corporations and American Adversarial Legalism* (Berkeley, 2000), on adversarial legalism; Austin Sarat and Stuart Scheingold, eds., *Cause Lawyering and the State in a Global Era* (New York and Oxford, 2001), on human rights and public interest lawyering; and Erik G. Jensen and Thomas C. Heller, eds., *Beyond Common Knowledge, Empirical Approaches to the Rule of Law* (Stanford, 2003), on the rule of law.

For the erosion of traditional professional controls and their supersession by external regulation, see Michael J. Powell, "Professional Divestiture: The Cession of Responsibility for Lawyer Discipline," *American Bar Foundation Research Journal* 1986, 31–54 and David Wilkins, "Who Should Regulate Lawyers?," *Harvard Law Review* 105 (1992), 801–87. For valuable historical-sociological accounts of the erosion of values and social supports sustaining traditional professionalism, see Steven G. Brint, *In an Age of Experts: The Changing Role of Professionals in Politics and Public Life* (Princeton, NJ, 1994); Elliott A. Krause, *Death of the Guilds: Professions, States, and the Advance of Capitalism, 1930 to the Present* (New Haven, CT, 1996); and Eve Spangler, *Lawyers for Hire: Salaried Professionals at Work* (New Haven, CT, 1986). Many jeremiads lament this decline: the best are Anthony T. Kronman, *The Lost Lawyer: Failing Ideals of the Legal Profession* (Cambridge MA, 1993); Sol Linowitz, *The Betrayed Profession: Lawyering at the End of the Twentieth Century* (Baltimore, 1994); and Mary Ann Glendon, *A Nation Under Lawyers: How the Crisis in the Legal Profession is Transforming American Society* (New York, 1994). For a contrasting celebration of the same trends, see Richard Posner, "Professionalisms," *Arizona Law Review* 40 (1998), 1–15; and for skepticism about nostalgia generally, see Marc Galanter, "Lawyers in the Mist: The Golden Age of Legal Nostalgia," *Dickinson Law Review* 100 (1996), 549–62. Among the many interesting treatments of lawyers' reputation and representations in popular culture, see Marc Galanter, *Lowering the Bar: Lawyer Jokes and Legal Culture* (Madison, WI, 2005) and Lawrence M. Friedman, "Law, Lawyers, and Popular Culture," *Yale Law Journal* 98 (1989), 1579–606.

CHAPTER 4: THE COURTS, FEDERALISM, AND THE FEDERAL
CONSTITUTION

EDWARD A. PURCELL, JR.

General

Surveys of twentieth-century American law include Lawrence M. Friedman, *American Law in the 20th Century* (New Haven, CT, 2002) and Austin Sarat, Bryant Garth, and Robert A. Kagan, *Looking Back at Law's Century* (Ithaca, NY, 2002), and the broad history of American constitutional law is recounted in Robert G. McCloskey, *The American Supreme Court* (2nd ed. rev., Chicago, 1994) and Alfred H. Kelly, Winfred A. Harbison, and Herman Belz, *The American Constitution: Its Origins and Development* (6th ed., New York, 1983). Studies of the influence of the justices' political and social attitudes on Supreme Court decisions include Lee Epstein and Jack Knight, *The Choices Justices Make* (Washington, DC, 1998) and Jeffrey A. Segal and Harold J. Spaeth, *The Supreme Court and the Attitudinal Model Revisited* (New York, 2002).

Federalism

David L. Shapiro, *Federalism: A Dialogue* (Evanston, IL, 1995) serves as an excellent introduction, as does William H. Riker, *Federalism: Origin, Operation, Significance* (Boston, 1964). Historical overviews together with more detailed analyses of twentieth-century developments are available in Joseph F. Zimmerman, *Contemporary American Federalism* (New York, 1992) and David B. Walker, *The Rebirth of Federalism: Slouching Toward Washington* (2nd ed., New York, 2000). Harry N. Scheiber surveys much of the relevant literature in two articles: "Federalism and Legal Process: Historical and Contemporary Analysis of the American System," *Law & Society Review* 14 (1980), 663 and "American Federalism and the Diffusion of Power: Historical and Contemporary Perspectives," *Toledo Law Review* 9 (1978), 619. Douglas T. Kendall, *Redefining Federalism: Listening to the States in Shaping "Our Federalism"* (Washington, DC, 2004) defends the idea of states as "laboratories of democracy," and Vincent Ostram, *The Meaning of American Federalism: Constituting a Self-Governing Society* (Lanham, MD, 1994) reviews the operations and theoretical foundations of the federal structure.

The increasing centralization of American government is criticized in Robert F. Nagel, *The Implosion of American Federalism* (New York, 2001) and John A. Ferejohn and Barry R. Weingast, *The New Federalism: Can the States Be Trusted?* (Stanford, CA, 1997). In contrast, Samuel H. Beer defends increasing nationalization and centralization in *To Make a Nation: The Rediscovery of American Federalism* (Cambridge, MA, 1993). Erwin Chemerinsky, "The Values of Federalism," *Florida Law Review* 47 (1995), 499 raises questions about the goals and significance of federalism, whereas Edward L. Rubin and Malcolm Feeley, "Federalism: Some Notes on a National Neurosis," *UCLA Law Review* 41 (1994), 903 mounts a broadside attack on its nature and utility. Normative constitutional theories of federalism are questioned in Frank B. Cross, "Realism About Federalism," *New York University Law Review* 74 (1999), 1304 and William N. Eskridge, Jr., and John Ferejohn, "The Elastic Commerce Clause: A Political Theory of American Federalism," *Vanderbilt Law Review* 47 (1994), 1355, whereas Edward A. Purcell, Jr., *Originalism, Federalism, and the American Constitutional Enterprise: An Historical Inquiry* (New Haven, CT, 2007) argues that the federal structure is intrinsically elastic, dynamic, and underdetermined.

Edward S. Corwin described "dual federalism" in "The Passing of Dual Federalism," *Virginia Law Review* 36 (1950), 1, an interpretation supported in Raoul Berger, *Federalism: The Founders' Design* (Norman, OK, 1987) and reinforced on economic principles in Richard A. Epstein, *How Progressives Rewrote the Constitution* (Washington, DC, 2006). Challenging that interpretation, Morton Grodzins maintains in *The American System: A New View of Government in the United States* (Chicago, 1966) that the nation's federalism is characterized not by sharp lines between state and national authority but by overlapping and "shared" functions. Extending Grodzins's analysis, Daniel J. Elazar argues in *American Federalism: A View from the States* (3rd ed., New York, 1984) and *The American Partnership: Intergovernmental Cooperation in the Nineteenth Century United States* (Chicago, 1962) that such "cooperative" federal-state relations were characteristic of American federalism during the nineteenth century.

More recently, some scholars have drawn on neo-classical economics to develop theories that stress the importance of limiting the central government and encouraging widespread "competition" among the states: Michael W. McConnell, "Federalism: Evaluating the Founders' Design," *University of Chicago Law Review* 54 (1987), 1484; James M. Buchanan, *Explorations into Constitutional Economics* (College Station, TX, 1989); Jonathan R. Macey, "Federal Deference to Local Regulators and the Economic Theory of Regulation: Towards a Public-Choice Explanation of Federalism," *Virginia Law Review* 76 (1990), 265; and Thomas R. Dye, *American Federalism: Competition Among Governments* (New York, 1990). Such "competitive" theories have drawn criticism: Don Herzog, "Externalities and Other Parasites," *University of Chicago Law Review* 67 (2000), 895; Lucian Arye Bebchuk, "Federalism and the Corporation: The Desirable Limits on State Competition in Corporate Law," *Harvard Law Review* 105 (1992), 1435; Jonathan Rodden and Susan Rose-Ackerman, "Does Federalism Preserve Markets?" *Virginia Law Review* 83 (1997), 1521; and Jules Coleman, *Markets, Morals, and the Law* (New York, 1998).

Herbert Wechsler advanced the modern theory that the political structure, not the Supreme Court, was the constitutional institution designed to protect decentralized government in "The Political Safeguards of Federalism: The Role of the States in the Composition and Selection of the National Government," *Columbia Law Review* 54 (1954) 543. That proposition is developed in Jesse H. Choper, *Judicial Review and the National Political Process* (Chicago, 1980) and John Hart Ely, *Democracy and Distrust: A Theory of Judicial Review* (Cambridge, MA, 1980). Larry Kramer has criticized the theory though not its basic conclusion in "Understanding Federalism," *Vanderbilt Law Review* 47 (1994), 1485 and "Putting the Politics Back into the Political Safeguards of Federalism," *Columbia Law Review* 100 (2000), 215, whereas Bradford R. Clark has explored other structural considerations in "Separation of Powers as a Safeguard of Federalism," *Texas Law Review* 79 (2001) 1321 and "Putting the Safeguards Back in the Political Safeguards of Federalism," *Texas Law Review* 80 (2001) 327. The thesis that the Court should not attempt to enforce federalism has been challenged on a variety of grounds: Stewart A. Baker, "Federalism and the Eleventh Amendment," *University of Colorado Law Review* 48 (1977) 139; Lewis Kaden, "Politics, Money, and State Sovereignty: The Judicial Role," *Columbia Law Review* 79 (1979) 847; Stephen G. Calabresi, "'A Government of Limited and Enumerated Powers': In Defense of *United States v. Lopez*," *Michigan Law Review* 94 (1995) 752; John C. Yoo, "The Judicial Safeguards of Federalism," *Southern California Law Review* 70 (1997), 1311; and Marci A. Hamilton, "Why Federalism Must Be Enforced: A Response to Professor Kramer," *Vanderbilt Law Review* 46 (2001) 1069.

States, Localities, and the National Branches
An understanding of American federalism requires an understanding of the ways in which states, localities, and the three branches of the national government interacted and changed over time. For the states, V. O. Key's classic study *Southern Politics in State and Nation* (New York, 1949) is outdated but remains valuable, whereas William E. Nelson, *The Legalist Reformation: Law, Politics, and Ideology in New York, 1920–1980* (Chapel Hill, NC, 2001) is an excellent study of legal developments in a single state. More general works include Jon C. Teaford, *The Rise of the States: Evolution of American State Government* (Baltimore, 2002) and G. Alan Tarr and Mary Cornelia Aldis Porter, *State Supreme Courts in State and Nation* (New Haven, CT, 1988). For the role of localities, see Jon C. Teaford, *City and Suburb: The Political Fragmentation of Metropolitan America, 1850–1970* (Baltimore, 1979); Roscoe C. Martin, *The Cities and the Federal System* (New York, 1965); Gerald E. Frug, "The City as a Legal Concept," *Harvard Law Review* 93 (1980), 1057; and Kenneth T.

Jackson, *Crabgrass Frontier: The Suburbanization of the United States* (New York, 1985).

On Congress, consult Nelson W. Polsby, *How Congress Evolves: Social Bases of Institutional Change* (New York, 2004); James L. Sundquist, *The Decline and Resurgence of Congress* (Washington, DC, 1981); David R. Mayhew, *America's Congress: Actions in the Public Sphere, James Madison Through Newt Gingrich* (New Haven, CT, 2000); David H. Rosenbloom, *Building a Legislative-Centered Public Administration: Congress and the Administrative State, 1946–1999* (Tuscaloosa, AL, 2000); R. Douglas Arnold, *The Logic of Congressional Action* (New Haven, CT, 1990); and Morris Fiorina, *Congress: Keystone of the Washington Establishment* (2nd ed., New Haven, CT, 1989).

For the presidency, general treatments are available in Stephen Skowronek, *The Politics Presidents Make: Leadership from John Adams to Bill Clinton* (Cambridge, MA, 1997) and Michael A. Genovese, *The Power of the American Presidency, 1789–2000* (New York, 2001), whereas studies focusing on twentieth-century developments include Sidney M. Milkis, *The President and the Parties: The Transformation of the American Party System Since the New Deal* (New York, 1993); Richard E. Neustadt, *Presidential Power and the Modern Presidents: The Politics of Leadership from Roosevelt to Reagan* (New York, 1990); Lewis L. Gould, *The Modern American Presidency* (Lawrence, KS, 2003); and Arthur M. Schlesinger, Jr., *The Imperial Presidency* (Boston, 1989).

For the Supreme Court, see Paul L. Murphy, *The Constitution in Crisis Times, 1918–1969* (New York, 1972); David P. Currie, *The Constitution in the Supreme Court: The Second Century, 1888–1986* (Chicago, 1990); and John E. Semonche, *Keeping the Faith: A Cultural History of the U.S. Supreme Court* (New York, 1998). The histories in the Oliver Wendell Holmes Devise series treat the Court and its development of constitutional doctrines at length. Only two volumes covering the years from World War I have been published: Alexander M. Bickel and Benno C. Schmidt, Jr., *The Judiciary and Responsible Government, 1910–21* (New York, 1993) and William M. Wiecek, *The Birth of the Modern Constitution: The United States Supreme Court, 1941–53* (New York, 2006). Three more, however, are scheduled for publication in the near future: Robert C. Post, *Constitutional Rights and the Regulatory State, 1921–30*; Richard D. Friedman, *The Hughes Court, 1930–41*; and Morton J. Horwitz, *The Warren Court and American Democracy, 1953–76*.

Studies examining the interrelationships among the national branches include Charles O. Jones, *The Presidency in a Separated System* (Washington, DC, 1994); Jon R. Bond and Richard Fleisher, *The President in the Legislative Arena* (Chicago, 1990); Henry J. Abraham, *Justices, Presidents, and Senators: A History of the U.S. Supreme Court Appointments from Washington to Clinton* (rev. ed., Lanham, MD, 1999); Louis Fisher, *Constitutional Conflicts Between*

Congress and the President (4th ed. rev., Lawrence, KS, 1997); Jessica Korn, *The Power of Separation: American Constitutionalism and the Myth of the Legislative Veto* (Princeton, NJ, 1996); Edward Keynes, with Randall K. Miller, *The Court v. Congress: Prayer, Busing, and Abortion* (Durham, NC, 1989); and Charles Gardner Geyh, *When Courts and Congress Collide: The Struggle for Control of America's Judicial System* (Ann Arbor, MI, 2006).

For discussions of federal-state intergovernmental relations, see Michael D. Reagan, *The New Federalism* (New York, 1972); Donald F. Kettl, *The Regulation of American Federalism* (Baltimore, 1983); and Deil Wright, *Understanding Intergovernmental Relations* (North Scituate, MA, 1978). Robert T. Golembiewski and Aaron Wildavsky consider the relative capacities of state and national government in *The Costs of Federalism* (New Brunswick, NJ, 1984), as does Paul Peterson in *The Price of Federalism* (Washington, DC, 1995) and Harold A. Hovey in *The Devolution Revolution: Can the States Afford Devolution* (New York, 1998). James L. Sundquist, with the collaboration of David W. Davis, examines the implementation of Lyndon Johnson's Great Society programs in *Making Federalism Work: A Study of Program Coordination at the Community Level* (Washington, DC, 1969), and David B. Walker, *Toward a Functioning Federalism* (Cambridge, MA, 1981) stresses the changes that the Great Society brought to American federalism. Timothy Conlan covers the years from the Nixon administration to the end of the twentieth century in two books, *New Federalism: Intergovernmental Reform from Nixon to Reagan* (Washington, DC, 1988) and *From New Federalism to Devolution: Twenty-Five Years of Intergovernmental Reform* (Washington, DC, 1998). Richard P. Nathan, Fred C. Doolittle, and Associates, *Reagan and the States* (Princeton, NJ, 1987) argue that the Reagan administration's federalism programs harmed the poorest and politically most vulnerable groups in American society.

Joseph F. Zimmerman, *Interstate Relations: The Neglected Dimension of Federalism* (Westport, CT, 1996) focuses on the often overlooked subject of relations between the states.

From World War I to the Great Depression
William M. Wiecek, *The Lost World of Classical Legal Thought: Law and Ideology in America, 1886–1937* (New York, 1998) discusses the evolution of American constitutional thinking up to the New Deal, while Christopher N. May, *In the Name of War: Judicial Review and the War Powers Since 1918* (Cambridge, MA, 1989) explores the centralizing impact of World War I on constitutional law. Walter F. Pratt, Jr., *Edward Douglas White, 1910–1921* (Columbia, SC, 1999) provides a useful introduction to the Court's work during and immediately after the war, and Alpheus Thomas Mason, *William Howard Taft: Chief Justice* (New York, 1965) provides a careful study

of the Court during the 1920s, a study that should be supplemented by Robert C. Post, "Chief Justice William Howard Taft and the Concept of Federalism," *Constitutional Commentary* 9 (1992), 199 and "Defending the Lifeworld: Substantive Due Process in the Taft Court Era," *Boston University Law Review* 78 (1998), 1498 and by Barry Cushman, "Formalism and Realism in Commerce Clause Jurisprudence," *University of Chicago Law Review* 67 (2000), 1089.

World War I and its aftermath were critical in spurring the gradual, if partial, move toward federal judicial protection of non-economic individual liberties, a major centralizing force in the twentieth century. Relevant studies include William Preston, Jr., *Aliens and Dissenters: Federal Suppression of Radicals, 1903–1933* (New York, 1963); Paul Murphy, *World War I and the Origins of Civil Liberties in the United States* (New York, 1980); Mark A. Graber, *Transforming Free Speech: The Ambiguous Legacy of Civil Libertarianism* (Berkeley, CA, 1991); John Braeman, *Before the Civil Rights Revolution: The Old Court and Individual Rights* (Westport, CT, 1988); David M. Rabban, *Free Speech in Its Forgotten Years* (New York, 1997); and Howard Gillman, "Preferred Freedoms: The Progressive Expansion of State Power and the Rise of Modern Civil Liberties Jurisprudence," *Political Research Quarterly* 47 (1994), 623.

From the Great Depression to the 1970s
Two excellent general histories are David M. Kennedy, *Freedom from Fear: The American People in Depression and War, 1929–1945* (New York, 1999) and James T. Patterson, *Grand Expectations: The United States, 1945–1974* (New York, 1996). Studies of the New Deal include Harvard Sitkoff, ed., *Fifty Years Later: The New Deal Evaluated* (Philadelphia, 1985); Steve Fraser and Gary Gerstle, *The Rise and Fall of the New Deal Order, 1930–1980* (Princeton, NJ, 1989); Alan Brinkley, *The End of Reform: New Deal Liberalism in Recession and War* (New York, 1995); Alonzo M. Hamby, *For the Survival of Democracy: Franklin Roosevelt and the World Crisis of the 1930s* (New York, 2004); and Sidney Milkis and Jerome M. Mileur, eds., *The New Deal and the Triumph of Liberalism* (Boston, 2002). James T. Patterson, *The New Deal and the States: Federalism in Transition* (Princeton, NJ, 1969) is a brief but useful examination of the New Deal's impact on the states. Suzanne Mettler, *Gender and Federalism in New Deal Public Policy* (Ithaca, NY, 1998) explores the New Deal's impact on women, and Harvard Sitkoff considers its impact on African Americans in *A New Deal for Blacks: The Emergence of Civil Rights as a National Issue* (New York, 1978). William H. Chafe, ed., *The Achievement of American Liberalism: The New Deal and its Legacies* (New York, 2003) traces the New Deal's continued impact through century's end.

The impact of the New Deal on constitutional law has remained a topic of vigorous debate. Michael E. Parrish, "The Great Depression, the New Deal, and the American Legal Order," *Washington Law Review* 59 (1984), 723 and the symposium "The Debate Over the Constitutional Revolution of 1937," *American Historical Review* 110 (2005), 1046 provide useful introductions. C. Herman Pritchett, *The Roosevelt Court: A Study in Judicial Politics and Values, 1937–1947* (Chicago, 1948) emphasizes the changes the Court made in constitutional doctrine in the decade after 1937, and William E. Leuchtenburg, *The Supreme Court Reborn: The Constitutional Revolution in the Age of Roosevelt* (New York, 1995) supports the claim that the New Deal effected a "constitutional revolution." Recent scholars have sought to qualify that view: Barry Cushman, *Rethinking the New Deal Court: The Structure of a Constitutional Revolution* (New York, 1998); G. Edward White, *The Constitution and the New Deal* (Cambridge, MA, 2000); and Richard D. Friedman, "Switching Time and Other Thought Experiments: The Hughes Court and Constitutional Transformation," *University of Pennsylvania Law Review* 142 (1994), 1891. Stephen Gardbaum argues that the New Deal Court did not merely expand national power but expanded state power as well in "New Deal Constitutionalism and the Unshackling of the States," *University of Chicago Law Review* 64 (1997), 483.

On the impact of World War II, see Daniel R. Ernst and Victor Jew, *Total War and the Law: The American Home Front in World War II* (Westport, CT, 2002) and the Round Table, "A Critical Moment: World War II and Its Aftermath at Home," in *Journal of American History* 92 (2006), 1211. Melvin I. Urofsky, *Division and Discord: The Supreme Court Under Stone and Vinson, 1941–1953* (Columbia, SC, 1997) covers the Court during and after the war, and the era's critical episodes involving civil liberties are examined in Greg Robinson, *By Order of the President: FDR and the Internment of Japanese Americans* (Cambridge, MA, 2001); Peter H. Irons, *Justice At War: The Inside Story of the Japanese American Internment* (New York, 1993); David Caute, *The Great Fear: The Anti-Communist Purge Under Truman and Eisenhower* (New York, 1979); and Stanley I. Kutler, *The American Inquisition: Justice and Injustice in the Cold War* (New York, 1982).

On *Brown* and civil rights, see the Round Table, "*Brown v. Board of Education*, Fifty Years After," in *Journal of American History* 91 (2004), 19; James T. Patterson, *Brown v. Board of Education: A Civil Rights Milestone and its Troubled Legacy* (New York, 2001); Michael J. Klarman, *From Jim Crow to Civil Rights: The Supreme Court and the Struggle for Racial Equality* (New York, 2004); Mary L. Dudziak, *Cold War Civil Rights: Race and the Image of American Democracy* (Princeton, NJ, 2000); Ira Katznelson, *When Affirmative Action was White: An Untold History of Racial Inequality in Twentieth-Century America* (New York, 2005); Michael R. Belknap, *Federal Law and Southern Order:*

Racial Violence and Constitutional Conflict in the Post-Brown South (Athens, GA, 1987); and Samuel Walker, *The Rights Revolution: Rights and Community in Modern America* (New York, 1998).

There are innumerable studies of the Warren Court. Morton J. Horwitz, *The Warren Court and the Pursuit of Justice* (New York, 1998), maintains that the justices exhibited an "expansive conception of the democratic way of life" and a special solicitude for "outsiders," suggesting that the *Carolene Products* case [*United States v. Carolene Products*, 304 U.S. 144 (1938)] "laid the groundwork" for much of the Court's constitutional jurisprudence. In contrast, Lucas A. Powe, Jr., *The Warren Court and American Politics* (Cambridge, MA, 2000) minimizes the significance of *Carolene Products* and finds the Court's roots in a dominant liberal nationalism that conducted "an assault on the South as a unique legal and cultural region" and "completed the eradication of federalism." Further discussions are available in Archibald Cox, *The Warren Court: Constitutional Decision as an Instrument of Reform* (Cambridge, MA, 1969); Mark Tushnet, ed., *The Warren Court in Historical and Political Perspective* (Charlottesville, VA, 1993); Bernard Schwartz, *The Warren Court: A Retrospective* (New York, 1996); Michael R. Belknap, *The Supreme Court Under Earl Warren, 1953–1969* (Columbia, SC, 2005); and "Symposium: The Jurisprudential Legacy of the Warren Court," *Washington and Lee Law Review* 59 (2002), 1055–1457.

From the 1970s to Century's End

Thomas M. Keck, *The Most Activist Supreme Court in History: The Road to Modern Judicial Conservatism* (Chicago, 2004) discusses the changes in the Court that followed the Warren era. Robert Mason, *Richard Nixon and the Quest for a New Majority* (Chapel Hill, NC, 2004) recounts Nixon's efforts to transform American politics and constitutional law, and Dean J. Kotlowski, *Nixon's Civil Rights: Politics, Principle, and Policy* (Cambridge, MA, 2001) examines his policies on race relations. In *The Rights Revolution: Rights and Community in Modern America* (New York, 1998) Samuel Walker evaluates conservative and communitarian attacks on the expansion of constitutional rights that occurred in the quarter-century after *Brown*.

For the Burger Court, consult Vincent Blasi, ed., *The Burger Court: The Counter-Revolution That Wasn't* (New Haven, CT, 1983); Charles M Lamb and Stephen C. Halpern, eds., *The Burger Court: Political and Judicial Profiles* (Urbana, IL, 1991); Earl M. Maltz, *The Chief Justiceship of Warren Burger, 1969–1986* (Columbia, SC, 2000); N. E. H. Hull and Peter Charles Hoffer, *Roe v. Wade: The Abortion Rights Controversy in American History* (Lawrence, KS, 2001); and Bernard Schwartz, ed., *The Burger Court: Counter-Revolution or Confirmation?* (New York, 1998). In "Does Doctrine Matter?" *Michigan Law Review* 82 (1984), 655 Frederick Schauer suggests the important role that precedent played in constraining the Burger Court, whereas Paul Bender, "Is the Burger Court Really Like the Warren Court?" *Michigan Law Review* 82 (1984), 635 stresses the substantial changes the Burger Court made in moving the law to the right. Albert W. Alshuler, "Failed Pragmatism: Reflections on the Burger Court," *Harvard Law Review* 100 (1987), 1436 emphasizes, and offers a variety of explanations for, the Court's apparent inconsistencies.

For the Rehnquist Court, see Martin H. Belsky, ed., *The Rehnquist Court: A Retrospective* (New York, 2002); Christopher E. Smith, *The Rehnquist Court and Criminal Punishment* (New York, 1997); James F. Simon, *The Center Holds: The Power Struggle Inside the Rehnquist Court* (New York, 1995); David G. Savage, *Turning Right: The Making of the Rehnquist Supreme Court* (New York, 1993); Tinsley E. Yarbrough, *The Rehnquist Court and the Constitution* (New York, 2000); Herman Schwartz, ed., *The Rehnquist Court: Judicial Activism on the Right* (New York, 2002); and the symposium in *Saint Louis University Law Journal* 47 (2003), 561–897. Dawn E. Johnsen, "Ronald Reagan and the Rehnquist Court on Congressional Power: Presidential Influences on Constitutional Change," *Indiana Law Journal* 78 (2003), 363–412 explores the efforts of the Reagan administration to alter constitutional law and influence the Rehnquist Court, and the "Symposium: Conservative Judicial Activism," *University of Colorado Law Review* 73 (2002), 1139 examines the meaning of judicial "conservatism" and "activism" in the twentieth century. Edward Lazarus, *Closed Chambers: The Rise, Fall, and Future of the Modern Supreme Court* (New York, 1999) provides an unusual clerk's eye view of the Court during its 1988–89 Term.

CHAPTER 5: THE LITIGATION REVOLUTION

LAWRENCE M. FRIEDMAN

Lawyers and non-lawyers have been complaining about American litigation and American litigiousness for at least a century and probably much longer. But there is surprisingly little actual study of rates of litigation over time. None of the studies are national; all of them are pretty much confined to one or two jurisdictions. This is not surprising. The work is slow and painstaking, and there are no historical statistics to speak of; each author has to dig out the material on his or her own. The earliest study was Francis W. Laurent, *The Business of a Trial Court: 100 Years of Cases* (Madison, WI, 1959), which was a study of Chippewa County, Wisconsin. Lawrence Friedman and Robert V. Percival, in "A Tale of Two Courts: Litigation in Alameda and San Benito Counties," *Law and Society Review* 10 (1976) 267 compared the work of two California courts, one urban and one rural, over time. Wayne V. McIntosh studied the work of courts in St. Louis, Missouri, in his book,

The Appeal of Civil Law: A Political-Economic Analysis of Litigation (Champaign, IL, 1990); other studies include John Stookey, "Economic Cycles and Civil Litigation," *Justice System Journal* 11 (1984) 282. A special issue of the *Law and Society Review* 24 (1990) was devoted to "Longitudinal Studies of Courts."

There have also been some historical studies of particular kinds of litigation, for example, tort cases, treated in Randolph Bergstrom, *Courting Danger: Injury and Law in New York City, 1870–1910* (Ithaca, NY, 1992) and Lawrence M. Friedman, "Civil Wrongs: Personal Injury Law in the Late 19th Century," *American Bar Association Research Journal* (1987) 351; Frank Munger, "Social Change and Tort Litigation: Industrialization, Accidents, and Trial Courts in Southern West Virginia, 1872 to 1940," *Buffalo Law Review* 36 (1987) 75; and David Engel, "The Ovenbird's Song.: Insiders, Outsiders and Personal Injuries in an American Community," *Law and Society Review* 10 (1976) 267. An important recent study is John Fabian Witt, *The Accidental Republic: Crippled Workmen, Destitute Widows, and the Remaking of American Law* (Cambridge, MA, 2004). The campaign against ambulance chasers is treated in Kenneth DeVille, "New York City Attorneys and Ambulance Chasing in the 1920s," *Historian* 59 (1997) 292. Robert Kagan has discussed the *decline* of one form of litigation, debt collection, in "The Routinization of Debt Collection: An Essay on Social Change and Conflict in the Courts," *Law and Society Review* 18 (1984) 323. There are also current studies of particular kinds of litigation, for example, medical malpractice, Neil Vidmar, *Medical Malpractice and the American Jury* (Ann Arbor, MI, 1997); another specialized study is James S. Kakalik et al., *Costs and Compensation Paid in Aviation Accident Litigation* (Santa Monica, CA, 1988). Jeff Yates, Belinda Creel Davis, and Henry R. Glick deal with more recent tort litigation rates in "The Politics of Torts: Explaining Litigation Rates in the American States," *State Politics & Policy Quarterly* 1 (2001) 127. On class actions, see Deborah Hensler et al., *Class Action Dilemmas: Pursuing Public Goals for Private Gain* (Santa Monica, CA, 2000).

One of the themes of the historical studies is whether or not there has been, in recent decades, a litigation explosion. Did the litigation rate go up in the late 20th century? Are Americans a litigious people? This issue is taken up in Marc Galanter, "Reading the Landscape of Disputes: What We Know and Don't Know (and Think We Know) About our Allegedly Contentious and Litigious Society," *UCLA Law Review* 31 (1983) 4. On federal litigation, see Terence Dungworth and Nicholas M. Pac, *Statistical Overview of Civil Litigation in the Federal Courts* (Santa Monica, CA, 1990). Robert Kagan's important study, *Adversarial Legalism: The American Way of Law* (Cambridge, MA, 2002) does argue for something distinctive about the uses of litigation in American society. On the social roots of the liability explosion (which is, of course, distinct from the alleged litigation explosion), see Lawrence M. Friedman, *Total Justice* (New York, 1985). There is also an argument that the litigation crisis has been largely manufactured; on this controversy, see Thomas F. Burke, *Lawyers, Lawsuits, and Legal Rights: The Battle over Litigation in American Society* (Berkeley, CA, 2002) and William Haltom and Michael McCann, *Distorting the Law: Politics, Media, and the Litigation Crisis* (Chicago, 2004). Further, on the campaign against lawsuits (mostly tort cases), and the results of the campaign, see Stephen Daniels and Joanne Martin, "It Was the Best of Times, It Was the Worst of Times: The Precarious Nature of Plaintiffs' Practice in Texas," *Texas Law Review* 80 (2002), 1781. On the campaign against lawyers, see Marc Galanter, "News from Nowhere: The Debased Debate about Civil Justice," *Denver University Law Review* 71 (1993) 77 and *Lowering the Bar: Lawyer Jokes and Legal Culture* (Madison, WI, 2005). On the relative role of individuals and corporations as litigants, see Marc Galanter, "Planet of the APs: Reflections on the Scale of Law and Its Users," *Buffalo Law Review* 53 (2006) 1369 and Terence Dunworth and Joel Rogers, "Corporations in Court: Big Business Litigation in U.S. Federal Courts, 1971–1991," *Law and Social Inquiry* 21 (1996) 497.

Litigation suggests trials to most people; but the trial is a complex process, and full-blown jury trials have been on the decline; see Marc Galanter, "The Vanishing Trial: An Examination of Trials and Related Matters in Federal and State Courts," *Journal of Empirical Legal Studies* 1 (2004) 459; on the background to this decline, see Lawrence M. Friedman, "The Day Before Trials Vanished," *Journal of Empirical Legal Studies* 1 (2004) 689. There is, however, a good deal of literature on the jury system in operation, beginning with the classic study by Harry Kalven Jr., and Hans Zeisel, *The American Jury* (Chicago, 1966); see also Valerie P. Hans and Neil Vidmar, *Judging the Jury* (New York, 1986).

The *avoidance* of litigation is an important subject in its own right. Here one might mention the classic study of Stewart Macaulay, "Non-Contractual Relations in Business: A Preliminary Study," *American Sociological Review* 28 (1963) 55. The study of the life-cycle of disputes, mentioned in the text, is discussed in Richard E. Miller and Austin Sarat, "Grievances, Claims, and Disputes: Assessing the Adversary Culture," *Law and Society Review* 15 (1980–81) 525. On out-of-court settlements, the classic study is H. Laurence Ross, *Settled Out of Court: The Social Process of Insurance Claims Adjustment* (1970; Chicago, 1980); see also Robert Mnookin and Lewis Kornhauser, "Bargaining in the Shadow of the Law: the Case of Divorce," *Yale Law Journal* 88 (1979) 950 and Herbert Kritzer, *Let's Make a Deal: Understanding the Negotiation Process in Ordinary Litigation* (Madison, WI, 1991) and *The Justice Broker* (New York, 1990).

CHAPTER 6: CRIMINAL JUSTICE IN THE UNITED STATES

MICHAEL WILLRICH

The literature on American criminal justice in the twentieth century is vast. An extraordinary range of disciplines take an interest in documenting, analyzing, and interpreting crime and criminal justice: journalism, film, law, criminology, sociology, anthropology, economics, political science, psychology, psychiatry, cultural studies, literature, and history, to name a few. This brief bibliographic note cites those works that have proved particularly useful to the writing of the essay.

For general historical overviews, see Lawrence M. Friedman, *Crime and Punishment in American History* (New York, 1993); Norval Morris and David J. Rothman, eds., *The Oxford History of the Prison: The Practice of Punishment in Western Society* (New York, 1996); and Samuel Walker, *Popular Justice: A History of American Criminal Justice* (2nd. ed., New York, 1998).

This essay has emphasized two historical themes: (1) the central importance of institutions to criminal justice history and (2) the role of criminal justice ideas and institutions (especially changing conceptions of criminal responsibility) in the development of American liberalism and the modern liberal state. For institutional approaches to recent criminal justice history, see Malcolm M. Feeley and Edward L. Rubin, *Judicial Policy Making and the Modern State: How the Courts Reformed America's Prisons* (New York, 1998) and Robert A. Kagan, *Adversarial Legalism: The American Way of Law* (New York, 2001). On criminal responsibility, see Thomas A. Green, "Freedom and Criminal Responsibility in the Age of Pound: An Essay on Criminal Justice," *Michigan Law Review*, 93 (1995), 1915–2053 and Gerald Leonard, "Towards a Legal History of American Criminal Theory: Culture and Doctrine from Blackstone to the Model Penal Code," *Buffalo Criminal Law Review*, 6 (2003), 691–832. In a previous work, I have examined both themes in the context of a study of criminal justice in early twentieth-century Chicago; see Michael Willrich, *City of Courts: Socializing Justice in Progressive Era Chicago* (New York, 2003).

For useful (though dated) overviews of early-twentieth-century developments in American criminal justice, see Livingston Hall, "The Substantive Law of Crimes," *Harvard Law Review*, 50 (1937), 616–53 and Sam B. Warner and Henry B. Cabot, "Changes in the Administration of Criminal Justice During the Past Fifty Years," *Harvard Law Review*, 50 (1937), 583–615.

On the Red Scare and the post-World War I civil liberties struggles, see Richard Polenberg, *Fighting Faiths: The Abrams Case, the Supreme Court, and Free Speech* (1987; Ithaca, NY, 1999); David M. Rabban, *Free Speech in its Forgotten Years* (New York, 1997); Melvin I. Urofsky and Paul Finkelman,

A March of Liberty: A Constitutional History of the United States, Vol. II: From 1877 to the Present (2nd ed., New York, 2002); and Samuel Walker, *In Defense of American Liberties: A History of the ACLU* (New York, 1990).

Historians have approached the Prohibition era from many angles. For general histories of Prohibition, see Norman H. Clark, "Prohibition and Temperance," in *The Reader's Companion to American History*, ed. Eric Foner and John A. Garraty (Boston, 1991), 871–75; Richard F. Hamm, *Shaping the Eighteenth Amendment: Temperance Reform, Legal Culture, and the Polity, 1880–1930* (Chapel Hill, NC, 1995); Thomas R. Pegram, *Battling Demon Rum: The Struggle for a Dry America, 1800–1933* (Chicago, 1998); and Ann-Marie E. Szymanski, *Pathways to Prohibition: Radicals, Moderates, and Social Movement Outcomes* (Durham, NC, 2003). On the local social and political dimensions of dry law enforcement, see Lizabeth Cohen, *Making a New Deal: Industrial Workers in Chicago, 1919–1939* (New York, 1990); Michael A. Lerner, "Dry Manhattan: Class, Culture, and Politics in Prohibition-Era New York City, 1919–1933" (Ph.D. diss., New York University, 1999); and Michael Willrich, "'Close That Place of Hell': Poor Women and the Cultural Politics of Prohibition," *Journal of Urban History*, 29 (2003), 555–74. On the politics of prisons during the period, see Rebecca McLennan, "Punishment's 'Square Deal': Prisoners and Their Keepers in 1920s New York," *Journal of Urban History*, 29 (2003), 597–619. On the cultural history of the gangster, see David E. Ruth, *Inventing the Public Enemy: The Gangster in American Culture, 1918–1934* (Chicago, 1996). And for a biographical study of one particularly significant prosecutor in America's first war on crime, see Mary M. Stolberg, *Fighting Organized Crime: Politics, Justice, and the Legacy of Thomas E. Dewey* (Boston, 1995).

The crime surveys of the 1920s and 1930s provide fascinating information about American criminal justice institutions and practices. For local and state surveys, see especially Roscoe Pound and Felix Frankfurter, eds., *Criminal Justice in Cleveland* (Cleveland, 1922); Missouri Association for Criminal Justice, *The Missouri Crime Survey* (New York, 1926); and Illinois Association for Criminal Justice, *The Illinois Crime Survey* (Chicago, 1929). For the Wickersham Commission reports discussed in the essay, see U.S. National Commission on Law Observance and Enforcement, *Report on Crime and the Foreign Born* (Washington, DC, 1931), *Report on Lawlessness in Law Enforcement* (Washington, DC, 1931), and *Report on Penal Institutions, Probation, and Parole* (Washington, DC, 1931). For additional information on the development of American prisons during this period, including Alcatraz, I consulted Edgardo Rotman, "The Failure of Reform: United States, 1865–1965," in *The Oxford History of the Prison: The Practice of Punishment in Western Society*, ed. Norval Morris and David J. Rothman (New York, 1995): 169–97.

The post-World War II era was an extremely rich and important era in American legal culture. See Mary Dudziak, *Cold War Civil Rights: Race and the Image of American Democracy* (Princeton, NJ, 2000); Morton J. Horwitz, *The Transformation of American Law, 1870–1960: The Crisis of Legal Orthodoxy* (New York, 1992); and Edward A. Purcell, *The Crisis of Democratic Theory: Scientific Naturalism & the Problem of Value* (Lexington, KY, 1973). The Model Penal Code has only begun to receive serious historical attention. See Markus Dirk Dubber, "Penal Panopticon: The Idea of a Modern Model Penal Code," *Buffalo Criminal Law Review*, 4 (2000), 53–100; Leonard, "Towards a Legal History of Criminal Law Theory"; and Charles McClain, "Criminal Law Reform: Historical Developments in the United States," in *Encyclopedia of Crime and Justice*, ed. Sanford H. Kadish (New York, 1983), vol. 2, 511–12. Essential primary sources include American Law Institute, *Model Penal Code: Official Draft and Explanatory Notes* (1962; Philadelphia, 1985); Herbert Wechsler, "The Challenge of a Model Penal Code," *Harvard Law Review*, 65 (1952), 1097–133 and "Symposium on the Model Penal Code: Foreword," *Columbia Law Review*, 63 (1963), 589–93; and Herbert L. Packer, "The Model Penal Code and Beyond," *Columbia Law Review*, 63 (1963), 594–607.

Since the 1920s, federal court decisions have extended (and in some cases largely repealed) constitutional protections to accused criminals, defendants, and prisoners. For useful general histories, see Anthony Lewis, *Gideon's Trumpet* (1964; New York, 1989); Melvin I. Urofsky and Paul Finkelman, *A March of Liberty*; and Walker, *Popular Justice*. On the (limited) impact of the early federal decisions in the South, see Michael J. Klarman, "Is the Supreme Court Sometimes Irrelevant?: Race and the Southern Criminal Justice System in the 1940s," *Journal of American History*, 89 (2002), 119–53. On the historical debates over "incorporation" of the Bill of Rights, see Akhil Reed Amar, *The Bill of Rights: Creation and Reconstruction* (New Haven, CT, 1998). The indispensable history of the post-1965 federal prison cases is Feeley and Rubin, *Judicial Policy Making*. On the recent era of judicial and Congressional conservatism with regard to prisoners' rights, see "Developments in the Law: The Law of Prisons," *Harvard Law Review*, 115 (2002), 1838–963. A useful study of federal crime policy in postwar America (from which I have drawn several presidential quotations) is Nancy E. Marion, *A History of Federal Crime Control Initiatives, 1960–1993* (Westport, CT, 1994).

The history of the severity revolution in late-twentieth-century America is just beginning to be written. For a comparative analysis, see James Q. Whitman, *Harsh Justice: Criminal Punishment and the Widening Divide Between America and Europe* (New York, 2003). See also Albert W. Alschuler, "The Failure of Sentencing Guidelines: A Plea for Less Aggregation," *University of Chicago Law Review* 58 (1991), 501ff; George Fisher, *Plea Bargaining's*

Triumph: A History of Plea Bargaining in America (Stanford, CA, 2003); and Jonathan Simon, "Sanctioning Government: Explaining America's Severity Revolution," *University of Miami Law Review*, 56 (2002), 217–53. On the role of the president and Congress, see Nancy E. Marion, *A History of Federal Crime Control Initiatives, 1960–1993* (Westport, CT, 1994). On the rise of new forms of prison labor, see Rebecca McLennan, "The New Penal State: Globalization, History, and American Criminal Justice, c. 2000," *Inter-Asia Cultural Studies*, 2 (2001), 407–19. For useful treatments of the Crime Drop of the 1990s, see Richard Rosenfeld, "The Case of the Unsolved Crime Decline," *Scientific American*, 290 (2004), 82ff and Alfred Blumstein and Joel Wallman, eds., *The Crime Drop in America* (New York, 2000). On the social and political context in which the severity revolution occurred, see especially Michael Katz, *The Price of Citizenship: Redefining the American Welfare State* (New York, 2001); Matthew D. Lassiter, "Suburban Strategies: The Volatile Center in Postwar American Politics," in *The Democratic Experiment: New Directions in American Political History*, ed. Meg Jacobs, William J. Novak, and Julian E. Zelizer (Princeton, NJ, 2003), 327–49; and Thomas J. Sugrue, *The Origins of the Urban Crisis: Race and Inequality in Postwar Detroit* (Princeton, NJ, 1996).

On the new "problem-solving courts," see Terry Carter, "Red Hook Experiment," *American Bar Association Journal* (2004), 36–42; Michael C. Dorf and Jeffrey A. Fagan, "Community Courts and Community Justice: Forward: Problem-Solving Courts: From Innovation to Institutionalization," *American Criminal Law Review*, 40 (2003), 1501–1511; and James L. Nolan, *Reinventing Justice: The American Drug Court Movement* (Princeton, NJ, 2001).

Finally, the following are full citations of cases discussed in the essay but not cited in the footnotes: *Powell v. Alabama*, 287 U.S. 45 (1932); *Norris v. Alabama*, 294 U.S. 587 (1935); *Brown et al v. Mississippi*, 297 U.S. 278 (1936); *United States v. Carolene Products Co.*, 304 U.S. 144 (1938); *Mapp v. Ohio*, 367 U.S. 643 (1961); *Gideon v. Wainwright*, 372 U.S. 335 (1963); *Cooper v. Pate*, 378 U.S. 546 (1964); *Miranda v. Arizona*, 384 U.S. 436 (1966); *In re Gault*, 387 U.S. 1 (1967); *Furman v. Georgia*, 408 U.S. 238 (1972); and *Gregg v. Georgia*, 428 U.S. 153 (1976).

CHAPTER 7: LAW AND MEDICINE

LESLIE J. REAGAN

As my chapter indicates, the field of law and medicine is vast once one looks beyond medical jurisprudence alone. I cite here only the main books, articles, and Web sites from which I have drawn material on specific subjects and cases.

An important introduction to the history of medical jurisprudence in general is James C. Mohr, *Doctors and the Law: Medical Jurisprudence in Nineteenth-Century America* (New York, 1993). For an analysis of physician involvement in the writing of state laws and the role of policymaking in professional development, see Mohr's *Abortion in America: The Origins and Evolution of National Policy, 1800–1900* (New York, 1978). For more focused discussions of malpractice, see Kenneth Allen De Ville, *Medical Malpractice in Nineteenth-Century America* (New York, 1990) and Chester R. Burns, "Malpractice Suits in American Medicine Before the Civil War," *Bulletin of the History of Medicine* 43 (1969). For a superb cultural and legal analysis of railroads and torts, see Barbara Young Welke, *Recasting American Liberty: Gender, Race, Law, and the Railroad Revolution, 1865–1920* (Cambridge, 2001). On abortion suits specifically, see Leslie J. Reagan, "Victim or Accomplice?: Crime, Medical Malpractice, and the Construction of the Aborting Woman in American Case Law, 1860s–1970," *Columbia Journal of Gender and Law* 10 (2001), 311–31. On licensing, see Richard Harrison Shryock, *Medical Licensing in America, 1650–1965* (Baltimore, 1967). On the changing role of medical experts in rape cases, see Stephen Robertson, "Signs, Marks, and Private Parts: Doctors, Legal Discourses, and Evidence of Rape in the United States, 1823–1930," *Journal of the History of Sexuality* 8 (1998), 345–88; Dawn Flood, "Proving Rape: Sex, Race, and Representation in Chicago Trials and Society, 1937–1969" (Ph.D. diss., University of Illinois, 2003) and her forthcoming book. For an example of how health law is now taught in law schools, see Barry R. Furrow et. al, *Health Law* (2nd ed., vols. 1 and 2, St. Paul, MN, 2000).

On medicine, the courts, and the press, see Mohr, *Doctors and the Law*; Charles E. Rosenberg, *The Trial of the Assassin Guiteau: Psychiatry and Law in the Gilded Age* (Chicago, 1968); Lisa Duggan, *Sapphic Slashers: Sex, Violence, and American Modernity* (Durham, NC, 2000); Regina Morantz-Sanchez, *Conduct Unbecoming a Woman: Medicine on Trial in Turn-of-the-Century Brooklyn* (New York, 1999); and Judith R. Walkowitz, *City of Dreadful Delight: Narratives of Sexual Danger in Late-Victorian London* (Chicago, 1992) on Jack the Ripper and newspaper interest in gynecological surgery and crime.

For an overview of the literature on the history of reproduction in the United States, see Leslie J. Reagan, "Medicine, Law, and the State: The History of Reproduction," in *A Companion to American Women's History*, Nancy A. Hewitt, ed. (Oxford, 2002), 348–65. On abortion and birth control, see Leslie J. Reagan, *When Abortion Was a Crime: Women, Medicine, and Law in the United States, 1867–1973* (Berkeley, 1997); Linda Gordon, *Woman's Body, Woman's Right: A Social History of Birth Control in America* (1976; rev. and updated, New York, 1990); James C. Mohr, *Abortion in America*; David J. Garrow, *Liberty and Sexuality: The Right to Privacy and the Making of*

Roe v. Wade (New York, 1994); and Rosalind Pollack Petchesky, *Abortion and Woman's Choice: The State, Sexuality, and Reproductive Freedom* (Boston, 1984). On before and after the Comstock Law, see also Helen Lefkowitz Horowitz, *Rereading Sex: Battles over Sexual Knowledge and Suppression in Nineteenth-Century America* (New York, 2003) and Janet Farrell Brodie, *Contraception and Abortion in Nineteenth-Century America* (Ithaca, NY, 1994). On Margaret Sanger, the birth control clinic movement, and the continuing availability of contraceptives, see Andrea Tone, *Devices and Desires: A History of Contraceptives in America* (New York, 2002) and Rose Holz, "The Birth Control Clinic in America: Life Within, Life Without, 1923–1973" (Ph.D. diss., University of Illinois, 2002). On the municipal court of Chicago and the use of the law to investigate and work to ameliorate social problems on an individual basis, see Michael Willrich, *City of Courts: Socializing Justice in Progressive Era Chicago* (Cambridge, 2003).

On sterilization, see Rosalind Pollack Petchesky, "Reproduction, Ethics, and Public Policy: The Federal Sterilization Regulations," *Hastings Center Report* 9 (1977), 29–42; Dorothy Roberts, *Killing the Black Body: Race, Reproduction, and the Meaning of Liberty* (New York, 1977); Philip R. Reilly, *The Surgical Solution: A History of Involuntary Sterilization in the United States* (Baltimore, 1991); W. Michael Byrd and Linda A. Clayton, *An American Health Dilemma, Vol. 2: Race, Medicine, and Health Care in the United States, 1900–2000* (New York, 2002), 65–76, 448–476; and Robert G. Weisbord, *Genocide? Birth Control and the Black American* (Westport, CT, 1975). For close studies of sterilization programs, see, on North Carolina, Johanna Schoen, *Choice and Coercion: Birth Control, Sterilization, and Abortion in Public Health and Welfare* (Chapel Hill, NC, 2005); on California, see Elena R. Gutierrez, "Policing 'Pregnant Pilgrims': Situating the Sterilization Abuse of Mexican-Origin Women in Los Angeles County," in *Women, Health, and Nation: Canada and the United States Since 1945*, Georgina Feldberg et al., eds. (Montreal, 2003), 378–403 and Wendy Kline, *Building a Better Race: Gender, Sexuality, and Eugenics from the Turn of the Century to the Baby Boom* (Berkeley, CA, 2001); on Minnesota, see Molly Ladd-Taylor, "Who is 'Defective' and Who Decides? The "Feebleminded" and the Courts," unpublished paper, 2003; on Puerto Rico, see Laura Briggs, *Reproducing Empire: Race, Sex, Science, and U.S. Imperialism in Puerto Rico* (Berkeley, CA, 2002).

For an excellent overview of the historical structure, achievements, and difficulties of public health, see Elizabeth Fee, "Public Health and the State: The United States," in *The History of Public Health and the Modern States*, Dorothy Porter, ed. (Amsterdam, 1994), Chapter 6, 224–75. On public health law, see Lawrence O. Gostin, *Public Health Law: Power, Duty, Restraint* (Berkeley, CA, 2000) and Lawrence O. Gostin, ed., *Public Health Law and Ethics: A Reader* (Berkeley, CA, 2002). On public health, the state, and police power, see Barbara Gutmann Rosenkrantz, *Public Health and the State: Changing Views in Massachusetts, 1842–1936* (Cambridge, MA, 1972) and William J. Novak, *The People's Welfare: Law and Regulation in Nineteenth-Century America* (Chapel Hill, NC, 1996).

On epidemics, quarantine, and isolation, see Charles E. Rosenberg, *The Cholera Years: The United States in 1832, 1849, and 1866* (Chicago, 1962); Judith Walzer Leavitt, *The Healthiest City: Milwaukee and the Politics of Health Reform* (Princeton, NJ, 1982); Gostin, *Public Health Law*; David F. Musto, "Quarantine and the Problem of AIDS," in *AIDS: The Burdens of History*, Elizabeth Fee and Daniel M. Fox, eds. (Berkeley, CA, 1988), 67–85; Lawrence O. Gostin, *The AIDS Pandemic: Complacency, Injustice, and Unfulfilled Expectations*, foreword by Michael Kirby (Chapel Hill, NC, 2004); and Paula A. Treichler, *How to Have Theory in an Epidemic: Cultural Chronicles of AIDS* (Durham, NC, 1999). On the 1894 Milwaukee incident, see Judith Walzer Leavitt, "Politics and Public Health: Smallpox in Milwaukee, 1894–1895," *Bulletin of the History of Medicine* 50 (1976), 553–68, reprinted in *Sickness and Health in America: Readings in the History of Medicine and Public Health*, Judith Walzer Leavitt and Ronald L. Numbers, eds. (2nd ed. rev., Madison, WI, 1985), 372–82. See also Judith Walzer Leavitt, "'Be Safe. Be Sure.' New York City's Experience with Epidemic Smallpox," in *Hives of Sickness: Public Health and Epidemics in New York City*, David Rosner, ed. (New Brunswick, NJ, 1995), 94–114, reprinted in *Sickness and Health in America: Readings in the History of Medicine and Public Health*, Judith Walzer Leavitt and Ronald L. Numbers, eds. (3rd. ed. rev., Madison, WI, 1997), 407–17. For examples of other mob actions in panicked reaction to epidemics of yellow fever, malaria, and cholera, see John Duffy, "Social Impact of Disease in the Late 19th Century," *Bulletin of the New York Academy of Medicine* 47 (1971), 797–811, reprinted in *Sickness and Health in America*, 3rd ed., 418–425. On the germ theory of disease and the reshaping of public health, see Nancy Tomes, *The Gospel of Germs: Men, Women, and the Microbe in American Life* (Cambridge, MA, 1998) and Judith Walzer Leavitt, *Typhoid Mary: Captive to the Public's Health* (Boston, 1996).

On medical examination, medical exclusion, and blame of immigrants for disease, see Leavitt, *The Healthiest City* and *Typhoid Mary*; Alan M. Kraut, *Silent Travelers: Germs, Genes, and the "Immigrant Menace"* (New York, 1994); Howard Markel, *Quarantine! East European Jewish Immigrants and the New York City Epidemics of 1892* (Baltimore, 1997); Alexandra Minna Stern, "Buildings, Boundaries, and Blood: Medicalization and Nation-Building on the U.S.-Mexico Border, 1910–1930," *Hispanic American Historical Review* 79 (1999), 41–82; and Nayan Shah, *Contagious Divides: Epidemics and Race in San Francisco's Chinatown* (Berkeley, CA, 2001).

On the history of venereal disease, see Allan M. Brandt, *No Magic Bullet: A Social History of Venereal Diseases in the United States Since 1880* (New York, 1985) and David J. Pivar, *Purity and Hygiene: Women, Prostitution, and the "American Plan,"* *1900–1930* (Westport, CT, 2002), especially Chapter 9. Two essential books on prostitution and venereal disease focus on the British C.D. Acts; see Judith R. Walkowitz, *Prostitution and Victorian Society: Women, Class, and the State* (New York, 1980) and Philippa J. Levine, *Prostitution, Race, and Politics: Policing Venereal Disease in the British Empire* (London, 2003).

On the public health response to tuberculosis and to specific groups identified as infectious, see Barron H. Lerner, *Contagion and Confinement: Controlling Tuberculosis Along the Skid Road* (Baltimore, 1998); Tera W. Hunter, *To 'Joy my Freedom: Southern Black Women's Lives and Labors After the Civil War* (Cambridge, MA, 1997), Chapter 9; Tomes, *The Gospel of Germs*; and Sheila M. Rothman, *Living in the Shadow of Death: Tuberculosis and the Social Experience of Illness in American History* (Baltimore, 1994).

On the history of health insurance proposals, see Paul Starr, *The Social Transformation of American Medicine* (New York, 1982) and Ronald L. Numbers, *Almost Persuaded: American Physicians and Compulsory Health Insurance, 1912–1920* (Baltimore, 1978). On the Sheppard-Towner Act and federal policies to provide health services to specific populations, by gender, age, income, or disease, see Molly Ladd-Taylor, *Mother-Work: Women, Child Welfare, and the State, 1890–1930* (Urbana, IL, 1994); Alisa Klaus, *Every Child a Lion: The Origins of Maternal and Infant Health Policy in the United States and France* (Ithaca, NY, 1993); Susan L. Smith, *Sick and Tired of Being Sick and Tired: Black Women's Public Health Activism in America, 1890–1950* (Philadelphia, 1995); and Laurie Kaye Abraham, *Mama Might Be Better Off Dead: The Failure of Health Care in Urban America* (Chicago, 1993).

On the Tuskegee Study, see Allan M. Brandt, "Racism and Research: The Case of the Tuskegee Syphilis Study," *Hastings Center Report* 8 (1978), 21–29; James H. Jones, *Bad Blood: The Tuskegee Syphilis Experiment* (New York, 1981); and Susan M. Reverby, ed., *Tuskegee's Truths: Rethinking the Tuskegee Syphilis Study* (Chapel Hill, NC, 2000). The Reverby collection is superb and includes a reprint of Brandt's article, many other scholarly pieces, and reprints of the original medical journal publications concerning the study, testimony from the government hearings including men who were in the study, the USPHS employee who brought the study to media attention, and the Clinton apology. Historian Susan Lederer notices that the Tuskegee study was careful to obtain consents for autopsy and suggests that the study was less about medical research than about human dissection; it was "a history in which racism figured prominently. The Public Health Service investigators . . . regarded their African American subjects neither as patients, nor as experimental subjects, but as cadavers, who had been identified while still alive." See Susan Lederer, "The Tuskegee Syphilis Study in the Context of American Medical Research," in *Tuskegee's Truths*, 266.

For analysis of administrative law, see Lucy E. Salyer, *Laws Harsh as Tigers: Chinese Immigrants and the Shaping of Modern Immigration Law* (Chapel Hill, NC, 1995). On the U.S. Food and Drug Administration (FDA), see Philip J. Hilts, *Protecting America's Health: The FDA, Business, and One Hundred Years of Regulation* (Chapel Hill, NC, 2003); J. P. Swann, "Sure Cure: Public Policy on Drug Efficacy before 1962," in *The Inside Story of Medicines: A Symposium*, G. Higby and E. Stroud, eds. (Madison, WI, 1997), 223–61; J. H. Young, "Sulfanilamide and Diethylene Glycol," in *Chemistry and Modern Society*, J. Parascandola and J. C. Whorton, eds. (Washington, DC, 1983); and Harry M. Marks, *The Progress of Experiment: Science and Therapeutic Reform in the United States, 1900–1990* (New York, 1997). On thalidomide, see Arthur Daemmrich, "A Tale of Two Experts: Thalidomide and Political Engagement in the United States and West Germany," *Social History of Medicine* 115 (2002), 137–58; Barbara Clow, "'An Illness of Nine Months' Duration': Pregnancy and Thalidomide Use in Canada and the United States," in *Women, Health, and Nation: Canada and the United States since 1945*, Georgina Feldberg et al., eds. (Montreal, 2003), 45–66; Insight Team of *The Sunday Times* of London, *Suffer the Children: The Story of Thalidomide* (New York, 1979); and Henning Sjostrom and Robert Nilsson, *Thalidomide and the Power of the Drug Companies* (Middlesex, England, 1972).

On health, the environmental movement, and the EPA, see Thomas R. Dunlap, *DDT: Scientists, Citizens, and Public Policy* (Princeton, NJ, 1981); Christopher Sellers, "Body, Place and the State: The Makings of an 'Environmentalist' Imaginary in the Post-World War II U.S.," *Radical History Review* 74 (1999), 31–64; Edmund P. Russell III, "Lost Among the Parts per Billion: Ecological Protection at the United States Environmental Protection Agency, 1970–1993," *Environmental History* 2 (1997), 29–51; and Leslie J. Reagan, "Spraying Forests, Farms, and Mothers: Reproductive Hazards, Lay Epidemiology, and the Environmental Protection Agency," paper in author's possession. For an important case study of industry's deliberate effort to hide information and deceive the state, the law, and the public about the dangers of lead and plastics, see Gerald Markowitz and David Rosner, *Deceit and Denial: The Deadly Politics of Industrial Pollution* (Berkeley, 2002). *Deceit and Denial* shows the significant health information documented in records that are held in private corporate hands and are generally unavailable. Through the legal process of seeking evidence in corporate papers and through depositions, the evidence of health issues and of deliberate corporate efforts to deprive the public of knowledge of health risks became apparent. Furthermore, as the authors made their findings public and the book went into print, several powerful companies (Dow, Shell, and Monsanto, for example) used their financial and legal muscle to undermine academic research and frighten scholars and their publishers. Industry attorneys deposed Markowitz and subpoenaed material from the University of California Press and peer reviewers. On the corporate response and for links to other reports on the industry and the book, see www.deceitanddenial.org for Markowitz and Rosner's "reply to the chemical industry's attacks" and to the report of a historian hired by the industry. Markowitz and Rosner's book underlines the importance of working against the sealing of legal materials in class action and other suits in the interest of public information sharing and public health.

For an introduction to the history of disabilities, see Paul K. Longmore and Lauri Umansky, eds., *The New Disability History: American Perspectives* (New York, 2001) and Catherine J. Kudlick, "Disability History: Why We Need Another 'Other,'" *American Historical Review* 108 (2003), 763–93. On the Americans with Disabilities Act, see "Americans with Disabilities Act Questions and Answers," http://www.usdoj.gov/crt/ada.

My discussion of recent cases concerning end-of-life issues and biomedical ethics only touches the surface of these issues and their medical-legal implications. Although my own analysis differs, the best place to start for a historical analysis of these issues is David J. Rothman, *Strangers at the Bedside: A History of How Law and Bioethics Transformed Medical Decision Making* (New York, 1991). On Quinlan, see "She Changed the Way People Looked at Life and Death," excerpts by Barbara Maneri as published in the *Sparta Independent*, January 6, 2000 at http://www.karenannquinlanhospice.org; Paul W. Armstrong, "Summary of *In the Matter of Quinlan*," Medical College of Georgia, 1979, www.lib.mcg.edu/drdilemma/consult/karenann.htm; *Matter of Quinlan* 70 N.J. 10 (1976). On Cruzan, see *Cruzan, by her Parents and Co-Guardians v. Director, Missouri Department of Health* 497 U.S. 261 (1990). On the Kowalski case, see Fred Pelka, *The Disability Rights Movement* (Santa Barbara, CA, 1997). My discussion of Schiavo is based on my reading of the coverage in the *New York Times* and BBC News and CNN online. See also George J. Annas, "'Culture of Life' Politics at the Bedside–The Case of Terri Schiavo," *New England Journal of Medicine* 352 (2005), 1710–15 and Timothy E. Quill, "Terri Schiavo – A Tragedy Compounded," *New England Journal of Medicine* 352 (2005), 1630–33. On the historical movement of the process of dying into the hospital and hospice care, see Susan L. Smith and Dawn Dorothy Nickel, "Nursing the Dying in Post-Second World War Canada and the United States" in *Women, Health, and Nation*, 330–354. For current information on HIPAA, see U.S. Department of Health and Human Services, http://www.hhs.gov/ocr/hipaa. For an example of how officially stated concerns about privacy and sterilization abuse have led to the destruction of historical records or to the removal of records from public research access, see the epilogue in Schoen, *Choice and Coercion*. As she observes, official public apologies for sterilization abuse have led to the closure of records that revealed the state's abuse.

On patient rights and the alliance between prosecutors and medicine to investigate the bodies of pregnant women, especially African American women as in South Carolina, see Dorothy Roberts, *Killing the Black Body*; Lynn M. Paltrow, "Background Concerning *Ferguson et al. v. City of Charleston et. al*, March 9, 2006, National Advocates for Pregnant Women, http://advocatesforpregnantwomen.org and related materials at this Web site; George J. Annas, "Testing Poor Pregnant Women for Cocaine – Physicians as Police," *New England Journal of Medicine* 344 (2001), 1729–32; and *Ferguson v. City of Charleston* 532 U.S. 67 (2001). See also Brian H. Bornstein, "Seize This Urine Test: The Implications of *Ferguson v. City of Charleston* for Drug Testing During Pregnancy," *Journal of Medicine and Law* 6 (2001), 65–79. For manslaughter charges against a Utah woman who refused a cesarean section, see http://www.cnn.com. On medicine, law, forced treatment, and the contemporary surveillance of pregnant women see also Cynthia R. Daniels, *At Women's Expense: State Power and the Politics of Fetal Rights* (Cambridge, MA, 1993) and Janet Golden, "'An Argument that Goes Back to the Womb': The Demedicalization of Fetal Alcohol Syndrome, 1973–1992," *Journal of Social History* 33 (1999), 269–98. On the law's conceptualization and use of the body for evidence, see Alan Hyde, *Bodies of Law* (Princeton, NJ, 1997).

CHAPTER 8: THE GREAT DEPRESSION AND THE NEW DEAL

BARRY CUSHMAN

General: Conditions and Responses

The era of the Great Depression and the New Deal was a period of extraordinary legal ferment, and the literature touching on various features of its legal and constitutional development is proportionately vast. For general histories of the Great Depression and the New Deal, see James MacGregor Burns, *Roosevelt: The Lion and the Fox* (New York, 1956); Arthur M. Schlesinger, *The Age of Roosevelt*, Vol. 1: *The Crisis of the Old Order, 1919–1933*; Vol. 2, *The Coming of the New Deal*; and Vol. 3, *The Politics of Upheaval* (Boston, 1957); Mario Einaudi, *The Roosevelt Revolution* (New York, 1959); William E. Leuchtenburg, *Franklin D. Roosevelt and the New Deal, 1932–1940* (New York, 1963) and *The FDR Years: On Roosevelt and His Legacy* (New York, 1995); Edgar Eugene Robinson, *The Roosevelt Leadership, 1933–1945* (New York, 1972); Frank B. Friedel, *Franklin D. Roosevelt: Launching the New Deal* (Boston, 1973) and *Franklin D. Roosevelt: A Rendezvous with Destiny* (Boston,

1990); Barry D. Karl, *The Uneasy State: The United States from 1915 to 1945* (Chicago, 1983); Robert McElvaine, *The Great Depression: America, 1929–1941* (New York, 1984); Harvard Sitkoff, ed., *Fifty Years Later: The New Deal Evaluated* (Philadelphia, 1985); Michael E. Parrish, *Anxious Decades: America in Prosperity and Depression 1920–1941* (New York, 1992); Alan Brinkley, *The End of Reform: New Deal Liberalism in Recession and War* (New York, 1995); David M. Kennedy, *Freedom from Fear: The American People in Depression and War, 1929–1945* (New York, 1999); and George T. McJimsey, *The Presidency of Franklin Delano Roosevelt* (Lawrence, KS, 2000).

On the Hoover Administration's response to the economic conditions of the Great Depression, see Harris Gaylord Warren, *Herbert Hoover and the Great Depression* (New York, 1959); Albert U. Romasco, *The Poverty of Abundance: Hoover, the Nation, the Depression* (New York, 1965); Jordan A. Schwarz, *The Interregnum of Despair: Hoover, Congress, and the Depression* (Urbana, IL, 1970); Martin L. Fausold and George T. Mazuzan, eds., *The Hoover Presidency: A Reappraisal* (Albany, NY, 1974); James Stuart Olson, *Herbert Hoover and the Reconstruction Finance Corporation, 1931–1933* (Ames, IA, 1977); and Martin L. Fausold, *The Presidency of Herbert C. Hoover* (Lawrence, KS, 1985).

On the approaches of the Hoover and Roosevelt Administrations to the problems of agriculture, see Edwin G. Nourse, Joseph S. Davis and John D. Black, *Three Years of the Agricultural Adjustment Administration* (Washington, DC, 1937); Murray R. Benedict, *Farm Policies of the United States, 1790–1950* (New York, 1953); Paul L. Murphy, "The New Deal Agricultural Program and the Constitution," *Agricultural History* 29 (1955), 160–68; M. S. Venkataramani, "Norman Thomas, Arkansas Sharecroppers, and the Roosevelt Agricultural Policies, 1933–37," *Mississippi Valley Historical Review* 47 (1960), 225–46; Christiana McFadyen Campbell, *The Farm Bureau and the New Deal: A Study of the Making of National Farm Policy, 1933–40* (Urbana, IL, 1962); Gilbert C. Fite, *American Agriculture and Farm Policy Since 1900* (New York, 1964); David E. Conrad, *The Forgotten Farmers: The Story of Sharecroppers in the New Deal* (Urbana, IL, 1965); Raymond Moley, *The First New Deal* (New York, 1966); Van L. Perkins, *Crisis in Agriculture: The Agricultural Adjustment Administration and the New Deal, 1933* (Berkeley, 1969); William D. Rowley, *M. L. Wilson and the Campaign for Domestic Allotment* (Lincoln, NE, 1970); Donald H. Grubbs, *Cry from the Cotton: The Southern Tenant Farmers' Union and the New Deal* (Chapel Hill, NC, 1971); Richard Kirkendall, "The New Deal and Agriculture," in John Braeman, Robert H. Bremner and David Brody, eds., *The New Deal* (Columbus, OH, 1975), Vol. 1: *The National Level*, 83–109; Peter Irons, *The New Deal Lawyers* (Princeton, NJ, 1982); Theodore Saloutos, *The American Farmer and the New Deal* (Ames, IA, 1982); Melvyn Dubofsky and Stephen

Burwood, eds., *Agriculture During the Great Depression: Selected Articles* (New York, 1990); and David E. Hamilton, *From New Day to New Deal: American Farm Policy from Hoover to Roosevelt, 1928–1933* (Chapel Hill, NC, 1991).

On the framing, implementation, and demise of the National Industrial Recovery Act, see Sidney Fine, *The Automobile Under the Blue Eagle: Labor, Management, and the Automobile Manufacturing Code* (Ann Arbor, MI, 1963); Ellis W. Hawley, *The New Deal and the Problem of Monopoly: A Study in Economic Ambivalence* (Princeton, NJ, 1966); Bernard Bellush, *The Failure of the NRA* (New York, 1975); Robert F. Himmelberg, *The Origins of the National Recovery Administration: Business, Government, and the Trade Association Issue* (New York, 1976); Peter Irons, *The New Deal Lawyers* (Princeton, NJ, 1982); and Ronen Shamir, *Managing Legal Uncertainty: Elite Lawyers in the New Deal* (Durham, NC, 1995).

On banking and securities regulation and reform, see Ralph F. De Bedts, *The New Deal's SEC: The Formative Years* (New York, 1964); Michael E. Parrish, *Securities Regulation and the New Deal* (New Haven, CT, 1970); Susan Estabrook Kennedy, *The Banking Crisis of 1933* (Lexington, KY, 1973); Joel Seligman, *The Transformation of Wall Street: A History of the Securities and Exchange Commission and Modern Corporate Finance* (Boston, 1982); G. J. Benston, *The Separation of Commercial and Investment Banking: The Glass-Steagall Act Revisited and Reconsidered* (New York, 1990); and Paul Mahoney, "The Stock Pools and the Securities Exchange Act," *Journal of Financial Economics* 51 (1999), 343–69 and "The Political Economy of the Securities Act of 1933," *Journal of Legal Studies* 30 (2001), 1–31.

On unemployment, see Stanley Lebergott, *Manpower in Economic Growth: The American Record Since 1800* (New York, 1964); John Garraty, *Unemployment in History: Economic Thought and Public Policy* (New York, 1978); and Alexander Keyssar, *Out of Work: The First Century of Unemployment in Massachusetts* (Cambridge, 1986). On Social Security, see Paul H. Douglas, *Social Security in the United States: An Analysis and Appraisal of the Federal Social Security Act* (New York, 1939); Frances Perkins, *The Roosevelt I Knew* (New York, 1946); Edwin E. Witte, *The Development of the Social Security Act* (Madison, WI, 1962) and "Organized Labor and Social Security," in Milton Derber and Edwin Young, eds., *Labor and the New Deal* (New York, 1972), 241–74; Arthur J. Altmeyer, *The Formative Years of Social Security* (Madison, WI, 1966); Roy Lubove, *The Struggle for Social Security, 1900–1935* (Cambridge, MA, 1968); Daniel Nelson, *Unemployment Insurance: The American Experience, 1915–1935* (Madison, WI, 1969); William Graebner, *A History of Retirement: The Meaning and Function of an American Institution, 1885–1978* (New Haven, CT, 1980); Bruce Allan Murphy, *The Brandeis/Frankfurter Connection: The Secret Political Activities of Two Supreme Court Justices* (New York, 1982); Wilbur J. Cohen and Thomas H. Eliot, "The Advent of Social

Security," in Katie Louchheim, ed., *The Making of the New Deal: The Insiders Speak* (Cambridge, MA, 1983), 159–68; and Saul J. Blaustein, *Unemployment Insurance in the United States: The First Half Century* (Kalamazoo, MI, 1993).

On developments in labor law, see Irving Bernstein, *The Lean Years: A History of the American Worker, 1920–1933* (Baltimore, 1960) and *Turbulent Years: A History of the American Worker, 1933–1941* (Boston, 1969); Melvyn Dubofsky, "Not So 'Turbulent Years': Another Look at the American 1930's," *Amerikastudien* 24 (1979), 5–20; Christopher Tomlins, *The State and the Unions: Labor Relations, Law, and the Organized Labor Movement, 1880–1960* (Cambridge, 1985); and Daniel Ernst, "The Yellow Dog Contract and Liberal Reform, 1917–1932," *Labor History* 30 (1989), 251–74. On the enactment, implementation, and interpretation of the National Labor Relations Act, see Thomas R. Fisher, *Industrial Disputes and Federal Legislation* (New York, 1940); Irving Bernstein, *The New Deal Collective Bargaining Policy* (Berkeley, CA, 1950); Leon Keyserling, "The Wagner Act: Its Origins and Current Significance," *George Washington Law Review* 29 (1960), 199–233; Richard C. Cortner, *The Wagner Act Cases* (Knoxville, TN, 1964) and *The Jones & Laughlin Case* (New York, 1970); R. W. Fleming, "The Significance of the Wagner Act," in Milton Derber and Edwin Young, eds., *Labor and the New Deal* (New York, 1972), 121–57; James A. Gross, *The Making of the National Labor Relations Board* (Albany, NY, 1974); Karl Klare, "Judicial Deradicalization of the Wagner Act and the Origins of Modern Legal Consciousness, 1937–1941," *Minnesota Law Review* 62 (1978), 265–340; Peter H. Irons, *The New Deal Lawyers* (Princeton, NJ, 1982); Thomas I. Emerson and Paul A. Herzog, "The National Labor Relations Board," in Katie Louchheim, ed., *The Making of the New Deal: The Insiders Speak* (Cambridge, MA, 1983), 205–18; and Kenneth Casebeer, "Drafting Wagner's Act: Leon Keyserling and the Pre-committee Drafts of the Labor Disputes Act and the National Labor Relations Act," *Industrial Relations Law Journal* 11 (1989), 73–131.

On the Hoover and Roosevelt administrations' relief efforts, see Josephine Chapin Brown, *Public Relief: 1929–1939* (New York, 1940); Searle F. Charles, *Minister of Relief: Harry Hopkins and the Depression* (Syracuse, NY, 1963); Paul A. Kurzman, *Harry Hopkins and the New Deal* (Fair Lawn, NJ, 1974); and Paul E. Mertz, *New Deal Policy and Southern Rural Poverty* (Baton Rouge, LA, 1978). On the Farm Security Administration, see Sidney Baldwin, *Poverty and Politics: The Rise and Decline of the Farm Security Administration* (Chapel Hill, NC, 1968). On the Tennessee Valley Authority, see C. Herman Pritchett, *The Tennessee Valley Authority: A Study in Public Administration* (Chapel Hill, NC, 1943) and Thomas McCraw, *TVA and the Power Fight, 1933–1939* (Philadelphia, 1971). On the Rural Electrification

Administration, see D. Clayton Brown, *Electricity for Rural America: The Fight for the REA* (Westport, CT, 1980). On Food and Drug reform, see the symposium on "The New Food, Drug, and Cosmetic Legislation," in *Law and Contemporary Problems* 6 (1939), 1–182. On bankruptcy reform, see David A. Skeel, Jr., *Debt's Dominion: A History of Bankruptcy Law in America* (Princeton, NJ, 2001). On the Indian New Deal, see Kenneth R. Philip, *John Collier's Crusade for Indian Reform, 1920–1954* (Tucson, AZ, 1977) and Graham D. Taylor, *The New Deal and American Indian Tribalism: The Administration of the Indian Reorganization Act, 1934–45* (Lincoln, NE, 1980).

On Congressional opposition to various features of the New Deal, see George Wolfskill, *The Revolt of the Conservatives* (Boston, 1962); James T. Patterson, *Congressional Conservatism and the New Deal: The Growth of the Conservative Coalition in Congress, 1933–1939* (Lexington, KY, 1967); Ronald Feinman, *Twilight of Progressivism: The Western Republican Senators and the New Deal* (Baltimore, 1981); and Clyde A. Weed, *Nemesis of Reform: The Republican Party During the New Deal* (New York, 1994).

On young lawyers in the administration, see, e.g., Donald Richberg, *My Hero: The Indiscreet Memoirs of an Eventful but Unheroic Life* (New York, 1954); Thomas E. Vadney, *The Wayward Liberal: A Political Biography of Donald Richberg* (Lexington, KY, 1970); Jerold S. Auerbach, *Unequal Justice: Lawyers and Social Change in Modern America* (New York, 1976); Peter Irons, *The New Deal Lawyers* (Princeton, NJ, 1982); Katie Louchheim, ed., *The Making of the New Deal: The Insiders Speak* (Cambridge, MA, 1983); Joseph Lash, *Dealers and Dreamers: A New Look at the New Deal* (New York, 1988); Thomas I. Emerson, *Young Lawyer for the New Deal: An Insider's Memoir of the Roosevelt Years* (Savage, MD, 1991); and Ronen Shamir, *Managing Legal Uncertainty: Elite Lawyers in the New Deal* (Durham, NC, 1995).

There is a rich biographical literature on the justices who sat on the Supreme Court during the New Deal crisis, particularly on the justices generally thought to be more liberal. On Chief Justice Hughes, see Samuel Hendel, *Charles Evans Hughes and the Supreme Court* (New York, 1951); Merlo J. Pusey, *Charles Evans Hughes* (New York, 1951); Dexter Perkins, *Charles Evans Hughes and American Democratic Statesmanship* (Boston, 1956); Paul Freund, "Charles Evans Hughes as Chief Justice," *Harvard Law Review* 81 (1967), 4–43; and David J. Danelski and Joseph S. Tulchin, eds., *The Autobiographical Notes of Charles Evans Hughes* (Cambridge, MA, 1973). On Justice Stone, see Samuel J. Konefsky, *Chief Justice Stone and the Supreme Court* (New York, 1945); Alpheus Thomas Mason, *Harlan Fiske Stone: Pillar of the Law* (New York, 1956); and Allison Dunham, "Mr. Justice Stone," in Allison Dunham and Philip B. Kurland, eds., *Mr. Justice* (Chicago, 1964). On Justice Cardozo, see Richard Polenberg, *The World of Benjamin Cardozo: Personal Values and the Judicial Process* (Cambridge, MA, 1997) and Andrew

L. Kaufman, *Cardozo* (Cambridge, MA, 1998). The literature on Justice Brandeis is immense. See, e.g., Alpheus T. Mason, *Brandeis: A Free Man's Life* (New York, 1946); Paul Freund, "Mr. Justice Brandeis," in Allison Dunham and Phillip B. Kurland, eds., *Mr. Justice* (Chicago, 1964); Melvin I. Urofsky, *A Mind of One Piece: Brandeis and American Reform* (New York, 1971) and *Louis D. Brandeis and the Progressive Tradition* (Boston, 1981); Lewis J. Paper, *Brandeis* (Englewood Cliffs, NJ, 1983); Philippa Strum, *Louis D. Brandeis: Justice for the People* (Cambridge, MA, 1984); and Nelson L. Dawson ed., *Brandeis and America* (Lexington, KY, 1989). Also helpful are Melvin I. Urofsky and David W. Levy, eds., *Letters of Louis D. Brandeis* (Albany, NY, 1978). The literature on Justice Roberts and the Four Horsemen is thinner, but useful nonetheless. On Justice Roberts, see Charles Leonard, *A Search for a Judicial Philosophy: Mr. Justice Roberts and the Constitutional Revolution of 1937* (Port Washington, NY, 1971). On Justice Sutherland, see Harold M. Stephens, "Mr. Justice Sutherland," *American Bar Association Journal* 31 (1945), 446–53; Joel F. Paschal, *Mr. Justice Sutherland: A Man Against the State* (Princeton, NJ, 1951); and Hadley Arkes, *The Return of George Sutherland: Restoring a Jurisprudence of Natural Rights* (Princeton, NJ, 1994). On Justice Butler, see Francis J. Brown, *The Social and Economic Philosophy of Pierce Butler* (Washington, DC, 1945) and David J. Danelski, *A Supreme Court Justice is Appointed* (New York, 1964). On Justice McReynolds, see James E. Bond, *I Dissent: The Legacy of Chief {sic} Justice James Clark McReynolds* (Fairfax, VA, 1992). There is not yet a published biography of Justice Van Devanter. See also Barry Cushman, "The Secret Lives of the Four Horsemen," *Virginia Law Review* 83 (1997), 559–646.

For general overviews of the legal and/or constitutional developments of the period, see Charles P. Curtis, Jr., *Lions Under the Throne* (Boston, 1947); Fred Rodell, *Nine Men: A Political History of the Supreme Court from 1790 to 1955* (New York, 1955); Thomas Reed Powell, *Vagaries and Varieties in Constitutional Interpretation* (New York, 1956); Bernard Schwartz, *The Supreme Court: Constitutional Revolution in Retrospect* (New York, 1957); Robert G. McCloskey, *The American Supreme Court* (Chicago, 1960); Walter F. Murphy, *Congress and the Court: A Case Study in the American Political Process* (Chicago, 1962); C. H. Pritchett, *The Roosevelt Court: A Study in Judicial Politics and Values, 1937–1947* (New York, 1963); Leo Pfeffer, *This Honorable Court: A History of the United States Supreme Court* (Boston, 1965); Alpheus Thomas Mason, *The Supreme Court from Taft to Warren* (rev. and enlarged ed., Baton Rouge, LA, 1968); William F. Swindler, *Court and Constitution in the Twentieth Century*, Vol. 2: *The New Legality, 1932–1968* (Indianapolis, IN, 1969–74); Paul L. Murphy, *The Constitution in Crisis Times, 1918–1969* (New York, 1972); Michael E. Parrish, "The Hughes Court, the Great Depression, and the Historians," *The Historian* 40 (1978), 286–308, "The Great Depression, the New Deal, and the American Legal Order," *Washington Law Review* 59 (1984), 723–50, and *The Hughes Court: Justices, Rulings, and Legacy* (2002); and Alfred H. Kelly, Winfred A. Harbison and Herman Belz, *The American Constitution: Its Origins and Development* (7th ed., New York, 1991). For contemporary accounts that had a powerful shaping influence on the interpretation of these developments, see Edward S. Corwin, *The Twilight of the Supreme Court* (New Haven, CT, 1934), *The Commerce Power Versus States Rights* (Princeton, NJ, 1936), *Court over Constitution* (Princeton, NJ, 1938), and *Constitutional Revolution, Ltd.* (Claremont, CA, 1941); Robert H. Jackson, The Struggle for Judicial Supremacy: A Study of a Crisis in American Power Politics (New York, 1941); Benjamin F. Wright, The Growth of American Constitutional Law (New York, 1942); and Carl B. Swisher, *American Constitutional Development* (Boston, 1943). For more recent accounts that continue to embrace an interpretation of these events cast in behavioralist terms, see Bruce Ackerman, *We the People*, Vol. 2: *Transformations* (Cambridge, MA, 1991); and William E. Leuchtenburg, *The Supreme Court Reborn: The Constitutional Revolution in the Age of Roosevelt* (New York, 1995). For revisionist interpretations that emphasize the importance of antecedent constitutional development, the quality and sophistication of government lawyering, and changes in Court personnel, see Peter Irons, *The New Deal Lawyers* (Princeton, NJ, 1982); Richard D. Friedman, "Switching Time and Other Thought Experiments: The Hughes Court and Constitutional Transformation," *University of Pennsylvania Law Review* 142 (1994), 1891–984; Barry Cushman, "The Hughes Court and Constitutional Consultation," *Journal of Supreme Court History* (1998), 79–111, *Rethinking the New Deal Court: The Structure of a Constitutional Revolution* (New York, 1998), and "Mr. Dooley and Mr. Gallup: Public Opinion and Constitutional Change in the 1930s," *Buffalo Law Review* 50 (2002), 7–101; and G. Edward White, *The Constitution and the New Deal* (Cambridge, MA, 2000). For a recent colloquy on these issues, see "Forum: The Debate over the Constitutional Revolution of 1937," *American Historical Review* 110 (2005), 1046–115.

Executive Authority and the Administrative State
On developments in administrative law, see James Landis, *The Administrative Process* (New Haven, CT, 1938); Robert E. Cushman, *The Independent Regulatory Commissions* (New York, 1941); Donald A. Ritchie, *James Landis*: Dean of the Regulators (Cambridge, MA, 1980); Thomas McCraw, Prophets of Regulation: Charles Francis Adams, Louis D. Brandeis, James M. Landis, Alfred E. Kahn (Cambridge, MA, 1984); Morton J. Horwitz, *The Transformation of American Law, 1870–1960: The Crisis of Legal Orthodoxy* (New York, 1992); George B. Shepherd, "Fierce Compromise: The Administrative Procedure Act Emerges from New Deal Politics," *Northwestern*

Law Review 90 (1996), 1557–683; and G. Edward White, *The Constitution and the New Deal* (Cambridge, MA, 2000). On executive reorganization, see Clinton L. Rossiter, "The Constitutional Significance of the Executive Office of the President," *American Political Science Review* 43 (1949), 1206–17; Barry D. Karl, *Executive Reorganization and Reform in the New Deal: The Genesis of Administrative Management, 1900–1939* (Cambridge, MA, 1963); Richard Polenberg, *Reorganizing Roosevelt's Government: The Controversy over Executive Reorganization, 1936–1939* (Cambridge, MA, 1966); A. J. Wann, *The President as Chief Administrator: A Study of Franklin D. Roosevelt* (Washington, DC, 1968); and Peri E. Arnold, *Making the Managerial Presidency: Comprehensive Reorganization Planning, 1905–1980* (Princeton, NJ, 1986). On regulation of the coal industry, see Ralph Baker, *The National Bituminous Coal Commission: Administration of the Bituminous Coal Act, 1937–1941* (Baltimore, 1941); Thomas C. Longin, "Coal, Congress and the Courts: The Bituminous Coal Industry and the New Deal," *West Virginia History* 35 (1974), 101–53; and James P. Johnson, *The Politics of Soft Coal: The Bituminous Industry from World War I Through the New Deal* (Urbana, IL, 1979). On the decisions and aftermaths of *Panama Refining* and *Carter Coal*, see Barry Cushman, "The Hughes Court and Constitutional Consultation," *Journal of Supreme Court History* (1998), 79–111 and *Rethinking the New Deal Court: The Structure of a Constitutional Revolution* (New York, 1998). On developments in foreign relations law, see G. Edward White, "The Transformation of the Constitutional Regime of Foreign Relations," *Virginia Law Review* 85 (1999), 1–150. On the Rules Enabling Act and the adoption of the Federal Rules of Civil Procedure, see Stephen B. Burbank, "The Rules Enabling Act of 1934," *University of Pennsylvania Law Review* 130 (1982), 1015–1197 and Stephen N. Subrin, "How Equity Conquered Common Law: The Federal Rules of Civil Procedure in Historical Perspective," *University of Pennsylvania Law Review* 135 (1987), 909–1002.

The Revolution in Due Process Jurisprudence

For studies of the relaxation of Fifth and Fourteenth Amendment constraints on economic regulation, see Virginia Wood, *Due Process of Law, 1932–1949: The Supreme Court's Use of a Constitutional Tool* (Baton Rouge, LA, 1951); Robert McCloskey, "Economic Due Process and the Supreme Court: An Exhumation and Reburial," *Supreme Court Review* (1962), 34–62; and Barry Cushman, "Lost Fidelities," *William & Mary Law Review* 41 (1999), 95–146 and "Some Varieties and Vicissitudes of Lochnerism," *Boston University Law Review* 85 (2005), 881–1000. On the controversy over the minimum wage decisions, see Felix Frankfurter, "Mr. Justice Roberts," *University of Pennsylvania Law Review* 104 (1955), 311–17; Erwin N. Griswold, "Owen J. Roberts as a Judge," *University of Pennsylvania Law Review* 104

(1955), 332–49; J. W. Chambers, "The Big Switch: Justice Roberts and the Minimum-Wage Cases," *Labor History* 10 (1969), 44–73; Merlo J. Pusey, "Justice Roberts' 1937 Turnaround," *Supreme Court Historical Society Yearbook* (1983), 102–07; Michael Ariens, "A Thrice-Told Tale, or Felix the Cat," *Harvard Law Review* 107 (1994), 620–76; and Richard D. Friedman, "A Reaffirmation: The Authenticity of the Roberts Memorandum, or Felix the Non-Forger," *University of Pennsylvania Law Review* 142 (1994) 1985–95.

On developments in contract clause jurisprudence, see Benjamin F. Wright, *The Contract Clause of the Constitution* (Cambridge, MA, 1938); Richard Maidment, "Chief Justice Hughes and the Contract Clause: A Reassessment," *Journal of Legal History* 8 (1987), 316–29; Samuel R. Olken, "Charles Evans Hughes and the *Blaisdell* Decision: A Historical Study of Contract Clause Jurisprudence," *Oregon Law Review* 72 (1993), 513–602; and James W. Ely, *The Contract Clause in American History* (New York, 1997). On the *Gold Clause Cases*, see John P. Dawson, "The Gold-Clause Decisions," *Michigan Law Review* 33 (1935), 647–84; John Dickinson, "The Gold Decisions," *University of Pennsylvania Law Review* 83 (1935), 715–25; Henry M. Hart, Jr., "The Gold Clause in United States Bonds," *Harvard Law Review* 48 (1935), 1057–99; and Gerald T. Dunne, *Monetary Decisions of the Supreme Court* (New Brunswick, NJ, 1960).

The Revolution in Federalism Jurisprudence

For developments in Commerce Clause jurisprudence, see Robert Stern, "The Commerce Clause and the National Economy, 1933–1946," *Harvard Law Review* 59 (1946), 645–93; Paul R. Benson, *The Supreme Court and the Commerce Clause, 1937–1970* (New York, 1970); and Barry Cushman, *Rethinking the New Deal Court: The Structure of a Constitutional Revolution* (New York, 1998) and "Formalism and Realism in Commerce Clause Jurisprudence," *University of Chicago Law Review* 67 (2000), 1089–150. Compare also Richard D. Friedman, "The Sometimes-Bumpy Stream of Commerce Clause Doctrine," *Arkansas Law Review* 55 (2003), 981–1008 and "Charting the Course of Commerce Clause Challenge," *Arkansas Law Review* 55 (2003), 1055–96 with Barry Cushman, "Continuity and Change in Commerce Clause Jurisprudence," *Arkansas Law Review* 55 (2003), 1009–54 and "Small Differences?," *Arkansas Law Review* 55 (2003), 1097–148. On *Erie*, see Henry J. Friendly, "In Praise of *Erie* – and of the New Federal Common Law," *New York University Law Review* 39 (1964), 383–422; Tony Freyer, *Harmony & Dissonance: The Swift & Erie Cases in American Federalism* (New York, 1981); and Edward A. Purcell, Jr., *Brandeis and the Progressive Constitution: Erie, the Judicial Power, and the Politics of Federal Courts in Twentieth Century America* (New Haven, CT, 2000). On regulatory taxation, see

R. Alton Lee, *A History of Regulatory Taxation* (Lexington, KY, 1973). On
the interpretation of the general welfare clause, see David Engdahl, "The
Spending Power," *Duke Law Journal* 44 (1994), 1–109; Theodore Sky, *To
Provide for the General Welfare: A History of the Federal Spending Power* (Newark,
DE, 2003); and Michele Landis Dauber, "The Sympathetic State," *Law and
History Review* 23 (2005), 387–442. On general developments in fiscal fed-
eralism, see V. O. Key, Jr., *The Administration of Federal Grants to States*
(Chicago, 1937); Henry J. Bitterman, *State and Federal Grants-in-Aid* (New
York, 1938); Jane Perry Clark, *The Rise of a New Federalism: Federal-State
Cooperation in the United States* (New York, 1938); and James T. Patterson,
The New Deal and the States: Federalism in Transition (Princeton, NJ, 1969).

On the Court-packing fight, see Merlo J. Pusey, *The Supreme Court Crisis*
(New York, 1937); Joseph Alsop and Turner Catledge, *The 168 Days* (Garden City, NY, 1938); Karl Lamb, "The Opposition Party as Secret Agent:
Republicans and the Court Fight, 1937," *Papers of the Michigan Academy of
Science, Arts, and Letters* 46 (1960), 539–50; Burton K. Wheeler, *Yankee from
the West: The Candid, Turbulent Life Story of the Yankee-Born U.S. Senator from
Montana* (Garden City, NY, 1962); William E. Leuchtenburg, "The Ori-
gins of Franklin D. Roosevelt's 'Court-Packing' Plan," *Supreme Court Review*
(1966), 347–400, "Franklin D. Roosevelt's Supreme Court 'Packing' Plan,"
in Harold M. Hollingsworth and William F. Holmes, eds., *Essays on the New
Deal* (Austin, TX, 1969) and "FDR's Court-Packing Plan: A Second Life, A
Second Death," *Duke Law Journal* (1985), 673–89; Leonard Baker, *Back to
Back: The Duel Between FDR and the Supreme Court* (New York, 1967); Lionel
Patenaude, "Garner, Sumners, and Connally: The Defeat of the Roosevelt
Court Bill in 1937," *Southwestern Historical Quarterly* 74 (1970), 36–51;
Gene M. Gressley, "Joseph C. O'Mahoney, FDR, and the Supreme Court,"
Pacific Historical Review 40 (1971), 183–202; William G. Ross, *A Muted
Fury: Populists, Progressives and Labor Unions Confront the Courts, 1890–1937*
(Princeton, NJ, 1994); and Barry Cushman, *Rethinking the New Deal Court:
The Structure of a Constitutional Revolution* (New York, 1998).

The Emergence of Modern Civil Rights
For overviews of legal and constitutional developments in the areas of civil
rights and civil liberties during this period, see Osmond K. Fraenkel, *The
Supreme Court and Civil Liberties: How Far Has the Court Protected the Bill
of Rights?* (New York, 1945); Harvard Sitkoff, *A New Deal for Blacks:
The Emergence of Civil Rights as a National Issue* (New York, 1978); and
Michael J. Klarman, *From Jim Crow to Civil Rights: The Supreme Court and
the Struggle for Racial Equality* (New York, 2004). For a revealing account
of the development of the famous Footnote Four of *Carolene Products*, see
Louis Lusky, "Footnote Redux: A *Carolene Products* Reminiscence," *Columbia*

Law Review 82 (1982), 1093–1110. For an explication of the precedential and theoretical foundations of Footnote Four, see Louis Lusky, "Minority Rights and the Public Interest," *Yale Law Journal* 52 (1942), 1–41. See also Alpheus Thomas Mason, "The Core of Free Government, 1938–1940: Mr. Justice Stone and 'Preferred Freedoms,'" *Yale Law Journal* 65 (1956), 597–629. On the application of various provisions of the Bill of Rights to the states, see Richard Cortner, *The Supreme Court and the Second Bill of Rights: The Fourteenth Amendment and the Nationalization of Civil Liberties* (Madison, WI, 1981). On *Brown v. Mississippi*, see Richard Cortner, *A "Scottsboro" Case in Mississippi: The Supreme Court and Brown v. Mississippi* (rev. ed., Baton Rouge, LA, 1986). On the *Scottsboro* litigation, see Dan T. Carter, *Scottsboro: A Tragedy of the American South* (Baton Rouge, LA. 1969). On the beginnings of the campaign to desegregate public education, see Daniel T. Kelleher, "The Case of Lloyd Lionel Gaines: The Demise of the Separate but Equal Doctrine," *Journal of Negro History* 56 (1971), 262–71; Genna Rae McNeil, *Groundwork: Charles Hamilton Houston and the Struggle for Civil Rights* (Philadelphia, 1983); and Mark V. Tushnet, *The NAACP's Legal Strategy Against Segregated Education, 1925–1950* (Chapel Hill, NC, 1987). On developments in First Amendment law, see Zechariah Chafee, Jr., *Free Speech in the United States* (Cambridge, MA, 1942) and G. Edward White, "The First Amendment Comes of Age: The Emergence of Free Speech in Twentieth-Century America," *Michigan Law Review* 95 (1996), 299–392. On *Herndon v. Lowry*, see Charles H. Martin, *The Angelo Herndon Case and Southern Justice* (Baton Rouge, LA, 1976). On civil liberties and the rights of organized labor, see Jerold S. Auerbach, *Labor and Liberty: The La Follette Committee and the New Deal* (Indianapolis, 1966) and Geoffrey D. Berman, "A New Deal for Free Speech: Free Speech and the Labor Movement in the 1930s," *Virginia Law Review* 80 (1994), 291–322. For detailed studies of the cases involving the civil rights and civil liberties claims of Jehovah's Witnesses, see David R. Manwaring, *Render unto Caesar: The Flag-Salute Controversy* (Chicago, 1962) and Shawn F. Peters, *Judging Jehovah's Witnesses: Religious Persecution and the Dawn of the Rights Revolution* (Lawrence, KS, 2000). On the development and activities of the Civil Rights Section of the Department of Justice, see Robert K. Carr, *Federal Protection of Civil Rights: Quest for a Sword* (Ithaca, NY, 1947); John T. Elliff, "Aspects of Federal Civil Rights Enforcement: The Justice Department and the FBI, 1939–1964," in Donald Fleming and Bernard Bailyn, eds., *Law in American History* (Boston, 1971) and *The United States Department of Justice and Individual Rights, 1937–1962* (New York, 1987); and Sidney Fine, *Frank Murphy: The Washington Years* (Ann Arbor, MI, 1984). On the peonage cases, see Pete Daniel, *The Shadow of Slavery: Peonage in the South, 1901–1969* (Urbana, IL, 1972) and Daniel A. Novak, *The Wheel of Servitude:*

Black Forced Labor After Slavery (Lexington, KY, 1978). For developments in voting rights law, see David Bixby, "The Roosevelt Court, Democratic Ideology, and Minority Rights: Another Look at *United States v. Classic,*" *Yale Law Journal* 90 (1981), 741–816 and Alexander Keyssar, *The Right to Vote: The Contested History of Democracy in the United States* (New York, 2000).

CHAPTER 9: LABOR'S WELFARE STATE

EILEEN BORIS

Interpretation of the New Deal has varied with the assessment of twentieth-century liberalism, itself subject to the political standpoint of historians themselves. Celebratory early accounts include Carl Degler, "The Third American Revolution," in *Out of Our Past: The Forces that Shaped Modern America* (1959; New York, 1970), 379–413. Liberal Arthur M. Schlesinger Jr. defends Roosevelt's expansion of government and regulation of the economy in his *Age of Roosevelt* trilogy: *The Crisis of the Old Order, The Coming of the New Deal,* and *The Politics of Upheaval* (Boston, 1956, 1958, 1960) Also writing as a participant in mid-century liberal politics, William E. Leuchtenburg provides a more critical evaluation that points to the limits of both structural economic reform and the new welfare state in *Franklin D. Roosevelt and the New Deal, 1932–1940* (New York, 1963).

New Left historians, like Barton Bernstein in "The New Deal: The Conservative Achievements of Liberal Reform," in *Towards a New Past: Dissenting Essays in American History* (New York, 1967), 263–68 are less sanguine about the consequences of the New Deal, charging that it reinforced capitalism rather than transformed the social order. For Colin Gordon, writing *New Deals: Business, Labor, and Politics in America, 1920–1935* (New York, 1994) nearly two decades later, business influence was significant, seeking to curb competition and generate market stability. In contrast, the collapse of welfare capitalism and ethnic benefit societies for Lizabeth Cohen in *Making a New Deal: Industrial Workers in Chicago, 1919–1939* (New York, 1990) opened the way for industrial workers to push for public pensions and social welfare. Jennifer Klein's *For All These Rights: Business, Labor, and the Shaping of America's Public-Private Welfare State* (Princeton, NJ, 2003) finds that both business, particularly the insurance industry and welfare capitalists, and industrial unions influenced New Deal "security," so that private and community-based benefits developed to supplement, if not substitute for, public ones. The U.S. welfare state forged in this era, then, took a mixed private-public form from the start.

Gabriel Kolko applied the concept of corporate liberalism to the New Deal in *Main Currents in Modern American History* (New York, 1976). Rejecting his terms, Theda Skocpol in "Political Response to Capitalist Crisis:

Neo-Marxist Theories of the State and the Case of the New Deal," *Politics and Society* 10 (1980), 155–201 offers a state-centered or policy-feedback approach to evaluating legislative and administrative programs. Stressing the significance of the Democratic party in the construction of a powerful state, David Plotke, *Building A Democratic Political Order: Reshaping American Liberalism in the 1930s and 1940s* (New York, 1996) shifts attention away from social movements and reformist business elites to the development of liberalism's political institutions and the interest group politics necessary to sustain them. His analysis counters those, like Frances Fox Piven and Richard Cloward in *Regulating the Poor: the Functions of Public Welfare* (New York, 1971), that view poor people's movements pushing political elites to gain relief or recognize unions.

Some overviews reconsider the New Deal in light of subsequent developments. The essays collected by Steven Fraser and Gary Gerstle in *The Rise and Fall of the New Deal Order, 1930–1980* (Princeton, NJ, 1989) reevaluate the period from the perspective of the Reagan Revolution. These essays conclude that the linkage of modern liberalism to an activist state led to ironic outcomes, and they lament alternatives, available at the time, that might have forged a more social democratic order. In *The New Deal: The Depression Years, 1933–1940* (New York, 1989), which is a generally balanced discussion of deficiencies and successes, Anthony J. Badger judges the period as "essentially a holding operation" (312), with World War II being the real engine of social change. On the other hand, David M. Kennedy considers these years as one distinct period in *Freedom from Fear: The American People in Depression and War, 1929–1945* (New York, 2001). Despite acknowledging programmatic inadequacies, Kennedy insists on the New Deal's liberal triumph, especially the bringing of "security" to workers, farmers, and others at risk.

Legal scholars emphasize the expansion of state power during the New Deal, although they disagree over its contours. Bruce Ackerman in *We the People: Foundations* and *We the People: Transformations* (Cambridge, MA, 1991, 1998) posits a living Constitution, transformed by the political will of the people in the legislative arena, a theory for which the New Deal becomes a prime example. This theory of constitution making stands apart from the internalist response to doctrinal statements and judicial philosophies put forth by Barry Cushman in *Rethinking the New Deal Court: The Structure of a Constitutional Revolution* (New York, 1998). Similarly G. Edmund White in *The Constitution and the New Deal* (Cambridge, MA, 2000) contends that the Supreme Court's 1937 upholding of the minimum wage represents the culmination of a gradual shift in standards of review that supported legislative regulation of the economy. Politics drops out of these accounts, unlike Peter Irons' *The New Deal Lawyers* (Princeton, NJ, 1982), which documents policymaking maneuvers in the executive branch as well as the judicial system. William E. Forbath, however, finds a more complicated legacy: New Dealers struggled for increased national power and against Lochnerism for the purpose of social citizenship. A "general Welfare Constitution" (166), he argues in "The New Deal Constitution in Exile," *Duke Law Journal* 51 (2001), 165–221, required a legislative and political struggle over expanding citizenship rights through collective bargaining and welfare measures.

Historians of the economic context, in which labor organized and labor law developed, stress different key components. Ellis W. Hawley interprets the NRA and subsequent economic policy in light of the battle between antitrust and planning in *The New Deal and the Problem of Monopoly* (Princeton, NJ, 1966). Stanley Vittoz in *New Deal Labor Policy and the American Industrial Economy* (Chapel Hill, NC, 1987) highlights the significance of the economic sector to explain the business response to different initiatives, finding only solid opposition in the case of the Wagner Act. He takes a middle ground between the defense of New Deal pluralism and the radical critique of its stabilization of capital. Michael Bernstein in *The Great Depression: Delayed Recovery and Economic Change in America, 1929–1939* (New York, 1987) deemphasizes specific policy initiatives to argue for long-term structural shifts in manufacturing to explain the persistence of the Depression.

Others focus on economic thought. Alan Brinkley in *The End of Reform: New Deal Liberalism in Recession and War* (New York, 1995) criticizes Keynesianism for stopping other reform innovations during the so-called Second New Deal, whereas Meg Jacobs in *Pocketbook Politics: Economic Citizenship in Twentieth-Century America* (Princeton, NJ, 2005) highlights how reformers sought economic recovery through enhanced purchasing power. This strategy meant strengthening the right to organize and to conduct collective bargaining through the Wagner Act, even though such a high-wage strategy generated tensions between different groups of workers and consumers. The politics of consumption, especially the increase in aggregate demand, stands at the center of Lizabeth Cohen's *A Consumers' Republic: The Politics of Mass Consumption in Postwar America* (New York, 2003), in which the New Deal marked the beginning of an organized consumer interest in the structuring of economic policy.

The standard narrative of the triumph of industrial workers remains Irving Bernstein, *The Turbulent Years: A History of the American Worker, 1933–1941* (Boston, 1969). For the rise of the Congress of Industrial Organizations (CIO), see also Sidney Fine, *Sit-Down: The General Motors Strike of 1936–37* (Ann Arbor, MI, 1969) and Art Preis, *Labor Giant Step: Twenty Years with the CIO* (New York, 1964). A more analytical discussion can be found in Robert H. Zieger, *The CIO, 1935–1955* (Chapel Hill, NC, 1995), a generally positive history that nonetheless laments "missed opportunities" (375) when it came to civil rights and blindness when it came to women. Zieger defends the organization against those, like Nelson Lichtenstein in *Labor's War at Home: The CIO in World War II* (New York, 1982), who locate in its growing bureaucratization and dependence on state authority a conservatizing lid on worker militancy.

Much of the scholarship on labor in the 1930s concentrates on local confrontations or specific sectors. Devra Weber in *Dark Sweat, White Gold: California Farm Workers, Cotton, and the New Deal* (Berkeley, 1994) charts the impact of the NRA and NLRB on Mexican agricultural labor. On the textile uprising of 1934, see Janet Irons, *Testing the New Deal: The General Textile Strike of 1934 in the American South* (Urbana, IL, 2000). Steve Fraser, *Labor Will Rule: Sidney Hillman and the Rise of American Labor* (New York, 1991) analyzes the garment industry and its system of collective bargaining. For transportation, see Joshua B. Freeman, *In Transit: The Transport Workers Union in New York City, 1933–1966* (New York, 1989). Melvyn Dubofsky and Warren Van Tine discuss mining in *John L. Lewis: A Biography* (New York, 1977).

Whether workers were even particularly militant during the 1930s has generated conflicting interpretations. Dubofsky's "Not So 'Turbulent Years': A New Look at the 1930s," in Charles Stephenson and Robert Asher, eds., *Life and Labor: Dimensions of American Working Class History* (Albany, NY, 1986), 205–23 argues that most did not partake of strike actions. He characterizes CIO leadership as often conservative. In contrast, Bruce Nelson, *Workers on the Waterfront: Seaman, Longshoremen, and Unionism in the 1930s* (Urbana, IL, 1988) stresses the flowering of radical class consciousness. In charting French Canadian organizing in *Working-Class Americanism: The Politics of Labor in a Textile City, 1914–1960* (Princeton, NJ, 2002), Gary Gerstle complicates this debate by introducing the saliency of ethnicity for class consciousness. He finds that socialists forged a strong union through ethnic notions of communalism, but that such radicalism fell prey to a new pluralist understanding of "Americanism." This in turn led to a less "anti-capitalist" stance. In contrast, Cohen in *Making a New Deal* finds earlier ethnic identities subsumed by a class identity forged in the process of organizing the CIO. Elizabeth Faue critiques the very terms of this debate by interrogating the gender ideology that shaped organizational forms in *Community of Suffering and Struggle: Women, Men, and the Labor Movement in Minneapolis, 1915–1945* (Chapel Hill, NC, 1991). By separating wage work from family labor, shop-floor unionization from neighborhood organization, Faue claims that national, highly centralized, and male-dominated labor federations vitiated an earlier community unionism, stymieing its militancy. Rather than the labor law or the World War II no-strike pledge then, Faue locates bureaucratization in the organizational separation of home from work. Conservative union leadership takes on a new meaning.

The centrality of the law for these trends has gained attention from labor historians as well as legal scholars. James A. Gross chronicles the NLRB in his two- volume account, *The Making of the National Labor Relations Board* (Albany, NY, 1974) and *The Reshaping of the National Labor Relations Board* (Albany, NY, 1981). Melvyn Dubofsky in *The State and Labor in Modern America* (Chapel Hill, NC, 1994) counters New Left and critical legal interpretations by arguing for the positive role of state agencies and labor law. His is the standard story with a more sophisticated understanding of the role of the state in advancing unionization. Written from the perspective of Trotskyist rank-and-file dissenters during World War II, Lichtenstein's *Labor's War at Home* judged the codification of an industrial relations regime through state boards and agencies as impeding the development of democratic and powerful trade unions. In *The State and the Unions: Labor Relations, Law, and the Organized Labor Movement in America, 1880–1960* (New York, 1985), Christopher L. Tomlins eschews a capitalist conspiracy to emphasize, much like the state-centered school of political sociologists, the relative autonomy of state actors whose legal instruments ensnarled unions in a set of rules that restricted their freedom of action. In defending AFL voluntarism, Tomlins convincingly portrays the Wagner Act and subsequent state regulation of collective bargaining as first favoring the CIO over the AFL and then channeling both into a maze of disciplining precedents, producing a "counterfeit liberty" (326).

Ruth O'Brien's *Workers' Paradox: the Republican Origins of New Deal Labor Policy* (Chapel Hill, NC, 1998) pushes back the development of "responsible unionism" that Tomlins finds within the doctrines of the National Labor Relations Board and Lichtenstein within the National War Labor Board to earlier administrative bodies and legal decisions, especially those regarding the railroads. Karen Orren in *Belated Feudalism: Labor, the Law, and Liberal Development in the United States* (New York, 1991) discovers that, in sustaining the Wagner Act, the Supreme Court broke with earlier master-servant doctrines, present in the same cases involving the railroads that O'Brien cites, and thus opened the way for a new liberal order in industrial relations.

Critical legal scholars especially have questioned the shaping of unions under the New Deal system. Karl E. Klare, in "Judicial Deradicalization of the Wagner Act and the Origins of Modern Legal Consciousness, 1937–1941," *Minnesota Law Review* 65 (1978), 265–339, labeled the Wagner Act the nation's most radical" (265) legislation, a response to the strike wave of 1934. But Klare concluded that subsequent Court interpretation disciplined such insurgency; through promoting economic rationalization through labor's own self-policing, the NLRB strengthened liberal capitalism. For Katherine Van Wezel Stone, in "The Post-War Paradigm in American Labor Law," *Yale Law Journal* 90 (1981), 1509–80, collective bargaining codified inequalities at work. In forging this system, a group of labor arbitrators relied on the philosophy of industrial pluralism. Thus, the outcome could have varied, a conclusion that David Brody disputes in "Workplace Contractualism: A Historical/Comparative Analysis," in Nelson Lichtenstein and Howell John Harris, eds., *Industrial Democracy in America: The Ambiguous Promise* (New York, 1992), 176–205. Brody argues that the structures of mass production, rather than any pluralist philosophy, generated the turn to workplace rules.

James B. Atleson's *Values and Assumptions in American Labor Law* (Amherst, MA, 1983), on the other hand, emphasizes belief systems. Judicial interpretation, he claims, depended on assumptions about economic life – the need to maintain production, the irresponsibility of employees, the duty of worker loyalty to employers, the sanctity of business ownership as a form of property, and the upholding of a right to manage industrial democracy. However, Atleson considers the NLRB a break with the previous industrial relations regime because of its attempt to balance the relative power of managers and workers; it was the courts that operated from pro-business assumptions and thus negated the promise of the Wagner Act. The turning point came with the limiting of the right to strike in *NLRB v. MacKay Radio and Telegraph Co.* 304 U.S. 333 (1938).

Other scholars consider the significance of the Commerce Clause for justifying state interference in the labor contract. Vivien Hart in *Bound By Our Constitution: Women, Workers, and the Minimum Wage* (Princeton, NJ, 1994) traces how previous court decisions led reformers to the Commerce Clause. James Gray Pope in "Labor's Constitution of Freedom" *Yale Law Journal* 106 (1997), 941–1028 and "The Thirteenth Amendment Versus the Commerce Clause: Labor and the Shaping of American Constitutional Law, 1921–1957," *Columbia Law Review* 102 (2002), 1–122 emphasizes how such grounding, when it came to the Wagner Act, failed to embed in the Constitution labor's right to organize. He excavates the Thirteenth Amendment as a more promising alternative but one rejected for undermining the power of policy experts and other elites. Forbath rejects such motives, pointing to the stream of New Deal thought that sought democratic control over economic and political institutions and feared judicial curtailment of social citizenship rights.

Hart's sympathetic study of protective labor laws extends the chronology of labor standards back to the Progressive era. So does Julie Novkov in *Constituting Workers, Protecting Women: Gender, Law, and Labor in the Progressive*

Era and New Deal Years (Ann Arbor, MI, 2001). Novkov pivots analysis of *West Coast Hotel* away from previous interpretations concerning legislative authority through a gender analysis that locates this key decision in debates about women's relationship to wage labor. Indeed, she claims that "the doctrinal framework for the modern interventionist state arose through battles over female workers' proper relationships with the state" (13). Sybil Lipschultz, "Hours and Wages: The Gendering of Labor Standards in America," *Journal of Women's History* 8 (1996), 114–36 differentiates between the industrial feminism of women advocates and the male lawyers who argued their cases. Landon R. Y. Storrs also labels as feminist the quest for labor standards, in contrast to previous interpretations that called such reformers maternalists in *Civilizing Capitalism: The National Consumers' League, Women's Activism, and Labor Standards in the New Deal Era* (Chapel Hill, NC, 2000). In these studies, legislation for women workers provides the basis for gender-neutral labor standards. Other historians are less sanguine about "protective" labor laws. See particularly Alice Kessler-Harris, *A Woman's Wage: Historical Meanings and Social Consequences* (Lexington, KY, 1990) and *In Pursuit of Equity: Women, Men, and the Quest for Economic Citizenship in 20th-Century America* (New York, 2001). In her later book, Kessler-Harris shows how major New Deal legislation – including the NRA, Social Security, Wagner Act, and the FLSA – incorporated male breadwinner ideology, denying women the legal basis for economic equity through employment. Similarly, economists Deborah M. Figart, Ellen Mutari, and Marilyn Power cast wage, hour, and unemployment policy as "a living wage for breadwinners" (91) in *Living Wages, Equal Wages: Gender and Labor Market Policies in the United States* (New York, 2002).

Suzanne Mettler in *Dividing Citizens: Gender and Federalism in New Deal Public Policy* (Ithaca, NY, 1998), like Kessler-Harris in *In Pursuit of Equity*, joins together analysis of the FLSA with social assistance for the elderly, unemployed, and poor children, rather than replicating a common historiographical separation of labor standards from Social Security. She considers structures of federalism – more than gender ideology – as the significant shaper of women's citizenship. Insofar as they failed to qualify for social insurance programs either from their own employment record or those of their male kin, women – whose usual occupations stood outside of labor law – came under more arbitrary and needs-tested social assistance administered on the state level. Eileen Boris, "The Racialized Gendered State: Constructions of Citizenship in the United States," *Social Politics* 2 (1995), 160–80 emphasizes how these gendered inequalities also were racialized, whereas Margot Canady, "Building a Straight State: Sexuality and Social Citizenship Under the 1944 G.I. Bill," *Journal of American History* 90 (2003), 235–57 reveals the heterosexual bias in these policies. A number of historians stress how gendered restrictions on military service and the inequalities of a Jim Crow army produced employment disadvantage. See Linda Kerber, *No Constitutional Right to Be Ladies: Women and the Obligations of Citizenship* (New York, 1998); Cohen, *A Consumer's Republic*; and David H. Onkst, "'First a Negro... Incidentally a Veteran': Black World War Two Veterans and the G.I. Bill of Rights in the Deep South, 1944–1948," *Journal of Social History* 31 (1998), 517–44.

Mary Poole, *The Segregated Origins of Social Security: African Americans and the Welfare State* (Chapel Hill, NC, 2006) and Linda Gordon, *Pitied But Not Entitled: Single Mothers and the History of Welfare* (New York, 1994) probe the policymaking that led to exclusions by race, gender, or racialized gender in labor standards and Social Security. Gwendolyn Mink, *The Wages of Motherhood: Inequality in The Welfare State, 1917–1942* (Ithaca, NY, 1995) emphasizes that the New Deal not only federalized previous mothers' pensions and other racialized maternalist policies but "also developed paternal social politics that tied men's economic security to fair wages, unions, and social insurance" (126), creating a fully gendered welfare state. Little research on carework as labor and its relation to employment and citizenship exists outside of discussions of welfare. Joanne L. Goodwin in "'Employable Mothers' and 'Suitable Work': A Re-evaluation of Welfare and Wage-Earning for Women in the Twentieth-Century United States," *Journal of Social History* 29 (1995), 253–74 particularly traces this connection. Ellen Reese, *Backlash Against Welfare Mothers Past and Present* (Berkeley, CA, 2005) compares the New Deal origins of AFDC with later developments in welfare reform.

Although not without disagreements among themselves, especially over the relative valuing of carework over women's employment, these historians show how gaps in coverage affected racial minorities, immigrants, and poor women. Such analysis challenges scholarship on Social Security, which has celebrated its achievement without interrogating its limits, such as Edward D. Berkowitz in *America's Welfare State: From Roosevelt to Reagan* (Baltimore, 1991). Gordon, *Pitied But Not Entitled* and Kenneth M. Casebeer, "Unemployment Insurance: American Social Wage, Labor Organization and Legal Ideology," *Boston College Law Review* 35 (1994), 259–348 also chart laborite alternatives to Social Security.

Jill Quadagno stresses the racial politics underlying Social Security and views the elimination of older workers from the labor force as one of the act's chief goals in *The Transformation of Old Age Security: Class and Politics in the American Welfare State* (Chicago, 1988). Similarly, in *Race, Money, and the American Welfare State* (Ithaca, NY, 1999) Michael K. Brown shows that the restrained fiscal policy of the New Deal programs exacerbated racial inequalities within the welfare state. In "Caste, Class, and Equal

Citizenship," *Michigan Law Review* 98 (1999), 1–91, William E. Forbath traces how Dixiecrat power and the Jim Crow system gave a "half-life" (76) to the New Deal's welfare constitution. Ira Katznelson, *When Affirmative Action Was White: An Untold History of Racial Inequality in Twentieth-Century America* (New York, 2005) demonstrates white advantage from the New Deal order.

African Americans critiqued the ways that the NRA, Social Security, and other New Deal measures discriminated against them, Dona Cooper Hamilton and Charles V. Hamilton explain in *The Dual Agenda: The African-American Struggle for Civil and Economic Equality* (New York, 1997). Public choice theorist David E. Bernstein argues in *Only One Place of Redress: African Americans, Labor Regulations, and the Courts from Reconstruction to the New Deal* (Durham, NC, 2001) that the New Deal labor regime strengthened workplace discrimination by allowing racially exclusive unions to flourish and led to black unemployment. Eric Arnesen documents the struggle against white exclusion in *Brotherhoods of Color: Black Railroad Workers and the Struggle for Equality* (Cambridge, MA, 2001). In "Class, Race and Democracy in the CIO: The 'New' Labor History Meets the 'Wages of Whiteness,'" *International Review of Social History* 41 (1996), 351–74, Bruce Nelson locates such internal racism as a major factor in the weakening of the trade union movement.

Eileen Boris, "'You Wouldn't Want One of 'Em Dancing with Your Wife': Racialized Bodies on the Job in WWII," *American Quarterly* 50 (1998), 77–108 shows these processes to be profoundly gendered with calls for economic equality heard as demands for social equality. Such responses seriously curtailed the work of the President's Committee on Fair Employment Practice (FEPC). Boris considers the FEPC as an extension of the New Deal labor standards regime in "'The Right to Work Is the Right to Live!' Fair Employment and the Quest for Social Citizenship," in Manfred Berg and Martin H. Geyer, eds., *Two Cultures of Rights: The Quest for Inclusion and Participation in Modern America and Germany* (New York, 2002), 121–41. The standard history of the FEPC is Merl E. Reed, *Seedtime for the Modern Civil Rights Movement: The President's Committee on Fair Employment Practice, 1941–1946* (Baton Rouge, LA, 1991), which chronicles the origins of this agency in African American militancy and views it as a shifting point in the civil rights struggle. Paul D. Moreno contrasts "race-conscious" measures like proportional employment during the 1930s with "a color-blind, disparate-treatment definition of discrimination" (4) during the FEPC years in a critique of Title VII efforts to end "disparate-impact" discrimination in *From Direct Action to Affirmative Action: Fair Employment Law and Policy in America, 1933–1972* (Baton Rouge, LA, 1997). The most positive assessment of black gains under the FEPC is Andrew Edmund Kersten, *Race, Jobs,*

and the War: The FEPC in the Midwest, 1941–46 (Urbana, IL, 2000). For its
limited impact in the Southwest, see Cletus E. Daniel, *Chicano Workers and
the Politics of Fairness: The FEPC in the Southwest, 1941–1946* (Austin, TX,
1990).

The literature on workers, predominantly men and women of color and
white women, excluded from the labor law is growing. For agriculture,
Cindy Hahamovitch, *The Fruits of Their Labor: Atlantic Coast Farmworkers
and the Making of Migrant Poverty, 1870–1945* (Chapel Hill, NC, 1997)
charts both farm worker unionism and state policies regulating labor supply. For the South, see Pete Daniel, *Breaking the Land: the Transformation of
Cotton, Tobacco, and Rice Cultures Since 1880* (Urbana, IL, 1985) and Jacqueline Jones, *The Dispossessed: America's Underclasses from the Civil War to the
Present* (New York, 1992). Neil Foley provides a broad analysis of race in
the making of agricultural labor and New Deal policy in *The White Scourge:
Mexicans, Blacks, and Poor Whites in Texas Cotton Culture* (Berkeley, CA,
1997). Mae M. Ngai, *Impossible Subjects: Illegal Aliens and the Making of Mod-
ern America* (Princeton, NJ, 2004) provides the most contextual discussion
of the *Bracero* Program, and Cindy Hahamovitch, "'In America Life is Given
Away': Jamaican Farmworkers and the Making of Agricultural Immigra-
tion Policy," in Catherine McNicol Stock and Robert D. Johnson, eds., *The
Countryside in the Age of the Modern State: Political Histories of Rural America*
(Ithaca, NY, 2001), 134–60 analyzes the creation of temporary H visas.
These unfree forms of labor, a new indentured servitude, joined linger-
ing peonage. In "The Thirteenth Amendment and the Lost Origins of Civil
Rights," *Duke Law Journal* 50 (2001), 1609–85 and 'Won't You Please Help
Me Get My son Home': Peonage, Patronage, and Protest in the World War
II Urban South," *Law & Social Inquiry* 24 (1999), 777–806, Risa L. Goluboff
recovers how the lawyers of the Civil Rights Section of the Department of
Justice turned to prohibitions against involuntary servitude to fight peonage and forge a labor-based civil rights law. She elaborates these arguments
in *The Lost Promise of Civil Rights* (Cambridge, MA, 2007).

Among those held against their will, Goluboff finds, were domestic servants. Questions of classification are at the center of scholarship on these and
other laborers outside of the law. The best history of household work in this
period remains Phyllis Palmer, *Domesticity and Dirt: Housewives and Domestic Servants in the United States, 1920–1945* (Philadelphia, 1989). Palmer
explores the exclusion of domestic workers from New Deal labor standards in "Outside the Law: Agricultural and Domestic Workers Under
the Fair Labor Standards Act," *Journal of Policy History* 7 (1995), 416–40.
Eileen Boris, *Home to Work: Motherhood and the Politics of Industrial Homework in the United States* (New York, 1994) shows how the division between
home and work denied the employment status of paid laborers in the home
in law as well as social policy; at best such laborers became classified as

"independent contractors" and thus placed outside the labor law. For babysitters as workers, see Miriam Formanek-Brunell, "Truculent and Tractable: The Gendering of Babysitting in Postwar America," in Sherrie A. Inness, ed., *Delinquents and Debutantes: Twentieth-Century American Girls' Cultures* (New York, 1998), 61–82. Paul K. Longmore and David Goldberger, "The League of the Physically Handicapped and the Great Depression: A Case Study in the New Disability History," *Journal of American History* 87 (2000), 888–922 discuss the struggle against official definitions of the disabled as not workers. Nelson Lichtenstein in "'The Man in the Middle': A Social History of Automobile Industry Foreman," in Nelson Lichtenstein and Stephen Meyer, eds., *On the Line: Essays in the History of Auto Work* (Urbana, IL, 1989), 153–89 shows the removal of foremen from the labor law in the Taft-Hartley Act to be a response to their attempt at unionization.

Taft-Hartley has yet to find its own historian. One place to start is "Taft-Hartley Symposium: The First Fifty Years," *Catholic University Law Review* 47 (1998), 763–1001. Although Tomlins and other critics of the Wagner Act view it as less of a break with the past than did commentators at the time, Lichtenstein's contribution to this symposium, "Taft-Hartley: A Slave Labor Law?," 763–89 characterizes the act as marking the time when the possibility of expanding the New Deal order ends: "After that date . . . labor and the left were forced into an increasingly defensive posture," he argues (765). For the demise of the social democratic promise, see Lichtenstein, *State of the Union: A Century of American Labor* (Princeton, NJ, 2002) and Theda Skocpol, *Social Policy in the United States: Future Possibilities in Historical Perspective* (Princeton, NJ, 1995). Nancy MacLean, *Freedom Is Not Enough: The Opening of the American Workplace* (Cambridge, MA, 2006) finds that the black freedom movement forced an expansion of job opportunities for women and other racial/ethnic groups before there occurred a conservative backlash to affirmative action. In addition to MacLean, for another historical study of Title VII and gender, see Alice Kessler-Harris, *In Pursuit of Equity: Women, Men, and the Quest for Economic Citizenship in 20th-Century America* (New York, 2001).

CHAPTER 10: POVERTY LAW AND INCOME SUPPORT: FROM THE PROGRESSIVE ERA TO THE WAR ON WELFARE

GWENDOLYN MINK, WITH SAMANTHA ANN MAJIC
AND LEANDRA ZARNOW

Although the development of the U.S. welfare state has enjoyed copious attention from scholars, attention to the development of poverty law has been spare. A legal arena for poor people's struggles for equity in the welfare state, poverty law received initial attention primarily from its own theorists and practitioners. Over the course of the past twenty years, however, both women's historians interested in the state and legal scholars interested in intersectional inequalities have raised the profile of poverty law as a cauldron of welfare state, constitutional, and social movement history and as a terrain for important struggles against gender, race, and class stratification and inequality.

Early studies considering the two-tier welfare system were completed by legal scholars, who were themselves participants in the burgeoning field of poverty law. These included Jacobus tenBroek, who explained how welfare law distinguished between the "deserving" and "undeserving" poor in his influential article, "The Impact of Welfare Law on the Family," *Stanford Law Review* 42 (1954), 458–85, and Ed Sparer, who first articulated the legal argument that welfare recipients should be granted the basic constitutional right to subsistence in "The Role of the Welfare Client's Lawyer," *UCLA Law Review* (1965) and also defined the role of poverty lawyers in "The Right to Welfare," in Norman Dorsen, ed., *The Rights of Americans* (New York, 1971), 81.

Legal scholars have since called this style of legal advocacy "cause lawyering," rooted in the tradition of legal realism. Jerold Auerbach traces the national bar's insincere commitment to representing underprivileged clients in *Unequal Justice: Lawyers and Social Change* (New York, 1976); Austin Sarat and Stuart Scheingold evaluate contemporary examples of cause lawyering in their edited collections, *Cause Lawyering: Political Commitments and Professional Responsibilities* (New York, 1998) and *Something to Believe In: Politics, Professionalism, and Cause Lawyering* (Stanford, CA, 2004).

Martha Davis examines the origins of 1960s poverty law in *Brutal Need: Lawyers and the Welfare Rights Movement, 1960–1973* (New Haven, CT, 1993), linking its development to the tradition of legal aid societies, legal realist thought, civil rights movement litigation campaigns, and the establishment of federally funded legal services in 1965. Marc Feldman, "Political Lessons: Legal Services for the Poor," *Georgetown Law Journal* 83 (1995), 1529 and Alan W. Houseman, "Political Lessons: Legal Services for the Poor – A Commentary," *Georgetown Law Journal* 83 (1995), 1669 offer brief historical overviews of the development of poverty law, drawing different conclusions about the continued effectiveness of legal services. Ruth Buchanan considers the aspects of 1960s poverty law that remain influential and locates the welfare rights movement as a significant corollary to the Office of Economic Opportunity Legal Services program in "Context, Continuity, and Difference in Poverty Law Scholarship," *University of Miami Law Review* 48 (1994), 999.

Contemporary histories of the welfare rights movement also illuminated poverty law, primarily by articulating and examining welfare rights claims.

Such works as Nick Kotz and Mary Lynn Kotz's *A Passion for Equality: George Wiley and the Movement* (New York, 1977) highlighted the contributions of male leaders. Other studies considered local welfare rights movement strategies and success, such as struggles in New York City to improve both welfare benefits and welfare distribution; see Larry R. Jackson and William A. Johnson, *Protest by the Poor: The Welfare Rights Movement in New York City* (Toronto, 1974).

Frances Fox Piven and Richard A. Cloward have contributed a uniquely first-hand and uniquely influential account of the welfare rights movement. They first explored the movement's strategy in *Regulating the Poor: The Functions of Public Welfare* (New York, 1971), which analyzed the logic and history of public relief and assessed the significance of welfare rights struggles for improving access to welfare benefits. Their superb follow-up book, *Poor People's Movements: Why They Succeed, How They Fail* (New York, 1979), situated the welfare rights movement within a larger study of poor people's movements during the twentieth century, with the underlying purpose of determining how poor people can force concessions from the state. They argued that the National Welfare Rights Organization (NWRO), the centerpiece of the welfare rights movement of the late 1960s and early 1970s, failed in that it did not successfully exploit welfare recipients' "unrest . . . to obtain the maximum concessions possible in return for quiescence" (353). According to Piven and Cloward, it was the rebelliousness of welfare recipients that won initial concessions; NWRO's focus on lobbying over agitation led to the organization's downfall.

Although low-income mothers were affected disproportionately by welfare policy and were the rank-and-file of the welfare rights movement, most early studies of poverty law and welfare rights ignored gender, whether as an empirical or an analytic factor. Beginning in the early 1980s, treatments of the welfare rights movement took more care to explore its gender dynamics, highlighting the role of poor women in developing NWRO's agenda and organizing strategy. Guida West's comprehensive study of NWRO, *The National Welfare Rights Movement: The Social Protest of Poor Women* (New York, 1981) stands out among these first works, especially for its placement of welfare recipients as central actors in the organization. Jacqueline Pope interviewed participants in the Brooklyn Welfare Action Coalition, the largest chapter of NWRO, for her book, *Biting the Hands That Feed Them: Organizing Women on Welfare at the Grassroots Level* (New York, 1989). Pope gave voice to participants' own accounts of the inequalities they experienced as impoverished women of color. Another study that illuminated the gendered dynamics of the welfare rights movement was sociologist Susan Handley Hertz's analysis of the movement in Minnesota, *The Welfare Mothers Movement: A Decade of Change for Poor Women?* (Lanham,

MD, 1981). One of Hertz's findings was that welfare rights and feminist organizing in Minnesota did not overlap, even though both movements affected women.

Among more recent scholarship, Martha Davis's *Brutal Need* (1993) remains the most thorough consideration of the legal arm of the welfare rights movement. Following West, Pope, and Hertz, Davis gives gender visibility in her work. But although she acknowledges the movement was led by "welfare mothers," her story is nonetheless one of the primarily male lawyers who supported recipients' efforts (3). She analyzes the litigation strategy employed by NWRO to promote a constitutional "right to live," showing how poverty lawyers pushed the courts to extend welfare recipients' entitlement to benefits, privacy, and fair hearings. She foregrounds the effectiveness of movement lawyers, who were "skill[ed] at translating recipients needs into legal or quasi-legal claims," giving their demands "a grounding and legitimacy" (142).

Taken as a whole, studies from West to Davis wrote women back into histories of the welfare rights movement, connecting both to the evolution of poverty law. Felicia Kornbluh carried this work further, tightening the connection between mothers' movement claims to welfare and their legal claims to rights. Kornbluh first examined NWRO in her astute article, "To Fulfill Their 'Rightly Needs': Consumerism and the National Welfare Rights Movement," *Radical History Review* 69 (1997), 76–113, in which she showed that welfare activists employed a language of rights, claiming benefits as their "rights as citizens, mothers, consumers, and human beings." The welfare rights movement politicized consumerism, she contends, in their demand for access to credit, their claims of income discrimination, and their articulation that "poverty itself endangered constitutional standards of equal protection" (89). Her work on women's poverty, welfare, and rights culminates in her 2007 book, *The Battle over Welfare Rights* (Philadelphia, 2007).

Studies of the welfare state also have benefited from increasing scholarly attention to gender beginning in the 1980s. The earliest description of gender and welfare actually dates to the mid-1960s – Winifred Bell's seminal and influential *Aid to Dependent Children* (New York, 1965) – but it took nearly two decades for concerted work on women and the welfare state to emerge. As women's historians and interdisciplinary historical scholars rediscovered the state during the 1980s, they led a reexamination of the welfare state that exposed its racialized and gendered structure and dynamics. During the 1980s, Mimi Abramovitz riveted attention to gender in her study of the functions and impacts of welfare, *Regulating the Lives of Women: Social Welfare Policy from Colonial Times to the Present* (Boston, 1988). During the 1990s, historical scholars from various disciplines debated the gendered origins of the welfare state. Key works include the following: Theda Skocpol, *Protecting Soldiers and Mothers: The Political Origins of Social Policy in the United States* (Cambridge, MA, 1992); Linda Gordon, *Pitied but Not Entitled: Single Mothers and the History of Welfare* (1994); Joanne Goodwin, *Gender and the Politics of Welfare Reform: Mothers Pensions in Chicago, 1911–1929* (Chicago, 1997); and Gwendolyn Mink, *The Wages of Motherhood: Inequality in the Welfare State, 1917–1942* (Ithaca, NY, 1995). More recent contributions to this vast area of scholarship include Anna Igra's 2006 book, *Wives Without Husbands* (Chapel Hill, NC, 2006), which revisits connections first drawn by tenBroek among poverty, family structure, and the family law of the poor.

Some of these works also deploy new theoretical frameworks that center inquiry on how intersecting inequalities of gender, race, and class have structured welfare policy, welfare discourse, and poverty politics. More recent scholars have elaborated and deepened the framework. Anne Valk, "Mother Power": The Movement for Welfare Rights in Washington, D.C., 1966–1972," *Journal of Women's History* 11 (2000), 34–58 considers how movement participants claimed rights as mothers while policymakers and popular discourse treated the motherhood of low-income women of color as dysfunctional. In *Storming Caesars Palace: How Black Mothers Fought Their Own War on Poverty* (Boston, 2005), Annelise Orleck demonstrates the racialized, gender consciousness among welfare mothers in Las Vegas who created a "new form of welfare reform – from the bottom up" from the early 1970s to the 1990s (5). In developing a self-run day care center, health clinic, and job training office, among other community services, she argues, welfare rights activists in Las Vegas crafted a model for fighting poverty that supported rather than demeaned poor people. In *Welfare Warriors: The Welfare Rights Movement in the United States* (New York, 2005), Premilla Nadasen contends that the welfare rights movement should be viewed as an integral strand of both the feminist and Black freedom movements since women struggled for their autonomy and crafted primarily a Black feminist politics. She also asserts that too much focus has been placed on NWRO, obscuring women's essential role in the movement's leadership and rank and file as well as the daily struggles and local activism that shaped movement claims. The ideological and tactical contributions of poor women of color to the welfare rights movement have been noted by legal scholars. William Forbath, "Constitutional Welfare Rights: A History, Critique and Reconstruction," *Fordham Law Review* 69 (2001), 1821–91 refutes constitutional scholars who suggest that constitutional welfare rights rulings were ordained by the logic of the Warren Court's Fourteenth Amendment case law and concern for the poor; instead, he argues that historical and social context – factors such as welfare rights organizers' campaign to expose the gendered, racialized welfare system – compelled the Court to act.

The repeal in 1996 of the Aid to Families with Dependent Children program spawned considerable scholarship that links legal developments more closely to policy and political developments in contemporary welfare law. Numerous legal scholars, most notably Dorothy Roberts, have laid bare the range of rights that are implicated by poverty policy. These rights include the right to welfare so famously asserted by the welfare rights movement of the 1960s and 1970s, but also extend to rights commonly protected for all citizens except those who receive welfare. Contemporary poverty law scholarship examines welfare policy's intrusions into low-income women's privacy rights, reproductive and sexuality rights, and family rights. Linda McClain's "Irresponsible Reproduction," *Hastings Law Journal* (1996), Gwendolyn Mink's *Welfare's End* (1998), Tonya Brito's "Welfarization of Family Law," *Kansas Law Review* (2000), and Anna Marie Smith's "Sexual Regulation Dimension of Contemporary Welfare Law," *Michigan Journal of Gender and Law* (2002) all examine the impact of specific welfare policy provisions on the legal rights of mothers who need welfare.

CHAPTER 11: THE RIGHTS REVOLUTION IN THE TWENTIETH CENTURY

MARK TUSHNET

Eric Foner, *The Story of Freedom* (New York, 1998) provides an overview of the rhetoric and substance of rights protection through U.S. history. Focusing on the Warren Court, Lucas Scot Powe, Jr., *The Warren Court and American Politics* (Cambridge, MA, 2000) places the first half of the rights revolution in its political context.

Charles A. Lofgren, *The Plessy Case: A Legal-Historical Interpretation* (New York, 1987) describes an early test-case strategy. Daniel Ernst, *Lawyers Against Labor: From Individual Rights to Corporate Liberalism* (Champaign, IL, 1995) presents an institutional and intellectual history of business litigation against labor unions in the early years of the twentieth century.

For the early history of the NAACP, see Charles Kellogg, *NAACP* (Baltimore, 1967), and for the ACLU, see Samuel Walker, *In Defense of American Liberties: A History of the ACLU* (Carbondale, IL, 1999). Peggy Lamson, *Roger Baldwin, Founder of the American Civil Liberties Union: A Portrait* (Boston, 1976) consists largely of Baldwin's memoirs; Robert C. Cottrell, *Roger Baldwin and the American Civil Liberties Union* (New York, 2000) is a more complete biography. Mark V. Tushnet, *The NAACP's Legal Strategy Against Segregated Education, 1925–1954* (Chapel Hill, NC, 1987), describes the development of the strategic litigation model, and his *Making Civil Rights Law: Thurgood Marshall and the Supreme Court, 1936–1961* (New York, 1994) carries the story through 1961. On the NAACP's challenge to capital punishment, see Michael Meltsner, *Cruel and Unusual: The Supreme Court and Capital Punishment* (New York, 1973).

Developments in procedural law are described in Edward A. Purcell, *Brandeis and the Progressive Constitution: Erie, the Judicial Power, and the Politics of the Federal Courts in Twentieth Century America* (New Haven, CT, 2000) and in Owen M. Fiss, *The Civil Rights Injunction* (Bloomington, IN, 1978). The background of the revised class action rules is described in Harry Kalven, Jr. and Maurice Rosenfeld, "The Contemporary Function of the Class Suit," *University of Chicago Law Review* 8 (1941), 684 and Benjamin Kaplan, "Continuing Work of the Civil Committee: 1966 Amendments of the Federal Rules of Civil Procedure (I)," *Harvard Law Review* 81 (1967), 356. The classic analysis of structural litigation is Abram Chayes, "The Role of the Judge in Public Law Litigation," *Harvard Law Review* 89 (1976), 1281. The extension of Chayes's analysis to mass civil litigation is described and criticized in Linda S. Mullenix, "Mass Tort as Public Law Litigation," *Northwestern University Law Review* 88 (1992), 579. The expansion of standing and the development of new forms of administrative review are described and given a largely political account in Richard Stewart, "The Reformation of American Administrative Law," *Harvard Law Review* 88 (1975), 1669.

Martha F. Davis, *Brutal Need: Lawyers and the Welfare Rights Movement, 1960–1973* (New Haven, CT, 1993) analyzes the poverty lawyers' "impact litigation." William N. Eskridge, Jr., *Gaylaw: Challenging the Apartheid of the Closet* (Cambridge, MA, 1999) combines advocacy with a description of the development of gay rights litigation. A more journalistic account is Joyce Murdoch and Deb Price, *Courting Justice: Gay Men and Lesbians Versus the Supreme Court* (New York, 2001). For a discussion of the rise of conservative strategic litigation groups, see Richard Delgado and Jean Stefancic, *No Mercy: How Conservative Think Tanks and Foundations Changed America's Agenda* (Philadelphia, 1996). Fred P. Graham, *The Self-Inflicted Wound* (New York, 1970) is a journalist's account of the criminal procedure revolution and the law-and-order backlash.

John Hart Ely, *Democracy and Distrust: A Theory of Judicial Review* (Cambridge, MA, 1980) elaborates the "footnote four" jurisprudence. Louis Lusky, "Footnote Redux: A Carolene Produces Reminiscence," *Columbia Law Review* 82 (1982), 1093 discusses the footnote's origins. A useful critique, developing though not endorsing the public choice version of footnote four jurisprudence, is Bruce Ackerman, "Beyond Carolene Products," *Harvard Law Review* 98 (1985), 713. There are many versions of the moral reading of the Constitution, but the primary articulations are Ronald Dworkin, *Taking Rights Seriously* (Cambridge, MA, 1977), and Ronald Dworkin, *Law's Empire* (Cambridge, MA, 1986). For the litigation developing the right of privacy, see David J. Garrow, *Liberty and Sexuality: The Right to Privacy and the Making of Roe v. Wade* (New York, 1994).

Owen M. Fiss, "Groups and the Equal Protection Clause," *Philosophy & Public Affairs* 5 (1976), 107 offers an early astute critique of the individualist orientation of equal protection law. For the development of affirmative action programs, see Hugh Davis Graham, *The Civil Rights Era: Origins and Development of National Policy, 1960–1972* (New York, 1990) and John David Skrentny, *The Ironies of Affirmative Action: Politics, Culture, and Justice in America* (Chicago, 1996).

Richard Cloward and Frances Fox Piven, *Poor People's Movements: Why They Succeed, How They Fail* (New York, 1977) describes the rights strategy for organizing the poor. On Clinton's medical insurance proposals, see Theda Skocpol, *Boomerang: Health Care Reform and the Turn Against Government* (New York, 1996) and Jacob Hacker, *The Road to Nowhere: The Genesis of President Clinton's Plan for Health Security* (Princeton, NJ, 1997). For an analysis of the Americans with Disabilities Act as social provision, see Samuel R. Bagenstos, "The Americans with Disabilities Act as Risk Regulation," *Columbia Law Review* 101 (2001), 1479. A partisan view of the debate between difference and sameness feminism is Catharine A. MacKinnon, *Feminism Unmodified: Discourses on Life and Law* (Cambridge, MA, 1987). Proponents of regulation describe the hate-speech controversy in Charles R. Lawrence III, Mari J. Matsuda, Richard Delgado, and Kimberle Williams Crenshaw, *Words That Wound* (Boulder, CO, 1993). Constitutional issues relating to immigration are explored in Gerald L. Neuman, *Strangers to the Constitution: Immigrants, Borders, and Fundamental Law* (Princeton, NJ, 1996).

Diverse challenges to the rights revolution are presented in the communitarian Amitai Etzioni, *The New Golden Rule: Community and Morality in a Democratic Society* (New York, 1996); the Republican Michael J. Sandel, *Democracy's Discontent: America in Search of a Public Policy* (Cambridge, MA, 1996); and the Christian social democrat Mary Ann Glendon, *Rights Talk: The Impoverishment of Political Discourse* (New York, 1991).

CHAPTER 12: RACE AND RIGHTS

MICHAEL J. KLARMAN

General

There is a substantial literature on the capacity of courts to produce social change. For a skeptical view, see Gerald N. Rosenberg, *The Hollow Hope: Can Courts Bring About Social Change?* (Chicago, 1991). For more optimistic assessments, see Jack Greenberg, *Crusaders in the Courts: How a Dedicated Band of Lawyers Fought for the Civil Rights Revolution* (New York, 1994) and

David J. Garrow, "Hopelessly Hollow History: Revisionist Devaluing of *Brown v. Board of Education,*" *Virginia Law Review* 80 (1994), 151–60. See also Michael W. McCann, *Rights at Work: Law and Politics of Pay Equity* (Chicago, 1994).

Rosenberg's controversial book has generated numerous responses and criticisms. See, e.g., David A. Schultz, ed., *Leveraging the Law: Using the Courts to Achieve Social Change* (New York, 1998); Peter Schuck, "Public Law Litigation and Social Reform," *Yale Law Journal* 102 (1993), 1763–86; and Michael W. McCann, "Reform Litigation on Trial," *Law & Social Inquiry* 17 (1992), 715–43.

On the general topic of the impact of Court decisions, see Stephen L. Wasby, *The Impact of the United States Supreme Court: Some Perspectives* (Homewood, IL, 1970); Joel F. Handler, *Social Movements and the Legal System: A Theory of Law Reform and Social Change* (New York, 1978); and Jeffrey A. Segal and Harold J. Spaeth, *The Supreme Court and the Attitudinal Model* (New York, 1993), 333–55.

For a sampling of the literature emphasizing the dependence of Court decisions on social and political context, see Robert G. McCloskey, *The American Supreme Court* (2nd ed., revised by Sanford Levinson; Chicago, 1994) and Robert A. Dahl, "Decision-Making in a Democracy: The Supreme Court as a National Policy-Maker," *Journal of Public Law* 6 (1957), 279–95. See also Barry Friedman, "Dialogue and Judicial Review," *Michigan Law Review* 91 (1993), 577–682. My own views on that topic are developed in Michael J. Klarman, "Rethinking the Civil Rights and Civil Liberties Revolutions," *Virginia Law Review* 82 (1996), 1–67.

Most of the themes and topics in this essay are further developed in Michael J. Klarman, *From Jim Crow to Civil Rights: The Supreme Court and the Struggle for Racial Equality* (New York, 2004). For criticisms of that work, see Paul Finkelman, "Civil Rights in Historical Context: In Defense of *Brown,*" *Harvard Law Review* 118 (2005), 973–1029; David E. Bernstein and Ilya Somin, "Judicial Power and Civil Rights Reconsidered," *Yale Law Journal* 114 (2004), 591–657; and David J. Garrow, "'Happy' Birthday, *Brown v. Board of Education?* Brown's Fiftieth Anniversary and the New Critics of Supreme Court Muscularity," *Virginia Law Review* 90 (2004), 693–729.

Still indispensable on the history of civil rights litigation in the Supreme Court is Richard Kluger, *Simple Justice: The History of* Brown v. Board of Education *and Black America's Struggle for Equality* (New York, 1976). Also very important are Greenberg, *Crusaders in the Courts* and Mark V. Tushnet, *Making Civil Rights Law: Thurgood Marshall and the Supreme Court, 1936–1961* (New York, 1994).

The briefs in many of the cases discussed in this chapter are collected in Philip B. Kurland and Gerhard Casper, eds. *Landmark Briefs and Arguments of the Supreme Court of the United States* (Washington, DC, 1975). The justices' conference notes in several of the cases are reproduced in Del Dickson, ed., *The Supreme Court in Conference (1940–1985): The Private Discussions Behind Nearly 300 Supreme Court Decisions* (New York, 2001).

Interwar Period

On the Court's race rulings during the *Plessy* era, see Owen M. Fiss, *Troubled Beginnings of the Modern State, 1888–1910*, Vol. 8 of *History of the Supreme Court of the United States* (New York, 1993), Chapter XII and Charles A. Lofgren, *The* Plessy *Case: A Legal-Historical Interpretation* (New York, 1987). On the Court's race rulings during the Progressive era, see Alexander M. Bickel and Benno C. Schmidt, Jr., *The Judiciary and Responsible Government 1910–21*, Vol. 9 of *History of the Supreme Court of the United States* (New York, 1984), Chapters 18 and 19; and Colloquium, "Rethinking *Buchanan v. Warley*," *Vanderbilt Law Review* 51 (1998), 787–1002.

On the Great Migration, see James R. Grossman, *Land of Hope: Chicago, Black Southerners, and the Great Migration* (Chicago, 1989). On World War I and rising black militancy, see Theodore Hemmingway, "Prelude to Change: Black Carolinians in the War Years, 1914–20," *Journal of Negro History* 65 (1980), 212–27; William Jordan, "'The Damnable Dilemma': African-American Accommodations and Protest During World War I," *Journal of American History* 81 (1995), 1562–83; and Steven A. Reich, "Soldiers of Democracy: Black Texans and the Fight for Citizenship, 1917–1921," *Journal of American History* 82 (1996), 1478–504.

On the origins and the early years of the NAACP, see Charles Flint Kellogg, *NAACP: A History of the National Association for the Advancement of Colored People*, Vol. 1: *1909–1920* (Baltimore, 1967). For good illustrations of what the organization was up against in the South in those early years, see Dorothy Autrey, "'Can These Bones Live?': The National Association for the Advancement of Colored People in Alabama, 1918–1930," *Journal of Negro History* 82 (1997), 1–12. On the political position of blacks at the national level in the 1920s, see Richard B. Sherman, *The Republican Party and Black America: From McKinley to Hoover, 1896–1933* (Charlottesville, VA, 1973). For a wonderful discussion of tensions in the North over residential integration, which culminated in the NAACP's most important case of the 1920s, see Kevin Boyle, *Arc of Justice: A Saga of Race, Civil Rights, and Murder in the Jazz Age* (New York, 2004). On the Klan and white resistance generally, see Leonard J. Moore, *Citizen Klansmen: The Ku Klux Klan in Indiana, 1921–1928* (Chapel Hill, NC, 1991).

For vivid portrayals of daily life for blacks under Jim Crow, see, for example, John Dittmer, *Black Georgia in the Progressive Era 1900–1920* (Urbana, IL, 1977); Grace Elizabeth Hale, *Making Whiteness: The Culture of*

Segregation in the South, 1890–1940 (New York, 1998); Leon Litwack, *Trouble in Mind: Black Southerners in the Age of Jim Crow* (New York, 1998); Neil R. McMillen, *Dark Journey: Black Mississippians in the Age of Jim Crow* (Urbana, IL, 1989); and George C. Wright, *Life Behind a Veil: Blacks in Louisville, Kentucky 1865–1920* (Baton Rouge, LA, 1990). For more contemporaneous accounts, see, for example, John Dollard, *Caste and Class in a Southern Town* (New Haven, 1937); Bertram Wilbur Doyle, *The Etiquette of Race Relations in the South: A Study in Social Control* (Chicago, 1937); Gunnar Myrdal, *An American Dilemma: The Negro Problem and Modern Democracy*, 2 vols. (New York, 1944); and Hortense Powdermaker, *After Freedom: A Cultural Study in the Deep South* (New York, 1939).

On blacks and the New Deal, see Ralph J. Bunche, *The Political Status of the Negro in the Age of FDR* (Chicago, 1973); John B. Kirby, *Black Americans in the Roosevelt Era: Liberalism and Race* (Knoxville, TN, 1980); Harvard Sitkoff, *A New Deal for Blacks: Emergence of Civil Rights as a National Issue*, Vol. 1: *The Depression Decade* (New York, 1978); Patricia Sullivan, *Days of Hope: Race and Democracy in the New Deal Era* (Chapel Hill, NC, 1996); Nancy J. Weiss, *Farewell to the Party of Lincoln: Black Politics in the Age of FDR* (Princeton, NJ, 1983); and Raymond Wolters, *Negroes and the Great Depression: The Problem of Economic Recovery* (Westport, CT, 1971). For recent revisionism on Roosevelt and race, see Kevin J. McMahon, *Reconsidering Roosevelt on Race: How the Presidency Paved the Road to* Brown (Chicago, 2004).

On competing approaches taken by black lawyers in the 1930s to the pursuit of social change, see Kenneth W. Mack, "Rethinking Civil Rights Lawyering and Politics in the Era Before *Brown*," *Yale Law Journal* 115 (2005), 256–354; Kenneth W. Mack, "Law and Mass Politics in the Making of the Civil Rights Lawyer, 1931–1941," *Journal of American History* 93 (2006), 37–62; and Charles H. Thompson, "Court Action the Only Reasonable Alternative to Remedy Immediate Abuses of the Negro Separate School," 419–34, in Yearbook (symposium): "The Courts and the Negro Separate School," *Journal of Negro Education* 4 (1935), 289–455. See also Beth Tomkins Bates, "A New Crowd Challenges the Agenda of the Old Guard in the NAACP, 1933–1941," *American Historical Review* 102 (1997), 340–77.

On the early criminal procedure cases, see Dan T. Carter, *Scottsboro: A Tragedy of the American South* (Baton Rouge, LA, 1979); Richard C. Cortner, *A "Scottsboro" Case in Mississippi: The Supreme Court and* Brown v. Mississippi (Jackson, MS, 1986 and *A Mob Intent on Death: The NAACP and the Arkansas Riot Cases* (Middletown, CT, 1988); and James Goodman, *Stories of Scottsboro* (New York, 1994). See also Leonard Dinnerstein, *The Leo Frank Case* (New York, 1968). Also helpful on lynch law are Anne S. Emanuel, "Lynching and the Law in Georgia, circa 1931: A Chapter in the Legal Career of Judge Elbert Tuttle," *William & Mary Bill of Rights Journal* 5 (1996), 215–48 and George C. Wright, "By the Book: The Legal Executions of Kentucky Blacks," in W. Fitzhugh Brundage, ed., *Under Sentence of Death: Lynching in the South* (Chapel Hill, NC, 1997), 250–70. See also Michael J. Klarman, "The Racial Origins of Modern Criminal Procedure," *Michigan Law Review* 99 (2000), 48–97.

On the white-primary cases, see Darlene Clark Hine, *Black Victory: The Rise and Fall of the White Primary in Texas* (Millwood, NY, 1979); Alan Robert Burch, "The NAACP Before and After *Grovey v. Townsend*" (master's thesis, University of Virginia, 1994); and Michael J. Klarman, "The White Primary Cases: A Case Study in the Consequences of Supreme Court Decisionmaking," *Florida State University Law Review* 29 (2001), 55–107.

There has been a great deal of recent scholarship on the phenomenon of lynching. Among others, see Brundage, *Under Sentence of Death* and *Lynching in the New South: Georgia and Virginia, 1880–1930* (Urbana, IL, 1993); and George C. Wright, *Racial Violence in Kentucky, 1865–1940: Lynchings, Mob Rule and "Legal Lynchings"* (Baton Rouge, LA, 1990). See also Arthur Raper, *The Tragedy of Lynching* (Chapel Hill, NC, 1933).

On the Mississippi Chinese and *Gong Lum*, see James W. Loewen, *Mississippi Chinese: Between Black and White* (Cambridge, MA, 1971) and Jeannie Rhee, "In Black and White: Chinese in the Mississippi Delta," *Journal of Supreme Court History* (1994), 117–32. On Northern school segregation during this era, see Davison M. Douglas, *Jim Crow Moves North: The Battle over Northern School Segregation, 1865–1954* (New York, 2005).

On *Gaines* and the NAACP's litigation strategy generally, see Mark V. Tushnet, *The NAACP's Legal Strategy Against Segregated Education, 1925–1950* (Chapel Hill, NC, 1987). See also Kevin M. Kruse, "Personal Rights, Public Wrongs: The *Gaines* Case and the Beginning of the End of Segregation," *Journal of Supreme Court History* (1997), 113–30. On the principal architect of that NAACP litigation strategy, see Genna Rae McNeil, *Groundwork: Charles Hamilton Houston and the Struggle for Civil Rights* (Philadelphia, 1983). Most of the cases of this era are usefully discussed in Bernard H. Nelson, *The Fourteenth Amendment and the Negro Since 1920* (Washington, DC, 1946).

World War II and Its Aftermath
On World War II and race generally, see Richard M. Dalfiume, *Desegregation of the U.S. Armed Forces: Fighting on Two Fronts, 1939–53* (Columbia, MO, 1969); Herbert Garfinkle, *When Negroes March: The March on Washington Movement in the Organizational Politics for FEPC* (Glencoe, IL, 1959); Phillip McGuire, *Taps for a Jim Crow Army: Letters from Black Soldiers in World War II*

(Santa Barbara, CA, 1983); Merl Reed, *Seedtime of the Modern Civil Rights Movement: The President's Committee on Fair Employment Practice, 1941–1946* (Baton Rouge, LA, 1991); and Neil A. Wynn, *The Afro-American and the Second World War* (New York, 1976). See also Jennifer E. Brooks, *Defining the Peace: World War II Veterans, Race, and the Remaking of Southern Political Tradition* (Chapel Hill, NC, 2004).

For the thesis that racial advance occurs only during war, see Philip A. Klinkner and Rogers M. Smith, *The Unsteady March: The Rise and Decline of Racial Equality in America* (Chicago, 1999). On rising black militancy during the war, see Rayford W. Logan, ed., *What the Negro Wants* (Chapel Hill, NC, 1944; New York, 1969). See also Kenneth R. Janken, "African-American Intellectuals Confront the 'Silent South': The *What the Negro Wants* Controversy," *North Carolina Historical Review* 70 (1993), 153–79; Lee Finkle, "The Conservative Aims of Militant Rhetoric: Black Protest During World War II," *Journal of American History* 60 (1973), 692–713; Gary R. Mormino, "G. I. Joe Meets Jim Crow: Racial Violence and Reform in World War II, Florida," *Florida Historical Quarterly* 73 (1994), 23–42; and Harvard Sitkoff, "Racial Militancy and Interracial Violence in the Second World War," *Journal of American History* 58 (1971), 661–81.

On the Cold War imperative for racial change, see Mary Dudziak, *Cold War Civil Rights: Race and the Image of American Democracy* (Princeton, NJ, 2000) and Brenda Gayle Plummer, *Rising Wind: Black Americans and U.S. Foreign Affairs, 1935–1960* (Chapel Hill, NC, 1996).

On local histories of the civil rights movement that emphasize the transformative importance of World War II, see John Dittmer, *Local People: The Struggle for Civil Rights in Mississippi* (Urbana, IL, 1994); Adam Fairclough, *Race and Democracy: The Civil Rights Struggle in Louisiana, 1915–1972* (Athens, GA, 1995); Robert J. Norrell, *Reaping the Whirlwind: The Civil Rights Movement in Tuskegee* (New York, 1985); Charles M. Payne, *I've Got the Light of Freedom: The Organizing Tradition and the Mississippi Freedom Struggle* (Berkeley, CA, 1995); and J. Mills Thornton, *Dividing Lines: Municipal Politics and the Struggle for Civil Rights in Montgomery, Birmingham, and Selma* (Tuscaloosa, AL, 2002).

On the growth of Southern liberalism, see Thomas A. Krueger, *And Promises to Keep: Southern Conference for Human Welfare, 1938–1948* (Nashville, TN, 1967). On Cleo Wright's lynching and the Justice Department's response, see Dominic Capeci, *The Lynching of Cleo Wright* (Lexington, KY, 1998). On the department's civil rights division and its new emphasis on the civil rights of blacks, see Robert K. Carr, *Federal Protection of Civil Rights: Quest for a Sword* (Ithaca, NY, 1947). The report of Truman's civil rights committee remains valuable; see *To Secure These Rights: The Report of the President's Committee on Civil Rights* (New York, 1947).

On *Smith* and its consequences see Hine, *Black Victory* and Steven F. Lawson, *Black Ballots: Voting Rights in the South 1944–1969* (New York, 1976), Chapter 2. See also Fred Folsom, Jr., "Federal Elections and the White Primary," *Columbia Law Review* 43 (1943), 1026–35.

On the higher education cases see Tushnet, *NAACP's Legal Strategy*, Chapter 7 and Jonathan L. Entin, "*Sweatt v. Painter*, The End of Segregation, and the Transformation of Education Law," *Review of Litigation* 5 (1986), 3–71. See also Ada Lois Sipuel Fisher, with Danney Goble, *A Matter of Black and White: The Autobiography of Ada Lois Sipuel Fisher* (Norman, OK, 1996). On the internal deliberations in the 1950 desegregation cases, see Dennis J. Hutchinson, "Unanimity and Desegregation: Decision Making in the Supreme Court, 1948–1958," *Georgetown Law Journal* 68 (1979), 1–87.

On desegregation in transportation, see Catherine A. Barnes, *Journey from Jim Crow: The Desegregation of Southern Transit* (New York, 1983). See also Joseph R. Palmore, Note, "The Not-So-Strange Career of Interstate Jim Crow: Race, Transportation, and the Dormant Commerce Clause, 1878–1946," *Virginia Law Review* 83 (1997), 1773–817.

On *Shelley* and the restrictive covenant litigation, see Clement E. Vose, *Caucasians Only: The Supreme Court, the NAACP, and the Restrictive Covenant Cases* (Berkeley, CA, 1959). On the legal reasoning in *Shelley*, see Mark V. Tushnet, "*Shelley v. Kraemer* and Theories of Equality," *New York Law Review* 33 (1988), 383–408 and Louis Henkin, "*Shelley v. Kraemer*: Notes for a Revised Opinion," *University of Pennsylvania Law Review* 110 (1962), 473–505. On government complicity in housing segregation, see Arnold R. Hirsch, *Making the Second Ghetto: Race and Housing in Chicago, 1940–1960* (Cambridge, 1983); Kenneth T. Jackson, *Crabgrass Frontier: The Suburbanization of the United States* (New York, 1985); Douglas S. Massey and Nancy A. Denton, *American Apartheid: Segregation and the Making of the Underclass* (Cambridge, MA, 1993); and Thomas J. Sugrue, *The Origins of the Urban Crisis: Race and Inequality in Postwar Detroit* (Princeton, NJ, 1996).

On Truman and race, see William C. Berman, *The Politics of Civil Rights in the Truman Administration* (Columbus, OH, 1970) and Donald R. McCoy and Richard T. Ruetten, *Quest and Response: Minority Rights and the Truman Administration* (Lawrence, KS, 1973). See also David McCullough, *Truman* (New York, 1992). On growing black political power at the national level, see Henry Lee Moon, *Balance of Power: The Negro Vote* (Garden City, NY, 1948). See also Michael J. Klarman, "The Puzzling Resistance to Political Process Theory," *Virginia Law Review* 77 (1991), 747–832.

On the incipient white backlash in the South, see Kari Frederickson, *The Dixiecrat Revolt and the End of the Solid South, 1932–1968* (Chapel Hill, NC, 2001); Julian M. Pleasants and Augustus M. Burns III, *Frank Porter Graham and the 1950 Senate Race in North Carolina* (Chapel Hill, NC, 1990); and

Samuel Lubell, *The Future of American Politics* (New York, 1952). On the relative failure of the Dixiecrats, see Alexander Heard, *A Two-Party South?* (Chapel Hill, NC, 1952).

On the Stone and Vinson Courts generally, see C. Herman Pritchett, *The Roosevelt Court: A Study in Judicial Politics and Values 1937–1947* (New York, 1948); C. Herman Pritchett, *Civil Liberties and the Vinson Court* (Chicago, 1954); Frances Howell Rudko, *Truman's Court: A Study in Judicial Restraint* (New York, 1988); Melvin I. Urofsky, *Division and Discord: The Supreme Court Under Stone and Vinson, 1941–1953* (Columbia, SC, 1997); and William M. Wiecek, *The Birth of the Modern Constitution: The United States Supreme Court, 1941–1953* (New York, 2006).

For excellent discussions of the internal deliberations in the race cases of this era, see Tushnet, *Making Civil Rights Law*.

On changing racial practices in the South, see Charles Johnson, *Into the Mainstream: A Survey of Best Practices in Race Relations in the South* (Chapel Hill, NC, 1947) and Morton Sosna, *In Search of the Silent South: Southern Liberals and the Race Issue* (New York, 1977). See also John T. Kneebone, *Southern Liberal Journalists and the Issue of Race, 1920–1944* (Chapel Hill, NC, 1985). On the desegregation of minor league baseball in the South, see Bruce Adelson, *Brushing Back Jim Crow: The Integration of Minor-League Baseball in the American South* (Charlottesville, VA, 1999). On the desegregation of major league baseball, see Jules Tygiel, *Baseball's Great Experiment: Jackie Robinson and His Legacy* (New York, 1983) and Arnold Rampersad, *Jackie Robinson: A Biography* (New York, 1997). On expanding federal control over Southern race relations, see Bruce J. Schulman, *From Cotton Belt to Sunbelt: Federal Policy, Economic Development, and the Transformation of the South, 1938–1950* (New York, 1991).

On the impact of McCarthyism on the political left and specifically on racial reform movements, see Martha Biondi, *To Stand and Fight: The Struggle for Civil Rights in Postwar New York City* (Cambridge, MA, 2003); Gerald Horne, *Communist Front? The Civil Rights Congress, 1946–1956* (Rutherford, NJ, 1988); and Wilson Record, *Race and Radicalism: The NAACP and the Communist Party in Conflict* (Ithaca, NY, 1964).

Brown v. Board of Education
There are numerous biographies of the unusually colorful group of justices who made this ruling. Among the best are Howard Ball and Phillip J. Cooper, *Of Power and Right: Hugo Black, William O. Douglas, and America's Constitutional Revolution* (New York, 1992); Mary Frances Berry, *Stability, Security, and Continuity: Mr. Justice Burton and Decision Making in the Supreme Court 1945–1958* (Westport, CT, 1978); John D. Fassett, *New Deal Justice: The Life of Stanley Reed of Kentucky* (New York, 1994); Linda C. Gugin and

James E. St. Clair, *Sherman Minton: New Deal Senator, Cold War Justice* (Indianapolis, IN, 1997); Bruce Allen Murphy, *Wild Bill: The Legend and Life of William O. Douglas* (New York, 2003); Roger K. Newman, *Hugo Black: A Biography* (New York, 1994); Michael E. Parrish, *Felix Frankfurter and His Times: The Reform Years* (New York, 1982); Bernard Schwartz, *Super Chief: Earl Warren and His Supreme Court – A Judicial Biography* (New York, 1983); James F. Simon, *Independent Journey: The Life of William O. Douglas* (New York, 1980); James E. St. Clair and Linda C. Gugin, *Chief Justice Fred M. Vinson of Kentucky* (Lexington, KY, 2002); Melvin I. Urofsky, *Felix Frankfurter: Judicial Restraint and Individual Liberties* (Boston, 1991); and G. Edward White, *Earl Warren: A Public Life* (New York, 1982). Robert Jackson is still awaiting a decent biography. In the meantime, there are a couple of useful articles: Gregory S. Chernack, "The Clash of Two Worlds: Justice Robert H. Jackson, Institutional Pragmatism, and *Brown*," *Temple Law Review* 72 (1999), 51–109 and Dwight J. Simpson, "Robert H. Jackson and the Doctrine of Judicial Restraint," *UCLA Law Review* 3 (1956), 325–59.

On the Court's internal deliberations in *Brown*, see Kluger, *Simple Justice*; Hutchinson, "Unanimity and Desegregation"; and Mark V. Tushnet, "What Really Happened in *Brown v. Board of Education*," *Columbia Law Review* 91 (1991), 1867–1930. There are several surviving sets of conference notes from *Brown I*. See Burton conference notes, Segregation Cases, 13 Dec. 1952, Box 244, Burton Papers, Library of Congress; Clark conference notes, *Brown v. Board of Education*, Box A27, Clark Papers, Tarlton Law Library, University of Texas; Douglas conference notes, *Brown v. Board of Education* and *Bolling v. Sharpe*, 13 Dec. 1952, case file: segregation cases, Box 1150, Douglas Papers, Library of Congress; and Jackson conference notes, 12 Dec. 1952, Box 184, Jackson Papers, Library of Congress. For an especially fascinating glimpse into Jackson's thinking about *Brown*, see Jackson draft concurrence, School Segregation Cases, 15 March 1954, case file: Segregation Cases, Box 184, Jackson Papers. See also Douglas memorandum for the file, Segregation Cases, 17 May 1954, Box 1149, Douglas Papers. On the internal deliberations in *Brown II*, see Warren conference notes, *Brown II*, case file: Segregation Cases, Box 574, Warren Papers; Burton conference notes, Segregation Cases, 16 Apr. 1955, Box 244, Burton Papers; Douglas conference notes, *Brown II*, 16 Apr. 1955, case file: Segregation Cases, Box 1149, Douglas Papers; and Frankfurter conference notes, *Brown II*, 16 Apr. 1955, File 4044, Box 219, Frankfurter Papers, Library of Congress. Also useful on the connection between *Brown I* and *Brown II* is Philip Elman, "The Solicitor General's Office, Justice Frankfurter, and Civil Rights Litigation, 1946–1960: An Oral History," *Harvard Law Review* 100 (1987), 817–52. On Justice Reed's tribulations, see John D. Fassett, "Mr. Justice Reed and

Brown v. Board of Education," *Yearbook of the Supreme Court Historical Society* (1986), 48–63.

On the post-*Brown* history of school desegregation, see James T. Patterson, Brown v. Board of Education: *A Civil Rights Milestone and Its Troubled Legacy* (New York, 2001) and J. Harvie Wilkinson, *From* Brown *to* Bakke: *The Supreme Court and School Integration: 1954–1978* (New York, 1979). On the support of most Northern whites for moderation in the wake of *Brown*, see Walter A. Jackson, "White Liberal Intellectuals, Civil Rights and Gradualism, 1954–60," in Brian Ward and Tony Badger, eds., *The Making of Martin Luther King and the Civil Rights Movement* (New York, 1996), 96–114.

On Little Rock, see Tony Freyer, *The Little Rock Crisis: A Constitutional Interpretation* (Westport, CT, 1984); Elizabeth Jacoway and C. Fred Williams, eds., *Understanding the Little Rock Crisis: An Exercise in Remembrance and Reconciliation* (Fayetteville, AR, 1999); John A. Kirk, *Redefining the Color Line: Black Activism in Little Rock, Arkansas, 1940–1970* (Gainesville, FL, 2002); and Special Issue, "40th Anniversary of the Little Rock School Crisis," *Arkansas Historical Quarterly* 56 (1997), 257–375. On Governor Faubus and his calculations, see Roy Reed, *Faubus: The Life and Times of an American Prodigal* (Fayetteville, AR, 1997).

On Eisenhower and race, see Stephen E. Ambrose, *Eisenhower*, Vol. 2: *The President* (New York, 1984) and Robert Fredrick Burk, *The Eisenhower Administration and Black Civil Rights* (Knoxville, TN, 1984). See also J. W. Anderson, *Eisenhower, Brownell, and the Congress: The Tangled Origins of the Civil Rights Bill of 1956–1957* (Tuscaloosa, AL, 1964). On Kennedy and race, see Carl M. Brauer, *John F. Kennedy and the Second Reconstruction* (New York, 1977) and Mark Stern, *Calculating Visions: Kennedy, Johnson, and Civil Rights* (New Brunswick, NJ, 1992).

On *Brown*'s direct impact (or lack thereof) on school desegregation, see Rosenberg, *Hollow Hope*. The *Southern School News* is vital for following post-*Brown* developments in Southern politics and school desegregation. Several books by contemporary journalists are also valuable: Benjamin Muse, *Ten Years of Prelude: The Story of Integration Since the Supreme Court's 1954 Decision* (New York, 1964); J. W. Peltason, *Fifty-Eight Lonely Men: Southern Federal Judges and School Desegregation* (New York, 1961); and Don Shoemaker, ed., *With All Deliberate Speed: Segregation-Desegregation in Southern Schools* (New York, 1957). See also Jack Bass, *Unlikely Heroes* (Tuscaloosa, AL, 1981).

On the anti-NAACP laws, see Walter Murphy, "The South Counterattacks: The Anti-NAACP Laws," *Western Political Quarterly* 12 (1959), 371–90. The ferocity of Southern white resistance to school desegregation is best captured in the Papers of the National Association for the Advancement of Colored People, microfilm collection, August Meier, ed. (Frederick, MD,

1982). Part 20 of the NAACP papers – on white resistance and reprisals – is especially useful in this regard.

On massive resistance generally, see Numan V. Bartley, *The Rise of Massive Resistance: Race and Politics in the South During the 1950s* (Baton Rouge, LA, 1969); Neil R. McMillen, *The Citizens' Council: Organized Resistance to the Second Reconstruction* (Urbana, IL, 1971); Benjamin Muse, *Virginia's Massive Resistance* (Bloomington, IN, 1961); Matthew D. Lassiter and Andrew B. Lewis, eds., *The Moderates' Dilemma: Massive Resistance to School Desegregation in Virginia* (Charlottesville, VA, 1998); Jeff Roche, *Restructured Resistance: The Sibley Commission and the Politics of Desegregation in Georgia* (Athens, GA, 1998); Bob Smith, *They Closed Their Schools: Prince Edward County, Virginia, 1951–1964* (Chapel Hill, NC, 1965); and Clive Webb, ed., *Massive Resistance Reconsidered* (New York, 2005). For the view that Southern politicians deserve much of the blame for massive resistance, see Anthony J. Badger, "The Forerunner of Our Opposition: Arkansas and the Southern Manifesto of 1956," *Arkansas Historical Quarterly* 56 (1997), 353–60 and "Southerners Who Refused to Sign the Southern Manifesto," *Historical Journal* 42 (1999), 517–34.

On *Brown*'s impact on Southern politics, see Numan V. Bartley and Hugh D. Graham, *Southern Politics and the Second Reconstruction* (Baltimore, MD, 1975) and Earl Black, *Southern Governors and Civil Rights: Racial Segregation as a Campaign Issue in the Second Reconstruction* (Cambridge, MA, 1976). See also James W. Ely, Jr., *The Crisis of Conservative Virginia: The Byrd Organization and the Politics of Massive Resistance* (Knoxville, TN, 1976); Helen L. Jacobstein, *The Segregation Factor in the Florida Democratic Gubernatorial Election of 1956* (Gainesville, FL, 1972); Robert Sherrill, *Gothic Politics in the Deep South: Stars of the New Confederacy* (New York, 1968); William C. Havard, ed., *The Changing Politics of the South* (Baton Rouge, LA, 1972); and George E. Sims, *The Little Man's Big Friend: James E. Folsom in Alabama Politics, 1946–1958* (Tuscaloosa, AL, 1985). The *Southern School News* also has extensive coverage of Southern elections in the post-*Brown* South.

On postwar and post-*Brown* violence in the South, see Michal R. Belknap, *Federal Law and Southern Order: Racial Violence and Constitutional Conflict in the Post-Brown South* (Athens, GA, 1987) and Gail O'Brien, *The Color of Law: Race, Violence and Justice in the Post-World War II South* (Chapel Hill, NC, 1999). On the most infamous postwar lynchings, see Howard Smead, *Blood Justice: The Lynching of Mack Charles Parker* (New York, 1986) and Stephen J. Whitfield, *A Death in the Delta: The Story of Emmett Till* (Baltimore, MD, 1988).

On the Montgomery bus boycott, see the valuable collection of original documents in Stewart Burns, ed., *Daybreak of Freedom: The Montgomery Bus Boycott* (Chapel Hill, NC, 1997) and the secondary accounts in David J.

Garrow, *Bearing the Cross: Martin Luther King, Jr., and the Southern Christian Leadership Conference* (New York, 1988) and Taylor Branch, *Parting the Waters: America in the King Years 1954–63* (New York, 1988). See also J. Mills Thornton, "Challenge and Response in the Montgomery Bus Boycott of 1955–1956," *Alabama Review* 33 (1980), 163–235.

On the conditions necessary for a successful civil rights movement, see Doug McAdam, *Political Process and the Development of Black Insurgency* (Chicago, 1982); Aldon D. Morris, *The Origins of the Civil Rights Movement: Black Communities Organizing for Change* (New York, 1984); Dennis Chong, *Collective Action and the Civil Rights Movement* (New York, 1991); and Donald Von Eschen, Jerome Kirk, and Maurice Pinard, "The Conditions of Direct Action in a Democratic Society," *Western Political Quarterly* 22 (1969), 309–25. See also James H. Laue, *Direct Action and Desegregation, 1960–1962: Toward a Theory of the Rationalization of Protest* (Brooklyn, NY, 1989).

There is a vast literature on the civil rights movement itself. Good places to start include Taylor Branch, *Parting the Waters*, *Pillar of Fire: America in the King Years, 1963–65* (New York, 1998), and *At Canaan's Edge: America in the King Years, 1965–68* (New York, 2006) and Garrow, *Bearing the Cross*. I have also relied heavily on the following: William H. Chafe, *Civilities and Civil Rights: Greensboro, North Carolina, and the Black Struggle for Freedom* (New York, 1980); James Farmer, *Lay Bare the Heart: An Autobiography of the Civil Rights Movement* (New York, 1985); Henry Hampton and Steve Fayer, eds., *Voices of Freedom: An Oral History of the Civil Rights Movement from the 1950s Through the 1980s* (New York, 1990); Louis E. Lomax, *The Negro Revolt* (New York, 1962); Andrew Michael Manis, *A Fire You Can't Put Out: The Civil Rights Life of Birmingham's Reverend Fred Shuttlesworth* (Tuscaloosa, AL, 1999); Manning Marable, *Race, Reform, and Rebellion: The Second Reconstruction in Black America, 1945–1990* (Jackson, MS, 1991); and Harvard Sitkoff, *The Struggle for Black Equality 1954–1992* (New York, 1993). On the sit-ins specifically, see Martin Oppenheimer, *The Sit-In Movement of 1960* (Brooklyn, NY, 1989) and Miles Wolff, *Lunch at the Five and Ten: The Greensboro Sit-Ins: A Contemporary History* (New York, 1970). On the Freedom Rides, see Raymond Arsenault, *Freedom Riders: 1961 and the Struggle for Racial Justice* (New York, 2005). Two books by Martin Luther King, Jr., remain important: *Stride Toward Freedom: The Montgomery Story* (New York, 1958) and *Why We Can't Wait* (New York, 1964). For reappraisals of the field, see the essays in Armstead L. Robinson and Patricia Sullivan, eds., *New Directions in Civil Rights Studies* (Charlottesville, VA, 1991).

On conflicts between the NAACP and the direct-action movement, see the essays by David Garrow and John Dittmer in Charles W. Eagles, ed., *The Civil Rights Movement in America* (Jackson, MS, 1986). One can also follow those conflicts as they developed in the NAACP Papers, especially

Part 21 – on the NAACP's relationship with the modern civil rights movement.

On other civil rights organizations, see, for example, Clayborne Carson, *In Struggle: SNCC and the Black Awakening of the 1960s* (Cambridge, MA, 1981); Adam Fairclough, *To Redeem the Soul of America: The Southern Christian Leadership Conference and Martin Luther King, Jr.* (Athens, GA, 1987); and August Meier and Elliot Rudwick, *CORE: A Study in the Civil Rights Movement, 1942–1968* (New York, 1973).

On the strategy of King and his lieutenants, see David J. Garrow, *Protest at Selma: Martin Luther King, Jr. and the Voting Rights Act of 1965* (New Haven, CT, 1978). On the Southern politicians who used *Brown* to their advantage, see Dan T. Carter, *The Politics of Rage: George Wallace, The Origins of the New Conservatism, and the Transformation of American Politics* (New York, 1995); Marshall Frady, *Wallace* (New York, 1968); William A. Nunnelley, *Bull Connor* (Tuscaloosa, AL, 1991); and Reed, *Orval Faubus*. See also Erle Johnston, *I Rolled with Ross: A Political Portrait* (Baton Rouge, LA, 1980).

On particular violent conflicts over school desegregation, see Liva Baker, *The Second Battle of New Orleans: The Hundred-Year Struggle to Integrate the Schools* (New York, 1996); E. Culpepper Clark, *The Schoolhouse Door: Segregation's Last Stand at the University of Alabama* (New York, 1993); William Doyle, *An American Insurrection: The Battle of Oxford, Mississippi, 1962* (New York, 2001); Morton Inger, *Politics and Reality in an American City: The New Orleans School Crisis* (New York, 1969); and Robert Pratt, *We Shall Not Be Moved: The Desegregation of the University of Georgia* (Athens, GA, 2002).

On Birmingham specifically, see Glenn T. Eskew, *But for Birmingham: The Local and National Movements in the Civil Rights Struggle* (Chapel Hill, NC, 1997) and David J. Garrow, ed., *Birmingham, Alabama, 1956–1963: The Black Struggle for Civil Rights* (Brooklyn, NY, 1989).

On Selma, see Charles E. Fager, *Selma, 1965* (New York, 1974); Garrow, *Protest at Selma*; and Stephen L. Longenecker, *Selma's Peacemaker: Ralph Smeltzer and Civil Rights Mediation* (Philadelphia, 1987).

On the 1960s civil rights legislation, see Hugh Davis Graham, *The Civil Rights Era: Origins and Development of National Policy, 1960–1972* (New York, 1990); Robert D. Loevy, ed., *The Civil Rights Act of 1964: The Passage of the Law that Ended Racial Segregation* (Albany, NY, 1997); and Charles and Barbara Whalen, *The Longest Debate: The Legislative History of the 1964 Civil Rights Act* (Cabin John, MD, 1985).

Post-Civil Rights Movement
On the Warren Court generally, see Lucas A. Powe, Jr., *The Warren Court and American Politics* (Cambridge, MA, 2000). For discussion of the Court's internal struggles over the sit-in cases, see Michael Klarman, "An Interpretative

History of Modern Equal Protection," *Michigan Law Review* 90 (1991), 213–318. On post-*Brown* desegregation developments, see Wilkinson, *From Brown to Bakke*; and Patterson, *Brown v. Board of Education*. On Goldwater and the 1964 election, see Bernard Cosman, *Five States for Goldwater: Continuity and Change in Southern Voting Patterns* (Tuscaloosa, AL, 1965). On the 1968 presidential election, see Theodore H. White, *The Making of the President, 1968* (New York, 1969).

On growing national resistance to school desegregation, see Kevin P. Phillips, *The Emerging Republican Majority* (New Rochelle, NY, 1969); Matthew D. Lassiter, *The Silent Majority: Suburban Politics in the Sunbelt South* (Princeton, NJ, 2006); and Ronald P. Formisano, *Boston Against Busing: Race, Class, and Ethnicity in the 1960s and 1970s* (Chapel Hill, NC, 1991).

On the Burger Court and race, see Paul Brest, "Race Discrimination," in Vincent Blasi, ed., *The Burger Court: The Counter-Revolution That Wasn't* (New Haven, CT, 1983). On *McCleskey*, see Stephen Carter, "When Victims Happen to Be Black," *Yale Law Journal* 97 (1988), 420–47 and Randall Kennedy, "*McCleskey v. Kemp*: Race, Capital Punishment, and the Supreme Court," *Harvard Law Review*, 110 (1988), 1388–1443. On *Armstrong*, see Richard McAdams, "Race and Selective Prosecution: Discovering the Pitfalls of *Armstrong*," *Chicago-Kent Law Review* 73, no. 2 (1998), 605–67. On the continuing influence of race on the criminal justice system today, see David Cole, *No Equal Justice: Race and Class in the American Criminal Justice System* (New York, 1999) and Randall Kennedy, *Race, Crime, and the Law* (New York, 1997).

On *Milliken*, see Eleanor Wolf, *Trial and Error: The Detroit School Desegregation Case* (Detroit, 1981). On the issue in *Washington v. Davis*, see Paul Brest, "Foreword: In Defense of the Antidiscrimination Principle," *Harvard Law Review* 90 (1976), 1–54 and Owen Fiss, "Groups and the Equal Protection Clause," *Philosophy & Public Affairs* 5 (1976), 107–177.

Lessons

For a skeptical view of the Supreme Court's contributions in the race field, see Girardeau A. Spann, *Race Against the Court: The Supreme Court and Minorities in Contemporary America* (New York, 1993).

On the conditions necessary for social reform litigation to be successful, see Charles R. Epp, *The Rights Revolution: Lawyers, Activists, and Supreme Courts in Comparative Perspective* (Chicago, 1998). See also Marc Galanter, "Why the 'Haves' Come Out Ahead: Speculations on the Limits of Legal Change," *Law & Society Review* 9 (1975), 95–160.

On the popular image of the Court as heroic defender of oppressed minorities and explanations for why this view exercises such a powerful hold on Americans' imagination, see Michael J. Klarman, "Rethinking the

Civil Rights and Civil Liberties Revolutions," *Virginia Law Review* 82 (1996), 1–67.

CHAPTER 13: HETEROSEXUALITY AS A LEGAL REGIME

MARGOT CANADAY

This essay integrates some major interpretations of sex, gender, sexuality, and law in twentieth-century America. Texts that I have drawn heavily from in constructing the overall narrative include Nancy Cott, *Public Vows: A History of Marriage and the Nation* (Cambridge, MA, 2000); Alice Kessler-Harris, *In Pursuit of Equity: Women, Men, and the Quest for Economic Citizenship in 20th-Century America* (Oxford, 2001); Linda K. Kerber, *No Constitutional Right to Be Ladies: Women and the Obligations of Citizenship* (New York, 1998); Linda Gordon, *Pitied but not Entitled: Single Mothers and the History of Welfare* (Cambridge, MA, 1994); Judith Baer, *Women in American Law: The Struggle Toward Equality from the New Deal to the Present* (New York, 1996); George Chauncey, *Why Marriage? The History Shaping Today's Debate* (New York, 2004); John D'Emilio and Estelle B. Freedman, *Intimate Matters: A History of Sexuality in America* (Chicago, 1997); John D'Emilio, *Sexual Politics, Sexual Communities: The Making of a Homosexual Minority in the United States, 1940–1970* (Chicago, 1983); David K. Johnson, *The Lavender Scare: The Cold War Persecution of Gays and Lesbians in the Federal Government* (Chicago, 2004); William N. Eskridge, Jr., *Gaylaw: Challenging the Apartheid of the Closet* (Cambridge, MA, 1999); and the Historians' Brief in *Lawrence v. Texas*.

More specifically, I am grateful to Stephen Robertson's discussion on the relationship between legal history and the history of sexuality (and his notion of the way that historians of sexuality read legal sources, as he says, "against the grain.") See Stephen Robertson, "What's Law Got to Do with It? Legal Records and Sexual Histories," *Journal of the History of Sexuality* 14 (2005), 161–85. On the potential of law as a bridge that can bring together subfields that are overly divided, see Barbara Y. Welke, "Willard Hurst and the Archipelago of American Legal Historiography," *Law and History Review* 18 (2000), 197–204. For an analysis of masculinity studies that argues that the tools of feminist history need to be re-integrated into the field (an argument that has strong parallels to the way I am characterizing the relationship between women's history and queer history) see Toby Ditz, "The New Men's History and the Peculiar Absence of Gendered Power: Remedies from Early American Gender History," *Gender and History* 16 (2004), 1–35. Gayle Rubin's call for a study of sexuality that is autonomous from feminism is articulated in "Thinking Sex: Notes for a Radical Theory of the Politics of Sexuality," in Carole Vance, ed., *Pleasure and Danger* (New York, 1984),

267–319. In that piece, Rubin explicitly distances herself from her earlier essay, "The Traffic in Women: Notes on the 'Political Economy' of Sex" in Rayna R. Reiter, ed., *Toward an Anthropology of Women* (New York, 1975), 197–210. This earlier essay argued powerfully that cultural prohibitions against homosexuality were tied to the subordination of women.

On the history of coverture, see Nancy Cott, *Public Vows*; Kerber, *No Constitutional Right*; Hendrik Hartog, *Man and Wife in America: A History* (Cambridge, MA, 2000); Michael Grossberg, *Governing the Hearth: Law and the Family in 19th-Century America* (Chapel Hill, NC, 1985); Reva Siegel, "The Modernization of Marital Status Law: Adjudicating Wives' Rights to Earnings, 1860–1930," *Georgetown Law Journal* 82 (1994), 2127–211; Norma Basch, "Marriage and Domestic Relations," Chapter 8 in Volume II of this *Cambridge History*; and the Historians' Brief in *Goodridge v. Massachusetts*. For two distinct but related essays that examine marriage by looking "outside" the institution, see Ariela Dubler, "Wifely Behavior: A Legal History of Acting Married," *Columbia Law Review* 100 (2000), 957–1021 and "In the Shadow of Marriage: Single Women and the Legal Construction of the Family and the State," *Yale Law Journal* (2003), 1641–715.

On the regulation of heterosexual deviance during the early years of the twentieth century generally see D'Emilio and Freedman, *Intimate Matters* and Mary E. Odem, *Delinquent Daughters: Protecting and Policing Adolescent Female Sexuality in the United States, 1885–1920* (Chapel Hill, NC, 1995). More specifically, Progressive era campaigns against prostitution are treated in Ruth Rosen, *The Lost Sisterhood: Prostitution in America, 1900–1918* (Baltimore, 1982). On anti-prostitution measures and provisions concerning "immoral purposes" within immigration law, see Cott, *Public Vows*; Martha Gardner, *The Qualities of a Citizen: Women, Immigration and Citizenship, 1870–1965* (Princeton, NJ, 2005); Eithne Luibhéid, *Entry Denied: Controlling Sexuality at the Border* (Minneapolis, MN, 2002); William Eskridge, *Gaylaw*; and Ariela Dubler, "Immoral Purposes: Marriage and the Genus of Illicit Sex," *Yale Law Journal* 115 (2006), 756–812. The latter also provides an interesting examination of the Mann Act. On the Mann Act, see also David J. Langum, *Crossing over the Line: Legislating Morality and the Mann Act* (Chicago, 1994). On attempts to control prostitution and venereal disease in the military during these years, see Nancy Bristow, *Making Men Moral: Social Engineering During the Great War* (New York, 1986) and Allan Brandt, *No Magic Bullet: A Social History of Venereal Disease in the United States Since 1880* (New York, 1985). On state regulation of obscenity before World War II, see Andrea Friedman, *Prurient Interests: Gender, Democracy, and Obscenity in New York City, 1909–1945* (New York, 2000). Readers interested in sexual violence (an important topic that I do not address in the text of the essay) will want to consult Stephen Robertson, *Crimes Against*

Children: Sexual Violence and Legal Culture in New York City, 1880–1960 (Chapel Hill, NC, 2005).

On the intensification of state homophobia during the 1930s and after, see D'Emilio and Freedman, *Intimate Matters* and Eskridge, *Gaylaw*. George Chauncey Jr. argues that local and state crackdowns occurred during the 1930s in *Gay New York: Gender, Urban Culture, and the Making of the Gay Male World, 1890–1940* (New York, 1994). The best treatment of sexual psychopath laws is Estelle B. Freedman, "'Uncontrolled Desires': The Response to the Sexual Psychopath, 1920–1960," *Journal of American History* 74 (1987), 83–106. See also George Chauncey Jr., "The Postwar Sex Crime Panic," in William Graebner, ed., *True Stories from the American Past* (New York, 1993), 160–178. On military policy regarding homosexuality during World War II, see Allan Bérubé, *Coming Out Under Fire: The History of Gay Men and Women in World War II* (New York, 1990) and Leisa D. Meyer, *Creating G.I. Jane: Sexuality and Power in the Women's Army Corps During World War II* (New York, 1988). For state repression during the early years of the Cold War, see especially John D'Emilio, *Sexual Politics/Sexual Communities*; David K. Johnson, *The Lavender Scare*; William Eskridge, *Gaylaw*; and the Historian's Brief in *Lawrence*. On the Johns Committee, see Stacey Braukman, "'Nothing Else Matters but Sex': Cold War Narratives of Deviance and the Search for Lesbian Teachers in Florida," *Feminist Studies* 27 (2001), 553–75. A contemporary account is Donald Webster Cory, *The Homosexual in America: A Subjective Approach* (New York, 1951). Moreover, while queer historians have mined legal sources to write local/community histories of gay life, we still lack a comprehensive understanding of local and state level policing aimed at sex/gender non-conformists. (We know a bit more about federal repression.) See "The Consenting Adult Homosexual and the Law: An Empirical Study of Enforcement and Administration in Los Angeles County," *UCLA Law Review* 13 (1966), 647–85.

On the channeling of state benefits to male breadwinners through work and marriage from the New Deal into mid-century, as well as the gender bias of Social Security, see especially Alice Kessler-Harris, *In Pursuit of Equity*; Nancy Cott, *Public Vows*; Linda Gordon, *Pitied but not Entitled*; and Linda Gordon, ed., *Women, the State, and Welfare* (Madison, WI, 1990). For the way Social Security built on the earlier gender bias of workmen's compensation, see John Fabian Witt, *The Accidental Republic: Crippled Workingmen, Destitute Widows, and the Remaking of American Law* (Cambridge, MA, 2004). On Civil War pensions and mothers' pensions see Theda Skocpol, *Protecting Soldiers and Mothers: The Political Origins of Social Policy in the United States* (Cambridge, 1995) and Sonya Michel, *Children's Interests/Mothers' Rights: The Shaping of America's Child Care Policy* (New Haven, CT, 1999). On the history of women at work in general, see Alice Kessler-Harris, *Out to Work:*

A History of Wage-Earning Women in the United States (New York, 2003) and Claudia Goldin (who also discusses differential marriage rates between European and American women), *Understanding the Gender Gap: An Economic History of American Women* (New York, 1990).

On tax policy, see Edward J. McCaffery, *Taxing Women* (Chicago, 1997); Carolyn Jones, "Split Incomes and Separate Spheres: Tax Law and Gender Roles in the 1940s," *Law and History Review* 6 (1988), 259–310; Alice Kessler-Harris, *In Pursuit of Equity*; and Lizabeth Cohen, *A Consumer's Republic: The Politics of Mass Consumption in Postwar America* (New York, 2003). For a consideration of taxation as a gendered obligation of citizenship, see Chapter 3 of Linda Kerber's, *No Constitutional Right to Be Ladies*.

On the exclusion from veterans benefits of soldiers discharged for homosexuality, see Margot Canaday, "Building a Straight State: Sexuality and Social Citizenship Under the 1944 G.I. Bill," *Journal of American History* 90 (2003), 935–57. On the relationship of race, class, and gender to the G.I. Bill more generally, see Lizabeth Cohen, *A Consumer's Republic*. (Cohen also details gender bias in access to mortgages and mortgage interest deduction.) On the deportation of aliens for homosexuality under the 1952 McCarran Walter Act, see Shannon Minter, "Sodomy and Morality Offenses Under U.S. Immigration Law: Penalizing Lesbian and Gay Identity," *Cornell International Law Journal* 26 (1993), 771–818 and Margot Canaday, "'Who Is a Homosexual?': The Consolidation of Sexual Identities in Mid-Twentieth Century American Immigration Law," *Law and Social Inquiry* 28 (2003), 351–87. The Quiroz case (involving the deportation of a Mexican lesbian) is analyzed in Eithne Luibhéid, *Entry Denied*. On the Boutilier case, see Siobhan B. Somerville, "Queer *Loving*," *GLQ* 11 (2005), 335–370 and Marc Stein, "*Boutilier* and the U.S. Supreme Court's Sexual Revolution," *Law and History Review* 23 (2005), 491–536. I have learned much from Stein's suggestion in his essay that one put together, conceptually, legal cases that would not normally be considered simultaneously by legal scholars conforming to more conventional doctrinal categories. Somerville's notion – that one look not *consecutively* for relationships between (in her case) the legal history of race and the legal history of sexual orientation but rather "*sideways* to consider how these categories were produced simultaneously" – is equally stimulating. The queer history of naturalization law is represented by a much smaller body of work (than queer immigration history), but see Siobhan B. Somerville, "Notes Toward a Queer History of Naturalization," *American Quarterly* 57 (2005), 659–75. On family reunification and mid-century immigration law, see Nancy Cott, *Public Vows*; Martha Gardner, *The Qualities of a Citizen*; and Eileen Boris, "The Racialized Gendered State: Constructions of Citizenship in the United States," *Social Politics* 2 (1995), 160–80.

On the particularly gendered nature of heterosexuality's legal regime, Michael Willrich's work on the way that welfare policy penalized men is illuminating: see Michael Willrich, "Homeslackers: Men, the State, and Welfare in Modern America," *Journal of American History* 87 (2000), 460–89. For a consideration of the way that state regulation not only targeted men but was authored and enforced by them (as an older tradition of female moral reform was supplanted by a growing state bureaucracy), see Friedman, *Prurient Interests*; Estelle B. Freedman, *Maternal Justice: Miriam Van Waters and the Female Reform Tradition* (Chicago, 1996); and Paula Baker, "The Domestication of Politics: Women and American Political Society, 1780–1920," *American Historical Review* 89 (1984), 620–47. An important companion piece to Willrich's – that emphasizes the costs that such breadwinner regulation exacted on women – is Anna R. Igra, "Likely to Become a Public Charge: Deserted Women and the Family Law of the Poor in New York City, 1910–1936," *Journal of Women's History* (2000), 59–81. An insightful analysis of the scale of postwar policing of sexual deviance is in Gayle Rubin's "Thinking Sex." See also Eskridge, *Gaylaw*.

On relative state indifference to lesbianism, see especially Alfred C. Kinsey, *Sexual Behavior in the Human Female* (Philadelphia, 1953), 484–85. See also Allan Bérubé, *Coming Out Under Fire*; David K. Johnson, *The Lavender Scare*; and Stacey Braukman, "'Nothing Else Matters but Sex.'" Regina Kunzel further argues that observers of women in prison at mid-century saw relationships among them as "essentially asexual." See Regina G. Kunzel, "Situating Sex: Prison Sexual Culture in the Mid-Twentieth Century United States," *GLQ* 8 (2002), 261. One localized but nonetheless important exception to state indifference to lesbianism was the campaign to shut down Broadway plays dealing with lesbian themes. These episodes are detailed in Friedman, *Prurient Desires*. Interestingly, Friedman also describes campaigns to shut down burlesque shows in New York in the first half of the twentieth century as driven by concerns about male disorderliness (rather than female performers).

On the racialization of the legal regime of heterosexuality, see Eileen Boris, "The Racialized Gendered State;" Alice Kessler-Harris, *In Pursuit of Equity*; Nancy Cott, *Public Vows*; Edward J. McCaffery, *Taxing Women*; and work cited above by Siobhan B. Somerville. David Onkst's treatment of African Americans under the G.I. Bill is also useful: "'First a Negro . . . Incidentally a Veteran': Black World War Two Veterans and the G. I. Bill of Rights in the Deep South, 1944–1948," *Journal of Social History* 31 (1998), 517–44. On the policing of black reproduction, see Dorothy Roberts, *Killing the Black Body: Race, Reproduction, and the Meaning of Liberty* (New York, 1997) and Joanna Schoen, *Choice and Coercion: Birth Control, Sterilization, and Abortion in Public Health and Welfare* (Chapel Hill, NC,

2005). On reproduction and law more generally, see Linda Gordon's revision of her classic work *Woman's Body/Woman's Right*, published as *The Moral Property of Women: A History of Birth Control Politics in America* (Urbana, IL, 2002); Leslie J. Reagan, *When Abortion Was A Crime: Women, Medicine, and Law in the United States 1867–1973* (Berkeley, 1997); Reva Siegel, "Reasoning from the Body: A Historical Perspective on Abortion Regulation and Questions of Equal Protection," *Stanford Law Review* 44 (1992), 261–381; and D'Emilio and Freedman, *Intimate Matters*.

On the federalism of family law, see Jill Elaine Hasday, "Federalism and the Family Reconstructed," *UCLA Law Review* 45 (1998), 1297–1400; Jill Elaine Hasday, "The Canon of Family Law," *Stanford Law Review* 57 (2004), 825–901; and Reva Siegel, "She the People: The 19th Amendment, Sex Equality, Federalism, and the Family," *Harvard Law Review* 115 (2002), 947–1046. On the relationship between miscegenation law and federalism, see Hendrik Hartog, "What Gay Marriage Teaches Us About the History of Marriage," *History News Network*, April 5, 2004, http://hnn.us/articles/4400.html; and Siobhan B. Somerville, "Queer *Loving*." On miscegenation law more generally, see Peggy Pascoe, "Miscegenation Law, Court Cases, and Ideologies of 'Race' in Twentieth-America," *Journal of American History* 83 (1996), 44–99.

On second-wave feminism's legal revolution, see Judith Baer, *Women in American Law*; Alice Kessler-Harris, *In Pursuit of Equity*; Linda K. Kerber, *No Constitutional Right to Be Treated Like Ladies*; Reva Siegel, "She the People"; and Cynthia Harrison, "Constitutional Equality for Women: Losing the Battle but Winning the War," in Sandra F. VanBurkleo, Kermit L. Hall, and Robert J. Kaczorowski, eds., *Constitutionalism in American Culture: Writing the New Constitutional History* (Lawrence, KS, 2002), 174–210.

On the perseverance of state benefits for marriage (including tax policy) in the last third of the twentieth century see David L. Chambers, "What If? The Legal Consequences of Marriage and the Legal Needs of Lesbian and Gay Male Couples," *Michigan Law Review* 95 (1996), 447–91; George Chauncey, *Why Marriage*; William Eskridge, *Gaylaw*; Nancy Cott, *Public Vows*; Edward J. McCaffery, *Taxing Women*; and Alice Kessler-Harris, *In Pursuit of Equity*. On state sanctions for homosexuality in the last third of the twentieth century, see George Chauncey, *Why Marriage*; the Historians' Brief in *Lawrence*; William Eskridge, *Gaylaw*; and Nancy Cott, *Public Vows*.

On gay marriage, see Peggy Pascoe, "Sex, Gender, and Same Sex Marriage," in Center for Advanced Feminist Studies, University of Minnesota, ed., *Is Academic Feminism Dead? Theory in Practice* (New York, 2000), 86–129; Mary Anne Case, "Marriage Licenses," *Minnesota Law Review* 89 (2005): 1758–98; George Chauncey, *Why Marriage*; Nancy Cott, *Public Vows*; Hendrik Hartog, "What Gay Marriage Teaches About the History of Marriage;" Peggy Pascoe, "Why the Ugly Rhetoric of Gay Marriage is Familiar to the Historian of Miscegenation," *History News Network*, April 19, 2004, http://hnn.us/articles/4708.html; Estelle B. Freedman, "Boston Marriage, Free Love, and Fictive Kin: Historical Alternatives to Mainstream Marriage," *OAH Newsletter* 32 (2004); and Nan D. Hunter, "The Sex Discrimination Argument in Gay Rights Cases," *Journal of Law and Policy* 9 (2001), 397–416. For an illuminating discussion of the involvement of historians in filing amicus briefs in recent abortion, sodomy, and same-sex marriage cases, see Estelle B. Freedman, "When Historical Interpretation Meets Legal Advocacy: Abortion, Sodomy, and Same-Sex Marriage," in *Feminism, Sexuality, and Politics* (Chapel Hill, NC, 2006).

I have also relied on my own research on the federal regulation of sex and gender non-conformity in immigration, military, and welfare policy in the early to mid-twentieth century United States. Primary source material throughout the essay, unless otherwise attributed, is drawn from my manuscript: Margot Canaday, *The Straight State: Sexuality and Citizenship in Twentieth Century America* (forthcoming from Princeton University Press). Finally, my ideas here have been shaped in conversation with Sandy Levitsky, Andrea Friedman, and Barbara Welke, and I am grateful for their insights.

CHAPTER 14: LAW AND THE ENVIRONMENT

BETSY MENDELSOHN

This essay does not present an exhaustive list of sources, but intends to direct the reader to good places to start exploring the insights of historians who have examined the historical relationship of law to environmental quality and management.

Information about the history of environmental law may be found primarily in legal history written about property and state power. Good starting places, therefore, are the key overviews of U.S. law, particularly Morton Horwitz, *The Transformation of American Law, 1780–1860* (Cambridge, MA, 1977) and Lawrence M. Friedman, *A History of American Law* (New York, 1986). However, so much legal action about the "commons component" of nuisance disputes among neighbors occurred in local courts, that most of the story is not integrated into secondary literature. Given the expense and logistical difficulty of appealing from county and other local courts during the pre-Civil War period, the historian should assume that there was a variety of law about nuisance that reflected local norms. It is therefore instructive to read Chapter 2 of Horwitz's *Transformation*, about eighteenth-century water law, in tandem with Gary Kulik's essay. "Dams, Fish and Farmers: Defense of Public Rights in Eighteenth-Century Rhode

Island," which is based on local records and appears in the important collection of essays edited by Steven Hahn and Jonathan Prude, *The Countryside in the Age of Capitalist Transformation* (Chapel Hill, NC, 1985), 25–50. As evidence of the local variety in the legal access of the public to rivers, this contrasting pair may be read with an important monograph that supports Horwitz's thesis for the locality of the industrialized Merrimack River: Theodore L. Steinberg, *Nature Incorporated: Industrialization and the Waters of New England* (Amherst, MA, 1991). Together, these publications reflect the essentially various and local experience of property law, as exercised over the environmental quality of the public interest in rivers. This variety must be emphasized for historians today; in our modern period the federal government has assumed responsibility for so much environmental law that the local origins of determining environmental quality have become hard to grasp.

A second resource for learning about the origins of environmental law is the law review literature. Since Lewis & Clark Law School began publishing *Environmental Law* in 1969, more than thirty law schools have begun reviews that publish occasional articles about the history of environmental law; other law schools with more general law reviews at times publish significant articles on its history. Looking for "environmental law" before 1969 is anachronistic, however, and investigating nuisance or natural resources is too broad. It therefore is helpful to look for articles about specifics – for example, fish, pollution, birds, drainage, dams, hunting, etc. – and also about general categories, such as navigable waters, police power, and municipal law. The older printed, multivolume indexes to law literature are a useful complement to the electronic databases such as *Lexis*. Related to the law review articles are the useful overviews of property law and environmental law to be found in casebooks written for law students. Of use for this chapter were Jesse Dukeminier and James E. Krier, *Property* (Boston, 1988); Frederick R. Anderson, Daniel R. Mandelker, and A. Dan Tarlock, *Environmental Protection: Law and Policy* (Boston, 1990); and Robert V. Percival et al., *Environmental Regulation: Law, Science, and Policy* (Boston, 1992). A caution about these books: their primary audience is law students, so their authors streamline the past to make their points.

For further investigation about private property land law and its relation to environmental problems, it is useful to read the elegant collections of essays by Carol M. Rose, *Property and Persuasion: Essays on the History, Theory and Rhetoric of Ownership* (Westport, CT, 1994) and Eric T. Freyfogle, *The Land We Share: Private Property and the Public Good* (New York, 2003). William Cronon, in his landmark first book about environmental history, delivered excellent insights into the exclusionary and pro-development consequences that flowed from the basic documents of property ownership and sale; see his *Changes in the Land: Indians, Colonists, and the Ecology of New England* (New York, 1983). John F. Hart, in several articles, has documented the contribution of colonial governments to the regulation of private land use; for example, see his substantial "Colonial Land Use Law and its Significance for Modern Takings Doctrine," *Harvard Law Review* 109 (1996), 1252–1300 and "Land Use Law in the Early Republic and the Early Meaning of the Takings Clause," *Northwestern University Law Review* 94 (2000), 1099–1156.

Several books could form a core library on the history of environmental law, drawn from law, history and economics. The ones useful to writing this chapter are arranged categorically below: wildlife, cities, water and wetlands, federal and state administration, and science and experts.

Wildlife

A thorough book about wildlife law was written by a lawyer with the Environmental Defense Fund, Michael J. Bean, *The Evolution of National Wildlife Law* (New York, 1977); its third edition, co-authored with Melanie J. Rowland (Westport, CT, 1997) truly is expanded. On the social origins of wildlife law in the nineteenth century, no book surpasses John F. Reiger, *American Sportsmen and the Origins of Conservation* (New York, 1975); its second edition (Corvallis, OR, 2000) likewise is truly expanded (to include fishermen, among other things). By focusing on the nineteenth century, Reiger does not fall into the trap of emphasizing only those developments that led to the modern, federal-dominated law landscape.

Since Reiger first established the importance of hunters and fishermen to creating conservation law, environmental historians have responded by examining how these laws were received in rural areas. Two books, in particular, describe hunting or conservation law as an imposition of state power on local communities: Louis Warren, *The Hunter's Game: Poachers and Conservationists in Twentieth-Century America* (New Haven, CT, 1997) and Karl Jacoby, *Crimes Against Nature: Squatters, Poachers, Thieves, and the Hidden History of American Conservation* (Berkeley, CA, 2001). For a focus on migratory animals, which energized the insertion of the federal government into existing state efforts to conserve wildlife around 1900, the key text is Kurkpatrick Dorsey, *The Dawn of Conservation Diplomacy: U.S-Canadian Wildlife Protection Treaties in the Progressive Era* (Seattle, WA, 1998). This appears in the important series of books funded by Weyerhaeuser and edited by one of the premier environmental historians, William Cronon.

A book that essentially stands alone for its analytical rigor, breadth, and depth, is Arthur F. McEvoy, *The Fisherman's Problem: Ecology and Law in the California Fisheries, 1850–1980* (Cambridge, 1986). McEvoy began with a central theory, drawn from economic theory and applied by natural resource managers to fish or timber: the calculation of "maximum sustainable yield." He then provides a history that traces the cultural, economic, and technological history of fishing and the scientific basis of knowledge about fish reproduction and wild populations. By linking knowledge, fishing practice, and state management of fisheries over a 130-year period, McEvoy generated a valuable method of environmental legal history. The most recent, comprehensive contribution to United States wildlife law is an interpretive casebook co-authored by law professors Dale D. Goble and Eric T. Freyfogle, *Wildlife Law: Cases and Materials* (Eagen, MN, 2002).

Cities
Because they have formed the environment of most U.S. residents for a century, cities are a primary focus of the history of environmental law. Here, it is useful to read about the history of municipal law, both its administration and the exercise of the police power. The key text on the role of municipal government, as a creature of the state, in regulating private activities that affect the public sphere is William J. Novak, *The People's Welfare: Law & Regulation in Nineteenth-Century America* (Chapel Hill, NC, 1996). Novak did not focus on environmental resources, but his book provides a powerful guide for environmental historians who wish to find law that was relevant to the "commons component" of private activities that were central to environmental quality. A useful complement is an in-depth study of the constitutionality of locally exercised police power, which looks not just at constitutional issues but also at the impact of constitutional changes on urban activities; see Ronald M. Labbé and Jonathan Lurie, *The Slaughterhouse Cases: Regulation, Reconstruction, and the Fourteenth Amendment* (Lawrence, KS, 2003). Focusing on cities explicitly, Jon C. Teaford describes the development of effective bureaucratic government to provide material, public services in the late nineteenth century; see his *The Unheralded Triumph: City Government in America, 1870–1900* (Baltimore, MD, 1984). A prize-winning history of urban waste practices has been published by the man who made that field, Martin V. Melosi, *The Sanitary City: Urban Infrastructure in American from Colonial Times to the Present* (Baltimore, 2000). Christine Meisner Rosen has published a significant article about nuisance trades in cities: "'Knowing' Industrial Pollution: Nuisance Law and the Power of Tradition in a Time of Rapid Economic Change, 1840–1864," *Environmental History* 8 (2003), 565–97.

Water and Wetlands
Wilderness has been used by historians to explain the cultural preoccupations of New England's colonists and has framed some questions important to the field of environmental history. Perry Miller established its allegorical

value for seventeenth- century Puritans in *Errand into the Wilderness* (Cambridge, MA, 1956). He identified themes of communitarian and personal moral trial not inconsistent with the nature preservation and nature recreation social movements reemerging in the late 1950s. As Roderick Nash noted in the introduction to the first edition of his *Wilderness and the American Mind* (New Haven, CT, 1967), many residents of the United States had come to see wilderness as emblematic of national character and its preservation as essential to retaining that character. Some publications have described the cultural values and legal doctrines that favored developed over wilderness landscapes. This pair of articles provide insight into the meaning of "waste": Nelson Van Valen, "James Fenimore Cooper and the Conservation Schism," *New York History* 62 (1981), 289–306 and Alan Taylor, "'Wasty Ways': Stories of American Settlement," *Environmental History* 3 (1998), 291–310.

Rivers occupy a special place in environmental law because navigable routes challenged assumptions that a landscape was comprised of contiguous, private land parcels. There are no significant secondary works for rivers in general, but a look at successive editions of Joseph Kinnicutt Angell's *A Treatise on the Common Law, in Relation to Navigable Waters*, which appeared in several editions beginning in 1824, shows how the law regarding public and private uses of watercourses changed in response to population growth and technological change. For wetlands, a collection of water features difficult to analyze because they have no legal category, the best guide is the award-winning book by Ann Vileisis, *Discovering the Unknown Landscape: A History of America's Wetlands* (Washington, DC, 1997), from which this chapter uses the term "commons component." A case study about the problems of surveying water features to lay down the original legal description of land by the General Land Office, may be obtained from Roger A. Winsor, "Environmental Imagery of the Wet Prairie of East Central Illinois, 1820–1920," *Journal of Historical Geography* 13 (1987), 375–97. A significant study of the legal process of drainage and landscape transformation along one river may be found in Daniel W. Schneider, "Enclosing the Floodplain: Resource Conflict on the Illinois River, 1880–1920," *Environmental History* 1 (1996), 70–96. For water law in the West, a topic not emphasized in this chapter, see Donald J. Pisani, *Water, Land, & Law in the West: The Limits of Public Policy, 1850–1920* (Lawrence, KS, 1996). Western water law, including its historical treatment, is covered extensively in law review literature.

Federal and State Administration

Federal administration of land and water surveying was established in the General Land Office, the comprehensive history of which is C. Albert White, *A History of the Rectangular Survey System* (Washington, DC, 1983). More interpretive histories by Paul W. Gates, Roy Robbins, and Vernon

Carstensen came out of the Wisconsin School in the 1960s. State administration must be understood in relation to the insights of James Scott,
*Seeing Like a State: How Certain Schemes to Improve the Human Condition Have
Failed* (New Haven, CT, 1998), although this text covers a great span of
time and culture. For the impact of the Civil War on governance and the
growth of administrative power in the states and federal government, in
general, see Richard Franklin Bensel, *Yankee Leviathan: The Origins of Central State Authority in America, 1859–1877* (Cambridge, 1990). The essential
statement on the relation of administrative government growth to the environment remains Samuel P. Hays, *Conservation and the Gospel of Efficiency: The
Progressive Conservation Movement, 1890–1920* (Cambridge, MA, 1959). A
companion case study, which dwarfs the Hays synthesis, is the incomparable
monograph by James Willard Hurst, *Law and Economic Growth: The Legal
History of the Lumber Industry in Wisconsin, 1837–1915* (Cambridge, MA,
1964). In addition to this secondary literature, it is always instructive to
consult Thomas McIntyre Cooley through the many editions of his treatise;
see *Treatise On the Constitutional Limitations Which Rest Upon the Legislative
Power of the States of the American Union* (Boston, 1868) and subsequent
editions.

Science and Experts
Science and expertise increasingly informed legal solutions to environmental problems, both in private law and in the administration of public law.
Tracing the growth of science and expertise in administrative government
is necessary to understanding how government made the transition from
using its information about natural resources to fuel economic progress to
using this information to sustain public health, or a sense of public welfare
broader than economic growth. A. Hunter Dupree, *Science in the Federal
Government: A History of Policies and Activities* (Baltimore, MD, 1986) provides the comprehensive overview. Other useful information may be found
in studies about particular environmental crises, such as hydraulic mining in California or the Dust Bowl. Case studies based on crisis events
typically trace how the public and economically interested sectors sought
legal and administrative solutions to resource scarcity or to great upsets
in property rights. A cluster of book-length examinations of agricultural
crises is particularly useful. For example, a fulsomely documented history
of the efforts of Massachusetts to confine a gypsy moth infestation may
be obtained from Robert Spears, *The Great Gypsy Moth War: A History of
the First Campaign in Massachusetts to Eradicate the Gypsy Moth, 1890–1901*
(Amherst, MA, 2005). There are many articles in *Isis, Journal of Agricultural
History, and Environmental History* that treat episodes of pest outbreak and
legal response. Two excellent articles that appeared in law reviews are Fred

P. Bosselman and A. Dan Tarlock, "The Influence of Ecological Science on American Law: An Introduction," *Chicago-Kent Law Review* 69 (1994), 847 and Fred Bosselman, "Four Land Ethics: Order, Reform, Responsibility, Opportunity." *Environmental Law* 24 (1994), 1439–1511.

CHAPTER 15: AGRICULTURE AND THE STATE, 1789–2000

VICTORIA SAKER WOESTE

Good surveys of the history of American agriculture include Murray Benedict, *Farm Policies of the U.S., 1790–1900* (New York, 1953); David Danbom, *Born in the Country: A History of Rural America* (Baltimore, 1995); and R. Douglas Hurt, *American Agriculture: A Brief History* (Ames, IA, 1994). Jonathan Hughes and Louis P. Cain, *American Economic History* (5th ed., Reading, MA, 1998) has chapters on agriculture in the colonial and post-Civil War periods. For a more recent synthesis, consult John Opie, *The Law of the Land: Two Hundred Years of American Farmland Policy* (Lincoln, NE, 1987). Wayne Rasmussen's four-volume edited collection of primary sources, including many federal statutes, is an indispensable starting place; see *Agriculture in the United States: A Documentary History* (New York, 1975).

Census and other sources of empirical data are essential to an understanding of agricultural expansion and change. In addition to published and manuscript census materials, see Donald B. Dodd, compiler, *Historical Statistics of the United States: Two Centuries of the Census, 1790–1990* (Westport, CT, 1993) and George Thomas Kurian, ed., *Datapedia of the United States, 1790–2005: America, Year by Year* (Lanham, MD, 2001).

For the colonial period, see Richard Lyman Bushman, "Farmers in Court: Orange County, North Carolina, 1750–1776," in Christopher L. Tomlins and Bruce Mann, eds., *The Many Legalities of Early America* (Chapel Hill, NC, 2001) and Brian Donahue, *The Great Meadow: Farmers and the Land in Colonial Concord* (New Haven, CT, 2004). Bruce H. Mann, *Neighbors and Strangers: Law and Community in Early Connecticut* (Chapel Hill, NC, 1987) anticipates Bushman's argument in non-agricultural contexts by examining the kinds of disputes that landowners commonly brought to court.

Many scholarly assessments of economic change between 1789 and 1865 focus on agriculture, rural life, and the commercial activities associated with farming. A good general introduction is Douglass North, *The Economic Growth of the United States, 1790–1860* (Englewood Cliffs, NJ, 1961). A more technical approach may be found in Lance E. Davis et al., *American Economic Growth: An Economist's History of the U.S.* (New York, 1972). Paul Gates' analysis of American agriculture in the first part of the nineteenth century has yet to be surpassed: *The Farmer's Age: Agriculture, 1815–1860*

(New York, 1960); he followed that book with one focusing particularly on the Civil War period, *Agriculture and the Civil War* (New York, 1965).

A spate of books chronicle the transition to market capitalism, revolving around agricultural production and commerce in the first third of the nineteenth century: Christopher Clark, *The Roots of Rural Capitalism: Western Massachusetts, 1780–1860* (Ithaca, NY, 1990); Winifred Barr Rothenberg, *From Market-Places to a Market Economy: The Transformation of Rural Massachusetts, 1750–1850* (Chicago, 1992); Charles G. Sellers, *The Market Revolution: Jacksonian America, 1815–1846* (New York, 1991); and the essays in Steven Hahn and Jonathan Prude, eds., *The Countryside in the Age of Capitalist Transformation: Essays in the Social History of Rural America* (Chapel Hill, NC, 1985).

Works of legal history bearing on themes addressed in this literature include Bruce Mann, *Republic of Debtors: Bankruptcy in the Age of American Independence* (Cambridge, MA, 2002); Morton Horwitz, *The Transformation of American Law, 1780–1860* (Cambridge, MA, 1977); and Charles W. McCurdy, *The Anti-Rent Era in New York Law and Politics, 1839–1865* (Chapel Hill, NC, 2001). For the earlier literature on the antebellum American state and regulation, see Louis Hartz, *Economic Policy and Democratic Thought: Pennsylvania, 1776–1860* (Chicago, 1968), which treats state-level political debates on transportation policy and gives particular attention to farmers' influence on legislatures; Oscar Handlin and Mary Frug Handlin, *Commonwealth: A Study of the Role of Government in the American Economy; Massachusetts, 1774–1861* (Cambridge, MA, 1969); Leonard Levy, *The Law of the Commonwealth and Chief Justice Shaw* (Cambridge, MA, 1957); J. Willard Hurst, *Law and the Conditions of Freedom in the Nineteenth-Century United States* (Madison, WI, 1956) and *Law and Economic Growth: The Legal History of the Lumber Industry in Wisconsin* (Madison, WI, 1984); and Harry N. Scheiber, "Property Law, Expropriation, and Resource Allocation by Government, 1789–1910," *Journal of Economic History* 33 (1973), 232–51. A more recent restatement of the general thesis developed in this body of work is William J. Novak, *The People's Welfare: Law and Regulation in Nineteenth-Century America* (Chapel Hill, NC, 1996).

No history of agriculture is complete without a serious consideration of its exploitation of labor. On slavery and agriculture, among many others, see Eugene D. Genovese, *Roll Jordan Roll: The World the Slaves Made* (New York, 1974); Dylan Penningroth, *The Claims of Kinfolk: African American Property and Community in the Nineteenth-Century South* (Chapel Hill, NC, 2003); and for a good historiographical overview, see Peter Kolchin, *American Slavery, 1619–1877* (reprint ed., New York, 2003). On race and migrant and tenant labor, see Sucheng Chan, *This Bittersweet Soil: The Chinese in California Agriculture, 1860–1910* (Berkeley, CA, 1986); Camille Guerin-Gonzalez,

Mexican Workers and American Dreams: Immigration, Repatriation, and California Farm Labor, 1900–1939 (New Brunswick, NJ, 1994); Vicki L. Ruiz, *Cannery Women/Cannery Lives: Mexican Women, Unionization and the California Food Processing Industry, 1930–1950* (Albuquerque, NM, 1987); and Cletus Daniel, *Bitter Harvest: A History of California Farmworkers, 1870–1941* (Ithaca, NY, 1981).

The Civil War is usually treated as a place marker, either as an endpoint or as the beginning of many books. A few historians have paid attention to the war period in its own right. In addition to Gates' *Agriculture in the Civil War*, which analyzes both Southern and Northern agriculture in addition to changes in federal policy, see Heather Cox Richardson, *The Greatest Nation of the Earth: Republican Economic Policies During the Civil War* (Cambridge, MA, 1997), which emphasizes federal regulatory expansion during wartime and its transformative effects on the market.

The period after the Civil War has attracted great interest, particularly for historians seeking to understand the scope and scale of economic change and farmers' participation in the process of industrialization. A good older survey that appeared with Gates' work in the Holt, Rinehart series on American economic history is Gilbert C. Fite, *The Farmer's Frontier, 1865–1890* (New York, 1966); the companion work is Fred Shannon, *The Farmer's Last Frontier: Agriculture, 1860–1897* (New York, 1945). Lee Benson, *Merchants, Farmers, and Railroads: Railroad Regulation and New York Politics, 1850–1887* (Cambridge, MA, 1955) spans the Civil War to analyze the policy arguments over the growth of the railroad industry. William Cronon's study of Chicago as the transportation nexus of the postbellum period, *Nature's Metropolis: Chicago and the Great West* (New York, 1991), is a masterful interdisciplinary study that owes a great deal to Fite, Benson, and Shannon. A good local study of changes in agriculture during this period is Marc Linder and Lawrence S. Zacharias, *Of Cabbages and Kings County: Agriculture and the Formation of Modern Brooklyn* (Ames, IA, 1999).

On public lands, the works of Paul Wallace Gates remain an essential touchstone; they include *History of Public Land Law Development: The Management of Public Lands in the United States, Report to the Public Lands Commission* (New York, 1968). Gates' essays, many of them exquisite studies of land policy and conflict in particular locales, may be found in *Land and Law in California: Essays on Land Policies* (Ames, IA, 1991). Also worth consulting are Benjamin Hibbard, *A History of the Public Land Policies* (Madison, WI, 1965) and Vernon Carstensen, *The Public Lands: Studies in the History of the Public Domain* (Madison, WI, 1962). A good, more recent study is Karen R. Merrill, *Public Lands and Political Meaning: Ranchers, the Government, and the Property Between Them* (Berkeley, CA, 2000).

The consequences of industrialization and the transformation of the modern regulatory state have drawn sustained attention from political scientists as well as historians. Elizabeth Sanders, *Roots of Reform: Farmers, Workers, and the American State 1877–1917* (Chicago, 1992) provides a useful analysis of the farm-labor alliance and how it dissolved by the end of the Progressive era. In *Alternative Tracks: The Constitution of American Industrial Order, 1865–1917* (Baltimore, 1994), Gerald Berk argues that local politics and political actors played significant roles in shaping law and reform during the late nineteenth and early twentieth centuries. Daniel T. Rodgers, *Atlantic Crossings: Social Politics in a Progressive Age* (Cambridge, MA, 1998) relates social and political change to industrialization in ways that illuminate the transformation of rural life. Arthur McEvoy, *The Fisherman's Problem: Ecology and Law in the California Fisheries, 1850–1980* (New York, 1986) implicates the administrative state in ecological depredation. Stephen Skowronek, *Building a New Administrative State: The Expansion of National Administrative Capacities, 1877–1920* (New York, 1982) does not treat agriculture, but is relevant for its analysis of regulatory expansion in other areas. Martin J. Sklar, *The Corporate Reconstruction of American Capitalism, 1890–1916: The Market, the Law, and Politics* (New York, 1988) is especially good on the legal and bureaucratic recognition of corporate power, combination, and monopoly during the Progressive era. The essays in Thomas K. McCraw, *Regulation in Perspective: Historical Essays* (Cambridge, MA, 1981), especially Ellis Hawley's on Hooverian associationalism and Morton Keller's on comparative regulation, remain useful. Kermit Hall treats agriculture and industrialization in his synthetic account of legal history, *The Magic Mirror: Law in American History* (New York, 1989).

On the history of farm movements, including Populism, refer to Solon Justus Buck, *The Granger Movement: A Study of Agricultural Organization and Its Political, Economic, and Social Manifestations, 1870–1880* (Cambridge, MA, 1913); Herman Steen, *Cooperative Marketing: The Golden Rule in Agriculture* (Garden City, NY, 1923); Steven Hahn, *The Roots of Southern Populism: Yeoman Farmers and the Transformation of the Georgia Upcountry, 1850–1890* (New York, 1984); and Edward L. Ayers, *The Promise of the New South: Life After Reconstruction* (New York, 1992), which revises Lawrence Goodwyn, *Democratic Promise: The Populist Moment in America* (New York, 1976), which is itself a revision of Richard Hofstadter, *The Age of Reform: From Bryan to F.D.R.* (New York, 1955). An accessible narrative focusing on the Populists' political fortunes is Robert C. McMath, Jr., *American Populism: A Social History, 1877–1989* (New York, 1993). For an analysis of the political theory of the Populists, consult Norman Pollack, *The Just Polity: Populism, Law, and Human Welfare* (Urbana, IL, 1987).

Twentieth-century agricultural history is generally represented in studies that focus either on the expansion of the administrative state or the rise of agribusiness or, in a few cases, on the two taken together. For good studies of social change resulting from mechanization and specialization in agriculture, see Hal Barron, *Mixed Harvest: The Second Great Transformation in the Rural North, 1870–1930* (Chapel Hill, NC, 1997); Pete Daniel, *Breaking the Land: The Transformation of Cotton, Tobacco, and Rice Cultures Since 1880* (Urbana, IL, 1985); and Mark Kramer, *Three Farms: Making Milk, Meat, and Money from the American Soil* (Boston, 1980).

On the administrative state and agriculture, see, among others, James H. Shideler, *Farm Crisis, 1919–1923* (Berkeley, 1957); David E. Hamilton, *From New Day to New Deal: American Farm Policy from Hoover to Roosevelt, 1928–1933* (Chapel Hill, NC, 1991); Morton Keller, *Regulating a New Economy: Public Policy and Economic Change in America, 1900–1933* (Cambridge, MA, 1990); Michael E. Parrish, *Anxious Decades: America in Prosperity and Depression, 1920–1941* (New York, 1992); Christine M. Campbell, *The Farm Bureau and the New Deal: A Study of the Making of National Farm Policy, 1933–1940* (Urbana, IL, 1962); Wayne D. Rasmussen, Gladys L. Baker, and James S. Ward, *A Short History of Agricultural Adjustment, 1933–1975* (Washington, DC, 1976); Theodore Saloutos, *The American Farmer and the New Deal* (Ames, IA, 1982); Grant McConnell, *The Decline of Agrarian Democracy* (New York, 1959); Gilbert Fite, *American Farmers: The New Minority* (Bloomington, IN, 1981); Catherine McNichol Stock and Robert D. Johnston, eds., *The Countryside in the Age of the Modern State: Political Histories of Rural America* (Ithaca, NY, 2001); and Victoria Saker Woeste, *The Farmer's Benevolent Trust: Law and Agricultural Cooperation in Industrial America, 1865–1945* (Chapel Hill, NC, 1998).

The literature on labor in agriculture is vast. On farmworkers and immigration in the West, see Cletus Daniel, *Bitter Harvest: A History of California Farmworkers, 1870–1941* (Ithaca, NY, 1981) and Sucheng Chan, *This Bittersweet Soil: The Chinese in California Agriculture, 1860–1910* (Berkeley, CA, 1986). On women farmers and farmworkers, see Deborah Fink, *Agrarian Women: Wives and Mothers in Rural Nebraska, 1880–1940* (Chapel Hill, NC, 1992) and *Cutting into the Meatpacking Line: Workers and Change in the Rural Midwest* (Chapel Hill, NC, 1998); and Mary Neth, *Preserving the Family Farm: Women, Community, and the Foundations of Agribusiness in the Midwest, 1900–1940* (Baltimore, 1995).

On combination and monopoly, see Bruce L. Gardner, *American Agriculture in the Twentieth Century: How It Flourished and What It Cost* (Cambridge, MA, 2002); Jon Lauck, *American Agriculture and the Problem of Monopoly: The Political Economy of Grain Belt Farming, 1953–1980* (Lincoln, NE, 2000); Linda C. Majka and Theo J. Majka, *Farm Workers, Agribusiness, and the State*

(Philadelphia, 1982); Deborah Fitzgerald, *Every Farm a Factory: The Industrial Ideal in American Agriculture* (New Haven, CT, 2003); and James B. Lieber, *Rats in the Grain: The Dirty Tricks and Trials of Archer Daniels Midland* (New York, 2000). For critiques of the post-World War II subsidy programs, see Adam D. Sheingate, *The Rise of the Agricultural Welfare State* (Princeton, NJ, 2001) and Joel Solkoff, *The Politics of Food: The Decline of Agriculture and the Rise of Agribusiness in America* (San Francisco, 1985).

A study of post-World War II pesticide use and government's irrational attachment to harmful chemicals unites an ecological perspective with a critique of agribusiness; see Pete Daniel, *Toxic Drift: Pesticides and Health in the Post-World War II South* (Baton Rouge, LA, 2005). A thoughtful treatment of Midwestern "survivors" of agribusiness is Dennis S. Nordin and Roy V. Scott, *From Prairie Farmer to Entrepreneur: The Transformation of Midwestern Agriculture* (Bloomington, IN, 2005). On the Nebraska wheat farmers' revolt against Monsanto, see Ted Nace, "Breadbasket of Democracy," *Orion* (2006), 1.

The farm debt crisis of 1980s is beginning to receive historical attention. See Neil Harl, *The Farm Debt Crisis of the 1980s* (Ames, IA, 1990) and Bruce L. Gardner, *American Agriculture in the 20th Century: How It Flourished and What It Cost* (Cambridge, MA, 2002).

CHAPTER 16: LAW AND ECONOMIC CHANGE DURING THE SHORT TWENTIETH CENTURY

JOHN HENRY SCHLEGEL

In thinking and writing about law and economic change in the United States in the short twentieth century one faces three problems. The first and hardest is simply coming to understand the relevant sequence of events, to pick out from the great mass of what are often only news stories those that seem to matter. This is especially true because most writers, whether reporters, essayists, popularizers, or scholars, write as if there still is a domestic economy with its problems and a separate international economy with its different set of problems. However plausible that belief was in 1920 or 1950, it is no longer plausible today, and so a serious reader constantly needs to supply the interrelationship between what are separately reported as domestic and international developments. This is not always easy.

For the eighties and beyond, matters become even worse. Little agreement is to be had on most significant questions because ideological presuppositions deeply color most of what has been produced by the popular press and there is little scholarly press. So, from time to time, when what I have read seems not to have made any sense, I have had to rely on feeble memories shared among friends here at Buffalo, even to garner hints of what it might be plausible to focus on. I cannot provide bibliographic references for such ephemeral sources.

And then there is the separable problem of understanding what seems to me and to others to be the key decade in the short twentieth century – the fifties. Though there is broad agreement on what happened to the economy in these years – virtually nothing – there is a significant split in understanding, among even scholars, about what those events mean. Persons of the Left see this decade as the epitome of a well-regulated economy of high wages and plentiful employment, unfortunately marred by a smotheringly conformist social structure and a politically repressive anti-Communist hysteria. Those of the Right see this decade as the epitome of a wholesome, family-centered social structure, a necessary anti-Communist vigilance, and a prosperous, but over-regulated, and so less prosperous than it might otherwise have been, economy. One always has to fight the opposed torques of these competing understandings of this period.

If a reader keeps all three problems in mind, I believe that what follows offers a sensible introduction to law and economic change, but with the following caveat. I have indiscriminately lumped together works of what are regularly denominated as separate sub-species of history – business, cultural, economic, intellectual, legal, political, and social – whether written by authors considered popular, scholarly, or in between, because I do not think that these categories make sense, even though they are the categories within which most authors have written. If, as I maintain, an economy is a persistent market structure, the fusion of an understanding of economic life and the patterns of behavior within economic, political, and social institutions that enact that understanding, then an ensemble of the various ways that historians traditionally carve up the past is the minimum necessary to understand any given economy and derivatively, economic change.

Thinking Well

Three authors seem to me to be extremely helpful whenever thinking about law and economic change. I hear Jane Jacobs, *The Death and Life of Great American Cities* (New York, 1961) and *The Economy of Cities* (New York, 1969), whenever I think or write on this topic. Willard Hurst, *Law and Economic Growth: The Legal History of the Lumber Industry in Wisconsin, 1836–1915* (Cambridge, MA, 1964) and *Law and Markets in United States History: Different Modes of Bargaining* (Madison, WI, 1982), echo as well. And, of course, there is Fernand Braudel, *Civilization and Capitalism 15th–18th Century*, 3 vols., Sian Reynolds, trans. (New York, 1981–84). Each of these works ought to remind any investigator into the economy to pay attention to the micro while striving to understand the macro.

At a more explicitly methodological level, I have learned a lot from Thomas G. Rawski, ed., *Economics and the Historian* (Berkeley, CA, 1996) and especially from Peter Lindert's essay in it, "International Economics and the Historian," 209–37. Douglass C. North, *Structure and Change in Economic History* (New York, 1981) was also thought provoking.

Economic Overviews

General sources are not as much help as one might hope. The relevant volume of Stanley L. Engerman and Robert E. Gallman, eds., *The Cambridge Economic History of the United States*, vol. 3 (Cambridge, 2000), can be a great store of information, should the information that one seeks be found therein, but the essays are at times obtuse in their single-minded devotion to measurement. I found the essays by Peter Temin, "The Great Depression," 301–28; Peter H. Linnert, "U.S. Foreign Trade and Trade Policy in the Twentieth Century," 407–62; Barry Eichengreen, "U.S. Foreign Financial Regulations in the Twentieth Century," 463–04; Louis Galambos, "The U.S. Corporate Economy in the Twentieth Century," 927–68; Richard H. K. Vietor, "Government Regulation of Business," 969–1013; and W. Elliot Brownlee, "The Public Sector," 1013–60 to be particularly helpful. The lovely essay by Christopher L. Tomlins, "Labor Law," 625–92, seems wholly out of place in this volume and, as a result, is likely to be missed by those who might profit from its clean lines. What is essentially a reader, Harold G. Vatter and John F. Walker, eds., *History of the U.S. Economy Since World War II* (Armonk, NY, 1996), presents much of the same material as the Cambridge history in a smaller scope and includes essays of similarly variable usefulness. Wyatt Wells, *American Capitalism 1945–2000: Continuity and Change from Mass Production to the Information Society* (Chicago, 2003) is a solid student text that can be of help to the general reader.

I found none of the large-scale economic histories of the United States to be as helpful as I expected, skewed as they are to disciplinary preoccupations. Still, Sidney Ratner, James H. Soltow, and Richard Sylla, *The Evolution of the American Economy: Growth, Welfare and Decision-Making* (2nd. ed., New York, 1993) seems to me to be the best of the available alternatives. In a smaller compass, Stuart Bruchey, *The Wealth of the Nation: An Economic History of the United States* (New York, 1988) has an extraordinarily strong overview in his final chapter. Adolf A. Berle, *The American Economic Republic* (New York, 1963) demonstrates the good judgment of this astute observer of the economy. Kenneth E. Boulding, *The Structure of a Modern Economy: The United States, 1929–89* (New York, 1993), though primarily a book of graphs and charts, still is a wonderful source.

Books of a more modest scope seem more helpful. Foremost is Herbert Stein, *The Fiscal Revolution in America: Policy in Pursuit of Reality* (2nd rev. ed., Washington, DC, 1996), but Harold G. Vatter, *The U.S. Economy in the 1950s* (New York, 1963); Michael French, *U. S. Economic History Since 1945* (Manchester, UK, 1997); Thomas K. McCraw, *American Business, 1920–2000: How It Worked* (Wheeling, IL, 2000); Samuel Rosenberg, *American Economic Development Since 1945* (London, 2003); Martin Feldstein, ed., *American Economic Policy in the 1980s* (Chicago, 1994); and Alberto Alesina and Geoffrey Carliner, eds., *Politics and Economics in the Eighties* (Chicago, 1999) were all quite helpful. Two books of essays added a certain flesh to these bones: Herbert Stein, *On the Other Hand... Essays on Economics, Economists, and Politics* (Washington, DC, 1995) and Donald N. McCloskey, ed., *Second Thoughts: Myths and Morals of U.S. Economic History* (New York, 1993).

The topic of growth/productivity deserves separate consideration. I found helpful Edward F. Denison, *Trends in Economic Growth, 1929–1982* (Washington, DC, 1985); William Baumol, Sue Anne Batey Blackman, and Edward Wolf, *Productivity and Leadership: The Long View* (Cambridge, MA, 1989); and Douglass C. North, *Institutions, Institutional Change and Economic Performance* (New York, 1990). Then there are the three volumes by John W. Kendrick, *Productivity Trends in the United States* (Princeton, NJ, 1961), *Postwar Productivity Trends in the United States, 1948–1969* (New York, 1973), and *Productivity in the United States: Trends and Cycles* (Baltimore, 1980). Also helpful is F. M. Scherer and David Ross, *Industrial Market Structure and Economic Performance* (Boston, 1990). Robert M. Collins, *More: The Politics of Economic Growth in Postwar America* (Oxford, 2000) is unusual for its combination of serious commitment to political analysis and its way of taking ideas seriously.

On a cautionary note, Mary O. Furner and Barry Supple, eds., *The State and Economic Knowledge: The American and British Experiences* (Cambridge, 1990) and Michael Bernstein, *A Perilous Progress: Economists and Public Purpose in Twentieth-Century America* (Princeton, NJ, 2001) raise sensible questions about the importance of economists in public policymaking that Theodore Rosenof, *Economics in the Long Run: New Deal Theorists and Their Legacies, 1933–1993* (Chapel Hill, NC, 1997) does not dissipate.

Other Overviews

There are dozens of these books, so any selection is destined to be idiosyncratic. I particularly like Howard Zinn, *Postwar America: 1945–1971* (Indianapolis, 1973), an absolutely wonderful left-wing rant, and as such a good antidote to all of the right-wing rants that one gets when reading about the economy. Similar in scope, though not in tone, is William E. Leuchtenburg,

A Troubled Feast: American Society Since 1945 (Boston, 1973). Gary A. Donaldson, *Abundance and Anxiety: America, 1945–1960* (Westport, CT, 1997) is a nice counterpoint to both. Other essential books of this genre include William E. Leuchtenburg, *Franklin D. Roosevelt and the New Deal, 1932–1940* (New York, 1963) and Otis L. Graham, *An Encore for Reform: The Old Progressives and the New Deal* (New York, 1967).

Douglas T. Miller and Marion Nowak, *The Fifties: The Way We Really Were* (Garden City, NY, 1977) is one of many books that combine social, political, economic, and cultural phenomena in a way that cries out for a television series on PBS. It contains a very useful chronology. David Halberstam, *The Fifties* (New York, 1993) is the best-known, and so already PBS-serialized, example of this genre; I found it really helpful in gaining an understanding of the lived experience of the associationalist economy. Such an understanding seems to me to be absolutely essential to writing about an economy in any time or place.

Of course, every author has his or her own understanding of what dates and topics are crucial, and so books such as these expand or contract and change focus somewhat arbitrarily. Useful, though of varying coverage, are John Brooks, *The Great Leap: The Past Twenty-Five Years in America* (New York, 1966); Geoffrey Perrett, *A Dream of Greatness, The American People, 1945–63* (New York, 1979); James Gilbert, *Another Chance: Postwar America, 1945–1968* (Philadelphia, 1981); J. Ronald Oakley, *God's Country: America in the Fifties* (New York, 1986); Jeffrey Hart, *From This Moment On: America in 1940* (New York, 1987); Lisle Abbott Rose, *The Cold War Comes to Mainstreet: America in the 1950s* (Lawrence, KS, 1999); and Eugenia Kaledin, *Daily Life in the United States, 1940–1959* (Westport, CT, 2000). James T. Patterson's Bancroft-Prize-wining, *Grand Expectations: The United States, 1945–1974* (New York, 1996) seems to me to focus a bit too much on political history, but, of course, that is what he does so superbly. John Patrick Diggins, *The Proud Decades: America in War and Peace, 1941–1960* (New York, 1988) seems a bit too concerned with high culture, but is still an wonderful, insightful book, with a stupendous bibliography and unusually apt illustrations, an oft-neglected part of the historian's craft in these days of tight university press budgets.

Peter Lewis, *The Fifties* (New York, 1978) is interesting because it demonstrates how, despite economic differences, the British social experience of these years was quite similar to the American. It also includes an interesting chronology.

Narrower Understandings
I have found books on politics at the federal level essential to understanding economic change, though infuriatingly tied to presidential administrations,

as if over any long period of time such modest alterations in policy as they may bring are not overwhelmed by longer term trends. In addition to the standard biographies, of which everyone has their favorite, I found helpful Ellis W. Hawley, Murray N. Rothbard, Robert F. Himmelberg, and Gerald D. Nash, *Herbert Hoover and the Crisis of American Capitalism* (Cambridge, 1973); William J. Barber, *From New Era to New Deal: Herbert Hoover, the Economists and American Economic Policy, 1921–1933* (New York, 1985); David M. Hart, "Herbert Hoover's Last Laugh: The Enduring Significance of the 'Associative State' in the United States," *Journal of Policy History* 10 (1998), 419–44; William J. Barber, *Design Within Disorder: Franklin D. Roosevelt, the Economists, and the Shaping of American Economic Policy, 1933–1945* (Cambridge, 1996); Susan M. Hartman, *Truman and the 80th Congress* (Columbia, MO, 1971); Alonzo L. Hamby, *Beyond the New Deal: Harry Truman and American Liberalism* (New York, 1973) and *Harry Truman and the Fair Deal* (Lexington, MA, 1974); Michael J. Lacey, ed., *The Truman Presidency* (Washington, DC, 1989); Charles C. Alexander, *Holding the Line: The Eisenhower Era, 1952–61* (Bloomington, IN, 1975); Robert Griffith, "Dwight D. Eisenhower and the Corporate Commonwealth," *American Historical Review* 87 (1982), 87–122; Michael S. Meyer, *The Eisenhower Presidency and the 1950s* (Boston, 1998); Allen J. Matusow, *Nixon's Economy: Booms, Busts, Dollars and Votes* (Lawrence, KS, 1998); and Gary M. Fink and Hugh Davis Graham, *The Carter Presidency: Policy Choices in the Post-New Deal Era* (Lawrence, KS, 1998).

Some books manage to escape the presidential fixation. Among them I have been helped by Michael D. Bordo, Claudia Dale Goldin, and Eugene Nelson White, eds., *The Defining Moment: Depression and the American Economy in the Twentieth Century* (Chicago, 1998) and especially, its essay by Douglas A. Irwin, "From Smoot-Hawley to Reciprocal Trade Agreements: Changing the Course of U.S. Trade Policy in the 1930s," 325–352; Donald Albrecht, ed., *World War II and the American Dream* (Cambridge, MA, 1995); Michael J. Bennett, *When Dreams Came True: The GI Bill and the Making of Modern America* (Washington, DC, 1996); Milton Greenberg, *The GI Bill: The Law That Changed America* (New York, 1997); Michael J. Hogan, *The Marshall Plan: America, Britain and the Reconstruction of Western Europe, 1947–52* (Cambridge, 1987); and Allen J. Matusow, *The Unraveling of America: A History of Liberalism in the 1960s* (New York, 1984);

Regional understandings, though, to my way of thinking, more likely to be able to avoid concentration on short-term political controversy, are harder to find. Most of the work has been done on the Northeast/Great Lakes Rust Belt, as if that were the only important region, but Gavin Wright, *Old South, New South: Revolutions in the Southern Economy Since the Civil War* (New York, 1986) is very helpful. A good book on the expansion of federal installations into the West during World War II is Gerald D.

Nash, *World War II and the West: Reshaping the Economy* (Lincoln, NE, 1990), while Ann Markusen, Peter Hall, Scott Campbell, and Sabina Detrick, *The Rise of the Gunbelt: The Military Remapping of Industrial America* (New York, 1991) looks at a broader picture. Pete Daniel, *Lost Revolutions: The South in the 1950s* (Chapel Hill, NC, 2000), a fine work of cultural history, nicely supplements books such as James C. Cobb, *The Selling of the South: The Southern Crusade for Industrial Development, 1936–1980* (Baton Rouge, LA, 1980). The more general idea of a Sunbelt is treated in Carl Abbott, *The New Urban America: Growth and Politics in Sunbelt Cities* (2nd ed., Chapel Hill, NC, 1987) and Raymond A. Mohl, ed., *Searching for the Sunbelt: Historical Perspectives on a Region* (Knoxville, TN, 1990).

A still different kind of overview is Alice Kessler Harris, *Out to Work: A History of Wage-Earning Women in the United States* (New York, 1982).

American Business
When attempting to gain an understanding of the American business corporation, one would be foolish not to start with Alfred D. Chandler, Jr., *The Visible Hand: The Managerial Revolution in American Business* (Cambridge, MA, 1977) and *Scale and Scope: The Dynamics of Industrial Capitalism* (Cambridge, MA, 1990). And yet it is important to remember that the triumph of this economic form was not just a matter of managerial/technological innovation, but that a certain amount of public relations was essential as well. On this subject, Elizabeth A. Fones-Wolf, *Selling Free Enterprise: The Business Assault on Labor and Liberalism, 1945–1960* (Urbana, IL, 1994) wears its heart on its sleeve, though is anything but wrong-headed in its illuminating analysis.

Much ink has been spilled on questions of government regulation of business. Although it is not a category of understanding that I find helpful, out of this vast literature two books stand out for what they have taught me: Ellis W. Hawley, *The New Deal and the Problem of Monopoly: A Study in Economic Ambivalence* (Princeton, NJ, 1966), and Louis Galambos and Joseph Pratt, *The Rise of the Corporate Commonwealth: U.S. Business and Public Policy in the Twentieth Century* (New York, 1988). Richard H. K. Vietor, *Contrived Competition: Regulation and Deregulation in America* (Cambridge, MA, 1994) tells its somewhat different story with great clarity and fairness. I also found helpful William G. Roy, *Socializing Capital: The Rise of the Large Industrial Corporation in America* (Princeton, NJ, 1997); Daniel Yergin and Joseph Stanislaw, *The Commanding Heights: The Battle Between Government & the Marketplace That Is Remaking the Modern World* (New York, 1998); and Wyatt Wells, *Anti-Trust and the Formation of the Postwar World* (New York, 2002). Jonathan J. Bean, *Beyond the Broker State: Federal Policies Toward Small Business, 1936–1961* (Chapel Hill, NC, 1996) bears reading by those interested in this subdivision of the broader topic.

Given that ours is a subspecies of capitalist economy, an understanding of labor and its regulation logically follows any discussion about capital. On this topic I have found useful Richard Edwards, *Contested Terrain: The Transformation of the Workplace in the Twentieth Century* (New York, 1979); Lizabeth Cohen, *Making a New Deal: Industrial Workers in Chicago, 1919–1939* (New York, 1990); Sanford M. Jacoby, *Modern Manors: Welfare Capitalism Since the New Deal* (Princeton, NJ, 1997); Andrew Wender Cohen, *The Racketeer's Progress: Chicago and the Struggle for the Modern American Economy, 1900–1940* (Cambridge, 2004); and Judith Stein, *Running Steel, Running America: Race, Economic Policy and the Decline of Liberalism* (Chapel Hill, NC, 1998). James B. Atleson, *Labor and the Wartime State: Labor Relations During World War II* (Urbana, IL, 1998) explains this quite crucial period clearly and carefully.

Specific industries regularly get separate treatment. On steel, John Hoerr, *And the Wolf Finally Came: The Decline of the American Steel Industry* (Pittsburgh, 1988) and Mark Reutter, *Sparrows Point: Making Steel – The Rise and Ruin of American Industrial Might* (New York, 1988) tell the story well, as does Christopher G. L. Hall, *Steel Phoenix: The Fall and Rise of the U.S. Steel Industry* (New York, 1997), though a different story.

John F. Stover, *American Railroads* (2nd ed., Chicago, 1997) is absolutely essential for understanding this aspect of transportation. Robert Barry Carson, *Main Line to Oblivion: The Disintegration of New York Railroads in the Twentieth Century* (Port Washington, NY, 1971) examines the details of railroading in one state, New York, and shows on a micro level how national problems play out. Good stories devoted to single roads can fill out details in another dimension. Examples are Joseph R. Daughen, *The Wreck of the Penn-Central* (Boston, 1971); Stephen Salsbury, *No Way to Run a Railroad: The Untold Story of the Penn Central Crisis* (New York, 1982); and H. Roger Grant, *Erie Lackawanna: Death of an American Railroad, 1938–1992* (Stanford, CA, 1994). John F. Stover, *The Routledge Historical Atlas of the American Railroads* (New York, 1999) is an wonderfully useful book given its quite modest scope.

An understanding of the housing industry is harder to capture, given that it has until very recently been a quite local, small-scale phenomenon. Gwendolyn Wright, *Building the Dream: A Social History of Housing in America* (New York, 1981) is still the basic book on this topic, but Gail Radford, *Modern Housing for America: Policy Struggles in the New Deal Era* (Chicago, 1996) provides great insight with respect to specific housing policy alternatives. Kenneth T. Jackson, *Crabgrass Frontier: The Suburbanization of the United States* (New York, 1985) is as basic a book as the Wright, though I think not sufficiently sympathetic to the postwar developments as they deserve. Bruce G. Carruthers and Arthur L. Stinchcombe, "The Social Structure of

Liquidity: Flexibility, Markets and States," *Theory and Society* 28 (1999), 353–82 has some good material on the development of the secondary market in home mortgages, as does Michael Lewis, *Liar's Poker: Rising Through the Wreckage of Wall Street* (New York, 1989).

An even more dispersed industry is agriculture, a topic that is most generally presented as a story about federal policy. Congressional Quarterly, *Farm Policy: The Politics of Soil, Surpluses, and Subsidies* (Washington, DC, 1984), has a wealth of information on this topic, as does U.S. Department of Agriculture, Economic Research Service, *History of Agricultural Price-Support and Adjustment Programs 1933–84: Background for 1985 Farm Legislation* (Washington, DC, 1985). Willard W. Cochrane and C. Ford Runge, *Reforming Farm Policy: Toward a National Agenda* (Ames, IA, 1992) brings this story forward with more of an analytic focus. John Mark Hansen, *Gaining Access: Congress and the Farm Lobby, 1919–1981* (Chicago, 1991) provides some explanation of how changes took place. Allen J. Matusow, *Farm Policies and Politics in the Truman Years* (Cambridge, MA, 1967) is helpful for this narrow period, as is Victoria Saker Woeste, *The Farmers Benevolent Trust: Law and Agricultural Cooperation in Industrial America, 1865–1945* (Chapel Hill, NC, 1998) on this other interesting topic. All of this policy analysis comes strikingly alive in an aptly named book, Richard Rhodes, *Farm: A Year in the Life of an American Farmer* (New York, 1989).

Public utilities seem not to be a subject given much examination. This is unfortunate, as is shown by Ronald C. Tobey, *Technology as Freedom: The New Deal and Electrical Modernization of the American Home* (Berkeley, CA, 1996), a meticulous depiction of how an important national initiative played out in one surprisingly representative place, Riverside, CA. It pays attention to questions of ethnicity and class without letting them overwhelm the rest of the story, an unusual strength. Peter Temin, with Louis Galambos, *The Fall of the Bell System: A Study in Prices and Politics* (New York, 1987) and Richard F. Hirsh, *Technology and Transformation in the American Electric Utility Industry* (Cambridge, 1989) are also helpful.

Richard H. K. Vietor, *Energy Policy in America Since 1945: A Study of Business-Government Relations* (New York, 1984) is more interested in oil and gas exploration and production as a regulated industry than as a part of the retail delivery of energy. On a related topic, two books on gas pipelines have come to my attention, again a matter of wholesale, not retail delivery of utility services: Christopher James Castaneda, *Regulated Enterprise: Natural Gas Pipelines and Northeastern Markets, 1938–1954* (Columbus, OH, 1993) and Clarence M. Smith, *Gas Pipelines and the Emergence of America's Regulatory State: A History of Panhandle Eastern Corporation, 1928–1993* (New York, 1996).

Miscellaneous books on industry segments include William R. Childs, *Trucking and the Public Interest: The Emergence of Federal Regulation, 1914–1940* (Knoxville, TN, 1985) and Eliot Sewell, *Networks of Innovation: Vaccine Development at Merck, Sharp & Dohme, and Mulford, 1895–1995* (New York, 1995).

Studies of technology are legion. Two good ones are David A. Hounshell and John Kenly Smith, Jr., *Science and Corporate Strategy: DuPont R&D, 1902–1980* (New York, 1988) and Margaret B. W. Graham and Bettye H. Pruitt, *R&D for Industry: A Century of Technical Innovation at Alcoa* (New York, 1990). No matter what the industry group in question may be, David F. Noble, *America by Design: Science, Technology and the Rise of Corporate Capitalism* (New York, 1977) and *Forces of Production: A Social History of Automation* (New York, 1984) and Clayton M. Christensen, *The Innovator's Dilemma: When New Technologies Cause Great Firms to Fail* (Boston, 1997) provide a caution for any technologically driven analysis.

The growth of the consumer economy is a hard thing to get a handle on other than by reading house histories of consumer products firms, in my experience a painful activity. I found Lizabeth Cohen, *A Consumers' Republic: The Politics of Mass Consumption in Postwar America* (New York, 2003) insightful when not distracted by contemporary issues. Richard S. Tedlow, *New and Improved: The Story of Mass Marketing in America* (New York, 1990) is also helpful. Lendol Calder, *Financing the American Dream: A Cultural History of Consumer Credit* (Princeton, NJ, 1999) illuminates this crucial subject.

Silently underlying all of these topics is James Willard Hurst, *The Legitimacy of the Business Corporation in the Law of the United States, 1780–1970* (Charlottesville, VA, 1970).

Finance

Money is both an industry and a topic. In exploring such, one might best begin with James Willard Hurst, *A Legal History of Money in the United States, 1774–1970* (Lincoln, NE, 1973), though much broader in scope and focused on earlier times. Along the way, it presents a sophisticated understanding of the role of the Federal Reserve Board in these years.

Public finance is a much-neglected subject. W. Elliot Brownlee, ed., *Funding the Modern State, 1941–1955: The Rise and Fall of the Era of Easy Finance* (Washington, DC, 1996) contains several very helpful essays, and his *Federal Taxation in America: A Short History* (New York, 1996) is a great entry point for the study of this narrower, but immensely complicated subject.

Robert Solomon, *The International Monetary System, 1945–1981* (New York, 1982) and *Money on the Move* (New York, 1999) are essential for anyone who wishes to understand American participation in the formalities of international finance. Scattered within the textbook form, Paul R. Krugman and Maurice Obstfelt, *International Economics: Theory and Policy* (5th ed., Reading, MA, 2000), 538–51, 557–64, 577–82, 586–600 is a great brief summary of American participation in international economic affairs since our Civil War. John Zysman and Laura Tyson, eds., *American Industry in International Competition: Government Policies and Corporate Strategies* (Ithaca, NY, 1983) has some helpful essays.

Jonathan Barron Baskin and Paul J. Miranti, Jr., *A History of Corporate Finance* (Cambridge, 1997) contains some very good work on this arcane, but crucial subject, whose modern treatment begins with Adolph A. Berle and Gardner C. Means, *The Modern Corporation and Private Property* (New York, 1932). However, most of what we know about corporate finance in action comes from books of a once topical nature. Of this literature I regularly found helpful the work of Martin Mayer, *The Bankers* (New York, 1974); *The Money Bazaars: Understanding the Banking Revolution Around Us* (New York, 1984); *Markets: Who Plays . . . Who Risks . . . Who Gains . . . Who Loses* (New York 1988); and *The Greatest Bank Robbery: The Collapse of the Savings and Loan Industry* (1990), even though internally these books can be of wildly varying quality. Other helpful books would include William Greider, *Secrets of the Temple: How the Federal Reserve Runs the Country* (New York, 1987); John Brooks, *The Takeover Game* (New York, 1987); Connie Bruck, *The Predators' Ball: The Junk Bond Raiders and the Man Who Stalked Them* (New York, 1988); Bryan Burrough and John Helyar, *Barbarians at the Gate: The Fall of RJR Nabisco* (New York, 1990); and James B. Stewart, *Den of Thieves* (New York, 1991).

Understanding Lived Experience
The suburban mindset is well understood by Tom Martinson, *American Dreamscape: The Pursuit of Happiness in Postwar Suburbia* (New York, 2000) and criticized in Stephanie Coontz, *The Way We Never Were: American Families and the Nostalgia Trap* (New York, 1992).

Karal Ann Marling, *As Seen on TV: The Visual Culture of Everyday Life in the 1950's* (Cambridge, MA, 1994) is a wonderful essay on the passing scene. Lynn Spigel, *Make Room for TV: Television and the Family Ideal in Postwar America* (Chicago, 1992), despite its title, focuses less on the visual than on the context of family living and its relationship to the television situation comedy. Both books make concrete one of the ways in which an economy is a lived experience.

At a more general level, Robert D. Putnam, *Bowling Alone: The Collapse and Revival of American Community* (New York, 2000) has some very helpful material about social change that has informed some of my observations, as has the slightly more directly relevant, but less factually dense, Bruce G. Carruthers and Sarah L. Babb, *Economy/Society: Markets, Meanings and Social Structure* (Thousand Oaks, CA, 2000).

Final, but Not After, Thoughts
Jeff Madrick, "How New is the New Economy?" *Working USA* 3 (1999), 24–47 and Roger Alcaly, "He's Got the Whole World in His Hands," *New York Review of Books* 46 (October 7, 1999), 35–39 provide a nice cautionary note with respect to the stability of the Impatient economy.

Pictorial sources are woefully ignored as central materials for understanding an economy's instantiation as social life. Two books stand out: Thomas Hine, *Populuxe* (New York, 1989) and Jim Heimann, ed., *50s: All-American Ads* (Köln, 2001), part of a series of large-format books by the German publisher, Taschen, that do nothing but reproduce ads from a relevant decade. The 30s, 40s, and 60s are also available. Douglas Dreishpoon and Alan Trachtenberg, *The Tumultuous Fifties: A View from The New York Times Photo Archives* (New Haven, CT, 2001), as the very best of the news photo books, shows the limits of such in a world where politics and celebrity so dominate the news.

CHAPTER 17: THE CORPORATE ECONOMY

GREGORY A. MARK

Legal history has always been regarded as a technical, almost arcane, branch of historical study. The legal history of the political economy has been regarded as all the more technical, involving as it does questions of economic practice and theory and the organization and operation of business entities, as well as seemingly dry questions of both private and public law. Unlike constitutional history, which touches on topics on which anyone who is well informed would be likely to have both questions and opinions – individual rights, the organization of the state, and the balance of state and federal responsibilities – these areas of law seem both obscure and not of immediate personal concern. Bypassed because of its technicality in the time when the study of great events and persons dominated historical study, it was equally bypassed in the era of social history as having little to do with everyday life. The historical literature is thus relatively thin, at least in comparison with other issues in legal history, not to speak of American history generally. It is no exaggeration to say that more historian's ink has been spilled on the Battle of Bull Run, to pick but one example, than on antitrust, much less the legal obligations of corporate managers or the Food and Drug Administration.

Any study of the twentieth century compounds the difficulty of historical understanding. Distance lends perspective and, with perspective, insight. Not for nothing has the past been called a foreign country. The twentieth-century United States, however, is both familiar and part of the felt experience of many. The United States and its modern institutions are ubiquitous; virtually everyone has grown up with both knowledge and opinions about both, especially the role of its law and its corporations. In that sense they are no more foreign than the United States is to Canadians. In a manner both more pervasive and misleading than in other realms, the historian's perspective is distorted by everyday experience. Assumptions are anachronistic, often completely unconsciously. The historical story, always subject to revision, should be at its most tentative, paradoxically nearly at the peak of available information.

To compound the paradox, although the historical literature is thin, the contemporary literature is voluminous. In the nineteenth century, America saw the flourishing of a robust and indigenous legal literature, written by and for the practicing bar. At the turn of the century it was augmented by law journals that developed as educational tools for law students in the newly burgeoning law schools. Thus, the twentieth century has two streams of legal literature, both deep and wide, which address all areas of law, including corporate law, antitrust, and administrative law. For those interested in sampling what practitioners were actually doing and what the commentators thought, both streams are surprising accessible – and remarkably under-researched.

The history of the laws that gave rise to the American corporation in the nineteenth century has been the subject of several jurisdiction by jurisdiction studies. The most famous of these are Oscar and Mary Handlin's *Commonwealth* (Cambridge, MA, 1947), which contextualized the rise of the corporate form in Massachusetts as a piece with the intimate involvement of the state government in the economy, and Louis Hartz's *Economic Policy and Democratic Thought* (Cambridge, MA, 1948), which dealt with Pennsylvania. Other studies, both in book and article form, have been published since the 1920s. The classic general work on the legal history of the political economy in the nineteenth century is J. Willard Hurst's *Law and the Conditions of Freedom in the Nineteenth-Century United States* (Madison, WI, 1956). On historiographical and other grounds these studies should be read alongside Morton Horwitz's *Transformation of American Law, 1780–1850* (Cambridge, MA, 1977) and Morton Keller's *Affairs of State* (Cambridge, MA, 1977), which both include excellent material on the early corporation.

The jurisprudential understanding of the modern corporation is set out in Gregory Mark, "The Personification of the Business Corporation in

American Law," *University of Chicago Law Review* 54 (1987), 1441, which traces the theoretical legal understanding of the corporation from the nineteenth through the twentieth century, and the chapter on the corporation in Morton Horwitz's *Transformation of American Law, 1870–1960* (New York, 1992). Herbert Hovenkamp's *Enterprise and American Law, 1836–1937* (Cambridge, MA, 1991) gives not just insight into the modern corporation's formative legal history but also ties the history to antitrust and other issues associated with regulating corporate behavior. Still the best history of twentieth-century corporate law issues, one that manages both distance and interpretive finesse notwithstanding the time in which it was written, is Hurst's *The Legitimacy of the Business Corporation in the Law of the United States, 1780–1970* (Charlottesville, VA, 1970). New Jersey's role in creating modern corporate codes is treated in some detail in Christopher Grandy, *New Jersey and the Fiscal Origins of Modern American Corporation Law* (New York, 1993). Joel Seligman has written a brief article-length treatment of Delaware's twentieth-century centrality in American corporate law: "A Brief History of Delaware's General Corporation Law of 1899," *Delaware Journal of Corporation Law* 1 (1976), 249.

The traditional understanding of the twentieth-century evolution of corporate law has been that of "the race to the bottom." That view is, for example, embodied in Seligman's work. The rationale for the downward slope was stated most famously by Adolph A. Berle, Jr. and Gardiner C. Means, *The Modern Corporation and Private Property* (New York, 1932), which developed the thesis of managerial exploitation caused by the separation of ownership from actual control. In the last quarter of the twentieth century that view was largely upended by the challenges of scholars in the neo-classical law and economics movement, who argued that the "race" was largely beneficent. Their work was not explicitly historical, but because it dealt with the evolution of legal institutions, it necessarily had an historical character. Progenitors of the movement included Henry Manne and Richard Posner, but in the field of corporate law the article by Ralph K. Winter, Jr., "State Law, Shareholder Protection, and the Theory of the Corporation," *Journal of Legal Studies* 6 (1977), 251 was among the first to suggest that competitive federalism resulted in optimal corporate codes. Roberta Romano's work, especially her *The Genius of American Corporate Law* (Washington, DC, 1993), carries that view out in some detail. This viewpoint has been tempered somewhat by a suggestion that competitive federalism is not a perfect market, as argued by Jonathan R. Macey and Geoffrey P. Miller, "Toward an Interest-Group Theory of Delaware Corporate Law," *Texas Law Review* 65 (1987), 469. In all of these works the distinction between history and policy analysis is evanescent, but no understanding of the history of corporate law is possible without knowing this interpretive tension.

Just as modern American corporate law was a development of the innovative impulses of the bar and business communities to provide a vehicle for business interests, modern antitrust grew from the impulses to contain the anti-competitive practices and tendency toward the gargantuan manifest in those vehicles. The work of James May is key to understanding state antitrust activity and the contemporary rise of federal antitrust, especially his "Antitrust Practice and Procedure in the Formative Era: The Constitutional and Conceptual Reach of State Antitrust Law, 1880–1918," *University of Pennsylvania Law Review* 135 (1987), 495. May's work suggests a more vigorous realm of state activity than Charles McCurdy, "The Knight Sugar Decision of 1895 and the Modernization of American Corporate Law, 1869–1903," *Business History Review* 53 (1979), 304. The legacy of the federalization of antitrust as purely a matter of consumer welfare, which became the dominant twentieth-century view, is probably best set forth in Robert Bork, *The Antitrust Paradox* (New York, 1978) and follows the theoretical model of neo-classical law and economics. That view cuts against the historical understanding of antitrust in general and the Sherman Act in particular, as both James Weinstein, *The Corporate Ideal in the Liberal State, 1900–1918* (Boston, 1968) and David Millon, "The Sherman Act and the Balance of Power," *Southern California Law Review* 61 (1988), 1219 have argued.

In the New Deal, however, the tension between economic welfare born of the economies of scale of the corporation and a political localism that might preserve relatively inefficient businesses was felt most keenly. That tension was reflected in the application of antitrust as Ellis W. Hawley, *The New Deal and the Problem of Monopoly* (Princeton, NJ, 1966) explained. The tension moderated the original trust-busting impulse and led to the more refined regulatory impulse. Thurman Arnold's role in, as Hawley has termed it, defining the "ambivalent" attitude towards antitrust is neatly set out in Alan Brinkley, "The Antimonopoly Ideal and the Liberal State: The Case of Thurman Arnold," *Journal of American History* 80 (1993), 557. Tony Freyer develops the regulatory perspective more completely in *Regulating Big Business: Antitrust in Great Britain and America, 1880–1990* (Cambridge, 1992) as does Rudolph J. R. Peritz, *Competition Policy in America, 1888–1992: History, Rhetoric, Law* (New York, 1996).

Administrative law and the administrative state are topics limited only by the limits of regulation itself. As William Novak has amply demonstrated in his *The People's Welfare: Law and Regulation in Nineteenth-Century America* (Chapel Hill, NC, 1996), the regulatory ambitions of government, whether expressed locally in the nineteenth century or nationally in the twentieth, are both deep and pervasive. No brief bibliography could do justice to the ambition. Stephen Skowronek, *Building a New American State:*

The Expansion of National Administrative Capacities, 1877–1920 (Cambridge, 1982), however, elegantly sets the stage for the nationalization of regulatory ambition that followed the Great Depression. The studies of the New Deal and the constitutional crises provoked by New Deal legislation are unending. Barry Cushman, *Rethinking the New Deal: The Structure of a Constitutional Revolution* (New York, 1998) is a careful and original analysis of the constitutional battles that legitimated the transfer of regulatory ambition from the states to the federal government. The key to constitutionality turned out to be ensuring that the lawmaking functions of the administrative state would be subject to review by traditional judicial organs, at the very minimum for procedural regularity and, no matter how attenuated the possibility, at least potentially for their substantive content. The Administrative Procedure Act was enacted in the immediate postwar period to bring that semblance of ordering principles to the jumble of novel bureaucracies created in the New Deal, each seemingly with its own law-creating body and process. Not surprisingly, this act itself was the product of the same political pressures that gave rise to and simultaneously tempered New Deal legislation, as made clear by George B. Shepard, "Fierce Compromise: The Administrative Procedure Act Emerges from New Deal Politics," *Northwestern University Law Review* 90 (1996), 1557.

The intellectual and practical difficulties posed by the process/substance distinction, so key to the legitimacy of the American national administrative state, have been well analyzed in several general studies. Among the most well known and cogent are Richard B. Stewart, "The Reformation of American Administrative Law," *Harvard Law Review* 88 (1975), 1667 and James O. Freedman, *Crisis and Legitimacy: The Administrative Process and American Government* (Cambridge, 1978). The attempts at the resolution of those difficulties form their own cottage industry, the history of which has not been really attempted.

Each area in which the administrative state developed a bureaucracy has its own history. The labor movement's relationship to the emerging federal regulatory apparatus, for example, has spawned a huge literature, which is treated elsewhere in this volume. Perhaps because the Great Depression is associated so closely with the stock market crash and perhaps because the manipulation of or state of the capital markets has always been a central concern to both political historians concerned with corruption and economists concerned with growth, respectively, the regulation of the securities markets has received somewhat more attention than other realms of the administrative state. Still the leading history with the most sophisticated attention to legal detail is Joel Seligman, *The Transformation of Wall Street: A History of the Securities and Exchange Commission and Modern Corporate Finance* (New York, 1995). It is a work of monumental detail. Michael E. Parrish,

Securities Regulation and the New Deal (New Haven, CT, 1970) nicely situates this aspect of the rise of the administrative state in the breadth of the New Deal's reformist cloak. Some economists, notably Milton Friedman, have questioned the efficacy of much of the New Deal and, directly and by implication, the regulation of the financial markets. Friedman, of course, was more concerned with the role of monetary policy than with securities regulation. Thus far, however, no sustained revisionist historical study of securities regulation has been mounted. Alongside the new federal regulation of the securities markets, of course, state law continued to regulate intra-corporate relations. The states also developed substantive regulations, the Blue Sky Laws. At least the beginnings of these understudied laws have been analyzed in Jonathan R. Macey and Geoffrey P. Miller, "Origin of the Blue Sky Laws," *Texas Law Review* 70 (1991), 348.

As the legacy of Berle and Means and even the title of Seligman's work suggest, any attempt to understand the evolution of the legal institutions of the corporate economy apart from some understanding of both corporations and the economy would ultimately be a sterile act. The works in business and economic history, as well as the biographies and prosopographies of people in business, are beyond the scope of this bibliography, but should not escape the attention of any person who would want seriously to understand the law of the corporate economy. Two notable works that have attempted to integrate a sophisticated understanding of financial institutions and the culture of American market capitalism demonstrate how rich a story can be told with that approach. From the perspective of business history, Morton Keller, *The Life Insurance Enterprise, 1885–1910 – A Study in the Limits of Corporate Power* (Cambridge, MA, 1963) brings together the story of an industry and its reach, the regulatory history of the states of the United States as well as other countries, and political history, including the history of scandal. More recently Mark Roe has attempted an even more ambitious study of the legal architecture of American finance. Roe is trained as a lawyer, not a historian, and his work is deliberately normative, but it nonetheless brings together strands of historical explanation rarely seen in this area of legal history. His *Strong Managers, Weak Owners: The Political Roots of American Corporate Finance* (Princeton, NJ, 1994) simultaneously touches on the Berle and Means thesis; the results of antitrust and regulatory actions that shaped the insurance, pension fund, banking, and mutual fund industries; and market forces in discussing how and why the American financial system evolved differently from other capitalist cultures.

No good history can ignore theory. Even seeming narration necessarily involves explanation. Alongside, or perhaps against, traditional lawyerly understandings of doctrinal development premised in analogic reasoning and the social context of legal development exemplified by Hurst and others, the law and economics movement suggests that the most powerful analytic tools that can be brought to bear in understanding the evolution of law are the tools of economics. As I have suggested, that approach has transformed contemporary (academic) understanding of antitrust law, where it was first applied; corporate law, its next important application; and ultimately the structure of the administrative state. If corporate law has seemed inaccessible to the law historian, the tools of law and economics seem doubly abstruse. Nevertheless, their utility and therefore their strengths and weaknesses as a substitute for temporal distance as a tool in aiding understanding need to be understood. An especially approachable work in this regard is Peter L. Bernstein, *Capital Ideas: The Improbable Origins of Modern Wall Street* (New York, 1992), which is a non-technical, almost breezy, contemporary chronology of the development of the tools of modern finance. The most detailed, indeed almost encyclopedic, if somewhat uncritical, history of law and economics, which puts in the context of general jurisprudence the evolution and application of neo-classical law and economics, is Neil Duxbury, *Patterns of American Jurisprudence* (Oxford, 1995).

Notwithstanding the seeming difficulty in approaching the history of a technical subject, the materials from which the history is written are easily available, especially for the twentieth century. Perhaps the largest single difference between the source material for legal history and the primary material for any other field is how accessible much of the material actually is. Accessibility of primary material renders its historical treatment all the more paradoxical. Not only are cases published, they are indexed and classified. Statutes and regulatory material, although somewhat less well organized for purposes of historical research, are all published. At the federal level even the formal background materials, such as hearings and governmental research, tend to be published and are generally archived when not published. While proceedings at other levels of government are much more spotty, contemporary coverage by way of professional publications in law, academic commentary, and published professional aids, such as form books, provides avenues into contemporary understanding rarely available in other fields. Indeed, nearly all of the academic commentary and much of the professional literature have had for decades their own index, the *Index to Legal Periodicals*. Virtually every twist and turn in corporate law, antitrust, and administrative law spawned commentary, all duly indexed. Even a casual perusal of the *Index* reveals much about contemporary understandings. It is as if an entire profession kept an analytic diary. Bridging all these sources are treatises, organizing and analyzing cases and other developments and giving insight into both what practitioners regard as a "better" approach and why, and the case books from which law students are taught, which reflect contemporary understandings of what is foundational and what is of contemporary importance. The history of the law of the political economy can be written. Just as war should not be left to the generals, the history should not be left to the lawyers.

CHAPTER 18: LAW AND COMMERCIAL POPULAR CULTURE
IN THE TWENTIETH-CENTURY UNITED STATES

NORMAN L. ROSENBERG

A growing number of "disciplinary encounters," involving an expanding array of different "research traditions" have enabled academic projects in law and culture. In a similarly interdisciplinary spirit, I have adapted the idea of a research tradition from David Bordwell's *On the History of Film Style* (Cambridge, MA, 1997) for this chapter's account of law and commercial popular culture (i.e., the products and images produced for and circulated in the commercial marketplace by the culture industry). For a suggestive overview of how encounters between the fields of law and social science shaped a research tradition in law and society, see Christopher Tomlins, "Framing the Field of Law's Disciplinary Encounters: A Historical Narrative," *Law & Society Review* 34 (2000), 911–72.

The research tradition in law and culture has drawn diverse perspectives from the fields of history, popular culture, American Studies, cultural studies, gender studies, cognitive studies and law and society. Naomi Mezey, in an important essay that has helped shape this chapter, draws on most of these perspectives: see "Approaches to the Cultural Study of Law: Law as Culture," *Yale Journal of Law and Humanities* (2001), 35–68. Mezey and Mark C. Niles, "Screening the Law: Ideology and Law in American Popular Culture," *Columbia Journal of Law & the Arts* 28 (2005), 91–185 builds on the frame of law as culture/culture as law and, in addition, nicely distinguishes the place of commercial culture, the primary of focus of his chapter, and of popular culture in legal studies. More broadly, Pierre Schlag's "The Aesthetics of American Law," *Harvard Law Review* 115 (2002), 1047–118 has also been important to how this chapter sees both legal history and of the role of culture.

Studies Relevant to Law and *Commercial Popular Culture*
Historical studies of commercial popular culture underscore the wide range of products and cultural forms that came to embrace (to invoke the law professor Karl Llewellyn's marvelously expansive and expressive phrase) "things legal." See Kurt Llewellyn, "Some Realism About Realism – Responding to Dean Pound," *Harvard Law Review* 44 (1931), 1222–56. The "penny presses" and "dime books" of the mid-nineteenth century offered, to use another Llewellyn-coined term, "jurisprudence for the millions." Dan

Schiller's *Objectivity and the News: The Public and the Rise of Commercial Journalism* (Philadelphia, 1981) and Andie Tucher, *Froth & Scum: Truth, Beauty, Goodness, and the Ax Murder in America's First Mass Medium* (Chapel Hill, NC, 1994) suggest how the early penny presses used stories about crime and court trials to attract readers and sell papers. Similarly, Michael Denning's *Mechanics Accents: Dime Novels and Working-Class Culture in America* (London, 1987) and Richard Slotkin's *Fatal Environment: The Myth of the Frontier in the Age of Industrialization, 1800–1890* (New York, 1985) detail how early dime novelists such as George Lippard, who had once covered court trials for the penny presses, made representations of things legal central to their fiction. Denning's *Mechanics Accents* also tracks the appearance of dime detective novels, often based on real-life legal conflicts, and on stories about "outlaw heroes," such as Jesse James, who challenged what they saw as a repressive legal order. See also Michael Schudson, *Discovering the News: A Social History of American Newspapers* (New York, 1978); Charles L. Ponce de Leon, *Self-Exposure: Human-Interest Journalism and the Emergence of Celebrity in America, 1890–1940* (Chapel Hill, NC, 2002); and Paul Starr, *The Creation of the Media: Political Origins of Modern Communications* (New York, 2004).

Historical accounts of crime and detective literature include Dennis Porter, *The Pursuit of Crime: Art and Ideology in Detective Fiction* (New Haven, CT, 1981); David Ray Papke, *Framing the Criminal: Crime, Cultural Work, and the Loss of Critical Perspective* (Hamden, CT, 1987); David Lehman, *The Perfect Murder: A Study in Detection* (New York, 1989); Martin Priestman, *Detective Fiction and Literature: The Figure on the Carpet* (New York, 1991); Karen Halttunnen, *Murder Most Foul: The Killer and the American Gothic Imagination* (Cambridge, MA, 1998); Claire Potter, *War on Crime: Bandits, G-Men, and the Politics of Mass Culture* (New Brunswick, NJ, 1998); Sean McCann, *Gumshoe America: Hard-Boiled Crime Fiction and the Rise and Fall of New Deal Liberalism* (Durham, NC, 2000); and Lawrence Friedman, and Issachar Rosen-Zvi, "Illegal Fictions: Mystery Novels and the Popular Image of Crime," *UCLA Law Review* 48 (2001), 1411–30.

J. Dennis Bounds traces the multimedia career of the twentieth century's most famous criminal lawyer in *Perry Mason: The Authorship and Reproduction of a Popular Hero* (Westport, CT, 1996). Norman Rosenberg's "Perry Mason," in Robert M. Jarvis and Paul R. Joseph, eds., *Prime Time Law: Fictional Television as Legal Narrative* (Durham, NC, 1998), 115–28 offers a brief overview of Mason's style of legal practice.

Perhaps the nation's most beloved lawyer, Atticus Finch of Harper Lee's *To Kill a Mockingbird* (novel, 1960; movie, 1962) gets praised, and also pummeled, in a series of essays. These include "Symposium: *To Kill a Mockingbird*," *Alabama Law Review* 45 (1994), 389–584; John Jay Osborn, Jr., "Atticus Finch – The End of Honor: A Discussion of *To Kill a Mockingbird*,"

University of San Francisco Law Review 30 (1996), 1139–42; Steve Lubet, "Reconstructing Atticus Finch," *Michigan Law Review* 97 (1999), 1339–62; Teresa Godwin Phelps, "Atticus, Thomas, and the Meaning of Justice," *Notre Dame Law Review* 77 (2002), 925; and Robert Battey, "Race and the Limits of Narrative: Atticus Finch: Boris A. Max, and the Lawyer's Dilemma," *Texas Wesleyan Law Review* 12 (2005), 389–425. Charles J. Shields, *Mockingbird: A Portrait of Harper Lee* (New York, 2006) seeks to illuminate the life of Finch's elusive creator. The best-selling novels of John Grisham are examined in Judith Grant, "Lawyers as Superheroes: *The Firm, The Client,* and *The Pelican Brief*," *University of San Francisco Law Review* 30 (1996), 1111–22 and John B. Owen's "Grisham's Legal Tales: A Moral Compass for the Young Lawyer," *UCLA Law Review* 48 (2001), 1431–42. See also Lawrence Friedman, "Law, Lawyers, and Popular Culture," *Yale Law Journal* 98 (1989), 1579–1606; Richard Posner, "The Depiction of Law in *The Bonfire of the Vanities*," *Yale Law Journal* 98 (1989), 1653–61; and Norman L. Rosenberg, "Young Mr. Lincoln: The Lawyer as Super-Hero," *Legal Studies Forum*, 15 (1991), 215–31.

Ray B. Browne, who has lovingly nurtured the study of commercial popular culture as an academic field, brought together a series of essays in Ray B. and Glenn J. Browne, eds., *Laws of Our Fathers: Popular Culture and the U.S. Constitution* (Bowling Green, OH, 1986) on the U.S. Constitution. In a similar vein, Maxwell Bloomfield's *Peaceful Revolution: Constitutional Change and American Culture from Progressivism to the New Deal* (Cambridge, MA, 2000) looks at constitutional imagery in various forms of popular culture. For brief overviews focused on the U.S. Supreme Court and constitutional law, see Bloomfield's "Popular Images of the Court," in Kermit Hall, ed., *The Oxford Companion to the Supreme Court of the United States* (New York, 1992), 655–60 and Norman L. Rosenberg, "The Supreme Court and Popular Culture: Image and Projection," in Christopher Tomlins, ed., *The United States Supreme Court: The Pursuit of Justice* (Boston, 2005), 398–422.

A number of potential cultural and cinematic themes in the representation of things legal in commercial motion pictures, radio, and television emerge from Robert B. Ray, *A Certain Tendency of the Hollywood Cinema, 1930–1980* (Princeton, NJ, 1985); Thomas Leitch, *Crime Films* (New York, 2002); Jack Shadoian, *Dreams and Dead Ends: The American Gangster Film* (New York, 2003); J. Fred McDonald, *Don't Touch That Dial: Radio Programming in American Life, 1920–1960* (Chicago, 1979); David Ray Papke, "The Public Prosecutor as Representational Image: Mr. District Attorney: The Prosecutor During the Golden Age of Radio," *University of Toledo Law Review* 34 (2003), 781–92; David Marc, *Demographic Vistas: Television in American Culture* (Philadelphia, 1985); Stephen Gillers, "Taking *L.A Law* More Seriously," *Yale Law Journal* 98 (1989), 1607–23; Kevin K. Ho, "'The

Simpsons' and Law: Revealing Truth and Justice to the Masses," *UCLA Entertainment Law Review* 10 (2003), 275–88; and the individual chapters in the earlier cited *Prime Time Law: Fictional Television as Legal Narrative*, edited by Robert M. Jarvis and Paul R. Joseph.

More specific studies of things legal in Hollywood movies began appearing during the late 1980s and early 1990s. The law professor John Denvir facilitated three collections of essays. These include a symposium entitled "Legal Reelism: The Hollywood Film as Legal Text," *Legal Studies Forum* 15 (1991), 195–263; *Legal Reelism: Movies as Legal Texts* (Urbana, IL, 1996); and "Symposium: Picturing Justice: Images of Law and Lawyers in the Visual Media," *University of San Francisco Law Review* 30 (1996), 891–1247. See also, Robert Post, "On the Popular Image of the Lawyer: Reflections in a Dark Glass," *California Law Review* 75 (1989), 379–89.

In *Reel Justice: The Courtroom Goes to the Movies* (Kansas City, MO, 2006) – a lively book that has attracted both a professional and popular audience – Paul Berman and Michael Asimow critique the "reality" of Hollywood motion pictures featuring courtroom sequences. They have also published a number of law review essays; see, e.g. Asimow, "When Lawyers Were Heroes," *University of San Francisco Law Review* 30 (1996), 1131–38l; "Bad Lawyers in the Movies," *Nova Law Review* 24 (2000), 533; and "Embodiment of Evil: Law Firms in the Movies," *UCLA Law Review* 48 (2001), 1339–92; and Bergman, "The Movie Lawyers' Guide to Redemptive Legal Practice," *UCLA Law Review* 48 (2001), 1393–1409. Asimow has also produced an edited version of the first law school textbook on motion pictures: Michael Asimow and Shannon Mader, eds., *Law and Popular Culture: A Course Book* (New York, 2004).

Anthony Chase has reworked and extended his earlier studies – such as "Lawyers and Popular Culture: A Review of Media Portrayals of American Attorneys," *American Bar Foundation Research Journal* (1986), 281–300 in *Movies on Trial: The Legal System on the Silver Screen* (New York, 2002). See also, Steve Greenfield, Guy Osborn, and Peter Robson, *Film and the Law* (London, 2001); Norman Rosenberg, "Hollywood on Trials: Courts and Films, 1930–1960," *Law & History Review* 12 (1994), 341–67 and "Law in Living Color" [Symposium], *Asian Law Journal* 5 (1998), 1–137; and a special issue edited by Robert M. Jarvis on "Admiralty Law in Popular Culture," *Journal of Maritime Law and Commerce* 31 (2000), 519–659.

Beginning with the penny presses themselves, accounts of "notorious trials" have done a brisk business. Erik Larson's *The Devil in the White City: Murder, Magic, and Madness at the Fair That Changed America* (New York, 2002) is a stunningly successful example of the ongoing commercial viability of accounts of the nineteenth-century crime scene. Specific studies of famous cases from the nineteenth and twentieth centuries include

"Symposium on Cases of the Century," *Loyola of Los Angeles Law Review* 33 (2000), 585–746; Amy Gilman Srebnick, *The Mysterious Death of Mary Rogers: Sex and Culture in Nineteenth-Century New York* (New York, 1995); Michael Grossberg, *A Judgment for Solomon: The D'Hauteville Case and Legal Experience in Antebellum America* (New York, 1996); Laura Hanft Korobkin, *Criminal Conversations: Sentimentality and Nineteenth-Century Legal Stories of Adultery* (New York, 1998); Patricia Cline Cohen, *The Murder of Helen Jewett* (New York, 1999); Richard Wightman Fox, "Intimacy on Trial: Cultural Meanings of the Beecher-Tilton Affair," in Richard Wightman Fox, ed., *The Power of Culture: Critical Essays in American History* (Chicago, 1993), 103–32; and Cara W. Robertson, "Representing 'Miss Lizzie': Cultural Convictions in the Trial of Lizzie Borden," *Yale Journal of Law & Humanities* 8 (1996) 351–416. An entry in the PBS "American Experience" series, *Murder of the Century* (1995, 2003), recovers the Thaw trial. A companion Web site – http://www.pbs.org/wgbh/amex/century/ – provides additional materials. The essays in Toni Morrison, ed., *Birth of a Nation'hood: Gaze, Script, and Spectacle in the OJ Simpson Case* (New York, 1997) provide some of the best looks at one of the most notorious trials of the late twentieth century.

Two important studies attempt to synthesize and evaluate the law *and* popular culture literature. Lawrence Friedman's "Lexitainment: Legal Process as Theater," *DePaul Law Review* 50 (2000), 539–58 surveys the changing role of popular legal forms. As the term "lexitainment" suggests, this essay sees jurisprudence for the millions blending education with amusement, but concludes that, over time, "didactic" elements have given way to an emphasis on marketing legal "spectacles as sheer entertainment." Richard Sherwin's jeremiad, *When Law Goes Pop: The Vanishing Line Between Law and Popular Culture* (Chicago, 2000) offers a highly critical analysis. It warns that the pyrotechnics of pop law, which seem to be spreading from the commercial culture industry to the nation's formal legal system, threaten the survival of traditional legal principles and values, particularly the idea that the practice of law provides a reasoned, principled path toward truth.

II. *Law* as *Culture/Culture* as *Law*

Jessica M. Silbey's review of *When Law Goes Pop* – "What We Do When We Do Law and Popular Culture," *Law & Social Inquiry* 27 (2002), 139–68 critically locates Sherwin's framework imagines both law and culture. Silbey's essay draws on research traditions that seek to map the complex interplay between the fields of culture and of law. As Naomi Mezey's earlier cited essay insists, law might be seen *"as culture and culture as law."* In its view, the new research tradition in law and culture might begin by viewing law "as one of signifying practices that constitute culture and vice-versa."

See also Costas Douzinas and Lynda Nead, *Law and the Image: The Authority of Art and the Aesthetics of Law* (Chicago, 1999); Rosemary J. Coombe, "Critical Cultural Legal Studies," *Yale Journal of Law & Humanities* 10 (1998), 463–84; and "Symposium: A New Legal Realism? Cultural Studies and the Law," *Yale Journal of Law & Humanities* 13 (2001), 3–171, edited by Austin Sarat and Jonathan Simon.

Providing one genealogy for this research tradition, Sarat and Simon see it emerging, toward the end of the 1980s, as one strand of the law-and-society movement begins to take "the cultural turn." See their broadly imagined "Introduction: Beyond Legal Realism? Cultural Analysis, Cultural Studies, and the Situation of Legal Scholarship," *Yale Journal of Law & Humanities* 13 (2001), 3–32. There is a vast body of scholarship on the legal-realist research tradition. On Thurman Arnold, one of the original realists most interested in cultural issues, see his own *The Symbols of Government* (New Haven, CT, 1935); Spencer Weber Waller, *Thurman Arnold: A Biography* (New York, 2005); Neil Duxbury, "Some Radicalism About Realism? Thurman Arnold and the Politics of Modern Jurisprudence," *Oxford Journal of Legal Studies* 10 (1990), 11–41; and Mark Fenster, "The Symbols of Governance: Thurman Arnold and Post-Realist Legal Theory," *Buffalo Law Review* 51 (2003), 1053–118. On Fred Rodell, see Neil Duxbury, "In the Twilight of Legal Realism: Fred Rodell and the Limits of Legal Critique," *Oxford Journal of Legal Studies* 11 (1991), 354–95. Laura Kalman, *Legal Realism at Yale, 1927–1960* (Chapel Hill, NC, 1986) provides a superb view of the academic context in which Arnold and Rodell worked.

Arguably, an earlier 1989 Symposium in the *Yale Law Journal*, entitled "Popular Legal Culture," might mark the point at which this turn became effectively legible. The lead essay by Stewart Macaulay – "Popular Legal Culture: An Introduction," 98 *Yale Law Journal* (1989), 1545–58 – offers an especially expansive framework for future scholarly work. At the same time, it teases out some of the implications of the claim that most people derive their "lessons" about the world of things legal – extending from practice in nation's formal court systems to policing practices on city streets and on to the various ways of avoiding state-imposed legal strictures – through a wide means of popular texts and activities.

Proceeding in this vein, Macaulay's colleague Marc Galanter has dissected jokes about lawyers, analyzing what this cultural form might say about law and legal practice. See *Lowering the Bar: Lawyers Jokes and Legal Culture* (Madison, WI, 2005); "Robert S. Marx Lecture: The Faces of Mistrust: The Image of Lawyers in Public Opinion: Jokes and Political Discourse," *University of Cincinnati Law Review* 66 (1998), 805–42; and "The Uri and Catherine Baker Memorial Lecture: Changing Legal Consciousness in America: The View from the Joke Corpus," *Cardozo Law Review* 23 (2002), 2223–40.

Invoking a broad view of the term "popular culture," Macaulay's essay also anticipated at least some of the many different directions the cultural turn has taken. Macaulay's own "Images of Law in Everyday Life: The Lessons of School, Entertainment, and Spectator Sports," *Law & Society Review* 21 (1987), 185–218 provides an early example of this kind of work, as does Barbara Yngvesson's "Inventing the Law in Local Settings: Rethinking Popular Legal Culture," *Yale Law Journal* 98 (1989), 1689.

During the late 1980s, a number of scholars associated with the law-and-society enterprise did begin looking at popular legal practices outside the formal policing and dispute settlement institutions of the liberal state. Drawing on French post-structuralist scholarship, especially the work of Pierre Bourdieu and Michel De Certeau, they talked about different "domains" of law and about law in "everyday life." See, e.g., Bourdieu, "The Force of Law: Toward a Sociology of the Juridical Field," *Hastings Law Journal* 38 (1987), 805 (R. Terdiman, trans.) and De Certeau, *The Practice of Everyday Life* (Berkeley, CA, 1984). The imaginative synthesis of theory and empirical work offered by Patricia Ewick and Susan S. Silbey – *The Common Place of Law out of the Ordinary: Law, Power, Culture, and the Commonplace* (Chicago, 1998) – provides a superb example of this kind of legal-cultural work. For a critical appreciation, see Naomi Mezey, "The Common Place of Law: Stories from Everyday Life [Review essay on Ewick and Silbey]," *Law & Social Inquiry* 26 (2001), 145–66.

Meanwhile, Austin Sarat and several co-editors began facilitating a series of volumes – under the title "The Amherst Series in Law, Jurisprudence, and Social Thought" – that bring a wide range of critical cultural insights into legal studies. These include *Law in Everyday Life* (Ann Arbor, MI, 1993), *Law in the Domains of Culture* (Ann Arbor, MI, 1998), and *Law on the Screen* (Stanford, CA, 2005).

Other examples of law-and-culture studies have enabled the particular project of this chapter by tracing how jurisprudence for the millions became embedded in the fields of commercial culture and law. Some seemingly borrow from the research tradition in law and literature and cross-examine narrative structures and imagery in popular legal texts with those found in more traditional legal discourse. See, for instance, two superb studies by Brook Thomas – *Cross-Examinations of Law and Literature: Cooper, Hawthorne, Stowe, and Melville* (New York, 1987) and "The Social Drama of an Antebellum Custody Case," *Law & Social Inquiry* 23 (1997), 431–56. See also Guyora Binder and Robert Weisberg, "Cultural Criticism of Law," *Stanford Law Review* 49 (1997), 1149–221.

In addition, studies focusing on visual texts have also looked to critical work in cultural and media studies. As Donald Black's *Law in Film: Resonance and Representation* (Urbana, IL, 1999) has usefully emphasized, however, too close a reliance on literary-oriented scholarship can result in studies that see visual texts as little more than illustrated print works rather than examples of the filmic and the televisual arts.

Leading examples of critical cultural scholarship on court trials include Shoshana Felman, *The Juridical Unconscious: Trials and Traumas in the Twentieth Century* (Cambridge, MA, 2002); Melissa J. Ganz, "Wicked Women and Veiled Ladies: Gendered Narratives of the McFarland-Richardson Tragedy," *Yale Journal of Law & Feminism* 9 (1997), 255–303; Robert Chang, "Dreaming in Black and White: Racial-Sexual Policing in *The Birth of a Nation*, *The Cheat*, and *Who Killed Vincent Chin?*," *Asian Law Journal* 5 (1998), 41–61; Rob Atkinson, "Liberating Lawyers: Divergent Parallels in *Intruder in the Dust* and *To Kill a Mockingbird*," *Duke Law Journal* 49 (1999), 601–747; David Ray Papke, "The American Courtroom Trial: Pop Culture, Courtroom Realities, and the Dream World of Justice," *South Texas Law Review* 40 (1999), 919; Orit Kamir, "Feminist Law and Film: Imagining Judges and Justice," *Chicago-Kent Law Review* 75 (2000), 899–931; Martha Merrill Umphrey, "The Dialogics of Legal Meaning: Spectacular Trials, the Unwritten Law, and Narratives of Criminal Responsibility," *Law & Society Review* 33 (1999), 393–423, "Media Melodrama! Sensationalism and the 1907 Trial of Harry Thaw," *New York Law School Review* 43 (1999–2000), 715–39, and "Fragile Performances: The Dialogics of Judgment in a Theory of the Trial," *Law & Social Inquiry* 28 (2003), 527–32; and Pnina Lahav, "Theater in the Courtroom: The Chicago Conspiracy Trial," *Cardozo Studies in Law & Literature* 16 (2004), 381–448.

The critical cultural literature on Hollywood motion pictures, radio, and television might be best approached through the Mezey and Niles essay, "Screening the Law," cited earlier. See also, Orit Kamir, *Framed: Women in Law and Film* (Durham, NC, 2006), which offers essays on several Hollywood and foreign-made movies, including *Anatomy of a Murder*, *Adam's Rib*, and *Nuts*; David Ray Papke, "Peace Between the Sexes: Law and Gender in *Kramer vs. Kramer*," *University of San Francisco Law Review* 30 (1996), 1199–1208, "Conventional Wisdom: The Courtroom Trial in American Popular Culture," *Marquette Law Review* 82 (1999), 471–89, and "Law, Cinema, and Justice: Hollywood Legal Films of the 1950's," *UCLA Law Review* 48 (2001), 1473; Carol Clover, "God Bless Juries," in Nick Browne, ed., *Refiguring American Film Genres* (Berkeley, CA, 1998), 255–77 and "Law and the Order of Popular Culture," in the earlier cited *Law in the Domains of Popular Culture*, 97–119; Marjorie Garber, "Cinema Scopes: Evolution, Media, and the Law," in *Law in the Domains of Popular Culture*, 121–59; Austin Sarat, "The Cultural Life of Capital Punishment: Responsibility and Representation in *Dead Man Walking* and *Last Dance*," *Yale Journal of Law & the Humanities* 11 (1999), 153–90 and "Exploring the Hidden

Domains of Civil Justice: 'Naming, Blaming, and Claiming' in Popular Culture," *DePaul Law Review* 50 (2000), 425–52; Rebecca Johnson and Ruth Buchanan, "Getting the Insider's Story Out: What Popular Film Can Tell Us About Legal Method's Dirty Secrets," *Windsor Yearbook of Access to Justice* 20 (2001), 87–109; Norman Rosenberg, "Looking For Law in All the Old Traces: The Movies of Classical Hollywood, the Law, and the Case(s) of Film Noir," *UCLA Law Review* 48 (2001), 1443–71; Rosenberg, "Constitutional History After the Cultural Turn: The Legal-Reelist Texts of Henry Fonda," in Sandra VanBurkleo, et al., eds., *Constitutionalism and American Culture: Writing the New Constitutional History* (Lawrence KS, 2002), 381–409; Susan Jeffords, "Popular Culture: 'Above the Law,'" *Indiana Law Journal* 77 (2002), 331–39; Susana Lee, "'These Are Our Stories': Trauma, Form, and the Screen Phenomenon of *Law and Order*," *Discourse* 28 (2002), 81–97; John Brigham, "Representing Lawyers: From Courtrooms to Boardrooms and TV Studios," *Syracuse Law Review* 53 (2003), 1165–99; Kimberlianne Podlas, "Broadcast Litigiousness: Syndi-Court's Construction of Legal Consciousness," *Cardozo Arts & Entertainment Law Journal* 23 (2005), 465–505; Elena Razlogova, "True Crime Radio and Listener Disenchantment with Network Broadcasting, 1935–1946," *American Quarterly* 58 (2006), 137–58; and Tom R. Tyler, "Viewing *CSI* and the Threshold of Guilt: Managing Truth and Justice in Reality and Fiction," *Yale Law Journal* 115 (2006), 1050–85.

Several motion pictures about things legal have attracted multiple essays. In addition to the earlier cited Rosenberg essays on *Young Mr. Lincoln* and Henry Fonda's films, see Virginia Wright Wexman's "'Right and Wrong: That's [Not] All There is to It!' and "*Young Mr. Lincoln* and American Law," *Cinema Journal* 44 (2005), 20–34. Norman Rosenberg, "Law Noir," in the earlier cited *Legal Reelism*, 280–302 addresses *Call Northside 777*, as does Jennifer L. Mnookin and Nancy West, "Theaters of Proof: Visual Evidence and the Law in *Call Northside 777*," *Yale Journal of Law & Humanities* 13 (2001), 329. There are several excellent essays on Clint Eastwood's *Unforgiven*, including William Ian Miller, "Clint Eastwood and Equity: Popular Culture's Theory of Revenge," in the earlier cited *Law and the Domains of Culture*, 161–201; Austin Sarat, "When Memory Speaks: Remembrance and Revenge in *Unforgiven*," *Indiana Law Journal* 77 (2002), 307–22; and Orit Kamir," "Honor and Dignity in the Film *Unforgiven*: Implications for Sociolegal Theory," *Law & Society Review* 40 (2006), 193–233.

On the gap between critical cultural legal studies literature and courtroom practice, see Jessica M. Silbey, "Judges as Film Critics: New Approaches to Filmic Evidence," *University of Michigan Journal of Law Reform* 37 (2004), 493–571 and "Filmmaking in the Precinct House and the Genre of Documentary Film," *Columbia Journal of Law & the Arts* 29 (2005),

107–80. Earlier discussions of documentary filmmaking in the context of things legal include Charles Musser, "Film Truth, Documentary, and the Law: Justice at the Margins," *University of San Francisco Law Review* 30 (1996), 963–84 and Bill Nichols, "The Unseen Jury," *University of San Francisco Law Review* 30 (1996), 1055–64.

Finally, there are several Web sites that track the intersection of law and culture. See, for example, "Picturing Justice: The On-Line Journal of Law and Popular Culture," at http://www.usfca.edu/pj. The materials on the "Famous Trials" Web site, edited by Douglas Linder, also offers perspectives of some of the "notorious" trials of the late nineteenth and twentieth centuries; see http://www.law.umkc.edu/faculty/projects/ftrials/ftrials.htm.

In addition, the Tarleton Law Library at the University of Texas provides e-texts of selected essays on law and various forms of culture, especially Hollywood movies: http://tarlton.law.utexas.edu/lpop/etext/index.html.

CHAPTER 19: MAKING LAW, MAKING WAR, MAKING AMERICA

MARY L. DUDZIAK

The literature on law and war is extensive and has expanded significantly since September 11, 2001. This essay cannot be comprehensive. Instead, my aim is to highlight particularly useful works in different relevant areas.

War and the Making of America

Scholars have focused on the way wars have helped "make" America in different ways, whether through the construction of American identity or through state-building. These works do not always have law at their center, but they are important for an understanding of the ways in which war has shaped American law.

On war and national identity, Jill Lepore, *The Name of War: King Philip's War and the Origins of American Identity* (New York, 1999) focuses on the way narratives of wars are constructed and helps us see that interpretations of wars infuse them with meaning that is drawn on in constructions of identity. For David Campbell, national identity and conceptions of national security are forged in relation to an "other," such as the Soviet Union during the Cold War: see *Writing Security: United States Foreign Policy and the Politics of Identity* (Minneapolis, MN, 1998). Works on historical memory focus on the ways the meaning of war is understood and functions over time. Some works on war and memory focus on the United States. See Marita Sturken, *Tangled Memories: The Vietnam War, the AIDS Epidemic, and the Politics of Remembering* (Berkeley, CA, 1997). Others focus on particular events involving the United States, such as the use of atomic weapons in World War II; see Michael J. Hogan, ed., *Hiroshima in History and Memory* (Cambridge,

1996). The focus of Susan Rubin Suleiman, *Crises of Memory and the Second World War* (Cambridge, MA, 2006), is global as well as national, because, she argues, the experience of the Holocaust was global and hence operated as a site of collective memory. The cultural production of war, including government efforts to generate support for war, is discussed in James R. Mock and Cedric Larson, *Words that Won the War: The Story of the Committee on Public Information, 1917–1919* (Princeton, NJ, 1939); Allen M. Winkler, *The Politics of Propaganda: The Office of War Information, 1942–1945* (New Haven, CT, 1978); Gerd Horten, *Radio Goes to War: The Cultural Politics of Propaganda During World War II* (Berkeley, CA, 2002); Walter L. Hixson, *Parting the Curtain: Propaganda, Culture, and the Cold War, 1945–1961* (New York, 1977); Thomas Doherty, *Projections of War: Hollywood, American Culture, and World War II* (New York, 1993); and Richard W. Steele, "Preparing the Public for War: Efforts to Establish a National Propaganda Agency, 1940–41," *American Historical Review* 75 (1970), 1640–53.

Although works on identity, memory, and culture have been the focus of historians and cultural studies scholars, writing about state-building has been done principally by political scientists. Robert Higgs, *Crisis and Leviathan: Critical Episodes in the Growth of American Government* (New York, 1987) sees war and other major crises, such as the Great Depression, as occasions for the expansion of the U.S. government. Central to his thesis is the idea of the ratchet. Once created by war or crisis, government powers do not fully recede after the war is over, but are turned to new uses in peacetime. Then government power expands again to meet the next crisis. Over time, government power ratchets up and is not cut back. Writing from a libertarian perspective, Higgs sees the expansion of government as a great threat to liberty, but the idea that war fuels state-building is not restricted to libertarian scholarship. Aaron Freidberg also notes that "the imminent threat of war produced pressures for the permanent construction of a powerful central state" in the United States, but he sees this dynamic as coming later, after World War II, and he emphasizes constraints. American "anti-statism," he argues, placed a break on excessive concentration of state power: Aaron L. Friedberg, *In the Shadow of the Garrison State* (Princeton, NJ, 2000). Historians Fred Anderson and Andrew Cayton take a broader view, seeing war and empire as central features of American history, in *The Dominion of War: Empire and Liberty in North America, 1500–2000* (New York, 2005). Ira Katznelson and Martin Shefter, eds., *Shaped by War and Trade: International Influences on American Political Development* (Princeton, NJ, 2002) examine war and international trade as two forms of international impacts on American state-building. The impact of World War II on the development of the administrative state and other areas is discussed in Daniel R. Ernst and Victor Jew, *Total War and the Law: The American Home*

Front in World War II (Westport, CT, 2002). See also Bartholomew Sparrow, *From the Outside In: World War II and the American State* (Princeton, NJ, 1996). For some scholars, in contrast, the American state is a "New Deal state," with its formative moments in "inter-war years" or peacetime. See Bruce Ackerman, *We the People, Vol. 2: Transformations* (Cambridge, MA, 1998). Works on law and government power in the New Deal era include Barry Cushman, *Rethinking the New Deal Court: The Structure of a Constitutional Revolution* (New York, 1998); William E. Leuchtenburg, *The Supreme Court Reborn: The Constitutional Revolution in the Age of Roosevelt* (New York, 1995); G. Edward White, *The Constitution and the New Deal* (Cambridge, 2000); and Laura Kalman, "The Constitution, the Supreme Court, and the New Deal," *American Historical Review* 110 (2005), 1052–80.

If war helped make America, what sort of nation did it make? For some scholars, war made the nation a "warrior state." Although some recoil from the expanse of government power inherent in a warrior state or worry about the implications of militarization for democracy, others see it as justifying an expansive role for the United States in the world. Supporting the warrior state argument is the pervasive engagement of the United States in military conflict, emphasized in Max Boot, *The Savage Wars of Peace: Small Wars and the Rise of American Power* (New York, 2002). For an argument that a warrior state is in tension with American constitutional values, see Mark E. Brandon, "War and the American Constitutional Order," in Mark Tushnet, ed., *The Constitution in Wartime: Beyond Alarmism and Complacency* (Durham, NC, 2005), 11–38. Michael Sherry's comprehensive study, *In the Shadow of War: The United States Since the 1930s* (New Haven, CT, 1995) does not use the "warrior state" language nor does it share Boot's embrace of American empire, but his argument that war and militarization have been central features of American life since the 1930s is consistent with the idea that war played a central role in building the twentieth-century American state.

War, Rights, and the Pendulum

The most classic works on law and war often focus on the impact of war on civil liberties. The focus is usually on the suppression of rights during wartime, although writers have different views about the degree to which this has been justifiable. Dominant throughout the literature is the idea of a pendulum that swings between rights and security. During wartime, the pendulum is thought to swing away from rights protection and toward more robust protection of security. When war is over, the pendulum is thought to swing in the other direction. Important to this conceptualization are assumptions shared by most writers: that American history can be divided into time zones (wartime and peacetime) and that wartime is exceptional and different from normal time. The idea of time zones is in tension, however, with some warrior state writers who see American military involvement as ubiquitous, rather than episodic.

A recent and helpful collection, Mark Tushnet, ed., *The Constitution in Wartime*, attempts to move beyond the standard framework for studying law and war by questioning traditional trade-offs between rights and security, even though the essays often work within the dominant conceptualization of war and American society: the idea that changes to the rights environment are turned off and on during periodic "wartimes." An example of scholarship that examines the impact of international pressures and security-related concerns on American law outside discrete "wartimes" is the work on the impact of fascism on American law before World War II. For example, David M. Bixby, "The Roosevelt Court, Democratic Ideology, and Minority Rights: Another Look at *United States v. Classic*," *Yale Law Journal* 90 (1981), 741–79 argues that concerns about fascism in Europe during Hitler's rise to power informed the thinking of American intellectuals, including members of the Supreme Court, on the weaknesses of a majoritarian form of government and the need for the courts to act as a bar to majority abuse of minority rights. See also Robert M. Cover, "The Origins of Judicial Activism in the Protection of Minorities," *Yale Law Journal* 91 (1982), 1287–1316.

An ambitious work challenging the dominant understanding that wartime has a negative impact on rights is Lee Epstein, Daniel E. Ho, Gary King, and Jeffrey A. Segal, "The Supreme Court During Crisis: How War Affects Only Non-War Cases," *New York University Law Review* 80 (2005), 1–116. These authors argue that a quantitative analysis of civil liberties cases during wartime shows that the impact of war on the Supreme Court is restricted to non-war-related cases. A limitation of this study is that it assumes that the boundaries of wartimes are discrete and discernible. World War II exists, for the authors, from the date of Pearl Harbor, December 7, 1941, to V-J Day, August 14, 1945, and they look for war-related impacts within that time period. But the nature of twentieth-century American warfare has made bright lines difficult to find. It is the case that, as Melvin Urofsky has shown, Pearl Harbor led to a greater level of overt engagement on the part of the Court with the U.S. war effort: Melvin I. Urofsky, "The Court at War, and the War at the Court," *Journal of Supreme Court History* (1996), 1–18. But the United States was engaged in the war long before Pearl Harbor. National security concerns related to the overseas conflict affected the nation before and after the formal dates of the war, surfacing in cases like *Minersville School District v. Gobitis*, 310 U.S. 586, 595 (1940) and *Woods v. Cloyd W. Miller, Co.*, 333 U.S. 138 (1948). Because Epstein et al. assume that war-related impacts turned off and on during discrete, formal wartimes, the article cannot provide a definitive answer to the question of whether war has an impact on civil liberties cases.

Within the traditional pendulum analysis lies much important work on law and war. An important work on the First Amendment is Geoffrey R. Stone, *Perilous Times: Free Speech in Wartime, From the Sedition Act to the War on Terror* (New York, 2004), which finds more repression during World War I than in later twentieth-century wars. Important developments in the First Amendment during and after World War I are addressed in David Rabban, *The First Amendment in its Forgotten Years, 1870–1920* (Cambridge, 1997) and Paul Murphy, *World War I and the Origins of Civil Liberties in the United States* (New York, 1979).

Paul Murphy, *The Constitution in Crisis Times, 1918–1969* (New York, 1972) remains a rich overview of much of the century. William H. Rehnquist, *All the Laws but One: Civil Liberties in Wartime* (New York, 1998) is principally on the Civil War, with twentieth-century chapters as well. It is perhaps most interesting as the work of a Supreme Court justice crafting a lesson from history that would then undoubtedly inform his own writing of law during wartime. Edward S. Corwin, *Total War and the Constitution* (New York, 1947) remains a classic. It may be most important as a primary source on the impact of World War II on legal thinkers, during what E. Blythe Stason in his introduction noted was a time in which Americans found themselves in a "scientific world" defined by the introduction of atomic energy, and yet "a bewildered and thoroughly chaotic world."

The greatest abuse of rights during World War II is often thought to be the internment of Japanese Americans. Two classic works detailing the history of anti-Asian sentiment in California and the role of prejudice in support for the internment program are Jacobus tenBroek, Edward Norton Barnhart, and Floyd W. Matson, *Prejudice, War and the Constitution: Causes and Consequences of the Evacuation of the Japanese Americans in World War II* (Berkeley, CA, 1970) and Roger Daniels, *The Politics of Prejudice: The Anti-Japanese Movement in California and the Struggle for Japanese Exclusion* (Berkeley, CA, 1962). Peter Irons, *Justice at War: The Story of the Japanese-American Internment Cases* (New York, 1983) details the history of internment, especially the litigation that would justify its constitutionality in *Korematsu* and related cases. Greg Robinson, *By Order of the President: FDR and the Internment of Japanese Americans* (Cambridge, MA, 2001) illuminates FDR's central role. The experience of internment is described in Yoshiko Uchida, *Desert Exile: The Uprooting of a Japanese-American Family* (Seattle, WA, 1982), and Jeanne Wakatsuki Houston and James D. Houston, *Farewell to Manzanar: A True Story of Japanese American Experience During and After the World War II Internment* (New York, 1973). Eric L. Muller, *Free to Die for Their Country: The Story of the Japanese American Draft Resisters in World War II* (Chicago,

2001) discusses prosecution of internees who were drafted while confined to camps, but some refused to serve a country that had imprisoned them. The imposition of martial law in Hawaii is the focus of Harry N. Scheiber and Jane L. Scheiber, "Bayonets in Paradise: A Half-Century Retrospect on Martial Law in Hawai'i, 1941–1946," *University of Hawaii Law Review* 19 (1997), 477–648.

Linda Kerber, *No Constitutional Right to Be Ladies: Women and the Obligations of Citizenship* (New York, 1998) considers women's citizenship rights in the context of women's exclusion from the obligation of military service, with chapters on jury service and veterans' preference policies, among other topics. Sandra F. VanBurkleo, *Belonging to the World: Women's Rights and American Constitutional Culture* (New York, 2001) is a helpful survey of women's constitutional rights. Philippa Strum, *Women in the Barracks: The VMI Case and Equal Rights* (Lawrence, KS, 2002) takes up an important 1996 equal protection case holding that exclusion of women from the Virginia Military Institute violated the Constitution.

Some scholars have focused on the impact of war or national security on the expansion of rights. Alexander Keyssar, *The Right to Vote: The Contested History of Democracy in the United States* (New York, 2000) finds that wartime has been the occasion for the expansion of voting rights. Phillip A. Klinkner with Rogers Smith, *The Unsteady March: The Rise and Decline of Racial Equality in the United States* (Chicago, 1999) argues that the only sustained progress on racial reform for African Americans has happened in the context of large-scale wars in which African Americans fought, when an ideology of democracy underlying the war was in tension with inequality and when a civil rights movement exploited this context. To make the thesis work, however, the authors collapse the years 1941–68, encompassing World War II, Korea, the Cold War, and part of Vietnam, into one long era when, they argue, all of their factors remained in play. The awkwardness of this periodization is apparent by the inability of their thesis to explain the falling off of reform efforts while African American troops continued to fight in an escalated war in Vietnam, illustrating, perhaps, that war matters, but that war-related time zones don't work. Nevertheless, Klinkner and Smith's effort to distill causal elements from history is important. A more focused work finding limited progress on civil rights during World War II is Daniel Kryder, *Divided Arsenal: Race and the American State During World War II* (Cambridge, 2000). Scholars have linked Cold War foreign relations to civil rights reform, as other nations argued that race discrimination undermined U.S. world leadership, thereby aiding the Soviet Union; see Mary L. Dudziak, *Cold War Civil Rights: Race and the Image of American Democracy* (Princeton, NJ, 2000) and Thomas Borstelmann, *The Cold War and the Color Line: American Race Relations in the Global Arena*

(Cambridge, MA, 2001). Richard A. Primus, *The American Language of Rights* (Cambridge, 1999) discusses the impact of anti-totalitarian thinking on American rights during and after World War II. Also important is Richard M. Dalfuime, *The Desegregation of the U.S. Armed Forces: Fighting on Two Fronts, 1939–1953* (Columbia, MO, 1969).

Law, War, and Government Power
A particular concern in the literature on law and war is the expansion of executive power; however, war has an impact on the powers of other branches of government as well. Scholarship on the impact of war on presidential power often tracks the assumptions about law and war in the traditional civil liberties literature. The assumptions are that wartime is exceptional and that in temporally discrete wartimes presidential power has expanded. An important difference in this area, as compared to the civil liberties scholarship, is the emphasis on change over time. Expansions of government power do not fully recede after a war, and most scholars see the expansion of presidential war power as having continued over time. For some scholars, this is a constitutional violation. For others, it is the embodiment of a constitutional vision of a "unitary executive," especially necessary after September 11. On the idea of states of exception, as they relate to executive power, see Georgio Agamben, *State of Exception*, Kevin Attell, trans. (Chicago, 2005).

For an historical survey of presidential war power, the standard work is Louis Fisher, *Presidential War Power* (Lawrence, KS, 1995). See also Edward S. Corwin, *The President: Office and Powers, 1787–1984*, 5th rev. ed. by Randall W. Bland, Theodore T. Hindson, and Jack W. Peltason (New York, 1984). A helpful, historically oriented collection of essays is edited by Demetrios Caraley, *The President's War Powers: From the Federalists to Reagan* (New York, 1984). Peter Irons, *War Powers: How the Imperial Presidency Hijacked the Constitution* (New York, 2005) is a critical survey. John Yoo argues for expansive powers in *The Powers of War and Peace: The Constitution and Foreign Affairs After 9/11* (Chicago, 2005). Jack L. Goldsmith examines battles over law and war within the Bush administration in *The Terror Presidency: Law and Judgment Inside the Bush Administration* (New York, 2007).

Francis D. Wormuth and Edwin B. Firmage, *To Chain the Dog of War: The War Powers of Congress in History and Law* (Urbana, IL, 1986) focuses on Congress and decries Congress's diminished role over time in declaring war. See also Louis Fisher, "How Tightly Can Congress Draw the Purse Strings?" *American Journal of International Law* 83(1989), 758–66; Thomas M. Franck, "Rethinking War Powers: By Law or 'Thurmaturgic Invocation'?" *American Journal of International Law* 83 (1989), 768; Harold Hongju Koh, "Why the President (Almost) Always Wins in Foreign Affairs: Lessons of the Iran-Contra Affair," *Yale Law Journal* 97 (1988), 1235–1342; and Ryan

C. Hendrickson, "War Powers, Bosnia, and the 104th Congress," *Political Science Quarterly* 13 (1998), 241–58. On initiating war, a useful collection, including essays on covert actions, is Gary M. Stern and Morton H. Halperin, *The U.S. Constitution and the Power to Go to War: Historical and Current Perspectives* (Westport, CT, 1994). See also John Lehman, *Making War: The 200-Year-Old Battle Between the President and Congress over How America Goes to War* (New York, 1992). On the impact of the United Nations on the power to go to war, see David Golove, "From Versailles to San Francisco: The Revolutionary Transformation of War Powers," *Colorado Law Review* 70 (1999), 1491–1523. On the meaning of war declarations and their absence, see Elaine Scarry, "The Declaration of War: Constitutional and Unconstitutional Violence," in Austin Sarat and Thomas R. Kearns, eds., *Law's Violence* (Ann Arbor, MI, 1993).

Christopher N. May, *In the Name of War: Judicial Review and the War Powers since 1918* (Cambridge, MA, 1989) focuses on the courts and argues that the judiciary should defer review of executive action during an emergency as a way of preserving an appropriate role for the courts related to wartime. Louis Henkin, *Foreign Affairs and the United States Constitution* (New York, 1997) is a classic work, and David Gray Adler and Larry N. George, eds., *The Constitution and the Conduct of American Foreign Policy* (Lawrence, KS, 1996) is a helpful collection with contributions by leading scholars.

Among the striking episodes in the exercise of presidential power in wartime was the use of a military tribunal to try German saboteurs during World War II. There is new interest in this episode due to the use of military tribunals after September 11, 2001. New work, detailing the history of military tribunals and addressing contemporary implications, is Louis Fisher, *Military Tribunals and Presidential Power: American Revolution to the War on Terrorism* (Lawrence, KS, 2005). On the World War II context, see Louis Fisher, *Nazi Saboteurs on Trial: A Military Tribunal and American Law*, (Lawrence, KS, 2005). For a shorter work, focusing on the Supreme Court's role, see David J. Danielsky, "The Saboteur's Case," *Journal of Supreme Court History* (1996), 61–82. President Harry S. Truman's seizure of the steel mills during the Korean War is another important episode. The best work on this remains Maeva Marcus, *Truman and the Steel Seizure Case: The Limits of Presidential Power* (New York, 1977). Helpful primary sources can be found in Alan F. Westin, *The Anatomy of a Constitutional Law Case: Youngstown Sheet and Tube Co. v. Sawyer, the Steel Seizure Decision* (New York, 1958).

Managing and Making War Through Law
The story of efforts to end war through law after World War I is told in Francis Paul Walters, *A History of the League of Nations*, 2 vols. (New York, 1952) and Warren F. Kuehl and Lynne K. Dunn, *Keeping the Covenant:*

American Internationalists and the League of Nations, 1920–1939 (Kent, OH, 1997). On Woodrow Wilson's role, see Thomas J. Knock, *To End All Wars: Woodrow Wilson and the Quest for a New World Order* (New York, 1992) and John Milton Cooper, *Breaking the Heart of the World: Woodrow Wilson and the Fight for the League of Nations* (Cambridge, 2001). On the Kellogg-Briand Pact, see Robert H. Ferrell, *Peace in Their Time* (New York, reprint ed., 1968).

U.S. involvement in the development of international human rights, including U.S. opposition, is detailed in Paul Gordon Lauren, *Power and Prejudice: The Politics and Diplomacy of Racial Discrimination* (Boulder, CO, 1996). See also Paul Gordon Lauren, *The Evolution of International Human Rights: Visions Seen* (Philadelphia, 1998). Eleanor Roosevelt's role is examined in Mary Ann Glendon, *A World Made New: Eleanor Roosevelt and the Universal Declaration of Human Rights* (New York, 2001). An important new work, stressing the importance of the Atlantic Charter, is Elizabeth Borgwardt, *A New Deal for the World: America's Vision for Human Rights* (Cambridge, MA, 2005). The creation of the United Nations and subsequent developments are discussed in Stanley Meisler, *United Nations: The First Fifty Years* (New York, 1997). On UN peacekeeping, see Brian Urquhart's memoir, *A Life in Peace and War* (New York, 1987). Also helpful is an edited collection, Adam Roberts and Benedict Kingsbury, eds., *United Nations, Divided World: The UN's Roles in International Relations* (New York, 1994).

For the development of the law of war and war crimes, see Howard Ball, *Prosecuting War Crimes and Genocide: The Twentieth-Century Experience* (Lawrence, KS, 1999) and Peter Maguire, *Law and War: An American Story* (New York, 2001). On war crimes tribunals, see Gary Jonathan Bass, *Stay the Hand of Vengeance: The Politics of War Crimes Tribunals* (Princeton, NJ, 2000). The problem of genocide in the late twentieth century is discussed in Samantha Power's critique of U.S. policy, *A Problem from Hell: America and the Age of Genocide* (New York, 2002). The problem of redress for victims of mass violence is addressed in Martha Minow, *Between Vengeance and Forgiveness: Facing History After Genocide and Mass Violence* (New York, 1998).

The U.S. role in the Nuremberg Trials is illuminated in Michael R. Marrus, *The Nuremberg War Crimes Trial, 1945–46: A Documentary History* (Boston, 1997). On the response to the My Lai massacre, see Michal R. Belknap, *The Vietnam War on Trial: The My Lai Massacre and Court-Martial of Lieutenant Calley* (Lawrence, KS, 2002). Elizabeth Lutes Hillman, *Defending America: Military Culture and the Cold War Court-Martial* (Princeton, NJ, 2005) illustrates the way that courts-martial during the Cold War helped produce a conception of military culture defined in part by race, gender, and heterosexuality. On the development of military justice in the United

States, see Jonathan Lurie, *Military Justice in America: The U.S. Court of Appeals for the Armed Forces, 1775–1980* (Lawrence, KS, 2001).

On the law of armed conflict, see Geoffrey Best, *War and Law Since 1945* (New York, 1994); Michael Reisman, *The Laws of War: A Comprehensive Collection of Primary Documents on International Laws Governing Armed Conflict* (New York, 1994); and Adam Roberts and Richard Guelff, eds. *Documents on the Laws of War* (New York, 2000). A recent, brief synthesis is Michael Byers, *War Law: Understanding International Law and Armed Conflict* (New York, 2005), and a new critical analysis is David Kennedy, *Of War and Law* (Princeton, 2006).

September 11 and the Law

The terrorist attacks on the United States on September 11, 2001, and the subsequent American "preemptive" war in Iraq have spurred a literature of their own. A common assumption is the idea that September 11 "changed everything," so that the rules of an earlier era no longer apply. Questioning this truism and exploring its implications is Mary L. Dudziak, ed., *September 11 in History: A Watershed Moment?* (Durham, NC, 2003), including essays by Marilyn Young and Ruti Teitel. Another helpful collection is John Strawson, ed., *Law After Ground Zero* (London, 2002). Among the many law review treatments of September 11-related topics is "Law and the War on Terrorism," including a foreword by Viet Dihn, "Freedom and Security After September 11," *Harvard Journal of Law and Public Policy* 25 (2002) 399. See also James F. Hoge and Gideon Rose, eds., *Understanding the War on Terror* (New York, 2005).

Although the Bush administration calls the post-9/11 era a "war" era, scholars debate this characterization. Many prefer to view it as an "emergency" and offer prescriptions for executive power in this context. See Kim Lane Scheppele, "Law in a Time of Emergency: States of Exception and the Temptations of 9/11," *University of Pennsylvania Journal of Constitutional Law* 6 (2004), 1001 and Bruce Ackerman, *Before the Next Attack: Preserving Civil Liberties in the Age of Terrorism* (New Haven, CT, 2006). Mark Tushnet raises the question of whether the "war on terror" should be regarded as an ongoing condition, rather than a temporally confined "emergency," requiring that long-term trade-offs over rights and security, rather than short-term emergency measures, should be contemplated: see Mark Tushnet, "Emergencies and the Idea of Constitutionalism," in Mark Tushnet, ed., *The Constitution in Wartime: Beyond Alarmism and Complacency* (Durham, NC, 2005).

There has been much debate about the legitimacy of executive branch actions pursuing hostilities in Iraq and in various programs related to what has been called the "war on terror." The legal authority underlying executive branch actions is thoughtfully examined in Curtis A. Bradley and Jack L. Goldsmith, "Congressional Authorization and the War on Terrorism," *Harvard Law Review* 118 (2005), 2047 and in responses to Bradley and Goldsmith, including Derek Jenks and Ryan Goodman, "International Law, U.S. War Powers, and the Global War on Terrorism," *Harvard Law Review* 118 (2005), 2653–62.

The PATRIOT Act has spawned its own literature. The U.S. government has made the act and related government reports available in a CD-ROM: 2006 *Complete Guide to the USA PATRIOT Act, Surveillance Tools Against Terrorism, and Domestic Spying* (2006). Among the most important critiques of Bush administration anti-terror policies is David Cole, *Enemy Aliens: Double Standards And Constitutional Freedoms in the War on Terrorism* (New York, 2003). The debate about whether September 11 made torture a legitimate government policy and the shocking disclosure of abuse of prisoners by American soldiers at Abu Ghraib prison in Iraq are documented in Karen J. Greenberg and Joshua L. Dratel, eds., *The Torture Papers: The Road to Abu Ghraib* (Cambridge, 2005) and Karen J. Greenberg, ed., *The Torture Debate in America* (Cambridge, 2005). A helpful pre-Abu Ghraib collection is Sanford Levinson, *Torture: A Collection* (New York, 2004).

CHAPTER 20: LAW, LAWYERS AND EMPIRE

YVES DEZALAY AND BRYANT G. GARTH

This chapter draws extensively on our jointly published works. Our first book, *Dealing in Virtue: International Commercial Arbitration and the Construction of a Transnational Legal Order* (Chicago, 1996), examined the development of international commercial arbitration in the period after World War II. The second, *The Internationalization of Palace Wars: Lawyers, Economists, and the Contest to Transform Latin American States* (Chicago, 2002), explored the transformation of the U.S. state since the 1960s and the transformation in globalization processes based on the import and export of U.S.-based technologies and approaches – including legal ones. Our discussion of the role of large law firms draws especially on "The Confrontation Between the Big Five and Big Law: Turf Battles and Ethical Debates as Contests for Professional Credibility," *Law & Social Inquiry* 29 (2004), 615–38.

The chapter is also based on work in progress that focuses more specifically on the rise of the foreign policy establishment and the role of law in U.S. colonial ventures, especially in the Philippines. These different research projects share an approach that links domestic political and economic developments to those that take place internationally. "Palace wars" for control over the national state are often fought on international terrain. Our exploration of the rise, decline, and revival of the FPE shows how its members used their expertise and contacts in foreign affairs to build their position within the United States.

The approach in this chapter comes from the sociology of the late Pierre Bourdieu, succinctly explained in Pierre Bourdieu and Loic Wacquant, *An Invitation to Reflexive Sociology* (Chicago, 1992). It does not focus on motives and ideologies, but rather on the strategies of particular groups, most notably the FPE. Accordingly, "strategy" refers to activities shaped by fields of practice and not necessarily to self-conscious activities with any particular instrumental design, such as building an empire or becoming a FPE. The approach also emphasizes that the role of law in the United States and elsewhere is always contested by competing forms of authority – including other disciplinary approaches, such as economics. This kind of approach is developed also in Christopher L. Tomlins, "Law's Disciplinary Encounters: A Historical Narrative," *Law & Society Review* 34 (2000), 911.

The literature that informs this chapter can be divided into four broad categories. The first focuses on the late nineteenth and early twentieth centuries and the early history of the lawyers who became the FPE. The setting for that development is chronicled in Sven Beckert, *The Monied Metropolis: New York City and the Consolidation of the American Bourgeoisie* (New York, 2001), which depicts the world of lawyers and business. The work on the legal profession of that time owes a major debt to Robert Gordon, who develops the notion of elite lawyer "schizophrenia." His approach is developed in "The Ideal and the Actual in the Law: Fantasies and Practices of New York City Lawyers, 1870–1910," in Gerald Gawalt ed., *The New High Priests: Lawyers in Post-Civil War America* (Westport, CT, 1984). We employ the term, but tend to see both the service to clients and the public service as part of one strategy that serves both lawyers and clients. Another helpful examination of the bar at the turn of the century is Michael J. Powell, *From Patrician to Professional Elite: The Transformation of the New York City Bar Association* (New York, 1988). The mix of activities is well apparent in Nancy Lisagor and Frank Lipsius. *A Law Unto Itself: The Untold Story of the Law Firm Sullivan & Cromwell* (New York, 1988). The foreign policy that emerged in full force in the Philippines is portrayed in Stanley Karnow, *In Our Image: America's Empire in the Philippines* (New York, 1989). The mix of idealism and realism is seen theoretically in Martin Sklar, *The United States as a Developing Country* (New York, 1992) and in practical terms in the memoir of George A. Malcolm, *American Colonial Careerist* (Boston, 1957).

The second category of literature focuses on the institutions created around this time and their activities over the course of the century – in particular, philanthropic foundations and the Council on Foreign Relations (CFR), as well as related organizations such as the American Society for International Law and the American Law Institute. The history of the

CFR is given generally in Peter Grose, *Continuing the Inquiry: The Council on Foreign Relations from 1921 to 1996* (Washington, DC, 1996). Helpful examinations of these institutions and the role of the FPE within them include Harold Berman, *The Ideology of Philanthropy: The Influence of the Carnegie, Ford, and Rockefeller Foundations on American Foreign Policy* (Syracuse, NY, 1983); Ellen Condliffe Legemann, *The Politics of Knowledge: The Carnegie Corporation, Philanthropy, and Public Policy* (Chicago, 1989); Leonard Silk and Mark Silk, *The American Establishment* (New York, 1980); and Judith Sklar, ed., *Trilateralism, the Trilateral Commission, and Elite Planning for World Management* (Cambridge, MA, 1980).

The third literature is biographical, focusing either on individuals or close-knit groups whose activities span decades. Of particular interest are Kai Bird, *The Chairman: John J. McCloy, the Making of the American Establishment* (New York, 1992); Kai Bird, *The Color of Truth: McGeorge Bundy and William Bundy, Brothers in Arms* (New York, 1998); William H. Harbaugh, *Lawyers' Lawyer: The Life of John W. Davis* (Charlottesville, VA, 1990); Geoffrey Hodgson, *The Colonel: The Life and Wars of Henry Stimson* (New York, 1990); Walter Isaacson and Evan Thomas, *The Wise Men: Six Friends and the World They Made* (New York, 1986); Geoffrey Kabaservice, *Kingman Brewster, His Circle, and the Rise of the Liberal Establishment* (New York, 2004); Ralph Eldin Minger, *William Howard Taft and United States Foreign Policy: The Apprenticeship Years 1900–1908* (Urbana, IL, 1975); and Warren Zimmerman, *First Great Triumph: How Five Great Americans Made Their Country a World Power* (New York, 2002).

The fourth body of literature chronicles the developments in human rights and in trade law. The human rights literature is especially rich, including Ann Marie Clark, *Diplomacy of Conscience: Amnesty International and Changing Human Rights Norms* (Princeton, NJ, 2001); William Korey, *NGOs and the Universal Declaration of Human Rights: A Curious Grapevine* (New York, 1998); William Korey, *The Promises We Keep: Human Rights, the Helsinki Process, and American Foreign Policy* (New York, 1993); Jonathan Power, *Like Water on Stone: The Story of Amnesty International* (Boston, 2001); and Howard Tolley, Jr., *The International Commission of Jurists: Global Advocates for Human Rights* (Philadelphia, 1994). Biographies of major participants here are also very useful, including Jeri Laber, *The Courage of Strangers: Coming of Age with the Human Rights Movement* (New York, 2002) and Aryeh Neier, *Taking Liberties: Four Decades in the Struggle for Rights* (New York, 2003). A good discussion of how human rights became institutionalized is Tamar Jacoby, "The Reagan Turnaround in Human Rights," *Foreign Affairs* 64 (1986), 1071–72. On matters of trade, we have relied heavily on Steve Dryden, *The Trade Warriors: USTR and the American Crusade for Free Trade* (New York, 1995). Recent developments in trade law are shown persuasively in Peter

Drahos and John Braithwaite, *Information Feudalism: Who Owns the Knowledge Economy?* (New York, 2002).

The sources for quotations not specifically referenced in the text are as follows (for complete bibliographic references see above): Kingman Brewster's comment about "on to law school" comes from Kabaservice, *Kingman Brewster*, p. 99; the quotation about Cyrus Vance's reasons for moving into corporate law is from Kabaservice at p. 306. The first quotations describing William Howard Taft's mission in the Philippines come from Minger, *William Howard Taft*, p. 2.; those about building the Philippines in the U.S. image and holding the Philippines for the benefit of the Filipinos come from Karnow, *In Our Image*, p. 197. The statement about the Council on Foreign Relations (CFR) and its attack on isolationism comes from Hodgson, *The Colonel*, p. 385. The statement about the anti-Communist threat as a source of the power of the establishment comes from Silk and Silk, *The American Establishment*, p. 200. McCloy's statement about recruiting from the CFR is from the same source, p. 202. Bird's statement about McCloy and the U.S. establishment is from Bird's biography of McCloy, *The Chairman*, p. 18; the description of McCloy's positions is from the same source at pp. 18–20. Kabaservice's comment about Brewster's project at Yale is in Kabaservice, *Kingman Brewster*, p. 289. The statement from the founders of the International Commission of Jurists that they feared the other side in the Cold War had "stolen the great words" comes from Tolley, *The International Commission of Jurists*, p. 29; the quotation on the new approach of the ICJ is from the same source, p. 51. The statement that human rights was a "moral mask" for trilateralism is from Sklar, *The United States as a Developing Country*, p. 29. Dryden, *The Trade Warriors*, p. 37, provides the statement from Heinz about his mistreatment by the State Department. The description of the approach of George Ball is from Dryden, *The Trade Warriors*, p. 42; the opinion of William Eberle and Harold Malmgren is from the same source, p. 165. Dryden also provides the description of the boom for alumni of the U.S. Trade Representative's office, at p. 344.

NOTES ON CONTRIBUTORS (IN ORDER OF APPEARANCE)

DANIEL R. ERNST is Professor of Law at Georgetown University Law Center

WILLIAM W. FISHER III is Hale and Dorr Professor of Intellectual Property Law at Harvard Law School

ROBERT W. GORDON is Chancellor Kent Professor of Law and Legal History at Yale Law School

EDWARD A. PURCELL, JR., is Joseph Solomon Distinguished Professor of Law at New York Law School

LAWRENCE M. FRIEDMAN is Marion Rice Kirkwood Professor of Law at Stanford Law School

MICHAEL WILLRICH is Associate Professor of History at Brandeis University

LESLIE J. REAGAN is Associate Professor of History and Medicine, and of Law and Gender & Women's Studies, at the University of Illinois, Urbana-Champaign

BARRY CUSHMAN is Percy Brown, Jr. Professor of Law and History at the University of Virginia Law School

EILEEN BORIS is the Hull Professor of Women's Studies, and Professor of History and of Law & Society at the University of California, Santa Barbara

GWENDOLYN MINK is Charles N. Clark Professor in the Program for the Study of Women & Gender at Smith College. Research for her chapter was assisted by SAMANTHA ANN MAJIC and LEANDRA ZARNOW

MARK TUSHNET is William Nelson Cromwell Professor of Law at Harvard Law School

MICHAEL J. KLARMAN is James Monroe Distinguished Professor of Law and Professor of History at the University of Virginia

MARGOT CANADAY is a Cotsen-Perkins Postdoctoral Fellow at the Princeton University Society of Fellows

BETSY MENDELSOHN is Director, Science, Technology and Society Programs at the University of Maryland, College Park

VICTORIA SAKER WOESTE is a Senior Research Fellow at the American Bar Foundation, Chicago. Research for her chapter was funded by the American Bar Foundation

JOHN HENRY SCHLEGEL is Roger and Karen Jones Faculty Scholar and Professor at the University at Buffalo Law School, State University of New York

GREGORY A. MARK is Professor of Law at Rutgers School of Law, Newark

NORMAN L. ROSENBERG is DeWitt Wallace Professor of History at Macalester College

MARY L. DUDZIAK is Judge Edward J. and Ruey L. Guirado Professor of Law, History and Political Science at the University of Southern California

YVES DEZALAY is a Principal Member of the Centre de Sociologie Européenne (CSE) located in the École des Hautes Études en Sciences Sociales in Paris, where he is Director of Research CNRS (Centre National de la Recherche Scientifique)

BRYANT G. GARTH is Dean and Professor of Law at Southwestern Law School, Los Angeles, and Director Emeritus of the American Bar Foundation. Research for his chapter with Yves Dezalay was funded by National Science Foundation Grant No. SES-9818796, "International Strategies, Law, and the Reconstruction of Asian States," and by the American Bar Foundation.

INDEX

New Deal (*cont.*)
  antitrust law during, 628–629
  associationalism and, 568
  banks, regulation of, 629–630
  bibliographic essays, 802–808
  Bill of rights, incorporation to states
    during, 309–310
  civil liberties during, 308–309
  civil rights during, 308–309
  collective bargaining, 287–288
  Commerce Clause during, 142, 294
  competing judicial philosophies
    regarding, 291–294
  contract law and, 143
  corporations during, 627–628, 632
  Court decisions regarding, 12
  criminal law and, 209–210
  currency inflation, 289–290
  Democrats and, 269–270
  economic change, role of law in,
    570–571
  economic reform measures, 273–274
  federalism, impact on, 138, 140,
    144–145
  gold clause and, 289–290
  historical background, 137–138
  Hughes Court and, 13, 138–139, 291,
    292, 293
  injunctions and, 11–12
  international affairs during, 142
  judicial authority, growth of, 141–142
  judicial resistance to, 290
  judiciary, changing role of, 268
  justiciability doctrine and, 308
  labor law and, 274–275, 321–323, 351
  legal issues regarding, 276
  legal profession during (*See* Legal
    profession)
  legal realism and, 661
  local governments, role of, 269
  mechanisms for, 269
  minimum wage laws, 284–287
  mortgage debt relief, 288–289,
    290–291
  NAACP during, 406, 411
  national government, growth in power
    of, 140–141, 268–269
  Native Americans and, 275
  negative Commerce Clause and,
    142–143
  overview, 268, 270, 317–318

  political coalition supporting, 269–270
  post-World War II period, survival into,
    145–147
  preemption and, 142–143
  President
    changing role of, 268
    growth of authority during, 141
  rate regulation, 284
  recovery measures, 273
  redevelopment measures, 275
  relief measures, 272–273
  resistance to, 11–13, 14–15
  spending power and, 307
  states, role of, 269
  substantive due process and, 143
  survival of, 13–14
  Taft Court and, 276
  taxpayer standing doctrine and,
    307–308
  Tenth Amendment and, 142
  voting rights during, 315–317
  war analogy, 692–693, 698
  welfare during, 363–367
New Left. *See* Liberalism
New Panama Canal Company, 95
"New property" concept, 369–371
New Right. *See* Conservatism
New York Convention, 750
New York Stock Exchange, 568, 623, 631
Newlands Act, 492, 496
Newman, Frank, 737–738, 752–753, 754
NGOs. *See* Human rights organizations
NHTSA. *See* National Highway Traffic
    Safety Administration
Niebuhr, Reinhold, 728
9/11
  bibliographic essays, 897–898
  Cold War compared, 714
  Guantánamo Bay, 715
  historical context, in, 714–715
  Korean War compared, 714
  military event, treatment as, 713–715
  military tribunals and, 709
  overview, 683
  responses to, 714
  world reaction to US response, 715
1968 Democratic Convention, 665, 737
Nineteenth Amendment, 132, 254, 445,
    703
NIRA. *See* National Industrial Recovery
    Act

Tort law (*cont.*)
  liability "explosion" in, 182
  mass torts
    complexity of, 186
    concentration of law firms, 119–120
    growth in, 119
    historical background, 118
    overview, 118, 186
    problems in, 120
  medical malpractice, 185–186, 191
  products liability, 119, 183, 639–640
  Rehnquist Court on, 171
  rights "revolution," tort reform and, 387
  strict liability, 185
  welfare *versus*, 190
Tort reform movement
  historical background, 190–191
  impact of, 191
  overview, 190
  Republicans and, 191
Tourgee, Albion, 379
Townsend, Willard, 326
Townsend Movement, 337
Toxic waste disposal. *See* Hazardous waste
    disposal
Toxics Release Inventory, 518
Trade Act of 1974, 746
Trade Agreements Act, 747
Trading with the Enemy Act of 1917, 692
Transportation, Department of, 152
Transportation, segregation in, 416–418
Treaties, environmental law under, 482,
    495–496
Trials, decline of, 180–181
Triangle Shirtwaist Fire, 118
Triborough Bridge and Tunnel Authority,
    606
Trilateral Commission, 734, 739, 740,
    744, 745
Truman, Harry S.
  administrative state, and reform of, 22
  civil rights laws, on, 413, 416
  Cold War, on, 709
  Congressional oversight of
    administrative state and, 18
  free trade and, 744
  health care, on, 16, 255, 395, 396
  Korean War and, 687
  loyalty review boards and, 17
  post-World War II period, removal of
    wartime controls during, 698
  steel mills, seizure of, 636, 698–699

  Stimson and, 726
  war and, 687
Trust Indenture Act of 1939, 569, 570,
    571, 631
Trusts. *See* Antitrust law
Tuberculosis, 253–254
Turner, Frederick Jackson, 496, 499, 617
Tuskegee Syphilis Study, 255–257
TVA. *See* Tennessee Valley Authority
Tversky, Amos, 53
Twain, Mark, 664
Twenty-First Amendment, 143, 204, 311
Twenty-Fourth Amendment, 316
"Typhoid Mary," 250–251

UCC. *See* Uniform Commercial Code
Umphrey, Martha Merrill, 668, 670
Unemployed Councils, 337
Unemployment insurance, 307, 336,
    338–339
Unfair labor practices, 17
Unger, Roberto, 65
Uniform Commercial Code (UCC), 38, 89,
    568
Uniform Crime Reports, 210, 220, 225
Uniform Sales Act, 89
Unilateralism in war, 714
Unions. *See* Organized labor
United Automobile Workers, 107, 349
United Electrical Workers, 349
United Kingdom, access to legal services
    in, 86–87
United Mine Workers, 287, 323, 326, 327
United Nations, 572, 685
United Nations Charter, 685
United Nations Security Council, 687
United States Steel Corporation, 330, 622
Universal Declaration of Human Rights,
    736
Universities. *See also specific university*
  hate speech and, 399
  segregation in, 381, 410–411, 414–415
Urban League, 337, 348, 366
U.S. Conference of Mayors, 157
USA PATRIOT Act, 714

Vaccination, mandatory, 249
Van Devanter, Willis
  "Court-packing" plan, on, 299
  New Deal and, 276
  retirement of, 278, 298
  unemployment compensation, on, 307